The Palgrave Handbook of Theatre and Migration

Yana Meerzon • S. E. Wilmer
Editors

The Palgrave Handbook of Theatre and Migration

Editors
Yana Meerzon
Department of Theatre
University of Ottawa
Ottawa, ON, Canada

S. E. Wilmer
School of Drama, Film, and Music
Trinity College Dublin
Dublin, Ireland

ISBN 978-3-031-20195-0   ISBN 978-3-031-20196-7 (eBook)
https://doi.org/10.1007/978-3-031-20196-7

© The Editor(s) (if applicable) and The Author(s), under exclusive licence to Springer Nature Switzerland AG 2023

This work is subject to copyright. All rights are solely and exclusively licensed by the Publisher, whether the whole or part of the material is concerned, specifically the rights of translation, reprinting, reuse of illustrations, recitation, broadcasting, reproduction on microfilms or in any other physical way, and transmission or information storage and retrieval, electronic adaptation, computer software, or by similar or dissimilar methodology now known or hereafter developed.

The use of general descriptive names, registered names, trademarks, service marks, etc. in this publication does not imply, even in the absence of a specific statement, that such names are exempt from the relevant protective laws and regulations and therefore free for general use.

The publisher, the authors, and the editors are safe to assume that the advice and information in this book are believed to be true and accurate at the date of publication. Neither the publisher nor the authors or the editors give a warranty, expressed or implied, with respect to the material contained herein or for any errors or omissions that may have been made. The publisher remains neutral with regard to jurisdictional claims in published maps and institutional affiliations.

This Palgrave Macmillan imprint is published by the registered company Springer Nature Switzerland AG.
The registered company address is: Gewerbestrasse 11, 6330 Cham, Switzerland

Acknowledgements

We wish to thank Eileen Srebernik, the commissioning editor at Palgrave Macmillan, for her enthusiasm and support for this project, and Immy Higgins, Editorial Assistant—Books Editorial Service Team (BEST), Springer Nature, for her editorial help in bringing this project to fruition.

We would like to acknowledge financial assistance of the Research and Publications Fund of the Faculty of Arts, University of Ottawa, Social Sciences and Humanities Research Council (SSHRC), Canada, and the Trinity College Association and Trust at Trinity College, Dublin.

We would also like to say a special thank you to Alessandro Simari, Orla McGinnity, and Fraser Stevens who spent hours working on the stylistic editing and copyediting of the chapters in the book.

We would also like to express our gratitude to the Victoria and Albert Museum for the right to reproduce the image of Ira Aldridge and the Israeli Centre for the Documentation of the Performing Arts, Tel Aviv University for permission to reproduce the image of Arye Elias.

Above all, we would like to thank all the contributors for their excellent work.

Contents

1	Theatre and Migration: Defining the Field Yana Meerzon and S. E. Wilmer	1
Part I	Theatre and Migration: Themes and Concepts	29
2	The Eternal Immigrant and the Aesthetics of Solidarity Silvija Jestrović	31
3	'A Real State of Exception': Walter Benjamin and the Paradox of Theatrical Representation Freddie Rokem	43
4	Theatre as Refrain: Representations of Departure from the Terezín/Theresienstadt Ghetto Lisa Peschel	55
5	Refugees and the Right to Have Rights S. E. Wilmer	67
6	Postmigrant Theatre and Its Impact on Contemporary German Theatre Azadeh Sharifi	79
7	Interculturalism and Migration in Performance: From Distant Otherness to the Precarity of Proximity Brian Singleton	91

8 Cosmopolitanism: The Troublesome Offset of Global Migration 103
   Yana Meerzon and Julija Pešić

9 Indigenous Migrations: Performance, Urbanization, and Survivance in Native North America 115
   Sara Pillatzki-Warzeha and Margaret Werry

10 Migratory Blackness in *Leave Taking* and *Elmina's Kitchen* 131
   Harvey Young

11 Climate Migration and Performance 143
   Paul Rae

12 Theatre's Digital Migration 157
   Matthew Causey

Part II Early Representations of Migration 169

13 Theatre and Migration in *Gilgamesh* 171
   Martin Worthington

14 Migration and Ancient Indian Theatre 183
   H. S. Shivaprakash and J. Sreenivasa Murthy

15 Fated Arrivals: Greek Tragedy and Migration 195
   Rush Rehm

16 Migration in Greek and Roman Comedy 207
   C. W. Marshall

17 Migrating Souls and Witnessing Travellers in the Dramaturgy of Nō Theatre 219
   Miki Iwata

18 The Things She Carried: The Vertical Migrations of Lady Rokujō in Japanese Theatre 229
   Carol Fisher Sorgenfrei

19 The Stranger's Case: Exile in Shakespeare 243
   Miranda Fay Thomas

20 The 'English Comedy' in Early Modern Europe: Migration,
    Emigration, Integration   255
    M. A. Katritzky

21 Migrations and Cultural Navigations on Early Modern
    Italian Stages   267
    Erith Jaffe-Berg

Part III   Migration and Nationalism   279

22 Immigration and Family Life on the Early
    Twentieth-Century Argentine Stage   281
    May Summer Farnsworth

23 Sonless Mothers and Motherless Sons or How Has
    Polishness Haunted Polish Theatre Artists in Exile?   291
    Kasia Lech

24 All Our Migrants: Place and Displacement on the Israeli Stage   303
    Sarit Cofman-Simhon

25 Shylock Is Me: Aryeh Elias as an Immigrant Jewish-Iraqi
    Actor in the Israeli Theatre   315
    Naphtaly Shem-Tov

26 Emerging, Staying, or Leaving: 'Immigrant' Theatre
    in Canada   327
    Art Babayants

27 Migrant Artists and Precarious Labour in Contemporary
    Russian Theatre   339
    Mark Simon and Varvara Sklez

28 Chicano Theatre and (Im)migration: *La víctima*   353
    Jorge A. Huerta

29 Staging War at the Home Depot: Yoshua Okón's *Octopus* and
    the Shadow Economy of Migrant Labour   365
    Natalie Álvarez and Jimena Ortúzar

30 From Emigrant to Migrant Nation: Reckoning with Irish
    Historical Duty   377
    Charlotte McIvor

31 Dwelling in Multiple Languages: The Impossible Journeys
    Home in the Work of Sidi Larbi Cherkaoui and Akram Khan   389
    Guy Cools

Part IV Migration, Colonialism, and Forced Displacement   401

32 The Theatre of Displacement and Migration in Southern
    Africa: Zimbabwe and South Africa in Focus   403
    Samuel Ravengai

33 From the Yoruba Travelling Theatre to the Nobel Prize in
    Literature: Nigerian Theatre in Motion   415
    Bisi Adigun

34 Migratory Subjectivities and African Diasporic Theatre:
    Race, Gender, and Nation   427
    Nicosia Shakes

35 Immobile Relegations and Exiles: Creation and Migration
    in French Theatre Between 1980 and 2020   439
    Selim Rauer

36 Storying Home: Retracing the Trail of Tears to Restore
    Ekvnvcakv   451
    Christy Stanlake

37 Diasporic Trauma, Nativized Innovation, and Techno-
    Intercultural Predicament: The Story of *Jingju* in Taiwan   463
    Daphne P. Lei

38 Our Life Together: War, Migration, and Family Drama in
    Korean American Theatre   475
    Ju Yon Kim

39 Chronicles of Refugees Foretold   487
    Hala Khamis Nassar

40 Ukrainian Theatre in Migration: Military Anthropology
    Perspective   499
    Robert Boroch and Anna Korzeniowska-Bihun

Part V Refugees   511

41 Spaces and Memories of Migration in Twenty-First-Century
    Greek Theatre: Station Athens's *I_Left* (*Ε_Φυγα*)   513
    Marilena Zaroulia

42 Troubled Waters: The Representation of Refugees in
    Maltese Theatre   525
    Marco Galea

43 Staging Borders: Immigration Drama in Spain, from the
    1990s to the Present   537
    Andrés Pérez-Simón

44 Performance and Asylum Seekers in Australia (2000–2020)   549
    Caroline Wake

45 *Ramadram*: Refugee Struggles, Empowerment, and
    Institutional Openings in German Theatre   561
    Anika Marschall

46 To Come Between: Refugees at Sea, from Representation
    to Direct Action   573
    Emma Cox

47 Theatre, Migration and Activism: The Work of Good
    Chance Theatre   587
    Alison Jeffers and Ambrose Musiyiwa

48 Theatre and Migration in the Balkans: The Death
    of Asylum in Žiga Divjak's *The Game*   599
    Milija Gluhovic

49 Theatre of the Syrian Diaspora   611
    Edward Ziter

50 The Finnish National Theatre, Refugees, and Equality   623
    Pirkko Koski

Part VI Itinerancy, Traveling, and Transnationalism — 637

51 Transnationality: Intercultural Dialogues, Encounters, and the Theatres of Curiosity — 639
Pavel Drábek

52 German Theatre and August von Kotzebue's Theatrical Success and Pitfalls in Russia — 651
Maria Berlova

53 The Itinerant Puppet — 663
John McCormick

54 Fin-de-siècle Black Minstrelsy, Itinerancy, and the Anglophone Imperial Circuit — 675
Kellen Hoxworth

55 Actor Migration to and from Britain in the Nineteenth Century — 687
Jim Davis

56 Migration and Marathi Theatre in Colonial India, 1850–1900 — 701
Kedar A. Kulkarni

57 *The Dybbuk*: Wandering Souls of The Vilna Troupe and Habimah Theatre — 713
Ina Pukelytė

58 Indian Circus: A Melting Pot of Migrant Artists, Performativity, and Race — 725
Aastha Gandhi

59 Contemporary (Post-)Migrant Theatre in Belgium and the Migratory Aesthetics of Milo Rau's Theatre of the Real — 739
Janine Hauthal

60 Belarus Free Theatre: Political Theatre in Exile — 751
Margarita Kompelmakher

Index — 763

Notes on Contributors

Bisi Adigun joined Bowen University Iwo in 2019, having previously worked as Adjunct Lecturer in African Theatre and Performance Studies at the Creative Arts Department of Trinity College, Dublin. He is also a playwright, director, and creative producer. In 2003, he founded Arambe Productions, Ireland's first African theatre company for which he produced and directed over 25 productions. Adigun's first volume of plays, *An Other Playboy: Home Sweet Home!, The Butcher Babes*, was published by Universal Books UK in 2018. He is also the co-editor, with Duro Oni, of *The Soyinka Impulse: Essays on Wole Soyinka* (BookCraft, 2019).

Natalie Álvarez is Associate Dean, Research and Professor of Theatre and Performance Studies in The Creative School at Toronto Metropolitan University (formerly Ryerson). She is author, co-editor, and editor of four award-winning books, most recently: *Sustainable Tools for Precarious Times: Performance Actions in the Americas* (Palgrave Macmillan, 2019), and *Immersions in Cultural Difference: Tourism, War, Performance* (2018). Her most recent book, *Theatre & War* was released by Bloomsbury in 2023. Her work on immersive performance in the public sphere, Latina/o/x contemporary performance, and performance activism has been published widely in international journals and essay collections.

Art Babayants is a multilingual artist-scholar who lives and works in Canada. Babayants' directing credits include musicals, contemporary Canadian drama, opera, and collectively devised performances. He holds a PhD in Theatre and Performance Studies from the University of Toronto and publishes on the issues of stage multilingualism, diasporic/immigrant theatre, queer dramaturgy, applied theatre, and contemporary musical theatre. Babayants has also co-edited *Theatre and Learning* (2015) and the special issue of *Theatre Research in Canada/Les recherches théâtrales au Canada* (Fall 2017) dedicated to multilingual theatre in Canada.

Maria Berlova is an independent scholar who holds two PhDs, from both the Russian Academy of Theater Arts (GITIS, Moscow) and Stockholm University. In 2018, Berlova published her book, *Theater of the King. Gustav III and the Formation of the Swedish National Stage* (in Russian). In 2021, Routledge published Berlova's second book, *Performing Power: The Political Secrets of Gustav III (1771–1792)*. It focuses on the tight link between theatre and politics during the Enlightenment in Sweden and other European countries. Berlova specializes in eighteenth- and nineteenth-century European and Russian theatre, as well as theatre perception.

Robert Boroch is a socio-cultural and military anthropologist. Boroch holds a PhD in Social Sciences (Security Studies), a PhD in Humanities (Literary Theory), and an MA in Theatre Studies.

Matthew Causey is Fellow Emeritus at Trinity College Dublin where he served as Head of School of Creative Arts and Director of the Arts Technology Research Laboratory. He is author of *Theatre and Performance in Digital Culture* (2009), and co-editor of *Performing Subject in the Space of Technology: Through the Virtual Towards the Real* (Palgrave Macmillan, 2015) and *Performance, Identity and the Neo-political Subject* (2015). His theoretical writings on digital culture and theory are published in many journals including his essay 'Postdigital Performance' (*Theatre Journal* 68, 2016).

Sarit Cofman-Simhon is a theatre researcher interested in performative practices in diverse Jewish languages, communities, and historical periods, and has written extensively on these topics. She is based jointly at the School of Performing Arts, Kibbutzim College, Tel Aviv and Emunah Faculty of Fine Arts, Jerusalem, where she is Head of the Theatre Department. She holds a PhD in Theatre Arts from the University of Minnesota. Her book on Jewish languages in Israeli theatre has been published in 2023 in Hebrew.

Guy Cools is a Belgian dance dramaturge. He taught at the Universities of Ghent and Ottawa and the Fontys School of Arts in Tilburg. In 2023, he will take up a professorship in the dance department of the University of Québec in Montréal. His most recent publications include *In-between Dance Cultures: On the Migratory Artistic Identity of Sidi Larbi Cherkaoui and Akram Khan* (2015); *Imaginative Bodies, Dialogues in Performance Practices* (2016); *The Choreopolitics of Alain Platel's les ballets C de la B* (2019); co-edited with Christel Stalpaert and Hildegard De Vuyst; and *Performing Mourning: Laments in Contemporary Art* (2021).

Emma Cox is Reader and Head of Department of Drama, Theatre and Dance at Royal Holloway, University of London. She is the author of *Performing Noncitizenship: Asylum Seekers in Australian Theatre, Film and Activism* (2015), *Theatre & Migration* (Palgrave Macmillan, 2014), and editor of the play collection *Staging Asylum* (2013). Cox's writing has been published internationally in journals such as *Theatre Journal* and *Theatre Research International*.

She is co-editor of the interdisciplinary volume, *Refugee Imaginaries: Research Across the Humanities* (2020).

Jim Davis is Professor of Theatre Studies at the University of Warwick. His most recent books are *Comic Acting and Portraiture in Late-Georgian and Regency England* (2015), *Theatre & Entertainment* (Palgrave Macmillan, 2016), and *Dickens Dramatized* Volume II (2017). He is also joint-author of *Reflecting the Audience: London Theatre-going 1840–1880* (2001) and has edited a book on Victorian pantomime (Palgrave Macmillan, 2010). He has many published book chapters and articles on nineteenth-century theatre to his credit. He is an editor of the refereed journal *Nineteenth-Century Theatre and Film*.

Pavel Drábek is Professor of Drama and Theatre Practice at the University of Hull, UK. He has published on Early Modern theatre, theatre theory, and translation: *Transnational Connections in Early Modern Theatre* (2020; co-edited with M.A. Katritzky, 2020); *Performance Cultures of the English Restoration 1660–1737* (2021; co-edited with Klára Škrobánková); and contributed to *The Routledge Companion to Theatre and Performance Historiography* (2021). He has edited Pamela Howard's *What Is Scenography?* (2019; third edition) and co-authored *The Art of Making Theatre* (2022), and he is writing *Adapting and Translating for the Stage*. He is a theatre maker, playwright, and translator.

May Summer Farnsworth teaches Spanish and Latin American literature at Hobart and William Smith Colleges in Geneva, NY. Her articles on feminist theatre and narrative have appeared in *Latin American Theater Review*, *South Atlantic Review*, *MIFLC Review*, *Romance Notes*, and *e-misférica*. She has co-edited a two-volume anthology of Latin American theatre by women, *Escrito por mujeres*. Her book, *Feminist Rehearsals* (2023), explores the relationship between theatre and the women's rights movements in Mexico and Argentina.

Marco Galea is Head of the Theatre Studies Department at the University of Malta. He has published on different aspects of theatre-making in Malta and on postcolonial theatre. Recent publications include *Redefining Theatre Communities* (2020; co-edited with Szabolcs Musca) and 'Who Gets to Represent the Past and Why Should They Bother? Maltese Political Theatre in the 1980s' in *World Political Theatre and Performance* (2020; edited by Mireia Aragay et al.).

Aastha Gandhi is Assistant Professor at Ambedkar University, Delhi. She holds a PhD in theatre and performance studies from Jawaharlal Nehru University (JNU), Delhi. Her thesis studied Indian circus history and performance, and its negotiations with state, popularity, and laws. As a trained dancer, her practice cultivates an understanding towards performative and phenomenological bodies. A degree in law adds to her investigations of performers in the eyes of the state. She was a researcher for the University of Warwick/JNU projects 'Cultures of the Left,' and 'Gendered Citizenship,' and was a Doctoral Fellow at the Cluster of Excellence, Freie University, Berlin. She is currently the Student Representative to the Executive Committee of the International Federation for Theatre Research.

Milija Gluhovic is Reader in Theatre and Performance Studies at the University of Warwick. His publications include *A Theory for Theatre Studies: Memory* (2020), *Performing European Memories* (Palgrave, 2013) and co-edited volumes *The Oxford Handbook of Politics and Performance* (2021), *International Performance Research Pedagogies* (Palgrave, 2018), *Performing the Secular* (Palgrave, 2017), and *Performing the 'New' Europe* (Palgrave, 2013). He is a member of the IFTR Executive Committee and the EASTAP Journal editorial board. Currently, he serves as the Director of International Partnerships at the School of Creative Arts, Performance and Visual Cultures at Warwick University.

Janine Hauthal is Assistant Professor of Intermedial Studies at the Vrije Universiteit Brussel in Belgium. Her postdoctoral research focused on British and settler Anglophone 'fictions of Europe' and was funded by the Research Foundation Flanders (FWO). Other interests include postdramatic theatre (texts), contemporary British and postcolonial literatures, metadrama/-theatre, genre theory, and cultural/transmedial narratology. Her most recent articles feature in *Modern Drama, English Text Construction, Antipodes*, and the *Journal of Postcolonial Writing*. Her latest FWO-funded project investigates 'Self-Reflexivity and Generic Change in twenty-first-Century Black British Women's Literature.'

Kellen Hoxworth is Assistant Professor of Theatre at the University at Buffalo. His work has been published in *American Quarterly, Contemporary Theatre Review, Journal of Dramatic Theory & Criticism, Modern Drama, Performance Research, TDR, Theatre Journal*, and *Theatre Survey*. His essay 'The Many Racial Effigies of Sara Baartman' received the 2018 Errol Hill Award for outstanding research in African American theatre and performance studies. His monograph *Transoceanic Blackface: Empire, Race, Performance* (Northwestern University Press, forthcoming) traces the transnational circulations of blackface minstrelsy and related forms of racialized performance from the pre-revolutionary circum-Atlantic world through the nineteenth-century Anglophone imperium.

Jorge A. Huerta is Chancellor's Associates Professor of Theatre Emeritus at the University of California, San Diego. He joined the faculty in 1975 and retired from UCSD in 2009. Huerta has directed in regional theatres throughout the United States and is a leading authority on contemporary Chicanx and Latinx theatre who has lectured throughout the US, Latin America, and Western Europe. He has published many articles and reviews in journals and anthologies and has edited three collections of plays. Huerta published the first book about Chicano theatre, *Chicano Theater: Themes and Forms* (Bilingual

Press, 1982), as well as *Chicano Drama: Performance, Society and Myth* (Cambridge University Press, 2000).

Miki Iwata is Professor of English at Rikkyo University, Japan. She received her PhD from Tohoku University on W. B. Yeats's drama and Irish cultural nationalism. Her research interests widely cover British as well as Japanese drama. Her recent publications include *Kyodai genka no Igirisu-Airurando engeki* [The Rival Brothers in British and Irish Drama] (Shohakusha, 2017; in Japanese), 'Brothers Lost, Sisters Found: The Verbal Construction of Sisterhood in *Twelfth Night*' (2019), and 'Tony Lumpkin in and out of Sweet Auburn: The Literary Topography of Oliver Goldsmith in *She Stoops to Conquer*' (2020).

Erith Jaffe-Berg is a professor at the Department of Theatre, Film and Digital Production at the University of California, Riverside. Her research focuses on the commedia dell'arte and performances by minority groups in Early Modern Italy. She has authored two books: *Commedia dell'Arte and the Mediterranean: Charting Journeys and Mapping 'Others'* (2015) and *The Multilingual Art of Commedia dell'Arte* (2009), among other essays and articles. She is currently completing a book on the Jewish theatre tradition in Early Modern Mantua. She is a member of the Son of Semele Theatre Ensemble and Theatre Dybbuk.

Alison Jeffers is Senior Lecturer in Applied Theatre and Contemporary Performance at the University of Manchester. She has researched and written widely on the subject of theatre and migration focusing on applied theatre and participatory arts practices with groups of refugees and asylum seekers in the UK. Her monograph *Refugees, Theatre and Crisis: Performing Global Identities* was published by Palgrave Macmillan in 2012, and she has made many contributions to journals and other edited collections on this subject. She is currently working with PhD researcher Ambrose Musiyiwa, in collaboration with Community Arts Northwest, on the work of refugee artists in the UK.

Silvija Jestrović is Professor of Theatre and Performance Studies at the University of Warwick, UK. She is the author of *Performing Authorial Presence and Absence: The Author Dies Hard* (Palgrave Macmillan, 2020), *Performance, Space, Utopia: Cities of War, Cities of Exile* (Palgrave Macmillan, 2012), *Theatre of Estrangement: Theory, Practice, Ideology* (2006). Her co-edited volumes include *Performance, Exile, and 'America'* (Palgrave, 2009; with Yana Meerzon) and O*xford Handbook of Politics and Performance* (2020; with Shirin Rai, Milija Gluhovic, and Michael Saward). She is currently the senior editor of *Theatre Research International*.

M. A. Katritzky is Barbara Wilkes Research Fellow in Theatre Studies and Director, Centre for Research into Gender and Otherness in the Humanities, in the Faculty of Arts & Social Sciences, The Open University, Milton Keynes, UK. Books include *Healing, Performance and Ceremony in the Writings of Three Early Modern Physicians: Hippolytus Guarinonius and the Brothers Felix and Thomas Platter* (2012), *Women, Medicine and Theatre 1500–1750: Literary*

Mountebanks and Performing Quacks (2007), *The Art of Commedia: A Study in the Commedia dell'Arte 1560–1620 with Special Reference to the Visual Records* (2006), and *Transnational Connections in Early Modern Theatre* (2020; co-edited with Pavel Drábek).

Ju Yon Kim is Professor of English at Harvard University. Her research and teaching interests include Asian American literature and theatre; modern and contemporary American theatre; and cross-racial and intercultural performance. Her first book, *The Racial Mundane: Asian American Performance and the Embodied Everyday* (2015), received the 2016 New England American Studies Association's Lois P. Rudnick Book Prize. Her articles have appeared in *Theatre Journal, Modern Drama, Journal of Transnational American Studies, Modernism/modernity, Theatre Survey*, and *Journal of Asian American Studies*. She is currently completing a manuscript titled *Paper Performance: Suspicion and the Spaces of Asian American Theater*.

Margarita Kompelmakher is a scholar, theatre instructor, and Director of Community Partnerships and Engagement at the Alliance Theatre in Atlanta, Georgia. She holds a PhD in Theater Historiography from the University of Minnesota-Twin Cities, where she wrote her dissertation on human rights theatre based on a critical case study of the Belarus Free Theatre. Her writing appears in *Modern Drama*, and the anthologies *Captured by the City: New Perspectives in Urban Culture* (2013) and *Staging Post-Communism* (2020).

Anna Korzeniowska-Bihun is a military anthropologist and literary and audiovisual translator. She holds a PhD in Humanities (Ukrainian Dramaturgy), MA in Theatre Studies, and MA in Ukrainian Studies.

Pirkko Koski is Helsinki University's Professor Emerita of Theatre Research. She has specialized in theatre performance analysis and historiography, as well as the historical analysis of Finnish theatre. She has written and edited several articles and books for the domestic and international market. Her most recent monographs include *Finland's National Theatre 1974–1991*(2022), *Suomen Kansallisteatteri ristipaineissa* [The Finnish National Theatre Caught in the Crossfire] (2019), and *Näyttelijänä Suomessa* [Being an Actor in Finland] (2013).

Kedar A. Kulkarni is Associate Professor of Literary and Cultural Studies at FLAME University in Pune, India. His book, *World Literature and the Question of Genre in Colonial India: Poetry, Drama, and Print Culture 1790–1890* (2022), won the American Comparative Literature Association's Helen Tartar First Book Subvention Grant.

Kasia Lech is a scholar, actor, storyteller, puppeteer, and Associate Professor of Global Performance Histories at the University of Amsterdam. She received her PhD from University College Dublin. Her research and creative practice explores theatre through practice-based and traditional scholarship, and she primarily focuses on theatre in the context of multilingualism, actor training, verse, and transnational experience. She authored *Dramaturgy of Form: Performing Verse in Contemporary Theatre* (2021). Her second book, *Multilingual Dramaturgies: Towards New European Theatre* is forthcoming with Palgrave. Lech performed internationally and co-founded Polish Theatre Ireland—an intercultural theatre company based in Dublin. She is an Executive Director at TheTheatreTimes.com.

Daphne P. Lei is Professor of Drama, at the University of California, Irvine. She has published and lectured widely on Chinese opera, Asian American theatre, intercultural, transnational, and transpacific performance in major journals and anthologies and in many different countries. She is the author of three monographs: *Operatic China: Staging Chinese Identity across the Pacific* (Palgrave Macmillan, 2006), *Alternative Chinese Opera in the Age of Globalization: Performing Zero* (Palgrave Macmillan, 2011), and *Uncrossing the Borders: Performing Chinese in Gendered (Trans)Nationalism* (2019; Finalist of the 2019 Theatre Library Association's George Freedley Memorial Book Award and the Finalist of the 2020 Outstanding Book Award of Association for Theatre in Higher Education). She is also the co-editor of *The Methuen Drama Handbook of Interculturalism and Performance* (2020; co-edited with Charlotte McIvor). Lei is the former president of American Society for Theatre Research (2015–2018) and the 2018 ASTR Distinguished Scholar.

Anika Marschall is Assistant Professor at Utrecht University, Netherlands. She holds a PhD from the University of Glasgow and her research interests are concerned with theatre, migration, and human rights. Anika has previously published about artistic interventions into asylum and statelessness, including performance works by Akira Takayama, Lawrence Abu Hamdan, Centre for Political Beauty, and Claudia Bosse. Anika is co-editor of the *Scottish Journal of Performance* and co-founder of the network Neue Kritische Theaterwissenschaft. Her monograph *Performing Human Rights* is forthcoming with Routledge.

C. W. Marshall is Professor of Greek in the Department of Ancient Mediterranean and Near Eastern Studies at the University of British Columbia, in Vancouver, Canada. He is also a Fellow of the Royal Society of Canada. His books include *Aristophanes: Frogs* (2020), *Aeschylus: Libation Bearers* (2017), *The Structure and Performance of Euripides' Helen* (2014), and *The Stagecraft and Performance of Roman Comedy* (2006). His work has been generously supported by the Social Sciences and Humanities Research Council of Canada.

John McCormick is a graduate of Trinity College Dublin (doctoral thesis on Gaston Baty). He was Lecturer in French at TCD from 1970 to 1984 and became the first director of the Drama Department in 1984. An active amateur puppeteer, his publications include *Popular Theatres of Nineteenth-Century France* (1993), *Popular Puppets in Europe 1800–1914* (1998; co-authored with Bennie Pratasik), *The Victorian Marionette Theatre* (University of Iowa Press, 2004), *The Italian Puppet Theater – A History* (2010), *Pupazzi—Glove Puppets and Marionettes in the Castello dei Burattini Museo Giordano Ferrari in Parma*

(2015; co-authored with Paolo Parmiggiani), and *The Holdens: Monarchs of the Marionette Theatre* (2018).

Charlotte McIvor is Senior Lecturer and Head of Discipline in Drama and Theatre Studies at the University of Galway, specializing in contemporary Irish performance, interculturalism, migration, race, gender, sexuality, and practice-as-research. She is the author of *Contemporary Irish Theatre: Histories and Theories* (Palgrave Macmillan, 2024, with Ian R. Walsh); *Migration and Performance in Contemporary Ireland: Towards A New Interculturalism* (Palgrave Macmillan, 2016); the co-editor of *The Methuen Drama Handbook of Interculturalism and Performance* (2020; with Daphne P. Lei), *Interculturalism and Performance Now: New Directions?* (Palgrave Macmillan, 2018; with Jason King), *Devised Performance in Irish Theatre: Histories and Contemporary Practice* (2015; with Siobhán O'Gorman), and *Staging Intercultural Ireland: Plays and Practitioner Perspectives* (2014; with Matthew Spangler); and has published in multiple journals and edited collections.

Yana Meerzon is Professor of Theatre Studies at the University of Ottawa. She is the author of three books, most recently *Performance, Subjectivity, Cosmopolitanism* (Palgrave Macmillan, 2020). She co-edited seven collections of articles, including *Migration and Stereotypes in Performance and Culture* (Palgrave Macmillan, 2020; with David Dean and Daniel McNeil). This book is a recepient of the Patrick O'Neill 2022 Award, honorable mention, with Canadian Association for Theatre Research (CATR). Her current research project is entitled 'Between Migration and Neo-Nationalism(s): Performing the European Nation — Playing a Foreigner,' which has been funded by the Social Sciences and Humanities Research Council of Canada (SSHRC).

J. Sreenivasa Murthy is retired Professor of Sanskrit, MES College, Bangalore and Director, Mahabhodi Society, Bangalore, India. He is currently working on a book about Indian concepts of translations and is actively engaged in Kannada theatre with great stalwarts like Sri Ranga and B.V. Karanth. He is the Resource Person at National School of Drama, Bangalore Chapter. He has translated and directed Sanskrit plays; been a member of the Board of Studies, Presidency University, Kolkata; lectured and taught classes on Natyashastra and Indian Aesthetics at several Indian Universities including JNU, New Delhi; been involved in translations of Buddhist Trepitikas from Pali into Kannada; and has participated in many national and international conferences on Sanskrit studies.

Ambrose Musiyiwa is a PhD researcher on a collaborative doctoral programme with the Drama Department at the University of Manchester and Community Arts Northwest (CAN). His research project 'Listening to the voice of refugee artists' examines the performance practices of artists from refugee backgrounds who are living and working in the UK. He has a background in the intersection between activism, migration, community action and coordinates Journeys in Translation, an international, volunteer-driven project translating *Over Land, Over Sea: Poems for Those Seeking Refuge* (Five Leaves Publications, 2015) from English into other languages. His recent anthology is *Black Lives Matter: Poems for a New World* (2020).

Hala Khamis Nassar is Associate Professor of Education at Bethlehem University, Palestine. Her research *and teaching interests include Palestinian Literature and theatre; and her first book is Mahmoud Darwish: Exile's Poet* (Interlink Books, 2007). Her articles on different historical periods of Palestinian theatre appeared in book chapters and in *Theatre Journal, Modern Drama, Theatre Survey*, and *The Columbia Encyclopedia of Modern Drama*.

Jimena Ortúzar is a Postdoctoral Fellow with 'Hemispheric Encounters: Developing Transborder Research-Creation Practices' at York University's School of the Arts, Media, Performance and Design. Her research explores transnational labour and migration through the lens of performance and gender studies. Her writing appears in international journals and essay collections on art and activism, contemporary theatre, and Latino/a/x performance. She is also a contributor to 'Gatherings: Archival and Oral Histories of Performance,' a project for preservation and study of performance histories in Canada.

Andrés Pérez-Simón teaches English literature and literary criticism at the Universidad Autónoma of Madrid. He is the author of *Baroque Lorca: An Archaist Playwright for the New Stage* (2020) and *Drama, literatura, filosofía: Itinerarios del realismo y el modernismo europeos* (2015). Pérez-Simón is also the editor and translator of *Despistemes: La teoría literaria y cultural de Emil Volek (Antología de textos)* (2018).

Lisa Peschel is a senior lecturer (associate professor) in theatre in the School of Arts and Creative Technologies at the University of York, UK. Her articles on theatrical performance in the Terezín/Theresienstadt ghetto have appeared in journals in the US and the UK as well as Czech, German, and Israeli publications. She has reconstructed and restaged scripts from the ghetto in the US, the UK, the Czech Republic, Australia, and South Africa. Her anthology of rediscovered scripts, *Performing Captivity, Performing Escape: Cabarets and Plays from the Terezín/Theresienstadt Ghetto*, was published by Seagull Books in 2014 (Czech- and German-language edition 2008).

Julija Pešić is a PhD candidate at the University of Toronto. Her doctoral dissertation investigates cultural specificity and global dynamics in the performance art of Marina Abramović, a Belgrade-born, New York City-based performance artist, now best known for her record-breaking 2010 MoMA retrospective. Julija's doctoral project has been funded by a Social Science and Humanities Research Council Doctoral Fellowship, an Ontario Graduate Scholarship, and a Helen Krich Chinoy Dissertation Fellowship granted by the American Society for Theatre Research. Julija is an alumna of Harvard University's Mellon School of Theatre and Performance Research.

Sara Pillatzki-Warzeha (Dakota) is a PhD candidate at the University of Minnesota. Her research is centred on Indigenous performance and storytelling, with specific interests in Indigenous feminisms as a dramaturgical lens, Indigenous/settler artistic collaborations, and decolonizing the theatre. She is also a full-time theatre artist working in directing and theatre education throughout the Midwest. She is an enrolled member of the Sisseton Wahpeton Oyate.

Ina Pukelytė is associate professor at the Theatre Studies Department of the University of Vytautas Magnus (Kaunas). She is a member of the International Federation of Theatre Research (IFTR/FIRT). She is former Head of Kaunas State Drama Theatre. Her research interests are Lithuanian theatre history, cultural policies, and management. Her monograph *Žydų teatras tarpukario Lietuvoje* [Jewish Theatre in Lithuania in the Period Between the Two World Wars] was published in 2017. She published a novel *Girls from Laisvės Alėja* in 2020 for which she was awarded a national Grigory Kanovich prize.

Paul Rae is Head of the School of Culture and Communication and Associate Professor in Theatre Studies at the University of Melbourne, Australia. He is the author of *Theatre & Human Rights* (2009), and *Real Theatre: Essays in Experience* (2019). From 2015–2018, he was Senior Editor of the journal *Theatre Research International*, and has published widely on contemporary theatre and on Asia-Pacific performance.

Selim Rauer is a teaching fellow at the Institute for Theatre Studies at the Sorbonne Nouvelle University in Paris and was research fellow and junior faculty at the Vidal Sassoon International Center for the Study of Antisemitism at the Hebrew University of Jerusalem. His work examines the territorialities of foreignness as well as traumatic and post-traumatic memories related to colonialism and the Shoah in French and Francophone contemporary literature and drama. He has published in various literary and academic peer-reviewed journals such as *La revue littéraire*, *Modern Drama*, and *Research in African Literature*.

Samuel Ravengai is Professor of Theatre Studies at Wits University. He holds an MA and PhD in Theatre and Performance from the University of Cape Town. He is former Head of the Department of Theatre and Performance and the current Head of Postgraduate Studies at Wits School of Arts. He is particularly interested in the interconnection of race, nation, empire, migration, and ethnicity with cultural production. His most recent published works include the collection *Theatre from Rhodesia to Zimbabwe: Hegemony Identity and a Contested Postcolony* (Palgrave Macmillan, 2021; co-edited with Owen Seda), *Decolonising African Theatre* (forthcoming), and several book reviews in high-profile journals. He is the current Editor-in-Chief of the *South African Theatre Journal*.

Rush Rehm is Professor of Theatre and Classics at Stanford University, and the author of *Euripides' Electra; Understanding Greek Tragic Theatre; Radical Theatre: Greek Tragedy and the Modern World; The Play of Space: Spatial Transformation in Greek Tragedy; Marriage to Death: The Conflation of Weddings and Funerals in Greek Tragedy*, and *Aeschylus' Oresteia: A Theatre Version*. Founder and Artistic Director of Stanford Repertory Theater, he has worked as an actor or director in Europe and Australia, and at many regional theatres in the United States.

Freddie Rokem is Professor (Emeritus) in the Department of Theatre at Tel Aviv University, where he was the Dean of the Faculty of the Arts (2002–2006). His more recent books are *Philosophers and Thespians: Thinking Performance* (2009); *Strindberg's Secret Codes* (2005), and the prize-winning *Performing History: Theatrical Representations of the Past in Contemporary Theatre* (2000). He was the editor of *Theatre Research International* (2006–2009) and a founding co-editor of the Palgrave/Macmillan book series 'Performance Philosophy' (2012–2017). He has been a visiting professor at many universities in the United States, Germany, Finland, and Sweden, and is also a practicing dramaturg.

Nicosia Shakes is an assistant professor in the Department of History and Critical Race & Ethnic Studies at the University of California, Merced. Her book, *Women's Activist Theatre in Jamaica and South Africa: Gender, Race, and Performance Space*, won the 2017 National Women's Studies Association/University of Illinois Press First Book Prize and is forthcoming in 2023 from the University of Illinois Press. Some of her publications appear in *Signs: Journal of Women in Culture and Society, The Black Scholar*, the *C.L.R. James Journal*, and the *Jamaica Journal*. Alongside her scholarship, she has been a theatre artist for many years. She holds a PhD in Africana Studies from Brown University.

Azadeh Sharifi is a visiting assistant professor at the Department of Germanic Languages and Literature, University of Toronto. Her work engages with (post)colonial and (post)migrant theatre history, theatre and performance by Black, Indigenous, and peoples of colour, and the intersections of race, class, and gender in contemporary European performances. She is currently working on her second book on the history of migrant and minority artists in Germany since 1955 (post-migrant German theatre history). She was previously a visiting professor at the University of Fine Arts (UdK) Berlin, postdoctoral researcher at LMU Munich, and fellow at Interweaving Performance Cultures, an international research centre at FU Berlin.

Naphtaly Shem-Tov is Senior Lecturer and the Head of Literature, Language, and the Arts Department at the Open University of Israel. His research interests are social aspects of Israeli theatre, festivals, applied performance, and education drama. Currently, he is researching Mizrahi (Middle Eastern) Jewish artists and their ethnic identity on the Israeli stage. He has published articles on these topics in several journals, including *The Drama Review, Theatre Research International, Contemporary Theatre Review, New Theatre Quarterly,* and *Research in Drama Education.* His books are *Israeli Theatre: Mizrahi Jews and Self-Representation* (2021), *Acco Festival: Between Celebration and Confrontation* (2016), and *Improvisational Teaching* (2015; in Hebrew).

H. S. Shivaprakash is a well-known poet, playwright, translator, and critic both in Kannada and in English. His plays are widely staged across India and USA. He is a former Dean and Retired Professor, School of Arts & Aesthetics, JNU, New Delhi. He is the former Editor of *Indian Journals* (a journal published by National Academy of Letters, New Delhi); a former Fellow in the School of Letters, University of Iowa, USA; and the former Director of the Cultural Centre, Indian Embassy, Berlin. Shivaprakash has authored thirteen volumes of poetry, twelve plays, seven critical works both in English and Kannada, and edited two anthologies of essays on Indian Theatre—*Indian Theatre in 2000* (2011) and *Ins and Outs of Indian Theatre* (2021).

Mark Simon is a research fellow at the Institute of Cultural Anthropology/European Ethnology at the Georg-August-Universität Göttingen, with a PhD in political science. Until recently, he worked for the Moscow School of Social and Economic Sciences. In recent years, he has been studying the artistic practices of migrants in European countries and in Russia and has published on this topic in such journals as *The Journal of Social Policy Studies* (2020), *Laboratorium* (2020), *Neprikosnovennyi zapas* (2020, 2018), *Sotsiologiia vlasti* (2017), and *Logos* (2016).

Brian Singleton is Samuel Beckett Professor of Drama and Theatre at Trinity College Dublin. His publications on orientalism and intercultural performance in European Theatre include analyses of the work of Artaud, Mnouchkine, Oscar Asche, and Lily Brayton. His monographs on Irish theatre include *Masculinities and the Contemporary Irish Theatre* (Palgrave Macmillan, 2011) and *ANU Productions: The Monto Cycle* (Palgrave Pivot, 2016). He co-edited with Janelle Reinelt the award-winning 40-volume book series 'Studies in International Performance' (Palgrave Macmillan, 2005–2014), and with Elaine Aston he co-edits the book series 'Contemporary Performance InterActions' (Palgrave Macmillan, 2014–2022). His current book project is *Performance and Neoliberal Ireland*.

Varvara Sklez is a PhD candidate in the Department of Theatre and Performance Studies at the University of Warwick. Her PhD dissertation focuses on issues of memory and protest in contemporary Russian theatre. She is a co-editor of *Politics of Affect: Museum as a Public History Site* (New Literary Observer, 2019), a participant in the 'Memories of the Soviet Peasant Rebellions of 1920–1921' project (2018), and a co-founder of the Public History Lab.

Carol Fisher Sorgenfrei is Professor Emerita of Theatre at UCLA and Research Fellow Emerita at the Institute for Interweaving Performance

Cultures, Free University, Berlin, Germany. She writes on post-war Japanese and cross-cultural performance and is also a translator, director, and playwright. The author of *Unspeakable Acts: The Avant-Garde Theatre of Terayama Shūji and Postwar Japan* (2005) and co-author of *Theatre Histories: An Introduction* (3rd ed. 2016), she has written over 100 articles and reviews, and presented over 150 papers and keynotes. She is Associate Editor of *Asian Theatre Journal* and Editor of the *Association for Asian Performance Newsletter*.

Christy Stanlake is a Professor at the United States Naval Academy. She works as both a scholar and a practitioner of Native Theatre. Her publications include *Native American Drama: A Critical Perspective* (2009) and *Critical Companion to Native American and First Nations Theatre: Indigenous Spaces* (2020; co-authored with Jaye Darby and Courtney Elkin Mohler). Christy has used Native theatrical theories to direct Lynn Riggs's *Green Grow the Lilacs* and JudyLee Oliva's national, equity production of *Te Ata*; both plays toured to the National Museum of the American Indian, Washington D.C.

Miranda Fay Thomas is Assistant Professor of Theatre and Performance at Trinity College Dublin. They are the author of *Shakespeare's Body Language: Shaming Gestures and Gender Politics on the Renaissance Stage* (2020) and editor of *The Tempest* (2021). They are currently editing *The Taming of A Shrew* for the New Oxford Shakespeare Alternative Versions, co-editing a collection of essays on the idea of the Shakespearean actor, and conducting research for a new monograph on casting practices and identity politics in twenty-first century performances of Shakespeare.

Caroline Wake is Senior Lecturer in Theatre and Performance at UNSW Sydney, with a longstanding interest in performance and migration. Her research in the area has been published in the special issue 'Envisioning Asylum/Engendering Crisis' of *RiDE: The Journal of Applied Theatre and Performance* (2018), which she co-edited with Emma Cox, as well as in *Performance Research*, *Modern Drama*, and *Text and Performance Quarterly*, among other journals.

Margaret Werry is Associate Professor of Theatre Arts and Dance at the University of Minnesota. She is the author of *The Tourist State: Performing Leisure, Liberalism, and Race in New Zealand* (2011), *Theatre & Tourism* (Palgrave Macmillan, forthcoming), and articles on pedagogy, immersive performance, intercultural theatre, indigenous performance history, museums, and climate change activism in the island Pacific. She is currently working on another project (*The Performing Dead: Public Culture at the Borders of the Human*) concerning the way we treat, trade, and display human remains in museums and popular culture.

S. E. Wilmer is Professor Emeritus at Trinity College Dublin, where he was Head of the School of Drama, Film, and Music. He has served on the executive committees of ASTR and the IFTR, as a visiting professor at Stanford University and the University of California at Berkeley, and as research fellow at the Freie Universität Berlin. He recently co-edited a special topic on 'Theatre and Statelessness in Europe' for *Critical Stages* in 2016. His latest books are *Performing Statelessness in Europe* (Palgrave, 2018), *Deleuze, Guattari and the Art of Multiplicity* (2020), and *Life in the Posthuman Condition* (2023).

Martin Worthington is Al-Maktoum Associate Professor in Middle Eastern Studies at Trinity College Dublin. His latest book is *Ea's Duplicity in the Gilgamesh Flood Story* (2019).

Harvey Young is Dean of the College of Fine Arts at Boston University, where he is also Professor of English and Professor of Theatre Arts. He is the author or editor of nine books, including *Embodying Black Experience* (2010), *Theatre & Race* (Palgrave Macmillan, 2013), and *The Cambridge Companion to African American Theatre* (2012).

Marilena Zaroulia is Senior Lecturer in Performance Arts at The Royal Central School of Speech and Drama, University of London. Her research focuses on theatre, performance, and the cultural politics of post-1989 Europe. She is the co-editor of *Performances of Capitalism, Crises and Resistance: Inside/Outside Europe* (Palgrave, 2015). Her work has appeared in international journals, including articles on performance and migration in *Performance Research* (2016) and *RIDE* (2018). Her monograph *Encountering Europe on British Stages: Performances and Politics since 1990* is forthcoming.

Edward Ziter is a theatre historian and professor in the Department of Drama at New York University. He is the author of *Political Performance in Syria: From the Six-Day War to the Syrian Uprising* (Palgrave Macmillan, 2014) and *The Orient on the Victorian Stage* (2003). He served as Middle Eastern area editor for the *Cambridge Encyclopedia of Stage Actors and Acting* (2015). His current research focuses on nationalist performance during the Arab Renaissance (the late nineteenth to early twentieth centuries) focusing on Arabizations of Romantic drama and Shakespeare.

List of Figures

Fig. 2.1	Sculpture of 'The Eternal Immigrant' by Ilya and Emilia Kabakov. (Photo: Ilya and Emilia Kabakov)	32
Fig. 11.1	A performer presents a dance form called 'Te Kaimatoa', in the town of Bairiki on South Tarawa, Kiribati, in July 2019. (Photo: Paul Rae)	148
Fig. 15.1	Suppliant women, with hands outstretched, seek help from Athens; from Euripides' *Suppliant Women*, Stanford Repertory Theater, 1993, directed by Rush Rehm. Photo: John B. Wilson	200
Fig. 25.1	*Shirei Humash* (Singing HaHomesh songs)—from left to right Arye Elias, Shlomo Artzi, Shoshana Damari, Edna lev; from Itzik Manger's Sherei HaHomesh, HaTeatron HaAmami, 1971, directed by Shmuel Boonim. (Photo: Yackov Agor. Photo courtesy of The Israeli Center for the Documentation of the Performing Arts, Tel-Aviv University)	316
Fig. 49.1	*Antigone of Shatila* (Beirut 2014). Director Omar Abusaada. (Photo: Dalia Khamisy)	619
Fig. 50.1	*Paper Anchor* (2011), Finnish National Theatre, directed and choreographed by Hanna Brotherus. In the first row, Alexandros Kotsopoulos. (Photo: Nico Backström)	627
Fig. 55.1	Ira Aldridge as Othello in *Othello* by William Shakespeare, Oil on canvas. Unknown artist c. 1848. Museum Number S.1129–1986. URL https://protect-eu.mimecast.com/s/Vj2fCL8N8UN MvnliB4TtD/	691

CHAPTER 1

Theatre and Migration: Defining the Field

Yana Meerzon and S. E. Wilmer

With the arrival of over a million refugees into Europe in 2015 and millions of displaced Ukrainians in 2022, the topic of migration has become a major source of public concern and discussion. Wars, failed states, authoritarian governments, abuses of human rights, marauding drug cartels, climate change, and poverty have recently caused citizens in many parts of the world to flee their countries. The number of displaced persons has now reached a record 100 million and is still growing. However, rather than being welcomed abroad like many from Ukraine, refugees frequently encounter closed borders, nationalist restrictions, detention camps, or deportation. Nations have been finding new ways to avoid processing asylum claims, while the human rights of non-citizens are ignored, with thousands of refugees dying en route, trying to cross the Mediterranean, the English Channel, or other dangerous territories. Because the need for asylum has been increasing and the problem has not been solved by political means, artists have been using theatrical performance to intervene in the political arena to offer insight and new perspectives.

However, migration is not a new topic. From earliest recorded time, individuals and populations all over the world have migrated to achieve a better life or escape subjection and the threat of violence. The theatre has continually addressed this theme both in its dramaturgy and in its performance practices.

Y. Meerzon (✉)
Department of Theatre, University of Ottawa, Ottawa, ON, Canada
e-mail: ymeerzon@uottawa.ca

S. E. Wilmer
School of Drama, Film, and Music, Trinity College Dublin, Dublin, Ireland
e-mail: swilmer@tcd.ie

By tradition, theatre artists have been mobile and always striven to find new audiences. Through the centuries, peripatetic artists have taken their work on the road in a variety of forms and manifestations such as pageant wagons, *commedia dell'arte*, touring shows, puppetry, opera, circus, dance, legitimate theatre, and mixed media. The stories they have told have regularly dealt with the theme of migration. Playwrights worldwide have explored the pathos of the homeless, the excluded, and the forcibly displaced to question the meaning of life.

This book brings together a range of scholarship focusing on many eras of performance, as well as various geographical and social conditions, to offer an understanding of the complexities of theatre and migration. It puts forward the idea that making theatre can reflect the multidimensional social, ethnic, cultural, and linguistic landscape of mobile subjects. In acts of live and active encounter between the artist and their audiences, performing arts can hold unparalleled emotional power over its spectators. They can make urgent the impersonal events of modern history such as wars, migration, and climate change, and they can use empathy to make this history important to each of the members of the audience. Performing arts can also act as a mechanism of warning: they can mobilize communities and speak of the disastrous outcomes caused by political injustice and the violation of human rights.

The State of the Field—Theatre and Migration

The academic field of theatre and migration has been developing since the early 2000s. It includes many important contributions. Marc Maufort (2003), Helen Gilbert and Jacqueline Lo (2007), Silvija Jestrović (2013), Emma Cox (2014, 2015), Charlotte McIvor (2016), S. E. Wilmer (2018), Szalbosc Musca (2019) and Yana Meerzon et al. (2020) wrote extensively on the theme of theatre and migration. Alison Jeffers (2013), Michael Balfour (2013), Mark Fleishman (2015), Azadeh Sharifi and Wilmer (2016), Cox and Caroline Wake (2018), and Anika Marschall (2018) focused their studies on theatre and refugees. Jestrović and Meerzon (2009), Meerzon (2012), Judith Rudakoff (2017), and Elena Marchevska (2017) wrote on theatre and exile, whereas Paul Rae (2006), Gilbert and Jacqueline Lo (2007), Dan Rebellato (2009), Barry Freeman (2017), and Meerzon's latest study (2020) added to this topic asking how globalization, tourism, professional exchanges, and advances in technology are reshaping the world of today into the image of cosmopolitan communities, with this image variously projected on stage.

The work on intercultural theatre (Pavis 1996; Tuan 2010; Knowles 2010, 2017, 2021; Tan 2012; Fischer-Lichte 2014; McIvor and Spangler 2014; Lei and McIvor 2020, Bharucha 2000; to name a few) is also instrumental in how we study and understand the politics and the aesthetics of theatre that reflects global movements. Guy Cools (2015), Royona Mitra (2015), and Lise Uytterhoeven (2019) collectively examine how migration and the sense of multiple belongings affect new work in choreography and contemporary dance.

This list is far from being comprehensive, as it only references books and some articles published in English, omitting many similar works produced worldwide. Despite considerable literature on theatre and cultural nationalism—such as Loren Kruger (1992), Günter Berghaus (1996), Jeffrey Schnapp (1996), Jeffrey D. Mason and J. Ellen Gainor (1999), Wilmer (2001, 2004, 2008), Lionel Pilkington (2001), Helka Mäkinen et al. (2001), Kiki Gouniardou (2005), Jen Harvie (2005), Gerwin Strobl (2007), Jason Shaffer (2007), Manfred Beller and Joep Leerssen (2007), Sonja Arsham Kuftinec (2009), Nadine Holdsworth (2010, 2014), Erin Hurley (2011), David Wiles (2011), and Dariusz Kosinski (2019)—we would like to argue that there is a serious deficiency of academic work addressing the political, educational, and artistic roles that theatre and performance arts can play in resisting nationalist and xenophobic discourses and practices. This handbook stems from our desire to fill the gap and to contour the directions of future research—this aim is reflected in the diverse content of this collection and its layout.

Initial Objectives

We started working on this project in the fall of 2019, aiming at augmenting the historical and multiple geographical dimensions of the conversation on migration and performance arts. One of the objectives was to establish the notion of migration as an umbrella term to discuss very different conditions, roots, and stories of peoples' movement across continents and in various periods of history. Each chapter reflects this idea and so proposes a new and unique reading of migration as it applies to its chosen case study. At the same time, when the COVID pandemic hit, we realized that many assumptions we shared about global migration—its hardships but also, in some cases, its advantages—were to be re-evaluated in the face of this new global disaster. Suddenly, social, racial, cultural, and geographical inequalities that migration reveals have re-emerged. With the introduction of COVID rules and restrictions, many countries—both in the west and in the east, in the north but also in the south—reverted to the worst practices of geo- and biopolitics. Countries began shutting down their borders, refusing medical attention and vaccines for refugees, and abandoning people who had already been thrown into the limbo of displacement when it came to their battle with the pandemic. Once again, COVID revealed that, in the face of humanitarian catastrophe, migrants, asylum seekers, and exiles fall victim to governmental regulations, threats, and politics.

This realization hit us even further in February 2022 when Russia began its unlawful invasion of Ukraine. With more than 5 million people fleeing Ukraine in the first weeks of this war, the issues of asylum seeking, protection, hospitality, compassion, and solidarity rose once again. On 2 March 2022, Slavoj Žižek, published an article 'What Does Defending Europe Mean?' (2022) in which he acknowledged an unprecedented rise in solidarity and empathy that the European governments and citizens demonstrated towards the Ukrainian refugees, the type of solidarity that the European continent, or the world in general, has not seen since the end of the Second World War. At the same time, Žižek warned that 'throughout the region, two species of refugee have emerged.' He reported that the Slovene government had sent a tweet the day after the invasion announcing that '[t]he refugees from Ukraine are coming from an environment which is in its cultural, religious, and historical sense something totally different from the environment out of which refugees from Afghanistan are coming' (quoted in Žižek). The Slovenian government's tweet revealed its own prejudices, and Žižek notes that '[a]fter an outcry, the tweet was quickly deleted, but the obscene truth was out: Europe must defend itself from non-Europe' (2022).

As co-editors of this collection, we find it necessary to keep Žižek's warning in mind and bring back into this discussion Hannah Arendt's statement on the right of any human being for protection and belonging, our 'right to have rights' (1968, 296). This book insists on equality—racial, gender, or age—when it comes to the protection of refugees, as well as on the hospitality and solidarity that each person in flight deserves.

At the same time, migration—and the war in Ukraine specifically—brings to the forefront the extraordinary resilience of theatre artists worldwide. While the theatre in Mariupol was bombed causing hundreds of deaths, theatre artists in Kiev and Odessa looked for new opportunities to perform and resurrect their activities. In Meerzon's interview in June 2022 with Alex Borovenskiy, an artistic director of ProEnglish Theatre in Kyiv, the question of resilience emerged. At the start of the invasion, Borovenskiy and several members of the company decided to stay in Kyiv. Their relocated theatre, which happened to be in the basement of their building, doubled as a shelter for about 25 Kyivites to hide during attacks. They also prepared, played, and streamed two productions on Facebook: Harold Pinter's 1991 play *The New World Order* and a new play called *The Book of Sirens*, which is based on Markus Zusak's 2002 *The Book Thief* and Hector Abad Faciolince's *The Oblivion We Shall Be*. These events not only exemplified the artists' personal bravery; they also were tributes to the power of performance to stand above the reality of horror, to bring people together, and to give them hope. Reflecting this stance, Borovenskiy said when interviewed that his company has adopted 'a new artistic and life motto': 'Art is not an Escape; it is a Statement of Life' (Meerzon 2022). Art, Borovenskiy says, can remind

> theatre makers and their audiences, in Kyiv and around the world, that during the times of war, calamities, natural disasters and any humanitarian crisis, performance arts remain the place of refuge. It is possible that many theatre makers today might feel that their professional skills are not adequate for a war combat, but live theatre can fight differently: it can allow its audiences to seek asylum from the everyday horrors, maybe only for a bit, for an hour or so, but it can give people hope and help them stay in touch with their own humanity. (Meerzon 2022)

Similarly, doing theatre in another land—in a detention camp or for the members of one's community—and using it as an instrument for political struggle or seeking justice, constitutes an act of civil, moral, and artistic responsibility. This book wishes to record, describe, examine, and celebrate these acts. However, before focusing on the specifics of this volume and how the terms 'migration' and 'performance' are treated across its chapters, we would like to speak to the role of the nation-state in limiting the rights of migrants, asylum seekers, and refugees, and examine the ways in which refugees can empower themselves through the arts. With more than 100 million refugees worldwide, it becomes our imperative to give a special space to this concept of empowerment in the book.

Refugees

We emphasize the proliferation of refugees in the twenty-first century as a main topic in the book. As we shall see later in this chapter, the UN has provided its own definition for the term 'refugee,' but the concept is quite vague because of the multiple possibilities for needing refuge. Arendt remarked in 1943 after the German government deprived Jews of their citizenship,

> A refugee used to be a person driven to seek refuge because of some act committed or some political opinion held. Well, it is true we have had to seek refuge; but we committed no acts and most of us never dreamt of having any radical political opinion. […] Now refugees are those of us who have been so unfortunate as to arrive in a new country without means and have to be helped by refugee committees. (Arendt 2007, 264)

Perhaps the same could be said of Ukrainian refugees in 2022.

The causes for becoming a refugee differ significantly from one individual or family to another, and the circumstances are not only diverse but are often in flux. The reasons for leaving home can include religious persecution, sexual violence, ethnic violence or ethnic cleansing, poverty, hunger, war and particularly civil war, climate change, loss of home or habitat, intimidation, threats of violence, fear, dispossession, loss of legal rights, loss of employment, disappearance, death or debilitation of a family member, alteration of national boundaries, imposition of hostile or punitive laws, etc. Likewise, reasons for moving to another place can result from the success of friends and family elsewhere, the prospect of job opportunities, higher wages, better housing, social support, a more favourable climate, a more welcoming environment to practise one's religion or express one's sexual orientation, more equitable laws, more possibilities for integration, naturalization, and citizenship, an opportunity to reunite with family, friends, religious, or ethnic group, or simply to escape danger. In some cases, decisions to move are taken by individuals and in other cases encouraged or enforced by authorities who organise coordinated evacuations as a result of uninhabitable conditions produced by military conflict, nuclear disaster, volcanic eruption, flood, wildfires, landslides, drought, chemical or biological contamination, or by the redrawing of political or ethnic boundaries or government policies of resettlement. Furthermore, refugees can pay huge sums to traffickers seeking to make money from guiding or transporting them across borders. Women and children are particularly vulnerable to sexual exploitation in return for 'safe' passage to another country. Refugees can also be exploited by governments (such as Belarus) as pawns in provocative geopolitical attacks, enticing refugees to cross into neighbouring countries that will not accept them. Refugees can be differentiated, for instance, by their ethnicity, gender, age, mobility, health, language, sexual orientation, nationality, skills, financial resources, employability, and size and age of family members. Thus, we can say that refugees are highly differentiated individuals and not just statistics.

Moreover, terms such as nomad, migrant, displaced person, asylum seeker, stateless person as well as refugee are often misleading categories and tend to converge. For example, in reviewing the period after the First World War, Giorgio Agamben observed, '[m]any refugees, who were not technically stateless, preferred to become such rather than return to their country' (2000, 17). In a 'Treatise on Nomadology' from *A Thousand Plateaus*, Gilles Deleuze and Félix Guattari tried to differentiate between nomads and migrants:

> The nomad distributes himself in a smooth space; he occupies, inhabits, holds that space; that is his territorial principle. It is therefore false to define the nomad by movement. Toynbee is profoundly right to suggest that the nomad is on the contrary *he who does not move*. Whereas the migrant leaves behind a milieu that has become amorphous or hostile, the nomad is one who does not depart, does not want to depart. […] If the nomad can be called the Deterritorialized par excellence, it is precisely because there is no reterritorialization *afterward* as with the migrant […]. (1987, 420–21, emphasis original)

However, contrary to what Deleuze and Guattari argue, migrants do not always succeed in reterritorializing and nor do refugees. The refugee sometimes succeeds only in deterritorializing because the process of reterritorialization may be too long and arduous or too difficult to achieve, and possibly endless. Often, the refugee is stopped at national borders, deported, or held in a refugee camp or detention centre, or dies on route. Moreover, nomads can also reterritorialize by evolving into today's settled citizens as their conditions for survival and employment become more sedentary or governments impose restrictions on their movement or force them to migrate to the cities or to other places. Likewise, forcibly displaced persons, who are more numerous today than ever, reaching more than 100 million in 2022 (UNHCR 2022), can behave more like nomads in certain circumstances, wanting to return home when the current danger has passed rather than settling in another location, as with those internally displaced by the wars in Syria and Ukraine. Thus, Deleuze and Guattari's distinction between the migrant and the nomad does not necessarily hold true because the lives of such individuals (including refugees and displaced persons) are in flux and evolving, rather than static.

Also, refugees sometimes move with others for self-protection as heterogeneous groups of different nationalities and languages, as in the processions of refugees from Greece towards Western Europe in 2015 and from Latin America towards the United States in 2019. Such processions form and reform. Individuals and families drop out while others continue. They move at different paces, some trying to keep up, others falling away or taking different routes. Thus, arguably, rather than being distinct, the trajectories of the migrant, the refugee, the stateless person, and the nomad overlap. In a sense they are all minority-becomings, transforming cultural roles and social norms, and sometimes merge into each other.

Terminology: From Migration to Exile

The Palgrave Handbook on Theatre and Migration is envisioned with these ambiguities in mind. It presents a wide survey of theatre and performance practices related to the experience of global movements. The title of the book focuses on the word 'theatre,' but the contributions in this volume look at many varieties of performing arts, including puppetry, street and cultural performances, immersive theatres, performance activism, dance, and circus. These performance forms all go beyond the notion of 'theatre' as a designated space for the encounter between the stage and the audience. Each contributor has adopted their own definition of theatre arts in relation to their individual projects.

When it comes to the term 'migration,' we have likewise opted for the most capacious understanding of this word. According to UNESCO's *Glossary of Migration Related Terms*, the word 'migration' refers to

> the crossing of the boundary of a political or administrative unit for a certain minimum period of time. It includes the movement of refugees, displaced persons, uprooted people as well as economic migrants. Internal migration refers to a move from one area (a province, district or municipality) to another within one country. International migration is a territorial relocation of people between nation-states. […]
>
> The dominant forms of migration can be distinguished according to the motives (economic, family reunion, refugees) or legal status (irregular migration, controlled emigration/immigration, free emigration/immigration) of those concerned. (*Glossary*)

Stephen Castles distinguishes between 'internal migration' as movement of people within one country 'from one area to another' and 'international migration as 'crossing of frontiers' of different countries (2000, 269). Accordingly, migration—both internal and international—is the major factor of today's globalization and creation of multi-ethnic states. But, Castles notes, it can be very difficult to come up with any conclusive, inclusive, or even accurate definition of migration, since such movements can be 'the result of state policies, introduced in response to political and economic goals and public attitudes' (2000, 270). Thus, international migration is often understood as problematic: 'something to be controlled and even curbed' (Castles 2000, 270). Different countries and their governments create extensive systems of control and navigation of peoples' movements, all recognized under the umbrella concept of international migration. Such systems differentiate between temporary labour migrants, highly skilled and business migrants, irregular migrants (or undocumented/illegal migrants), refugees, asylum seekers, people on the move from forced migration, but also migrants who come to unite with their families and even return migrants: 'people who return to their countries of origin after a period in another country' (Castles 2000, 271). Using 'migration system theory,' Castles concludes that migration is not only the major factor of globalization, but that it is also a force that can be seen as 'eroding the power of the nation-state' (2000, 278). Consequently, the state finds it more and more difficult to control peoples' movement, which results in increased security measures and border-control functions. The failure on the part of nation-states to accommodate and integrate large numbers of people within their territory and economic systems leads to the phenomenon of 'statelessness' (Castles 2000, 279). Together with climate change and war conflicts, this phenomenon functions as a major catalyst for creating 'refugees' and 'asylum seekers.'

When it comes to governing systems dealing with other types of migrants, some countries opt to using such terms as permanent residents, immigrants, or skilled workers.

For example, in a country like Canada, whose economic growth has been reliant on importing a foreign workforce since the country's independence in 1867, newcomers can seek a status of 'permanent residents' within four major streams of migration. These streams are (1) economic migration, which welcomes 'economic immigrants [who] come through federal high-skilled worker programs'; it is based on a point system 'that gives preference to younger candidates with job offers and high levels of education, experience, and language proficiency (i.e., English and French)'; (2) the Provincial Nominee Program, which invites foreigners to apply for their resettlement in a specific province, 'which choose[s] candidates who fill their economic needs'; (3) the family class that refers to 'spouses, partners, and children joining family members already living in Canada. Under this program, legal permanent residents apply to sponsor their relatives, who must also apply for permanent residency'; and, finally, (4) 'protected persons and refugees,' which can be either government-assisted or privately sponsored (Cheatham 2022). In Canada, 'Government-assisted refugees are referred by the UN High Commissioner for Refugees based on their location and vulnerability, and receive government assistance during their transition. Privately sponsored refugees, who accounted for more than half of resettled refugees in 2020, are brought to Canada by government-approved citizens and organizations that assume legal and financial responsibility for them' (Cheatham 2022).[1]

Migration is (of course) political, and (therefore) we should see the state's categorization of would-be migrants not as just factual categorizing of people like a grocer (we have three apples, four oranges, two bananas, and one tangerine), but ideological and political ones, bound up with both political economic concerns and modelling liberal forms of good citizenry in imagined communities. The contributors of this book offer, amongst other critical contributions, ways of problematizing categories of migration that appear, at first glance, stable and well-defined.

However, for centuries, people talked about migration in terms of exile. According to the Cambridge English Dictionary, 'exile' means either a person or a condition of 'being sent or kept away from their own country, village, etc., especially for political reasons.' In Biblical terms, exile refers to a condition of living away from one's own country; for example, a group (like the Israelites) who were forced to leave their homeland and are waiting to return. In ancient Greece, the Athenian democratic law shaped the political identity and the immunity of its polis. It used exile as a form of punishment and as a mechanism of self-defence: it helped the city to conceptualize 'what the Athenians "were not" with an actual act of physical separation, thus vividly enacting the creation of community through the exclusion of an "other"' (Forsdyke 2005, 7).

Political exile—an act of removal and banishment—remains one of the most powerful paradigms of physical, spatial, and temporal separation from one's native land. Accordingly, the word 'exile' evokes the meanings of trauma, muteness, impossibility of reconciliation, and the deficiency of any personal or collective closure. But it also signifies a displacement and a falling out of time phenomenon. Following this tradition, Edward Said defines exile as a metaphor of death and suggests a view of the exilic journey as a crossing of the River Styx from the world of the living (the homeland) to the world of the dead (the new land) (Said 2000, 174). In his definition, Said reinforces a long-standing tradition of seeing exile as regret, doubt, sorrow, and nostalgia.

Today, the word 'exile' does not really appear within the legal vocabulary of nation-states. Neither the Human Rights nor Refugee Conventions refer to it. We tend to think of 'exile' in emotional and psychological terms, and we often use it to speak about peoples' personal experiences and collective memory, and to create conditions of solidarity and compassion. Exile, we might want to suggest, invites the work of reflection: it encourages one to think of the history of mankind and its current moment, as one of history's variables: the gaze of an exilic artist, as Joseph Brodsky would state, is simultaneously turned into one's past and one's future (Brodsky 1995, 27).

In this book, case studies refer to numerous variants of peoples' movement and displacement, both in their involuntary and voluntary forms. Many

---

[1] As a result, in 2021 Canada granted the status of permanent residency to more than 400,000 foreign subjects, with the majority being skilled professionals from India (Cheatham 2022).

chapters speak of refugees and asylum seeking, whereas others focus on exile (internal and external) and emigration/immigration, but also environmental and climate migration, slavery as forced relocation, as well as cosmopolitan travel and self-identification. Once again, every chapter carefully crafts its own focus point on migration and provides a theoretical framework and methodology to study the chosen phenomenon. Collectively the book indicates more than 150 ways in which we can speak of migration today, and it is structured in six sections.

Section One (Theatre and Migration: Themes and Concepts) is devoted to the major theoretical concepts related to peoples' movement, including exile, refuge, displacement, asylum seeking, colonialism, human rights, globalization, and nomadism, to name a few. The subsequent sections contain case studies across various geographies and time periods that highlight, describe, and analyse different theatre practices related to migration.

We open the book with 'The Eternal Immigrant and the Aesthetics of Solidarity' in which Silvija Jestrović discusses well-known tropes and experiences of exile, such as internal rift and disconnect that mark individual experiences. At the same time, Jestrović focuses our attention on how the ongoing crisis of migration, and specifically the worldwide crisis of refugee movements, impacts our discussions, imaginings, responses, and representations of the exilic figure. Speaking of exilic matrix and exilic heterotopia, she considers the aesthetic of solidarity as a set of strategies to destabilise the symbolic mise-en-scene of exile.

Freddie Rokem continues this conversation by working with the notion of exile as a state of exception, as put forward by Walter Benjamin in his famous essay 'On the Concept of History,' which he wrote to reflect his own experience as a refugee at the beginning of the Second World War. To Benjamin 'the state of exception'—which speaks both to the principles of authoritarianism and displacement—has become the norm and is no longer an exception, and thus, Benjamin hopes for a real state of exception, for example, that of not being persecuted.

An extreme example of the state of exception is the German judicial system imposed on Jews during the Holocaust. Lisa Peschel recalls the performances developed in the desperate conditions of the Terezín/Theresienstadt ghetto to which theatre artists had been deported by the Nazi government. Despite the woeful circumstances, theatre artists tried to keep the inmates' hopes alive by scripting and performing imaginary and utopian futures for their audiences.

Steve Wilmer's chapter 'Refugees and the Right to Have Rights' puts the conversation on exile, refugees, and the state of exception in the context of Human Rights, as it was discussed and critiqued by Hannah Arendt, Giorgio Agamben, and Jacques Rancière. The philosophers collectively and variously argue, as Wilmer outlines, that, while the nation-state privileges the rights of its citizens, it arbitrarily undermines the status of the refugee. In his chapter, Wilmer examines the ways in which theatre performances can oppose the disenfranchising actions of the nation-state.

Azadeh Sharifi continues this dialogue on migration, refugees, and the nation-state, now in application to what is called a postmigrant theatre and second- and third-generation migrants. Sharifi's geographical focus is contemporary German theatre, in which this artistic movement emerged. She names and analyses artistic strategies of resistance to the homogenizing narrative of the nation-state as developed in postmigrant theatre.

Brian Singleton brings the conversation on resisting homogenous narratives to the question of blending different styles of theatre. He surveys the history of intercultural theatre practices as an example of seeking new languages of performance to express multiple encounters between people on the move, and more importantly how these political and artistic processes relate to the practices of migration. Singleton offers a widely and carefully conceived overview of the term 'interculturalism.' By acknowledging multiple contestations of the binarism inherent in the term 'interculturalism,' and a shift in focus from aestheticism to subjectivities (Fischer-Lichte 2014; Mitra 2015), Singleton reveals the proximity between intercultural performances and migration.

Following Singleton's lead to connect politics and aesthetics, Meerzon and Julija Pešić turn to another contested term, 'cosmopolitanism,' which they define as 'the troublesome offset of global migration.' The authors invite us to think about cosmopolitanism as one's worldview, an ethical behaviour based on modes of mobility and responsibility for the other. The chapter recognizes that advocating for cosmopolitanism can be problematic in today's world, but it invites readers to consider cosmopolitanism as a state of non-belonging, which produces anxiety in settled populations, and fosters simultaneity, relationality, and a-temporality; all of which define the subjectivity of a contemporary migrant.

The next several chapters focus on aspects of theatre and migration that have been significantly overlooked and undertheorized till now. With the active calls for decolonization, anti-racism, and the need for better work on diversity, the field of theatre and migration studies is now seeking new understandings of how colonialism contributed to migration. Sara Pillatzki-Warzeha and Margaret Werry address the issues of Indigenous migrations and the practice of survivance by indigenous North Americans. They argue that despite some popular assumptions of Indigenous identity as 'a continuous attachment to specific, ancestral territory, and to traditional lifeways rooted in that place,' making migrancy and indigeneity a difficult (if not impossible) tension to resolve, more recent scholarship, to which this chapter further adds, proposes to consider mobility as one of the integral features that make Indigenous modernities. Situating performance practices of the Indigenous diasporas in North America within this theoretical framework, the authors activate the criticism of such colonial assumptions and operations of power. By introducing the discourse of migration studies into their discussion of the construction of Indigeneity, the authors focus on those theatres of the US urban centres that investigate Indigenous experiences of exile and challenge our assumptions about settler-colonialism to enable the politics and the ethos of survivance.

Focusing on the theatre work by Winsome Pinnock and Kwame Kwei Armah, Harvey Young not only moves the conversation on migration and colonialism forward; he also introduces the notion of 'migratory blackness' to discuss the movements, experiences, and perspectives of black migrants in predominantly white places. Young uses the Windrush generation and their descendants as his case study and demonstrates how the violent heritage of colonialism continues for many racialized people who continue struggling with anti-Black racism in the United Kingdom. Young reminds us that the impact of colonialism has been unfolding through the twentieth century and has not stopped today. But, as he demonstrates, the landing of a thousand Jamaican migrants in England in June 1948 represented a shift in the colonial logic of the British Empire. As newcomers to the United Kingdom, they faced hardships similar to those of other migrants, but their encounters with the culture of the colonizer, now in the colonizer's own land, mobilized grassroots activism about race, national identity, and belonging.

The last two chapters that comprise this section take the conversation of performance and migration into new directions related to climate change and digital realities. Paul Rae, in his contribution 'Climate Migration and Performance,' studies a range of traditional performance forms of the central Pacific nation of Kiribati. Echoing the contribution by Pillatzki-Warzeha and Werry, Rae carefully studies how closely and deeply Kiribati performance is linked to their land and seas. He outlines strategies of resistance and activism as found in the Pacific region, which actively pushes back against the idea of climate migration; but at the same time, he puts forward difficult questions about survival, should the situation emerge when the people of Kiribati find themselves in need to leave their homeland and assume the role of eternal exile. With this image, we circle back to Jestrović's argument on our need to re-think the concepts of exile, migration, and solidarity, to realize that the climate threats in the Pacific are as urgent as in many other parts of the world, and hence make migration a feasible scenario for their future survival.

Matthew Causey focuses on another unprecedented cause for migration as prompted by the economic and technological developments in the twenty-first century. He argues that we have entered the epoch of the digital and the virtual, which also enables the performance of self via social media. These digital dislocations, he asserts, are 'no less real because of their virtuality.' Intensified by the global pandemic, these digital migrations present both threats and advantages to how we have been making and experiencing theatre for ages.

Section Two (Early Representations of Migration) includes essays on some of the ancient forms of drama. They illustrate how migration has always featured as a theme in theatrical practice and dramaturgy. The first article concerns perhaps the earliest known performance text, the Babylonian epic poem *Gilgamesh*, which has been adapted over the years into many theatrical forms such as opera, ballet, drama, and recently (by the Akram Khan company) as contemporary dance. Martin Worthington, a specialist in Babylonian and

Assyrian literature, who acted as a consultant for the use of Babylonian in the Marvel Studios 2021 superhero film production of *Eternals*, reveals how *Gilgamesh* depicts epic journeys and inhuman transformations. The hero transgresses the barriers between the earthly and the superhuman, encounters strange creatures, and undergoes mystical adventures, ultimately returning home after a fruitless quest to become immortal. Despite a fanciful plot, Worthington shows how contemporary theatre—like the Irish company Macnas that turned their theatrical version of the epic into a film during the COVID pandemic—can avail of Babylonian mythology to comment on contemporary issues today, such as the anthropogenic destruction of the planet.

Moving from ancient Babylon to ancient India, H. S. Shivaprakash and J. Sreenivasa Murthy discuss the *Natyashastra*, the Indian equivalent of Aristotle's *Poetics*. This Sanskrit text provides a mythological origin to the art of theatre, with gods and humans arguing over what should be performed and reaching a compromise. Shivaprakash and Murthy describe the proliferation of ancient theatrical practices such as their themes, forms, and languages in various regions of India. Pointing out that the rigid caste system did not prevent different castes working together, the chapter provides many details of early touring and performance practices, noting how they spread across the vast area of India and beyond.

Turning to ancient Greece, Rush Rehm points out that various characters in ancient Greek tragedies such as Oedipus, Philoctetes, Medea, Orestes, and Heracles suffer from exile. He also observes that many characters and members of choruses are slaves who have been forced to live far from home, such as Cassandra who becomes a sexual slave of Agamemnon. Rehm argues that these plays often contained political messages for their huge Athenian audiences that still resonate today. For example, the Athenian population prided themselves in their practice of welcoming strangers and demonstrated support for the notion of hospitality (*philoxenia*) in their dramas. Thus, Aeschylus's *Suppliant Women*, about Egyptian women threatening to hang themselves if not accorded protection, are saved by a vote from the citizens of Argos, a favourable allusion to the democratic system newly introduced in Athens. Likewise, *Sons of Heracles* by Euripides, about children fleeing for their lives, portrays a successful appeal for sanctuary. Moreover, when the malevolent character who had pursued them is tried, the Athenians refuse to execute him because they regard the murder of war-captives as illegal—a stance apposite to the current Russian invasion of Ukraine.

Departing from tragedy, C.W. Marshall reviews the theme of migration in many ancient Greek and Roman comedies. He considers the influence of the Peloponnesian War which motivated many of the comedic moments in ancient Greek comedy, such as the draft dodgers and prisoners of war in Aristophanes's *Acharnians* and *Birds*. Like Rehm, Marshall takes a particular interest in the themes of abduction, sexual slavery, and female trafficking which played a large role in Roman comedies, such as Plautus's *The Menaechmi* and *Rudens*. Marshall also points out the surprisingly sympathetic characterization in

Terence's *Andria* of a female migrant who becomes a prostitute to avoid poverty.

Far from the physical realities of asylum seekers and female victims, Miki Iwata takes us to a more nebulous and purgatorial world in ancient Japan where unsettled and migrating spirits in Japanese nō plays wander in search of solace. Iwata discusses the origins of nō theatre as a travelling art form featuring migration as a major theme. Often in these plays a travelling Buddhist monk encounters a person who turns out to be a disconsolate ghost oscillating between their past life and their present death, longing to find rest from past calamities.

Moving forward in time, Carol Sorgenfrei demonstrates the vertical migration of nō texts from the medieval era to the present. She examines the various transformations of *The Tale of Genji*, an eleventh-century novel by the female writer Murasaki Shikibu that was adapted as a nō play, and has been variously reinterpreted by male authors more recently, Sorgenfrei explains the context and social meaning of the original novel within a patriarchal society and demonstrates how later interpretations of the play have not successfully reflected the coping strategy of the protagonist and the viewpoint of the original author.

Miranda Fay Thomas observes that most of Shakespeare's plays are set abroad. While there are many variations on the theme of migration, such as shipwreck in *Twelfth Night* and *The Tempest* and abandonment in *King Lear*, Thomas analyses notions of exile that feature in his oeuvre, as in the ever-popular *Romeo and Juliet* and the lesser-known *Pericles*. Thomas considers the inclusion of diverse characters such as Othello, Caliban, and Shylock as well as the characterization of females and argues that Shakespeare's plays tended to gratify a white male public and reinforced both class entitlement and social prejudices—concerns that persist today and have been explored in recent productions.

M. A. Katritzky demonstrates how the rise of professional theatre in the German-speaking regions of Early Modern Europe reflected the touring practices of theatre, specifically when mixed-gender French and Italian acting troupes joined the migrant actors of all-male English companies. As Katritzky argues, comedy, and specifically stage clowns, like Pickelhering, were the most popular among itinerant troupes and genres. Their humour happened to be relatable to various European audiences and hence it mobilized further the ideas and the practice of theatrical transnationalism.

Erith Jaffe-Berg continues this conversation on transnational trade practices with a survey of itinerant performances, migrations, and cultural navigations on the Early Modern Italian stages. Specifically, she studies the ways Christian *commedia dell'arte* performers and non-Christian performers, including Jewish and Turkish itinerant artists, interacted with each other on stage.

As we can see in these early forms, migration has been an important theme and practice from the earliest days of theatre. Whether in comedy or tragedy, migration has appeared as an area of common concern, reflecting the social issues of the day. Whether it was the role of leadership in *Gilgamesh*, the questioning of the Indian caste system in the *Natyasastra*, the importance of hospitality in *Suppliant Women*, or the representation of females in *Tale of Genji* and Shakespearean drama, these plays all reflect their social context and reveal ideological prejudices about migrating people as opposed to settled populations.

Section Three (Migration and Nationalism) moves on from ancient, medieval, and renaissance worlds to more recent times to assess the link between nationalist politics and governmental control of migration. We have witnessed this especially with the financial collapse of western banks and institutions in 2008 and particularly since the flight of refugees from the Syrian war in 2015. In the last decade nationalist politics has produced some disturbing results such as the British exit from the European Union (Brexit), the increasing influence of anti-immigration politicians in many parts of Europe (especially France and Austria), the elections of right-wing leaders such as Donald Trump in the United States, Jair Bolsonaro in Brazil, Viktor Orbán in Hungary, the Law and Justice party in Poland, and the Russian invasion of Ukraine on the premise that Ukraine is Russian. The chapters in this section relate to the perception of immigrants, the conditions of exile, and the question of national identity in various countries.

May Summer Farnsworth recounts the changing role of *criollo* (native-born Argentinian) and *gringo* (European immigrant) characters on the Argentinian stage as a reaction to social change and assimilation pressures in the late nineteenth and early twentieth centuries. She shows how the plays in the early years tended to make fun of different stereotypes, but later these comparisons took on a darker tone as the characters and their difficulties in their social environment became more realistic.

Kasia Lech discusses the role of Polish nineteenth-century artists in exile and their deployment of the theme of the mother (of the nation) and her son who longs for a country which has been destroyed by imperial forces, as in the work of Adam Mickiewicz (*Forefathers' Eve*) and Juliusz Słowacki. Lech also demonstrates how this nationalist theme has influenced more recent artists such as Sławomir Mrożek, Janusz Głowacki, and Martyna Majok.

Sarit Cofman-Simhon analyses the theatrical output in Israel-Palestine concerning three types of migrating people and their relative status in the nation-state: European Jews migrating to Israel amidst the Holocaust, Palestinians displaced after the 1948 war, and the recent arrival of African migrant labourers and refugees. She shows that African immigrants rarely feature on the main stages and, when they had appeared, they were presented in a light-hearted way that did not make the audience feel guilty for neglecting their needs.

The next group of chapters reveal the problems for people whose immigrant cultural background does not accord with the prevailing notion of national identity, thereby impeding their access to leading theatre venues. Naphtaly Shem-Tov considers the precarious position in Israel of the immigrant actor from an Arab country. He focuses on Aryeh Elias who emigrated from Iraq and whose Arabic accent prevented him from being cast as a major protagonist on the main Israeli stages. Although popular in films and as a character actor, Elias always regretted not being able to land more substantial roles on the stage such as Shylock in *The Merchant of Venice*. Like Shem-Tov, Art Babayants considers the question of access by immigrant artists. He questions the terminology of 'immigrant artist' as it applies in the context of Canadian theatre, observing the difficulties for theatre workers who do not conform to the French or English norm and are relegated to fringe theatre productions. In the light of Russia's nationalist (as well as imperialist) policies, Mark Simon and Varvara Sklez survey the problems for migrant artists from other regions of the former Soviet Union to find work in Moscow's theatres. Generally, Russian nationalist policies have impeded migrant theatre artists and discouraged themes about the migration of ethnic minorities from being presented on the main drama stages. Their chapter indicates, however, that, despite the general resistance to migrant theatre makers, the policies of Teatr.Doc in Moscow have offered an unusual avenue for their work.

Turning to the United States, Jorge Huerta demonstrates the divisive impact of US immigration policies on Mexican families. Long a source for migrant labour in the United States, Mexicans have often suffered from arbitrary changes in governmental border policies depending on whether their labour was required or not. As an expert on Chicano/a drama, Huerta reviews the role that Chicano theatre has played in challenging US government practices. He focuses on *La Víctima*, a play developed by El Teatro de la Esperanza, that represents the tragic result when the son of a Mexican woman becomes a US border guard and deports his own mother. Natalie Álvarez and Jimena Ortúzar also comment on the difficulties for Latin Americans coming to the United States. They describe a provocative performance in the parking lot of a Home Depot store in Los Angeles, where migrant labourers re-enact scenes of urban warfare to call attention to the horrendous conditions in their homes in Guatemala. As the shoppers go about their daily chores in the mall, they encounter the Guatemalans exposing the violence that has impelled them to flee their country.

With their well-known greeting 'céad míle fáilte' (a hundred thousand welcomes), the Irish might be expected to have integrated refugees enthusiastically, especially given that Ireland had been an emigrant nation for two centuries before numerous immigrants from Europe and Africa started arriving around 2000. However, Charlotte McIvor points out that Irish society has failed to appreciate its own increasing complexity. The Irish theatre has tended to repeat a trope of historical duty to integrate foreigners by focusing on the asylum seeker from the global south rather than acknowledging the arrival of other types of immigrants. Focusing on the recent productions of *Mouth of a Shark* by Maeve Stone and Oonagh Murphy and *The Beach* by Brokentalkers, which emphasize the failure of the nation and the people to support the needs of victimized minorities, McIvor suggests that other stories are waiting to be told.

This section concludes with Guy Cools's contribution on multilingualism, migration, and homecoming in the work of two prominent European choreographers: the Belgian-Moroccan Sidi Larbi Cherkaoui and the

British-Bangladeshi Akram Khan, whose work, Cools stipulates, is considered exemplary for many contemporary European artists who grew up in-between cultures. Cherkaoui and Khan spent years to investigate and celebrate their multiple identities. In their artistic work they not only problematize the notion of 'second generation migrants,' but also engage with the idea of cosmopolitan roots, echoed in one's search for the 'antithetical notion of "home."' Heteroglossia and in-betweenness characterize their artistic language, which envisions dialogue as the only positive way forward that migration—be it exile, freely chosen travelling, or asylum seeking—can make possible.

The chapters in this section consider prevailing notions of identity in different countries and how they have affected the representation and employment of immigrants. Natphtaly Shem-Tov, Art Babayants, and Varvara Sklez and Mark Simon demonstrate the difficulties that immigrant theatre makers encounter in seeking to appear on the main stages in Israel, Canada, and Russia. Jorge Huerta and Natalie Álvarez and Jimena Ortuzar illustrate the survival tactics for Latin American migrant labourers in the United States, while Charlotte McIvor and Guy Cools reveal the complex problems for immigrant theatre workers trying to represent their own personas despite normalized perceptions of national identity in Ireland, the United Kingdom, and Belgium.

Section Four (Migration, Colonialism, and Forced Displacement) focuses on the difficult tension between migration and colonialism. It speaks to a variety of peoples' movements related to this tension, including colonial conquests and travelling, inspired by ideas of geographical discovery but also ambitions for imperial expansion. It also addresses the tragic aspects of colonization, including racism, slavery, human trafficking, and different forms of nationalist and ethnic prejudice.

Samuel Ravengai examines theatrical performances reflecting the displacement of populations in southern Africa. His chapter provides a comprehensive survey of how European immigrants moved to what we know today as South Africa and Zimbabwe. Looking at a variety of plays, which responded differently to these movements, Ravengai introduces notions of liberatory nationalism (Europhobia), African indigenes, and Afrophobia to study turbulences that took place during the moments of encounter between European immigrants and indigenous people in Africa, and by Africans migrating more recently to South Africa.

Bisi Adigun continues this conversation with his contribution to Yoruba travelling theatre and the work of Wole Soyinka. He argues that migration within Nigeria and across the borders of the country, but also the practices of migration into Nigeria, have widely shaped Nigerian theatre, particularly, from the era of the Yoruba travelling theatre to the year Soyinka received the Nobel Prize in Literature.

In her chapter 'Migratory Subjectivities and African Diasporic Theatre: Race, Gender, and Nation,' Nicosia Shakes dismantles the myths of migration by focusing on how race, gender, and colonialism contribute to the formation of intersecting identities based on peoples' experiences and accounts of relocating into the new lands. Using the framework of Black and decolonial feminism as well as African Diasporic theories, Shakes builds her arguments in relation to Carole Boyce Davies's (1994) concept of 'migratory subjectivities' and Jamaican experiences with migration. Grappling with the racialized meaning of such terms as 'immigrant,' 'emigrant,' and 'expatriate,' and obvious difficulty in framing slavery and slave within the discourses of migration studies, Shakes recognizes this context as 'the main historical system that [...] initiated the major composition of the modern African Diaspora.' In her analysis of several plays and productions that stage the experience of Jamaican migrants in England and the United States, Shakes provides a fierce critique of the oppressive conditions of race, gender, nationality, and sexuality that Black women have experienced and continue experiencing through international travel.

Selim Rauer takes this discussion of migration and colonialism further, centring his analysis on the history of colonization by France in Africa and the Middle East. He begins his survey from 1981, the year François Mitterrand was elected as President of the French Republic. With a leftist government, Rauer demonstrates, a new generation of artists and activists from Caribbean, North-African, and sub-Saharan backgrounds came onto the French theatre scene. These artists addressed the notion of the 'Grande Nation' with its imperialistic memory and post-colonial present, as well as what Rauer calls 'immobile relegation' as socio-historical and artistic experiences that fostered the production of new hybrid identities such as Afropeanism and Marronage culture.

Christy Stanlake brings yet another geography into this discussion of migration and colonization. In her chapter 'Storying Home: Retracing the Trail of Tears to Restore *Ekvnvcakv*,' Stanlake studies the traumatic history of settler-colonialism in the United States, which resulted in Indigenous peoples' mass displacement. This displacement continued through several decades and took many forms, including the Trail of Tears, when Native Americans were forcefully removed from their ancestral homelands in the eastern United States. Using the theoretical framework of Native American authors, including US Poet Laureate Joy Harjo (Muscogee Creek) and Yvette Nolan (Algonquin), Stanlake criticizes the application of the term 'exile' to these experiences; instead, she studies how Native theatre practices transform the legal language and meaning we associate with sovereignty into a specific cultural practice, when a theatre performance turns into a ceremonial space of one's re-connection with their homeland and a chance of healing to everyone who was ever pushed away from it.

Moving focus to Asia, Daphne Lei recounts the forced migration from mainland China to Taiwan at the end of the Chinese civil war and the attempt to preserve cultural values. She investigates the preservation of *Jingju* (Beijing opera, Peking opera) which the military troops brought to Taiwan. Unaffected by the Cultural Revolution in mainland China that abandoned the form, *Jingju* thrived and developed new aspects in Taiwan.

While South Koreans have been lauded for their entrepreneurial skills, Ju Yon Kim recalls the multiple displacements and hardships for Korean Women as a result of the Japanese occupation, the Second World War, the American military occupation, and the Korean War. She recounts the social issues that emerged such as the stigma of prostitution and miscegenation, and the abandoned children of mixed-race marriages, and she reveals the waves of emigration by Koreans to the United States. Undermining the stereotypes of hapless Korean women being saved by Americans, she analyses the theatrical work that has exposed the lives of Korean American families and the misogyny, racism, and violence that affect the women.

Hala Khamis Nassar laments the Israeli practice of settler colonialism and their occupation of Palestinian lands that has resulted in thousands of forcibly displaced Palestinians. Nassar recounts the history of Palestinian disenfranchisement and dispossession since the *naqba* (catastrophe), and she demonstrates the importance of theatre in educating the current population about this history, especially conveyed in recent docudramas such as *Taha* and *The Alley*.

In 'Ukrainian Theatre in Migration: Military Anthropology Perspective,' Robert Baroch and Anna Korzeniowska-Bihun discuss the difficulties for the performing arts during the ongoing war in the Donbas since 2014 and the Russian invasion in 2022. They investigate the efforts of theatre to counter the effects of Russian propaganda and address the needs of displaced people from eastern Ukraine, focusing on the work of two groups: the Theatre of Displaced People (TDP) and the Luhansk Regional Theatre (LRT). The TDP has worked as a therapeutic organization trying to bring together young audiences and youth groups affected by the division of the Donbas region, and the LRT has been mounting more conventional performances while being forced to move twice to escape the encroaching war. Their article demonstrates the realities of war-time theatre in ever-changing circumstances as an aggressive Russian government tries to reassert its control over an independent country.

The chapters in this section consider the role of theatre makers amongst oppressed populations trying to reassert their dignity and power. Ravengai notes how South African performances today revise dominant narratives of colonial history. Shakes and Kim reveal the continuous struggle for empowerment by Jamaican and Korean-American women, and Rauer points out the oppressed conditions and 'immobile relegation' of immigrants to France from former colonies as conveyed in recent drama. Lei witnesses the survival of Jingju theatre traditions in Taiwan by the forced evacuation of performers from mainland China. Stanlake and Nassar consider the legacy of settler-colonialism in the United States and Israel and the effort of American Indian and Palestinian theatre makers to reassert their place in society despite the efforts of colonial powers to remove them. Likewise, Ukrainian theatre makers, as discussed by Baroch and Korzeniowska-Bihun, are resisting Russia's efforts at imperial expansion by claiming their own right to sovereignty. This conversation about forced displacement anticipates our next section in the book, focused on the experiences of refugees and how theatre practices can be reflective of them.

Section Five (Refugees) reveals the vast array of dramatic work portraying refugees. These chapters reflect the role that the nation-state plays in controlling the movement of people within and across their borders. As Thomas Nail writes,

> the migrant has been predominantly understood from the perspective of *states*. Since the state has all too often written history, the migrant has been understood as a figure without its own history and social force. 'In world history,' as Hegel says, 'we are concerned only with those peoples that have formed states [because] all the value that human beings possess, all of their spiritual reality, they have through the State alone.' (Nail 2015a, 4, emphasis original)

The chapters in this section address this neglected history, demonstrating the precarious status of the non-citizen who is often dependent on voluntary support, artistic or otherwise. Many of the chapters concern activist and politically motivated work. While some address perennial concerns, others reflect particularly difficult social conditions.

Marilena Zaroulia considers the juxtaposition of two periods of migration in Greek history as they come together in a site-specific performance of *I Left* by the Station Athens theatre group: the displacement of the Greek and Turkish populations resulting from the war between Greece and Turkey after the First World War, and the 2015 influx of refugees from the Middle East and Africa, both of which raise questions about the immigrant as foreign other.

Marco Galea points out the reluctance of Maltese theatre to deal with the thorny political issue of refugees, given the relatively easy access to this small island state for African and Middle Eastern migrants crossing the Mediterranean. He discusses two exceptions to this trend, one of which is a one-man street performance sympathetic to the plight of the refugees, and the other is a more mainstream and less empathic opera financed by the state.

Andrés Pérez-Simón illustrates the advent of African immigrant characters in Spanish drama from the 1990s influenced by the work of the French playwright Bernard-Marie Koltès. Pérez-Simón reviews various plays written by both male and female Spanish playwrights that have depicted African immigrants in Spain, and especially Angélica Liddell's satirical performance of *And the Fish Rose Up to Make War Against Mankind* about fish arriving in Spain after consuming dead migrants in the sea.

Caroline Wake analyses the changing strategies of Australian theatre practitioners to contest the governmental treatment and detention of asylum seekers. She shows how early performances favoured documentary forms whereas more hybrid approaches were later employed to confront the issue. More recently, Wake proposes, theatre makers have tended to question the efficacy of theatre, given that the government has tended to repeat the same harsh measures for dealing with migration, despite the numerous performances that have challenged these.

Anika Marschall investigates the work of the Migrantpolitan at the Kampnagel theatre centre in Hamburg, Germany, that has supported and defended refugees, such as those from Lampedusa who fled across the Mediterranean from war-torn Libya. She contrasts the often-ignored legacy of the German colonial policies in Africa and the government's restrictive practices regarding asylum with the decolonial practices at the Kampnagel art centre.

Emma Cox examines the concept of 'intervention' in relation to activist performances about refugees. Distinguishing extreme types of intervention from symbolic ones, she highlights the work of British graffiti artist Banksy who decorated a ship as an artwork and deployed it in the Mediterranean, where it served to rescue African refugees.

Alison Jeffers and Ambrose Musiyiwa analyse the work of the Good Chance Theatre which established a geodesic dome outside Calais in the migrant camp known as 'the jungle.' The dome was used for entertaining and keeping up the spirits of the migrants who were living in desperate conditions. The Good Chance Theatre project later evolved into the play *The Jungle*, which became a West End and Off-Broadway success.

Referencing the Balkan route for refugees in 2015, Milija Gluhovic examines *The Game*, a devised theatre production that ironizes the struggle of asylum seekers to overcome the impediments created by governments to prevent their migration. The piece reveals numerous tactics by nation-states to deny refugees access to asylum procedure while demonstrating the possible counter-tactics by refugees to circumvent these practices.

Reflecting on the effects of the civil war in Syria, Edward Ziter reviews the plethora of Syrian dramas that comment on the ongoing struggle for survival. In particular, Ziter focuses on Omar Abusaada's trilogy of ancient Greek plays as performed by Syrian refugees with no previous acting experience. He observes how these performances elicit autobiographical reflections from the actors, especially women, on their difficult lives.

Pirkko Koski records the role of the Finnish National Theatre in highlighting governmental resistance to the influx of asylum seekers in their series of performances with refugees from Iraq and Afghanistan. She discusses the supervisory work of Jussi Lehtonen and especially his production of *Other Home*, which brought together Finnish and Arab actors to address the perilous position of asylum seekers in Finland at a time when many faced deportation.

These chapters focus on efforts by theatre makers in various parts of the world to present performances which call attention to the conditions of refugees and the restrictions imposed on them by different governments. Most of these chapters refer to plays that create sympathy for asylum seekers, such as Zaroulia on Greece, Wake on Australia, Pérez-Simón on Spain, Jeffers and Musiyiwa on the Jungle in Calais, Ziter on displaced Syrians, Gluhovic on the Balkans, and Koski on the Finnish National Theatre. Cox chooses the unusual case of Banksy who took direct action on behalf of refugees by creating an artwork that served as a rescue vessel in the Mediterranean. In general, these chapters question the role of different governments for neglecting the needs of refugees, emphasizing the arbitrary decisions of nation-states to create their own rules about who can enter and who can't.

The concluding section of the book—Section Six (Itinerancy, Travelling, and Transnationalism)—looks at migration as a feature of the theatre trade, focusing on travelling companies and itinerant artists. It examines several modes of transnational encounter that reflect practices of local and global migrancy. Pavel Drábek's opening chapter comments on the history of cultural dialogues in theatre, as reflected in the concept of 'transnationality.' Zooming in on a variety of theatre genres—from morality plays to civic comedy and baroque opera—Drábek argues for a different perspective on theatrical itinerancy and transnationality, including intercultural encounters of individual artists and metaphysical dialogues that arise within these meetings.

Maria Berlova describes nineteenth-century St. Petersburg as an intersectional cosmopolitan zone, with French, Italian, and German theatres prospering in the city. August von Kotzebue not only worked for St. Petersburg's German Theatre from 1781–1783, but his plays also formed the core of its repertoire. Kotzebue's life trajectory as a European settler in imperial Russia constitutes the focal point of Berlova's chapter.

John McCormick calls puppetry one of the oldest migratory professions, a way for the very poor to survive. From Russian *skomorokhs* to Venetian *bagatellieri*, itinerant puppeteers made their living by professional travelling. Rarely of high respect, these artist-migrants were often seen by the authorities as possible criminals, vagrants, and socially dangerous elements. As McCormick states, therefore, 'migrancy did not so much modify the profession of puppetry as shaped it,' which eventually led to the transformation of its tools and practices.

Kellen Hoxworth looks at another type of professional migrancy in connection to Black Minstrelsy and the Anglophone imperial circuits. He focuses on post-Civil War America, studying the ways that African American performers established themselves as popular rivals to white companies of blackface minstrelsy. As Hoxworth demonstrates, Black Minstrelsy's performers used their signature appeal: '"authentic" blackness.' Some critics of Black minstrelsy saw it as a popular form that confirmed and even mobilised 'the racist figurations of blackness common to the white blackface repertoire'; other scholars recognize Black minstrelsy as 'a charged site for performing vernacular Black humour, Black music, and the complex racial politics of blackness, freedom, and modernity,' with Robert C. Toll's special emphasis on mobility and itinerancy as the fundamental feature of the early Black performance. These Black minstrelsy troupes developed extensive travelling routes not only in the United States but also in the United Kingdom and its colonies, including southern Africa, South Asia, Australia, and New Zealand, on what was known as the Anglophone imperial circuit.

Jim Davis's chapter 'Actor Migration to and from Britain in the Nineteenth Century' focuses on several colonial realities of the nineteenth century and studies actors' migration to and from Britain. Specifically, this chapter considers two case studies: the migration to Britain of black American actor Ira Aldridge (1807–1867), whose move away from America was racially determined, with no professional prospects for a black actor in the United States at the time; and the migration of British and Irish actors to Australia, including G. V. Brooke (1818–1866) and George Coppin (1819–1906), for whom migration was rather accidental in the sense that it was an outcome of their touring practices. This migration varied in terms of the artists' economic or professional success, but unlike for Aldridge it was a matter of their choice not an impact of racism.

Kedar Kulkami draws an interesting map of theatrical migrations as established by the Marathi theatre in Colonial India. Speaking of professional travelling in three dimensions: urban migration (from smaller settlements to large cultural hubs), transformation of performance genres due to this travelling, and professionalization of theatre at the time, Kulkami presents Marathi theatre practices as migratory and cosmopolitan as they 'borrowed freely from and also influenced other traditions in its proximity, especially the Parsi theatre.'

Ina Pukelytė studies the notion of migration as practices of transmigration, migrating identities and nomadic theatre. She uses the most famous Jewish play *The Dybbuk* by An-sky to demonstrate how the idea of migration drives the conflict of the play forward and how it was reflective of An-sky's own complex identity. Pukelytė extends her discussion of migration and dybbuk by surveying the nomadic lifestyle of two Jewish theatre companies: The Vilna Troupe and Habimah.

In her chapter 'Indian Circus: A Melting Pot of Migrant Artists, Performativity, and Race,' Aastha Gandhi also examines the economics of migration in colonial and post-colonial India, but now within the interdisciplinary structures of Indian circus. Recognizing many international, colonial, and post-colonial influences that formed economic practices, lifestyle, training, and artistry of Indian circus, Gandhi—echoing Kulkami's argument to a certain extent—proposes the notion of 'cosmopolitanism' as a defining category of the complex subjectivity and identity of an artist from the Indian circus.

Janine Hauthal discusses the transnational choreographic practices in Belgium as well as the intermedial work of Milo Rau. Hauthal notes the intertextuality and multilingualism of Rau's 'migratory aesthetics,' which integrates film and live theatre in such productions as *Empire*, bringing together actors from different national environments to reflect on their work and their personal difficulties.

Rita Kompelmakher discusses the transnational work of the Belarus Free Theatre (BFT) that addresses both British and Belarussian audiences in asserting opposition to the regime of Alexander Lukashenko. Created in a gesture of resistance to Lukashenko's version of nationalism, the BFT manifests the problems in trying to communicate with audiences from different cultural and political backgrounds in Minsk and London who understand the same performance differently. She concludes with a discussion of their 2022 production of *Dogs of War*, a timely warning of Russia's expansionist ambitions.

Conclusion

Migration—as we see today—has become a permanent constant of our world. With many disruptions around the globe, which include local war conflicts, economic expansions, neo-colonial aspirations, climate change, and cultural shifts, peoples' forced and voluntary movements are increasing and will continue to do so. As Nail observes, 'Today there are over 1 billion migrants. Each decade, the percentage of migrants as a share of total populations continues to rise. […] What is more, the percentage of total migrants who are nonstatus or undocumented is also increasing, thus posing a serious challenge to democracy and political representation' (Nail 2015b, 187). These migrations have already re-shaped and will continue reshaping problematic relations between states, but also between nations and people, and between citizens and the *sans papiers*. They will keep forcing the hosts to interrogate their understanding of hospitality, shaping communities and solidarity as necessary practices of our collective being. And they will put forward difficult, if not impossible, questions of choice for people: to run or not to run, to relocate or not to move, to provide sanctuary and asylum, or to promote detention and exclusion. None of us—as this book shows—should become a victim of forced migration, but none of us has the luxury, privilege, or right of knowing this future in advance. The questions about border crossing and border protection, but also about peoples' integration into their new societies—and thus about the long-lasting definitions of nations and nationhood as well as the status of the undocumented—will be mobilized again and again. And hence we must remember the collective but also individual responsibility of each of us to keep our minds and our hearts open: those who serve as hosts today might turn into migrants tomorrow or vice versa.

Theatre artists, as this book demonstrates, have already and will undoubtedly 'continue to challenge nationalistic and xenophobic attitudes, empower themselves by actions of solidarity in overcoming restrictive practices, provide support and pathways for the dispossessed and inform audiences about their responsibility to find solutions' (Wilmer 2018, 211). Theatre artists resist the authoritarian myths of homogeneity as fostered by nation-states (Wilmer 2018, 209).

However, this Handbook can only serve as a mapping out exercise of performative practices and dramatic forms that speak to these processes of global movement. The co-editors are grateful to each contributor to this book for making this mapping a viable exercise and invite readers of this book to engage with the same labour of identifying similar and/or omitted questions and case studies related to migration that they would want to address both in their everyday life and professional work. A forthcoming book series on Performance and Migration that Yana Meerzon and Steve Wilmer will be developing with Palgrave is a new venue to continue this dialogue.

REFERENCES

Agamben, Giorgio. 2000. *Means without End: Notes on Politics*. Trans Binetti and Casarino. Minneapolis: Minnesota Press.
Arendt, Hannah. 1968. *The Origins of Totalitarianism*. New York: Harcourt
———. 2007. 'We Refugees.' In *The Jewish Writings*, ed. J. Kohn and R. Feldman New York: Schocken.
Balfour, Michael, ed. 2013. *Refugee Performance: Practical Encounters*. Bristol: Intellect.
Beller, Manfred, and Joep Leerssen, eds. 2007. *Imagology: The Cultural Construction and Literary Representation of National Characters: A Critical Survey*. Amsterdam: Rodopi.
Berghaus, Günter, ed. 1996. *Fascism and Theatre: Comparative Studies on the Aesthetics and Politics of Performance in Europe, 1925–1945*. Providence: Berghahn.
Bharucha, Rustom. 2000. *The Politics of Cultural Practice: Thinking through Theatre in an Age of Globalization*. Hanover: Wesleyan University Press.
Boyce-Davies, Carole. 1994. *Black Women, Writing and Identity: Migrations of the Subject*. New York: Taylor & Francis Group.
Brodsky, Joseph. 1995. 'The Condition We Call Exile.' In *On Grief and Reason: Essays*, 22–35. New York: Farrar, Straus, and Giroux.
Castles, Stephen. 2000. 'International Migration at the Beginning of the Twenty-First Century.' *International Social Science Journal*, 52 (165), 269–81.
Cheatham, Amelia. 2022. 'What Is Canada's Immigration Policy?' *Council On Foreign Relations*, February 9, 2022. https://www.cfr.org/backgrounder/what-canadas-immigration-policy.
Cools, Guy. *In-between Dance Cultures: On the Migratory Artistic Identity of Sidi Larbi Cherkaoui and Akram Khan*. Amsterdam: Valiz, 2015.
Cox, Emma. 2014. *Theatre and Migration*. Basingstoke: Palgrave Macmillan.
———. 2015. *Performing Noncitizenship : Asylum Seekers in Australian Theatre, Film and Activism*. London: Anthem Press
Cox, Emma, and Caroline Wake, eds. 2018. 'Envisioning Asylum/Engendering Crisis: or, Performance and Forced Migration Ten Years On,' *Research in Drama Education: The Journal of Applied Theatre and Performance*, 23 (2), 137–47.
Deleuze, Giles, and Félix Guattari. 1987. *A Thousand Plateaus: Capitalism and Schizophrenia*. Trans. Brian Massumi. London: Continuum.
Fischer-Lichte, Erika. 2014. *The Politics of Interweaving Performance Cultures*. New York: Routledge.
Fleishman, Mark, ed. 2015. *Performing Migrancy and Mobility in Africa: Cape of Flows*. Basingstoke: Palgrave.
Forsdyke, Sara. 2005. *Exile, Ostracism, and Democracy: The Politics of Expulsion in Ancient Greece*. Princeton: Princeton University Press.
Freeman, Barry. 2017. *Staging Strangers: Theatre and Global Ethics*. Montreal: McGill-Queen's University Press.
Gilbert, Helen, and Jacqueline Lo. 2007. *Performance and Cosmopolitics: Cross-Cultural Transactions in Australasia*. Basingstoke: Palgrave Macmillan.
Glossary of Migration Related Terms. 2017. UNESCO. https://wayback.archive-it.org/10611/20180705022135/http://www.unesco.org/new/en/social-and-human-sciences/themes/international-migration/glossary/
Gouniardou, Kiki, ed. 2005. *Staging Nationalism: Essays on Theatre and National Identity*. Jefferson: McFarland.

Harvie, Jen. 2005. *Staging the UK*. Manchester: Manchester University Press.
Holdsworth, Nadine. 2010. *Theatre and Nation*. Basingstoke: Palgrave Macmillan.
———. 2014. *Theatre and National Identity: Re-Imaging Conceptions of Nation*. London: Routledge.
Hurley, Erin. 2011. *National Performance: Representing Quebec from Expo 67 to Céline Dion*. Toronto: University of Toronto Press.
Jeffers, Alison. 2013. *Refugees, Theatre and Crisis: Performing Global Identities*. Basingstoke: Palgrave Macmillan.
Jestrović, Silvija, and Yana Meerzon, eds. 2009. *Performance, Exile and 'America'*. Basingstoke: Palgrave Macmillan.
Jestrović, Silvija. 2013. *Performance, Space, Utopia: Cities of War, Cities of Exile*. Basingstoke: Palgrave Macmillan.
Knowles, Richard Paul. 2010. *Theatre & Interculturalism*. Basingstoke: Palgrave Macmillan.
———. 2017. *Performing the Intercultural City*. Ann Arbor: University of Michigan Press.
———, ed. 2021. *International Theatre Festivals and Twenty-First Century Interculturalism*. Cambridge: Cambridge University Press.
Kosinski, Dariusz. 2019. *Performing Poland: Rethinking Histories and Theatres*. Aberystwyth: Performance Research Books.
Kruger, Loren. 1992. *The National Stage: Theatre and Cultural Legitimation in England, France and America*. Chicago: University of Chicago Press.
Kuftinec, Sonja Arsham. 2009. *Theatre, Facilitation, and Nation Formation in the Balkans and Middle East*. Basingstoke: Palgrave Macmillan.
Lei, Daphne P., and Charlotte McIvor, eds. 2020. *The Methuen Drama Handbook of Interculturalism and Performance*. London: Bloomsbury Methuen.
Mäkinen, Helka, S. E. Wilmer, and W. B. Worthen, eds. 2001. *Theatre, History and National Identities*. Helsinki: University Press.
Marchevska, Elena. 2017. *The Displaced & Privilege: Live Art in the Age of Hostility*. London: Live Art Development Agency.
Marschall, Anika. 2018. 'What Can Theatre Do About the Refugee Crisis?: Enacting Commitment and Navigating Complicity in Performative Interventions,' *Research in Drama Education: The Journal of Applied Theatre and Performance*, 23 (2), 148–66.
Mason, Jeffrey D., and J. Ellen Gainor, eds. 1999. *Performing America: Cultural Nationalism in American Theater*. Ann Arbor: University of Michigan Press.
Maufort, Marc. 2003. *Transgressive Itineraries: Postcolonial Hybridizations of Dramatic Realism*. Bruxelles: Peter Lang.
McIvor, Charlotte, and Mathew Spangler, eds. 2014. *Staging Intercultural Ireland*. Cork: Cork University Press.
McIvor, Charlotte. 2016. *Migration and Performance in Contemporary Ireland: Towards a New Interculturalism*. Basingstoke: Palgrave.
Meerzon, Yana. 2012. *Performing Exile—Performing Self: Drama, Theatre, Film*. Basingstoke: Palgrave.
———. 2020. *Performance, Subjectivity, Cosmopolitanism*. Basingstoke: Palgrave Macmillan.
———. 2022. '"Art is Not an Escape; It Is a Statement of Life." Interview with Alex Borovenskiy,' *Critical Stages/Scènes Critiques*, 25. Accessed July 16, 2023. https://www.critical-stages.org/25/?s=borovenskiy.

Meerzon, Yana, David, Dean, and Daniel McNeil, eds. 2020. *Migration and Stereotypes in Performance and Culture*. Basingstoke: Palgrave Macmillan.
Mitra, Royona. 2015. *Akram Khan; Dancing New Interculturalism*. Basingstoke: Palgrave Macmillan.
Musca, Szabolcs, ed. 2019. "Theatre and Migration between Ethics and Aesthetics" (Special Issue), *Performing Ethos: International Journal of Ethics in Theatre & Performance*, 9 (1).
Nail, Thomas. 2015a. *The Figure of the Migrant*, Stanford: Stanford University Press.
———. 2015b. 'Migrant Cosmopolitanism.' *Public Affairs Quarterly*, 29 (2), 187–99.
Pavis, Patrice. 1996. *The Intercultural Performance Reader*. London: Routledge
Pilkington, Lionel. 2001. *Theatre and the State in Twentieth-Century Ireland: Cultivating the People*. London: Routledge.
Rae, Paul. 2006. 'Where is the Cosmopolitan Stage?' *Contemporary Theatre Review*, 16 (1), 8–22.
Rebellato, Dan. 2009. *Theatre and Globalization*. Basingstoke: Palgrave Macmillan
Rudakoff, Judith, ed. 2017. *Performing Exile: Foreign Bodies*. Bristol: Intellect.
Said, Edward. 2000. *Reflections on Exile and Other Essays*. Cambridge: Harvard University Press.
Schnapp, Jeffrey T. 1996. *Staging Fascism: 18 BL and the Theater of Masses for Masses*. Stanford: Stanford University Press.
Shaffer, Jason. 2007. *Performing Patriotism: National Identity in the Colonial and Revolutionary American Theatre*. Philadelphia: University of Pennsylvania Press.
Sharifi, Azadeh, and S. E. Wilmer, eds. 2016. 'Theatre and Statelessness in Europe.' *Critical Stages/Scènes critiques*, 14.
Strobl, Gerwin. 2007. *The Swastika and the Stage: German Theatre and Society, 1933–1945*. Cambridge: Cambridge University Press.
Tan, M.C.C. 2012. *Acoustic Interculturalism: Listening to Performance*. Hampshire: Palgrave Macmillan.
Tuan, Iris Hsin-Chun. 2010. *Intercultural Theatre: Adaptation and Representation*. Mauritius: LAP.
UNHCR. 2022. 'UNHCR: Ukraine, other conflicts push forcibly displaced total over 100 million for first time.' *UNHCR*, May 23, 2022. Accessed July 18, 2022. https://www.unhcr.org/en-ie/news/press/2022/5/628a389e4/unhcr-ukraine-other-conflicts-push-forcibly-displaced-total-100-million.html
Uytterhoeven, Lise. 2019. *Sidi Larbi Cherkaoui: Dramaturgy and Engaged Spectatorship*. Cham: Palgrave Macmillan.
Wiles, David. 2011. *Theatre and Citizenship: The History of a Practice*. Cambridge: Cambridge University Press.
Wilmer, S. E. 2001. *Theater, Society and the Nation: Staging American Identities*. Cambridge: Cambridge University Press.
———., ed. 2004. *Writing and Rewriting National Theatre Histories*. Iowa City: Iowa University Press.
———., ed. 2008. *National Theatres in a Changing Europe*. Basingstoke: Palgrave Macmillan.
———. 2018. *Performing Statelessness in Europe*. Basingstoke: Palgrave Macmillan.
Žižek, Slavoj. 2022. 'What Does Defending Europe Mean?' *Project Syndicate*, March 2. Accessed March 20, 2022. https://www.project-syndicate.org/commentary/europe-unequal-treatment-of-refugees-exposed-by-ukraine-by-slavoj-zizek-2022-03; https://www.project-syndicate.org/commentary/europe-unequal-treatment-of-refugees-exposed-by-ukraine-by-slavoj-zizek-2022-03.

PART I

Theatre and Migration: Themes and Concepts

CHAPTER 2

The Eternal Immigrant and the Aesthetics of Solidarity

Silvija Jestrović

Ilya and Emilia Kabakovs' model for the sculpture *Eternal Immigrant* (1995/2004) depicts a body lumped over a wall's edge, upper-half on one side, lower-half on the other—neither able to cross over, nor to fall back. Running away from precarity and towards a promise of the good life, the *Eternal Immigrant* is forever stuck in the liminal space of her journey. Resilient, wounded or even lifeless, the 'eternal immigrant' has become a recurring figure of twentieth-century exile and has entered the twenty-first on an overcrowded makeshift boat, her body washed ashore on sandy beaches to the astonishment of sunbathing holiday makers. We have seen various reiterations of the wall, too. Some have crumbled, their pieces sold as tourist memorabilia. New ones have mushroomed—in concrete, as electrical fences, or as barbed wire (Fig. 2.1).

I met the eternal immigrant myself in September 1987 at the border between Slovenia and Austria. I was in my late teens, travelling with friends for pleasure and cultural experiences on the cheap—to Paris by bus. As we were checking in for our overnight stay in a small hotel by the border, he was making frantic phone calls by the reception desk. He was a doctor from Lebanon, fleeing the civil war with his wife and three children. They had been stranded in this border hotel, with no country willing to take them in. Do we, by any chance, know anyone who could help? The next morning, we were on the road again, swiftly crossing various European borders with our red Yugoslavian passports,

S. Jestrović (✉)
University of Warwick, Coventry, UK
e-mail: S.Jestrovic@warwick.ac.uk

© The Author(s), under exclusive license to Springer Nature Switzerland AG 2023
Y. Meerzon, S. E. Wilmer (eds.), *The Palgrave Handbook of Theatre and Migration*, https://doi.org/10.1007/978-3-031-20196-7_2

Fig. 2.1 Sculpture of 'The Eternal Immigrant' by Ilya and Emilia Kabakov. (Photo: Ilya and Emilia Kabakov)

no visas required, en route to Paris for the first time. The incomplete story of the Lebanese doctor, his wife, and three children has unfolded in my imagination in all its possible variations, yet the image of the man in a border hotel waiting to cross over remains frozen in place. The *Eternal Immigrant*—balancing the invisible line between Western Europe and a country that is no more.

Curiously enough, it must have been only a few weeks before this encounter when I had first heard someone commenting on the political situation in my native Yugoslavia: 'Mark my words, this country will be the next Lebanon.' Even though I found the analogy powerful, in that sun-kissed autumn of 1987, the Highway of Brotherhood and Unity, taking us from Belgrade to Zagreb and then further to the border hotel in Slovenia, was as busy and boring as ever and the man from Lebanon, with no place to go, emerged from such a different reality that he might as well have been a protagonist in a novel. The road we travelled down was built after WWII, stretching diagonally through the whole of Yugoslavia, hence its name. Little did I know that it was my last trip on it. A few years later in 1991, after a short war, Slovenia proclaimed independence from Yugoslavia. Croatia followed, but that war was not a short one; Bosnia was next. Yugoslavia was falling apart in a bloodbath, the Lebanon analogy becoming very real, with Sarajevo—the city of braided cultures and ethnicities—arguably resembling Beirut. The man from Lebanon with no home and no country no longer resembled a fictional hero. Rather, he could not have become more real and he was everywhere fleeing the war in Croatia, running from the snipers in Sarajevo, waiting for the decision on his immigrant visa at the Canadian embassy in Belgrade. That autumn of 1987 in the lobby of the small border hotel he was the sign of things that were yet to come. And the future he announced has continued to unfold, while he, the *Eternal Immigrant*, is sailing on an overcrowded boat approaching Lampedusa, is running to jump on a truck to take him across the English Channel, and is waiting for the day when his train to elsewhere will arrive.

Exilic Heterotopia and Exilic Matrix

In his seminal 1984 essay, the 'Reflections on Exile,' Edward Said, who shared the exilic condition after being forced to leave his native Palestine as a child, wrote:

> The difference between earlier exiles and those of our time is, it bears stressing, scale: our age—with its modern warfare, imperialism, and the quasi-theological ambitions to totalitarian rulers—is indeed the age of the refugee, the displaced person, mass immigration. (Said 2000, 174)

Stephen Wilmer's book, *Performing Statelessness*, opens with an epigraph from Said's essay and an introductory passage that also foregrounds the continuous unprecedented scale of exile in the twenty-first century:

> Ongoing wars in the Middle East and Africa, poverty and authoritarian or unstable rule in Sub-Saharan African states have made many people flee. [...] The number of refugees drowning in the Mediterranean while trying to get to Europe has steadily increased (with more than 5000 dying in 2016) and the total of displaced people in the world has reached a record 65 million. (Wilmer 2018, 1)

Even though the numbers must have been different in 1984, when Said wrote his essay, it is striking that both the twentieth and twenty-first-century discourses on exile have this sense of scale and magnitude in common.

The exilic figure and the border shaped through the semiotics of various political imaginaries that often foreshadow physical spaces, as well as the sense of the unprecedented scale of modern migration, have become the recurring tropes in the *exilic matrix*—where different bodies, numerous borders, and various means of crossing them become morphed and interchangeable—elegantly sublimated in Kabakovs' model of the *Eternal Immigrant*. This recurring, repeating, morphing of bodies, spaces, numbers, experiences, and feelings that the figure of the *Eternal Immigrant* synthesises simultaneously enable us to make new connections and see analogies in less obvious places and yet by the same token, they muddle and oversaturate our vision—they create *exilic heterotopias*. The *exilic heterotopia* contains what Yana Meerzon recognises as the multitudes of migrations, negotiating degrees of displacement expressed through various legal and institutional terms with individual experiences, and we might add, in different time/space constellations. The vague, umbrella term *exile* gains specific currency in this constellation. Echoing Emmanuel Levinas, Meerzon stresses the importance of remembering that:

> The word exile not only allows us to identify foreigners and strangers in the bodies of refugees and immigrants, but also makes us recognise their fundamental eminence as human beings and as Other. The word exile forces us to acknowledge and accept our own responsibility towards this Other; it makes us see the Other within ourselves. (Meerzon 2017, 30)

This *exilic heterotopia* foregrounds analogy and comparison, as openings in the matrix of modern exile, not only to compassion but also to identification and solidarity—not only to feel for the *Other* but to find the stranger in ourselves.

Nevertheless, the *exilic heterotopia* also emanates a sense of no escape from the matrix of displacement. Repetition of the exilic tropes, at the heart of this matrix, poses a threat of oversaturation, or as the Russian Formalist scholar Viktor Shklovsky put it, of automatising or habitualising our perception. During his short exile in Berlin following the Russian Revolution, Shklovsky wrote letters to Elsa Triolet that turned into the epistolary novel *Zoo: Or Letters Not About Love*. There he quotes Triolet—'Quit writing about HOW, HOW, HOW much you love me, because at the third "how much," I start thinking about something else'—and the definition of habitualisation of perception emerges (Shklovsky 2012, 102). After how many bodies washed ashore on Mediterranean beaches do we start thinking about something else? Shklovsky, like his fellow exile Brecht, believed that making the familiar strange is a way of counteracting habitualisation of perception and, hence, the main role of art. To find the crack in the matrix is to look for *differences*—it is indeed a defamiliarisation strategy.

Differences

There is an additional figure in the Kabakovs' model of the *Eternal Immigrant*—the one standing opposite, looking at the body frozen in the act of climbing the wall. Who is this figure that is watching? A hostile guard? A kind host about to extend a helping hand? Another immigrant who has managed to make the crossing? The synthesis the model offers is a theatrical situation that could also be described as: *a* is doing while *b* looks on (Bentley 1965, 158). There is a relational dimension that the second figure brings, her gaze opens to a variety of interpretations. I see in this dialectic between watching and doing an opening to search for the differences in the exilic matrix. The framework of theatre and performance is particularly well suited to this quest, because of its capacity to make the familiar strange and also to heighten tensions and paradoxes between doing and watching and between uniqueness and repetition.

There are three kinds of *differences* I would like to foreground here when it comes to the notion of exile along the rough and meandering lines that separate the twentieth century from the twenty-first: *the disciplinary, the artistic*, and *the politico-existential*. Through this strategy of spotting the differences, I will further attempt to identify the potential of exilic theatre and performance to formulate an *aesthetic of solidarity*.

The Disciplinary

In 2002, the Russian-Canadian Yana Meerzon, Czech-Canadian Veronika Ambros, French-Canadian Danielle Couture, English-Canadian Joanne MacKay Bennett, and I put together a conference at the University of Toronto entitled *Theatre and Exile* that subsequently led to a special issue of *Modern Drama*. The conference was inspired by our own experiences of uprootedness and of the exilic heterotopia, but also by a kind of cross-cultural encounter that our intellectual camaraderie enabled us to build on. Hannah Arendt and Edward Said's work, George Lemming's postcolonial critique *Pleasures of Exile*, and Svetlana Boym's *The Future of Nostalgia* were among the works that offered some conceptual points of departure. However, most of our theoretical frameworks at that time, with some exceptions in the area of applied theatre, were coming from other disciplines including cultural studies, literature, and philosophy. Our disciplinary vocabulary was relying on borrowed language that we were negotiating in search of our own. However, Yana Meerzon's subsequent book, *Performing Exile/Performing Self* (2012), followed that trajectory as it was charting its bespoke performance analysis framework.

In 2008 Helen Gilbert and Sophie Nield organised the *Performance and Asylum* conference at Royal Holloway University in London, out of which followed the special issue in *Research in Drama Education* (*RiDE*) offering a comprehensive overview of a range of exilic theatre and performance practices, including verbatim and documentary theatre, and a matching spectrum of scholarly responses on aesthetic, ethical, and legal issues concerning theatre and asylum. Questions of citizenship, trauma, and memory emerged to a different degree in the works of Alison Jeffers, Sophie Nield, Milija Gluhović, and others, beginning to further map the theatre and performance studies scholarship on exile.

A new issue of *RiDE, Envisioning Asylum/Engendering Crisis* has emerged with the aim of revisiting the state of play in the area of performance and asylum ten years on. Edited by Emma Cox and Caroline Wake, this collection demonstrates how the scholarship on exile has grown in our field, including performance-specific concepts and vocabularies, and how it has been shaped within the current global geo-political landscape. Cox has coined the term 'processional aesthetics' as an analytical tool to understand modes of representation and ways of responding to the refugee crisis, but also to critically engage with the danger of over-aestheticising political issues (Cox 2017, 477–496).

Marilena Zaroulia's terms 'aesthetics of obscenity' and 'aesthetics of sincerity' add to the conceptual vocabulary a critical lens to ask what is the ethics of these responses, and do they resist or perpetuate the neoliberal system (Zaroulia 2018, 186)? Mark Fleishmann's work on *Performing Migrancy and Mobility in Africa* (2015) and Janelle Reinelt's and Bishnuprya Dutt's project *Gendered Citizenship: Manifestations and Performances* (2016) have been among the contributions that expanded the geographical scope and perspectives of exilic scholarship including issues of new mobilities, migrant labour, and human trafficking. These, together with more recent works of Cox, Meerzon, Wilmer, Rudakoff, and others, are just some examples that show how the seemingly empty space—between the figure trying to climb the wall and the one watching from the other side of the Kabakovs' model—has been mapped, performed, and problematised as the scholarship on exile developed in our field. The 2018 IFTR conference, *Theatre and Migration*, further demonstrated that this body of scholarship has developed to the extent that we might begin to talk about *exilic theatre and performance* as a subfield, in line with categories such as *political theatre* or *feminist theatre*. Exile and exilic performance are no longer theorised in a borrowed language of literary and social sciences, but rather through our own inherently interdisciplinary vocabulary and conceptual paradigms.

The Artistic: Talking Back and Responding To

Even though some forms have been continuously deployed to grapple with socially engaged representations of exilic experiences such as verbatim and documentary theatre, Forum theatre, and Playback, I argue that there has been a shift both in aesthetics and in perspectives that have emerged with and from the events known as the refugee and migrant crises. To explain this—in no way categorical—delineation, I would call the former mode *talking back* and the latter *responding to*.

The mode that I have named *talking back* is mainly formulated through the body of work of artists, thinkers, and scholars who have used their own exilic experience as a point of departure. This does not imply that the artistic and critical discourse is necessarily emerging in the autobiographical mode, but that some level of first-hand experience of displacement becomes an epistemological tool to renegotiate the relationship between—to return to Kabakovs' model—the one looking on and the other climbing the wall. The *talking back* mode often challenges the gaze. The term *responding to* is coined to describe the work of artists and thinkers who are approaching exilic issues from the position of the onlooker rather than a first hand-experience (even when they problematise their own privileged perspective). These works are about exilic experiences, often prompted by the refugee and migrant crisis, and are at times co-created with migrants and refugees. The *responding to* mode is deeply rooted in the moral and political consciousness of the authors with the aim of destabilising the pre-existing perspectives on these issues, raising awareness of the plight of displaced people, and opening cultural, social and political spaces for change and solidarity.

The term *talking back* paraphrases the postcolonial strategies of writing back and returning the gaze, often by taking the construction of the Other as a point of departure. Exilic talking back deploys a variety of aesthetic strategies, including imploded cultural stereotypes, intertextuality, linguistic macaroni and heteroglossia, *subversive body* acts—(to borrow from Butler), yet not only of gender but also of ethnicity—various forms of space mappings and interventions, humour, and other means of subverting expectations. Theatrical works in that mode range from Janusz Glowacki's play *Hunting Cockroaches* (1987) that depicts a Polish émigré couple in their cockroach-infested New York city apartment, confronting expectations and constructions of otherness as it unmasks liberal token gestures of compassion, to Guillermo Verdechia's *Fronteras Americanas* (1993) that through ethnic 'subversive body acts' (Butler) constructs the pan-Latino Other as a strategy of counter-stereotyping.

Viewed against Kabakovs' *Eternal Immigrant* model, exilic talking back emerges from the space in between the figure trying to cross over and the onlooker at the other side—destabilising both positions. From there, exilic experience starts to emerge as a critical perspective and as a source of creativity, where, as Said puts it, 'Seeing the entire world as a foreign land makes possible the originality of vision' (Said 2000, 186).

Nevertheless, in the face of the ongoing refugee crisis, *exilic talking back* has been replaced with a mode of *responding to* that is often marked by a great sense of urgency. This comes in a variety of forms. We can find it in Andreas Lustgarden's didactic play *Lampedusa* (2015), which offers a lesson in hospitality through the representation of rigid, xenophobic protagonist, who strikes up an unlikely friendship with a refugee. The Young Vic's production *The Jungle* (2017)—written by Joe Murphy and Joe Robinson, who had set up a theatre in the actual refugee and migrant camp in Calais known as The Jungle—has been a big success and has transferred to London's West End. This performance uses an immersive theatre strategy set in a ramshackle Afghan restaurant to bring the stories, atmosphere, and political duplicity of the camp's subsequent demolition closer to the audience's experience—this performance is about responses to the refugee and migrant crisis as much as it is about The Jungle in Calais.

The ongoing socially engaged project *Refugee Tales* has the structure of a pilgrimage inspired by Chaucer's *Canterbury Tales,* whereby activists and artists walk to call an end to indefinite immigration detention. Two volumes have already emerged featuring short stories by some of the leading UK writers and are based on interviews with refugees. The Centre for Political Beauty's intervention *The Dead Are Coming* was a funeral procession from Sicily to the outskirts of Berlin that took actual refugee bodies for burial. Shock tactics like these, belonging to Zaruilia's repertoire of 'the obscene,' have been frequently used as modes of *responding to*. Other examples include Ai Weiwei's *Lotus* installation made of refugees' life jackets, and his even more controversial recreation of the image of the drowned Syrian child refugee Alan Kurdi.

All these works involve a certain illustrative or mimetic dimension, despite their various stylised conceptual frameworks. They curate the exilic experience and voices, even if actual migrants and refugees are placed on stage. These are often performances that aim to bring the hardship and precarity of the experience closer to the privileged observer, to awaken conscience, solidarity, and even communal action. Some are more successful in that than others, some are ethically less problematic than others, some offer provocative aesthetic choices, and others illustrate the situation, reiterating what is already well known. However, if applied to the constellation of Kabakovs' model, they are all asking, in one way or another: Who is this figure on the other side of the wall watching? Ethics, politics, activism, anger, and compassion of the onlooker are at the centre of these responses, while the one climbing the wall becomes an amalgam of bodies, voices, and stories often predictable even when geographies and political conditions are vastly different. The space in between the two figures and their positions remains undisturbed, even if the one standing on the other side is stretching out a helping hand.

There is nothing inherently wrong though in asking who this figure on the other side is. Given that the figure on the other side of the wall is enigmatic and could hold a contrasting range of positions—from the radically liberal calling for a utopian abolition of borders to the disturbingly right-wing responses—to interrogate the plurality of that figure, rather than to merely demonstrate compassion, might be paramount. Still why this shift from *exilic talking back* to *responding to*? Why has it become so difficult for the exilic figure to speak beyond the narratives that the one standing at the other side expects to hear?

The Politico-Existential or the Good Life

In another of Kabakovs' works there is a deserted train station. Walking into this installation gives an eerie sense that the last train has just left. On the wall above the tracks, a neon inscription says: 'Not everyone will make it to the future.' This brings numerous associations to mind: the trains of progress for which some get tickets, while others are left behind, and the ghost trains en route to Nazi concentration camps and Soviet gulags of the twentieth century. These days, however, we read into this installation the migrants and refugees, the large number of bodies trying desperately to jump on that train that would take them away from precarity and closer to their dream of a good life. Confronted with the alarming numbers, not only of the displaced but also of those who will never make it, we are perhaps more than ever acutely aware that 'not everyone will make it to the future.' This is also one of the reasons why some exiles cannot talk back. It is hard to talk back from the position of bare life (although, and I disagree with Agamben here, not impossible). A certain degree of safety and some basic existential needs must be met before the exilic plurality of vision can emerge to give 'rise to an awareness of simultaneous dimensions, an awareness […] that is *contrapuntal*,' as Said put it (Said 2000, 186). As for the figure from the other side of the wall, the conscious understanding that these destinies are shaped by economic and political factors, rather than by some mysterious esoteric design, poses a vexing political and ethical challenge: What does it mean to live a good life?

The constellation of figures in Kabakovs' model—the space between the person stuck in her attempt to get to the other side of the wall and the one standing opposite—charts a demarcation line, a rift, a gap, sometimes even a minefield between precarious life and good life. How do we speak about ourselves and the *Other* from this position, with this gaping hole between us—the rift between the *Eternal Immigrant* and the relative safety of being at the other (presumably) better side of the wall? This is not only about how we relate to the *Other* in solidarity, but also about defining the *good* in good life.

Shirin Rai asks: 'When we think of the good life, whose life are we thinking of and who is the agent of change?' (Rai 2018, 6). This involves obligations of justice, redistribution of resources, and holding the private and public together in shaping the good life as a life of solidarity, 'requiring us to imagine new ways of thinking about resistance and change through alliances of the excluded' (6). So, how can theatre and performance work as a site of such re-imaginings in the context of exile? How can they play simultaneously, with various registers of *talking back* and with different modes of *responding to*, perhaps even move beyond the binary that these modalities suggest towards an *aesthetic of solidarity*?

THE AESTHETIC OF SOLIDARITY

I propose that we think of exilic theatre and performance as means to exercise the *aesthetic of solidarity*, inspired by Peter Weiss' *aesthetic of resistance*. In his eponymous novel, written against the backdrop of rising fascism in the 1930s, Weiss asserts that art is the means of finding new modes of political action and new forms of social understanding. In his foreword to the novel, Fredric Jameson describes it as 'a proletarian Bildungsroman, a pedagogy of the subaltern' (Jameson 2005, x). Likewise, the *aesthetic of solidarity* is not so much an attempt to formulate an aesthetic theory, but rather a sketching out of an aesthetic pedagogy. This pedagogy is about the emergence and modification of existing models of art, culture, and collectivity—a process of learning solidarity as the re-imagining of a shared good life in the context of bad life. *Aesthetic of solidarity* is conscious of the difference in exilic experiences and of the position of relative privilege from which it has been formulated. In its name already, the *aesthetic of solidarity* implies that the aesthetic is inseparable from the political, that *form is content*.

In sketching out the *aesthetic of solidarity*, the following four modes might offer potential paradigms for further development: (1) *intervention/disturbance*, (2) *form-made-difficult*, (3) *ready-made direct action*, and (4) *being there*. In this final section, I will briefly mention works that I find evocative of these paradigmatic modes.

1. Christophe Schlingensief's well-known project *Please Love Austria*, where he placed a group of alleged asylum seekers in a container at the Herbert-von-Karajan Square in the heart of Vienna, is the epitome of an *intervention/disturbance* mode of the *aesthetics of solidarity*. On the top of the container a huge banner proclaimed *AUSLÄNDER RAUS!* (FOREIGNERS OUT!) Back in 2001, the performance was conceptualised in the style of reality TV show *Big Brother*, where the audience could vote the asylum seekers out of the country via an internet platform. The last one to remain was promised a monetary prize and marriage to an Austrian citizen to get immigration papers. This project was a reaction to a series of electoral successes of Austria's far-right Freedom Party, whose strong anti-immigration stand defined their election campaign (1999/2000). The performance, however, has never ceased to be eerily relevant, not only within the context of the current and ongoing migrant and refugee crisis in Europe, but also with the global rise of the Right. Schlingensief calls for rethinking both the forms of self-righteous political activism and political theatre rooted in show-me-your-wounds strategies. The performance intervenes into the fabric of the public sphere, mobilising publics that would not normally go to the theatre, disturbing previously held positions, putting the issues of asylum centre stage, whereby the city square became the agora—a site of debate and dissensus.
2. *The form-made-difficult* comes from the Russian Formalist concept of *zatrudnennaya forma* (form made difficult), which is also a strategy of making the familiar strange. This is not a means to bring the meaning closer to our understanding, but the exact opposite, to make the reception process laborious and prolonged—to subvert audience expectations and their stock responses—to take us to new levels of meaning-making, that confront rather than confirm what we know. Elfriede Jelinek's writing exemplifies this strategy, as in her version of *The Supplicants* (2013), inspired by asylum seekers from Afghanistan and Pakistan, who in a gesture that unintentionally echoed Schlingensief's intervention, left the detention centre at the outskirts of Vienna and occupied the Votiv-Kirche in the historic centre of the city. Jelinek's dramaturgy does not have designated speakers, the voices change sometimes mid-sentence, her punctuation follows the rules of musical annotation, while conflicting views have been woven together to further problematise the material. Intertextuality is among her key strategies for making-the-form-difficult: the lines from Aeschylus's tragedy, mixed with trivia and media headlines, her own authorial voice, and occasional parodies of Heidegger. The text is approached as an open-ended process, not only for theatre makers that take upon the challenge of its staging, but also for the writer herself.

3. *Immigrant Movement International*, the ongoing project of the Cuban performance artist Tanya Bruguera, epitomises the *ready-made direct action* as a mode of the aesthetic of solidarity. Bruguera also calls it *Arte Util* (Useful Art). *Immigrant Movement International* located in Queens, New York, is designated to offer practical support to immigrants in America (legal and illegal) in learning their rights and building stronger networks amongst themselves, while working on a range of social projects including art-making workshops for children, free consultations with immigrant lawyers, language classes, and so on. Bruguera, however, frames her social initiatives as a work of art-in-progress—a kind of *ready-made* socially engaged practice. She sees her work as an expended aesthetics about the role of artists in society, whereby *Art Util* 'transforms the condition of viewer into one of citizenry' (Mansour 2011).

4. *Being there* as a form of *aesthetics of solidarity* has been inspired by the ongoing project of artist Carmen Wong called *Breakfast Elsewhere*. In Wong's project there is no overt agenda to either empower the marginalised or teach hospitality, but there is no overt declaration of solidarity either. Yet *Breakfast Elsewhere* is a prime example of the *aesthetic of solidarity* in carving out time and space to do something simple together, yet in a somewhat unusual way—to perform the everyday in a not so everyday setting. The *Breakfast* I attended in 2017 was taking place in the evening, in a Theatre studio at Warwick University. We, a diverse group of participants, were asked to cook together and we made a Middle Eastern breakfast of hummus and pita. The recipe came from a Syrian refugee living in Coventry. The instructions were pre-recorded and communicated to a volunteer through headphones, who then shared them with all of us. The originator of the recipe was observing and then joined us as we sat on the floor to drink tea, eat, talk, and listen to one another. There were no stories of hardship, nor gestures of compassion, no token *Others* either. Our *Breakfast Elsewhere* unfolded as a ritual of simple communal intimacy, of slowness and of listening.

These very different modes all demonstrate that the *aesthetic of solidarity* is never purely reactive. Hence, the art emerging from the *aesthetic of solidarity* is neither a charitable gesture nor a vehicle for single-issue movements advocating the plight of migrants and refugees. *Aesthetic of solidarity* can only truly take place within the broader context of political resistance and with the artist's full awareness of what that context is. Current global right-wing populism has placed border protection, national unity, and the threat of the Other in the form of a migrant, a refugee, a Muslim at the centre of its identity formations and political agendas. In his article 'We Can't Address the EU Refugee Crisis Without Confronting Global Capitalism,' Slavoj Žižek writes about managing the refugee crisis in a solidaristic fashion:

> The ultimate cause of refugees is today's global capitalism itself and its geopolitical games, and if we do not transform it radically, immigrants from Greece and other European countries will soon join African refugees. When I was young, such an organised attempt to regulate commons was called Communism. Maybe we should reinvent it. Maybe, this is in the long term our only solution. (Žižek 2016)

Even if the trope of the *Eternal Immigrant* speaks to the notion of *exilic heterotopias* and transcends diverse experiences of displacement, the sculpture, just like the artistic pair that made it, might have been born out of the dissident figure escaping oppressive communist regimes of the twentieth century, climbing the wall towards the promise of freedom and abundance that capitalist Western democracies had to offer. At this junction in time, however, the exile is often not only the victim of local regimes and conflicts, but also of a cynical global political landscape, governed by the neoliberal economy, within which freedom and abundance in one part of the world feed off cheap labour and extreme inequality elsewhere. Like Peter Weiss' *aesthetic of resistance*, formulated in its own time against the backdrop of growing fascism, the *aesthetic of solidarity*, within the current neoliberal regime and the global rise of the Right, has no other choice but to speak from the Left.

References

Bentley, Eric. 1965. *The Life of Drama*. London: Methuen, 1965.
Cox, Emma. 2017. 'Processional Aesthetics and Irregular Transit: Envisioning Refugees in Europe.' *Theatre Journal*, 69 (4), 477–496.
Jameson, Frederic. 2005. 'Forward: A Monument to Radical Instants.' In *The Aesthetic of Solidarity* by Peter Weiss, Trans. Joachim Neugroschel, vi–xlix. Durham: Duke University Press.
Mansour, Chris. 2011. 'On the Fallacies of Useful Art: Tanya Bruguera's Immigrant Movement International.' *Seismopolite: Journal of Arts and Politics* 2 (December). http://www.seismopolite.com/on-the-fallacies-of-useful-art-tania-brugueras-immigrant-movement-international
Meerzon, Yana. 2017. 'On the Paradigms of Banishment, Displacement and Free Choice.' In *Performing Exile: Foreign Bodies*, edited by Judith Rudakoff, 19–35. Bristol: Intellect.
Rai, Shirin. 2018. 'The Good Life and the Bad: Dialectics of Solidarity.' *Social Politics* 25 (1), 1–19.
Said, Edward. 2000. *Reflections on Exile*. Cambridge, MA: Harvard University Press.
Shklovsky, Viktor. 2012. *Zoo or Letters not about Love*, translated by Richard Sheldon. London: Dalkey Archive Press.
Wilmer, S. E. 2018. *Performing Statelessness in Europe*. London: Palgrave Macmillan.
Zaroulia, Marilena. 2018. 'Performing That Which Exceeds Us: Aesthetics of Sincerity and Obscenity During "The Refugee Crisis."' *RiDE: Research in Drama Education*, 23 (2), 179–92.
Žižek, Slavoj. 2016. 'We Can't Address the EU Refugee Crisis Without Confronting Global Capitalism.' *In These Times*, September 9, 2016. http://inthesetimes.com/article/18385/slavoj-zizek-european-refugee-crisis-and-global-capitalism.

CHAPTER 3

'A Real State of Exception': Walter Benjamin and the Paradox of Theatrical Representation

Freddie Rokem

As the Second World War broke out in September 1939, Walter Benjamin, who had mostly been living in exile in Paris since the Nazi takeover of power in Germany in February 1933—no longer as a *flaneur* but a refugee—was incarcerated at the Clos-Saint-Joseph internment camp in Nevers, south of Paris. He was released in November 1939 and returned to Paris. However, as the German army invaded France, in June 1940, Benjamin first fled to Lourdes and then to Marseilles, preparing his escape over the Pyrenees, through Spain, to the US. During these last months in Paris—the city which more than any other represented modernity—Benjamin wrote what was to become his final work, the collection of aphoristic theses, 'On the Concept of History' (*Über den Begriff der Geschichte*). These texts were made public soon after his suicide in September 1940 and are considered to be a cornerstone of his philosophy of history. At the same time as these short texts present his Marxist/materialist understanding of historical processes, they are also very personal, both 'reflecting' and 'reflecting on' the developments in Europe, and in Germany in particular, from the First World War to the gradually approaching catastrophe of the Second World War.

My contribution to the handbook on theatre and migration will focus on the eighth thesis from 'On the Concept of History,' quoted in full here, because what follows is basically a reading of this text:

> The tradition of the oppressed teaches us that the 'state of exception' in which we live is not the exception but the rule. We must attain to a conception of history

F. Rokem (✉)
Tel Aviv University, Tel Aviv, Israel
e-mail: rokem@tauex.tau.ac.il

© The Author(s), under exclusive license to Springer Nature Switzerland AG 2023
Y. Meerzon, S. E. Wilmer (eds.), *The Palgrave Handbook of Theatre and Migration*, https://doi.org/10.1007/978-3-031-20196-7_3

that accords with this insight. Then we will clearly see that it is our task to bring about a real state of exception, and this will improve our position in the struggle against fascism. One reason fascism has a chance is that, in the name of progress, its opponents treat it as a historical norm.—The current amazement that the things we are experiencing are 'still' possible in the twentieth century is *not* philosophical. This amazement is not the beginning of knowledge–unless it is the knowledge that the view of history which gives rise to it is untenable. (Benjamin 2003, 392; modified; quotation marks and emphasis in original)

This is perhaps the most personal of the short texts in 'On the Concept of History,' not in the sense of being private or autobiographical, but clearly relating to his experience during this time—an experience which he shared with many of his fellow refugees, and has since then reoccurred with numerous variations, up until our own time—arguing that 'the state of exception' in which 'we live'—in the first person plural—has become the rule. Therefore, Benjamin concludes, in order to 'improve *our* position in the struggle against fascism,' it is necessary to create what he terms 'a *real* state of exception' (emphases added). In what follows I want to suggest that this struggle has a performative dimension and that Benjamin's ideas and formulations are both informed by and have in turn informed dramatic writing and the practices of theatre and performance.

War and persecution, including confrontations with real and imagined threats as well as personal insecurity during times of crisis, frequently leading to migration and exile, are some of the manifestations of what has been termed a state of exception, in German *Ausnahmezustand*. This notion, first coined in 1922 by Carl Schmitt—jurist, political theorist and eventually a prominent member of the Nazi Party—aimed at defining the constitutional aspects of a legal sovereign's right to transcend the rule of law in the name of the public good, which could of course also include the establishment of dictatorship. Schmitt coined this term in his book *Political Theology*, partly in response to Walter Benjamin's 1921 essay 'Towards a Critique of Violence,' examining concrete situations challenging constitutional governance with *Gewalt*, a word which in German besides violence also refers to 'power' and 'force.' Benjamin concludes this essay by introducing the notions of mythical and divine violence, taking the reader beyond the limits of rationality to confront expressions of violence (Rokem 2018). Schmitt, arguing for the right of the sovereign to declare a state of exception, coins this term to regulate and integrate what for Benjamin was chaotic and irrational, even deplorable. While both Benjamin and Schmitt were critical of the liberalism practiced in the Weimar Republic, their critique emanated from diametrically opposed ideological positions.

Benjamin's eighth thesis—written almost 20 years after the notion of the *Ausnahmezustand* was coined—presents a very different perspective, beginning by referring to the 'tradition of the oppressed' and their experience of a 'state of exception'—drawing attention to what must be learned from this experience. Benjamin laments that the 'state of exception' has become the rule.

This creates an amazement 'that the things we are experiencing are "still" possible in the twentieth century'—with both 'state of exception' and 'still' appearing in quotation marks—distancing himself, even mockingly from Schmitt's position. This amazement, Benjamin concludes, is non-philosophical, certainly aware that amazement or wonder (*Thaumazein* in Greek) was traditionally considered to be the beginning of philosophical thinking, not a scandalous impasse of despondency and despair.

Already 15 years before writing 'On the Concept of History,' Benjamin had referred briefly to Schmitt's ideas of the *Ausnahmezustand* in his study of the Baroque mourning play, *Origin of the German Trauerspiel*, published in 1928. However, the possibility that Benjamin had been in agreement with Schmitt over these issues, which has frequently been claimed (e.g. by Agamben 2005, Chap. 4) is hardly plausible. Benjamin distanced himself from Schmitt, who was on the side of the victimizers. At this point, following the conventions regarding arguments about such matters within the public sphere of the Weimar Republic, before the Nazi takeover of power in 1933, they were in a polite disagreement. The letter that Benjamin sent to Schmitt, along with a copy of the *Trauerspiel*-book that Benjamin wrote for his second doctorate, demonstrates how formal politeness can reflect profound disagreement. In his study of the German Baroque mourning play, intending to promote his academic career—an intention which never materialized—Benjamin formulates his critique of Schmitt very cautiously, pointing out that the most important function of the Baroque ruler is to avert a state of exception, claiming, no doubt with direct reference to Schmitt's ideas, but without mentioning him by name, that this was 'more spiritual and more profound than its modern reconception' (Benjamin 2019, 49).

The scant evidence from the 'exchange' of ideas between Benjamin and Schmitt has been examined and discussed at great length (e.g. by Agamben 2005; Bredekamp 1999; Hasan-Rokem 2008; Kahn 2014; Weber 1992). Without going into further detail here, it is also important to add that this 'debate' was renewed by Schmitt more than 15 years after Benjamin's death, in 1956, in the polemical pamphlet *Hamlet or Hecuba: The Intrusion of the Time into the Play*. Besides criticizing Benjamin's *Trauerspiel*-book, Schmitt argued that Shakespeare's play is first and foremost a veiled representation of the historical reality in which King James—whose mother, Mary Stuart, had been an accomplice in the killing of James' father and had married the murderer—ascends the throne (Schmitt 2009). Even if this raises some interesting issues with regard to the interactions between a historical situation and a contemporary work of art, Schmitt's reading can under no circumstances clarify why Shakespeare's play has achieved its extraordinary canonical status. Nor can it make us overlook Schmitt's role within the Nazi movement which he never really regretted. Instead, I hope to show here how Benjamin's idea of a 'real state of exception' accounts for the inspiration we get from plays like *Oedipus Tyrannus* and *Hamlet*, without attaching their significance to a specific event or situation or by suppressing their remarkable openness and agility to relate to many different states of exception.

Benjamin's basic claim in the eight thesis is that the situation 'in which we live,' immediately after the outbreak of the Second World War, when the state of exception has become the rule, is both unphilosophical (***kein philosophisches***—with the word *kein* emphasized in the original) and untenable (*nicht zu halten*) (quoting original German in Benjamin 1991, 697). Therefore, it is 'our task' (*Aufgabe*)—a term Benjamin frequently mobilizes as the incentive for beginning a critique—to induce or bring about what he calls 'a real [or true/actual] state of exception' (*die Herbeiführung des wirklichen Ausnahmezustands*). This, he claims, will change our understanding of historical processes, creating new forms of knowledge which can in turn even improve 'our position in the struggle against fascism.' The traditional amazement as the source for philosophical knowledge has collapsed into a state of hopelessness and despair, while at the same time pointing out a possibility for confronting this situation. The question I want to address here is what does Benjamin mean by such a real state of exception. How and where is it possible to induce or create such a state of exception? And how can it become effective in the fight against the injustices of fascism as well as improve the situation of the potential victims of such situations?

I want to suggest that the *real* state of exception is induced by being staged in the theatre; or to be more specific: a state of exception becomes 'real' by being performed on a stage. By highlighting the aesthetic dimension of such exceptional situations, by performing them, they re-enter the domain of philosophy. This line of thinking—based on Benjamin's commitment to bridge the gap between philosophy and performance (Rokem 2010)—assumes that by being staged an aspect of historical processes is revealed which those who are experiencing a state of exception as victims are incapable of fully understanding. This is in particular true when such a state of exception has become the rule and is taken for granted. Paradoxically, by being staged, the state of exception becomes 'real,' in the sense of being more palpable, more fully transparent than the direct experience of ongoing states of exception. The lack of transparency in states of exception is in fact one of their defining features which has ironically even increased with the more recent media developments, constantly feeding us with an uncanny combination of facts and fake news.

In his Kafka essay, which was published in 1934, Benjamin argues that the unintelligible dimension in Kafka's writing, what he terms their 'code of gestures which surely had no definite symbolic meaning for the author from the outset,' derive their meaning from their 'ever-changing contexts and experimental groupings,' for which, as Benjamin concludes '/t/he theatre is the logical (*gegebene*/given) place' (Benjamin 1999, 801). This in effect means that the incomprehensible states of exception described in Kafka's writings, which for Benjamin are what he calls their 'cloudy spot'—referring in particular to the short parable 'Before the Law' (which is a part of his novel, *The Trial*) about the man from the country who is kept waiting his whole life outside the gate to the law—will ultimately receive their full ideological or philosophical significance by being staged in the theatre. Such a process, through which the theatre (and different performative activities) can at least potentially bestow meaning to what is otherwise unintelligible, is in fact an important aspect of Kafka's writing which no doubt influenced Benjamin and has in turn influenced the theatre. Obvious examples are the final moments in his novel *The Trial*, when K. immediately asks the two men who have come to carry out his death-sentence in which theatre they are playing; or in the 'Nature Theatre of Oklahoma' [*sic!*], in the novel *Amerika* (*The Man Who Disappeared*), where the moment of individual death is configured as a theatre where everybody is invited to become an actor, retrospectively at least endowing their individual lives with meaning.

Benjamin draws attention to such a performative reading of his eighth thesis by using an expression which has completely slipped away from the English translation of his text. He writes that by accepting the 'task to bring about a real state of exception,' it is in fact positioned 'in front of the eyes:' *vor Augen stehen*, literally meaning 'stand before the eyes.' This expression more generally means to 'envision' or 'show,' but the German-language text emphasizes that the task he presents is to position or situate the real state of exception before our eyes, as a performance. In order to clarify in which sense such a real state of exception is both performative and philosophical and can give rise to a new understanding of history, I first want to demonstrate briefly how Benjamin activates the language of his own writing—with German being more directly available for such a meta-performative dimension than English—making the words on the page literally 'perform' his arguments.

The frequently quoted opening sentence of his academic thesis *On the Origin of the German Trauerspiel* is an excellent example of this performative strategy. Here Benjamin has integrated the inherent linguistic performativity with the claim that this sentence makes about a work of art: "*Es ist dem philosophischen Schrifttum eigen, mit jeder Wendung von neuem vor der Frage der Darstellung zu stehen*" (Benjamin 1972, 7). Howard Eiland's English translation of this sentence reads: 'It is peculiar to philosophical writing to be confronted anew at every turn with the question of presentation' (Benjamin 2019, 1). Philosophical writing is characterized by repeatedly facing or being confronted with the question of *Darstellung*, a key term in German aesthetics, literally meaning something which is positioned or situated, prefixed by *dar*, as in *darauf* (thereon) or *darüber* (about that); thus also, as in the eighth thesis pointing at something situated 'in front of the eyes,' *vor Augen stehen*.

Darstellung generally refers to a work of art which can either be seen as a 'presentation,' as something which is shown or presented as in Eiland's translation; or is a 'representation,' the term in Osborne's translation (Benjamin 2009), as something which imitates (represents) through *mimesis*, by applying or developing a certain aesthetic practice. The German term *Darstellung* means both or even designates something between them, emphasizing the self-referentiality of the opening sentence of the *Trauerspiel*-book, literally 'performing' itself through its language; depicting/performing how philosophical writing faces or confronts the 'question' of re/presentation, serving as a model for the mutual interactions and inter-dependencies between art and its critique; between doing and thinking.

This dialectical procedure, Benjamin adds, is repeated 'with every turn'—*mit jeder Wendung*—which both means with every new phrase (or turn) of the language used, but also by personifying philosophy as literally 'turning' towards the arts through the multi-layered choreography of the writing itself. Such a situation, with philosophical writing facing the question of re/presentation, also alludes to how Oedipus faces the sphinx, supposedly providing the 'correct' answer to its philosophical riddle-text defining what it means to be human. With its changing number of legs while the voice is one, the riddle-text is a *Darstellung* of a human. Oedipus's answer grants him the right to enter Thebes as its new ruler and the husband of his mother, Queen Jocasta. His solution of the riddle puts an end to the interregnum and the state of exception caused by the death of King Laius, killed by Oedipus himself. However, many years later, the fact that the person who killed Laius has not yet been identified gives rise to the new state of exception with which Sophocles' play opens. Benjamin's *Trauerspiel* book is an extended exploration of how his own philosophical writing 'faces' a broad range of enigmatic theatrical representations—in particular the *Trauerspiel*, the mourning play itself, but also Ancient Greek and Elizabethan tragedy, constantly turning in new directions.

In the eighth thesis of 'On the Concept of History,' written almost 15 years after the *Trauerspiel*-book, Benjamin returns to the scenario of facing the question of *Darstellung*, but with an unexpected turn. Here his point of departure is the inability of philosophy to cope with the state of exception which has become the rule. Therefore, this state of exception has to be replaced by or transformed into a *real* state of exception leading to new forms of knowledge about history which—as Benjamin implies—can re-ignite the performative dimensions of philosophical discourse/writing as well as the art of performance/theatre itself; while attempting to integrate the incomprehensibility and lack of transparency of a state of exception as essential components of this real state of exception which a work of art like Sophocles' tragedy enables us to approach.

For Benjamin himself, the last years of the Weimar Republic and the burning of the *Reichstag*, followed by the Nazi takeover of power in February 1933 and finally leading to the Second World War, had been an unphilosophical and unacceptable state of exception. For those living in such 'dark times' (*finstere Zeiten*, an expression frequently used by Benjamin's close friend Bertolt Brecht), it was impossible (or at least very difficult) to grasp the larger contexts for their own experiences as they were unfolding and in particular how to prevent becoming victimized by this ongoing state of exception. Benjamin and Brecht as well as many others left Germany immediately after the Nazi takeover. Benjamin himself experienced the uncertainty and the threat of such a state, as an inherent component of the exception itself, finally leading to his suicide in September 1940 after the difficult crossing of the Pyrenees by foot to the small Spanish border-town Portbou. In fact, we do not know the exact circumstances of his suicide nor whether he believed, assumed or actually knew that the policemen on guard outside his hotel room where he was spending the night would hand him over to the Nazis on the French side of the border the following morning.

Before continuing the discussion of Benjamin's eighth thesis it is important to point out that the frequently used English translation of *Ausnahmezustand* as 'state of *emergency*' misses an important point, because the opposite of 'emergency' is not 'rule.' Even if emergency laws are activated during a state of exception and Schmitt often used the term *Ernstfall* (which means 'emergency' or 'special case') as a synonym for *Ausnahmezustand*, for Benjamin the antithesis between 'exception' and 'rule' is what really matters for his understanding of such states. The weight of the antithesis exception/rule was reinforced by the historical fact that the initial *Ausnahmezustand* declared by Hitler when he took over the power in 1933 was never cancelled.

The dialectics between 'exception' and 'rule' has also received attention in other performative contexts. It is possible that Benjamin with his interest in surrealism was aware of Alfred Jarry's novel *Exploits and Opinions of Dr. Faustroll, Pataphysician*, from 1898, introducing the science of Pataphysics, bringing poetry and science closer to each other in playful or ludic constellations. According to Jarry,

> Pataphysics will be, above all, the science of the particular, despite the common opinion that the only science is that of the general. Pataphysics will examine the laws governing exceptions, and will explain the universe supplementary to this one /and/ will describe a universe which can be—and perhaps should be—envisaged in the place of the traditional one, since the laws that are supposed to have been discovered in the traditional universe are also correlations of exceptions, albeit more frequent ones, but in any case accidental data which reduced to the status of unexceptional exceptions, possess no longer even the virtue of originality. (Jarry 1996, 21–2)

Jarry's own play *King Ubu* demonstrates that it is possible to find humour, albeit absurd humour, in exploring the laws which govern exceptions.

There could however be no doubt that Benjamin was familiar with Bertolt Brecht's 'learning play' *The Exception and the Rule* (*Die Ausnahme und die Regel*), written in 1930, about a year after Benjamin and Brecht had become close friends. It was only published in Moscow in 1937, when both Benjamin and Brecht were living in exile, and it was first performed in Hebrew at Kibbutz Givat Haim, in what was then British Mandatory Palestine. It was directed by another German exile, Alfred Wolff, for the First of May celebrations at the kibbutz in 1938, at a time the tensions between Jews and Palestinians had just reached an additional stage of mutual mistrust and violence (Rokem 2015, 2016). Ten years later, in 1948, as a response to the events of the Shoah, Israel was declared an independent state, creating new states of exception, which are still (in 2022) unresolved as Israel refuses to recognize the rights of the Palestinian refugees or support the establishment of a Palestinian state.

Brecht's learning play presents a different form of exception from the one defined by Schmitt. Brecht depicts the unexpected outcome of a trial against a rich man who has killed his servant after they got lost in a desert trying to reach the village where oil has been found, where the rich man was supposed to sign a contract for extracting the 'riches' of the earth, to increase his wealth. The rich man was however brought to trial after shooting the servant, and claimed, in his defence, that he had understood the servant's gesture in the dim light of a setting sun as an attempt to shoot him with a pistol while the servant was in fact offering him a bottle of water to relieve the thirst brought about by the desert heat. Even if the evidence presented to the court unambiguously shows that the servant wanted to assist his thirsty master, the verdict is 'not guilty' because, as the judge explains, it is unlikely that a servant who has been mal-treated would not want to shoot his master. The rich man's cruel behaviour was logical from a socio-economic perspective, while the servant acted on the basis of human kindness, which under the existing circumstances was simply inconceivable.

The dialectics between the 'exception' and the 'rule' in Benjamin's eighth thesis—overcoming a state of exception which has become the rule by creating a real state of exception—is based on a somewhat different scenario. Instead of showing how justice is distorted, as Brecht did in his play, Benjamin draws attention to how states of exception are experienced by the 'victims' when they occur, unable to understand their situation. Brecht's focus is on the 'logical' conclusion of the verdict, however distorted; while for Benjamin, the less the historical subjects can grasp the dangers they experience—unable to give a rational or philosophical account of their own situation—the more threatening these dangers become. And the realization that such instances are constantly reoccurring intensifies the sense of threat and fear, sometimes with disastrous consequences, while in other instances, rescuing the victim through some unexpected stroke of luck or by a supernatural intervention, which is also possible, at least in the theatre.

Benjamin emphasizes the irrationality of states of exception, while Brecht shows how the 'criminal' behaviour of the wealthy businessman receives legal recognition by distorting not only justice, but the facts as well. For Benjamin, however, the facts are not without ambiguities. Benjamin in fact rejects an empirical approach, that the past can be understood through the 'common-sense' Enlightenment approach introduced by Leopold von Ranke (1795–1886), one the leading historians of the time and the founder of modern, source-based historiography. In the sixth thesis of 'On the Concept of History,' Benjamin declares that 'articulating the past historically does not mean recognizing it "the way it really was"' (*wie es denn eigentlich gewesen ist*), as Ranke had done; instead, he maintains, that understanding the past 'means appropriating a memory as it flashes up in a moment of danger,' claiming that historical materialism 'wishes to hold fast that image of the past which unexpectedly appears to the historical subject in a moment of danger. The danger threatens both the content of the tradition and those who inherit it' (Benjamin 2003, 391). Besides the irrationality of a dangerous moment in the present, as it is experienced, it also serves as the key which can unfold a chaotic moment in the past, creating a composite image of past and present.

Benjamin also explored such a multi-dimensional approach, formulated in theatrical terms, establishing connections between a present moment of danger and a previously unrecognized or distinctly meaningful past. In the *Arcades Project* he points out how the interaction between two or several discrete events in time establishes a view of history where 'each "now" is the now of a particular recognizability,' described as the formation of an image, which

> is that wherein what has been comes together in a flash with the now to form a constellation. In other words: image is dialectics at a standstill. For while the relation of the present to the past is purely temporal, the relation of what-has-been to the now is dialectical: not temporal in nature but figural [*bildlich*]. Only dialectical images are genuinely historical. (Benjamin 2002, 463)

On the one hand this creation of a standstill is related to Benjamin's description of the sudden appearance of a stranger, opening the door to the room where some form of violence is taking place. Benjamin used this image in several instances as he was explaining the use of the gesture of an interruption (*Unterbrechung*) in Brecht's epic theatre, which I have explored in detail at a previous occasion (Rokem 2019).

At the same time, just as Benjamin's performative enactment of philosophical writing in the opening sentence of the *Trauerspiel*-book alludes to a canonized dramatic source—Sophocles' *Oedipus Tyrannus*—the connection between two points in time, creating an image-constellation of two moments of exception, giving us a 'full picture' from which a philosophical discourse springs, directs us to another canonized drama with which Benjamin was occupied, Shakespeare's *Hamlet*. This play, which as *Oedipus Tyrannus* focuses on finding the assassin of a legal sovereign, is also situated between two interregnum exceptions: the aftermath of the death of Old King Hamlet and the crowning of Claudius, with which the play opens, and the expected crowning of Fortinbras, with which it ends.

Here I will only focus on the first appearance of the ghost—literally a figure from the past demanding to be remembered—making the past visible through what can be understood as a specific 'now' of recognizability. The first appearance of the ghost in the play itself is a moment when we can literally see how 'the time is out of joint,' as Hamlet remarks after he has encountered the ghost himself at the end of the first act (Shakespeare 2019; 1.5.189). The play itself opens with a gradually growing sense of anxiety—with the ominous question 'Who's there?' (1.1.1)—fuelled by the contradictory perceptions of what the guards have already experienced since a few nights with the appearance of the ghost. After the first 40 lines of the play the ghost—who has by then been referred to as 'this thing,' 'this dreaded sight' and 'this apparition' (1.1.21, 25, 28)—actually appears. Before this happens, Marcellus quotes Horatio, who 'says 'tis but our fantasy, / And will not let belief take hold of him' (1.1.23–4). However, as Marcellus adds, should it appear again, Horatio, who has already taken on a key role in interpreting what they are experiencing (and will be appointed for this task by Hamlet in the last scene, to tell Hamlet's story after his death), 'may approve our eyes and speak to it' (1.1.28), because—as we learn when the ghost appears—Horatio is a scholar who knows how to 'question it' (1.1.45).

After Horatio's sceptical dismissal of the ghost is repeated in his own voice—'Tush, tush, 'twill not appear' (1.1.29)—when Barnardo describes what he and Marcellus had seen the previous night, 'When yond same star that's westward from the pole / Had made his course t'illume that part of heaven / Where now it burns,' adding how 'The bell then beating one—' (1.1.35–9), Marcellus interrupts Barnardo's narrative, exclaiming 'Look where it comes again' (1.1.35–40). As Bernardo describes the previous appearance of the ghost it reappears, superimposing two discrete moments (or events), showing metatheatrically through a scenic image (or stage event) that 'The time is [literally] out of joint' (1.5.189). It is no longer possible to distinguish between the present moment of danger and the past event. They have, according to Benjamin's depiction of the real state of exception, become a composite image-constellation through which similar, discrete moments of crisis become superimposed.

The states of exception are staged very differently in *Oedipus Tyrannus* and in *Hamlet*. But they are both concerned with the legitimacy of political power during times of crisis and transition and the consequences such situations have for the characters involved, giving the spectators an opportunity, at least after the performance, to reflect on the situations inducing fear and anxiety. The medium of the theatre, through which these possibilities are communicated, is based on the fluidity between the direct involvement in a moment of uncertainty, on the one hand, and retrospective reflection, on the other. This fluidity can bridge the epistemological gap of stage representations between the direct experience of fear, persecution and displacement, on the one hand, and retrospective reflections and presentations of the more general characteristics of such shattering experiences, on the other. For those who experience the appearances of the ghost, it is no doubt a confusing and distressing experience, while a retrospective theatrical representation of these events on the stage would ideally strive to present a more synoptic understanding of such threatening situations, repeating them in different constellations, even trying to enlighten them within a causal or rational framework, by framing them aesthetically.

The paradox of theatrical representation, wavering between the unsettling experience of catastrophic events in the past, and the 'now' of the performance itself, framing those events aesthetically, moving freely between different time frames, involving supernatural agents or external narrators who explain to the spectators what the significance of those events is and how to express the out-of-jointness of time cannot be described on the basis of a simple formula. What I have been suggesting here is that this paradox is an expression of a 'real' state of exception, something for which we need a stage to make it re/presentable, or realizing what in Benjaminian terms is its 're/present-ability.' One of the basic tasks of the theatre is to address this paradox, setting up the spatio-temporal framework which can accommodate the chaotic and threatening experiences of the individuals who are appearing as dramatic characters in a stage performance, on the one hand, while at the same time enabling the spectators to understand and form an opinion concerning these unsettling experiences and even find ways to protest or take action against injustices and expressions of human failure, on the other. Such a strategy could even 'improve our position in the struggle against fascism' and other forms of injustice.

References

Agamben, Giorgio. 2005. *State of Exception*. Chicago: Chicago University Press.
Benjamin, Walter. 1972. *Ursprung des deutschen Trauerspiels*. Frankfurt am Main: Suhrkamp Taschenbuch Verlag.
———. 1991. 'Über den Begriff der Geschichte.' In *Gesammelte Schriften*, vol. 1, edited by Rolf Tiedemann and Hermann Schweppenhäuser, 693–704. Frankfurt am Main: Suhrkamp Taschenbuch Verlag.
———. 1999. 'Franz Kafka: On the Tenth Anniversary of his Death'. In *Selected Writings*, vol. 2, edited by Michael W. Jennings, Howard Eiland, and Gary Smith, translated by Harry Zohn, 794–818. Cambridge: Harvard University Press.
———. 2002. *The Arcades Project*. Translated by Howard Eiland and Kevin McLaughlin. Cambridge: Harvard University Press.
———. 2003. 'On the Concept of History.' In *Selected Writings*, vol. 4, edited by Howard Eiland and Michael W. Jennings, translated by Harry Zohn, 389–400. Cambridge: Harvard University Press.
———. 2009. *The Origin of German Tragic Drama*. Translated by John Osborne. New York: Verso Books.
———. 2019. *Origin of the German Trauerspiel*. Translated by Howard Eiland. Cambridge: Harvard University Press.
Bredekamp, H. 1999. 'From Walter Benjamin to Carl Schmitt, via Thomas Hobbes.' *Critical Inquiry*, 25(2): 247–66.
Hasan-Rokem, Galit. 2008. 'Carl Schmitt and Ahasver. The Idea of the State and the Wandering Jew.' *Behemoth. A Journal on Civilisation*, 2: 4–25.
Jarry, Alfred. 1996. *Exploits and Opinions of Dr. Faustroll, Pataphysician*. Translated by Simon Watson Taylor. Boston: Exact Change.
Kahn, Victoria. 2014, *The Future of Illusion: Political Theology and Early Modern Texts*. Chicago: University of Chicago Press.
Rokem, Freddie. 2010. *Philosophers and Thespians: Thinking Performance*. Stanford: Stanford University Press.
———. 2015. 'The Aesthetics of Learning: Bertolt Brecht's *Die Ausnahme und die Regel* (*The Exception and the Rule*).' *Theatre Topics*, 25(1): 57–66.

———. 2016. 'The Archives of *The Exception and the Rule*; Brecht in Kibbutz Givat Haim 1938 and 2013.' In *Beyond Evidence: Das Dokument in den Künsten*. 225–42. Paderborn: Wilhelm Fink.
———. 2018. 'On [the limits of] Affirmation: Benjamin and Wittgenstein.' *Performance Research*, 23(4/5): 134–40.
———. 2019. '"Suddenly a Stranger Appears": Walter Benjamin's Readings of Bertolt Brecht's Epic Theatre.' *Nordic Theatre Studies*, 31(1): 8–21.
Schmitt, Carl. 2009. *Hamlet or Hecuba: The Intrusion of the Time into the Play*. Translated by David Pan and Jennifer R. Rust. New York: Telos Press Publishing.
Shakespeare, William. 2019. *Hamlet, Prince of Denmark*. Third Edition. Cambridge: Cambridge University Press.
Weber, Samuel. 1992. 'Taking Exception to Decision: Walter Benjamin and Carl Schmitt.' *Diacritics*, 22(3/4): 5–18.

or to go out oneself, in order to 'open onto a future' (1987, 311). Perhaps surprisingly, little attention has been paid to the refrain as a theoretical resource for mobilities research, even though the concept aligns with some of the most-quoted studies in the field. For example, the refrain's focus on practice is echoed in Sheller and Urry's 'new mobilities paradigm' when they argue against an 'ontology of distinct "places" and "people"' and for a 'complex relationality of places and persons connected through performances' (2006, 214). Similarly, the notion of the refrain resonates with the views of Ahmed et al. (2003) on home and migration as acts of 'uprooting' and 'regrounding', which they regard as 'simultaneously affective, embodied, cultural and political processes' (2). They urge us to 'avoid assuming that home has an essential meaning, in advance of its making' (8); similarly, Deleuze and Guattari view 'home' as something that 'does not pre-exist: it was necessary to draw a circle around that uncertain and fragile center, to organize a limited space' (311). They also acknowledge that those practices have an explicitly affective dimension: their opening metaphor portrays a child, 'gripped with fear', using a familiar song as a 'rough sketch of a calming and stabilizing [...] center in the heart of chaos' (311).

Although perhaps too metaphorical, even metaphysical, to be embraced by the social sciences, the concept of the refrain has great potential to explicate the Terezín/Theresienstadt prisoners' cultural practices as a form of regrounding within the chaotic space of the ghetto. Such practices enabled the prisoners to go 'from chaos to the threshold of a territorial assemblage' and to organize territories within the ghetto according to familiar models (Deleuze and Guattari 1987, 312). In this study, however, I will focus on the third aspect of the refrain: when one imaginatively leaves the territorial assemblage to open onto possible futures. I will examine Czech and German-language scripts that enacted a form of virtual uprooting, allowing the prisoners, from within a calm and stable territory established through familiar theatrical practices, to explore their uncertain future by representing their departure from Terezín/Theresienstadt.

Migration and the Terezín/Theresienstadt Ghetto

These scripts were written in an environment created by very unusual conditions of forced migration. Below I describe the conditions that allowed the prisoners to continue their pre-war theatrical practices in the ghetto and why, in their scripts, they created both eagerly anticipated and greatly feared versions of their future.

As Raul Hilberg documented decades ago, the Nazis set up an elaborate network of transportation—a vast system of mobility—to carry out their mission of destruction. A key role in this network was played by transit camps such as Terezín/Theresienstadt: they served as places to gather the Jews of Europe before sending them on to the death camps and slave labour camps. Although Terezín/Theresienstadt served other functions as well, most famously as a

CHAPTER 4

Theatre as Refrain: Representations of Departure from the Terezín/Theresienstadt Ghetto

Lisa Peschel

The application of theories of migration to the history of the Holocaust is still in its early stages. In his recent study, *Journeys from the Abyss: The Holocaust and Forced Migration*, historian Tony Kushner argues that those fleeing Nazi persecution 'can be meaningfully set alongside refugee movements from before and after the Nazi era' (2017, 12). He also points to other recent works that have applied migration theory to complicate the view of Holocaust journeys, such as Tim Cole's examination of movement both into and out of the Hungarian ghettos (2011) and Simone Gigliotti's interpretation of testimony about train deportations 'through the prism of cultural geography, and theories of mobility and transit' (2009, 65). As geographer Etienne Piguet succinctly states, 'it seems less and less justified to treat forced migration as incompatible with migration theory in general' (2018, 24).

In the following essay I will consider the Terezín/Theresienstadt ghetto as a site within a system of forced migration and will interpret theatrical performances by the prisoners through Deleuze and Guattari's notion of 'the territorial refrain' as a way that territories are constituted through practice. In brief, the refrain has three aspects: using a familiar practice to establish a 'calm and stable' centre point in a chaotic environment, using known landmarks and practices to organize a space of 'home' around that point and using that 'home' as a stable point from which to 'join with the world'—to let outside forces in,

L. Peschel (✉)
University of York, York, UK
e-mail: lisa.peschel@york.ac.uk

© The Author(s), under exclusive license to Springer Nature Switzerland AG 2023
Y. Meerzon, S. E. Wilmer (eds.), *The Palgrave Handbook of Theatre and Migration*, https://doi.org/10.1007/978-3-031-20196-7_4

model ghetto displayed to visitors from the International Red Cross in the summer of 1944 to mislead them about the nature of the concentration camps, its underlying function was always to facilitate deportations. Tables of arriving trains (from November 1941 until April 1945, mainly from Czechoslovakia, Germany and Austria) and departing transports (from January through October 1942 to various destinations, but after October 1942, mainly to Auschwitz) reveal the transitory nature of life in the ghetto (Lagus and Polák 1964, 334–348). Nevertheless, against this backdrop of constant mobility, some prisoners remained in the ghetto for months or even years: long enough to establish a cultural life, and long enough to share intense hopes and fears about how their time in the ghetto would end.

The Czech Jews, the largest of the national groups in the ghetto and the first to arrive, underwent what could be called a forced internal migration. Although certainly a traumatic and disorienting break with their former lives, these transports to the ghetto were not the 'hidden Holocaust' inside cattle cars that Gigliotti describes (2009, 2), but rather, passenger trains taking them to a known destination in their own country: the small, historical fortress town of Terezín/Theresienstadt, located 40 miles northwest of Prague.

The ghetto, although fraught with dangers, was structured according to familiar principles. The Nazis forced representatives of the Prague Jewish community to plan and establish the ghetto, and an organizational chart of the so-called Jewish Self-Administration from 1941–1942 includes, for example, departments of labour, youth care, health services and even recreation (Hájková 2020, Fig. 1.2). According to Rabbi Erich Weiner, leader of the *Freizeitgestaltung* (Office of Leisure Time Activity) when it was established in February 1942, the prisoners themselves organised the first cultural activities in December 1941. These programmes of recitations and light music featured poetry performed in the languages most frequently spoken by the Czech and German Jews: Czech and German (Weiner 1999 [1943], 210–11). From these humble beginnings the cultural life expanded, and by July 1944 the *Freizeitgestaltung* included sections for theatre, music, lectures, several sports and a library (Adler 2005 [1960], 239–40).

All of this activity, however, took place against acute awareness that their stay in the ghetto was temporary. Successful escapes were exceedingly rare; therefore, there were only three ways that prisoners could realistically contemplate leaving the ghetto: liberation, deportation or death. Regarding liberation, prisoners pinned their hopes on a short war—so short that, in one script, they mocked their own optimistic estimate of six weeks (Peschel 2014, 214). The possibility of death in the ghetto, perhaps surprisingly, was not a great danger for the young authors of the plays I will examine. Most of the approximately 33,000 prisoners who perished in Terezín/Theresienstadt were over 60 years of age; the mortality rate for Czech Jews born after 1900 was less than 10 per cent (Hájková 2020, 116, Table 2.1). For this group, fear of death was mainly associated with transports leaving the ghetto. Announcement of an outgoing transport inspired fear, even crippling panic; most prisoners did not know their destination, but they suspected it would be much worse (Hájková 2020, 201, 231). Prisoners were not completely powerless in the face of this threat. The ghetto's Jewish leaders were able to protect certain groups until the autumn of 1944, and those who found themselves on a transport list could petition to be removed (Hájková 2020, 215). Nevertheless, the irregular pattern of departure and unknown destination of the transports made them a constant source of anxiety.

Thus, for the young Czech Jews, Terezín/Theresienstadt was familiar in many ways. The forces of chaos, however, were only weakly contained: the rules of the ghetto, and even its Jewish leadership, changed on Nazi whim, and the prisoners faced hunger, overcrowding and illness, the death of loved ones, and the ever-present threat of the outgoing transports.

Theatre in the Ghetto as Refrain

Thrust into the chaotic environment of the ghetto, the prisoners brought the familiar practice of theatrical performance with them. There that practice, along with many others imported from pre-war life, functioned, in Deleuze and Guattari's terms, as a 'song' that established 'the beginning of order in chaos' (311) by imposing familiar administrative practices, as well as embodied practices of theatrical performance and attendance, upon the ghetto. The prisoners sometimes engaged in completely escapist performances, blocking out the ghetto to experience temporary relief from constant anxiety, especially by performing familiar works from the pre-war period. In their original scripts, however, the young Czech-Jewish prisoners often engaged with the ghetto itself, taking 'something from chaos across the filter or sieve of the space that has been drawn' and confronting their hopes and fears within an environment under their control (311).

The most common 'filtering' mechanisms were familiar forms of humour. In my anthology of plays written in the ghetto, from which I will draw all the following examples, ten of the twelve scripts are comedies (Peschel 2014). In effect, with these comic plays, they domesticated dangerous events in the ghetto by placing them within familiar narratives and aesthetic forms and associating them with laughter rather than fear. This enabled them not only to gain temporary relief inside the theatre, but also to face the reality of the ghetto itself with less fear (Peschel 2018).

To explore departure from the ghetto, they also wrote scripts that sent a 'thread of a tune' into the future (Deleuze and Guattari 1987, 311). In these plays they used a wider variety of filtering techniques: sometimes they represented anticipated or threatening events as comic, or contained them within familiar forms; sometimes they constructed metaphors or allegorical narratives that enabled them to regard possible futures from a safe distance. In the rest of this overview of theatre in the ghetto, I will engage briefly with several representations of leaving Terezín/Theresienstadt. In the more detailed case studies below, I will explore the only two non-comic scripts that have, thus far, come to light, reading both as allegories for the moment of departure.

Liberation, in most cases, is represented in humorous and optimistic ways. For example, the duo Felix Porges and Vítězslav Horpatzky created a Czech-language musical revue (a cabaret with scenes held together by an overarching plot) based on a familiar comic refrain: the style of the tremendously popular interwar Liberated Theatre of Jiří Voskovec and Jan Werich (Taussig 2001 [1944], 313). In *Smějte se s námi* (Laugh with Us), rather than constructing an extended metaphor, they quite literally perform their hoped-for future. The first and last scenes take place in the present of the ghetto, with the duo welcoming their spectators and then bidding them farewell, but most of the revue is spent guiding them through an imagined postwar Prague, identical to the one they left behind.

The specific moment of departure is represented by a single sentence. The penultimate scene of the revue takes place in a Prague city park, even further in the postwar future. Horpatzky, in this scene playing a pensioner rather than simply a postwar version of himself, explains the ghetto to Porges, who plays a much younger man asking about the strange insignia on the pensioner's jacket: the yellow star. At the end of a long, comic dialogue about life in the ghetto, the young man remarks 'it must have been a total madhouse there. I'm surprised you didn't try to escape'. The pensioner replies simply, 'That wasn't necessary; it was dissolved' (Peschel 2014, 214). This moment, narrated from a distant postwar future, is remarkable in its brevity and nonchalance: in the pensioner's memory, the end of the ghetto was so uneventful that it was not even worth describing.

Young Zionist Walter Freud employed a similar strategy to represent liberation but began by constructing an allegory based upon a different type of familiar refrain. For centuries, comic performances called *Purim shpiels*, or Purim plays, have been used to mark the Jewish holiday of Purim, which celebrates the Jews' victory over their enemies as described in the biblical Book of Esther. In Freud's German-language *Purimspiel*, a cabaret-like collection of comic scenes, he first introduced the notion of liberation allegorically. In a scene that places seemingly modern-day characters in biblical times, a character named Frau Mueller tells another named Herr Schoen that the battle between the Jews and their enemies has been cancelled, 'and now we'll go free' (Peschel 2014, 299). Two subsequent scenes set in biblical times are interrupted by Herr Schoen rushing in to announce 'Friends, we are saved' (302) and 'We're free again—the whole thing's been resolved' (305). His final appearance, however, takes place in the ghetto. He leads a celebratory procession past a young Zionist worker named Aaron, saying simply, 'If I say it, you can believe it!' One of Aaron's fellow Zionists then calls out to him from the procession, 'You're going to miss Aliyah. Hey, come with us …' (312). In this scene, which abandons the allegory of the Purim story to represent the prisoners' own idealized vision of departure from the ghetto, Freud establishes an affective territory that goes beyond simply controlling fear with a familiar song: he represents not just calm but the relief, even euphoria, of freedom. Regarding the post-departure future, rather than the longed-for return to Prague that is represented in such detail in *Laugh with Us*, Freud looks past the moment of liberation towards the Zionist goal of making Aliyah: to return to the land of their forefathers and create a Jewish state.

Other plays explored the possibility, not of liberation, but of deportation and even death. *Laugh with Us* engaged briefly with the much-feared outgoing transports, using the filtering technique of humour to bring this element of chaos safely into their theatrical space. In the middle of the park scene, the pensioner briefly describes the outgoing transports as a prize that children compete for, 'since only selected people were allowed to leave on such a transport' (Peschel 2014, 208). Thus, Porges and Horpatzky placed this threat within a familiar framework and attempted to make it, temporarily, a source of laughter rather than fear.

Prince Bedridden, a Czech-language musical revue with the German title *Prinz Bettliegend*, briefly acknowledged the fear that deportation evoked, representing it in a way that actors and audience could manage rather than attempting to replace it with another affect. Although only the songs were preserved, survivor testimony reveals that this comic fairy tale by Josef Lustig satirized corruption and favouritism in the ghetto regarding protection from transports. It drew not only upon the style of the Liberated Theatre but also upon literal refrains: prisoner František Kovanic set his ghetto-specific lyrics to melodies by Jaroslav Ježek, Voskovec and Werich's beloved composer. Most were humorous, but the comic mood was suspended in one song called 'My Suitcase and Me' (*Kufr a já*), set to Ježek's pensive melody 'The World Inside Out' (*Svět naruby*). The lyrics establish the suitcase as a metaphor for the singer:

> Just a number, not a name, thin skin covering a frame
> In weather foul or fair, delivered here and there
> That's my suitcase—and that's me

The song ends with this verse:

> A thorny uphill path, a long road full of hurt for my suitcase, me as well
> If I'm lucky I'll just lose my shirt, if I'm not I'll lose myself. (Peschel 2014, 129)

In 'My Suitcase and Me', the metaphor did not create safety through distance; the singer and the suitcase are repeatedly, explicitly conflated and both potentially face destruction. But the form within which the lyrics were set—the calming, even if melancholy, melody—contained the threat within a familiar refrain, enabling the prisoners to contemplate this possible future. For the brief duration of a single song, they could safely acknowledge and experience their fear without being overwhelmed by it.

Case Studies: *The Smoke of Home* and *Orpheus*

Both of the full-length non-comic plays that have come to light thus far represent the moment of departure from the ghetto. Unlike Kovanic's metaphor of the suitcase, however, the allegories constructed by the authors of these plays establish a degree of distance from the prisoners' own experience. One play engages with liberation as a moment when they will be forced to confront almost unimaginable loss, and the other with the possibility of death.

Dým domova (The Smoke of Home) represents the moment of liberation through the allegory of a historical drama. This Czech-language script was written by two young authors, Zdeněk Eliáš and Jiří Stein. In brief, it is a one-act play about four soldiers imprisoned in a tower in Marburg, in the German Protestant state of Hessen, during the Thirty Years' War. The characters spend much of the play conversing about their homes as they imagine returning to the pleasures of their former lives. Near the end of the play, in a moment of conflict triggered by an opportunity to escape, the character Casselius reveals to the other three the information that he has been keeping from them: that their homeland has been utterly destroyed in the war. In the moment when their dreams of home are dashed, bells ring to mark the declaration of peace.

The allegory that distances this negative view of the end of the war from their own experience—the historical setting—simultaneously contains the event within a familiar narrative. The history of the Thirty Years' War was well known to Czechs: in their national master narrative, that war led to defeat by the forces of the Catholic Habsburgs and centuries of Germanization that ended only with the establishment of independent Czechoslovakia in 1918. The authors also drew on a familiar source of inspiration. Rainer Maria Rilke's prose poem *The Song of Love and Death of the Cornet Christoph Rilke* was tremendously popular during this period in both the original German and in various Czech translations. *The Smoke of Home* starts with a prologue that echoes the beginning of Rilke's poem, both works take place against the backdrop of a seventeenth-century battle, and Eliáš and Stein's main character is also a cornet (standard-bearer). The name of that character, Christian, and the fact that the protagonists are German Catholics from Bavaria rather than Protestant Czechs, may have served as additional distancing devices for the Czech-Jewish prisoners. The elements of familiarity within this refrain, however, organized a territory within which to explore the possibility that liberation would not be a moment of joy and relief.

The authors prepared the audience for the vicarious experience of loss by portraying vividly each character's attachment to his home. Each identifies with a specific location and landscape, and a specific emotional or sensual touchstone. Their descriptions convey not only a sense of place but of movement through it: young Christian envisions his fiancée running down the lane to meet him; the old soldier von Waldau looks forward to riding and hunting, drinking and carousing on his ancestral lands, Catholic priest Father Anselm imagines peaceful walks in the parsonage garden. Casselius, however, refuses to be drawn into nostalgic conversations. He laughs when they ask him where his home is; he simply gestures in a circle around himself.

The moment when the others must face the magnitude of their losses is triggered by an opportunity for only two of them to escape. To stop the violent conflict that breaks out, Casselius reveals to the other three the information that he has been keeping from them about their home village of Rain, von Waldau's ancestral lands and Christian's family estate:

> Casselius: There are no stones left standing in your Rain—today your church and parsonage, Father Anselm, are shattered ruins [...] [Waldau] has long since stopped smoking amidst the trampled and ruined fields! And you, Christian, were you to go from Rain up to Stetten, at the crossroads by the three firs you would see a thread of smoke from the conflagration where Stetten used to stand! (Peschel 2014, 165)

Allegorically, by forcing the characters to confront the losses caused by the war, the authors enable their spectators to do the same: to prepare themselves for the possibility that the homes to which they longed to return, and the loved ones with whom they hoped to be reunited would be destroyed or irrevocably changed. This confrontation, however, did not take place through performance. According to a handful of survivors, Eliáš and Stein decided such an ending, even in allegorical form, would be too devastating for prisoners who needed hope above all else. Rather than staging the play, they shared the manuscript with friends young enough to bear the thought that they would have to build completely new lives after the war (Peschel 2014, 147).

The German-language verse drama *Orpheus*, written by young poet Georg Kafka, a distant relative of Franz Kafka, portrays a lesser-known aspect of the mythical figure: the end of his life. In brief, the script begins with a monologue to the audience by a shepherd boy, Alkaios, about Orpheus' fate after the death of Eurydice: he has chosen to live as a 'simple shepherd, like us' (Peschel 2014, 337). As the curtain opens, the other shepherds lament the poet's deep melancholy; without his music, the earth refuses to bear fruit. But a visit by the god Hermes, bearing a mysterious gift from the underworld, finally sets in motion the chain of events that leads to his re-engagement with his music and to his death.

As with *The Smoke of Home*, the allegory that both evoked the possibility of death and distanced it from the prisoners' own experience was based upon a familiar narrative: the well-known myth. Kafka placed the intensely emotional content within a carefully structured form, alternating throughout most of the poem between iambic pentameter and hexameter (I have preserved the metre in my blank-verse translations). What I will mainly examine here, however, is the evolution in Orpheus' attitude towards death. As the play begins, he is virtually paralysed with grief. Although the shepherds beg him to play for them again, he is consumed by a profound sense of isolation. He has destroyed his lyre, silencing his own artistic voice, and he both fears and longs for death. He shares a premonition with Alkaios:

> For just above your head, my slim young shepherd boy,
> I hear the wings of my destiny beating. (Peschel 2014, 346)

When Hermes arrives from the underworld with a gift from Eurydice, a mysterious object wrapped in black, Orpheus is initially overwhelmed by its association with death. When he finally reaches out to open it, his mother, from whom he has been estranged, appears. She begs him to give it to her instead, but he refuses. As she walks away, it appears that he has severed his last tie to the world of the living. But in the moment that he chooses death by unwrapping the gift, 'a golden harp, entwined in black laurel', his voice as an artist is restored:

> Oh evening of my lifetime! Symbol of fulfilment
> My lyre, it has now returned to me
> I am no longer mute. (356)

As he begins to play, his melancholy evaporates. Even the metre of the verse changes to irregular dactylic feet, capturing the dizzying rhythm of his song:

> Everywhere happiness, gone is all loneliness!
> Finally the end is in sight, open the door into light!
> Tear all things stable apart, spirit in verse! (358)

He summons the Bacchantes, and the myth takes its course: in a frenzy of dancing, they kill him. But in the final moments of his life, everything from which he has been alienated is restored to him. The shepherds not only embrace him but perpetuate his art: Alkaios exhorts the others to 'gather up his early-orphaned verses' (359), and they recite brief echoes of Orpheus' poetry until they are interrupted by the voice of Eurydice. He responds to her call lovingly, and with his last breath he reaches out to his mother, imploring the shepherds to tell her 'she should weep no more…' (360).

Within the carefully structured world of the play, Kafka makes the thought of death bearable by representing it not only as an act of agency, but as a choice that reunites Orpheus with Eurydice, restores all his ties to his loved ones and ensures his immortality as an artist. Very few prisoners literally chose death through suicide (Hájková 2020, 148), but they may have drawn parallels with their own situation by reading death as a metaphor for transport. Just as it was possible to appeal to be taken off a transport list, it was possible to volunteer for one. When Georg Kafka's mother was deported in May 1944, he chose to join her.

Unlike *The Smoke of Home*, *Orpheus* did have a modest production: it was performed as a dramatic reading by a single actor. Perhaps the mythical setting provided enough distance for the audience to bear the allegory; one survivor even interpreted it as 'without reference to Theresienstadt or the period' (Adler 2005 [1960], 759).

The Final Departure

Within the ghetto, all three aspects of Deleuze and Guattari's 'territorial refrain' played out through theatrical practice. With their performances, the prisoners established calm centre points in the chaos of the ghetto. Around these points they created virtual territories defined by familiar practices. From within these safe spaces, some of their scripts sent a 'thread of a tune' into the future, exploring and preparing for departure from Terezín/Theresienstadt.

Porges and Horpatzky's version of the future in which the ghetto was simply 'dissolved', however, did not come to pass. Of all the authors presented here, only Porges remained in the ghetto until it was liberated by the Soviet army in May 1945. Josef Lustig died of an illness in January 1944. Eliáš and Kafka were deported in May 1944. Four months later, on 28 September, mass transports began. The SS took over organization of the lists and no one was safe. Two-thirds of the ghetto's population, including Horpatzky, Freud, Kovanic and Stein, were sent to Auschwitz in a single month. Only Eliáš survived.

The Smoke of Home foreshadowed many prisoners' postwar fates. Those Czech Jews who survived and attempted the internal migration back to their homes returned to a social and cultural version of the physical destruction that the character Casselius had described. Although most towns and cities had remained unscathed, Czech society had radically changed during six years of Nazi occupation. Many survivors, having lost most or all of their family members, faced new forms of antisemitism and a very difficult process of regrounding (Peschel 2012).

Although, in Georg Kafka's play, Orpheus perished, the script also opened onto a possible future in which someone might gather up the poet's 'early-orphaned verses'. That possible future has been realized by postwar artists and scholars, who have used the prisoners' refrains to create new territories of commemoration and pedagogy. Some works, like *The Smoke of Home*, were preserved complete, and needed only to be reanimated through performance. Others, surviving as fragments, inspire more complex practices of co-creation that generate new works of art (Peschel and Sikes 2020). When we perpetuate their refrains through our own theatrical practices, we venture from home on the thread of a tune that links their voices and ours, hoping to craft a safer territory within our own uncertain future.

References

Adler, H.G. 2005 [1960]. *Theresienstadt: das Antlitz einer Zwangsgemeinschaft.* Göttingen: Wallstein.

Ahmed, Sara, Claudia Castañeda, Anne-Marie Fortier, and Mimi Sheller, eds. 2003. *Uprootings/Regroundings: Questions of Home and Migration.* Oxford, New York: Berg.

Cole, Tim. 2011. *Traces of the Holocaust: Journeying in and out of the Ghettos.* London, New York: Continuum.

Deleuze, Gilles and Félix Guattari. 1987. *A Thousand Plateaus: Capitalism and Schizophrenia.* Translated by Brian Massumi. Minneapolis, MN: University of Minnesota Press.

Gigliotti, Simone. 2009. *The Train Journey: Transit, Captivity, and Witnessing in the Holocaust.* New York: Berghahn Books.

Hájková, Anna. 2020. *The Last Ghetto: An Everyday History of Theresienstadt.* New York, NY: Oxford University Press.

Kushner, Tony. 2017. *Journeys from the Abyss: The Holocaust and Forced Migration from the 1880s to the Present.* Liverpool: Liverpool University Press.

Lagus, Karel and Josef Polák. 1964. *Město za mřížemi.* Prague: Naše vojsko.

Peschel, Lisa, 2012. '"A Joyful Act of Worship": Survivor Testimony on Czech Culture in the Terezín Ghetto and Postwar Reintegration in Czechoslovakia, 1945–48.' *Holocaust and Genocide Studies* 26 (2), 209–228.

———, ed. 2014. *Performing Captivity, Performing Escape: Cabarets and Plays from the Terezín/ Theresienstadt Ghetto.* Calcutta: Seagull Press.

———, ed. 2018. 'Laughter in the Ghetto: Cabarets from a Concentration Camp.' In *Theater unter NS-Herrschaft: Theatre under Pressure*, edited by Brigitte Dalinger and Veronika Zangl, 271–283. Vienna: Vienna University Press.

Peschel, Lisa and Alan Sikes. 2020. 'Pedagogy, Performativity and "Never Again": Staging Plays from the Terezín Ghetto.' *Holocaust Studies* 26 (2), 259–281.

Piguet, Etienne. 2018. 'Theories of Voluntary and Forced Migration'. In *Routledge Handbook of Environmental Displacement and Migration*, eds. Robert A. McLeman and François Gemenne, 17–28. London, New York: Routledge.

Sheller, Mimi and John Urry. 2006. 'The New Mobilities Paradigm'. *Environment and Planning A* 38 (2), 207–226.

Taussig, Josef. 2001 [1944]. 'O terezínských kabaretech'. In *Terezínské studie a dokumenty 2001*, edited by Miroslav Kárný, Jaroslava Milotová and Eva Lorencová, 310–46. Prague: Academia.

Weiner, Erich. 1999 [1943]. 'Freizeitgestaltung in Theresienstadt.' In *Theatrical Performance during the Holocaust: Texts, Documents, Memoirs*, edited by Rebecca Rovit and Alvin Goldfarb, 209–30. Baltimore: Johns Hopkins University Press.

CHAPTER 5

Refugees and the Right to Have Rights

S. E. Wilmer

The notion of universal human rights has proved to be an illusion for refugees. Referencing the work of Hannah Arendt and Giorgio Agamben, this chapter will review the uneasy position of non-citizens, often reduced to what Agamben calls 'bare life' (1998, 6–9). It will contrast the ancient Athenian moral value of *philoxenia* (hospitality) with the legal powers of the modern state to determine who can enter and remain in the country and under what conditions. It will reveal how the theatre (as well as other art forms) can play an important role in empowering refugees to challenge the restrictions imposed by the nation-state and demonstrate how specific forms of theatre can heighten awareness about various aspects of human rights. For example, Maxi Obexer's *Illegal Helpers* explores deportation procedures in German-speaking states, highlighting methods by which ordinary citizens can circumvent legal measures to enable refugees to remain in their countries. Many plays, such as *The Charges* by Elfriede Jelinek, emphasize the moral obligations of citizens and governments to offer hospitality to refugees arriving in their country. Moreover, as in the case of Refugee Club Impulse's *Letters Home* and their campaign 'My Right is Your Right,' refugees themselves use theatre and performance to claim their rights.

S. E. Wilmer (✉)
School of Drama, Film, and Music, Trinity College Dublin, Dublin, Ireland
e-mail: SWILMER@tcd.ie

Defining Human Rights

In the eighteenth century, American and French revolutionaries attempted to define the notion of human rights, such as 'Life, Liberty and the pursuit of Happiness' in the USA and the 'Declaration of the Rights of Man and of the Citizen' in France. However, it immediately became clear that what were supposedly universal human rights did not apply to everyone, such as women, slaves, those without property, or members of particular ethnic minorities.

In the twentieth century, a renewed effort to define the concept of human rights evolved as a result of the massive number of displaced persons from two world wars. According to Giorgio Agamben,

> the first appearance of refugees as a mass phenomenon occurred at the end of World War I, when the collapse of the Russian, Austro-Hungarian, and Ottoman empires, and the new order created by peace treaties, profoundly upset the demographic and territorial structure of Central and Eastern Europe. In just a short time, a million and a half White Russians, seven hundred thousand Armenians, five hundred thousand Bulgarians, a million Greeks, and hundreds of thousands of Germans, Hungarians, and Romanians left their countries and moved elsewhere. (Agamben 1995, 16–17)

Regarding this inter-war period, Hannah Arendt wrote, 'we became aware of the existence of a right to have rights ... only when millions of people emerged who had lost and could not regain these rights because of the new global situation' (1968, 296–97).

In order to define human rights, politicians encountered a major structural impediment. Following the First World War and the dissolution of empires into nation-states, the new states established militarized border posts marking off the boundaries of their newly created countries and restricting entry. According to Arendt, 'suddenly, there was no place on earth where migrants could go without the severest restrictions, no country where they would be assimilated, no territory where they could found a new community of their own.... It was a problem not of space but of political organization' (1968, 293–94). She argued that the control of national borders by newly created nation-states had established a new order that protected its own citizens but denied the rights of others: 'Nobody had been aware that mankind, for so long a time considered under the image of a family of nations, had reached the stage where whoever was thrown out of one of these tightly organized closed communities found himself thrown out of the family of nations altogether' (1968, 294).

Following the Second World War, the United Nations tried to establish international conventions about human rights which would, amongst other measures, protect refugees fleeing from persecution. In 1948 the General Assembly of the United Nations adopted the *Universal Declaration of Human Rights* which proclaimed: 'Everyone has the right to seek and to enjoy in other countries asylum from persecution' (UN 1948, Article 14). In 1951, under the auspices of the United Nations, 26 states concluded a new convention, the

Convention relating to the Status of Refugees 1951, article 1A (2), which defines a refugee as 'someone who is unable or unwilling to return to their country of origin owing to a well-founded fear of being persecuted for reasons of race, religion, nationality, membership of a particular social group, or political opinion' (UNHCR 2010, 3). This Convention also clarified certain important rights for refugees. Article 33 prohibited host nations from the *refoulement* of refugees: 'No Contracting State shall expel or return ("refouler") a refugee in any manner whatsoever to the frontiers of territories where his life or freedom would be threatened on account of his race, religion, nationality, membership of a particular social group or political opinion' (UNHCR 2010, 30). Also, Article 31 proclaimed that refugees should not be punished for arriving illegally in the host country.

Circumventing Human Rights

However, such efforts to establish international conventions on human rights have been only partially successful. Nation-states have developed various methods to curb the influx of refugees, often infringing these conventions. Despite the 1951 UN convention on refugees stating explicitly that countries 'shall not impose penalties, on account of their illegal entry or presence, on refugees' (UNHCR 2010, 29), many states treat them and those assisting them as criminals because they have entered illegally (see EU Monitor 2002). Furthermore, rather than welcoming refugees, countries around the world have been building fences and walls to keep them out. The United States has been stepping up control of their borders since 9/11, extending a wall along the southern border with Mexico since 2008, and more than 100,000 'illegal aliens' have been deported annually. Similarly, the EU has tried to discourage or impede refugees, other than those fleeing from Ukraine during the current war, thereby gaining the reputation of 'fortress Europe.' Many European countries have closed their borders, reinforced and extended their border defences, banned air and sea travel for those without visas, and introduced intimidating practices. In addition, the EU Dublin regulation requires refugees to have their asylum applications processed in the first country they enter in the EU, and this has resulted in the backlog of huge numbers of refugees along the Mediterranean coast (e.g. in Cyprus, Greece, Italy, Malta and Spain), especially on the island of Lesbos.

Moreover, governmental authorities frequently deport refugees back to the country from which they have fled without first determining whether they have a legitimate claim for asylum. Frontex, the European Agency for Management of the External Borders created by the EU in 2005 (and now the agency with the largest budget in the EU), has often assisted in the return of refugees who were in boats on their way to the Canary Islands or across the Mediterranean from Africa. Rather than safeguarding the rights of refugees, it has focused its efforts on their interception and deportation (see Cross 2011, 58). For example, in 2006 Frontex launched Operation Hera to prevent migration from

Africa. With the help of the Spanish, Portuguese, Italian, and Finnish governments and 'following bilateral agreements between Spain and Senegal and Mauritania, including repatriation agreements' (Frontex 2017), Frontex used planes and boats and 'the installation of the SIVE maritime surveillance system' (Frontex 2017) to intercept boats leaving the African coast, thereby reducing the number of migrants from 32,000 in 2006 to a mere 170 by 2012.

The EU has also subsidized internment camps and other forms of accommodation outside the EU to deter refugees from entering. Turkey houses more than three million refugees, and when the Turkish government threatened to help them cross the borders into the EU in 2016, the EU agreed to pay it six billion euro to support the cost of housing them (European Commission 2020). The advantage to the EU for supporting refugee camps outside its borders is that the asylum seekers will never actually set foot in the EU, and thus their application for asylum may never have to be processed. The idea for these camps has been very appealing to Member States, but it has raised complaints from human rights organizations that they function like concentration camps. Nation-states have sponsored these camps so that they don't have to take direct responsibility for refugees and have encouraged the development of a non-governmental industry to cater for them. As Seyla Benhabib writes, 'The elaborate game of head counting, status granting, and legal classification [...] has spawned a transnational set of institutions, treaties, and litigations, as well as creating armies of aid-workers, humanitarians, camp directors, and international lawyers in addition to hundreds of NGOs and INGOs' (Benhabib, 2017, p. 115).

In 2013, after the fall of Muammar Gaddafi and the ensuing civil war, the Libyan coastguard was unable to patrol its borders. As a result, the Italian government launched a programme called *Mare Nostrum* to patrol the sea off the Libyan coast. In addition to forcing refugee boats back to Libya, it assisted in many rescues, enabling refugees to land in Italy. When this programme ended, the EU refused to continue it, and NGOs came to the assistance of refugees in the Mediterranean, helping them to enter Europe. Recently, however, Member States have impeded such activities and the EU has instead funded Operation Sophia to help the Libyan coastguard (also funded by the EU) return refugees to overcrowded and dangerous Libyan detention centres (Michael et al. 2019; Johnson 2021). According to a report in the *Guardian*,

> in late 2017, decision-makers in Brussels were split between a group of hardliners who wanted Europe's migration control outsourced to Libya and a reduction in sea crossings at all costs, and others who argued that [Operation] Sophia and the NGO ships should be allowed to continue rescue operations. The hardliners won out. Now, more than two years later, the presence of European rescue ships in the central Mediterranean is minimal. (Howden et al. 2020)

By contrast with their current welcoming attitude towards Ukrainians fleeing their country in 2022, Central and Eastern European countries have tended to be hostile towards refugees. Prime Minister Viktor Orbán announced a state of emergency, built border fences, reinforced border patrols, and warned that anyone (including children) trying to enter Hungary illegally would be detained in converted shipping containers on their borders. In 2021 the Belarusian government used refugees as pawns in a geopolitical game of retaliation for EU sanctions against their country. Belarusian travel agencies promoted flights from the Middle East for people from Iraq, Turkey, and other countries. On arrival, they were transported from the airport into the forests, and told where they could safely cross unpatrolled borders into EU member states. With many thousands of refugees suddenly coming across their borders, Poland, Latvia, and Lithuania all declared states of emergency; deployed soldiers, police, and border guards to guard the borders; erected razor-wire fences; and in some cases pushed back refugees entering their countries. In response, the Belarusian parliament passed a law enabling the country to refuse the re-entry of refugees from Poland, Latvia, and Lithuania, thus leaving the refugees stranded at the border. According to an Editorial Board opinion piece in the *Washington Post* (2021) in October 2021,

> the BBC found a group of men from African countries shivering in a forest in the border region. One Nigerian said they had been pushed between the two countries like a football. Belarusian border guards have been forcing them across the barbed wire. On Sept. 19, three men were found dead on the Polish side of the border after suffering from hypothermia and exhaustion; a woman was found dead on the Belarusian side, one meter from the border.

Rather than protecting refugees in accordance with UN conventions, nation-states around the world operate detention facilities to incarcerate them or pay foreign countries to detain them. For example, Australia has maintained a policy of mandatory detention of asylum seekers and frequently deports them to the island states of Nauru and Papua New Guinea. These policies have led asylum seekers to engage in such protests as 'hunger strikes, throwing themselves on razor-wire fences, or sewing their lips together to draw attention to their corporeal experiences of state power' (Gilbert and Lo 2007, 18). More recently, the Danish government passed legislation in 2021 in favour of creating a detention centre in a country outside the EU to which Denmark can export asylum seekers to be processed (Milne and Schipani 2021). Likewise, in 2022, the British Home Office proposed deporting asylum seekers to Rwanda to be processed. As Arendt predicted, 'the danger is that a global, universally interrelated civilization may produce barbarians from its own midst by forcing millions of people into conditions which, despite all appearances, are the conditions of savages' (1968, 302).

In addition to the possibilities of detention or deportation, the conditions for asylum seekers inside Member States of the EU have also been severely restricted. In most EU states, educational and work opportunities are limited, movement from place of residence prohibited, and cooking one's own food restricted. The length of time for an asylum claim to be processed varies enormously from one country to another. In Ireland it is not unheard of for it to take up to ten years for the government to make a final decision, resulting in a refugee unable to progress in their career or be useful to the community for much of their adult life. Although not normally detained, those who have entered Ireland looking for sanctuary have been restricted in their activities. Defined as homeless, they have been assigned temporary accommodation in Direct Provision centres where, impeded from accepting paid employment, they have often felt isolated and were often forced to wait an indefinite period to discover their fate. Their inability to work has also rendered them vulnerable to accusations of laziness: 'Asylum-seekers note that their legally imposed status undermines their willingness to contribute to their host society as workers and tax-payers while confining them to the position of social welfare recipients, a position with which many are deeply uncomfortable' (Galvin 2000, 208). As in other EU countries, unaccompanied minors were normally deported from Ireland when they reach the age of 18, a practice that caused a sensation when a Nigerian student, who was preparing to take his state exams in 2005, was deported to Lagos, apparently wearing his school uniform. However, the Irish government has announced that they intend to abolish direct provision centres in the next couple of years.

The welcome given to Ukrainian refugees by neighbouring states during the current war puts into relief the arbitrary decisions made by nation-states to decide who can enter and under what conditions. Countries in Europe, which earlier refused entry to refugees from the Middle East and Africa, are now welcoming hundreds of thousands of Ukrainians under an EU Temporary Protection Direction. 'Among the entitlements the directive provides is permission to reside in a member state for a period of one year, but this may be extended for up to three years. It also provides for full access to the labour market and access to accommodation if needed, as well as access to medical care, social welfare supports and education' (Sanz 2022, p. 14). Slavoj Žižek has compared the reception of Ukrainians with refugees who were earlier refused entry when fleeing the war in Afghanistan. Quoting a Slovenian government tweet that stated, 'The refugees from Ukraine are coming from an environment which is in its cultural, religious, and historical sense something totally different from the environment out of which refugees from Afghanistan are coming' (Žižek 2022). Žižek concluded, 'Two species of refugee have emerged […] The obscene truth [is] out: Europe must defend itself from non-Europe' (Žižek 2022). While some Ukrainian women and children have been subject to sexual abuse, trafficking, exploitation, and extortion (Lamb 2022, p. 9), in general, Ukrainian refugees have been provided the dignity of a kind welcome to the European Union that has largely been denied to African and Middle Eastern refugees.

The Role of Theatre in Claiming Rights

Having seen how certain types of refugees are left disempowered by the nation-state, we can now turn to the role of the arts in re-empowering the refugee. The ancient Greeks emphasized the ritual of *hiketeia* (supplication) and the importance of *philoxenia* (hospitality) as religious practices and social duties. The Greeks stressed the moral obligation of the host for their guest, of welcoming the outsider to the community. Ancient Greek drama drew attention to such moral responsibilities. For example, in *Oedipus at Colonus*, Oedipus has become a refugee, exiled from Thebes, and begs King Theseus for the right to end his days in Colonus on the outskirts of Athens. Theseus allows him to remain, and it is then revealed that, because of his hospitality, the gods will protect Athens in the future. The play thereby emphasizes the potential benefit of looking after asylum seekers. Similarly, in *The Suppliants* by Aeschylus, when 50 women from Egypt arrive in Argos to ask for protection, King Pelasgos, despite being faced with dangerous consequences from the men who are pursuing the women, consults with his community and agrees to grant them sanctuary (1992, pp. 38–39). Thus, these plays and others underline the moral responsibilities of Greek citizens for foreigners and refugees, like hosts for their guests. Hospitality has also been stressed as fundamental to ethics by modern philosophers such as Emmanuel Levinas (1991a) and Jacques Derrida (Derrida and Dufourmantelle 2000, 151). As Judith Butler writes, 'Emmanuel Levinas offers a conception of ethics that rests upon an apprehension of the precariousness of life, one that begins with the precarious life of the Other' (Butler 2004, xvii–iii).

The ancient Greek dramas easily lend themselves to the issue of refugees today and have often been appropriated by modern theatre artists to promote sympathy for refugees. In 2013, the Austrian Nobel laureate, Elfriede Jelinek wrote *Die Schutzbefohlenen* (The Charges) a play that emphasized the notion of hospitality. Austria is one of the many countries in Europe that has regularly detained asylum seekers (see Amnesty International 2008). Jelinek was inspired to write a version of an ancient Greek play because of an occupation of the Votive Church in Vienna in 2012 by refugees who went on hunger strike to demand better conditions. Refusing the demands by the hunger strikers, the Austrian authorities persuaded them to move to a monastery from which many were deported.

Using Aeschylus's *The Suppliants* as a starting point for the play, Jelinek focused on the present-day needs of refugees in Austria and, by contrast with the welcome given by King Pelasgos, she exposed the intolerant attitudes of Austrian society and its politicians. For the first presentation of the play by the Thalia Theatre in Hamburg in 2014, director Nicolas Stemann included in the cast a group of asylum seekers who had been rescued from the Mediterranean near Lampedusa. Although it was illegal in Germany to employ asylum seekers, Joachim Lux, the head of the theatre, received permission from the Mayor of Hamburg to enable this to happen. Thus, it presented on stage those whose human rights were in jeopardy. It provided an unusual experience for Hamburg residents, coming face-to-face with refugees who were seeking their hospitality. The spectators were given the opportunity to meet the refugees personally in an after-show discussion and enquire about their conditions. Thus, the production of *Die Schutzbefohlenen* (The Charges) encouraged the local population to wrestle with their conscience in deciding how to respond to what Levinas calls 'the proximity of one to the other' who is in a state of 'vulnerability' (Levinas 1991b, 15). Faced with a group of refugees in their own city of Hamburg, the audience was put in the position of the King and citizens of Argos. The production evoked a sense of moral responsibility towards those on the stage who gazed at the audience and asked for a place to live. The performers were not just actors but people who did not have the right to remain in the country and could be deported at any time. The encounter compelled an affective and ethical response. During the after-show session that I attended, spectators asked how they could assist the refugees.

Many productions around the world have evoked sympathy for refugees such as *The Jungle* (2017) developed by Joe Murphy and Joe Robertson of the Good Chance Theatre in collaboration with the National Theatre and staged at the Young Vic in London. *The Jungle* recreated events that had taken place in the Calais jungle where refugees trying to get to England had been surviving appalling conditions. Likewise, the six-hour performance of *Le Dernier Caravansérail* (The Last Caravan Stop) by the Théâtre du Soleil in Paris in 2003 portrayed refugees trying to escape hazardous conditions in many parts of the world. Some plays have dealt more with legal issues, such as Maxi Obexer's *Illegale Helfer* (Illegal Helpers) in 2016 that questioned the justice of EU laws for refugees, asking whose interests they served and explaining how to circumvent them, and Anestis Azas' *Case Farmakonisi or the Justice of the Water* (2015) that investigated the judicial procedures related to an incident in which a boatload of refugees were possibly drowned by the Greek coastguard while trying to turn them back. Other plays have concentrated more on moral obligations such as Ice and Fire Company in England that frequently perform versions of *Asylum Monologues* (2006) and *Asylum Duologues* (2008) with professional actors playing the parts of refugees.

In addition, some companies have provided a space for refugees to express their own concerns. The Maxim Gorki Theater in Berlin created a seven-member 'exile ensemble' of actors from Syria, Afghanistan, and Palestine to perform such pieces as *Winterreise* (Winter Journey) (2017) about their personal difficulties of coming from the Middle East and encountering racism and hostility in Germany. According to Marike Janzen, 'the Gorki's efforts to assert exile, and being in exile, as the normative mode of being human even within the context of national culture and state cultural programs presents a noteworthy rebuke to a state system keeping refugee bodies out of their territories and beyond their sphere of protection' (2020, 247).

Similarly, refugees have initiated their own productions. A remarkable example is George Seremba's autobiographical one-man play *Come Good Rain* (1993). As a university student in Kampala, Seremba had been an opponent of

Ugandan government policies. One day he was abducted from the campus, tortured, sentenced to death by firing squad, taken into the forest, blindfolded, shot many times, and left for dead 1993. Miraculously he survived and was discovered by sympathetic villagers who kept him hidden and helped him to recover. He managed to escape to Kenya, and applied for resettlement in Canada, where he wrote *Come Good Rain* about his experiences in Uganda, starting from his early schooling and leading up to his escape from the country. During the performance, in an extraordinary moment that brings home the reality of his story, Seremba removes his shirt and reveals the many scars on his body from the bullet wounds. These wounds had provided an extreme form of physical evidence that he required protection from persecution and enabled him to gain asylum and later come to Trinity College Dublin to earn his PhD. Seremba has performed this play, which, as he says, displays the 'ferocious resilience, qualities which many an asylum seeker has to have in abundance,' to call attention to the plight of asylum seekers (Seremba 2008).

The Refugee Club Impulse was one of the most successful theatre initiatives by refugees in Germany. Prior to forming the group in 2013, the asylum seekers were living in a shelter in the Spandau area of Berlin and participated in acting exercises as a form of recreation. Following this, they adopted the name Refugee Club Impulse, and with the help of German advisers and a professional immigrant director, devised a play called *Letters Home* (2014). The framing device for *Letters Home* was a classroom situation where the refugees are learning about German culture and politics. When the teacher notices that they are having personal difficulties, she asks them to write letters home to convey their concerns. In developing the script for the play, the amateur actors, who came from many different countries including Pakistan, Afghanistan, Iraq, Syria, and Gambia, wrote personal letters that they could plausibly have sent to their relatives in their home countries, identifying some of their difficulties in trying to gain asylum and settle in Berlin. *Letters Home* also included scenes conveying earlier experiences of oppressive conditions in their home countries that forced them to flee. The actors were filmed reading their letters and these filmed episodes were interspersed into the play along with choreographed movements and devised scenes reflecting the specific problems that the refugees were encountering in Germany, such as difficulties in finding employment or establishing friendships. At the end of the play, the students come back together in the classroom, and they decide with the teacher that they should take their concerns to the German parliament. When the play was first performed at the Haus der Kulturen der Welt in November 2014, the actors encouraged the audience to join them in marching out of the theatre towards the German parliament, a short walk away, as a symbolic protest against the conditions under which asylum seekers live in Berlin. Because of the success of their initial performance at the Kulturen der Welt, the Maxim Gorki Theater and the Schaubühne later hosted performances by the company.

As an extension of their work, they started a campaign called 'My Right is Your Right' in 2014. Many Berlin theatres (such as the Deutsches Theatre,

Ballhause Naunynstrasse, Maxim Gorky, Grips, and the Schaubühne) supported this campaign, and it was prominently featured in the 2015 Theatertreffen which encouraged nightly announcements on its behalf at the end of many of the different festival performances. In March 2016 'My Right is Your Right' and the Refugee Club Impulse organized an outdoor carnival demonstration in support of the rights of refugees. According to Samee Ullah, an asylum seeker from Pakistan, who helped to organize the event, 'it was a historical thing. Seven state theatres came into the streets to demonstrate for refugee rights on the refugee day against racism with five thousand people.... Each float had one demand: right of work, right of education, life and dignity, right to stay here' (Ullah 2016). By organizing a carnival through the streets of Berlin, the refugees were staging what Jacques Rancière calls a 'dissensus'—that is, 'a division inserted in "common sense." ...They acted as subjects of the Rights of Man in the precise sense that ...[t]hey acted as subjects that did not have the rights that they had and had the rights that they had not' (Rancière 2010, 69). As in the conventional sense of carnival in which the world is turned upside down, the refugees were claiming equality with those around them who had the rights of citizens. The title of their movement 'my right is your right' implied that 'your right is my right.' As refugees with no rights (*sans papiers*), they were also claiming the right to have rights.

Conclusion

In conclusion it is difficult to assess to what degree theatre can affect government policy or policy makers. Similarly, we can acknowledge that the position of refugees from the global south has tended to deteriorate in the current century with ongoing wars, religious conflicts, terrorist activities, hate speech, and xenophobia, and with the ever-burgeoning border fences, refugee camps, and detention centres. We can guess that the current treatment of Ukrainian refugees is an anomaly and that the walls of fortress Europe will close again in front of other refugees. The notion of universal human rights remains a myth. As Arendt forewarned, 'the Rights of Man, supposedly inalienable, has proved to be unenforceable–even in countries whose constitutions were based upon them–whenever people appeared who were no longer citizens of any sovereign state' (Arendt 1968, 293).

Nevertheless, we can say that refugees are not always totally impotent (as 'bare life') or without resources. As we have seen in examples from various parts of the world, theatre has frequently elicited sympathy for refugees. Some performances stress legal issues, some present moral arguments, and some offer the opportunity for refugees to claim the rights which they have been denied. Thus, theatre has served as a powerful and empowering organ: a forum to uphold the equality of refugees as human beings, justifying the claim for their 'right to have rights.'

References

Aeschylus. 1992. *The Suppliant Maidens*. In *Aeschelus II*, trans. Seth G. Benardete, eds. David Grene and Richard Lattimore, 1–42. Chicago: University of Chicago Press.

Agamben, Giorgio. 1995, *Means without End: Notes on Politics*, translated by Vincenzo Binetti and Cesare Casarino. Minneapolis: University of Minnesota Press.

———. 1998. *Homo Sacer: Sovereign Power and Bare Life*, translated by Daniel Heller-Roazen. Stanford: Stanford University Press.

Amnesty International. 2008. 'Austria—Amnesty International Report 2008.' Accessed December 29, 2010. http://www.amnesty.org/en/region/austria/report-2008.

Arendt, Hannah. 1968. *The Origins of Totalitarianism*. New York: Harcourt.

Benhabib, Seyla. 2017. *Exile, Statelessness, and Migration*. Princeton: Princeton University Press.

Butler, Judith. 2004. *Precarious Life: The Powers of Mourning and Violence*. New York: Verso.

Cross, Mai'a K Davis. 2011. *Security Integration in Europe: How Knowledge-based Networks Are Transforming the European Union*. Michigan: University of Michigan Press.

Derrida, Jacques and Anne Dufourmantelle. 2000. *Of Hospitality*, translated by Rachel Bowlby. Stanford: Stanford University Press.

European Commission. 2020. 'EU signs final contracts under the €6 billion budget of the Facility for Refugees in Turkey.' Press release, December 17, 2020. Accessed November 4, 2021. https://ec.europa.eu/commission/presscorner/detail/en/ip_20_2487.

EU Monitor. 2002. 'Legal provisions of JAI (2000)22—Initiative of France with a view to the adoption of a Council Directive defining the facilitation of unauthorised entry, movement and residence.' *EU Monitor*, August 3, 2000. Accessed October 29, 2021. https://www.eumonitor.eu/9353000/1/j9vvik7m1c3gyxp/vi8rm2ypr4yp.

Frontex. 2017. 'Western African Route'. Press release, 2017. Accessed April 29, 2017. http://frontex.europa.eu/trends-and-routes/western-african-route/.

Gilbert, Helen and Jacqueline Lo. 2007. *Performance and Cosmopolitics: Cross-Cultural Transactions in Australia*. Palgrave Macmillan: Houndmills.

Howden, Daniel, Apostolis Fotiadis and Zach Campbell. 2020. 'Revealed: the great European refugee scandal.' *Guardian*, March 12, 2020. Accessed October 29, 2021. https://www.theguardian.com/world/2020/mar/12/revealed-the-great-european-refugee-scandal.

Janzen, Marike. 2020. 'The Maxim Gorki Theater's "Exil Ensemble" as State-Sponsored Repudiation of Citizenship.' In *Writing Beyond the State: Post-Sovereign Approaches to Human Rights*, eds. Alexandra S. Moore and Samantha Pinto, 243–63. Cham: Palgrave.

Johnson, Sarah. 2021. 'Fresh Evidence of Violence at Libyan Detention Centres as Boats Turned Back.' *The Guardian*, July 15. Accessed October 30, 2021. https://www.theguardian.com/global-development/2021/jul/15/fresh-evidence-of-violence-at-libyan-detention-centres-as-boats-turned-back.

Lamb, Christina. 2022. 'Predators Exploit Lack of Checks to Drag Women and Children Into a New Hell.' *Sunday Times*, April 3, 2022, p. 9.

Levinas, E. 1991a. *Totality and Infinity: An Essay on Exteriority*, translated by Alphonso Lingis. Dordrecht: Kluwer.

———. 1991b. *Otherwise Than Being*, translated by Alphonso Lingis. Dordrecht: Kluwer.

Michael, Maggie, Lori Hinnant, and Renata Brit. 2019. 'Making Misery Pay: Libya Takes EU Funds for Migrants.' *Associated Press*, December 31, 2019. Accessed October 29, 2021. https://apnews.com/article/united-nations-tripoli-ap-top-news-international-news-immigration-9d9e8d668ae4b73a336a63.6a86bdf27f.

Milne, Richard and Andres Schipani. 2021. 'Danish Parliament Approves Law to Process Asylum Seekers Outside Europe', *Financial Times*, 3 June, https://www.ft.com/content/7917b3e5-8dd9-4bb6-9d5d-81506c38c9c4, accessed 10 December 2022.

Rancière, Jacques. 2010. *Dissensus: On Politics and Aesthetics*, edited and translated by Steven Corcoran. London: Continuum.

Sanz, Catherine. 2022. 'Confusion and Questions Over Best Options for Protection for Fleeing Ukrainians'. *Sunday Business Post*, 20 March.

Seremba, George. 1993. *Come Good Rain*. Blizzard Publishing Ltd.

———. 2008. Personal communication with author, September 14, 2008.

Ullah, Samee. 2016. in *One in a Million* film, privately held.

UN. 1948. *Universal Declaration of Human Rights*.

UNHCR. 2010. *Convention and Protocol relating to the status of refugees*.

Washington Post. 2021. 'Opinion: Lukashenko is exploiting migrants as a weapon against his neighbors. The E.U. must stop him.' *Washington Post*, October 2, 2021. Accessed October 28, 2021. https://www.washingtonpost.com/opinions/2021/10/02/lukashenko-is-exploiting-migrants-weapon-against-his-neighbors-eu-must-stop-him/.

Žižek, Slavoj. 2022. 'What Does Defending Europe Mean? *Project Syndicate*, March 2. Accessed March 20, 2022. https://www.project-syndicate.org/commentary/europe-unequal-treatment-of-refugees-exposed-by-ukraine-by-slavoj-zizek-2022-03.

CHAPTER 6

Postmigrant Theatre and Its Impact on Contemporary German Theatre

Azadeh Sharifi

History and Politics

Postmigrant theatre as an artistic movement and an aesthetic practice is deeply rooted in the historical, political, and cultural circumstances of Germany in the twenty-first century. Germany's successful rehabilitation after the Second World War was only possible through the recruitment of migrant workers from Southern Europe, North Africa, and the Middle East. They were called 'Guest-Workers' because they were expected to leave once the rebuilding of the country had been fulfilled. The rise of Germany to become an economically and politically important global nation was amongst other things possible through the exploitation of these (million) underpaid workers who were also heavily restricted and denied access to social, political, and economic participation, for example, by the complicated procedure to German citizenship, the denial of the right to vote, and so on.

When in 2001 the citizenship law finally changed from *ius sanguinis* (right of blood) to *ius soli* (right of soil), it enabled descendants of former migrants to become German citizens. But simultaneously a new terminology, *Mensch mit Migrationshintergrund* (person with a migration background), was generated. This phrasing identified and divided those Germans who were of German descent and those who have become German citizens. Nevertheless, the paradigmatic shift in the German legislation sparked a social and cultural shift.

A. Sharifi (✉)
University of Toronto, Toronto, ON, Canada
e-mail: dr.azadeh.sharifi@gmail.com

© The Author(s), under exclusive license to Springer Nature Switzerland AG 2023
Y. Meerzon, S. E. Wilmer (eds.), *The Palgrave Handbook of Theatre and Migration*, https://doi.org/10.1007/978-3-031-20196-7_6

It is within these changes that the movement of postmigrant theatre could emerge. Until the beginning of the twenty-first century, most migrant artists and artists of marginalized communities were only able to produce theatre in small fringe venues and out of their own pocket. Although Germany's theatre institutions are highly subsidized, migrant artists and artists of colour were often disqualified from receiving funding either due to their legal status or their lack of artistic 'quality.' Here, the interweaving of a hegemonic discourse and its colonial traces (or its coloniality of power) become evident. Prevailing hegemonic discourse ruled (and in some ways is still ruling) who was considered legitimate as an artist, and the possibility that artists of colour could produce 'valuable' art did not enter the German discourse for a long time. But the assertion that artists of colour lack 'quality' is an ongoing structural issue that is not confined to Germany and/or artists of colour in Germany (Vanden Heuvel 2021, 88).

Postmigrant theatre was established in 2008 and later became a movement. It has paved the way for structural changes not only in German theatres, but also in other art sectors like film, media, and art museums. As a label and an artistic strategy of resistance against a hegemonic narrative of Germany and Germanness, it can be understood as an intervention not only into German theatre, but also into German politics and its approach to migration and migrants.

This article defines the history and politics of the postmigrant theatre movement and its artists. It contextualizes why postmigrant theatre has emerged and why it has deeply changed German theatre. To emphasize how postmigrant theatre has been a platform for artistic and political resistance, the performance *Krieg der Hörnchen* (War of the Squirrels) which premiered in 2012 at Kulturfabrik Löseke Hildesheim by Simone Dede Ayivi will be examined as a fitting example. Ayivi's performance reveals the complex, politically charged and pseudo-scientific discussion on migration and racism in Germany.

Beyond Belonging: Postmigrant Theatre

Artists of colour have been producing art in Germany since at least the 1960s, but they were not formally recognized until the beginning of the twenty-first century. Similarly, German theatre studies didn't engage with their art since theatre work produced by migrant artists was seen as amateur and not 'relevant' for the German theatre (Brauneck 1983). These artists came from various regions, had different class and family backgrounds, and distinct cultural and theatrical heritage, but they were identified as migrants or even 'foreigners' and put into a kind of racialized 'box' which kept them from entering drama schools and theatre programmes, getting funding for their art or even producing and playing on the main stages. The same is true for German minorities like black Germans, Romani, and Sintize (German Romani), and German Jews who were barely present in German theatres after the 1960s. And even if some of these artists entered the art institutions like drama school or state and city theatres, they mostly played stereotypical roles like refugees, 'pimps' and 'prostitutes,' 'trash collectors,' or 'cleaning staff' (Thiele 2010, 184).

Today, the hierarchy of race and the intentional exclusion of artists of colour can be observed through under-representation in the ensembles and/or even critical dismissal in theatre reviews where the art and artists are racialized, but it is rare that it is openly named. Schlossparktheater that was caught in 2012 in a controversy using blackface on a white actor for the role of an African American character, stated publicly the following: 'Our casting of the "black American" with a "white actor" follows a long tradition in German-speaking countries that is not racist. There is hardly an ensemble in a German, Austrian or Swiss theatre that includes black actors. Simply because the theatre's repertoire cannot offer them many roles in a season that justifies a permanent engagement' (Wissert 2014, 7–8). The idea that artists of colour, especially actors and directors, can only represent their own race or ethnicity while white actors and directors are free to choose every topic, story, or even character, has been an unquestioned practice until recently.

And since the racialized discourse in Germany running through conversations regarding migrants, 'visible' minorities, and Others intersects with class and economic background, one of the main reasons that racialized and minoritized artists are under-represented in German theatre has been justified with social circumstances and education. For example, when Karin Beier became the artistic director of Schauspiel Köln in 2008, she fired most of the actors of colour in the company's diverse ensemble the following year, arguing that it was difficult to find fitting actors of colour; she further implied that it was a 'social' issue and that due to their social—mainly working-class—background that they were not able to become good actors (Pilz 2011).

Conversations about race and racism in Germany have, for a long time, only been discussed in relation to the Nazi regime and the Holocaust. German society perceives itself as redeemed from its atrocities and racism, and especially antisemitism, as no longer part of the society. Michal Bodemann (1996) problematizes how in the German remembrance of the Holocaust, which he calls *Gedächtnistheater* (remembrance theatre), Jewish people play a very particular role: that is being the victims of Germany and accepting the German vindication. Therefore, most of public and political debates on race and racism were reframed under 'xenophobia' as a fear of the 'foreign.' As Maria Alexopoulou has outlined, 'German historiography does not consider "race" an appropriate analytical concept for studying the practices and discourses that target and produce migrant Others on the basis of origin, culture, or religion' (2018). But the public and academic conversation has been successfully changed by Jewish, black, migrant, and other scholars (and activists) of colour who have mapped out the continuity of structural racism and antisemitism (El-Tayeb 2016; Steyerl and Gutierrez Rodriguez 2003; Czollek 2018).

This is also the case for German theatres. The discussion on race, racism, and cultural diversity entered German theatres through the success of the postmigrant theatre movement and its activist artists. In 2003, Matthias Lilienthal became the artistic director of Hebbel am Ufer which united three independent small venues in Berlin Kreuzberg. Since this area of Berlin had been traditionally a district of migrant residents, he decided to invite the neighbourhood and its local artists into the theatre. For this project, he invited Shermin Langhoff to curate a festival with mainly young Turkish-German artists. Langhoff—who had until then worked in the film sector, and famously as an assistant to Fatih Akin—programmed with other artists like Tuncay Kulaoglu the festival *Beyond Belonging: Migration*[2], which took place for the first time in 2006. Langhoff expressed her curatorial vision as follows: 'Beyond the currently dominant discourse on integration and constructed (national or ethnic) affiliations, as well as the everyday (and structural) racism which is part of the cultural and media industry, we want to welcome artists (of colour) coming from film, literature, fine arts and music to the forum of theatre' (Hebbel am Ufer 2006). The title of the festival, Beyond Belonging: Migration[2], addressed the main idea of rejecting the nation-bound cultural frame. And it highlighted that migrant artists and artists of colour do produce high-quality art that goes beyond cultural borders and national ideas of what art, theatre, and artists are or might look like. The festival that was produced twice at Hebbel am Ufer, and the third time as part of the newly founded Ballhaus Naunynstrasse, was very well received by the audience as well as the press.

After the second edition of the festival in 2007, Langhoff and her colleagues started planning a platform for a new venue. They envisioned a theatre that would operate in 'contrast with already established theatres as an exploratory concept with respect to the artists involved and their narrative and aesthetical aspirations' (Nobegra 2011, 94). In 2008, the city government of Berlin decided to fund a venue dedicated to postmigrant theatre but for the price of defunding another traditional venue, Tiyatrom, which was established by Turkish actors who previously were part of Peter Stein's Turkish Ensemble. Between 1979 and 1984 Peter Stein, who was at that time the artistic director of Schaubühne am Hallenschen Ufer, founded the Türkisches Ensemble. The Turkish artists of this ensemble founded Tiyatrom, where they produced and performed Turkish plays.

In 2008, Ballhaus Naunynstrasse, which had been a production house for independent groups who were mostly migrants and people of colour at least since 1983, became the foundation for postmigrant theatre. The venue is dedicated to artists who were labelled migrants but were mainly Germans of colour, as well as second-, third-, or even fourth-generation descendants of migrants. There, the artists developed and presented their work without being put in a box, racialized, or labelled as the *Other*. Postmigrant theatre re-opened the box and enabled these artists to produce art that challenged the hegemonic narrative of German theatre and allowed them simultaneously to search for their own artistic language and form. The postmigrant theatre is what Stuart Hall would have called a 'creative force in emergent forms of representation amongst hitherto marginalised peoples' (1989, 69).

In the beginning, the postmigrant theatre movement was belittled by other German artists, theatre critics, and even scholars. Wolfgang Schneider, for example, acknowledged that there might be an under-representation of migrants and people of colour, and that the culturally diverse society of Germany hadn't been present and/or was misrepresented in theatre, but he still regarded it as unnecessary to have a dedicated or 'special' venue or even movement for these artists (Schneider 2011, 9). Langhoff had to publicly and repeatedly defend Ballhaus Naunynstrasse, emphasizing that it wasn't a 'Ghetto-theatre' (Fanizadeh 2009), but an approach to make the artists on the margins visible within the mainstream German theatre (Nobegra 2011, 100).

In fact, the term postmigrant can be seen as a direct result of the stigma that migrants and artists of colour have experienced. Originally, it was used by German scholars in the US to capture the complexity and intertextuality of literature by migrant writers in Germany (Lornsen 2001, 8). Shermin Langhoff and her colleagues picked up the term and enriched it with new meaning. Langhoff has stated that postmigrant theatre represents 'the stories and perspectives of those who have not immigrated but who have the migration background as part of their personal knowledge and collective memory' (Langhoff et al. 2011, 400). The main claim of postmigrant theatre is that migration is not only part of the experience of those who have migrated (or their descendants) but rather it has become part of German society. In a broader sense, German society has been profoundly transformed through migration, immigration as well as emigration (Foroutan 2019). As an unknown and 'unwritten' label, postmigrant theatre became an umbrella under which theatre and performance could be produced as a challenge to the internalized double consciousness (Du Bois 1903) that most of these artists experienced. Postmigrant theatre established an aesthetic and intellectual space for subaltern artists to speak for themselves, in their own voices, and thus to produce new theatrical discourses. Racialized and marginalized artists could stage their own plays, author their own narratives, and forge their own aesthetics.

The theatre's strategy, especially in its early years, involved staging experiences of migration, displacement, and life in the diaspora, as well as critically examining German society, both historically and today. Despite all the success, not only on a national but also on an international level, Langhoff stated that 'we bark from the third row' and spoke of a cultural hegemony that defines and simultaneously excludes artists of colour and minority artists (Nobegra 2011, 94): 'Who has the right to say That is Art. And that is not Art. How art should be or not be. Or what is part of art and what is not part of it. There is a power of labelling, that is not outside of our reach, a power of interpretation that is (ironically) not completely in our own hands' (Freitext 2013, 9). To draw here from Fred Moten and Stefano Harney's critical engagement with the *Undercommons* in hegemonic and racialized spaces like academia, there is a parallel at least with the beginning of postmigrant theatre (Harney and Moten 2013). Although Ballhaus Naunynstrasse and the postmigrant theatre received only a fraction of funding that other German theatres receive from the German government and wasn't hardly able to maintain its institutional integrity (Nobegra 2011), it found ways of solidarity and fugitive modes of interventions. And despite these diminutions and limitations, it became highly successful after only one season through sold-out shows, through productions that received multiple awards, by challenging German theatre tradition, and by filling the gaps in the culturally diverse society.

A good example for this approach and its success is *Verrücktes Blut* (Mad Blood): an adaption of a French movie *La journee de la Jupe* (2008), directed by Jean-Paul Lilienfeld, where a female teacher is confronted with unruly (and violent) students and who uses a gun in the classroom to enforce good behaviour and to force French (or European) culture on them. In the version for Ballhaus Naunynstrasse, which was directed by Nurkan Erpulat, the teacher played by Sesede Terziyan seems to be white and her students are migrants played by Nora Abdel-Maksoud, Hassan Akkouch, Emre Aksızoğlu, Murat Dikenci, Pınar Erincin, Adrian Saidi, Hasan H. Taşgın, and Paul Wollin. The students are forced at gunpoint by the teacher to read the 'Aesthetic Education of Man' by Friedrich Schiller. In this text, Schiller analyses the violent circumstances of the French revolution in order to emphasize that the main purpose of art and aesthetic education in society is as a force for liberating and enabling humans, so that they can learn about the nation-building of the German society and 'integrate' themselves into German society. The play however untangles different layers of racism and discrimination that are projected towards the students in the play as well as the actors of colour on stage. It becomes more and more apparent that Schiller's aesthetic education, although equally flawed in many ways, enables the students to liberate themselves from the hegemonic narrative and empowers them to be who they are on stage. Even the white teacher 'comes out' as non-white and Turkish. The production of *Mad Blood* was invited to the highly prestigious Berliner Theatertreffen in 2011 and has since then become part of the German repertoire.

From 2008 until 2013, the Ballhaus Naunynstrasse (under the leadership of Langhoff) produced many successful plays and performances. Productions such as *Schwarze Jungfrauen* (Black Virgins) by Feridun Zaimoglu in 2006, *Lö Bal Almanya* (The German Ball) by Nurkan Erpulat and Tuncay Kulaoglu in 2010, as well as several youth productions by *Akademie der Autodidakten* (Academy of the Autodidacts), deal with the experience of migration and postmigration, its success and its failure, as well as experiences of Othering (and Orientalization) and structural racism. Besides artistic and aesthetic exploration, postmigrant theatre and its artists were always interested in engaging in social and political discourses and debates. They successfully brought issues of different marginalized communities to the centre of attention. For example, they supported the refugee movement which fought against restricting laws (e.g. 'Residenzpflicht') for asylum seekers (Wilmer 2018, 192). This collaboration was rooted in the shared and lived experiences of the artists and the refugee activists. For example, in 2014, the youth project Academy of the Autodidacts undertook the project *Refugee Strike & Beyond* in which five inhabitants of the protest camp at Oranienplatz worked with the filmmakers Llaima Sanfiorenzo and Simon Paetau to produce five short films. The short videos show the lives of the five refugees and their struggles.

In 2013, Langhoff became the new artistic director of Maxim-Gorki-Theater in Berlin, making her one of the first women of colour to be in a leading position at a Stadttheater (city theatre), which is fully subsidized by the German government. There, she decided not to use the term postmigrant theatre anymore. Since 2013, Wagner Carvalho has become the artistic director of Ballhaus Naunynstrasse and he has put the focus on Black and Afro-German perspectives, artists, and aesthetics under the umbrella of postmigrant theatre. Both venues often cooperate and co-produce plays and events and have created a network for artists to become more visible within the German theatre.

Artistic Resistance and Political Platform

The artistic and aesthetic exploration started by the postmigrant theatre movement has always been connected to the experiences of racialized and marginalized artists as well as marginalized communities. This includes Jewish, Roma, black, (former) refugee and (former) migrant (including e.g. Eastern European or Russian) artists. One of the main objectives was to tell the stories and histories of these individuals and groups from their own perspectives and points of view, decentring narratives that consider Germany and Germanness from a solemnly nationalistic and ethnic orientation and moving towards a narrative of nation-building that includes colonialism, slave trade, imperialistic aspiration, migration, flight, and asylum as well as the histories of ethnic, race, religious, and linguistic minorities. In that sense, the postmigrant theatre is a platform of artistic and political resistance. The performance *Krieg der Hörnchen* (War of the Squirrels) by the Afro-German artist Simone Dede Ayivi, which premiered in 2012 in Kulturfabrik Löseke Hildesheim and was presented at Black Lux festival in 2013 at Ballhaus Naunynstrasse, uses a playful strategy to question the debates on migration and integration and reveal their racist pseudo-scientific (social Darwinist) rhetoric and colonial roots. The performance questions—through its only black female performer—the whiteness of the aesthetic space (i.e. the German theatre) and politicizes the stage by using real documents and actual material from the German debate but using them to the point of absurdity. Dede Ayivi's performance uncovers the roots of structural racism in Germany and puts a finger into its core.

The performance *War of the Squirrels* is about brown squirrels who have lived peacefully in the German forests until the invasion of the grey North American squirrels. In the booklet for the performance, the storyline is presented as follows:

> What do you think of those who accuse you of only coming here to eat the acorns of other squirrels?
> There is a war in the animal kingdom. A new breed is spreading across Europe. The American grey squirrel is stronger, more resilient, more potent and will sooner or later oust our red squirrel. The other will dominate our forests. (Ayivi 2012)

The introduction in the performance booklet emphasizes that the story is about the 'fear of change, fear of foreign infiltration and the longing for everything to stay as it always has been' (Ayivi 2012) and that the performance is an allegory for the ongoing German debates around migration and race and the infiltration by foreigners.

War of the Squirrels begins with a performer coming on stage holding a tape recorder with which she records the date, time, and place of the performance, as well as the number of spectators in the audience and the theatre's sponsors. After recording this information, she rewinds the tape, presses play, and then goes behind a white cupboard offstage, where she places the tape recording so that it is no longer visible to the audience. Ayivi is playing with ideas of history, witnessing, evidence, and truths. The audience has seen her make the recording, and they can testify to the truth of the information: date, time and place, number of audience members, and the sponsors. If she plays the tape, there is no reason to doubt what is said on the tape. But the tape doesn't stop with previous recorded information, it continues to tell a brief history of the universe from a squirrel perspective. The audience has no reason to doubt that history either, because this information is presented under the disguise of the recorded objective truth. The recounted history is packed with an audio documentary about a mythical German forest as well as radio clips reporting on the threat and the possible extinction of German squirrels. While the audio clips are played to the audience, images of a replica of a forest are screened on stage. The replica forest is green, healthy, and peaceful. The first part of the performance creates an atmosphere of a brown homogenous squirrel society that has been cultivated and advanced but is now under attack by the aggressive and 'barbaric' grey squirrels that endanger the forest that is their home.

In the next scene, the performer plays with the tape recorder, looking for a radio station where snippets of an interview on the theatrical use of blackface in Germany are discussed. The interviewee (it's the voice of the author Michael Laages) refers to blackface as a neutral theatrical masquerade, especially because, as he claims, Germany has no colonial history and no (or not enough) black (German) actors. Both statements (neither of which are true) are not questioned or invalidated but presented as part of a cacophony of noises. When the performer changes the radio station again, a grey squirrel is being interviewed. The reporter asks the squirrel if it is still connected to its home and if it feels foreign in the German forest. The squirrel answers the questions in a thick German local (Hesse) dialect by denying that it knows any other home than the German forests. The reporter doesn't give up asking biased questions; for example, why doesn't the grey squirrel want to integrate into the society, if it has plans to leave soon, etc. The questions are, in fact, questions that are posed towards migrants and people of colour and which many racialized Germans face every day.

While listening to the radio, the performer prepares cookies in the background that she then places on a tray and offers to the spectators by bending down and making clicking noises as if they were squirrels she was trying to lure.

When the audience doesn't respond, she throws the cookies at them. This interaction is accompanied by laughter from the audience, but it also contains a switch in the roles and the power dynamic between a single black subject and a predominantly white audience. The black performer has the power to navigate and dominate the interaction and set the parameters of communication which is in many ways returning the colonial gaze.

After a short break, the performer slips into the costume of a brown (local) squirrel. She then brings forward a flip chart with magnets in the shape of squirrels. She counts the squirrel-magnets and then starts performing the eradication and decimation of the brown squirrels. Some die of natural causes, some are murdered. The performer re-enacts their death on stage: one by one, she takes down the magnets and then makes funny faces and falls to the ground. She repeats this sequence over and over again, until all brown squirrel-magnets are eliminated. After the death of the brown squirrels, the performer slips out of the costume and brings the vintage tape recorder back on stage. Then she starts recording the audio, which is a cacophony of the different radio stations, and replaying through the tape recorder but this time she uses headphones and repeats what she hears. The audio becomes one linear narrative of a division of 'us' and 'them,' the brown squirrels (us) and the grey squirrels (them); us, who want the traditional German theatre, and them, who want to 'change' it by erasing blackface and including people of different ethnic backgrounds. The performance ends with the performer repeating the last argument of those in favour of blackface (as a neutral theatrical device) which is that the freedom in decision-making by artistic directors by enabling blackface will be threatened because other artistic staff (i.e. people that are lower in the hierarchy in the German theatre) and the audience might want to participate in the artistic decisions. Here, the performer stops the tape recorder and her repetition of the recording. She looks at the audience and addresses them: 'We will work hard to achieve that!'

The performance *War of the Squirrels* includes several aesthetic elements of postmigrant theatre that are essential. It focuses on a black female performer and narrates a story on migration and reacts to a political debate that is on the incompatibility of the migrants and the natives, their culture and way of living, the overpopulation through those migrants, and how this is a threat to the 'natural' habitat (i.e. the German nation). And as in many other performances of postmigrant theatre, Ayivi uses counter-narrative and humour as a strategy of resistance. Here, the squirrels serve as an allegory for the contemporary political debates. But it also goes beyond that. Priscilla Layne suggests that interrogating the performance from a posthuman perspective allows one to see the debate from the outside. From a posthuman perspective, the humanist understanding of the world is decentralized and understandings of the native (or the subject), identity, and belonging are decolonized (Layne 2022). The struggle of the squirrels that is presented in the performance discloses how the imperial (and colonial) European idea of life and living is even projected onto the wildlife and told as a 'natural' way of history. The play's absurd narrative conceit—that is, the 'war of the squirrels'—facilitates for the audience the ability to see beyond ethno-nationalist (and pseudo-scientific) rhetoric. And finally, the performance discusses and navigates the intersection of race, gender, identity, and migration on stage, enabling an intervention into the white-centred German theatre to produce new aesthetic and artistic practices.

Not Beyond Strategic Essentialism Yet!

The uniqueness of the postmigrant theatre movement is intertwined with the history of a resistance by artists of colour and minority artists who have fought against exclusion and marginalization; it is also intertwined with the resistance of activists from various social movements who have fought for social, political, and cultural changes. And the movement is not only spreading in Germany but also in Europe since migration has radically changed many European societies. But the rise of the Far-right, racism, anti-Muslim sentiments, antisemitism, and attacks against migrants, people of colour, and Jewish people, leaves German society divided. And some of the necessary critical discussions are still being held as lip service with no effective consequences.

While discussions on postcolonial critique and decolonial practices have entered many artistic spaces and art institutions through, amongst others, the postmigrant theatre movement, they still do not translate into radical transformation and sustainable modes of inclusion. As Eve Tuck and K. Wayne Yang have powerfully argued, decolonization is not a metaphor (Tuck and Wayne Yang 2012). The question remains how to engage in academic or intellectual debates while subjects and communities that are affected and have fought to bring these discussions forward are systematically excluded. Forced (economic, political, and social) migration is still rooted in European colonial desires and imperial exploitation and has now been translated into 'cultural appreciation'—a euphemism for 'cultural appropriation' since the majority of art institutions like theatre are predominantly white and racialized, and minoritized subjects still serve as tokens. And the German artworld is not able to uphold their ethical responsibilities as in the case of the Humboldt Forum, a new museum in Berlin that came under scrutiny because of the colonial history of its artefacts like the Benin Bronzes (Sarr and Savoy 2019). In an article for the French newspaper *Le Monde*, Achille Mbembe reacts to the French government's 'hesitance' to make a restitution of African artefacts. He makes clear how the racialized subjects, and in this case all Africans, are still made 'incapable' to be the 'safeguard of universal heritage' (Truong 2018). And here again, the myth of the unqualified racialized subjects emerges, a trope that has been used also to disqualify artists of colour in Germany. But this hasn't stopped (or has maybe even empowered) the artists and activists of colour to debunk the myth of the unqualified racialized body. The artists are uncovering the coloniality of power Mignolo 2007 in German theatre; not only in its artistic leadership and artistic practices but also in its spectators and the gaze, its language, gestures, and other theatrical devices.

And the institutions are slowly crumbling as more and more artists no longer accept abusive behaviour. More and more artists are stepping forward and demanding the end of racism, sexism, ableism, classism, and other forms of discrimination and maltreatment that have been occurring in these institutions on stage as well as within its structures (Sharifi 2019). The correlation between the postmigrant movement and the uprising of various social groups and communities against discrimination and marginalization in German theatres lies in the strategic alliances that have been created throughout the last decade. Gayatri Spivak's politically motivated term 'strategic essentialism' is employed by minoritized subjects and communities acting on the basis of a shared identity in the public arena in the interests of unity during a struggle for equal rights (Landry and MacLean 1996, 214). This temporary essentialism can help to create solidarity, a sense of belonging, and identity for social action.

The postmigrant theatre movement has provided such alliances as well as an umbrella for many minoritized subjects and communities to demand and claim access and space in art institutions and theatres. And it continues to inspire other artistic and activist movements that aim for a radical change within the theatre field.

References

Alexopoulou, Maria. 2018. 'Producing Ignorance: Racial Knowledge and Immigration in Germany,' *History of Knowledge*, July 25, 2018. Access October 14, 2021. https://historyofknowledge.net/2018/07/25/producing-ignorance-racial-knowledge-and-immigration-in-germany/.
Ayivi, Simone Dede. 2012. *The War of the squirrels*. Programme. Berlin.
Bodemann, Michael Y. 1996. *Gedächtnistheater. Die jüdische Gemeinschaft und ihre deutsche Erfindung*. Hamburg: Rotbuch Verlag.
Brauneck, Manfred. 1983. *Ausländertheater in der Bundesrepublik Deutschland und in West-Berlin*. Hamburg: Hamburg Universität.
Czollek, Max. 2018. *Desintegriert euch!* München: Carl Hanser Verlag.
Du Bois, W.E.B. 1903. *The Souls of Black Folk*. Chicago: A. C. McClurg & Co.
El-Tayeb, Fatima. 2016. *Undeutsch. Die Konstruktion des Anderen in der postmigrantischen Gesellschaft*. Bielefeld:Transcript.
Fanizadeh, Andreas. 2009. Wir inszenieren kein 'Ghetto-theatre.' *Taz*, April 18, 2009. Access June 29, 2021. https://taz.de/!674193/.
Foroutan, Naika. 2019. *Die postmigrantische Gesellschaft: Ein Versprechen der pluralen Gesellschaft*. Bielefeld: transcript Verlag.
Freitext. 2013. 'Im besten Fall stürzt das Weltbild ein.' *Freitext, Kultur- und Gesellschaftsmagazin*, 22, 6–14.
Hall, Stuart. 1989. 'Cultural Identity and Cinematic Representation.' *Framework: The Journal of Cinema and Media*, 36, 68–81.
Harney, Stefano, and Fred Moten. 2013. *The Undercommons. Fugitive Planning & Black Study*. New York: Minor Compositions.
Hebbel am Ufer. 2006. *Beyond Belonging*. Programme. Berlin.
Landry, Donna, and Gerald MacLean, eds. 1996. *The Spivak Reader*. New York: Routledge.

Langhoff, Shermin, Tuncay Kulaoglu, and Barbara Kastner. 2011. 'Dialoge I: Migration dichten und deuten: Ein Gespräch zwischen Shermin Langhoff, Tuncay Kulaoglu und Barbara Kastner.' In *Das Drama nach dem Drama: Verwandlungen dramatischer Formen in Deutschland seit 1945*, edited by Artur Pelka and Stefan Tigges, 399–408. Bielefeld: transcript Verlag.

Layne, Priscilla. 2022. 'From Postmigrant to Postnational: Exposing and Resisting the Absurdity of Nationalism in Simone Dede Ayivi's Posthumanist Performance *War Between Squirrels* (2013).' *The Drama Review* (forthcoming).

Lornsen, Karin. 2001. *Transgressive Topographien in der türkisch-deutschen Postmigrantenliteratur*. Waterloo: University of Waterloo.

Mignolo, Walter. 2007. 'Delinking: The Rhetoric of modernity, the logic of coloniality and the grammar of de-coloniality,' *Cultural Studies*, 21 (2), 449–514.

Nobegra, Onur. 2011. 'We Bark from the Third Row': The Position of the Ballhaus Naunynstrasse in Berlin's Cultural Landscape and the Funding of Cultural Diversity Work.' In *50 Jahre türkische Arbeitsmigration in Deutschland*, edited by Seyda Ozil, Michael Hofmann, and Yasemin Dayioglu-Yücel, 91–112. Göttingen: V&R unipress.

Pilz, Dirk. 2011. 'Man muss bestimmte Menschen meiden.' *Berliner Zeitung*, April 4, 2021. Accessed October 14, 2021. https://www.berliner-zeitung.de/karin-beier-demnaechst-intendantin-am-hamburger-schauspielhaus-ueber-erfolg-und-gutes-theater-man-muss-bestimmte-menschen-meiden-li.63023?pid=true.

Sarr, Felwine and Bénédicte Savoy. 2019. *Zurückgeben. Über die Restitution afrikanischer Güter*. Berlin: Matthes & Seitz.

Schneider, Wolfgang. 2011. *Theater und Migration. Herausforderungen für eine neue Kulturpolitik*. Bielefeld: transcript Verlag.

Sharifi, Azadeh. 2019. 'German Theatre: Interventions and Transformations.' *Critical Stages*, 20. Accessed July 26 2023. https://www.critical-stages.org/20/german-theatre-interventions-and-transformations/.

Steyerl, Hito and Encarnación Gutiérrez Rodríguez (eds.). 2003. *Spricht die Subalterne deutsch? Migration und postkoloniale Kritik*. Münster: Unrast Verlag.

Thiele, Rita. 2010. 'Schauspiel Köln. Theater für eine multikulturelle Stadt.' In *Zwischenspiele. Neue Texte, Wahrnehmungs- und Fiktionsräume in Theater, Tanz und Performance*, 183–190. Bielefeld: transcript Verlag.

Truong, Nicolas. 2018. 'Achille Mbembe : La restitution des oeuvres est l'occasion pour la France de réparer et de réinventer sa relation avec l'Afrique.' *Le Monde*. https://www.lemonde.fr/idees/article/2018/11/28/achille-mbembe-la-restitution-des-uvres-est-l-occasion-pour-lafrance-de-reparer-et-de-reinventer-sa-relation-avec-l-afrique_5390009_3232.html

Tuck, Eve, and K. Wayne Yang. 2012. 'Decolonization is Not a Metaphor.' *Decolonization: Indigeneity, Education & Society*, 1 (1), 1–40.

Vanden Heuvel, Mike. 2021. 'American Theatre Ensembles. 1995–Present.' In *American Theatre Ensembles*, volume 2, edited by Mike Vanden Heuvel, 35–94. London: Bloomsbury Publishing.

Wilmer, S. E. 2018. *Performing Statelessness in Europe*. Cham: Palgrave Macmillan

Wissert, Julia. 2014. *Schwarz.Macht.Weiß.Eine künstlerische Recherche zur Frage nach strukturellem Rassismus auf deutschsprachigen Bühnen*. Salzburg: Universität Mozarteum.

CHAPTER 7

Interculturalism and Migration in Performance: From Distant Otherness to the Precarity of Proximity

Brian Singleton

Throughout the nineteenth and twentieth centuries and in the first two decades of the twenty-first century the performance of the Other and otherness on European stages has always been predicated on migration. But that migration did not always intersect with representation on the stage that we would consider intercultural today. Setting migration in its historical and socio-political contexts is crucial to an understanding of what prefigured the notion of the intercultural in performance, how the term interculturalism emerged and to what kind of performance it was applied. Further, in a globalized world, how did economic migration along with conflict migration, particularly from Africa and the Middle and Near East, come to challenge previous notions of interculturalism in a new and highly unstable world order? And still further, in the twenty-first century, why was intercultural theatre positioned by theorists in the milieux of migrants who had arrived, settled and were processing their experiences of transnational migration and being Other in cosmopolitan world cities?

I will come to how the term interculturalism emerged in performance in the late 1970s and 1980s and the types of migration with which it intersected, but first I need to go back to its precursors to demonstrate the contextual differences but artistic similarities between the 1980s and cultural representation a

B. Singleton (✉)
Trinity College Dublin, Dublin, Ireland
e-mail: BSNGLTON@tcd.ie

© The Author(s), under exclusive license to Springer Nature Switzerland AG 2023
Y. Meerzon, S. E. Wilmer (eds.), *The Palgrave Handbook of Theatre and Migration*, https://doi.org/10.1007/978-3-031-20196-7_7

century before. Nineteenth-century Orientalist painters from Delacroix to Gérome considered themselves realists as they explored North Africa and the Middle East often accompanying military campaigns. Their art work had an enormous influence on wider culture throughout Europe as art began to pictorially represent the Orient of Empire under military protection as an experience of both anxiety and desire. The artists' gaze wavered often from the military to depictions of taboo subjects such as sex and religion. Of intense interest stood the harem (often depicted as a guard protecting the entrance to the women unseen), and the trance-like dancing of the mystic Sufis (commonly known as whirling dervishes) representing an embodied and transcendental religiosity. These oriental subjects emerged in broader European cultures similarly mapping anxieties and desires onto other races and religions but crucially experienced at home and at a safe remove from its subjects.

Such mapping of European anxieties and desires onto other races and religions crossed over into theatre in the last two decades of the nineteenth century when musical comedy and light opera repositioned domestic settings in an imagined Orient and gave licence to greater freedom in representation particularly in relation to sex and religion. The *Arabian Nights* tales had made a huge impact particularly on children's literature but also on the various forms of popular theatre to derive from it. Plays such as *Kismet*, pantomimes such as *Aladdin* and the light operas of Gilbert and Sullivan (*The Mikado*) forged a major paradigm shift throughout all forms of culture in wider British society, creating a consumer market for all things oriental, from fashion to shoe polish. British theatre goers never had to leave home in order to experience this thinly disguised Orient of Empire, two dimensional and largely pictorial. And the melodramas of Dion Boucicault, such as *Jesse Brown, or the Siege of Lucknow* (1858), within a matter of days, staged the real event, placing the women of England in peril against native insurrection in India but rescued by a Scotsman who signalled the benefits of a United Kingdom. The migrants of Empire were lauded and applauded.

At the helm of theatrical orientalism in London was Australia-born actor Oscar Asche who dominated the West End stages through First World War and after which his versions of the pantomime spectacular, often replete with authentic stage properties, picked up in the markets on his travels by ship to and from his native Australia. His jingoistic songs and nationalistic tableaux pandered to nationalist wartime fervour. But his fashion parades and drunken orgies on stage revealed how orientalism worked as a theatrical trope: the characters depicted were not English and not *not* English at the same time. Asche's *Chu Chin Chow* (1916–1921) and *Cairo* (1921–1922) dominated the West End up until the syndication of theatres took hold in the 1920s and the popular audiences for orientalism shifted into cinemas, and the theatre took a more modern and upper-middle-class turn. Though Asche had direct experience of Arab and African cultures on his travels and tours, he was a traveller consumer of all things foreign and was only interested in migrating inanimate objects back to his stages and reconfiguring and reimagining the cultural forms he happened to encounter, though the forms and the people who performed for him were left behind.

As orientalism on the stage waned, its premise in other cultural forms such as cinema and opera encapsulated the orientalist moment and lived on as replicable cultural artifacts. But representing others in a decolonizing Europe ran aground when after the Second World War migrants from the formerly colonized nations came to Britain and joined the workforce in the rebuilding of the country. Concomitantly scholarship was forging new ground in postcolonial theory, and the seminal work of Edward W. Said, *Orientalism* (1978), contested the term as a pursuit of knowledge of the other and reconfigured it as misrepresentation. The search for and fascination with the other, however, never ceased and with increasingly affordable global travel a new impetus emerged to seek out other cultural forms, to embrace or appropriate them for a new postmodern theatre. And for that impetus and emergence a new term was coined: interculturalism.

Theoretical and Cultural Contexts

While cinema continued to travel the world in search of the foreign throughout the twentieth century with increasing realism, theatre retreated to the drawing room until the Second World War, subsequently challenging British society in particular with its declining Empire and its war-time poverty. But it also brought about a political shift in the academy, a shift to the left, that allowed for the emergence of new subjects such as sociology, cultural studies, theatre studies and anthropology. And it was in the nexus of the latter in an interdisciplinary experiment at New York University that director Richard Schechner invited anthropologist Victor Turner and his scholarship into the rehearsal room. The search was on for something new. This was in the late 1970s when the art world had refracted into a postmodern condition, believing French postmodern theorists such as Jean-François Lyotard that grand narratives had to be broken down and everything had been said before, and Jean Baudrillard who saw before him a culture of copies, simulacra that ghosted the original to the point where the original was no longer extant. Postmodern theory is crucial to an understanding of what Schechner proposed with his first use of the term intercultural in that theatre's use of the rituals of other cultures and religions as source materials would only ever be simulacra and a replacement for the voracious appetite of the Western cultural consumer. Interculturalism emerged in the 1970s, therefore, in a postmodern context of bricolage a re-assembly of previous cultural materials, but still firmly rooted in the binarism of late-orientalism, exposing the migrant artist still as the visionary of an imagined other.

While Schechner and others were studying rituals for their postmodern performance and travelling the world to encounter them, European theatre practitioners were also engaged in a form of new cosmopolitanism, as they too unlike their fairly benign predecessors (Yeats, Artaud, Dullin) travelled East in search of a new theatrical form. This search dominated European theatre for most of the twentieth century as the modernists sought to escape the trap of realism that cinema could do better. Two European theatre directors led the charge, the English director Peter Brook, who in 1970 established the International Centre for Theatre Research at the Bouffes du Nord theatre in Paris, and French theatre director Ariane Mnouchkine who had risen to fame with her highly popular and political theatre forms in her Théâtre du Soleil company's home, a former ammunitions factory, La Cartoucherie, in the Vincennes forest. While Brook's intercultural period was dominated by an adaptation of *The Mahabharata* (1985) using a variety of actors from around the world, his version was very much Orientalized in terms of image and sound to the point where some might say Christianized at points. The cosmopolitan Brook spent many months in India researching, seeing productions and promising work for local actors that never materialized. The criticism against his production was vehement and led Indian scholar Rustom Bharucha to excoriate Brook's practice of cultural appropriation:

> Peter Brook's *Mahabharata* exemplifies one of the most blatant (and accomplished) appropriations of Indian culture in recent years. Very different in tone from the Raj revivals, it nonetheless suggests the bad old days of the British Raj, not in its direct allusions to colonial history, but in its appropriation of non-western material within an orientalist framework of thought and action, which has been specifically designed for the participant, Brook has created a so-called international market. (1652)

Bharucha went on to berate Brook for assembling a group of actors from all over the world and from their own performing traditions but not allowing those traditions space to exist within the homogenized English or French parameters of the production. Only one actor was from India, to add insult to injury, and Bharucha thus raised a crucial ethical dimension to Brook's brand of interculturalism: 'Unavoidably, the production raises the questions of ethics, not just the ethics of representation, which concerns the decontextualisation of an epic from its history and culture, but the ethics of dealing with people (notably Indians) in the process of creating the work itself' (646). While migration was central to Brook's creation of a universalist approach to an Indian religious text, in his own journeys east, and the journeys of actors from around the world to Paris, the expected migration of Indian practitioners with their cultural forms never materialized. The inequity of the relationship between the elite European cosmopolitan artist and his appropriation of a source culture and its exponents calls into question this form of interculturalism, revealing how little it differs from earlier orientalist practices where the European elite artist did not need to travel at all in order to appropriate another culture.

Ariane Mnouchkine wisely steered clear of religious texts of other cultures but was still fascinated by the dance forms of Asia to the point where she not only travelled East consuming Asian cultures but invited practitioners of many dance forms back to Paris to teach members of her company. From 1981 onwards, Mnouchkine has used this paradigm of representing Western cultural texts using corporeal and other forms derived from other cultures. Patrice Pavis was at the forefront of analysing this form of interculturalism using his hourglass model of sifting culture from one space to another through a theatrical funnel. In his book *Theatre at the Crossroads of Culture* (1992) Pavis sets out to investigate 'how a target culture analyses and appropriates a foreign culture and how this appropriation is accompanied by a series of theatrical operations' (4). And he goes on to suggest the hourglass is continually turning as culture sifts and transforms what comes before into new cultural contexts. It appears as a permanently turning world of appropriating cultures in which postmodern theory fits symbiotically. In most respects his theory matched Mnouchkine's intercultural theatre practice though it did not quite clarify that the original culture was largely divorced from its source culture by the time it had reached its target.

Such was Mnouchkine's success with her intercultural productions of Shakespeare (1981–1984) and after, that she attracted actors from all over the world who joined her company and produced work in French, though also in other languages at times, using voices and accents of a world theatre. Here was interculturalism in a globalized form in which the actors were imported to Paris for training and rehearsals and then were exported on world tours of the Théâtre du Soleil's highly sought-after productions on the supranational festival circuit. And while Mnouchkine continues to see theatrical cultural forms as universal the politics of world culture has shifted so significantly that the kind of practice the Théâtre du Soleil continues to embody is seen to be predicated on the tenets of orientalism though in a new guise and in a version of the term intercultural which by the end of the first decade of the twenty-first century had lost its valence and value.

Not all scholars and critics were taken in by this form of interculturalism. Writing in *Performing Arts Journal*, art and film critic Daryl Chin laid bare the project of the type of interculturalism as represented by Brook and Mnouchkine:

> To put this in the most extreme, stringent terms: the Eurocentric ego declares that, if recognition of the validity of 'otherness' must be accorded, then there is total equivalence, an absolute breakdown of distinction. The Eurocentric ego is making a declaration, which is: if it can no longer claim dominance and superiority, if equity must be awarded, if the Eurocentric ego can no longer presume on self-importance, then nothing is important.
>
> Hidden in the agenda of postmodernism is, I think, a rebuke, an insult, a devaluation. Instead of recognizing the status of 'the other' as an equal, there is the undermining of 'the other' by a declared indifference to distinction, while attempting to maintain the same balance of power. (Chin, 165)

Thus, what is missing in intercultural theatre in the 1980s and 1990s is the voice and the body of the people whose cultures have been transposed. While

Brook and Mnouchkine worked with international casts, the source culture, as Pavis would say, was not simply passed through an hourglass to emerge in French culture as something other; it emerged as neither autochthonous nor even French, but universal, with universalist impulses and drives, images and sounds. Chin calls out this drive thus:

> The idea of interculturalism as simply a way of joining disparate cultural artifacts together has a hidden agenda of imperialism. When is interculturalism a valid expression of the postmodern crisis in information overload, and when is it merely a fashion statement of the ability to buy and sell anything from any culture? (167)

And so, with the onslaught of criticism by the turn of the millennium, intercultural theatre was beginning to wane in both practice and scholarship, though it did not cease. Erika Fischer-Lichte, who had been one of the first scholars to put forward a theorization of interculturalism in Europe, along the sociosemiotic lines of Patrice Pavis, established the International Research Center 'Interweaving Performance Cultures' at the Freie Universität in Berlin. From 2008 over the course of the next ten years, invited international scholars and practitioners to the Center debated, researched, presented and published new scholarship on the broad spectrum concept of interweaving. Criticized by some for evacuating the political in the meeting of cultures, interweaving found a usefulness in the contest of cultures in postcolonial contexts.

In North America, however, interculturalism re-emerged with a prevailing politics that matched the experiences of migrants struggling to establish themselves in global cities. This paradigm shift in configuring interculturalism was effected primarily by Ric Knowles in his several interventions in the debate: *Theatre & Interculturalism* (2010), a special issue on Theater & Interculturalism for *Theater Journal* (2011), and later in his monograph *Performing the Intercultural City* (2017). His principal argument is premised on seeking what he calls 'interculturalism from below'. His search focuses on theatre and performance in the destination cities of global migration in which displaced persons connect their embodied culture with their lived experience of relocation. This shift was significant in that it moved completely away from intercultural performance as cultural appropriation along a post-colonial axis, to emergent cultures of *trans*national migrants at destination points. The influence of the paradigm shift was significant in that a slew of new books collecting examples of performances of this new interculturalism emerged, such as Charlotte McIvor and Jason King (eds.) *Interculturalism and Performance Now: New Directions* (Palgrave Macmillan, 2019|) and Daphne P. Lei and Charlotte McIvor (eds.) *The Methuen Drama Handbook of Interculturalism and Performance* (Bloomsbury Methuen, 2020). In the latter's Introduction, Lei began by excoriating European theatrical interculturalism of the 1980s–2000s, the like of whose work in 2011 in *Theater Journal* she had termed Hegemonic Intercultural Theatre. In the *Methuen Drama Handbook* in 2020, however, Lei begins with a personal anecdote of how, while watching recordings, her three-year old son could understand that the cultural appropriation of Peter Brook's *The Mahabharata* was wrong, and of how Mnouchkine was the only woman in a list of directors of the same period as 'notorious' (1). However, at the same time as North American scholarship was emphatically denouncing hegemonic interculturalism in theatre, its European practitioners continued to provide it with a home and a major platform.

A Short Overview of Theatrical Practices

Despite the denunciation of hegemonic interculturalism by others, I would still argue that Mnouchkine and the Théâtre du Soleil's contribution to the intercultural debate (particularly in her productions of Shakespeare's plays in the 1980s and of ancient Greek tragedy in the 1990s) achieved what many of her predecessors of modern French theatre (Dullin & Artaud among others) had only aspired to do, namely to create a new form for theatre to counter realism. And their 2003 production of *Le Dernier Caravansérail (Odyssées)* was a seething critique of Western societies for inciting financial inequity and political instability and then enacting draconian policies to keep out of fortress Europe (and Australia) the victims of economic and conflict migration and protect their economies. Further, *Les Naufragés du Fol Espoir* (2010) looked back to an earlier modernity and onstage to a live mimed replication of the creation of early cinema, with a focus on the dangers of European nationalism manifesting itself in global colonialism, exploitation and oppression. We watched how cinema of a century ago wavered in how to tell the story of the dangers in the rise of nationalism that led to the First World War and focused instead on how the pan-European thirst for adventure deposited its unwanted criminals in the furthest reaches of the earth while at the same time seeking to bring back to Europe the riches it discovered there. It was an excoriating attack on the new colonialism that emerged in Britain and France at the end of the nineteenth century, shifting from a benign form of trade in its global outposts, to trade on a mass scale with military enforcers. Despite its temporal location it was very much a critique of contemporary globalization.

But with the global recession from 2007 onwards, globalization itself came under greater attack for creating a gig economy of precarity for migrant and indigenous citizens alike, as multinational companies uprooted their manufacturing and services to ever-lower wage economies, leaving economic catastrophe in their wake at a time when banks were pumping money in to inflate poor economies only to increase their indebtedness and their risks. In the crash that followed, intercultural theatre of aesthetics and form had lost its socio-political hinterland, even though productions such as *Caravansérail* were on message with migrant representation, and the rise in populist nationalism as the converse of globalization had been prefigured in *Les Naufragés*. And this is the moment that intercultural theory turned its attention from globalized theatrical interculturalism, skipped over the us/them binary of the national and focused on local communities in world cities where migrants themselves performed from below.

And it was in this context of anti-hegemonic rights to self-representation, Mnouchkine gave refuge to Canadian director Robert Lepage's cancelled production of *Kanata* after a public letter in Le Devoir, 'Encore une fois, l'aventure se passera sans nous, les Autochtones?' (2018), attacked the white director for appropriating the concerns and representations of Indigenous people of Canada's First Nations without their input. His work, like Mnouchkine's, had moved away from the supranational HIT variety, but moved into the territory of the European colonizer and his colonized subjects. And so, later that year by invitation of Mnouchkine the production was remounted at the Théâtre du Soleil with a new title, *Kanata—Episode 1—the Controversy*, telling the intended story of Indigenous peoples through the lens of Lepage's own victimization. Two of the world's leading theatre practitioners of the intercultural playing and defending the white victim smacked of tone-deaf privilege. In *The Methuen Drama Handbook of Interculturalism and Performance* Charlotte McIvor and co-author of the 'Conclusion', Justine Nakase write of directors of these HIT performances in the era post-globalization, where interculturalism retains as its premise the essentialism of culture, but in a new world order where post-globalization politics calls out appropriation, silencing and othering: 'And they have too often been undergirded by privilege earned by colonial legacies and neoliberal bankrolls which mask their provenance with claims of unity, universality, and transcendence. But these limited and/or problematic practices also largely began or are sustained by earnest intentions' (253).

Writing from Ireland as a European scholar who analysed and published on such privileged 'hegemonic intercultural theatre', and not writing about a city with a long tradition of inward migration, as Ric Knowles writes about Toronto, Canada, I have found that 'new interculturalism' does not always appear 'from below'. The experience of living in Dublin, Ireland, since 1990, in a monocultural, white and predominantly Catholic society was challenged by an economic boom between 1997 and 2007. Economic success attracted economic migrants from Eastern Europe and also from Africa, some claiming asylum. In those first decades representation of and by new migrants was scarce. Polish and African theatre companies emerged from diasporic communities both attempting to integrate practitioners and spectators from outside their communities. The African Arambe Productions made the biggest impact as the work was prolific and one of their adaptations of Irish canonical plays, for which they had made a name (J. M. Synge's *The Playboy of the Western World*, co-written by Arambe's director Olabisi Adigun and Booker Prize winning novelist, Roddy Doyle), transferred to the Abbey Theatre, Ireland's national theatre in 2007. The new arrivals in the play (Christy Mahon and later his father) were African in the adaptation and arrived on the all-white stage where the justice meted out to the new African characters made for, at times, uncomfortable viewing. This type of interculturalism was of a clash not a mixing and so stereotypes of the African male as sexual object or warrior emerged from the casting and staging. But the production wrongly is remembered more for a dispute between the authors and the theatre, with Adigun suing the theatre and his co-writer for changes made and royalties not paid in the production's revival. Adigun won his case but at a cost to his place in Irish theatre. Just as the ice-cold reception of the African migrants in the adapted play, speaking to some degree the words of the original play, as a metaphor for the experiences of migrants in real life, so too in real life beyond the theatre, the African writer was forced to use the court system to obtain what was rightfully his in pecuniary terms as well as reclaim ownership of this manifestation of a hybrid cultural artifact.

In 2014, ANU Productions concluded a tetralogy of performances of the communities of north inner-city Dublin with a production of *Vardo*, premised on a Traveller family that lived there. Their research and experience of living and working in the area revealed a good deal more about what was actually happening in the area in the form of people trafficking in and out of modern apartment blocks with great regularity. The production thus shifted on its axis from the Traveller family in a settled community, to an unsettled community of migrants on the axes of global criminal networks. At the southern end of the quarter-square mile of inner-city Dublin that was their source material for four years lay Busáras, the central bus station, a transient place from city to country but with a new international dimension since the inward migration of globalization that had occurred during the economic boom of 1997–2007. Here was a nodal point of connection with migrants in performance in intercultural transactions with local spectators in an immersive context where it was not clear who was an actor or bus passenger, and what if anything the spectator could do to stop the trafficking in plain sight, acted or not.

In the underground locker room, an East European-sounding woman implored each spectator in turn throughout the day to help her escape an international prostitution ring into which she had been duped and trafficked. East European is deliberately vague as the woman never reveals a nationality and brings into question in a white European context the role of *acoustemological interculturalism* as conceived by Marcus Tan in signifying representations of otherness 'that neither negate or homogenize differences but permanently destabilize and invalidate authoritative claims to authenticity' (Tan 2020, 16). Rather than fetishize her difference by scopic viewing, the woman's secret performance in the basement locker room offers 'a way of escaping the visibility of the intercultural and thus its identitarianism, by considering the possibility of listening to it instead' (Singleton, 2021, pp. 303–4). She asked me to help her find her passport and the fragility of this tenuous relationship between me and an East European other heightened the precarity of her situation. But it also heightened the spectator's. Thrown into situations without context or pretext, I as spectator struggled to do the right thing, as the situation called on spectators to act ethically to help the woman escape, not knowing the consequences of my action, but certainly knowing hers. Eventually the moment to help evaporates and her enforcer with a strong working-class Dublin accent takes control of the situation. I move away and am joined by a Nigerian man who invites me to hear his own story. The actor is Kunle Animashaun, replicating his own experience of being a migrant in Ireland, and he shows me images of his character's father on his mobile phone. His father has died and he is unable to return home as this would render his application for asylum null and void. In 'ANU Productions and the Performance of Otherness' (2021) I explain how the migrant is seen as spectacle in the bus station and how his actions, accosting individual spectators with regularity, caught the suspicious eyes of passengers and even security (even though they had been briefed and his performance had permission). Replicating his own migrant experience in his performance doubled the extent of the precarity of an African man in a bus station that served the nation and not the migrant.

While Kunle was a spectacle of otherness, the trafficked East European migrant could only be read in acoustemological terms. Upon leaving the bus station spectators are forced into a car with the fleeing East European woman going towards a fate she knew but we didn't. The car was driven by a woman with a middle-class Irish accent and our destination was a modern apartment which served as a brothel, and the spectator's role was switched to consumer. The acoustemology of this encounter pitted self and other in terms of languages and accents, as visible difference was not secure, and implicated Irish citizens at differing social levels in international criminal activities. When the performance was over I remained on the street and, prompted by director Louise Lowe, began to observe a Mercedes car with blacked-out windows parked on one side of the street, while another Mercedes slowly turned a corner. Here was real-life trafficking in action, and like in performance, I did nothing but observe. And so to what extent thus far has there been an intercultural exchange, if interculturalism is predicated on adjoining two or more cultures? The actual exchange is between actor playing foreign and spectator invariably playing self. And the intercultural encounter is predicated on the spectator desirous of acting in the intercultural exchange but in reality frozen in fear of doing so by not being allowed deliberately to know the context of the situation played out in public space. In the globalized city that is contemporary Dublin here was a performance that asked spectators to act and to intervene in the criminal and immoral transaction that globalization engenders.

Unlike the earlier postmodern interculturalism of the 1980s and onwards, of the HIT variety, in which the replicated culture has been processed into Western culture as otherness as opposed to the Other, ANU Productions' *Vardo* asks the spectator to align with the Other and to perform that alliance publicly. In it, Kunle, the Nigerian migrant, is lamenting his inability to return to Nigeria for his father's funeral, revealing the precarity of the migrant in the context of seeking asylum. Also, the East European trafficked migrant has no desire to remain and is desperate to return home. Their performances in the very public space of Dublin's central bus station, engaging with a single spectator repeatedly over a long duration, play into the othering of the migrant by the unwitting passengers in the bus station whose gaze clearly marked the migrant as a stereotype of illegal activity. And it was my interpretation of their negative reading of Kunle that prompted me to protect him from their gaze and from being stereotyped. The dichotomization of Self/Other, own/foreign, on which much intercultural theory in the twentieth century was predicated and on which Daphne P. Lei's notion of Hegemonic Intercultural Theatre is predicated, here breaks down as the spectator is not only immersed in the plight of the migrant other but is also implicated by association in the co-creation of the intercultural migrant from below. Implied thus, the spectator has to choose whether to passively ignore the scopic and hostile gaze of the unwitting bus passengers or take action to protect the migrant from that gaze. This production not only gives voice to the migrants 'from below', but positions the spectators 'below' as well, and invites spectators to align with the plight of the migrants as allies who listen to their words, thoughts, desires and fears (and to engage with them one-to-one in a form of acoustic interculturalism), and then go further to protect the intercultural encounter from being read unknowingly as a negative stereotype of otherness in public space.

References

Bharucha, Rustom. 1988. 'Peter Brook's "Mahabharata": A View from India.' *Economic and Political Weekly* 23:32 (6 August): 1642–1647.

Chin, Daryl. 1989. 'Interculturalism, Postmodernism, Pluralism.' *Performing Arts Journal*, 12 (1), 163–175.

Fischer-Lichte, Erika, Torsten Jost, Saskya Iris Jain, eds. 2014. *The Politics of Interweaving Performance Cultures: Beyond Postcolonialism*. New York: Routledge.

Knowles, Ric. 2010. *Theatre & Interculturalism*. Houndmills: Macmillan international/Red Globe Press.

———. 2017. *Performing the Intercultural City*. Ann Arbor: University of Michigan Press.

Lei, Daphne P. 2011. 'Interruption, Invention, Interculturalism: Robert Wilson's HIT Productions in Taiwan.' *Theater Journal* 63: 4 (December): 571–586.

Lei, Daphne P. & Charlotte McIvor, eds. 2020. *The Methuen Drama Handbook of Interculturalism and Performance*. London: Bloomsbury Methuen.

McIvor, Charlotte, 2016. *Migration and Performance in Contemporary Ireland*. London: Palgrave Macmillan.

McIvor, Charlotte & Jason King, eds. 2019. *Interculturalism and Performance Now: New Directions?* London: Palgrave Macmillan.

Mitra, Royona. 2015. *Akram Khan: Dancing New Interculturalism*. Houndmills, UK & New York: Palgrave Macmillan.

Patrice, Pavis. 1992. *Theatre at the Crossroads of Culture*. Translated by Loren Kruger. London: Routledge.

Singleton, Brian. 2021. ANU Productions and the Performance of Otherness. *Orbis Litterarum*, 76: 301–310. https://doi.org/10.1111/oli.12325

Tan, Marcus. 2020. '(Re)Sounding Universals: The Politics of Listening to Peter Brook's *Battlefield*.' In *The Methuen Drama Handbook of Interculturalism and Performance*, edited by Daphne P. Lei & Charlotte McIvor, 13–27. London: Bloomsbury Methuen.

specific and singular to each of us, our need to come to terms with our mortality is a universal encounter, and hence it is not surprising that death becomes one of the central subjects for many cosmopolitan artists to investigate.

The life trajectory and the work of a performance artist Marina Abramović exemplify these philosophical and political tendencies of today's cosmopolitanism. Born in 1946 in the Socialist Federal Republic of Yugoslavia (hereafter referred to as SFR Yugoslavia), Marina Abramović brought the history of her troubled land and the story of her own biography to the aesthetics of cosmopolitan performance, and thus she made her work intrinsically political. In her recent works Abramović turned to the questions of home, belonging, and her own future death and burial. She began to use the narrative structures of *autothanatography*—a genre of literature that describes the author's autobiographical experiences related to the act of dying—to queer the idea of death as a tragic end in the life of an individual, of an artist, but also of a nation. A pioneer of performance art, Abramović uses her body as a vehicle of energy, politics, and artistic expression. Engaging with the ritual of staging her own death and the death of others on stage, Abramović re-defines *autothanatography* as a type of performative testimony, and she questions the relationships 'between writing, the self and death' (Sorin and Vallas 2017). The 1997 video installation and live performance *Balkan Baroque*, performed at the 47th Venice Biennale, the 2011 *The Life and Death of Marina Abramović* (later dubbed *The Life*) directed by Robert Wilson for the Manchester International Festival, and the 2020 *The 7 Deaths of Maria Callas, an Opera Project* directed and designed by Abramović (with music by Marko Nikodijević in collaboration with the Bavarian State Opera) present the most compelling examples of this practice, and hence constitute the case study of this chapter. Before we examine these works, we will briefly sketch what we see as the essence of a cosmopolitan worldview and behaviour, in which the work of Abramović is immersed.

Cosmopolitanism: A Philosophical Condition of Social Behaviour, Personal Ethics, and Artistry

Supporting cosmopolitanism—a moral ideal based on 'the idea of equal human dignity' and 'respect for humanity,' which is 'at the root of much of the international human rights movement' and which holds 'a formative role in many national legal and constitutional traditions' (Nussbaum 2019, 3)—has become a necessity in a world defined by global wars, mass migration, rise of xenophobia, and nationalism. Theatre is well positioned to address these issues. Using empathy, affect, and telling personal stories of displacement through embodied encounter between the actor and their audience, performance arts can serve as a training ground for social behaviours. In the centre of this encounter is a new cosmopolitan: a person of divided origins and cultural heritage, someone who speaks many languages and claims different countries as their home or place of belonging. This new cosmopolitan claims multiple belongings and acquires multiple points of view. Together with refugees, asylum seekers, and political exiles, these new cosmopolitans—sometimes economic migrants and expatriates, sometimes jet-setters and tourists—add to the making of a collective 'we,' the heterogeneous populace of today's urban environments, which has come to defy the definitions of the nation-state that are rooted in the homogeneity of national language(s), religion, and ethnicity. Not surprisingly, cosmopolitan practices have also added to the rise of new nationalism, with its calls for religious fundamentalism, ethnic purity, preservation of national languages and cultures, closing borders, and stripping people of dual citizenship.

The etymology of the Greek word *cosmopolis*, from which today's 'cosmopolitanism' stems, implies an unresolved paradox. *Cosmos* refers to a universal order as established by nature; *polis* speaks of the order as made by people. Positioned between the state and the cosmos, cosmopolitanism signifies negotiation across differences. The tactics of dialogue, listening, and compromise form the basis of these mediations; they define a cosmopolitan worldview and inform artistic practices that focus on the figure of a cosmopolitan subject, constantly interrogating oneself and the world.

Even though cosmopolitanism was popular with the early Christians, the concept has only gained momentum since the Enlightenment. Philosophers of the time from Diderot to Hume and Voltaire to Jefferson subscribed to an 'attitude of open-mindedness and impartiality' (Kleingeld & Brown), and, accordingly, a journey into a foreign land was understood as an opportunity for discovery of oneself and of others. The emergence of the pejorative narratives of cosmopolitanism as a juxtaposition between a trustworthy, sedimentary patriot and a suspiciously mobile foreigner arose in the early nineteenth century. These narratives were mobilized and widely supported by the ideologies of the nation-state. Yet, as Julia Kristeva reminds us, these narratives can also be found in the 1789 *Declaration of the Rights of Man and Citizen*, the foundational document of the Western democracy: 'the Declaration shifts from the universal notion–"men"–to the "political associations" that must preserve their rights, and encounters the historical reality of the "essential political association," which turns out to be the nation' (148). In this context, a private person acquires a lesser value than a citizen; the citizen turns into a political object, whose 'national identification is the essential expression of his sovereignty' (Kristeva 1991, 149). Categorized as 'citizen,' Kristeva argues, the individual was now defined by their duties towards the nation, whereas any foreigner, who 'does not belong to the group' (95) and 'who does not have the same nationality' (96), becomes a stranger. This foreigner, in other words, can now be easily denied the privileges that come with this citizenship. Theories of cosmopolitanism continue to grapple with the incumbent consequences of identity and social behaviour when individuals are categorized in accordance with their position in relation to the nation-state.

When it comes to theorizing the figure of 'foreigner,' a famous saying of the German nineteenth-century sociologist Georg Simmel comes to mind: to him a stranger is someone who 'comes today and stays tomorrow' (Simmel 1950, 402).

A disturbing foreign entity, the stranger moves from the social periphery to its centre, and so they can be regarded as dangerous. But 'strangeness' also presupposes freedom: the stranger's acceptance of both the anxiety and the excitement to be on the road. To Simmel, however, mobility turns a reliable citizen into an uncontrollable engine of change (403–405), a fear that many populist governments and ideologists exploit today.

Thinking of the paradoxes of movement, Zygmunt Bauman constructed a new theory of *liquid modernity* rooted in the consciousness and practices of international mobility, with the free but somewhat irresponsible individual, the person of power and privilege, at its centre. In his definitions, Bauman distinguished between 'solid modernity' as an 'era of mutual engagement' in contrast with a 'fluid or liquid modernity' as 'the epoch of disengagement, elusiveness, facile escape and hopeless chase' (2000, 120). In his thinking, Bauman echoes Simmel's concern about wandering turned into settlement and how it can be destructive to the well-being of the nation-state, its political structures, and economy.

Walter Benjamin's philosophy of *flaneur* and Edward Said's conceptualization of the *intellectual in exile* build towards this theory of international mobility and cosmopolitanism as well. Benjamin's flaneur—a detached observer of their day and history—stems from the tenets of European Modernism. Flaneur comes from the place of economic stability, but their appearance is also connected to industrialization, exile, and banishment of the inter-war period of the twentieth century (Benjamin 1983, 35–36). The figure of un-settlement, the flaneur is a pensive traveller and a narrator of historical destructions: someone who is not simply positioned outside history but also actively seeks to stay on the margins. The flaneur is a distant cousin to Said's *intellectual in exile*—someone who is never 'fully adjusted, always feeling outside the chatty, familiar world inhabited by natives' (Said 1994, 53). This exile is like a new cosmopolitan, who makes up the core membership of what Beck defines as a newly imagined community of global risk (2011, 1348). This new cosmopolitan emerges as the result of the 'global interconnectivity' between people and states, and so endorses 'the end of the "global other"' (1348). Neither social condition nor a recognized political order, new cosmopolitanism is a process that takes place 'behind the façade of persisting national spaces, jurisdictions and labels, even as national flags continue to be raised and national attitudes, identities, and consciousness remain dominant' (Beck 2011, 1348). For Beck, the emergence of the 'global other' raises the following question: 'How can strangers—constructed as members of imagined national communities—be turned into neighbours?' (1349) This question invites an interrogation of our personal ethics and responsibilities towards the other, and it also suggests that cosmopolitanism is a phenomenon of 'mind crossing borders,' a *work-in-progress*, and a *work-in-process* (Bhabha 2014, 262). It produces a new *cosmopolitan subjectivity*. Defined by the sense of internal rupture, this *cosmopolitan patriot* carries their cultural roots from one place to another, equally loving all their homelands as the evidence of one's 'loyalty to humankind' (Appiah 1997, 622).

New cosmopolitans are open to dialogue and constant re-adjustment of their personal values, ready to take their moral, ethical, and political stand.

In her 2020 book *Performance, Subjectivity, Cosmopolitanism*, Yana Meerzon proposes a definition of the politics and the aesthetics of the *theatre of cosmopolitanism* (15–17), which constitutes an intersection of a social-political phenomenon and an aesthetic condition. Meerzon takes inspiration from Rebecca Walkowitz's work on *critical cosmopolitanism* in literature (2006), which 'identifies critical cosmopolitanism as a type of philosophical and artistic practice' (Meerzon 2020, 15). Critical cosmopolitanism 'reflects cosmopolitan artists' personal conditions of movement, be it the experience of a refugee displaced by war, an asylum seeker, or an economic migrant. [It] encourages these artists' adoption of a transnational position and multiple points of view' (15). From here a new theory of cosmopolitan theatre emerges. As a social phenomenon, Meerzon posits that 'cosmopolitan theatre is marked by the economic situation and personal mobility of its makers' (16); and as an artistic practice, cosmopolitan theatre addresses what Dan Rebellato describes as 'the fundamental gap between representation and re-enactment, questioning the encounter principle that motivates any type of live performance' (2009, 78). Frequently, 'its dramatic investigation is centred on an individual in crisis—someone in the midst of a physical and existential journey, to whom the state of personal liminality has become the new norm' (Meerzon 2020, 17). Many cosmopolitan theatre makers present their work at international theatre festivals for international audiences; they often 'use dramaturgical tactics of fragmentation and deconstruction, uncanny and vertigo, multilingualism, space/time simultaneity, audience displacement, and immersion' (18) to evoke the state of vulnerability and internal rift, in which these works are produced.

Marina Abramović: The Case of Cosmopolitanism

An impressive international reputation and a privileged socio-economic position on the world art scene and market make Marina Abramović a prime example of today's cosmopolitan nomad. Living without a permanent address in a technologically globalized world, Abramović's work constantly returns to the place of her origin. In so doing, she rethinks the status of the artist's body and its belonging to the local, global, and digital worlds. Abramović's transnational career spans over almost five decades, and it is defined by a trajectory from being a radical artist at home to a renowned art-world celebrity in the West, whose work is intimately linked to no fewer than three urban hubs (Belgrade, Amsterdam, and New York) and four continents (Europe, Australia, Asia, and North America). In her interview with Adrian Heathfield, the artist says: 'My nomadic nature allows me to make work in different locations around the world. Every place I go, every city, every country, I create that home. Ideas appear to me anywhere, and I can develop these ideas in different locations as I travel' (Abramović 2019, 26). This thinking of geographical and cultural nomadism is reflected in Abramović's work, in which the artist experiments with almost every sub-genre of performance arts and media. It makes Abramović one of the most renowned, successful, and internationally celebrated performance artists of her generation. The figure of 'Marina Abramović' emerges from an irresolvable tension between growing up in the atmosphere of strict personal discipline, the daily performativity of the Socialist regime, and her nomadic life practices, whereas her experiment in fostering *presence*—energy exchange between the performer and the audience—defines the core of her aesthetics. Using her own body as 'a laboratory for experiments in consciousness,' pain, and suffering, Abramović works on eradicating consciousness from her body in public, 'emptying out and erasing self' (Phelan 2004, 572). She explores the notion of death or internal stasis through the lens of her own philosophy of art, which she calls 'The Abramović Method,' and seeks a cathartic purification of self as other (Richards 2010, 77). Death—as movement versus stasis—is a central theme to many of her works. For example, in the video-works *Cleaning the Mirror I, II, III* (1995) and *Nude with Skeleton* (2005), the plastic and gypsum skeleton, a metonymy of a deceased body, is positioned alongside Abramović's living body, so the artist's living self turns into 'a *memento mori* in herself' (Westcott 2010, 243). These video-installations serve as Abramović's laboratory to creatively explore her own mortality and place in the world, and they also thematically resonate with one of her major projects, 1997 *Balkan Baroque*, which features Abramović both irreversibly linking herself to the troubled history of her homeland and declaring herself a cosmopolitan citizen of the world.

Presented at the 47th Venice Biennale, the multimedia project *Balkan Baroque* consists of a live performance and a video installation, which serve as commemoration of the Yugoslav wars and of the artist's absence from her country. At the time, the Balkan region was in a vulnerable place. The peace accord known as the Dayton Agreement (1995) had recently been signed, and it brought a tenuous closure to the three-and-a-half year long Bosnian conflict. Years of civil war, the international embargo, and political isolation established by the UN Security Council left SFR Yugoslavia in a precarious position. This complex and conflicted situation gave Abramović's project a region-specific meaning: it linked *Balkan Baroque* to the disintegration of the Yugoslav state body.

At the same time, the project's aesthetics was insistently self-referential: it relied on the devices of artistic self-renewal and self-preservation. The live performance unfolded in a dark basement filled with cow bones. The artist was placed in the centre of this composition, immersed in the act of repetitive cleaning of these bones. Using a metal brush to clean 1500 bloody bones, Abramović performed this act of cleaning for six hours per day over four consecutive days. The stench of the disintegrating bones, which accompanied the performance, enhanced the eschatological meaning of the project. The bones and the blood, along with Abramović's performative act of purification, made the concept of death tangible and real. This visceral and olfactory presence of death evoked the aesthetics of the baroque, in which amassing of styles and artistic conventions were accompanied by a morbid and erotic fascination and fear of death. In this performative setting, Abramović's body became a source of ambiguity and a synonym for *Balkanness*, standing (ironically) for what the Western audiences viewed as atavistic, pagan, barbaric, stuck, antimodern, and regressive (Pejić 2019, 254). It staged a problematic tension between Abramović's individual narrative of her family and country's past, and it linked the death of a single body to the destruction of the Yugoslav state.

Thinking through Edward Said's notion of *Orientalism*, historian Maria Todorova claims that the Western consciousness always imagined the Balkans as something unstable and unpredictable: the East is configured as the violent, regressive, and primitive antithesis to the rational, progressive, and civilized West (Todorova 1997, 13). Todorova's argument draws upon the Balkans' historical and geographical positioning, and its complex cultural and political relationship to the West and the East that transpires from it. In this scheme, the Balkans arises as a liminal, transitional, and 'in-between' territory—a 'semi-primitive/semi-civilized other'—which bridges and juxtaposes East and West at the same time (13). Abramović's work exemplifies Todorova's argument. *Balkan Baroque* manifests the artist's inner conflict: it reveals her cosmopolitan world view, which embraces both her rational/scientific/Western self and her irrational/atavistic/Balkan self.

A triptych of video portraits—Marina's father, mother, and Marina herself—accompanies Abramović's live performance. It comments on the ideologically shaped public image of Abramović's parents—that is, communists whose lives and careers coincided with the rise and decline of SFR Yugoslavia. The centrally positioned, life-size video portrait of Abramović herself further contributes to this project's ambiguity. This image simultaneously evokes and rejects the canons of Orthodox Christian iconography: Abramović's body suggests the image of Christ, but it does not appear in a tranquil state as the conventions of this genre dictate. In it, Abramović emerges in the process of visual and metaphorical transformation: from an image of Abramović as a rational scientist, bespectacled and wearing a white lab coat, to an image of a carnivalesque female dancer. The visual and semantic contrast of two Abramovićs refers to the clichéd West/*Balkanness* dichotomy, and thus illustrates how skilfully Abramović manipulates the Western gaze. She entrenches the gaze of the 'Others'—of the West—within the frame, which is itself also the subject of critique and question.

Unlike *Balkan Baroque*, which explored the death of the Yugoslav state and Abramović's personal war trauma, which she has internalized even without having experienced this war directly (MoMA 2021), her 2011 autobiographical project *The Life and Death of Marina Abramović* ponders the artist's own death. It stages Marina's future funeral, during which three bodies of the artist—three Marinas—are to be simultaneously buried in the three cities that determined her artistic trajectory, namely Belgrade, Amsterdam, and New York. Much like *Balkan Baroque*, which is based on a re-enactment of a ritual and exemplifies cosmopolitan aesthetics, *The Life* is a ceremonial performance. It presents the figure 'Marina Abramović' as a citizen of the country that does not exist today, as her mother, and as three other female figures or Marina's doubles—'the warrior one, the spiritual one, and the bullshit one' (Abramović 2016, 338). This 'curious doubling of narrator and narrative object—the twinning of the living and the dead,' with the artist living through her own death and funeral (Secomb 2002, 42)—capitalizes on Abramović's search for the sense of the real and illustrates her deep distrust of theatre as something 'fake' (Abramović 2016, 337). The production reflects Abramović's desire to use her posthumous body as a type of 'memorabilia and monument' (Racanović 2019, 201). It pre-enacts the impossible: in the moment of her death the artist's body will multiply and through the act of three entombments it will re-enforce Abramović's contribution to the cultural history of the three cities in which she lived and to the history of performance art.

Using elements of *autothanatography*—the author's 'promise and a warning of the death to come' (Secomb 2002, 42)—this production emphasizes liveness as physicality of experience; and so, it mobilizes Abramović's presence as marked and unmediated, framed through the theatricalization of her own self. It stages Marina's funeral, in which 'the survivor lives on […] awaiting the death interrupted and suspended' (Secomb 2002, 42). Performing her *autothanatography*, in which Abramović's traumatic memories about her parents blend with the broader socio-political and cultural context in which she grew up, the artist redefines not only her own past and anticipated future but also her family's past and the traumatic history of her home country. Standing centre stage and holding her own death-mask as her final double, Abramović enacts Levinas's affirmation of alterity as one's 'responsibility invoked by the face of the other in the face-to-face relation' (Secomb 2002, 39). This image presents Abramović's spectators with an 'opportunity to dwell within their own memories' and past experiences (Phelan 2004, 576); and it invites them to recognize 'the other' within their own selves. Once again, *The Life* positions Abramović's work as inherently pluralistic and autobiographical. At the same time, expensively made and internationally promoted at Manchester Theatre Festival, Luminato Theatre Festival in Toronto, Teatro Real in Madrid, the Single Theatre in Antwerp, and the Park Avenue Armory in New York (Abramović 2016, 338), this production also speaks to the paradox of cosmopolitanism. On one hand, it is situated within economic, financial, and movement-related global privilege; on the other hand, it capitalizes on the authenticity of the performer's scenic presence, deeply connected to the wound of separation from her native land.

In contrast to the previous two projects, Abramović's most recent work as of this writing—*7 Deaths of Maria Callas*—seems to be less autobiographical. It explores death as enacted by an internationally celebrated opera diva Maria Callas. This multimedia spectacle consists of seven death scenes, which Callas used to perform, and an eighth one: a tragedy of Callas's own death as interpreted by Marina Abramović. While seven opera singers dressed like Callas's maid Bruna sing their numbers on stage, seven silent films (directed by Nabil Elderkin) are projected on a screen. In these films, Marina Abramović and Willem Dafoe re-perform the same death scenes using additional references to Callas's own unhappy love affair with the Greek magnate Aristotle Onassis. Abramović's re-enactment of Callas's work as *prima donna assoluta* draws on many biographical parallels between them. Both artists had complex relationships with their mothers, experienced intense suffering because of unrequited love, explored specific attitudes towards their own bodies as unwanted and ugly, and survived heart attacks. Abramović's embodiment of Callas as someone reckless and abandoned, who dies in exile, desperate and alone, achieves its dramatic climax in the final scene. In it, once Callas's mortal body leaves the stage, all that remains is her empty apartment in Paris in 1977. Like a deceased body in many cultures, the apartment needs to be literally and metaphorically cleansed in preparation for a final ceremony and, symbolically, the eternal state of tranquillity and stasis. The act of cleaning is performed by the opera singers in the last scene literally and metaphorically—seven Brunas clean Callas's apartment after her death. This act of cleaning, at the same time, enables once again Abramović's philosophy of art rooted in the process of cathartic purification and cleansing of emotions through art, and so is transnational and universal. On stage, she collapses Callas-the-person and Callas-the-soprano. As such, they become one body, one entity. 'Life for art and art as a passion and fate' (Maria Callas 2010, 0:18) are the most significant points that connect these two performers. They use their bodies as the main source of their artistic power: the body that produces the voice of Maria Callas and the body that produces the performative presence of Marina Abramović.

Yet *7 Deaths of Maria Callas* is much more than just an homage to Callas's life and talent. Based on numerous quotations from Abramović's previous works, it helps the artist to re-enact her own artistic journey. The scene of strangulation in *Otello*, as interpreted by Abramović, is exemplary of this self-referential practice. On screen, Abramović re-enacts and references her own video cycles, *Dragon Heads* (1990–1994) and *Snake Whisper* (2019). In these videos, Abramović's head is framed by a close-up shot as she remains motionless, on the verge of death, while a snake slithers around her neck and body—an image which broadly resonates with *Otello*. As a chthonic being in many mythologies, the snake is symbolically associated with the underworld. As such, the scene embodies not only the idea of death and the awareness of the temporality of human existence, but also Abramović's idea about the *cathartic* nature of art.

Conclusion

Marina Abramović's work, her focus on death and eternal stasis, we argue, helps us better understand the anxieties, the experiences, and the fears of a cosmopolitan nomad. In *Balkan Baroque*, death signifies the collapse of the world in which Abramović was born and grew up; in *The Life and Death of Marina Abramović*, the performer stages her own funeral, through which she intends to control her legacy as an individual and as an artist; and, in *The 7 Deaths of Maria Callas*, Abramović re-enacts death as a performative experience and theatrical endeavour produced by another artist and in another time. In all her works Abramović remains an advocate for human dignity. The autobiographical body of the performer, which undergoes various forms of artistic experimentation and psycho-physical transformation, serves as a symbolic capsule of Abramović's personal history. Abramović's artistic project also exemplifies how a philosophical call for moral equality and a call for more equitable international laws in human rights can be concretized through the field of performance arts; it makes her work unmistakably cosmopolitan.

References

Abramović, Marina. 2019. 'Liquid Knowledge—In Conversation with Adrian Heathfield.' In Marina Abramović–The Cleaner, 26–34. Belgrade: Publicum.
———. 2016. *Walk Through Walls: A Memoir*. New York: Crown Archetype.
Appiah, Kwame Anthony. 1997. 'Cosmopolitan Patriots.' *Critical Inquiry*, 23 (3), 617–639.
Bauman, Zigmunt. 2000. *Liquid Modernity*. Cambridge: Polity Press.
———. 2004. *Wasted Lives: Modernity and Its Outcasts*. Cambridge: Polity Press.
———. 2017. 'Symptoms in Search of an Object and a Name.' In *The Great Regression*, ed. Heinrich Geiselberger, 13–25. Cambridge: Polity Press.
Beck, Ulrich. 2011. 'Cosmopolitanism as Imagined Communities of Global Risk.' *American Behavioral Scientist*, 55 (10), 1346–1361.
Benjamin, Walter. 1983. 'The Flaneur.' In *Charles Baudelaire: A Lyric Poet in the Era of High Capitalism*. Translated by Harry Zohn, 35–66. New York: Verso.
Bhabha, Homi K. 2014. 'Epilogue: Global Pathways.' In *The Politics of Interweaving Performance Cultures, Beyond Postcolonialism*, eds. Erika Fischer-Lichte, Torsten Jost, and Saskya Iris Jain, 259–277. London and New York: Routledge.
Bharucha, Rustom. 2014. 'Hauntings of the Intercultural: Enigmas and Lessons on the Borders of Failure.' In *The Politics of Interweaving Performance Cultures, Beyond Postcolonialism*, eds. Erika Fischer-Lichte, Torsten Jost, and Saskya Iris Jain, 179–201. London and New York: Routledge.
Kleineld, Pauline, and Eric Brown. 2014. 'Cosmopolitanism,' In *The Stanford Encyclopedia of Philosophy*, ed. Edward N. Zalta. Stanford: Stanford University; https://pure.rug.nl/ws/portalfiles/portal/14454370/plato.stanford.pdf
Knowles, Ric. 2010. *Theatre and Interculturalism*. Basingstoke: Palgrave Macmillan.
Kristeva, Julia. 1991. *Strangers to Ourselves*. Translated by Leon Roudiez. New York: Columbia University Press.

"Maria Callas—Vissi d'arte (Puccini, Tosca)." *YouTube*. Uploaded by anes1001, 4 April 2010, https://www.youtube.com/watch?v=NLR3lSrqlww

McIvor, Charlotte, and Jason King. eds. 2019. *Interculturalism and Performance Now: New Directions?* Basingstoke: Palgrave Macmillan.

Meerzon, Yana. 2020. *Performance, Subjectivity, Cosmopolitanism*. Basingstoke: Palgrave Macmillan.

MoMA. 2021. 'Marina Abramović. *Balkan Baroque*. 1997.' Accessed July 9, 2021. https://www.moma.org/audio/playlist/243/3126

Nussbaum, Martha C. 2019. *The Cosmopolitan Tradition: A Noble but Flawed Ideal*. Cambridge: Harvard University Press.

Pejić, Bojana. 2019. 'And Now, Let's Remember … Yugoslavia.' In *Marina Abramović—The Cleaner*, 250–260. Belgrade: Publicum.

Phelan, Peggy. 2004. 'Marina Abramović: Witnessing Shadows,' *Theatre Journal*, 56 (4), 569–577.

Racanović, Svetlana. 2019. 'Hoće li Marina Abramović umrijeti?' In *Marina Abramović—Od reza do šava*. Editor-in-chief Vladislav Bajac, 199–202. Beograd: Geopoetika.

Richards, Mary. 2010. *Marina Abramović*. London and New York: Routledge.

Said, Edward. 1994. 'Intellectual Exile: Expatriates and Marginals.' In *Representations of the Intellectual: The 1993 Reith Lectures*, 47–65. London: Vintage.

———. 2000. *Reflections on Exile and Other Essays*. Cambridge: Harvard University Press.

Schiller, Nina Glick, and Noel B. Salazar. 2013. 'Regimes of Mobility Across the Globe,' *Journal of Ethnic and Migration Studies*, 39 (2), 183–200.

Secomb, Linnell. 2002. 'Autothanatography.' *Mortality*, 7 (1), 33–46.

Simmel, Georg. 1950. 'The Stranger.' In *The Sociology of Georg Simmel*, edited by Kurt H. Wolff, 402–408. Glencoe: Free Press.

Sorin, Claire, and Sophie Vallas. 2017. 'Introduction,' *E-rea*, 15 (1), 1–6.

Todorova, Maria Nikolaeva. 1997. *Imagining the Balkans*. New York: Oxford University Press.

Westcott, James. 2010. *When Marina Abramović Dies: A Biography*. Cambridge, MA: The MIT Press.

CHAPTER 9

Indigenous Migrations: Performance, Urbanization, and Survivance in Native North America

Sara Pillatzki-Warzeha and Margaret Werry

In popular discourse, there is a tension between the Indigenous and the migrant. In this thinking, Indigeneity is defined by a continuous attachment to specific, ancestral territory, and to traditional lifeways rooted in that place; to be a migrant is, then, to become less Indigenous, to compromise one's identity. This essay challenges this set of assumptions. Such assumptions not only misrepresent Indigenous experiences of identity, migration, place, and belonging. They also serve an ongoing settler-colonial operation of power that attempts to eliminate Indigenous peoples by simultaneously displacing them and undermining the ground of their sovereignty and identity. In contrast, we focus on the ways in which performance and theatre by Indigenous artists reveal the unique complexity of Indigenous experiences of migration. After briefly introducing some of the key ideas that are necessary to understand the contexts and consequences of Indigenous migration, we narrow our scope to a specific instance: the urbanization of Native peoples in the USA. The work of urban US theatre and performance makers represents Indigenous experiences of exile, dispossession, dislocation, trauma, healing and homecoming, guesting on others' territory, reclaiming one's own, and making relations with other migrants. These Native artists explore new configurations of old genealogies and cosmographies, inter-tribal or trans-national forms of belonging, and revitalize forms of ceremony, community-building, and place-making. Their body

S. Pillatzki-Warzeha • M. Werry (✉)
University of Minnesota, Minneapolis, MN, USA
e-mail: sarapw@umn.edu; werry001@umn.edu

of work offers a profound critique of the imbrication of migration with the violence of settler-colonialism, while also enacting a politics and ethos of survivance, that is, the active, creative, performative process of thriving in the face of attempted elimination. They help illustrate what is meant by a 'land-based dramaturgy,' a dramaturgy that acknowledges the 'ongoing [ancestral] relationship between people and land' (Joseph 2019, 144), that is targeted by colonialism but is inalienable to Indigenous peoples, whether migrants or original inhabitants.

Indigeneity and Migration

First, what do we mean by the term 'Indigenous,' and how does this term stand in relation to the identities, experiences, and politics of migration? Indigeneity is an identity term of relatively recent genesis. The contemporary definition of the term was forged in the crucible of post-WWII supra-national governance bodies (such as the UN), where representatives of original peoples began to advocate for collective recognition, finding common cause with nationalist movements from the decolonizing third world, and civil rights struggles in the first world (Niezen 2003). Rather than Aboriginal, autochthonous, Native, tribal, First Nations, or Indian (which are local, national, colonial, or universalizing terms), Indigenous is a category that operates at a global scale, establishing a commonality between diverse peoples based on their descent from the 'earliest populations in an area' (Sissons 2005, 22) and their shared experience of encounter with colonial capitalism: settler invasion and occupation, dispossession, and minoritization in the settler nation-states where their ancestral territories are located. Indigeneity also invokes the extraordinary movements for self-determination, cultural revitalization, and 'Indigenous becoming' (Clifford 2013, 8) that have flourished in the last five decades in response to these conditions, that Leanne Betasamosake Simpson has termed the 'radical resurgence' of Indigenous peoples (2017).

It is important to note that this definition, by foregrounding not only the anteriority of Indigenous populations but also their relation to settler states, excludes nativists or ethnic minorities who often try to claim the mantle of autochthony in struggles for advantage, casting themselves as the original people and others—often migrants—as aliens. Further, Indigeneity is not a racial or ethnic designation, even though Indigenous populations are frequently racialized or framed as ethnic minorities within settler nation-states. It is important to note also that Indigenous is an identity term rejected by many Native communities and individuals who prefer to self-identify by tribe, clan, or family, hewing to endogenous ways of determining membership and belonging. Likewise, some embrace collective terms (such as Māori or Kanak or Indian) that refer to solidarities that are national rather than transnational in scale, even as others see these same terms as artifacts of colonial (mis)recognition. In short, in the Indigenous world, the terminology of identity is complex terrain.

Indigeneity, it should be clear from this history, is an identity term that has come about in the context of—and in part as a result of—the increased mobility and cosmopolitan consciousness of Indigenous peoples. And it denotes neither a fixed classification nor shared essence as much as a 'heuristic framework' (Gilbert 2017, 174) for thinking about the commonality of diverse groups. In fact, central to the constitution of Indigenous as a term is a respect for the irreducible diversity of histories, experiences, and current political circumstances of different communities. The cultural politics of indigeneity is deeply local, rooted in specificity of different groups' relations and struggles with settler states, their ancestries, thought systems, lifeways, and practices. Moreover, Indigenous protocols regarding knowledge also constrain generalizations and 'objective' epistemological frameworks (Tuhiwai Smith 2012). There is no view from above or elsewhere, only situated perspectives and sovereign singularities.

At the same time, many of those who identify as Indigenous feel that their commonality also inheres in culture, in a shared relationship to land, origins, and genealogies. The term that Dene scholar Glen Coulthard uses to describe this ethos is 'grounded normativity,' the 'place-based foundation of Indigenous decolonial thought and practice,' and 'the modalities of Indigenous land-connected practices and longstanding experiential knowledge that inform and structure our ethical engagements with the world and our relationships with human and nonhuman others over time' (2014, 14).

This aspect of Indigenous attachment to land might be taken to indicate the incommensurability of migrancy and Indigeneity: if Indigenous identity is conceptually embedded in place and past, is it deauthenticated, threatened, or compromised by migration? Does Indigeneity then stand outside modernity? Nothing could be further from the fact.

Firstly, from an Indigenous perspective, place-based identity does not depend on uninterrupted residence; it means participating in a 'system of reciprocal relations and obligations' that are nondominating and nonexploitative (Coulthard 2014, 13). Those relations can be maintained at a distance, and new relations entered into with new places and peoples. In fact, the spatial and temporal extension of this relationship to land is crucial to many understandings of Indigenous identity. For Leanne Betasamosake Simpson grounded normativity refers to a mesh of 'radiating responsibilities' that originate in land (*Aki*, in Nishanaabe) and radiate both outwards creating networks of connections to other nations and beings, past and future, and inwards, such that Indigenous bodies are 'networked vessels' that contain this original land-based knowledge (2017, 21). In another example, Māori grounded normativity is anchored by the term *whakapapa*, which refers to both the geological strata of land and the genealogical webs that link people with each other and with land, forests, water, and all other entities; *whakapapa* thus defines your origins, your place in the world, and your responsibilities to others.

Likewise, commitment to 'grounded normativity' does not mean living close to the earth. Such romanticizing eco-primitivist rhetoric can as easily be used to delegitimize Indigenous rights claims and lifeways (particularly urban ones) as to argue for them (Sissons 2005, 16). Nor does grounded normativity imply legal ownership. An Indigenous-centred view of sovereignty (a key term in Indigenous politics) is not about control of territory, and certainly not about the ownership of land as property (although in practice it may require both). As Sheryl Lightfoot (Anishanaabe) argues, Indigenous frameworks resist the (neo-)liberal state's norms and forms of territoriality (2016). Instead, sovereignty is what empowers people to honour their relations and obligations. Indigenous thinkers mobilize the term sovereignty to refer to rights to self-determination, as well as the rights to nurture the cultural practices that sustain grounded normativity, as in language sovereignty or food sovereignty. As numerous Indigenous scholars have argued, because sovereignties are nurtured, developed, and expressed through embodied practices (such as storytelling (Howe 1999; Carter 2016), dancing (Simas and Bodhran 2019), or navigation (Diaz 2019)) resurgence is sustained by performance, and it can take place anywhere, not only on ancestral territory. Thus, while the place-based foundation of Indigenous identity is rooted in deep, ancestral, and cosmological time and specific lands, it is also highly contemporary, adaptable, and mobile; it is what Miller has termed a '*competing mode* of modernity' (2019, 11).

The idea that Indigenous identity is rooted in past and place in a way that would be compromised by migration is a pernicious product of settler-colonial ideology and is—like enforced migration itself—part of a suite of techniques that settler-colonialism deploys to disrupt and disavow the intimate connections of grounded normativity that are the source of Indigenous resilience. As Patrick Wolfe (2006) has argued, colonialism is a structure not an event: it is not something that happened in the past, with unfortunate contemporary consequences; it is an ongoing process the impetus of which is to eliminate Indigenous peoples in order to supplant them. These strategies of elimination are many and varied: territorial dispossession, resource extraction, outright genocide, the destruction of ecologies, sustenance and lifeways (such as the eradication of buffalo), family separation (from residential schooling to foster care), outlawing of language and cultural practices, the over-policing of Indigenous communities, and under-policing of white violence against them. It also includes the governmental or legal manipulation of Indigenous belonging through blood quantum or descent rules, in ways that diminish the membership of Indigenous communities over time by declaring those of mixed descent to be not real Indigenous people.

This attempted alienation can also take symbolic form, and again performance is pivotal. Indigenous autochthony is appropriated by settlers 'playing Indian' (Deloria 1998) and Indigenous people are often disappeared through structures of feeling that associate Indigeneity with the historical past, rendering the expression of Indigenous identity in the context of modernity comically anomalous (Deloria 2004) or illegitimate (O'Brien 2010). Modern Indians, settlers pronounce, cannot be 'real Indians.'

These histories of settler-colonialism make the conjunction of Indigeneity and migration complex terrain. In a way, communities have become Indigenous (as opposed to, say, Ohlone or Tuhoe or Mapuche) through the migrations of colonists, the 'transits of empire' that have thrown original peoples into motion and into relation with each other in a liminal space of 'suspicion and unintelligibility' (Byrd 2011, xv) with respect to settler politics. Many have been subjected to enforced mobility, a strategy of biopolitical regulation designed to induce them to 'give up lands and give up themselves' (Simpson 2014, 16). In the US this has taken the form of forced relocations between states or onto reservations, or the violent transection of Native territories by national borders, making migrants out of people in place. For instance, the Mohawk nation Kahnawà:ke to which Audra Simpson belongs is divided by the US/Canada border; to receive the supposed gift of either American or Canadian passports, and thus freedom of movement, tribe members must repudiate their own nationhood. Many refuse. Colonization by biopolitics has also taken the form of policies promoting or compelling urban migration, which we will focus on in the second half of this paper.

Attention to forced Indigenous migrations has obscured older forms of voluntary Indigenous mobility: until recently, white scholars largely hewed to primitivist assumptions about the static rootedness of Indigenous peoples, while Indigenous scholars focused on confronting ongoing territorial dispossession. Yet, historically, many Indigenous people were prodigious travellers, practicing nomadic or seasonal migration, maintaining wide trade networks, and undertaking journeys of exploration, diplomatic or military missions. Many, like Māori, anchor their identities in origin stories of migration, of ancestral canoes and heroic navigators, as well as in creation stories that describe their emergence from the land.

A recent generation of Indigenous scholars focuses on mobility as a constitutive feature of Indigenous modernities. Jace Weaver (2014), for instance, coined the term Red Atlantic to name the hemispheric space produced by the circulation of Native American ideas, goods, and culture from the fourteenth century to the present, by diplomats, scholars, artists, traders, and adventurers plying the Atlantic. David Chang (2018) has written about the global consciousness and world-girdling philosophies of Native Hawaiian whalers and globe-trotters from the eighteenth century. For many Indigenous travellers, the pull of adventure and opportunity was shadowed by the push of colonial violence. Storyteller and historian Dovie Thomason describes the Lakota performers of Buffalo Bill's Wild West Show, whose years-long sojourns in Europe reenacting their military defeat at the hands of the US Army were a way to escape the confinement and poverty of the reservation system and provide for their families (see also Thrush 2017; Kroes 2012). For these performers, 'transmotion' was a technique of survivance (Vizenor et al. 2008), of active presence and sovereignty. For others, modern migrations are a continuation of centuries-old world-making practices. Tongan theorist, Epeli Hau'ofa, for instance, famously described the way the vast and vibrant diaspora of Pacific Islanders in the cities of the US, New Zealand, Australia, and Europe extends their ancient 'sea of islands' into an expansive, dynamic network in which people, ideas, remittances, goods, and arts ceaselessly circulate, genealogically incorporating new peoples and places (2008, 27–40).

In the title of his influential essay, 'Varieties of Indigenous Experience,' settler anthropologist James Clifford points to the scholarly project that stems from a recognition that Indigenous belonging thrives in motion as well as in place. He advocates for a focus on not only Indigenous roots, but also on Indigenous routes and returns, acknowledging that people are always 'improvising new ways to be native,' always engaged in dynamic processes of 'uprooting and rerooting, waxing and waning of identities' (2013, 69). Other scholars, such as Chickasaw theorist Chadwick Allen, explore the methods that best capture this variety, 'transindigenous' methods that through studying diverse texts or forms alongside each other 'acknowledge the mobility and multiple interactions of Indigenous peoples, cultures, histories, and texts' (2012, xiv).

URBAN MIGRATION AND INDIGENOUS SURVIVANCE

Urbanization is the largest global migration in human history, and in the last century it has swept up Indigenous peoples along with other rural populations. The vast majority of Indigenous people in the US, Australia, New Zealand, and Canada now live in cities. And a growing number of Indigenous peoples from Latin America, Asia, and Africa are gravitating to cities both within and outside their own countries. Some seek opportunity, but most are driven by dispossession of their lands and livelihoods through logging, mining, or agricultural land theft, and other factors such as climate change impact, extreme poverty, persecution, or armed conflict; most face redoubled structural discrimination in cities (see United Nations 2009).

In the US, urbanization was pursued as a governmental policy that aimed at elimination by assimilation. Before we survey the histories, policies, and outcomes of Indigenous urbanization in the US, however, we should state clearly that *all* cities are Native spaces, originally and irrevocably. All US cities are located on Indigenous land and required the displacement of Indigenous people for their foundation. The city from which we write, Minneapolis/St. Paul, is located in the birthlands of the Dakota people. Following conflict with the United States in the US-Dakota Wars of 1862, Dakota people were largely exiled from Mni Sota Makoce, herded onto reservations in South Dakota or fleeing across the border to Canada. When a hundred years later, descendants of those people were pushed back into the cities of Minnesota by federal urban relocation policies aimed at cultural erasure, it was an ironic homecoming for some of them. The Sisseton Wahpeton Oyate, from which one of the authors of this essay, Sara, comes is a Dakota community located in Northeast South Dakota on the Lake Traverse Reservation. When we speak of home, is the home we are referring to the reservations where a large concentration of our people still reside? Or the lands here in Mni Sota Makoce, the lands of our people's birth? Likely, it is both.

Not only are all cities Native spaces, but Native Americans have always been part of their migrant populations, from the 19C Mohawk ironworkers who plied the skyscrapers of New York (Simpson 2014) and Indian vaudeville performers who played its stages (Mojica 2009), to the Native Americans who migrated during WWII to support the war effort in shipyards and munitions factories (Miller 2019). The largest migration to US cities, however, took place between 1948 and the 1970s, when approximately 15,500 Native people relocated to American urban centres (Rosenthal 2012, 50). While many were drawn by the post-war boom, seeking opportunities beyond the poverty of the reservation system, many were pushed by federal policies: the Voluntary Relocation Program (1952), the Indian Relocation Act of 1956, and the Bureau of Indian Affairs' Adult Vocational Training program (AVT). These policies were aggressively assimilationist, co-joining urbanization and termination, that is the withdrawal of federal recognition for tribes and of federal funding for social services such as medical care and food assistance. The AVT sold disenfranchisement as opportunity, with a promise of training that would lead to socioeconomic stability; but many Native folk had little option but to move.

Federally sponsored relocations worked (like previous colonial policies) to eliminate Native peoples: disrupting community and familial ties, alienating Indigenous people from the land, lifeways, and support systems. The so-called social services offered by the BIA included forced sterilization, incarceration, and foster and adoption programmes that removed children from kin: the traumatic effects continue generations later. Many Native people found themselves in inferior housing, with insecure, seasonal, or low-waged work and a sense that they had been 'abandoned by a paternalistic federal government' (Miller 2019, 2). Their economic marginalization was compounded by structural racism, as they were lumped in with a 'growing racialized mass' of Black, LatinX, and other minorities in declining cities at a moment when white residents were fleeing for the suburbs (132). The result was the disproportionately high levels of poverty, homelessness, incarceration, ill-health, and mortality in urban Native communities that have endured to this day.

This negative picture, however, does not account for deep resilience of Indigenous migrants: despite the efforts of the federal government to assimilate them, the confluence of different tribal populations in cities spurred the emergence of new solidarities. As a generation raised in cities came of age in the late 1960s and early 1970s, common experiences of discrimination, disillusionment, and disenfranchisement coalesced in urban-originated movements such as Indians of All Tribes (IOAT), survival schools, and the American Indian Movement (AIM). These multi-tribal movements, inspired by decolonization struggles elsewhere in the world and the Black Power movement at home, had a flair for the performative, staging symbolically resonant actions that challenged the state's sovereign claims, such as the occupation of Alcatraz island

(1969–71). Where Native Americans previously resided on the fringes of the national imaginary, they now visibly occupied its core (Sissons 2005, 66).

Now in their fourth generation since these early waves of migration, urban Native communities are continually inventing new ways to be Native. Urban residents who live in multi-tribal communities are more likely than their rural counterparts to have complexly mixed heritage and multiple attachments, and scholars have coined new terms to describe the forms of identity that this has produced, such as 'ethnic Indian' (Deloria and Lytle 1984), supratribal, pan-tribal, or pan-Indian, while urbanites have invented their own names to capture their unique identities, such as NDN, or 'Indigenous' itself (Lobo 1998; Lawrence 2004). Some Native commentators fear these multi-tribal solidarities complicate the sovereign claims of the original inhabitants of urban regions, such as the Ohlone in the Bay Area, or the Lenape in NYC (Ramirez 2007). More recently Native critics, activists, and artists have begun to grapple with the relationship between Indigenous and Black experiences of compelled urbanization (including the Great Migration), showing that anti-Indigenous and anti-Black settler logics are deeply intertwined, and calling out Native movements that have failed to acknowledge this fact for their complicity in anti-Blackness (Justice 2018).

From the earliest days of the migration wave, Native migrants created cultural institutions to build community, from newcomer support centres to the language nests, radio stations, sporting leagues, and eventually dance and theatre companies that sprang up in numerous cities in the 1980s. These organizations not only brought migrants from different tribes together, but also sustained links between urban populations and rural kin. Performance is a pivotal facet of urban survivance practices: powwows, traditionally ritual spaces for dance and singing, have endured in urban spaces and have innovated to support multiple communities and needs in the form of university powwows, sobriety powwows, or 2-Spirit [LBGTQI] powwows. And increasingly, Native urban networks are forgings links with other urban immigrant populations, especially Indigenous ones. For example, anthropologist DeLugan has studied the alliances formed between Guatemalan Maya and Native US migrants in the San Francisco Bay Area where both communities celebrate Mayan New Year/Waqxaqi' B'atz' together with a syncretic ceremony that helps rally Native American support for migrant rights activism.

Native cultural resurgence in cities participates in the 'long process of reimagining Indian Country' (Rosenthal 2012, 12), where Indian Country denotes any place or social setting in which Native Americans exist. The complex forms of migrant belonging that urban Native Americans have developed, however, are subtly different to those of other migrant groups. *Diaspora* often presupposes distance from the place of origin, a sense of loss and longing; *exile*, an enforced expulsion with a thwarted expectation of return; *transnational*, a crossing of state borders; *cosmopolitanism*, a transcendence of the local. For urban Native Americans, however, being part of a diaspora may mean circular migration between homeland and city or being connected to 'multiple sites and communities [and nations]…maintaining all of these relationships simultaneously' (Ramirez 2007, 11). Likewise migrants can move between or belong to different nations without crossing borders, or without moving at all; they can experience powerful feelings of exile while still being free to move home; and lead profoundly cosmopolitan lives while being intimately anchored in specific lands and places (DeLugan 2010).

Theatre, Performance, and Urbanization

Urbanization was catalytic for the growth of Native scripted drama in the US, which thrived in urban production venues, community centres and colleges, and multi-tribal companies. This work often reflected on the urbanization process: Native playwrights embraced theatre as an art of urban tribalography (Howe 1999), a labour of storytelling that theorizes, heals, and guides as it narrates.

Collectively, urban Native plays challenge one of the US's deepest settler mythologies. This mythos codes cities as modern, white places and Native Americans as rural and traditional, confined to history, and it maps this distinction onto the modernist teleology of irreversible, inevitable progress. Rural to urban migration thus figures as a journey into modernity and away from Indigeneity, leading to a 'narrative estrangement that renders urban and Indigenous realities as somehow mutually exclusive' (Thrush 2017, 111). This powerful mythos, which dominates settler media, renders urban Indigenous peoples either invisible, illegible, or tragic, 'husks, shells, ghosts, and otherwise inauthentic manifestations of some lost past' (111). It has spawned the genre of settler *poverty porn*, full of pathologizing stereotypes of urban Natives as desperate, doomed, and crying out for white rescue. By contrast, Native plays that address urbanization hold the traumatic legacies of colonial violence and the ongoing discrimination faced by Native urbanites in tension with the dimensional presence of Native characters engaged in the struggle for self-determination. They innovate an urban 'land-based dramaturgy' (Joseph 2019, 144) that balances the need to grieve and protest the damage of dislocation with the desire to represent the vitality of Indigenous urban survivance and (re)build the relational bonds between places of origin and migrant homes, original peoples, and newcomers.

A longer version of this chapter would trace this important genealogy of Native theory-praxis, beginning with Hanay Geiogamah's (Kiowa) *Body Indian* (1980 [1973]), set in a rented room on the outskirts of an Oklahoma city. The play stages an allegory for the dismemberment of the Indian body politic at the hands of the settler-state. Yet while *Body Indian* paints a bleak picture of urban dislocation and lateral violence, its production wove together rural and urban Native communities, and made vibrant Native social and cultural worlds present in settler-dominated spaces. Bruce King's (Turtle Clan of Hodenausaunee-Oneida Nation) *An Evening at the Warbonnet* (King 2007 [1989]), set in an urban Indian bar, suggests that the ground for resilience lies in the emerging common culture of urban Indian Country. King's city is a space of exile and refuge for the alienated, deracinated collateral damage of settler-colonialism. But ultimately, his characters find salvation in two trickster figures, their presence a sign that Native community 'has the potential for regeneration… to continually take new forms and thus endure' (Lobo 1998, 427).

This genealogy also includes the late Assiniboine/Nakota playwright William S. Yellow Robe Jr. whose work often centres characters pulled between reservation and city, facing alienation and isolation in the city while struggling to feel fully part of their ancestral communities. In plays such as *Frog's Dance*, Yellow Robe Jr. offers resources for reintegration and healing, showing how individual and community well-being depend on resilient, inextinguishable relational bonds that are continually 'made and remade' (Yellow Robe Jr 2020; Furlan 2017, 3) through performative reunions between city and reservation dwellers. Finally, the innovative stage idiom of playwrights such as Marie Clements places reservation-to-city migration very explicitly in the context of ongoing colonial attempts to eliminate Native people. Her play *The Tombs of the Vanishing Indian* (2012), for instance, alternates between the original moment of colonial dispossession in the early nineteenth century; 1955, when a mother and her three daughters move to Los Angeles as part of an urban relocation programme; and 1973 where we see the consequences of the eliminatory violence faced by each of the grown sisters: assimilative adoption, forced sterilization, violently negating stereotypes, incarceration, and mental illness. Yet like these other dramatists, Clements' dramaturgy is not purely tragic. The play drives towards a climax in which a retributive flood of Indian tears wipes the city clean, resuturing bonds between generations, original inhabitants and Indigenous migrants, homeland and city, restoring a web of relations that transcends the severing, amnesiac violence of colonization.

Contemporary Native performance artists, in contrast to these dramatists, work not only at level of theatrical representation, but also by creating social architectures and ritual processes in their work to sustain grounded normativity in urban spaces. We are moved, in particular, by two multidisciplinary artists who create in urban centres far removed from their own homelands, but who create in ways that honour the people from whom they come, the peoples on whose lands they reside, and the myriad others who make their homes there. They explore how the performative protocols of 'guesting' as a migrant—Indigenous *or* non-Indigenous—can support the ongoing work of decolonization (Koleszar-Green 2019).

The first of these is Seattle-based maker and educator Dakota Camacho, whose family hails from Låguas (Guåhan, and the Northern Mariånas), Guam. For more than a century, the US has regarded Guam as one of its territories, and like many of Guam's Indigenous CHamoru, Camacho's family were displaced by the islands' occupation and militarization, and now reside in Seattle in the mainland US. Camacho's work MALI'E' | Tåno' Uchan (which one of us saw during Weesageechak Festival 32 at Native Earth Performing Arts in Toronto, 2019) layers spoken word poetry, Pasifika dance, hip hop, video projections, and stage ceremony to evoke *yo'ña* (their) own layered diasporic identity: the language, influences, and land of Coast Salish tribes with whom Camacho shares a home, the Black and LatinX urban culture that permeates Seattle's spaces, the diverse communities of migrants from the island Pacific, and a larger, planetary Indigenous awareness. (Comacho uses gender neutral Fino' CHamoru pronouns, *yo'ña* (possessive) and *guiya* (third person). In Comacho's words, they align *guiya* 'with my ancestors' vision of being a being.') An empty stage is washed by a sound that could be waves against the shore or a person's deep breathing, and Camacho enters carrying a canvas tote bag emblazoned with the words 'Good Medicine.' From it Comacho pulls and carefully unwraps and offers up objects specific to *yo'ña* Oceanic heritage, the bag reminding us that the things the migrant carries are medicine, memories, and offerings to those *guiya* now joins. Beginning with a low chant, *yo'ña* vocalizations evolve from CHamoru incantations to hip hop poetry and rap, in English, Spanish, and Fino' CHamoru. Behind Comacho, a video projection shows *guiya* as a child learning a traditional dance, intercut with clips of other Pasifika dancers (Hawaiian, Tahitian, Māori) performing in what looks like a pan-Pacific community festival.

In this piece, and others (such as *Etak* (2021)), Camacho's guiding method and metaphor are the embodied Pasifika art of navigation, an art that draws on cosmography and genealogy to integrate people and places through movement (Diaz 2019). Comacho's act of unpacking tells us that things from home—languages, dances, songs, and migrant bodies—are not lost in transit, but replanted in new ground. *Yo'ña* lyrics in their swiftly propulsive, rhythmic succession of images, laminate together body, language(s), other peoples, and the elements of land itself to anchor 'Native diasporic consciousness' (Ramirez 2007, 11):

> While blood's pulsing through my drumbeat…
> Lukas past the skywalking horizons, catwalking with Africans, Zapotecs, Crees, Jews, and Mayans…
> I'm of Native stock, and yes I'm made of rock…
> Dakota es my nombre. Tacoma is the mountain
> I'm sailing in the Salish and navigating what my sound is.
> You know that I will own this, I was born near the Snohomish
> Tying tight songlines between coconuts and cedar trees. […]

In this last stanza, Comacho's poetry resembles the forms of ritual greeting in some Island cultures, in which a newcomer announces their ancestry (including their non-human ancestors such as rivers or mountains) while acknowledging that of their hosts; the gesture lays the ethical ground of the encounter between guest and host. As Dakota writes: 'The Navigator journeys through their own family history, dancing rituals of *respect and reciprocity* with the territories and cultures of Oceanic, Black, & Native Turtle Island communities that have guided their canoe back home, despite the colonial lie that home/culture has been lost' (Camacho 2019).

Where Dakota conceives of performance work as an exchange of gifts that establishes relations of humility and gratitude, Yup'ik dancer and creator Emily Johnson likewise fosters a creative process that inquires into the ethics of 'guesting' (Chelsea Vowel, qu Johnson and Recollet 2019, 18) on others' homelands. Her work is itself migratory, performed in cities around the US and the world. However, she seeks cities that have original Indigenous populations, aiming to bring audiences together, as guests, to support and uplift those Indigenous communities and lands on which they reside. Defying the standard commodity model of touring performance, Johnson's work often takes the form of durational, site-specific, outdoor gatherings of audiences and performers, both engaged in processes of making that 'build relationships with the land upon which they visit and live [that] extend to responsibility, care, reciprocity, and anti-colonial understandings of love' (Johnson and Recollet 2019, 18).

Her project *Shore* (Johnson 2014), which has been performed in several cities including Naarm/Melbourne, Lenapehoking/NYC, and Minneapolis, is (in her words) one such 'care procession.' In each site, the multi-day community event is a social choreography composed of a variety of experiences: readings, dance performances that move between sites and venues, volunteering (on wetland restoration projects, for instance), and the cooking and sharing of a meal. Building on years of advance work in establishing relationships with local organizations, communities, and leaders, and germinating deep commitments to activist causes beyond the local (such as the water-protector movement), it operates as a kind of embodied land acknowledgment. It moves beyond the now-standard symbolic nod to (supposedly) former inhabitants, and into the realm of ethical responsibility: seeking (rather than presuming) permission to stay; collaborating with ancestral inhabitants on projects of concern *to them*; and paying rent to original peoples. Decolonization, she proposes, is never a mere metaphor or value claim (Tuck and Yang 2012) but is an active practice that unsettles colonial arrangements in the past, present, and future.

Conclusion

Urban migration, we have argued, does not portend the loss of Indigeneity. It is, rather, another way of *being* Indigenous, as valid, vital, and modern as those ways rooted in ancestral places. Urbanization is a colonial process that Indigenous people have endured and survived; it is also a path chosen to expand, reinvent, and sustain Indigenous worlds, as Indigenous people have always done (Simpson 2017). And theatre and performance have played a vital part in both processes: theorizing, exposing, mourning, and healing the trauma of dislocation, dismantling colonial myths, nurturing connections to land and ancestry, building new-old networks of relations, upholding the rights and obligations of original peoples, and working towards a mutual thriving.

References

Allen, Chadwick. 2012. *Trans-Indigenous Methodologies for Global Native Literary Studies*. Minneapolis: University of Minnesota Press.
Byrd, Jodi A. 2011. *The Transit of Empire: Indigenous Critiques of Colonialism*. Minneapolis: University of Minnesota Press.
Camacho, Dakota. 2019. 'MALI 'E'.' Accessed July 13, 2021. https://www.dakotacamacho.com/malie.
Carter, Jill. 2016. 'Sovereign Proclamations of the 21st Century.' In *Performing Indigeneity*, edited by Yvette Nolan and Rick Knowles. Toronto: Playwrights Canada Press.
Chang, David. 2018. *The World and All the Things Upon It: Native Hawaiian Geographies of Exploration*. Minneapolis: University of Minnesota Press.
Clements, Marie. 2012. *Tombs of the Vanishing Indian*. Vancouver: Talonbooks.
Clifford, James. 2013. *Returns: Becoming Indigenous in the Twenty-First Century*. Cambridge: Harvard University Press.
Coulthard, Glen. 2014. *Red Skin, White Masks: Rejecting the Colonial Politics of Recognition*. Minneapolis: University of Minnesota Press.
Deloria, Phillip. 1998. *Playing Indian*. New Haven: Yale University Press.
———. 2004. *Indians in Unexpected Places*. Lawrence: University Press of Kansas.
Deloria, Vine, Jr., and Clifford M. Lytle. 1984. *The Nations Within: The Past and Future of American Indian Sovereignty*. New York: Pantheon.
DeLugan, Robin Maria. 2010. 'Indigeneity across Borders: Hemispheric Migrations and Cosmopolitan Encounters.' *American Ethnologist*, 37 (1), 83–97.
Diaz, Vincente. 2019. 'Oceania in the Plains: The Politics and Analytics of Trans-indigenous Resurgence in Chuukese Voyaging of Dakota Lands, Waters, and Skies in Miní Sóta Makhóčhe.' *Pacific Studies*, 42 (1/2), 1–44.
Furlan, Laura M. 2017. *Indigenous Cities: Urban Indian Fiction and the Histories of Relocation*. Lincoln: University of Nebraska Press.
Geiogamah, Hanay. 1980. *New Native American Drama: Three Plays*. Norman, OK: University of Oklahoma Press.
Gilbert, Helen. 2017. 'Introduction.' In *In the Balance Indigeneity, Performance, Globalization*, edited by Helen Gilbert, J.D. Phillipson, and Michelle H. Raheja, 1–23. Liverpool: Liverpool University Press.
Hau'ofa, Epeli. 2008. *We Are the Ocean: Selected Works*. Honolulu: University of Hawai'i Press.
Howe, LeAnne. 1999. 'Tribalography: The Power of Native Stories.' *Journal of Dramatic Theory and Criticism*, 14 (1), 117–125.
Johnson, Emily. 2014. 'Shore.' Accessed July 13, 2021. http://www.catalystdance.com/shore.
Johnson, Emily, and Karyn Recollet. 2019. 'Kin-dling and Other Radical Relationalities.' *Movement Research Performance Journal* 52/53 (Fall): 18–23.
Joseph, Dione. 2019. 'Cradling Space.' In *Performing Turtle Island*, edited by Jesse Rae Archibald-Barber, Kathleen Irwin, and Moira Day, 131–145. Regina: University of Regina Press.
Justice, Daniel Heath. 2018. *Why Indigenous Literatures Matter*. Waterloo: Wilfred Laurier University Press.

King, Bruce. 2007. *Evening at the Warbonnet* in *Evening at the Warbonnet and Other Plays*. UCLA American Indian Studies Center.

Koleszar-Green, Ruth. 2019. 'What Is a Guest? What Is a Settler?' *Cultural and Pedagogical Inquiry*, 10 (2), 166–177.

Kroes, Rob. 2012. *Buffalo Bill in Bologna: The Americanization of the World, 1869–1922*. Chicago: University of Chicago Press.

Lawrence, Bonita. 2004. *"Real" Indians and Others: Mixed-Blood Urban Native Peoples and Indigenous Nationhood*. Lincoln: University of Nebraska Press.

Lightfoot, Sheryl R. 2016. *Global Indigenous Politics: A Subtle Revolution*. Routledge.

Lobo, Susan. 1998. 'Is Urban a Person or a Place? Characteristics of Urban Indian Country.' *American Indian Culture and Research Journal*, 22 (4), 89–102.

Miller, Douglas K. 2019. *Indians on the Move: Native American Mobility and Urbanization in the Twentieth Century*. Chapel Hill: University of North Carolina Press.

Mojica, Monique. 2009. 'Stories from the Body: Blood Memory and Organic Texts.' In *Native American Performance and Representation*, edited by S. E. Wilmer, 97–109. Tucson: University of Arizona Press.

Niezen, Ronald. 2003. *The Origins of Indigenism: Human Rights and the Politics of Identity*. Berkeley: University of California Press.

O'Brien, Jean. 2010. *Firsting and Lasting: Writing Indians Out of Existence in New England*. Minneapolis: University of Minnesota Press.

Ramirez, Renya K. 2007. *Native Hubs: Culture, Community, and Belonging in Silicon Valley and Beyond*. Durham: Duke University Press.

Rosenthal, Nicolas G. 2012. *Reimagining Indian Country: Native American Migration & Identity in Twentieth-Century Los Angeles*. Chapel Hill: University of North Carolina Press.

Simas, Rosy, and Ahimsa Bodhran. 2019. 'Sovereign Movements: Building and Sustaining Native Dance and Performance Communities—A Dialogue.' *Movement Research Performance Journal* 52/53 (Fall): 4–6.

Simpson, Audra. 2014. *Mohawk Interruptus: Political Life Across the Borders of Settler States*. Durham: Duke University Press.

Simpson, Leanne Betasamosake. 2017. *As We Have Always Done: Indigenous Freedom Through Radical Resistance*. Minneapolis: University of Minnesota Press.

Sissons, Jeffrey. 2005. *First Peoples: Indigenous Cultures and Their Futures*. London: Reaktion.

Smith, Linda Tuhiwai. 2012. *Decolonizing Methodologies: Research and Indigenous Peoples*. 2nd ed., Zed Books; Dunedin: University of Otago Press.

Thrush, Coll. 2017. 'Placing the City: Crafting Urban Indigenous Histories.' In *Sources and Methods in Indigenous Studies*, edited by Chris Andersen and Jean O'Brien, 110–117. New York: Routledge.

Tuck and Yang. 2012. 'Decolonization is Not a Metaphor.' *Decolonization: Indigeneity, Education, and Society*, 1 (1), 1–40.

United Nations Department of Economic and Social Affairs, Secretariat of the Permanent Forum on Indigenous Issues. 2009. "State of the World's Indigenous Peoples." (https://www.un.org/esa/socdev/unpfii/documents/SOWIP/en/SOWIP_web.pdf)

United Nations Economic and Social Council. 2021. Update on the Promotion and Application of the United Nations Declaration on the Rights of Indigenous Peoples, E/C.19/2021/6. New York: United Nations HQ.

Vizenor, G., et al. 2008. *Survivance: Narratives of Native Presence*. Lincoln: University of Nebraska Press.

Weaver, Jace. 2014. *The Red Atlantic: American Indigenes and the Making of the Modern World, 1000–1927*. Chapel Hill: University of North Carolina Press.

Wolfe, Patrick. 2006. 'Settler Colonialism and the Elimination of the Native.' *Journal of Genocide Research*, 8 (4), 387–409.

Yellow Robe, William S. 2020. *Frog's Dance* in *Restless Spirits: Plays*. Excelsior Editions, an Imprint of State University of New York Press.

CHAPTER 10

Migratory Blackness in *Leave Taking* and *Elmina's Kitchen*

Harvey Young

On 22 June 1948, the ocean liner Empire Windrush arrived at Tilbury, a seaport town on the outskirts of London. Carrying more than one thousand Jamaican migrants, the ship represented a shift in the colonial logic of the British Empire. For more than two centuries, white men had sailed the seas in search of regions to conquer, claim and settle. They had indentured, enslaved, raped and murdered people—mostly nonwhite people of colour—in pursuit of imperial ambitions. The arrival of the Windrush marked a shift, a dramatic redirectional flow, in the movement of people. Jamaicans had travelled to England to assert their legal status as British subjects. They were newcomers to the United Kingdom but not unfamiliar with UK culture. Playwright Winsome Pinnock remembers her parents' stories about celebrating Empire Day as children in Jamaica: 'when their schools distributed British flags and lollipops' (2018, 4). The Windrush voyagers were arriving at a familiar destination where they had never been but thought they knew. For the next fifteen years, tens of thousands of West Indians, the Windrush generation, would travel to the United Kingdom and, in the process, catalyse debates and activism concerning race, national identity and belonging in the metropole.

This chapter introduces the concept of *migratory blackness* to address the movements, experiences and perspectives of the Windrush generation and their descendants. It engages Winsome Pinnock's *Leave Taking* and Kwame Kwei-Armah's *Elmina's Kitchen* to reveal how the *after empire* crossings of West Indians to Great Britain helped to reorient and revise the imperial logic of the

H. Young (✉)
Boston University, Boston, MA, USA
e-mail: harveyy@bu.edu

© The Author(s), under exclusive license to Springer Nature Switzerland AG 2023
Y. Meerzon, S. E. Wilmer (eds.), *The Palgrave Handbook of Theatre and Migration*, https://doi.org/10.1007/978-3-031-20196-7_10

West. It demonstrates how theatre stages Black British life, including entanglements with anti-Black racism as well as everyday efforts to remain connected with the cultures of the West Indies.

Migratory Not Exilic

The fascination at the arrival of the Empire Windrush was not only the thrill of seeing a ship emerge from the horizon and representing the expanse of British influence. The appearance of the ship also was a signal that England's future would be profoundly different than its past. The Windrush brought Black people as free citizens to Great Britain in numbers never before seen. It raised the question of whether the United Kingdom could (and would) embrace these brave voyagers. To stand along Tilbury's shore as the Windrush approached was to witness diaspora in action. For those spectators not mesmerized by the size of the vessel, the scene offered a lesson: migrations are first and foremost about the movements of people.

There is not an African diaspora without the rupture that was the shipping of human bodies, as cargo in the holds of ships across an ocean. The diaspora was both movement and the cleaving apart families and communities. Although much has been written about the preservation of Africanist elements in New World Black cultural creations, their reclamation or restoration (which is certainly indebted to a reimagination) does not erase the violence of relocation nor the trauma of dislocation. The survivors of these past journeys, according to theatre historian Errol G. Hill, 'were the people of Africa, known first as slaves, then blacks, then Afro-Caribbeans.' Hill writes, 'For centuries they constituted that section of the population for whom the Caribbean was the only home they knew; that other home from which their ancestors were torn long ago survived only in racial memory' (1991). The sites of arrival became home but not homeland.

Rooted in the past journeys of ancestors, the Black diasporic experience can be anchored in a feeling of uncertain stasis that occurs with the realization that *I have arrived*. Racial harassment, profiling, and violence erupt not as abstractions but in response to the physical presence of individuals whose perceived and assumed difference triggers outrage, anxiety, and/or fear. The black body is not the disruptive agent. Rather, it is the other person, the racist (who masquerades their hate as heightened nationalism or community-minded vigilance) who seeks to destroy and displace. We can imagine the Black family who moves into a new neighbourhood and encounters crosses burning on their lawn or unwelcoming stares in grocery stores. We can picture the Black athlete on the pitch being subjected to taunts and jeers of alleged fans whose conception of nation has no place for people with brown complexion. Of course, Blackness is more than skin deep. It anchors itself in the stories passed down across generations which, regardless of complexion, informs subjectivity and perspectives on the world. It is connected to the ways in which folks have been socialized. It is rooted in the daily dramas (and celebrations) of living and being Black.

Once challenged for being limiting and potentially essentialist, the concept of the black body has been redeemed as a result of numerous incidents of police violence against African Americans within the United States. Tamir Rice, age 13, was shot to death on the playground playing with a toy in 2014. Breonna Taylor, age 26, was shot to death in her apartment in 2020. These among dozens of other contemporary cases launched an awareness that earlier imaginings of post-Blackness or efforts to identify Blackness as no longer influenced by the stark restrictions of the past (captivity and, later, segregation) were premature. When people are profiled, incarcerated and murdered simply for being Black, embodied experiences are difficult to ignore. The reembrace of the body has inspired a new generation of scholars to theorize the experience of migration (either voluntary or by force) in the flesh and bones on the move. Among the more inspired of these is the framing of the black body as *vessel*, an analytic that accounts for its materiality (a physical presence that contains an experience) and a metaphor calling to mind images of the ships that criss-crossed oceans sailing triangular routes. Iyanna Hamby, for example, asserts that the 'corporeal nature of the vessel additionally transports the fugitive nature of blackness that could be reembodied in performance' (2021). For Hamby, the concept of the vessel invites consideration of both the traumatic episodes of the past (captives shackled on ships) and the liberating potential of their descendants (and those who remember them) to embrace performance to revisit the past.

The idea of the vessel informed by phenomenological understandings of embodied being aligns the diasporic imaginary with the essence of theatre-making. In both, the expired and past event is remembered and revived. Nostalgia looms large. In the theatre, characters are given breath and life. A production run that has stopped and ended can be relaunched. Audiences bring their own assumptions, memories and projections to the theatre and liberally map them across the play to give the staged work new, personal meaning. It is for this reason that an array of performance scholars, including Joseph Roach, Richard Schechner, Marvin Carlson and Rebecca Schneider, have offered similar perspectives on the *return* in theatre—variously described in terms of surrogacy, not not, haunting and remains—which metaphorically straddles the line between past and present, life and death. Referring to 'this sense of something coming back in the theatre,' Carlson writes, 'one might argue that every play is a memory play' (2003, 2). Andrew Sofer offers, 'Our pleasure in seeing the relic revived, the dead metaphor made to speak again, is the very reason we go to the theater to see a play we already know well' (2010, 3). Black theatre and performance frequently engage the diasporic imagination to write into history the achievements and experiences of ancestors denied their rightful place in the archive. More consistently than a history book, the stage presents Black life to be seen, encountered, learned from and shared with others. It resurrects the dead, restages the past (and passed) and presents experiential Blackness as a *refrain* to be reencountered, reengaged and remembered. The scholarly investigations of Sandra L. Richards on slave tourism and historical sites as well as Harry J. Elam, Jr.'s explorations into historical memory in the work of August Wilson underscore the imbrication of diasporic imagination and Black performance.

Movement is endemic to the enterprise of theatre making which has a long history of artists on tours, traveling circuits and uprooting to the big city. It is not difficult to see how live performance served as an extension of colonizing efforts. The stage enabled opportunities for culture—language, religion, history, manners and more—to be relayed and repeated over decades (and centuries) reifying the influence of imperial regimes. Theatre historian Errol G. Hill notes, 'The art of theatre of Europe had helped to inculcate a love of stage plays in Caribbean audiences... Although its repertoire included some plays that dealt with universal human problems, such plays did nothing to solve their problem of cultural identity' (1991). Inspired by the structure of imported plays by William Shakespeare among others while conscious of the exclusion of Black stories (and/or racist representations of Black characters), an explosion of amateur little theatres was created in the mid-twentieth century in the Caribbean. These include Hill's Whitehall Players in 1946 and Derek Walcott's Trinidad Theatre Workshop in 1959. Both sought to insert a Black subjectivity into the staging of classic plays in addition to presenting new works by regional playwrights such as Douglas Archibald and Clifford Sealy (Charles-Farray). The community of artists that formed during the Windrush years assumed leadership roles in the remaking of theatre on both sides of the Atlantic. The look of Black Caribbean theatre varied depending on the coast. Folk traditions were reclaimed in the islands. Narratives of Black experience were inserted into conventionally structured Western plays in Great Britain. Of course, the two influenced each other as individuals and their families crisscrossed the Atlantic.

Reflecting on present day theatre in Jamaica, Thomas Trainer notes, 'Jamaican theatre is a product of postcolonialism' (2018, 2). He writes,

> During the anticolonial movement of the mid-20th century, African folk traditions rose to the forefront of Jamaican public life blending with traditional European standards of artistic excellence. After independence in 1962, Jamaican politicians, intellectuals and artists alike saw theatre as a means to reclaim cultural hegemony and establish a unified national identity that can be part and parcel to the development of industry, stable political institutions, and socioeconomic prosperity. (3)

The flows of cultural influence continued in the decades post-Windrush as Black Caribbean immigrants in the United Kingdom remained connected with friends and family in the West Indies. Victoria Saab Sams, in her study on postcolonial theatre in London, observes, 'The seventies were a boom time for the establishment of theatre companies committed to producing drama by and for Black British artists and audiences' (2001, 24). This new theatre, led by innovators such as Jimi Rand, Yvonne Brewster, Derek Walcott as well as Keskidee Arts Center dramatists, aspired to reflect the realities and cultures of Black life in the United Kingdom rather than striving to erase those differences as part of an assimilationist effort. The stories sought to stand apart—to signal the uniqueness of the Black British experience and, in so doing, to write Black history.

The Windrush years, as both actual migrations and, later, nostalgic referent, inspired storytelling. It was a time of optimism and possibility. Equally importantly, it gave Black folk access to the narratives of aspirational journeys resembling those available to non-Black people whose ancestors voluntarily sailed oceans in search of adventure and new opportunities. In *Beyond Windrush*, J. Dillon Brown and Leah Reade Rosenberg observe,

> 'Windrush' stands metonymically as a marker for the emergence of an increasingly multicultural national polity, in which the old self-understanding of Englishness as racially white gradually cedes prominence to a newer conception of Britishness—one that strives to include the burgeoning populations of citizens who trace their heritage back to the once-colonized spaces of the British Empire. (2015, 3)

The arrival of the ship spurred the establishment of cultural pluralities within the United Kingdom. Whereas Brown and Rosenberg contend that this new perspective inside but also outside of British culture establishes the Black 'writer as exile' (7), this framing does not apply entirely to theatre artists. Rather than the exilic, I offer a simple formulation—*migratory blackness*—to account for this sense that home and, perhaps, homeland comprise multiple points (and, potentially, multiple places) along a journey. All of those places remain available to go to (or return from). Although the exilic can exist as a romantic concept with which to talk about the in-between state of the immigrant, it does not apply to this study of Black drama because the freedom to move (and to return at will) for the playwrights and their characters is never in dispute. The experience of migratory blackness is the understanding that the places encountered, stopped at and settled exist simultaneously as home, as *a* home, and as not home. It is informed by the rupture of the African slave trade in which ancestral connections were sharply severed. The absence of an identifiable place of ancestral origin—the ability to name a town in a region within a particular country—transforms all subsequent landing places along the journey as potential homes (and homelands for subsequent generations). These stops invite return and opportunities to reconnect with and imaginatively experience the past. Unlike an exilic state of mind, the perspective informed by migration enables the writer or artist to appreciate the volitional state of their present stand as well as their agency in shifting locations perhaps today, tomorrow or at some point in the future whenever they choose. Migratory blackness, like a ship, is anchored but equipped to travel.

The experience of migration is not easy, especially for marginalized and minoritized racial and ethnic groups. The challenges of acceptance (even if the goal is not assimilation) are evident in immigration studies about how certain groups became (over time) a part of the mainstream, majority culture. The difficulties were (and remain) especially acute for Black migrants. Lewis R. Gordon, in *Her Majesty's Other Children*, succinctly writes, 'Whether it be Queen Isabella, Queen Victoria, or the White House and Capitol Hill, Her Majesty has never had concern for children like my grandmother's children' (1997, 6). It was this lack of concern as well as the necessity to address the ills of colonialism that inspired the 1956 World Congress of Black Writers and Artists in Paris, midway through the Windrush years. Hortense Spillers commenting on the significance of the assembly writes, 'Black writers and artists—in short, black intellectuals—had come together…to assess the future of global 'black cultures,' now that colonialism itself was apparently at an end' (2012, 932). The artists assembled, 'readying themselves to throw off, at long last, the shackles of colonialism and the horrors of racism that had provided engines of European wealth and prosperity in the modern world and rendered America a nation divided' (934). They committed to speak back to dominating imperial cultures and to articulate the experience of Blackness. Inherent within theatres of migration is a critique of the larger social world. The characters, always within an in-group setting consisting of other marginalized individuals, speak their truth and disclose the everyday prejudices that they face.

Inherent in speaking back is the act of confronting and challenging the power dynamics of imperialism. Migratory blackness reframes and revises the authority of the West. It reminds us that the West was always a fiction. In 'The West and the Rest: Discourse and Power,' Stuart Hall writes, 'the "West" is a *historical* not a geographical construct.' It exists as a shorthand for 'the type of society that is developed, industrialized, urbanized, capitalist, secular and modern' (2018, 142). It is also a construct indelibly associated with whiteness resulting from sustained, imperialist efforts to deny non-white people of colour access to technological, industrial and financial resources. That idea had a material and indeed geographical dimension as it structured and determined colonial relationships. The Windrush generation (and their descendants) challenged this formulation through their movements. Those aboard the Windrush sailed east to reach the West. When they longed for home (after having settled in Great Britain), they looked westward. Their migratory movements were not simply a retracing of previous trade routes but rather fundamental revisions of a previously held imperial logic. Migration became a rupture that marked their status as distinctly *after empire* and resistant to the binarial frameworks of 'center-periphery, metropole-colony, colonizing nation-colonized people' (Geigner and Young 2021, 2). The plays created by the Windrush generation and their descendants spotlight, as Edward Said identified it, the 'flexible *positionality*' of the West (2014, 7). They call out the existence and the persistence of anti-Black racism in Great Britain while also affirming a new British identity no longer separable from Blackness.

Staging Jamaica

Winsome Pinnock, as Lynette Godard writes, 'is undoubtedly Britain's leading black woman playwright of the 1980s and 1990s' (2015, xii). In most accounts of Black British theatre, scholars point to the production of Pinnock's play, *Leave Taking*, as the first play penned by a Black British playwright to be staged by the National Theatre (in 1994) more than thirty years after the prominent theatre company opened its doors. The milestone exists more as a fact of history rather than a metaphorical opening of the floodgates. A quarter-century later, Black British playwrights continue to be infrequently produced at the most recognizable theatres in the country. Pinnock remarked in 2020, 'Look at the number of plays by black playwrights in any institution at any given time and that will tell you about institutional racism' (Akbar 2020). She added, 'There are theatres in this country that have never produced a play by a black British playwright' (2020).

A first-generation Londoner, Pinnock remembers, 'I grew up in Islington, in the poor bit, in a single-parent household and I was educated in the inner city' (Gardner 2018). Her Jamaican mother shared her memories, stories of and pride in her Caribbean heritage. This maternal (and island) influence would play a determining role in the aspiring playwright's outlook on life. Pinnock proudly states, 'I am a Windrush baby…the child of people from the Windrush generation, and this country owes that generation so much' (Gardner 2018). As a student, she gravitated to the theatre. It was an unconventional path for a first-generation student with her social class background. Pinnock reflects, 'I was the only black woman in my year at Goldsmith and I was one of two working-class people' (Akbar 2020). Whereas her privileged classmates could be out and open about their interests in drama, Pinnock was the opposite. 'I wrote in secret,' she remembers. Fortunately, the young artist was not shy about sharing her early writings. She knew that her voice—and her experience—needed to be seen on the stage. Pinnock recalls, 'I sent a short piece called *Saturday Night* to the Royal Court young writers group, then led by Stephen Warelam and Hanif Kureishi. Stephen wrote back and said, "Come join our group"' (Akbar 2020). She did.

A heightened awareness of her mother's experience as a part of the Windrush generation informs the dramaturgy of Winsome Pinnock. She seeks to create theatre that reflects or, at least, acknowledges the stories and histories shared by Black Britons like herself. In a 2018 interview, she declared, 'It's not enough that you now have black actors playing parts not necessarily written for them' (Gardner 2018). Although the increasing presence of Black actors on British stages is progress in itself—as evidenced by director Paulette Randall's 2003 observation that 'it's still a political act to put a black person on stage,' visibility onstage without the ability to share an authentic experience is a hollow achievement (Griffin 2006, 11). What Pinnock strived (and still strives) to do was to create dramas that acknowledged and celebrated the everyday happenings in the lives of Black Britons onstage. This ambition appears neither herculean nor radical until one acknowledges the currents of resistance that Pinnock faced simply to render migratory blackness visible within mainstream British theatrical culture. In their introduction to *Modern and Contemporary Black British Drama*, editors Mary F. Brewster, Lynette Goddard and Deidre Osbourne remind their readers that 'it should be remembered that in the context of migration and racism, the audiences and attendees were overwhelmingly white' (2015, 9). Pinnock faced the challenge of convincing non-Black audiences to appreciate the fact that the stories and, indeed, lives of Black folk mattered decades before international activism would champion such an outlook.

The tolls of being Black British are exemplified by an unseen character in Winsome Pinnock's 1987 play *Leave Taking*. A family friend, Broderick, tells Viv, the younger daughter of the play's protagonist, about Gullyman who often appeared on the 'street no shoes, no socks, shirt open down to him navel. In the cold. Man a walk an' shake' (2018, 28). Gullyman emigrated to England from the West Indies with only 'two dollar in him pocket' (28). Within two years, he had made (and saved) enough money to buy a car and a house. Broderick remembers, 'Gullyman forget everybody—all him friends, him people back home, just cut everybody off.' He also assumed an affected English accent—'always correcting people, "Don't say wartar man. Say wortur"' (29). However, his attempts to assimilate were unsuccessful despite his self-made accomplishments because his new countrymen refused to accept him as an equal: 'One mornin Gullyman wake up to him lovely car covered in shit an a message on him door read "wogs out"' (29). Broderick says that Gullyman was heartbroken by the incident. His 'mind crack[ed]' and 'now he can hardly talk broken English' (29). Not having been seen for a '[l]ong time now,' Gullyman may be dead (28). Gullyman exists as an extreme example of the challenges facing Black immigrants. However, all of the characters within Pinnock's play reveal the ways in which they have been discriminated against within the United Kingdom.

Leave Taking tells the story of a working-class single mother, Enid, who is raising two daughters in London. Enid leaves Jamaica when her boyfriend, who had previously emigrated to England, sends her a transoceanic passenger ticket. The relationship eventually crumbles. Temporally, the play takes place long after the marriage has disintegrated and Enid, with her daughters, has fled what became a physically abusive situation. Her daughters, Viv and Del, are now seventeen and eighteen, fledgling adults who are striving for independence from their mother. Not financially secure in Great Britain, Enid equally does not feel at home in Jamaica, which she last visited five years earlier. Although she struggles to make ends meet in England, works two jobs and still wears shoes with holes in them, Enid is considered a success by her kin in Jamaica to whom she represents the West. Reflecting on her financial struggles, she laments that her relatives 'don't imagine how we live over here' (2018, 39). Nevertheless, Enid prefers life in Great Britain even with its racial and working-class biases. She reveals to the audience that the imperial logical of the West has been embraced by her family. As a result of colourism, her mother prefers

Enid's lighter complexioned sister. It is this uncritical embrace of the West that motivates her to tell Viv to 'Forget about Jamaica' (39). In choosing to move east and, equally importantly, to remain in London, Enid dispels the mythology of the West (at least to herself).

The experience of migration saturates the play. The characters understand that their present stand in England was enabled by prior voyages across the Atlantic (both westward and eastward). Movement defines them as much as their Blackness in their new country, especially since Blackness in the United Kingdom exists as a marker of migration. Although one could assert that the characters never find home and, as a result of white nationalism and prejudice remain in a state of unease which disallows ever being at rest, such an emphasis on the exilic discounts the ability that Black folk have to build a life even in the most hostile settings while preserving the right to return *home*. There is agency in choosing to settle here or there, in deciding to remain or leave a city, country or continent. This is evident in the 2003 play *Elmina's Kitchen* by Kwame Kwei-Armah, a Black British playwright who has identified his mother's 1962 ticket from Grenada to England as his most 'treasured possession' (Greenstreet 2018).

In *Elmina's Kitchen*, the action takes place in a 'West Indian takeaway restaurant in "Murder Mile" Hackney' (Brewer et al. 2015, 123). The play centres on the protagonist Deli, who owns the establishment and his efforts to maintain his struggling business against the threats of street gangs. Conventional in its single location setting, the play succeeds in presenting Caribbean (and also transatlantic Black American) influences in Great Britain. This is a place where the music, food and iconography of the islands live. It is both home and homeland. Black British men (primarily) of the Windrush generation gather to talk, joke and form community. Here, West Indian and British cultures blend together, which is perhaps best represented by the character Digger, a gangster and friend of Deli: 'Digger's accent swings from his native Grenadian to hardcore Jamaican to authentic black London' (Brewer et al. 2015, 124). There is a naturalness and fluidity in the way that he code switches. His everyday speech as well as his heightened performances of self (e.g. exaggerating an accent on a phone call) reveal his amalgam of influences.

Until Deli elects to change menus with an eye towards attracting a different (white) clientele and a tragic act of violence occurs in the final act, Elmina's Kitchen (the restaurant) is a safe haven, a landing spot, from the disruptive influences of life in greater England. As a place apart, it is also where critiques of anti-Black racism in England can be freely expressed. The truth teller, history bearer and griot in this instance is Clifton, an amateur calypso singer and Deli's father, who 'uses his eastern Caribbean accent to full effect when storytelling' (Brewer et al. 2015, 152). Clifton sings,

> History is a funny thing,
> History is a funny thing,
> Listen to me, people,

> Cos is about football me ah sing.
> Clive Best the greatest
> Baller West Ham ever had,
> But from the stands they'd shout each game,
> Go home you black bastard.
> [...]
> Oh England, what a wonderful land,
> In England what you must understand,
> Is whatever you do, wherever you rise,
> Please realise, you could never disguise,
> You's a black man in a cold cold land. (173)

Clive Best, a professional soccer player originally from Bermuda and a leading scorer for West Ham United, was subjected to intense racist taunts and jeers throughout his decade long career with the team beginning in the late 1960s. The song is cautionary, alerting the listeners in the story world as well as those attending the play itself of the persistence of anti-Black racism in the United Kingdom. Doubtful that Black British folk will be accepted within the United Kingdom, Clifton advocates for an adherence to and maintenance of Jamaican cultural values, including (self-servingly) a heightened sense of respect and responsibility for elders. Eventually cast out by his son, the patriarch as sooth-sayer departs with a warning: 'All you generation is a curse. You go rot, mark my words' (209).

Across *Leave Taking* and *Elmina's Kitchen*, common themes emerge related to the experience of migratory blackness. First, the dramas offer compelling portraits of protagonists who have established a sense of home within a new country even in the face of racism. Although the characters certainly are aware of the ways in which they are seen as outsiders, it is notable that they have established a place in which they have anchored their sense of self as Black Britons. They are not exiles. They are a people who have travelled and who understand their past movements as core to their identities. Second, they privilege the maintenance of West Indian culture within these new national settings. Island culture migrated to the United Kingdom with/in the voyagers on those boats. In addition to references to island spirituality, music and food, the plays embrace island dialect to underscore the fact that aspects of the West Indies remain embodied within characters despite their change in location. The tragedy of Gullyman was that he sought to abandon his roots and assimilate. Enid, despite her strained relationship with her mother, does not actually forget Jamaica. Throughout the play, she remains connected to island culture through her frequent visit to Mai, an obeah woman or spiritualist. Third, the dramas created by West Indian playwrights in the United Kingdom offered a portrait into embodied experiences not previously seen on regional and national theatre stages. Mary Brewer, Lynette Godard and Deirdre Osbourne write, 'Black British writers...have provoked a revolution in dramatic language and form that is equitable with the impact attributed to the Angry Young Men in (re)defining theatre history' (2015, 13). Their works invite a consideration of citizenship and national identity not from a perspective of anxiety or anger but rather pragmatism, revealing both the promises and the failures of the West. The reality check of these works—the realization that imperialism was, as Broderick asserts in *Leave Taking*, actually vampirism—'They suck the blood outta the island, suck them dry' (Pinnock 2018, 28)—forces a national reckoning of the history and ongoing social effects of colonialism. This is the work of migratory blackness in the theatre.

References

Akbar, Arifa. 2020. 'Winsome Pinnock meets Jasmine Lee-Jones.' *The Guardian*, June 26, 2020. https://www.theguardian.com/stage/2020/jun/25/winsome-pinnock-meets-jasmine-lee-jones-some-uk-theatres-have-never-staged-a-black-british-play.

Brewer, Mary F., Lynette Godard, and Deidre Osborne, eds. 2015. *Modern and Contemporary Black British Drama*. London: Palgrave Macmillan.

Brown, J. Dillon and Leah Reade Rosenberg. 2015. *Beyond Windrush: Rethinking Postwar Anglophone Caribbean Literature*. Biloxi: University Press of Mississippi.

Carlson, Marvin. 2003. *The Haunted Stage: The Theatre as Memory Machine*. Ann Arbor: The University of Michigan Press.

Charles-Farray, Janine. 2017. 'Reunion Honours Company of Player.' *Trinidad Guardian*, March 9, 2017. https://farray1.rssing.com/chan-8443028/latest-article9.php.

Gardner, Lyn. 2018. 'Winsome Pinnock: 'I Used to Think We Needed Change – Now We Need a Revolution.' *The Guardian*, May 23, 2018. Accessed July 26, 2023. https://www.theguardian.com/stage/2018/may/23/winsome-pinnock-leave-taking-bush-theatre.

Geigner, Megan E. and Harvey Young, eds. 2021. *Theatre after Empire*. London: Routledge.

Gordon, Lewis R. 1997. *Her Majesty's Other Children: Sketches of Racism from a Neocolonial Age*. Oxford: Rowman and Littlefield Publishers.

Greenstreet, Rosanna. 2018. 'Kwame Kwei-Armah: 'I Have My Mother's 1962 Ticket from Grenada to England in a Frame,' *The Guardian*, October 18, 2018. Accessed July 26, 2023. https://www.theguardian.com/lifeandstyle/2018/oct/13/kwame-kwei-armah-mother-grenada-1962-southall-riots.

Griffin, Gabriele. 2006. 'Theatres of Difference.' *Feminist Review*, 84, 10–28.

Hall, Stuart. 2018. "The West and the Rest: Discourse and Power [1992]." In *Essential Essays, Volume 2: Identity and Diaspora*, Stuart Hall, David Morley, 141–184. New York, USA: Duke University Press.

Hamby, Iyanna. 2021. Conversation with the Author. Unpublished.

Hill, Errol G. 1991. Perspectives in Caribbean Theatre: Ritual, Festival, and Drama. College of Fellows of the American Theatre. https://www.thecollegeoffellows.org/wp-content/uploads/2015/12/HillErroll-Caribbean-Theatre-1991.pdf.

Pinnock, Winsome. 2018. *Leave Taking*. London: Bush Theatre/Nick Hern Book.

Said, Edward W. 2014. *Orientalism*. New York: Knopf/Doubleday.

Sams, Victoria Saab. 2001. 'No Place Like Home: Staging Displacement in Postcolonial Theatre in London.' PhD diss., University of California, Los Angeles.

Sofer, Andrew. 2010. *The Stage Life of Props*. Ann Arbor: University of Michigan Press.

Spillers, Hortense. 2012. 'A Transatlantic Circuit: Baldwin at Mid-Century Opening Keynote Address.' *Callaloo*, 35 (4), 929–938.

Trainer, Thomas. 2018. 'Performing Postcolonialism: Developments in Sociopolitical Commentary in Jamaican Theatre' (MA Thesis), Villanova University.

CHAPTER 11

Climate Migration and Performance

Paul Rae

Most people who follow current affairs will know of climate migration: forced and often permanent displacement resulting from anthropogenic climate change. However, while environmental factors do indeed drive large-scale human movement globally, strictly speaking, climate migration is only beginning. One reason is that the really severe projected impacts of climate change lie in the future: in its *Sixth Assessment Report* (2021), the United Nations' Intergovernmental Panel on Climate Change (IPCC) painted a range of alarming scenarios stretching to 2100 and beyond, stating unequivocally but still hopefully: 'Global warming of 1.5° C and 2° C will be exceeded during the 21st century unless deep reductions in CO_2 and other greenhouse gas emissions occur in the coming decades' (in press, SPM-17). Another reason climate migration remains an emergent phenomenon is that the practical drivers of migration are rarely reducible *only* to climate change, which often amplifies existing social and economic problems. Debates are ongoing about whether it is useful or even possible to isolate climate change as a cause of migration. This is compounded by the fact that existing international instruments are poorly equipped for formally recognizing climate refugees and migrants, or for establishing the obligations that states and other entities bear them. Numerous initiatives grant protections to climate migrants, such as the Nansen Initiative's 'Protection Agenda' (2015, signed by 109 countries) and the UN's 'Global Compact for Safe, Orderly and Regular Migration' (2019, 164 countries). But these are non-binding by comparison with the 1951 Refugee Convention (and

P. Rae (✉)
University of Melbourne, Melbourne, VIC, Australia
e-mail: paul.rae@unimelb.edu.au

© The Author(s), under exclusive license to Springer Nature Switzerland AG 2023
Y. Meerzon, S. E. Wilmer (eds.), *The Palgrave Handbook of Theatre and Migration*, https://doi.org/10.1007/978-3-031-20196-7_11

the 1967 Protocol, which extended its scope), which defines a refugee as someone unable to return to their country of origin for fear of persecution on the basis of race, religion, nationality, membership of a particular social group or political opinion (UNHCR 2010, 14). In short, the very questions of whether climate refugee is a useful designation, or who is a climate migrant, remain open and contested.

This is not to deny the disruptive impacts of environmental change. As the UNHCR reports, between 2009 and 2019, 'weather-related events triggered an average of 21.5 million new displacements each year—more than twice as many as displacements caused by conflict and violence' (UNHCR n.d.). A 2018 World Bank report on internal migration in Sub-Saharan Africa, South Asia and Latin America predicts that without decisive climate action there could be over 143 million climate migrants within those regions alone by 2050 (World Bank Group 2018, xix). Reflecting these concerns, in 2020 the UN Human Rights Committee made a landmark judgement in reviewing the case of Ioane Teitiota, who from 2013–2015 had sought unsuccessfully to claim refugee status in New Zealand on the basis of climate change threatening his home country of Kiribati in the central Pacific. The Committee upheld New Zealand's decision to deport Teitiota, but it nevertheless affirmed that 'environmental degradation, climate change and unsustainable development constitute some of the most pressing and serious threats to the ability of present and future generations to enjoy the right to life' (OHCHR 2020a, 9). A legal scholar quoted in the accompanying press release noted that 'this ruling sets forth new standards that could facilitate the success of future climate change-related asylum claims' (OHCHR 2020b) because it expands the basis on which a claimant's right to life must be assessed.

Phenomena of such scale and complexity may seem a far cry from the traditional concerns of theatre and performance. To date, a global picture of climate migration is more readily available through the media, government and NGO reports, or hard and social science research than in the theatre. Yet such a picture will inevitably be partial and rather abstract: it may give some indication of the causes, scale and future of climate migration, but not what it means at ground level, what it looks and feels like to those impacted or how it implicates those who may presume themselves distant from it. Performance offers no panacea for this, but a brief survey of some of the growing range of works dealing with environmentally driven migration does help establish a baseline understanding of where and how it might sit in relation to the broader phenomenon.

First, with most climate migrations yet to take place, theatre and performance can provide a mechanism for anticipating that future, prompting audiences to imagine what it may hold. This seems particularly important at present, where reluctance by some governments and citizens to take decisive climate action is born in part of an unwillingness or inability to imagine the future impacts of present *in*action, which may lead to greater human displacement and social instability.

Accordingly, some performance-makers have sought to bring home these prospects by giving them form on stage. In *The Jungle Book Reimagined* (2022) by British-Bangladeshi choreographer Akram Khan, the child Mowgli is a climate refugee from India, who arrives in a London deserted and overgrown by the jungle that forms the setting of the play (Akram Khan Company 2021). This neatly inverts a classic work of imperial children's literature: the exotically tropical setting of Rudyard Kipling's *Jungle Book* (1894) now folds back upon the hitherto temperate environment enjoyed by its original readership. If Khan repurposes a work from the past, then *This Liquid Earth: A Eulogy in Verse* (2019), by the South African playwright Amy Jephta, looks back upon the present from the future. Set in 2080, climate migrants from Europe and the Americas converge on 'the last place able to sustain human life', the southernmost tip of Africa (Jephta n.d.). With readings presented at London's Royal Court theatre and the Edinburgh Festival in 2019 in a season of international plays on the climate crisis, *This Liquid Earth* explored a reversal of the direction of migratory travel explored in *The Jungle Book Reimagined*, asking its UK audiences to imagine their own displaced future, as they seek refuge in the Global South.

A second way of thinking about the relation of performance to climate migration stems from the fact that performance is adaptable and often highly mobile, and therefore subject to its own migrations. This can take various forms. One entails travelling where migrants cannot—at least not yet. In 2018, Britain's Royal National Theatre collaborated with the Environmental Justice Foundation to present portraits of individuals from climate-threatened environments in the Arctic and Bangladesh. Projected onto the exterior wall of the theatre's fly tower, the resulting films remain available online. Actors voice monologues of up to ten minutes in length derived from interviews with the individuals, who gaze levelly into the camera (Royal National Theatre 2018). Their experience of the challenging environments they inhabit and the combination of hope and anxiety their stories express are etched onto their faces. The sustained visual and verbal address both asserts the subjects' humanity and implicates the viewer in a relationship of ethical responsibility: theatrically informed public address as early warning system.

Equally, however, performance can travel with migrants, or find them where they settle. *Masters of the Currents* (2018), by Los Angeles-based Teada Productions, drew on research with Micronesian communities living in Hawai'i to tell the story of three young people who 'have fled their island nations due to environmental and economic pressures, and who must now overcome conflicts of identity to be accepted by their peers [...] while still holding onto the history and rich cultural traditions of their ancestral islands' (Teada Productions 2020). Such works are able simultaneously to give voice to experiences of climate migration, and to provide a mechanism by which participating communities may assert their subjectivity and agency in the host environment, laying claim to a sense of belonging in the process.

The third contribution of performance to climate migration sits in a complex relation to the first two, because it acknowledges the complexities of performance itself, and how they reflect the unstable and ambiguous status of climate migration today. Broadly stated, we are on the cusp of a changing reality that implicates people worldwide in many different ways. Individuals are challenged to change their way of life, and how they interpret and express their experience of the world as a result. We are asked to recognize urgent and unique human needs against a backdrop of long-term and often unpredictable global transformations; to acknowledge the relationship between mundane features of daily life and significant effects in distant places; to recognize both that environmental factors have long driven migration by humans and other animals and that for the vast majority such upheavals are a last resort; and to appreciate the changing status of individuals and peoples on the move, even as we seek to mitigate or avoid such outcomes. As a compressed and compelling activity of long standing in many cultures, one that can speak with intimate knowledge of a people or place, even as it invents new responses to fast-changing circumstances, performance is a field of expression that maintains the capacity to hold these contrasting and sometimes contradictory qualities within it.

The ensuing sections in this essay stage these complexities by examining in greater detail two contrasting ways of thinking about performance and climate migration. First, I speculate on the role of performance in a future where climate migration takes place. Second, in a necessary paradox, I analyse some recent performances aimed at reducing the likelihood of climate migration. My examples are drawn from Oceania, a region known both for its vibrant performance cultures and for crystallizing numerous tensions relating to climate change. Australia's economic reliance on fossil fuels and a pervasive strain of climate denialism in its domestic politics means it has a poor record on climate action. Currently, Australia is the seventh largest per capita emitter of greenhouse gasses globally (ahead of the US and China) (World Bank n.d.), and the fifteenth largest emitter overall (Greenpeace 2021, 16). By contrast, the fourteen Pacific island nations emit only 18% of Australia's total between them (Greenpeace 2021, 16). They include low-lying atoll nations such as Kiribati, the Marshall Islands and Tuvalu, which are sometimes described as the canaries in the coalmine of climate change. In the early 2000s, then-Kiribati President Anote Tong became a high-profile representative of climate-threatened states on the global stage, pressuring industrialized nations to act decisively on global warming. Conjuring the spectre of entire populations displaced, he spoke of 'migration with dignity' for his people, and Kiribati's purchase of a large parcel of land in Fiji in 2014 was widely seen as a future refuge for I-Kiribati (people from Kiribati) climate migrants.

For good and ill, then, Oceania provides a distinctive and dynamic environment for thinking about the relationship between performance and climate migration. In what follows, I focus first on a speculative example, informed by the case of Kiribati. I then consider a number of counter-examples with international reach and address.

Performance for Climate Migrants

Let us say that large-scale climate migration starts to happen and is recognized as such. What would it look like? Drawing on an indicative selection of the scholarly literature (Biermann 2018; Skillington 2017; Wewerinke-Singh 2018; Wyman 2017), we can hope it would include some or all of the following features. Affected communities would have a high level of self-determination in how and when they leave their homelands, and where they go—something planned well in advance and taking place progressively. Migrants will be permanently resettled and enjoy residency rights in their new locations, while remaining free to express their shared identity and cultural traditions. They may assert their collective rights by organizing themselves socially and politically, and, where possible, maintain some form of sovereignty over their place of origin. They will be supported by the receiving state or region, and by an international community that recognizes its moral and material obligations to peoples who are almost certainly among the least directly responsible for their predicament, and among the most vulnerable to it.

Of course, this is an abstract and perhaps idealized vision of climate migration: when it happens, it will reflect specific local environmental, cultural and political circumstances. And where performance is integral to a culture, it will have a central role to play in these upheavals. This can be well illustrated by the case of Kiribati, whose territory spans an enormous stretch of the Pacific Ocean, but whose land consists largely of thin slivers of coral atoll, few more than a couple of hundred metres in width or rising more than three metres above sea level. It is hard to over-state the intimacy of the relationship between traditional dance in Kiribati and its islands, lagoons, and surrounding ocean. Traditionally, everything the dancers wear comes from the land and sea, from pandanus skirts and sashes to coconut and seashell belts, to flower garlands and the glistening coconut oil with which they anoint their skin (Fig. 11.1).

By comparison with the easeful undulations of some well-known Pacific dances like the Hula, the movements of Kiribati dance are rigid and forceful. The arms are held out perpendicular to the body, from which they describe intricate choreographies and descend into powerful thigh slaps. This is accompanied by darting movements of the head and short, quick steps, whose avian effect recalls the movements of the frigate bird, the national bird of Kiribati, and an inspiration for much of the choreography (for a sample, see teimatoa9april 2012). The dancers' bodies are conceived as continuous with the land (represented by the torso) and sea (the hips). The repertoire is large: there are sitting and standing dances; men's, women's and mixed dances; and narrative, abstract, and game-like dances. All are accompanied by the multi-part harmonies of rousing choral songs, and between them the words and gestures speak through arcane and contemporary references to life on the islands, the many

Fig. 11.1 A performer presents a dance form called 'Te Kaimatoa', in the town of Bairiki on South Tarawa, Kiribati, in July 2019. (Photo: Paul Rae)

activities it entails, and the flora and fauna found there. As one male ex-dancer wryly put it as we watched a rehearsal in Bairiki township on South Tarawa in June 2019: 'it has fishing in it; how to win a [canoe] race in it; how to do magic; how to get your wife back'.

For I-Kiribati to be uprooted and relocated as a result of climate change would be an appalling and radically destabilizing experience. Unfortunately, however, the I-Kiribati are no strangers to such upheavals. In the 1930s, the British colonial authorities attempted to relocate Gilbertese (as they were known) communities from one island group to another to address drought-induced food shortages. This failed, and in the 1950s those communities were relocated once again to the Solomon Islands. Similarly, in the 1940s, the population of the Kiribati island of Banaba, which had been ruinously mined for phosphate by the British and Australians, was relocated to Fiji. As Tabe (2019) and Teaiwa (2015) have explained, respectively, both cases underscored the importance of land and place to the Kiribati sense of self and community, and the role of cultural practices in offsetting some aspects of this wrenching deracination. This would only be intensified by the wholesale migration of the population and helps frame a broader account of what it might achieve.

To begin with, we can say performance is an important practice which migrants will carry with them when they leave their homeland: as the uniquely concentrated expression of an indigenous culture, it is a vector for transporting knowledge. Dancing will conserve a relation to the environment; teaching dance will transmit cultural memory; making costumes will sustain core skills—such as weaving pandanus strips into baskets, clothes and mats—that are intensified in the intricacies of dance costumes.

Moreover, the centrality of dance to community life means each presentation is an opportunity for asserting collective identity. This is important for strengthening ties that may be threatened by other aspects of the migrants' new lives, for affirming claims they make to their rights as residents, and perhaps to the sovereignty afforded by their homeland. One complex area of international law arising from the prospect of wholesale climate migration is whether there can be a state without a territory. What *is* Kiribati if its islands are no longer habitable, or are underwater? Can the I-Kiribati still lay an exclusive economic claim to the 3.4 million km^2 of ocean to which its paltry but widely distributed 811 km^2 of land currently entitles it? Would they retain a seat at the United Nations? Could they have a government, with accompanying international representation, protection, standing and so on? Performance cannot answer these questions. But Kiribati culture is overwhelmingly oral and performative: what makes someone I-Kiribati is integrally bound up with the stories they tell about who they are and where they come from. It is hard to imagine those thorny questions being settled *without* reference to the collective identity, agency, history and land ownership that song and dance assert.

Concurrently, as the existing repertoire is adapted to the new location, and new dances are created, new forms of belonging will be forged. This will help the community to interpret their newfound circumstances, folding them into the lifeworld they brought with them: how to be a different kind of body, or to incorporate new experiences into previous ways of knowing. New forms may specifically focus on the migration experience, telling how and why the community was uprooted and resettled. Grief will be the overwhelming emotion during this period, and dance, as an emotive outlet (especially when paired with song), would no doubt serve to express and perhaps process it.

But dance is not only an inwardly focused community activity. In Kiribati as elsewhere, it has long served as an interface with outsiders, be they from another village, island or nation. Through the exchange of dance and the formalities performance enables, communities are able to learn how to *be* guests, residents, and hosts. Dance thereby serves a mediating role in the new location: between us and you; there and here; and between the vast, swirling forces causing this situation, and the human scale at which it is processed and enacted. Again, however, we must ask: is such an outcome inevitable?

Performance Against Climate Migration

Speculations about the future tell us as much—if not more—about the present; and sometimes this can cause the future to work out differently. What do these speculations mean for climate migration and performance *now*? Posing such a question brings us into a much more granular world than the one described above. What the prospects for climate change and migration mean on a daily basis in climate-threatened Pacific islands is varied and contested. First, there are more immediately pressing matters, like earning a living, raising children and staying healthy. As elsewhere, climate change awareness is uneven there, and the relationship between climate change and observable phenomena easily misinterpreted. And while the headline news of climate change is king tides, contamination of fresh water lenses or reduction in rainfall, on a daily basis it may be experienced more as a tugging anxiety, or fatalistic resignation.

At the same time, many practices foster adaptation and resilience. Religion—particularly Christianity—provides a prism through which many in the Pacific confront or indeed reject climate change. Governments, often collaborating with international agencies, are implementing adaptation strategies through infrastructure development, coastal erosion prevention and food security initiatives. Local and traditional knowledge is also being harnessed, sometimes in dialogue with climate science and development studies, to address issues such as water conservation and food security. And the long, regionally networked, history of climate adaptation and environmentally motivated seaborne migration provides a source of resilience and a more robust framework for facing change than those, often formulated outside the region, that figure Pacific peoples as vulnerable victims.

Accordingly, Pacific nations are pushing back against the assumption that climate change is *their* problem. As a 2020 report by the Marshall Islands government puts it: 'Climate change poses a direct affront to our right to self-determination and adaptation is our response: our assertion of the continued collective right to self-determination inherent in our nationhood' (RMI 2020, 1). The inalienable right to remain is the first pillar of the Marshall Islands' approach. This is not to deny the possibility of migration, rather: 'Preserving our citizens' right to choose whether and when to migrate is paramount' (26). The report also echoes many other statements from the region calling on wealthier nations to reduce greenhouse gas emissions.

Performance has many roles to play here, most not about climate migration as such, but its avoidance. For instance, performance activism seeks to bring local conditions to international attention. In 2009, the Maldives government invited reporters to an underwater meeting of its cabinet to highlight rising sea levels, and the champion I-Kiribati weightlifter David Katoatau famously dances after each final competition lift to bring attention to the climate crisis. Perhaps the most media-savvy regional activists are the Pacific Climate Warriors. They draw deeply on the performance aesthetics and costumes of the region to provide a powerful visual identity to their protests and social media campaigns—arresting evidence of their assertion that 'We are not drowning. We are fighting!' (2015).

An aligned but extended version of this strategy is represented by the Marshallese poet Kathy Jetñil-Kijiner. She came to international prominence at the United Nations in 2014, where she delivered 'Dear Matafele Peinem', an impassioned poem addressed to her young daughter, reflecting on a future impacted by climate change. Since then, Jetñil-Kijiner has continued to make speeches, presentations and short films that combine spoken-word poetry with images and contextualizing backdrops. For example, in the six-minute film *Rise: From One Island to Another* (2018), Jetñil-Kijiner collaborates with Greenland poet Ava Niviâna to stage both extremes of global heating: melting glaciers on an arctic island and rising sea levels threatening a tropical one. Addressing each other as, respectively, 'Sister of ocean and sand' and 'Sister of ice and snow', the film shows Jetñil-Kijiner and Niviâna exchanging totemic gifts with each other in Greenland—shells from the Marshalls and stones from the glacier. They embody myths the poets recount to explain their indigenous relations to their land. Cutaway images show members of their communities, and of Jetñil-Kijiner floating in a Marshallese lagoon. As stirring music builds, the poets cease describing their separate environments to each other and join voices to address the world at large:

> From these islands
> we ask for solutions.
> From these islands
>
> we ask
> we demand that the world see beyond
> SUVs, ACs, their pre-packaged convenience
> their oil-slicked dreams, beyond the belief
> that tomorrow will never happen, that this
> is merely an inconvenient truth.

Revising 'we ask' as 'we demand' marks a shift to a performative mode, seeking to bring about the transformations described through the very making of the demand, on film. By the conclusion, a further shift has occurred—the second-person singular 'you', followed in the excerpt above by the second-person plural 'their' is now superseded by the first-person plural 'we':

> …these issues affect each and every one of us
> None of us is immune
> And…each and every one of us has to decide
> if we
> will
> rise…

The poem's central challenge resides in its final word. At the outset, the title *Rise: From One Island to Another* appears to describe how melting ice on one island causes sea level rise on another. By the end, the term has been repurposed: now people are called upon to 'rise', precisely so sea levels will not, and all the better for Jetñil-Kijiner to make good on her commitment in the poem that 'we will not leave…/We will choose/ to be rooted in this reef/ forever' (Mainspring Media 2018).

Staging the costs of climate change and challenging the inhabitants of high emissions countries to consider their entanglement with those facing climate migration find a different inflection in the work of Tongan-Australian performance artist Latai Taumoepeau, who seeks to sensitize her fellow Australians to the situation in the region of her heritage and ancestors. Climate change has long been Taumoepeau's focus. In durational performances such as *i-Land X-isle* (2013), *Repatriate* (2015), and *Ocean Island…Mine!* (2016), she pitted her body against large amounts of ice and water to highlight both the strengths and vulnerabilities of humans' interconnectedness with their environments. More recently, she has sought to make explicit the connections between local audiences in Australia and conditions in the neighbouring region. As part of *Refuge*, a six-year multi-disciplinary project by Melbourne's Arts House focusing on scenario planning for a range of disasters, Taumoepeau used the drills and language of domestic emergency preparedness in Australia to anticipate climate crisis in the Pacific. Her contribution *MASS MOVEMENT* (2021), which took the form of an audio walk along the shoreline and waterways of Melbourne, culminated in *MASS MOVEMENT FOLAU: The Arrival*, an open-air participatory performance that began with Taumoepeau welcoming the audience with a series of questions:

> How and why does one depart their home?
> Who is at the destination?
> Who has always been there and how do we attune to the First Peoples?
> How do we learn to love Country?
> What did we bring with us?
> What do we have to do when we get there?
> What needs to happen so we may remain at home?

Accompanied by drummers of Cook Islands heritage, and artists and emergency service personnel involved in the larger *Refuge* project, Taumoepeau then led the audience through a syncopated choreography of arm movements and claps. Framed, for the purpose of pedagogy, around movements named after tropical fruits, it gradually became apparent the movements were linking participants' bodies to the waves of the sea, and that variations in pace and energy reflected the changing behaviour of the oceans. On a topic prone to didacticism, Taumoepeau's performance was subtle. Participants could draw their own connections between the framing questions, the cultural context of the work, and the embodied experience of participating in a mass representation of oceanic activity.

These connections were quickened, at the performance in Melbourne in May 2021 at Flagstaff Gardens, a park in the CBD, by a traffic accident in the background. A tram collided with a car, and the emergency services soon arrived. The appearance of fire engines, sirens, bystanders, and so on seemed to intensify the focus of the performance on climate emergency (which is often diffuse until suddenly it isn't), and to bear out Taumoepeau's intuition that disaster preparation has standard operating procedures, and performance might take its place among them. The fact that personnel from the State Emergency Service, in attendance at the performance as Taumoepeau's collaborators, broke away to help manage the traffic incident, underscored the point. We might even draw a relation between the percussion of the F7 Soul Drummers group, and the single, massive impact of the tram upon the car. This seems an absurd connection to make. But it is not unreasonable. The final question in Taumoepeau's list, above—'What needs to happen so we may remain at home?'—has two contrasting meanings: what needs to happen (in Australia) so that we (potential climate migrants) may remain at home; and what needs to happen (in terms of climate migration) so that we (high emissions-producing Australians) may remain (safely) at home? Making a link between the community drumming of *MASS MOVEMENT FOLAU* and a tram T-boning a car reminds us that progressive action following a participatory climate performance now is far preferable to the dangerous and costly destruction of infrastructure further down the track.

Conclusion

Climate migration will be a defining feature of the global picture for at least the next century. We have barely begun to grapple with its realities and must do so, even as we redouble our mitigation efforts. And though its scale seems far to exceed theatre's sphere of operations, its impacts will nevertheless be experienced and interpreted at the human level. For cultural geographer Carol Farbotko, climate migration 'is not […] a fixed "out there" phenomenon. Rather, it is emergent in practices, including those that attempt to know and govern a set of subjects called "climate migrants"' (2017, 67). She discusses a 2014 New Zealand court case where a Tuvaluan family sought residency on climate change grounds. Residency was ultimately justified in more broadly humanitarian terms, but Farbotko notes that using climate-related arguments pointed to a larger possibility: that 'through a performative combination of representation [here, self-identifying as "climate migrants"] *and* practice [a court case], an abstract notion of "climate migration" can become "real" for particular individuals, at least at a particular legal moment' (80).

Farbotko's minimalist reasoning provides a useful corrective to the often moralistic tone of public climate discourse. Nevertheless, it is clear there will be countless moments when 'climate migration' becomes 'real' for individuals and communities, raising the question of what other 'performative combinations of representation and practice' might enable it. Farbotko's argument that the seemingly vast phenomenon of climate migration is made at the scale of activity theatremakers know well, using the—to them—familiar mechanisms of representation and practice, provides a way of understanding how performance can participate in the larger project of formulating the meanings of climate migration as if it will happen, even while performers act in hope that it will not.

References

Akram Khan Company. 2021. 'Jungle Book Reimagined.' https://www.akramkhan-company.net/productions/jungle-book-reimagined/. Accessed 20 July 2021.

Biermann, Frank. 2018. 'Global Governance to Protect Climate Refugees.' In *Climate Refugees: Beyond the Legal Impasse?*, edited by Simon Behrman and Avidan Kent, 265–277. London: Routledge.

Farbotko, Carol. 2017. 'Representation and Misrepresentation of Climate Migrants.' In *Research Handbook on Climate Change, Migration and the Law*, edited by Benoît Mayer and François Crépeau, 67–81. Northampton: Edward Elgar.

Greenpeace. 2021. 'Te Mana o Te Moana: The State of the Climate in the Pacific 2021.' https://act.greenpeace.org.au/pacific-climate-report. Accessed 27 September 2021.

Intergovernmental Panel on Climate Change. In Press. 'Summary for Policymakers.' In *Climate Change 2021: The Physical Science Basis.* Cambridge: Cambridge University Press.

Jephta, Amy. n.d. 'This Liquid Earth.' https://www.amyjephta.com/this-liquid-earth. Accessed 19 July 2021.

Mainspring Media. 2018. *Rise: From One Island to Another.* https://vimeo.com/289482525. Accessed 20 July 2021.

OHCHR. 2020a. 'Views Adopted by the Committee under Article 5 (4) of the Optional Protocol, Concerning Communication No. 2728/2016.' https://tbinternet.ohchr.org/_layouts/15/treatybodyexternal/Download.aspx?symbolno=CCPR/C/127/D/2728/2016&Lang=en. Accessed 27 September 2021.

OHCHR. 2020b. 'Historic UN Human Rights Case Opens Door to Climate Change Asylum Claims.' https://www.ohchr.org/EN/NewsEvents/Pages/DisplayNews.aspx?NewsID=25482. Accessed 27 September 2021.

Pacific Climate Warriors. 2015. 'We Are Not Drowning. We Are Fighting!' https://world.350.org/pacificwarriors/2015/07/15/we-are-not-drowning-we-are-fighting/. Accessed 20 July 2021.

RMI. 2020. *Adaptation Communication.* Republic of the Marshall Islands: Climate Change Directorate.

Royal National Theatre. 2018. 'Nowhere to Call Home: Climate Change and Forced Migration.' https://www.nationaltheatre.org.uk/your-visit/exhibitions/nowhere-to-call-home. Accessed 19 July 2021.

Skillington, Tracy. 2017. *Climate Justice and Human Rights.* New York: Palgrave Macmillan.

Tabe, Tammy. 2019. 'Climate Change Migration and Displacement: Learning from Past Relocations in the Pacific.' *Social Sciences.* https://doi.org/10.3390/socsci8070218

Teada Productions. 2020. 'Masters of the Currents.' http://www.teada.org/masters-of-the-current-1. Accessed 19 July 2021.

Teaiwa, Katerina. 2015. *Consuming Ocean Island: Stories of People and Phosphate from Banaba.* Bloomington: Indiana University Press.

teimatoa9april. 2012. 'Kiribati Dance 1.' https://www.youtube.com/watch?v= Yfu5pw5Uib0. Accessed 27 September 2021.

UNHCR. n.d. 'Displaced on the Frontlines of the Climate Emergency.' https://storymaps.arcgis.com/stories/065d18218b654c798ae9f360a626d903. Accessed 19 July 2021.

UNHCR. 2010. *Convention and Protocol Relating to the Status of Refugees.* Geneva: UNHCR.

Wewerinke-Singh, Margaretha. 2018. 'Climate Migrants' Right to Enjoy Their Culture.' In *Climate Refugees: Beyond the Legal Impasse?*, edited by Simon Behrman and Avidan Kent, 194–213. London: Routledge.

World Bank. n.d. 'CO2 Emissions (metric tons per capita).' https://data.worldbank.org/indicator/EN.ATM.CO2E.PC. Accessed 27 September 2021.

World Bank Group. 2018. *Groundswell: Preparing for Internal Climate Migration.* Washington: World Bank.

Wyman, Katrina M. 2017. 'Ethical Duties to Climate Migrants.' In *Research Handbook on Climate Change, Migration and the Law*, edited by Benoît Mayer and François Crépeau, 347–375. Northampton: Edward Elgar.

CHAPTER 12

Theatre's Digital Migration

Matthew Causey

Contemporary theatre practices within developed economies and communities with advanced technological infrastructures are experiencing their own *migration* from the live and the present to the digital and the virtual. The traditional performance of self in the *real world* in *real time* is likewise displaced within electronic communications of social media. The multiple transitions to electronic communications and platforms, underway for nearly a quarter of a century, represent a digital diaspora not yet fully understood. The situation is identified as a postdigital condition, in which technologized cultures are 'fully familiarized and embedded in electronic communications and virtual representations, wherein the biological and the mechanical, the virtual and the real, and the organic and the inorganic approach indistinction' (Causey 2016, 432). These dislocations, or migrations, no less real because of their virtuality, are exacerbated by the Covid-19 pandemic and resulting legislated social distancing, closures and lockdowns. As Slavoj Žižek suggests the pandemic has created a situation in which 'the basic coordinates of the everyday lives of millions are disintegrating, and the change will affect everything, from flying to holidays to simple bodily contact' (Žižek 2020, 90). The focus of this chapter is to bracket those assertions and to question what happens to a postpandemic postdigital theatre and its audience now relocated from their traditional material home. How will the data-subjects of postdigital culture represent their identity within the migration of the theatre and the self to the screens of virtual environments? This chapter acts as something of an afterword, or coda, to the book as a whole and moves the discussion further to consider a migration whose 'virtual, but

M. Causey (✉)
Trinity College Dublin, Dublin, Ireland
e-mail: CAUSEYM@tcd.ie

© The Author(s), under exclusive license to Springer Nature Switzerland AG 2023
Y. Meerzon, S. E. Wilmer (eds.), *The Palgrave Handbook of Theatre and Migration*, https://doi.org/10.1007/978-3-031-20196-7_12

real' world affects and effects are shaping our global communications and communities, politics and ideologies, knowledge, ethics and aesthetics.

In the midst of a postdigital culture and the ubiquitous presence of virtual environments, electronic communications and the presentation of the self in social media and via digital avatars, the theatre maintains its claim to *liveness* and consistently privileges the experience of the corporeal 'here and now'. Nonetheless, for many years, theatre makers who are privileged enough to gain access to new technologies have experimented with performance strategies shaped by computational interventions which allow theatre experiences which are decidedly *not-here* and *not-now* and which occur asynchronously, telepresently, and virtually, augmenting reality in hybrid forms. As noted above, the Covid-19 pandemic and the resulting institutional and governmental states of exception to enforce lockdowns, social distancing, and self-isolation further alienate the theatre from its dependency on the present here and now and accelerate the theatre's continuing migration to the digital. As audiences are banned outright or placed in new forms of *splendid isolation* the theatre has had to rethink its insistence on the live and face-to-face and reconstruct its ontological grounds and aesthetic models. The digital migration is a result of the necessities of public health during the pandemic as well as the desire to explore the potential of art and technology.

The stretching of the meaning of migration to include the transition to the digital is admittedly troubling and can be critiqued as a metaphorical use of the word. It is true that the digital migration is a phenomenon limited to advanced technological cultures. It may also be argued that such a strategy is a manner of culture appropriation attaching to the condition of disenfranchised people physically migrating as a result of violence, climate change, and economic and political upheavals. The *actual* global migrations represent a humanitarian crisis of critical importance and political urgency demanding societal action and solutions and equating the situations is inappropriate, inaccurate, and historically ignorant. However, migrant populations do not escape the postdigital condition and become unwitting data-subjects as they are under surveillance and digitized for tracking, policing, and control. There is something to be learned from the linkage of digital and actual migrants as the two phenomena do not necessarily cancel each other out. The very real phenomena resulting in the transitions and translations to the virtual and the digital which while certainly less materially challenging are decisive for the future of technologized cultures and the multitudes of data-subjects living in the postdigital condition. My contention is that the journey from the physical to the virtual accelerated by the pandemic represents one of the most significant performances of migration in contemporary global culture. The digital migration is taking place in part as a result of the many public health initiatives such as the closures of live theatres and cinemas, universities and secondary schools, restaurants and hospitality establishments, shoppes, and retail outlets across the world following wherever the pandemic reaches. The economy is kept alive by virtual home offices and friends and family remain in contact electronically with primary communications facilitated via video-conferencing and tele-present systems. It is not hyperbole to suggest that these reconfigurations of the presentation of self and the circulation of information via digital communications dwarf even the seismic shift of Gutenberg's printing press. These real-world lived experiences are not metaphors. Even as the pandemic in vaccinated population centres is abated and there is a 'return to normality' the residue of the isolations will remain. The insistent drive (capitalistic and psychological) towards virtualizing communication, culture, subjectivities, politics, and power accelerates.

I will first discuss the debates and resistance surrounding the global lockdowns and granting of emergency powers to local and national governments which give rise to an urgent move towards digitizing and virtualizing culture. I argue that a postdigital theatre and performance will be a necessary aid for our understanding of the current crises of pandemic and digital migration. Secondly, I will analyse two recent theatre works which are exemplary of the digital migration and postdigital performance as they respond to the social distance requirements of the pandemic while utilizing new performance technologies that extend the boundaries of theatre performance and spectatorship within virtual spaces. I will consider *To Be a Machine* presented by Ireland's Dead Centre Theatre Company and UK's Royal Shakespeare Company's *Dream*, an interactive and virtual adaptation of *Midsummer Night's Dream*. I have chosen these work not because they are representations of the global migration crisis but because they are, in fact, an enactment of an actual migration to the digital.

Emergency Powers, the Pandemic, and the Postdigital

If, in fact, we have experienced a genuine global emergency or crisis as a result of the coronavirus pandemic of 2020/21, then it is a crisis which, as they say, has not gone to waste. Many governments of various countries have instituted states of exception and been granted unprecedented emergency powers to control their citizen's movements, work practices, and social lives. Examples of such control systems include surveillance drones which are being used across Europe to monitor populations. Tracking apps are designed to follow movements of those infected. Politico reports that, 'In the European Union, home to the world's strictest privacy regimen, leaders have taken the unprecedented step of asking telecoms companies to hand over mobile phone data so they can track population movements and try to stop the spread' (Manancourt et al. 2020). As noted above, closures and restriction of public and private methods of association are widespread. Nonetheless, in some areas the success of the vaccinations and public health initiatives are allowing a lifting of lockdowns, while in other areas such as Argentina, India, and Melbourne (as of mid-2021) restrictive measures to curtail the virus are still required. Complicating matters, there is a constant threat of new variants of the virus developing.

While recognizing the need to combat the genuine peril the virus represents to the world, some public intellectuals, politicians, and activists have noted the lack of significant challenges to the encroachments of basic human rights of movement, assembly, and privacy. An uncomfortable and unusual agreement arose in 2020 between reactionary conservative populations across North America and Europe and some leftist philosophers such as Giorgio Agamben and Slavoj Žižek who questioned the political overreach and curtailment of basic human rights within the lockdowns. Even some popular musicians such as Van Morrison and Eric Clapton joined the protest composing and recording songs of resistance to the lockdowns (Clapton 2020). In many cases the opposition to the public health directives and restrictions was widely criticized as irresponsible. Taking a more nuanced but no less controversial approach, Agamben, referring to the lockdown in Italy, wrote,

> The first thing that the wave of panic that has paralyzed the country obviously shows is that our society no longer believes in anything but bare life. It is obvious that Italians are disposed to sacrifice practically everything—the normal conditions of life, social relationships, work, even friendships, affections, and religious and political convictions—to the danger of getting sick. (Agamben 2020)

Similar to the case against the lockdown protests, there has been considerable push-back to Agamben's argument from significant philosophers including Jean-Luc Nancy who sees in Agamben's resistance a naïve refusal of common-sense communal practices to respond to the pandemic and save much unnecessary suffering (Nancy 2020).

Žižek, in his book on the topic of the pandemic, worries over a more fundamental effect of the pandemic, writing,

> The catch is that, even if life does eventually return to some semblance of normality, it will not be the same normal as the one we experienced before the outbreak. Things we were used to as part of our daily life will no longer be taken for granted, we will have to learn to live a much more fragile life with constant threats. We will have to change our entire stance to life, to our existence as living beings among other forms of life. In other words, if we understand "philosophy" as the name for our basic orientation in life, we will have to experience a true philosophical revolution. (Žižek 2020, 78)

Perhaps, Agamben is correct and we are risking a loss of basic human rights in our panic to preserve 'bare life'. Perhaps, Žižek is right and the situation demands a radical reconfiguration of culture, thinking, our relation to the earth and life itself. Finding a fair balance between health, human rights, and economics is not easy. No matter how you read the current exceptional state of exception, the politics of the pandemic, and the chosen strategy of lockdowns and mass surveillance there is one element which seems incontrovertible, namely, the victory of the virtual. A victory at least for those able to afford access to the hardware required to live a virtual life, but a 'philosophical revolution' sure enough. The virtual is the modality of communication and commerce par excellence in the age of self-isolation. Make contact but do not convene. Go shopping, but don't leave the house. The quick transition to life in virtual environments, although well-established before the pandemic, is being realized in the test-runs of asynchronous classrooms, Zoom meetings, online performances, VR visits to the art galleries, electronic shopping 'til we're dropping. The migration is underway towards a postdigital, post-pandemic global culture which will challenge fundamental human rights while altering our basic relation to life. A clarifying, resistant, and motivating post-digital, post-pandemic theatre seems inevitable.

Postdigital theatre can be understood as theatre and performance that

> incorporates the discourse and ideologies of the digital, and questions the significant issues involved in negotiating being in a postdigital culture while working toward effective political engagements. Performance works that draw on the structures and strategies of the digital, whether analogue, digital, or hybrid, are potentially well-positioned and programmed to engage the challenges of devising resistant forms of contemporary performance. The structural elements and logic of the digital that are being incorporated into performance include, but are not limited to, asynchronicity and multidimensionality, the transmedial and trans-identities, bugs and glitches, malware and hacking, copy and paste, and the reality of the virtual. The incorporation of these phenomena into performance practice is to think digitally, returning the system back against itself. A postdigital performance thinks digitally in order to resist, or at least understand, the systems of electronic and computational control. (Causey 2016, 432)

A postdigital performance practice thinks digitally and its technologies of representations draw on the logic of the internet. Postdigital performance is, as is the case for any significant or responsive art, historically informed, and, in some cases, history-making, being shaped by and shaping the most current technologies of representation. The tiring prefix of *post* in postdigital does not refer to an end of the digital but rather an absorption of the digital into all manners of life. Similarly, a post-pandemic culture will need to acclimate to the demands of the virus. We may be finished with the virus but the virus, in all likelihood, is not finished with us. Inevitably, the world will restart, in one way or another, and in different manners, in different regions, at different speeds. What will remain within the post-pandemic culture is yet to be determined. What art will emerge in the post-pandemic period will tell us much about what is to remain and what might matter amongst the ruins.

Postdigital, Post-pandemic Theatre

During the Covid-19 pandemic many theatre companies, located amongst population centres with ready access to digital technologies, established online presences and streamed pre-recorded or live performances of traditional theatre works. Necessitated by social distancing requirements theatres attempted to sustain their artists and maintain a connection with their audiences by delivering their works virtually. For the most part, these virtual offerings were traditional theatre presentations simply recorded or streamed live on digital platforms. Other theatre makers such as Ireland's Dead Centre Theatre Company and the Royal Shakespeare Company of the United Kingdom created more adventurous forays into digital theatre using forms and technologies that are hybrid, augmented, and virtual. Their works engaged experimental forms and a research ethos in order to explore new models of theatre production and audience configurations and reception opportunities. The performances introduced, either directly as in the case of Dead Centre or by proximity, an accident of the access to the technologies, as demonstrated in the work of the RSC, the philosophical revolution confronting our postdigital, postpandemic condition.

Dream

The Royal Shakespeare Company's *Dream*, inspired by Shakespeare's *Midsummer Night's Dream*, is a live, online performance created with motion capture technologies. The script works off several scenarios built around Shakespeare's characters from the original play including Puck and his companions, the fairies of the forest, Cobweb, PeaseBlossom, Moth, and Mustardseed. The presentation is streamed online, and members of the audience are allowed (at an extra cost) a modicum of interaction by remotely controlling the movement of fireflies who travel around the characters in the virtual forest. The streamed performance transitions from *live scenes* of the actors in their motion capture suits (dark tights with attached sensors at key body points, helmets, and radio microphones) in the motion capture space (darkened grid floor in front of a wide projection screen with multiple hanging cameras tracking the movement) to the virtual forest and the digitally designed characters and environment streamed to the audience's computer devices. The running time is fifty minutes and the narrative seems less focused on plot as opposed to taking the opportunity to explore the technological potential and challenges of live motion capture and creating virtual characters in virtual environments.

The technology necessary for such a performance is expensive and complex. Forty-eight cameras are required for the motion capture alone not including the live cameras which are filming the action for streaming. Motion capture (mo-cap) is a well-established and common process in Hollywood filmmaking, gaming design, and experimental theatre and dance. Mo-cap tracks the sensors attached to the actors and translates that information to the computer creating digital figures in real time which are then programmed into the virtual forest and projected upon the screen in the theatre space or streamed online to the various computers, smart phones, and tablets of the audience. The RSC's *Dream* is a collaboration with the Audience of the Future research group with funding from various sources including the UK Research and Innovation through the Industrial Strategy Challenge Fund. The collaborators of the Audience of the Future include 'fifteen specialist organisations and pioneers in immersive technology [who] have brought together their expertise in theatre and performance, the music industry, video production, gaming and the research sector to explore what it means to perform live using technologies such as virtual reality, augmented reality and mixed reality' (Dream.online 2021a). The combination of academics, artists, technologists, game designers, computer programmers, and venture capitalists is a necessary consortium to realize such a costly and time-consuming project. Such projects are necessarily outside the budgets and resources of most commercial or independent theatres and artists.

The first challenge for the reception of the work is to assure the audience that the show is, in fact, live. The hybridity of the event presents an interesting dilemma for the producers as the claims to liveness and the here-and-now are not so readily perceived. In an attempt to assure any perspective audience that what they will view online is indeed live the producers write on their website that *Dream* is 'performed live by actors in a motion capture space at Portsmouth Guildhall. You will see both the actors themselves and their avatars in the virtual forest. The avatars are driven by the movements of the actors in real time' (Dream.online 2021b). The reminders that the performance is taking place in real time do require some foregrounding for the audience as the virtual imagery is easily confused with what is actually live, what is pre-recorded, what is digitally stored for playback, and what is spontaneous and what is re-enacted. This unintended zone of indistinction between the organic or live and machinic and digital is a key modality in postdigital culture where the perceived differences between the virtual and the real are considered merely an aesthetic.

In offering an enhanced audience interaction and experience the RSC sells an Audience Plus ticket which allows the ticket holder interactive and remote control of 'fireflies, helping to light the forest and interacting using their mouse, trackpad or touchscreen. The actors respond to audience interaction and direction, making each performance unique' (Dream.online 2021b). Such website descriptors and promotions prompt the perspective audience to recognize liveness, spontaneity, and uniqueness. If an event is to be framed as a piece of theatre while being presented on screens its only recourse to that claim is to maintain a hold on uniqueness and foreground liveness facilitated primarily by computerized interactivity. What cannot be denied is that presence, the here and now, and corporeality are absent. The migration of theatre to the digital cannot have it both ways as the live and the virtual are not discrete units. Postdigital theatre *is* both live and digitized, but functions as a third way in a techno-performativity. It is a theatre that is like the live theatre, only different.

To Be a Machine

Founded in 2012 and based in Dublin and London, the Dead Centre Theatre Company works under the artistic direction of Bush Moukarzel and Ben Kidd. Their previous theatre works including *Hamnet*, *LIPPY*, and *Chekhov's First Play* were premiered in Ireland, but have toured extensively to New York, Hong Kong, Russia, China, Australia, France, Estonia, Holland, Romania,

Germany, and throughout the UK. During the pandemic in Dublin in 2020 and as part of that year's Dublin Theatre Festival, Dead Centre presented a performance piece based on the 2017 non-fiction book *To Be a Machine: Adventures Among Cyborgs, Utopians, Hackers, and the Futurists Solving the Modest Problem of Death* by Mark O'Connell. The book surveys the topic of transhumanism, a posthuman philosophy and practice which theorize the body as obsolete and an obstacle to be extended, altered, and hacked by such tactics as uploading the brain's contents into computers, cryopreservation, radical life extension, increased mental capacity, prosthetics, and genetic modification. The author questions the contemporary obsession with technology, the rise of artificial intelligence, and considers how humanity is being shaped by linking to these machines. O'Connell links his own existential concerns and anxieties to these larger issues.

Dead Centre's performance adaptation of the book is a truly original approach to the theatre and for reasons both philosophical (transhumanism) and practical (pandemic) is a work developed as a 'live-audience-upload-experience'. The company describes the work on their website,

> In the midst of a global pandemic, where our bodies have become biohazards, transhumanists offer a way into a disease-free digital age. We follow Mark from cryonic storage facilities to basement biohacking labs as he meets the prophets of our techno-future. We use the theatre to hold a wake for the very idea of congregating together in a room, and a meditation on humanity's attempt to solve the modest problem of death. (Dead Centre 2021)

The one-man performance featuring Jack Gleeson performing the role of the book's author Mark O'Connell was streamed live from the Projects Art Centre in Dublin. At each seat in the theatre is an iPad supported on a column with various power adaptors and USB cables attached. Before the performance the audience is asked to upload a video of themselves to be streamed on each of the iPads individually. The audience is literally uploaded into the theatre and given a digital presence in the space. The live streamed performance is viewed by the spectators on computers at their remote locations while their pre-recorded video images on the tablets in the actual theatre are both *witness* and *performer* before and within the live performance. The online spectator views the performance and themselves both watching and participating in the performance. Described by theatre reviewer Helen Meaney in the *Guardian* newspaper, Gleeson,

> stands on a bare stage speaking remotely, by livestream, to an audience that is both there and not there. As the lights go up on the empty auditorium, each viewer from home can make out their own face glowing on a tablet screen from the rows of seats. These pre-recorded images of disembodied heads prove to be an apt metaphor for an excursion into transhumanism, and for the creation of a theatre performance when we can't be in a room together. (Meaney 2020)

The performance has many uncanny moments but none more so than when the live camera turns to the audience and the rows of faces on iPads, which seem so tragically isolated, trapped, and deathlike. The scene is like looking across a field of digital tombstones. Each person is visible but absent, electronically present but untouchable and unable to sense the other spectators. The performance plays adroitly with the here-and-not-here and the now-and-not-now of electronic communications and duplications. The first image of the performance is a close-up talking head of Gleeson/O'Connell which when the live camera pulls back reveals the actor to be an image on an iPad and the *actual* actor is standing next to the tablet. But, of course, the *actual actor* is really, for the computer watching spectator, just another screened image. The layered technological illusions playing amongst what is real and what is not are the substance of what generates the angst running through the work.

Gleeson as O'Connell insists from the start of the performance, not unlike the RSC's website for *Dream*, that what you are seeing is live. Speaking directly to the camera and by extension the audience, 'This is happening live!' he declares. The breaking of the fourth wall never seemed so desperate, distressed, and anxiety-ridden. The desire and longing to be part of a community and to assemble altogether as an audience in one space at one time permeate the digital performance. Gleeson asks the audience what they miss most about going to the theatre. A functioning chat box is opened and with some cueing from the technical staff the audience answers. Replies such as 'darkness', 'reality', 'other people' are typed quickly. The audience seems to wish for the promise of future social gatherings, community, presence, and all the moments that make theatre theatre.

Gleeson, working his way through the re-enactment of the book's concerns, considers the transhumanist interest in being freed of the body and its terminal limitations. He relates those issues to the birth of his son who appears as a crying infant on a suspended iPad. The baby's cries are amplified and the sound begins to compete with Gleeson's monologue. A mildly agitated Gleeson attempts to turn down the sound of the iPad and knocks the tablet to the floor. Multiple lines of misapprehension, technological artifice, and emotional anxieties are drawn together at this moment as it seems the actual baby is in jeopardy from the fall, which of course is untrue either in the stage illusion or reality. The iPad shows a cracked screen, which is similarly shown not to be true. It is at this point that the performance begins to unravel and reveal its profoundly hollow centre. There is no there there, or for that matter, no here here. The final scenes of the play take place in front of a green screen in order to project the character to various locations where he had met and interviewed the various transhumanists. Eventually Gleeson appears back in the theatre but now even that space is likewise digitally generated and unreal. Where is the actor, the theatre, the audience? Somewhere in a digital loop, or nowhere at all. The claim to liveness is abandoned. The work accepts its postdigital condition.

Dead Centre's performance of *To Be a Machine*, while ostensibly about our journey, or our migration to the digital, is actually not about the anxiety of being alone online, but rather the anxiety of *Being*. It is *Being* itself that haunts the piece. Technology is just another way of experiencing our essential homelessness, our uncanny being. Whether or not it is within an electronic setting or a material one, the problem remains one of *Being* and its opposite, *not-Being* (or, death). The directors and writer do seem to hold out some potential for the theatre to relieve the many absences and loneliness of existence. However, the fact that the final images of the performance seem to suggest that the theatre in which all of this is taking place is just another green screen projection may even place that forlorn hope in doubt. Ironically, the anxieties of being a terminal, corporeal body are aggravated by the depths and debris of the multiple electronic illusions which seem to distance the subject even further from that body. The further we venture, or migrate, towards dwelling in virtual environments the deeper our doubts of what is genuine and authentic intensify. Negotiation, ownership, and acceptance of the new dwelling place is a task of the postdigital condition.

The performance of *To Be a Machine* works within a postdigital condition, thinking digitally and uploading the audience who is downloading the performance in a virtual and perpetual loop. The play and the thought of this hybrid theatre is that the performing subject is both data and lived body, drawing our attention to the fact that the lived body *is* data, and that data *is* lived.

Conclusion

While many of the world's migrants grapple with the real-world traumas, injustices, and challenges of their situation and the world itself attempts to come to terms with the changes necessary to guarantee the rights of these people, the digital migration continues and accelerates. As mentioned earlier, the equating of the situations is inappropriate, inaccurate, historically ignorant, and politically suspect. But what the digital transition might learn from the migrant is the knowledge that what is lost in any migration is, primarily, one's homeland. To leave one's home is to risk one's safety, history, family, connections, knowledge, ownership, meaning, and purpose. As the theatre's dwelling place will be at times, more or less, abandoned for digital realms the risks are real for the journey from home. What may be lost may not be easily regained, rebuilt, or returned. This fact is already well known to the real-world global migrants whose struggle endures. And, yet the possibility exists that a new home awaits.

References

Agamben, Giorgio. 2020. 'Giorgio Agamben: Clarifications.' Translated by Adam Kotsko. *An und fur sich Blog*, March 17, 2020. https://itself.blog/2020/03/17/giorgio-agamben-clarifications/.

Causey, Matthew. 2016. 'Postdigital Performance.' *Theatre Journal* 68 (3): 427–441. https://doi.org/10.1353/tj.2016.0074.

Clapton, Eric. 2020. 'Stand and Deliver.' Written by Van Morrison. The state51 Conspiracy. December 18, 2020. Music Video, 4:33. https://www.youtube.com/watch?v=tMkV4vYr_ik.

Dead Centre. 2021. Dead Centre.org. *To Be a Machine*. Accessed May 25, 2021. https://www.deadcentre.org/tobeamachine.

Dream.online. 2021a. 'Audience of the Future.' *Dream.online*. Accessed May 24, 2021. https://dream.online/audience-of-the-future/.

Dream.online. 2021b. 'FAQ.' *Dream.online*. Accessed May 24, 2021. https://dream.online/faq-location/lobby/.

Manancourt, Vincent, Janosch Delcker, Mark Scott, and Laurens Cerulus. 2020. 'In Fight against Coronavirus, Governments Embrace Surveillance.' *Politico.eu*, March 24, 2020. https://www.politico.eu/article/coroanvirus-covid19-surveillance-data.

Meaney, Helen. 2020. 'Dublin Theatre Festival Review.' *The Guardian*, October 9, 2020. https://www.theguardian.com/stage/2020/oct/09/dublin-theatre-festival-review-citys-players-adapt-to-age-of-covid.

Nancy, Jean-Luc. 2020. 'Epidemic Paradoxia.' *Antinomies: Writings and Images*. Last modified February 27, 2020. https://antinomie.it/index.php/2020/02/27/eccezione-virale/.

Žižek, Slavoj. 2020. *Pandemic: Covid-19 Shakes the World*. London: Or Books.

PART II

Early Representations of Migration

CHAPTER 13

Theatre and Migration in *Gilgamesh*

Martin Worthington

Gilgamesh is not a play, and it does not explicitly deal with migration in the sense of 'movements by groups' (indeed, it is generally less concerned with groups than with individuals). And yet, 'theatre' and 'migration' are, both singly and conjointly, useful lenses through which to view this ancient Babylonian narrative. I will therefore deal with the two themes in turn, then discuss their interrelations in a specific performance.

Gilgamesh was a legendary king of Uruk, about whom several poems existed in both Sumerian and Babylonian. They are known from manuscripts (clay tablets) from c. 1800 BC onwards (the stories in Sumerian are suspected to be older). This paper concentrates on the 'Standard Version' of the Babylonian poem, which is the best-preserved and most widely known. The date of redaction of the Standard Version is unknown, but the manuscripts date to the first millennium BC. By far the best and fullest edition is that of Andrew George (2003), which includes extensive and authoritative introductory matter. The text and translation are also accessible online, with updates by other scholars, via the electronic Babylonian Library project (https://www.ebl.lmu.de).

The poem comprised c. 3000 lines, of which 2000+ are currently known. It is divided into eleven chapters or cantos, each of which was written on a single clay tablet. The chapters are therefore also known as 'Tablets' and are referred to with Roman numbers. There is further a twelfth Tablet (not treated here), which is prose rather than poetry, and which contradicts the main plot.

The essentials of the story are these: Gilgamesh's rule is overbearing, so the people of Uruk complain to the gods. These send a purpose-made creature, Enkidu, to calm Gilgamesh down. After first living Mowgli-like with gazelles,

M. Worthington (✉)
Trinity College Dublin, Dublin, Ireland
e-mail: WORTHINM@tcd.ie

Enkidu is humanised by the prostitute Shamhat, and becomes Gilgamesh's bosom friend. Together they mount an expedition to the Cedar Forest, killing its guardian Humbaba. Then they kill the Bull of Heaven, sent by Ishtar, goddess of sex and war, because Gilgamesh refuses her offer of marriage. The gods are angered, and Enkidu must die. In despair, Gilgamesh goes in search of immortality, journeying to the faraway Babylonian Noah (Uta-napishti), encountering magical beings along the way. But Uta-napishti explains that he became immortal because of the Flood, and the circumstances cannot be replicated. Hence, in Tablet XI, Gilgamesh returns to Uruk unsuccessful but, it is implied, wiser. (In the prose Tablet XII, Enkidu is still alive.)

Translations differ widely both in accuracy and in faithfulness to the original Babylonian. Moreover, as new fragments of tablets are found, translations need updating. At the present time, George (2003) or his volume in Penguin Classics can be particularly recommended.

GILGAMESH AND THEATRE

Dramatisations of Gilgamesh

When one takes into account small productions, staged dramatisations of *Gilgamesh* (as distinct from even more numerous readings)[1] are legion. Here is a selection, culled from Theodore Ziolkowski (2012) and online searches:

- the ballet-pantomime *Gilgamesz* by the Polish composer Augustyn Block (1968)
- the 2-hour poetic drama *Gilgamesh* by Michel Garneau, premiered at the *École nationale de théâtre* (1974); reperformed in 1996 at the *Théâtre entre chien et loup* in 53 minutes
- the circus-like performance for children *Ombra di Luna* by Marcello Chiarenza, premiered at the *Festa Internazionale del Circo Contemporaneo di Brescia* (2001) (see also Chiarenza's *Labirinto Mare* and *Visioni*)
- the 'homosexuelle Lovestory' *Gilgamesch und Enkidu* by Andreas Stadler, first performed in Zurich in 2004, and awarded the *Kulturpreis* of the *Verein Network*
- the 80-minute, 3-actor performance *Gilgamesh* by Christian Leavesley and Phil Rolfe (originally developed by the Australian ensemble Uncle Semolina) at Sydney Opera House
- the comedy hip-hop show *Rapconteur* by Baba Brinkman, premiered at the Edinburgh Fringe (2010), which mixed *Gilgamesh* with *Beowulf* and Chaucer's *The Merchant's Tale*
- the part-acted, part-puppet performance *Gilgamesh and Me* by the Babolin Theatre ensemble at the Edinburgh Fringe festival (2019)
- the ballet *Outwitting the Devil* by the Akram Khan Company (2019)

---

[1] Among the tellings (rather than staged performances) it is worth singling out the project *Gilgamesh 21* by the Enheduanna Society (in 2016), which promoted tellings of the story among young people, many of them of Iraqi descent.

The above selection illustrates the great variety in dramatisations of *Gilgamesh*, which differ in duration, genre, size and age of cast and audience, and degrees to which they aim to be faithful to the original story. *Gilgamesh*, then, enthrals modern performers. But how does this relate to what would have happened to the story in antiquity?

Gilgamesh and Orality, Ancient and Modern

Ancient experiences of *Gilgamesh* were in many ways probably closer to the modern experience of Theatre than to the modern practice of reading. For, though *Gilgamesh* survives from antiquity in written form, Mesopotamia was—even long after the invention of writing, and after literacy became important for all sorts of reasons—a largely oral world. There is no evidence that people in Ancient Mesopotamia read for pleasure.

Through the fictive claim to be the wording which Gilgamesh himself inscribed on a stele, the poem presents itself as a written product. But this claim happens only in the Prologue, which was probably added secondarily (some scholars, e.g. George (2003, 28-33), think in the late second millennium BC). Nowhere else in the preserved portions of the poem do we have a reference to writing, nor does any part of the plot rely on writing. In this, the world of the poem resembled many people's experiences of the world around them.

Hence, though today we confront a written poem, this is likely to be but a fragment of what *Gilgamesh* meant to people in Ancient Mesopotamia. When Gareth Brereton (n.d.) wrote that a visitor to Nineveh should not miss 'the weekly shows of the Epic of Gilgamesh, performed by dancers and acrobats acting out the hero's adventures,' he probably captured the spirit of the thing even if we have no positive evidence for such a scenario.

Oral stories circulate in varying degrees of specificity: some people know only the 'core facts,' some know details and variant traditions arise. Further to the considerable evidence assembled to this effect by George (2003, 59-70), Cynthia Jean comments that 'the character of Gilgamesh' is likely to have travelled more, and further, than the written poem associated with him (2014, 114). The perception (not found in the poem) that Gilgamesh was a god of the Underworld (George 2003, 124–135) reflects wider traditions.

Paradoxically, therefore, modern performers, in all their variety of responses to the *Gilgamesh* story, may be closer to the original's 'spirit' than modern philologists (present writer included) who labour over the details of the written poem's wording.

Dramatisation and the Poem's Unsaids

The poem leaves much unsaid. In particular it is very short on 'stage directions,' such as where characters should stand, how they deliver their lines, how they are dressed, what the background looks like and so on. Even a director who wanted to dramatise the production as 'faithfully' as possible would have to cut a great number of Gordian knots. Taking the written poem on its own terms, this would have applied in antiquity as much as today.

For example, consider Gilgamesh's age. This is likely to have a significant effect on how the audience perceives him. Western traditions tend to make senescent kings wise or careworn, while younger specimens tend to carry connotations of heroism or belligerence. So, is Gilgamesh old or young, or does he grow older as the story advances? Here we run into the problem that the poem's timeline is—as with many works of Babylonian literature (Foster 1996, 27–8)—hopelessly blurry (North and Worthington 2012, 194–99): though we meet references to specific numbers of days, adding them up leaves so many gaps that the overall duration is uncertain. The tone suggests it is unlikely to be two weeks or two months, but whether it is five years or fifty years is unclear, and a precise duration may not be how ancient audiences thought about the matter.

More generally, it is a feature of Babylonian literature as a whole that characters are not described as growing older (though they do grow wiser).[2] A director who wishes to honour this trend might be compelled to have a young Gilgamesh at the end of the story, where a modern audience would be more comfortable with an older person.

Parts Versus Whole

Considerably shorter than both the *Iliad* and the *Odyssey*, the full *Gilgamesh* poem is still rather long. While there are modern audiences trained to enjoy performances as long as Wagner's *Ring Cycle*, many adaptors will be keen to abridge. This may be more within the spirit of the ancient poem than is first apparent.

Writing was in ancient Mesopotamia by no means as pervasive as in our world, where many books might turn up almost anywhere. *Gilgamesh* manuscripts usually stem from 'libraries' somehow associated with institutions. The largest and most famous of these are the Ninevite collections of the Assyrian king Ashurbanipal (seventh century BC), who evidently strove to document all parts of all compositions equally well. Outside of Ashurbanipal's Libraries, however, there is a noticeable tendency—shared with other Babylonian compositions (see Driver 1948, 69)—for *Gilgamesh* manuscripts to dwindle the further one gets into the poem: apparently, people started copying at the beginning, and did not get all the way through. Compare graffiti at Pompeii, where the part of the *Aeneid* cited most frequently is the first line (Harris 1989, 261; Milnor 2014, 237-53), probably because (then as now) this is the one which most people knew.

---

[2] Foster (1996, 29), with reference to a Russian work by I. S. Klotchkoff. The point was made for gods also by Bottéro (2001, 61).

It seems likely, therefore, that many collections held incomplete 'sets' of *Gilgamesh* tablets. To us this is jarring, but it might have been less so in antiquity if each Tablet of the composition was recognised as a self-standing episode in its own right. This scenario is lent plausibility by A.D. Kilmer (2006)'s argument that the most important line in each tablet of Babylonian poetry was placed in the centre of the clay tablet.

Migration in the Poem

Let us first survey migration in the world in which the poem was created and transmitted, and then migration-related themes in the poem itself.

Mesopotamian Migrations

The world of Ancient Mesopotamia was no stranger to the movement of peoples.[3] The details of course vary hugely across time and place, but overall trends are likely to have been characteristic of most periods.

For a start, a good part of the population at any given time would have been nomadic pastoralists (see survey in Castillo 2005). This was not without influence on Mesopotamian *belles lettres*. Jean-Robert Kupper (1961) convincingly argued that the Sumerian poem *The Marriage of Martu*,[4] an 'origin myth' for the Amorite god Martu/Amurru, was created by settled Mesopotamians in response to the arrival of Amorite nomads in the early second millennium BC.

But there were many other types of people movement. It no doubt happened with refugees from wars—a phenomenon increased in the first millennium BC by first the Neo-Assyrians' and then the Neo-Babylonians' practice of forced deportation (which led to the Jewish Exile in Babylon). Nebuchadnezzar's Egyptian wars in the Levant brought Egyptians to Babylonia in the late 600s BC (Hackl and Jursa 2015). Even without wars, families could relocate owing to political turbulence (an example is discussed by Wiggermann 2008).

On the positive side, then as now there were no doubt migrants moved by economic opportunity. The excavation of cuneiform archives at Kanesh in central Turkey has demonstrated the presence of a resident colony of Assyrian traders there in the early second millennium BC (survey in Larsen 2015). This is unlikely to have been the only such case (cf. Harris 1976, 149-51).

The Poem's Journeys

There is a lot of movement in *Gilgamesh*—a point highlighted in the title of Eric Leed's book *The Mind of the Traveller: From Gilgamesh to Global Tourism*

---

[3] A survey of the topic is Beckman (2013). An insightful study of the *historiography* on this topic is Wiedemann (2020).

[4] Translated at https://etcsl.orinst.ox.ac.uk/section1/b171.htm. This poem is so far extant on a single damaged tablet of the early second millennium BC.

(1991). The two biggest journeys, which between them take up a large chunk of the poem, are the expedition to the Cedar Forest and Gilgamesh's quest for immortality. There are (unsurprisingly) also many other movements of various kinds, including 'the land Uruk' gathering around the newly arrived Enkidu (II 103-104), 'the kings of the earth' gathering in Uruk for Enkidu's funeral (VII 143 / VIII 87) and men who live at various removes from the city coming to it to frequent harlots (VII 154-155).

Nonetheless, the written poem seems to drive home the message that where people belong is at home in the city (van de Mieroop 1999, 44): the two big journeys both end badly, and Gilgamesh himself ends up back in Uruk, where he started out. He has thus changed his original plan, which was that if he could not reach Uta-napishti he would roam the wild (X 76-77 and 153-154): the quest has 'tamed' him, and, wittingly or unwittingly, he ends up following Shiduri's advice (X 91) that, if the quest cannot be achieved, he should go back whence he came. His return seems to be decided by Uta-napishti's nameless wife (XI 217, cf. 275), who together with Shiduri has a very influential, if understated, role. In keeping with this outcome, George (2012) has observed that, at the end of the poem, the grammar transitions from motion to stasis.

Even the journeys' geography agrees with the poem's preference for city life: since the big rivers in Iraq flow South-Eastwards, they are not much help in getting *to* the Cedar Mountain (in Lebanon): boats would have to be towed upstream, sometimes crossing from one bank to the other (Comfort and Ergeç 2001, 23). Sure enough, we hear nothing in *Gilgamesh* about riverine transport on the outbound journey: it seems to have been a long thirsty trek. But, once the cedars have been successfully felled, the Euphrates provides an easy way of transporting them back. The menfolk of Uruk probably had this in mind when they voiced the wish that Gilgamesh should come back safe and sound to the city's *quay* (III 215). The quest for immortality is similar: difficult though the outbound journey proves (along the path of the Sun, no less!), on the way back it seems to be a single boat ride from Uta-napishti's realm direct to Uruk. Overall, the natural world is used and described in such a way that it is easier to return to Uruk than it was to leave it.

All this presumably reflects the viewpoint of the literate elites who created and transmitted the written poem. Oral and rural narratives about Gilgamesh could have had different emphases.

Displacement

Several characters in the poem have been 'displaced.' In Tablet X we meet the enigmatic figure of Shiduri, who lives 'by the sea-shore.' Her name is written with the divine determinative, and she is also referred to as a 'female tavern-keeper' (*sābītum*), a profession well known from the early second millennium BC (see references in Worthington 2010). Gilgamesh himself apparently has no inkling of her divinity, addressing her as *sābītum*. How she came to be dwelling where she does, and how she deals with the isolation, we are not told.

Also displaced are Uta-napishti and his spouse, who survived the Flood. They live 'at the mouth of rivers,' having been placed there by the chief god Enlil (XI 205). They enjoy the services of a ferryman.[5] We get no particular sense they are unhappy. Ur-shanabi himself brings Gilgamesh to Uruk, apparently for the first time. He too is displaced, but Gilgamesh expects him to be impressed by the city (XI 323-328). The poem does not say whether he remained there or went back to the 'mouth of rivers.'

In Tablet VII, Enkidu addresses the door made from the wood procured by the expedition to the Cedar Forest. Apparently (the context is broken) Enkidu regrets its having gone to the temple of Enlil in Nippur, wishing it had instead gone to the temple of Shamash in Sippar. Though neither the door nor its wood are characters in the conventional sense, Enkidu's address is striking. The wood has undergone the most violent and forcible dislocation of any recounted in the poem, and also it has transitioned from its wild state to being part of 'civilisation.' Perhaps Enkidu singles it out because, as well as his own part in its fate, he recognises something of himself in it. The wood's story is untypical of most migrations, for, as a highly prized commodity, cedar was highly valued where it ended up.

Gilgamesh the Wayfarer

Gilgamesh's long journey in search of immortality changes him. When he approaches the scorpion-folk in Tablet IX, they recognise him as part-god from his physical features (lines 48-51). But by the time he comes to Shiduri (much of the intervening narrative is lost), he looks different: though the narrator reminds us that he has the 'flesh of the gods' (X 7), his face is 'identical to that of one who has journeyed far' (X 9), and Shiduri takes him for a 'hunter of wild bulls,' locking her door (X 13). The gut reactions of further characters to Gilgamesh's appearance are lost, but they are unlikely to have been more refined. Several characters, not least Uta-napishti (X 216), ask him the same questions, including 'Why is your face identical to that of one who has journeyed from afar?'

One gets the impression that this part of the poem is set in a world where travellers arouse suspicions. One of Uta-napishti's first thoughts on seeing Gilgamesh is 'he is no man of mine' (X 189), and even the scorpion folk, who recognise Gilgamesh's part-divinity, seem (the lines are broken) to have questioned him closely. This no doubt has to do with the inaccessibility of the relevant places to ordinary people: their denizens are not used to seeing strangers, and the scorpion folk were there to 'guard' the location (X 39, 45).

---

[5] His name, Ur-shanabi, suggests he may have been supplied by their protector, the god Ea (who first alerted Uta-napishti to the impending Flood): 'Ur-shanabi' is Sumerian for 'Dog (i.e. servant) of two-third,' and 'two-third' alludes to Ea's mystical number 40, which is two thirds of Mesopotamia's 'ideal number,' sixty.

Migrants in the Poem?

Whether migrants in a conventional sense feature in *Gilgamesh* is unclear and depends on one's definition. Generally, the poem seems to be more interested in drawing a line of division between 'city dwellers' and 'others' than between 'settled people' and 'people who move.'

Thus it is one of the poem's 'unsaids' whether the hunter who first meets Enkidu in Tablet I was settled or nomadic: though going to the city is apparently not routine for him (I 148), we do not know if he lives in a stationary settlement or in a nomadic community. When he goes to his 'father' for advice, the word 'father' could also mean 'sheikh' or 'tribal leader,' and it is possible that some audiences understood it thus. Either way, the advice of the 'father' to go and ask king Gilgamesh for Shamhat contains an implicit acknowledgment of the city's superiority: only it has the means to tame the wild Enkidu.

Similar considerations apply to the shepherds to whom Shamhat leads Enkidu in Tablet II. The prejudices of city-dweller audiences might have led some to assume settlement from the reference to the shepherds having a *tarbāṣu* 'animal pen,' but Enkidu moving from utter wilderness to city life via the shepherds as nomads or transhumant pastoralists would strengthen George's idea of this step as a 'half-way house' (2003, 455). Either way, when the shepherds first see Enkidu they compare him to 'battlements,' and deduce from this that he must have been born in the mountains. Even though they dwell outside the city, their instinctive frame of reference for hugeness and magnificence puts city life first, and natural world second.

Enkidu's 'Migration'

The most conspicuous *metaphorical* migration in the poem occurs in Tablet I, where Enkidu passes from the realm of beasts to that of humans—a move which later, in Tablet VII, he regrets (though at the Sun God's behest he goes on to acknowledge that it had its plusses).

The principal catalyst for the transformation, that which enables him to talk like a human, is the six days and seven nights of sex with the prostitute Shamhat (sometimes, I think wrongly, understood as a priestess). While this might reflect a metaphysical interest in the transformative-initiatory power of sex, it could also, more prosaically, reflect a historical reality that outsiders' (including migrants') integration into a new group was facilitated by marriage to locals.

A transformation opposite to Enkidu's is alluded to in Tablet VI, when Gilgamesh turns down an offer of marriage from the goddess Ishtar: detailing how she ill-treated her previous lovers, he says that she turned a shepherd into a wolf, to be attacked by his own assistants and dogs. In this metamorphosis—a rarity in Babylonian written literature (Sonik 2012)—we have an early instalment of the long cultural history of the demonisation of the wolf, who has often been used as a hostile metaphor for migrants (see Arnds 2021, 2 and passim). (Though Ea pairs the wolf and lion as person-killers (XI 189-192), the wolf but not the lion is named in the lists of animals that mourn Enkidu (VIII 16-17) and Gilgamesh kills on his travels (X 259-260).)

Dramatisation as Migration

A particularly interesting crucible for reflecting on the relation between dramatisation and migration is afforded by the *Gilgamesh* produced by the performance group Macnas as part of the celebrations for 'Galway City of Culture 2020.' The work was originally intended to be a staged production, but morphed into a film owing to the Covid-19 pandemic. The result is a film of 24-and-a-bit minutes, which uses land- and cityscapes of present-day Ireland.

The Macnas *Gilgamesh* is a free adaptation of the ancient poem: while it features many of the characters (Gilgamesh, Enkidu, Uta-napishti, Ishtar, Ninsun, Enlil) and their attributes (e.g. Gilgamesh's desire for immortality, Enkidu's connection to gazelles), it ploughs its own creative furrow, moving in a visually dark, slow-moving and dream-like world whose occurrences it portrays elliptically. All lines are spoken as characters' thoughts: the actors never move their lips.

The film juggles antiquity and modernity in complex ways, so that it is not always clear which is which. For example, the opening scene features a winged Enlil (chief god of the pantheon in early Mesopotamia) looking down from the heavens, with surtitles that read 'I remember when we galloped across the heavens on stallions. When the land was new and gorgeous in her first coat of green. That was then and this is now.' While 'then' clearly refers to the time when the world was created, it is less clear what Enlil's 'now' means: is he talking at the time of Gilgamesh's adventures, or in the viewer's own present? This ambiguity runs through much of the production.

Some of Enlil's utterances fit our present at least as well as the Mesopotamian past. For example, 'No-one prays to me any more. No-one mentions my name. This … is how gods die' makes at least as good a sense for today as for the era in which the *Gilgamesh* poem is set. There is a strong ring of modernity also in Uta-napishti's complaint: 'Those gods have done more damage than good. Isn't that the crux of the whole sorry saga?'

Yet the Macnas production also closely ties Enlil to the world of the *Gilgamesh* poem. It implies that Enlil's fall from supremacy was at least partly due to Gilgamesh's expedition to the Cedar Forest (which destroyed what the film's Uta-napishti calls 'Enlil's sanctuary since time began'). Uta-napishti recounts that his boatman brought Enlil to him, clutching 'cedar children' whom Gilgamesh had killed.

How much time has passed between this and other parts of the film is unclear. Different characters may be using the present tense to refer to different points in time. If some of Enlil's relate to our present, at least one of Uta-napishti's does not: 'Gilgamesh needs rain.' A sense of temporal indeterminacy thus arises which chimes with that of the original poem.

There is also a sense in which it is not necessary to define the relation between the two temporal spheres, ancient and modern. When Enlil says 'The rivers rise again. The air smells of rot and decay. The animals fewer. The skies darken. All as it was before, all ready (or: already) to happen again,' these have an emphasis on environmental change, which is significant for contemporary audiences, regardless of when we should understand Enlil to be speaking to them. The same applies to Enlil's mournful utterance about humans: 'I made them for nature—not this, not this.'

Likewise, Ninsun mentions the Celtic goddess 'Ursula of the Silver Host' alongside a list of Mesopotamian deities. This evinces integration between two worlds (Ancient and Medieval), but the nature of this integration is left allusively hazy.

All in all, the Macnas *Gilgamesh* affords viewers an elegant disorientation (experienced also by Uta-napishti, who asks rhetorically 'What century am I in?'). It is not only the poem which has been 'migrated' from clay tablets to film: cut adrift from secure anchor points, viewers themselves become migrants between the different planes the film interweaves.

Concluding Remarks

The written *Gilgamesh* poem ('standard version') is more interested in travel than in migration, not least because (like much Mesopotamian literature) it is chauvinistically urban. But the legends of Gilgamesh no doubt circulated more widely than the written tablets we know them from, and probably with variations which would surprise us. Modern performers who adapt the story to their own ends might well be in sympathy with many an ancient storyteller. Modern dramatisers have long been enthused by the story's antiquity, polysemy, relatability and variety of moods, and will no doubt continue to do so. It would not be surprising if, in an age of increasing ecological-mindedness, future years saw an increasing focus on the poem's complex treatment of the animal kingdom and natural world, and of the different ways in which humans relate to them.

References

Arnds, Peter. 2021 *Wolves at the Door: Migration, Dehumanization, Rewilding the World*. London: Bloomsbury.

Beckman, Gary. 2013. 'Foreigners in the Ancient Near East.' *Journal of the American Oriental Society*, 133: 203–15.

Bottéro, Jéan. 2001. *Religion in Ancient Mesopotamia*. Chicago: Chicago University Press.

Brereton, Gareth. n.d. 'Historical city travel guide: Nineveh, 7th century BC.' https://blog.britishmuseum.org/historical-city-travel-guide-nineveh-7th-century-bc/

Castillo, Jorge S. 2005. 'Nomadism through the Ages.' In *A Companion to the Ancient Near East*, edited by Daniel Snell, 126–40. Malden: Blackwell.

Comfort, Anthony and Rifat Ergeç. 2001. 'Following the Euphrates in Antiquity: North-South Routes around Zeugma.' *Anatolian Studies*, 51: 19–49.
Driver, Godfrey R. 1948. *Semitic Writing from Pictograph to Alphabet*. London: Geoffrey Cumberlege.
Foster, Benjamin R. 1996. *Before the Muses: An Anthology of Akkadian Literature*. Second Edition. Bethesda: CDL Press.
George, Andrew R. 2003. *The Babylonian Gilgamesh Epic: Introduction, Critical Edition and Cuneiform Texts*. 2 vols. Oxford: Oxford University Press.
———. 2012. 'The Mayfly on the River: Individual and Collective Destiny in the Epic of Gilgamesh'. *KASKAL*, 9: 227–242.
Hackl, Johannes and Michael Jursa. 2015. 'Egyptians in Babylonia in the Neo-Babylonian and Achaemenid Periods.' In *Exile and Return: The Babylonian Context*, edited by Johannes Stöckl and Caroline Waerzeggers, 157–180. Berlin: De Gruyter.
Harris, William V. 1989. *Ancient Literacy*. Cambridge: Harvard University Press.
Harris, Rivkah. 1976. 'On Foreigners in Old Babylonian Sippar.' *Revue d'Assyriologie*, 70: 145–52.
Jean, Cynthia. 2014. 'Globalization in Literature: Re-Examining the Gilgameš Affair.' In *Melammu: The Ancient World in an Age of Globalization*, ed. Markham J. Geller, 111–16. Berlin: Max Planck Institute for the History of Science.
Kilmer, A. D. 2006. 'Visualizing Text: Schematic Patterns in Akkadian Poetry.' In *If a Man Builds a Joyful House: Assyriological Studies in Honor of Erle Verdun Leichty*, edited by Ann K. Guinan et al., 209–21. Leiden: Brill.
Kupper, Jean-Robert. 1961. *L'iconographie du dieu Amurru dans la glyptique de la Ire dynastie babylonienne*. Brussells: Palais des Académies.
Larsen, Mogens T. 2015. *Ancient Kanesh: A Merchant Colony in Bronze-Age Anatolia*. New York: Cambridge University Press.
Leed, Eric I. 1991. *The Mind of the Traveller: From Gilgamesh to Global Tourism*. New York: Basic Books.
Milnor, Kristina. 2014. *Graffiti and the Literary Landscape in Roman Pompeii*. Oxford: Oxford University Press.
North, Richard and Martin Worthington. 2012. 'Gilgamesh and Beowulf: Foundations of a Comparison.' *KASKAL*, 9: 177–217.
Sonik, Karen. 2012. 'Breaching the Boundaries of Being: Metamorphoses in the Mesopotamian Literary Texts.' *Journal of the American Oriental Society*, 132: 385–93.
van de Mieroop, Marc. 1999. *The Ancient Mesopotamian City*. Oxford: Oxford University Press.
Wiedemann, Felix. 2020. 'Migration and Narration: How European Historians in the Nineteenth and Early Twentieth Centuries Told the History of Human Mass Migrations or Völkerwandlungen.' *History and Theory*, 50: 42–60.
Wiggermann, Frans A. M. 2008. 'A Babylonian Scholar in Assur.' In *Studies in Ancient Near Eastern World View and Society Presented to Marten Stol*, edited by Robartus J. van der Spek, 203-34. Bethesda: CDL Press.
Worthington, Martin. 2010. 'Schankwirt(in).' In *Reallexikon der Assyriologie*, vol. XII, edited by Michael P. Streck, 132–34. Berlin: De Gruyter.
Ziolkowski, Theodore. 2012. *Gilgamesh Among Us: Modern Encounters with the Ancient Epic*. Ithaca: Cornell University Press.

CHAPTER 14

Migration and Ancient Indian Theatre

H. S. Shivaprakash and J. Sreenivasa Murthy

INTRODUCTION

As explicated in ancient texts, pre-modern Indian understanding of what constitutes 'theatre' is dynamic. Its conceptual appearance and evolution has coincided with periods of upheaval, generated in social-political milieus replete with the movements and migrations of people and groups resulting from natural calamities like floods and famines, man-made disasters like wars and conflicts, and/or in response to new developments like the rise and fall of monarchies and dynasties as well as the rise of towns and cities. In this respect, migration has been one of the most important shaping influences on Indian theatre from ancient times to the present. Sanskrit theatre—together with dramaturgical texts and evolutions of traditions concerning style, language, and performance modes—presents itself as a valid historical entry point to understanding the migrations of people across geographical, cultural, and linguistic domains. This chapter will focus on changes in cultural-theatrical practices as well as artistic expression in relation to the migratory movements of theatre styles and artists in ancient India. Specifically, this chapter examines the evolution in linguistic approaches, *shailīs* (styles), physical descriptors, and musical and dance traditions that became integral parts of theatrical development in ancient India. Beginning with a cultural overview of ancient Indian theatre, this chapter will explore the patterns of migrations, as well as their causes and

H. S. Shivaprakash (✉)
Jawaharlal Nehru University (JNU), New Delhi, India

J. S. Murthy
Mahabhodi Society, Bangalore, India

effects, as evidenced in Sanskrit dramaturgy, examining the elements of texts, languages, styles, and people across classical, regional, written, and oral performance traditions.

The Nature and Context of Sanskrit Drama

Pre-modern Indian society was characterized by caste-hierarchy, which involved exogamous social groups. Despite this, drama and theatre were spaces of convergence of disparate caste groups. Sanskrit theatre, which is considered the chief glory of the ancient period, provides a special fictional space in which 'migrations' from one caste to another were envisioned.

In Sanskrit drama, the protagonist is mostly a *Kshatriya* (the warrior class) or in some cases *Vaiśya* (the merchant class), who constitute the top rungs of the caste pyramid. The *śūdras* (the worker class) performed the dance forms. The *Vidūṣaka* (the jester) was a Brahmin, or someone from the priestly class. In some cases, lower-caste characters were explicitly portrayed. For instance, the character Vasantasenā—the female protagonist of the play *Mrichchakatikam* (The Clay Cart) by *Śūdraka*—is a prostitute. There are plays with dramatic situations in which a character is elevated from a low caste to a higher caste in a dramatic plot, a form of social mobility that arises from cross-caste collaboration; for instance, *The Clay Cart* concludes with Vasantasenā (a courtesan) marrying Chārudatta (the merchant protagonist). A courtesan is thus 'upgraded' to be the legal spouse of a man from a higher caste. On the contrary, in the play *Avimārakam* by Bhāsa, the Kshatriya protagonist becomes an untouchable because of a curse. In spite of this, his love affair with the Kshatriya princess goes on. When the curse is lifted, he takes the princess in marriage (see Varadpande 2005, 68).

The *Nāṭyaśāstra* (*NŚ*), the oldest available text on drama and theatre in ancient India (dated variously between 500 BCE and 500 CE), is ascribed to Bharata, who is not an author but a compiler. Bharata is a common noun referring to an itinerant group of actors. In the absence of a singular historiographical text of Indian theatre, it is not unreasonable to assume that the *NŚ* evolved out of a compilation of various linguistic, cultural, musical, and other traditions that originated in different regions and then migrated to other parts of the Indian subcontinent. Although the following will focus primarily on NŚ, the exact nature of ancient Indian drama cannot be fully understood unless we recognize movements and counter-movements of various regional and inter-regional modes of performing traditions. The narratives in Sanskrit drama are normally taken from inter-regionally shared narratives like the *Rāmāyana*, *Mahābhārata*, and *Brühatkathā* in the classical and non-classical traditions. The dramaturgical text indicates the members of different professions and sub-castes coming together in enacting a play. And *Nāṭya* itself, which is Bharata's concept of the composite art of theatre, understands the resulting art as arising from the convergence of many arts and artisans.

The NŚ, holding a similar position in the Indian dramatic tradition as Aristotle's *Poetics* does in the Western tradition, is a manual and multifaceted reference book containing theatrical practices of the period, and it offers readers a mythological narrative about the emergence of theatre. Perhaps reflecting the itinerant experiences of Bharata, theatre itself is conceived of in the NŚ as a 'migratory' art form that travels from the sphere of the gods to the human world. In the first place, theatre is framed as a moral apparatus that is provided to humans as a divine gift from the gods, who also guide theatre's formal development as different gods contribute to the new dramatic forms and theatrical structures. The NŚ mentions that *Nātya* (total theatre) arose in response to increasing ills and evils in the world. To re-establish the good and help mankind to follow *dharma* (the path of virtue) and desist from evil, the creator-god Brahma taught the art of theatre to Bharata and his children. Later, the great god Shiva watched a theatrical piece consisting of action and narration; to make the art more pleasant, he added music and dance to it. In the very first staging of a mythical drama to an audience of gods and demons, the demons were irritated by the unfair treatment meted out to them in the play and rebelled against the gods and caused disturbance during the enactment. Brahma placated them, saying that it was all a show. Brahma later devised a series of purifying rites and rituals to protect the acting area from further trouble. When Bharata staged the amended play before Lord Shiva, Shiva suggested that the play be prefixed with *pūrvāranga*—a series of preludes consisting of rituals of sanctifying the acting area, propitiating the local deities, and opening benedictory verses authored by the playwright. This is further followed by the introduction of the theme through a song written by the playwright or improvised by the actors and enacted through *nritta* (the pure dance to be explained later).

This mythical account of the descent of drama from the realm of gods to the human world suggests a milieu of discord between different classes of being. In Indian cosmology, there is a recognition of different classes of beings *viz asuras* (demons), *devas* (divine beings), *manushya* (humans), *gandharvas* (celestial musicians), and so on: a classification based on inherent qualities that can be seen across the spectrum of human nature in the phenomenal world. Theatre, in this conceptual respect, is a process and a product of migration. At the ideational level, the gods create things and so they create the arts, and both theatre and art are picked up by the sages and given to mortals who use it as an offering to the gods. Thus, the cycle is completed.

The mythological origins of *Nātya* (i.e., theatre) as a form emerging from cosmological migration is mirrored in ancient textual narratives regarding dance. Brahma created drama and taught Bharata who in turn taught the gods and mortals the art of theatre called *Nātya*. This is the first part of the mythography in the *Nātyaśāastra*. Similarly, parents of the universe Śiva and Pārvati created the terrible and the beautiful dances called *Tāndava* and *Lāsya*, which mark the dismantling and recreation movements. When Bharata showed the Drama that was created to Śiva, he suggested the inclusion of *pūrvāranga* (preparing the stage) abounding in *nritta* (pure dance), and it came into the world through his follower *Nandikeshvara*. The Apsarās (water nymphs) are the promoters of *Nātya*, and Urvashi taught to the mortals in the king Pururavā's court. This narrative, covered in the last chapter of *NŚ*, establishes dance as a similarly migratory form that is disseminated from the gods to the court.

Brahma fashioned drama by borrowing from all the four sacred *Vedas* (sacred books of ancient Indians) and other systems of knowledge. Shiva added to these two forms of dance—*lāsya* (elegant) and *tāndava* (vigorous). Though born amidst distress and discord, it was an art of synthesis depicting *trilokya* (all three worlds): the world above, the demonic below, and the human in between. It was meant for all classes of being, unlike earlier sacred knowledge texts meant for only higher classes. Explicating the nature of *Nātya* to gods and demons, Brahma explains, '[t]his art is not just the expression of you people (gods and demons) alone, but the sympathetic exposition of the goings-on in all the three worlds' (Ch. 1, 117–119).

Though ancient Indian drama was also born out of a world of strife, like Greek theatre, it did not foreground conflict but emphasized reconciliation between the worlds. Unlike Greek theatre—which emphasizes the unities of time, place, and action—the events of Sanskrit drama are spread over not only different times and places but also move to-and-fro between the three worlds, reflecting Sanskrit theatre's interest in migration itself as both dramatic content and form. For instance, in the last chapter of *NŚ*, Bharata's children, who were the vehicles of drama, later became so arrogant that they started ridiculing the sages. The angered sages cursed and relegated them to the lower class of *śūdras*, barring them and their art form access to divine realms. However, the curse was later mitigated at the request of Nahusha, the noble king. The progeny of Bharata came down to earth with their women. Drama continued to flourish again as their numbers proliferated. Thus, traversing and depicting all the worlds fraught with conflicts and relieved by truces and compromises, *Nātya* was an art and space for rest in a restless world and reconciliation amidst conflicts. Consider also the case of famous female protagonists like Sītā, Śakuntalā, and Urvashi, each of whom are of divine or semi-divine origins. The protagonists of Sanskrit drama like Dushyanta in *Śākuntalam* and Urvashi in *Vikramōrvaśīyam* (Vikrama and Urvashi) traverse between the three worlds. In *Shakuntalā*, the final reconciliation of the male and female protagonists Dushyanta and Śakuntalā happens in the sacred groves of the sage Kaśyapa, located at the meeting point of the earth and the sky.

Thus, when it comes to one possible connection of migration and theatre, we argue that while there was a great emphasis on harmony and reconciliation in Sanskrit drama, its action was set in the restless movement of people from place-to-place and up-and-down the ladder of social hierarchy, and in different stages of socio-political evolution from the tribal to urban society. All of this impacted and shaped the course of the evolution of drama and theatre in the ancient period.

Drama: Site of Convergence and Divergence of Styles and Contents

A close look at the evolutions and amalgamations of various dramatic styles and techniques offers an understanding of the possible patterns of migrations in the ancient period. The emergence of the composite art of *Nātya* was preceded by two critical stages, which are still seen in the surviving forms of acting and enactment. The most primeval form of enactment in the parlance of NŚ is called *nritta* (pure dance). The tribal and folk dances like *Dollina Kunita* (drum dance) of Karnataka, *Bihu* (harvest dance) of Assam, *Thābal Chongba* (moonlight dance) of Manipur are all examples of *nritta*. Nritta as a dramatic form upholds the distinctiveness of dance forms across the geographical and linguistic terrains covering the southern peninsula to the north-eastern hills of the Indian subcontinent. These dance forms have survived the onslaughts of invasions, colonization, and modernity to uphold dramatic traditions from the ancient times, and they have evolved both out of folk/tribal traditions and intercultural influences. For instance, similarities can be seen in dance forms across northeast India with cultural contexts ranging across to China, Mongolia, and parts of South-East Asia. Between Sanskrit, Tibetan, and Mongolian, translations, interpretations and cross-cultural adaptations are evident in lived cultural traditions and rituals, especially in masked dances, *jātrās* (processions), and other rituals of birth and death.

The next stage brings in the *nritya* that involves the enactment of a narrative—for example, *Lai Haraoba* of Manipur, which is the enactment through song and dance of the cosmogonic myth of the Meitei tribe. These are dance dramas that involve an elaborate narrative and its performance. It is a kind of *nritta* and due to its narrative feature, it is seen as a *nātya*-enactment of drama through dance and music. *Nātya*, whose target audience is the city dweller (*nāgarika*), is more of an enactment centred on towns and cities (*nagara*). Thus, the migration and transmutation of the tribal and rural into the urban form of enactment is referred to as *nātya*, which involves the communication, not only of a storyline but also of archetypal aesthetic emotions, *rasa*. The *nritta* and *nritya* make for stylization in a drama called *nātyadharmī* as against the realistic expressions following the ways of day-to-day life known as *lokadharmī*. The stylization and recontextualization of narrative to urban domains of performance (*nātya*) involves the movement of people from rural and forest habitats to urban centres leading to a theatrical vocabulary necessarily involving multicultural traits and features. The progressive transformation of *nritta* into *nritya* and later into *nātya* reveals a process of movement from folk/tribal milieu to the urban context. We can illustrate this pattern called *dandi* in North and *kolata* in South India. This rural *nritta* form was embedded in a *nritya*, which, in turn, is a part of an urban classical play *Panchrātra* (Five nights) by Bhāsa.

The movement of tribal and folk enactments into the urban areas is not unilateral. The standardized urban genres travelled back to rural areas with a margin of adaptation and popularization. This kind of to-and-fro movement is still found in Indian dance and theatre to this day. As examples of how the regional and non-classical elements are absorbed into the classical theatre, we can mention *Brūhatkathā*, a compilation of hundreds of folktales emanating from a tribal community called Vidyadharas in the Vindya region around the ancient city of Ujjain. One of the famous stories of this compilation is that of Udayana, the king of Vatsa country, who elopes with Vasavadatta, the princess of Avanti. This story of love and war was so widely popular that the great classical poet Kālidāsa refers to it in his poetic work *Meghadūtam*: '[y]ou will reach the land of Avanti where you will be treated to the tales of Udayana by the village elders well-versed in it' (*Meghadūtam* 32). The same regional story of Udayana had already travelled back before Kālidāsa into the two famous classical plays by Bhāsa about Udayana, *Pratijna Yougandharayana* (The Vow of Yougabdharayans), and *Svapna-Vasavadattam* (Dream of Vasavadatta). The same story was to become the theme of two classical plays *Ratnāvali* and *Priyadarśikā* by Shri Harsha (2000, 2004).

Similar movements from the regional into the trans-regional are found in several other plays. A folk ritual of *dohada* by virtue of which a virgin kicks a barren tree into full flowering, becomes a crucial part of the action in Kālidasa's *Mālavikāgnimitram* (Malavika and Agnimitra). Regional theatre texts and practices became naturally trans-regional with translations, adaptations, and recreations across linguistic and literary traditions. The great enactment poem of Sanskrit *Gita Govindam* (The Song of the Cowherd Lord) by Jayadeva (circa 11 century CE) became so famous in all the regions of the subcontinent that it was adapted for enactments in various regional forms of dance and drama for several centuries—Sourastra in the west, Kerala and Andhra Pradesh in the South, Mathura in the North, and Manipur in the Northeast. Often in these adaptations, folk performance elements combine with stylized urban elements or classical texts and are recreated in folk performance vocabulary, as can be seen with the Mahabharata narrative and the Pandavani performance in north India.

The *mārga* (classical/trans-regional) and *desī* (folk/regional) are not to be understood as hierarchical but in a lateral spectrum that highlights differences and distinctions not evaluations. These descriptive categories pertain to dance (*nritta* and *nritya*) as well as drama (*nātya*) and highlight inter-regional movements and exchanges in performative art forms. In the Sanskrit play *Venīsamhāra* (The Killer Braid) by Bhatta Nārāyana (circa 800 CE), a ferocious form of tribal dance is introduced during the prelude to the entry of the protagonist of Bhima. The same dance is also included in the denouement of the play where the protagonist takes revenge on the villain. Having thus become a component of a classical play, this dance travelled back to the folk theatrical form Yakshagana in the far-off coastal region of the south after almost nearly 900 years. In the Yakshagāna play based on the same theme, the protagonist Bhima is given the costumes of the demonic tribals and made to perform the same dance.

Theatre of Itinerant Artists: Forms and Conditions of Migration

The theatre of the ancient period was subject to divergence caused by calamities like flood, famine, war, and other man-made calamities. Such developments caused the actors to travel from region to region along with specialized forms of enactments. The itinerant theatre artists of ancient Indian theatre were semi-nomadic tribal actors known by diverse names such as *Kuśīlava*, *ŚhakāŚhailūṣ*, and *Bharata*. These were the best-known performing groups in the northern part of the Indian subcontinent, where Indo-Aryan languages and dialects were spoken. The ancient epic of the *Rāmāyana* was supposed to have been sung with gestures by Kusha and Lava in the court of Rama and in the penance groves and on the streets. In the southern part of India during the Sangam Age (circa 200 CE), the performers of oral poetry called *Pāṇars* went from court to court to sing and narrate the exploits of Tamil kings. The migration of performing communities and theatrical forms did not end after 700 CE, the date which Indian historians consensually agree as the end of the ancient period. Even today, some of the performing groups from ancient and medieval times are still extant. They are semi-nomadic like the *Bhawāi* performers of Gujarat and *bahuroopiās* from different regions of the subcontinent.

In *Shilappadikaram* (The Anklet Story), the most ancient Tamil dramatic poem ascribed to Ilango Addigal, cowherd actors put on a pastoral dance on the theme of Krishna's love for cowherd girls. They were members of a pastoral community that had migrated to Madurai of South India from the banks of the river Yamuna in North India. They had travelled all the way to the far-off city looking for a better livelihood. In the same text, the dance of the courtesan Mādhavi is described elaborately. It begins with the setting up of the flag of Indra (king of gods) in the dance space. In *Nātyaśāstra (NŚ)*, this commemorates the vanquishing of demons that disturbed the first performance. This is a convention that is in keeping with *NŚ*, which had obviously travelled from North to South. The sophisticated dance of Mādhavi comes from the predominantly *mārga* (classical) stream of enactment. In contrast, the dance of the cowherd is an example of the regional migration of a *desī* (non-classical) form of enactment. These textual traditions are distinctive in their blending of classical and folk elements and serve as repositories of artistic narratives which evolved as they migrated from one region to another. The dance of Madhavi is created according to the conventions of the *NŚ*, compiled in the far-off northern parts of India, whereas the dance of the cowherd is derived from folk performance traditions from the banks of the Yamuna from where the performing pastoral tribes had migrated to the prosperous city of Madurai for their livelihood.

The Anklet Story also narrates another form of ritualistic dance by a tribal dancer who belongs to a nomadic tribe that lives on attacking and robbing wealth from wayfarers. The wealth so earned was offered to their goddess *Kotravvai* (a fierce tribal deity considered to be the prototype of goddess *Durgā* of the later Hindu pantheon). These examples from the most ancient

Dravidian epic illustrate that different migratory modes were factored into different kinds of theatre at different stages of evolution from *desī* to *mārga*.

Limitations were sometimes imposed on the migrating troupes of actors. The ancient Indian classic on statecraft *Arthaśāstra* prescribed that the actors belonging to the semi-nomadic tribe could perform only during lean seasons so as not to interfere with agricultural processes (*Arthaśāstra* 2.19). Before they travelled outside their own provinces, they had to obtain due permission from *Antapala Durga* (the Border Security Office). In Kālidāsa's first play *Malavika and Agnimitra*, the female protagonist Mālavikā had to get such permission. She was sent to the queen Dharini by the latter's half-brother from a low-caste wife of Dharini's father.

The entire troupe of actors was a loose-knit family also consisting of prostitutes and their offspring. The social status of these female performers made them outcasts and subject to different types of migration. The *sūtradhāra* (stage manager) of ancient drama who sets the action going was the head of such a family. This is the reason why he is the first to appear on the stage. The actress whom he calls upon the stage addresses *sūtradhāra* as *Āryaputra* (husband). Other artistes of the troupe were called *Bhavuka* (brother-in-law)—a common address heard in the brothel of those days. Artisans, particularly actors, were often joined by those exiled from the community and the offspring of inter-caste marriages in a lower caste. This is reflected in actors being dubbed as outcastes in the *Arthaśāstra* (I: 13). It assigns the task of artists and actors to *śūdras*, who are enjoined to learn these arts. According to the *Baudhāyana Dharmasūtra*, another book on ethical codes, 'A Brahmin who gives up Brahmanical obligations shall be made a śūudra; and Brahmin who takes to work like cattle rearing, artisanship, acting, etc. is a *śūdra*' (*Baudhāyana Dharmasūtra* II. 4: 7-15, I 5.10.24). Vidūṣaka, the Brahmin jester in Sanskrit, exemplifies such caste demotion by describing himself as a snail among cobras. Moreover, the people who were excommunicated for their sexual and other crimes would end up joining a troupe of itinerant actors. The last chapter of NŚ tells a story of the ex-communication of actors who are later absorbed back into the community—a case of cyclical movement, and an important dimension of different kinds of migration related to ancient Indian theatre.

Migration of People, Theatre, and Texts

The significance of migration in ancient India not only pertains to and involves the migration of performers. The migration of communities and specific sections of the communities like the merchants also significantly impacted the annals of ancient theatres. The kind of composite theatre described in NŚ is conditional upon the emergence of urban culture. The spectator in NŚ is known as *Nāgarika*, meaning a city dweller. The rural people frequently migrated to cities in search of jobs and merchandise. The rural rich would go to cities seeking entertainment. In rural and urban areas, merchants (called *sārtha*) were the significant theatre patrons. Always on the move, they would give a fillip to the migration of the artists and genres of theatre.

Similarly, an even more comprehensive picture of ancient theatre can be obtained by extending the idea of migration to the manifold and cyclic divergence and convergence of texts, theories, narratives, and styles of performances. There was constant movement between the dominant and subordinate, the *mārga* (classical, inter-regional) and *desi* (folk, regional, non-classical), as well as the oral and the written traditions. The Sanskrit plays contain written dialogue with stylized movements. The regional folk performances have a tradition of stylized acting but no written script. But there are to-and-fro influences as well. The actor who improvises extempore in a folk play has a wide knowledge of the relevant texts not necessarily by reading but through oral transmission since there was a tradition of oral recitals of the classics. Therefore, in many Sanskrit plays, we find a combination of classical elements along with folk elements contextual to regions. The movement of performative texts clearly indicates the inter-regional and inter-cultural migrations of people who bring stylizations and influences with them.

Convergence of the Regional and the Trans-Regional

By the time *Nātyaśāstra* (*NŚ*) was written or conceived, the theatre practices from different geographical regions had converged at the major cities and the Sanskrit dramas also clearly suggest a confluence of regional practices and dialects. The *NŚ* speaks of *vrittis and pravrittis*. *Vrittis* can be understood as dominant enactment modes while *pravrittis* are regional adaptations of such modes. *Vrittis* stand for a typology of acting styles based on general human behaviour modes and *are* of four kinds:

1. *ārabhati*—that has prominence for a strong physical movement
2. *Bhārati*—which is predominantly verbal.
3. *Sātvati*—that is abounding in psychological play with controlled physical movement.
4. *Kāiśhikī*—which is a happy blend of these three elements of acting.

The first three types represent acting that make up *natya* (physical, verbal, and emotional) and the fourth combines the previous three in proportion to the regional needs and requirements. Their combination results in *pravritti*, which are regional styles (*NŚ* xiv/xiii, 36–54). There are four kinds of *Pravrittis*, namely *Āvanti*, *Dākshinātya*, *Pānchali*, and *Odra-Magadhi*, each representing different regions of the subcontinent in the ancient period. This can be illustrated through the example of two regional varieties of *yakshagāna* a well-known and popular genre of traditional drama characteristic of the coastal area in the southern region of Karnataka. This form, though based on more or less the same principles of theme and stylized enactment, has two different presentation modes corresponding to the northern and southern parts of this area. The northern style emphasizes the component of the verbal acting (bhārati), whereas the southern style emphasizes the components of the physical acting (ārbhati). The permutations and combinations of *vrittis* to get the required regional mix called *pravritti* indicate how ancient Indian drama was trying to achieve a reconciliation of the regional *vrittis* and trans-regional *pravrittis*.

The director of a play was expected to synchronize the various conventions in diverse ways, depending on the *parishad*, the audience, the place, and time of enactment.

Such statements in the *Nātyaśāstra* (*NŚ*) are to be understood along with similar things mentioned in the chapters on *pūrvāranga* (Ch. V, 173). All four regional forms use the *pūrvāranga*, an introductory piece of benediction with ritual, music, songs, and dance. This is reminiscent of the drama's ritual role, which is practiced with a local touch.

The Movements and Migrations Between the Written and the Oral

In Sanskrit dramaturgy, one comes across elaborate denominations and descriptive elements of performance, especially those pertaining to the delivery of the spoken word. The written texts vis-a-vis the dramatic texts were open to improvisations and adaptations depending on the regional variations and styles. Some texts, like *Mrichhkatikam*, are already elaborate in the range of characters with different linguistic styles. The oral tradition of speech is therefore crucial to understanding how written dramatic texts were adapted on the stage and how the treatise of the *NŚ* reflects these elements. The written drama's prologue at the end of the *pūrvāranga* is a connecting point between the written drama and the performing tradition.

While the training for these performances was, in general, acting, applying it to a drama was specific to the performer for a specific audience. In the *Kūdiyāttam* tradition, the notes prepared for the performance of a play were called *āttaprakāram*. Like the region-based acting style, the use of regional prakrit also indicates the confluence of regions in Sanskrit drama. *NŚ* speaks of *tatsama*—common to Sanskrit and Prākrit—and *Tadbhava*, which mean derivatives of Sanskrit words and Desi, the non-Sanskrit words. Further, it also speaks of *atibhāshā* (for gods, abounding in Vedic usages), *āryabhāshā* (for royal persons and elite), different *jātibhāshā* (the language of different communities including *mlecchabhāshā* or foreign languages), and *anyatarēbhāshā* (in-between language) of the rural and tribal languages (XVII, 27–30). The last one includes sounds of birds and beasts that are to be communicated through stylization, *nātyadharmi* (31). Jāti bhāshā itself is made of Sanskrit and Prākrit (32). Women speak *Mahārāshtri*, but *Apasarās* (goddesses of water and clouds) may use Sanskrit. *Māgadhi, Āvanti, Prāchya, Shurāseni, Ardhāmāgadhi, Bāhlika* are the main *Prākrits* coming from respective regions.

Less-known dialects such as *Ābhīra, Chandala, Drāvida*, and *Odhra* are also mentioned. Of them, the first two are community languages and the other two are regional (45–61). The *chāndālī* is also for *pulkāsa* (53), which refers to a community called *domba* (acrobats). According to the early chronicler Abhinavagupta, these Dombas are acrobats and performers known for tricks, tightrope walking, and other athletic feats. The regional dialects are appropriated for different types of characters. These varieties can be seen in the extant Sanskrit plays. The producers may use *desabhāshās* (regional dialects) as they deem fit.

In drama, the literary flavour arises from different languages from different lands: *nānādeshāsamuttham hi kāvyam bhāvati nātake* (47). After a detailed list, Bharata says that what is not said here at all should be known from the world or people (*lokādgrāhyam*). Thus, it was open-ended and always capable of integrating everything into itself. In this way, we see how linguistic registers, variants, and styles were amalgamated in ancient Indian dramaturgy and theatre to highlight the inter-regional migrations of actors, musicians, and performers in general.

The sections on *pravritti* and language refer to *mlecchas* (a general term for foreigners) and *yavanas* (mostly referring to western countries in general and Greece in particular). Commenting on this, Abhinavagupta says *parvātakāccha* (Indo-Tibetan regions) and other *mlecchas* are to be avoided and hence not mentioned openly (Abhinavagupta on *NŚ* XIII, 41). It is to be noted in later parts of the same text, while mention is made of *pragjyotisha* and *kāmarūpa* (regions of the northeastern parts of the subcontinent and beyond, right up to Cambodia), Abhinava mentions *turúska* (Turkey), *āratta* (Arabia), *kakhāsa* (Caucasian regions), and others are included (XIII, 50). This demonstrates that the ancient Indian theatre was in dialogue not only with different prākrits (regional languages on the Indian subcontinent) but also with languages of other foreign lands (*mlecchas*).

Conclusion

The brief account given about ancient Indian drama reveals the dynamic nature of the drama and theatre of the period in a socio-political situation full of changes resulting from the rise and falls of kingdoms and the migrations of artists and people. There were other kinds of migration as well of styles of drama and theatre between tribal, rural, and urban contexts. There were also convergences and divergences resulting from the interface between regional and trans-regional forces. After the end of the ancient period, several new developments throughout the subcontinent were occasioned by the emergence of Bhakti (devotional) cultures and other sartorial schools of *yoga* and *tantra*.

All this altered the directions and dynamics of pan-Indian theatre. The period following the ancient times further saw the migration of Indian narratives and performances to different regions of South-East Asia, which is borne out by different versions of Rama-centric dance theatres throughout South-East Asia, as migrations of theatres within India and between India and the neighbouring South-East Asian regions continued for many centuries.

References

Bhasa. 1991. *Thirteen Plays of Bhasa*. Translated by A. C. Woolner and Lakshman Sarup. Delhi: Motilal Banarsidass Publishers.

Bhasa. 2005. *Svapna-Vasavadattam: The Dream of Vasavadatta*. Edited by S. Tiwari. Translated by A.C. Woolner. New Delhi: Global Classics.

Harsha. 2000. *Priyadarśikā*. Translated by G.K. Nariman and A. V. Williams Jackson. Cambridge: Parentheses Publications.

———. 2004. *Ratnāvali*. Translated by C. Sankara Rama Sastri and Ramji Thakur. New Delhi: Global Classics.

Kalidasa. 2006. *The Recognition of Shakúntala*. Translated by Somadeva Vasudeva. New York: New York University Press.

Nagar, R.S., ed. 2009. *Natyashastra with Commentary Abhinavabharathi by Abhinavaguptaacharya*. New Delhi: Parimal Publication.

Rajan, Chandra, ed. 1997. *The Complete Works of Kālidāsa: Volume One Poems*. New Delhi: Sahitya Academi.

Rangacharya, Adya. 2003 [1986]. *The Nātyaśāstra: English Translation with Critical Notes*. Bangalore: IBH Prakashana.

Tawney, C.H. 1875. *The Mālavikāgnimitram: A Sanskrit Play by Kalidasa*. Calcutta: Thacker, Spink & Co.

Varadpande, M.L. 2005. *History of Indian Theatre*. Delhi: Abhinav Publications.

CHAPTER 15

Fated Arrivals: Greek Tragedy and Migration

Rush Rehm

> Great is the wrath of Zeus, god of suppliants.
> Aeschylus, *Suppliant Women*

Although the migration of large groups of people does not appear in Greek tragedy, the acceptance of people on the move—strangers, asylum-seekers, exiles, refugees, outcasts, orphans, suppliants—plays a central role. No theatrical genre has treated that subject more frequently and with greater complexity than Greek tragedy.

Under the protection of the gods (at least in principle), travellers, wanderers, strangers, and suppliants in ancient Greece merited *philoxenia*, love/friendship for guests/strangers (the opposite of our xenophobia). In Hesiod's *Works and Days* (324–27), 'the gods blot out ... whoever does wrong to a suppliant or a guest'. Hospitality offered or denied provides the major theme of Homer's *Odyssey*, as the incognito Odysseus makes his way home after the Trojan War. On Ithaca, Odysseus first claims to be a shipwrecked foreigner who went to sea as an economic migrant: 'Nothing is worse than wandering for mortals; / but because of their cursed bellies men endure evil woes, / when wandering and suffering and pain come upon them' (*Odyssey* 15:343–45). The swineherd Eumaeus offers him food, clothing, and shelter, for he himself had been captured and sold into slavery as a young boy: 'It is not right to mistreat a stranger / .... For every beggar / and wanderer comes from Zeus' (*Odyssey* 14.56–58). We might compare the passage in *Hebrews* (xiii, 20), some 700

R. Rehm (✉)
Stanford University, Stanford, CA, USA
e-mail: mrehm@stanford.edu

© The Author(s), under exclusive license to Springer Nature Switzerland AG 2023
Y. Meerzon, S. E. Wilmer (eds.), *The Palgrave Handbook of Theatre and Migration*, https://doi.org/10.1007/978-3-031-20196-7_15

years after Homer: 'Be not forgetful to entertain strangers: for thereby some have entertained angels unawares.'

The treacherous nature of ancient travel encouraged *philoxenia*. Unexpected arrivals invoke the idea of reciprocity, for one day the host might find himself in similar straits, needing food and shelter. The origin of many tragic myths involves the arrival of a foreigner, who overcomes deadly challenges to establish a dynastic line. Tantalus from Asia Minor settles in the Peloponnese; his son Pelops has two sons, Atreus and Thyestes, and their children—Agamemnon, Menelaus, Aegisthus—play important roles in Aeschylus' *Oresteia*, Sophocles' *Electra* and *Ajax*, and Euripides' *Electra*, *Orestes*, *Iphigenia in Aulis*, and *Helen*. The mythical founder of Thebes, Cadmus, originally came from Phoenicia (now Lebanon) or Egypt; his grandson Pentheus suffers a terrible fate in Euripides' *Bacchae*, when he fails to welcome 'the Stranger' (the god Dionysus in disguise) along with his Asian followers.

Tragedy emerged as a hybrid performance genre in Athens at roughly the same time (508/7 BC) that the city adopted the radical political system called *demokratia* (*demos* + *kratos*, people power). Performed each year at the festival of the City Dionysia, Greek tragedies used the mythic past to explore the tensions in democratic Athens. The city fostered citizen equality, while exploiting non-citizen slaves;[1] it opened its doors to innovation and outside influences while exercising imperial control over other Greek cities; Athens celebrated civic loyalty and service while producing some outrageously self-serving leaders. Important to its self-image, the city took pride in helping refugees, asylum-seekers, and suppliants, and the subject finds its way into the many Greek tragedies.

Oedipus of Thebes provides the tragic paradigm for the fate of the homeless refugee. Aeschylus, Sophocles, and Euripides all wrote tragedies based on the story, but only those of Sophocles survive. In *Oedipus Tyrannus*, a prophecy warned Laius and Jocasta that their new-born son would grow up to kill his father, so they expose the infant Oedipus on Mt. Kithairon. The shepherd assigned the task takes pity and gives the helpless child to a fellow herdsman from Corinth, as they move their flocks up to mountain pastures in the summer. Known as transhumance, this migration for animal grazing ignores political borders, just as the two shepherds forget blood ties and kinship when they rescue the baby.

Given to the childless king and queen of Corinth, who rear him as their own son, Oedipus comes to question his parentage. Learning from the Delphic oracle that he will kill his father and father children with his own mother,

---

[1] Slavery in the fifth-century BC Greek world usually involved war captives, both Greeks and 'barbarians' (the onomatopoetic word for non-Greek speakers whose speech sounded like 'bar-bar' to the Greeks). Domestic slaves (part of the *oikos*, 'household', 'family') appear frequently in tragedy: male tutors, manservants, bodyguards, maidservants, nurses and wet nurses. We never meet industrial slaves, like those who worked in the deadly silver mines in Attica. At the City Dionysia, a pre-performance proclamation named the year's manumitted slaves, making the audience witnesses to their new status.

Oedipus flees from Corinth. On the road an arrogant traveller attacks him with an animal goad, and the enraged Oedipus slays him. Arriving at Thebes, Oedipus solves the Sphinx's riddle and becomes king by marrying Laius' widow, Jocasta. Years later, Thebes suffers a devastating plague caused by the unsolved murderer of Laius. In his effort to find the killer and save the city, Oedipus uncovers the truth about himself. Choosing a punishment that fits his failure to see what was in front of him, Oedipus blinds himself. A political exile and social pariah, he wanders the wilds of Mount Kithairon, where he was saved as an infant.

Sophocles returns to the story in *Oedipus at Colonus*, posthumously produced at the City Dionysia in 403 BC. Led by his daughter Antigone, Oedipus—blind, and stateless—arrives at the grove of the Furies in Colonus, near Athens. The Athenian leader Theseus grants the old man's request for asylum:

> I myself was reared in exile, just
> like yourself, and I had to fight for my life
> in foreign lands, more than any man—
> so, I would never turn away a stranger
> like yourself, refusing to help him to safety.
> I well know that I am a human, and tomorrow
> my lot could be no better than yours.
> (*Oedipus at Colonus* 562–68)

In a typical Sophoclean twist, Oedipus reveals a prophecy that the city that holds his buried body will prosper in the future. The accursed exile now finds himself pursued by the Theban ruler Kreon, who wants to bring him back to the city that drove him out. A war ensues between Athens and Thebes, and Theseus' army prevails. With Oedipus' final resting place secure, his body will mingle with the soil of Colonus, where Sophocles himself was born, only two and a half miles from the theatre of Dionysus. One would be hard pressed to find a more compelling fated arrival, one that bestows mysterious benefits for the city that accepts a once-abhorred refugee.

In ancient Greece, a ritualized version of mutual hospitality called *xenia* (guest-friendship) could bind together landed families, where past hospitality entailed reciprocity in the future. We see *xenia* at work in several tragedies, most importantly in Euripides' *Alcestis*. When Heracles arrives unexpectedly, the Thessalian king Admetus welcomes his friend, but does not confide that he is in mourning for the death of his wife Alcestis. Discovering the truth, Heracles wins the dead woman back from underworld and restores her to her husband. In *Alcestis*, *xenia* takes precedence over marital grief, and it results in a fairy-tale-like triumph over death

The violation of *xenia* lies at the heart of the most famous Greek myth, that of the Trojan War. When visiting the Spartan ruler Menelaus, the Trojan prince Paris steals (or seduces) Menelaus' wife Helen and takes her back to Troy.

Paris' transgression angers the gods as well as the Greeks, as the Chorus in Aeschylus' *Agamemnon* make clear:

> I trust and fear in Zeus,
> the god of guests and hosts [*xenion*]
> ...
> Paris suffered as Zeus ordained.
> Who says the gods do not care
> if we trample untouchable things?
> (*Agamemnon* 362–63, 370–72)

The guarantor of the guest-host relationship, Zeus punishes Paris and his city for violating the norms of hospitality, culminating in the Greeks' destruction of Troy.

Xenia plays a role in the story of exiles as well as guests. Aeschylus' *Oresteia* and Sophocles' *Electra* tell the story of Orestes, exiled from Argos by Aegisthus and Clytemnestra, the murderers of his father. Orestes finds asylum with his father's guest-friend Strophius, king of Phocis (near Delphi), who raises the orphan with his own son. Orestes eventually returns home, murders the usurpers, and regains his patrimony and rule in Argos. Euripides offers a less triumphant account in his *Electra*. After returning from exile and taking vengeance on Aegisthus and Clytemnestra, Orestes faces permanent banishment from Argos as a matricide. His sister Electra also must abandon her home, leaving for Phocis as the bride of Pylades. The two siblings bitterly mourn what lies ahead, cut off from each other and from their native city. In a society that prized kinship, shared ritual, and civic attachment, exile seems the cruellest of punishments. We find this confirmed in the fatal decision of Socrates, described in Plato's *Phaedo*. Condemned to death if he remains in Athens, the philosopher Socrates prefers suicide to leaving the city of his birth.

Exiles appear time and again in Greek tragedy, and sometimes—as in *Oedipus at Colonus*—those who have driven them off later try to secure the exile's return. In Sophocles' *Philoctetes*, the Greeks sailing for Troy maroon the warrior on a deserted island, because of the gangrenous stench of his wounded leg. Abandoned by his comrades and in extraordinary pain, Philoctetes survives nine miserable years on Lemnos. When the Greeks discover they cannot win the war without him, they send Odysseus and Neoptolemus back to the island to force him to re-join the campaign. *Philoctetes* exposes the callousness of the Greek leaders who exploit a lonely man deprived of human community, even as it questions the validity of the war that will deliver Philoctetes from his infirmity.

The title character of Euripides' *Medea* suffers a double exile. Helping Jason steal the golden fleece, Medea abandons her native town of Colchis on the Black Sea and flees with him to Greece. After living as Medea's husband for some years in Corinth, Jason discards her so he can marry into the royal family. Fearing Medea's potential revenge, Kreon, the king of Corinth, banishes her from the city. The fortuitous arrival of the Athenian ruler Aegeus prompts

Medea to beg him for asylum, and Aegeus promises her a safe haven in his city. After killing Jason's fiancée and her father Kreon, Medea slays her two young sons to get back at their father. She departs for Athens, borne aloft in a chariot of the sun-god Helios, her divine grandfather.

In the play's 'Ode to Athens', the Chorus warn against accepting a child-killing foreigner into the city. The women praise Athens for its beauty, civility, and love of the arts, but in an abrupt shift, they express that Athens would welcome this exiled murderess. Other tragedies (including Euripides' lost *Aegeus*) tell how Medea later turned against the city that gave her asylum, trying to kill Aegeus' young son Theseus. He survives to perform labours like those of Heracles, until he himself becomes the legendary king of Athens.

In Euripides' *Heracles*, the fates of these two heroes intertwine. After rescuing Theseus from the underworld, Heracles reaches his adopted home in Thebes just in time to save his family from the vicious tyrant Lycus. In an act of divine cruelty, the goddess Hera drives Heracles mad, and he mistakenly murders the wife and children he has just saved. Returning to his senses, Heracles rejects the gods who could act so cruelly, and he contemplates suicide. Theseus arrives and persuades his friend to accept asylum in Athens. Unlike Medea, Heracles spills kindred blood through no fault of his own, and—like Oedipus at his death in Sophocles' play—his living presence delivers great benefit to the city that took him in (Fig. 15.1).

Theseus appears as the protagonist in Euripides' *Suppliant Women*, a tragedy that explores the duty of democratic Athens to honour suppliants and guarantee rituals owed to the dead. The mothers of the Argive 'Seven Against Thebes' seek Athens' help to recover their sons' bodies, denied burial by the Theban ruler Kreon. The suppliant women appeal to Aethra, the mother of Theseus, and she urges her son to take up the women's cause. When the Thebans refuse to return the Argive bodies, Theseus leads the Athenian army to secure their burial. Although victorious, Theseus refuses to sack the city, intent only on restoring the Argive dead so that their mothers and orphaned sons can perform funeral rites. In Euripides' play, Theseus and Athens defend the panhellenic norm that the dead—whether ally, enemy, or stranger— deserve burial:

> Let the dead by buried in the earth,
> and let each element return from whence it came
> into the light of day—the spirit to the upper air
> and the body to the earth. We do not possess
> our bodies forever; we live our lives in them,
> and then the earth that nourished us takes them back.
> (*Suppliant Women* 531–36)

Theseus understands that no one is an exile from death, that the earth takes everyone in the end, no matter who they are, where they came from, or what they have done.

Fig. 15.1 Suppliant women, with hands outstretched, seek help from Athens; from Euripides' *Suppliant Women*, Stanford Repertory Theater, 1993, directed by Rush Rehm. Photo: John B. Wilson

Foreigners who took up long-term residence in Athens became metics (from *meta + oikos*, after-dwelling or changed dwelling), somewhat like resident aliens today. Metics came from both within and beyond the Greek-speaking world, and the category also included slaves freed by their Athenian masters. Although denied citizen status, required to register with an Athenian patron, and subject to special taxes and regulations, Athenian metics could amass great wealth and influence. Aspasia, the partner of the Athenian general Pericles, was a foreign-born metic, as was their son, Pericles the Younger. The historian Herodotus, the sophist Protagoras, the orator Lysias, and the philosopher Aristotle were all metics in Athens.

Non-citizen residents played a particularly significant role in Athenian theatrical life. An *aulêtês* (player of the *aulos*, something like a clarinet) accompanied the choral lyric, and almost all these musicians were not born in Athens but were metics or slaves. Only 3 per cent of ancient Greek tragedies survive in full, but we know the titles of many more, and some of the authors were not from Athens: Pratinas from Phlius, Ion of Chios, Achaeus of Eretria, Neophron of Sikyon, Theodectes of Phaselis, and Aristarchus of Tegea. We also know of non-Athenian prize-winning actors: Mynniskos of Chalkis (who acted for Aeschylus), Neoptolemus of Scyros, Aristodemus of Metapontum (on the Black Sea), and Polus of Aegina (perhaps the first method actor, who used an urn with his own son's ashes for the mourning scene in Sophocles' *Electra*). Given the long rehearsal periods for the City Dionysia, we can assume that these foreign-born playwrights and actors were Athenian metics.

We find many references to metics in tragedy. The funeral oration in Euripides' *Suppliant Women* includes the following passage: 'As befits all foreign inhabitants [*metoikountas xenous*], / Parthenopaeus caused no trouble or envy, nor incited / discord with his language, the worst quality in both / foreigner and citizen' (*Supp.* 892–95). In Euripides' lost *Erechtheus* (fr. 360, 11–13), Praxithea conveys the difficulty of adapting to a new home: 'Whoever settles in one city from another, / resembles a peg fitted badly in a piece of wood—/ a citizen in name, but not in fact'. Tragic characters also use 'metic' metaphorically, to suggest profound existential displacement. Exiled at the end of Euripides' *Bacchae*, Cadmus laments that he must 'go among foreigners, / an aging metic [*metoikos*]' (*Ba.* 1354–55). Sentenced to a living death, Sophocles' Antigone describes herself as a 'metic [*metoikos*], / neither a mortal nor a shade / among the shades … / …/ a metic [*metoikos*], accursed / and unmarried' (*Ant.* 850–52, 867–68).

On a brighter note, at the end of Aeschylus' *Eumenides*, Athena offers the Furies permanent residence in Athens (*metoikois*, *Eum.* 1010), promising them sacrifice at marriage and childbirth. The Furies embrace their new home, encouraging all Athenians to 'show reverence / for our presence as metics [*metoikian*]' (1018–19), and they don the robes worn by actual metics during the great Athenian festival of the Panathenaia (1028).[2] Although not citizens of Athens, these primal divinities are given a home, and their ongoing presence as outsiders reminds Athenians of the need to include different perspectives as their struggle to secure justice and prosperity.

In the ancient world, forced migration included those captured or sold into slavery, the situation of several female Choruses in tragedy: Euripides' *Helen* (Greek maidens enslaved in by the Egyptian ruler Theoclymenus), *Iphigenia among the Taurians* (Greek slaves in the service of the Taurian king Thoas), *Phoenician Women* (women from Tyre sent as temple slaves to Delphi), and *Hecuba* and *Trojan Women* (captive Trojan women, destined for slavery in Greece). Aeschylus' *Choephori* has a Chorus of palace slaves from Asia Minor, as well as Orestes' old Nurse Cilissa, a native of Cilicia, now southern Turkey.

Tragedy also features foreign slaves as main characters, frequently women who must serve their masters sexually. In Aeschylus' *Agamemnon*, the Greek commander returns home with the Trojan princess Cassandra, now his war-bride. Euripides' *Andromache* dramatizes the story of Hector's widow, seized at the sack of Troy to become the slave/concubine of Achilles' son Neoptolemus. Andromache bears him a bastard son, arousing the jealousy of Neoptolemus' Spartan wife Hermione, who tries to murder both mother and child. In

---

[2] Carved roughly 15 years after the premiere of Aeschylus's *Oresteia*, the Parthenon frieze depicts the Panathenaic procession and may have included metics, although the relevant blocks are damaged.

Sophocles' *Women of Trachis*, Heracles sacks the city of Omphale to seize the princess Iole. Heracles' wife Deianeira expresses both jealousy and sympathy for this young woman, taken from her home and forced into sexual slavery.

Sophocles shows us the narrow path for survival that a captured slave must walk. In *Ajax* the title character suffers such humiliation from his fellow Greeks during the Trojan War that he considers suicide. His war-bride/wife Tecmessa—a Phrygian captured by Ajax—knows what will happen to her and their child if her husband kills himself:

> There is no greater evil for humans
> than fate imposed by compulsion …
> Should you die, and abandon me,
> know on that day the Greeks
> will take me, have their way by force,
> and then I and our son will live as their slaves.
> (*Ajax* 485–86, 496–99)

Tecmessa faces the horrible reality of living in a world where male violence rules, and where the weak may have to depend on those who victimize them. The situation of sex-trafficked women today—both used by, and dependent on, their exploiters—has its parallels in Greek tragedy.

Let us look at two very different tragedies—Aeschylus' *Suppliant Women* (ca. 467 BC) and Euripides' *Children of Heracles* (ca. 426 BC)—that deal with refugees, suppliants, foreigners, and captive slaves. The first play shares aspects of contemporary asylum seekers fleeing their homeland out of fear of sexual abuse and exploitation. The second looks at refugees trying to escape political and military violence, a scenario all too common today. Both plays champion the civilized duty of cities (states, in the modern scenario) to receive and protect those seeking asylum, even if extending that protection leads to unexpected, and sometimes even brutal, results.

In Aeschylus' *Suppliant Women*, the Chorus of Egyptian Danaids (daughters of Danaus) come to Argos seeking protection from their Egyptian cousins (sons of Aegyptus, Danaus' brother), who are determined to marry them against their will. Guided by their father, the women supplicate the Argive king Pelasgus, claiming descent from the Argive race. They trace their genealogy back to Io, who was driven out of Argos two generations before, wandering over much of the known world before making her way to Egypt.[3]

Rare for a Greek tragedy, skin colour plays an important part in *Suppliant Women* (the adjective 'dark-skinned' for Ethiopians occurs in two fragmentary plays of Euripides). The Danaids describe themselves as a 'dark-skinned / sun-beaten race' (*Supp.* 154–55), and the Greek Pelasgus likens them 'not to those in our country, / but to the women of Libya; / the Nile, too, might bear such

---

[3] Aeschylus—or more probably his son, the playwright Euphorion—tells her story in *Prometheus Bound*, where Io hears from Prometheus the strange journey that lies ahead before she reaches her new home.

fruit' (*Supp.* 279–81). In spite of their physical difference, the Chorus claim that their blood kinship entitles them to the protection of the city of Argos. They also appeal to the rights of all suppliants, for Zeus 'feels sympathy for human exiles' (215). Pelasgus admits that 'the wrath of Zeus, lord of suppliants, weighs heavily' on him (347), but he knows that defending the women may lead to a war with Egypt. The Chorus plead with the Argive king, reminding him of his own words:

> Look at me, a suppliant, a wandering fugitive,
> like a calf fleeing a wolf, high up
> the steep rocks, lowing in fear,
> yet trusting the herdsman will save them. ... /
> The wrath of Zeus, lord of suppliants, endures ... /
> Do not dare watch suppliants
> dragged off, a violation of justice.
> (*Supp.* 350–53, 385, 429–30)

By calling the suppliant maidens 'citizen-foreigners' (*astoxenoi* 356), Pelasgus honours their Argive descent. But he fears his subjects will suffer if the ensuing war ends in defeat, that 'honouring these foreigners will destroy the city' (401). When the desperate Danaids threaten to pollute the gods' sanctuary by hanging themselves, Pelasgus calls an assembly and delivers an impassioned speech on the refugees' behalf. The Argive citizens (all male) vote unanimously to defend the suppliants.

An Egyptian vessel lands a troop of men ('their black limbs / set off clearly against their white robes', 719–20) who try to drag the suppliant women from the sanctuary. Pelasgus arrives to stop them, but the Egyptians insist they have every right to marry their cousins. They point out that the women have no legal standing, and that Argos has no business interfering in the affairs of another country. We hear similar arguments today that ethical norms do not apply across cultures, although this position contravenes the UN Declaration on Human Rights, signed by all UN members). Undeterred, Pelasgus invokes the role of the gods—especially Zeus—in defending suppliants, as well as the support of the Argive citizens.[4]

We know from fragments and other evidence that Aeschylus told the story in a connected trilogy. In the next play, *Danaids*, the Egyptians have married their cousins (one assumes the Argives lose the battle with the sons of Aegyptus). On their wedding night, the Danaids take revenge: each one murders her husband, except Hypermnestra, who refuses. She is tried for her apostasy from sisterly solidarity, but the goddess Aphrodite intervenes on her behalf. Hypermnestra and her husband Linceus initiate the Danaid line, culminating

---

[4] The United Nations 1951 Refugee Convention asserts the principle of non-refoulement—refugees should not be returned to a country where they face persecution, including serious threats to their life or freedom. In Aeschylus's play, the appeal to the rights of suppliants alone does not guarantee their protection; the claim of shared kinship and descent also plays an important role.

generations later in the birth of Perseus, the mythical founder of Mycenae. The unexpected outcome does not minimize or resolve the challenges of offering foreigners asylum, for Aeschylus exposes the complex interplay of racial and cultural difference, patriarchy, misogyny, female resistance, solidarity, individual choice, democratic decision-making, domestic abuse, and interstate violence.

Euripides' *Children of Heracles* also deals with refugees, asylum, servitude, and revenge. Eurystheus, the king who forced Heracles to perform his labours, pursues the hero's orphaned children, fearing that one day they might avenge their father. Iolaus—Heracles' faithful companion, now an old man—leads the children to Zeus' altar at Marathon to beg for asylum in Athens. Like the Danaids in Aeschylus' *Suppliant Women*, Iolaus appeals to kinship ties, and also to the *xenia* that binds the Athenian king Demophon (through his father Theseus) to the children (through their father Heracles). Demophon grants the refugees protection, even though it means war with Eurystheus and his army. An oracle promises an Athenian victory, but only if a maiden is sacrificed before the battle. Heracles' daughter Makaria (Blessed One) volunteers, pointing out the hypocrisy of asking foreign citizens to risk their lives without the suppliants themselves being willing to die (*Hcld*. 500–34).

Following Makaria's sacrifice, Iolaus insists on joining the fray in spite of his age. A slave of Heracles' mother Alcmene brings the news of victory, including Iolaus' miraculous rejuvenation in battle and the capture of Eurystheus. Elated, Alcmene grants the slave his freedom (in Athens this means elevation to metic status), and she demands that Eurystheus be put to death. The law forbids the murder of war-captives, and the Athenians refuse. Crazed for vengeance, Alcmene says that *she* will kill Eurystheus and take on the guilt and pollution herself. Condemned to death but unrepentant, Eurystheus reveals a prophecy that, once buried in Athenian soil, he will protect Athens from future invasion by the descendants of Heracles' children. Given the play's date (430 BC), the prophecy apparently refers to the impending invasion of Athens by the Spartans (ostensibly descendants of Heracles) in the early stages of the Peloponnesian War.

The dizzying reversals in *Children of Heracles* challenge interpretation and frustrate any simple moral. Suffice it to say, the play supports the Athenian decision to protect the suppliants, even though the city learns that later generations of those they helped will become their foe. Eurystheus, the very man who waged war to kill Heracles' children, will become an 'enemy hero' of Athens and help the city ward off that invasion. In the process, a brave girl dies so that her siblings can go free, an old man regains his youth in the bloodshed of battle, a slave wins his freedom, and a grandmother proves a vicious avenger. As evidenced in *Suppliant Women* and *Children of Heracles*, Greek tragedy dramatizes issues of migration, refugees, and asylum with intensity and passion, and without easy simplification

By the end of the fifth century, Athenian tragedy proved popular in northern Greece, Sicily, and southern Italy. In the late-fourth, early-third century BC, interest in these performances expanded, in part due to the conquests of Alexander the Great, who spread Greek culture (as well as death and destruction) as far as the Danube to the north, the Hindu Kush to the east, and south to the Sudan. In response to this upsurge in cultural production, theatre artists incorporated themselves into guilds called artists of Dionysus (*technêtai Dionysiou*). Including playwrights, actors, musicians, mask-makers, and other practitioners, these guilds were organized on the model of a small city, or *polis*. They negotiated festival contracts, handled the logistics (and dangers) of travel, arranged lodging in the different locales, sent official representatives hither and yon, issued honorary decrees, demanded immunity from local taxation and military service, and so on.

These professional artists resembled a band of theatrical mercenaries, responding to the best offer. With the end of democracy in Athens in 338 BC, tragedy became an increasingly cosmopolitan phenomenon, with celebrity and spectacle replacing the civic-driven self-exploration of fifth-century Athens. While the artists sold their wares wherever they could, including in the service of the hero-tyrants of Hellenistic cities, their guilds proclaimed that they worked first and foremost for the theatre god Dionysus. The parallels with market-driven artistic production in the twenty-first century seem sadly inescapable. More importantly, the underlying causes of forced migration and the flood of immigrants, refugees, and asylum seekers that we see today find their tragic precedents in our earliest formal theatre.

REFERENCES AND FURTHER READING

Aeschylus. 2008. *Tragedies*. Edited and translated by A.H. Sommerstein. 1–3 vols. Loeb Classical Library. Cambridge, MA: Harvard University Press.

Csapo, Eric. and Peter Wilson. 2021. *A Social and Economic History of the Theatre to 300 BC, in three volumes. Volume II: Theatre Beyond Athens*. Cambridge: Cambridge University Press.

Easterling, Pat. 2011. 'Sophoclean Journeys.' In *Tradition, Translation, Trauma: The Classic and the Modern*, edited by J. Parker and T. Mathews, 73–90. Oxford: Oxford University Press.

Easterling, Pat, and Edith Hall, eds. 2002. *Greek and Roman Actors: Aspects of an Ancient Profession*. Cambridge: Cambridge University Press.

Collard, C., M.J. Cropp, K.H. Lee, com., ed., and trans. 1995. *Euripides, Selected Fragmentary Plays, Vol. I*. Warminster: Aris &Phillips

Euripides, Tragedies. Edited and translated by D. Kovacs.1–6 vols. Loeb Classical Library. Cambridge, MA: Harvard University Press, 1994–2002.

Fisher, N.R.E. 1993. *Slavery in Classical Greece*. London: Bristol Classical Press/ Duckworth.

Garlan, Y. 1988. *Slavery in Ancient Greece*. Revised, edited, and translated by J. Lloyd. Ithaca: Cornell University Press.

Gould, J. 1973. 'Hiketeia,' *Journal of the Hellenic Society* 93: 74–103.
March, Jenny. 2014. *Dictionary of Classical Mythology*. Oxford: Oxbow Books.
Rehm, Rush. 2016. *Understanding Greek Tragic Theatre*. London: Routledge.
Roisman, Hannah M., ed. 2014. *Encyclopedia of Greek Tragedy*. Chichester: Wiley-Blackwell.
Sophocles, Tragedies. Edited and translated by H.L. Jones. 1–3 vols. Loeb Classical Library. Cambridge, MA: Harvard University Press, 1994–1996.

CHAPTER 16

Migration in Greek and Roman Comedy

C. W. Marshall

In Aristophanes' lost comedy *Babylonians* (426 BCE), the chorus probably represented refugees from the Persian empire following the fall of Babylon, enslaved and living in Athens (Welsh 1983). Stereotypes likely played into established tropes of cowardice and effeminacy for foreigners, which made their learning to serve in the Athenian navy appear ridiculous. The young men in the chorus adopt the role of forced migrants trying (and failing) to adopt expected Athenian citizen wartime behaviour. Migrants are mocked. This goes beyond merely 'othering' the barbarians: Aristophanes calls attention to their economic (and potential military) contributions to the *polis* even as they are disparaged, all safely framed within public citizen performance. Ancient scholars suggest these figures are coded analogues to those enslaved during the Samian War (441–439). Unlike Babylonians, however, the residents of Samos were Greek: when Aristophanes compares the Babylonian chorus to 'the Samian people, how many-lettered' (*Babylonians* fr. 71), he reinforces a complex negotiation of power relationships, acknowledging Athens's intellectual debt to the island's cultural exports (Athens had taken its 24-letter alphabet from Samos), while simultaneously commenting on the owl tattoos the Athenians had placed on the foreheads of the enslaved POWs, which claimed them permanently as Athenian prisoners; Samians had apparently done the same to Athenian captives with a tattoo of a distinctive ship (Henderson 1998–2007, 5.146–149). Implicitly, the Babylonian chorus is likewise tattooed and likewise wretched, as owls on the foreheads of their masks proclaim Athenian cultural hegemony and deny the integration of wartime refugees.

C. W. Marshall (✉)
University of British Columbia, Vancouver, BC, Canada
e-mail: toph.marshall@ubc.ca

With one line, Aristophanes reveals how some migrants to Athens are forever branded. Further, the play's success depends on appealing to a Dionysia festival audience which itself contained non-Athenians.

The realities of ancient migration are represented throughout ancient comedy, at times with sympathy and nuance, and at times with scathing cruelty. In drawing on familiar aspects of Athenian (and later Roman) life, comedy encompasses the complex realities of migration in all its forms: 'Whether it is thought in terms of individuals (immigrant, expatriate, temporary worker, exile, refugee, itinerant, cosmopolitan nomad, et cetera) or collectives (colonial settlement, diaspora, slave or convict transportation, trafficking, displacement), migration is, at its heart, about encounters with foreignness' (Cox 2014, 3). Garland (2014, 239–243) wrestles with some of the problematic terminology of migration in the ancient Greek context. Different migrant groups manoeuvre their position within the *polis*, negotiating a complex range of intersectional identities. What is presented on stage is usually free of such nuance. Athenian comedy, through distortion and exaggeration, reduces the intersectional complexities of the migrant experience.

There is a presumed homogeneity of audience response in Greek comic narratives, focalized through a certain *polis* (usually Athens). This ideological composition of the audience is different from the reality, where a heterogeneous audience—including metics (free, non-citizen residents; often migrants or descendants of migrants), non-resident foreigners, enslaved persons, and so on—must be presumed to accept the normative imposition of the citizen perspective, unless they somehow choose to introduce a resistant reading. At the City Dionysia, a series of cultural ceremonies which accompanied the theatrical contests were uniformly aimed at inculcating and normalizing this citizen perspective (Goldhill 1990). Later, in the Roman republic, the heterogeneity of the audience was even more extreme, widening the ambit for resistant readings further. Richlin persuasively frames these comedies as 'slave theatre' (2017, though see Brown 2019 for a challenge concerning audience composition).

This chapter traces significant themes pertaining to migration through an examination of representative plays. In the first section, 'Flight,' Aristophanes and his contemporaries reveal examples of those who have experienced forced migration and the economic hardships that attend it. In the second, 'Plight,' the plays of Menander (at the end of the fourth century) and the Latin playwrights Plautus and Terence (in the early second century) provide examples of the separation of families and the traumatic consequences of that, demonstrating how economic migration operates as a social force.

There is always a question of scale, and the applicability of specific fictional examples to the lived experience of individuals in the ancient Mediterranean. Dramatic narratives typically focus on a limited number of individuals and yet can represent wider migratory practices. A playwright distorts, selects, and magnifies, but audience engagement depends on an identifiable point of contact. Meaning is found in specifics. Theatre preserves plausible conversations between migrant characters which are otherwise unavailable in the historical record. That they are invented does not reduce their interpretative value. Greek and Roman comedy show how migration was and could be conceived and provide tools to recognize factors that shaped the realities for historical populations.

Flight

Against the background of the Peloponnesian War (431–404 BCE), several Athenian plays present individuals or groups who have been displaced. The comic poet Eupolis' play *Helots* (possibly 429–428 BCE; Storey 2011, 2.128–133) presented a chorus of runaway Spartan labourers seeking sanctuary at the temple of Poseidon at Sounion. In the early years of the Peloponnesian War, such a plot would flatter Athenian self-image as providing a democratic home to those fleeing the enemy. Aristophanes' *Farmers* (424–422 BCE; Henderson 1998–2007, 5.160–173) evidently focused on the Athenians displaced from the countryside during wartime—forced local migration of the economically dispossessed to unsanitary and diseased conditions in urban Athens (Thucydides 2.16).

Aristophanes' *Acharnians* (425 BCE) presents Dikaiopolis as one of these internally displaced farmers. As an evacuee from the countryside (*Ach.* 32–33), he is one of the internally displaced for whom living conditions can be especially desperate (Garland 2014, 106, and 224–225; Koser 2016, 65–66 and 101). As today, those settled in refugee camps, even internally, are subject to violence and abuse, and these foster dependency and economic isolation, and create lasting psychological trauma (MacDowell 1995, 46–48; Koser 2016, 70–71). Aristophanes' *Knights* 792–794 (424 BCE) suggests such evacuees were treated poorly and had endured loss of property continually since 431, even if they still had more to eat than those who stayed in the countryside (Eupolis' *Demes* fr. 99.11–20).

Weary of wartime privations, Dikaiopolis negotiates a personal peace treaty with Sparta which allows him to trade with foreign cities. As he opens his personal market (*agora*; *Ach.* 719–728), he identifies Peloponnesians as being particularly welcome. This indicates the actual lack of free movement for individuals between cities during the war. The first visitor is a Megarian, from the nearby *polis* Megara, which was allied with Sparta. The Megarian decree of c. 432 had banned trade, with the result that Megarians were 'starving at a quick march [i.e. gradually but inevitably]' (535; see Olson 2002, xxxii–xxxvi). This decree was considered one of the causes of the war, and Aristophanes' Megarian reveals his desperation. The scene (729–835) is uncomfortable to read: the Megarian has brought his two daughters in a sack, whom he intends to sell in a foreign market. Aristophanes works a complex visual pun, whereby each daughter is disguised as a piglet (*choiros*, a sacrificial animal), but *choiros* is also a slang term for hairless vulva (Henderson 1991, 131–132). They are sold as a sacrifice to Aphrodite and will be given a tail/penis (784–796). These elaborate enacted images present sexual enslavement in a neighbouring *polis* as an alternative to starvation (734), and the girls are clearly miserable when they are made to 'oink' (780, 800–803 *koï, koï*).

This humour is just barely a double-entendre, and is politically problematic:

> If Aristophanes wants us to sympathize with the Megarian, we might expect the hero Dikaiopolis to express sympathy. In fact, the Megarians' predicament prompts only jokes. (Carey 1993, 248)

Though features of this scene may draw on the cruder comic drama of Megara itself, metatheatrically importing a foreign kind of comedy into Athens (Konstantakos 2012, 126–149), the extreme situation presented is designed to encourage the audience to revel in the discomfort and desperation of the migrant. The Megarian sells his daughters for some salt and garlic (traditional Megarian staples), and apparently leaves content. Disentangling the metaliterary and voyeuristic from the social commentary is not possible.

As with *Babylonians*, Aristophanes has created another complex staged metaphor that generates humour but fails to reinforce the actual suffering of migrants. Instead, the focus appears to be on litigious exploitation: a self-appointed prosecutor, or sycophant, appears to extend the euphemisms for genitalia to figs (818–828); subsequently a Theban arriving at the private market and looking to purchase a distinctive Athenian commodity is sold a sycophant (860–958; MacDowell 1995, 71–75). Both the Megaran and the Theban speak their local dialects (Olson 2002, lxx–lxxv), mocking their foreignness and maintaining their status as outsiders within the community.

Eupolis' *Draft-Dodgers* (c. 414–412; Storey 2011, 2.62–67) appears to present flight from military service as a subject of humour. The play's alternate title 'Men-Women [*Androgynai*]' suggests draft evasion may have involved crossdressing, a strategy the mythical Achilles had attempted to avoid fighting at Troy. While in reality draft evasion likely involved the manipulation of legal exemptions (Christ 2004, 36–43), comedy presents the theme in terms of flight. Another lost comedy, Cratinus' *Female Runaways* (430s; Storey 2011, 1.296–301), also appears to involve cross-dressing men (fr. 60). Aristophanes' plays *Daedalus* (Henderson 1998–2007, 5.198–205, set on Crete) and *Cocalus* (280–287, set in Sicily) presented the mythical craftsman Daedalus as an asylum-seeker from Athens, fleeing legal consequences and pollution of manslaughter. *Danaids* (228–237) seems to have parodied the tragic narrative of the daughters of Danaus seeking protection in Argos following their forced marriage to the sons of Aegyptus. *Phoenician Women* (372–375) was another paratragic narrative, this one featuring enslaved foreign women in Greece (Euripides' tragedy with this title is set in Thebes).

Finally, Aristophanes' *Birds* (414 BCE), roughly contemporary with *Draft-Dodgers*, presents two Athenians fleeing Athens. The natural assumption for spectators would be that Peisetairos and Euelpides are fleeing the war, even though the given reason is the excessive legal apparatus of the city, which Euelpides describes:

we, being of good standing in tribe and clan, solid citizens, with no one trying to shoo us away, have up and left our country with both feet flying. Not that we hate our city *per se*, as if it weren't essentially great and blest and open to everybody to come and watch their wealth fly away in fines. No, it's that the cicadas chirp on their boughs for only a month or two, whereas the Athenians harp on their lawsuits their whole lives long. That's why we're trekking this trek [...] in search of a peaceable place, where we can settle down and pass our lives. (*Birds* 33–45; tr. Henderson 1998–2007, 3.17–19)

These Athenians seek to escape the responsibility of jury-duty and debt-repayment (*Birds* 109–110, 115–116), and by framing themselves as political refugees fleeing a harsh and uncompromising regime, the characters recognize the complexities of migration as a multidirectional issue.

After contemplating and rejecting other city-states (120–154), the Athenians decide to found their own city among the birds. Migration becomes colonization, and with the eventual founding of the new city, Nephelokokkugia ('Cloudcuckooland', 809–850) a new destination for migrants is created (for colonialism and migration see van Dommelen 2012). Migrants are attracted to the new city, both named individuals and generic representatives of a profession. A priest, a poet, and an oracle collector all present means of affirming the new *polis* and are all sent away (859–991). The next visitors escalate the threats to the city's welfare (992–1055): the geometer Meton offers to survey the area but is dispatched as a charlatan; an overseer (*episkopos*) arrives attempting to force the new city into the Athenian empire but leaves when bribed to return to Athens to advocate for Persians (an enemy of Athens); a decree-seller offers advice on the formulation of new laws. Each of these is an opportunist, and their presence seeks to prey upon the disenfranchised (MacDowell 1995, 209–212). None is received in the new city, which is simultaneously coded as a para-Athenian alternative, and an anti-Athenian opposite. Other visitors—messengers, heralds, and ambassadors (both human and divine)—are received and sent away. There is no successful migration to Cloudcuckooland.

A final trio of Athenian refugees confirm this pattern (1337–1468). The promise for new wings allowing citizens to fly offers a rich metaphor for enfranchisement, but those seeking wings are all morally compromised and rejected (MacDowell 1995, 212–216). A father-beater presents himself as a political refugee (1344–1345, 'I want to live with you and I yearn for your laws'), since domestic assault is a crime among humans but not apparently among birds. Cinesias, a poet known for his florid and degenerate musicality, wants wings to allow his verse to be elevated, as it were. Finally, another sycophant appears wanting wings to allow him to seek individuals to be sued among the island cities dependent upon Athens (1424–1425). Each of these represents a migrant class familiar today—a political refugee, a social migrant, and an economic migrant—and each is ascribed a negative valence that prejudices the predominantly Athenian audience against any resident foreigners (*Ach.* 508 had disparaged metics 'the useless part of the *astoi* [local population]'). *Birds* concludes with a diplomatic marriage between Peisetairos and Basileia ['Royalty'], Zeus's daughter, as a type of elite migration (1706–1765). Aristophanes' *Birds* demonstrates an awareness of the complexities of migration even as it re-inscribes Athenocentric values that privilege citizens above other inhabitants of the city.

PLIGHT

In the years immediately following the death of Alexander the Great (323 BCE), as the Greek world expanded across the Eastern Mediterranean, overseas trade facilitated human trafficking. There are no ancient definitions of trafficking, but the practice as understood today was nevertheless widespread. The UN definition provides a standard by which to evaluate the representation of trafficking in ancient comedy:

> The recruitment, transportation, transfer, harbouring or receipt of persons, by means of the threat, or use of force or other forms of coercion, of abduction, of fraud, of deception, of the abuse of power or of a position of vulnerability or of the giving or receiving of payments or benefits to achieve the consent of a person having control over another person, for the purpose of exploitation. (UN Protocol to Prohibit, Suppress, and Punish Trafficking in Persons 2000)

Ancient comedy presents narratives premised on individual trauma, and ancient enslavement of humans regularly involved transnational trafficking. Enslavement was legally permitted, and was facilitated through the forced migration of individuals, particularly of children. Comedies testify to the variety of experience, even within their formulaic romantic narratives. The examples that follow demonstrate the social and economic precarity of child and female migrants in particular as presented in comedy (and this corroborates the important analysis of Làpe 2021).

Menander's *Sikyonioi* presents Philoumene, four-year-old daughter of the Athenian Kichesias, kidnapped by pirates along with her enslaved minder Dromon (*Sik.* 3–15, 354–357). They are taken to Mylasa in Caria (modern southwest Turkey), which serves as a point of transit, where they are sold to a soldier from Sikyon, who brings them back enslaved to the Greek mainland. The transfer from Greece to war-torn Asia Minor and back allows the traffickers to obscure the victims' city of origin, perpetuating an accepted fiction of ignorance of the trafficked individual's former home. The soldier Stratophanes, himself a mercenary fighting in Caria (136–137), returns with Philoumene and Dromon (or possibly it was his foster-father and namesake, which reduces the age gap between the eventual couple). This is a romanticized representation of real-life child abductions and offers the foundation for a plot whereby both Stratophanes and Philoumene will be revealed over the course of the dramatic action to be Athenian-born, and therefore marriageable to each other. Stratophanes' military service marks him as an economic migrant who maintains his civic identity, whereas Philoumene and Dromon lose their identities.

Precise details of the plot are lost because so little of Menander's play survives, and all this is prologue to the dramatic action.

In *Sikyonioi*, Philoumene has fled enslavement and sought refuge in Eleusis, which serves geographically and ideologically as a midpoint between Sikyon and Athens (see Garland 2014, 230–231 for runaway slaves). Because she claims to be a freeborn Athenian, Philoumene is granted asylum. The play indicates that Stratophanes did not use her sexually when she was in his care (fr. 4 'he brought her up apart, as fits a girl who's free' [tr. Arnott 1979–2000, 3.303, adapted]), but the vulnerability of a trafficked child over a period of more than ten years is not to be discounted: Stratophanes' kindness (if it is that) is exceptional. In Eleusis, a debate between the two would-be lovers presents Stratophanes as democratic and Athenian, and the rival lover Moschion as oligarchic and Macedonian. This portrayal prejudicially favours Stratophanes, despite Athens's diminished political importance in the late fourth century (Lape 2004, 215–219). Moschion is described as pale and beardless (*Sik*. 200–201), which are 'signs of political and gender deviancy' (Lape 2004, 223, and see 222–231). Stratophanes additionally has a creditor from Boeotia seeking to gain control of his supposed property, a detail which raises the risk of further forced movement for Philoumene.

Though the plot recuperates Stratophanes for an Athenian audience, the underlying vulnerability of Philoumene meets the UN definition for human trafficking. Comedy invents such traumatic situations, and in the artificiality of the dramatic resolution it emphasizes how different fiction can be from lived experience. Trafficking is not simply a plot convenience: it is consistently presented accurately, with journeys of multiple legs, that facilitate increased isolation and removal of status for trafficked individuals, enabling enslavement and sexual exploitation (Marshall 2013, 179–182).

Sometimes, the individual being trafficked is not a child, and in these cases, comedy works to allay audience anxieties for non-enslaved women. In Menander's *Leukadia*, the Leucadian woman of the title is apparently shipwrecked, removing human agency from at least part of the transportation (*Leuk*. 34–36). In Plautus' *Persa* ('The Persian') a slavedealer named Dordalus believes he is buying an enslaved woman from most remote Arabia (*Pers*. 541), through the agency of a Persian trafficker. This situation demonstrates that the presumptive value of an enslaved woman derives from her vulnerability and her distance from legally authoritative demonstrations of her natal status. The audience knows that both the trafficker and the Arabian woman are actually Athenian residents (the former enslaved, the latter a free but poor unmarried woman). Their scheme is designed to entrap Dordalus into illegally purchasing an Athenian. No sympathy is offered for the slave dealer, but the presumption of vulnerability and exploitation of forced migrants is evident throughout and is instrumental in the maintenance of dramatic tension.

The plays of Plautus (fl. c. 205–188) and Terence (fl. 166–160) are Latin adaptations of the Greek comedies by Menander and his contemporaries. As adaptations, they may preserve Greek plot details but can equally be freely adapted for narrative and contextual reasons. Specific details in these Roman plays may overlap with their lost Greek originals but must be presumed to be meaningful in the first instance to audiences in Rome in the early second century BCE, in the years following the protracted Hannibalic (Second Punic) War.

The moral worlds of Hellenistic Greece and Republican Rome are equally challenging. Plautus' *Menaechmi* presents a narrative of a male child being trafficked (*Men.* 17–33): a Syracusan merchant takes one of his twin sons to Tarentum (from Sicily to South Italy), where the child gets separated and is found by a merchant from Epidamnus (in modern Albania). With an unsettling neutrality, the same word, *mercator* (17, 32), is used for both men; there is no word in Latin for trafficker (*leno* is used for figures like Dordalus, the legal but disreputable dealer in enslaved persons for sexual exploitation). The action of *Menaechmi* is set many years later, with the Syracusan brother arriving in Epidamnus, having sought his brother in many Mediterranean ports for more than five years (230–250). The separation of migrant families is familiar today, and the premise of the play depends on an audience in postwar Rome accepting the need to recover and repatriate trafficked family members. Again, a comic plot seeks to resolve the plight of these trafficked individuals, restoring them to their natal family.

Similar themes emerge in Plautus' *Poenulus* ('The Puny Punic'). As a child aged seven, Agorastocles was kidnapped (*Poen.* 66 *surrupitur*) from Carthage and transported to Calydon in western Greece, where he was adopted by a childless old man (64–74). Separately, another trafficker kidnapped (87 *surrupuit*) two girls aged five and four from a Carthaginian suburb and transported them to Anactorium, also in western Greece (just over 100 km from Calydon), where they were sold to a *leno* who subsequently moved with them to Calydon (83–95). The play therefore begins with abducted Carthaginian cousins living next door to one another, unaware of their common heritage until the girls' father Hanno arrives (930). Hanno has been searching for his children in brothels across the Mediterranean (104–115). The play concludes with Hanno reunited with his daughters and (in the extant, later version of the play's ending) Agorastocles engaged to his cousin Adelphasium (1356–1358). All will return to Carthage together (1419–1420).

There is a lot to unpack in this challenging plot. The presentation of Carthaginians, transplanted to Greece and subject either to forced movement or working to recover family members lost through transportation, normalizes the trauma associated with melodramatic comic plots. Even though these characters are 'part of a nation that had always been a rival of Rome,' their portrayal is mostly sympathetic and 'the play contains practically no racial or ethnic slurs' (De Melo 2011–13, 4.11, 12). Franko (1995) isolates the implications of incest in Hanno's search for his daughters, but the plight of the children is comparable to that found for Greek characters in other plays. Though the cousin-marriage implied at the end is unique, 'marriage between cousins was legal and carried no social stigma in Roman society' (Shaw and Saller 1984, 433). Hanno's opening speech is in Punic (a language unknown to most in the

Roman audience), and yet his quest to recover his daughters is at heart as earnest as that of the Syracusan brother in *Menaechmi*. Though he knows other languages (*Poen*. 112), his Punic presentation is the choice of a man asserting and re-affirming his natal identity through cultural performance. Cox stresses how theatre can use language to express migrant subjectivity, stressing that language on stage can contain meaning even if it does not convey it (2014, 13–14). Conversely, I would add, it can convey meaning without requiring audience comprehension: tone, gesture, and delivery shape audience perceptions of the Carthaginian characters. Though having a foreign character speaking another language might be unsettling for an audience, the tenor of his search is consistently affirmed as positive. What these characters mean for Roman spectators c. 189–187 BCE, however, as the city continues to recover from the Hannibalic War, will be fundamentally different than what it might have meant for the audience of the Greek play on which it is based.

Poenulus is a story of familial restoration, with the promise of return migration, back to home and safety, a central theme for theatre and migration (Cox 2014, 77). Home becomes both a promise and a destination, even if it is not a destination that can always be reached. Other comedies maintain the absence of values associated with home, acknowledging persistent cultural differences between the enslaved and the slaveowners. In Menander's *Aspis* ('The Shield'), the enslaved Daos acknowledges differences to his owner Smikrines:

> I come from Phrygia. Much that you approve
> Appals me—and the converse. (*Asp*. 206–207, tr. Arnott 1979–2000, 1.37)

This self-awareness demonstrates 'that Daos must have been captured and reduced to servitude as a young adult (if not later), if he can plausibly avow his Phrygian acculturation' (Konstan 2010, 40).

Many of these themes come together in Plautus' *Rudens* ('The Rope'), which is uniquely set on a remote African coastline, near Cyrene. Two women being trafficked for sex had been kidnapped as children by pirates (*Rud*. 39–42, 106), and years later are shipwrecked while travelling to be sold by a *leno*. The women arrive at the house of an Athenian exile, who has migrated to North Africa due to poverty and debts:

> Over there lives Daemones, in the farm and farmhouse so close to the sea, an old man who came here as an exile from Athens, not a bad person; what's more he is deprived of his homeland not on account of any offense, but in rescuing others he entangled himself and lost his well-earned fortune through his kindness. (*Rud*. 33–38, tr. De Melo 2011-13, 4.409)

Daemones' poverty is relative—his household includes his wife and at least four men he keeps enslaved—and one of the women enslaved by the *leno* will prove to be Daemones' daughter, kidnaped long before. The play does not provide details of the legal proceedings that drove Daemones from Athens, nor does it suggest he will return to Athens at the play's conclusion. Though he is not a tax exile in the modern sense, his financial hardships have made him an economic migrant, even if his lifestyle remains comparatively privileged. In contrast, his daughter may be expected to return to Athens once she marries the young man Plesidippus, who is a kinsman (1214 *cognatum*) of Daemones.

Hardship does not require extreme and fanciful events at their root. Terence's *Andria* (165 BCE) presents, with sympathetic detail, a woman named Chrysis migrating from the island of Andros to Athens and adopting sex work as a free non-citizen in order to avoid poverty. An Athenian named Simo provides a moving account that suggests a reality familiar to the Roman audience:

> Meanwhile, about three years ago, a woman moved into the neighbourhood, driven here by poverty and the indifference of her family, a most beautiful woman in the prime of life. ... At first she lived a virtuous life, sparing and thrifty, earning her living by spinning wool. But when a lover approached her offering money, first one and then another, human nature always being inclined to prefer pleasure to toil, she accepted the offers and took up the profession. (*And.* 69–72, 74–79, tr. Barsby 2001, 1.55)

Economic hardship and a lack of financial and other support from her extended family (71 *cognatorum*) brings Chrysis to a larger urbanized economic centre. Her initial occupation as a weaver (75 *lana et tela victum quaeritans*, literally, 'seeking food with wool and web') points to the struggles a new non-citizen migrant might typically face. The transition to sex work is presented as almost inevitable.

Simo, as an Athenian male citizen with property, offers a normative moral view on this development, stressing that she initially lived virtuously (74 *pudice*, 'modestly') and the transition to sex work was 'from work ['honest work'] downhill to pleasure' (78 *ab labore proclive ad lubidinem*). It is a condescending and contemptuous perspective—*ad lubidinem* can also suggest 'on a whim'—that ignores the genuine struggle this change would have entailed for her in a society that regulated female sexuality rigidly. The model of sex work presented here is different from that in the previous examples, where the women were enslaved. In those cases, the slave-owner (*leno*) profits from the sale or short-term use of the women he enslaves. Here, a non-citizen but free woman makes contracts for herself. In Latin, both relationships label the woman as a *meretrix* (prostitute), but the economic distinction and difference of agency are substantial (Marshall 2013, 174–177). Chrysis maintains relationships with multiple clients (four are mentioned at 86–88), and in that position earns enough to maintain other women, including Glycerium, who the dramatic action will reveal to be a freeborn Athenian. This model of sex work is found elsewhere in Roman comedy (e.g. Phronesium in Plautus' *Truculentus*, Thais in Terence's *Eunuchus*) and is typically condemned by the men in the play.

Even within the patterns of Greek and Roman comic narratives, a woman in Chrysis' situation will never be identified as an Athenian citizen through the course of the plot and will not be married by the end of the play. For these economic migrants, for whom sex work becomes a viable profession because of their non-citizen status, the normative happily-ever-after outcome towards which the plots conventionally drive is simply not available. Women living apart from their natal communities had limited opportunities.

Conclusion

Beginning in the last decade of the fifth century, Athenian comic competitions began to attract migrant playwrights from other cities, and the period of Middle Comedy in the early fourth century is filled with names of non-Athenians. This includes 'some of the most influential and productive poets … [whose] ideas would have brought fresh ideas and a broader, less parochial, approach to comedy, even contributing features from native comic traditions' (Hartwig 2014, 218, who also provides a list). The influence of foreign artistic practice was already being felt in the musical innovations in drama at the end of the fifth century, and this paved a way for the more active involvement of non-Athenians within the contests (Wilson 2002, 47–49). This internationalization of drama continued into the Hellenistic period, when many playwrights came to Athens hoping for dramatic success: Alexis, for example, whose *Karchedonios* ('The Carthaginian') was the source play for *Poenulus*, came from Thurii in South Italy, and Diphilus, who wrote the original for *Rudens*, came from Sinope on the Black Sea to make a career in Athens. Actors became professional, with guilds managing itinerant performers that travelled the Mediterranean. In Rome, the extant comic playwrights are both outsiders as well: Plautus came from an Oscan-speaking area not controlled by Rome, and Terence from North Africa, and both may at one time have been enslaved.

The comic drama presented in the Greek and Roman worlds was grounded in the real lives of its spectators. Migration in its many forms is depicted in a way that recognizes the harsh realities of those who leave or are taken from their natal communities. The displacement of individuals through warfare, enslavement, or economic need provides a shifting centre around which Greek and Roman comedy was created.

References

Arnott, W. G. 1979–2000. *Menander*, 3 vols. Cambridge, MA: Harvard University Press.
Barsby, John. 2001. *Terence*, 2 vols. Cambridge, MA: Harvard University Press.
Brown, Peter. 2019. 'Were There Slaves in the Audience of Plautus' Comedies?' *Classical Quarterly* 69(2), 654–671.
Carey, Christopher. 1993. 'The Purpose of Aristophanes' *Acharnians*.' *Rheinisches Museum für Philologie* 136(3–4), 245–263.

Christ, Matthew R. 2004. 'Draft Evasion Onstage and Offstage in Classical Athens.' *Classical Quarterly* 54(1), 33–57.

Cox, Emma. 2014. *Theatre & Migration*. Basingstoke: Palgrave Macmillan.

De Melo, Wolfgang. 2011–13. *Plautus*, 5 vols. Cambridge, MA: Harvard University Press.

Franko, George F. 1995. 'Incest and Ridicule in the *Poenulus* of Plautus.' *Classical Quarterly* 45(1), 250–252.

Garland, Robert. 2014. *Wandering Greeks: The Ancient Greek Diaspora from the Age of Homer to the Death of Alexander the Great*. Princeton and Oxford: Princeton University Press.

Goldhill, Simon. 1990. 'The Great Dionysia and Civic Ideology.' In *Nothing to do with Dionysos? Athenian Drama and Its Social Context*, edited by J. J. Winkler and F. I. Zeitlin, 97–129. Princeton: Princeton University Press.

Hartwig, Andrew. 2014. 'The Evolution of Comedy in the Fourth Century.' In *Greek Theatre in the Fourth Century BC*, edited by Eric Csapo, Hans Rupprecht, J. Richard Green, and Peter Wilson, 207–227. Berlin: De Gruyter.

Henderson, Jeffrey. 1991. *The Maculate Muse*, 2nd ed. Oxford: Oxford University Press.

———. 1998–2007. *Aristophanes*, 5 vols. Cambridge, MA: Harvard University Press.

Konstan, David. 2010. 'Menander and Cultural Studies.' In *New Perspectives on Postclassical Comedy*, edited by Antonis K. Petrides and Sophia Papaioannou, 31–50. Newcastle Upon Tyne: Cambridge Scholars Publishing.

Konstantakos, Ioannis. 2012. '"My Kids for Sale": The Megarian's Scene in Aristophanes' *Acharnians* and Megarian Comedy.' *Logeion* 2, 121–166.

Koser, Khalid. 2016. *International Migration: A Very Short Introduction*, 2nd ed. Oxford: Oxford University Press.

Lape, Susan. 2004. *Reproducing Athens: Menander's Comedy, Democratic Culture, and the Hellenistic City*. Princeton and Oxford: Princeton University Press.

———. 2021. 'Mobility and Sexual Laborers in Menander's *Dis Exapaton* and Plautus' *Bacchides*.' *Ramus* 50, 25–42.

MacDowell, Douglas M. 1995. *Aristophanes and Athens: An Introduction to the Plays*. Oxford: Oxford University Press.

Marshall, C. W. 2013. 'Sex Slaves in New Comedy.' In *Slaves and Slavery in Ancient Greek Comic Drama*, edited by Ben Akrigg and Rob Tordoff, 173–196. Cambridge: Cambridge University Press.

Olson, S. Douglas. 2002. *Aristophanes: Acharnians*. Oxford: Oxford University Press.

Richlin, Amy. 2017. *Slave Theater in the Roman Republic*. Cambridge: Cambridge University Press.

Shaw, Brent D. and Richard P. Saller. 1984. 'Close-Kin Marriage in Roman Society?' *Man* 19(3), 432–444.

Storey, Ian C. 2011. *Fragments of Old Comedy*, 3 vols. Cambridge, MA: Harvard University Press.

van Dommelen, Peter. 2012. 'Colonialism and Migration in the Ancient Mediterranean.' *Annual Review of Anthropology* 41, 393–409.

Welsh, D. 1983. 'The Chorus of Aristophanes' *Babylonians*.' *Greek, Roman, and Byzantine Studies* 24(2), 137–150.

Wilson, Peter. 2002. 'The Musicians among the Actors.' In *Greek and Roman Actors: Aspects of an Ancient Profession*, edited by Pat Easterling and Edith Hall, 39–68. Cambridge: Cambridge University Press.

CHAPTER 17

Migrating Souls and Witnessing Travellers in the Dramaturgy of Nō Theatre

Miki Iwata

The idea of migration is deeply rooted in the historical development of the genre which we now know as Nō drama. In this area of theatre, several different, though overlapping, kinds of 'migration' can be identified. Firstly, early performers were originally nomadic travellers who were tax-exempted but, at the same time, deprived of the rights granted to settled residents. Secondly, their nomadic circumstances are reflected in the typical plot structure of Nō, in which a travelling Buddhist priest meets a strange figure who is discovered to be a ghost in the latter half of the play. Here, it is important to note that not only the witnessing priests but also the ghosts can be thought of as exiles, in that they are displaced from their natural course from life to afterlife, or from this to the other world. In other words, in the dramaturgy of Nō theatre it is only travellers who can hear the dead speak and see them dance, because they are both outside the ordinary way of life, while the audience is permitted to observe that otherworldly encounter on stage, thanks to the priest's function as a medium.

To consider the idea of migration in Japanese Nō theatre, it is important that we first discuss how Nō theatre was constructed in the historical context. Originating in China around the eighth century as *sangaku* (miscellaneous dance and music), Nō theatre developed its basic forms in the late fourteenth century under the patronage of Ashikaga Yoshimitsu (1358–1408), the third shogun of the Muromachi shogunate. At that time, the genre was called *sarugaku* (a corrupt pronunciation of *sangaku*; the *kanji* character representing *ape*

M. Iwata (✉)
Rikkyo University, Tokyo, Japan
e-mail: mikiiwata@rikkyo.ac.jp

© The Author(s), under exclusive license to Springer Nature Switzerland AG 2023
Y. Meerzon, S. E. Wilmer (eds.), *The Palgrave Handbook of Theatre and Migration*, https://doi.org/10.1007/978-3-031-20196-7_17

was applied for the sound *saru,* as an indication of its humorous or mimetic theatrical performance). It is generally understood that the more sophisticated name Nō (probably derived from the Japanese word that stands for expertise or accomplishments) was adapted by Zeami Motokiyo (1363–1443), who started his career as Yoshimitsu's protégé and later came to be the most important actor, playwright and theorist in the whole history of Nō.

When Ernest Fenollosa (1853–1908) introduced Nō theatre to the Western world in the early twentieth century, Nō plays were described as 'only for the few; for the nobles; for those trained to catch the allusion' (Fenollosa and Pound 1916 / 1999, 5). However, this is likely the case only for the more recent, fully developed version of Nō theatre after it was formally assigned as the official ceremonial ritual for the samurai class by the Tokugawa shogunate in the early seventeenth century. Indeed, in what is allegedly the oldest book on theatre written in Japanese, *Shin sarugaku ki* (New Records on Sarugaku) in the mid-eleventh century, *sarugaku* is clearly distinguished from *bugaku* (dance and music). Unlike *sarugaku, bugaku* was a classical form patronised by Emperor and aristocrats in Kyoto and covered almost any secular performative art including pantomime, acrobatics, and juggling. As Seki Kobayashi and Shozo Masuda point out, the formation of Nō theatre can be described as 'the process in which the *sarugaku* in a narrow sense was developed from this early *sarugaku* in a broader sense' (Kobayashi and Masuda 1976, 39).

In this chapter, I will investigate how these complex ideas of *migration* work in Nō theatre in the time of Zeami. After explaining the historical background and emergence of Nō from *sarugaku* along with analysing the structure of the subgenre of *mugen* (dream vision) Nō, which was shaped through Zeami's works, I will examine one of the representative *mugen* Nō plays by Zeami, *Izutsu* (The Well Cradle), to illustrate Nō's dramaturgy.

THE GRADUAL FORMATION OF NŌ THEATRE FROM *SARUGAKU*

In the twelfth century, *sarugaku* began to be used in the performances linked to religious rituals held in large Buddhist temples. Among the most famous of those rituals was *shuni-e* (February service), where 'the emergence of the topsy-turvy, the carnivalesque, was demanded in order to secure the peace of the new year' (Matsuoka 2009, 115). The concluding part of *shuni-e*, which was called *tsuina* and was a ceremony for driving out demons who carried plague, was entrusted to *sarugaku* players. This participation in *shuni-e* was crucial to *sarugaku*'s gradual transformation from miscellaneous popular entertainment to religiously charged ritualistic theatre, and the use of masks was a central feature. For example, the oldest existing Nō play, *Okina* (An Old Man), is less a play than a dance performed by a player wearing a mask of an old man, which symbolises a celebration of (or a prayer for) peaceful longevity. *Okina* is a rare surviving example from this early phase of the Nō's development.

After Buddhist temples became active in large-scale fund-raising events called *kanjin* in the mid-thirteenth century, *sarugaku* rapidly became closer to what it is now recognised as Nō. Actors began to tour widely, beyond the region under the direct control of the organising temple, to perform didactic plays about how the sinful would suffer in hell after their death. Beyond this instructional use, these events had another important role in the lives of the lay people of the day. According to Shinpei Matsuoka, '*kanjin* was not simply an occasion for soliciting contribution. Frankly speaking, it offered the space for a memorial service for the repose of the dead' (Matsuoka 2009, 121). Through their participation in those events, it was thought that financial contributors could help their dead relatives and friends enter Nirvana. This creation of a special space for an encounter between the living and the dead later became an essential quality of Nō theatre.

In this era, playscripts were normally written by Buddhist priests and intellectuals from the elite class, while *sarugaku* players were instruments of the organisers of *kanjin* events. However, beginning in the early fourteenth century, performers began writing plays for themselves. Around the time of Kan'ami Kiyotsugu (1333-84), Zeami's father and a great pioneering figure in the formation of Nō, it was no longer unusual for a player to also be a playwright for his company. Kan'ami himself had a high reputation as both author and performer. Yet, as the change happened gradually, he often depended on pre-existing works for his plays' source materials. It is known, for example, that *Kayoi-Komachi* (The Courtship of Lady Komachi) a play written by Kan'ami and later revised by Zeami, was originally derived from an *ur-play* about the same story by a Buddhist preacher.

As *sarugaku* became more influential and distinct from other performing arts of the day, such as *dengaku* (rice field dancing: popular rituals in association with rice planting in farming communities), it attracted the attention of the political authorities of the Muromachi shogunate. Since the establishment of the first regime by the samurai class in the late twelfth century (the Kamakura shogunate), the national polity of Japan had been in a curious state of dual rule by the emperor and the shogun. As the Muromachi shogunate was a relatively new political power, the third shogun, Yoshimitsu, wanted to be equipped with some cultural capital that could rival *bugaku*, the ceremonial dance and music officially sanctioned by the imperial court. Haruko Wakita maintains that, while performing artists in medieval Japan were in general socially marginalised people, who were often referred to as 'river-beach beggars' because of their nomadic lifestyle, 'it is probably only the *sarugaku* players who succeeded in extricating themselves from a marginal position not only as exceptional individuals but as a whole group' (Wakita 2013, 245). This was a result of *sarugaku*'s selection as the shogunate's equivalent to *bugaku*. However, the secret of *sarugaku*'s unusual success started with a few exceptional individuals, especially Kan'ami and Zeami, who acquired special favour from Yoshimitsu.

At the time of the advancement of the Kanze troupe (the company headed by Kan'ami and, after his death, by Zeami) under the patronage of Yoshimitsu, *sarugaku* companies began to settle in the capital city Kyoto. The four leading companies among them—the Kanze, the Konparu, the Kongō, and the Hōshō—were called 'the Yamato four' because they were originally based in Yamato region. Indeed, we can trace a direct line of succession from them to the modern Nōgaku Performers' Association, established in September 1945, immediately after Japan's surrender to the Allies. Evidenced by the historical record, we can understand how crucial and important this period of the Yamato Four was to the development of what we now know as Nō theatre.

Even after settling in Kyoto, the Kanze troup did not stop touring around the country. In fact, Kan'ami died in Suruga (the old name for Shizuoka) in 1384 after his company made a guest performance, at the invitation of Asama Shrine in Suruga. That they continued their touring even in the sixteenth century can be clearly traced from historical documents, such as a notice of a temporary levy issued in 1557 by the Asakura clan in Echizen (the old name for Niigata) in order to raise funds for a performance of the Kanze in their province (Wakita 2013, 28-29).

The continuation of their touring might have been due to its positive economic effect for them. However, at the same time, maintaining the remnant of a travelling company must have been important for their dramaturgy, since the sense of being out of place and alienated from the settled community is quintessential for the typical structure of Nō plays, in which a traveller (often a Buddhist monk on a pilgrimage) encounters a spirit who is bound to a place associated with feelings of remorse stemming from their life. For example, in analysing Zeami's play *Yōrō*, Akio Torii notes that the travelling monk's opening speech addresses his distance from the capital under Emperor Yūryaku (a legendary emperor in the fifth century). Torii argues that by setting the play's time and place as remote from those in audience during Zeami's time, the Nō stage paradoxically achieves a profound duality that merges 'the present and the past, the centre and the border, awakening and sleeping, and the conscious and the unconscious' (Torii 1999, p. 23).

In order to dig into this duality in Zeami's dramaturgy, the next section will focus on both Zeami's theoretical treatises on Nō theatre and his plays, which are of equal importance in explaining how the idea of migration is embedded in the heart of Nō.

Zeami's Theory of Nō Through His Treatises and Plays

When Kan'ami died at the age of 51 in 1384, Zeami was forced to take over the Kanze troupe at approximately 22 years of age. Since his first performance as a boy actor in front of Yoshimitsu ten years before that, Zeami, renowned for his extraordinary beauty, had been enjoying the shogun's favour. However, now past his blooming youth and having just reached adulthood, Zeami likely felt difficulties in leading his father's troupe in his early years as the company's head. Even though little is known about Zeami in that period, he set about writing theoretical treatises from his late thirties on, and continued with it as his lifework, even after his retirement from the management of the Kanze in 1422.

The first and most famous among these treatises is *Fūshikaden* (Teachings on style and the flower), completed around 1400, in which, as well as in his later writings, *the flower* is a symbol of the quintessence of the art of Nō. The first chapter of the book is devoted to matters that require attention from players, according to their age group. Zeami describes a boy actor at the age of 11 or 12—the age when Zeami was first presented to Yoshimitsu—as one whose 'appearance, no matter in what aspect, will produce the sensation of Grace', but importantly, he reminds the reader that 'this Flower is not the true Flower. It is only a temporary bloom' (Rimer and Yamazaki 1984, 5). Furthermore, at the end of Chap. 3, he declares the purpose in writing this book as follows: 'In order to support our house, and because I have such a deep respect for our art, I have pondered deeply over things that my late father told me, and I am recording here those major points' (Rimer and Yamazaki 1984, 30). From these words, it is not difficult to see a talented early bloomer, who lost his father and mentor after the initial stage of what was to be a long career, struggling to grasp the essence of their family vocation. Ironically, this cutting short of Kan'ami's personal guidance led to our great fortune in possessing Zeami's treatises, thanks to which posterity can appreciate the theoretical foundation of Nō theatre in the time of its formation.

Nevertheless, these theoretical works of Zeami were never written for the general public. They were confidential private manuscripts exclusively for his direct descendants. These writings were passed from generation to generation only within the head families of the Kanze and the Komparu, originating with Zeami's son-in-law, until they were first edited and published by the historical geographer, Togo Yoshida, in 1909. It is no exaggeration to say that serious modern scholarship on this esoteric theatrical art is founded on the publication of *Zeami jūroku bu shū* (Sixteen Books by Zeami).

Like Zeami's treatises, the word Nō (as a name for the genre) only gained wide circulation in modern times. In spite of Zeami's endeavours to make the *sarugaku* of the day appear more genteel by using a different *kanji* character to represent the sound *saru* (ape) or calling this art *nō* (though *nō* and *sarugaku* were not entirely interchangeable in Zeami's usage), neither contrivance was received well in society and the genre continued to be generally called *sarugaku* until the Meiji Restoration of imperial power in 1868. Having lost the patronage of the (deposed) Tokugawa shogunate, *sarugaku* players had to modernise their profession in order to survive those turbulent times. When they established their trade association in 1881, it was designated as *nōgaku sha* (the *nōgaku* society) rather than *sarugaku sha* because the founding members thought, according to the descriptions of the prospectus for the scheme, the word *sarugaku* sounded 'vulgar and inappropriate' (Kobayashi and Masuda 1976, 93). Since then, this theatrical genre has been widely known as Nō. In brief, our modern idea of Nō theatre depends on the achievements of Zeami in great measure. Non-experts tend to think about Nō as something timeless or accomplished from the outset, but it is important that we understand the historical context of this modernisation of the old genre before discussing Nō theatre in the time of Zeami.

As Akiko Baba maintains, the preface of *Fūshikaden*, in which Zeami explains the origin of Nō, illustrates his intention to 'conduct a revolution in the tradition of *sarugaku*' (Baba 1984 / 2003, 13) by looking back to prehistoric myth, redefining the art not as a descendant of comic entertainment but as high art with a spiritual aura. At the same time, it is his plays themselves that form the most important expression of his dramatic theory, as is clearly shown in the opening sentence of Chap. 6 of *Fūshikaden*: 'Writing texts for the nō represents the very life of our art' (Rimer and Yamazaki 1984, 43).

Zeami as a playwright repeated the above-mentioned common dramatic structure of Nō, in which a travelling priest encounters an earth-bound spirit in a two-part structure. In the first part, a travelling figure meets a stranger who tells the traveller about a local, often tragic, anecdote of old. In the latter, the stranger betrays his/her true identity (in the traveller's dream) as a ghost of the protagonist of the previously told story. In short, the two-part structure—named by Kentaro Sanari as *mugen Nō* (Dream Vision Nō) in the early twentieth century—highlights that it is the encounter of two different kinds of exiles that reveals the spiritual dimension of the play on stage.

After the ghost reveals itself in the traveller's dream, a *mugen* Nō play reaches its climax, which is a dance of the spirit. Just as Torii defines Nō theatre as 'the dramatic art of redemption through speech and dance' (Torii 1999, 37), the dance which evokes the otherworldly and the spiritual on stage is at the core of the dramaturgy of Nō, and the dancer is endowed with special significance in it. The player who performs the spirit and dancer wears a mask and is called *shite* (performer)—an appellation that makes many Nō specialists identify Nō as essentially a one-man show—while the player featured as the witnessing traveller does not put on a mask and is called *waki* (bystander). In the performance practice of Nō theatre, these roles are strictly divided and *waki* players can only perform *waki* characters in any play.

In this long-standing system, one may wonder why everybody does not want to be a *shite* rather than a *waki*. One of the answers is that individuals could not choose their roles before the Meiji Restoration. When someone was born into a family of a *waki* school, they would naturally be brought up as a *waki* player, and the family specialty would be handed down from generation to generation. Indeed, many *waki* schools, having lost their stable financial support from the Tokugawa shogunate, went to ruin and disappeared in the late nineteenth century. Even now, when each school of *shite*, *waki*, *jiutai* (chorus), and *hayashi* (musicians) remain open and exclusive family businesses no longer exist, but are a kind of guild open to outsiders as well, individuals cannot change their first choice as to what school they belong to, and this immobility makes *waki* schools look somewhat less attractive.

Nevertheless, Noboru Yasuda, a Nō critic and *waki* player, maintains that the role of *waki* is indispensable for Nō's dramaturgy concerning the revelation of the spiritual on stage. He calls attention to the fact that *mugen* Nō plays often begin with reference to the melancholic state of mind of a wandering *waki* character, as notably shown in the opening speech of the priest in the anonymous play, *Kumasaka*: 'These weary feet that found the World | Too sad to walk in, whither | Oh whither shall wandering lead them?' (Waley 1922 / 1998, 60). The travelling life of a *waki* character suggests that he suffers alienation from the lifestyle of people in the permanently settled community and their lifestyle. The displaced status of *waki* works as a catalyst for his chance meeting with the spiritual who are migrating between the past/life and the present/death, failing to belong to either of them.

Yasuda takes up *Kakitsubata* (Iris; attributed to Komparu Zenchiku) as an example for his discussion. The play is based on an episode from *Ise monogatari* (The Tales of Ise), a collection of *waka* poems and related narratives dating from the Heian Period (794–1185). In the play, a wandering priest comes across a place called *yatsuhashi* (eight bridges) and is impressed by the beautiful irises growing there. Then, a woman comes and informs him that this place is remembered in connection with Ariwara no Narihira (825-80), the historical personage and protagonist of *Ise monogatari*, who left the capital with no particular destination due to his unrequited love and, reaching here, composed a *waka* poem using the characters *ka-ki-tsu-ba-ta* to form an acrostic. Later in the play, the woman reveals that she is not a human but a spirit of the iris, and tells him about her cherished memories of Narihira and the enormous influence of his poem on her. Although this is not a typical *mugen* Nō play, Yasuda argues, the basic structure is the same. For the audience in the Muromachi period (1336–1573), the wandering priest is contemporary with them. In contrast, the spirit of the iris still dwells in the days of Narihira, about 400 years before the time of the audience. In the dramatic form of *mugen* Nō,

> there is a corporeal exile with a solid, living body on the one hand, and there is the protagonist whose soul both remains in one place and perpetually migrates at the same time, on the other. When the two encounter each other over time and space, there emerges an other world on stage. Nō theatre is nothing less than the story of the other world made accessible to us. (Yasuda 2011, 160)

We may then summarise the quintessence of Nō as the sympathetic interaction between two different kinds of migration, one physical and the other spiritual; the former functions as a medium, through which the audience can gain access to the otherwise intangible. Behind the dramaturgy is the idea that there is a sphere which settled people can never reach, and a travelling *waki* character, as a kind of surrogate, sets out on a trip not only to the countryside but also to that spiritual *terra incognita*.

Dramaturgy That Makes the Invisible Visible in *Izutsu*

Critics almost unanimously agree that *The Well Cradle* is the supreme masterpiece among Zeami's *mugen Nō* plays, partly because he himself commends the play as his best in *Sarugaku dangi* (An account of Zeami's reflections on *sarugaku*), the collection of the reflections of Zeami in his late years recorded by his second son, Motoyoshi. Addressing the composition of Nō plays and admitting that there are superior as well as inferior ones among his own works, Zeami estimates that 'In terms of the levels of excellence, *Izutsu* can be said to be on the highest level, that of the Flower of Peerless Charm' (Rimer and Yamazaki 1984, 214). In the final section, I will analyse this play and illustrate the working of Zeami's dramaturgy in terms of the above-mentioned physical and spiritual migrations.

Like *Iris*, *The Well Cradle* is also based on *The Tales of Ise* (Episode 23). It is crucial for a Nō play to be based on a well-known old story so that the audience can sense the dramaturgical duality of the past and the present. In the source material, a couple who exchanged *waka* songs of love (an act equivalent to a promise of marriage) at a nearby well in their childhood becomes estranged from each other after the marriage and the husband begins to frequent another woman. The husband, suspecting that the wife may also have a lover, because she seems indifferent, conceals himself in the house to watch her. However, the wife, supposing that now she is alone, sadly sings a *waka* song of concern for the absent husband, which makes the husband stop visiting his mistress. Even though their names are never specified in the book, they were generally interpreted as the historical figures of Narihira and his wife (the daughter of Kino Aritsune) in medieval Japan. Haruo Nishino notes that 'this attitude is not necessarily the same as modern interpretation of *The Tales of Ise* (Nishino 1998, 460), but the narrative frame of Zeami's *The Well Cradle* is based on this presupposition.

As is often the case with Nō plays, *The Well Cradle* begins with the soliloquy of the wandering Buddhist monk. He happens to be near the temple that was allegedly built on the site of the old residence of Narihira and his wife, and prays for them. Following this, the monk encounters a woman who draws water from the well to offer to the old grave of Narihira, singing as follows: 'I would not wish to live on and on without my waiting for him, though it is in vain. Everything in this world leads to memories, and indeed memories outlive the one whom I have been waiting for' (my translation: Japanese text, Nishino 1998, 461). This is one of the best-known lines of the play, and is an early indication that she is the ghost of the wife of Narihira. She was called 'a lady who waits' (Nishino 1998, 464) because Narihira was known as a womaniser who had extra-marital affairs with several women. Even after both of them were dead, the spirit of the wife stays in their old abode, waiting for the husband to return, which ironically prevents her from having the chance to meet him again in heaven. The monk notices that she must be somebody related to Narihira and, after their exchange concerning the man of hundreds of years ago and the famous well, she confesses her identity and disappears behind the well.

In the second part of the play, the monk goes to sleep in the expectation that he may meet her again in a dream. The woman indeed appears in his dream (as is represented, of course, on stage), but this time in male attire. She now wears Narihira's kimono that was kept as a memento and begins to dance in imitation of the husband's dance. The dancer and *jiutai* (the chorus), in a *hemistichomythic* way, recite the *waka* song which young Narihira sent to her as a token of love at the old well. During the dance, *jiutai* chants that 'it is the man in his own headdress and kimono. It is not the woman but the man, the face of Narihira' (Nishino 1989, 464). As Tom Hare tersely summarises that 'Zeami's *mugen* plays most characteristically treat the interior life of a ghost' (Hare 2008, 16), *The Well Cradle* penetrates so deep into the intense wish of the ghostly wife to meet her husband once again that she not only reveals herself through the sympathetic communication with the wandering monk but, at the play's climactic moment, even embodies onstage what she has long yearned after.

Impressed by the scene, and describing it as a surprisingly modernistic stage effect, Shozo Masuda contends that:

> What is at stake now on stage is not a beautiful woman in male attire but Narihira himself. Before the audience knows it, the character has been changed from one to the other. It is something like a cinematographic technique of a double exposure. The stage effect is all the more powerful because of the further twist that the woman is in fact a male actor in female dress. (Masuda 1971, 67)

At this climactic point, the woman looks into the well and finds the one whom she has been waiting for so long, reflected in the water. She then sings her last line, 'I see the dear old face—how dear it is to me' (Nishino 1989, 464). Following this, the chorus takes over her line and sings the concluding lines in which the perspective of the speaker(s) ambiguously move from the spirit of the wife to the awakened monk:

> CHORUS. How dear it is to me, though it is me—the dead woman disappears, but like a withered flower whose flavour still lingers after all hues are gone. ... The dream is broken and now I am awakened; the dream is broken and the dawn has come. (Nishino 1989, 464-65)

In these concluding lines, all three characters—the travelling priest, the wandering spirit, and even the lost husband—melt away into an inclusive dramatic catharsis. The dream is now over, the ghost slowly recedes from the stage over a bridge into the greenroom, the ordinary world where this kind of sympathetic encounter between the living and the dead is normally impossible.

Crossing the Bridge

In the time of Zeami, the layout of the Nō stage was different from the modern stage. While the structure of the contemporary Nō stage can be traced back to the ones that were built in Buddhist temples' precincts in the late sixteenth century, it was originally a simple temporary stage. And yet, one important thing has remained unchanged up until now: a bridge is crossed between the greenroom and the main stage. As we have seen, epiphanic moments of a migrating soul in *mugen* Nō plays are made possible through the medium of a wandering *waki* character. Neither of them is part of the settled community; they come and go before the audience over the bridge.

For local spectators, those early Nō performances were played by travellers who came from nowhere and set up an ad-hoc stage. After the performance, both the players and the stage disappeared again, much like the spirit in the play. In the play, only a traveller could encounter the spirit who lingered in a certain place over time, and the settled local spectators could only have that vicarious spiritual experience through the travelling players. It is this state of *exilic being* that makes the invisible visible on stage in Nō theatre, the art of dramatic paradox.

References

Baba, Akiko. (1984) 2003. *Koten wo yomu, 'Fūshikaden'* [Reading classics: *Fūshikaden*]. Tokyo: Iwanami Shoten.
Fenollosa, Ernest, and Ezra Pound. (1916) 1999. *'Noh' or Accomplishment: A Study of the Classical Stage of Japan*. Gretna: Pelican Publishing.
Hare, Tom, trans. 2008. *Zeami: Performance Notes*. New York: Columbia University Press.
Kobayashi, Seki, and Shozo Masuda. 1976. *Nō no rekishi* [The history of Nō theatre]. Tokyo: Heibonsha.
Masuda, Shozo. 1971. *Nō no hyōgen, sono gyakusetsu no bigaku* [Expressions of Nō theatre: the aesthetics of paradox]. Tokyo: Chūko Shinsho.
Matsuoka, Shinpei. 2009. 'Nō Kyōgen no seiritsu no haikei' [The backgrounds behind the establishment of Nō and Kyōgen]. In *Nihon no dento geino kouza: buyo, engeki* [Lectures on Japanese traditional performance art: dance and drama], edited by Yukio Hattori, 87-130. Kyoto: Tankōsha.
Nishino, Haruo, ed. 1998. *Yōkyoku hyakuban* [One hundred Nō plays]. Tokyo: Iwanami Shoten.
Rimer, J. Thomas, and Masakazu Yamazaki, trans. 1984. *On the Art of the Nō Drama: The Major Treatises of Zeami*. Princeton: Princeton University Press.
Torii, Akio. 1999. *Shokuzai no Chusei* [The idea of redemption in Medieval Japan]. Tokyo: Perikansha.
Wakita, Haruko. 2013. *Nōgaku kara mita Chūsei* [Medieval Japan from the viewpoint of Nō theatre]. Tokyo: Tokyo daigaku shuppankai.
Waley, Arthur, trans. (1922) 1998. *The Nō Plays of Japan: An Anthology*. New York: Dover Publications.
Yasuda, Noboru. 2011. *Ikai wo tabi suru nō, waki to iu sonzai* [The journey to the other world in Nō drama: the meaning of *waki*]. Tokyo: Chikuma Shobo.

CHAPTER 18

The Things She Carried: The Vertical Migrations of Lady Rokujō in Japanese Theatre

Carol Fisher Sorgenfrei

SITUATING JAPAN

'Theatre and Migration' is a rich and complex topic that is fraught with passion and the awareness of incalculable suffering. Humans (and animals) have migrated from place to place—sometimes willingly, sometimes under great duress—since well before the time imagined by the author of the Hebrew Bible, when God expelled Adam and Eve from paradise. Simply typing 'theatre and migration' into Google on September 19, 2021, yielded over twenty-six million hits. Where to begin?

Discussions of migration and theatre often focus on dramaturgical strategies such as the content and casting of plays about the plight of migrants fleeing war, famine or economic meltdown, and their experiences of welcome or rejection in their new countries. Other key areas include the debate over mono- or multi-lingual performance; whether the representation of one ethnicity or race by actors of another ethnicity or race is appropriate or ethical; who the intended audience is; how and when to use cultural markers such as clothing, music, or theatrical style; and so on.

Theatre scholars (and producers) have also become aware of the profound difficulties facing migrating creative personnel: actors, directors, playwrights and designers. How and in what ways can these migrating artists participate in theatre in their new homes? What happens when their language skills diverge from those of native-born artists? Can artistic practices or styles that would be normal in their countries of origin be transported to a new culture with

C. F. Sorgenfrei (✉)
University of California, Los Angeles, Los Angeles, CA, USA

© The Author(s), under exclusive license to Springer Nature Switzerland AG 2023
Y. Meerzon, S. E. Wilmer (eds.), *The Palgrave Handbook of Theatre and Migration*, https://doi.org/10.1007/978-3-031-20196-7_18

different expectations? Will/should migrating practices become 'naturalized' in the new home, or will their use contribute to cultural stereotypes? Who constitutes the audience—other migrants from their homeland, members of their new country, or both? Such debates are made more complex by the dilemmas of ethical practice.

In contrast, Japanese theatre artists have never been persecuted or forced to migrate, and migration into Japan remains quite limited. Foreign workers, especially those from the Philippines, Taiwan or Indonesia, face many legal and cultural obstacles, including discrimination. However, their situation has not yielded a significant body of theatrical representation.

The most visible aspect of Japanese theatrical migration has been the West's fascination with stage practices derived from traditional genres. Conversely, Western realism has impacted modern Japanese theatre. Certain Japanese stage directors (and director-playwrights) such as Ninagawa Yukio, Suzuki Tadashi, Miyagi Satoshi, Terayama Shūji and others (Japanese names appear in Japanese order, with family name first) are highly visible in Euro-American, Asian and Australian festivals. All such artists and intercultural or fusion practices, in both directions, have been extensively analysed by theatre scholars.

The Past Is a Foreign Country

In this chapter, I would like to present an aspect of theatrical migration that has seldom been sufficiently discussed—what I call 'vertical migration'. I take my cue from that memorable quote from L. B. Hartley's 1953 novel *The Go-Between*: 'The past is a foreign country; they do things differently there'.

When people, animals, cultural products, ideologies, and so on migrate between cultures—whether by choice or not—the result is 'horizontal migration'. Soldiers, merchants, travellers, artists, performers, the dispossessed, and other migrants carry cultural/historical memories as well as aspects of native performance to distant shores, importing songs, dances, stories, gestures, and so on. Horizontally migrating theatrical practices mingle with 'native' arts, creating new intercultural forms.

In contrast, 'vertical migration' is the chronological movement, transmission, and retrieval of knowledge, skills, and historical/cultural memory—either worldwide or within a specific cultural heritage. Vertical migrants include both tangibles such as ruins and artefacts and intangibles such as arts, crafts, languages, religious/philosophical systems, survival skills, and scientific/mathematical discoveries. Vertical migrants transmitted via printed, digital, or visual format comprise what Diana Taylor (2003) calls 'the archive'. Performative events, physical and vocal acting style, dance, musical skills, and other transient non-archivables comprise Taylor's 'repertoire'. Some cultural/historical memories (the Holocaust, the atomic attacks, genocides, etc.) are so traumatic that, even when documented, neither archive nor repertoire can adequately contain them. The broader concept of vertical migration, which is peripherally aligned with memory studies, can embrace such orphans.

Intertextuality is a subset of vertical migration. When James Joyce quipped that professors would argue over *Ulysses* for centuries, he assumed a 'universal' pool of intertextual knowledge spanning Indo-European languages, cultures and histories. What happens when vertical migrants (intertextual or otherwise) fail to be 'universal', but are confined to a specific, insular culture? Whether as large as a national or linguistic group, or as small as a family, each insular culture transmits its own vertical migrants. Insiders understand vertically migrated, non-'universal' references and memories; most outsiders don't.

Japan is one such insular culture. Crucially, its language is unrelated to most (possibly all) other languages. Chinese written characters migrated to Japan in the fifth century CE, forming part of a complex writing system. However, the two languages differ grammatically. Over the millennia, Japan accepted and naturalized those Asian and Western cultural influences that seemed useful; however, prior to the US Occupation following World War II, Japan had never been invaded, defeated, or colonized. Consequently, despite the rapid horizontal migration of literary, cultural, and scientific influences since 1868, native culture was never obliterated. Whether the country was totally isolated or inundated with horizontal cultural migrants, Japanese artists have always employed complex modes of vertical migration.

For example, Japanese poets traditionally employed *honkadori*, literate allusions to older poems. Seventeenth- and eighteenth-century *kabuki* playwrights, forbidden from discussing political issues, substituted analogous historical or literary situations (*mitate*)—fooling no-one but pleasing the censors. Such insular vertical migrations demand copious footnotes for non-Japanese readers/viewers. Even when vertical migration is intentionally 'universal', as in Suzuki Tadashi's Greek plays or Ninagawa Yukio's Shakespeare productions, huge swathes of Japan's vertically migrating repertoire (and in Suzuki's case, parts of the archive) remain insular.

The story of Lady Rokujō, a fictional character created by the female author Murasaki Shikibu in *Genji Monogatari* (The Tale of Genji) (c. 1004 CE), remains primarily insular, despite the novel's status as a 'world classic'. This essay highlights the vertical migration of Rokujō's sexual jealousy and spirit possession in the work of four male playwrights. Whether fourteenth-century *nō* practitioners or post-war experimental theatre artists, these playwrights use vertical migration to respond to cultural trauma. All also harbour fears of a potential female invasion/migration into shakily defended male territory.

Murasaki Shikibu's *The Tale of Genji*

The Tale of Genji (Murasaki 1978), a long prose narrative sometimes dubbed the world's first novel, was written by a Japanese noblewoman conventionally called Murasaki Shikibu (c.978–c.1014). It narrates the amorous and political adventures of the fictional Prince Genji, the Emperor's son by a low-level courtesan. One of his many affairs is a long, passionate liaison with Lady Rokujō, who is seven or eight years older. As the widow of the Crown Prince, Rokujō is deprived of becoming Empress. When Genji rejects her to reconcile with his young wife Aoi, Rokujō is devastated. She is further humiliated when Aoi's carriage rudely pushes hers aside. Jealousy and anger possess her; without her knowledge or intent, her living spirit leaves her body and torments the pregnant Aoi. Despite prayers and exorcistic rites, Aoi dies after giving birth to Genji's son. When Rokujō finally suspects her own guilt, she turns to a life of religious penance.

For many female readers today, several of Genji's night-time escapades read as rape perpetrated by a powerful male on a voiceless female, usually without her consent, and occasionally on a woman whose identity is not clear to Genji. However, Murasaki depicts Genji not as a sexual predator, but as a desirable, charming, handsome partner who undergoes many tribulations. The female characters with whom he interacts—including Lady Rokujō, whose relations are consensual—have minimal ways to express their emotions or process their experiences. Murasaki was writing for other Heian court ladies, who, like her female characters, were required to submit their bodies and their children to the political/social demands of a patriarchal, essentially polygamous system. Doris G. Bargen, reading the novel with a feminist sensibility, suggests the prevalence of female spirit possession as a coping strategy:

> It appears that this female author wanted to articulate precisely that which her female characters were forbidden to articulate [...]. Since the possessed women in the *Genji* cannot openly verbalize grievances they are not supposed to hold, a number of them [...] stage their social and psychological conflicts as performances in which possessing spirits give voice to their anguish and their anger [...].My study proposes [...] [a] dynamic between the possessed woman and her charismatic, empowering spirit – a dynamic that is no longer defined as an antagonism (the male viewpoint) but as an alliance (the female viewpoint). (Bargen 1997, 27)

Bargen is suggesting that the dominant viewpoint typical of patriarchal, Chinese-originated 'either/or' Buddhism cannot fully submerge the powerful, gynocentric 'both/and' viewpoint typical of pre-Buddhist, Shintō/shamanistic Japan. Today, these conflicting ideologies join Westernization in a complex balancing act of three-way 'both/and' thinking.

Zeami Motokiyo's *Aoi no Ue*

Nō theatre appeared around four centuries after Murasaki's time. The Imperial Court had been badly weakened by years of devastating clan warfare, earthquakes, fires, and plagues. By the mid-fourteenth century, a new Shōgun (military ruler) enforced peace, usurping most imperial powers. The new rulers, uncultured samurai responsible for the deaths of famous warriors and imperial family members, promulgated laws displacing former aristocrats and disadvantaging their widows. Continuing plagues, earthquakes and fires were blamed on the angry ghosts of the losing side; prayers and rituals abounded. Various theatrical genres, both native and immigrant, religious and secular, vied for popularity. Some performances ended in riots. Although officially outcasts, the best performers were idolized. One less raucous troupe was led by the father of actor/playwright Zeami Motokiyo (c.1363–c.1443). Captivated by the eleven-year-old Zeami's beauty, the brash, seventeen-year-old Shōgun invited the entire troupe to live in his palace. There, in an ultimately successful ploy to minimize the young Shōgun's wilder proclivities, former Imperial courtiers tutored Zeami in refined, courtly arts. It was in this traumatic, complex, and dangerous milieu that Zeami perfected his art, ultimately creating nō. For a significant number of nō plays, historical or literary memory (often conveniently revised) is a crucial component.

Although some nō plays depict contemporary characters, such as distraught mothers of kidnapped children, most plots derive from literary or historical narratives. Nō features elegant poetry, literary allusion, and the transformation or release of the protagonist's anguished spirit by Buddhist prayer. In the most characteristic plays, the central character—whether living or dead—remembers/relives an emotional past moment, appearing first in illusory or disguised form, then reappearing as themselves. Nō texts and performance practices are transmitted directly from master to disciple, while printed scripts are consulted by the audience. Today, few actors or audience members fully comprehend the archaic language. Masks are ancient, revered objects; smaller than the face, their tiny eyeholes make vision difficult. Some actors maintain that being semi-blinded by the mask results in spiritual awakening or even possession by the character's spirit.

Although *Aoi no Ue* (Lady Aoi), attributed to Zeami, is the most iconic of several nō plays about Rokujō, it differs radically from Murasaki's original. The sickly Aoi is not enacted; she is represented by an empty kimono on the stage floor. A shamaness conjures the living spirit of Lady Rokujō, who recites her grievances and jealousy: 'Present vengeance is the retribution/ Of past wrongs you did to me./ […] Do you not feel the fury of my anger?/ You shall feel the fulness of its fury./ This loathsome heart!/ This loathsome heart!/ My unfathomable hate/ Causes Lady Aoi to wail in bitter agony' (Zeami 1959, 97). When the shamaness fails to defeat the demonic spirit, a male Buddhist ascetic is summoned. Rokujō re-enters wearing a horned demon mask, representing her true nature (or that of the spirit possessing her). She challenges the ascetic, saying, 'Return at once, good monk, return at once/ Else will you be burdened with regret'. Side notes in the printed script describe the action, stating, '[He] [t]urns toward ROKUJŌ and tries to vanquish ROKUJŌ by his incantation, but she puts her brocade outer-kimono around her waist and takes a defiant attitude' (Zeami 1959, 100-101). They battle as he chants prayers. Finally, his exorcistic rites quell the demon possessing Rokujō. Aoi lives; Rokujō accepts Buddhist teaching and attains Nirvana.

Unlike the original, Prince Genji does not appear and Aoi is reduced to an empty kimono. The conflict now is between supernaturally empowered opponents—a demonic (or demonically possessed) female and a saintly male ascetic. In the novel, Rokujō does not intend to harm Aoi and is unconscious of her spirit's behaviour; in the nō, she acts with clear intentionality. In the novel, once Rokujō realizes what she has done, she is horrified, repents, and chooses piety; in the play, she is forced to submit to Buddhist tenets. The novel shows the failure of all religious efforts to save Aoi; the play shows the incompetence of female-performed Shinto/shamanistic rites and the success of male-performed Buddhist rituals. In the novel, Aoi dies. In the play, she lives. In the novel, Aoi is pregnant, and though she dies, she gives birth to Genji's son. In the play, she is not pregnant. If Genji and his desired heir are banished from the play, Aoi is hardly more visible, being reduced to a symbolic kimono lying on the stage floor.

Why might Zeami so radically revise a beloved classic? Steven Brown suggests that Zeami's fascination with dispossessed, mad, and aged female characters (the protagonists of many plays) reflects a shift in political and cultural power. The formerly elite classes were traumatized by their defeat in lengthy clan wars that had turned their world upside-down. At the Emperor's court, once dominant, cultured aristocrats were displaced by newly victorious (brash, uncultured) samurai; formerly wealthy, aristocratic widows were denied the right to inherit. The victors, unused to aristocratic ways, became obsessed with pacifying the ghosts of their enemies. Continuing earthquakes, floods, fires, droughts, and plagues supported fears of supernatural retribution. For Brown, these fears are concretized in the reversal of gender politics. He maintains that *Aoi no Ue* is 'an active reconfiguration of power relations between men and women staged before the same Muromachi audience that had witnessed the utter disinheritance of women'. He suggests that '[t]he absence of Genji [...], along with the omission of his guilt, [...] shifts the blame for Rokujō's possession of Aoi from the man's neglect to the woman's jealousy' (Brown 2001, 77–78).

Female possession, an expression of forbidden emotions in Bargen's view of the Heian court, has become a demonic force in the nō. Brown suggests that Rokujō's tale—a female story rewritten by a male for a primarily male audience—is tied to the newly implemented, patriarchal legal system, to be enjoyed by that system's male beneficiaries. As the story migrated vertically over four centuries, its meaning migrated from the valorization of supernatural possession as a force empowering a voiceless, female audience to the need to vanquish dangerous, supernaturally possessed females by a controlling (but fearful) male audience. Pregnancy—a hoped-for future—is irrelevant. The female body, reduced to an empty kimono, disappears. By obliterating female emotions and female bodies, Zeami reinvents Murasaki's novel for his male audience as the victory of stoic, martial samurai over effeminate, aristocratic courtiers.

Historical Interregnum: Kabuki

During the period of kabuki's development and flowering (seventeenth through mid-nineteenth centuries), Murasaki's masterpiece is conspicuously absent. One would expect stories like Rokujō's to be made into dance pieces or powerful emotional plays featuring popular *onnagata* (female role specialists). Samuel L. Leiter (2009) suggests this lacuna may result from a prohibition on depicting the Imperial family. Since that prohibition no longer obtains, post-war kabuki plays based on *The Tale of Genji* are performed, but none focuses on Lady Rokujō. Although media and social intoxication with the current royal family may engender imagined parallels to the cloistered, beautiful, and sometimes scandalous Heian court (Leiter, footnote 137), most contemporary Japanese are as unfamiliar with *Tale of Genji* as Americans are with *The Canterbury Tales*.

Mishima Yukio's *Aoi no Ue* (aka *The Lady Aoi*)

Six centuries later, in 1954, Mishima published *The Lady Aoi*. It was a mere nine years after Japan's ignominious defeat in World War II and two years after the end of the seven-year US-led Occupation. Despite rapid transformation from near total devastation to extraordinary prosperity, the horrors of war and the atomic attacks on Hiroshima and Nagasaki could not be easily forgotten. The rapid migration into Japan of Western ideologies, codes of behaviour, and dress—and the continuing presence of American military—were both welcomed and feared.

Among the disenchanted was novelist and playwright Mishima Yukio (1925–1970). Mishima longed for the samurai spirit of *bushidō* ('The Way of the Warrior', an ethical code of conduct for the feudal samurai class that emphasized military prowess, honour and supreme obligation to one's lord, even if it meant personal or familial suffering). He mourned a lost time when the emperor was God and Japan a powerful empire. Paradoxically, he admired Western art and culture, wore the finest Western suits, and lived in a Western-style mansion. Although married, he was a homosexual infatuated with S&M. His spectacular, militaristic suicide by disembowelment and pleas for the nation to turn back the clock often overshadow his literary and theatrical output, including nine one-act plays using plots from nō. Misleadingly termed 'modern nō plays', they are often lyrical one-acts in shingeki style. Shingeki, the offspring of various horizontally migrating Euro-American theatrical genres, developed in the early twentieth century. By the early post-war period, shingeki (especially psychological realism) had become the dominant form of Japanese theatre.

Mishima's play takes place late at night in Aoi's room in a modern psychiatric hospital. As in many nō plays, time expands and the past is relived. Hikaru (i.e., 'The Shining Prince', one of the novel's sobriquets for Genji) has just returned from a business trip. During his absence, an elegant woman in a shining, silver car visited Aoi each night. The mysterious woman, of course, is Rokujō, and the silver car is her carriage. She always brings Aoi invisible, thorn-covered 'flowers of pain' that exude 'a loathsome odour.' (Mishima 1967, 153)

Tonight, her goal is to make Hikaru love her again. Hikaru easily succumbs, and they relive a memorable yacht trip, during which she threatened to send her living spirit to murder her rival if Hikaru should abandon her. In her bed, the present Aoi moans. When Hikaru escapes the memory, Rokujō has vanished. Confused, he telephones her home. While still speaking to Rokujō by phone, he hears her living spirit calling from outside the door, asking him to bring out her gloves. As though hypnotized, he takes the gloves, sets down the still live phone, and leaves. From the phone, we hear Rokujō's confused voice asking why he telephoned in the middle of the night. Aoi reaches for the phone, shrieks in pain, collapses, and dies. There is no suggestion that she is pregnant. The spirit behind the door and the woman on the phone are clearly separate beings. The focus is on the spectral Rokujō of the past's emotional control over Hikaru, rather than on freeing either woman from possession. In the end, it is Hikaru who is possessed (literally and symbolically).

Mishima was closely allied to the Japanese romantic/decadent writers (*Nihon rōmanha*) of the early to mid-twentieth century. Their goal was to 'overcome modernity', that is, the effects of Westernization—a practice demanding the wilful revision and erasure of historical memory. Like them, Mishima revelled in nostalgia for what he imagined to be a lost, militaristic past and is often called 'the cruelty of beauty'. Hikaru rejects the very real and present body of a young Aoi; instead, he embraces the cruel but beautiful sexuality of an older, ghostly, and clearly superior Rokujō. Aoi is not pregnant because she represents the sterility of contemporary Japan. Rokujō's goal is to destroy a sickly, insane present and to return Hikaru to the beautiful sanity of the past, a lost idyll represented by the elegant yacht safely navigating calm waters. The living Aoi and Rokujō's ghostly spirit—the past and the present—are rivals for Japan's love. A corporeal Rokujō holds no interest for Hikaru. As Bargen suggests, this 'either/or' separation of the females conforms to the traditional male view of possession—two distinct beings at war.

Mishima's reversal of Zeami's decision to eliminate Genji, the hero (or antihero?) of Murasaki's novel, is ironic because like Zeami, Mishima imagined a male audience wishing to rediscover a lost sense of male Japaneseness. Hikaru (Japan) is weak because he has chosen to love Aoi (the youthful, modern West). Aoi must die so that the glorious past can be reborn. Thus, Hikaru (Japan) abandons her in favour of Rokujō (the illustrious Japan of the past).

Kara Jūrō's *Two Women*

Just nine years after Mishima's spectacular suicide and twenty-five years after his *The Lady Aoi*, Kara Jūrō (b. 1940) produced *Futari no Onna* (Two Women, Kara 1992). This 1979 work treats Mishima's play as a virtual ur-text, barely referencing versions by either Murasaki or Zeami. Kara was writing for a generation born into ignominious defeat and national abjection. Unlike Mishima's cohort, they harboured no illusions about Japan's militaristic past. Rather, they were deeply distressed by the ongoing presence of US troops and by Japan's transformation into a staging ground for US wars in Southeast Asia. Kara joined the massive, unsuccessful protests in 1960 and 1970 against renewing the US–Japan security treaty (*Anpo*). Like protesters worldwide, Japanese demonstrators also advocated ending the Vietnam War, increasing civil rights, and making drastic changes to education, government, and society at large; and like their international counterparts, the Japanese suffered excessive police violence. Kara was among the founders of angura (underground) theatre. Angura is a post-war genre that simultaneously rejects shingeki and embraces episodic, shocking, counter-cultural elements. Angura's distinctive ethos thus reflects both vertical migration from kabuki's early, outcast days and horizontal migration from Euro-American experimental and avant-garde theatre. Kara's *Two Women* is antithetical both politically and theatrically to Mishima's work.

Referencing Mishima, *Two Women* begins in a psychiatric hospital located by the sandy beach at Izu. Koichi—the avatar of Genji—is a psychiatrist. To Pat Boone's 1957 hit song 'Love Letters in the Sand', he composes a love letter in the sand to his fiancée Aoi. The song and its singer, who was second only to Elvis Presley in popularity at the time of the song's release, clearly suggest American cultural hegemony; but the sea will erase the sand-written letters (and US influence?). Reversing Mishima, Rokujō is now the psychiatric patient. She is obsessed with an ant circus, a part of the complex colony of sand ants to which she longs to belong. A former radical activist, she conflates Koichi (who did not participate in the protests) with the activist lover who abandoned her. Koichi notices a striking resemblance between Rokujō and Aoi; in fact, they are played by the same actress, emphasizing both the contrast to Mishima's play and conformity to Bargen's idea of a unifying 'both/and' (or complicit) force.

The hospitalized Rokujō gives Koichi a key. Later, the cured Rokujō's car collides with that of the pregnant Aoi. Both the pregnancy and the car collision reference Murasaki's novel while repudiating Mishima's play. Aoi, suffering from morning sickness, finds the key and is consumed with jealousy. Her jealousy reverses both previous versions of the tale. Aoi suffers a psychotic break, turns into Rokujō, and is hospitalized. She escapes and follows Koichi to Rokujō's apartment. In Koichi's mind, the two women have merged. Aoi-Rokujō leaps from the rafters, dangling dead in mid-air with a broken neck. Koichi goes mad, returns to the hospital but is refused entry to Rokujō's old room, number six. The room number is an insular reference to Murasaki's novel: Rokujō (aka 'The Lady of the Sixth Ward') is so-named because she lives in Kyoto's sixth ward ('roku' means 'six'). Rokujō finds him on the beach composing love letters in the sand to Aoi. In their renewed passion, they transform into ants burrowing in the sand.

Like Mishima, Kara suggests that Japan suffers from insanity, but a very different kind of insanity than Mishima's vision. Kara laments the lost idealism of the 1960s to early 1970s while questioning the protests' rationale. He mourns the transformation of both formerly idealistic youths like Rokujō and formerly complacent middle-class students like Koichi into anonymous worker-ants populating the circus that is contemporary corporate Japan. Both idealism and indifference are ultimately buried by the sands of time and senseless passion.

Kara depicts the two women as aspects of one woman, representative of Japan's failure to confront both past and present. By being complicit in their emotional revenge on Koichi/Genji, they conform to Bargen's notion of Heian female possession as a weapon against male power. For Kara, however, this weapon is toothless. As a psychiatrist who sleeps with women who are (or become) psychotic, Koichi's unprofessional behaviour mirrors what many contemporary female readers perceive as Genji's sexual predation. If Koichi/Genji represents the ideal Japanese male (as Genji does for Murasaki), Kara suggests that the national soul is in deep trouble. The play is unremittingly pessimistic.

Kawamura Takeshi's *Aoi*

A quarter century separated Mishima's *The Lady Aoi* from Kara's *Two Women*. Another vertical migration of twenty-four years brings us to Kawamura Takeshi's (b. 1959) 2003 *Aoi*.

Kawamura's generation, like those of Zeami, Mishima, and Kara, faced political, social, and environmental traumas. Three events rocked 1989: the fall of the Berlin Wall, the Chinese crackdown on democracy advocates at Tiananmen Square, and the death of Hirohito (the Showa Emperor). This last event ended a sixty-three-year reign that began in 1926. During that time, Japan's militaristic expansion into Asia had devolved into the devastation of the Second World War and its aftermath. The nation had transformed from an exporter of cheap trinkets into an international powerhouse. When the 'bubble economy' collapsed in 1991, a decade of economic stagnation and massive unemployment ensued. Two horrors made 1995 memorable: the Kobe earthquake (resulting in 6,000 deaths, 30,000 injuries, and the destruction of much of the city) and the doomsday cult Aum Shinrikyo's deadly sarin gas attack on Tokyo's subways. As Japan's Asian neighbours continued to demand apologies for wartime atrocities, a right-leaning government financially aided the United States' Gulf War; in 2003, Japanese troops joined international efforts to rebuild Iraq, raising troubling constitutional questions.

Kawamura's play depicts this chaotic, rapidly transforming milieu. Unlike Mishima's and Kara's plays (both set in psychiatric wards), *Aoi* takes place in a beauty salon owned by Hikaru, the Genji character. Hikaru's apprentice is practising cutting long, female hair on a wig mounted on a manikin. Kawamura, nodding to both Mishima and Kara, depicts Aoi as an escaped mental patient. The apprentice has been forbidden from cutting her hair. When Hikaru enters, he sees Aoi and the piles of hair. He accuses the 'country bumpkin' apprentice of disobedience. He calls Aoi 'a sublime sickness that no one can cure' (Kawamura 2011, 174). Rokujō's reflection appears in the mirror demanding a haircut and Aoi's body flies off. The Rokujō-reflection reminds Hikaru of their past as illicit lovers and co-murderers of her husband, to whom Hikaru had been apprenticed. Rokujō says, 'You belonged to my husband [...]. He was the master. You and I, we were both [...] [s]laves to that jiggling body of his, the fat swollen [...] to his lust for control' (Kawamura 2011, 183). They relive the husband's murder on a 'long, hot night in August [...] when the air was yellow as if it were filled with a toxic gas [...] the sky was stained with such a deep red it seemed as though a neighbouring town has been bombed and was on fire [...]. Imagine—after that bombing, everyone living like empty shells' (Kawamura 2011, 186). After murdering the Master, they douse his body with sulphuric acid. As the body dissolves, Rokujō says, 'Look. Our empire is melting away [...]. Hikaru, make love to me' (Kawamura 2011, 188). Back in the present, Rokujō's reflection demands a final haircut before leaving forever. The stage directions read, 'There is a bizarre sound and huge amounts of hair fall from the sky and obscure the two. Darkness. When the lights come up, Hikaru is on the ground' (Kawamura 2011, 193).

The dazed Hikaru awakens and sweeps the piles of hair. The physical Rokujō enters, saying that she and the Master have just returned from a six-month journey. Hikaru is confused. Aoi, who was supposedly back in hospital, re-enters, sees Rokujō and says, 'I'm ready for my execution, Hikaru' (Kawamura 2011, 196). Hikaru grabs her hair, but it comes off—it is a wig. Aoi is completely bald. As she becomes hysterical, confusing Hikaru with the father she claims abused her, Rokujō takes the apprentice in her arms, promising to help his career just as she did for Hikaru. They leave. Aoi feels 'reborn' (Kawamura 2011, 197). Hikaru prepares to cut her non-existent hair, saying 'I'll never let you go…Your hair, it's so beautiful'. The stage directions read, 'a gentle breeze blows through the mountains of hair' (Kawamura 2011, 197). Translator Peter Eckersall notes that in production, '[s]oft, billowing strands of hair that soon become tangled are projected on the stage, symbolizing the threat of violence and intense memories merging with the present' (Kawamura 2011, xxiv).

Past and present are entangled. The script clearly references the atomic bombings of August 1945 that ended World War II and both the literal and symbolic death of the emperor/master and his swollen empire. Sickness, pollution, insanity, and spirit possession are equated with contemporary political and cultural phenomena. If Kara began (incompletely) to approach a more female-centric view by conflating the two women's identities, Kawamura seems to reject the female perspective entirely. As in many Japanese horror films, thick, long, black female hair is both sexually alluring and terrifying, evocative of madness and death. Female sexuality and possession are tied to the polluted, disgusting world evoked by earlier, misogynistic forms of Buddhism, including that of Zeami's victorious ascetic. There is no pregnancy, no intimation of new life or renewal. The memories of rape and betrayal by father/husband/master are allegorical and political. The female characters have no interior lives; they exist only to control or create havoc for males. Spirit possession (Bargen's female weapon, traditionally practiced in Shintō and shamanism) here becomes a justification for highly theatrical, horror-film staging effects. The audience—like Hikaru—is left in a state of psychic paralysis. Kawamura seems to suggest that past and present are equally insane, so we might as well just enjoy the show.

Conclusion

Murasaki's female response to a patriarchal world has migrated vertically for over a thousand years. Male playwrights hijacked the tale to explain their own incomprehensible times. For Zeami, this meant eliminating Genji and emphasizing the power of Buddhist exorcism to reconcile demonically dangerous, often female, ghosts with the brash new samurai 'boys' club' now in power. In contrast, all three post-war playwrights reclaimed Genji, but none reaffirmed Murasaki's vision. Mishima's Hikaru retreats into a glorious past, leaving the sickly female present to die; his Rokujō is not a demon but a saviour. The left-leaning, anti-establishment Kara's Koichi refuses his duty to cure an insane world, dooming him to life as a sand-burrowing worker-ant. Kawamura is even more pessimistic. His Hikaru may be aware of the past, but he neither ignores it (like Kara's character) nor embraces it (like Mishima's). He simply buries himself in mounds of sexually alluring, suffocating, demonic female hair.

Each of these playwrights claims the past as his own; each transforms memory into whatever he needs it to be. Nevertheless, the power of the female-created original never wanes. Every Japanese knows the name of Murasaki Shikibu, but only the cognoscenti recognize the names of these male playwrights.

Acknowledgements Earlier versions of this chapter were presented as '"An Endless River of Blood:" Theatricalizing Lady Rokujō from *Nō* to the Present' at the International Federation for Theatre Research, Stockholm, Sweden, 2016 and at *Enacting Culture(s): Theatre and Film Across Disciplines,* Peter Wall Institute for Advanced Studies, University of British Columbia, Vancouver, Canada, 2018. I am indebted to comments at those meetings and to suggestions from J. Thomas Rimer and Andrea Labinger.

References

Bargen, Doris G. 1997. *A Woman's Weapon: Spirit Possession in 'The Tale of Genji'*. Honolulu: University of Hawai'i Press.
Brown, Steven. 2001. *Theatricalities of Power: The Cultural Politics of Noh*. Stanford, CA: Stanford University Press.
Kara, Jūrō. 1992. 'Two Women.' Translated by John K. Gillespie. In *Alternative Japanese Drama: Ten Plays*, edited by Robert Rolf and John Gillespie, 293-324. Honolulu: University of Hawai'i Press.
Kawamura, Takeshi. 2011. 'Aoi.' Translated by Aya Ogawa. In *Nippon Wars and Other Plays*, edited by Peter Eckersall, 168-197. Calcutta: Seagull Books.

Leiter, Samuel L. 2009. 'Performing the Emperor's New Clothes: *The Mikado, The Tale of Genji*, and Lèse Majesté on the Japanese Stage'. In *Rising from the Flames: The Rebirth of Theater in Occupied Japan, 1945-1952,* edited by Samuel L. Leiter, 125-171. Lanham, MD: Lexington Books.

Mishima, Yukio. 1967. 'The Lady Aoi.' In *Five Modern Nō Plays*. Translated and edited by Donald Keene, 143-171. Tokyo: Tuttle.

Murasaki, Shikibu. 1978. *The Tale of Genji*. Translated and edited by Edward G. Seidensticker. New York: Knopf.

Taylor, Diana. 2003. *The Archive and the Repertoire: Performing Cultural Memory in the Americas*. Durham, NC: Duke University Press.

Zeami, Motokiyo. 1959. 'Aoi no Ue.' In *Japanese Noh Drama* v. II. Translated and edited by Japanese Classics Translation Committee, 87-102. Tokyo: Nippon Gakujutsu Shinkōkai.

CHAPTER 19

The Stranger's Case: Exile in Shakespeare

Miranda Fay Thomas

Migration and exile are one of Shakespeare's most persistent preoccupations. *Twelfth Night*'s opening shipwreck sees Viola washed up on a strange shore where she must re-negotiate her identity for success in a new land; Coriolanus is banished from Rome when he refuses to meet the people's expectations of him; *The Merchant of Venice* and *Othello* depict the mistreatment of outsiders in the Mediterranean; *Richard II*'s banishment of Bolingbroke sets in motion the usurpation of the king himself. Why does Shakespeare focus so much on themes of displacement? Social concerns aside, the topic simply makes good theatre. Banishment is crucially theatrical, 'dramatic almost to excess' (Kingsley-Smith 2003, 1): inclusion and exclusion are performative processes that require en-action. But more than this, Shakespeare's dramas of exile enable a considered examination of the relationship between home and identity. His work demonstrates how being an outsider 'is a relative identity and not a fixed position' (Novy 2013, 1); fortunes and circumstances are capable of being reversed (we might note how, in French, *hôte* can refer to a guest *or* a host). There is a curious moment of confusion in *The Merchant of Venice* that speaks to this. In Shylock's final scene, Portia asks, 'Which is the merchant here, and which the Jew?' (Shakespeare, *The Merchant of Venice*, 4.1.170) This might be treated as a comedic statement, as the performed markers of religious and cultural difference should make it obvious which of the men is Antonio and which is Shylock, but the fact that the question is asked raises the possibility that the distinction might not be so obvious as we might think. Portia's query may—whether it means to or not—draw attention to how difference might be constructed

M. F. Thomas (✉)
Trinity College Dublin, Dublin, Ireland
e-mail: THOMASMF@tcd.ie

through its very expectation and easily re-drawn. Shakespeare's plays present 'the precarious instant [...] between hospitality or inhospitality' (Schülting 2013, 24), creating the heightened drama of welcome or rejection which—for some characters—might be a matter of life or death.

This chapter introduces the contexts and theatrical practices of exile in Shakespearean drama before considering two case studies in greater depth: *Romeo and Juliet* and *Pericles*. The former play addresses the theme of banishment through Romeo's punishment to leave Verona after killing Tybalt, setting into motion the play's tragic finale of fatal confusion; *Pericles* is a play that addresses not one separation, but many: the plot revolves around the necessity and dangers of travel, but due to its generic expectations and Pericles' social status as prince, all ends well. The chapter assesses the literal and figurative language of exile, and how language itself helps to create the conditions necessary for the process of exile to occur. Additionally, it situates these themes within the context of Shakespeare's cultural capital by interrogating the idea of canonical inclusion: the first published quarto of *Romeo and Juliet* was not printed with Shakespeare's name attached, and *Pericles*—co-authored with George Wilkins—was not acknowledged as having Shakespearean authorship until 1664. In this way, the primacy of language to the theme of exile is developed yet further through a consideration of exile in—and out of—the canon itself.

Migration and Exile in the Age of Shakespeare

At the time Shakespeare was writing, accounts of travel and experiences abroad influenced colonial projects (such as the English voyages to America and Ireland) as well as offering new material for the theatrical imagination. These journeys prompted a reflection upon both the individual self and the nation at large, for as Lloyd Kermode writes, 'the alien excursion *supports* and *confirms* rather than instigates self-scrutiny, self-discovery, and the subsequent assertion of Englishness' (2009, 89). On a practical level, this manifested in an acceleration of map-making. 'What the Elizabethan subject of cartography finds on the horizon, at the edges and limits of its maps, threatens the organisation of the subject's own position' (Armstrong 2000, 147–8), and encounters with people and places now theorised as 'the Other' had a profound effect on how one viewed one's own place in the world. More than that, it made people much more aware of the mappable limitations of their own existence. 'Not for nothing', notes Lisa Hopkins, 'does Queen Elizabeth in *Richard III* lament that "I see, as in a map, the end of all"' (Hopkins 2005, 2). The borders of England itself were in flux: Elizabeth had lost territory in France and remained Queen there in name only (6). Moving into the seventeenth century, the reign of James united England with Scotland, but prior to this, the highlands had 'seemed so alien from England that there had been considerable doubt over whether he was eligible to succeed' (7). Indeed, as Ruth Norrington points out, 'because of the Alien Act, which stated that the heir to the throne had to be born on English soil, James's hereditary pretension to the throne was not acknowledged or ratified by Parliament until March 1604, a fact he would find hard to forget' (Norrington 2002, 103).

The Early Modern period saw changes in population that resulted in terms like 'strangers' and 'aliens' being used to describe immigrants, many of whom were re-settling to avoid military operations and violence, as well as religious persecution. Due to increased migration, travel, and trade, London became known as a 'world city'. Indeed, the interplay of cultural exchange and the emergence of capitalism led Thomas Dekker to observe in 1630 that 'This World is a Royall Exchange, where all sort of Men are Marchants' (qtd. in Bartolovich 2000, 14). The impact of this hit London culturally and socially, as well as economically: the area around St Paul's Cathedral was referred to by John Earle as 'the whole world's map […] with a vast confusion of languages' (16). But this was not universally viewed as a positive development. Bartolovich reminds us of the concern that 'such exchanges tended to transform their participants', with this process enabling 'an allegory of moral corruption' (16–17); Kermode too notes that in the earlier years of Elizabethan drama, 'English-alien contact is represented as causing infection, "deformation", or corruption by the presence of real alien bodies and influences' (Kermode 2009, 4). The population of London was growing rapidly, but not merely due to foreign immigrants; issues such as crop failure and unemployment within elsewhere in England brought many to London (Griffin 2014, 14). By 1600, London had sixteen times the population of Norwich, the second most populous town in the country (Kermode 2009, 2). For some, this brought positives: trade flourished as new skills were brought to the city, and landlords were able to rent out cheap accommodation to new immigrants. However, these newcomers were seen as taking away jobs from the locals; furthermore, 'they clustered and traded among themselves, sent money abroad instead of reinvesting it in England, and practised religion that was influenced by extremists and attracted good members away from the Church of England' (1). But it is important that we look at the statistics and place them in context, with 'the contemporary censuses (the Returns of Strangers) show[ing] a proportional *decrease* in the Continental alien presence in the latter half of the century: from 12.5 per cent in 1553, to 10 per cent in 1571, falling to between 5 and 6 per cent in 1593' (2).

Despite this, during the reign of Elizabeth I, banishments were proclaimed for the Irish, Scots borderers, Anabaptists, 'Egyptians', and 'Negroes' and 'blackamoors' (Kingsley-Smith 2003, 11, 13). 'Many in the government tried to respond by having all foreigners register; some wanted to forbid merchants from other countries from selling their wares. Libellous fliers were posted, and in 1593 a member of the Privy Council proposed expelling all foreigners within three months' (Novy 2013, 6). Perhaps the real source of resentment was that England was becoming increasingly dependent on the wealth and skills of those who came from outside its borders (Griffin 2014, 25; citing Pettegree 1986, 293–4). Above all, the drama of this period reveals how 'the presence of immigrants often reveals more about the host society than it does about the immigrant him/herself' (Espinosa and Rutter 2014, 5). As we will see, Shakespeare's drama is an affective one often rooted in the shifting of previously firmly-held positions. What is sometimes termed Shakespeare's essential ambivalence may be re-read as a flexible lens of relativity that opens up the potential for relatability on multiple sides, sometimes reactionary, sometimes progressive. Indeed, Shakespeare has been deployed as a rhetorical tool at both ends of the political spectrum.

Migration and Theatre Practices in Shakespeare's Age

The vast majority of Shakespeare's plays are set somewhere other than England. Indeed, Thomas Platter wrote that audiences could go to plays in London to 'learn [...] at the play what is happening abroad [...] [M]en and womenfolk visit such places without scruple, since the English for the most part do not travel much, but prefer to learn foreign matters [...] at home' (quoted in Bartolovich 2000, 17). The creation of the Globe theatre in 1599 deliberately evoked exoticism, transporting people who saw the theatre to another space and time. The exterior of the building would have been completely whitewashed as 'a considered adaptation of the classical Roman amphitheatre' (Day 1997, 95): the exposed beams that are a feature of the London Globe replica today are an inaccuracy pandering to the modern visitor's expectation of a Tudor style, whereas a crucial feature of the original Globe theatre(s) was that it stood out from the surrounding Early Modern buildings. The Globe, like other public playhouses of the period, was located outside of the City of London's walls associating these theatrical sites with other venues of danger and immorality such as plague hospitals, asylums, and brothels. In fact, the 1574 decision by the City to move the theatres into the Liberties was described as a 'banishment' in a later petition of 1596 (Kingsley-Smith 2003, 19). The ban on performances during outbreaks of plague was also described in these terms: in 1572, Harrison records that 'plays were banished for a time out of London, lest the resort unto them should engender a plague' (19).

Touring was regular and necessary not just in times of plague, when the purpose-built theatres in London were closed: touring was a 'normal requirement' of companies, and according to Greenfield, 'provincial records of visits by companies like the Queen's Men, the Lord Admiral's Men, and the Earl of Worcester's Men reveal no increases in touring activity because of the plague' (Greenfield 1997, 252). Travel was a common occurrence for companies, not just within England, but also in Europe. The English acting troupes were especially popular in Germany, where the locals attended performances despite not knowing English, because they understood the story through the gestures that were exhibited (Astington 2010, 181). However, touring was not always a successful endeavour: in 1593, Pembroke's Men toured after their shows were stopped by the London plague, but with expenses outweighing profit 'they returned to London, sold their wardrobe to cover their debts, and ceased to function as a company' (Greenfield 1997, 251).

Touring was a practice that emerged far earlier than the building of the London theatres, and was less of a novelty and more of a continuation of traditions from the thirteenth and fourteenth centuries, that only clearly declined in frequency in the 1610s and 20s (Greenfield 1997, 252–3). This was due to the royal monopoly of 1603, that decreed companies could only receive patronage from members of James I's royal family, in addition to a more concerted effort by local authorities to oppose the visits of touring players (265). Consequently, over time, some towns 'began to recognize a distinction between players who had royal patrons and those who did not, a distinction that allowed them to prevent the latter from performing', in addition to shutting out traveling troupes who might increase the spread of plague (266–7). One persistent perception of traveling troupes was that they were thought of as 'little better than roving vagabonds' (251). But while we have evidence of how these traveling companies entered into disputes, with some places even paying them *not* to play, 'such records make up less than 5 percent of the more than three thousand records concerning performance by touring companies during Shakespeare's lifetime' (251–2). This doesn't mean that the immoral associations with roving players didn't remain. Despite the companies being blessed with aristocratic patronage, players were still regarded as being 'outside or at least on the margin of the social hierarchy and thus viewed as a threat to the social order' (258). Dramatic licence translated to other freedoms: their practices were associated with festivals, where normal obligations would be suspended. In this way, migrating companies evoked a wider sense of the period's social mobility, both its advantages and its dangers.

Banishment and/as Death in *Romeo and Juliet*

The tension of *Romeo and Juliet* is rooted in spaces and boundaries. We see the Montagues and Capulets crossing lines of social decorum, showing up to parties they aren't invited to, and even climbing up to the bedroom of their rival's daughter. We also see the difficulty of being a teenager and trying to negotiate for your own place within society, as we see in Romeo's banishment from Verona.

After Romeo has slain Tybalt, the Prince is looking to restore law and order, and Romeo's father desperately advocates for death not to be used as punishment. The argument here is that there has been too much death already: the day has already made corpses of Tybalt and Mercutio, so Romeo's body will be sent into exile rather than the afterlife. Despite this, Romeo's banishment is still equated with death, as we see in the following scene where the newly married Juliet is awaiting news from her Nurse. Even though Juliet is unaware that Romeo has just been banished, she enters 3.2 alone musing on the interconnections of time and space, wishing for mastery over both:

> Gallop apace, you fiery-footed steeds,
> Towards Phoebus' lodging. Such a wagoner
> As Phaeton would whip you to the west
> And bring in cloudy night immediately. (Shakespeare, *Romeo and Juliet*, 3.2.1–4)

Her desire to bend time and space to her will is an eerie foreshadowing of what she does not yet know, but what we already do: that she will be separated by great distance from her husband. While the barriers between them up until this point have been challenging to overcome, they have been ultimately surmountable (practically, if not socially). But Romeo's banishment introduces a whole new level of difficulty for their relationship, so much so that it seems akin to a living death. In romantic literary terms, this is somewhat apt, as Kingsley-Smith notes how 'exile was commonly associated with death in Elizabethan love poetry. *Romeo and Juliet* takes this association further by endorsing the lovers' exile/death wordplay with action' (Kingsley-Smith 2003, 47).

Juliet's reaction to banishment—as a concept, even as a word—is extreme. She reflects that the word is 'worser than Tybalt's death / That murdered me' (Shakespeare, *Romeo and Juliet*, 3.2.108–9). She goes on to bewail:

> Tybalt is dead and Romeo banished.
> That 'banished', that one word 'banished'
> Hath slain ten thousand Tybalts. (Shakespeare, *Romeo and Juliet*, 3.2.112–4)

The intense repetition of 'banishment' in these lines has the effect of semantic satiation: the word is repeated so many times in the scene (there are far more examples than the ones included here) that it almost becomes almost nonsensical. Her speech demonstrates 'a sense of linguistic failure', with the usually articulate Juliet only able to repeat herself (Kingsley-Smith 2003, 47). This mirrors Juliet's lack of comprehension or ability to accept what is happening, and thus her conflation of one banishment with the deaths of many: 'To speak that word / Is father, mother, Tybalt, Romeo, Juliet, / All slain, all dead' (Shakespeare, *Romeo and Juliet*, 3.2.122–124). Her conception of banishment is one that contains both everything *and* its annihilation: 'There is no end, no limit, measure, bound, / In that word's death' (Shakespeare, *Romeo and Juliet*, 3.2.125–6). For Juliet—and, as we shall see, for Romeo—banishment might as well be death; for if she cannot see her spouse, he might as well not exist: she has been denied his company, and in their separation, there is an emptiness akin to the destruction of life itself. What many first note about this play—its tendency towards melodrama—is perfectly apt in this scene: the play *is*, after all, *Romeo and Juliet* (with the emphasis on the *and*). If they are separated, the play cannot continue, and the whole world of the play, including its other characters—father, mother, Tybalt—will all vanish. Contained within the title itself is the central drama of this play: a story that in itself becomes hysterical over its need to be told.

In the next scene, 3.3, Romeo learns of his fate. His reaction mirrors Juliet's:

> Ha, banishment? Be merciful, say 'death'
> For exile hath more terror in his look,
> Much more, than death. Do not say 'banishment'. (Shakespeare, *Romeo and Juliet*, 3.3.11–13)

Why is Romeo not relieved at being banished rather than killed for his crime? Because, to his mind:

> There is no world without Verona walls
> But purgatory, torture, hell itself.
> Hence banished is banished from the world,
> And world's exile is death; then 'banished'
> Is death mistermed [...]
> [...] Heaven is here
> Where Juliet lives, and every cat and dog
> And little mouse, every unworthy thing,
> Live here in heaven and may look on her,
> But Romeo may not. (Shakespeare, *Romeo and Juliet*, 3.3.17–23; 29–33)

The sheer immaturity of these lines—the lack of imagination of worlds beyond Verona—reminds us how young and naive Romeo actually is. At least in death he would not have to wait out the minutes away from her, because neither time nor space will continue to exist for him in the mortal sense. Yet, coupled with this youthful impatience is a meditation on the egotistical nature of performance. To be in a play and have your character banished from the stage is a kind of death for the actor. Romeo is behaving like an actor who wants a bigger role, refusing to leave the stage graciously. What we read in these lines is a temper tantrum that others will get to see Juliet while he will not; perhaps the comment that 'every unworthy thing / [...] may look on her' refers to the fact that the groundlings by the actor's feet will still be able to see Juliet onstage, but Romeo will be denied both his view of her and of his capacity, as actor, to be centre of attention. The theatrical scaffold upon which Romeo rants and raves is both Verona—*where* he exists—and the stage—*how* he exists—and the overlap of these spaces deepens our understanding of how death and exile operate as a physical and semantic nexus. After 3.5, when the young lovers say their farewells, Romeo is off-stage until 5.1, where we see him in Mantua receiving the false news of Juliet's demise. Until then we are not treated to lengthy scenes of Romeo wandering around in exile, presumably as they are not dramatically necessary to the plot, but this is precisely the premise of exile in *Romeo and Juliet*: it is a banishment from the world of the stage, and one's place within literal and imagined theatrical communities.

As the lovers bid farewell in the morning light, Juliet experiences a feeling of uncanniness:

> O God, I have an ill-divining soul!
> Methinks I see thee now, thou art so low,
> As one dead in the bottom of a tomb. (Shakespeare, *Romeo and Juliet*, 3.5.54–56)

Juliet's prescience is correct: 3.5 is the last time that they will both be theatrically alive in each other's presence (they are reunited in the tomb in Act 5, but while Romeo is alive Juliet appears dead, and it is only when Romeo dies that

Juliet awakes). This means that Romeo and Juliet were, in fact, correct in their hysteria: when Romeo leaves Verona, death will inevitably follow. The equation, in this case, of exile and mortality, while initially seen as hyperbolic, turns out to be literal. As Shakespeare will go on to write in Hamlet, death is 'the undiscovered country, from whose bourne / No traveller returns'.

The Painful Adventures of *Pericles*

Whereas in *Romeo and Juliet*, migration is a means of advancing the plot, in *Pericles* migration could be said to be the plot in its entirety. The play is riddled with treacherous voyages, families separated, and the need to rely on the mercy of strangers in new lands. The play's first act alludes to Christianity's very first story of exile. Pericles sees the beautiful daughter of Antiochus, commenting:

> You gods that made me man and sway in love,
> That have inflamed desire in my breast
> To taste the fruit of yon celestial tree
> Or die in the adventure, be my helps,
> As I am son and servant to your will,
> To compass such a boundless happiness. (Shakespeare, *Pericles*, 1.1.20–25)

Evoking the banishment of Adam and Eve from Eden, and the verb 'compass' foreshadowing the travels ahead, Pericles' predicament in the first act is the need to escape from dangerous knowledge: the beautiful daughter is entrapped by the incestuous love of her father, and Pericles' life is in danger if he reveals the truth. This sets his first voyage in motion: he is advised by Helicanus 'go travel for a while' (Shakespeare, *Pericles*, 1.2.104). He sails to Tarsus, where Cleon governs, and Pericles brings corn to feed the starving citizens. Introducing himself, Pericles acknowledges that a strange ship approaching Tarsus may be a cause for concern, with the governor fearing the boats 'Are like the Trojan horse was stuffed within / With bloody veins expecting overthrow' (Shakespeare, *Pericles*, 1.4.91–2), but the example set is one of mutualism and symbiosis (at least, until Act 4, when Pericles' daughter is entrusted to Tarsus only for Cleon's wife Dionyza to plot her murder). However, no good deed goes unpunished, and Pericles becomes shipwrecked at Pentapolis. There, he falls on the mercy of some generous fishermen, who—ignorant of Pericles' noble birth—treat him well, offering him garments and sustenance, before telling him of a tournament hosted by King Simonides. Pericles wins the tournament before revealing his true identity, and wins the hand of the King's daughter, Thaisa. From here, the plot multiplies into further strands of voyage, confusion, and loss: Thaisa appears to die in childbirth, the daughter grows up away from her father, and Pericles ages into loneliness. But all ends well, with the family reunited in Mytilene.

Critical views on the play take a variety of approaches. Suzanne Gossett reminds us that Shakespeare's romance plays are often seen 'as representations of the human journey', but that in *Pericles*, 'voyage is not merely metaphor but the central and repeated action' (Gossett 2005, 26). Other critics have focused less on metaphor and more on the play's treatment of place. Peter Holland ponders the precise location of Pentapolis, which seems to be part of Greece in the play, but according to the story *Pericles* is based on (the adventures of Apollonius of Tyre) may be more accurately located in North Africa (Holland 2005, 14). Shakespeare's inaccuracy is more kindly described by Gossett as 'imaginative geography' (2006, 229), an analysis which evokes the value of a combined geographical and narrative plausibility: the re-location of Pentapolis enables Shakespeare and Wilkins to confine the action of the play to 'the northern and eastern shores of the Mediterranean' (Holland 2005, 14) and therefore to areas Shakespeare's audience may have been more familiar with. Critics also comment on the play's political parallels with Jacobean England: Constance Jordan relates Pericles' political problems to James I's difficulties with the House of Commons and suggests that the eventual union of Tyre and Pentapolis shadows the creation of Great Britain (1997, 36–56).

But while the play fixates on the dangerous realities of migration and travel, it is worth reflecting: just how much is Pericles' luck in surviving all of these voyages down to the artificial safety of being a prince in a romance genre? Class privilege here begets narrative privilege. Pericles often receives a noble welcome, even before his hosts know who he is, and the success or failure of travel in Shakespeare's plays is 'to some extent prescribed by the genre' (Schülting 2013, 31). As Schülting notes, 'Despite his obscure identity which he does not disclose to his host, Pericles is granted abundant hospitality at Simonides's court, which goes far beyond the basic needs of a castaway [....] Simonides gives freely to those who have come to honour his sovereignty and, one should add, who "by nature" deserve it' (35). This idea—of the 'deserving' visitor— reinforces the all-too familiar concept of the 'good immigrant': migrants who are seen as more 'acceptable' to the host country for their provision of highly valued skills, services, and other traits seen as beneficial, including a noble birth.

Two twenty-first century productions situate *Pericles* within current sociopolitical contexts. A collaboration between the Royal Shakespeare Company and Cardboard Citizens (The Warehouse, 2003) cast both 'RSC actors and performers from refugee backgrounds', and interpolated immigrants' testimonies into the script (Cox 2014, 15). The theatrical space, in Southwark, London:

> was deliberately evocative of a detention centre akin to Calais's now-closed Sangatte and was the site of the previous year's Crisis at Christmas event for the homeless. *Pericles* was an ambitious promenade work that used several vast interiors, including an entry zone where audiences could peek into tents and see performances of testimonies on TV screens; a room set up like a forbidding exam hall in which audience members, seated at desks, were confronted with convoluted refugee application forms; a fisherman's shore overflowing with pegged clothing and washing machines; an austere arrangement of blue camp beds; and

a Temple of Diana dominated by a bright, kitschy image of the late Princess Diana. (16–17)

A different approach was taken by Cheek By Jowl, whose 2018 production was performed in French:

> *Périclès* took place on a detailed set built around a single character—a patient in a psychiatric hospital (Grégoire). While the comatose patient's family were visiting him, the patient came to life as Périclès, and the play took over the bodies and objects that inhabit the ward: during his shipwreck, for instance, Périclès emptied a bedpan over himself, and the fishermen that rescued him were the doctor and nurses of the ward, patiently changing his bed and pyjamas and washing him down, before placing him into a straightjacket that served as the 'armour' for the jousting. (Kirwan 2019, 184)

Both productions used realistic sets to establish a firm sense of place, and notably, both adopted the theme of institutionalisation (a detention centre and a hospital), emphasising the wider structural politics shaping how the story is imagined for modern audiences. *Pericles* and its recent productions serve as stark reminders not just of the physical turmoil of refugee travel, but the emotional and psychological cost.

In the play's prologue, Gower—the chorus-figure—says of this 'old' tale that 'lords and ladies in their lives / Have read it for restoratives' (Shakespeare, *Pericles*, 1.0.7–8); in other words, it's a story meant to make us feel better. To what extent is this the case? It is worth noting a detail from the RSC/Cardboard Citizens production, wherein testimonies from refugees were interrupted by

> a formally dressed man [who] came forward to pronounce, '[t]hose are all the stories we have time for. Now, in future, please try to avoid stories which are too long, too complicated, too difficult to believe, too culturally specific, or too painful to listen to.' He was followed by a teacher figure who 'educated' the audience about how universal Shakespeare is. (Cox 2014, 16–17)

The inclusion of this moment served to satirise the over-used opinion that Shakespeare's writing can speak to the entire human experience. Shakespeare's stories of migration can certainly speak to our modern concerns; but they have limitations. Novy argues that Shakespeare's outsiders have been used for multiple purposes by many different groups across time: 'Shylock, Othello, and many others have occasioned attacks on Shakespeare for his biases, praises of Shakespeare for being really on their side, and re-writings by authors who use them to articulate post-Shakespearean ideas about minority, female, or colonial experience' (2013, 1). Shakespeare is regularly celebrated both as England's national poet and the most famous playwright in the world. But we must note that, if Shakespeare can be said to be universal, it is because the way universality is modelled has been shaped in the image of white, English-speaking men like him. Shakespeare's stories of migration have lasted long in the public imagination, but we must also remind ourselves of their cultural specificity. If these stories, as Gower says, are read 'for restoratives', then this has mostly been for white privileged audiences to make themselves feel better, restoring the status quo.

References

Armstrong, Philip. 2000. *Shakespeare's Visual Regime: Tragedy, Psychoanalysis and the Gaze*. Basingstoke: Palgrave.

Astington, John. 2010. *Actors and Acting in Shakespeare's Time*. Cambridge: Cambridge University Press

Bartolovich, Crystal. 2000. '"Baseless Fabric": London as a "World City".' In *The Tempest and Its Travels*, edited by Peter Hulme and William H. Sherman, 13–26. London: Reaktion Books.

Cox, Emma. 2014. *Theatre & Migration*. London: Palgrave Macmillan.

Day, Barry. 1997. *This Wooden 'O': Shakespeare's Globe Reborn*. London: Oberon Books.

Espinosa, Ruben, and David Rutter eds. 2014. *Shakespeare and Immigration*. Surrey and Burlington: Ashgate.

Gossett, Suzanne. 2005. 'Political *Pericles*.' In *World-Wide Shakespeares: Local Appropriations in Film and Performance* edited by Sonia Massai, 23–20. Oxon: Routledge.

Greenfield, Peter H. 1997. 'Touring.' In *A New History of Early English Drama*, edited by John D. Cox and David Scott Kastan, 251–268. New York: Columbia University Press.

Griffin, Eric. 2014. 'Shakespeare, Marlowe, and the Stranger Crisis of the Early 1590s.' In *Shakespeare and Immigration*, edited by Ruben Espinosa and David Ruiter, 13–36. Surrey and Burlington: Ashgate.

Holland, Peter. 2005. 'Coasting in the Mediterranean: The Journeyings of Pericles.' *Angles on the English-Speaking World* 5: 11–29.

Hopkins, Lisa. 2005. *Shakespeare on the Edge: Border-crossing in the Tragedies and the Henriad*. Hampshire and Burlington: Ashgate.

Jordan, Constance. 1997. *Shakespeare's Monarchies: Ruler and Subject in the Romances*. New York: Cornell University Press.

Kermode, Lloyd Edward. 2009. *Aliens and Englishness in Elizabethan Drama*. Cambridge: Cambridge University Press.

Kingsley-Smith, Jane. 2003. *Shakespeare's Drama of Exile*. Hampshire and New York: Palgrave.

Kirwan, Peter. 2019. *Shakespeare in the Theatre: Cheek By Jowl*. London: Arden Bloomsbury.

Norrington, Ruth. 2002. *In The Shadow of the Throne: The Lady Arbella Stuart*. London: Peter Owen.

Novy, Marianne. 2013. *Shakespeare and Outsiders*. Oxford: Oxford University Press.

Pettegree, Andrew. 1986. *Foreign Protestant Communities in Sixteenth-Century London*. Oxford: Clarendon Press.

Schülting, Sabine. 2013. 'What Country, Friends, is This? The Performance of Conflict in Shakespeare's Drama of Migration,' In *Shakespeare and Conflict: A European Perspective*, edited by C. Dente and S. Soncini, 24–39. Hampshire and New York: Palgrave.

Shakespeare, William. 2012. *Romeo and Juliet*. Edited by René Weis. London: Arden Bloomsbury.
———. 2013. *The Merchant of Venice*. Edited by John Drakakis. London: Arden Bloomsbury.
———. 2006. *Pericles*. Edited by Suzanne Gossett. London: Arden Bloomsbury.

CHAPTER 20

The 'English Comedy' in Early Modern Europe: Migration, Emigration, Integration

M. A. Katritzky

In sixteenth- and seventeenth-century Europe, migrancy was a fact of life for professional performers. The rudimentary stage and organizational skills of some professional performers hardly differentiated them from peddlers or beggars, often limiting them to touring alone, or in small family groups, within their own local region. Talent and business know-how generated the commercial success enabling renowned travelling performers to migrate across multiple national borders, with large troupes capable of staging full-length dramas supported by music and acrobatics (Katritzky 2007, 79–115). Beginning in the 1580s, mixed gender French and Italian acting troupes were joined on mainland Europe by migrant English troupes, while professional Dutch and German acting troupes only became a viable economic threat during the seventeenth century. Although French, and especially Italian, actresses excited enormous interest, touring provided many challenges. Unpredictable weather conditions, geographic and linguistic barriers, and political and religious considerations lessened the commercial appeal of Northern tours for their troupes. Thus, the first professional migrant acting troupes to dominate the German-speaking regions were English. The Thirty Years' War (1618–1648) brutally devastated central Europe's population and culture, and increasingly damaged Germany's reputation as an attractive, lucrative hub for migrant performers. Even so, English-born actors toured and performed in Northern and Central Europe for nearly a century, influencing the rise of professional theatre in the German-speaking regions with their multi-talented style of performing.

M. A. Katritzky (✉)
The Open University, Milton Keynes, UK
e-mail: m.a.katritzky@open.ac.uk

© The Author(s), under exclusive license to Springer Nature Switzerland AG 2023
Y. Meerzon, S. E. Wilmer (eds.), *The Palgrave Handbook of Theatre and Migration*, https://doi.org/10.1007/978-3-031-20196-7_20

Many migrant English actors maintained home bases in England. However, in comparison with other nationalities, English actors were more likely to emigrate and integrate into mainland European communities through marriage and theatrical contracts with local women and performers. Although the dozen or so performers of each full-sized English troupe were exclusively male until the 1650s, dependents travelling with them were routinely assigned professional responsibilities in sales, costume, or other non-performing areas. A document dating to 1615 awarding the troupe leader John Spencer the citizenship, protection and patronage of the city of Cologne, following his conversion to Catholicism, along with that of his entire acting troupe and entourage, including his wife and children, suggests that Spencer habitually toured with his family (Chambers 1923, 90; Haekel 2004, 65–68). Another exceptional document, sentencing two mercenaries to choose between heavy fines or immediate banishment for seriously injuring Spencer's heavily pregnant wife during an argument at Rothenburg Town Hall in Bavaria in 1613, reveals that it was her responsibility to collect the entrance money for the troupe's performances from spectators (Katritzky 2008, 42).[1]

Not all migrant English actors toured with English dependents, and ample opportunities to meet mainland women are graphically indicated in Fynes Moryson's travel account of the 1590s:

> When some of our cast dispised Stage players came out of England into Germany, and played at Franckford in the tyme of the mart [...] the Germans, not vnderstanding a word they sayde, both men and women, flocked wonderfully to see theire gesture and action. [...] When some cast players of England came into those partes [the Low Countries], the people not vnderstanding what they sayd, only for theire action followed them with wonderfull Concourse, yea many young virgines fell in loue with some of the players, and followed them from Citty to Citty, till the magistrates were forced to forbid them to play any more.[2]

Thomas Sackville, whose troupe was performing in German by 1596,[3] and one of his actors, John Bradstreet, were two of many migrant English actors touring with foreign dependents (Katritzky 2008, 41–42). During Sackville's 1597 Frankfurt season, he and Bradstreet successfully petitioned for their wives, German-born Elisabeth Smidts and Danish-born Katharine Brasen (personal chambermaid to Duchess Elisabeth of Braunschweig-Lüneburg), to be allowed to stay on as private lodgers for several weeks while they left Frankfurt.[4] Around 1602, Sackville, creator of the popular English stage fool John Posset, retired from the stage to concentrate on his cloth-dealing business interests. This work funded construction of the imposing half-timbered family house still standing

---

[1] Rothenburg Stadtarchiv, AA 536/I, ff. 11^{r-v}, 13^r-17^v.
[2] Oxford Corpus Christi College, MS.CCC94, 470, 520–1.
[3] Frankfurt, Stadtarchiv, Burgermeisterbücher 1595, f.231^r (23.3.1596).
[4] Frankfurt, Stadtarchiv, Ratsprotokolle 1597, ff.39^v, 41^r, Burgermeisterbücher 1597, ff.107^r, 110^v (27 & 29.9.1597).

at 1 Kanzleistrasse, just off Wolfenbüttel's main market square, where Sackville lived until his death in 1628 with his German-born second wife, Elisabeth Francken (Zimmermann 1902, 38–44, 54–55). Here, he welcomed touring English performers, such as in September 1620 when William Taylor, a long-term actor and lutenist at the Saxony court of Count Ernst III zu Holstein-Schaumburg in Bückeburg and his brother John Taylor (London's self-styled 'water poet'), visited Sackville for two days en route to a court christening in Prague (Taylor 1620, sig.B4^v). This increasing integration of English actors into German-speaking communities during the seventeenth century contributed to a significant theatrical transmigration: the establishment of the so-called 'English Comedy' in Germany. Central to the touring English actors' multi-talented and spectacular performing style were their distinctive stage clowns, especially Pickelhering. The earliest professional touring German actors based their style of acting on skills passed down by migrant English actors—whether at first hand, via local performers with experience of English troupes, or less transparently. The English style of acting was so foundational to the origins and progression of German professional acting that well into the eighteenth-century German troupes habitually toured under the rubric of English comedians.

HISTORICAL, GEOGRAPHICAL, AND CULTURAL CONTEXT

In order to understand why English actors toured Early Modern Germany, and how they became so successful and popular that they dominated early professional German theatrical style, we must remind ourselves of the uneven rise of professional acting. Performing was an important part of medieval life in every European region. But wandering minstrels faced harsh economic challenges, including widespread church disapproval and legal constraints. Calendar regulations restricted the activities of performers to specific dates and seasons centred around the major Church Feasts, strictly excluding Lent and other fasting days. Medieval-organized theatre largely consisted of amateur performances by men and boys attached to schools and universities, city guilds, church congregations, or courts. By the mid-sixteenth-century, some amateur performers were attempting to establish more economically secure long-term career prospects for themselves by signing contracts to band together in formal groups with ambitious cultural and economic aims. Widespread opportunities for long-term co-ordinated professional acting were only developed in Europe during the sixteenth century. These were facilitated by actors who introduced the significant features of Early Modern commercial drama, including year-round availability of performances, the participation of female as well as male actors, and above all migrancy.

Not every European region produced equally successful professional players. During the late sixteenth and early seventeenth centuries, German-speaking Europe imported, rather than exported, professional drama. While Jesuit drama and other school productions, folk theatre, civic religious plays, and court festivals flourished, German professional actors only flourished after 1648. The German speaking regions offered wealthy courts, Europe-wide Habsburg cultural contacts and highly profitable international business centres such as Danzig, Leipzig, or Frankfurt. These advantages established central Europe as the great contact zone for itinerant professional acting troupes until 1618. Additional economic activity was important for travelling performers. The touring Italians often pursued healthcare related options; by contrast, English actors enjoying court patronage often had diplomatic duties or non-medical commercial interests. Some dealt in cloth (Oppitz-Trotman 2020, 115–54), arms, musical instruments, or luxury goods, either between courts or at trade fairs.

Within Early Modern Europe, profitable transregional circulation of professional theatre mainly involved performers from two language areas, and audiences in two host regions. Firstly, from the mid-sixteenth century onwards, when mixed gender commedia dell'arte actors from the Italian peninsula toured mainly Mediterranean regions, and secondly, from the 1580s onwards, when English itinerant professional all-male acting troupes exported their 'English Comedy' to mainland Northern Europe for over a century. The long expensive journeys associated with overseas touring required considerable financial incentives; players who travelled had to flexibly accommodate local regulations, confessional practice, and linguistic barriers. Like the Italians, the English troupes developed innovative promotional strategies for challenging the traditional restrictions of the Christian festive year, and for encouraging prominent court and civic patrons to finance their travel expenses. Royal or noble patronage provided two essential ingredients for successful touring actors: a secure haven for the winter months and the diplomatic weight to persuade city councils to permit public performances.

Familial ties between the London royal court and North European courts provided touring English troupes with a ready-made patronage network. Queen Anna, wife of King James I of England, was the sister of King Christian IV of Denmark. Three of Anna's sisters respectively married Duke Heinrich Julius of Braunschweig-Lüneburg (Elisabeth), second cousin Christian II, Elector of Saxony (Hedwig), and John Adolf, Duke of Holstein-Gottorp (Augusta). Although considerations of distance, language, and politics primarily confined them to Protestant northern Europe, patronage was key. Wealthy Habsburg-connected patrons warmly recommended the rare openly Catholic English troupes to each other. For example, on 18 March 1617, Archduke Karl, Prince-Bishop of Breslau, recommended the English troupe of John Green to Franz von Dietrichstein, Archbishop of Olomouc, that had delighted his Habsburg family in Graz in 1608 and was now at his court in Neisse, after performing for several months at the court of his brother-in-law Zygmunt III, King of Poland (Soffé 1888). Local civic regulations also played their part, as troupes typically supplemented court engagements with public touring. They would gain a licence to play in a particular city by submitting a signed supplication to its magistrates in advance of their visit (Haekel 2004, 43–6). Decisions on licensing, level of entrance fee, and length of stay (usually three consecutive weeks with no Sunday performances) were often finalized after the mayor and councillors had watched a complimentary performance. Robert Browne's formal supplication of 1602 to Frankfurt's magistrates acknowledges the importance of making sure that this performance was seemly and modest, and a marginal addendum suggests that invited dignitaries routinely brought their wives, children, and other guests to them.[5]

Theatrical Practices Related to Migration

The English actors abroad made a lasting impact on the theatrical cultures of mainland Europe. While they did present versions of London plays, it is anachronistic to approach their performances purely, or even primarily, from the perspective of the surviving corpus of manuscript and printed play texts. These texts do not reflect a representative image of their activities; gradually, a broader perspective is shifting scholarly attention to the importance of a rich web of continuing mutual influences between European and English play texts, puppet theatre, novellas and folk tales, and religious sources, such as the vernacular bibles of Luther and King James I (Bosman 2004; Haekel 2004; Drábek and Katritzky 2016; Drábek 2020). Archival researches increasingly contextualize the English comedians within the traditions of court and popular culture; Jesuit, Piarist, and Lutheran school theatre; and hagiography, Easter plays, and other religious ceremony and performance.

Archival records only rarely identify performers by name, theatrical role, or by their exact performance skills. Typically, their skills were much broader than those now associated with the modern acting profession. Overseas, as in England, English touring performances habitually supplemented drama with a high element of music and spectacle. During the 1590s, even English actors in reputable London-based companies, such as The Queen's Men, often shared their stages with acrobats (McMillin and MacLean 1998, xii). Overseas, the entertainments for which they were employed at court, or paid by public spectators, sometimes involved no scripted drama. Germany shared England's widespread interest in music and English performers became popular in Europe as professional court musicians even before they toured as actors (Wikland 1977; Spohr 2009). English actors were often referred to as players, or in German *Instrumentisten*, ambiguous terms that denoted musicians as well as actors—performers who were institutionally perceived as being engaged in the same activities. For example, when Will Kempe, a future partner of William Shakespeare in the London-based acting troupe the Lord Chamberlain's Men, performed at King Frederick II of Denmark's court at Kronborg Castle in Elsinore for several months in 1586, the Danish accounts identified him as 'Wilhelm Kempe Instrumentist' (Wikland 1977, 129).

Substantial overlap of the Early Modern performing professions obscures attempts to interpret known records unambiguously, or to conclusively

---

[5] Frankfurt, Stadtarchiv, Ratssupplikationen 1602, ff.265r-266v [7.9.1602].

distinguish between migrant English troupes staging plays, and those limiting their activities only to music and spectacle (Vander Motten and Abbing 2020, 14–15). Overseas audiences valued the English actors as multi-talented performers, whose acting featured highly skilled non-verbal elements lacking, or inadequately represented, in local amateur and church-sponsored productions. Hugely popular with both public and court audiences, fencing, singing, dumb shows, dancing, rope-dancing, acrobatics, and above all the clowning and improvised speeches of their distinctively costumed, often German-speaking, stage fools, were crucial to their commercial success. Records such as one noting that on 19 July 1585, English performers received payment from the city of Leipzig for a performance enlivened with acrobatics and all manner of entertainments, repeatedly emphasize their wide and varied range of theatrical and musical skills.[6]

Outside the context of longer court and civic engagements, the limitations of touring restricted the English troupes in Europe to simple stages, few costumes and props, a narrow repertoire repeatedly recycling similar elements, and heavy reliance on improvised vernacular clowning and non-verbal spectacle. Further central principles, not simply dictated by the constraints of overseas touring but fundamental to their popularity and influence, can also be identified. They include a reduction to essentials in terms of scripts, their immediately recognisable comic clown figures (notably Pickelhering), their focus on shared contemporary socio-political concerns, and their broad diversity of performative skills, in terms of music, dancing, and acrobatics, as well as acting. Overseas, the English actors defined their brand through positive characteristics developed directly from the necessary economies and commercial priorities of transnational migrancy, primarily enhancing their crowd-pleasing reputation with multi-talented, non-scripted performing skills.

From the 1580s until their gradual assimilation into German professional troupes in the later seventeenth century, around 12 full-sized English-led acting companies and many smaller groups of English performers variously toured the Spanish Netherlands, Germany, and Central European Habsburg Lands. Some also toured the Mediterranean or Baltic regions, even venturing as far as Ljubljana, Venice, Helsinki, Königsberg, or Riga. Queen Elizabeth I's 1572 Vagrancy Act defined as 'Sturdy Beggers' all 'Fencers Bearewardes Comon Players in Enterludes & Mynstrels Juglers' without a patron or 'Lycense of two Justices of the Peace at the leaste' (Haekel 2004, 21). These vagrancy laws were aimed at unsalaried masterless men and travelling minstrels, and would not have motivated trained musicians employed at court or in secure civic positions to consider emigrating. While *The Run-Away's Answer*, a pamphlet of 1625 attributed to Thomas Dekker, hints at a connection between actors venturing abroad, and a rise in social status and suggests poverty, lawsuits, and the plague as possible reasons for leaving London, viable acting troupes rarely left England

---

[6] 'Thaler den englischen Spielleuten, so ufm Rathaus ihr Spiel mit Springen und allerlei Kurzweil getrieben' (quoted: Chambers, II, 272).

simply as the less skilled overspill of a crowded London stage (Bosman 2004, 561–62; Spohr 2009, 28; Drábek and Katritzky 2016, 1528–29).

Credible reasons for touring abroad include the political, religious, and economic. Noble and royal patrons referenced their culture, connections, and wealth by circulating their performers not just around England but also across the Channel. Migrant performers supplemented their seasonal court remuneration through public shows and non-theatrical economic activities. During the Interregnum (1642–1660), escalating English Protestant disapproval of the theatre led to the complete closure of London's public theatres by the Puritan parliament. Some English actors touring Europe were openly Catholic; many were suspected of being Catholic spies. Resurrection plays, such as civic Easter mystery plays, St George plays, or Lazarus plays, represent a significant sector of Early Modern European performance culture. Certain saints' plays and other religious dramas indicated by the English comedians' extant play titles suggest evidence for the progressive integration of Catholic content into religious stage traditions then outlawed in England but flourishing in Europe. Before risking expensive transnational tours with unpredictable outcomes, English actors would have informed themselves of mainland conditions and commonalities between English and German court and civic performance culture. They would also have acquired appropriate patronage, knowledge of German markets, and confidence in their English product.

Clearly, the English actors' early overseas tours were organized around special occasions with ready-made audiences willing to pay for entertainment and celebration. Generally, these were court festivals such as weddings or christenings, or internationally renowned trade fairs such as the biennial Frankfurt Book Fair. English performances at Elsinore in 1585 were staged in the context of a diplomatic undertaking instigated by Robert Dudley, first earl of Leicester. English diplomatic connections also surround the prolonged Swedish engagement of another troupe of twelve actors and musicians in 1592, to perform in Nyköping, at the wedding of the future King Charles IX of Sweden to Princess Christina of Holstein-Gottorp, sister of John Adolf (Wikland 1977, 34). In August 1596, the prominent guest list for the Copenhagen coronation of King Christian IV included his sisters Anna and Elisabeth and their husbands, King James VI of Scotland (the future King James I of England), and Duke Heinrich Julius of Braunschweig-Lüneburg. Greatly impressed by the English actors and musicians at the festivities for his own marriage in Copenhagen in 1590, Heinrich Julius had been supporting (and writing plays for) English comedians and acrobats at his Wolfenbüttel court since 1592. Although like James VI unable to attend in person, Heinrich Julius sent 18 English performers to perform at Christian IV's coronation (Wikland 1977, 133).

Actors dependent on patronage and the box-office cannot afford to lose touch with the wishes of their audience. The extent to which *Engelische Comedien und Tragedien Sampt dem Pickelhering*, a collection of German play texts named after the most popular English stage clown, directly reflects professional performance practice, is unclear (Anonymous 1620). Perhaps intended to guide German school actors, English actors are credited with introducing to Germany this publication's representative selection of comedies, tragedies and sung comic interludes (the new genre of Pickelhering jigs or *Singspiele*). These showcase the English stage clown's special features. Generally named Pickelhering, he often spoke German and his singing, dancing, and acrobatics required no translation; he exploited the fool's licence for religious, political, and social criticism; his ability to corrupt words, even plots, and act as a calculated theatrical disturber in an otherwise evenly flowing medium, served to mediate between audience and action; his distinctive costume enhanced his status as an iconic trademark image for the English actors, enabling them to promote a wide variety of works to their audiences under his name (Katritzky 2007, 291–97; Katritzky 2014).

Engelische Comedien und Tragedien Sampt dem Pickelhering caters to court and city tastes with a balanced mixture of sacred and profane; naturalism and magic; plots borrowed from Bible stories, legends, royalty and merchant adventurers, and clowning jigs. Its plays involve a limited range of stock characters: the ruler, wise father, prodigal lover, crafty servant and cuckold, the marriageable young girl and strong-willed woman, allegorical figures of Good, Evil and Fortuna, devilish villain, and clown, Pickelhering. A companion volume of play texts to *Engelische Comedien und Tragedien Sampt dem Pickelhering* (1620) was published in 1630. A surprising degree of un-Englishness is indicated by these two volumes and by other surviving repertory and play title lists and manuscript play texts evidencing the dramaturgy of the English players in Europe. Johann Georg Gettner's *Die Heylige Martyrin Dorothea*, in effect a shortened German translation of the 1690s of Phillip Massinger and Thomas Dekker's *The Virgin Martyr* (1620), is one such play text powerfully demonstrating the influence of English Renaissance drama on the German Baroque stage (Mikyšková 2017). As a brand name, the 'English Comedy' referred not to a fully exported theatre culture, but to the migrant actors' idiosyncratic spectacle-based performing style. The great strength of their plots is not originality, but suitability for performance. They incorporate gritty realism, social immediacy and exciting scenes into sparse scripts creating space for improvisation. Above all, the most influential contribution of the migrant English players to the early Baroque dramaturgy of vigorous European theatre traditions was not play texts, but London performance techniques innovatively modified through the experience of long-term migrancy (Drábek 2020).

Case Study: George Jolly's Troupes

The systematic introduction of actresses into dramatic performances in German-speaking Europe was pioneered by George Jolly's migrant English troupes (Katritzky 2007, 275–78, 2008, 43–44). During the 1650s, when most English-born actors had permanently returned to Britain, Jolly's troupe toured Germany. Publicized as English, it included many European actors and staged plays featuring German-born actresses, rather than English boys or men, in the female roles. In the late 1640s and 1650s, after the London theatres had closed, Jolly toured the Low Countries, France, Germany, and Austria, first with the Prince of Wales's Company, then variously with John Wayde, William Rowe, and his own troupe (Alexander 1978, 40–5). Rowe, who settled his family in Utrecht by 1645, has been identified as the probable father of Jolly's wife, named in archival records as 'Maria di Roy von Utrecht in Holland' (Riewald 1960, 86–91; Worp 1911, 128). Jolly habitually cited the heavily pregnant state of his wife when requesting extensions to his troupe's playing licences (e.g. Frankfurt, 1657; Nuremberg, 1659). During the 1660s, Jolly punctuated English provincial tours with occasional overseas visits. As late as 1671, he is recorded in Dresden with his largely German troupe (Limon 1985, 11, 124), albeit as 'Gideon Gellius'. More so than most migrant English performers, numerous international variants of Jolly's name have considerably obstructed scholarly enquiries into his activities (Astington 2001, 2–3).

Following a financially disastrous tour of 1650 to Danzig, terminating with the loss of their costumes and props, Jolly radically restructured his troupe. Wishing to strengthen his market appeal in Germany, he largely replaced his English and Netherlandish players with German actors. The importance of singing to his repertoire of pastorals and dramas provided a major impetus to introduce actresses. In 1647, Jolly's players included two women, the young widow Maria Ursula Cärer (or Harer, neé Leopold), who married Jolly's actor Johann Ernst Hofmann, and 'Catrin', probably Catharina Fasshauer, wife of Jolly's actor Johann Georg Encke and daughter of English-trained troupe leader Johann Fasshauer (Jakubcová 2007, 157–58, 163–65; Rudin 2018, 478; Alexander 1978, 35–36). Women were no temporary addition to Jolly's troupe. Actresses are specifically noted in Jolly's supplication of 15 January 1654 to the authorities of Basel, and in playbills such as one date 9 December 1654. In this, Jolly, styling himself as the 'genuine English Picklehering', offers to delight the citizens of Rothenburg with 'lovely English music, frequent scene and costume changes, and genuine women, after the French fashion'. A playbill for Jolly's 1669 Rothenburg season still promotes as a novelty the onstage participation of 'genuine women' (Rudin and Kurz 1988, 36, 42). Already in 1656, four of Jolly's brightest stars, self-styled '*Englischer Comoediant*' ('English actor') Hofmann and his wife Cärer, and Peter and Rebekka Schwarz, had acrimoniously left to establish their '*Hochteutschen Compagni Comoedianten*' ('High-German Acting Company') (Rudin 2018, 471, 481). Between tours, this first longstanding professional German troupe wintered at court, first in Heidelberg with Prince Charles Louis, Elector Palatine (grandson of King James I and Anna of Denmark), and later at Innsbruck. In 1658, Charles Louis writes of the irascible Jolly: 'Master George the comedian has arrived in our regions [Heidelberg], but in a miserable state, because his company has broken up completely, and split into two, even the women have left him' (Alexander 1978, 31).

Jolly's pupil Maria Ursula Hofmann is the first of a long line of accomplished English-trained actresses who led professional German troupes. They included Catherina Elisabeth Velten, a prominent English-trained German actress who became sole leader of a troupe in widowhood, and Germany's most celebrated eighteenth-century actress, Caroline Friederike Neuber (Katritzky 2007, 264–65). Although the mainland activities of Jolly and his predecessors were transitory and amorphous, their impact on the development of German professional theatre was decisive. It is no exaggeration to directly attribute the rise of secular German professional theatre to that exported by successive waves of English troupes who toured Germany from the 1580s. German actors trained with migrant English troupes and assimilated their repertoires and stage skills. They continued to label themselves English comedians and to base their productions on the English style of acting for decades, even after the last British-born actors had left Germany. The more commercially successful aspects of English professional stage business increasingly dominated German professional acting. Their clown-centred, medley style of performing is reminiscent of the contrasting acts of nineteenth-century English music-hall. Based around comic jigs of the type that traditionally concluded English plays, but were increasingly marginalized on London stages, it remained popular in German-speaking Europe into the eighteenth century (Drábek 2020, 142). Despite having learned her trade with English-trained performers, Neuber dealt the German legacy of the migrant actors its greatest blow. In 1737, Neuber reacted against the Italian and English troupes' spectacle-based style of acting by symbolically calling for their iconic clowns to be banished from German stages. In a complex, variously interpreted public performance, she heavily censored their improvised bawdiness, and is even said to have ostentatiously burned a Harlequin puppet (Lande 2018, 94; Oppitz-Trotman 2020, 19). However, long after the popular clowns influenced by the migrant troupes had left their stages, great German professional actors (Kreuder 2020, 162–3), dramatists (Lande 2018, 302), and writers (Katritzky 2007, 291–8) continued to draw inspiration from the clown-based blood and thunder style of performing developed by the migrant English actors.

'NOT LESSER BUT DIFFERENT'

By comparison with London actors, English players overseas are sparsely documented by performance venues or play texts. They staged scripted drama, but also dancing, singing, acrobatics, and less easily categorized forms of spectacle. Other aspects of their multi-talented work, which can only be fully understood in terms of the demands of touring theatre and urban audiences, include their minimal staging, stereotypic characterisations, tendency towards the improvised rather than the written text, and the excitement and spectacle on which their repertoire is founded. Current literary and historical approaches to Early Modern English performance practice in Europe increasingly suggest that it drew on influences from a wide range of central European as well as English sources. Literary as well as dramatic sources were adapted to reflect contemporary performance pressures, such as didactic content dictated by specific courts, religious and civic concerns, and generic, commercially successful, audience pleasing stage routines. Surviving play texts such as *Engelische Comedien vnd Tragedien* (Anonymous 1620) are intertextual records, mediating between the English and mainland pre-texts and performances they reference. Multicultural, polyglot, and hybrid, neither tightly scripted Jacobean plays nor florid German baroque performances, the 'English Comedy' was a 'theater in between' (Bosman 2004, 564), a 'nexus of transnational influences' (Drábek 2020, 140–1), whose music, improvisation, clowning, and spectacle should be viewed as 'not lesser but different' (Holland 2007, 32; Drábek and Katritzky 2016, 1532).

References

Anonymous. 1620. *Engelische Comedien vnd Tragedien [...] Sampt dem Pickelhering*. Leipzig. [Modern edition: Manfred Brauneck, ed. 1970. *Engelische Comedien und Tragedien (Spieltexte der Wanderbühne* I). Berlin: de Gruyter.]

Alexander, Robert J. 1978. 'George Jolly [Joris Joliphus], der wandernde Player und Manager: Neues zu seiner Tätigkeit in Deutschland (1648–1660).' *Kleine Schriften der Gesellschaft für Theatergeschichte* 29/30: 31–48.

Astington, John H. 2001. 'Two Seventeenth-Century Actors: New Facts.' *Theatre Notebook* 55 (1): 2–5.

Bosman, Anston. 2004. 'Renaissance Intertheater and the Staging of Nobody.' *English Literary History* 71 (3): 559–85.

Chambers, E. K. 1923. *The Elizabethan Stage*. 2 vols. Oxford: Clarendon Press.

Drábek, Pavel. 2020. 'Why, Sir, Are There Other Heauens in Other Countries? The English Comedy as a Transnational Style.' In *Transnational Connections in Early Modern Theatre*, edited by M. A. Katritzky and Pavel Drábek, 139–161. Manchester: Manchester University Press.

Drábek, Pavel and M. A. Katritzky. 2016. 'Shakespearean Players in Early Modern Europe.' In *The Cambridge Guide to the Worlds of Shakespeare, vol. II: The World's Shakespeare, 1660–Present*, edited by Bruce R. Smith, 1527–1533. Cambridge: Cambridge University Press.

Haekel, Ralf. 2004. *Die englischen Komödianten in Deutschland: eine Einführung in die Ursprünge des deutschen Berufsschauspiels*. Heidelberg: Winter.

Holland, Peter. 2007. 'Shakespeare Abbreviated.' In *The Cambridge Companion to Shakespeare in Popular Culture*, edited by Robert Shaughnessy, 26–45. Cambridge: Cambridge University Press.

Jakubcová, Alena, ed. 2007. *Starši divadlo v českých zemích do konce 18. stoleti—Osobnosti a dila*. Prague: Divadelní Ústav.

Katritzky, M. A. 2014. '"A Plague o' These Pickle Herring": From London Drinkers to European Stage Clown.' In *Renaissance Shakespeare: Shakespeare Renaissances. Proceedings of the Ninth World Shakespeare Congress*, edited by Michael Procházka, Michael Dobson, Andreas Höfele, Hanna Scolnicov, 159–168. Newark: University of Delaware Press.

Katritzky, M. A. 2008. 'English Troupes in Early Modern Germany: The Women.' In *Transnational Exchange in Early Modern Theater*, edited by Robert Henke and Eric Nicholson, 35–46. Aldershot: Ashgate.

Katritzky, M. A. 2007. *Women, Medicine and Theatre 1500–1750: Literary Mountebanks and Performing Quacks.* Aldershot: Ashgate.

Kreuder, Friedemann. 2020. 'The Re-inspired and Revived Bernardon: Metamorphoses of Early Modern Comedy in Eighteenth-Century Bourgeois Theatre.' In *Transnational Connections in Early Modern Theatre*, edited by M. A. Katritzky and Pavel Drábek, 162–178. Manchester: Manchester University Press.

Lande, Joel B. 2018. *Persistence of Folly: On the Origins of German Dramatic Literature.* Ithaca: Cornell University Press.

Limon, Jerzy. 1985. *Gentlemen of a Company: English Players in Central and Eastern Europe, 1590–1660.* Cambridge: Cambridge University Press.

McMillin, Scott, and Sally-Beth MacLean. 1998. *The Queen's Men and their Plays.* Cambridge: Cambridge University Press.

Mikyšková, Anna. 2017. 'Translation as a Means of Dramatic Exchange: St Dorothy's Play in the 17th Century.' *Czech and Slovak Linguistic Review* 1/2: 159–168.

Oppitz-Trotman, George. 2020. *Stages of Loss: The English Comedians and their Reception.* Oxford: Oxford University Press.

Riewald, J. G. 1960. 'New Light on the English Actors in the Netherlands, c.1590–c.1660.' *English Studies* 41: 65–92.

Rudin, Bärbel and Hans-Joachim Kurz. 1988. 'Pickelhering, rechte Frauenzimmer, berühmte Autoren: zur Ankündigungspraxis der Wanderbühne im 17. Jahrhundert.' *Kleine Schriften der Gesellschaft für Theatergeschichte* 34/35: 29–60.

Rudin, Bärbel. 2018. '"Zwei Mal in der Wochen Komödie": Das erste deutsche Hoftheater in Heidelberg. Zur ortsfesten Subventionierung professioneller Schauspielkunst seit 1656.' *Daphnis* 46: 467–503.

Soffé, E. 1888. 'Eine nachricht über englische komödianten in Mähren.' *Anglia: Zeitschrift für englische Philologie* 10: 289–290.

Spohr, Arne. 2009. *"How Chances It They Travel?": Englische Musiker in Dänemark und Norddeutschland 1579–1630.* Wiesbaden: Harrassowitz.

Taylor, John. 1620. *Taylor his Trauels: From the City of London in England, to the Citty of Prague in Bohemia.* London: Henry Gosson.

Vander Motten, J. P. and Michiel Roscam Abbing. 2020. 'Seventeenth-century English Rope Dancers in the Low Countries.' *Theatre Notebook* 74 (1): 8–31.

Wikland, Erik. 1977. *Elizabethan Players in Sweden 1591–92 &c.* 3rd ed. Upssala: Almqvist & Wiksell.

Worp, J. A. 1911. 'Die englischen Komödianten Jellifus und Rowe.' *Shakespeare Jahrbuch* 46: 128–9.

Zimmermann, Paul. 1902. 'Englische Komödianten am Hofe zu Wolfenbüttel.' *Braunschweigisches Magazin* 8: 37–45, 53–7.

CHAPTER 21

Migrations and Cultural Navigations on Early Modern Italian Stages

Erith Jaffe-Berg

The theatre and performances created in the Italian peninsula by actors in the *commedia dell'arte*, as well as by groups of Jewish and Ottoman Turkish performers grappled with migration in a number of ways. Actors in the *commedia dell'arte* embodied movement and journeys in their itinerant lifestyle, as they travelled between the different states of the Italian peninsula and toured different European countries. The experience of migration seeped into plot lines in the many scenarios of the *commedia dell'arte*, which, thematically, reflected the actors' and audiences' experiences of cultural exchanges and confrontations. These encounters were the inevitable results of Early Modern mercantile economies as well as of immigration and migration, brought on by agricultural crises, plagues, military incursions, and religious persecution. Migration shaped not only the themes explored on stage but the multilingual composition of the performances themselves. In *commedia dell'arte*, several dialects and languages were spoken by different character types, each of whom was associated with a different region in the Italian peninsula or the European horizon (Jaffe-Berg 2009). The Christian *comici* were not the only Italian performers to enact migration, and migrant groups of Ottoman Turks as well as long-established communities of Jews also performed, and in their theatrical work, they reflected their own traditions and their own perception of intercultural navigations and exchanges (Jaffe-Berg 2015). These performance examples serve us in identifying the ways in which the *commedia dell'arte* reflected their audiences'

E. Jaffe-Berg (✉)
University of California, Riverside, Riverside, CA, USA
e-mail: erithj@ucr.edu

© The Author(s), under exclusive license to Springer Nature Switzerland AG 2023
Y. Meerzon, S. E. Wilmer (eds.), *The Palgrave Handbook of Theatre and Migration*, https://doi.org/10.1007/978-3-031-20196-7_21

confrontations with the hardship of cultural migration, as a challenging, sometimes thrilling, and inevitable aspect of early modernity.

In this chapter, I explore how cultural migrations and navigations were undertaken by *commedia dell'arte* performers. Then, I shift the focus to how cultural minority groups, specifically Muslim Ottoman Turks and Jews, performed themselves on Early Modern Italian stages. I contextualize the ways in which the Christian *commedia dell'arte* represented these cultural minorities in comparison with how they represented themselves. I study the dangerous, daredevil acts of Ottoman Turkish acrobats hired to perform in Venice and Rome during Carnival time. I also present the case of Jewish actors, who were allowed to travel, performing in the style of the *buffoni* and of the *comici* while living openly as Jews. As this essay shows, ranging from *commedia dell'arte* performances' exoticizing others' appearance and languages to enabling non-Christian actors to take up common performance modes, Early Modern Italian performances presented a complex spectrum of both inclusion and distance, reflecting their audiences' ambivalence towards migration.

Cultural Migration in the Italian Peninsula and in *Commedia Dell'arte*

The Early Modern Italian peninsula grappled with issues of migration that Italy, as a nation, is still confronted with today (Fogu 2020; Olivito 2016). Migration is defined as a permanent change in residence, driven by a diversity of motives, with the aim of improving one's material, social or political circumstances (Massey et al. 1988, 1). In this essay, since the focus is on the Early Modern period, I extend the definition of *migration* to also encompass the actors who led a continuously nomadic life, travelling, and touring. The Italian Peninsula, surrounded by the Mediterranean Sea—the Adriatic, Tyrrhenian, Ligurian, and Ionian Seas—with ample fluvial bodies within it, then and now, is a veritable liquid conductor, allowing transportation of people and goods in all directions. The Mediterranean itself has, for millennia, served as a pelagic body, a repository of ocean life, a liquid bridge between continents, and a threshold for seafaring expeditions (Braudel 1966; Horden and Purcell 2020; Abulafia 2011). Mediterranean historians have considered in detail issues of captivity, piracy, and exchanges within the Mediterranean that result from this geography (Rothman 2009; Greene 2010; Dursteler 2011). Cultural and literary critics have applied this historical research to their understanding of literary and cultural developments in the Italian peninsula (Vitkus 2003; Matar 1999; Chambers 2008; Fogu 2020; Matvejević 1999). Recently, critical race studies have refocused attention on the construction of race, charting its beginning in the Middle Ages and tracing it through the Early Modern period (Heng, 4). One consequence of pre-dating the focus on race is that it impacts our view of the history and politics of migration in Italy and elsewhere. Mediterranean studies and critical race studies of the Middle Ages and

Early Modern period refocus attention on the way in which migration—understood as the movements of peoples across nation-state borders—have influenced how cultures are navigated in this highly porous region that often functions as a contact zone (Pratt 1992). It also means acknowledging the contribution of other religious, ethnic, and racial groups beyond what had been considered primarily in terms of a Christian Europe. Geraldine Heng has been instrumental in changing the discourse on race, locating it starting in the Middle Ages, in order to consider a longer history of racializing Jews, Muslims, blacks, and other groups, and she has argued for using the full critical tool set of analysing how the mechanisms of racialization functioned in defining, representing, branding, and otherwise subjugating peoples of non-white races.

> [I]n addressing the nested discourses formative of race in the European Middle Ages, it was particularly important to note that religion—the paramount source of authority in the medieval period—could function both socioculturally and biopolitically: subjecting peoples of a detested faith, for instance, to a political theology that could bioligize, define, and essentialize and entire community as fundamentally and absolutely different in an interknotted cluster of ways. (Heng 2018, 3)

In addition to Heng's work, critical race studies are redefining the ways in which we frame the exceptional and urge scholars to look back again at the marginalized, often relegated to footnotes in theatre history books. As Ayanna Thompson reflects, since Imtiaz Habib's *Black Lives in the English Archives, 1500–1677* (2008), it is no longer possible to overlook the presence of African, American, and Indian blacks in sixteenth and seventeenth-century England, while Nabil Matar's work 'palpably demonstrates that there are always (at least) two sides to every economic, diplomatic, and religious encounter in the early modern world' (Thompson 2021, 9–10). Summarizing the important work of recent scholars influenced by critical race studies, Heng asserts: 'Scholars who are invested in the archaeology of a past in which alternative voices, lives, and histories are heard, beyond those canonically established as central by functionalist studies, are thus not well served by evading the category of race and its trenchant vocabularies and tools of analysis' (Heng, 5). When we look again—as Heng, Thompson, Noémie Ndiaye, and others have urged us to do—we reassess the true contribution and importance of these marginalized Early Modern groups, such as Jews and Muslims, among others, and find a more complex picture of theatre production and performance emerges.

Migrations and Journeys of the *Comici*

The *commedia dell'arte* performers were especially well-positioned to capture the themes of travel and migration; Roberto Tessari goes so far as to identify the migratory passages as constitutive of the *commedia dell'arte* (Tessari 2013, 64). After all, the *comici* were, themselves, itinerants and, in many cases, migrants, repeatedly travelling from place to place with hardly a base or static location (Ferrone 2018; Katritzky 2006; Henke 2008; Jaffe-Berg 2015). As Kenneth Richards puts it, itineracy was 'a given for late Italian Renaissance professional theatre companies' (Richards 2015, 47). The lack of centralization in the Italian peninsula meant that the region was divided into separate principalities and republics, with few major urban centres to rival the size of London, Paris or Madrid (Richards 2015, 47; Henke 2002, 11). By necessity, troupes travelled inter-regionally, responding to invitations by patrons and searching for new audiences, following the seasonal periods in which performance was allowed, especially the period of Carnival (Henke 2008, 21). As Henke explains, the repertoire of each troupe 'was not sufficient to entertain one urban public all year round,' making it necessary for them to tour (Henke 2002, 11).

Though the companies toured of necessity, this apparent constraint was also creatively generative. Siro Ferrone has long emphasized the importance of journeys and migration; as he explains it, the journeys of the *comici* functioned 'as an enzyme triggering the creativity of actors and eliciting unexpected emotional responses from audiences being confronted with actors from various geographical contexts' (Ferrone 2018, 67). For the *comici*, creativity and ingenuity were based in travel, which was reflected in the regional heterogeneity of characters, in multilingualism, and in the plots, which were about travel and adventure. Part of the experience of migration was that the actors were always outsiders in the minds of the audience (Ferrone 1993, 18; Henke 2002, 9; Jaffe-Berg 2015, 32). The foreign status of the actors—their distinctive language and manner of behaviour—was one of the draws of the *commedia dell'arte*. 'Whatever the differing civil and social statuses of these troupes, the reasons for the success of their performances were most likely found not only in the quality of the texts they performed, but especially in the fruitful gap between the expectations of local audiences and these "foreign" actors with their alien linguistic, rhythmic and emotional expressions' (Ferrone 2018, 68). That position of alterity meant, for the actors, a loyalty more to their art than to any state, and it opened the door for them to forge networks with unexpected partners from other marginalized groups, such as the Jews who often supplied the *comici* with costumes, props, and financial services (Jaffe-Berg 2020, 360–361).

The multilingual composition of *commedia dell'arte* was an essential part of the draw of their performances (Clivio 1989; Jaffe-Berg 2009; Carlson 2006). It was one of the ways in which this type of performance reflected the inherent plurality and diversity of the peninsula, in which the regions were defined by separate cultures, dialects or languages, and political structures. As Claudio Fogu puts it: 'Commedia dell'arte identified Italian-ness itself with linguistic diversity and gestural communication compensating for the absence of a unifying language' (Fogu 2020, 63). On stage, the set characters (Pantalone, the Dottore, the Innamorato/a, the Capitano, the Zanni) embodied different regions along the peninsula and spoke the regional dialects or languages. They also altered words, in the explanation of Roberto Tessari, adding a comic filter to their performance in order to draw attention to linguistic variation and purposefully corrupt the literary language (Tessari 1969, 256).

Representations of Migration and Displacement in *Commedia Dell'arte*

As we have seen, accelerated travel and migration were parts of life for Italian merchants and traders, not to mention, soldiers, explorers, and pirates, as well as a significant number of captive people who were abducted for ransom or enslaved. This movement, conveying new groups of people, meant that these racialized others sometimes permanently settled within the Italian peninsula. Different groups, such as *Italiani* Jews and Roma people, had been part of the Italian peninsula for centuries and millennia. The Ottoman Turks came and remained as foreigners, living in the peninsula for shorter periods. They found themselves represented in literature and on stage by artists who, like their audiences, were grappling with how to live with these communities. The positive, as well as the negative aspects of travel and migration, especially in the Mediterranean, were subject of the many plays or play scenarios (abbreviated plots used by the actors) collected and published in the main collections of the *commedia dell'arte*: Flaminio Scala's *Il teatro delle favole rappresentative* (1611), as well as the Corsini, Locatelli and Correr collection, among other scenarios. These scenarios record travel and migration, with all their implications: love and riches, as well as kidnapping, ransom, conversion, danger, and poverty. The collections of scenarios feature diverse characters from across the Mediterranean and suggest settings that are equally far-reaching. They reflect on the fantasies of Early Modern audiences, but they also reflect on the harsh realities (captivity, violence, hunger, death) that audience members lived through and spoke of. Frequently, the *innamorato* (male lover type) travelled across the Mediterranean, where he took on various roles—merchant, adventurer, student or lover. His travel often entangled him with lovers who were non-Christians. In these instances, the scenarios explored the more extreme aspects of migration, including kidnapping and conversion, in which the boundaries and limits of acceptable migratory experiences were stretched and explored. For example, the second scenario in the Scala Collection, *La fortuna di Flavio* (Flavio's Luck), offers a veritable mapping of the Mediterranean, dotted by key ports and points of interest for the audience (Scala in Andrews 2008, 19–30). The scenario depicts the *innamorato* Flavio, the son of the Venetian Pantalone, who resides in Rome and is kidnapped by pirates in the Mediterranean and, as described in the *argumento*, is sold as a slave in Constantinople. There, he befriends the son of the pasha, who is allured by the promise of Christianity and decides to escape Constantinople with Flavio and convert to Christianity. They set off, but mayhem ensues, whereupon Flavio is lost at Sea while the Pasha's son is saved, converted, and brought to Rome. Meanwhile, Flavio continues to crisscross the Mediterranean, is washed on the island of Pantelloria (in the Straight of Sicily), sails to Bari, in South-Eastern Italy, along the Adriatic Sea, makes his way to Milan, stopping in Rome where he is reunited with his family and his friend, the Pasha's son. The sheer volume of locations is overwhelming, as are the stunning turns or conversions from one culture and religion to another.

As in *La fortuna di Flavio*, the scenarios reflect the many cultures encountered in travel and immigrant communities living among Italians. The representation of migrant communities was true not only of the Scala collection but also the Corsini collection. In the Corsini, housed in Rome, at least three scenarios depict Ottoman Turks: *Le due schiave* (The Two Slave-Girls), *La schiava* (The Slave Girl) and *Elisa Alii Bassà: Opera turches[ca]* (Elisa Alii Bassà: A Turkish Work) (Jaffe-Berg 2015, 59). Elsbeth Aasted dates the collection to the late sixteenth century while Stefano Mengarelli dates it to the 1620s, accepting that the scenarios inscribed performances from a few decades earlier (Aasted 1992; Mengarelli 2008). The title character is a Muslim girl named Elisa who is beloved by Alii. By the end of the scenario, it becomes evident that both presumed Muslim characters are, in fact, long-lost Christian siblings (Flavia and Orazio) who were captives taken along the Peloponnesian coast. While Elisa knows she was born a Christian, and even reveals herself to two other women, Angelica and Franceschina as such, Alii embraces his Muslim Turkish identity, oblivious to the fact that he, too, was born Christian (Testaverde 2007, 482). As a presumed Turk, Alii acts in the ways the audience expects a Turk to behave—he is combative, violent, easy to be agitated, and always with a sword in hand (482–3). On the other hand, Elisa is compassionate, caring for anyone around her who is hurt and often laments other peoples' troubles (Testaverde 483). However, when Alii catches the eye of his long-lost father, he seems to recognize their kinship, and at that very moment 'Alii laments, father and son discover one and other' (*Alii si lamenta, si scoprono padre e figliolo*) (484). The magical ways of *commedia dell'arte* facilitate both the reunion and recognition. However, the changed behaviour, from violence to compassion, indicated a deeper transformation which is supported by the racialization of Turks as violent and Christians as compassionate and noble. The scenario enacts how the once hot-headed and fearsome Alii becomes, by the end of the scenario, the pacific son and future husband of Christians (485). Viewed with Heng in mind, the performance of *Elisa Alii Bassà* is a powerful example of the recurrent ways *commedia dell'arte* enacted a racialized view of Muslims.

All the characters perform migrations—travelling over the Mediterranean ocean in search of a loved one or to escape parental control and seek one's fortune. For some of the characters, travel is precipitated by love and leads to conversion and the permanent migration, taking up residence in the Ottoman lands (as happened in *La fortuna di Flavio*). For others, the travel is forced on them as the result of kidnapping and ransoming. These migrations and cultural navigations are found not only in the Correr but in the other collections as well. 'In the complex Mediterranean crossings that pervade the 1611 scenarios of Francesco Andreini's colleague Flaminio Scala, especially in the romance-type *argomenti* that provide the plot backgrounds for the unity-bound plays, the regular *arte* characters are conveyed, against their will, by Ragusan, Turkish, Arabic, and Algerian ships across the Mediterranean' (Henke 2008, 21). The recurrent subjects of travel, piracy, captivity, and conversion within the Mediterranean was commonly staged in the *scenari*.

The plots of the *commedia dell'arte* performances embraced intra-peninsular movement by depicting characters who migrated from one Italian region or state to another. How else would it be possible to explain the coterminous existence of a Dottore from Bologna, a young man from Florence, a merchant from Venice and a servant from Bergamo? The movement of dispossessed farmers from the hills of Bergamo to the port city of Venice were represented in the relationship of the impoverished and ever hungry *zanni* (a servant type) and his wealthy employer, Pantalone. The intrusive Spanish or Swiss Capitano appeared ubiquitously in a number of scenarios, in recognition of the ever-presence of mercenary soldiers within the peninsula. These were not fictional realities, however fantastical and stylized the performance may have been, they were reflections of the migratory patterns of the people within the Italian peninsula and from other places. The plots were also the result of the movements of the actors themselves, who often came together as a troupe reflecting a mosaic of regions, dialects, and cultural experiences that reflected the diversity of their characters on stage. Finally, the plots reflected the reality that the *commedia dell'arte* audiences, especially those in the piazza, were often regionally displaced residence themselves. Henke argues that the economic shift from an artisan to a nascent manufacturing and merchant economy by the sixteenth century catalysed migratory phenomena leading to a large degree of vagrancy and poverty resulting from migration from within the Italian peninsula (from hill towns of Bergamo to Venice) and outside of the peninsula (migrations from Greece, Germany and elsewhere) (Henke 1997, 2). 'This urban influx catalysed the new professional theatre […] in creating a critical audience mass for the *commedia dell'arte* troupes, who required piazza and hall (stanza) audiences as much as they needed the better documented courtly venues' (Henke 1997, 2). These very displaced migrants were often the hungry consumers of the comic staging of the migratory experiences.

In addition to the trans-regionality of *commedia dell'arte* staple characters, there was also a recurrent and significant presence of Mediterranean minority characters such as Arabs, Armenians, Jews, Greeks, Roma people, and Turks (Jaffe-Berg 2015). The stereotypical roles each took on in the different scenarios suggest the ways the ethnic groups they represented were viewed, depending on the locale. For example, variations in the treatment of Jews, Turks, and Armenians reflected distinctive roles each group had within the Mediterranean mercantile economy. At the same time, in certain scenarios, the interchangeability of Jews and Muslims as Levantines suggests that the representations could also be stereotypical (Jaffe-Berg 2015, 10–11; 101–104). Nevertheless, the recurrent presence of these characters asserts the *commedia dell'arte* as a Mediterranean, as much as an Italian form (Fogu 2020, 63). As such, the Mediterranean characters in the *commedia dell'arte* are an important indication that the theatrical form was invested in representations of migration.

NON-CHRISTIAN PERFORMERS IN THE ITALIAN PENINSULA: OTTOMAN TURKS AND JEWS

The Italian peninsula also invited many performances by these members of cultural minorities who were either foreign or permanent residents of the peninsula. These examples stand out for the ways their performances reflected on the experiences of migration and cultural navigation in this Early Modern period. The seasonal performance known as *Il volo del Turco* (The Flight of the Turk), which Turkish acrobats were hired to perform, was used to open the carnival season in Venice. It is recorded pictorially in an original engraving on paper (c. 1548) and through archival mentions in local state archives that still house the letters of exchange (dated 1564 and 1565) about spectacular events and performances that took place and were considered noteworthy enough to record (Battista 1564; Muir 1981, 171; Chaganti et al. 2017, 28–29). In the performance, a Turkish acrobat performed a walk on a tight rope strung above the Venetian lagoon and ended up crossing towards the Doge's palace, supplicating at the Doge's feet. The performance was both virtuosic and awe-inspiring in terms of the acrobat's ability, and, simultaneously, degrading, in making the acrobat, ultimately, kneel before Venetian power. It was a symbolic articulation of Venetian ambivalence towards their enemy and mercantile partner, the Ottomans. Other Ottoman Turkish acrobats performed elsewhere in the peninsula, and, while we don't have many specific names of performers, a few came down to us, including one known as Ali who performed in Rome in 1547 (Carboni 2007, 332).

Another case of non-Christian performances within the Italian peninsula were the Jews who frequently staged plays in Mantua, Ferrara, Pesaro, and Venice (Jaffe-Berg 2015, 121–144). Theirs was a rich theatre tradition of staging plays for their own community and, as a tribute and form of taxation, for the Christian rulers. Among the many instances in which the Jews performed, there is one that stands as a counterpart to the daring Turkish acrobat. This was Samuel 'Shlumiel' Basilea, who performed solo performances, with various persona, throughout the Northern Italian region. Basilea, who functioned as an itinerant performer, in the shadow of other *comici* and even of the Venetian *buffoni*, performed linguistic transformations that reflect on larger cultural patterns of transition and change. He was noted for being able to enact a whole performance with many different characters emphasizing the distinct characters with vocal variations (License for Simone Basilea to perform, 1612). In his solo performance style, Basilea resembled the Venetian *buffoni* tradition of earlier in the sixteenth century in Venice. While these two examples stand out, they are clearly not unique, and suggest these are the few recorded performances among what is likely to have been a much wider set of ongoing performances staged in various places in the peninsula by non-Christian performers whose very presence reflected on the cultural migrations that were inherent to this time and place.

THE PERILS AND CHALLENGES OF MIGRATION

For all of these performers—Christians, Muslims, and Jews—migration and movement spelled danger, as they could be stopped at any moment by regional authorities, since itineracy itself was suspect. In addition, there were the natural dangers of travel—inclement weather, as well as the wear and tear of travel, which translated to broken wagons, sick horses or mules, and illness and plague along the way (Ferrone 2018, 69). Plagues periodically overtook cities, and performers, who were already away from their homes or lacking those, were dislodged because of it (Henke 2002, 11). Such was the case when the Sack of Mantua (1630) led to forced exile of the Jewish actors and their relocation to Venice from where they needed to escape when the plague of 1631 caught up with them there (Harrán 2001, 229).

Movement and migration as recurrent motifs in the plots point to a paradox—while the troupes moved, and while the plots often involved travel, the audiences depended on the performance being anchored in set and recognizable characters. Thereby, the performance instantiated a type of stasis (familiarity of characters, plots, and endings) even while the actors were constantly on the go. The audience could always expect that when they met a Pantalone, he would always be recognizable, if not ever, exactly the same. The plot depended on the characters being consistent, but the surface-level circumstances and plots changing. In its stasis or familiarity of characters, the *commedia dell'arte* belied the movement and constant change experienced by its *comici* and by audiences. It also promised an unchanging world that was different from the one lived by the inhabitants of the Early Modern Italian peninsula, prone to wars, changes of leadership, the onslaught of famine, plague, which often necessitated exile and movement, not to mention the waves of newcomers, immigrants, and different communities of people who came to reside among the Christian residents.

The journeys and migrations depicted in *commedia dell'arte* reflected the regionally and linguistically varied peninsula. Performances thereby reflected the constant negotiation of inhabitants of the peninsula as to how to view others living among them—a spectrum ranging from acceptance to discomfort to aggression. For the Jewish and Ottoman Turkish inhabitants of the peninsula, performance meant a shared experience but also an opportunity to reconnect with rituals and performances that were culturally distinct. The complexities of cultural confrontation were never far from the *commedia dell'arte* or Jewish or Turkish performers—they lived them, explored them onstage, and provided audiences with sometimes reassuring and sometimes unsettling pictures of migration and cultural navigation.

REFERENCES

Aasted, Elsebeth, 1992. 'What the Corsini Scenari Can Tell Us About the Commedia dell'Arte.' *Analecta Romana Instituti Danici* 10:159–82.

Abulafia, David. 2011. *The Great Sea: A Human History of the Mediterranean.* Oxford: Oxford University Press.

Anon. *Alisa Alii Bassà. Opera turches[ca].* In Testaverde, ed. *I canovacci della commedia dell'arte.* 481–86.

Braudel, Fernand. (1966) 1995. *La Méditerranée et le Monde Méditerranéen à l' Époque de Philippe II.* Translated by Siân Reynolds. Berkeley: University of California Press.

Carboni, Stefano, ed. 2007. *Venezia e l'Islam 828—1797.* Exhibition catalogue Palazzo Ducale Venice. Venice: Marsilio.

Carlson, Marvin. 2006. *Speaking in Tongues: Language at Play in the Theatre.* Ann Arbor: University of Michigan Press.

Chaganti, Seeta, Noah Guynn, and Erith Jaffe-Berg. 2017. 'Institutional Frameworks.' Vol. 2 of *A Cultural History of Theatre in the Middle Ages*, edited by Jody Enders, 17–38. London: Bloomsbury.

Chambers, Iain. 2008. *Mediterranean Crossing: The Politics of an Interrupted Modernity.* Durham and London: Duke University Press.

Clivio, Gianrenzo P. 1989. 'The Languages of the commedia dell'arte.' In *The Science of Buffoonery: Theory and History of the Commedia dell'Arte*, edited by Domenico Pietropaolo, 209–237. Toronto: Dovehouse Editions.

Dursteler, Eric R. 2011. *Renegade Women: Gender, Identity, and Boundaries in the Early Modern Mediterranean.* Baltimore: The Johns Hopkins University Press.

Ferrone, Siro. 1993. Republished 2011. *Attori, mercanti, corsari: La Commedia dell'arte in Europa tra Cinque e Seicento.* Turin: Giulio Einaudi Editore.

Ferrone, Siro. 2018. 'Journeys.' In *Commedia dell'Arte in Context.* Edited by Christopher B. Balme, Piermario Vescovo, and Daniele Vianello, 67–75. Cambridge: Cambridge University Press.

Fogu, Claudio. 2020. *The Fishing Net and the Spider Web: Mediterranean Imaginaries and the Making of Italians* London: Palgrave Macmillan.

Greene, Molly. 2010. *Catholic Pirates and Greek Merchants: A Maritime History of the Mediterranean.* Princeton: Princeton University Press.

Harrán, Don. 2001. *Jewish Musical Culture: Leone Modena in the Jews of Early Modern Venice.* Edited by Robert C. Davis and Benjamin Ravid, 211–230. Baltimore and London: Johns Hopkins University Press.

Heng, Geraldine. 2018. *The Invention of Race in the European Middle Ages.* Cambridge: Cambridge University Press.

Henke, Robert. 1997. 'The Italian Mountebank and the *Commedia dell'arte*.' *Theatre Survey*, 38 (2), 1–29.

Henke, Robert. 2008. 'Border-Crossing in the *Commedia dell'Arte*.' In *Transnational Exchange in Early Modern Theater*, edited by Robert Henke and Eric Nicholson, 19–34. Aldershot: Ashgate.

Henke, Robert. 2002. *Performance and Literature in the Commedia dell'Arte.* Cambridge: Cambridge University press.

Horden, Peregrine and Nicholas Purcell. 2020. *The Corrupting Sea: A Study of Mediterranean History.* Oxford: Wiley-Blackwell.

Jaffe-Berg, Erith. 2015. *Commedia dell'arte and the Mediterranean: Charting Journeys and Mapping 'Others'.* Ashgate: Farnham, Surrey, 2015. Republished by Routledge 2016.

———. 2009. *The Multilingual Art of Commedia dell'Arte*. New York and Ottawa: Legas.

———. 2020. 'Towards an Expansive Historiography of Jews and Creative Collaborators and Hired Contractors in Early-Modern Italian Theatre and Performance.' In *The Routledge Companion to Theatre and Performance Historiography*, edited by Tracy C. Davis and Peter W. Marx, 348–363. London: Routledge.

Katritzky, M.A. 2006. *The Art of Commedia: A Study in the Commedia dell'Arte 1560–1620 with Special Reference to the Visual Records*. Amsterdam and New York: Rodopi.

Letter from Giovanni Battista to the Duke of Mantua dated June 3, 1564. Archivio di Stato di Mantova (ASMn), Archivio Gonzaga (AG) 1497:1 cc.188–9.

License for Simone Basilea to perform granted by the Duke Vincenzo Gonzaga of Mantua, 1612, ASMn AG Libri Mandati. Busta 47 vol 98 c 14. Archivio di Stato Mantova, Archivio Gonzaga (State Archives of Mantua, Gonzaga Archives), Mantua, Italy.

Massey, Douglas S., Joaquín Arango, Graeme Hugo, Ali Kouaouci, Adela Pellegrino, and J. Edward Taylor. 1988. *Worlds in Motion: Understanding International Migration at the End of the Millennium*. Oxford: Clarendon Press.

Matar, Nabil. 1999. *Turks, Moors & Englishmen in the Age of Discovery*. New York: Columbia University Press.

Matvejević, Predrag. 1999. *Mediterranean: A Cultural Landscape*. Translated by Michael Henry Heim. Berkeley: University of California Press.

Mengarelli, Stefano. 2008. 'The Commedia dell' Improvviso Illustrations of the Corsini Manuscript: A New Reading.' *Early Theatre*, 11 (2), 212–226.

Muir, Edward. 1981. *Civic Ritual in Renaissance Venice*. Princeton, NJ: Princeton University Press.

Ndiaye, Noémie. 2021. 'Off the Record: Contrapuntal Theatre History.' In *The Routledge Companion to Theatre and Performance Historiography*, edited by Tracy C. Davis and Peter W. Marx, 229–248. London: Routledge.

Olivito, Elisa. 2016. *Gender and Migration in Italy: A Multilayered Perspective*. London and New York: Routledge.

Pratt, Mary Louise. 1992. *Imperial Eyes: Travel Writing and Transculturalism*. New York and London: Routledge. Second Edition. 2008.

Raccolta di Scenari Più scelti D'istrioni. MS 45.G. 5/6, Biblioteca dell'Accademia Nazionale dei Lincei e Corsiniana, Rome.

Richards, Kenneth. 2015. 'The Commedia dell'Arte acting Companies.' In *The Routledge Companion to Commedia dell'Arte*, edited by Judith Chaffee and Olly Crick, 43–54. Routledge: London and New York.

Rothman, Natalie E. 2009. 'Interpreting Dragomans: boundaries and Crossings in the Early Modern Mediterranean.' *Comparative Studies in Society and History*, 51 (4), 771–800.

Scala, Flaminio. 2008 'Flavio's Luck (La Fortuna di Flavio).' In *The Commedia dell'Arte of Flaminio Scala: A Translation and Analysis of 30 Scenarios* edited and translated by Richard Andrews, 19–30. Lanham: The Scarecrow Press.

Testaverde, Anna Maria, ed. 2007. *I canovacci della commedia dell'arte*. Transcribed and annotated by Anna Evangelista. Turin: Giulio Einaudi.

Tessari, Roberto. 2013. *La Commedia dell'arte: Genesi d'una società dello spettacolo*. Rome: Gius. Laterza & Figli.

Tessari, Roberto. 1969. *La Commedia dell'Arte nel Seicento—'Industria" e "arte giocosa" della Civiltà baroccà*. Florence: Leo S. Olschki.

Thompson, Ayanna. 2021. 'Did the Concept of Race Exist for Shakespeare and His Contemporaries? An Introduction.' In *The Cambridge Companion to Shakespeare and Race*, edited by Ayanna Thompson, 1–16. Cambridge University Press.

Vitkus, Daniel J. 2003. *Turning Turk: English Theater and the Multicultural Mediterranean, 1570–1630*. New York: Palgrave Macmillan.

PART III

Migration and Nationalism

CHAPTER 22

Immigration and Family Life on the Early Twentieth-Century Argentine Stage

May Summer Farnsworth

From the late 1800s to the mid-1900s, the Argentine stage offered diverse representations of the nation's large-scale immigration experiment. Dramas, romances, and comic sketches reflected the dynamic political/social/cultural tensions between *criollos* (native-born Argentines) and *gringos* (European immigrants). Nineteenth-century political theorist, Juan Bautista Alberdi (1810–1884), famously proclaimed, 'to govern is to populate' (*'gobernar es poblar'*), and argued that European immigration held the key to Argentina's future progress (1914, xv). Yana Meerzon, drawing from Sarah Ahmed's *Promise of Happiness*, identifies Western drama's tendency to depict either 'happy migrants' or 'melancholic migrants' (Ahmed 2010: 123, 142; Meerzon 24). Likewise, in turn-of-the-century Argentina, a collection of characters emerged along a happy-melancholic continuum. Some early immigration-themed plays presented comic and romantic portrayals of delusional newcomers, hopeful mothers, nostalgic *criollos*, and wealthy *gringos*. Often these characters drove didactic, moralistic plots that affirmed Alberdi's vision for social progress—and national happiness—through immigration. Several later works took a more pessimistic turn, presenting recurring conflicts and communication breakdowns between selfish swindlers, ungrateful children, and preoccupied migrant fathers. Playwrights José Podestá, Justo López de Gomara, Florencio Sánchez, Francisco Defilippis Novoa, Armando Discépolo, and Enrique Santos Discépolo presented variations of these emblematic characters in nationally celebrated *gringo-criollo* dramas.

M. S. Farnsworth (✉)
Hobart and William Smith Colleges, Geneva, NY, USA
e-mail: FARNSWORTH@hws.edu

Cocoliche: The Delusional Newcomer

More than five million immigrants moved to Argentina between the 1860s and the 1930s. By 1914, foreigners outnumbered native-born Argentines in many parts of the country, including Buenos Aires, where three-fourths of the adult population were foreign-born (Scobie 1964, 33). Italians comprised roughly half of the immigrant population; Spaniards made up a third of the new arrivals (Germani 1966, 167). Tensions between native Argentines and European immigrants ran high, as Ana Cara-Walker explains, 'the groups especially threatened by the new arrivals and the ensuing changes were rural and urban non-elite *criollo* men who had to compete for housing, jobs, women, and social status with an overwhelming, mostly male influx of foreigners' (1987, 40).

A stereotypical delusional newcomer, Cocoliche, first appeared in the 1886 circus spectacle *Juan Moreira* by Argentine playwright and performer, José Podestá (1858–1936). Podestá's script was an adaption of a cowboy (*gaucho*) adventure novel written by Eduardo Gutiérrez in 1879. *Juan Moreira* perpetuated a sentimental nostalgia for *criollo* tradition at a time when modern feats of engineering, many of which were brought by foreigners, such as industrial fences and railroads, endangered the *gaucho* way of life. The *gaucho* hero was a man of strong convictions juxtaposed with Cocoliche's nonsensicality. Cocoliche delivered comic monologues in a baffling and highly entertaining mixture of Spanish and Italian. He made fun of the process of assimilation using humour and exaggeration. For example, Cocoliche bumbled through basic national cultural practices, all the while affirming his *criollo* authenticity. Argentine actress, María Padín, recalled having seen the clownish Cocoliche botch the art of sipping mate: 'he pulled out the metal *bombilla* and ate the yerba mate leaves' (Qtd. in Castagnino 1982, 31). Thus, Cocoliche falls into a category Meerzon calls the 'comedic migrant … a theatrical simpleton … unable to communicate their wishes, looking out of place and acting differently to the accepted social and cultural norms of the majority' (2020, 25). One commentator in 1910 described the Cocoliche as an 'uncultured and ridiculous European … the Napolitano-Criollo' (Rossi 1910, 130). Immigrant performers reimagined the role, however, presenting a clever and eccentric Cocoliche who also poked fun at *criollos*, according to Cara-Walker:

> The entire phenomenon embodied a paradox: Cocoliche the character was neither gaucho nor Italian, yet at the same time he was both. As the 'gaucho,' he mocked the immigrants' language and behavior, and as the 'Italian,' he celebrated Argentine culture and tradition, leaving foreigners no alternative but to want to become 'native.' In this manner, Cocoliche's double identity allowed for not only the survival but also the control of both cultural 'faces.' (1987, 43)

Social clubs in Buenos Aires hired Cocoliches as carnival clowns. Their performances mocked idealizations of manliness and made light of *criollos*' anti-immigrant anxieties. As Micol Seigel explains, 'Cocoliche embodied a sexually licentious, ambigendered mother-father figure with proliferating progeny, taking over the nation through uncontrollable reproduction' (2000, 63). In this way, the stereotypical happy migrant ridiculed criollo insecurities.

Hopeful Mothers, Nostalgic Criollos, and Wealthy Gringos

A few *fin de siècle* romance plays by immigrants to Argentina countered the Cocoliche narrative and became national classics. The Spanish-born, Justo López de Gomara (1859–1923), and the Uruguayan, Florencio Sánchez (1875–1910), featured optimistic mothers-to-be, old-fashioned *criollos* and industrious foreigners. Theatre critic Willis Knapp Jones considered this a pivotal cultural moment: 'the gaucho had become anachronism to the progress of Argentina. Serious dramatists pondered the character of the hard-working *gringos*, and seeing them taking over the old homes and fortunes of the Creoles, wondered about them upsetting the homogeneity of the nation' (1966, 118). López de Gomara's foreigners surpassed their *criollo* counterparts in finance, agriculture, and engineering. In *Gauchos y gringos* (1884), a cross-cultural love affair unfolds during a contentious railroad construction project on the Argentine countryside. Finally, the father gives away his daughter and asks for a grandchild in return, imagining that 'the criollo and the immigrant will form a giant race' (López de Gomara 1963, 48). In Florencio Sánchez's *La gringa*, which debuted in Argentina in 1904, the son of an old-fashioned *gaucho* falls in love with a wealthy immigrant's daughter. 'Look at the beautiful couple,' one character comments, 'a daughter of pure gringos … a son of pure criollos … they will bring forth the race of the future' (Sánchez 1945, 178). Here again, the young mother-to-be transmits a message of optimism that aligns with Alberdi's Eurocentric immigration discourse. Argentina's future success, these plays suggest, entails uniting hard-working *criollos* with victorious wealthy foreigners. Marriage and wealth typically serve as Western Culture's 'happiness indicators,' as Ahmed reminds us (2010, 6). The patriarchal *gringo-gaucho* romance trope continued in numerous twentieth-century plays, including *Al campo* (To the Countryside) by Nicolás Granada (1902), *Misia Pancha la Brava* (Lady Pancha the Fierce) by Alberto Novión (1915), and *Las minas de Caminiaga* (The Pretty Girls of Caminiaga, 1935) by Alberto Vacarezza (Jones 1966, 123).

Daily Struggles, Sainetes, and the Grosteco

In contrast to the nationalistic formulas for happiness popularized by Podestá, López de Gomara, and Sánchez, many playwrights from the 1910s to 1930s preferred to dramatize the daily struggles of poor immigrant labourers, small business owners, social activists, and concerned parents. *Almafuerte* (1914), by Salvadora Medina Onrubia (1894–1972), for example, revealed the struggles of immigrant factory workers fearing deportation. The play presents a love match between a Galician (*gallego*) factory worker and a *criolla* seamstress. The lovers negotiate small cultural differences, such as the immigrant's preference for coffee over mate, as they fight for better work environments and more hygienic living conditions. In 1912, theatre critic Rodolfo Fausto Rodríguez saw the struggling immigrant as a mainstay on the national stage:

> So, it is easy to see that these individuals, by adapting to our environment, struggling to assimilate our customs, forming families, will inspire the artists to insert them into his work on more than one occasion. And we will always have some foreigners, some 'gringos', in our productions. But that does not mean that they are not national. (1912, 77)

A series of short farces called *sainetes* illustrated the sharp divide between the language and customs of immigrants and the nation's expectations for assimilation. *Sainetes* were typically staged in public meeting places, such as *conventillos* (tenement housing). Donald Castro explains: 'the patios of slum tenement houses in Buenos Aires ... brought together all of the porteño ethnic types and also cut along class lines' (2004, 127). These spaces illustrate what Mary Louise Pratt calls 'contact zones,' as they represent diverse groups living in 'conditions of coercion, radical inequality, and intractable conflict' (1992, 7). The public delighted in the *sainetes*' depiction of urban language, culture, and settings, as Roberto F. Giusti observed in 1920: 'Their success is more often derived from colourfully drawn scenes: the characters, the music, the working-class dances, the expressions and new slang, everything that represents the *conventillo*' (1920, 15). Still many *sainetes* also transmitted a message of continual ethnic engineering; Adriana Bergero argues that 'the *sainete* proposes encounters, truces, and hopes, metamorphized in the racial and linguistic mix found in the *conventillos*, from which Argentina's *razza forte* (mighty breed) will emerge' (2008, 81). Immigrant-*criollo* relations in the *sainete* included a cast of unhappy characters, such as hostile criollos, cruel swindlers, ungrateful offspring, and preoccupied fathers. Mid-century theatre critic, Domingo S. Casadevall, maintained that the theatre industry drew inspiration from popular tango lyrics, which frequently depicted themes of desperation, resentment, and '*la mala vida*' ('the bad life') (1957, 15). Francisco Defilippis Novoa and the Discépolo brothers, Armando (1887–1971) and Enrique Santos (1901–1951), brought the plight of the alienated working-class immigrant to the fore through innovative, avant-garde *sainetes grotescos* (grotesque *sainetes*). Filled with communication failures and 'linguistic uncertainty,' the *sainete grotesco* presented a pessimistic view of immigrant life (Romano 1986, 31). 'The dark areas, the irrational and self-conscious, appear for the first time,' Claudia Kaiser-Lenior argues, calling the *grotesco* 'a fracture in the *sainete*'s structure' (1977, 48). David Viñas describes the typical *grotesco* protagonist as alienated, dehumanized, and marginalized in financial and linguistic contexts (1997, 42–65). These short farces typically began with misunderstandings and ended in turmoil and tragedy. According to Kaiser-Lenoir, the individual crisis found in the *grotesco* plot echoes larger social crises: 'ultimately, the source of frustration lies in the system in which they live' (1977, 22).

The Discépolo brothers specialized in undermining the simplistic happiness formulas of earlier plays. Born in Buenos Aires to Italian immigrants, they contributed extensively to national popular culture. Armando authored numerous celebrated plays and Enrique Santos—nicknamed *Discepolín*—was a beloved actor, dramatist, and composer of popular tangos (Kaiser-Lenoir 1977, 22). Armando Discépolo's appropriately titled farce, *Babilonia* (1925), depicts disgruntled immigrant servants living in a constant state of disharmony in a rich, hostile *criollo* family home. Spanish, Italian, and German workers clash interpersonally, professionally, and linguistically, all the while facing disapproval from native Argentines. Discépolo paints an unforgiving, unglamorous, and decidedly unhappy portrait of the immigrant experience. As Teresa Sanhueza argues, 'the microcosm of the house represents the macrocosm of Argentine society … life in Argentina is like a potpourri in which all kinds of people—thieves, victims, artists, merchants, the ignorant, teachers—are mixed together' (2003, 13). While popular *sainetes* tended to depict public spaces, such as tenement courtyards, the *grotesco* highlighted spaces of confinement and incomprehension, which 'contributes to the anxiety prompted by claustrophobia' (Bergero 2008, 39).

Selfish Swindlers, Preoccupied Fathers, and Ungrateful Children

The Discépolo brothers' co-written tragi-comic piece, *El organito* (the Organ Grinder, 1925), presents an immigrant father who is also a shameless swindler. Saverio works the streets grinding a steel hand organ while his brother-in-law begs for money at his side. Soon, Saverio replaces his brother-in-law with a more persuasive beggar: 'He plays up the *l'idiota* routine, you know? (*imitating him soberly*) Ah, ah! …. Ah, ah! … he laughs, he dances, he jumps … It's quite a spectacle' (Discépolo and Discépolo 1958, 188). When Saverio criticizes his adult children for failing to inspire enough pity, his oldest son, Nicolás, complains that he never asked for a life of misery:

> And if you had told me: *Che*, Nicolás: you'll play the hunchback, the gimp, the blind man, you'll beg for money all your life; *Che*, Nicolás, come into the world: broken, dirty, depreciated, you'll have to spend your life making people feel pity in order to eat and if you don't, it's off to the scrap heap! Nicolás, come into the world! … Do you really think I would've wanted to be born? (Discépolo and Discépolo 1958, 193)

Saverio also refuses to provide for his family. He denies food to his children as punishment for their unconvincing performances of poverty. The children's refusal to participate in their father's perverse idea of family harmony brings to mind Ahmed's description of the role of coercion in the construction of happiness: 'Happiness involves both reciprocal forms of aspiration … and forms of coercion that are exercised and concealed by the very language of reciprocity' (Ahmed 2010, 91). Saverio's unhappy children refuse to play along. They stop swindling, stop complying with their father's demands, and insist that they owe him nothing. Nicolás and his brother, Humberto, stand up to Saverio when they become thieves instead of beggars. Wielding bricks as weapons, they make Saverio their first victim. Their sister (Florinda) runs away from home with nothing but her body to sell. As Bergero argues, signs in the *grotesco* point to the decline of the social order and the home (2008, 81). The Discépolo brothers present a dysfunctional family structure and, by extension, a nation in desperate need of reform, but their script stops short of proposing alternatives.

Francisco Defilippis Novoa (1890–1929) was born in Paraná, Entre Ríos, where he worked as a schoolteacher and a journalist before debuting a series of plays in Rosario and Buenos Aires. He translated works from Italian to Spanish and authored numerous original scripts, including *sainetes grotescos* and motion-picture screenplays. *Los inmigrantes* (1921) shows a family caught between a selfish swindler and a preoccupied father. Italian shoemaker, Vicente, plays the role of an earnest, though unsuccessful, newcomer. He has moved to Buenos Aires to go into business with Antonio, a wealthy and selfish man from his home village. Vicente and his wife, Teresa, have a ward, Pascualín, who suffers from a cognitive disability. Unable to speak, Pascualín expresses emotion through gestures and grunts. Pascualín has followed Vicente to the new world in search of safety and compassion:

> He probably came from a closed-off family in the mountains who sent him to town, in order to rid themselves of a useless burden … Boys threw stones at the poor thing and made him a laughing stalk … He loved me like a dog too … When I had the chance to marry … I was so happy and I forgot my faithful dog, Pascualín. But on the high seas, from the most hidden corner of the ship, the sailors pulled him out with a broom. … The captain released him in Buenos Aires so as not to throw him into the sea or take him back … So I tied him to my destiny. Providence, or whatever, asked me to care for and protect him. (Defilippis Novoa 1921, 4)

Teresa was already pregnant (with Antonio's baby) when she married Vicente. After years of negligence, Andresito's biological father demands recognition of his paternity. Nevertheless, Vicente continues to play the role of father to his chosen family; he works hard and provides a stable home for Andresito and Pascualín. In scene two, Andresito, now sixteen years old, longs for assimilation and acceptance. He blames Pascualín him for the cruelty of others:

ANDRESITO: This imbecile, whenever he finds me, he follows me. When I am leaving school, when I am out on the street, everywhere.
VICENTE: So what?

ANDRESITO: My schoolmates mock me. Some call him my brother, others call him my uncle. To some, he's my father. I've had to fight double for him … because they called me the son of Quasimodo … (*furious*). And I can't take it anymore, you know! I can't stand it. If he doesn't stop following me, I'll hit him until he learns to talk again. (Defilippis Novoa 1921, 14)

A silent, pitiful, and dependent creature, Pascualín constantly reminds Andresito of the stigma of immigration. Andresito has not absorbed Vicente's capacity for selfless nurturing. Seeing how Andresito mistreats Pascualín, Vicente fears the future:

VICENTE: … Your lack of affection saddens me, and it scares me to think that tomorrow you could treat me the same way.
ANDRESITO: Dad!
VINCENTE: Yes, son, your father was a poor soul in Europe. Here he made his fortune by depriving himself. Sometimes, he would go without eating. His work has given him a crushing fatigue.
ANDRESITO: You have said this to me many times.
VICENTE: And I'll keep telling you, so you don't get overwhelmed by the taunting of your companions. I am very worried about your ingratitude, because one always has to forgive in life, and you don't forgive, do you? Am I right? (Defilippis Novoa 1921, 15)

Vicente has worked hard to maintain family happiness and unity in Argentina, but assimilation pressures accumulate and secrets from the past haunt him. The father worries that the son will resent him, especially when he learns the story of his origins. In the end, Antonio returns and threatens to tell Andresito the truth. Sensing Vicente's anxiety, Pascualín impulsively attacks Antonio, killing him instantly. Vicente and Teresa see their tenuous family structure dissolve. Andresito witnesses the murder of his biological father, adding trauma to the shame he already feels about his family. Pascualín will almost certainly be institutionalized. Like *The Organ Grinder*, *Los inmigrantes* leaves spectators with a sense of dread and national disharmony, which diverges from the happy national discourses of earlier decades.

He visto a Dios, by Defilippis Novoa, also presents a preoccupied immigrant father, an ungrateful son, and a selfish swindler. Hardworking Carmelo has sent his son, Chicho, to school and saved money for his future. Chicho, however, has decided that he would rather gamble, drink, and socialize than work or study. Since his son refuses to help, Carmelo hires Victorio to work in his jewellery store, but he pays him a pittance. Carmelo's only friend is a bible salesman who would rather talk about God than make money. *He visto a Dios* relies heavily on Italian words and expressions. Victorio says, for example, 'I'm alone in *l'America.*' 'I want my wife, I want my child,' he exclaims, using 'voglio' instead of the Spanish word, *quiero* (I want). He says 'mío figlio' instead of *mi hijo* (my son). 'I earn' (*gano*) becomes 'guadagno' and 'five thousand pesos' (*cinco mil pesos*) becomes 'cinque mila pesi' (Defilippis Novoa 1958, 227). Italo-Spanish dialogues dominate all three scenes in the play, recalling the Cocoliche of Juan Moreira and carnival. Clearly, Victorio would like to provide for his son the way Carmelo has provided for Chicho. Sadly and ironically, however, Chicho obstructs his own child's path to happiness and success. When Chicho realizes that his girlfriend, Nuncia, is pregnant, he refuses to take responsibility. When Chicho dies at the hands of mafiosos, Victorio devises an elaborate scheme to steal Carmelo's savings and split the money with Nuncia's father. Victorio puts on a fake white beard and visits Carmelo pretending to be God. Victorio calls Carmelo a sinner and an abuser ('pecatore' and 'osorero') and commands him to hand over his money: 'dame tutu cuanto guarda in tasca' (242). Comically, Carmelo never wonders why God speaks the immigrants' mixture of Italian and Spanish. Eventually, the bible salesman arrives and exposes the sham. But Carmelo decides he would rather have a relationship with God than money. He gives all of his wealth to the pregnant Nuncia, instead of the swindlers, so long as she agrees not to have an abortion; 'women were born to give birth,' he tells her (247). Once again, a woman assumes the role of reproductive labourer, in this case reluctantly, while the men negotiate financial power and responsibility amongst themselves. In this way, Defilippis Novoa's messaging aligns somewhat with nationalist playwrights from earlier decades by poking fun at unsuccessful migrants and exalting hopeful mothers, but it also follows the *grotesco* tendency to depict moral ambiguity, communication failures, and uncertain futures. As was the case with *El Organito*, the younger immigrant's struggle to wrest money and power from the older immigrant takes centre stage in *He visto a Dios*. The negative depictions of older gringos may subtly promote assimilation into the dominant culture. According to Casadevall, many tangos and *sainetes* authored by second-generation Argentines joined *criollos* in caricaturing *gringos*. In particular, they laughed at 'the ignorance and greed of their elders' (1957, 17). As Ahmed has noted in the context of British film in the twenty-first century the immigrant child protagonist may subtly promote the ideal of 'the happiness of integration' by rejecting their parents' culture (2010, 137).

Argentina's turn-of-the-century playwrights offer myriad dramatic interpretations of Alberdi's words, 'gobernar es poblar,' and their implication for the Argentine family writ large. Popular romances and *sainetes* offered comic portrayals of immigrant characters along a happy-melancholic continuum, from *Juan Moreira*'s laughable Cocoliche to *El organito's* ruthless Saverio. The characters populating canonical immigration-themed plays—the delusional newcomer, the hopeful mother, the ungrateful child, the selfish swindler, and the preoccupied father—emphasize the family's symbolic role in cultural mixing, depict myriad communication failures between *gringos* and *criollos*, and reveal intergenerational conflicts and assimilation pressures. While many plays from the late 1900s to the 1920s project happy outlooks for the nation and celebrate ethnic mixing, the *grotesco criollo* avoids formulaic plotlines and eschews happy endings, highlighting instead powerful social anxieties and ethical impasses faced by immigrants and their children.

References

Ahmed, Sarah. 2010. *The Promise of Happiness.* Durham: Duke University Press.
Alberdi, Juan Bautista. 1914. *Bases y puntos de partida para la organización política de la República Argentina.* Buenos Aires: Francisco Cruz.
Bergero, Adriana. 2008. *Intersecting Tango: Cultural Geographies of Buenos Aires, 1900–1930.* Pittsburg: University of Pittsburgh Press.
Cara-Walker, Ana. 1987. 'The Art of Assimilation and Dissimulation Among Italians and Argentines.' *Latin American Research Review*, 22 (3), 37–67.
Casadevall, Domingo F. 1957. *El tema de la mala vida en el teatro nacional.* Buenos Aires: Editorial Guillermo Kraft.
Castagnino, Raúl Hector. 1982. *Circo: teatro gauchesco y tango.* Buenos Aires: Instituto Nacional de Estudios de Teatro.
Castro, Donald S. 2004. 'The Palomas and Gavilanes: Gender in the Sainetes of Alberto Vacarezza.' *Latin American Theatre Review*, 38 (1), 127–43.
Defilippis Novoa, Francisco. 1958. 'He visto a Dios.' In *Siete sainetes porteños,* edited by Luis Ordaz, 217–249. Buenos Aires: Losange.
Defilippis Novoa, Francisco. 1921. 'Los inmigrantes.' *Teatro Argentino.* 42: 2–23.
Discépolo, Armando and Enrique Santos Discépolo. 1958. "El organito." In *Siete sainetes porteños,* edited by Luis Ordaz, 181–215. Buenos Aires: Losange.
Germani, Gino. 1966. 'Mass Immigration and Modernization in Argentina.' *Studies in Comparative International Development* 11: 165–82.
Giusti, Roberto F. *Florencio Sánchez: Su Vida y su obra.* 1920. Buenos Aires: Agencia Sudamericana de Libros.
Jones, Willis Knapp. 1966. *Behind Spanish American Footlights.* Austin: U of Texas P.
Kaiser-Lenior, Claudia. 1977. *El grotesco criollo: estilo teatral de una época.* Havana: Casa de las Américas.
López de Gomara, Justo. 1963. *Gauchos y gringos.* Universidad de Buenos Aires, Facultad de Filosofía.
Medina Onrubia, Salvadora. 1914. 'Almafuerte.' *Nuestro Teatro.* 1.9: 2–26.
Meerzon, Yana. 2020. 'Precarious Bodies in Performance Activism and Theatres of Migration.' In *Migration and Stereotypes in Performance and Culture,* edited by Yana Meerzon, David Dean, and Daniel McNeil, 21–38. London: Palgrave Macmillan
Pratt, Mary Louise. 1992. *Imperial Eyes: Travel Writing and Transculturation.* New York: Routledge.
Rodríguez, Rodolfo Fausto. 1912. *Contribución al estudio del teatro nacional.* Buenos Aires: Natalio Moscardini.
Romano, Eduardo. 1986. 'Grotesco y clases medias en la escena argentina.' *Hispamérica*, 15 (44), 29–37.
Rossi, Vicente. 1910. *Teatro nacional rioplatense.* Río de la Plata, Imprenta Argentina.
Sánchez, Florencio. 1945. *Obras completas.* Edited by Darío Cúneo. Buenos Aires: Claridad.

Sanhueza, Teresa. 2003. 'Italian Immigrants in Argentina: Some Representations on Stage.' *Italian Americana*, 21 (1), 5–21.
Scobie, James. 1964. *Argentina: A City and a Nation*. Oxford: Oxford University Press.
Seigel, Micol. 2000. 'Cocoliche's Romp: Fun with Nationalism at Argentina's Carnival.' *TDR: The Drama Review*, 44 (2), 56–83.
Viñas, David. 1997. *Grotesco, inmigración y fracaso. Armando Discepolo*. Buenos Aires: Corregidor.

CHAPTER 23

Sonless Mothers and Motherless Sons or How Has Polishness Haunted Polish Theatre Artists in Exile?

Kasia Lech

Between 1795 and 1989, Poland spent 173 years out of 194 in a situation of bondage. From 1795 until 1918, the previous Polish-Lithuania Commonwealth territories were divided between Russia, Prussia, and Austria; in 1939, Nazi Germany and Soviet Russia attacked Poland, starting WWII, and post-war Poland was a part of the Soviet bloc until 1989. These were periods of fastidious censorship that intensified at times of political upheaval. At the same time, these moments called for public debate. With theatre in Poland seen as an important platform for such discussions, Polish playwrights in exile took a formative role concerning Polish theatre and discourses on Polishness. Without contemporary technologies like the internet, artists relied on their relatively easy access to printing and mobility of the written word to construct and interrogate Polishness. The chapter focuses on how these art projects from the Romantic era to the present have engaged with 'motherhood' as a metaphorical vessel for performances of personal and communal bondage, exile, and freedom.

The connections between exile, motherhood, and nation are central. Gendered imagining of a nation is common in cultures faced with nation-building (Boehmer 2005). In Poland, this has intersected with the tropes of exile as 'coerced homelessness' (Rumbaut and Rumbaut 2005, 331). For Dragan Todorovic, 'home ceases to exist after one goes into exile' (2019, 21).

K. Lech (✉)
University of Amsterdam, Amsterdam, Netherlands
e-mail: k.k.lech@uva.nl

© The Author(s), under exclusive license to Springer Nature Switzerland AG 2023
Y. Meerzon, S. E. Wilmer (eds.), *The Palgrave Handbook of Theatre and Migration*, https://doi.org/10.1007/978-3-031-20196-7_23

In the context of national bondage, 'home ceases to exist' both before and after one emigrates. For the artists discussed in this essay, the national 'homelessness' underpinned their subsequent individual and communal exilic experiences of 'homelessness.' In Poland's patriarchal tradition, which dominates its national liberation movement, home has been a space of mothers, evoking links between bondage, exile, and motherlessness, particularly in the context of 'Matka Ojczyzna.'

'Matka Ojczyzna' first appears in sixteenth-century Polish writings. Directly translated, it means 'Mother Fatherland' but connotes 'Mother Homeland.' Before it became associated with 'homeland,' the word 'ojczyzna' referred to an inheritance from a father ('ojciec'), evoking the tropes of origin, belonging, land, and home. However, 'matka,' 'ojczyzna,' and 'Matka Ojczyzna' have a grammatically feminine gender. The term's irony brings to the fore and frames the different associations of motherlands and fatherlands. These are, respectively, 'birth, hearth, home, roots, [and] the umbilical cord' in contrast with 'filial duty, the bonds of fraternity, and paternity' (Boehmer 2005, 27). The connotation of 'Mother Fatherland' is the homeland as the sanctified mother of all Polish people, and the need for unified effort and sacrifice of Polish women and men with clearly assigned gender roles under male leadership. Maria Janion argues that 'Polish national culture is remarkably masculine' (2006, 266), which is evident in the works of the predominantly male artists discussed in this essay.

Critical synergies within the migration-motherhood-nation nexus are time-related. Yana Meerzon observes that '[t]he gaze of someone in exile is turned simultaneously into their past and their future, so the condition of exile might carry a shadow of privilege, essentialism, and metaphor' (2021, 199). Rumbaut frames these intersecting temporal frames within exilic experiences as a need 'to resolve dual crises: a "crisis of loss"—coming to terms with the past—and a "crisis of load"—coming to terms with the present and immediate future' (2005, 338–39). For the artists discussed in this chapter, the pasts, presents, and futures refer to themselves, but above all to Poland and its communities. Motherhood fulfils the need for metaphor and essentialism that Meerzon mentions as a junction of temporal structures. Motherhood connotes intersections of past, present, and future, perhaps most evident in the moment of birth. It evokes various individual and communal belonging discourses, including an unbreakable bond between a person and their mother(land). This essay discusses motherhood as a complex allegorical platform for several personal, artistic, political, ideological, and spatial negotiations between the self and Poland. These negotiations are underpinned by the experiences of personal and communal loss and the need to imagine the future. The new exilic identity of the artists considered here arises above all from their physical and spiritual proximity to their mothers and/or Poland as 'Mother Fatherland,' its culture, and its community. The majority of their works are created in Polish and, with some exceptions, directed at Polish audiences at home and abroad. While the focus of this chapter is on the expression of Polishness in exilic drama, my analysis will undertake such considerations in view of the non-dramatic writings of their authors.

The first part of the discussion focuses on the *Wielka Emigracja* ('Great Emigration'). The term refers to Polish migrants who found themselves abroad, mainly in France, after the fall of the 1830–1831 November Rising, an unsuccessful attempt to regain the country. The 'Great' recognizes their impossible to overestimate role in the Polish cultural and socio-political past and present. Romantics politicized motherhood and the mother-son bond, setting up the scene for a migrant artist to become 'the soldiers of rising [Mother] Fatherland' (Mickiewicz 1832, 52). The soldier metaphor operates here in a broad context that includes artistic activities. This chapter then moves to focus on how later artists in exile authored works in dialogue with Romantic notions of Polish national and cultural identity—returning to, adopting, and demythologizing Romantic tropes of migration-motherhood-nation to reflect on Polishness in times of political uncertainty.

By shedding light on the synergies between migration, motherhood, and nation across time, the chapter reveals how individual and communal exilic experiences are written into Poland's collective memories as 'the relationship that a society constructs with its past' (Rusu 2013, 261–62) and its politics of memory. It also signals how the migration-motherhood-nation discourses have paradoxically contributed to marginalization of Poland's ethnic minorities. Peter J. Verovšek defines politics of memory as a 'communicative paradigm' and transtemporal processes by which collective memories are created, sustained, and used, and come into 'conflict with other narratives that are present within society at large' (2016, 535). Thus, in its final section, the chapter turns to how, in today's Poland, migration-motherhood-nation continues to be a model for performances of Polish communities regardless of their exilic experiences or lack thereof. In doing so, it follows Dariusz Kosiński's use of 'Polish theatres' as performative practices within the Polish socio-political-cultural space (2010, 19–22). Kosiński's work has been criticized for homogenous engagement with Polishness (Wilmer 2021). But it is relevant here because of it as an example of how deeply the migration-motherhood-nation nexus is rooted in Polish discourses. Unless stated differently, all translations from Polish are mine.

How Did the Great Migrants Plan to 'Birth' Poland?

Poland lost its independence as Johann Gottfried von Herder's ideas of 'national spirit' and the need to define one's national identity spread across Europe. However, Prussia, Russia, and Austria took over Polish institutions and controlled the public spaces in which a debate on Polishness would have otherwise happened (Prokop 1991, 414). Poles had to turn to arenas less controlled by the three empires, like theatre. As Kosiński explains, the socio-political, legal, religious, and cultural attempts to define the Polish community stretch back at least to the sixteenth century, have been highly performative, and have the theatre as an important platform (2010, 21, 211). In the early 1800s, this meant looking for gaps in censorship, playing with allegories and historization, and departing from earlier performances of Polishness that recognized the country's multicultural and multireligious communities.

However, the November Rising resulted in several repressive measures. One of them was censorship of the theatre, whereby the performance of tragedies was forbidden (Kosiński 2010, 242). Influential Romantics like Adam Mickiewicz propagated the idea that comedy and related genres such as farce were not art and could not deal with Poland's tragedy; these were the genres allowed on the Polish stages. The Great Emigration was ideologically and politically divided on the reasons for the insurrection's failure and possible future actions. Internationally, the Polish quest for freedom provoked hostility and laughter. Europe was not ready to pay the price of another continent-wide war against the three empires for a politically unified and independent Poland (Davies 2005, 13–14, 241). Polish writers in exile were in an ideal position to change the discourse, unite Poles, and keep up the belief in freedom. European Romanticism presented poets as communal leaders and focused on the past through its historicism and interests in the spirits of the deceased. The former via the medium of theatre was central in defining Polish post-partition identity and facilitating belief in Poland's future freedom. Mickiewicz already had socio-political and cultural authority as a poet strongly connected with the national liberation movement.

Motherhood was the perfect vessel to bring different tropes that occupied the Great Migrants. Polish mothers were at the heart of the Polish cause, rendered as those responsible for passing on Polish heritage, both spiritually and physically, to the new generation of Poles. This linked with the tropes of Fatherland as a mother, sanctified by the status of Holy Mary as the Queen of Poland and mother of Poles, rooted in the Middle Ages. One implication of this cultural framing was that one had only one mother and, therefore only one Mother Fatherland, encouraging homogenous discourses of the nation. Another implication was that one should love Poland like one's mother. The Great Emigration's artists expanded these tropes and their intersections into sacred symbols of motherless sons and sonless mothers. The tension between these two symbols speaks to what Edward W. Said describes as 'the unhealable rift' that exile puts 'between a human being and a native place, between the self and its true home' (2001, 173). In Polish Romantics' work, another layer arose from the national bondage: 'the unhealable rift' between the Polish people and their Mother Fatherland.

The Great Migrants' exilic gaze reinforced their authority as spiritual leaders and framed their narrations of the Polish past and foretelling of Poland's future, setting ways to heal the rift. In 1842, Mickiewicz announced himself as '*wieszcz*' (1874, 255). Later, scholars applied the term to selected writers of the Great Emigration. The word '*wieszcz*' comes from Polish and Ukrainian folk traditions and translates into English as 'bard.' However, etymologically, it connects to the words 'to know' ('*wiedzieć*') and 'to lead' ('*wieść*'). '*Wieszcz*' denotes someone who foretells the future. Mickiewicz's announcement and appearances of '*wieszcz*' figures in Romantic dramas reflected Polish Romantics' version of the exilic gaze and spoke to the need for metaphor that they found in motherhood.

The Great Migrants left behind their loved ones. The images of homeland overlapped with images of homes, mothers, and lovers, becoming a vital creative resource (Prokop 1991, 415). In the opening of Mickiewicz's epic poem *Mr Tadeusz* (1834), adapted numerous times for stage and screen, nostalgia for the lost Mother Fatherland' intersects with childhood memories of Holy Mary healing him from sickness and bringing him back to his mother's arms. Juliusz Słowacki wrote poems and letters to his mother Salomea. Written regularly for two decades, the letters recorded his life and most intimate experiences. They were an 'identity project' as Słowacki negotiated his identity through a dialogue between his nostalgia for his mother and the past and future (Sikora 2018, 268, 280–82). Słowacki's experiences of exile and motherlessness intersected and informed his exilic gaze on self in the world. Similarly, the Great Migrants used tropes of motherhood to shape their narratives on exile and national bondage.

Elżbieta Ostrowska observes brotherhoods that Polish Romantics created. She argues that, typically for nationalistic contexts, Polish national liberation culture has been dominated by homosocial bonding that idealizes motherhood and desexualizes women (apart from the reproductive function) (2004, 216–19). The homosocial bonding leads to an enhanced sense of national solidarity as a brotherhood with one mother, further strengthening homogenous national discourses. In this sense, the loss of Poland through the partition and exile has been an experience of (homo)communal motherlessness. This sentiment is evident in Mickiewicz's 1832 *The Books of the Polish People and Polish Pilgrimage*, which presents Polish migrants as 'the Soul of the Polish Nation.' The booklet reflects on the Polish past and future and presents exiles as pilgrims to emphasize their sanctified role in leading the nation towards spiritual and political freedom (1832, 24). At the same time, the ghost of Mother Fatherland (often bloodstained) appears in various pre-Romantic and Romantic Polish poetry, says Janion. She recalls the famous finale of *Mr Tadeusz* in which Mickiewicz mourns 'Mother Poland' (Janion 2006, 264–65; Mickiewicz 1885, 399).

In the works of Polish Great Migrants, the cure to communal and individual motherlessness is the sacred 'blood and milk' oath connecting Poles and Mother Fatherland. The latter can be resurrected, explains Maria Janoszka, through its children's and enemies' blood (2014, 102–4). The embodiment of the oath is the figure of a sonless Polish Mother. Through the present acts of birthing and raising children (or rather sons), she bridges Poland's past and future. Or, more bluntly, she births, feeds with breastmilk made of her blood and raises sons, so that they may die for Poland's freedom, as Mary raised Jesus to die for humanity.

These tropes are particularly striking in the third part of Mickiewicz's play *Dziady* (Forefathers' Eve), completed in 1832 and accompanied by a poem 'To The Polish Mother' that both laments and glorifies the fate of Polish Mother(s) and her son(s). *Forefathers' Eve* reinforces the ideas that suffering is necessary for salvation. It is an artistic interpretation of Polish messianism: the Polish nation has been chosen by God to be sacrificed for the freedom of the world, as Jesus Christ was sacrificed to redeem humanity. It plays on the connotation of Mother Fatherland and Holy Mary as the mother(s) of all Poles.

Forefathers' Eve's main character is the poet-lover Gustaw that transforms from a Romantic lover into Konrad: the son and lover of Mother Fatherland. The act emphasizes the particular 'thanatotic and incestuously-perverted' overtones that metaphors of mothers take in Poland's traditions (Ostrowska 2004, 221; Janion 2006, 273–74). Another example is the so-called Great Improvisation, in which Konrad reveals he is like a mother feeling the pain of his foetus (Mickiewicz 1864, 147), speaking to how the Great Migrants wish to 'birth' Mother Fatherland (Siwicka 1993, 71). Birth or resurrect her through enemies' blood as in the so-called 'Vengeance Song' that dramatizes the 'blood and milk' oath. Konrad sings it with a brotherhood of (male) prisoners (Mickiewicz 1864, 137–38).

Forefathers' Eve personifies the 'sonless' Polish Mother. Mrs Rollinson is a blind elderly widow who comes to Senator Novosilcov (the representative of the Tsar in Poland) begging for her son's freedom. Mickiewicz layers precarious contexts as a contrasting background for Mrs Rollinson's (ostensible) 'agency' and patriotic 'activism' and strengthens homogenizing discourses on Poland. Novosilcov and the devils are the play's only multilingual characters, reflecting on Poles' long and desperate fight against Russification and Germanization. Novosilcov pretends to agree to free her son but gives orders to kill him 'accidentally.' When Mrs Rollinson returns filled with vengeance, Novosilcov runs away terrified. Her appearance manifests a shift as the events start following the earlier vision by Priest Peter, who foretells Poland's freedom. The suggestion is that Poland's independence will come true if mothers follow the male lead.

Kosiński and others have described *Forefathers' Eve* as 'matecznik' of Polish theatre (2010, 117), which means 'backwoods' but comes from 'mother' ('matka'), presenting it as the 'source' for Polish theatre. The impact of the Great Migrants in general on Polish socio-political-cultural spheres is unarguable. And their engagement with the migration-mother-nation nexus contributed to discourses that equated national independence with homogeneity. This included ignoring Mickiewicz's transnational identity (Polish, Lithuanian, Belarusian). The 1918 Kielce pogrom is an example. As Poland regained freedom, the Jewish community was violently attacked for speaking Yiddish after a meeting in a theatre about the future of the Jewish community in independent Poland. Throughout 1920s and 1930s, the Romantic migrants continued to play symbolically central role. The 1928 transfer of Juliusz Słowacki's ashes from Paris to the Wawel Cathedral (the royal burial site) was a pilgrimage and the country-wide celebration. His ashes travelled on a river ship 'Mickiewicz' (!) through Poland. The country's leader Józef Piłsudzki 'welcomed' Słowacki home.

During WWII, multiple Polish theatres operated in Lithuania, Palestine, Canada, and Germany, amongst others. Actress Jadwiga Domańska, who led the Dramatyczny Theatre at the 2nd Polish Corps, saw it as serving 'the common, national cause' (Braun 1996, 289). Following the 1945 open letter to Polish migrants by literary and theatre critic Tymon Terlecki, calling Poles abroad to 'amplify Polishness' (2003, 31), the Polish Instytut Literacki in Rome published Mickiewicz's *The Books of the Polish People* and various theatre activities appeared abroad. As pointed out by Dobrochna Ratajczakowa, these works were aimed at Polish communities abroad and seen as a direct continuation of the Great Migrants' work. The displacement, characteristic of exilic experience in general, was imposed on Mother Fatherland. For Poles abroad, the 'real' Poland was in exile. The broad Polish communities abroad, regardless of their generational status, became 'Polonia' (in Latin Poland). Poland at home had been overtaken by 'foreign' and toxic values (Ratajczakowa 1994, 271–73). Significantly, the works written in exile at that time have had minimal impact on Polish stages (Ratajczakowa 1994, 271–73). The exceptions are the authors with a formative role in Polish theatre: Witold Gombrowicz, Sławomir Mrożek, and Janusz Głowacki. I will focus on Mrożek's and Głowacki's works, in which exile as motherlessness interrogates individual and communal experiences of exile and Poland.

MOTHERLESS-EXILE AS DIAGNOSIS OF POLISH EXPERIENCES

Mrożek's *Pieszo* (On Foot) was written in 1980, nearly two decades into Mrożek's emigration, in a critical time for Poland. Communist power weakened, and the Solidarność movement was about to appear and defeat it (Davies 2005, 470–508). As Communism got close to becoming the past, and the future had not yet appeared, Mrożek reflected on a similar moment a few decades before. *On Foot* happens during the last days of WWII and the first days under Communist rule. In Mrożek's words, the play speaks about the moment when 'biological beginning blends into historical ones' (2000, 130). Mrożek uses the analogy to refer to his own coming of age in 1945; he was then fifteen. In the context of *On Foot*, the metaphor concerns images of motherhood in the exilic and national liberation discourses.

In *On Foot*, Father and Son walk behind the front line to find the boy's sick mother, setting up a perfect allegory for Poland in 1945. On their 'pilgrimage,' they meet characters awaiting a better life in free Poland. They all evoke 'the cultural patterns' underpinning the moods and ideas of Polish society in 1945 (Stephan 1989, 46). One of them is a pregnant Girl, raped by soldiers, evoking tropes of raped motherlands in cultures with bondage experiences. Girl's lines are limited to short responses, and Son's mother never appears. The latter only exists in two lines delivered by Father near the beginning and the end of the play (1983, 26, 62). However, symbolically, the Girl and Son's motherlessness are central to Mrożek's reflection on Polish communities and himself in 1945 and 1980. According to stage direction, just before *On Foot*'s Epilogue, Son lies next to Girl 'not as a man, but as a child. He presses against her arm like a child, as if she were his mother. Girl wakes up and reacts as if she were his mother, protectively stroking his hair.' This is the first time the play shows her in a 'motherly' role. Son moans: 'I don't want to,' referring to Superiusz's suicide and the haunting sound of a train that has just passed them, described by a character as 'Transport,' recalling the Holocaust. *The Internationale*, the national anthem of the USSR, announces the start of the Epilogue set in the first days of Communist rule (Mrożek, 1983, 55–56).

The embrace between Son and Girl symbolizes the birth of a mother, evoking Romantic tropes and conveying hopes for the future in 'a new' Poland. At the same time, the scene connotes exile, especially given that Son's turn to another mother is temporary. In the end, Father and Son continue to walk, looking for Son's mother. To paraphrase Mrożek (2000, 130), the embrace moment blends biological beginnings and endings with historical turning points. The latter can be both beginnings and endings or just part of the wheel of history, particularly given that the play leaves the characters still searching. Through the tropes of motherhood, Mrożek captures the essence of his own and Polish experiences in 1945 and 1980, trapped in a moment between past and future that is filled with hope and fear. The temporal proximity between 1945 and 1980 emphasizes multiple crises within these experiences. To recall Rumbaut's ideas (2005, 338–39), the 1980s exilic experiences are underpinned by crises arising from coming to terms with the past and the futures that were hoped for in 1945 but never happened. These layered losses frame the coming to terms with the present and immediate future in the 1980s, suggesting that the wheel of history is turning, the migration-mother-nation nexus is its axis, and freedom may never be achieved.

Despite Mrożek's dark vision, in 1989, Poland regained its independence. The exilic artists no longer needed to speak for Poland's freedom and were free to return, but not all did so. The perspective of the artists abroad at that moment was captured in *Antigone in New York* by Janusz Głowacki. Commissioned and subsequently staged by the Arena Stage in Washington D.C., the play applies Romantic tropes in a transnational context. *Antigone in New York* was named as one of the best plays of 1993 by *Time* magazine (Trojanowska 2003, 279), and in 1992 as one of the three most critical recent Polish plays by Jan Kott (1992, 155). The play takes place in New York City's Tompkins Square Park during the night preceding its closure in June 1991, when hundreds of police forcibly removed around 200 people living in the park. Głowacki stages multiple identities: Irish-American policeman Murphy, Puerto Rican Anita, Russian Jew Sasha, and Polish Flea (continuing his *Hunting Cockroaches*' mocking association of Polish migrants with pests). The last three are homeless, motherless, and branded by Murphy as foreign (Głowacki 1997, 1.1, 8). Intersecting these tropes, the play evokes the precarity that escapes national and social boundaries. The aim is to speak about society in crisis at a particular moment in New York's social history. Yet, the Polish character, clearly referencing Głowacki, continues an irreverent dialogue with Romantic tropes.

Flea is an unwanted child whose mother tries to drown him when he is born (1997, 1.2.17–18). The suggestion is that giving birth to him was a sin, probably as she was unmarried. Here Głowacki mocks the Virgin Mother cult in Poland. It also operates as a reflection on the early 1990s debate on making abortion illegal in Poland and the potential consequence of such a law. On another level, the image of a mother drowning her child mocks an iconic Polish Mother: if one is raising a son so he can die, one might as well kill him straight away. Moreover, it works as a metaphor for Poland under the Communist regime. The connections between rejecting mother and country are signalled in Flea's fear of returning home. When his girlfriend Jola comes to the United States, he hides in the bushes, which can be read as Głowacki's irreverent self-reflection. The sexualized image of Jola with 'blonde hair, big tits' (1997, 1.2, 22) replaces Mother Fatherland and her 'blood and milk' as a symbol of 1990s Poland and its post-censorship mass-sexualization or pornification. It also plays on the Gustaw-Konrad transformation, evoking 'incestuously-perverted' tropes of motherhood in the Polish tradition (Janion 2006, 273–74).

Pulitzer-winning Martyna Majok and her 2020 play *Sanctuary City* 'freed' the metaphor of exile as motherlessness from specifically Polish and nationalistic overtones. Majok belongs to the so-called 'one-and-a-half' generation of migrants, children born in the country of their parent(s) but 'free of the impulse for self-justification that drives their parents' exilic vision' (Rumbaut and Rumbaut 2005, 331, 338). That freedom feeds into Majok's play, which uses motherlessness as a metaphor of banishment from society and complicates interconnections between exile and movement, bringing the former into broader debates on inequality in the contemporary United States (Majok 2020). However, the intersections between the tropes of migration, motherhood, and nation still play a part in Majok's work. Her 2014 *Ironbound* is inspired by her mother's story and the invisibility of her experience as a Polish migrant. As Majok says, '[w]hen she saw it opening night at Round House, she witnessed 300 people in a huge theatre stand up for a story that she knew in her heart is hers. That meant more to me than anything in my career that, that night, she felt seen and valued' (Majok 2016, 11).

Conclusion

The migration-motherhood-nation nexus has functioned as a creative and political resource for facilitating and interrogating individual and communal performances related to Poland. The playwrights discussed in this essay used their exilic gazes to illuminate critical synergies between exile, motherhood, and the Polish nation. These exilic gazes were multifocal. They focused on individual and communal pasts and futures, and they looked at different presents in Poland and abroad as well as at futures imagined by the pasts. While the artists' ideas on individual and national freedoms shifted in response to their unique circumstances, the trope of motherhood remained the manifestation of an unbreakable bond between the self, Poland, and Polish communities across time. The bond did not necessarily have a nationalistic overtone and for some artists it was a burden. Nevertheless, for 200 years, the artists in exile wrote the migration-motherhood-nation nexus into intergenerational experiences of Polishness. In the 2020s, three decades after Poland regained freedom, it continues to play a major part within Polish politics of memory.

The motherlessness-exile link underpins calls by far-right organizations for repatriating Polish exiles and/or their descendants. The current far-right government prides itself on Polish migrants returning 'home.' The migration-motherhood-nation nexus also models the voices from the centre and left. During the October 2021 protest defending Polish membership in the European Union, numerous speakers linked a potential Polexit with displacement and exile. Politician Donald Tusk, actress Maja Ostaszewska and others said, 'You will not walk us out of Europe,' echoing the official hashtag *#ZostajeMywEU* (We are staying in the EU). Europe worked as a metonymy of the EU. WWII veteran Wanda Traczyk-Stawska ended her speech: 'I am a soldier who remembers the spilling blood, the dying friends. I am here to speak in their name. No one will ever walk me away from my (Mother) Fatherland, which is Poland, but also Europe. Because Europe is also my Mother' (Zakrocki 2021). In doing so, she used the past experiences of exile and WWII to frame her redefinition of Mother Fatherland to include the European Union as an act that protects Poland's future. Mrożek was right. The wheel of Polish history is turning, and the migration-mother-nation nexus continues as its axis.

References

Boehmer, Elleke. 2005. 'Motherlands, Mothers and Nationalist Sons: Theorizing the En-Gendered Nation.' In *Stories of Women: Gender and Narrative in the Postcolonial Nation*, edited by Elleke Boehmer, 22–41. Manchester: Manchester University Press.

Braun, Kazimierz. 1996. *A History of Polish Theater, 1939-1989: Spheres of Captivity and Freedom*. London: Greenwood Press.

Davies, Norman. 2005. *God's Playground: A History of Poland*. Two vols. Oxford: Oxford University Press.

Głowacki, Janusz. 1997. *Antigone in New York*. New York: Samuel French.

Janion, Maria. 2006. *Niesamowita Słowiańszczyzna: Fantazmaty Literatury*. Kraków: Wydawnictwo Literackie.

Janoszka, Maria. 2014. '"Beniowski" We Krwi: O Kilku Wymiarach Symboliki "Cieczy Osobliwej" w Poemacie Juliusza Słowackiego.' In *Granice Romantyzmu: Romantyzm Bez Granic?*, edited by Marek Piechota, Marta Kalarus, and Oskar Kalarus, 100–115. Katowice: Wydawnictwo Uniwersytetu Śląskiego.

Kosiński, Dariusz. 2010. *Teatra Polskie: Historie*. Warszawa: Wydawnictwo Naukowe PWN.

Kott, Jan. 1992. 'Antygona Powiesiła Się w Tompkins Square Park.' *Dialog*, 10, 153–55.

Majok, Martyna. 2016. 'Ten Questions with Martyna Majok.' *The Dramatist*, 19 (1), 10–11.
Majok, Martyna. 2020. 'Sanctuary City.' Unpublished manuscript.
Meerzon, Yana. 2021. 'From Exile to Migration.' In *The Oxford Handbook of Politics and Performance*, edited by Shirin Rai, Milija Gluhovic, Silvija Jestrović, and Michael Saward, 198–212. Oxford: Oxford University Press.
Mickiewicz, Adam. 1832. *Księgi Narodu Polskiego i Pielgrzymstwa Polskiego*. Paris: A. Pinard.
———. 1864. *Dziady*. Wrocław: H. Skutsch.
———. 1874. 'Przemówienie Na Posiedzeniu Towarzystwa Literackiego Polskiego w Paryzu, 3 May 1842.' In *Korespondencya*, 254–56. Paris: Księgarnia Luxemburgska.
Mrożek, Sławomir. 1983. *Pieszo*. Warszawa: Czytelnik.
———. 2000. *Małe Listy*. Warszawa: Noir sur Blanc.
Ostrowska, Elżbieta. 2004. 'Matki Polki i Ich Synowie. Kilka Uwag o Genezie Obrazów Kobiecości i Męskości w Kulturze Polskiej.' In *Gender: Konteksty*, edited by Małgorzata Radkiewicz, 215–27. Kraków: Rabid.
Prokop, Jan. 1991. 'Kobieta Polka.' In *Słownik Literatury Polskiej XIX Wieku*, edited by Józef Bachórz and Alina Kowalczykowa, 414–417. Wrocław: Ossolineum.
Ratajczakowa, Dobrochna. 1994. 'Światło Duszy i Lampy Rozumu.' In *Teatr i Dramat Polskiej Emigracji 1939-1989*, edited by Izolda Kiec, Dobrochna Ratajczakowa, and Jacek Wachowski, 265–81. Poznań: Wydawnictwo Acarus.
Rumbaut, Ruben D., and Rubén G. Rumbaut. 2005. 'Self and Circumstance: Journeys and Visions of Exile.' In *The Dispossessed: An Anatomy of Exile*, edited by Peter I. Rose, 331–55. Amherst: University of Massachusetts Press.
Rusu, Mihai. 2013. 'History and Collective Memory: The Succeeding Incarnations of an Evolving Relationship.' *Philobiblon*, 18, 260–82.
Said, Edward. 2001. 'Reflections on Exile.' In *Reflections on Exile and Other Literary and Cultural Essays*, 173–86. London: Granta Books.
Sikora, Agata. 2018. 'Nostalgia Za Przyszłością: Życie Jako Opowieść w Listach Juliusza Słowackiego Do Matki.' *Teksty Drugie*, 6, 267–82.
Siwicka, Dorota. 1993. 'Ojczyzna Intymna.' *Res Publica Nowa*, 7-8, 70–72.
Stephan, Halina. 1989. 'Sławomir Mrożek: From Satire to National Drama.' *The Polish Review*, 34 (1), 45–56.
Terlecki, Tymon. 2003. *Emigracja Naszego Czasu*. Lublin: Wydawnictwo UMCS.
Todorovic, Dragan. 2019. 'We Are Who We Are Not: Language, Exile, and Nostalgia for the Self.' In *Dramaturgy of Migration: Staging Multilingual Encounters in Contemporary Theatre*, edited by Yana Meerzon and Katharina Pewny, 20–29. London: Routledge.
Trojanowska, Tamara. 2003. 'Many Happy Returns: Janusz Głowacki and His Exilic Experience.' In *Living in Translation: Polish Writers in America*, edited by Halina Stephan, 259–87. Amsterdam: Rodopi.
Verovšek, Peter J. 2016. 'Collective Memory, Politics, and the Influence of the Past: The Politics of Memory as a Research Paradigm.' *Politics, Groups, and Identities*, 4 (3), 529–43.
Wilmer, S.E. 2021. 'Performing "Polishness".' *Pamiętnik Teatralny*, 70 (2), 165–69.
Zakrocki, Maciej. 2021. 'Transmisja Wystąpień z Pl. Zamkowego. Protest w Obronie Obecności Polski w UE.' TOK FM.

CHAPTER 24

All Our Migrants: Place and Displacement on the Israeli Stage

Sarit Cofman-Simhon

In December 2019, a few weeks before COVID-19 shut down all of the theatres in Israel, a new musical opened at Haifa Theatre; *Gently*, by Shiri Nadav Naor, directed by Moshe Naor to lyrics of Sha'anan Street and with a score by Amir Lekner, was a musical about a family of African refugees living in Tel Aviv, struggling with the everyday difficulties of immigration. Some of the actors were refugees too. This was quite surprising, since mainstream Israeli theatre has otherwise so far failed to voice the problems of Africans in Israel, including those of Ethiopian Jews who are Israeli citizens. No show treating the latter's experiences of living in the country has been staged in mainstream spaces. For a short time, before the theatre had to close because of the pandemic, the issue of asylum seekers was represented on a main stage.

A major thematic concern of Israeli theatre is its response to the experience of migration, which is part of the collective memory of almost all of its spectators: nearly every Israeli citizen has experienced displacement—if not first-hand, at least through their parents. For Israeli Jews, to tackle migration means triggering both the myth of the Exodus from Egypt and the memory of the devastation of the Holocaust. The consciousness of needing to care for refugees is unambiguously present in the Hebrew Bible, rooted in the Israelites' experiences in Egypt:

> But the stranger that dwelleth with you shall be unto you as one born among you, and thou shalt love him as thyself; for ye were strangers in the land of Egypt: I am the LORD your God. (Leviticus 19: 34)

S. Cofman-Simhon (✉)
The School of Performing Arts, Kibbutzim College, Tel Aviv and Emunah Faculty of Fine Arts, Jerusalem, Israel

The year 2018, says Maya Buenos, a young Israeli theatre director, can be seen as catalysing the comparison between asylum seekers in Israel and Jewish refugees in the past (Unpublished interview, 2021). That was the year in which the Israeli government attempted to relocate some of its asylum seekers to various African states. Many Israelis protested, declaring they would hide the African refugees in their own homes (Kershner 2018). The government abandoned the project. The presence of refugees has occasioned a heated debate in Israel: now that Jews finally have a home and a state, and are not forced to move from place to place, should they not show compassion towards today's refugees? 'They aren't refugees,' said Prime Minister Benjamin Netanyahu in 2017 to the Israeli inhabitants of a poor neighbourhood in Tel Aviv, who were protesting about the many African refugees living in their vicinity, 'Or at least most of them aren't. Most of them are looking for jobs,' he added (Surkes 2021). African migrants are granted temporary visas in Israel, they generally work in marginal spaces (washing dishes in restaurants, cleaning houses), beyond the law and without statutory safeguards. The Hotline for Refugees and Migrants (HRM), a not-for-profit organization, defends their rights.

I would like to explore here three types of representation of displacement on the Israeli stage: two that have been extensively researched, and one that is rather new and under-researched. First is the Holocaust survivor: as Joseph Carens writes, 'The catastrophe of the Holocaust became paradigmatic to the responsibility of states to welcome those in critical need' (Carens 2013, 194). Second, the Palestinian exile, following the establishment of the State of Israel in 1948, represented in Israeli theatre in both Hebrew and Arabic. Finally, the representation of African refugees of the 2000s, which contributes to the ongoing debate in Israel: one camp claiming that since we are all migrants, we should be more empathic towards today's asylum seekers, and the other demanding they be deported.

Place and Displacement in the Making of the State of Israel and Israeli Theatre

For centuries, Jews have been practically migrants: even if settled on a certain land for a long period of time, their relation to the land was different from those around them who did not have a history of movement. The place they occupied was always intermediate, or secondary to the principle of returning home to the Land of Israel, aka the Holy Land. The notion of a holy land complicates all discussion of place and displacement with theological ideologies. After all, the Crusaders did not come to the Holy Land for lack of somewhere to be at home, or with straightforwardly imperialist intentions, but rather to fight in a religious war against the Muslims who controlled the Holy Sepulchre and the land that they believed to be holy (Cohen 1985).

For Jews, diaspora was complemented by the belief in redemption, associated with the return to a utopic, promised land (Genesis, 15:18–21). Their national and religious founding myth has been basically a story of refugees who escaped slavery (the biblical Exodus of the Israelites from Egypt led by Moses) and sought asylum, wandering in the Sinai desert for forty years and establishing a new, monotheistic religion (Numbers, 34:1–12). When they finally reached the Promised Land, they fought and conquered parts of Canaan, which they viewed as God's fulfilment of the promise (Deuteronomy, 1:8). The Jews lived there for more than a millennium, the majority being expelled by the Romans in the first century CE to a long-lasting diaspora.

In the late nineteenth century, there began a migration of Jews to the land known from Roman times as Syria-Palaestina and, under the Ottoman Empire, as Palestine (Beška and Foster 2021). This movement of people accelerated after WWI during the British Mandate. It culminated in the years after the establishment of the State of Israel in 1948, which was supposed to put an end to Jewish cosmopolitanism, offering them a utopian home (Cofman-Simhon 2020).

On November 29, 1947, the UN voted for the end of the British Mandate in Palestine and for a two-state solution. The Jewish leadership accepted this UN resolution, but the Palestinians and all Arab states rejected it. Half a year later, when the British left, local Jewish leaders declared the establishment of an independent state—Israel. A war broke out which involved Egyptian, Jordanian, Syrian, and Iraqi armies, against the newly established Israeli army. The war lasted more than a year and ended with armistice agreements. During the war the newly born Israeli state enlarged its borders that were initially voted for by the UN. In Israel, this war is commonly called the War of Independence, while for the Palestinians it is the Nakba (catastrophe): between 1947 and 1949, at least 750,000 Palestinians out of a population of 1.9 million became refugees (Ben-Ami 2006). Some of these were displaced within Israeli borders. Many others and their descendants live to this day in the Gaza Strip and the West Bank, Jordan and Lebanon, and view themselves as refugees, waiting for the right of return to the villages and cities they (or their parents) inhabited before 1948. Those who remained within the borders became Israeli citizens and constitute today about 21% of Israel's population. At its most basic level, the conflict between Israelis and Palestinians is over place and displacement; over who gets what land and how that land is controlled.

Prior to 1948 and during the first years of the state, Hebrew theatre extensively tackled the issue of land: the book *Adama, Adam, Dam* (Earth, Man, Blood) (1980) by Gideon Ofrat analyses the image of land (and blood) in those plays, and is subtitled 'the myth of the pioneer and the rite of earth in settlement drama.' Shimon Levy, too, writes about the complex relation to land in Hebrew theatre:

> Plays such as [...] *Dan ha-shomer* (Dan The Guard) (1940) by Sheen Shalom and even *Ha-adama ha-zot* (This Land) (1942) by Aaron Ashman, represent a relatively harmonious community whose major task is to find their roots in their newly-gained long Promised Land. [...] Another motif also apparent in the Israeli

drama of those years is a religious, though not Halachic [according to Jewish religious laws] or denominational, attitude toward the land itself and to physical work on it as a substitute for the holiness of Jewish Law, presumably less important now, when 'we have our own land again.' (Levy 2019)

In 1967, Egypt, Syria, and Jordan went to war against Israel, upon which Israel took over Egyptian, Jordanian, and Syrian territories along with their Palestinian populations, whom it has controlled ever since. For more than five decades, while politicians on both sides have failed to find a peaceful solution, Israeli theatre has been taken up less with the question of land and more with a suffering and hostile population in the occupied territories: 'Relationships with the neighbor/enemy are a frequent topic in Israeli drama' (Levy 2019), and one may add that there is a particular focus on the effects of the occupation on Israeli politics, economy, culture and psyche.

THE HOLOCAUST IN ISRAELI THEATRE

Leah Goldberg's *Ba'alat Ha-Armon* (The Lady of the Castle, 1955), Ben-Zion Tomer's *Yaldey Ha-Tzel* (The Children of the Shadows, 1961), Aaron Megged's *Hannah Szenes* (1958), Yehoshua Sobol's *Ghetto* (1983) and Motti Lerner's *Kastner* (1984), to mention only a few, are Israeli plays which deal with issues of survival during the Holocaust (Taub 1996). They culminated with David Ma'yan's *Arbeit Macht Frei In Teutland Europa* (1992), mounted by the Akko Theater Group, a performance which was critical of the way the Holocaust had been represented in Israeli culture. *Third Generation/Dritte Generation* (2008) by Yael Ronen tells about the grandchildren of the Holocaust: Germans, Israelis, and Palestinians who 'grapple with memory, guilt and the roles of perpetrators and victims, with a high level of self-irony' (Wikipedia 2022).

As a case study, one of the most canonical Israeli plays tackling the Holocaust is *Ha'Yeled Holem* (The Child Dreams, 1993) by Hanoch Levin. The play was inspired by the story of the ocean liner S.S. St. Louis, on which the film *Voyage of the Damned* (1976), directed by Stuart Rosenberg, was based: 'Levin's masterpiece is a journey to a distant land, to the unknown, a flight from a menacing past to a consoling future' (Isra-Drama 2018). The film, and the book of the same title written by Gordon Thomas and Max Morgan-Witts in 1974, were based on historical facts and chronicled the events:

> In the wake of the bloody events of Kristallnacht on 13 May 1939, the S.S. St. Louis set sail from Hamburg bound for Cuba with 936 Jewish refugees on board. The Cuban immigration authorities refused the refugees entry. The hounded vessel sailed from port to port hoping to find a country that would agree to accept its passengers. (Isra-Drama 2018)

The ship returned to Europe. More than 600 of the 936 passengers were murdered in Nazi concentration camps.

The plot of *The Child Dreams* begins in a house with a father, mother, and their sleeping child. The family idyll is interrupted when a wounded violinist, covered in blood, bursts into their home, followed by a platoon of soldiers. The soldiers order them all to get out. The father is shot in front of the family. The commander then allows the child and mother to go free, they flee and run to the harbour, where a large ship is at anchor. They beg the captain to let them board the ship. At first he disagrees, but eventually he blackmails the mother, proposing that she have sex with him in exchange for permission for the two to board the ship. She accepts. The ship sets sail and reaches an island where it puts down anchor, but the military there do not let the passengers disembark. They are declined in other ports too. In the last act of the play we see a pile of dead children, eagerly waiting for one more child to die in order to complete the quota of dead children, after which the Messiah is expected to arrive and restore them to life. The mother brings her dead child to the pile.

The Child Dreams can serve as a prototype for the treatment of place and displacement in Israeli theatre. In 2018, when the Israeli government attempted to relocate some of its asylum seekers to various African states, the play was staged again, by Israel's National Theatre Habima, and prompted reactions such as:

> When the play was first staged in 1993, we could read it in the local context—wrapped in memories we heard from Holocaust survivors, and from the harsh images the occupation [of Arab territories] provided to the newscasts. Today, following the bloody war in Syria, the death journeys of Sudanese and Eritrean refugees through Sinai to Israel in an attempt to seek refuge, and the waves of refugees trying to reach Europe, the show takes on universal dimensions—testifying to the horrors of war in the twenty-first century. (Yaari 2018)

Indeed, in 1993, the Israeli audience took the play mainly at face value, but in 2018, as the critic Helen Kaye wrote, it could be seen as 'at once a searing indictment of man's ghastly inhumanity to man and an anthem to mercy, even hope' (2018).

In a similar vein, Glenda Abramson indicates that *The Child Dreams* has acquired a sort of medieval theological dimension due to it being structured around an existential journey, where the refugees' quest brings about allegorical religious disillusionment (Abramson 1998, 222). The play includes human typology and each of its four acts is 'corresponding to one of the stations of suffering, similar in intent to *The Pilgrim's Progress*. Each stop implies a challenge or a test for the play's characters' (Abramson 1998, 222). Eventually, 'everyone is denounced in this play: God, the Messiah, and humankind' (Abramson 1998, 223). Humankind is cruel, God does not rescue and the Messiah does not arrive.

Palestinian Displacement in Israeli Theatre

Contrary to the Jewish view of a promised land, the Palestinian narrative relates to place and land in a most concrete fashion. Since 1976, March 30 has been known to Palestinians as Land Day, 'a major commemorative date in the Palestinian political calendar and an important event in the Palestinian collective narrative—one that emphasises Palestinian resistance to Israeli colonisation and sumud (steadfastness)' (Hawari 2018).

Land, place, and displacement have been pivotal thematic and poetic aspects of theatre in Arabic staged by Israeli Palestinian artists. In Suhayl Abu Nuwara's play *Zughrudat al-Ard* (The Joyous Cry of the Land, 1976), an old, sick father wants to stay on the land, while his educated children want to go away to a better life abroad. *Jalili, ya Ali* (Ali the Galilean, 1981), written and staged by Al-Hakawati Company, presents the adventures of a Palestinian villager in Tel Aviv, 'the very heart of the occupiers' country. A circus-like burlesque style is used to portray a series of episodes in Ali's life, as refugee and stranger in his own country' (Snir, 1995, 46). Imil Habibi's *Umm al-Rubdblkiyd* (The Junk Dealer, 1985), based on one of his stories, tells about—

> Hind, a junk dealer who, following the 1948 War, refused to emigrate to Lebanon with her husband and children but chose to stay in her home in Wadi al-Nisnas in Haifa. She recalls her memories of childhood interwoven with feelings of blame for the Palestinians who left their homeland as well as for those who chose to stay. (Hawari 2018, 49)

A case study of a more recent production acted by Israeli Palestinians in both Arabic and Hebrew is *Ga'aguyim* (Longing, 2003), directed by Yigal Azaraty and staged by the Arab-Israeli Theatre in Jaffa-Tel-Aviv. It was a compilation of the Jewish and Palestinian actors' personal monologues. The play began with the line '*Watnee hakiba*' ('my homeland is a suitcase') from a poem by the *de facto* national Palestinian poet Mahmoud Darwish (2016): 'My homeland is a suitcase. I am a traveler' was the opening statement of the show. The Israeli Palestinian actress Rauda Saliman recited the poem in Arabic and in Hebrew on a small stage, surrounded by the standing audience. This line was the initial text written by Mahmoud Darwish and she delivered it as such. But in the next few weeks, a furore arose around the poem, following fierce criticism from the Israeli Palestinian audience, and Darwish decided to rewrite the line as 'My homeland is not a suitcase / I am not a traveler.'

The audience's insistence on not accepting the suitcase and the wandering as a settled condition suggests that the Israeli Palestinian spectators, in a painful inverted symmetry with Israeli Jews, do not view themselves as eternal wanderers in exile from their homeland, but rather as refugees clinging to a concrete land as their physical homeland. The condition of carrying a lost homeland in a suitcase indeed became part of Jewish consciousness (in Israel and elsewhere), but this is not the case with the Palestinian spectators (Cofman-Simhon, 2020).

Although Darwish himself lived with the sense of being untethered to place, he agreed to rectify his poem for the sake of his Israeli Palestinian audience. The suitcase thus became a rhetorical tool. Loaded with the meaning of homelessness, it became a mental refuge, a symbol of the sense of deterritorialization, even for those who did not experience physical displacement. The Palestinian artists viewed themselves as refugees without physical exile: 'Exile is not only a political fate—it can be a state of mind, a cultural and inner exile, either imposed or chosen' (Nasrallah and Perlman 2011, 141).

Another play about Palestinian homelessness is *Memory* (2006) by the Israeli Druze Palestinian playwright Salman Natour:

> Natour was a warrior in the battle of narratives. He was fixated on documenting oral Palestinian history and telling the human stories of three Palestinian generations as they physically and emotionally oscillated between home and exile. (Hassan 2016)

Memory is the first part of Natour's trilogy *Sixty Years: A Desert Journey*, published between 2006 and 2009. In the play, the controversy over land, place and displacement is characterized by a scene in which the narrator tells of a Palestinian man, Abu Salah:

> One day when I was walking in a market in Nazareth, I saw the [Jewish] merchant from Romania. I asked him: 'Where are you from, Mr. Birinbaum?'
> He looked down on me and said in Arabic: 'I am from Saffuriya [Tzipori in Hebrew]. And where are you from, you Sheikh?'
> Abu Salah looked down on him and immediately replied, 'I am from Romania.'
> [Birinbaum] was astonished and replied 'Is that possible?!'.
> 'Look, if it is possible that Mister Birinbaum is from Saffuriya, how can it not be that Mister Abu Salah is from Romania?' (Natour 2006)

For Natour, the Jewish narrative of enduring memory and homecoming after two millennia of exile was an absurdity. Ironically enough, he seems to contradict himself when concomitantly emphasizing the importance of the persistent Palestinian memory of displacement. In his play, one of the characters says: 'If we lose our memory, hyenas will eat us' (Natour 2006), demonstrating the analogy between Jewish and Palestinian memories of land. The painful symmetry between the Palestinian and Jewish senses of displacement is stunning.

Representing African Refugees in Israeli Theatre

Given the complexity of the Israeli relationship with displacement, the representation of African asylum seekers in Israeli theatre is a case study of the attitude of a host population towards people seeking refuge.

The geographical location of Israel makes it the only land bridge between Africa and Europe via the Sinai Peninsula. The border between Egypt and Israel has been functioning as the nightly conduit for contraband drugs, and until 2014, the trafficking of African people too, mainly male (Loveluck 2013). In 2014, Israel built a wall along the border, and the trafficking has stopped. A few thousand of those who crossed the border clandestinely eventually made it to Turkey and from there to Europe. According to the Israeli Population Authority, since the early 2000s, almost 70,000 people illegally crossed the border from Egypt into Israel, the vast majority remaining in Israel, many receiving temporary work permits, others working illegally. Most live in south Tel Aviv. They came mainly from East Africa: Darfur, Ethiopia, Eritrea, and Somalia (Lidman 2018).

Yaffa Schuster was one of the first Israeli theatre directors to initiate shows about and with asylum seekers. In 2010, she founded the African-Israeli Stage, an NGO with the declared intention of staging a 'repertoire [that] portrays African plays focusing on contemporary and classical creation of African playwrights and authors, as well as plays portraying the experience of immigration' (African-Israeli Stage 2023). The show *Shnot Galut* (Years of Exile, 2014) was the result of her joint work with refugees from Darfur and Sudan about their daily life and absorption in Israel. The show was accompanied by original music from Sudan and Arabic singing, and acted in Arabic and Hebrew. Schuster wrote the play with Adam Ahmad and Yasser Abdullah who had studied theatre in Sudan, and it was accompanied by professional musicians, all of them asylum seekers. In 2019, the company began to present another play by Adam Ahmad, called *Ha'palit Ha'metoraf* (The Crazy Refugee), at the Arab-Hebrew Theatre in Jaffa-Tel Aviv. An article about the show read: 'It's really funny, unbelievable that after everything they went through to get to Tel Aviv they all sit together and laugh about it' (*Time Out* 2019). Schuster has continued to work with African refugees and in 2022 staged with them the play *Ha'Derech* (The Road) by the Nigerian Nobel Prize laureate Wole Soyinka. Even though it is not a production about refugees, this is one of the rare occasions in Israel in which the actors are Africans without Israeli citizenship (with the exception of one Israeli Ethiopian actress).

Another Israeli theatre director, Chen Alon, together with filmmaker Avi Mograbi, formed the theatre company Holot Legislative Theatre (HLT) with a group of illegal African asylum seekers from Holot (Sands) detention centre. The centre opened in 2013, 'following a number of government decisions aimed at reducing the concentration of asylum seekers in cities' (Lidman 2018). It was shut down after four years. Alon and Mograbi would visit Holot one day a week and engage a group of asylum seekers using Augusto Boal's Theatre of the Oppressed method. HLT emerged from an eighteen-month process of development. Some of the participants have remained with the company and act in HLT shows to this day. Most are now living and working in Tel Aviv and the surroundings, 'having been tolerated by the state, while also triggering demographic and labor anxieties among some in the Israeli public' (Kuftinec 2019, 167). The company numbers around eighteen actresses and actors, about half of them Israelis.

In the Legislative Theatre methodology, actors and audience retain the right to discuss and rectify various legal decisions and 'change' the laws (Salvador 2014). Sonja Kuftinec describes:

> Based on the refugees' testimonies and personal stories, these performances offer a rereading of the 1951 UN Refugee Convention, aiming to arouse public and legal debate leading to political transformation [...]. Scenes incorporate up-to-the-minute legislative developments around refugee status and switch out different personal scenarios. (Kuftinec 2019, 167–9)

The shows always end with a forum discussion 'where the audience is invited to directly intervene in the stage action' (Kuftinec 2019, 171). HLT has performed throughout Israel at the invitation of various communities.

Gently (2019), the only show about refugees on a mainstream stage in Israel, was in fact not about people seeking refuge, but rather about racism. The expensive and elaborate production of this musical by Shiri Nadav Naor, directed by Moshe Naor to lyrics by Sha'anan Street and a score by Amir Lekner, employed actors and singers whose status demonstrated the hierarchy of immigrants in Israel. The announcement of auditions read 'We are looking for: actors, dancers and singers with an African look who have the ability to play, sing and dance' (Haifa Theatre 2019). The result was that the leading roles were distributed to Jewish Israelis of Ethiopian origin, and since some of the other actors and singers were not Israeli citizens, it was impossible to gather them together again after the months of lockdown due to the first wave of COVID-19. The plot tells of 'an itinerant musician, the very charismatic [Israeli Ethiopian singer] Gili Yalo who charms his way through the character of Malachi Gently' (Carmi 2020). His wife Miriam, played by Israeli Ethiopian singer Esther Rada, has recently delivered a white baby—the actual delivery scene being a very effective company number to the Hebrew translation of *Amazing Grace*. When the cops see the white baby, they arrest Miriam. In desperation, Malachi turns to TV celeb Michael Fried, who has a *tour de force* of his own, keeping his foot permanently in his trying-to-be politically correct mouth. Incidentally, Miriam is his cleaning lady. Fried's intervention does the trick. Miriam and baby are released.

As we can see, the theme of the show was neither the status of refugees, nor the ongoing discrimination against Ethiopian Israelis. A musical about African refugees was apparently easier to digest and supposedly allowed the spectators to remain within their comfort zone where they could feel compassionate for unfortunate non-citizens, rather than critically looking at themselves *vis-à-vis* Israeli citizens who experience racism.

As opposed to the works analysed above, the last show I would like to explore invests the stage with a more symbolic rendition of the refugee issue: in 2019, Maya Buenos, Israeli actress, director and member of the Holot Legislative Theater, staged a production about and with asylum seekers: *Hof Mivtahim, Concerto Le'palit ve'Tizmoret* (Safe Shore, Concerto for Refugee and Orchestra), in collaboration with the Raanana Symphonette Orchestra. Describing the project, Buenos explains that:

> I started researching at the universal level: according to the UN every 2 seconds someone in the world becomes a refugee. I wanted to make the refugee crisis resurface on stage. Around the same time, I was approached by Raanana Symphonette who wanted to do something together. So I decided that the orchestra would represent an inflatable boat. (Unpublished interview, 2021)

Even though one of the actors in this production was an African asylum seeker, Buenos's work was primarily a response to the excruciating images of the body of the three-year-old Syrian toddler Aylan Kurdi washed up on the coast of Turkey in September 2015. The characters in the play were well known refugees, such as the Syrian piano player Iyam al-Ahmad and the Yazidi Nobel Peace Prize winner Nadia Murad. Buenos had met Murad when she visited Israel under the auspices of IsraAID, a humanitarian aid NGO based in Israel, which had sent a delegation to rescue captive Yazidi women from Iraq. The images of refugees standing at the gates of a country begging for asylum appeared again and again in the media of the time, and the show staged that moment in front of the gate, showing the longing for a safe shore and, in many cases, rejection from it. In front of the audience, the musicians produced a rickety ship aiming to reach the shore of refuge. Buenos explains that the play was based on letters from Holocaust refugees: Jewish actresses and actors who wrote applications for work permits to Habima theatre in Tel Aviv, such as a soprano singer who wrote that she was ready to work in the theatre's sewing shop. 'Meskin [the manager] signed the refusal letter. It was in the power of the theatre to save lives and they did not do it' says Buenos (Unpublished interview, 2021). *Safe Shore* opened first in Jerusalem, as a site-specific performance in the archaeological location of the Tower of David. The walls of the Old City of Jerusalem reflected a sense of no specific place, and at the same time, an impenetrable wall, like the diverse shores from which the boat was expelled.

Conclusion

In 2018 the Israeli government attempted to relocate some of its asylum seekers to various African states, resulting in numerous protests around the country. Concomitantly, the number of theatre productions tackling the refugee issue has doubled. Israeli artists have spoken about how they identify with refugees because of their Jewish past: 'I hold on to my Jewish identity through the feeling of refugee' says Maya Buenos (Unpublished interview, 2021). Chen Alon and Avi Mograbi had refugee grandparents (Kuftinec 2019). HLT even enacted a scene from *The Child Dreams* where one of the characters asserts: 'What happened to the Jewish people in the Holocaust must not happen again. We must define the duty of the countries of the civilized world to give asylum to refugees' (Kuftinec 2019, 166). Newspapers wrote about these shows as stirring up the collective memory of the Israeli public. A memory that answers what seems to have been forgotten—the experience of refugees. On the other hand, the analogy between Palestinian and Jewish displacement is fraught with divergent political meanings.

REFERENCES

Abramson, Glenda. 1998. *Drama and Ideology in Modern Israel*. Cambridge: Cambridge University Press.

African-Israeli Stage. 2023. 'African-Israeli Stage'. https://theatrestage.wixsite.com/africanisraelistage. Accessed 1 June 2023.

Ben-Ami, Shlomo. 2006. *Scars of War, Wounds of Peace: The Israeli-Arab Tragedy*. Oxford: Oxford University Press.

Beška, Emanuel and Foster, Zachary. 2021. 'The Origins of the Term "Palestinian" ("Filasṭīnī") in Late Ottoman Palestine, 1898–1914'. *Academia Letters*, Article 1884. https://doi.org/10.20935/AL1884. Accessed 26 July 2023.

Carens, Joseph H. 2013. *The Ethics of Immigration*. Oxford: Oxford University Press.

Carmi, Noga. 2020. 'Premiere of the Musical Gently at the Haifa Theater.' *Haipo*. https://haipo.co.il/item/172862. Accessed 13 February 2022.

Cofman-Simhon, Sarit. 2020. 'The Suitcase as a Neurotic Container in the Israeli Theatre: The Return of the Wandering Jew.' *Migration and Stereotypes in Performance and Culture*, edited by Yana Meerzon, David Dean and Daniel McNeil, 77–99. London: Palgrave Macmillan.

Cohen, Richard. 1985. *Vision and Conflict in the Holy Land*. Jerusalem: Yad Ben-Zvi; New York: St. Martin's Press.

Darwish, Mahmoud. 2016. 'Diary of a Palestinian Wound.' *The Palestine Project*. https://thepalestineproject.medium.com/diary-of-a-palestinian-wound-2b75f3bacf63 Accessed 17 May 2022.

Haifa Theatre. 2019. 'Auditions for the New Musical of the Haifa Theatre – "Gently"'. *Facebook*, 6 June 2019. https://www.facebook.com/haifacity/?locale=he_IL. Accessed 1 June 2023.

Hassan, Budour Youssef. 2016. 'Preserving Memory Amid a War That Still Rages.' *The Electronic Intifada*, February 22. https://electronicintifada.net/content/preserving-memory-amid-war-still-rages/15756. Accessed 25 February 2022.

Hawari, Yara. 2018. 'Palestine Land Day: A Day to Resist and Remember.' *Aljazeera*, March 30, 2018. https://www.aljazeera.com/opinions/2018/3/30/palestine-land-day-a-day-to-resist-and-remember. Accessed 26 February 2022.

Isra-Drama. 2018. 'The Child Dreams by Hanoch Levin.' *The Hanoch Levin Institute of Israeli Drama*. https://exposure.dramaisrael.org/2018/the-child-dreams/. Accessed 22 December 2021.

Kaye, Helen. 2018. 'Revival of Hanoch Levin's "The Child Dreams" is Mandatory Viewing.' *The Jerusalem Post*, June 19. https://www.jpost.com/israel-news/culture/revival-of-hanoch-levins-the-child-dreams-is-mandatory-viewing-560370. Accessed 13 December 2021.

Kershner, Isabel. 2018. 'Israel Moves to Expel Africans. Critics Say That's Not Jewish.' *The New York Times*, February 2. https://www.nytimes.com/2018/02/02/world/middleeast/israel-migrants-african.html. Accessed 18 May 2022.

Kuftinec, Sonja. 2019. 'Holot Legislative Theatre: Performing Refugees in Israel.' *TDR: The Drama Review*, 63 (2), 166–172.

Levy, Shimon. 2019. 'The Development of Israeli Theatre – a Brief Overview.' *The Theatre Times*, March 15. https://thetheatretimes.com/the-development-of-israeli-theater-a-brief-overview/. Accessed 26 February 2022.

Lidman, Melanie. 2018. 'Large Migrant Detention Center to Close at Midnight Amid Deportation Plan.' *The Times of Israel*, March 12. https://www.timesofisrael.com/large-migrant-detention-center-to-close-at-midnight-amid-deportation-plan/. Accessed 20 January 2022.

Loveluck, Louisa. 2013. 'Egypt's Sinai: Trafficking, Torture and Fear.' *Aljazeera*, December 6. https://www.aljazeera.com/features/2013/12/6/egypts-sinai-trafficking-torture-and-fear. Accessed 3 January 2021.

Nasrallah, Aida and Perlman, Lee. 2011. 'Weaving Dialogues and Confronting Harsh Realities: Engendering Social Change in Israel through Performance.' *Acting Together I: Performance and the Creative Transformation of Conflict: Resistance and Reconciliation in Regions of Violence*, edited by Cynthia E. Cohen, Roberto Gutiérrez Varea and Polly O. Walker, 123–144. Oakland, CA: New Village Press.

Natour, Salman. 2006. *Memory*. Unpublished text [Hebrew, translation mine].

Ofrat, Gideon. 1980. *Earth, Man, Blood*. Cherikover, Tel Aviv [in Hebrew].

Salvador, Eduardo. 2014. 'Legislative Theatre: Art for Community Conflict Resolution. From Desires to Law.' *Journal of Conflictology*, 5 (1), 3–12.

Snir, Reuven. 1995, June. Palestinian Theatre: Historical Development and Contemporary Distinctive Identity.' *Contemporary Theatre Review*, 3 (2), 29–73.

Surkes, Sue. 2021. 'Offered Little Hope, African Migrants Despair of Israel as a Refuge.' *The Times of Israel*, September 5. https://www.timesofisrael.com/offered-little-hope-african-migrants-despair-of-israel-as-a-refuge/. Accessed 1 April 2022.

Taub, Michael. 1996. *Israeli Holocaust Drama*. Syracuse, New York: Syracuse University Press.

Time Out. 2019. 'Ken Lehiot Sha'anan: Festival Yom ha'Palit Itkayem be 'Neveh Sha'anan'' (To be tranquil: the refugee's day to take place in Neveh Sha'anan). Time Out, June 19. https://timeout.co.il/%D7%99%D7%95%D7%9D-%D7%94%D7%A4%D7%9C%D7%99%D7%98/. Accessed 1 June 2023.

Wikipedia. 2022. 'Yael Ronen.' *Wikipedia*. https://second.wiki/wiki/yael_ronen. Accessed 13 Feb 2022.

Yaari, Nurith. 2018. 'Hanoch Levin, Ha-yeled holem' [translation mine] *Habima Website*, http://archive.habima.co.il/showPage/?itemId=1188. Accessed 4 Feb 2022.

CHAPTER 25

Shylock Is Me: Aryeh Elias as an Immigrant Jewish-Iraqi Actor in the Israeli Theatre

Naphtaly Shem-Tov

Aryeh Elias (1921–2015) was a famous and beloved Israeli stage and screen actor. Born in Iraq, he studied acting at the Institute for Fine Arts in Baghdad prior to immigrating to Israel in 1949. Throughout his long acting career in Israel, he auditioned for many roles in the artistic and prestigious public theatres but, in most cases, he did not land a role. His conspicuous Iraqi accent was the primary reason he was rejected. Both directors and theatre managers viewed it as 'problematic' and 'ridiculous,' because it was an Arabic accent that evoked the Arab enemy and it diverged radically from the standard Hebrew accent that Zionism identified with the 'New Israeli Jew.' This orientalist and Eurocentric outlook made it impossible for Elias to realize his dream of performing classical roles on stage, especially the role of Shylock in Shakespeare's *The Merchant of Venice* that he had a particular interest in performing. Therefore, he mostly performed in commercial theatre, in film, and on television (Fig. 25.1). In these productions, his accent and his Middle Eastern appearance constituted part and parcel of the characters that he played. They

---

This research was supported by The Open University of Israel's Research Fund (grant no. 510395).

N. Shem-Tov (✉)
Open University, Ra'anana, Israel
e-mail: naphtalysh@openu.ac.il

Fig. 25.1 *Shirei Humash* (Singing HaHomesh songs)—from left to right Arye Elias, Shlomo Artzi, Shoshana Damari, Edna lev; from Itzik Manger's Sherei HaHomesh, HaTeatron HaAmami, 1971, directed by Shmuel Boonim. (Photo: Yackov Agor. Photo courtesy of The Israeli Center for the Documentation of the Performing Arts, Tel-Aviv University)

were mostly comedies in which he played 'likeable Mizrahi'[1] characters; sometimes he performed the ethnic identity in a stereotypical fashion, and sometimes he performed them in other complex and moving ways. These Mizrahi roles gained Elias many admirers. Over time, he became one of Israel's most beloved actors and even won acting prizes. Nonetheless, the ongoing refusal to award him more than a few significant roles in Israeli public theatre wounded him, and it pained him throughout his life.

For an immigrant actor, the accent can be a serious and problematic obstacle, especially in the national and Eurocentric context of Israel. Definitely, Elias was a well-known and well-loved Israeli actor but the story of his immigration to Israel never ended. His Mizrahi identity, appearance, and especially his Iraqi accent led to 'likeable Mizrahi' typecasting. Only on the margins of the cultural field—as a director and actor in the Arab theatre—did he manage to create beyond the limits of his typecasting. The fact that Elias was cast as an ageing gay man in *Gerushim Meuharim* (A Late Divorce)—a character who was so different and far from the 'likeable Mizrahi'—shows how colour-blind casting gave us a brief glimpse of Elias's abilities which, over the years, could have

---

[1] Mizrahi, an adjective meaning 'Eastern' in Hebrew, is also used as a noun referring to Jews whose family origins are in the Middle East and North Africa. Mizrahim is the masculine plural noun form.

embodied diverse, deep, and fascinating roles were it not for the rigid limits of the politics of casting in the Israeli theatre.

This chapter focuses on how an immigrant actor with a foreign accent copes with the obstacles of the theatre field in a national context. First, in order to understand Elias's story and especially his rejection because of his foreign accent, I historically contextualize the Israeli theatre as part of Zionist nation building. Second, I follow how Elias copes with his rejection while having a general discussion about the accent of an immigrant actor. Third, I draw upon Israeli theatre's casting politics to contextualize my analysis of Elias's acting career and his accent, and I show how this Middle Eastern immigrant actor responded to a Eurocentric theatre.

Context: Zionist Movement, Israeli Theatre, and Mizrahi Jews

The Zionist movement grew in late-nineteenth-century Europe similar to the rise of the idea of nationalism among other nations in Europe and as a solution to rising anti-Semitism on the continent—pogroms in Eastern Europe and racism in the western countries against Jews, such as the Dreyfus affair, culminating in the Holocaust. During the first half of the twentieth century, the Zionist movement became established in Palestine controlled by the British Mandate. Following the UN decision to divide the territory into a Jewish state and an Arab state, Israel was established in 1948.

The Zionist project aspired to create a Jewish nation-state that would be a home to every Jew, and efforts to realize this dream have made Israel into a society composed of Jewish immigrants and their descendants from all over the world. This has created the connection between Israel's cultural identity and the various traditions of Jewish immigrants a matter of debate. Zionism aspired to create a unified culture for all Jews through erasure of all Jewish traditions and cultures that was not in accord with a secular and Eurocentric Zionist outlook. European nationalist images of a strong, powerful, and brave light-skinned man served as a model for the 'New Jew' Zionism sought to construct. This model is orientalist because it treats the Arab world around Israel as inferior, against the backdrop of the Arab-Israeli conflict.

Israeli theatre is centralized and largely publicly subsidized. Seven large public theatres, four located in Tel Aviv, constitute its core: Habima, The Cameri, Beit Lessin, Gesher, the Jerusalem Khan Theatre, Haifa Municipal Theatre, and Beersheba Theatre. These theatres constitute the central artistic platform, while commercial theatre is comparatively marginal. The main repertoire of these theatres includes Western canonical drama, American and British popular contemporary plays, and mostly original Hebrew plays. Thematically, the repertoire deals with social and political issues, such as the Palestinian-Israeli conflict and religious-secular struggle, though these conflicts are approached from a very moderate political perspective that is in line with the views of the Israeli establishment that funds these mainstream theatres. Aesthetically, the performances are mostly conservative realism which suit Israeli audience TV viewing habits.

In addition, since the end of the twentieth century, Israeli fringe theatre, which is comprised of experimental, alternative, and political troupes receiving small subsidies from the state and whose performances are produced on shoestring budgets, has grown significantly: it proves aesthetically and politically fascinating (Shem-Tov 2016). From its inception, Hebrew theatre has been part of the Zionist project and, in practice, it has adopted Zionism's cultural values as its own. Hebrew drama and translated Western drama have been given favoured status within its repertoire, and its performative language has been influenced by Western theatre. Although Israel is a geographical part of the Middle East, its theatre is Eurocentric, as is Israeli culture in general.

In the 1950s, there was a massive migration of about half a million Mizrahim—Jews from the Middle East and North Africa to Israel. Zionist Orientalism perceived these immigrants as a primitive and inferior uncivilized population in contrast to the Eurocentric model of the New Jew. This racist perception was the basis for discriminatory policies towards Mizrahim in all areas of life: education, health, employment, housing, culture, art, and more. The Mizrahim were excluded from Israel's social and cultural centres of power and became the lower class in Israel.

Because the Mizrahim diverged from the Zionist model, they were compelled to erase their original identity and culture to adapt to a Western-oriented Hebrew culture. Those who had been involved in Arabic theatre prior to their immigration to Israel, in places such as Iraq, Egypt, and Morocco, were kept out of Israeli theatre. Their accents, their physical appearance, and a lack of faith in their professionalism contributed to prejudice and prevented them from achieving a place in Israeli theatre. Even though Elias encountered obstacles trying to find work in the public theatre, he is a quintessential example of an immigrant Mizrahi actor who did not give up and who found different ways to perform on stage and screen.

Trials in Theatre: From the Centre to the Margins

In Israeli theatre and cinema, Elias never performed different types of 'likeable Mizrahi.' For example, he never played characters with sexual passion, courage, and valour, or tortured characters who thought deeply about human existence. Complex characters of classic drama that he played in Baghdad in the 1940s (Elias 2005; Moreh 1985), such as evil Iago and Faust who sells his soul to Satan, were radically different from the 'likeable Mizrahi' characters that had shaped Elias's career. Theatre directors, who argued that Elias's Iraqi accent was too thick for the Israeli ear, denied his dream of playing Shylock from *The Merchant of Venice*. This claim proves ironic because most of the Hebrew theatre's founders and early actors had also immigrated to Israel and had recognizable East European accents. In her discussion of Mizrahi actors' casting, Ella

Shohat argues that the refusal to cast Elias as Shylock was unfortunate, 'because a talented director might have used the "marginal" accent as a way to underline Shylock's own marginality within Christian Venice' (1989, 55). Shohat notes that accent was something used to bar many actors, as it had blocked Elias, and commercial theatre and Bourekas[2] cinema were the only frameworks in which they could appear. Yet, even there, they were quite frequently called upon to reproduce Mizrahi stereotypes.

Elias's Iraqi accent became the organizing principle of a life story filled with missed opportunities and pain. Generally, the proper accent and pronunciation of Hebrew were both major issues in Hebrew theatre in the early twentieth century. For 2000 years, Hebrew had been a holy language for religious purposes only. As part of the Zionist project, Hebrew was renewed as a daily spoken language, therefore, the question of the correct pronunciation and proper accent arose. Jews from different parts of the world had different accents when using Hebrew as a holy language, so Zionism aspired to a uniform accent, and only in the 1930s and 1940s did a Hebrew accent take shape among Jews born in Israel. In practice, on the Hebrew stage, most of the actors were immigrants with Eastern European accents, which were not perceived as problematic while an Arabic accent like Elias's was perceived as foreign and ridiculous.

An accent is most often noticed in an immigrant actor, as the Serbian-born writer and media artist Dragan Todorovic formulates: 'Even the best amongst us are like diesel engines—under the rich vocabulary and the proper grammar, always that hum betraying a second language, that constant tremor of accent' (2020, 23). Indeed, the accent of an immigrant actor may block communication in the encounter with the audience, but it can also be a unique theatrical sign and become meaningful in the performance itself through postdramatic dramaturgical devices which are sensitive to multilingualism and multiculturalism (Meerzon and Pewny 2020).

Diana Manole argues that 'accent as a national identity marker [...] signals the distinction between natives and non-natives' (2015, 256). An accent is a sign of alienation that carries prejudices and stereotypes about the alleged inferiority of the accent holder. Hence, on stage, the actor's accent has a negative emotional impact on the audience more than the content of their words. Therefore, strongly accented actors are usually excluded from the mainstream: this can be called 'accent discrimination.' Manole also claims: 'When accented performers choose to work in mainstream dramatic theatre in their new countries, they are usually forced to accept ghettoization in "ethnic" characters' (261). Nonetheless, Manole shows successful development through careers of immigrant Canadian actors who have foreign accents: 'Accented actors may evolve from being perceived and even perceiving themselves as displaced/misplaced outsiders to gaining (or regaining) the status of transnational artists who feel at home on any stage in the world, Canada included' (257).

---

[2] Popular comedies and melodramas, common in the 1960s and 1970s, centered on the tension between Mizrahi and Ashkenazi Jews.

Yana Meerzon (2012) and Emma Cox (2014) stress that a foreign accent, like the body itself, characterizes the immigrant actor as a foreigner whose belonging is cast in doubt. Yet, this fact can sometimes become a source of strength that immigrant actors exploit for different and alternative types of performance. Acknowledgement of this allows us to look at the story of Elias's place in Israeli theatre differently. It can be understood as one of a movement from a lack of belonging and rejection based on his accent towards belonging, excitement, and mutual understanding that began with his rediscovery of Arabic theatre in Israel.

Elias explains how he auditioned at the national theatre Habima soon after immigrating to Israel. His career shocked the casting panel: 'For years, that was the way they responded to me. They laughed at the very idea that I was going to perform a Shakespearean monologue in Arabic translation. After they finished laughing, they would start asking questions. Did you come to Israel on a donkey? Is there really a drama school in Baghdad?' He concluded, saying 'Hamlet could have a Russian accent but he could not have an Arabic one' (quoted in Peled 2003). 'Shakespeare in Arabic' and the possibility of professional Arab theatre subverted the idea of Westernization and provided another option of artistic theatre planted in the Middle East. Therefore, the ridicule and rejection of the casting panel towards Elias echoed the threat from other alternatives that integrated Western and Eastern cultures, and it completely clashed with the Zionist Eurocentric perception. The inability to even imagine that Baghdad had an academy for the arts and the way that the casting panel poked fun at the very idea of a Shakespearean monologue delivered in Arabic, as if it was an oxymoron, testify to the Orientalist character of Israeli casting politics.

The Politics of Casting in Israeli Theatre Understood Through Elias's Career

Elias's case points to a central problem in a society that has immigrant actors and culturally distinct minorities (Shem-Tov 2013). Casting, as we know, is not just a question of typecasting where one checks to see how well the actor matches the physique of the character and how much talent they bring to the role. Casting is connected to an actor's public image as well as to the memory of their previous roles and their social identity (Carlson 2003). Sometimes identity is marked or embedded in the body. Therefore, skin colour, accent, and diction, for example, mark ethnic identity and a whole host of cultural markers, stereotypes, and prejudices associated with it. Hence, casting does not just have artistic meaning. It also carries social and political meanings.

Starting in the 1980s, a conversation about casting began in the West. Black and Hispanic actors pointed out discrimination and how they were being cast in fewer and fewer roles on stage and screen. The expression 'traditional casting' refers to the assigning of roles to actors based on their social identities and in accordance with the expectations of the mainstream hegemonic audience, such that the default choice is white. In contrast, non-traditional casting is casting in opposition to these expectations and the granting of equal opportunities to actors at auditions. One can distinguish four different approaches to non-traditional casting (in the following explanation, my examples are drawn from Israeli theatre):

1. Colour-blind casting: An actor can play any character without connection to their ethnic identity. This approach works best in plays where the character's identity is not explicitly stated. Hamlet and King Oedipus, for example, can be dark-skinned. The actress Ruti Asarsai, who is an Ethiopian Jew, was cast in the role of Lady Macbeth in performances of *Macbeth* directed by Omri Nitzan (The Cameri Theatre 2013).
2. Conceptual casting: An actor is intentionally cast for a specific role, so that their ethnic identity can aid them in providing a complex and unique interpretation of the play. In 1987, Gdalya Besser staged Strindberg's *Miss Julie* and cast the Palestinian actor Yussuf Abu-Warda in the role of Jean, the servant and lover of Ms. Julie. The complex relations between Jean and Julie which play out against the background of class and gender also take on a political dimension due to inequality between Jews and Arabs in Israel. In other words, Abu-Warda's Palestinian identity offers the Israeli audience a political message that is not inherent in the original play.
3. Societal casting: Every actor plays a role that is suited to them based on their social identity. For example, a Black actor plays a Black figure. Until the 1970s, Ashkenazic actors also played the roles of Mizrahim and Arabs in Israeli theatre. Today, in most productions, Arabs play Arabs and Mizrahim play Mizrahim.
4. Cross-cultural casting: The fictional world of the play is transferred to a different culture. Therefore, all the characters undergo cultural modification. In 1985, Ilan Ronen directed *Waiting for Godot* (Haifa Theatre) and employed cross-cultural casting. The Arab actors Makram Khoury and Yussuf Abu-Warda play Didi and Gogo as if they were Palestinian constructions workers waiting either for the Palestinian revolution or a just peace that is slow in arriving.

Since the beginning of the current millennium, battles have been waged and changes have begun in the field of Israeli theatre that have again raised issues related to multiculturalism, in general, and critical Mizrahi discourse, in particular. Mizrahi artists have staged performances and plays that touch upon their Mizrahi identity, such as autobiographical performances (Shem-Tov 2018), historical plays (Shem-Tov 2019a, b), and plays performed in Judeo-Moroccan Arabic (Shem-Tov 2019c). Yet, despite these changes, non-traditional casting remains relatively rare in mainstream Israeli theatre. Sarit Cofman-Simhon argues that even when such casting is employed today, for example, in the case of Jewish actresses of Ethiopian origin, the stereotype of the 'exotic black woman' is used to frame it (Cofman-Simhon 2019). As someone who has managed the Khan Theatre, Jerusalem's public theatre, and, as a director with unique political and artistic vision, Ofira Henig sharply criticizes the politics of casting in Israeli public theatre:

> Israeli theatre favors white Israeliness. It is a generation behind television and cinema. Most of the cultural managers continue to cast according to color, race, religion, and sex, not noticing that Peter Brook had already started the revolution when he cast a black man in the role of Hamlet, and that for quite some time now, even in the English theatre, which is very popular here—actors of African or Indian origin are cast in the role of Henry V—the ultimate English king. In most cases, my casting choices are met with mumbling and hushed opposition if only to avoid accusing me, God forbid, of the very same racism. (2013, 7)

In the 1950s, Elias succeeded in getting work at The Cameri Theatre. After two small roles, he played the muezzin in *Taalulei Nasir al-Din* (The Pranks of Nasir al-Din) by Yosef Milo (1953). Since this was a play about the Islamic world, Elias's Iraqi accent helped him land this central role. He received positive reviews. It was a musical consisting of 45 performers including a Bukharan band. The space was a colourful and exotic market designed from an orientalist perspective. Because the performance's materials were oriental, the audience received Elias's Iraqi identity as a resource that contributed to the creation of the fictional world on stage. The critique emphasized Elias's accent, and especially his Eastern unique vibrational mode of singing. Yet, after the production closed, he was let go due to budgetary problems at the theatre. Only 40 years later would he return to work at The Cameri Theatre again, when he played the role of a Mizrahi rabbi and spiritual leader in *Tikun Hatzot* (Midnight Rite) by Rami Danon and Amnon Levi (1996). In fact, these were the only two meaningful roles that Elias played in Israeli public theatre, and they were roles that fall into the category of 'conceptual casting' because the Arabic accent and Middle Eastern identity were the basis for shaping the characters he embodied. Elias's Middle Eastern identity, accent, and physical appearance were the 'lens' through which the audience experienced Elias's acting.

Arabic theatre was the only place in Israel where Elias could perform. He and other immigrant actors from Iraq created Arabic radio plays to perform on Kol Yisrael (Israel's public domestic and international radio service). Kol Yisrael's radio channel in Arabic was almost the only professional site where Jewish artists from the Middle East could create in Arabic. This channel was intended for the Arab population in Israel and the Arab cultural capital of these artists was therefore an important resource, whereas in other Israeli cultural and artistic sites, these artists were excluded because their cultural capital was perceived as worthless from an orientalist perspective.

Together with the Iraqi actors from Kol Yisrael, Elias formed the Ur Ensemble that went on to produce the play *Majnun Layla* (Mad about Layla) by the Egyptian playwright Ahmed Shawqi (Shem-Tov 2020). The play had a triumphant run in Arab towns and in areas of Israel with large pockets of Mizrahi Jews. The production succeeded and it received excellent reviews. Due to their prejudices, members of the Israeli establishment were surprised to learn that there were talented theatre personnel amongst the immigrants from Islamic lands. For example, this is what Shmu'el Salmon, the director of the Ministry of Education's Department for Arab Education and Culture, had to say after going to see the play with low expectations and coming out surprised:

> To tell you the truth, I went to the show, because, as a public official, I felt obligated. I expected to leave a tasteless, cheap and sentimental performance disappointed. Without going into details, I want to say that the ensemble should congratulate itself on an amazing artistic effort. Many elements of the performance were artistically wrought, the speaking was good and only very rarely was there empty recitation, and good taste was never impaired. The actors kept my attention throughout the performance. (ibid, 393)

Due to budgetary problems, the ensemble disbanded. Elias went to Paris to study for three years. While there, he worked with Marcel Marceau and performed at the Comédie-Française. He returned to Israel in the early 1960s and, despite his studies and the recommendations that he received, he did not find work in the public theatre. Again, he was told this was due to his accent.

During the 1960s, Elias produced Arabic theatre with amateur actors in northern Israel. Following this, some of these actors, such as Adib Gahashan and Yussuf Ferah, studied to become professional actors and became well-known actors in Israeli theatre. In practice, Elias's work contributed to the rehabilitation of Palestinian theatre that had suffered a devastating blow during the 1948 war, just like other areas of Palestinian culture (Snir 2005). Elias's work preceded theatre projects promoting co-existence between Jews and Arabs by a decade or more and his approach proved innovative. Elias operated as an Arab-Jewish artist (Shohat 2017; Shenhav 2006): a Jew by religion and an Arab by culture and language, Elias employed Arab culture as a common denominator and he produced theatre with Palestinian actors that blurred national boundaries. Elias had this to say about that period in his life: 'Hebrew theatre rejected me due to my language and I suddenly discovered the Arab villages. It gave me and them food for the soul' (quoted in Peled 2003). Even after his movie roles made him famous, Elias continued this work. He established a theatre in East Jerusalem and produced a number of Arabic language performances with Palestinian actors. In the 1980s, he ran a community theatre program for inmates at Maasiyahu Prison and they produced several dramas that dealt metaphorically with issues of subjugation and oppression. For this work, Elias received the Presidential Award for Volunteerism.

In 1983, Elias was cast in a role that had him playing a character quite different from the 'likeable Mizrahi,' and it testifies to his range as an actor. This was the first time Elias was chosen through colour-blind casting—according to his talent, detached from his ethnic identity. The theatre director and Israel Prize laureate Nola Chilton was staging a theatrical adaptation of A. B. Yehoshua's novel *A Late Divorce* at the Neve Tzedek Theatre. Although it was fringe theatre, it employed some of Israeli theatre's best artists. The producer Miriam Etzioni suggested that Chilton cast Elias as Calderon, an aging homosexual banker with a young lover. Elias said the following about the role: 'I almost never reject a film or theatre role because I know how to offer what a role needs. Look at *A Late Divorce*. I played a homosexual in it. In the play, I arrive home and I see my young man with somebody else. I began to cry on stage' (quoted in Zilkha 2002). Elias received critical acclaim for this role and he won an acting award. Since this figure was a radical deviation from the 'likeable Mizrahi,' Elias amazed the critics. Yet, he responded ambivalently: 'At the age of sixty, I am sick of getting discovered. I would like a meaty role in a repertory theatre. Why do they not give me the role of Polonius in one of the productions of *Hamlet* that will be staged in the theatre?' (quoted in Noy 1983). Following his success in *A Late Divorce*, Elias turned to Habimah and proposed the idea of adapting one of the novels of Sami Michael (an Israeli author of Iraqi descent). He was brushed off. Furthermore, the theatre manager insulted him, proposing that he emigrate from Israel and try his luck elsewhere.

Conclusion

As an immigrant, Aryeh Elias was one of the first actors who dealt with the white default choice advanced in the casting politics of Israeli theatre and fought for 'non-traditional casting.' Elias almost realized his dream in 1986 when the Beit Lessin public theatre decided to cast him in the role of Shylock in *The Merchant of Venice*. Unfortunately, after a month of rehearsals, budgetary problems led the theatre not to proceed with the performance. In an interview towards the end of his career, Elias summed up what happened as follows:

> The Jew Shylock is my greatest disappointment. This is because Shylock is not a role. Shylock is who I am. Shylock is a person who looks for honor and wants to get what he deserves, and I, an Arabic-accented actor in Israel who wants to perform, felt like Shylock in my soul. 'If you prick us, do we not bleed, and if you poison us, do we not die?' (Peled 2003)

References

Carlson, Marvin. 2003. *The Haunted Stage: The Theatre as Memory Machine*. Ann Arbor: University of Michigan Press.

Cofman-Simhon, Sarit. 2019. 'The New Belle Juive Onstage: Ethiopian Actresses in Israel.' *Nashim: A Journal of Jewish Women's Studies & Gender Issues*, 34, 146–167.

Cox, Emma. 2014. *Theatre and Migration*. London: Palgrave Macmillan.

Elias, Aryeh. 2005. *Dvash Tmarim*. Ramat-Gan: Shlomi Hizki Ot Le-Mofet.

Henig, Ofira. 2013. 'The Director's Way.' *Teatron—An Israeli Quarterly for Contemporary Theatre*, 36, 4–10.
Diana Manole. 2015. 'Accented Actors: From Stage to Stages via a Convenience Store.' *Theatre Research in Canada*, 36 (2), 255–273.
Meerzon, Yana. 2012. *Performing Exile, Performing Self: Drama, Theatre, Film*. London: Palgrave Macmillan.
Meerzon, Yana, and Katharina Pewny. 2020. 'Introduction—Dramaturgy of self: Language, authorship, migration.' In *Dramaturgy of Migration: Staging Multilingual Encounters in Contemporary Theatre*, edited by Yana Meerzon and Katharina Pewny, 1–5. New York: Routledge.
Moreh, Shmu'el. 1985. 'The Jewish Theatre in Iraq in the First Half of the Twentieth Century.' *Pe'amim*, 23, 64–98.
Noy, Adi. 1983. 'Talk of the Town.' *Yedi'ot Ahronot*, July 1.
Peled, Asefa. 2003. 'I am Shylock.' *Yedi'ot Ahronot*, November 14.
Shem-Tov, Naphtaly. 2013. 'Black Skin, White Pioneer: Non-Traditional Casting in an Israeli School.' *Research in Drama Education*, 18 (4), 346–358.
———. 2016. *Acco Festival: Between Celebration and Confrontation*. Boston: Academic Studies Press.
———. 2018. 'Displaying the Mizrahi Identity in an Autobiographical Performance: Body, Food and Documents.' *New Theatre Quarterly*, 34 (2), 160–175.
———. 2019a. 'Performing Iraqi-Jewish History on the Israeli Stage.' *Theatre Research International*, 44 (3), 248–261.
———. 2019b. '"In Sorrow Thou Shalt Bring Forth Children": Docu-Poetic Theatre in Israel.' *TDR/The Drama Review*, 63 (3), 20–35.
———. 2019c. 'Celebrating of Jewish-Moroccan Theatre in Israel: Production, Repertoire, and Reception.' *Contemporary Theatre Review*, 29 (1), 56–70.
———. 2020. 'The Jewish-Iraqi Theatre—Ur Ensemble: *Majnūn Laylā* as Interweaving Performance Cultures.' *Journal of Modern Jewish Studies*, 19 (3), 382–404.
Shenhav, Yehouda. 2006. *The Arab Jews: A Postcolonial Reading of Nationalism, Religion, and Ethnicity*. Stanford University Press
Shohat, Ella. 1989. *Israeli Cinema: East/West and the Politics of Representation*. Austin: University of Texas Press.
———. 2017. *On the Arab-Jew, Palestine, and Other Displacements*. London: Pluto Press
Snir, Reuven. 2005. *Palestinian Theater*. Wiesbaden: Reichert Verlag
Todorovic, Dragan. 2020. 'We Are Who We Are Not: Language, Exile, and Nostalgia for the Self.' In *Dramaturgy of Migration: Staging Multilingual Encounters in Contemporary Theatre*, edited by Yana Meerzon and Katharina Pewny, 20–29. New York: Routledge.
Zilkha, Ben. 2002. 'An Eye Laughs an Eye Cries.' *Ma'ariv: Zeman Tel Aviv*, October 4, 2002. [In Hebrew].

CHAPTER 26

Emerging, Staying, or Leaving: 'Immigrant' Theatre in Canada

Art Babayants

When analysing theatre created by immigrants it is important to recognize that some artists may willingly accept the title of immigrant, while others may well resist it. For instance, two Quebecois playwrights of Lebanese origin, Wajdi Mouawad and Abla Farhoud, have clearly expressed dissatisfaction with the limiting immigrant label (Charafeddine 2018, 13). To recognize the problematic nature of the term 'immigrant', here and throughout this chapter I will be putting the term 'immigrant' theatre in quotation marks. Arguably, Canadian 'immigrant' theatre could be easily called 'the theatre created by first generation Canadians' (or New Canadians/Nouveaux Canadiens, as they are officially called by the Canadian government), and yet, Canadian theatre researchers almost never use this more legally correct term.

It is interesting to be analysing Canadian 'immigrant' theatre after the Black Lives Matter (BLM) movement peaked in the summer of 2020 and, subsequently, pushed more white-dominant organizations to open up space for creators of colour, including immigrants (Nestruck 2020). This kind of change has been mostly visible in bigger urban centres with a higher degree of population diversity, for instance, in Toronto, Ontario. Toronto's three most prominent indie theatres (Theatre Passe Muraille, Tarragon, and Factory), which have historically had white male artistic directors, are now run exclusively by people of colour, one of whom is a daughter of Hong Kong immigrants to Canada.

The more traditional racial makeup of Canadian theatre is critiqued in the classic one-man show *Fronteras Americanas* (Verdecchia 2013/1993), written

A. Babayants (✉)
Bishop's University, Sherbrooke, QC, Canada

© The Author(s), under exclusive license to Springer Nature Switzerland AG 2023
Y. Meerzon, S. E. Wilmer (eds.), *The Palgrave Handbook of Theatre and Migration*, https://doi.org/10.1007/978-3-031-20196-7_26

by Guillermo Verdecchia, a celebrated Argentina-born Toronto-based theatre artist. Verdecchia at one point stops his performance and asks for the house lights to come up. Then he, or rather his character, invites the audience to take an evaluative look around and discover that the theatre public in Toronto, a city often touted as the most multicultural city in the world, generally happen to be almost exclusively white. Verdecchia's metatheatrical gesture provides an important context for understanding the position of 'immigrant' theatre, especially theatre produced *by* and *for* those who come from minoritarian racial, ethnic, cultural, and/or linguistic backgrounds.

One relative exception to this rule is Quebec, the French-speaking province of Canada, recognized as a 'nation within a nation' (Reference 2014), where immigrants, including artists of colour, do occasionally occupy some positions of power and even become major representatives of Quebecois culture. For instance, scholar Nadine Charafeddine points out that celebrated playwright Wajdi Mouawad, originally from Lebanon, has led several large theatre institutions in the country including the French Theatre of the National Arts Centre (Ottawa), while playwright Miguel Retamal, who immigrated from Chile after Pinochet's coup d'état in 1973, was once the director of le Théâtre de Rimouski in the Bas-St Laurent region of Quebec (Charafeddine 2018, 11). Immigrant theatre creators are now included in Quebec's most comprehensive historiographic volume entitled *Le Théâtre contemporain au Québec, 1945–2015* (Contemporary Quebec Theatre. 1945–2015). Its authors acknowledge that the first allophone voices (in Canada, especially in Quebec, *allophone* signifies someone who doesn't speak English or French as their mother tongue) appeared in Quebec theatre in the 1980s starting with Italian-born Quebecois Marco Micone, who wrote domestic dramas which largely relied on the realist conventions popular in Quebec theatre ten years prior (David et al. 2020, 252–253). The authors of *Le Théâtre contemporain au Québec* also recognize that in Montreal specifically there have been periods of a more significant immigrant influence: for instance, the 1990s are labelled as a *décennie russe* (Russian decade)—a partial misnomer emphasizing the large number of emigré artists from the former USSR and the Eastern Block who settled in Quebec's largest cultural centre (Guay et al. 2020, 359). Generally speaking, Quebec presents a different cultural context from English Canada, which requires a chapter in its own right.

Returning to the 2020–2021 radical wave of change, it is clear that the issue of power redistribution has become absolutely vital; therefore, in this chapter, I have chosen to provide a bird's eye view of Canada's 'immigrant' theatre through the concept of *power*. My goal is, first, to elucidate which social, political, economic, cultural, and linguistic contexts shape power relations as they pertain to 'immigrant' theatre and, second, to identify which power positions immigrant theatre creators, especially people of colour and allophones, occupy in the models of creation common for 'immigrant' theatre. I acknowledge that my focus will be largely on English Canada and on the work created within the last 20 years, although it is important to recognize that immigrants have been involved in amateur and professional theatre creation in Canada over the entire course of the country's history (see, for instance, Filewod 2019).

'Immigrant' Theatre: Canadian/Quebecois Contexts and Beyond

Modern Canada, a descendant of New France (1534–1755), the British Empire (1755–1867), and the Dominion of Canada (1867–1960s), is the world's second largest country, occupying vast territories of the Indigenous peoples that have lived there for millennia. Remaining loyal to its colonial roots, often in opposition to the U.S., Canada 'achieved independence', not through a revolution, but rather 'in a sequence of acts in several different legislatures over decades' (Filewod 2004, 149). Canada now represents 'a postcolonial fiction that provides legal and infrastructural cohesion to a country that has never succeeded in enlisting its citizens in a common nation principle' while navigating between 'anglophone and francophone nationhoods' and forcing 'a governing narrative of hybrid multiculturalism' (Filewod 2004, 149). The Canadian Multiculturalism Act, which received Royal Assent in 1988, has reshaped immigration to the country, making it more diverse than ever before and, in a way, pushing against the blatantly racist immigration laws of the past (for instance, the Head Tax applied to Asian immigrants from 1896 to 1923).

Theatre artists come to English Canada and Quebec—the francophone province that oversees its own immigration programme targeting specifically French-speaking migrants—as refugees and immigrants. Edward Said distinguishes between the refugee and the immigrant: while both go through an exilic experience, it is the refugee that invariably faces ostracism—immigrants, on the other hand, possess an 'ambiguous status' as they do not necessary deal with ostracism in their country of origin (Said 2008, 250). Additionally, moving to Canada can be a planned experience or a last-minute emergency: for instance, in the devised production *In Sundry Languages*, Ahmed Moneka, a Baghdad-born performer tells his story of arriving in Canada as a participant in the Toronto International Film Festival and receiving an unexpected call from home advising him to claim refugee status, as he would likely face legal prosecution in Baghdad for playing a gay character in an Iraqi film if he returned (Toronto Laboratory Theatre 2019, 35–36).

Another set of contexts is related to the infrastructures of the host country, whose legal peculiarities may or may not provide certain *affordances* only to certain newcomers. For instance, a student from France who moves to Quebec and decides to pursue a degree in theatre or theatre studies will pay low domestic student fees—all of that thanks to an agreement between Quebec and France. Access to education is vital for immigrant artists as a means to gain cultural and human capital in a new country or province: for instance, young actor Santiago Guzmán came to Canada from Mexico City as an international student. He chose Newfoundland's Memorial University because their acting programme fees were the most affordable in the country (Babayants 2021). These affordances and circumstances find their way into numerous solo shows exploring each immigrant's unique life trajectory: Guzmán's *Altar* (2020) speaks about his experience as a gay man looking for love in his new country, while Korean-Canadian Maki Yi's *Suitcase Stories* (2016) reveals her experience with her first Canadian landlady who turned out to be exploitative and abusive. Some solo shows focus specifically on the country of origin—for instance, George Seremba's celebrated play *Come Good Rain* (1993) speaks about his own botched assassination conducted by Uganda's military intelligence.

Another major affordance is language: research shows that the mastery of one's second language is one of the two biggest predictors of an immigrant's economic success in Canada (Bonikowska and Hou 2015). Allophone performers, that is, those who do not speak English or French as their first language, are acutely aware of how their language skills or their 'accentedness' can become a major impediment to being cast in Canadian productions (Manole 2015; Babayants 2017). This is particularly common in English Canada, which generally favours text-based realism and, thus, pushes 'accented' actors to the margins by only allowing them to appear in productions as 'ethnic' characters with a foreign accent (Manole 2015). In multilingual Montreal though, a marked accent on one's French can also become an aesthetic: for instance, Peter Batakliev, who emigrated from Bulgaria in 1990, is often praised for using 'his pronounced accent to good effect' (Charlebois 2020). However, Batakliev's case may be an exception rather than the rule.

On the other side of the spectrum are those immigrants who arrive with full command of one of the official languages of Canada: in their case, language can become a major advantage for their artistic careers. It is perhaps not surprising that Quebec's most celebrated 'immigrant' theatre artist, Wajdi Mouawad, though multilingual, is first and foremost a French speaker. Similarly, Djanet Sears, a celebrated Toronto-based playwright whose Guyanese-Jamaican family immigrated to Canada from Britain when she was young, is first and foremost an English speaker. Contrary to Mouawad and Sears, those who do not have sufficient mastery of English and/or French will certainly experience more difficulty creating work for mainstream venues and may eventually suffer ghettoization. This lack of linguistic competence in English and/or French can also impede immigrant artists' success rate when applying for federal, provincial, or municipal art funding, which all require English or French.

Another important peculiarity that Canada, specifically English Canada, bestows upon its immigrants is identified by Canadian theatre historian Alan Filewod in his article "Settlers, Immigrants and Theatre in Fictive Canada" (2019), where he questions the very notion of an immigrant and, specifically, how that notion is applied as one of the means to Other certain newcomers. He explains that white immigrants of British ancestry (settlers) do not normally see themselves as immigrants while labelling others, for instance, accented newcomers, as immigrants (Filewod 2019, 29). It is this perceived centrality or, rather, the default nature of white British ancestry that pushes Canadian immigrant theatre artists to either fit in—if they are white-passing—or be Othered.

Filewod's observations are consonant with Tony Nardi's critique of English Canada's theatre and culture in general in his solo performance/reading *Two Letters and Counting: Letter Three*, which was part of the Festival Transamérique in 2014 (Montreal). Nardi, born in Calabria, came to Quebec as a child and worked across Canada in Calabrian, Italian, French, and English. When explaining how English Canadian culture prioritizes the Anglophone colonial mentality, he asserts: 'English Canada shamelessly promotes the glories and virtues of British or American theatre and film in all media at the expense of its homegrown talent and art' (Nardi 2013). At the same time, he also questions the virtues of Canadian ethnic communities, or ghettos, when it comes to contemporary Canadian theatre creation, as those communities fail to adequately support theatre unless it glorifies nostalgia for the homeland. If we extrapolate Nardi's critique to Canada's 'immigrant' theatre in general, we can place 'immigrant' theatre creation between two polar opposites: the default English/Anglo identity and the conservative, nostalgia-oriented ethnic community. Consequently, an immigrant artist creating outside of the accepted Anglo Canadian stage conventions or against the nostalgic leanings of their ethnic or linguistic community is unlikely to obtain financial support, substantial media coverage, or public recognition.

Nardi's critique resonates with Mayte Gómez's analysis of Verdecchia's *Fronteras Americanas*. In her 1995 article, Gómez takes a strong stand on the diversity issue arguing that despite its legal commitment to multiculturalism, Canada in fact erases difference though the 'ideology of acculturation': 'Elsewhere I have argued that all aspects of Canadian life, but most obviously the arts, have been affected by what I have called "the ideology of Multiculturalism", an apparently liberal discourse of "integration" of and respect for all cultures underneath which lies a reality of acculturation into a mainstream' (1995, 26). Speaking of the inescapable influence of acculturation on minority artists, Gómez asserts that 'whether they [the artists] reproduce it [acculturation] or attempt to consciously subvert it, they are bound to be framed by it, and often they comply with it and challenge it at the very same time' (1995, 26).

The consequences of this adjustment, acculturation or, as Babayants and Moosavi call it, 'domestication' (2019, 259), could vary from tragic to absurd: for instance, celebrated Iranian playwright Mohammad Yaghoubi, whose work had been translated into a multitude of languages and performed in dozens of countries, after his arrival in Toronto received advice from a fellow immigrant director to deliberately modify his writing style by adding copious stage directions in order to fit the conservative Canadian standard of playwriting and eventually please the jury of a local theatre festival (Babayants and Moosavi 2019, 259). A few years later Yaghoubi received an *emerging* artist residency at Canadian Stage, Toronto's largest independent theatre company (Babayants and Moosavi 2019, 266). While it could be seen as a cause for celebration for a newcomer to the country, here I interpret it more as an absurd situation given that the previous artist residents were primarily recent local theatre school graduates with no international cachet. This *downshifting process* is familiar to many established immigrant artists as they have to transition to their 'emerging' status in Canada. Some accept their new diminished positionality, and others, after years of frustration, may choose to leave, as their access to production resources and lack of connections outside of their ethnic or first language community would be extremely limited, especially when compared to the resources in their country of origin which may boast a large number of state-owned theatres, as is the case in France, Germany, Iran, Poland, or Russia.

There are, certainly, other specifically Canadian contextual peculiarities that affect immigrant artists: Quebec's independence project, the government-imposed bilingualism versus the *de facto* multilingualism, the ongoing oppression of the First Nations, and the lack of funding for newcomer artists compared to large amounts of money available for established Anglo- and Francophone companies and festivals. Some of those have been addressed by ongoing research in the field (for instance, Knowles 2017, 27–30). There are, however, two more general, not Canada-specific, elements that need to be considered when talking about theatre creation among immigrant artists: first, it is the presence/absence of a large first language community and, second, the first-to-second-generation immigration spectrum.

Regarding the presence/absence of a first language community, Ric Knowles observes that 'the geography of contemporary downtown Toronto facilitates working across differences. [...] Downtown neighborhoods are mixed. They flow into one another, allowing for the performance of intercultural exchange and intercultural identities not pre-scripted by official multilingualism' (2017, 40–41). Contrary to that, outside of its downtown core, Toronto is replete with ethnic, linguistic, or cultural silos. Knowles also cites the curious case of Nina Lee Aquino, who in 2006 was the artistic director of fu-GEN Asian Canadian Theatre Company. Aquino, an immigrant herself, refused to take up residency in one of the Toronto suburbs 'in fear of ghettoization' knowing that fu-GEN's public resides in proximity to downtown Toronto (Knowles 2017, 41). This ghettoization issue is not exclusively Canadian, though—it happens in many multicultural urban centres around the world. In Canadian urban centres, it divides the mainstream English or French theatre and the so-called ghetto theatre, which I will introduce below.

In regards to the first-to-second-generation spectrum, migration research also offers a useful set of terms: first (those who immigrated as adults), 1.5 (those who immigrated as children), and second-generation immigrants (those who were born in Canada). In English Canada, it is usually the 1.5 and second-generation artists who become more noticed, while first-generation artists find it hard to penetrate the theatrical mainstream. The first generation may also see things through different lenses and be less interested in the aesthetics dominating English Canadian stages. For instance, playwright Deniz Başar, who has lived in Izmir, Istanbul, Toronto, and Montreal, through the words of her character Derya, an immigrant from Turkey, pushes against the solipsism of artistic clichés produced by immigrants' children:

> [...] why should I care about your step mother, or your coming out to your family, and ha-ha immigrant families who don't get things—which creeps me out because it means that in the best case scenario in a couple of decades I will be the butt of the joke in my future children's stand-up routines to feed the hunger of more white audiences for minstrelsies. (Başar 2020, 18)

In addition, a significant number of first-generation artists arrive with a hybrid identity that often gets lost in a default dual hybridity that only considers the points of departure and arrival. For instance, Soheil Parsa, a Toronto-based theatre director, belonged to a persecuted religious minority (Bahá'í) in his home, Iran, where Islamic law has been woven into the fabric of the state since the Islamic Revolution of 1979. He is nevertheless often simply labelled Iranian-Canadian without any mention of his minoritarian identity. Arguably, immigrants who come from minoritarian and/or oppressed backgrounds and who are used to navigating between the majority culture (language, religion, ethnicity, or race) and their own, find the transition to a new, but still minoritarian status in Canada a not entirely new struggle. In contrast, those who come from majoritarian backgrounds must learn to transition to a minoritarian status for the first time. In Canada, they become a visible and/or audible minority (i.e., due to an accent)—something that may cause difficulty and even anger, which often resurface as themes in their theatre work. For instance, this dissatisfaction with the lost ability to be non-accented, hence, unmarked, led Cynthia Ashperger (pseudonym: Lola Xenos), an immigrant performer and acting teacher from the former Yugoslavia, to create the musical *Foreign Tongue* (Xenos 2019).

With these contexts in mind, let us look at the common models within which immigrant theatre is created in Canada.

Model 1: Immigrant Excluded but Represented

The first type of 'immigrant' theatre can directly or indirectly address the immigration theme while only representing one's migration experience. This model is particularly popular when it comes to second-generation immigrants creating shows based on the stories of their parents' immigration. Meanwhile, actual immigrants are completely excluded or included only tangentially in the process of creation.

One of the most famous examples of this kind of theatre is *Kim's Convenience* (first produced at Toronto Fringe in 2011), the most commercially successful production in the history of Soulpepper Theatre Company (Toronto's largest repertory theatre). The comedy revolves around a 1980s convenience store owned by first-generation Korean immigrants with two grownup children. While this specific play was seen as a major breakthrough in Canadian theatre in terms of the representation of people of colour, it was written by a second-generation Canadian (Ins Choi) and adhered to most conventions of English Canadian mainstream theatre: primacy of spoken text, stage realism, a linear structure of a well-made play, a tokenistic use of an immigrant language (Korean), and a didactic nature—qualities that have been criticized by avant-garde theatre artists (Tannahill 2015). In French Canada, Dynamo Theatre produced a physical theatre piece called *Inner Migrant*, where 'a Montreal actor steps into the shoes of a Portuguese migrant and takes the stage with a musician' (Dynamo Theatre Website n.d.). While the theatre genres and styles of *Inner Migrant* and *Kim's Convenience* are different, both represent a mode of production where actual immigrant creators are not included in the creative process.

Model 2: Immigrant Siloed and/or Erased

Most immigrants to Canada settle down in large cities where they find significant communities speaking their first language: for instance, Toronto boasts six Chinatowns, Little Italy, Little India, Little Portugal, and Little Jamaica, among many others. What often emerges within those communities is *ghetto* or *ethnic theatre* (Berger et al. 2011), where performances happen in the community's first language. In his book *Staging Strangers*, Barry Freeman provides a detailed history of such a company—Nové divadlo, a Czech and Slovak church basement theatre located in Toronto. Nové divadlo has produced over 150 shows and yet, has been mainly invisible to mainstream Canadian theatre critics and audiences (Freeman 2017, 41). Similar theatres emerge and disappear in smaller cities, too: for instance, Regina, Saskatchewan has recently seen the birth of Lexeme Theatre performing in Urdu primarily for the growing Pakistani community of Saskatchewan's capital.

According to Filewod, ghettoized theatre creators tend to suffer a sort of historiographic erasure, at least in English Canada. He specifically describes the case of Myroslav Irchan, a Ukrainian playwright who lived in Winnipeg, Manitoba in the 1920s and eventually became one of the most produced playwrights in the country. Despite his incredible popularity Irchan was never included in English Canadian theatre history (Filewod 2004, 146–147).

Model 3: Immigrant Paired

This model refers to a situation when power is shared between a first-generation immigrant and a local collaborator (usually, a white collaborator) who has access to and understanding of the local cultural capital. Bea Pizano, originally from Columbia, works with her life partner Trevor Schwellnus. Pizano and Schwellnus co-run Aluna Theatre, Toronto's LatinX company, which shares their rehearsal space with Modern Times Theatre. Modern Times was also originally a partnership—its leaders Soheil Parsa (mentioned above) and Peter Farbridge met at York University where they studied theatre. While Aluna and

Modern Times usually produce different kinds of work, both companies are committed to hiring immigrants and people of colour without reducing their roles to one single culture or country of origin. For instance, in Lorca's *Blood Wedding* (2015) directed by Soheil Parsa, immigrant performers Bea Pizano (from Columbia), Carla Melo (from Brazil), among others, performed roles that had nothing to do with their ethnicity or origins—something that Kelly Nestruck, a theatre critic of a major national newspaper called 'a quintessentially Canadian approach to the classics—one that isn't about a nebulous idea of diversity, but simply emphasizes the individuality of the performers' (Nestruck 2015).

Model 4: Immigrant Supervised—The Subaltern Position

This type of theatre, or rather production, involves first-generation immigrants who are directed or sometimes dramaturged or guided in one way or another by non-immigrant Canadians. This kind of theatre often involves a collaboration between non-professional immigrant performers and a professional Canadian director where the power generally remains in the hands of the director although its distribution could vary. Examples would include the bilingual production *Polyglotte (2015)* directed by Montreal's Olivier Choinière (a francophone Québécois), and *Brimful of Asha* (2012) directed by Toronto's Ravi Jain (a second-generation Anglophone Canadian).

The *Polyglotte* director explains that the production allows audiences 'to see ourselves collectively in 2015 through the gaze of the immigrant, of that Other who is part of us, is necessary. It is through him or her [a new immigrant] that I [Olivier Choinière; non-immigrant, white, male, Quebecois] can get beyond my own clichés' (Meerzon 2015, 185). Yana Meerzon explains that 'in its political and artistic statements […] *Polyglotte* continued the work of theatre-artist immigrants, such as Mani Soleymanlou in Quebec or Carmen Aguirre in English Canada, who have made serious attempts to bring the immigrant topics out of the "minority theatre" box, the box created by the cultural and economic policies of multiculturalism, and to personally integrate in what we would call "a mainstream Canadian theatre"' (2015, 185). While *Polyglotte* does use immigrant performers, mostly amateur actors, to educate Canadians about their own country, what remains unclear is the ethical question of how those immigrant performers benefited from being in that production and revealing their stories of becoming Canadian citizens.

In *Brimful of Asha*, produced by WhyNotTheatre (Toronto), the director's mother, Asha Jain, a first-generation immigrant from India, occupies the stage with Ravi Jain to discuss the matters of her son's arranged marriage. As the conversation between Mother and Son develops, a cultural clash between the first- and second-generation immigrants occurs. While Asha Jain was probably being guided by her director son throughout the development of the show dramaturgy, her stern views and cultural perspectives end up acknowledged and respected throughout the text and her authorship is recognized in the show programme.

Model 5: Immigrant Unleashed

This last type of 'immigrant' theatre refers to first-generation immigrants running their own companies, occupying positions of power, and producing theatre beyond their ethnic or linguistic communities. For instance, Mohammad Yaghoubi and Aida Keikhaii, both first-generation immigrants from Iran, created Nowadays Theatre (Toronto) and have been producing contemporary Iranian and Canadian repertoire for both Persian and English-speaking audiences. Another example is the Toronto Laboratory Theatre's production of *In Sundry Languages* (originally a quote from Thomas Kidd's *Spanish Tragedy*), a collectively devised performance that included untranslated text in many languages spoken by its immigrant performers (Meerzon 2020). Such productions assert the right of immigrant artists to create work in their first language(s), promote a diversification of theatre audiences, and involve the use of a multilingual dramaturgy, which defies translation into the languages of power.

It is important to recognize that unlike the first model, where the actual immigrants are excluded from the production, the Immigrant Unleashed model remains on the fringes of Canadian theatre, not becoming a commercial success or receiving large amounts of government funding. Moreover, the very existence of this model can sometimes be simply an act of desperation. For instance, Santiago Guzmán, mentioned earlier, turned to playwriting and producing because he, as a newcomer from Mexico, realized that he would not fit the roles available in the local theatre in his home province, Newfoundland. Guzmán, like many before him, created his theatre company, TODOS Productions, dedicated to performers of colour and queer artists (Babayants 2021).

The five models above are certainly flexible entities meant to be challenged. For instance, Vancouver's Rice-and-Beans Theatre unites a diverse group of first-, 1.5, and second-generation immigrants that are mostly people of colour. This company, co-led by Derek Chan and Perdro Chamale, explores very common Canadian 'immigrant' theatre issues, such as the hybrid identity of second-generation immigrants (*DBLSPK: Mother Tongue* produced in 2021) who lost or never properly learned their first language. At the same time, Rice-and Beans also creates boundary pushing performances, for instance, *Yellow Objects* (2021), which directly responds to Chinese government-induced oppression of freedom in Derek Chan's native Hong Kong (Smith 2021).

In conclusion, I would like to share a short anecdote that reveals Canada's persistent commitment to the country's colonial mentality, which, among other things, keeps immigrant creators mostly on the margins:

EUROPEAN SCHOLARS:
We don't really know much about Canadian theatre. Who is the most famous Canadian playwright?
CANADIAN COLLEAGUE:
William Shakespeare.

A lot of time has passed since the 1980s, when this running gag originated, specifically since 1988, when the Canadian Multiculturalism Act, which 'instigated the study of ethnic, multicultural, and intercultural theatre practices' (Meerzon 2015, 181), was passed. Today, despite the official multiculturalism and the tentative gains of the positions of power by immigrant artists and/or artists of colour, William Shakespeare is still arguably a much more prominent figure in English Canadian theatre than any of the first-, 1.5, or even second-generation Canadian theatre creators.

References

Babayants, Art. 2017. '"In Unknown Languages": Investigating the Phenomenon of Multilingual Acting.' PhD Dissertation. University of Toronto.
———. 2021. Telephone interview with Santiago Guzmán. August.
Babayants, Art and Marjan Moosavi. 2019. 'Moments of Encounter: Iranian Canadian Immigrant and Diasporic Theatre.' In *Theatre and (Im)migration. New Essays on Canadian Theatre*, edited by Yana Meerzon, 244–266. Toronto: Playwrights Canada Press.
Başar, Deniz. 2020. *Wine & Halva*. A Play. Unpublished Script.
Berger, Jeniva, Jean Yoon, and Katherine Foster Grajewski. 2011. 'Multicultural Theatre.' *The Canadian Encyclopedia*. https://www.thecanadianencyclopedia.ca/en/article/multicultural-theatre. Accessed 22 February 2022.
Bonikowska, Aneta, and Feng Hou. 2015. 'Which Human Capital Characteristics Best Predict the Earnings of Economic Immigrants?' *Statistics Canada*. https://www150.statcan.gc.ca/n1/pub/11f0019m/11f0019m2015368-eng.htm. Accessed 22 February 2022.
Charafeddine, Nadine. 2018. 'La théâtralisation de l'exil dans la dramaturgie migrante au Québec (1980–2010).' PhD Dissertation. Département des littératures de langue française, Université de Montréal.
Charlebois, Gaétan. 2020. 'Peter Batakliev.' *Canadian Theatre Encyclopedia*. https://www.canadiantheatre.com/dict.pl?term=Batakliev%2C%20Peter. Accessed 22 February 2022.
David, Gilbert et al. (Eds). 2020. *Le théâtre contemporain au Québec, 1945–2015. Essai de synthèse historique et socio-esthétique*. Montréal: Les Presses de l'Université de Montréal.
Dynamo Theatre Website. n.d. 'Inner Migrant.' https://dynamotheatre.qc.ca/en/spectacles/inner-migrant/. Accessed 22 February 2022.
Filewod, Alan. 2004. 'Named in Passing: Deregimenting Canadian Theatre History.' In *Writing and Rewriting National Theatre Histories*, edited by S.E. Wilmer, 146–175. Iowa City: University of Iowa Press.

———. 2019. 'Playing on Indigenous land: Settlers, immigrants and theatre in fictive Canada.' In *Theatre and (Im)migration. New Essays on Canadian Theatre*, edited by Yana Meerzon, 27–55. Toronto: Playwrights Canada Press.

Freeman, Barry. 2017. *Staging Strangers. Theatre and Global Ethics*. Montreal and Kingston: McGill-Queen's University Press.

Gómez, M. 1995. 'Healing the Border Wound: *Fronteras Americanas* and the Future of Canadian Multiculturalism.' *Theatre Research in Canada / Recherches théâtrales au Canada*, 16 (1), 26–39.

Guay, Hervé, assisted by Gilbert David, Patrick Lerous with the collaboration of Erin Hurley and Yannick Legault. 2020. 'Percées internationals et horizons incertains (1990–1999).' *Le théâtre contemporain au Québec, 1945–2015. Essai de synthèse historique et socio-esthétique*, edited by Gilbert David, et al. Montréal: Les Presses de l'Université de Montréal.

Knowles, Ric 2017. *Performing the Intercultural City*. Ann Arbor: University of Michigan Press.

Manole, Diana 2015. 'Accented Actors; From Stage to Stages via a Convenience Store.' *Theatre Research in Canada*, 36 (2), 255–273.

Meerzon, Yana. 2015. 'Theatre and Immigration: From the Multiculturalism Act to the Sites of Imagined Communities.' *Theatre Research in Canada*, 36 (2), 181–195.

———. 2020. *Performance, Subjectivity, Cosmopolitanism*. Houndsmills, Basingstoke: Palgrave Macmillan.

Nardi, Tony. 2013. *Two Letters and Counting. Letter Three*. Performance. https://www.youtube.com/watch?v=pBmdElK1j98. Accessed 22 February 2022.

Nestruck, Kelly. 2015. 'Blood Wedding: A Quintessentially Canadian Approach to Classics.' *The Globe and Mail*, March 17, 2015; https://www.theglobeandmail.com/arts/theatre-and-performance/blood-wedding-takes-a-quintessentially-canadian-approach/article23504015/. Accessed 26 July 2023.

———. 2020. 'Why a Single Artistic Director is Still Enough?' *The Globe and Mail*, December 1, 2020; https://www.theglobeandmail.com/arts/theatre-and-performance/article-why-a-single-artistic-director-is-still-enough/. Accessed 22 February 2022.

Reference re Supreme Court Act, ss. 5 and 6, 2014 SCC 21, para. 49.

Said, W. Edward. 2008. *Réflexions sur l'exile et autres essais*. Arles: Actes Sud.

Smith, Janet. 2021. 'Theatre Artist Derek Chan Stages a Lament for Hong Kong in Multifaceted Yellow Objects.' *Stir. Arts and Culture*. Vancouver. April 19. https://www.createastir.ca/articles/derek-chan-yellow-objects-rice-and-beans?fbclid=IwAR2jnZRCTAv4bnmMq8fYPEsi-xMg34ERvUQURaGm0Vq4Bd6wffx9Ik8dXuk. Accessed 22 February 2022.

Tannahill, Jordan. 2015. *The Theatre of the Unimpressed: In Search of Vital Drama*. Toronto, ON: Coach House Books.

Toronto Laboratory Theatre. 2019. 'In Sundry Languages.' In *Canadian Theatre Review. Radical Hospitalities*, edited by Brian Batchelor, Hanna Rachow, and Denis Rogers Valenzuela with Jenn Stephenson. Winter: 31–39.

Verdecchia, G. (1993) 2013. *Fronteras Americanas*. Electronic edition by Alexander Street Press. Retrieved from http://solomon.nadr.alexanderstreet.com.myaccess.library.utoronto.ca/cgi-bin/asp/philo/navigate.pl?nadr.1453.

Xenos, Lola. 2019. 'Foreign Tongue. The Musical.' In *Scripting (Im)migration: New Canadian Plays*, edited by Yana Meerzon, 243–333. Toronto: Playwrights Canada Press.

CHAPTER 27

Migrant Artists and Precarious Labour in Contemporary Russian Theatre

Mark Simon and Varvara Sklez

INTRODUCTION

Looking closely at the migration in post-Soviet Russia, one can discover a variety of forms of precarious labour, including artistic work which remains largely underexplored. Although today, people from Uzbekistan, Tajikistan, and Kyrgyzstan make up the bulk of the migration inflow to Russia, theatrical productions with artists of Central Asian origin are rare, especially those dedicated to labour migration. This situation is due to the relative insensitivity of Russian theatre to acute social issues, on the one hand, and to the tacit racialized division of labour within professional theatrical institutions, on the other. Under these conditions, building a career for a migrant artist on the Russian stage—here referred to as a person of a visible minority originally from Central Asia—is a precarious effort.

In this chapter, which was written prior Russia's full-scale invasion of Ukraine in February 2022, we focus on three theatrical projects, each of which provides a distinct example of an artistic rendering of a career path in theatre related to migratory experience. The first example is *Aqyn-Opera*, staged at Teatr.doc in 2012. It featured three professional Pamirian actors and musicians who were forced to give up their artistic careers at home and moved to Russia as odd-jobbers. The second case is the play *Plakha* (The Place of the Skull), based on Chingiz Aitmatov's novel, staged at the Moscow Youth Theatre with

M. Simon
Institute for Cultural Anthropology and European Ethnology,
University of Göttingen, Göttingen, Germany

V. Sklez (✉)
University of Warwick, Coventry, UK

the participation of amateur Kyrgyz actors from the theatre group Ayan. Our final case study is the witness performance *Neformat* (Non-Standard) directed by Anastasia Patlay, written by Nana Grinshtein, and performed by professional actors of non-Russian ethnic origin.

We argue that each of these three cases (artists who became migrant workers; migrant workers who seek to be artists; and artists with migration biographies employed in the creative industry) addresses the problem of precarity of artistic labour in connection to migration. This problem is related to racialization, which manifests itself in aspects such as conformity to the canon and typecasting in the field of cultural production. It also reflects the generally vulnerable position of an artist in the post-Soviet reality, in relation to the market, the society, and the state.

Onur Kömürcü-Nobrega, in her work on postmigration theatre in Berlin (2014), develops Sara Ahmed's concept of the cultural politics of emotion (2004). She argues that migrant artists are often involved in affective labour through performing acts of memory, which is widely illustrated by three examples we chose. Kömürcü-Nobrega focuses on how the artists' acts of remembrance counteract the neglect of migrant stories in the cultural landscape of the 'host country' and question 'hegemonic, static and reductive historical accounts' (2014, 29). We aim to expand Kömürcü-Nobrega's ideas of emotional labour and remembrance. First, we will differentiate between the acts of personal and collective memory before turning to comment on the complexity of their relationship to the hegemonic symbolic order(s). Then, we will address the issue of the commodification of an artistic act of remembering and migration on the Russian stage today.

Immigration to Russia in the Post-Soviet Period: Major Milestones

During the three decades of post-Soviet history, the migration inflow to Russia has transformed several times. Each of these transformations influenced the trajectories of the integration of migrants from the former Soviet republics into Russian society, including their presence in the cultural sphere. To contextualize the theatrical projects which feature migrants and (or) are dedicated to the topic of migration, we will briefly outline the milestones of modern migration to Russia.

The first years after the collapse of the Soviet Union were characterized by the nation-building processes that took place in each of the former Soviet republics, and the transformation of migration from internal (from one republic to another) to external or international. Many persons from the 'non-titular' population, including ethnic Russians, who used to live in those republics fearing the rise of ethnic nationalism, decided to resettle in their so-called historical homelands (see Mukomel 2005, 12).

During the second half of the 1990s, political factors faded into the background, and economic motivations began to play a dominant role in post-Soviet migrations. Russia became the main magnet for labour migration in the territory of the former USSR, and temporary workers from member countries of the Commonwealth of Independent States (CIS) started to dominate the migration inflow to Russia.

Although the need to promote the benefits of long-term migration has been symbolically recognized by Vladimir Putin's government, law-enforcement practices discourage migrants from settling permanently. The Russian migration policies often push migrants into a semi-legal position, which reflects the interests of federal and regional governments, security agencies, and large enterprises (Reeves 2013; Malakhov 2014).

Migrants from Central Asian countries, primarily from Uzbekistan and Tajikistan, occupy the least privileged position in the Russian labour market. The situation with migrants from Kyrgyzstan is slightly better because Kyrgyzstan is a member of the Eurasian Economic Union. (Unlike citizens of Uzbekistan and Tajikistan, they do not need to apply for a work permit.) Despite their increased social and economic presence in large Russian cities, these migrants still face numerous obstacles due to the tacit racist attitude of bureaucrats and police officers.

Theatrical Context

After the collapse of the USSR, Russian theatres actively implemented dramaturgy and aesthetics which were out of political favour in Soviet times. One such aesthetic was verbatim theatre, which had reached Russian theatre makers via a series of seminars organized by the Royal Court Theatre in Moscow in 1999–2000. Though some of the theatre artists in Soviet and post-Soviet times raised difficult questions about the past and present, the verbatim method lent itself well to the exploration of the challenges and inequalities of contemporary society. It was only natural that Teatr.doc—one of the key venues for the development of *Novaya drama* (the New Drama) and documentary theatre in Russia—happened to be the first Russian theatre company to address the issue of post-Soviet migrations. In 2003, this theatre staged Alexander Rodionov's play *Voyna moldovan za kartonnuyu korobku* (The War of the Moldovans for the Cardboard Box), based on a criminal incident that happened to migrants from Moldova in one of the Moscow markets.

The next two performances on this topic appeared nine years later, in 2012, also thanks to Teatr.doc. The first one was a documentary one-man play *Uzbek*, created by Talgat Batalov, a Tashkent native who began his career at the famous Ilkhom theatre. His play embodied the journey of a migrant in Russia who must pass through a Kafkaesque bureaucracy, in which one's legal documents (such as passport, registration at the place of residence, and work permit) play the most significant role as a marker of one's identity (Flynn 2016, 20–21). Another performance staged by Teatr.doc was *Aqyn-Opera*, to which we will return later. It was the first production in the history of Russian theatre to feature migrant workers.

Since the second half of the 2010s, a few theatre productions have been staged that focused on the issue of labour migration or involved people with migrant experiences. Several examples include *Svan*, a play in verse written by Ekaterina Troepolskaya and Andrey Rodionov, and directed by Yuri Kvyatkovsky (Meyerhold Centre, 2015), *Non-Standard* by Anastasia Patlay and Nana Grinshtein (Teatr.doc, 2020), and *Respublika* (The Republic) written by Sergey Davydov and directed by Aleksandr Kudryashov (Etnoteatr, 2020).

At the end of 2010s, the broader artistic community's sensitivity to the issues faced by migrants had increased; some institutions (theatres, museums, galleries) refashioned their policies and practices with regards to accessibility for foreigners, multilingualism, and relationships with employees of Central Asian origin in a bid to be more inclusive, though determining how they could successfully reach out to migrant audiences remained a challenge. At the same time, migrants (especially the younger generation who had come from big cities) became more involved in the entertainment sphere (particularly in stand-up comedy). Nevertheless, contemporary theatre (and migrant theatre, correspondingly) still occupies a relatively small segment in Russian theatre. While the performances dedicated to labour migration have never been subjected to direct persecution from the authorities, there are still a number of political, economic, and aesthetic factors that reduce the visibility of migrant artists and their stories in Russian theatre. Moreover, migration is not often referred to even within experimental theatre due to the lack of initiative from migrant artists and communication with migrant communities. In the following sections, we will explore these controversies in more detail, focusing our approach through the subject of artistic labour.

Aqyn-Opera: Between Individual and Cultural Memory

Context

The play *Aqyn-Opera* is a unique example of migrant theatre artists returning to the professional stage. Abdumamad Bekmamadov, Pokiza Kurbonaseinova, and Ajam Chakaboev, all natives of the Pamirs (Tajikistan), used to be professional performers at home but, in 1999, decided to migrate to Russia as handymen to provide for their families. Since their departure, they had not performed on stage and rarely played musical instruments.

Thanks to Vsevolod Lisovsky—a Russian theatre director, TV producer, and screenwriter, who began his theatrical career at Teatr.doc—the trio was given the opportunity to appear on the Russian professional stage. Lisovsky invited the three Pamirians to create a documentary script based on their experiences as migrant workers in Moscow and to use traditional Pamirian songs to frame this narrative. The term *aqyn* that features in the title of the play—a title provided by Lisovsky—refers to the traditions of storytelling and improvised singing, widespread both in the Caucasus and in Central Asia. The difficulty, however, was that during the day these artists were engaged in physically exhausting and precarious work, and so they had rare spare hours to collect any material for the play and rehearse. Because acting in an independent theatre could not serve as a fully-fledged source of income for Abdumamad, Pokiza, and Ajam, performances were often cancelled and postponed. In addition, after one of the artists had to suddenly return home, Lisovsky found himself in search of new participants. He visited one of the informal recruitment points for migrants, where he held up a poster, saying: 'Collecting stories of migrants for the theatre. This work is paid for.' Based on this search, he created *Aqyn-Opera 2* (Aizman 2014; Simon 2020).

For the Pamirian artists, this theatrical comeback came at a certain price. To participate in this work, they were asked to share their recollections and experiences as migrant workers with the audience of Teatr.doc. These recollections turned into a 'commodity' or 'product,' which ironically did not bring them any tangible material dividends, and thus less than three years after its opening, the *Aqyn-Opera* project came to an end. Nevertheless, the project gained recognition from the Russian theatrical community when it received the Golden Mask award in 2014.

Text

The text of the play is based on the stories told by Pamirian artists about the vicissitudes of their fate. It testifies to the life of migrant workers in Moscow in the first decade of the twenty-first century. The play consists of four main plots: Abdumamad's arrival to Moscow and his constant transitions from one hard labour to another; the artistic biography of Pokiza, who left her new-born son with her parents to become an actress and later went to Moscow; stories about migrants' encounter with death; and the story of Abdumamad's return to his homeland after 10 years of absence. The tragic episodes from the lives of these characters are interspersed with anecdotes about Abdumamad working different jobs. Ironic storytelling style makes it possible to avoid the feeling that the characters complain about their fate in front of their Moscow audiences, which allows them to avoid a 'victim' position.

In its consideration of the theme of memory, the play oscillates in its focus between cultural memory (expressed in the desire to preserve a Pamirian identity) and the individual memories of people whose biographies are marked as special because of both their migrant and artistic backgrounds. Despite references to traditional Pamirian culture (through songs), Abdumamad and Pokiza appeared in the play as people whose life paths are difficult to reconcile with the patriarchal attitudes common among some Central Asian communities. Due to the desire to build an artistic career, they often could not meet the expectations of their relatives. Their migration to Russia, on the one hand, left a heavy imprint on the loss of their respective social status, but, on the other hand, allowed them to continue to lead an independent lifestyle.

Performance

Curiously, almost no immigrant spectators attended *Aqyn-Opera*, despite Lisovsky's many attempts to invite them. There are several explanations for this. First, in the early 2010s, it was physically dangerous for Central Asian migrants to travel via public transport in Moscow. For example, on the eve of one of the performances, Abdumamad himself was beaten in the metro by nationalists and had to play on stage with his head bandaged. Second, Teatr.doc is a small theatre company and it cannot accommodate many spectators. Third, for the migrants, unlike regular Moscow audiences, the stories told in the play were by no means a revelation, but a part of their everyday life.

Lisovsky was obsessed with the idea of making a social project out of *Aqyn-Opera*. He dreamed of playing it in places where migrants usually gathered—at construction sites, in dormitories, and at meetings of migrant trade unions. However, almost all of his attempts to take the performance outside Teatr.doc failed. Several years later, Lisovsky admitted that the project's social mission was ultimately fulfilled by itself, without his help. If in the early 2010s migrants were a 'visual irritant' for Russians, by the end of the decade the situation had changed. Muscovites had already become accustomed to the presence of immigrants from Central Asia, and horizontal ties had been established between migrants and the host society (Lisovsky, personal interview, 13 December 2018).

Aqyn-Opera reveals three dimensions of the precariousness of migrant labour. The first dimension involves the problem of low wages for artists in post-Soviet countries, ultimately forcing them into changing their profession. The precedent of the participation of Pamirian artists in the project of a Russian independent theatre also proved that acting could not bring them sufficient income. The second dimension refers to the text of the play, which reflected the conditions of precarious labour for the Tajik migrants in Russia. Nevertheless, as a performance, *Aqyn-Opera*, both institutionally and aesthetically, did not become a place of reconciliation between migrant communities and the Moscow theatre audience.

AYAN THEATRE: FROM MIGRANTS TO ARTISTS THROUGH OBLIVION

Context

Ayan is the first theatre company in Russia created by migrant workers. It started with Ainash Kozubaeva, a former teacher of Russian, who had been working in Russia for more than 15 years. In 2018, together with the theatre director Sadyr Sagynbaev, she began to train young Kyrgyz workers to act. Ayan theatre company opened with the play *Igra v Tzaria* (Playing the Tsar) by Tajik playwright Dzhuma Kuddus, directed by Sagynbaev. The company prepared through rehearsals in parks and cafes, culminating in a premiere that took place at an NGO resource centre in a residential area of Moscow. Members of the Kyrgyz community received an invitation for opening night, and they were astonished by what was staged: they did not expect to find non-professional Kyrgyz actors in Moscow, and they could not imagine that a company like Ayan would open with a play written in Russian by a Tajik playwright and translated into Kyrgyz. Some Kyrgyz public figures criticized this work because they believed that it was the company's duty to begin its activities by staging one of the works by the famous Kyrgyz writer Chingiz Aitmatov (1928–2008), a laureate of numerous Soviet state awards.

However, despite all the difficulties, Ayan began to perform at different venues (renting them at their own expense). Shortly thereafter, Vyacheslav Spesivtsev, the head of the Moscow Youth Theatre, who also happened to be close friends with Aitmatov and had staged his novel *The Place of the Skull* in the late 1980s, invited the Ayan artists to create a studio at his theatre. Within this studio, novice actors had the opportunity to take acting classes. After several months of work, a decision was made to revive the staging of *The Place of the Skull*, making it a bilingual, Russian-Kyrgyz performance.

Thus, young people from Kyrgyzstan, deprived of the chance to master a theatre profession at home due to the need to provide for their families, ended up on the stage of one of the Russian state theatres. Moreover, Ayan changed the symbolic status of its members from migrant workers, employed in physically demanding and low-paying jobs, to artists.

Text

Chingiz Aitmatov's novel *The Place of the Skull* illustrates the gap that lies between nature and modern mankind. Driven by spiritual quests, the protagonist of the novel, Avdiy Kallistratov, a former seminarian, travels to the Chuy Valley (stretched along the border of Kazakhstan and Kyrgyzstan) to write an article about hemp traders. Upon trying to understand the motives of young people involved in drug trafficking, Avdiy infiltrates a gang of cannabis hunters and falls prey to his good intentions to save them. The parallel storyline of the novel revolves around the misadventures of the she-wolf Akbara, who links together the two main characters—the spirit seeker Avdiy and Boston, an exemplary family man and a worker at a Kyrgyz collective farm. Like Avdiy, Boston is forced to suffer for the sins of others. Boston's envious neighbour Bazarbai steals cubs from Akbara's lair and leaves them in Boston's house. In retaliation, Akbara drags off Boston's young son. Trying to save the baby, Boston accidentally shoots him.

Performance

In 1987 when *The Place of the Skull* was published, it did not comply with official Soviet ideology, since it criticized the idea of the subordination of nature to humanity. Nevertheless, the adaptation of Spesivtsev's staging, made together with Ayan, largely conveys nostalgia for the Soviet past. The performance contains idyllic scenes with marches of pioneers, estrada (official pop-songs) songs of the 1980s, and, at the end of the performance, a sort of Aitmatov mausoleum appears on the stage.

Among the performers of the Ayan theatre, only one actress played a role that was not related to her ethnic origin. The rest of the migrant artists were dressed in ethnic costumes, portraying members of Boston's family and his neighbours. Such a stage representation, built on the folklorization of people from Central Asia, reflects current Russian cultural policy (Simon 2021). At present, the Russian bureaucratic institutions responsible for the management of diversity in the country propose to combine ethnic and Soviet symbols in the public representation of the peoples of the former USSR. For example, at the annual celebration of Victory Day on 9 May 2021, during the Immortal Regiment march, people of Central Asian descent dressed in ethnic costumes and carried portraits of war heroes.

The Place of the Skull, in other words, reproduced the Soviet ideological framework of *Druzhba narodov* (Friendship of Peoples), according to which each of the 'fraternal peoples' attains access to cultural participation through an appeal to ethnic origin. Such a representation inevitably presupposes a collective oblivion to the fact that the Soviet Union has collapsed.

The joint work of the Moscow Youth Theatre and Ayan reveals the phenomenon of oblivion on several levels. Our interviews conducted with young Kyrgyz artists demonstrate that getting on stage changes their symbolic social status as migrants. They receive recognition from the audience as artists, which allows them to forget for a brief moment that they are precarious workers in Russia. As a text, Aitmatov's novel conveys the message that a rupture with nature and the abandonment of roots always leads to tragedy. In the performance, the connection between the characters and their 'roots,' which, according to Aitmatov, was cut off by Soviet policy, is paradoxically restored through an appeal to an imaginary 'Soviet' ideal. Pastoral pictures of Soviet life depicted in the production, despite the tragic content of the play, seem to reconcile the ethnic Kyrgyz heritage with the current Russian patriotic narratives about the great past. Such a reconciliation becomes possible only thanks to the collective oblivion of the fact that the USSR no longer exists, and former fellow citizens have turned into migrants. Thus, *The Place of the Skull* is an embodiment of a collective fantasy of a common past, which blocks individual reflection about the present with its economic and symbolic inequality.

Non-Standard: Actor as a 'Perfect' Migrant

Context

In the summer of 2020, director Anastasia Patlay and playwright Nana Grinshtein started to conduct interviews with migrants. While they talked to people of different professional backgrounds, they realized that the careers of migrant actors were particularly affected by their journey. Having noticed this tendency, they interviewed more actors, including those who moved to Moscow from other Russian regions and shared a non-Russian ethnic background.

The life stories of five actors (Nargis Abdullaeva, Aziz Beyshenaliev, Feruza Ruzieva, Dzhan Badmaev, and Rafael Durnoyan) made the text of the play. Coming from non-Russian families, all of them had to face racial stereotypes, especially after they moved to Moscow. Their personal trajectories differ. Beyshenaliev is from an Uzbek/Kyrgyz family; he was raised in Turkmenistan and Uzbekistan, studied acting and worked in Tashkent before moving to Moscow in 1997. He lives in Kazakhstan now. Abdullaeva, who is of Tajik/Bukharian Jewish/Crimean Tatar descent, studied and worked in Tashkent in the Ilkhom theatre and moved to Ukraine and then to Russia in the early 2010s. Ruzieva is from an Uzbek/Iranian family; she studied acting and worked in Tashkent, and also moved to Moscow in 2009. Durnoyan comes from an Armenian family who has lived in Russia for more than a century, and Badmaev is from a Kalmyk family in Russia. Both moved to Moscow in the early 2010s and graduated from The Russian Institute of Theatre Arts.

It is important to emphasize that the actors who had arrived from Central Asia (Abdullaeva, Beyshenaliev, Ruzieva) belonged to the Russian-speaking cultural space which existed across all the national republics in the late-Soviet Union. Both Patlay and Grinshtein talked about the feeling of belonging to the Russian culture that was common among Russian-speaking inhabitants of cosmopolitan Tashkent and Baku (where they themselves come from), as well as the feeling of a shared mixed background, commonplace for many dwellers in these cities (Patlay and Grinshtein, personal interviews, 24 May 2021). Their position changed dramatically after the collapse of the USSR when the former republics became nation-states, and the Russian-speaking population in these respective countries lost the privileges it had enjoyed.

All these artists' histories share a lot in common in terms of precarious labour. Firstly, some of them had to take on various jobs after they had moved to Moscow. It is particularly striking in the case of Nargis Abdullaeva who was a star of the world-renowned Ilkhom Theatre, but had to work as a cleaner (among other jobs) after moving to Moscow. Secondly, almost all of their theatrical work took place in independent theatres, which did not provide enough income. Finally, the existing stereotypes made it arduous for them to get leading roles in mainstream theatres or films.

Nevertheless, the very emergence of *Non-Standard* gives reason for optimism. Created in Teatr.doc and supported by the Heinrich Böll Foundation, the performance was invited to remain in the Meyerhold Centre, where it was able to address a wider audience, who, in turn, responded to the theme in a lively manner. This demonstrates that the topic of migration and the related problems are 'in the air,' as Patlay put it. She added that, unlike their experience with another witness performance of *Vne teatra/A chto esli ya ne budu …* (Outside Theatre/What If I Won't Be …), Grinshtein and herself did not exactly need to look for performers for *Non-Standard*. They were already surrounded by actors with a relevant background.

Text

The play represents the issue of precarious labour as a problem of personal history while addressing xenophobia, racial typecasting, and social and economic changes in a post-Soviet space. Starting from the stereotypes these actors faced throughout their careers, the play turns to the exploration of these stereotypes in their biographies. For example, for the artists with mixed ethnic backgrounds, migration creates more of a burden as they discover that they belong neither at home nor elsewhere. The inclusion of two migrant characters who come from within Russia problematizes the issues of identity, power, and labour throughout the whole post-Soviet space. For example, the ethnic Armenian Rafael is accused of both not living in his 'own' country and not knowing Armenian. The fact that his family has lived in Russia for longer than a century, and even his parents do not speak Armenian, does not seem to suit those who articulate such stereotypes.

Another layer for depicting the 'unsettlement' that the actors experienced is their family histories and some key moments of their biographies that do not necessarily deal with xenophobia and ethnicity-related stereotypes. By drawing attention to these moments, the play underlines that each story is unique and worth telling in its entirety, not limiting it to the boundaries of a single group (ethnic, national, migrant, etc.). Therefore, in the play, the stereotypes that the actors faced in their professional lives become the cause for revisiting their biographies, traumas, and ways of coping with such adversities. Overcoming these stereotypes means finding one's own identity anew. By bringing these stories together and organizing them as a group discussion (the actors often ask each other questions), the play creates a space where difference is cherished, and, at the same time, empathy is provoked through this diversity. A poetic finale represents this process as never-ending, utopian, and complete only during brief moments of a sublime experience.

The representation of the 'migrant artist' in this play reflects the difficulties of adapting oneself to the turbulent processes within post-Soviet societies as both a person of non-Russian ethnic background and an actor. By discussing the migrant story as a story of personal (though shared) unsettlement, the play goes further in its reflections about what makes up the acting profession. Aziz's story about his autism, with which he has been recently diagnosed, occupies a significant role in this thinking. He suggests that acting was only natural to him because, through performances, he could finally act in the world he imagined. Therefore, acting may be regarded not only as a means of production for him (as he uses his mind, body, and acting skills for work) but also as a means of living his life more wholly. Actors become the face of migration not only because their professional success depends on their appearances but also because it implies the unending process of being different, being 'non-standard.'

Performance

Composed of acts of individual memory, the performance of *Non-Standard* creates a model of social memory not bound by an ethnic/national/migrant framework. It suggests possibilities for sharing experiences about being different, unsettled, and hurt. The cinematic optics provided both in Shamshad Abdullaev's poems, slow motions of the performers who play table tennis without a ball (a reference to *Blow-Up*), and their video portraits demonstrated on the screens, mediates the stories told by the witnesses (as they 'play' table tennis while retelling them). While Abdullaev uses cinematic optics to transform a 'shapeless' space of Fergana Valley to spaces renowned in world culture—and to let them be inhabited by this space (Korchagin 2014), Patlay uses such an optics to problematize verbatim stories as a means of immediate access to migrant experience. This experience is presented as always-already eluded (like a migrant artist identity), affected (as it is involved in power relations), and mediated (by artistic method).

Conclusion

All three cases analysed in this chapter demonstrate precarity of labour and migration in contemporary Russian theatre. The participants of *Aqyn-Opera* were not able to proceed with their careers in their home countries and had to move to Moscow and change their occupation; even after their return on stage in Teatr.doc, they found themselves in the position shared by so many artists working in independent theatres who find theatre labour to rarely be a sufficient source of income. The Ayan theatre emerged as a grassroots initiative with the participation of labour migrants from Kyrgyzstan who did not have a professional theatrical background; they later developed their initiative into a theatre studio that co-created the bilingual production *The Place of the Skull*, which was staged at the Moscow Youth Theatre. The participants of *Non-Standard* are professional actors who moved to Moscow from various places across the former USSR and pursued their careers; the controversy of the precarious labour of migrant artists was explored in this performance in relation to racial typecasting in Russian theatre and the film industry, and with regards to the issues of xenophobia, nationalism, and family history.

Our arguments are partly in line with the ideas of Onur Kömürcü-Nobrega, who explored how the artists' acts of remembrance counteract the neglect of migrant stories in the cultural landscape of the 'host country.' This is particularly true for *Aqyn-Opera*, which was the first performance in Russia where labour migrants testified to their experience. While *Aqyn-Opera* oscillates between individual memory and cultural memory and makes visible both the challenges of living in post-Soviet Moscow and the life of traditional Pamirian culture, the performance turned out not to be appreciated by a diasporic audience (until it was awarded the prestigious Golden Mask prize in 2014), and the participants were not able to fully resume their acting careers. At the same time, *The Place of the Skull*, which was welcomed by the Kyrgyz community, ignores the individual memories and migrant background of its Kyrgyz participants. References to ethnic Kyrgyz heritage are framed by current Russian patriotic narratives about the great past which shades the tragic contents of the novel as well as the fact that the USSR has collapsed. Nevertheless, the performance is important for Kyrgyz actors in terms of a change of status (from labour migrants to artists) and gives them a chance to perform as someone other than migrants.

Herein, a set of problematic questions arises. While Russian independent/experimental theatre is clearly more responsive to the issue of migration and the artists with a migrant background, what kind of stories are expected from them? Should these stories be about their migration experiences only, as Russian documentary theatre tended to be focused on the experience of particular social groups (Beumers and Lipovetsky 2009, 227)? Is it possible to give a voice to these artists without limiting their experience to a migrant one, but not avoiding it? *Non-Standard* seems to refer to these concerns, as it gives a voice to actors with a migrant background and does not limit their stories to it. Their performance explores the very idea of being a migrant artist in a post-Soviet context.

Overall, these cases demonstrate that the precarity of migrant labour in today's Russia goes hand-in-hand with the precarity of artistic labour on its stage.

References

Ahmed, Sara. 2004. *The Cultural Politics of Emotion*. New York: Routledge.
Aizman, Ania. 2014. 'Documenting Migrant Labour in Moscow's Teatr.doc.' *Maska*, 30(172–174): 116–125.
Beumers, Birgit, and Mark Lipovetsky. 2009. *Performing Violence: Literary and Theatrical Experiments of New Russian Drama*. Bristol: Intellect.
Flynn, Molly. 2016. 'Show Us Your Papers: Performing Post-Soviet National Identity in Talgat Batalov's Uzbek.' *Problems of Post-Communism* 63(1): 16–26.
Kömürcü-Nobrega, Onur. 2014. 'Postmigrant Theatre and Cultural Diversity in the Arts: Race, Precarity and Artistic Labour in Berlin.' PhD diss., Goldsmiths, University of London.
Korchagin, Kirill. 2014. 'Prostranstvo i vremya ferganskogo filma (O poezii Shamshada Abdullayeva).' *Noviy mir*, 5: 184–189.
Malakhov, Vladimir S. 2014. 'Russia as a New Immigration Country: Policy Response and Public Debate.' *Europe-Asia Studies*, 66(7): 1062–1079.
Mukomel, Vladimir I. 2005. *Migratsionnaya politika Rossii. Postsovetskiye konteksty*. Moscow: Dipol-T.
Reeves, Madeleine. 2013. 'Clean Fake: Authenticating Documents and Persons in Migrant Moscow.' *American Ethnologist*, 40(3): 508–524.

Simon, Mark. 2020. 'Staging Urban Diversity: Migrants on Theatrical Stages in Berlin and Moscow.' *Laboratorium: Russian Review of Social Research*, 12(1): 15–47.

———. 2021. 'Why Manizha's 2021 Eurovision Entry Touched a Raw Nerve in Russia.' *ZOiS Spotlight*, May 12, 2021. Accessed May 28, 2021. https://en.zois-berlin.de/publications/why-manizhas-2021-eurovision-entry-touched-a-raw-nerve-in-russia.

CHAPTER 28

Chicano Theatre and (Im)migration: *La víctima*

Jorge A. Huerta

The focus of this chapter is on the development of two bilingual (Spanish-English) docu-dramas that deal specifically with (im)migration: *Guadalupe* and *La víctima* (The Victim), created by members of the Chicano theatre troupe, *El Teatro de la Esperanza* (The Theatre of Hope) in Santa Barbara, California in 1974 and 1976, respectively. I focus on these two plays to illustrate the importance of theatre that educates the public about the history and impact of (im)migration within Mexican and Mexican-American or Chicano communities. Both *Guadalupe* and *La víctima* have been performed by Latinx theatre companies as well as colleges and universities over the decades. In fact, proving the play's lasting significance, *La víctima* was produced in 2019 in Los Angeles, California, inspired, in part, by the man who launched his presidential campaign by declaring that Mexicans were rapists, thieves and drug dealers and vowing to build a wall across the US-Mexico border. I return to these two plays in order to unpack the state of Chicano theatre in California during the mid-1970s, when the study and development of Chicano theatre was just beginning to be acknowledged by a handful of theatre departments in the Academy.

The theme of migration between Mexico and the US has been a constant in popular culture by Mexicans and Mexican-Americans for generations. In 1848, when the Treaty of Guadalupe Hidalgo was ratified, the Mexicans, mestizos, African and indigenous populations suddenly became foreigners in their own lands. The geographical and culture clash(es) that were exacerbated by Manifest Destiny gave the Anglo colonizers the right to invade the lands and marginalize

J. A. Huerta (✉)
University of California, San Diego, La Jolla, CA, USA
e-mail: jhuerta@ucsd.edu

© The Author(s), under exclusive license to Springer Nature Switzerland AG 2023
Y. Meerzon, S. E. Wilmer (eds.), *The Palgrave Handbook of Theatre and Migration*, https://doi.org/10.1007/978-3-031-20196-7_28

the people who had lived in these territories for centuries. This sense of internal colonization and displacement led to the historical moment and the sociopolitical climate that this chapter explores.

The period under consideration begins in the mid-1960s, when Mexican-American high school students began to organize and fight for their rights, rebelliously self-identifying as Chicanas (female) and Chicanos (male), in a blatant rejection of the hyphen in Mexican-American. These social protest efforts mirrored the Civil Rights Movement and were also inspired by the late Cesar Chavez and Dolores Huerta, struggling to establish a farmworkers' union in California. The students' anger and frustration led to school walkouts calling for better schools that included their history, not his/story and demanding access to higher education. The war in Vietnam was also an urgent issue as thousands of Chicanos and Puerto Ricans were being drafted and killed or injured in numbers exceeding their percentage of the US population. This was the beginning of what would be called the Chicano Movement.

HISTORICAL, GEOGRAPHICAL AND CULTURAL CONTEXT

It was during this period that Chicano high school and university students formed a national coalition called MEChA, acronym for *El Movimiento Estudiantíl Chicano de Aztlán* (Chicano Student Movement of *Aztlán*). *Aztlán* is the Aztecs' (*Nahuatl*) term for their ancestral lands to the north, leading Chicanos to adopt the identifier to indicate the Southwest and beyond. In 1968 I was a high school drama teacher when I first witnessed the Teatro Campesino, an event that changed my life. Eager to know more about this troupe and the history of Chicano theatre, I enrolled in the Doctoral programme in Dramatic Art at the University of California, Santa Barbara (UCSB) in 1970. My wife, our two toddlers and I arrived to UCSB and a baptism by fire; we were immersed in the Revolution on August 29, 1970, when we joined with students, staff and faculty from UCSB to attend the Chicano Moratorium on the War in Vietnam in East Los Angeles. Tens of thousands of people from all corners of the country marched, chanting slogans and waving posters that read 'Hell no! We Won't go!' and '*Raza sí, Guerra no!*' (People yes! the war no!). It was a peaceful demonstration until we saw busloads of Los Angeles County Sheriffs arriving in full riot gear. We jumped into a passing stranger's car and escaped before the officers started a police riot, shooting teargas into the crowd. Three people were killed, including Ruben Salazar, a *Los Angeles Times* reporter. The event echoed the historic farmworkers' march of 1966 when union strikers travelled 360 miles from Delano to Sacramento, the capitol of California. The marchers were encouraged and motivated by the Teatro Campesino's performances and protest songs every evening. Unfortunately, teatro performances at the Moratorium were cancelled when the violence broke out but that did not dissuade the members of the teatros across the country to continue in their quest for social justice through street theatre.

Theatrical Practices Related to Migration in the Historical Period and Geography

This discussion of Chicano theatre begins with Luis Valdez and the Teatro Campesino. Born in 1940 in a migrant farm labour camp in Delano, California, Valdez earned a scholarship to San Jose State College, where he saw his first full-length play, *The Shrunken Head of Pancho Villa* produced in 1964. After graduating he worked with the San Francisco Mime Troupe and returned to Delano in 1965, hoping to form a farmworkers' theatre. With Chavez and Huerta's blessings, he gathered a group of farmworkers and persuaded them to demonstrate events that had happened on the picket lines. They were armed with masks and signs that indicated who each character represented, such as '*Campesino*' (farmworker), '*Esquirol*' (scab or strike-breaker), '*Coyote*' (farm labour contractor) and '*Patrón*' (Boss). When he placed a pig face mask on the worker portraying the Boss, the others laughed enthusiastically. As Valdez stated, 'We use comedy because it stems from a necessary situation—the necessity of lifting the morale of our strikers. ... This leads us into satire and the underlying tragedy of it all—the fact that human beings have been wasted in farm labor for generations' (Bagby 1967, 77). The group created what Valdez would call '*actos*,' short satirical sketches that they would perform on the picket lines at the edges of the fields, under the watchful eyes of the wealthy growers' hired guns.

Most importantly, the *actos* were created collectively, through improvisations that pitted the humble *Campesino* against the greedy and despised growers and their henchmen. The *actos* were modern morality plays, allegories of Good versus Evil. Valdez became the director and playwright for this raggletaggle troupe and the Teatro Campesino was born. Within a matter of months, they broadened their reach, performing at universities, union halls and community centres, bringing the Cause to the general public and earning revenue for the Union. The year, 1965, was the beginning of the 'Great Grape Boycott,' a movement that reached across the country and abroad. The *actos* were simple but not simplistic, clearly showing how the public could support the Union by boycotting table grapes.

By 1967 Valdez and the Teatro left the Union in order to focus on their theatre. In those formative years Valdez described the Teatro as 'somewhere between Brecht and Cantinflas' (Bagby 1967, 77). Valdez had studied Brecht's aesthetics and politics and he was well aware of the physical humour of the popular Mexican stage and film character, Cantinflas, an iconic underdog similar to Charlie Chaplin's Little Tramp. The *actos* combined these elements, along with protest songs that gave the striking farmworkers and enthusiastic audiences a sense of purpose and hope. The Teatro expanded their repertoire to include issues that spoke to urban problems, including worker's rights, education, police brutality, injustice on the streets and in the courts and the war in Vietnam. Wherever the Teatro Campesino performed, especially on college campuses, enthusiastic students were inspired to form their own teatros. Aware that these groups could use some guidance, Valdez and his Teatro hosted the first Chicano Theatre Festival in their storefront theatre in Fresno, California in 1970 and the Chicano Theatre Movement was born.

What made the early Chicano Theatre Movement unique was the fact that the people who were forming their own teatros did not have an aesthetic framework upon which to base their theatrical efforts. In relation to theatre training, with the exception of a few individuals, there was little or no access to 'the means of production,' to apply a Marxist dictum to formal theatrical facilities and training. Chicanas and Chicanos, by virtue of their working-class, marginalized subjectivity were not usually exposed to theatre and certainly not to Chicano theatre beyond the Teatro Campesino. The majority of these students were the first to attend college and had no intention of going into the theatre as a profession. UC Santa Barbara was unique in that a Chicano doctoral student was teaching a workshop in Chicano theatre in a Department of Dramatic Art.

I taught my first Chicano theatre workshop during my first semester at UCSB. We discovered that a majority of the students in the class had been advised by their high school counsellors or teachers not to go to college, so I asked them to improvise scenarios I termed 'The High School Counsellor.' As in any improvisation, the characters have distinct objectives: the Chicana wants to apply to college and the Counsellor or Teacher can only picture her as a wife, homemaker and mother. As for the male students, the idea of a Chicano aspiring to college was so remote that the counsellor or teacher could only offer: 'You people work well with your hands,' or 'what about the military; don't you want to serve your country?' These brief improvisations were not realistic; the villain was an exaggerated buffoon, allowing the students to laugh at this grotesque reality.

Aside from teaching, I would work with the members of the campus's Teatro Mecha creating short pieces that the students created collectively or individually, which we would perform for campus rallies. However, by the end of that academic year the campus Mecha organization split into two factions. The newly formed student organization, called *La Raza Libre* (The Free People), became a part of a new community centre in Santa Barbara's *barrio* (Mexican community) called *La Casa de la Raza* (The House of the People). I and six undergraduates left Mecha and joined with La Raza Libre to become the cultural arm of La Casa de la Raza. We named our newly liberated troupe *El Teatro de la Esperanza* (The Theatre of Hope).

In 1971 *Teatro de la Esperanza* performed at the Second Chicano Theatre Festival and invited representatives of the other teatros to meet at UCSB that spring. Under Valdez's guidance a national coalition of Chicano theatres was born, called *El Teatro Nacional de Aztlán* (The National Theatre of Aztlán), or by its acronym, *TENAZ*, which means tenacious in Spanish. In support of these new coalition-building efforts the Teatro Campesino offered their newly published actos to any teatro who wanted to produce them, royalty-free. Sadly, all of those actos are as relevant today as they were in the 1960s and one of the most popular actos is *Los vendidos* (The Sellouts), which ridicules Mexican-Americans who deny their heritage; an important theme in the two docu-dramas discussed below.

GUADALUPE: THE FIRST DOCU-DRAMA ABOUT MEXICAN IMMIGRANTS

Working on campus and at *la Casa*, I and my wife, Ginger, guided members of the Teatro de la Esperanza in the troupe's aesthetic, musical and political growth. By the fall of 1973 we had a core group of six serious undergraduates and one graduate student who had coalesced into the collective that would create one of the hallmarks of early Chicano theatre, *Guadalupe*, named for the town of Guadalupe. The practical knowledge that the theatre majors in the group had acquired during their studies was important, as were the knowledge and hands-on experience acquired through TENAZ festivals and workshops with world-renowned directors, playwrights and collectives from the US, Mexico and Latin America. We were greatly influenced by the movement termed Theology of Liberation, active in Latin and Central America, which became an important touchstone for our emerging political awareness. These experiences informed our path towards a theatrical statement that would be about immigrant Mexicans and Chicana/os in the US.

In actuality, we did not look for the town of Guadalupe; Guadalupe came to us when the Teatro members were asked to sing protest songs during a demonstration at the Santa Barbara County Courthouse in early 1974. Based on actual incidents in 1972–1973, *Guadalupe* revolves around a group of Mexican farmworkers and their (US born) children in the town, an hour's drive from campus. In this agricultural town of about 1000 inhabitants, the schools were not serving the majority Mexican and Chicano students with respect, punishing them for speaking Spanish, offering no bilingual education and offering no Spanish-speaking teachers. When a Parents' Committee was formed, the local powers fought their efforts, to the point of arresting three of the parents who had organized a protest against the school board. The US Commission on Civil Rights investigated the situation and published a scathing report titled 'The Schools of Guadalupe: A Legacy of Educational Oppression.' The Teatro members had found the subject matter for the production that would introduce the docu-drama to Chicano theatre.

We gathered material for the play in a kind of ethnographic theatre, visiting the town several times, interviewing the parents and others who had been affected by the neglect and/or abuse of the power brokers. The town of Guadalupe was a microcosm of all of the problems Mexicans and Chicana/os face in the broader society, including political corruption, police brutality, drug and alcohol abuse as well as overt scare tactics to keep the farmworkers from organizing. We attended mass at the Roman Catholic parish to hear what the priest, a Spanish missionary, had to say. Aware that we were in his church, he admonished his congregants: '¡*Vds. que siguien a Cesar Chavez irán directatamente al infierno!*' ('Those of you who follow Cesar Chavez will go directly to Hell!') (Huerta 1977, 238).

Another person we were told about was a Mexican-American used car salesman who personified a *vendido* (sell-out), so the play begins when the actor playing this character runs onto the stage shouting for guards to be placed at the doors. His first lines clearly identify him: 'My name is Marcos Cortez and I've come here to talk about the truth behind the Chicano Movement.' After vilifying the Parents' Committee, Cortez states: 'This type of action ... makes me ashamed to call myself Spanish' (Huerta 1977, 218). Throughout his diatribe, actors are shouting at him from the audience, mocking him. By calling himself 'Spanish,' he reflects those Mexican-Americans who deny their Mexican heritage believing it is preferable to be European. This emotional scene introduces the members of the Parents Committee as they exchange insults with Cortez. The debate ends with shouts of '*Viva Cesar Chavez*!' Suddenly a drumbeat stops the action, everybody freezes and an actor, still in the audience, addresses the audience in Spanish. Her lines are repeated in English by the actor playing Cortez: 'This parent-teacher meeting took place on February 16, 1972 in Guadalupe, California. The following events led up to this meeting' (Huerta 1977, 219). The actors then sing a popular Mexican *corrido* with the lyrics changed to introduce the town of Guadalupe. The re-writing of the lyrics to a well-known *corrido* becomes a kind of Brechtian *verfremdungseffekt or* distancing, listening to something unfamiliar in a familiar context.

In thirteen scenes framed by choral transitions, the Teatro told the story of a community under siege. We knew that this play would tour to mostly non-theatre venues and thus it was simply staged on an empty space framed by benches or chairs where the actors sat, watching the unfolding story as they prepared to play the various roles. The transitions were often physical transformations. For example, the brief scene in the church begins with the parents on their knees in Mass while the priest spews his rhetoric. The actors, still on their knees, turn around and transition to their labour in fields, as the musical narrative continues.

Most importantly the play reflected the fact that women were very strong leaders in the Parent's committee. The play premiered on Cinco de Mayo of 1974 at the University of California, San Diego in a lecture hall. After a successful tour of Southern California and the provinces of Mexico with *Guadalupe*, it was time for my wife and me to step aside. I took a position in the Theatre Department at the University of California, San Diego, eager to continue directing, researching and writing about a movement in motion. We were confident that the Esperanza members would continue to create exciting and necessary theatre.

LA VÍCTIMA RESPONDS TO THE CYCLE OF MASS DEPORTATIONS OF MEXICANS

It is no great revelation that a capitalist economy has always depended on a cheap pool of labour. However, when the US economy crashed in 1929, the government chose to repatriate Mexicans. Two generations later, in the mid-1970s, the US economy was in trouble and again the government blamed Mexicans, deporting them to Mexico by the tens of thousands. The Teatro members saw this as an urgent story to expose, bringing the events of the past face-to-face with the present. In the words of Mark S. Weinberg, 'The company had begun to explore a more clearly defined Marxist analysis of history and was developing a class consciousness, that, while recognizing the uniqueness of Chicano culture was also cognizant of the exemplary nature of the Chicano working experience' (Weinberg 1992, 73–74). Weinberg then quotes one of the founders of the teatro, the late José Guadalupe Saucedo, who told me, 'We're trying to show the Chicanos and Mexicans in this country that they are scapegoats for capitalism' (Huerta 1977, 44).

By 1975, the teatro members were ready to collectively create and direct their own docu-drama titled *La víctima* (The Victim). In this piece they created a fictitious account of a Mexican family caught in the throes of three major events: the Mexican revolution of 1910–1920, the Mass Deportations of the 1930s and culminating in the mass deportations in the late 1970s. The family was fictitious, but the motivating events were factual. Because the teatro members would be generating income by touring this production, they kept the same minimalist style as in *Guadalupe*. The playing area is an empty space framed by benches stage left and right. Downstage, framing the acting area are two easels with placards that announce the title of each scene. The first placards announce the title of the play. The nine actors remain onstage throughout the production, sitting on the sidelines, watching the action and changing minimal costume or prop accessories while a new scene unfolds and an actor stands next to the placard to recite the narrative quote.

There are many victims in the play but the focus is on the lives and losses of Amparo and her son Sammy, who is separated from her as they are boarding the train back to Mexico. He is adopted by another Mexican family and grows up to become an Immigration and Naturalization System (INS) agent. The actors relate this sequence of events in fifteen scenes, each scene introduced by a *corrido*. With the exception of the actor playing Sammy, the other eight actors play multiple roles, adding to the theatricality of the piece. The characters are all real people, and the actors must give each character his or her unique persona. To give the reader a sense of how the play functions in a Brechtian, transformational style I will discuss the first few scenes.

Setting the narrative tone, the play begins with the following Prologue recited by an actor: 'The Chicano is a victim of a subtle and complex form of oppression which differs from traditional forms yet results in same end: The exploitation of one group for the benefit of another.' After reciting the narrative, the actor reveals a placard that reads: 'Northern Mexico late night 1915. The mass migration' (Huerta 1977, 326). While this placard indicates the time, place and action, it is underscored by a *corrido* informing the audience that the Mexican Revolution is forcing thousands of Mexicans to flee to the north, looking for a better life and to escape the violence of the Revolution.

As the *corrido* is sung, four actors cross to centre stage: Amparo as a young girl, her older brother and their parents, ostensibly sitting at the side of the railroad tracks. We don't yet know that this will be Amparo's story but the mood of the scene clearly establishes the pathos that will ensue. Because this scene takes place in Mexico, the characters speak Spanish, establishing why the family is leaving. Most importantly, the father is adamant that this move is only temporary; he believes the Revolution will end soon and they will return to their *ranchito* (little ranch) in their beloved homeland. The train, indicated by a whistle blow, arrives, and the actors rush to the sidelines, as if to board the train, to prepare for the next scene.

The next *corrido* relates how the family settled in the city and found jobs. The lyrics also tell the audience that Amparo, now a young woman, is about to meet her future husband, Julian. The Narrator recites: 'Los Angeles, 1922. During the 1921 economic crisis the Mexican national became the scapegoat for the failures of the American economy. Mexican workers bore the burden through deportations, establishing a pattern which continues to this day' (Huerta 1977, 327). The placard reads: 'The first deportation.' Humour has always been an important element in Chicana/o theatre, and after the scene in Mexico, we are immersed in the contradictions of a new life for Mexicans in the US. The following scene takes place in a dance hall, where we find Amparo, her friend, Lupita, her father and two young Mexican men eager to meet the girls. It is a classic scene, made humorous when the girls speak in *Spanglish* (a term that identifies the Chican/ao as bilingual). Amparo runs into the scene and yells, 'Lupita, Lupita, hurry, hurry!' Lupita responds, '¿*Que*, Amparo, what happened?' Amparo replies, '*Es que me quiero ver bien* gut, *pa' cuando venga* you know who' ('I want to look really good for when you-know-who arrives') (Huerta 1977, 328). The scene gives the necessary exposition about the growing loss of jobs for Mexicans and prepares us for Amparo and Julian's marriage. As foretold by the placard, the scene ends when INS officers raid the dance. The next *corrido* tells us that Amparo married Julian and now has a young son named Sammy.

The placard for the following scene reads: 'Los Angeles. Amparo's home.' The narrator states: 'At the height of the Depression the American labour force suffered a 25% unemployment rate. For the Chicano worker, the unemployment rate rose to a staggering 80%. The placard reads: The Depression, 1930s' (Huerta 1977, p. 338). We now find Amparo, pregnant, talking with Sammy, who is upset because his best friend's family has returned to Mexico. Amparo consoles Sammy by singing a Mexican lullaby that her mother would sing to her, assuring her that she would always be with her daughter, even when separated. This poignant lullaby presages the next scene as well as the final moments of the play. Julian comes home and announces that he has been laid-off and that they have to take advantage of the free passage back to the Homeland.

The following scene is brief but hits at the core of the (im)migration problem: the separation of families. The Narrator states, 'Train station. Los Angeles. In 1932 during his election campaign, incumbent President Hoover promises to rid the country of Mexicans' (Huerta 1977, 336). The placard reads, 'The Repatriation 1935.' In this riveting and emotional scene, Amparo is separated from Sammy at the train station. Holding her baby girl in her arms she screams for her boy, '*Mi'jo!*' (my son) who is on the other side of the stage, looking for her and screaming '*Mamá!*' (Huerta 1977, 336). Freeze. Sound of a train. A guitar strums and another *corrido* informs us that fifteen years have passed and Amparo has never forgotten the horror of being separated from her son. The lyrics also tell us that Sammy was adopted and loved by the Mendozas and that he is now a young man. The Narrator states: 'Los Angeles, Clara's family porch. Emerging from WWII as one of the most decorated of ethnic groups, the Mexican-American mistakenly considered himself to be a full-fledged American. Consequently, young Chicanos enlisted for the Korean War believing it to be a way out of the barrio, and an avenue for social mobility.' The placard reads: 'The first Mexican-American' (Huerta 1977, 337).

The play follows the same structural pattern, with placards and quotes that set the tone. As the plot unfolds, we find that Sammy and Clara are becoming acculturated as Mexican-Americans. The action moves between Los Angeles, Korea and Mexico; the thematic threads intertwined between languages, cultures and aspirations. The next scene focuses on correspondence between Clara and Sam who is in Korea where he learns 'to kill the communists!' The action then returns to Mexico where we meet Amparo as a mature woman and learn that her husband, Julian, is ill and that their *ranchito* is not producing crops. Antonia, who was a baby when they were deported and lost Sammy, lives in the US and has returned to persuade her parents to move back to the US. But Amparo adamantly refuses, declaring that she will never return to the country that separated her from her son, Sammy. The youngest son, Meño, wants to move to the US with Antonia and their parents finally agree to let him join her in order to send more money home.

The remaining scenes split the action between distinct locations as we learn that Antonia and Meño are working in a factory where the workers are planning to strike. She is in favour of unionizing; Meño, who is undocumented, is opposed. Meanwhile, we discover that Sammy is being promoted as an INS field officer, conducting immigration raids. His conscience is shaken when his college-age daughter, who calls herself a Chicana, questions what he does for a living while Clara defends Sammy. The crises pile-up when Julian dies and Antonia returns to Mexico to bring Amparo back across the border. Later, we're now in Los Angeles and find Antonia, and Meño arguing about the strike. Amparo tells them the poor are poor because they don't unite against the rich, motivating them to go to the picket line. Amparo follows them, only to find the INS agents led by Sammy, rounding everybody up, including 'the old lady' who, we can tell, instinctively recognizes her long-lost son.

In the penultimate scene, we find Sammy interrogating Amparo. He knows that she realizes he is her son but when she brings this truth to the fore he shouts in Spanish '¡Sáquenla!' ('Get her out!') (Huerta 1977, 362). In the next and final scene the Narrator recites, 'Mendoza's home. Los Angeles. The individual who chooses to take part in the dehumanizing of others inevitably begins the process of his own dehumanization.' The Placard reads, 'The Victim' (Huerta 1977, 363). Sammy is in bed with Clara and awakens from a nightmare. He tells her that he thinks 'the old lady' was his mother but Clara tries to persuade him that she wasn't. Sobbing in his wife's arms he repeats 'She's not my mother!' trying to appease his guilt. Opposite, Amparo appears and sings the lullaby she sang to him as a little boy a generation ago. He sees her and shouts 'I hate you! I hate you!' (Huerta 1977, 365). Freeze, music begins and the ensemble gathers to sing a rousing *corrido* of liberation. After a successful premier at the University of California, San Diego in 1976, the production toured the US, and performed in Poland, Yugoslavia and Sweden. The play has been performed across the country and abroad several times over the decades.

* * *

When *The Victim* was produced in 2019, Trump was still in office, spewing his xenophobic tropes, while migrant children were being taken from their parents and placed in what looked like cages. Given the graphic imagery and the repetition of history, José Luís Valenzuela knew it was time to re-visit *The Victim*. Mexican-born, Valenzuela is the Founding Artistic Director of the Latino Theatre Company in Los Angeles, and Distinguished Professor of Theatre, *Emeritus* at UCLA. Valenzuela knows the play well, having produced it with his professional company in 1997 and 2010. He expanded the cast to sixteen undergraduate students from East Los Angeles Community College and UCLA, giving more students an opportunity to participate in this production. The premier was staged in the Los Angeles Theatre Centre, followed by a tour to schools and colleges throughout southern California. In the words of Gad Guterman, 'The play thus offers a most compelling case against an immigration system that often hinders reunification' (Guterman 2014, 107) This statement confirms the argument that *The Victim* is a testament to the Chicanos' commitment to the very urgent and continuing cause of reforming an immigration system that continues to separate families. The play transformed the lives of the students, many of whom became activists. Valenzuela told me, 'Everywhere we went it was the first time the students had seen anything like this. *The Victim* is one of the masterpieces of the American theatre that will live forever.' And it has.

REFERENCES

Bagby, Beth. 1967. 'El Teatro Campesino: Interviews with Luis Valdez.' *Tulane Drama Review*, 11, 70-80.

Guterman, Gad. 2014. *Performance, Identity, and Immigration Law: A Theatre of Undocumentedness*. London: Palgrave Macmillan.

Huerta, Jorge A. 1977. 'El Teatro de la Esperanza: Keeping in Touch With the People.' *The Drama Review*, 21 (1), 37-46.

Teatro de la Esperanza. 1989a. 'Guadalupe.' In *Necessary Theatre: Six Plays About the Chicano Experience* edited by Jorge A. Huerta, 208-257. Houston: Arte Público.

———. 1989b. *La víctima*. In *Necessary Theatre: Six Plays About the Chicano Experience* edited by Jorge A. Huerta, 316-365. Houston: Arte Público.

Weinberg, Mark S. 1992. *Challenging the Hierarchy: Collective Theatre in the United States*. Westport: Greenwood.

CHAPTER 29

Staging War at the Home Depot: Yoshua Okón's *Octopus* and the Shadow Economy of Migrant Labour

Natalie Álvarez and Jimena Ortúzar

On a typical day in Los Angeles, California, undocumented day labourers of Indigenous Maya from Guatemala wait in the parking lots of box stores like Home Depot for employers to come by with offers of by-the-hour construction jobs for below market rates of pay. As contractors, landscapers, and homeowners arrive, the day workers jostle with other undocumented migrants from Mexico and Central America for job opportunities, negotiating wages on the spot and hoping that employers honour them at the end of the day. In Yoshua Okón's 2011 *Octopus*, however, Mayan day workers engage in a different kind of labour by activating a Home Depot parking lot to stage a reenactment of their experiences fighting in Guatemala's Civil War (1960–1996). A bright orange shopping cart becomes a surveillance vehicle; the workers body-roll along the asphalt dodging imaginary gunfire and take cover in mounds of grass; others lie still, arms and legs splayed, as casualties of war. Shoppers pass by this scene unfazed, sauntering to their parked cars without noticing the action unfolding around them. For them, it is a typical day in Los Angeles where migrant labour is always already invisible.

N. Álvarez (✉)
Toronto Metropolitan University, Toronto, ON, Canada
e-mail: natalie.alvarez@torontomu.ca

J. Ortúzar
York University, Toronto, Canada
e-mail: jimena@nyu.edu

© The Author(s), under exclusive license to Springer Nature Switzerland AG 2023
Y. Meerzon, S. E. Wilmer (eds.), *The Palgrave Handbook of Theatre and Migration*, https://doi.org/10.1007/978-3-031-20196-7_29

More than a decade earlier, on a day that was anything but typical in Guatemala City, survivors of Guatemala's Civil War gathered inside the National Theatre to hear the results of a United Nations truth commission, which concluded that the US-backed Guatemalan military had committed genocide against the Mayan population during the country's 36-year civil war. Although the terror waged against Mayan peoples was widely known, this occasion was the first time an internationally supported body held the Guatemalan government and its military allies responsible for the bloodshed. Those inside the theatre erupted in tears and chants of '¡Justicia!' as the report's conclusions were read (Navarro 1999). Outside the theatre, Mayan women held signs showing the massacres committed against their communities. Shortly after this event, former US president Bill Clinton gave an official apology expressing regret for the role the US played in the brutal anti-guerrilla campaign that caused the deaths of thousands of civilians.

By transplanting scenes from Guatemala's Civil War onto a commercial parking lot in Los Angeles, *Octopus* reappropriates the tradition of war reenactments in the US to tell the unfinished history of US foreign policy in Latin America and the story of 'the war' that is, as Okón insists, 'not over' for Mayans facing the pervasive violence against immigrants in the US (quoted in Hernandez 2011). Documented on video and presented in gallery installations and virtual exhibits, *Octopus* invites an examination of reenactment as a record of undocumented lives produced by US intervention in Guatemala and relegated to a shadow economy where they circulate unseen to the benefit of citizen-consumers and the US economy at large. By placing spectators in the curious position of seeing their fellow citizen-consumers *not see* as migrant workers turn a Home Depot parking lot into a theatre of war, *Octopus* reveals something fundamental about viewers' own entanglements as the beneficiaries of this shadow system that relies on an exchange economy of visibility and invisibility, seeing and not seeing.

The Tentacles of US Intervention

Guatemala's Civil War was one of the longest and most brutal armed conflicts in Central America, which killed an estimated 200,000 people. Among those killed or disappeared were entire Mayan communities seen as allies of leftist guerrillas fighting to overthrow the ruling military junta. Hundreds of villages were attacked and burned, their inhabitants tortured and slaughtered. The Commission for Historical Clarification, which was set up as part of the peace accord that ended the war in 1996, confirmed that the US government had supported the war by providing both funding and training to the Guatemalan military. According to the commission's report, US training in counterinsurgency tactics 'had a significant bearing on the human rights violations during the armed confrontation' (1999, 19). Even more disturbing was evidence that the US had known of the genocide at the hands of the Guatemalan military and yet continued its support.

US involvement in Guatemala began well before the civil war when the Central Intelligence Agency (CIA) orchestrated a *coup d'état* in 1954 to oust the popular and democratically elected president Jacobo Árbenz Guzmán.

Árbenz was responsible for agrarian reforms that redistributed land to the rural poor, which in turn affected the largest landowner in Guatemala: the United Fruit Company. The multinational corporation (now called Chiquita Brands) was also Guatemala's largest employer and controlled the country's railroads and ports, its power largely the result of concession-laden contracts with previous regimes (Castañeda 2014, 3). It was thus known among Guatemalans as *el pulpo* (the octopus), 'a hateful and insatiable octopus' whose tentacles were everywhere sucking the sweat and blood of the people (Árbenz qtd in Castañeda 2014, 3). In response to land reforms, United Fruit urged Washington to intervene and waged an anti-Árbenz campaign painting the government as a communist threat, a highly effective move amid the Cold War when hostility to US companies was seen as a sign of communist infiltration (Schlesinger and Kinzer 1983, 78–90). (Curiously, the Americans themselves were invoking the figure of the octopus in their references to communism.) Many Guatemalans saw the coup largely as a result of United Fruit's anger towards the Árbenz administration (Castañeda 2014, 3). A succession of US-backed military regimes and ongoing support for counterinsurgency operations ensured that the country would remain an 'archaic and unjust socioeconomic structure' (Tomuschat 1999) in which US multinationals like United Fruit could continue to grow, further extending their tentacles to profit from cheap labour and unlimited resources.

By taking the moniker 'Octopus' for the title of a reenactment of the Guatemalan Civil War on US soil, Okón draws attention to United Fruit Company's role in the coup as well as the close link between corporate interests and government policy (every US policy maker involved in the decision to topple the Guatemalan government had family or business ties to United Fruit Company). This connection is by no means exclusive to Guatemala; it is at the core of US foreign policy, which is 'designed to create and maintain an international order in which US-based businesses can prosper' and a world of 'societies open to profitable investment, to expansion of material and human resources on the part of US corporations and their local affiliates' (Chomsky 1999, 6–7). By the 1980s, Guatemala's neighbours had become targets of US intervention in Central America, which left 80,000 dead during the Salvadoran civil war when the US trained and funded right-wing death squads; 50,000 in the Contra war waged by the US against the Sandinista government in Nicaragua; and thousands kidnapped and executed by security forces in Honduras and Panama. US destabilization in the region played a defining role in creating the political and economic conditions that exist in these countries today, precipitating the ongoing waves of migration to the US southern border.

Knowing that the US was not an innocent bystander to the war that ravaged Guatemala but rather a sponsor and mastermind of state terror that decimated the country's Indigenous populations changes the contextual circumstances in which *Octopus* takes place. It means the shoppers of Home Depot are not innocent bystanders to the war scene unfolding in its parking lot. As US citizens and consumers, they bear some responsibility for their government's actions, or at least some responsibility for holding their government accountable. The shoppers become, as curator Noor Alé suggests, the protagonists of this work just as much as the war survivors-turned-migrant workers they fail to see (2020). Their indifference to the Mayans reenacting their experiences of war becomes the subject of *Octopus*, which symbolically performs the US's longstanding pretence of being just that, a bystander to the wars it helped create. It is this indifference that confronts the viewer watching from the gallery along with the inequality of relations conveyed by the stark contrast of Home Depot shoppers and undocumented day workers inhabiting parallel realms in the same shared parking lot.

Pushed into the Shadows

The long civil war led to a significant rise in transnational migration beginning in the late 1970s and continuing in the post-war years as Guatemalans faced social violence and increasing inequality. Guatemalan Mayans, whose communities were devastated by war and poverty, fled their homeland and made their way to Mexico and the US. By 2010, the year before *Octopus* was staged, Guatemalans had become the fourth largest group of Latin American-born immigrants, driving a rapid growth in the US migrant population, which rose from less than one million in 1960 to roughly 19 million (Tienda and Sanchez 2013, 48). As in the case of Guatemala, the flows of migration from Latin America surged after 1970 when country after country experienced tumultuous revolutionary activity, authoritarian backlash, military coups, and brutal dictatorships often supported by the US government. This surge in migration coincided with a revival of day labour in the US as part of a larger process of informalization that began with the dismantling of internal labour markets and the weakening of employment protections in the early 1980s. Thus, as the US was increasing its military assistance to Guatemala under the Reagan administration, which in turn led to an increase in migration northwards, Americans were experiencing a revolution of neoliberal reforms at home, which impacted low-wage sectors of the economy. Contrary to the formalization of the US's reliance on migrant labour with the establishment of the Bracero Program, a 'guest worker' program in operation between 1942 and 1964 that drew largely upon Mexican men to fill short-term agricultural contracts, the informal or shadow economy in the US grew as a consequence of aggressive neoliberal restructuring that, in the name of labour market flexibility, rolled back government regulations, eroded labour protections, and undermined trade unionism (Theodore 2006, 253). Informalization enabled the incorporation of migrants into local labour markets with day labour emerging as an extreme form of labour market flexibility (Peck and Theodore 2012, 744; Theodore 2006, 251, 257).

Watching the Mayan workers combat crawl across the Home Depot parking lot, viewers are not only confronted with the violence of the past but also compelled to reckon with ongoing violence against migrants that condemns them to highly exploitative labour. If one of the consequences of US foreign policy in Guatemala was the mass migration of Mayans to the US, one of the consequences of US immigration policy was to push undocumented migrants into the shadow zones of the labour market. Immigration reforms in the 1980s and 1990s imposed sanctions on employers that knowingly hired undocumented workers and curtailed public assistance and government services, making migrants ever more dependent on shadow work and increasingly vulnerable to threats of deportation. Immigration enforcement surged in the late 1990s and gained momentum after 9/11 when immigration and counterterrorism policies were often conflated (Jonas 2013). The number of Guatemalans deported from the US increased from 1763 in 1995 to a record 30,313 in 2011 when *Octopus* was made (Jonas 2013). For these migrant workers waiting in parking lots morning after morning, the threat of deportation is real. As Okón relays, the performers in *Octopus* were 'more afraid of immigration than talking about the war' (quoted in Hernandez 2011). In this respect, the performance action Okón stages in the Home Depot parking lot is as much about the US as it is about the war they fled. 'The war is not over,' Okón maintains, 'the war is over there' in the US where Guatemalan Mayans are fighting daily for scraps of work while evading immigration raids (quoted in Hernandez 2011). Their reenactment, then, has a dual effect on the viewer: it reinscribes the Guatemalan Civil War into the history of the US and simultaneously establishes the US as the new war zone where Guatemalan Mayans remain brutally affected by state and market violence.

Rewriting the Narrative Through Reenactment

In transplanting the Guatemalan Civil War onto US soil, Okón irreverently draws on the tradition of American Civil War reenactments in which thousands of enthusiasts and hobbyist historians gather each year to stage sham battles with diligent attention to detail—a tradition that dates back to the time of the Civil War itself (1861–1865). As early as 1861, a year when over 4,000 men had been killed on the front-lines of the Civil War, groups of citizens gathered to simulate the conflicts unfolding on the battlefield (Eisenfeld 2015). The practice of Civil War reenactments was reinvigorated in the 1960s, animated by the war's centennial and efforts to keep the memory of the war alive as those who experienced it first-hand passed away (Schneider 2011, 8). In his engagement with non-actors, that is, Mayans who had themselves fought in the Guatemalan Civil War, Okón indirectly gestures to the early history of American Civil War reenactments in which war veterans, in the immediate wake of the war, were conscripted to participate in sham battles to commemorate the conflict in which they themselves had fought (Eisenfeld 2015). If the Civil War reenactment is driven by an 'effort to play one time in another' and 'keep the past alive' (Schneider 2011, 10), *Octopus* cheekily summons this animating force to domesticate the Guatemalan Civil War on US soil. By playing 'one time in another' and staging the ongoing present of the war Guatemalan Mayans continue to fight, the reenactment troubles the *out-of-sight, out-of-mind* quintessence of US foreign policy, which maintains its myth of innocence in relation to its military interventions in Latin America.

The palimpsest of the *Octopus* reenactment on the Home Depot parking lot gives the lie not only to the US myth of innocence but also to its immigration discourse and policies (such as Arizona Senate Bill 1070 and the ramped-up efforts of the US Immigration and Customs Enforcement or ICE under the Trump administration), which have criminalized the waves of undocumented immigrants that its military interventions across Latin America have produced. This is, according to Okón, one of the principal aims of *Octopus*: Okón observed that many of the conversations about undocumented workers in Los Angeles viewed the issue of migration as a domestic one, rarely turning to its root causes (Okón 2021). *Octopus*, then, opens up these wider geopolitical entanglements to view, shifting viewers' perspective from a bounded and bordered perspective of immigration to one that recognizes US foreign policy as the primary driver of the so-called 'migrant invasion,' a phrase Donald Trump used in reference to the 2018 *Viacrucis del Migrante* or migrant caravans composed of migrants from Guatemala, Honduras, Nicaragua, and El Salvador seeking asylum in the US.

While some Home Depot parking lots had previously become battlegrounds over the presence of migrant day labourers, attracting both anti-immigrant protests and support from city councillors and immigrant rights organizations (Greenhouse 2005), the parking-lot-as-battle ground in *Octopus* suggests that migrant labour has become normalized to such an extent that shoppers see neither the workers nor the battle they enact in full public view. For undocumented workers, remaining invisible is normally a matter of safety to avoid encounters with authorities that might result in detention or deportation. But their invisibility also suggests their presence is tolerated only insofar as they fill undesirable jobs at less-than-subsistence wages and remain excluded from the public sphere as rights-bearing members of society. In his push for immigration reform, former US president Barack Obama repeatedly referred to migrants from Mexico and Central America as the people who 'pick our fruit,' 'make our beds,' and 'mow our lawns' (Obama 2014a, b), thus reminding American citizens that, without immigrants, daily life would cease to function smoothly (this scenario was imagined in a 2004 mockumentary, *A Day Without a Mexican* by Sergio Arau, that shows just how quickly the lives of Californians descend into chaos when immigrants mysteriously disappear). Clearly, Obama intended for his audience to recognize the indispensable labour that migrants perform, but nowhere does he mention the role of the US government in creating the conditions that have forced thousands of people in Central America to migrate north. This missing history is precisely what Okón is inviting viewers to recognize in *Octopus*.

By bringing a historical and geopolitical dimension to the politics of immigration, Okón's *Octopus* in Los Angeles contributes to an extensive body of contemporary performance in California that stages actions (or, in the Latin American tradition, *acciones* of politico-aesthetic intervention in galleries and public spaces) designed to make visible an otherwise invisible migrant workforce—a performance genealogy that can be traced back to the interventions of Luis Valdez and El Teatro Campesino, a farm workers theatre troupe formed in 1965 in Delano, California. El Teatro Campesino toured migrant camps to inform labourers about their rights and galvanize them to join the efforts of civil rights activists Dolores Huerta and Cesar Chavez to unionize farm workers. Performing at sites where undocumented day labourers gather throughout the Los Angeles area, Teatro Jornalero Sin Fronteras (TJSF), or Day Labor Theater Without Borders has, since 2008, extended El Teatro Campesino's legacy by using theatre to educate migrant workers about their rights within hostile work environments and an increasingly anti-immigrant climate. *Secos y Mojados*, or the dry and wet ones, a name that refers to the clandestine movement of migrants across borders, is a San Francisco-based collective, comprised of transnational immigrants Violeta Luna, David Molina, and Roberto Varea, whose work integrates theatre, music, and performance art and draws on interviews with undocumented community members to find an expressive place for migrant experience in a 'more inclusive social imaginary' (Creative Capital). A desire for collaborative, participatory performance that activates border communities while calling attention to the plight of migrant workers undergirds the curatorial aims of the sprawling inSITE art event, which has featured public actions along the Tijuana/San Diego border since 1994 (Klein 2019, 181). The aims of the inSITE event can be seen as an outgrowth of prolific art-activist collectives in the Tijuana/San Diego region, such as The Border Arts Workshop/Taller de arte fronterizo (BAW/TAF), founded in 1985 by Guillermo Gómez-Peña, David Avalos, Emily Hicks, and Michael Schnorr, whose work moved 'from art show to street theater, and from activism to farce' as it centred on migration and the 'bicultural vision' of undocumented workers (Fusco 1989, 602).

In San Diego proper, where high concentrations of undocumented workers experience intense discrimination, a local performance group comprised of artists Elizabeth Sisco, Louis Hock, and David Avalos created the controversial *Arte Reembolso/Art Rebate,* funded by the National Endowment for the Arts (NEA), in which they redistributed the entirety of their $4,500 artist fee as $10 'tax rebates' to 450 workers as they waited in parking lots to be picked up for day labour at sub-minimum wages. Encouraging media coverage, the artists turned the spotlight on these otherwise invisible sites of the shadow economy and the contradictions of the political moment that witnessed strident calls to secure the border even as US businesses continued to profit from the porosity of its border regions, which enabled a steady supply of cheap, migrant labour. Upon receiving the $10, the workers were given a flyer that acknowledged the taxes they pay to the US government whenever they eat in a restaurant or shop at the local K-Mart store, and thanked them for their contributions to the US economy, which is 'indifferent to national borders' (quoted in Montgomery 2017, 61). The action sparked a far-reaching debate about immigration and a political firestorm: *Arte Reembolso* became a central figure of the culture wars of the 1990s, listed among the infamous artists and 'NEA Four' (Karen Finley, Tim Finley, John Fleck, and Holly Hughes) by Republican senators and Christian organizations calling on Congress to defund the National Endowment for the Arts.

In its efforts to make migrant lives visible within a broader geopolitical context of US accountability, *Octopus* places the migrant workers in the foreground, making them 'protagonic,' in the sham battle they stage in the Home Depot parking lot through elaborately choreographed scenarios that collide with the mundane movements of shoppers who stroll by on their way to and from their cars (Hammer Museum 2011). In the development process, Okón and the Mayan day labourers used a vacant parking lot next to the Home Depot as their rehearsal space, where the men showed Okón the repertoire of tactical movements they had engaged in battle. As Okón soon discovered, this tactical repertoire further revealed the tentacles of US foreign policy interests that had inscribed themselves on the bodily memories of these Mayan migrants through a genealogy that can be traced back to the School of the Americas (SOA). Since its founding in 1946 in the US-controlled Panama Canal Zone before moving to Fort Benning in Columbus, Georgia in 1984, SOA has trained more than 60,000 officers, cadets, non-commissioned officers, and military leaders from across Latin America in combat skills and counterinsurgency warfare. Despite the training it allegedly offered in human rights, SOA provided the curricular foundation for US empire-building and state-sponsored violence that ravaged Latin America, producing graduates who would go on to become enforcers of brutal political oppression and war crimes widely documented by international human rights organizations. In an effort to recover from this tarnished reputation, SOA changed its name in 2001 to the Western Hemisphere Institute for Security Cooperation (WHINSEC), although its curriculum and training manuals remained unchanged. While the Mayan labourers had been conscripted on both sides of the Guatemalan Civil War—some with leftist rebel groups, some with the state military only to learn later that the US had funnelled arms to both in an effort to foment the conflict—they had no interest in honouring those positions in *Octopus*. They shared, after all, the same tactical repertoire—a repertoire that was ultimately choreographed by SOA and one that continues to define the war they fight today in the US.

The tactical repertoire of movements the Mayan migrants summoned during the rehearsal process gradually took the shape of a series of scenarios, which Okón storyboarded, detailing camera angles, positioning, and transitions between scenes. The storyboard ultimately generated a tightly rehearsed script that would be inserted into an otherwise improvised and somewhat unpredictable frame determined by the quotidian activity of Home Depot shoppers, traffic, and the potential appearance of store security. The juxtaposition between the tightly scripted choreography of Mayan performers and the mundane movement of shoppers creates an unsettling tension, as 'two parallel realities in the same place and the same time' unfold before the viewer: 'two dimensions that are kind of co-existing and almost not touching' which, for Okón, becomes a 'metaphor for undocumented human beings' (Okón qtd. in Alé and Okón 2020).

The tension between the two parallel realities is, in moments, distressingly comic, often as a result of the choreographic flourishes that throw the collision between these two dimensions into heightened relief: the Mayan performers take cover behind the ornamental grass in the parking lot, which becomes a site of camouflaged surveillance; they cascade over the trunks of cars in a series of body-rolls while holding invisible M16s; and a shopping cart is turned into a battle tank with a Mayan performer poised in a state of mission-readiness, on the lookout while he is pushed through the parking lot at a cautious pace by a fellow performer. Impatient with the artworld's tendency to equate solemnity with profundity, Okón intently pursues the dark comedy elicited by these contrasting realities. For Okón, comedy is an effective way to unveil the brutality of structural violence that is so often concealed from view, and to ensnare viewers in their complicity: once viewers laugh, Okón contends, they are irrevocably and inextricably implicated in the scenario unfolding before them (Hammer Museum 2011).

Seeing, Not Seeing

But if Okón set out to make the Mayan day labourers visible as protagonists of this reenactment, the live performance seemingly failed to achieve this objective. The shoppers and employees passed by these choreographic abstractions of counterinsurgency warfare unperturbed and unfazed, which also suggests a failure in being seen: migrant workers have been rendered invisible to such an extent that they simply blend into the background despite the artist's efforts to bring them out of the shadows. Nowhere is this more evident than in a scene in which a worker appears sprawled across the parking lot, apparently dead, as another presumably wounded worker crawls on his back to reach him, eventually collapsing beside him. The two casualties lie still as people pass by the bodies splayed out on the ground. A Home Depot worker walks by, turns his head to look at them, and continues walking. A woman follows and then a man, slowly pushing a cart full of potted plants; they each look at the workers and then causally continue walking. Several cars and pickup trucks drive by, slowing down to go over a speed bump just in front of the workers and then speeding up again, undaunted by the lifeless-looking bodies. What is perhaps more disturbing about this scene is that Okón, who had been asked to leave the premises by security guards, hid the camera in a car in order to film the workers' die-in, erasing any sign of production from the event as a performance. This part of the war reenactment, then, was inadvertently made possible through invisible theatre, which paradoxically confirmed the workers' invisibility. Whether dead or alive, remaining still or acting out, the unsuspecting spectators failed to see the workers or simply ignored them.

It is not until the performance is migrated into a four-channel video installation, first screened at the Hammer Museum in Los Angeles in January 2011, that the viewer's gaze is actively arrested. Standing in the centre of the gallery space, the footage of the reenactment jumps from wall to wall, compelling onlookers to pivot, making them conscious of their gaze and the act of looking as they follow the moving images that surround them. The self-consciousness of this act of looking is intensified by the disparity produced by the looks of their surrogates on screen who do not see: the indifferent shoppers whose gazes are so habituated to the larger structural practices of un-seeing that ensure undocumented lives remain invisible. The gallery-goers, in effect, see themselves not seeing. What they do see, in turn, is how that un-seeing sustains their positions as beneficiaries of the shadow economy that renders some lives invisible for the conveniences, comforts, and privileges of others.

That the migrant workers are only seen once the performance is framed as a war reenactment and placed under the controlled conditions of the gallery raises questions about the limits of performance, particularly as a tactical event and 'ephemeral appropriation of public space' that, in its synthesis of the aesthetic and the political, produces a 'critical encounter between performers and spectators' (Fuentes 2019, 13). As a record of the live event, *Octopus* suggests that performance alone is insufficient in its capacity to make undocumented migrants visible. It may be that for migrant workers to be seen, performance has to be reconfigured for the viewer, in this case through its documentation and exhibition that extends the spatio-temporal dimension of the event. Indeed, despite his efforts to make the workers 'protagonic,' Okón had anticipated that customers would ignore them and initially conceived the project as a multiple channel video installation (Okón 2021). Inside the dark viewing space of the gallery surrounded by screens, time slows down considerably, the bodies of the workers move in and out the frames, the noises of the parking lot are amplified against the contemplative silence and stillness of the gallery space, and in one scene the voices of the performers are clearly heard speaking in their native language as their feet shuffle along the pavement.

Through this altered time and space, Okón creates an immersive experience that demands a different kind of attention from the viewer, one that disrupts the accelerated pace with which experiences are consumed and re-sensitizes the onlooker to the surroundings of daily urban life. The performance, as Philip Auslander and Christopher Bedford might argue, does not ontologically precede its documentation or its discourse; it is produced and animated by them (2006, 5; 2012, 78). *Octopus* as a performance, then, (re-)occurs through the interplay of migrant bodies and bystanders onscreen and through the presence of the spectators whose act of viewing becomes itself a laborious endeavour, one that unveils just how much their own lives and histories are entangled with those of migrants and the ways in which not-seeing participates in the social, political, and economic forces that uphold structural violence.

References

Alé, Noor and Yoshua Okón. 2020. 'Latin American Speaker Series 2020: Yoshua Okón.' Co-presented by Sur Galley and Vtape, Toronto. February 2020.
Arau, Sergio, dir. *A Day Without a Mexican.* 2004; Altavista Films; Televisa Cine. Film.
Auslander, Philip. 2006. 'The Performativity of Performance Documentation.' *Performing Arts Journal*, 28 (3), 1-10.
Bedford, Christopher. 2012. 'The Viral Ontology of Performance.' *Perform, Repeat, Record: Live Art in History*, edited by Amelia Jones and Adrian Heathfield, 78-87. Bristol: Intellect.
Castañeda, Ingrid Yulisa. 2014. 'Dismantling the Enclave: Land, Labor, and National Belonging on Guatemala's Caribbean Coast, 1944–1954.' PhD diss., Yale University.
Chomsky, Noam., and Heinz Dieterich. 1999. *Latin America: from Colonization to Globalization* Melbourne: Ocean Press.
The Commission for Historical Clarification. 1999. *Guatemala: Memory of Silence.* https://hrdag.org/wp-content/uploads/2013/01/CEHreport-english.pdf.
Creative Capital. 'Secos y Mojados.' https://creative-capital.org/artists/secos-mojados/.
Eisenfeld, Sue. 2015. 'The Birth of Civil War Reenacting.' *New York Times*, January 8, 2015.
Fuentes, Marcela A. 2019. *Performance Constellations: Networks of Protest and Activism in Latin America.* Ann Arbor: University of Michigan Press.
Fusco, Coco. 1989. 'Border Art Workshop-Taller de Arte Fronterizo.' *The Nation*, 248 (17), 602.
Greenhouse, Steven. 2005. 'Day Laborer Battle Runs Outside Home Depot.' *New York Times*, October 10, 2005; https://www.nytimes.com/2005/10/10/us/day-laborer-battle-runs-outside-home-depot.html. Accessed 26 July 2023.
Hammer Museum. 2011. 'The Making of Yoshua Okón's *Octopus*.' https://hammer.ucla.edu/exhibitions/2011/hammer-projectsyoshua-okon.
Hernandez, Daniel. 2011. 'A Place Where Guatemalan Day Laborers are Survivors of War.' *Los Angeles Times*, November 24, 2011; https://www.latimes.com/archives/blogs/world-now/story/2011-11-24/a-place-where-guatemalan-day-laborers-are-survivors-of-war. Accessed 26 July 2023.
Jonas, Susanne. 2013. *Guatemalan Migration in Times of Civil War and Post-War Challenges.* Migration Policy Institute. https://www.migrationpolicy.org/article/guatemalan-migration-times-civil-war-and-post-war-challenges
Klein, Jennie. 2019. 'Sustainable Practices on the US-Mexico Border: inSITE_05, Intervention, and Precarious Communities'. *Sustainable Tools for Precarious Times: Performance Actions in the Americas*, edited by Natalie Álvarez, Claudette Lauzon, and Keren Zaiontz, 177-199. London: Palgrave Macmillan.
Montgomery, Harper. 2017. 'Immigration, Not Money: The True Meaning of *Arte Reembolso/Art Rebate*.' *Diágolo*, 20 (1) 59–72.
Navarro, Mireya. 1999. 'Guatemalan Army Waged "Genocide," New Report Finds.' *New York Times*, February 26, 1999; https://archive.nytimes.com/www.nytimes.com/library/world/americas/022699guatemala-report.html. Accessed 26 July 2023.
Obama, Barack. 2014a. 'Remarks by the President in Address to the Nation on Immigration.' Obama White House Archives, November 20. https://obamawhitehouse.archives.gov/the-press-office/2014/11/20/remarks-president-address-nation-immigration.

———. 2014b. 'Remarks by the President on Immigration.' Obama White House Archives, November 21. https://obamawhitehouse.archives.gov/the-press-office/2014/11/21/remarks-president-immigration.

Okón, Yoshua. 2021. Personal Communication. May 28.

Peck, Jamie, and Nik Theodore. 2012. 'Politicizing Contingent Work: Countering Neoliberal Labor Market Regulation… from the Bottom Up?' *South Atlantic Quarterly*, 111 (4), 741-761.

Schlesinger, Stephen C., and Stephen. Kinzer 1983. *Bitter Fruit: the Untold Story of the American Coup in Guatemala*. New York: Anchor Press/Doubleday.

Schneider, Rebecca. 2011. *Performing Remains: Art and War in Times of Theatrical Reenactment*. London: Routledge.

Theodore, Nik. 2006. 'Closed Borders, Open Markets: Immigrant Day Laborers' Struggle for Economic Rights.' *Contesting Neoliberalism Urban Frontiers*, edited by Helga Leitner, Jamie Peck, and Eric Sheppard, 250-265. New York: Guilford Publications.

Tienda, Marta and Susana Sanchez. 2013. 'Latin American Immigration to the United States.' *Daedalus*, 142 (2), 48-64.

Tomuschat, Christian. 1999. 'The Atrocity Findings: "The Historic Facts Must Be Recognized."' *New York Times*, February 26. https://www.nytimes.com/1999/02/26/world/the-atrocity-findings-the-historic-facts-must-be-recognized.html. Accessed 26 July 2023.

CHAPTER 30

From Emigrant to Migrant Nation: Reckoning with Irish Historical Duty

Charlotte McIvor

This chapter surveys contemporary Irish theatre's response to the Republic of Ireland's post-1990s transition from an emigrant nation to one re-shaped by significant inward-migration. The mainstream professional Irish theatre industry's reaction to these demographic shifts over the last 25 years has been often reactive. For example, newcomers to Ireland have been chronically represented as asylum seekers in productions fronted by white Irish artists and/or production companies despite those seeking asylum being a small minority of those who have recently emigrated to Ireland. This activity has run parallel to nascent but consistent efforts to establish theatre companies led by those from backgrounds of migration and/or with minority ethnic identities (Arambe Productions, Camino de Orula Productions, Polish Theatre Ireland, Outlandish Theatre Platform) often at the intersection between community and professional practice as well as active individual artists including FeliSpeaks (Felicia Olusanya), Dagogo Hart, Mirjana Rendulic, and George Seremba who write and perform. In addition, minority ethnic actors living in Ireland from backgrounds of personal or family migration have been employed on prominent stages such as the Abbey, Ireland's national theatre, most notably now international film star Ruth Negga, but also Mojisola Adebayo, Alicja Ayres, George Seremba, and Kwaku Fortune.

This chapter presents two recent case studies: Oonagh Murphy and Maeve Stone's *The Mouth of a Shark* (2018) and Brokentalkers' *This Beach* (2016). Both were created in the immediate aftermath of the 2015 intensification of

C. McIvor (✉)
University of Galway, Galway, Ireland
e-mail: charlotte.mcivor@nuigalway.ie

© The Author(s), under exclusive license to Springer Nature Switzerland AG 2023
Y. Meerzon, S. E. Wilmer (eds.), *The Palgrave Handbook of Theatre and Migration*, https://doi.org/10.1007/978-3-031-20196-7_30

the ongoing global refugee crisis which also prompted the European Union to draft new policy documents and reports about the role of the arts as a site of intercultural dialogue in these conditions (see McIvor, 2018, 230–247). Both of these productions were led by white Irish-born theatremakers, although both productions also involved collaboration with individuals seeking asylum or with refugee status in the development, creation and/or performance phases of the works and featured minority ethnic actors resident in Ireland in major roles.

These case studies were chosen because they both replay *and* critique contemporary Irish theatre's representational patterns regarding migration and migrant experiences in Ireland since the mid-1990s. This chapter argues Irish approaches have been overdetermined over time by a persistent focus on individuals seeking asylum—a limited perspective that obscures the wider diversity in circumstances of those from migrant backgrounds living in Ireland.

Also, key to both case studies is their use of what Steve Garner has termed Irish 'historical duty' as a central framing device (2004, 185). Irish 'historical duty' describes feelings of particular responsibility towards migrants, refugees, and asylum seekers due to our own histories of emigration under economic duress as well as during the Great Famine of 1845–1852. Irish playwrights and theatremakers have returned to historical duty again and again as a theme and/or plotting device over the past 20 years as in productions including Donal O'Kelly's *Farawayan* (1998) and *The Cambria* (2005), Jim Minogue's *Flight to Gross Ile* (Mountjoy Theatre Project, 1999), Upstate Theatre Project's *Journey From Babel* (2009), Fiona Quinn's Voyage of the Orphans (County Limerick Youth Theatre, 2009), and Sonya Kelly's *How To Keep An Alien* (2015). This uniquely Irish dramaturgical strategy does dramatize how the unequal economic and cultural economies of the past experienced by white Irish-born people when emigrating are shared by individuals coming to Ireland from the African continent, Middle East, and/or Global South in particular (i.e., non-white and formerly resident outside the European Union). But what are the representational and ethical risks of repeatedly presenting the stories (and lives) of refugees, those seeking asylum, migrant and/or minority ethnic individuals and groups on Irish stages *only* as they intersect with white Irish histories of parallel hardship? This is the line of argument I pursued at length in *Migration and Performance in Ireland: Towards A Contemporary Interculturalism* (McIvor 2018, 117–152), but its urgency has only been amplified by the continuation and intensification of historical duty as a thematic/dramaturgical strategy in some key post-2016 works such as *The Mouth of a Shark* and *This Beach*.

Geographical and Cultural Context

Over the last three decades, the Republic of Ireland underwent an economic boom (the so-called Celtic Tiger) and bust in parallel with the Maastricht Treaty's creation of the Eurozone in 1993 and the European Union's expansion since then from 11 to 27 nations (following the United Kingdom's departure in 2020). In addition, the Republic negotiated the ongoing fallout of the Troubles in Northern Ireland including the formalization of the Belfast Agreement in 1998, and, more recently, the United Kingdom's exit (or Brexit) from the European Union. But it is inward-migration that arguably has had the biggest impact on contemporary Ireland's evolving social and cultural identities from allegedly monocultural to multi- or intercultural. Apart from a brief period in the 1970s, net emigration dominated Irish life for more than 200 years, but then 'as prosperity took hold from the mid-1990s, net immigration has become the norm, except for the post-crash years 2010–2014' (FitzGerald 2020), a shift that has had enormous implications for the racial and ethnic diversity of the Republic of Ireland. The Celtic Tiger almost immediately resulted in increased flows of economic migrants from outside the European Union as well as individuals of Irish birth or descent returning to Ireland, but also higher numbers of individuals seeking asylum which led to the creation of the first Irish state system for processing those seeking asylum, the highly controversial Direct Provision system founded in April 2000 (Loyal and Quilley 2018; O'Reilly 2018).

As of the most recent 2016 Irish Census, 17.3% of the population was born abroad, with 11.6% reporting as 'non-nationals' from outside the European Union, figures that stand in sharp contrast to the 2002 Census which recorded a less than 5% non-national population. The largest groups by nationality in 2016 other than Irish were Polish, United Kingdom, Lithuanian, Romanian, Latvian and Brazilian (CSO 2017a) The 2016 figures are more or less in line with the 2011 Census (a very slight decrease from 12.2% in 2011), suggesting that there was not a mass exodus of 'non-nationals' during the temporary reversal of net migration identified above as between 2010 and 2014. And tellingly, there was a 14.7% increase in 'mixed Irish and non-Irish households' since 2007, and 'one in three of those with African ethnicity (38.6%) were born in Ireland (22,331 persons), as were 31.3 per cent (2,126) of those with other Black backgrounds' (CSO 2017b). Taken together, these recent figures suggest profound transformation within the Republic's demographic profile within the space of a generation, decisively changing what can or should be assumed about the racial and/or ethnic identity of someone living in Ireland and identifying as Irish today.

Overview of Theatrical Practices Related to Migration

From the early to late 2000s, there was a semi-regular appearance of professional Irish theatre productions on the theme of migration and/or featuring minority ethnic and/or migrant characters as produced by companies including the Abbey Theatre, Arambe Productions, Calypso Productions, Camino de Orula Productions, Fishamble: The New Play Company, Polish Theatre Ireland, Storytellers Theatre, Upstate Theatre Project among others. Some of these companies were migrant-created and led, such as Arambe Productions,

Camino de Orula Productions, and Polish Theatre Ireland, whereas in the other cases these productions were presented by white-Irish led companies, albeit with the work sometimes created in consultation with minority ethnic and/or migrant artists as in the work of Calypso Productions and Upstate Theatre Project in particular (see McIvor 2014, 341–349; McIvor 2016, 181–200; King 2005; King 2004).

But the 2008 economic crash and following recession heavily impacted the arts sector across the island, resulting in lower overall funding and for an extended period, a deprioritization of cultural diversity strategies in the arts. As King details, 'emergent immigrant and minority ethnic arts practitioners' were 'devastated by the economic collapse and largely disappeared from the professional Irish theatre scene' (2016, 73), only recently beginning to re-emerge prominently through the rising profiles of individuals like FeliSpeaks (Felicia Olusanya) (poet/performer/playwright) and Dagogo Hart (poet/performer/playwright) who often work at the intersection of art forms including music, visual art, and poetry.

Post-2008, the independent companies and practitioners named above and also including Outlandish Theatre Platforms and Terra Nova Productions in the North (see McIvor 2019, 343–371) have created important works that have kept issues of migrant and minority ethnic representation on independent theatrical stages often with great struggle in terms of funding and sustainability of individual or company practice. But one consistent pattern pre- *and* post-Celtic Tiger has been that migrant and minority ethnic characters have remained most likely to appear onstage as characters seeking asylum ('asylum seeker') or with refugee status if they are represented at all ('refugee') (see Ahmed 2004, and Jeffers 2011, for critiques of the dehumanizing potential of these labels).

THE MOUTH OF A SHARK (2018) AND THIS BEACH (2016)

The use of 'asylum seeker' or 'refugee' character types as the stand-ins for demographic social change has been true from the earliest contemporary Irish play to directly address this contemporary wave of inward-migration, Donal O'Kelly's *Asylum! Asylum!* (premiered at the Abbey, Ireland's national theatre in 1994). This pattern repeated in O'Kelly's *Farawayan* (Calypso Productions 1998), Charlie O'Neill's *Hurl* (Barabbas 2003) all the way through to Bisi Adigun and Roddy Doyle's *Playboy of the Western World: A New Version* (2007), where the main character Christopher Malomo attempts to claim asylum in Ireland while on the run from murdering his father in Nigeria—a plot convolution that defied all logical sense and international humanitarian law in the most seminal and controversial production in this subgenre due to a subsequent legal dispute involving Adigun versus Doyle and the Abbey over rights (McIvor 2016, 64–73). These representations of the 'asylum seeker' and 'refugee' may intend to raise awareness amongst (white) Irish(-born) audiences about the survivors of humanitarian crises living on our own shores and in need of justice, but their accumulation in the absence of a comparable number of migrant and/or minority ethnic characters *not* from this background over the same period also subtly implies that the only reason a migrant and/or minority ethnic person might settle in Ireland or be welcome to settle here is if they are literally stateless.

The end of the Celtic Tiger in 2008 brought a brief end to this theatrical trend for the better part of a decade, but significantly, contemporary Irish theatre's chronic use of the figure of the asylum seeker/refugee reignited as a pattern post-2015. Key productions as part of this wave include Brokentalkers' *This Beach* (2016), Fionnoula Gygax's *Hostel 16* (2016), Outlandish Theatre Platform's *Megalomaniac* (2016), Martin Sharry's *Playboyz* (2018), and Maeve Stone and Oonagh Murphy's *The Mouth of a Shark* (2018).

However unlike the first wave of contemporary Irish theatre productions pre-2015 which focused on asylum and refugeeness, this cluster of productions is unified not in a general reaction to Ireland's seemingly sudden diversification but rather more specifically either in a critique of Ireland's state-run but privately managed Direct Provision system for processing asylum seekers (*Hostel 16, Playboyz*) or in considered engagement with the wider European and worldwide escalation of a humanitarian crisis for displaced people fleeing conflict zones including but not limited to Syria (*Megalomaniac, This Beach, The Mouth of a Shark*). Taken together, Murphy and Stone's *The Mouth of a Shark* and Brokentalkers' *This Beach* expose the limitations and possibilities of contemporary Irish theatre's reliance on the intertwined figures of the contemporary asylum seeker/refugee and historical Irish emigrant.

Subtitled '*A theatrical song-cycle about migration*,' Murphy and Stone's *The Mouth of a Shark* is a documentary musical that juxtaposes fragmented accounts of LGBTQ+ individuals who left the Republic of Ireland and Northern Ireland by choice for political or cultural reasons (mostly in the 1970s and 1980s) with accounts of those who have come to Ireland seeking asylum more recently in response to persecution by their family and/or society due to their sexual orientation. *The Mouth of a Shark* therefore very intentionally makes use of the Irish historical duty trope, however, this time it also exposes the limits of Irish tolerance by highlighting circumstances in which Irish-born people were pushed to emigrate through the cruelty and abuse of other Irish people. In making this move, the production makes complex use of quite recent Irish histories of social exclusion to problematize complacency about Ireland as an unproblematically welcoming and tolerant home for LGBTQ+ individuals following a decisive 2015 majority vote to legalize marriage equality.

The Mouth of a Shark was presented as part of the 2018 Dublin St. Patrick's Day Festival as a collaboration between THISISPOPBABY, 'a theatre and events production company that rips up the space between popular culture, counter culture, queer culture and high art' (THISISPOPBABY, 2021) and Change of Address, a 'collective formed by artists Moira Brady, Oonagh Murphy and Maeve Stone to increase visibility and raise awareness of the experiences of refugees and asylum seekers in Irish society' (Change of Address, 2021). These production contexts add layers of deeper meaning to the performance itself, as the Dublin St. Patrick's Day Festival was strategically rebranded post-Celtic Tiger and with constant strategic attention to the contributions of minority ethnic and migrant communities to Irish society, such as through the long-running City Fusion group who performs as part of the parade featuring multi-racial and ethnic participants and white Irish-born community groups performing together after months of collaboration (see McIvor 2016, 213–254). In addition, Change of Address not only generates artistic work but has also spun-out community-led offerings like the Identity LGBT Support Group, which was initiated at the request of members as a 'peer to peer support network grew in partnership with the Irish Refugee Council' from 2018 and now run by LGBT Ireland (Change of Address, n.d.) Therefore, *The Mouth of a Shark* does not simply stand on its own as a singular production but is instead implicated in these other networks of tourism/heritage practices, community organizing and the wider landscape of socially engaged contemporary Irish theatre and other art forms such as the emergent Irish spoken word scene from which *The Mouth of a Shark* performer Yemi Azamosa joined the project as the founder of the Fried Plantains Collective (Fried Plantains Collective, 2021).

Performed by four actors from diverse racial and ethnic backgrounds (Yemi Azamosa, Daryl McCormack, Michelle O'Rourke, and Ashley Xie), *The Mouth of a Shark* continuously weaves between the 1970s/1980s and the present day, often within the space of a single musical stanza, referencing events that took place in Ireland, Northern Ireland, the Irish diaspora, the United States, Zimbabwe, South Africa, France, and other unnamed locations. The documentary musical takes its name from Somali-British poet Warshan Shire's poem 'Home' which 'says that people only leave their home if that home is the mouth of a shark' (Amnesty International, 2022). This documentary musical is entirely sung over eight movements that are interspersed with spoken audio clips from the community interviews that informed the project. The four performers remain onstage the entire time, with no costume changes, and only four blocks as set pieces, supporting each other as a chorus even in brief solo moments.

The Mouth of a Shark's dramaturgical strategy of blending pieces of individual's stories across time intentionally blurs the experiences of Irish individuals living abroad and individuals living in Ireland now from various backgrounds of migration (voluntary and forced). Murphy and Stone effectively use shared moments of lyric and song throughout to amplify the connections across these disparate and fragmented experiences, with the performers delivering unison lines about cross-cutting emotions throughout to drive this home: 'Just needed to get away,' 'You get to a place where you're so tired of fighting/with people/you get to a place where you're so tired' (Murphy and Stone, 5). This has the effect of deliberately suspending the audience in a version of theatrical time where the Irish/global present is co-implicated in the past and vice versa, with references to transnational colonial histories throughout. To performatively merge these convergent histories, the actors employed what might be described as an affect-less or deadpan style of acting delivery throughout. In performance, this manifested as lack of differentiation between 'characters' portrayed by individual performers over the course of the musical—a very powerful strategy given the diversity of the ensemble which resulted in minority ethnic performers getting to voice the (white) Irish stories of an older generation, potentially communicating a shared contemporary ownership of this history by all now living in Ireland including those from backgrounds of migration. And indeed, *The Mouth of a Shark* concludes with an even larger multi-racial and ethnic chorus joining the four performers onstage from a door that was opened behind the audience, a performative gesture that made manifest the ongoing multiplication of diverse individuals and communities within Ireland with the performance's final lyric deployed as an invitation but also a challenge to the audience: 'Whose hand are you going to take?' (Murphy and Stone, 27).

Despite these powerful strategies, the documentary musical's explicit emphasis on trauma (which is literally repeated as a lyric throughout but especially in moments narrating migrations *to* Ireland from non-Western locations) does raise some challenging questions. Non-Irish born characters recount instances of physical and sexual abuse, harassment by family members, and political persecution, but Irish-born characters' instances of trauma are left vaguer overall (albeit with one story of abuse within an Irish reform school). Additionally, non-Irish born characters are portrayed as being forced into migration as a matter of life and death, whereas Irish-born characters' journeys are to some extent positioned as a matter of choice.

Yet, one could argue that *The Mouth of a Shark*'s blending of stories and timelines is doing something more subtle than either directly equating the levels of trauma or violence experienced by individuals in different national contexts or making the non-Irish people's histories and experiences only digestible when disguised as Irish. Rather, it is forcing audiences to work harder to untangle Irish and other histories in order to understand better the constellation of factors that bring people to Ireland today and that have influenced Irish-born people's movements over generations.

This Beach's creators Feidlim Cannon and Gary Keegan leaned into magnifying rather than obscuring their own blind spots regarding migration in creating this work. Whereas *The Mouth of a Shark* applies documentary theatre methods to the creation of the musical, Keegan and Cannon consciously rejected this approach. After travelling to Germany to begin the project and being put in touch with 'a group of refugees in Spandau' with their own theatre group, Keegan and Cannon realised 'we were just one in a long line of white privileged artists who had come to visit them, thinking we could tell their stories.' Rather than looking to others for their stories, Keegan and Cannon 'turned the gaze back upon ourselves: we who are safe, we who are citizens, who own property, who have the experience of wealth' (Keating 2016), yet nonetheless featured a diverse cast and was presented in co-production with the Goethe Institute, Munich Kammerspiele, and Tiger Dublin Fringe, premiering in Munich (Brokentalkers, 2021). *This Beach* was also part of a European theatre and film project entitled 'Europoly' by the Goethe-Institut in cooperation with

Münchner Kammerspiele, Onassis Cultural Centre Athens, Sirenos—Vilnius International Theatre Festival, Teatro Maria Matos Lisbon, and Tiger Dublin Fringe.

Set on a dystopian beach that audiences should assume is somewhere in Europe and with action sometime near the present, *This Beach* follows a family who owns this beach after winning it through the spoils of war centuries earlier and is gathering for a wedding. They have confined themselves to this beach to protect this space and their other material assets, but must cope with an ever-increasing flow of people washing up dead on their shores, and one who washes up on shore still alive. *This Beach's* premiere in Germany signals the work's engagement with pan-European debates on migration and does not confine its meanings to either a German or an Irish context primarily.

This Beach is set in an English-speaking European location that is highly citational of very concrete locations within Europe and elsewhere where the 'the wealthy tourist from the Global North and the utterly disenfranchised refugee from the Global South' (Pugliese 2009, 671) cross paths daily but have these same paths of contact erased deliberately. The characters' relationships to one another are sketched only broadly in familial and kinship terms: we have the father, Daniel, and son, Ankur (the groom), a mother, Pom, and daughter, Dagmara (the bride), and Ankur's friend from military service, Carl. The characters' name are the same as the actors' names, and in the 2016 preview that I attended in Dublin prior to the German premiere, the production employed racially and ethnically transgressive casting in that the race/ethnicity of the parents and their children do not match, although Pom did speak Polish to Dagmara at one point in the play. Daniel Reardon and Pom Boyd are Irish-born actors, while Ankur Bahl is South Asian-American currently living in London and Dagmara Jerzak is of Polish descent but trained in Scotland and lives in Ireland.

After the wedding, the action focuses on the intrusion of a stranger, a young man named Neimhim who washes ashore still alive. In the Irish canon of plays concerning inward-migration, the formula of the stranger intruding into situations of domesticity as a microcosm of what the nation is experiencing through inward-migration is almost as familiar as historical duty (see Doyle's *Guess Who's Coming for the Dinner*, and Adigun and Doyle's *Playboy of the Western World: A New Version*). But in *This Beach*, this formula is warped as this actor is Irish-born—an insider cast against type as the outsider. Through Neimhim, we get the only fleeting reference to Irish histories of emigration as he reports of his old home that 'we grew potatoes' (Cannon and Keegan, 37), but are given no other concrete information that would lead audiences to believe that he is a ghost of the Famine. In fact, *This Beach* satirizes this very potential having Dagmara relate an exaggerated account of their conversation: 'The ancient fishing harbor is now a site of a mass exodus. The fishing boats are now overcrowded coffin ships' (Cannon and Keegan, 38).

This Beach throws up many themes—the expropriation of land from indigenous populations over generations through the family's ownership of the beach, the trauma of conflict and the residues of violence in majority ethnic populations through Ankur and Carl's experience as soldiers, the irony of Western Europe's obsession with its own history in the face of the erasure of the history of so many ejected from its shores through Daniel's excavation projects in his suitably petite sandbox, and, finally, the ambivalent and often harmful role of the artist in conflict and traumatic situations as played out through the character of Dagmara, who is a documentary filmmaker. Brokentalkers' conscientious thematic overloading of *This Beach* is a strategy meant to trouble the political efficacy of representation itself, artistic or otherwise, in working through the present circumstances of the European crisis. However, in pointing in so many directions at once, *This Beach* also suggests that myopic views of global migration patterns, from contemporary individual or nationalist perspectives, will only serve to accelerate the present crisis with the largest number of people displaced worldwide since the second world war as a reproduction of earlier interlinked historical moments. Their allegorical use of the beach as holiday site and graveyard instead aggressively claims *This Beach's* scene as the new European Union normal grounded in apathy while also problematizing the counter-possibility of sympathetic engagement with victims as a liberatory political catalyst.

This Beach ends on Ankur, Dagmara, Pom, and Carl freezing to death on a reduced shoreline. While this image could be read as a narcissistic appeal to Western European audiences to engage before the tables are turned on themselves, it could also be read as an exposure of the palimpsestic nature of history where following short-sighted contemporary concerns (as represented by the relentless pleasure consumption of those living on the beach over seeking a more equitable distribution of resources) results in a duplication of patterns of disenfranchisement and violence now and in the past. This reading is supported by the terms of Neimhim's departure from the play. Ankur and Carl's patience with Neimhim disintegrates, especially as Ankur sees him as a romantic rival for Dagmara (despite the fact that he reveals he is gay). Ankur and Carl want to kill him, Daniel wants to keep him as a worker, Pom wants him for company, and Dagmara wants him for the poetic potential of his narrative as a migrant/refugee/asylum seeker:

> Dagmara: On the one hand I want to keep him here, to work with him on his story, but him leaving is strangely beautiful, don't you think? If we force him to stay, we are denying him the opportunity to complete his story.
>
> Ankur: This is where his story ends.
>
> Dagmara: That's not a compelling ending. He needs to experience more hardship to be a true hero. We should let nature take its course. Send him away, allow him to fulfill his destiny. Who are we to deprive him of those exciting experiences? (Cannon and Keegan, 45)

Ankur's murderous intents are only slightly more revolting than the seething narcissism of the others who can see him only as psychological assist, labour asset, or flexible aesthetic trope. Meanwhile, Neimhim leaves unnoticed, prompting the ensemble to imagine him safely ensconced elsewhere within a neoliberal capitalist fantasy of fulfilment 'happy. Comfortable. In charge of his own life' with a 'spacious open plan kitchen' and a house with 'flat screen TVs in every room' and an 'integrated sound system' (Cannon and Keegan, 47). By animating Neimhim to leave the stage on his own terms but dramatizing how he still fuels the fantasies of the other characters in absentia, Brokentalkers decisively link the tropes of *how* we tell stories about migration and those migrating to characters' direct participation in reproducing the political and economic patterns that displace those on the move by participating in the telling of others' stories in the way that they do. In *This Beach*, Keegan and Cannon ultimately demand that the audience turn the gaze back on themselves rather than keeping it focused on characters like Neimhim.

The Republic of Ireland's rapid rate of social change within a generation means that its future is destined to be as a migrant rather than emigrant nation, regardless of the setback of the economic downtown at the end of the 2010s. Overall, the contemporary Irish theatre has not caught up to reflecting its living population on its live stages in terms of giving individuals from a background of migration an equal place to tell their stories on their own terms unencumbered by migration status/history (particularly if they have sought asylum) or by historical duty as the only legible point of translation. However, the future of Irish theatrical representation of experiences of migration is a story that is more than ready to be written, with emerging artists like FeliSpeaks and Dagogo Hart beginning to create a new wave of work that is challenging anew the too-long prevailing trends in this thematic area on the contemporary Irish stage.

References

Amnesty International. 'Home By Warshan Shire.' Accessed 11 February 2022. https://www.amnesty.ie/wp-content/uploads/2016/06/home-by-warsan-shire.pdf.

Ahmed, Sara. 2004. *Cultural Politics of Emotion*. Edinburgh: Edinburgh University Press.

Brokentalkers. *This Beach*. Accessed June 2, 2021. https://brokentalkers.ie/portfolio/this-beach/.

Cannon, Feidlim and Keegan, Gary. *This Beach*. Unpublished manuscript. January 26, 2016.

Central Statistics Office. 2017a. 'Census 2016-Migration and Diversity.' Accessed June 2, 2021. https://www.cso.ie/en/releasesandpublications/ep/p-cp7md/p7md/.

———. 2017b. 'Census of Population 2016- Profile 8- Irish Travellers, Ethnicity and Religion.' Accessed June 2, 2021. https://www.cso.ie/en/releasesandpublications/ep/p-cp8iter/p8iter/p8e/.

Change of Address. 'About.' Accessed June 22, 2021a. https://changeofaddresscollective.com/about.

Change of Address. 'Identity LGBT Support Group.' Accessed June 22, 2021b. https://changeofaddresscollective.com/about.

FitzGerald, John. 2020. 'Migration has been a brain gain for Ireland in recent decades.' *Irish Times*. 6 June. https://www.irishtimes.com/business/economy/migration-has-been-a-brain-gain-for-ireland-in-recent-decades-1.4401340.

Fried Plantains Collective. 'About Fried Plantains Collective.' Accessed June 22, 2021. https://friedplantainscollective.wordpress.com/home/

Garner, Steve. 2004. *Racism in the Irish Experience*. London: Pluto Press.

Jeffers, Alison. 2011. *Refugees, Theatre and Crisis: Performing Global Identities*. Basingstoke: Palgrave Macmillan.

Keating, Sara. 2016. 'Brokentalkers break their own free-form traditions.' *Irish Times*. September 12. https://www.irishtimes.com/culture/stage/brokentalkers-break-their-own-free-form-traditions-1.2784448.

King, Jason. 2016. 'Contemporary Irish Theatre, the new *Playboy* controversy, and the economic crisis. *Irish Studies Review* 24 (1): 67-78.

———. 2005. 'Interculturalism and Irish Theatre: The Portrayal of Immigrants on the Irish Stage.' *The Irish Review*, 33: 23-39.

Loyal, Steven and Quilley, Stephen. 2018. *State Power and Asylum Seekers in Ireland: An Historically Grounded Examination of Contemporary Trends*. Cham: Palgrave Macmillan.

McIvor, Charlotte. 2018. 'When Social Policy Meets Performance Practice: Interculturalism, the European Union, and the "Migratory and Refugee Crisis."' *Theatre Research International* 44 (3): 230-247.

———. 2016. *Migration and Performance in Contemporary Ireland: Towards a New Interculturalism*. London: Palgrave Macmillan.

———. 2014. 'White Irish-Born Male Playwrights and the Immigrant Experience.' In *Literary Visions of Multicultural Ireland: The Immigrant in Contemporary Irish Literature*, edited by Pilar Villar-Argáiz, 37-50. Manchester: Manchester University Press.

Murphy, Oonagh and Stone, Maeve. 2018. 'The Mouth of a Shark.' Unpublished manuscript.

Pugliese, Joseph. 2009. 'Crisis heterotopias and border zones of the dead.' *Continuum: Journal of Media & Cultural Studies* 23 (5): 663-679.

THISISPOPBABY. 'Home.' Accessed 22 June 2021a. https://thisispopbaby.com.

THISISPOPBABY. 'Where We Live 2018.' Accessed 22 June 2021b. https://thisispopbaby.com/shows/where-we-live-2018/.

CHAPTER 31

Dwelling in Multiple Languages: The Impossible Journeys Home in the Work of Sidi Larbi Cherkaoui and Akram Khan

Guy Cools

After World War II, an ambivalent attitude towards migration developed in Europe. Migrants were welcomed because recovering economies required large labour forces, but they were also treated as second-class citizens and even scapegoated in times of crisis. This stigmatisation was passed on to 'second generation immigrants,' which the EU glossary defines as 'persons who were born in and are 'residing in a country that at least one of their parents previously entered as a migrant' (European Commission, n.d.). In what follows I will discuss the problematic nature of this concept. Migrants frequently don't have easy access to basic amenities, let alone cultural experiences, particularly in the performing arts. Even at the beginning of the third decade of the twenty-first century, theatre institutions still have to be reminded to be more inclusive and present a more diverse artistic programme. At the same time, a generation of artists such as Sidi Larbi Cherkaoui and Akram Khan have used their own identity *in-between cultures* to create a new imaginary that places different (dance-)languages next to each other, without blending them, celebrating diversity.

G. Cools (✉)
Dance Department, Université de Québec à Montréal, Montréal, QC, Canada
e-mail: cools.guy@uqam.ca

Migration in Post-war Europe

In his exhaustive overview *The Unsettling of Europe: The Great Migration, 1945 to the Present* (2019), Peter Gatrell describes in detail the ambivalent policies of the European community and its member states towards migration. He illustrates how waves of migration were mobilised to support the rebuilding and further development of local economies, for example in the 1950s and 1960s, while at the same time, migrants were often wrongly scapegoated for economic recessions. The recession following the financial crash of 2008 highlighted how both attitudes can go hand in hand. On the one hand, there was 'a realization that Europe faced a reduction in its number of citizens of working age, and thus that a demographic "crisis" loomed in Europe to which migration seemed to provide an answer' (Gatrell 2019, 364). On the other hand, 'complaints about the financial crisis and the impacts of austerity were displaced onto migrants' (360). He also explains that the elimination of borders within the Schengen area went hand in hand with a closing off of *Fortress Europe* for refugees from outside Europe. The discourse around how migrants should interact with their host country has alternated between assimilation—which 'required that migrants adjust to the host society on its terms by forfeiting cultural attributes that stood in its way' (232)—and integration. He writes: 'Integration meant tolerating and enabling cultural diversity. Integration was about gain (…) assimilation was about loss' (233).

The problematic status of migrants is often passed on to successive generations, who grow up between two or more cultures. 'The emergence of a second generation, children of guest workers and other migrants, gave rise to further anxieties about a deprived and alienated underclass' (Gatrell 2019, 244). The notion of 'second generation immigrants' is misleading because they were in fact born in the places where they live. And yet, many European countries will deny them full citizenship unless at least one parent has already acquired citizenship of their host country. The journal *Comparative Migration Studies* has published a special issue on second-generation migrants from refugee backgrounds, which gives an overview of the literature on second-generation migrants. The editorial states that in Europe, this second generation represents more than 30% of the population, a very substantial percentage. The authors write that the category of 'second generation' is both 'a description as well as a marker of their exclusion' (Chimienti 2019, 2). They conclude that the notion of a 'second generation' is problematic, as 'it raises debates towards the socially constructed character of this category' (3), denying the diversity of the individuals' backgrounds and experiences. Past studies on second-generation migrants have tended to focus on their social, educational, economic, cultural and inter-generational lives, mainly analysing their level of integration or assimilation and the problems related to it, often in comparison with the first generation. 'More recent research also explores feelings of belonging and identity' (4). As to the latter, the authors assert that 'second-generation descendants of migrants are often described as having fractured or fluid identities, multiple belongings and contradictory notions of home' (8). In my analysis of the work of Sidi Larbi Cherkaoui and Akram Khan, I will focus on the latter.

In *The Unsettling of Europe*, Gatrell gives many examples of migrant experiences being documented, mainly in literature, film and music. In the field of European theatre, it was only in the first decades of the twenty-first century that the need for a more inclusive theatre and dance landscape, one that would give a voice to its migrant minorities, slowly became apparent. Even today, in 2021, this is still an important issue for which special policies and measures need to be developed. On 8 March 2021, International Women's Day, the European Theatre Convention published the results of a major study on gender equality and diversity amongst its members in 22 countries, looking at 4000 theatre employees and analysing 650 performances. The study concluded that it still found 'a "noteworthy" absence of people from minority backgrounds' (European Theatre Convention 2021) in the theatre staff and proposed to its members a code of conduct which includes the principle of reflecting gender and diversity across artistic creation and programming.

Two choreographers who have contributed substantially to a more inclusive contemporary dance scene on Europe's most important stages are the Belgian-Moroccan choreographer Sidi Larbi Cherkaoui and the British-Bangladeshi choreographer Akram Khan. They both celebrate their identity in-between cultures but also problematise the notion of being *second-generation migrants*.

THE PROBLEMATIC NOTION OF SECOND-GENERATION MIGRANTS

The biographies of Sidi Larbi Cherkaoui and Akram Khan share many similarities, but they are also fundamentally different. Both artists made their debuts on the European dance scene around the turn of the millennium. Their iconic contemporary dance practices integrate text and live music into an interdisciplinary performance practice. During the formative years of their careers, they consciously used their identity *in-between cultures* as a creative source for and explicit theme of their work. Their highly successful and often large-scale productions introduced a new imaginary to their audiences, deliberately combining different languages and dance techniques and offering a less Eurocentric perspective.

Akram Khan was born in 1974 into a Bangladeshi family of migrants, who had moved to London after Bangladesh's war of independence in 1971. In the discourse that Khan has developed about his artistic identity, he delineates the various influences he had to negotiate as a child: at school, among his peers who came from all kinds of cultural backgrounds but shared the same references and interests such as Michael Jackson or Bruce Lee, and at home with his family, who had their own daily rituals and cultural affinities. He has also reflected on the *con-fusion* of having to learn different dance languages—the

Indian kathak dance he trained in from a young age and the various Western dance techniques he acquired during his university training. It would become one of his most important creative tools. Khan rejects the notion of fusion, which suggests a blending together, eliminating and erasing the differences. *Con-fusion*, by contrast, allows the differences to co-exist and influence each other.

Depending on their own cultural origins, dance scholars have interpreted Khan's contribution in different ways. In his paper 'Contemporary Dance and the Performance of Multicultural Identities' (2004), Ramsay Burt argues that choreographers such as Khan are representative of a generation of artists whose work no longer relates to the host culture (i.e., contemporary Western art practices) in terms of accommodation or resistance but has the potential to contribute to and influence the host culture by creating 'an appreciation and openness towards difference' (Burt 2004, 2). Royana Mitra meanwhile, in her monograph *Akram Khan, Dancing New Interculturalism* (2015), continues to embed Khan's artistic journey in a diasporic account. She problematises the label 'contemporary kathak,' writing: 'Contemporary *kathak* implies a limiting encounter between classical *kathak* and Western contemporary dance training, where the only possible (and desirable) outcome is a contemporisation (and westernisation) of the non-Western classical dance form.' Mitra also acknowledges the creative potential of the physiological and creative tensions Khan had to negotiate, with 'the most unnerving and exciting of these tensions' being 'the clash between the *known* nature of his classical repertoire and the *unknown* nature of contemporary dance.' Mitra concludes her argument by saying that instead of Khan being an example of contemporary British South Asian Dance, he embodies 'explorations of new interculturalism and begins to transform the British contemporary dance in intercultural ways' (Mitra 2015, 73).

Sidi Larbi Cherkaoui was born in 1976 as the second son of a Flemish mother and a Moroccan father. At home they spoke Dutch, French and Arabic and he was taught the foundations of both the Catholic and the Muslim faith. Early on in his career, Cherkaoui developed a discourse in which he defined himself as a *metis*, who had to negotiate not only two family lineages but also multiple identities. In the 'State of the Union' address he gave at the annual Dutch and Flemish theatre festival in 2008, Cherkaoui explicitly referred to the text *In the Name of Identity* (1998) by the Lebanese author Amin Malouf. In it, Malouf discusses the multiple identities that all of us inhabit and which are activated by specific contexts. These identities can change over time or in dialogue with others. Malouf writes that certain aspects of these identities, such as nationality, race or religion, can become 'deadly identities' (which was also the original French title of the text). This happens when one identity takes over and suppresses all the others. People living on the edges of different aspects of their identity, as migrants do, have the potential to build bridges between the different communities and cultures they are part of, on the condition that they fully embrace and can live the diversity of their identity. Cherkaoui has embraced his multiple identities and has set himself the task of becoming all-inclusive in his stage language, embracing all cultures, traditions and dance techniques in a non-hierarchical way. In his 'State of the Union' address, he pleads for a theatre landscape that is 'totally inclusive,' 'for a theatre without hierarchies,' 'for a theatre language that includes all other languages' and 'for a migrating theatre' (Cherkaoui 2008).

Cherkaoui has often publicly questioned the problematic notion of 'second generation migrant.' He wrote amongst others a monthly column in the progressive internet magazine *MO*, which functions as a media platform for a number of NGOs, including Oxfam. One of his columns bore the title 'One Surname, a Lot of Future.' In it, Cherkaoui considered his recent nomination as one of the twenty-five most influential migrants in Belgium in one of the annual polls that are published at the end of the year. 'Migrant literally means coming from another country, in which case I should have been disqualified in the poll,' he reflects, 'since I was born here. My father, who migrated from Tangiers, Morocco, could have been nominated. But it seems the word "migrant" is transferable. It also sticks to your children.' (Cherkaoui 2014)

Akram Khan and Sidi Larbi Cherkaoui identify as British and Belgian citizens respectively, but in the reception of their work and in the public discourse that accompanies it, they are often still considered 'migrants.' In the first decade of their careers, they explored these contradictions both thematically and formally, celebrating the diversity of (dance) languages on stage or using the con-fusion that this created at the level of their own bodies as a creative source.

Impossible Journeys Home

The notion of the 'in-between' is central to the book *Entre-Deux: l'origine en partage* (1991) by the psychiatrist Daniel Sibony, who is himself of mixed Arabic, Jewish and French origin. It begins with a chapter on 'the migrant' and concludes with a chapter on 'travelling.' Sibony writes that 'the idea of travelling is not about the way, but the desire of wayfaring, to let oneself and the here be seduced by a there, the move in-between and to displace oneself' (Sibony 1991, 305).

For migrants, this act of travelling is not a single voyage but a constant coming and going between their country of origin and the place they are eventually able to settle in. Gatrell's book gives ample testimony of the journeys of many forced migrants and refugees, which are rarely straightforward, one-way trips but usually include many detours and long periods of waiting or being held in temporary shelters. Once resettled, migrants continue to travel between these two places, even if it is only in their imagination. As such the migrant experience remains a nomadic one, often antithetical opposed to the stable notion of 'home' the settler has. Migrants are 'unsettled settlers,' which is the title of Graham Huggan's contribution to *Essays in Migratory Aesthetics* (2007). Iain Chambers starts his book on *Migrancy, Culture, Identity* (1994) with a chapter on the 'impossible homecoming.' For Chambers the migratory experience is not 'an account of travel. For to travel implies movement between fixed positions, a site of departure, a point of arrival, the knowledge of an itinerary. It also intimates an eventual return, a potential homecoming.' The movement of migrancy according to Chambers is 'a movement in which neither the points of departure nor those of arrival are immutable or certain.' While 'the promise of homecoming (…) becomes an impossibility,' the migrant dwells 'in language, in histories, in identities that are constantly subject to mutation' (Chambers 1994, 5). Even if the economic and sociological living conditions of 'second generation migrants' such as Sidi Larbi Cherkaoui and Akram Khan are often very different from their parents, on the level of their identity formation, they experience a similar *con-fusion* of where they belong. In the first decade of their artistic careers, both artists frequently explored this theme, using the polarities of the voyage and home.

In the documentary film *Dreams of Babel* (2009), Cherkaoui remembers his family's annual car journeys to Morocco as a ritual initiation in different stages. 'I multiply my travels. (…) To move. It is without doubt the place where I feel most at ease to work, to transform, to feel free: at the margin or in transit' (Boisseau 2013, 20). In her monograph on Sidi Larbi Cherkaoui, the dance scholar Lise Uytterhoeven discusses how 'travel stories are a key dramaturgic interest of Cherkaoui's and were often generative sources for his early work' (Uytterhoeven 2019, 79).

Cherkaoui and Khan met early in their careers and began an artistic exchange. In 2005, this led to the iconic duet *zero degrees*, which they co-created and which I accompanied as a dramaturge. The backbone of *zero degrees* is an account of a journey that Khan undertook years earlier to India and Bangladesh, and the questions it raised for him about his own foreignness. Khan's narrative begins with the crossing of a border and him being asked to prove his identity. An identity that completely coincides with a document: his passport. It determines his identity and his mobility. As the train journey unfolds, Khan discovers that he is a foreigner in his country of origin. A foreigner who needs his cousin to explain the local customs to him and prevent him from getting into trouble because of his ignorance and his different ways of behaving: 'It is not my clothing, I don't think. It is just my mannerisms. They can identify that I am a foreigner. And maybe it is arrogance' (Performance text *zero degrees*). Writing about the significance of *zero degrees* in Akram Khan's artistic journey, Royana Mitra describes it as 'a formal and narrative exploration of the politics of border spaces as a metaphor for the transient nature of diasporic identity' (Mitra 2010, 40).

If journeys and the crossing of borders are important themes in Cherkaoui's and Khan's choreographic universes, often a real or imagined home has emerged as another core idea. Nobody has reflected more eloquently on how the notions of migration and home are deeply linked in our subconscious than John Berger. In *Our Faces, My Heart, Brief as Photos* (1984), Berger references Mircea Eliade when he writes: '[H]ome meant the center of the world—not in a geographical, but in an ontological sense' (Berger 1984, 55). Emigration always implies a dismantling of this centre and a 'move into a lost, disoriented one of fragments' (57). The new home that the migrant is eventually able to create will never fully recreate this centre. It will remain a partially improvised, temporary shelter and 'when the original home is lost and it is impossible to return, the mortar which holds the improvised 'home' together (…) is memory' (64).

For its opening season, the new museum Museé National de l'Histoire de l'Immigration (National Museum of the History of Immigration), in Paris, commissioned Sidi Larbi Cherkaoui to make a video installation with the French filmmaker Gilles Delmas. The museum, which opened in 2007, reused the Palais de la Porte Doreé, originally built for the International Colonial Exhibition in 1931. Cherkaoui was very aware of the paradoxical relationship between the history of the building and its new mission.

> The foundational idea behind this new institution is opposite to its original mission. The original project was based on an ethnocentric vision where Europe imposed itself on the periphery and talked about everything that came from elsewhere from a Western point of view. The new project affirms that we are no longer at the center (…) and this implies a process of relearning to think and to work. (Cherkaoui & Delmas 2007, 9–10)

Together with Delmas, Cherkaoui created the video installation *Zon-Mai* (2007), which is an anagram of and pun on the French word *maison* (house). On the four walls and the roof of an abstract house twenty-one short choreographic films are projected, presenting dancers from eighteen different countries, all migrants in their temporary homes. 'Dancers from very different backgrounds—geographically and artistically—with very distinct energies reunite under the same roof' (13).

In 2007, Akram Khan was commissioned to create a new work for the cultural programme leading up to the 2008 Summer Olympic Games in Beijing. *bahok* (2008) was named after the Bangla word for *carrier*. It refers to another Berger quote, from a text in which he discusses the experience of the Palestinian diaspora, *Hold Everything Dear* (2007). 'For nomads, home is not an address, home is what they carry with them' (Berger 2007, 129). Originally, Khan wanted to focus on the nomadic experience of contemporary dance artists and the diverse languages and dance techniques that come together in a contemporary dance company. The original cast of *bahok* was made up of nine dancers of seven different nationalities. 'How will strangers who speak different languages and master different dance techniques (from ballet, folk dance, and martial arts to more contemporary idioms) relate to each other?' (Cools 2015, 93). Early on in the research, Khan invited the dancers to tell a story about home and to his surprise everyone referred to their original childhood homes rather than their actual, current homes. For Eulalia Ayguade Farro, it was the unique quality of the Spanish rain that represented home. For Shanell Winlock, from South Africa, home was the smell of burnt car tyres in the townships, or of her father's shoes. South Korean Kim Young Jin mixed his memories of the rivers at home with the cliché of the 'spitting Chinese,' which came about because of the daily commercials that the group watched on Chinese television during their final residence in Beijing, in which the local population was reminded to clean up their behaviour for the foreign guests. In the final work, some of these stories are told in words (often in a performer's mother tongue) while others become the starting point for a danced solo. The notion of home emerges as the antithesis of the nomadic condition of contemporary dance artists, who meet in non-places (such as airports or train stations) where total strangers end up sitting next to each other, obliged to interact with each other.

In her analysis of *bahok*, Royana Mitra discusses 'this pluralistic embodiment of homes' (Mitra 2015, 130). She also contrasts the 'uprootedness' of Khan and his fellow 'travellers' with that of his parents. 'Khan is aware of the difference between mobility derived from the privilege of relocation and mobility experienced through enforced dislocation' (119). Mitra defines Khan's own mobility as both 'an economic condition of privilege and choice and a sociological condition that complicates the relationship between place and identity politics' (136). 'In other words, these subjects are new cosmopolitan elites, privileged, opportunity-seeking and upwardly mobile, who can become agents as citizens of the world if they so wish' (118).

bahok begins with a long, silent scene in which the dancers are simply waiting. Chairs and an old-fashioned analogue announcement board define the almost empty stage as a neutral transit zone. The board announces its messages with a soft clattering sound: 'Please Wait' or 'Delayed.' The first encounter between Meng Ningning (from China) and Eulalia Ayguade Farro (from Spain) immediately sets the tone. Meng first addresses Eulalia in Mandarin and then continues with the limited words of English that they both share, demonstrating a desire to communicate but also its difficulties. To Meng's question, 'Where does she come from?' Eulalia answers the obvious, 'I am not Chinese,' provoking immediate laughter in the audience. The comedy that often results from misunderstandings in intercultural dialogue re-emerges at several other moments in the performance, such as in a danced duet in which Meng tries to partner up with Indian dancer Saju Hari, matching her frivolous ballet moves and pirouettes to his more down to earth martial art technique of *kalaripayattu*.

bahok also repeats the metaphors of the journey and the border crossing. Shanell Winlock and Kim Young Jin depict yet another situation of being lost in translation: together they are being interviewed by an invisible customs officer. The comic effect of the misunderstandings is tempered here. There is a more serious undertone since it is clear that misunderstandings can potentially influence whether one is allowed to enter the country or not. At its creation in Beijing, *bahok* ended with Ayguade Farro speaking to her mother on the phone in her native tongue while the announcement board develops a life of its own, commenting on her situation: 'Are you lost? You look lost. Do you know where you are going? (...) What are you carrying? Body. Memories. Home' (Performance text *bahok*).

In 2010, Sidi Larbi Cherkaoui and his artistic partner Damien Jalet co-created *Babel* ⁽*words*⁾. It is a large-scale dance theatre production that explores—as the title suggests—the relationship between territory and language throughout the history of mankind, from prehistory to the contemporary megapolis. In the video documentary *All Dancers Are Migrants* (2011), Cherkaoui discusses 'how certain languages occupy a certain territory. And how as humans, we always create a certain territory. We need a space around our body. All other spaces are conventions between people. (...) Like all conventions they are temporal. They change.' In the dance performance these spatial transformations are constantly created by the dancers manipulating the large aluminium frames that are Antony Gormley's set design. A cityscape transforms into an enclosed boxing ring, which becomes a border control area at an airport. Similar to *bahok*, the latter is a non-place where travellers are in transit or are prevented from crossing territorial borders. In her analysis of *Babel* ⁽*words*⁾, Lise Uytterhoeven concludes that Cherkaoui 'foregrounds the travel story as a site where cultures clash in the "contact zone"' (Uytterhoeven 2019, 188).

In one of *Babel* ⁽*words*⁾ 's first scenes, all the performers mark out their 'territory' on stage with their hands while calling out the word 'land' in their multiple mother tongues. This polyphony of languages is later contrasted with a monologue that ironically celebrates English as 'the most widespread language in the world' (Performance text *Babel* ⁽*words*⁾). Throughout the production, Cherkaoui has performers speak in their mother tongues, without offering any translation, so that only part of the audience understands what they are actually saying. This refusal to translate the *heteroglossia* of languages is a deliberate strategy that he has used in many of his works.

Mikhail Bakhtin was the first to use the term *heteroglossia*. From its first use, the diversity of languages implies that there are different ways of conceptualising and experiencing the world. In *Speaking in Tongues: Language at Play in the Theatre* (2006), Marvin Carlson applies the concept to a wide range of historical and contemporary theatre practices combining multiple languages. Uytterhoeven, in turn, shows how Cherkaoui uses *heteroglossia* and non-translation as deliberate strategies for the creation of a more inclusive, less Eurocentric stage language 'that holds the potential to counter nationalism' (Uytterhoeven 2019, p. 132). Uytterhoeven argues that Cherkaoui's incorporation of a diversity of languages—including Russian, Arabic, Japanese and Hebrew—is very different from the *heteroglossic* theatre practices of other Belgian companies, such as Needcompany. Cherkaoui not only uses a much broader range of languages but also decides not to translate them. Uytterhoeven concludes that this dramaturgy of non-translation functions as a postcolonial critique. 'In the light of the politics of translation within postcolonialism, Cherkaoui rejects the burden of responsibility for translation, which is often put on the Other, the immigrant, to translate for the benefit of the dominant culture' (142). In her 'final reflections,' Uytterhoeven explicitly links Cherkaoui's approach to the concept of *cosmopolitanism*, 'which is based on the utopian notion that all human beings belong to the same community and have responsibilities of justice and hospitality towards each other beyond state boundaries' (211).

Cosmopolitan Artists Claiming Agency over Their Own Narratives

In *Performance, Subjectivity, Cosmopolitanism* (2020), Yana Meerzon analyses *Babel* $^{(words)}$ as an example of the contemporary chorus play, which 'stages cosmopolitanism and its singularities as being multiplied and diversified from within' (Meerzon 2020, 187). Meerzon's concept of a 'cosmopolitan artist,' which has also been used by both Mitra and Uytterhoeven, offers a valuable alternative to the reductive *second-generation* migrant label. It acknowledges that the self-chosen mobility of Cherkaoui and Khan, which they also portray in their travel narratives, is privileged compared to that of forced migrants. But it also doesn't deny that they still have to negotiate a fractured, 'hybrid and divided self' (Meerzon 2020, 22) that often feels it doesn't belong anywhere.

In the first decade of their careers, Sidi Larbi Cherkaoui and Akram Khan explored the complexities of their multiple identities: being native Europeans, being labelled *second-generation migrants*, claiming agency over their own narratives as *cosmopolitan artists*. They did so by narrating travel stories in which border crossings and cultural misunderstandings highlighted the difficulties of navigating a world still dominated by nation states and national identities. Although their mobility is economically more privileged than their parents,' they have experienced a similar sense of not belonging, which they articulate in multiple explorations of the theme of home. Formally, they celebrate *heteroglossia* and the co-existence of multiple dance languages and cultures on stage, each of which is valued equally.

References

Berger, John. 2007. *Hold Everything Dear*. London: Verso.
Berger, John. (1984) 2005. *and our faces, my heart, brief as photos*. London: Bloomsbury.
Boisseau, Rosita. 2013. *Sidi Larbi Cherkaoui*. Paris: Les Editions Textuel.
Burt, Ramsay. 2004. *Contemporary Dance and The Performance of Multicultural Identities*. https://www.akramkhancompany.net/wp-content/uploads/2016/01/kaash-essay.Pdf. Accessed 15 November 2021.
Chambers, Iain, 1994. *Migrancy, Culture, Identity*. London: Routledge.
Cherkaoui, Sidi Larbi. 2008. *State of the Union*. Theaterfestival. https://www.youtube.com/watch?v=OSHGFEZ7EP4. Accessed 26 July 2023.
———. 2014. *Een Achternaam, veel toekomst*. www.mo.be/artikel/een-achternaam-veel-toekomst. Accessed 26 July 2023.

Cherkaoui, Sidi Larbi and Delmas Gilles. 2007. *Zon-Mai, Parcours Nomades*. Arles: Actes Sud/Cité Internationale de l'Histoire de l'Immigration.

Chimienti, Milena, Alice Bloch, Laurence Ossipow and Catherine Wihtol de Wenden. 2019. 'Second Generation from Refugee Backgrounds in Europe.' Editorial. in: *Comparative Migration Studies* 7 (40), 1-15.

Cools, Guy. 2015. *In-Between Dance Cultures. On the Migratory Artistic Identity of Sidi Larbi Cherkaoui and Akram Khan*. Amsterdam: Valiz.

European Commission. n.d. 'Second-generation migrant.' Migration and Home Affairs. Accessed 11-15-2021 https://ec.europa.eu/home-affairs/pages/glossary/second-generation-migrant_en

European Theatre Convention. 2021. 'Diversity & Gender Equality in European Theatres – A Study.' Diversity and Gender (words) Equality. March 2021. https://www.europeantheatre.eu/page/advocacy/diversity-gender-equality-theatre.

Gatrell, Peter. 2019. *The Unsettling of Europe. The Great Migration, 1945 to the Present*. London: Penguin Random House.

Huggan, Graham. 2007. 'Unsettled Settlers: Postcolonialism, Travelling, Theory and the New Migrant Aesthetics.' In *Essays in Migratory Aesthetics: Cultural Practices Between Migration and Artmaking* edited by Sam Durrant and Catherine M. Lord, 129-143. Amsterdam: Rodopi

Meerzon, Yana. 2020. *Performance, Subjectivity, Cosmopolitanism*. Basingstoke: Palgrave Macmillan.

Mitra, Royona. 2010. 'Dancing Embodiment, Theorizing Space: Exploring The 'Third Space' in Akram Khan's zero degrees.' In *Planes of Composition: Dance, Theory and the Global* edited by André Lepeki and Jenn Joy, 40-63. New York: Seagull Press.

———. 2015. *Akram Khan. Dancing New Interculturalism*. Basingstoke: Palgrave Macmillan.

Sibony, Daniel. 1991. *Entre-deux. L'origine en partage*. Paris: Editions du Seuil.

Uytterhoeven, Lise. 2019. *Sidi Larbi Cherkaoui. Dramaturgy and Engaged Spectatorship*. Basingstoke: Palgrave Macmillan.

PART IV

Migration, Colonialism, and Forced Displacement

CHAPTER 32

The Theatre of Displacement and Migration in Southern Africa: Zimbabwe and South Africa in Focus

Samuel Ravengai

A survey of the most recent literature on the subject of migration projects the issue of movement as a preoccupation of African people keen to go to western countries and relocating to more prosperous African countries like South Africa. The literature completely writes off one of the major migrations in human history which was sanctioned at the Berlin Conference (1884/5). It is the migration of Europeans from their continent to Africa as an economic project, and their internal movements in Zimbabwe and South Africa in search of land, livestock, wild animals, grain and mineral resources. Major media houses are currently preoccupied with migrations of Africans as they cross the Mediterranean Sea in makeshift boats to find a new life in Europe. Eurocentrism has created a language which glorifies white migrations as investors while Africans are labelled as economic refugees. The treatment of Africans at ports of entry in Europe, even those with visas, is unpleasant while those of white people is gracious, a situation described by Cresswell (2010) as 'tunnelling'. The latest example is the terrible treatment of black students at Ukraine's border posts as they try to flee the Russia-Ukraine conflict. Guns are pointed at them by security forces as they are suspected of being insurgents. When they reach the check point or train station, they are told to go to the back of the queue to allow Ukrainian forced migrants to be served or board trains first. Africans are directed to walk to their preferred destinations.

S. Ravengai (✉)
Wits University, Johannesburg, South Africa
e-mail: Samuel.Ravengai@wits.ac.za

© The Author(s), under exclusive license to Springer Nature Switzerland AG 2023
Y. Meerzon, S. E. Wilmer (eds.), *The Palgrave Handbook of Theatre and Migration*, https://doi.org/10.1007/978-3-031-20196-7_32

In this chapter, I would like to focus on how playwrights and theatre makers captured these moments, including internal displacements, as in rural-urban migrations. These moments of encounter have caused pain to both parties and the agentive response has expressed itself in different forms including racism, liberatory nationalism (Europhobia), xenophobia and more recently, Afrophobia.

Historical and Cultural Context

Migration of peoples has been a characteristic feature of the demographics of southern Africa or perhaps the rest of humanity. From about 2000 BC, massive waves of Bantu people moved from Central and North Africa to occupy lands in southern Africa which had been hitherto thinly populated by the Khoi and San peoples. Some of these Bantu movements at times coincided with incursions of Persian, Chinese, Jewish, Arab, Indian and Phoenician merchants who were coming to trade in gold, ivory and slaves, some of them establishing families and staying permanently in southern Africa, such as the Lemba who can be linked to the Sabaean (Yemen) Jews (Gayre of Gayre 1972). New identities were formed through these contacts. Just after the peopling of southern Africa had somewhat settled, new European incursions began from 1503 on a temporary basis with the Portuguese sailor, Antonio Saldanha, landing at Table Bay, but more permanently from 1652 with the arrival of Jan van Riebeeck with the Dutch East India Company. He established a fort to develop a vegetable garden and other supplies to replenish ships rounding the Cape. By 1657, the company had begun to release some of its employees from service to become free burghers (free citizens). This created conflict with the Khoi Khoi over land and water, but the latter were subdued under the force of guns and forced to become servants in the new economy established by the settlers. It became customary that every Dutch white male had to have a farm and the free burghers began to migrate eastwards in search of water, land and livestock to loot from Africans. The Xhosa who had settled in the present-day Eastern Cape by between AD 580 and 760 slowly began to migrate eastwards towards the coast absorbing the Khoi Khoi within their ethnicity (Beach 1984). The pressures of trek Boers who were moving eastwards began to be felt, resulting in the first frontier wars with the Xhosa in the 1770s around present-day Gqeberha. Herbert Dhlomo's play, *Dingane*, which I will return to, captures moments like this.

In 1820, there was a massive migration of British settlers to the Cape Colony, numbering 4000 under an assisted emigration scheme passed by the British parliament. There was massive unemployment in the United Kingdom which various political proponents thought would be solved by migrations to colonies. The Voortrekker thought that the British were to be a solution to the conflicts between themselves and the Xhosa as they would be settled in a corridor between the trek Boers and the stolen lands of the Xhosa to create a buffer zone that would prevent direct contact with the Xhosas. However, the

Xhosa did not take kindly to seeing their land being parcelled out to the British settlers and this caused further tremors which are captured in Fatima Dike's play *The Sacrifice of Kreli*.

The arrival of the British caused further tensions between trek Boers and the British. The Dutch East India Company lost control of the Cape after the 1795 Battle of Muizenberg (Bredekamp 1995). The Cape effectively became a British colony. The trek Boers resented the Anglicization of the Cape, the banning in 1834 of the slavery on which they had relied for decades, the British liberalism which did not respect their interpretation of Calvinism which projected them as a 'Chosen People', landlessness among trek Boers, growing Afrikaner nationalism and several other factors, causing one of the greatest mass movements of white people on African soil. An estimated 6000 white trek Boers left the Cape between 1835 and 1846 and, if their servants and slaves are included, the estimate rises to 15,000 people who left the Cape at the time under what has been recorded in history as the Great Trek (SAHO 2019). These migrations established two Boer republics, Orange Free State and the Transvaal Republic, from which two Anglo-Boer wars were waged to defend the Boer republics from British imperialism in 1880 and 1899–1902. The re-enactment of the Great Trek was to take place in 1938 (Kruger 2020) and I will return to this shortly.

Cecil John Rhodes sponsored the migration of British colonialists under his company, the British South African Company (BSAC), to colonize Mashonaland and Matabeleland (renamed Southern Rhodesia), present-day Zimbabwe. Dubbed the Pioneer Column comprising the Pioneer Corps (PC) and the British South African Police (BSAP), the invasion column left Macloutsie in present-day Botswana in June 1890 with 250 men to colonize and map out the present-day Zimbabwe. On their way to present-day Harare, they contacted both Ndebele and Shona natives, resulting in armed conflict as captured in Robert Mshengu Kavanagh's *Mavambo* (1997). Upon arrival in then Salisbury (Harare) the Corps were to be disbanded and given 3000 acres of African land and 15 mining claims as compensation. This land had been occupied and effectively farmed by nearly half a million Africans who owned the territory at that time from about 200 AD. The ramifications of dispossession were to be felt for nearly a century.

During the Zimbabwean economic crisis starting from 1998 and reaching its climax in 2008, nearly 250,000 immigrants moved to South Africa. The Zimbabwean government's 2000 fast-track land reform programme dispossessed British colonial subjects of the land they had acquired during colonial conquest. This was an affront to the United Kingdom, which then mobilized the European Union and the United States to impose sanctions on Zimbabwe under the guise of punishing the postcolonial government for its alleged human rights violations. While a combative war did not ensue as in the Democratic Republic of the Congo (DRC), Angola and Mozambique, this was an economic war which plunged Zimbabwe into an economic crisis leading to thousands of professionals and unskilled labourers migrating to Canada, Australia,

UK, New Zealand and South Africa, with the latter hosting the highest number of Zimbabwean immigrants. Nkala's *The Crossing* (2011) and Hungwe and Karize's *Burn Mukwerekwere* (2018) capture the moments of black South African responses to these immigrants.

A Snapshot of Plays Dealing with Migration in South Africa and Zimbabwe

In the area of theatre and migration, South Africa is the most researched country in Southern Africa. Loren Kruger (2020) has a whole chapter devoted to the performance of pageants dedicated to celebrating the history of white immigrants in South Africa. The conflict between the English and trek Boers resulted in further migrations within South Africa as the Boers tried to avoid the English, forming two dominions in the process: Transvaal and Orange Free State. These republics were later collapsed in 1910 to form the Union of South Africa with other English dominions. The authorities decided to celebrate this union by performing a pageant, the 1910 Pageant of the Union. According to Kruger, this pageant began in Table Bay, Cape Town, and continued to the Cape Town City Council and Parliament. The organizers cast 5000 performers. In the performance, the arrival of European colonials is depicted, including the conquering of African lands as Herbert Dhlomo's *Dingane* will further reveal. For a pageant that was celebrating the unity of white people, some rough memories that had separated them in the past were left out: the Anglo-Boer wars. Kruger concludes that despite a cursory depiction of white women and people of colour, they were not given agency and the pageant glorified and valorized the heroic white males. According to Kruger this pageant was re-enacted in 1936 with a different script writer, Gustav Preller. Again, the focus was on migrations of Europeans to South Africa, labelled 'the beginning of history' (Kruger 2020, 29). The main characters are Europeans telling the story of migration from their perspective, the landing of van Riebeeck (1652), Simon van der Stel's exploits (1690), the occupation of the Cape by the British (1806), the arrival of British settlers (1820) and Nagmaal (holy communion) after the battle of Vegkop (1836). History is made by Europeans, and Africans were its objects to be tossed around without subjectivity. The pageant ends with the election of Paul Kruger as president of the Republic and the National Convention Assembly in Cape Town. The last part caused a feeling of nostalgia amongst Afrikaners who then decided to re-enact the Great Trek in 1938, which, according to Kruger, commemorated the century of the vow[1] taken at the Battle of Blood River in 1838 and a century of Boer resistance to the British. Nine ox-drawn wagons were used to retrace the trekkers' journey from Cape Town to Pretoria. Performers, men in farmer commandos and women in bonnet attire gathered at points along the path of South Africa. According to

---

[1] A vow taken by trek Boers on 16 December 1838 that they would build a church if God granted them victory against the Zulu and honour this day forever.

Kruger, 200,000 people assembled to welcome the performers in wagons and witnessed the unveiling of the cornerstone of the Voortrekker Monument in Pretoria on 16 December.

While Dhlomo focuses on the clashes between the Zulu and the Boers, Fatima Dike in *The Sacrifice of Kreli* (1976) focuses on the consequences of these frontier wars by shifting her gaze to a defeated Xhosa king of the Gcaleka tribe who has decided to live in a valley in Bomvanaland in the Eastern Cape. He is banished there with 300 soldiers and no women and children. This group of people has been living in this valley for seven years and they want the king to decide whether they should relaunch an offensive against the British or let them go back as a defeated nation to be with their families. The king is torn between these two positions. They have not been farming or living with their families to multiply their numbers. Thus, the encounter between the English migrants and Xhosa indigenes has brought about suffering of a scale never known to the Xhosa nation.

Magnet theatre conducted a project over a long period of time where it developed a repertoire of plays and performances which Fleishman called 'dramaturgies of displacement' (2015, 12). One of the co-directors of Magnet Theatre, Mandla Mbothwe, created performances on internal migrations specifically devoted to capturing the traumas of internal migrants as they travel from Eastern Cape along the N2 freeway to Cape Town. He created two works: *Inxeba lomphilisi* (The Wound of a Healer, 2010) and *Ingcwaba Lendoda Lise Cankwe Ndlela* (The Grave of the Man is Next to the Road, 2009).

The play *The Wound of a Healer* focuses on how performance makes visible the hidden everyday trauma of internal migrants of Xhosa extraction who use the N2 highway as the entry and exit points. The characters seen in the play are in fact spirits of the people who have died while attempting to make their way to Cape Town. In African cultures, these spirits must not be left to roam in the wilderness; they must be led back to their ancestral lands. The play features a healer who is trying to ritually collect these spirits so that they can rest in peace. It becomes an opportunity to learn about the traumas of these souls while they were still living and moving through this middle passage to a land where prosperity was assumed to be within reach. The chorus of these spirits physically perform this trauma.

Another Magnet Theatre play, *Every Year, Every Day, I am Walking* investigates the situation of refugees/migrants from other African countries resident in South Africa. In his play, *Every Year, Every Day, I am Walking*, Mark Fleishman (2015) tries to make the lives of migrants visible by creating a theatre that relies on the body for its realization. He avoids the strategies of what has been called Refugee Theatre, which tends to rely on verbatim techniques. He pursues what he calls a non-factual truthfulness. The play and characters follow three distinct stages of homeplace, the road and Cape Town. Through these phases the lives of migrants are explored.

Gina Schumkler's *The Line* is set in South Africa, with South African and Mozambican characters across the Afrophobic conflict divide. This is a verbatim theatre piece composed of six of the twelve testimonial monologues of people Schumkler interviewed in a period of five months after the Afrophobic attacks of 2008 and 2015 in South Africa. The play explores the trauma experienced by survivors, who are played by performers. This play captures the responses of black South Africans to the presence of the foreign other in the richest province of South Africa, Gauteng. The voices captured represent different categories of players during the Afrophobic attacks, such as instigators, attackers and those complicit with the violence through cheering the attackers (Maedza 2017). The narrative takes a verbatim approach which is however manipulated by the playwright in terms of rearranging the events. The performers directly address the audience, and the testimonies are interspersed with flashbacks of attack scenes. The character monologues are introduced by playing back voice-overs taken from the original interviews recorded by the playwright during the period of research. This play echoes the experiences of other characters in a different play, Blessing Hungwe's and Rumbidzai Karize's *Burn Mukwerekwere*, which captures the Afrophobic attacks of 2008 in Cape Town.

The Crossing was written by Jonathan Nkala while in exile in South Africa to record his experiences while travelling from Zimbabwe to South Africa. Nkala reveals sixteen encounters which he had while travelling from Zimbabwe to South Africa, ending in the city of Cape Town. Nkala's body carries with it the playing culture or underscore that has been ingrained into his being through playing, gaming, practice, performance, competition and watching others play in his Imbizo township of Kwekwe City. When he meets others on his journey, he shares this cultural capital to ease tensions and create work that could be sold for monetary rewards. While other plays written by immigrants in South Africa have sought sympathy through mobilizing the victimhood trope, Nkala deviates from this narrative and celebrates personal sacrifice and the joys of victory over forces that are against life and human dignity.

Writing and Performing Migration: Some Case Studies

I base this analysis on two plays written at different times but capturing the same period of colonization: one based on the South African experience written by Dhlomo and the other one based on the Zimbabwean experience workshopped by University of Zimbabwe theatre students with Kavanagh acting as a scribe. Herbert Dhlomo's *Dingane* and Kavanagh Mshengu's *Mavambo* (First Steps) capture the moments of European migration to Africa which suggest that their mission was not investment but plundering African resources and pacifying Africans through a corrupted religion.

Dingane opens with the death of Shaka, king of the Zulu, who himself instigated one of the greatest movements of Africans from South Africa to Zambia, Zimbabwe, Malawi and Tanzania during the time of *mfecane* (the crushing which caused massive migrations from South Africa to other Africans regions). Shaka dies at the hands of Mbopha, Shaka's principal servant, and two other assassins. As he dies, he orders his guard, Jeqe, to take action by reversing the coup by avenging his death and overthrowing the coup plotters. Jeqe escapes to join the Swazi king. Meanwhile Dingane, Shaka's brother who has now taken over the throne, receives news of the Boers who are 'homeless wanderers owing allegiance to no king' (Dhlomo 1985, 85). Bongoza, one of Dingane's chiefs (an *induna*), hatches a plan to defeat the Boers that is well received by the king. He would act as a deserter and meet the Boers in the valley of Ophathe. Two regiments would hide in the valley holding skin shields which Bongoza would show the Boers as cattle that they could loot for themselves. On advancing to the valley, they would be swarmed by the Zulu regiments and get killed.

In seeking land and wealth, the Boers decide to use peaceful means by visiting Dingane, led by Retief. Retief presents his plan to purchase land on which to settle. However, he is accused of having settled himself on the horizons of the Zulu Kingdom, to which he retorts, '[W]e found open spaces unoccupied' (89). This is contrary to Zulu custom that 'people receive the king's consent before they occupy any part of the land, from the sea to beyond the Khalamba' (89). This issue becomes a flash point during discussions. When the meeting ends King Dingane reflects on what has just happened and agrees to Bongoza's summation that 'the Boers have one aim only—land and cattle, the very things that are the soul of our race' (91).

Meanwhile Dingane has opted for war after getting counsel from his paternal aunt, Mkabayi, whose view about the Boers is: 'I abhor them! Heralds of strife! Thieves of our peace! Grabbers of our land! Usurpers of our sovereignty! Impeders of our efforts! Enslavers of our soul!' (97). Away from the African people, the Boers disparage them in racist language. It is this fight for resources that results in the manufacture of stereotypes to justify the occupation. On their own the Boers call the Zulus 'black monkeys' or 'children', 'cunning devils' and 'inhuman giants'.

The Boers collaborate with Mpande, the brother of Dingane, and launch an offensive against the Zulu regiments. Through the agency of the messenger, King Dingane is informed that most of his soldiers have been killed and the Ncombe River has been turned into blood. The Boers are celebrating the victory. As this message is being delivered, the Zulu army runs back to the king's court with the Swazi army in hot pursuit. Jeqe kills Dingane offstage and drags his body to the stage. An alliance between a Zulu prince, Mpande, Swazi regiments and the Boers dethroned Dingane to overturn the coup that killed Shaka, in order to establish an ethical Zulu administration. However, this is effected through the assistance of Boers, who will in future destroy the African state.

What is clear from this play is that at the moment of encounter with Africans, the white settler projects himself as superior and constructs a language to immortalize this relationship. Language becomes a reservoir of prejudices against Africans. The relationship is also characterized by a surface projection of rationality on the part of the Boers. When conversation and rational disputation does not bear the intended result, the immigrant resorts to violence to subdue the Africans and dispossess them of their land and cattle. In the case of Zimbabwe, the Pioneer Column established what was called the Loot Committee to collect the spoils of war. In the ensuing Matabele war, a herd of more than 200,000 cattle was looted under the oversight of John Meikles and distributed to the corps with members of the committee getting the lion's share of the loot. Colonial history projects Africans as the thieves who waged war to steal the white man's cattle. The plays written through the agency of black playwrights and Marxists like Kavanagh Mshengu choose to toe the line of historical truth as opposed to colonial discourse.

In 1890, the British colonialists moved in a convoy from present-day Botswana on their way to present-day Harare, establishing various forts as they marched north. The names of 250 white males recruited in the police force and the army are known. Yet when one looks at the pictures of the invading column, one notices the presence of undocumented African and Coloured servants who drove the oxen, pulling the wagons and serviced these vehicles. These have been completely written out of history. The voices of Africans whose land was being invaded are also missing. Robert Kavanagh's *Mavambo* (First Steps) and Danai Gurira's *The Convert* (2013) bring to the fore these voices.

The play *Mavambo* is divided into four compressions:[2] Sekuru's narration, Alexio's journey to Salisbury (as Harare was called), Alexio's experience of the Rhodesian racist system and finally Alexio's imprisonment and decision to join the liberation struggle. It is a play that tries to cover the history of Zimbabwe. The last three compressions do not deal much with migration and I will focus on the first compression, which is relevant to this chapter.

The story is told through the agency of the omniscient narrator, Alexio, who tries to recount the story of colonization as it was told by his paternal grandfather, Sekuru. The story took place in the village of Makosa. As Alexio reminisces over the story, the images of his memory are projected on the stage and with mbira music in the background. The *sarungano* (storyteller), Sekuru, appears on stage and tells the story as he told it to Alexio. The rest of the cast responds as audience/performers, as would be the case in traditional storytelling. The village of Makosa was headed by chief Chuma and it was invaded by the Cecil John Rhodes Pioneer Column on their way to the north to establish the final fort. This column was led by Jackson, who presented a request to the chief to rest his 24 oxen in exchange for a fresh span of the same number. He also wanted to recruit young men whom he promised would be employed by his column for wages. When this request was turned down by chief Chuma, Jackson mobilized his fighting men to shoot at the chief's warriors, who were keen to defend their families. The battle between guns and spears was

---

[2] 'Compression' is a word that I use in my new theory of Afroscenology to designate action units in African plays that do not use the western units of scenes and acts. They are named in this way because the action that unfolds exerts a lot of pressure in the unit without necessarily leading to a resolution. The action leads to deformation as opposed to formation of something new.

unbalanced and soon the warriors began to fall, prompting chief Chuma to stop the battle. Emerging as victors, Jackson no longer negotiated but demanded what he wanted, forcibly taking 24 oxen and 20 young men as slaves. Forty Makosa warriors lay dead and 11 wounded. At the chief's council, it was debated whether to pursue the invading column or not, and they passed the resolution that the captured young men would liberate themselves.

After a period of time, another white person was sighted and chief Chuma ordered him to be captured. What is narrated by Sekuru is then performed by players impersonating warriors, women, Muchinda (headman) and the white man, Reverend Mills. In the interaction, Rev Mills requested to establish a mission in Chuma's chiefdom. Chief Chuma was furious that people who looked like Rev Mills had decimated his village. Rev Mills further revealed that one of the captured boys from Makosa, Shonga, helped him to learn Shona. The other 19 boys were working for white men to dig minerals. Chief Chuma did not fully grasp the value of a mission station and western education which he said would alienate his subjects from their African culture. A plan was hatched to kill Rev Mills, but the chief took counsel from his soothsayers who advised that Rev Mills must not be killed as this would cause doom to the village. Rev Mills was expelled from the village and returned to his mission Mutoko station. There is a sense in which the narrative tries to highlight the way African democracy functioned in reaching a decision. The metaphysical world of Africans is projected in a positive light as it is not depicted as a source of evil used to destroy people, but as the source of the choice to save the life of a white missionary.

While Rev Mills was sleeping at his Mutoko mission station, without his white friends knowing that he had returned, something unpleasant happened. Shonga, who had been captured from Makosa village, was evangelizing to a group of Africans at a different village in Mutoko. Jackson, the leader of the invasion column, appeared and ordered that the unmarried women be moved to the church premises to sexually service four white males and that the rest of the church group was to go back home. Shonga is racially abused by Jackson when he tries to passively resist the order. Realizing the potential sexual abuse of young African women by white men, Shonga decided to dismiss everybody, provoking tantrums from Jackson. When the women started running away, the other white men ran after them and aimed guns at Shonga, at which point Rev Mills was awoken by the noise. He called his friends to order. In anger, Jackson pursued the villagers while dragging Shonga with a rope tied to a horse. The white gang torched the thatched dwellings of the villagers. The Mutoko warriors fiercely attacked the gang, causing Jackson's armed column to retreat. Shonga was killed in the scuffle together with an unidentified number of African men, including the white man whom Shonga strangled to death at the point of his own death.

While *Mavambo* deals with the conquest and proselytization of Africans by white immigrants, Danai Gurira's *The Convert* focuses on the life of African immigrants brought by the white colonialists from South Africa.

The Convert,³ a play written by Danai Gurira, focuses on the black colonists who came with the Pioneer invading column to illuminate how the local Shona population responded to their fellow African brothers who were advancing the colonial cause. Jackson's character in *Mavambo* matches that of Chancellor, Chilford Ndlovu's friend, in this play. He is a worldly replica of Chilford. He resembles Jackson in *Mavambo* while Chilford resembles Reverend Mills in the same play, except that in *Mavambo*, the domineering voices are white. Stolen from the blacks after the defeat and death of his father at the hands of white soldiers, he resides amongst the white community, seemingly enjoying the status of black colonists—the Cape boys.⁴ Chancellor has the same attitude towards blacks as that of Chilford. He sees them as kaffirs, primitive and savages. Whereas Chilford has reverence for God, Chancellor is the flipside of the same coin. He pursues the cravings of his flesh by drinking, fighting and sleeping around. In fact, at his death, many women came with his children claiming paternity. Chancellor does not hide his lust towards Jekesai even right under the nose of Chilford. He attempts to rape Jekesai but is stopped by Tamba and his uncle. In the ensuing conflict, he is killed by Tamba.

In his dealings with fellow black people, Chilford comes across as a black person with black skin who masks the white man in him. Anything African is inherently bad and evil, whilst anything white is inherently good and holy. When white people go out to kill and suppress the first Chimurenga uprisings, Chilford has no problems with that, yet when the self-same black people defend themselves by killing white people and their black accomplices, he denounces them. After a savage white attack on blacks in the Mazowe area, Tamba and his uncle flee to Salisbury, where they kill Chilford's friend, Chancellor, inside Ndlovu's house. Tamba and his uncle flee back to Mazowe and back to Salisbury when pursued by white colonialists. Tamba confesses to killing Chancellor. Even if his widow, Prudence, forgives Tamba and Mai Tamba and Ester plead with Chilford to let Tamba live, Ndlovu expels Tamba from his house. Tamba is killed 'like a chicken' by his white pursuers.

This missionary family was soon joined by Jekesai, Mai Tamba's niece from Mazowe. Jekesai becomes Chilford Ndlovu's most successful missionary project. She denounces her African name, Jekesai, and adopts Ester as her born-again name. She acquires an amazing level of competence in the English language and becomes literate in a short period of time. She devours volumes of scripture to a point where she resembles the critical consciousness of the biblical Berea Church. She engages a white missionary and corrects him on his biased interpretation of scripture. She is admonished by her master, Chilford,

---

³ I watched Danai Gurira's *The Convert* at the Prince Edward High School Beit Hall in the evening of 16 December 2013 and took notes from which this writing is based.

⁴ The so-called Cape Boys were a vibrant group of Xhosa, Hottentots and Coloured people (brought from South Africa by the invading column) with various skills in leather working, building, smithing, wagon repair, evangelism, transport riding and market gardening and earned £5/month as compared to £1/month paid to locals and in some cases 15 shillings per month (see Yoshikuni 2006).

for correcting a white priest. Her critical mind and her biblical application of scripture become a source of annoyance to her master, Chilford Ndlovu. Ndlovu's position is that the white man's culture must be absorbed without questioning. They are ordained by God to bring the natives from darkness to light.

By the end of the play Jekesai denounces her adopted name, Ester, and reverts to Jekesai. She throws away her European dress and adorns herself in her African costume and this time boldly stands before Chilford Ndlovu without shame, as if to mock his Christian sensibilities. At this time Chilford Ndlovu is deserted. Mai Tamba and Prudence have left. Chancellor is dead. There is war in the city and in the countryside. Ndlovu radiates a sense of regret, confusion and double feelings.

Using intertextuality as a reading method, a few issues are clear. Colonial discourse had successfully projected the black sign as a quintessence of negativity. The two plays reveal that not a single race can monopolize negativity. The white characters in *Mavambo* can perform dastardly acts, just like the black colonists in *The Convert*. Superiority is a social construct accepted and projected by both white and black colonials in colonial Rhodesia. It is the advancement of colonialism which caused mistrust, racism and recourse to violence to reclaim lost humanity. Colonialism dehumanized blacks through violence and blacks used the same method through liberatory nationalism to reclaim their personhood. While liberation struggles were acceptable as a last resort in the face of oppression, they have left a culture of violence which characterizes the kinds of xenophobic and Afrophobic attacks seen in contemporary plays on migration in Zimbabwe and South Africa.

References

Beach, D. N. 1984. *Zimbabwe Before 1900*. Gweru: Mambo Press.
Bredekamp, Henry C. Jatti. 1995. 'The Battle of Muizenberg (1795): The Moravian Missionaries and the Telling of Corps Pandouren History.' *Kronos*, 22, 36–53. https://journals.co.za/doi/pdf/10.10520/AJA02590190_329. Accessed 25 April 2022.
Cresswell, Tim. 2010. 'Towards a politics of mobility.' *Society and Space Journal*, 28 (1), 17–31. https://doi.org/10.1068/d11407. Accessed 26 July 2023.
Dhlomo, Herbert. 1985. 'Dingane.' In *H.I.E Dhlomo: Collected Works*, 1–50. Johannesburg: Ravan Press.
Dike, Fatima. 1976. *The Sacrifice of Kreli*. Alexandria, VA: Alexander Street Press.
Fleishman, Mark. 2015. 'Dramaturgies of Displacement in the Magnet Theatre Migration Project.' In *Performing Migrancy and Mobility in Africa: Cape of Flows*, edited by Mark Fleishman, 12–36. New York: Palgrave Macmillan.
Gayre of Gayre. 1972. *The Origin of the Zimbabwean Civilisation*. Salisbury: Galaxie Press.
Gurira, Danai. 2013. 'The Convert.' Performance watched at Prince Edward Beit Hall on 16 December 2013.

Hungwe, Blessing and Karize Rumbidzai. 2018. 'Burn Mukwerekwere.' *Southern African Plays Collection*, edited by Likongwe, Smith, 175–223. Lilongwe: Pan African Publishers.

Kavanagh, Mshengu Robert. 1997. *Making People's Theatre*. Harare: University of Zimbabwe Press.

Kruger, Loren. 2020. *A Century of South African Theatre*. London: Methuen Drama.

Maedza, Pedzisai. 2017. *Performing Asylum: Theatre of Testimony in South Africa*: African Studies Centre: University of Leiden.

Nkala, Khumbulani Jonathan. 2011. 'The Crossing.' In *Cockroach: A Trilogy of Plays*, 1–99. Cape Town: Junkets.

SAHO. 2019. 'Great Trek 1835–1846.' *South African History Online*. https://www.sahistory.org.za/article/great-trek-1835-1846. Accessed 8 February 2022.

Yoshikuni, Tsuneo. 2006. *African Urban Experiences in Colonial Zimbabwe: A Social History of Harare before 1925*. Harare: Weaver Press.

CHAPTER 33

From the Yoruba Travelling Theatre to the Nobel Prize in Literature: Nigerian Theatre in Motion

Bisi Adigun

While the history of theatre in Nigeria can be traced to the pre-colonial period, what brought it to the consciousness of various academies all over the world was when Wole Soyinka won the Nobel Prize in Literature in 1986. According to the Swedish Academy, the body responsible for awarding the yearly Nobel Prize for Literature, Soyinka is a writer, 'who in wide cultural perspective and with poetic overtones fashions the drama of existence' (Nobel Prize 1986). While he writes primarily in the English language for a worldwide audience, including the global north where all black people are considered the same, Soyinka's 'wide cultural perspective' is essentially African. However, when asked in an interview in 1985, 'Do you see yourself as a Yoruba writer?,' Soyinka's quick response was: 'Well, it's obvious that I am not an Igbo writer!' Then, he proceeded to explain how a Nigerian writer 'is a creature of formation,' due to the linguistic, religious, ethnic, and cultural diversity of Nigeria, before unequivocally declaring: 'There's no question at all about it in my mind, I'm primarily a Yoruba writer, just as you have Occitan writers in France, Welsh writers, Scottish Literature … even when it is written in English' (Wilkinson 2001, 149). In this chapter, I trace the development of Nigerian theatre, particularly, from the era of the Yoruba travelling theatre to the year Soyinka was awarded the Nobel Prize, with particular focus on how migration within and across the borders of Nigeria, as well as immigration into Nigeria, has shaped

B. Adigun (✉)
Bowen University, Iwo, Nigeria
e-mail: olabisi.adigun@bowen.edu.ng

this development. According to Ric Knowles, interculturalism—which, in my view, is a by-product of migration—'is an urgent topic in the twenty-first century' (2010, 3), and the reason he advances to reinforce his position is that:

> As cities and nations move beyond the monochromatics, as human traffic between nations and cultures (both willing and unwilling) increases, as hybridity and syncretism (the merging of forms) become increasingly characteristic of cultural production everywhere, and as nineteenth century nationalism gives way to twenty-first century *trans*nationalism, it becomes imperative that the ways in which cultural exchange is performed be critically re-examined. (Knowles 2010, 3; emphasis original)

Arguably, Soyinka is not only intercultural, but he is also a transnational writer bearing in mind that he is a Yoruba writer who writes in English. His aesthetics and theory of Yoruba tragedy, though significantly influenced by Greek tragedy, are predicated on the Yoruba myth of Ogun, who is the Yoruba god of war and iron. Furthermore, while elements of European theatre tradition are traceable in his drama, the Yoruba metalanguages—music, songs, proverbs, mime, incantations, and various other performance elements—he employs in his dramaturgy are also the hallmark of the practitioners of the Yoruba travelling theatre, such as Hubert Ogunde (1916–1990), Kola Ogunmola (1925–1973), Duro Ladipo (1931–1978), and many others. Thus, while the Yoruba cosmology and its attendant traditional religious festivals have provided the fillip for Soyinka's theorization of his Yoruba tragedy, further to carrying out extensive field research on various traditional festivals all over Nigeria, it is clearly the foundation laid by the Yoruba travelling theatre practitioners upon which Soyinka has built its aesthetics.

Migration: Within, Beyond, and into Nigeria

In 'A Theory of Migration,' Everett S. Lee defines migration broadly 'as a permanent and semi-permanent change of residence' (1966, 49). Thus, for Lee, migration is associated with the movement of humans from one space to another, regardless of the distance or geographical locations; and since humans are the practitioners and consumers of theatre, which, *vis-à-vis* migration, is the focus of this study, I propose to adopt Lee's simple definition to examine migration within, across, and into Nigerian shores from the period when Nigeria was a British colony until 1986. As a truly multicultural entity, Nigeria comprises mainly of the Hausa/Fulani people in the North, the Igbo in the Southeast, and the Yoruba in the Southwest. It was these three groups as well as all the various ethnic groups within them that the British brought together and named Nigeria in 1914. Migration as a phenomenon, on the other hand, is as old as human civilization. Thus, it is hardly surprising that when Nigeria was still a colony Nigerian subjects were always migrating from one part of the country to another for various reasons, be they war, education, persecution, transfer, marriage, service, or simply in search of greener pastures provided by the colonial enterprises in the urban areas of the country (Akinriade 2015, 66). Not unexpectedly, this trend continued after Nigeria gained its independence in 1960. For example, the 1966 coup against the Nigerian federal government (as well as its counter-coup responses) and the pogrom of thousands of Igbos in the North during this period led to over a million people within this group recorded as returning to their traditional territories in the Southeast.

However, the migration of Nigerian people is not limited to within the borders of what is known today as Nigeria. Nigerians can be found in numerous African countries, including Republic of Benin, Cameroon, Ghana, Sierra Leone, South Africa, and even beyond African shores. The first recorded presence of Nigerians in the UK can, for instance, be traced to over 200 years ago by virtue of the transatlantic slave trade. Olaudah Equiano (1745–1797), a former slave who was born in the Kingdom of Benin in the southeast of present-day Nigeria, lived in London and participated (alongside other Africans living in Britain) in the debate over the slave trade's abolition. Furthermore, Nigerians have always been travelling to the UK to holiday, study, work, or live. It is hardly surprising then that in 2019 the Office for National Statistics estimated Nigerian-born immigrants living in the UK to be over 215,000, making Nigerians one of the UK's largest immigrant groups, as is also the case in many other European countries, North America, South America, and in Asia. In short, wherever in the world there is life, you will find Nigerians.

The earliest known instance of non-African migration into what is known today as Nigeria can be traced to the Portuguese explorers who reached Benin about 1458; later on, other Europeans, such as the English and Dutch, arrived to exchange their mirrors, gunpowder, and liquor for tobacco, palm produce, and slaves. During the transatlantic slave trade, over a million slaves were shipped to the new world, particularly the Caribbean, through the Calabar and Bonny Ports in the southern coast. In the words of Nigerian journalist Adaobi Trici Nwauban, '[a]bout 1.5 million Igbo slaves were shipped across the Atlantic Ocean between the 15th and 19th Centuries' (2020). Apparently, the trading of slaves did not stop in Igbo lands until the 1940s, despite the abolition laws passed around the world many decades before. But aside from traders, many other Europeans arrived in the southern part of present-day Nigeria on missionary duties. History has recorded, for instance, the presence of Mary Slessor, a Scottish Presbyterian missionary, who (in 1819) stopped the killing of twins as was the hitherto custom among the Igbo people. As we will see anon, it is worthy to note that two main practitioners of the Yoruba travelling theatre—namely Ogunde and Ladipo—began their career as theatremakers in the church.

In the areas of arts and culture, particularly the development of theatre in Nigeria, a special mention must be made of Ulli Beier: a German Jew, who—along with his Austrian wife, Susan Wenger—arrived in Nigeria to teach phonetics at the University of Ibadan in 1956. Beier and Wenger lived in Ede, Ilobu, and Oshogbo—typical Yoruba enclaves, which made them become interested in traditional Yoruba arts and heritage. Consequently, Beier contributed immensely to the development of culture, modern arts, and theatre in Nigeria, and his contribution, particularly to the establishment of Duro Ladipo's travelling theatre in Oshogbo, cannot be overstated. Under the pen name Obotunde Ijimere, Beier wrote the play *The Imprisonment of Obatala* (1966) based on the myth of Obatala, the Yoruba archdivine creator god. Beier is also the author of *Eda* (1966), an adaptation of Hugo von Hofmanthal's *Everyman*, which Duro Ladipo performed to critical acclaim in Nigeria as well as in Germany, Austria, Belgium, and Switzerland. It was also Beier who drew Soyinka's attention to the historical event that inspired *Death and the King's Horseman* (1975).

Two other immigrants in Nigeria that must also be mentioned at this juncture, owing to their contributions to the development of theatre in the late 1950s to early 1960s, are English migrants Geoffrey Axworthy and Martin Banham. In 1956, Axworthy and Banham had arrived in Ibadan purposely to 'awaken public and official interest in drama and theatre as entertainment, as an art, and as an educational tool' (Axworthy 1972, 17). It was the Dramatic Society which Axworthy and Banham had initiated upon their arrival that would later present Soyinka's plays *The Swamp Dwellers* (1958) and *The Lion and the Jewel* (1959) as a double bill in 1959. These were the first plays by Soyinka ever seen in Nigeria. It is also worthy of note that it was this Dramatic Society that would subsequently evolve into the first School of Drama in any Nigerian university, when it received a grant of two hundred thousand dollars from the Rockefeller Foundation in 1962. 'That the University College Ibadan should be the object of philanthropic largesse,' in the words of Christopher Balme,

> was not surprising considering its position as Nigeria's premier, and until 1960, only university. Established in 1948 on the recommendation of the British government's Elliot Commission on Higher Education in West Africa as a University College, it was part of a network of new colonial universities in West and East Africa and the West Indies. They were staffed largely by British lecturers, awarded degrees through the University of London, and were designed by British architects. (2019, 8)

It was no sheer coincidence, therefore, that Soyinka eventually returned to Nigeria in January 1960, after his five-year sojourn in the UK, on a Rockefeller grant, and in the appointment of the School of Drama at University College Ibadan.

The Emergence of Professional Theatre in Nigeria

In *Drama and Theatre in Nigeria: A Critical Source Book*, Yemi Ogunbiyi suggests two broad classifications for Nigerian forms of drama, namely traditional and literary. The former he further sub-divides into Dramatic ritual, popular tradition, and Yoruba travelling theatre (2014, 11). The travelling theatre was greatly influenced by the first two categories of traditional forms of drama, on the one hand, and by European colonization, on the other. Further, it is important to reiterate here that it is the travelling theatre in particular that laid the foundation upon which Soyinka and other Nigerian first-generation writers, who are the pioneers of the literary form of drama, built their careers as dramatists. Hence Martin Banham's argument that 'it is a mistake to accept too uncritically a view of Wole Soyinka as being one of leader and led'; to do so, Banham contends, 'would be to overlook the considerable role of the folk opera company … who work mainly in Yoruba' (1972, 10). In light of Banham's contention, this discussion on how Soyinka's drama won him the Nobel Prize in Literature ought to begin with an appraisal of the emergence of the Yoruba travelling theatre.

The first professional Yoruba travelling theatre company, The Ogunde Concert Party, was founded in Nigeria in 1945 by Hubert Ogunde, whom many would regard as the 'founding father' of modern Nigerian theatre. Ogunde was a teacher for eight years in Ososa, his hometown in Western Nigeria, but would later become a policeman. His talents as a man of the theatre, however, came to the fore as the choirmaster of the Lagos-based Church of the Lord. He successfully presented selected biblical scenes in between songs that he was asked to compose and arrange for the Church's Service of Songs. The following year, Ogunde resigned from the police force and concentrated full time on doing theatre work. At first, he was performing religious plays, but within a short time he began to explore the social issues of the day. One of his earliest plays, *Strike and Hunger* (1945), was banned in some parts of Nigeria by the then colonial authorities because of their anxiety that the play could incite workers to go on strike. With a view to becoming a better playwright and showman, Ogunde travelled to England in July 1947 after gaining admission into the Buddy Bradley School of Dancing in London. 'During my stay there,' in Ogunde's words, 'I had the opportunity of visiting several theatres and film studios in the United Kingdom and later I went to Paris on a sight-seeing trip' (Lindfors 1976, 244). When he returned to Nigeria in September of the same year, it was with theatrical equipment worth two thousand pounds. More importantly, he introduced tap dance into his performances and wrote more plays, making him increasingly famous. In the year 1948, Ogunde toured to Ivory Coast and Ghana. One of his most famous plays, *Bread and Bullet* (1950), was inspired by an actual event in which some coal miners were shot. Furthermore, his *Yoruba Ronu!* (1965), literally a call for the Yoruba people to unite in order to be a force to reckon with, was banned by the then government of the Western Region of Nigeria who claimed the play foregrounded the cause of a rival party. Truly, Ogunde, who was eventually invited to be the director of the National Troupe when it was founded in 1986, as Soyinka has rightly observed, 'must be saying something really dangerous, or something worth listening to' (Gibbs 2001, 108). And, perhaps, something worth emulating, one may add, because by 1947 another travelling theatre troupe known as Ogunmola's Theatre Party was founded.

Kola Ogunmola was a former school teacher who concentrated more on the dramatization of biblical themes and fairy stories, thereby avoiding social or political issues. One of his famous plays is *Love of Money* (c. 1950), which tells the story of Adeleke who turns his back on his first wife and marries a younger wife only to be duped and dumped. But as great an actor and a producer as Ogunmola was, it was when Robert July, the representative of the Rockefeller Foundation in Nigeria, saw him perform in Oshogbo in 1955 that he had his break. Having been impressed by Ogunmola's performance, July negotiated a generous Rockefeller Foundation grant for him, coupled with a six-month residency with the Drama Department at the University of Ibadan, during which he was able to familiarize himself with more sophisticated stage techniques, interact with students, and work on the production of a new play. Consequently, his theatrical interpretation of Amos Tutuola's novel *The Palmwine Drinkard*, in which he also played the lead role and which he eventually took to Algiers, is still regarded as one of the most powerful performances ever given by Ogunmola in his short theatre-making career. 'In his praise song of the spirit of palm wine, he surpasses anything that has ever come on the local stage,' Segun Olusola wrote in *Nigeria Magazine* of Ogunmola's powerful performance. 'Whether he sings it or leads the chorus to recite it, his pauses, nuances, gestures, word association or the eloquent mimes when he puts his expressive face in full use,' Olusola concluded, 'you are witnessing a great performer in the act with a relish for the liquor that is easily transferable to the audience' (Quoted in Beier 2014, 406). Upon completing his six-month residency, Ogunmola, with the aid of the Rockefeller grant, became fully professional and thenceforth, 'his popularity rose fast and his perfection grew steadily (Beier 2014, 407).

For a few years, Ogunmola's troupe and Ogunde's remained the most popular until Duro Ladipo founded his own theatre company, which became the most 'artistically ambitious' (White 1974, 150) of all these travelling theatre troupes. Duro Ladipo, like Ogunde, began his career in the church as a music composer. But in 1960, he caused a controversy in his church when he introduced Yoruba drums, which church members associated with pagan worship, into his music composition. As a result, he began to present his composition outside the church and his idea of incorporating traditional Yoruba drums into his music was one of the things that ultimately set him apart from his predecessors and peers. Also, for drawing upon Yoruba historical legends, Ladipo became the first writer of Yoruba tragic operas. He recruited traditional performers such as 'drummers, dancers and singers and proceeded to immerse himself in the serious study of classical Yoruba music, poetry and history.' Ogunbiyi goes on to note that

'The end-result was a different kind of Yoruba theatre, self consciously traditional [...], invigorating, intense and with a charm of its own. Imbued with a genuine sense of cultural revivalism, Ladipo reached beyond the morality plays characteristic of the forerunners of Yoruba travelling theatre, into the new territory of Yoruba historical drama.' (2014, 423)

Aside from specializing in historical drama, as is exemplified by his plays *Oba Moro* (1962), *Oba Koso* (1963), *Oba Waja* (1964), *Moremi* (1966), and many others, another way in which Ladipo distinguished himself was by setting up in Oshogbo town a cultural centre called Mbari Mbayo. The centre, which opened on March 17, 1962 with a performance of *Oba Moro*, became a hub not only for performances but also for fine artists. It is important to note that the idea to set up the centre was born when Ladipo was invited to perform a Christmas Cantata at the Mbari Club in Ibadan, which itself was set up in June 1961 by a group of writers, including Wole Soyinka, JP Clark, DO Fagunwa, Christopher Okigbo, Demas Nwoko, and Uche Okeke, as well as Ulli Beier and South African Ezekiel Mphalele. That said, one peculiarity common to these three travelling theatre troupes under discussion here is that they all performed in the Yoruba language and therefore significantly helped 'the strengthening and confirmation of the cultural identity of the Yoruba people' (Fischer-Lichte 1990, 17), which, one can argue, is also Soyinka's preoccupation in his corpus of drama, though he writes in English. In other words, although we can recognize Soyinka as the Nobel Laureate, the foundation of his work has been created by the so-called travelling theatre practitioners. In an interview with James Gibbs in 2001, Soyinka makes this point more eloquently:

> Well, you can imagine what an exciting, absolutely unpredictable, un-uniform theatre this was and this is the tradition on which we, the so-called modern dramatists, in various forms, have attempted to build—not non-consciously, but this material was there, and we tried as much as possible to make use of it. (Gibbs 2001, 76)

Thus, if one carefully analyses Soyinka's theatre, one is bound to see the influence of the travelling theatre practitioners on it. The idea of participating as an actor in his Orisun Theatre productions of his plays can, for instance, be likened to how Ogunde, Ogunmola, and Ladipo ran their individual theatre troupes as writers, directors, and performers. Then, the similarity between the titles of Ogunde's opera, *The Black Forest* (1945), and Soyinka's first Yoruba tragic drama, *A Dance of the Forest* (1960), is noteworthy. Although Ogunde's opera was first produced in 1945, its re-staging at the Glover Memorial Hall in Lagos in 1950 marked an important milestone in Ogunde's career. In the re-staging, Ogunde thrilled his audience not only with native opera, but also 'with refined African music played on foreign and native instruments combined' (Quoted in Clark 2014, 378). Furthermore, Ogunde had rearranged the opera to include an ancient Yoruba dance as well as dialogue rendered in Yoruba. Therefore, the performance marked the beginning of what is now known as the Yoruba Concert Party. Extracts from Soyinka's play, on the other hand, were first produced with the title *A Dance of the African Forests* in 1959 as part of the 'Without the Decor' programme at the Royal Court Theatre in London. However, when he produced the play, re-titled *A Dance of the Forests*, with his 1960 Masks theatre group, he incorporated the daredevil, well-choreographed, energetic display of the Atilogwu dancers from the East.

Regarding how Ladipo influenced Soyinka, this can undoubtedly be observed in the rearranging of historical materials for dramaturgical purposes. While Ladipo relies heavily on Samuel Johnson's *History of the Yoruba* as source of material for his historical plays, he often 'reworked the materials, adding new dimensions and sometimes sacrificing strict chronological details for dramatic effect' (Ogunbiyi 2014, 425). In other words, Ladipo would research a pertinent Yoruba history and alter it to suit his dramaturgy. For instance, Ladipo's *Oba Koso* was inspired by the tragic fall of Sango, the third and most feared Alaafin of Oyo, who was famous for spitting fire when angered. However, Ladipo deemed it dramatically necessary to include the battle between two Oyo warriors Timi and Gbonka, even though that conflict did not actually occur during the reign of Sango. This same aesthetic technique can be observed, for instance, in the depiction of the real event of a District Officer, one Captain J. A. MacKenzie, who prevented Alaafin's Horseman, Olokun Esin Jinadu, from carrying out his traditional duty of committing a ritual suicide in order to lead the deceased king to the world of the dead in Soyinka's *Death and the King's Horseman* (1975). As Soyinka has made clear in his Author's Note for the play, the setting of his play, 'for minor reasons of dramaturgy' (1984, 144), has been pushed back from 1946 by a couple of years in order to coincide with the Second World War. Also, while, Muraino, the last-born son of the Horseman who returned home and eventually took his own life in place of his father, according to the historical account, was a trader in Ghana, Soyinka makes him the first-born son of Elesin Oba, as well as a medical student in Britain in his play. It is not only the Yoruba travelling theatre tradition that shaped Soyinka's artistic outlook, however. The fact that he was an immigrant in the UK between 1954 and 1960 and on a self-imposed exile again in the UK between 1971 and 1974 unarguably contributed immensely to his aesthetics and dramaturgy, particularly his Yoruba tragedy, which would eventually earn him the Nobel Prize in Literature.

Soyinka Back in Nigeria and on His Way to Becoming a Nobel Laureate

In *Becoming Intercultural*, Young Yun Kim argues that when one migrates to another country, even for a short while, when one returns (if one returns), one is not the same as one was before one left. 'Indeed, the process of crossing cultures challenges the very basis of who we are as cultural beings,' writes Kim,

> It offers opportunities for new learning and growth. Being 'uprooted' from our home brings us understanding not only of people and their culture in our new environment, but of ourselves and our home culture. (Kim 2001, 9)

If viewed through the lens of Kim's analysis, it was not the same Soyinka who entered Britain at the age of twenty to study at Leeds University that returned to Nigerian soil on the first of January 1960. He had become five years older; a husband to a white woman; a father of a mixed-race boy; a holder of an Honours BA in English; a career playwright; and above all a professional theatre director/producer. So, no sooner had Soyinka arrived in Nigeria than he promptly began his theatre work and research. Within ten months of arriving in Nigeria, he founded the 1960 Masks, arguably the first semi-professional English-speaking theatre group, with which he produced his first tragic play, *A Dance of the Forests*, though its official staging was cancelled by the organizing committee who had selected it to celebrate Nigeria's independence. It was this theatre group that would, in 1964, metamorphose into the Orisun Theatre with which Soyinka produced a number of his new plays as well as several political sketches and revues collectively published under the titles *Before the Blackout* (c. 1971) and *Before the Blowout* (1978). Thus, within a period of five years, Soyinka had established himself as a dramatist and theatre director of repute both at home and abroad. Some of the plays he wrote during this period include *The Strong Breed* (1964), *Kongi's Harvest* (1964), and *The Road* (1965), the latter of which had its world premiere at the London Commonwealth Festival the same year it was written.

It was not only through his theatre work that Soyinka kept himself occupied, however. In between writing plays and teaching at the then University of Ife, he was also travelling the length and breadth of Nigeria with his Rockefeller research grant witnessing various traditional festivals for the purpose of redefining tragedy from an Afrocentric point of view. It was this extensive research that culminated in Soyinka's essay, 'The Fourth Stage: Through the Mysteries of Ogun to the Origins of Yoruba Tragedy,' written in 1967 in honour of his former lecturer at Leeds, G. Wilson Knight. In Biodun Jeyifo's opinion, the essay 'remains probably the most important and the most richly suggestive of Soyinka's theoretical writing' (1993, xvii–xviii). However, by the time it was published, the Nigerian civil war had started, and Soyinka had been imprisoned by General Yakubu Gowon for allegedly gunrunning for the Biafrans. Although Soyinka was never tried, he was detained between August 1967 and October 1969, a year and ten months of which he spent in solitary confinement. It was, unarguably, the most traumatic experience that Soyinka had undergone for the sake of his country. Consequently, after a year during which he returned to his position as the director of the School of Drama at the University of Ibadan and wrote his absurd play *Madmen and Specialists*, Soyinka took a leave of absence and went on a self-imposed exile to Britain, saying, '[H]e wanted to get away from it all,' as Olumuywa Awe recalled, 'to get something out of his system' (2005, 79). It was during the early part of this exile period that Soyinka wrote his prison memoir, *The Man Died* (1972), the publication of which made Awe realize what Soyinka meant by 'getting something out of his system.' In Awe's words, '[t]he amount of bottled-up rage, contempt and disgust relating to events in the country, to persons and their pretensions is evident on every page' (ibid.). Subsequently, the National Theatre of Great Britain also commissioned Soyinka to write *The Bacchae of Euripides: A Communion Rite*, which had its world premiere in 1973.

Finally, and most importantly, towards the end of his self-imposed exile, Soyinka also wrote *Death and the Kings Horseman*. *Horseman* is not only Soyinka's quintessential Yoruba tragedy, it is arguably the only play of his in which migration is cardinal and immigrants play important parts. Based on a real event, as already stated above, the play dramatizes how Elesin Oba, the King's Horseman, is prevented by the British colonial Officer, Simon Pilking, from carrying out his traditional duty of committing suicide in order to lead his master the Alaafin of Oyo, who died thirty days prior, into the world beyond. Meanwhile, upon receiving the notice of the death of the former King, Olunde, Elesin's first son, who is a medical student in Britain, has promptly returned home to perform the necessary rites on his father before his burial. Shortly before Olunde realizes that his father has shirked his responsibility, he tries to explain to Jane Pilking, the wife of the Colonial Officer, the importance of his father's suicide. When Jane tries to persuade him that the act of committing suicide for the sake of leading a dead king to the world beyond is feudal and barbaric, Olunde's response is: 'You forget that I have now spent four years among your people. I discovered that you have no respect for what you do not understand' (Soyinka 1984, 192). Clearly, it was Soyinka's experience as an immigrant in the UK that manifested himself in the character of Olunde, who eventually laid down his life to save his people from the calamity that would have been the consequence of his father's failure to carry out his duty. One can indeed stretch the argument further that Olunde is the 'return of the repressed' (à la Sigmund Freud), bearing in mind that Soyinka spent a little over four years in the UK and the real-life person upon which the character of Olunde is based, to reiterate, was a trader in Ghana and not a medical student in the UK. It is not Olunde who is the only immigrant in *Horseman*, however. Simon Pilking and his wife are also immigrants in Nigeria, according to Lee's definition of migration. Thus, the conflict of the play hinges on the lack of understanding of the Yoruba worldview by the British immigrants in Nigeria and the understanding of the ways of the whites by a Nigerian immigrant in Britain. In spite of Soyinka's warning in his Author's Note to would-be producers that they should not reduce his play to 'a clash of culture,' scholars like Adebayo Williams have found that 'by exploring the sacred terror of ritual suicide within the context of the cynicism and cultural desiccations of the colonialists, Soyinka is engaged in nothing less than a sublime cultural battle' (1993, 72). Hence, and as it relates to my earlier claim that interculturalism is a by-product of migration, Soyinka's trajectory as a man of culture can be seen as undergoing constant transformation through migratory movements: he was essentially *intra*cultural (due to Nigeria's multiculturalism) before he travelled to Britain as an immigrant and (following Kim's argument, referenced above) he became *inter*cultural upon his return to Nigeria. These migrations, and the cultural perspectives generated from them, were essential to sending Soyinka on his way to winning the Nobel Prize.

Conclusion

Due largely to colonization, Nigeria, which was an invention of the British, has succeeded in producing the first ever African Nobel Laureate in Literature in the same way, I would argue, that Kenya, another British former colony, has produced the first ever black president of the United States. The fact is that Barack Obama would not have been who he is today had his Kenyan-born father not travelled to America to study in the late 1950s. Migration therefore is a defining factor in the making of Obama, the first black POTUS, as is the case with the making of Soyinka, the first black Nobel Laureate of Literature. When Soyinka returned to Nigeria after his five-year sojourn in the UK, he was a Rockefeller research fellow and an affiliate of the Dramatic Society at University of Ibadan, which would not have come into existence but for the efforts of two English immigrants. Not only that, another European immigrant in Nigeria drew Soyinka's attention to a historical event which would later be the source material for his most important play, *Horseman*. So, migration and immigrants have immensely influenced Soyinka's career as a dramatist. Be that as it may, it is this chapter's conclusion that without the foundation that was laid by the Yoruba travelling theatre tradition, particularly its deployment of the cultural paradigms of the Yoruba people of Southwest Nigeria that Soyinka has successfully built upon, it is highly unlikely that he would have won the Nobel Prize in Literature. However, the travelling theatre practitioners themselves would not have been sources of inspiration for Soyinka had they not been influenced one way or the other by internal or external migration as well as European immigrants within Nigeria. So, an analysis of Nigerian theatre would be incomplete without due regard to the immense contributions that both internal and international migration have made to its development.

References

Akinriande, S. 2015. '"He is Not One of Us': Nigeria – Indigeneship, Otherness and the Ethical Dimension of Citizenship." In *Ethical Dimensions of Citizenship*, edited by M.A. Makinde, 62-91. Ibadan: NAL Occasional Publication.

Awe, Olumuyiwa. 2005. 'Before My Very Eyes' . In *Before Our Very Eyes: Tribute to Wole Soyinka, Winner of the Nobel Prize for Literature*, edited by Dapo Adelugba, 56-85. Ibadan: Spectrum Books Limited.

Axworthy, Geoffrey. 1972. 'The Performing Arts – A Footnote.' *New Theatre Magazine*, XII(2), 17-18.

Balme, Christopher. 2019. 'Building Theatrical Epistemic Communities in the Global South: Expert Networks, Philanthropy and Theatre Studies in Nigeria 1959–1969.' *Journal of Global Theatre History*, 3(2): 3-18.

Banham, Martin. 1972. 'Playwright/Producer/Actor/Academic: Wole Soyinka in the Nigerian Theatre'. *New Theatre Magazine*, XII(3): 10.

Beier, Ulli. 2014. 'E. K Ogunmola; A Personal Memo.' In *Drama and Theatre in Nigeria: A Critical Source Book*, edited by Yemi Ogunbiyi, 398-411. Ikeja: Tanus Books Limited.

Clark, Ebun. 2014. 'Ogunde Theatre: The Rise of Contemporary Professional Theatre in Nigeria 1946-72.' In *Drama and Theatre in Nigeria: A Critical Source Book*, edited by Yemi Ogunbiyi, 364-97. Ikeja: Tanus Books Limited.

Fischer-Lichte, Erika. 1990. 'Theatre Own and Foreign. The Intercultural Trend in Contemporary Theatre.' In *The Dramatic Touch of Difference: Theatre Own and Foreign*, edited by Erika Fischer-Lichte, Josephine Riley, and Michael Gissenwehrer, 11-19. Tübingen: Gunter Narr Verlag.

Gibbs, James. 2001. 'Soyinka in Zimbabwe: A Question and Answer Session.' In *Conversations with Soyinka*, edited by Biodun Jeyifo, 68-128. Jackson: University Press of Mississippi.

Jeyifo, Biodun. 1993. 'Introduction: Wole Soyinka and the Tropes of Disalienation.' In *Wole Soyinka. Art Dialogue and Outrage; Essays on Literature and Culture*, ix-xxx. London: Methuen.

Kim, Yun Young. 2001. *Becoming Intercultural: An Integrative Theory of Communication and Cross-Cultural Adaptation*. London: Sage Publications.

Knowles, Ric. 2010. *Theatre and Interculturalism*. Palgrave Macmillan.

Lee, Everett S. 1966. 'A Theory of Migration.' *Demography*, 3(1): 47-57.

Lindfors, Bernth. 1976. 'Ogunde on Ogunde: Two Autobiographical Statements.' *Educational Theatre Journal*, 28(2): 239-46.

'The Nobel Prize in Literature 1986.' Accessed January 18, 2022. https://www.nobelprize.org/prizes/literature/1986/summary/.

Nwaubani, Adaobi Trici. 2020. 'My Nigerian Great-Grandfather Sold Slaves.' *BBC*, July 19, 2020. Accessed November 17, 2021. https://www.bbc.com/news/world-africa-53444752. Accessed 17 November 2021.

Ogunbiyi, Yemi. 2014. 'Introduction – Nigerian Theatre and Drama: A Critical Profile.' In *Drama and Theatre in Nigeria: A Critical Source Book*, edited by Yemi Ogunbiyi, 2-67. Ikeja: Tanus Books Limited.

Soyinka, Wole. 1984. *Death and the King's Horseman*. In *Soyinka Six Plays*, 143-220. London: Methuen.

Wilkinson, Jane. 2001. 'Wole Soyinka.' In *Conversations with Soyinka*, edited by Biodun Jeyifo, 143-66. Jackson: University Press of Mississippi.

Williams, Adebayo. 1993. 'Ritual and the Political Unconscious: The Case of Death and The King's Horseman.' *African Urban Quarterly*, 8(4): 67-79.

White, Anthony Graham. 1974. *The Drama of Black Africa*. London: Samuel French.

CHAPTER 34

Migratory Subjectivities and African Diasporic Theatre: Race, Gender, and Nation

Nicosia Shakes

INTERROGATING MIGRATION THROUGH RACE AND GENDER

How are people's experiences of migration shaped by their race and gender? And, in what ways do theatre artists generate knowledge about these intersecting identities based on their and others' accounts of leaving their birth countries and settling in others? In this chapter I engage these questions drawing on Black and decolonial feminist cultural analyses, and African Diasporic theories about the role of culture in shaping Black/African (Africana) identities and communities globally. I begin by discussing some key points to consider in the analysis of race and gender, travel and mobility. Then, I apply Carole Boyce Davies's (1994) concept of *migratory subjectivities* to two plays that represent Jamaican experiences with migration in different time periods and places. I will employ the terms African/Black and African-descended interchangeably depending on geographic context. And my use of the term migrant encapsulates the descriptors *immigrant, emigrant,* and *expatriate* to describe people who are in the process of migrating and anyone who lives in a country that is different from where they were born, regardless of citizenship status. I recognise that these terms are very racialised. For example, the term immigrant is usually reserved for people from the Global Majority of countries in Africa, Asia, the Caribbean and Latin America, or the poorer countries of Europe. It can be juxtaposed against the word expatriate, which is typically utilised to describe migrants from wealthy White majority countries, with a presumption

N. Shakes (✉)
University of California, Merced, Merced, CA, USA
e-mail: nshakes@ucmerced.edu

that they are the only ones who maintain economic and political affiliations with their birth countries and have the desire to return. I avoid reproducing this racial-ethnic hierarchy by using the term immigrant when necessary, to describe people of any race and nationality who have settled long term in countries in which they were not born.

For Africana people, the concepts of travel, migration and mobility have distinctly violent racial implications that one has to unpack prior to describing their migrant histories. While Africans have moved to other parts of the world for millennia, it is impossible to discuss their global dispersion without considering the trans-Atlantic and Indian Ocean trades in enslaved Africans, and centuries of European colonialism in the Americas and Africa. Regarding how we frame slavery and slave trades in this history, the use of the term migration is a bit dubious. While it generally denotes any process in which people move from one place and settle in another, it seems euphemistic as a descriptor for slavery even if prefaced by the word forced, because of the capacious violence of that system and its function as human trafficking. Notwithstanding the difficulties in classifying slavery in migration studies, it is the main historical system that uprooted and brought large communities of Africans into other parts of the world—mainly the Americas—and initiated the major composition of the modern African Diaspora. The legacies of slavery and colonialism continue to drive Africana people's migrations from their birth countries to other parts of the world. In Africa, Latin America and the Caribbean the massive inequalities, poverty and search for employment and educational opportunities in mainly wealthy countries in Europe and North America are the results of five centuries of European domination precipitated by racist conquest and genocide. Older colonial legacies endure alongside newer iterations (such as the existence of overseas departments and territories of European countries and the United States in Africa, Asia, the Americas and the Pacific). These are compounded by contemporary imperialism through White majority countries' exploitation of the natural and human resources of most parts of the world, often in the service of wealthy citizens and corporations.

Historically, the nuances of gender did not receive adequate attention in accounts of slavery and colonialism. For example, slave narratives have been crucial to the study of Black experiences of displacement, refuge, and migrations during the seventeenth to nineteenth centuries; however, most of these canonical narratives published as monographs, some of which have inspired plays and movies, are written by men (Brown 2007; Cugoano 1999; Douglass 2021; Equiano 2016; Northup 2019). The dearth of published narratives by women is mainly due to differences in mobility between Black men and women during and after slavery and limited access to White-owned publishing resources. Mary Prince's *The History of Mary Prince* and *Incidents in the Life of a Slave Girl* by Harriet Jacobs are two exceptions to the rule (Jacobs 2001; Prince 2001). In 2004, I directed a performance of slave narratives from the Americas for a symposium I planned called *Sankofa: Slavery and Its Impact on Contemporary Jamaica,* organised by Liberty Hall: The Legacy of Marcus

Garvey. While conducting the research for the performance, I had such a difficult time finding published slave narratives by women that I had to forego the monographs (with the exception of Mary Prince's), and rethink how I approached the subject to include excerpts from formerly enslaved people in anthologies and unpublished archival sources.

Narratives around post-slavery migration have also been skewed along gender lines. In the late 1800s to the twentieth century, in the decades after the end of trans-Atlantic slavery and following European colonisation of most of Africa, the wave of Caribbean and African migration was mostly by men who fought in the two world wars and/or sought educational opportunities in Europe. These gendered mobilities, that is, differences in patterns of travel based on gender, impacted literature and other published stories about migrants. For example, in the former British colonies in Africa and the Caribbean, for many years the dominant representations of migrants were in novels and prose about men. Women novelists like Buchi Emecheta, Andrea Levy, Zadie Smith and others would begin to change this tendency in the latter part of the twentieth century, interrupting the tendency for men's gender positionality to be normalised as representative of all African/Black migrant experiences.

Though novels continue to dominate the artistic archives that give insight to race, gender and migration in the African Diaspora, some of the most profound representations of these themes are in dramatic writing and/or theatre. Among these are stories that take place in Black majority spaces. For example, Ama Ata Aidoo's 1965 play, *Dilemma of a Ghost*, explores the ethnic conflicts between Black/African people in the Diaspora and Africans on the continent in a plot about a Ghanaian man's return home with his Black American wife, whom his family looks down on as a descendent of slaves (Aidoo 1995). The themes of ethnocentrism and xenophobia are also present in some sections of The Mothertongue Project's *Uhambo: Pieces of a Dream*, staged in 2004, which addresses the silencing of women's experiences during South Africa's first ten years of democracy after apartheid. *Uhambo* includes vignettes on the xenophobia directed at migrants from other African countries (Matchett and Okech 2015). Other plays like my own *Afiba and Her Daughters* staged in 2016 and *A Vigil for Roxie*, which premiered in 2011 and is co-authored by Amba Chevannes, Carol Lawes, Honor Ford-Smith and Eugene Williams, feature women characters who leave their birth countries and struggle to manage transnational responsibilities (see Ford-Smith 2015).

One play which allows a glimpse into a real historical woman's experience is *Marys Seacole* by Jackie Sibblies Drury, which premiered in 2019. The play is based on the life of the famous Jamaican businesswoman, nurse and healer who travelled the world and is best known for establishing a hotel for wounded and sick soldiers during the Crimean War. The daughter of a free Black Jamaican woman and a White Scottish man, Seacole defied the racial and gender codes of the Victorian era with her travels and work, and her story is a rare narrative of a nineteenth-century migrant Black woman who influenced the majority-White spaces through which she moved despite racism (see Stewart 2019). Among fictional stories based on the history of Jamaican migrants in the twentieth century, Una Marson's *London Calling* is a landmark production (Marson 2002). The play was first staged in Kingston, Jamaica, in 1937, and set in London. It is a critique of the racist anxieties and Black stereotypes in Britain during the early twentieth century in reaction to the wave of migrations of African and Caribbean people there. *London Calling* is among the earliest stories about this era by an Afro-Caribbean writer. One of the play's successors in this respect is Andrea Levy's repertoire of novels set in England, and, in particular, the 2019 theatre adaptation of her novel, *Small Island*, written by Helen Edmundson. I will next discuss *Small Island* alongside Staceyann Chin's *MotherStruck!* which is based on her life as a Black Jamaican lesbian navigating U.S. and Jamaican society in the contemporary world. I engage these plays using Carole Boyce Davies's concept of migratory subjectivities and place them within an African Diasporic frame that explores their transnational resonances.

Migratory Subjectivities and the Nexus of Race and Gender

In *Black Women, Writing and Identity: Migrations of the Subject* Carole Boyce Davies (1994) uses the concept of *migratory subjectivities* to define the work of a group of African and African Diasporic women writers. She asserts that their writings demonstrate that Black women's identities are complex and fluid, not always in 'harmony', and existing in multiple spaces. Most importantly, Boyce Davies emphasises that Black women's experiences are not simply characterised by domination and oppression, but also by resistance and agency:

> Migrations of the subject refers to the many locations of Black women's writing, but also to the Black female subject refusing to be subjugated. Black female subjectivity then can be conceived not primarily in terms of domination, subordination or "subalternization", but in terms of slipperiness, elsewhereness. Migratory subjects suggests that Black women/'s writing cannot be located and framed in terms of one specific place, but exist/s in myriad places and times, constantly eluding the terms of the discussion. (Boyce Davies 1994, 26)

Like the authors whose work Boyce Davies explores, Chin's and Levy's migrant identities are reflected in the formats and contents of their stories. Chin is a Jamaican-American who moved to the United States in her early 20s while Levy was a Black British woman, born to Jamaican parents in England. She passed away in 2019 leaving a legacy of five critically acclaimed novels and an anthology of short stories, inspired by her family history. *Small Island* is her most renowned novel, with the widest media circulation. Alongside the 2019 stage adaptation, there was a 2009 BBC One adaptation as a miniseries with the same title under the direction of John Alexander, from a teleplay by Paula Milne and Sarah Williams. It was later acquired by the Public Broadcasting

Station (PBS) and featured in the Masterpiece Classics series. *Small Island* and most of Levy's other stories are set during the period after World War II when Britain was the primary site of emigration from Jamaica given the country's status as a British colony during that period. These stories are therefore a generation older than Chin's, whose novel *The Other Side of Paradise* (2010) and *MotherStruck!* are situated within more contemporary patterns of migration from Jamaica to North America, which intensified in the 1980s to 2000s.

MotherStruck!

MotherStruck! is an autobiographical monodrama/one-person play. Since its 2015 premiere Off-Broadway under the direction of Cynthia Nixon, it has only been performed by Chin and remains unpublished, though it has been staged in many countries. The versions I analyse here were performed at the 2017 Black Lavender Festival organised by the Department of Africana Studies/Rites and Reason Theatre at Brown University and in 2019 at The College of Wooster in Ohio as part of a transnational performance series I co-organised. *MotherStruck!* chronicles Chin's life in Jamaica, including her experiences growing up poor and dealing with childhood abuse, her embrace of her sexuality and the backlash that followed. Following an anti-lesbian sexual assault by a group of men, she left Jamaica for New York in 1997. There she became part of an active LGBTQ community and artistic scene, honed her poetry at the Nuyorican Poets Café and other spaces and eventually became a mother to a daughter after years of trying to get pregnant via in vitro fertilisation (IVF).

As a lesbian she found a more accepting sexual environment in New York than in her home country. However, as a mixed-race woman of obvious African and Asian descent with a very strong foreign accent from a Black majority country, U.S. racism and sexism became part of her daily life intersecting with homophobia despite legal and other protections for LGBTQ people. Moving between Jamaica and the United States requires navigating these different layers of her identity. For instance, Jamaica is a Black majority country in which people are socially defined according to skin colour and other phenotypes such as hair texture, and colourism is perhaps the most ubiquitous manifestation of racism. Thus, in Jamaica the question of her Africanness vis-à-vis her Asianness often emerges, and her aesthetic power in relation to dark-skinned Black women is more pronounced than in the United States where colour-based divisions among Black people are less palpable than the Black-White racial hierarchy. While she acknowledges her biracial heritage, she primarily sees herself as Black, based on her family history of being raised by Black people (and not the Chinese-Jamaican side of her family), the prevalence of anti-Blackness among Asian communities and her rooting within Black identity and activism. In a conversation with me she stated, 'I'm happy to be seen as a Black person because then I can use whatever bullhorn I have to bellow whatever contentions that Blackness might have with White supremacist patriarchal supremacy in the U.S. or elsewhere' (personal communication 2021).

As her racial identity gets defined within the geographic and cultural spaces she occupies and by her activist politics, so too do her levels of engagement with the Jamaican and Caribbean diaspora from her location in Brooklyn. The borough has one of the largest populations of Caribbean-descended people in the United States; and throughout a century of migration, Caribbean people have recreated and evolved their cultures there, blending them with native-born Black American and other cultures, and originating celebrations such as the annual West India Day Parade (also called Brooklyn Carnival). Thus, Chin's geographic and cultural positioning in one of the main locales of the Jamaican diaspora shows that it is not always useful to set up neat binary distinctions between immigrants' home countries and adopted countries when they live in an enclave heavily steeped in the culture of the birth country or ancestral homeland. Instead, the geographies that immigrants navigate are never fixed, but often involve multiple sites of belonging, alienation, empowerment, and oppression.

Still, there is a longing for the geography of Jamaica which constitutes part of Chin's migrant subjectivity. Her frequent travels back there allow her to forge a different relationship with her birth country and to assess its transformations from the outside. Thus, *MotherStruck!* includes scenes in which she observes the changes in Jamaican society, such as the widening of more accepting spaces for LGBTQ people. For example, in scene eighteen on one of her trips to the country, she is shocked when she sees a group of gender non-conforming 'teenagers in male bodies dressed completely in women's clothes' confidently 'sashaying' through a supermarket 'laughing, loud and unafraid' without being harassed (Chin 2017, 42). Alongside Chin's articulation of her relationship to Jamaica almost three decades after she left, the climax of the play is when she becomes a mother, which was made difficult by her statuses as a poor artist struggling to make a living, single and a lesbian. Her decision to become a mother was transgressive considering all of the ways in which she was curtailed by her sexual orientation and economic, national and marital statuses. In her analysis of *MotherStruck!* Valerie Palmer-Mehta (2016) notes, 'Discourses of motherhood can be particularly problematic because, although varied iterations of motherhood have emerged over time, such articulations invariably assume heteronormativity while requiring women's all-encompassing time and effort and their subservience either to men, children, or the state' (35). Additionally, notwithstanding the increases in media visibility for families with gay parents, heterosexual motherhood within the bounds of marriage is still celebrated by mainstream culture as a marker of good citizenship. In the context of the United States this version of motherhood is still distinctly raced as White, sexed as heterosexual and conceived within ethno-national norms as American-born. While the play culminates in the birth of her daughter Zuri, and the resolution focuses on her settlement into motherhood, the story is essentially about Chin finding her voice as a poet, author, activist, lesbian, migrant, and sole parent; and her resolution of all of these positionalities. She forged her own home space away from Jamaica by building a family and a community for herself. But the story does not end with this resolution. Chin adds another layer of complexity to it by remarking on a contemporary tendency in the patterns of migration in New York City—gentrification and its displacement of Black and other People of Colour: 'the more gay white couples move into my building, the less Black families I see in my elevators. It's only a matter of time before Zuri and I are missing from these elevators too' (Chin 2017, 40). The final scene ties together all of these conflicting experiences with a statement on the kind of life she wants to give Zuri—one in which she can explore multiple possibilities without constraint. Among these multiple possibilities is Zuri's appreciation for her Jamaican heritage through long sojourns in Jamaica, not simply short-term visits. Chin views these long stays in Jamaica as crucial to her daughter's embrace of her Black identity: 'I want her to be around Black people. I wanted the pilot to be Black, I wanted the Prime Minister to be Black, the person who washed her clothes weekly to be Black, I wanted the aunties to be Black, I wanted her to be surrounded by Black people; and the bonus is that she gets to hear the accent I grew up with' (personal communication 2021). Thus, *MotherStruck!* and Chin's experiences display an approach to family and community building that is transnational and crosses borders, bridging the country of origin and the country of immigration.

Small Island

The theme of family and community-making amid alienating national contexts also runs throughout *Small Island*. Adapted for the stage by Helen Edmundson, the play premiered in 2019 at the Royal National Theatre in London under the direction of Rufus Norris. It tells the story of the Windrush generation: Caribbean people who sailed to England on the SS *Empire Windrush* in 1948 and subsequent journeys, and settled there under the Nationality Act. They had responded to England's call for labour to rebuild the country following the ravages of World War II. The play, like the novel on which it is based, features a large ensemble of characters with a main focus on two couples: one Black Jamaican and the other White English. The Jamaicans Hortense Joseph (née Roberts) and Gilbert Joseph rent a room in Queenie and Bernard Bligh's house after their migration to England. Gilbert, who first met Queenie during the war, is more at ease with this living situation than Hortense, who came to England with idealised expectations. Interwoven with their stories is that of Michael Roberts, Hortense's second cousin and first love interest, whose brief affair with Queenie produced a child whom she named Michael, after his father. The play begins with Hortense's life in Jamaica, her ambitions to become an English lady and, later, her marriage of convenience to Gilbert. The characters' gendered mobilities are reflected through their conjugal relationships: Both Hortense and Queenie marry in order to achieve a middle-class English social status. Hortense does so by funding Gilbert's migration to England with the promise that he will send for her because 'A single woman cannot travel on her own—it would not be respectable. But a married woman can go anywhere she pleases' (Edmundson and Levy 2020, 60). Similarly, Queenie marries Bernard because she needs his economic support in order to live an urban English life, and not have to return to her parents' pig farm in the countryside.

The men characters are more mobile largely due to their involvement in World War II. This mobility becomes part of the conflict in Bernard and Queenie's relationship when he does not immediately return home from India following the war. For the Black men, World War II was the catalyst for their migration as well as their first encounter with British racism. Though they never met each other, both Gilbert and Michael served as soldiers in the war from the base in England. After returning to Jamaica Gilbert realised the extent of his home country's poverty and yearned to go back to the much richer society in England despite the racism there. While the characters do not mention the root of the hardships in Jamaica, it is implicit in the story that Jamaica's impoverishment is the result of three centuries of British colonialism. Furthermore, the country's economy suffered after World Wars I and II because Jamaicans were taxed by Britain to pay for these wars in which they had very few stakes. More explicit commentaries on race, class, and colonialism emerge through the relationships among the characters, especially the rampant racism suffered by Gilbert, Hortense, and other Black Caribbean migrants.

Hortense, in particular, exhibits the naïveté of many Caribbean people about how they would be perceived in Britain (see Evelyn 2013, 130). She believed that England would welcome her because she is well-educated, relatively light-skinned and proficient in English culture. However, these beliefs get unfulfilled in her interactions with English people, especially when she finds out from a group of condescending White women at the Education Department that she cannot immediately become a teacher in England, because they do not recognise her Jamaican education. Ethnicity, race and gender also interlock with sexuality in the characters' relationships. Queenie has a sexual fascination with Black men, which gets fulfilled when she has an affair with Michael Roberts and falls in love with him after he shows up to rent a room from her while her husband is away at war; Michael himself is sexually fascinated by White women but quickly moves on to Canada after his affair with Queenie; Hortense initially looks down on Gilbert as a dark-skinned working-class man and does not have sex with him until the end of the story; and there are ongoing sexual anxieties among the English people—particularly White men—about relationships between White women and Black men. In act two, scene three, when Gilbert is being harassed at work by a group of White men he tries to play these anxieties against them by responding, 'I not fucked your wife yet', after they ask him when he is going back to the jungle (74). However, he quickly apologises when they threaten him with violence. This scene shows the ultimate power of even working-class White men to humiliate and physically assault Black men with impunity.

Among the major characters the one who embodies these racist tendencies is Queenie's husband, Bernard. He is outraged to come home after the war to find that his wife has rented their upstairs rooms to Black people and is humiliated when she gives birth to a biracial baby—the product of her affair with Michael. By making London the point of contact for the major characters, as well as the point of origin for a biracial affair and child, the story essentially challenges the notion of a homogenously White Britain. Corrine Duboin (2011) writes that Andrea Levy seeks to redress the attachment of Britishness to ethnicity by giving 'a complete picture of post-war London as a problematic "contact zone"[;] from different vantage points, she gives voice to both "mainstream" white Londoners and black newcomers' (28). The story also decolonises British White nationalism by emphasising that the multi-racial, multi-ethnic environment of post-war London emerged from Britain's racist conquests in Africa, Asia, and the Caribbean.

The birth of Queenie and Michael's biracial baby is concurrent with Hortense and Gilbert's preparations to move out of their room in Queenie's and Bernard's house to their own home in another part of London. Queenie begs Gilbert and Hortense to take her baby with them, because she is unable to protect him from the racism she knows will eventually come from her husband and her community; though Bernard tries to convince her otherwise. In the final scene of the script the handing over of baby Michael to Hortense and Gilbert and then to other characters is depicted in a religious-mythic way that seemingly evokes the story of the biblical Moses being sent in a basket down the river Nile towards Pharaoh's daughter. In contrast to the playscript, the 2019 National Theatre production, the novel and the BBC One TV adaptation have realistic endings. The 2019 stage play concludes with Hortense and Gilbert cuddling the baby and surrounded by the full cast with the ocean in the background, the novel ends when they move into their new house, and the final scene in the miniseries features baby Michael as a middle-aged man telling his grandchildren his parents' story (Alexander 2010; Levy 2004; Norris 2019). The playscript's mythic ending seems a bit unwieldy when considered in relation to the others. Nevertheless, it contains a profound commentary on how the baby might navigate social contexts that are different from and/or similar to those of his parents. The basket travels into infinity and the directions state: '*The lights fade down until there is only a spotlight on this baby—made by all us—floating into an uncertain world*' (Edmundson and Levy 2020, 101). The baby's biracial, biethnic heritage, and his adoption by Black people arguably places him in a more liminal space than that of the other Black characters (see Duboin 2011). That space is located in, but not quite belonging, and yet to transition to full citizenship within a nation.

It is significant that the play premiered in 2019 a year after the beginning of the *Windrush Scandal* in which hundreds of people belonging to the Windrush generation who migrated after World War II were targeted by the British government. They were wrongfully detained, harassed, denied healthcare, deported or threatened with deportation because they did not have up-to-date citizenship paperwork. The scandal was just the most blatant contemporary example of Caribbean people being told by agents of the British state and British people that they do not belong there (Lammy 2020). While White immigrants from other European countries also face discrimination in Britain, race plays a role in framing experiences of xenophobia and national belonging. Thus, the play's irresolute ending hints at the contributions that migrants from former British colonies made to Britain's development as well as the impending clash between White British nationalism and a view of a multi-racial nationalism. Importantly, the play also includes women as major characters in the story of this conflict.

As previously stated, most of the canonical stories about this era from the perspective of Black migrants feature male protagonists. Among them are Lamming's novel *The Emigrants*, first published in 1954, and Samuel Selvon's novel *The Lonely Londoners*, which appeared in 1956 (Lamming 1994; Selvon 1989). Considering this, it would have been justifiable for Levy and later Edmundson to have only Black women as major characters. The play centres Hortense a bit more than the other protagonists by beginning with her childhood experiences in Jamaica. However, because the major commentary is on British society and nationalism writ large the story goes beyond according visibility to women. By including major characters of varied positionalities, the dynamics of gender, race, and class are able to play themselves out in different points of contact: rural and urban spaces in Jamaica; rural and urban spaces in England and during pre-World War II and post-World War II time periods.

CODA: THEATRE'S EMBODIMENT OF MIGRANT IDENTITIES

Small Island and *MotherStruck!* when analysed together display similar tendencies in migratory subjectivities: space and positionality shifts; intersecting sometimes conflicting identities and Black agency amid victimisation. Migratory subjectivities are also discernible in the writers' critiques of their birth countries' suppression of people on the basis of gender and sexuality. While 1940s Jamaica is figured as passive due to its status as a British colony in *Small Island*, in *MotherStruck!* Chin focuses on postcolonial Jamaica's suppression of LGBTQ people—albeit while having to manoeuvre around North American and European imperialist tendencies to single out Africa and the Caribbean as sites of inordinate homophobia. Much like Gloria Anzaldúa's (2012) critiques of Mexico and the United States in *Borderlands—La Frontera*, Chin calls out both the home/ancestral country and the White majority adopted country for their ascriptions to racial, gender, sexual, and other hierarchies that curtail women. While there are time differences and variations in their commentaries on race, sexuality, and gender; *MotherStruck!* and *Small Island* essentially show that ethno-national ties are contestable and can often be in conflict with one's aspirations to a good life. More broadly the experiences on which they are based represent 'agency and the processes of Black self-making' that are constitutive of the African Diaspora (Gordon 2006, 94).

In *Difficult Diasporas: the Transnational Feminist Aesthetic of the Black Atlantic*, Samantha Pinto (2013) argues for a view of the African Diaspora as not only a 'set of physical movements but also of aesthetic and interpretive strategies' (3). Among these interpretive strategies is a recognition of the role of movement, travel, displacement, and settlement in how Africana people's identities are shaped across different times and spaces. As the 'medium of representation par excellence' (Migraine-George 2008, 1) theatre allows for more profound embodiments of these tendencies than are available in the global news media, in governmental debates, and in policy-based research around how to address migration.

References

Books and Essays

Aidoo, Ama Ata. 1995. *Dilemma of a Ghost and Anowa*. London: Longman.
Alexander, John, dir. 2010. *Masterpiece Classic: Small Island*. Arlington: Public Broadcasting Station. DVD.
Anzaldúa, Gloria. 2012. *Borderlands/La Frontera: The New Mestiza*. 4th ed. San Francisco: Aunt Lute Books.
Boyce Davies, Carole. 1994. *Black Women, Writing and Identity: Migrations of the Subject*. New York: Taylor & Francis Group.
Brown, William Wells. 2007. *The Escape or, A Leap for Freedom*. New York: Cosimo Classics.
Chin, Staceyann. 2010. *The Other Side of Paradise: A Memoir*. New York: Scribner.
Chin, Staceyann. 2017. '*MotherStruck!*' Unpublished playscript. Microsoft Word file.
Cugoano, Quobna Ottobah. 1999. *Thoughts and Sentiments on the Evil of Slavery*. Illustrated edition. New York: Penguin Classics.
Douglass, Frederick. 2021. *Narrative of the Life of Frederick Douglass: The Original 1845 Edition*. Independently published.
Duboin, Corinne. 2011. 'Contested Identities: Migrant Stories and Liminal Selves in Andrea Levy's Small Island.' *Obsidian* 12 (1): 14–33.
Edmundson, Helen, and Andrea Levy. 2020. *Small Island*. London: Nick Hern Books.
Equiano, Olaudah. 2016. *Interesting Narrative of the Life of Olaudah Equiano: Written by Himself*. 3rd ed. Boston: Bedford/St. Martin's.
Evelyn, Kim. 2013. 'Claiming a Space in the Thought-I-Knew-You-Place: Migrant Domesticity, Diaspora, and Home in Andrea Levy's "Small Island."' *South Atlantic Review* 78 (3/4): 129–49.
Ford-Smith, Honor. 2015. 'Theatre Performance: "A Vigil for Roxie."' *Memory, Urban Violence and Performance in Jamaican Communities*. Accessed September 20, 2021. https://forevermissed.wordpress.com/
Gordon, Edmund T. 2006. 'The Austin School Manifesto: An Approach to the Black or African Diaspora.' *Cultural Dynamics* 19: 93–97.
Jacobs, Harriet. 2001. *Incidents in the Life of a Slave Girl*. Reprint edition. Mineola: Dover Publications.
Lamming, George. 1994. *The Emigrants*. Reprint edition. Ann Arbor: University of Michigan Press.
Lammy, David. 2020. 'Two Years after Windrush, We're Deporting People Who've Only Known Britain as Home.' *Guardian*, February 10, 2020. https://www.theguardian.com/commentisfree/2020/feb/10/windrush-deporting-people.
Levy, Andrea. 2004. *Small Island*. London: Headline Review.
Marson, Una. 2002. *Pocomania and London Calling*. Kingston: Blue Banyan Books.

Matchett, Sara, and Awino Okech. 2015. '"Uhambo: Pieces of a Dream": Waiting in the Ambiguity of Liminality.' In *Performing Migrancy and Mobility in Africa: Cape of Flows*, edited by Mark Fleishman, 110–24. New York: Palgrave Macmillan.

Migraine-George, Thérèse. 2008. *African Women and Representation: From Performance to Politics*. Trenton: Africa World Press.

National Theatre. https://video.alexanderstreet.com/watch/small-island. Accessed January 24, 2022.

Norris, Rufus, dir. 2019. *Small Island*. Script by Helen Edmundson. London: Royal.

Northup, Solomon. 2019. *Twelve Years A Slave (Annotated): The Original 1853 Manuscript*. Independently published.

Palmer-Mehta, Valerie. 2016. 'Subversive Maternities: Staceyann Chin's Contemplative Voice.' *QED: A Journal in GLBTQ Worldmaking* 3 (1): 34.

Pinto, Samantha. 2013. *Difficult Diasporas: The Transnational Feminist Aesthetic of the Black Atlantic*. New York: New York University Press.

Prince, Mary. 2001. *The History of Mary Prince*. Edited by Sara Salih. Penguin Classics edition. New York: Penguin Classics.

Selvon, Samuel. 1989. *The Lonely Londoners*. Harlow: Longman Publishing Group.

Stewart, Zachary. 2019. 'Marys Seacole and the Black Female Caretakers Who Make the World Go Round.' *Theater Mania*. Accessed October 17, 2021. https://www.theatermania.com/off-broadway/reviews/marys-seacole-and-black-female-caretakers_87924.html.

CHAPTER 35

Immobile Relegations and Exiles: Creation and Migration in French Theatre Between 1980 and 2020

Selim Rauer

Part One: Exile, Migration, and Immobility in Postcolonial France

Given the social, cultural, and political invisibility suffered by many French citizens of foreign origin, whose traumatic and post-traumatic memories hinge upon a French history of colonization, deportation, and slavery, we can now, in the postcolonial era, see in metropolitan France a new form of spiritual and physical demotion. Within this era, one can witness the ongoing notion of relegation, which here refers to an exilic experience which does not lead to the loss of civil or political rights. I qualify this reality, described in various contemporary dramas or scenic approaches as an *immobile relegation*, as a form of physical and spiritual demotion imposed on people living in specific peri-urban localities due to their origins, skin colour, or name—a reality of the colonial imaginary which remains active in metropolitan France today. As Achille Mbembe asserts in his article 'La république et l'impensé de la race' ('The Republic and the Unthinking of Race'), this postcolonial period has not allowed for a decolonization process, one which should have transformed perceptions and practices within the reality of a multicultural French society (Mbembe 2006, 194–198). The sociocultural and economic constraints of French suburbs, or so-called *banlieue*, undoubtedly signify one of the most

S. Rauer (✉)
Sorbonne Nouvelle University, Paris, France
e-mail: selim.rauer.1@sorbonne-nouvelle.fr

© The Author(s), under exclusive license to Springer Nature Switzerland AG 2023
Y. Meerzon, S. E. Wilmer (eds.), *The Palgrave Handbook of Theatre and Migration*, https://doi.org/10.1007/978-3-031-20196-7_35

tangible expressions of this immobile relegation—a new form of exile endured by the portion of the French population who were born and raised in France but with an immigrant background. These suburbs have become theatres of confrontation and fracture within the establishment—policed spaces of exile by the French government. Artificially planned suburbs have reinforced a troubling component of French culture: much of the French population is forced to endure a degraded socio-economic reality, which re-actualizes the colonial past and practices of the country and re-exiles a significant portion of French society (Lapeyronnie 2017, 296–298). This colonial legacy and urban reality have created a situation of social fracture and can be blamed for unleashing the 2005 French uprising, which took place in the poorest peripheries of the major French cities. As I will demonstrate, this immobile relegation, from which at least two generations of French citizens have suffered, has been highlighted and denounced through different methods in contemporary French theatre. This artistic dialogue can be explained through the sociological and political evolutions of the last 40 years, which have allowed for new approaches and debates concerning French identity and migration to play out in the public sphere. French writers, dramatists, artists, and performers—some with immigrant heritages or of intersectional or multicultural identities—have off-and-on experienced hopes of recognition of a modern multi-ethnic and integrative society within the larger cultural-historical narrative of the Grande Nation.

In this chapter, I will address the case of French dramatist Bernard-Marie Koltès (1948–1989), who at the dawn of the 1980s shed light on this situation of immobile relegation, which otherwise remained concealed in most public debates. I will then turn to the Franco-Ivorian writer Koffi Kwahulé (1956–) to envision the representation of an Afropean and Afro-descendant imaginary. This case study creates a new horizon and greater visibility for artists, dancers, and performers who identify in their productions with multiculturalism and what we may call a *border identity* at the crossroads of different narratives, imaginaries, nations, and memories, as best exemplified by French choreographer Bintou Dembélé (1975–). But first, we must interrogate the broader postwar historical context which produced a new theatrical reality through sociopolitical changes at work in 1981, due in no small part to the election of the first socialist president in the Fifth Republic's history, François Mitterrand (1916–1996).

Some Great Expectations

On 10 May 1981, given the occasion of François Mitterrand's election as the first socialist to access the French presidency in the history of the Fifth Republic founded by General de Gaulle (1890–1970), great expectations arose for social revolution. This rupture marked a profound democratic change: the desire to amend republican institutions, and to liberate a distinctive national imaginary and discourse. Mitterrand and his leftist union believed that the emancipation of popular classes went hand-in-hand with a universal desire for structural reform.

During the 1980s the country rediscovered itself as a land of migration and a territory in which different cultures, imaginaries, and realities coexisted in order to produce a new, multi-faceted identity. Lasting works like Bernard-Marie Koltès' *Combat de nègre et de chiens* (Black Battle with Dogs) (1983), *Quai Ouest* (Quai West) (1985), *Dans la Solitude des Champs de Coton* (In the Solitude of the Cotton Fields) (1986), and *Retour au désert* (The Return to the Desert) (1988) attest to this spirit. The campaign slogan, 'Changing Life', marked voters' hopes for a better future—especially those of constituents who sought greater visibility in the French society after 27 years of conservative policy. These constituents represented a broad tapestry of life experience, largely including that of low-income workers and citizens with immigrant backgrounds. 'Changing lives' also signified a different form of governmentality: it meant appealing to new practices, different words, new political actions through legislative power, and invoking a change of mindset.

Unfortunately, after 1983 and the so-called austerity turning point, François Mitterrand's political action, and even more so that of the conservative governments which succeeded him, failed in maintaining this new cultural horizon. The increasing domination of neo- or ultraliberal practices, which imposed themselves on a global scale with the fall of the Berlin Wall and the dissolution of the Eastern Bloc, did not allow for the emergence of a true alter-globalization—that is to say, that of renewed cultural, economic, and political practices deriving from a proper multiculturalism and replacing the neocolonial and capitalist paradigm, in which borders and identities are no longer locations of sovereignty, identity, and power (Hardt and Negri 2009, pp. 103, 104, 105). By banning the word *race* from its constitution in 2018, the French State, while seeking to deny an ethnicist conception of the state, in fact rejected any visibility of the racial question and of the French colonial imaginary. And yet, such visibility would theoretically enable a more effective approach to combatting racial prejudices at the root of hiring, housing, or schooling discrimination in France, all of which are the products of (neo)colonial thought and the practices of marginalization (Talpin et al. 2021, 19–30). This occultation of the racial question has condemned entire sections of the Black, Arab, Muslim, and Caribbean communities to an immobile relegation in France—to an internal confinement within its own borders, producing an insular identity in which the traumatic memory continues to update the colonial past in real time (Rauer 2020, 63–79). This new form of exile—this immobile relegation to a postcolonial no-man's-land—also affected theatre artists, dramatists, actors, dancers, performers, and directors with immigrant backgrounds.

Bernard-Marie Koltès, or the Centralization of Margins

Contemporary French theatre—its administration and its prevailing imagination—is not only the product of a history of domination, but also the reflection of practices and imaginaries manufacturing social realities and statuses within the realm of race. Being Black or a person of colour in France is neither an essence nor a culture: it is the product of a cultural construction, imposing a situation of social downgrading over the racialized individual (Ndiaye 2009, 83). Today, an aspect of French postcolonial tragedy relies on the fact that a good number of French citizens undergo a migrant's imaginary status connected to their name, skin colour, or religion (mainly Islam), thus becoming, despite themselves, foreigners within their own country. As Pierre Bourdieu recalls in his preface to *The Suffering of the Immigrant* by sociologist Abdelmalek Sayad: 'the immigrant is *atopos*, without home, out of place, unclassifiable. [...] Neither citizen, nor foreigner, neither on the side of the Same nor totally on the side of the Other, he is in this indefinable place of which Plato refers as the border between social and non-social being' (Sayad 1999, 8). By becoming prisoner of this indefinable place or border, French citizens of foreign origins are constantly relegated to a past, an origin, a stigma affixed to their culture or skin colour. They have reached the status of symbolic and affective statelessness, exposing them to a state of psychological, legal, and sometimes even physical fragility because a broader cultural-historical imagination and series of practices push them back to an uninhabitable faraway. And if there is any place capable of materializing this faraway or beyond—this non-space bordering reality and fiction, life and death, past and present—it is indeed theatre. Or, more precisely, the stage itself considered as the place of emergence and vanishment. In theatre, the material world—a social and historical reality—can be summoned, as Brecht reminds us in/through the estrangements of his didactic theatre. But this reality, transformed by theatrical action and aesthetics, magnifies a metaphysical consciousness of being through which the spectator can see a spectral double on stage: the singular and essentialized Other acting in the sanctified space of theatre; this man, woman, or child who becomes, as Artaud states, 'a perpetual specter in which forces of affectivity radiate' (Artaud 1964, 169). It is this double, this Other considered as a brother or a sister condemned to an endless exile, which emerged in Bernard-Marie Koltès' theatre in the 1980s.

Koltès' writing is sophisticated and yet transparent—almost colloquial. It surfaces as an amplifier of the torment of ostracized and racialized others, men and women from the postcolonial time. He updates in his own way a question famously raised by Gayatri Chakravorty Spivak: can the subaltern speak? Koltès dramatizes a crucial political subject: he represents the exploited Other, the one reduced to silence. From a rather Marxist perspective, he 'stands for' *(vertreten)* the invisibilized ones (Spivak 2010, 56). Alboury in *Black Battle with Dogs* (1983); Abad in *Quai West* (1985); the Dealer in *In the Solitude of the*

Cotton Fields (1986); and Mathilde Serpenoise, Fatima, Aziz, or Saïfi in *The Return to the Desert* (1988)—each of these characters bears witness to an exilic burden linked to the history of French domination and postcolonial migrations to France. What Koltès succeeds in highlighting (as revealed in a small number of interviews granted to the media about his work) is how the migrant emerges as an ontological threat—a shadow, something almost dehumanized. We see this clearly in *Black Battle with Dogs*? Alboury, a character who spends his time moving and sliding like a ghost in the twilight near a bougainvillea during the first portion of the play. This exilic experience taking the shape of an insular relegation is perhaps best reflected in this drama. A worker, called Nouofia, has been shot dead, then thrown into the latrine and lost in the river. This racist felony has been perpetrated by a French foreman named Cal. Nouofia's alleged brother, Alboury, illegally penetrates the French company's enclosure to claim the body from Horn, the site manager. The women from the village occupy the ancient Greek role of suppliants—those who plea to those in authority—and keep wailing in anticipation of the return of a body which cannot be returned. This absent corpse seems to hold power over the unfolding drama, and in the consciousnesses of each character this 'desire for apartheid' and the 'fantasy of extermination' specific to the colonial world is crystallized (Mbembe 2019, 48). The horror expressed by this tragedy, which seems to be a modern recreation of Sophocles' *Antigone* set in the postcolonial era, is that of enmity—of a constructed representation of the Other as metaphysical foe. Incapable of returning Nouofia's body, the foreman must attempt to buy off and then kill Alboury before deciding to sacrifice the foreman responsible for the first instance of bloodshed. Locked in this site, which becomes a metaphor for the camp, former colonists perpetuate an imaginary and a praxis of predation over territories and bodies considered as properties and resources—something to be mastered, or eventually substituted or destroyed. Here, the corporate world and its transgressions against underpaid workforces from former colonies puts into perspective a global hegemony based on class, gender, or race biases. In such a context the reader or spectator understands that decolonization does not mean the end of the colonial world and its practices. Its imagination, through the theological and political figure of the enemy, has been conveyed from the biological to the socio-economic space, which allows racism to be rendered invisible but also for an integration of any other form of discrimination (Hardt and Negri 2009, 191). Koltès paints a grey zone in which a spiritual experience of banishment is accomplished by characters dispossessed of their own lives in a world that buries unresolved past traumas and hatred.

The body of the one who is considered to be a foreigner or a migrant is not only a racialized body, but an enemy. The migrant is not only somebody carrying out this movement from the outside to the inside—they are not only the migrant crossing a border—they are also, in this case, the threshold delimiting stage and backstage, reality and drama. In postwar and postcolonial France, the migrant is secluded in a binary understanding of migration, which is on the one hand a resource (for instance, the labour force needed for the reconstruction of the country), and on the other, a danger, a sort of contagion spreading physical and cultural alteration and insecurity, re-actualizing the Schmittian concept of the political (i.e., the rudimentary agon separating the Friend from the Enemy). Whoever finds themselves prisoner of this status is therefore also captive to a memory as a moral and historical condemnation which refers to the concept of the Zone defined by Frantz Fanon. The Zone encompasses the inside and the outside of the colonial world—it is not only a delimitation but a sphere of enmity, encapsulating perception and identity (Fanon 2002, 42). Bernard-Marie Koltès' dramaturgy allows for a centralization of margins by bringing back to the centre of the stage a reality which otherwise remains in the blind spot of official French national narratives today.

Koffi Kwahulé: Afropeanism and Migration

Afropeanism can be understood as the merging of one or many north- or sub-Saharan cultures or imaginaries with any kind of European identity, hence allowing for the creation of a new cross-cultural identity specific to the postcolonial era. Koffi Kwahulé is a Franco-Ivorian writer and dramatist. Born in 1956 in Abengourou (Ivory Coast), he has spent most of his life living and writing in France. He is one of the rare inheritors, along with Kossi Efoui, Sony Lab'ou Tansi, or more recently Léonora Miano, of the political and postcolonial theatre that unfolded in the 1980s with Koltès. Koffi Kwahulé gives to his characters a dramatic intensity which reverberates the strange experience—or experience of strange(r)ness—which originates from a multicultural identity positioned at the intersection and/or overlap of various borders. Kwahulé stages an open identity that challenges values deriving from the forces, structures, and formations of patriarchy, capitalism, and cultural fetishism, disclosing how multidirectional memories and identities become the threshold of a new relation to a contemporary French society fashioned by the history of migrations. In effect, his work shatters the cultural and territorial assignments manufactured by a pervasive nation-state perspective. In such a postcolonial, or even neocolonial context—in a world globalized by capitalism—Kwahulé exposes how mere existence, habits, and cultural hybridity become spaces of political resistance against an inclination to mastery through uniformization. Here the subjective voice of the character or actor standing alone on stage becomes the representation of a collective consciousness testifying to an experience of reality.

The topic at the heart of Kwahulé's theatre—that is, migration—raises both the question of the migrant's status passing through a symbolic and geographic border, and that of the gaze affixed to him/her by an alleged cultural or moral authority (that of the *majority*) creating a stranger identity and imaginary. The migrant is everywhere in Koffi Kwahulé's dramaturgy. Migration refers here to a physical and spiritual experience, which cannot be compared to an Odyssey (implicating a return to a homeland), but rather to an exile—a tragic path with no destination. In the most Heideggerian perspective, the exilic character epitomizes a *Dasein* type of authenticity as 'being-towards-death' (Heidegger 2010, 242). The experience of most of Kwahulé's characters (as is the case with Koltès) is the existential experience of homelessness—of something essential having been revoked through threat of death over the living being with no place to settle, no security, and no justice, thus exposing the migrant to an endless exodus. The migrant's burden is a never-ending attempt to comply with the injunction of integrating in one society—one language, one land—while surviving on a border. Kwahulé's characters go through revelatory rites of passage which transform their lives, bringing them to their existences' limits—to death itself. This death does not mark an end or a milestone, but signals the crossing of a new threshold on stage. This initiation ritual occurs in plays such as *Big Shoot* or *P'tit-souillure* (2000), as well as in the confined female prison of *Misterioso 119* (2005), a play of extraordinary violence whose final scene, titled 'Eucharist', shows female prisoners literally dismembering and ingesting a body and reminding us, perhaps more than of the Catholic liturgy, of the sacrifice of Pentheus orchestrated by the god of exile, Dionysus in Euripides' *Bacchae*.

The question of the social, cultural, and sexual assignments which enable specific spaces of seclusion and control that respond to a long patriarchal tradition of nation-statism surfaces in most of Kwahulé's plays. Kwahulé shows how patriarchy and nation-statism have fashioned a praxis of power through human division which has basically structured capitalism and one of its deviations—colonialism—as a system of exploitation based on the colourification and sexualization of bodies (Mies 2014, 11). This aspect comes through in a play entitled *Jaz*, published in 1998, but also later in a drama titled *La mélancolie des barbares* (The Barbarians' Melancholy), first published in 2009. The work puts into perspective the mechanisms of an immobile relegation deriving from the paradoxes of a French postcolonial reality which is not freed from a past imperial imaginary. What Kwahulé divulges here are the logics of cultural hegemony condemning the Other to a situation of psychological and physical captivity which has been unconsciously internalized. Patriarchy as a social system remains an overarching background unifying all other forms of domination. A man, perhaps in his 50s, called the Komissari, has been appointed to a suburb to restore order and stop illegal drug and sex trafficking. This violent man marries a woman named Monique, nicknamed Baby Mo. The Komissari forces her to wear a veil to be 'spared from the world's defilement' (Kwahulé 2013, 10). Baby Mo secretly loves Zac, a drug dealer. The Komissari will take this young man under his wing while ignoring the relationship his wife has formed with him. Kwahulé works into this drama an inversion of norms, which at first seems to blur borders. However, this inversion of predominant logics of power and their modes of representation in this dramaturgy allows for an *unveiling* of truth in a Hegelian sense (Hegel 1988, 55). To evoke the relegation to which many immigrants and French Muslims (often Arabs) have found themselves condemned in France since decolonization, Kwahulé shows a man of indefinite identity, a holder of the so-called monopoly of legitimate violence. We see a senior police officer veiling a woman he allegedly loves and handling her as a mere object—as a property and not a person. Highlighting this desire to cover the female body permits the author to denounce another obsession—one just as violent—which consists of unveiling her body with the same frenzy. Here, Koffi Kwahulé illustrates in a properly Kantian way that what conforms to reality is above all the moral intention with which we provide our actions, as much as our actions themselves. We fully understand here that in the name of a pretended French secularism, we are making secularism a state religion, more than a tool of expression of freedom of conscience. Kwahulé's strength precisely resides in his ability to deterritorialize French or Western hegemonic imaginaries (white, male, and Christian identities, chiefly) towards territories generally associated with cultures identified as minorities and problematic—that is to say not integrated into the so-called national cultural centre or majority. In this drama, violence is no longer ascribable to an ethnic or religious category connected to a postcolonial reality and integration issues. Violence, the *thingification* of others, the dominating impulses deriving from degraded modes of existence, and a particular socio-economic environment are perceived in all their crudity precisely by removing the racialized ethnical or cultural mask, thus allowing for the production of segregationist discourses. Monique, Judikaël, Lulu, and Zac are the few names with European and biblical sounds from this text. Responding to a baroque gesture of folds (Deleuze 1993, 16–18), Kwahulé proceeds to another ruse or strategy derived from Marronage, which consists in shifting the alleged representatives of a legitimate place of power from the centre to the margin, thus demonstrating the way disparities and class tensions have survived beyond any ethno-centred cleavages in France at the beginning of the twenty-first century.

Bintou Dembélé: Marronage as a Strategy

> Going to Senegal and discovering I was not considered Senegalese has been a violent experience. I was more often than not referred to as a white (*toubab*). I guess the most hurtful thing was discovering that part of my Africanity was rejected in my country of origin, rather than seeing me not accepted as French in France. It's like being permanently quartered. (Niang and Nielsen 2017)

These words by Bintou Dembélé, a French performer and choreographer of African descent, born in 1975 in Bretigny-sur-Orge, describe a situation of permanent exile and relegation which most French citizens with migrant origins have had or still have to withstand. Dembélé's father was part of the first wave of sub-Saharan migrants who came to work during the 1960s in France. Born and raised in a Parisian suburb, like many others from her generation, Dembélé integrates the French postcolonial consciousness of the Mitterrand generation. Finding herself at the point of imbrication of several cultures and identities, Dembélé exemplifies through her life and work that so-called notion of 'Oceanic Africas' or 'Liquid Africa' (Vergès 2016, 50–59). This identity refers to the multiple cultural and territorial realities of Black men and women whose traumatic and post-traumatic memories and pasts are connected to the history of slaves' deportation across seas and continents. Some of these reckonings have taken place in theatre and urban performances, as shown by Dembélé. The importation of hip-hop culture and break-dancing in France during the 1980s played a major function in this trans-identitary construction. This connection with African American diasporic communities, with their music, performances, and language has been an inspiration to an entire generation of young French citizens who felt stuck at a distant remove—alienated from the National Narrative—on account of their skin colour, faith, or place of residence. The African American ethos and its celebration of hybridity and cross-border identity appeared to restate in a post-industrial and postcolonial society a Marronage strategy, which dates back (at least) to seventeenth-century plantation culture and society. Marronage refers to the escaped slaves who found shelter at the top of the hills, in mountains or in forests and recreated there a new life and community (Roberts 2015, 13).

In 1989, Dembélé joined the *Concept of Art* group and became familiar with House Dance, Breaking Dance, and New Style. She eventually performed in urban areas in the centre of Paris, in districts and places such as Chatelet-Les-Halles, the Pompidou Centre esplanade, the Place du Trocadéro, or in the (at the time) recently erected business district of La Défense. Moving from the street to the stage in 1996, she joined the Contemporary Dance Theater (Théâtre Contemporain de la Danse, also known as TCD). After many collaborations with the *Käfig* company and the famous French rapper MC Solaar (1969–), in 2002 she created her own company, *Rualité*, which challenged colonial and identity issues and legacies through three different productions: *L'Assise* (2005), *LOL* (2009), and *Mon appart' en dit long* (My Apartment Says a Lot) (2010). Following the aesthetic and identitary dynamics initiated by a generation of dramatists and writers such as Koffi Kwahulé, Kossi Efoui, and Maryse Condé, Bintou Dembélé crafted an identity by referring to Edouard Glissant's logics of creolization. Originating from the Caribbean world, the concept of creolization comes close to a Marronage aesthetic in its reference to a process of hybridization of different languages, practices, and cultures. Regarding this historical reality specific to the Caribbean or Guyana, Marronage and creolization refer today to the identity and cultural emancipation of French citizens with foreign ancestries who have associated their culture of origin with that of their metropolitan birth through their practices and discourses, thus creating a new multi-faceted identity and culture (Glissant 1997, 34). This creative process can be found in Bintou Dembélé's stage work, particularly in her choreography of Jean-Philippe Rameau's *Les Indes Galantes* (The Amorous Indies) (1735), the libretto of which, composed by Louis Fuzelier (1672–1752), exploits a traditional exotic or orientalist representation of the world, featuring the encounter between the Western civilization and distant, uncivilized wild worlds. Clément Cogitore (1983–), a visual artist and videographer in charge of this production, invited Bintou Dembélé to orchestrate the choreography for this show in 2017. The choreographer's desire was to bring this work up to date with the urban and political reality of her time. She succeeded in representing the racialized Other as a foreigner, as someone coming with a potentially threatening different culture from the other side of a border, in this case beyond the ring road—beyond the centre.

This image of Dembélé dancing on the Opéra Garnier stage has fused different practices and imaginaries stemming from a diverse array of languages and cultures, combined with the prejudices of French imperialism. As their native grandparents and parents, they have been assigned a symbolic space—that of the savages. At the beginning of the twenty-first century, they remained consigned to a different subcategory of citizenship. Thus, the representation of the so-called savages dance in the fourth scene of the production is organized by Dembélé as a tribal dance by a group of young suburban people forming in a circle, trying to capture the alienating and essentializing gaze of the centre, of the majority, of the West; producing beauty through body, gesture through thought. As Dembélé mentions in the show's programme: 'artistic forms are generated by History' (Dembéle 2019). In this way she proposes that her performers adopt hip-hop and KRUMP (Kingdom Radically Uplifted Mighty Praise) dances. KRUMP was born in Los Angeles' poorest ghettos following the riots that shook the city after the beating by the police of Rodney King, an African American man who was stopped by police after speeding on the freeway. Dembélé stages maroon bodies achieving Marronage aesthetics as an emancipation strategy for those who found themselves prisoners of a hegemonic and violent gaze in the time and space of the colony and beyond, in the postcolony. Dembélé's choreography became a celebration of Afropeanism as a space of freedom where multidirectional imaginaries and identities allow for empowerment and sovereignty, but also shattered centres, margins, and categories—the very concepts of the camp and the Zone. Another complicating dimension is that such a production was staged in one of the most conservative theatrical bastions of the French capital, if not culture—the Garnier National Opera House—thus asserting Dembélé's capacity to perform and impose a *Marronage* culture on a traditional audience unaccustomed to this type of performance and paradigm shift.

Dembélé's thought, sensibility, and theatrical practice exemplify a certain layering of culture, as well. Like the Cameroonian writer Léonora Miano, born in 1973 and living in France since 1991, Dembélé has prevailed in fusing her sub-Saharan roots with her French identity by summoning her own specific Afropeanity as a transnational culture which defies borders and nation-state assignations, separation, and delimitations (Miano 2012, 25). For these Afro- or Arab-descendant authors and artists, Marronage, Afropeanism, and creolization represent a way to fashion what French philosopher Michel Foucault characterized as a heterotopia: a cultural or institutional space that is 'other' (Foucault 1994, 752). The theatrical space—the stage—epitomizes an absolute elsewhere, both utopian and recreational, enabling reality and imagination beyond cultural limitations. What unites dramatists and artists such as Koltès,

Kwahulé, and Dembélé is their ability to produce a catharsis of exile through theatre. Here, border crossing is no longer a symbol of banishment, but the translation of an appropriation of the world and its diversity within a hybrid identity and language that salves trauma and memory.

References

Artaud, Antonin. 1964. *Le théâtre et son double (Oeuvres complètes IV)*. Paris: Gallimard.
Deleuze, Gilles. 1993. *The Fold: Leibniz and the Baroque*. Translated by Tom Conley. Minneapolis: Minnesota UP.
Dembéle, Bintou. 2019. 'Les indes galantes: C̶h̶o̶r̶é̶g̶r̶a̶p̶h̶i̶e̶r̶ Rameau.' In *Opéra de Paris Magazine*, interview with Simon Hatab and Katherina Lindekens, 7 October. https://www.operadeparis.fr/magazine/rameau. Accessed 11 March 2022.
Fanon, Frantz. 2002. *Les damnés de la terre*. Paris: La découverte.
Foucault, Michel. 1994. *Dits et écrits IV (1980–1988)*. Paris: Gallimard.
Glissant, Edouard. 1997. *Poetics of Relation*. Translated by B. Wing. Ann Arbor: Michigan UP.
Hardt, Michael & Negri, Antonio. 2009. *Commonwealth*. Cambridge: Harvard UP.
Hegel, Georg Wilhelm Freidrich. 1988. *Aesthetics*. Translated by. T.M. Knox. New York: Clarendon Press / Oxford.
Heidegger, Martin. 2010. *Being and Time*. Translated by J. Stambaugh. Albany: SUNY.
Kwahulé, Koffi. 2013. *La mélancolie des barbares*. Paris : Éditions Théâtrales.
Lapeyronnie, Didier. 2017. 'The Banlieues as a Colonial Theater, or the Colonial Fracture in Disadvantaged Neighborhoods.' In *The Colonial Legacy in France: Fracture, Rupture, and Apartheid*. Edited by Dominic Richard David Thomas, Pascal Blanchard, and Nicolas Bancel. 144–152. Bloomington: Indiana University Press.
Mbembe, Achille. 2006. 'La république et l'impensé de la race.' In *La fracture coloniale*, edited by Pascal Blanchard, Nicolas Bancel et Sandrine Lemaire, 137–153. Paris: La Découverte.
———. 2019. *Necropolitics*. Translated by Steven Corcoran. Durham: Duke UP.
Miano, Léonora. 2012. *Habiter la frontière*. Paris: L'Arche Éditeur.
Mies, Maria. 2014. *Patriarchy and Accumulation on a World Scale: Women in the International Division of Labour*. London: Zed Books.
Ndiaye, Pap. 2009. *La condition noire: essai sur une minorité Française*. Paris: Gallimard.
Niang, Mame-Fatou, & Nielsen, Kaytie. 2017. *Mariannes Noires*. Production: Round Room Image.
Rauer, Selim. 2020. 'Rethinking French Insularities: Marie NDiaye's *Rosie Carpe*.' *Research in African Literatures*, 51 (2), 63–79. Bloomington: Indiana UP.
Roberts, Neil. 2015. *Freedom as Marronage*. Chicago: Chicago UP.
Sayad, Abdelmalek. 1999. *La double absence*. Paris: Seuil.
Spivak, Gayatri Chakravorty. 2010. *Can the Subaltern Speak?* Edited by. R.C. Morris. New York: Columbia UP.
Talpin, Julien et al. 2021. *L'épreuve de la discrimination*. Paris: P.U.F.
Vergès, Françoise. 2016. 'Les Afriques liquides.' In *Penser et écrire l'Afrique aujourd'hui*, edited by Alain Mabanckou, 50–59. Paris: Seuil.

CHAPTER 36

Storying Home: Retracing the Trail of Tears to Restore *Ekvnvcakv*

Christy Stanlake

Constructing the United States relied greatly upon displacing the land's Indigenous peoples, whose ancient homesites, towns, and trade routes became the foundations of settler-colonial homesteads, cities, and roads. This systematic appropriation of Indigenous homelands occurred in various forms across many decades and remains a contemporary struggle, as evidenced by the 2020 Supreme Court decision in *McGirt v. Oklahoma* reaffirming Muscogee jurisdiction over lands reserved for the Muscogee (Creek) Nation. In American history, one of the most infamous exiles of Native Americans remains the Trail of Tears, Andrew Jackson's forced-march removal of the Cherokee, Chickasaw, Choctaw, Seminole, and Muscogee Nations from their ancestral homelands in what is now the southeastern quadrant of the United States to land in Indian Territory (presently Oklahoma). Across the 1830s, between 9000 and 16,000 Native Americans lost their lives during this exile. The term 'exile' reflects the genocidal nature of the Trail of Tears, which was a politically motivated expulsion of Native nations from their homelands administered by the US Army, which treated the Native men, women, children, and elderly as prisoners.

While the Trail of Tears backgrounds this chapter's analysis, the chapter's focus considers a contemporary, visionary form of migration: a retracing of the Trail of Tears by Native American women authors descended from survivors and whose writings serve as a migratory healing ceremony for their communities, Native homelands, and all who dwell upon them. Some of these writers have literally walked the Trail, while all the writers use the Trail of Tears to

---

C. Stanlake (✉)
United States Naval Academy, Annapolis, MD, USA
e-mail: stanlake@usna.edu

© The Author(s), under exclusive license to Springer Nature Switzerland AG 2023
Y. Meerzon, S. E. Wilmer (eds.), *The Palgrave Handbook of Theatre and Migration*, https://doi.org/10.1007/978-3-031-20196-7_36

frame their journeys back to their nations' homelands. In doing so, they critically examine the relationships between Native American sovereignty and US federal law, demonstrating that law and history are byproducts of a deeper cultural understanding of sovereignty, one that is spiritual and liberatory, generating a sense of wholeness in oneself and healing across communities.

General understandings of Native American sovereignty emerge from the 1832 Supreme Court case of *Worchester v. Georgia*, decided during the Cherokee Nation's fight to retain its self-governance and homelands and designating Native American nations as 'domestic dependent nations' that reside within the United States. Significantly, this concept of sovereign Native nations also lies at the core of the United States' creation, during which America obtained land through numerous treaties that US representatives negotiated with various Native nations. Not only did these treaties allow for the physical establishment of the United States, the Constitution designates their importance, calling treaties the 'supreme Law of the Land' (art. VI, §2). Legally, sovereignty is the right of a people to govern themselves; thus, Native nations should have the right to determine laws within their own lands' boundaries. That has not been the case due to federal laws that criminalized Native religious traditions, policies that removed Native children from their homes in order to annihilate Native cultures, and numerous instances in which the federal government broke treaties with Native nations. Because of these attacks on Native sovereignty, as well as differences between Native American and Western worldviews, Native communities view sovereignty as something more than self-governance. Sovereignty is embodied and cultural: the right to retain one's language, to practice one's spiritual traditions, to rear one's children, and to structure community upon Indigenous worldviews. Though Native nations vary greatly, one of the central worldviews shared by many is that law does not originate with people; rather, governance comes directly from the earth, from one's specific homelands, which contain a nation's origin stories, a nation's spiritual root. These stories demonstrate how beings can live in a healthy manner with one another. Treaties may have given settler-colonizers lands, but Indigenous homelands and the stories that emerge from them give Native nations community, culture, language, governance, and health—sovereignty.

The writings of contemporary descendants of Trail of Tears survivors demonstrate how the legal concept of sovereignty is an external manifestation of a more complex set of relationships pertaining to a person's right to engage in Native cultural expressions, especially those concerning ceremony, language/storytelling, and homelands. These writings reveal overlaps between law and storytelling, both of which use language to generate material effects in the world. Native theatre further transforms the legal concept of sovereignty into a cultural practice of sovereignty, as the theatre space becomes a ceremonial space where the performance of language reestablishes the connection to one's homelands, reorienting the performers and audience to earth-centred principals. Ultimately, this rebalancing offers healing to everyone gathered together for the performance.

Methodology and Performance Practices

This study uses Native American intellectual traditions as the basis for its critical examination of works by Native authors (Warrior 1995). The choice to eschew Western traditions of literary criticism in favour of theoretical analysis drawn from Native American and First Nations epistemologies is the standard for Native Studies across the United States and Canada. In *American Indian Literary Nationalism*, Jace Weaver (Cherokee), Craig Womack (Muscogee/Cherokee), and Robert Warrior (Osage) call for 'scholarship that draws on theoretical and epistemological models that arise from indigenous languages and literatures, as well as the many, varied, complex, and changing modes in which Native nations have operated on the ground, in particular places, over a wide expanse of time' (2006, 244). The emphasis on experiences Native communities have with their homelands across time resonates deeply with plays that address the Trail of Tears' relationship to contemporary descendants.

Joy Harjo (Muscogee), Poet Laureate of the United States, uses her title to advocate for a concept called *Ekvnvcakv*, a Muscogee word that articulates a spiritual and embodied understanding of interrelatedness provided by the earth. This relationality encompasses all living beings, not just humans, but animals, plants, water, air, and spirits. Part of this relationality is the concept that language comes from the earth and so offers a reciprocal way for humans to connect to one's sacred homelands, to attain balance with one's relations, and to express sovereignty. Extending this philosophy, art becomes more than aesthetics; art is also spiritual, political, communal, and capable of producing material effects in the world—including sustaining cultural and physical survival.

Harjo calls Native artists to return the United States to *Ekvnvcakv*, not only for the benefit of Indigenous peoples, but for all Harjo's relations. She challenges Native artists to 'be ready to reopen the wound, and even open to revising the [American] story' to lead a new movement towards understanding 'in that immense field of meaning, that connects us to each other, to the plant people and the animal people, to the spirit and to the earth, *Ekvnvcakv*' (Harjo 2020, 9). In both an ecological and a political sense, Harjo warns that without *Ekvnvcakv* the very existence of the United States is at stake: 'If this country is to integrate spiritually, creatively, and profoundly, we must nourish the roots. There is no America without Native nations, arts, cultures, languages, and humanities. Without the acknowledgement and inclusion of Indigenous roots, a land—a country—is unmoored, without stability' (7). Harjo's *American Sunrise* exemplifies how Native arts can heal the wounds of history, the divisions across communities, and the dangerous imbalance between humans and the living world (Harjo 2019a). A descendent of Trail of Tears' survivors, Harjo uses the book to chronicle her literal journey from Oklahoma back to Muscogee homelands. A prayer honouring the earth, closes the book proclaiming, 'Bless us, these lands, said the rememberer. These lands aren't our/lands.

These lands aren't your lands. We are this land'—words that supplant Manifest Destiny's human-centred perspective with the Native philosophy of *Ekvnvcakv* (Harjo 2019b, 108).

Playwright Yvette Nolan (Algonquin) explains that Native theatre is particularly well suited to both communicating and materially producing interconnections through its live, communal medium. In *Medicine Shows*, Nolan asserts:

> Indigenous theater artists make medicine by reconnecting through ceremony, through the act of remembering, through building community, and by negotiating solidarities across communities. The act of staging these things reconnects who we are as Indigenous people with where we have come from, with our stories, with our ancestors [..., making] the Indigenous artist a conduit between the past and the future. Ceremony. Remembrance. Making Community. Survivance. (2015, 3)

Accordingly, Native American playwrights who enact ceremonies of remembrance through retracing the Trail of Tears combine the theatre's healing/good medicine potential with Harjo's call for Native artists to return to wounds to re-envision the American story in ways that nurture life's meaning through *Ekvnvcakv*.

Like *American Sunrise*, contemporary plays by women whose families survived the Trail of Tears journey back through time and place in order to offer healing. Moreover, live theatre produces this healing through literal ceremonies of remembrance that performers and audiences engage in together, while Native dramaturgy enacts earth-centred philosophies. The following examination demonstrates how Native American philosophies of interrelatedness—articulated through concepts of land, time, language, and healing—shape the dramaturgy of two different plays. Each play begins with ceremony; next, the plays shift into scenes that demonstrate paths to healing within their Native communities; finally, the plays invite all viewers/beings into an act of ceremonial healing based upon earth-centred philosophies. Throughout these three layers of action, each play incorporates staging choices that viscerally demonstrate concepts of *Ekvnvcakv*. Both plays function in ceremonial time, meaning the worlds of the ancestors and contemporary characters interrelate and, sometimes, interact with one another. Similarly, both plays convey the literal power of one's homelands through the physical use of soil from those lands, connecting the characters to both place and ancestors. The interconnections amongst land, language, and sovereignty are featured when both plays emphasize specific, geographical places where—as the ancestors' stories record—Native sovereignty was challenged. Finally, both plays convey the story of the Trail of Tears for vital reasons: to heal their Native communities; to transform American History through Native stories; and to offer all audience members earth-centred philosophies of healing in place of national narratives about dominating the land and Indigenous people.

Journeying Back Through the Trail of Tears

Sovereignty by Mary Kathryn Nagle (Cherokee) and *And So We Walked* by DeLanna Studi (Cherokee) are contemporary plays written by women who carry the stories of their ancestors. Both plays intervene in the national narrative by using the Trail of Tears as a vehicle to place Native American peoples and philosophies at the centre of the US origin story. Though they 'reopen the wound' of American genocide, the plays do this to offer healing: to give visibility to Native American presence, both past and contemporary; to enact Indigenous values of interconnectedness; and to root human experience within the spirit of the earth through storying.

In addition to being a professional playwright, Nagle is an attorney who specializes in constitutional law and its relationship to tribal law; she has argued in federal and the US Supreme Court to protect and extend tribal sovereignty (Pipestem 2021). In 2018, Washington, DC's Arena Stage premiered Nagle's *Sovereignty*, a play that connects the contemporary battle for tribal governments to prosecute non-native perpetrators of violence against Native people on tribal lands to the issue of tribal sovereignty affirmed by *Worcester v. Georgia* (1832).

DeLanna Studi is an actor, writer, and activist, who serves as the Artistic Director of Native Voices at the Autry. Studi's one-woman show is based on her six-week, 900-mile trek from her ancestral homelands to Oklahoma. Studi travelled alongside her father, Thomas, who speaks fluent Cherokee and helped Studi talk with elders (Robinson 2017). The play recounts the new understanding Studi and Thomas gathered along their journey. Studi's 'Author's Note' states that the play also 'seeks to make social innovation by dragging the Trail of the Tears out of the past. It is a story that is part of the fabric of America, but […] is often forgotten as a central piece of our shared American History' (2017b, ii).

Entering the Ceremony of Remembrance

Paula Gunn Allen (Laguna Pueblo/Sioux) defines ceremony as the 'enactment of a specialized perception of a cosmic relationship,' one that functions to integrate all relations and to 'support the sense of community that is the bedrock of tribal life' (1992, 61, 63). Accordingly, *Sovereignty* and *And So We Walked* begin in ceremony: dramatic action that places their main characters in sacred locations, providing connections across the generations. In both plays, the words of the ancestors are literally heard through either sound effects or interweaving storylines from different eras. This use of ceremonial action emphasizes how time in these plays functions as a spiral, placing moments in the past adjacent to—and sometimes alongside—the present. Accordingly, viewers can visualize the interrelatedness of place, time, and action, ideas Nagle expressed to the Association for Theatre in Higher Education (ATHE): 'We understand that when we walk on the land, we walk with our ancestors, and what happens today is a reflection of what happened then, and what happened then is a reflection of what's happening today' (Nagle 2021).

Sovereignty's Ceremonial Time

Sovereignty opens with Sarah Ridge Polson, a talented young attorney, visiting the Ridge family cemetery in Oklahoma. Sarah pours a jar of dirt, collected from her family's homelands during her travels through Georgia, over the grave of John Ridge, her great-great-great grandfather, a legal scholar who helped attorneys win *Worcester v. Georgia*. Sarah tells her aunt that she is moving back to Oklahoma to continue advancing Cherokee sovereignty by working for the Cherokee Nation's Attorney General's Office (Nagle 2020, 5–6). Thus, Scene One draws a direct connection between Sarah and her ancestor, John Ridge, through their blood and shared advocacy for sovereignty. Their interrelatedness is literally displayed through Sarah's ritualized delivery of sacred earth to 'bring a little bit of their old home to their home here' (6). This soil represents the Cherokee people's homelands and sovereignty that John Ridge spent his life attempting to protect before his nation's exile to Indian Territory. As the play develops, interconnections between the past and present grow through scenes that juxtapose Sarah's fight for jurisdictional rights over non-native offenders with scenes from the 1800s depicting John Ridge and his father, Major Ridge, working to secure Cherokee Nation sovereignty and homelands. These past scenes include attempted negotiations with President Jackson, John Ridge's drafting the brief that won *Worcester v. Georgia*, and the Ridge family's decision to sign the controversial Treaty of New Echota (1835). Signed by members of the Treaty Party, the Treaty of New Echota agreed to give up Cherokee homelands in exchange for five million dollars and lands in Indian Territory that the federal government agreed to never claim and upon which the Cherokee Nation would continue to exercise sovereignty. The Treaty Party signed the document based on Jackson's declaration he'd remove the Cherokee people in defiance of the Supreme Court's ruling supporting the Cherokee Nation's sovereign right to its homelands. Although Principal Chief of the Cherokee Nation, John Ross, and the much larger National Party protested the treaty, the US Government used the document to legally justify the exile of the Cherokee people. *Sovereignty* portrays that the Ridge family's agreement to sign stemmed from their assessment that the treaty best 'preserves our exclusive jurisdiction over Cherokee lands' and sovereignty; moreover, the treaty promised other provisions, including a seat in the US House of Representatives for the Cherokee Nation (121–22). The federal government broke many of the treaty's promises, but the act of signing a legal agreement with the Cherokee Nation continued US recognition of the nation as a sovereign political entity, a status that Georgia's continued violence against Cherokee people and Jackson's promised military exile threatened to destroy. Indeed, the treaties signed by the five 'civilized' nations whom the Trail of Tears exiled are documents the 2020 Supreme Court used to uphold Native sovereignty over tribal lands across Oklahoma in *McGirt v. Oklahoma*.

Sovereignty's use of ceremonial time not only draws connections between the Cherokee people's homelands and present-day Oklahoma; it also demonstrates how the Cherokee Nation's fight to retain and extend their sovereignty is ever-present. John Ridge's work provides precedent for legal arguments Sarah continues to make. Significantly, this spiralling of time is more than a dramaturgical convention theatricalizing philosophical and generational interconnections; it is also semiautobiographical. Nagle's portrayal of the nineteenth-century Ridge family is her family's story. Nagle, like her character Sarah, is John and Major Ridge's direct descendant whose career literally continues the legal arguments for Cherokee sovereignty her ancestors began crafting almost two centuries ago (Nagle 2020, back cover).

And So We Walked*'s Remembrance*

Studi's play begins in the ceremony of prayer, demonstrating how Native concepts of language reconnect people to sacred places and the ancestors whose spirits reside there. Upon her seven-sided stage, Studi offers words to the Creator, immediately interweaving art/spirituality, past/present, and language/homelands through *Ekvnvcakv* (Studi 2017a, 1). The stage geometrically represents the Cherokee people's original seven clans' connection to the earth, mirroring how, in Cherokee gatherings, clans encircle the sacred, eternal flame of the Cherokee Nation. Upon her earth-centred stage, Studi transitions to storyteller, relating how her narrative is 'written in blood,' referencing her ancestors' deaths along the Trail of Tears (1). Place and prayer, then, enable time's spiral to connect Studi's present world to her ancestors, dramatized by whispers the audience hears from Studi's grandmothers who speak to her of *Tsalaqwa Wevti*, Cherokee for 'the "old homeplace." Kituwah in North Carolina' (4).

Studi organizes the plot around interactions with sacred places she and her father literally visited as they retraced the Trail of Tears. They first encounter 'Qualla Boundary […] home of the Eastern Band of Cherokee Indians […] in North Carolina,' marking both Studi's reunion with Cherokee homelands and the location where exile divided the Cherokee into three bands: Eastern, Western (Studi's nation in Oklahoma), and Keetoowah (Studi 2017a, 22). TJ Holland, their 'Eastern Band cultural liaison,' points towards a mountain where Earth reveals her people's rupture: 'over there—straight up the mountain—is the Trail your family walked. This is where our people were torn from each other. What you're looking at is a *scar*' (22). While one might perceive the scar as metaphor, Native dramaturgy suggests a visceral connection: just as the Cherokee Nation was ripped apart, their homeland physically experiences that painful rift as a wound: earth, Cherokee individuals, and the bands bear the same scar. TJ prays with Studi, then offers her a handful of earth, soil she carries on stage (22–23). The ceremonial structure of *And So We Walked*—from its opening action, to its supporting sound and set design, to Studi's first interaction with Cherokee homelands—materially represents the interrelated concepts of *Ekvnvcakv*.

Healing Across Native Communities

Once these plays position both dramatic action and audience into a world that is not just aesthetic, but one deeply rooted in Native American philosophies, they begin to work towards healing—the theatrical medicine Nolan speaks of that builds and restores relationships. Both *Sovereignty* and *And So We Walked* embark upon migrations of ceremonial remembrance to heal not just the plays' characters, but also painful divisions existing across the Cherokee community. Studi's play mentions the literal rending of the Cherokee Nation into three, but both plays demonstrate further injuries incurred across community after the Treaty Party and National Party's debate became entrenched, causing Cherokee people to turn against one another. The Treaty Party was villainized as those who sold Cherokee homelands and caused the Trail of Tears; consequently, National Party loyalists assassinated John and Major Ridge after the nation settled in Indian Territory. *Sovereignty* shows that Ridge family descendants were equally disparaged; Sarah is warned to keep secret about her Ridge ancestry when she's in Oklahoma (Nagle 2020, 6). Studi's play extends this Ross/Ridge animosity to further political splintering. Such divisions strike at the core of Cherokee identity and belonging, increasing the wound first marked at Qualla Boundary.

Community Healing: Sovereignty

Sovereignty offers good medicine to Cherokee people by showing John Ross and the Ridge family's interrelatedness through their fierce battles to sustain Cherokee sovereignty. Nagle reveals this positive connection between families after having first addressed the historic Ross/Ridge dispute in *Sovereignty*'s opening scene, where Aunt Flora warns Sarah that the attorney general's office is 'controlled' by Rosses (Nagle 2020, 5). Although almost two centuries have passed, Flora views the conflict in present terms, declaring, 'The moment [contemporary Attorney General John Ross] finds out you're a Ridge, he'll do whatever he can to undermine your work [...]. The day you trust a Ross is the day they kill you' (6).

Contrasting such intratribal factions, *Sovereignty*'s 1800s scenes are dominated by Ridge/Ross collaborations to win *Worchester v. Georgia* and fight the backlash of Georgians' violence against Cherokee people. We learn that Ross served as Major Ridge's translator, and that Major Ridge fulfilled a fatherly role for Ross, whose father was white. Ross confides in John Ridge, 'I wanted to speak our language. When I was a boy. But every time I tried, my father scolded me. Speaking Cherokee was "uncivilized." So I spoke English. Until I met your father' (Nagle 2020, 27). Establishing this kinship, Nagle dramatizes the trauma enacted upon the Cherokee Nation when its leaders, both committed to Cherokee survival and sovereignty, divide their community based upon *how* to protect their nation. Ross proclaims, 'Our land is who we are. It's what makes us Cherokee'; while John Ridge questions, 'What use will our land be once we've all been killed? […] If we agree to move west, we'll lose our lands, but we'll preserve the nation' (91).

In *Sovereignty*'s present-day scenes, Jim Ross and Sarah retrace their grandfathers' footsteps fighting for Cherokee Nation sovereignty. Their shared commitment to Cherokee community offers a way to heal the old divisions across land and time. Accordingly, Jim invites Sarah to represent their grandfathers' shared mission by delivering to the US Supreme Court their nation's argument for Cherokee jurisdiction over non-native perpetrators of domestic violence against Cherokee people on Cherokee lands. Significantly, Sarah is a survivor of such an assault; the correlation allows her oral argument to relate her body to the Cherokee people's bodies, sovereignty, history, and homelands—all of which endured violent assaults after Jackson flouted the Supreme Court in his 'mission to erase tribal jurisdiction and, ultimately, Tribal Nations' (Nagle 2020, 125).

Community Healing: And So We Walked

Studi explores communal wounds concerning belonging, especially for later generations of Cherokee people raised away from their original homelands. When Thomas is invited to a Stomp Dance near Medicine Creek, he brings his daughter to this significant site of healing. Studi's doubt about her own belonging and value to the community has grown as she's witnessed crowds embrace her father—a full-blood Cherokee—as their beloved son. She worries that her half-Cherokee blood quantum and unfamiliarity with the language will prevent her from connecting to her people. Thomas tells Studi that 'The *Ga-ti-yo*, Stomp Dance, is a sacred event,' which the Cherokee protected by practicing it in secret for over a century when federal laws banned the exercise of Native American religions until 1978's American Indian Religious Freedom Act restored such rights (Studi 2017a, 30). During the ban, Native traditions continued at great peril ensuring that people could maintain relationships across generations, communities, homelands, and the spirit world. Studi's father recounts how Cherokee people on the Trail of Tears literally 'carried the embers of the First Fire from North Carolina to Oklahoma'; he then reveals, 'one hundred and fifty years after the Trail, my Cousin John and some others brought that fire back here, from Oklahoma' (30).

The evening's dance at Medicine Creek occurs where Studi's family returned the First Fire, the emblem of Cherokee community and survival. As women prepare Studi for the dance, they remind her, 'We, Cherokee, know women are sacred. Powerful. We keep the culture alive. We create the next generation of Cherokee' (Studi 2017a, 33). Studi's experience of dancing at Medicine Creek is healing; it physically manifests concepts of interrelatedness across members of the community, Cherokee homelands, their sacred fire, stories of the ancestors, and Studi's own realization of her acceptance and value. Like the fire her ancestors returned, Studi—a Cherokee woman—fulfils a sacred role, keeping Cherokee culture alive. This sense of belonging is medicine to Studi's soul, reflecting the women's assertion: 'That's why we go to stomp. *Nv wo' ti*. For medicine' (34). As Studi reenacts this scene for her audiences, she embodies her continued connection to Cherokee homelands and people, literally fulfilling—through theatre/story—the Cherokee woman's role of maintaining cultural traditions.

Ekvnvcakv: Transforming the American Story

Harjo's call to Native American artists is more than a request to include Native representation in the country's national narrative; it is a declaration that Native stories and art can salvage America's people and ravished lands—all beings—through the transformative power and revered understanding *Ekvnvcakv* provides. Accordingly, *Sovereignty* and *And So We Walked* lead all viewers on a visionary migration towards interrelatedness by inviting them into a ceremonial place where actions evoke a core concept—the story not only belongs to the storyteller, but to all those who hear it. One of the material effects of storytelling lies in this understanding that listeners share responsibility with the storyteller in honouring the story, sharing it with others, and continuing the process of weaving interconnectedness.

Sovereignty

In her address to ATHE, Nagle explained that Native theatre is more than entertainment: 'Storytelling is how we survived' (2021). Recounting the significance of Cherokee survival, *Sovereignty* roots the United States and its federal laws in Native homelands, sovereignty, and earth-centred philosophies that reveal the intertwining histories of the United States and Native America. Nagle's portrayal of 1800s Cherokee life demonstrates the commonalities between Cherokee people and settler-colonialists, placing national 'founding fathers' on equal footing with Cherokee leaders, who have studied law, Latin, and British literature; who regularly send representatives to negotiate with world leaders, including the King of England (Nagle 2020, 30); and who publish *The Cherokee Phoenix*, a national newspaper covering world events in Cherokee and English languages (46). Moreover, *Sovereignty* portrays the initial friendship between Jackson and Major Ridge. As compatriots, they lead their respective forces to victory at the Battle of Horseshoe Bend, where Jackson gave the Cherokee orator the name 'Major,' in tribute to Ridge's leadership (44). This history exposes the toxic roots of the 'primitive Indian' stereotype permeating US national narratives when Nagle unveils how Jackson corrupts both Cherokee and American values by using white-supremacist language to justify theft of Native homelands. Betraying his political ally and personal friend, Jackson tells John Ridge, 'I say this as your friend. You find yourselves established in the midst of a superior race, and although you do not appreciate the cause of your inferiority, if you do not yield to the force of progress or civilization and move west, you will disappear' (46).

Nagle's audiences must weigh Cherokee narratives against settler-colonial myths of superiority when Sarah delivers her Supreme Court argument in the form of direct-audience-address that collapses theatre/Supreme Court and viewers/justices. This dramaturgical move connects Native and non-native audience members to the Cherokee story of the Trail of Tears, as everyone—now sharing the same country—witness a descendant of John Ridge proclaiming that 'Tribal jurisdiction over non-Indians predates the United States Constitution. So tribal jurisdiction isn't unconstitutional. It's preconstitutional' (Nagle 2020, 125). Sarah's statement invites theatregoers to envision Cherokee sovereignty as foundational to the United States, a central concept of liberty expressed through interconnectedness. In *Sovereignty*'s DC premiere, this moment profoundly resonated with *Ekvnvcakv* because Arena Stage is a brief walk away from the US Supreme Court.

And So We Walked

Studi's *And So We Walked* also ends with an emphasis on interconnections across generations, stories, land, and beings, including the audience. Studi shares an ancestral story about the Cherokee Nation's hope in the midst of genocide: 'When Chief John Ross heard about the removal, he told the Cherokee to plant their corn that season, to show Creator, the US Government, and each other that we had no intention of leaving' (Studi 2017a, 66). Thomas explains that, although the Trail of Tears would prevent the Cherokee people from seeing the corn mature, 'we know when we plant seeds that we may never get to see them sprout, but some future generation will. We hold on to hope. That's why we have the Green Corn Ceremony every year to forgive and begin anew' (66). The story demonstrates how rooting human spirit and actions in one's relationship to the earth—and, by extension, all one's relations—creates resilience. The grandmothers echo this by telling Studi that 'hope of the future' kept them walking along the Trail (67). Studi—standing upon the stage—presents the embodiment of her grandmothers' hope, which she releases into the audience's future through storytelling. Embracing her ancestors' knowledge and hope for a healthier world, Studi faces her audience to deliver her final line: 'And so we walked …' (68). Her play ends with this sense of motion, walking upon the earth, as Studi transforms the Trail of Tears—an exile intended to break Native sovereignty through dividing people from their homelands—into a storied path to home, to *Ekvnvcakv*. Part of the healing extends to Studi's audience, people who now carry the stories of Studi, her grandmothers, and their homelands.

* * *

Harjo attests that motion is one of the signs of a nation's vitality: 'A healthy cultural system is marked by diversity and movement. Diversity ensures that life creates and continues creatively [...]. Artists and purveyors of cultural knowledge, keepers of earth, know this—we move toward that which has been unimagined to make fresh avenues of meaning, avenues by which we can move understanding' (Harjo 2020, 8). Although the Trail of Tears is a scar upon the earth, a crime against US law, and a sin against humanity, Native women authors—keepers of cultural memory and the land's stories—are accomplishing the unimagined. They are retracing the Trail to transform its meaning, creating possibility out of the interrelatedness of time, generations, earth, and stories. Through theatre's live medium, Native playwrights are working to heal deep wounds, inviting the world to join this ceremony of making good medicine that roots all communities, understanding, and health in the Indigenous earth—*Ekvnvcakv*.

References

Gunn Allen, Paula. 1992. *The Sacred Hoop: Recovering the Feminine in American Indian Traditions*. Boston: Beacon Press.
Harjo, Joy. 2019a. *An American Sunrise: Poems*. New York: W. W. Norton.
———. 2019b. 'Bless this Land.' In *An American Sunrise*, 106–108. New York: W. W. Norton.
———. 2020. 'Keynote Address.' In *Native Arts and Culture: Resilience, Reclamation, and Relevance Conference Program*, 6–9. Washington, DC.
Nagle, Mary Kathryn. 2020. *Sovereignty*. Evanston: Northwestern University Press.
———. 2021. 'Keynote Address: A Conversation with Ty DeFoe and Mary Kathryn Nagle.' *Association for Theatre in Higher Education 2021 Conference*. August 5, 2021.
Nolan, Yvette. 2015. *Medicine Shows: Indigenous Performance Culture*. Toronto: Playwrights Canada Press.
Pipestem 2021. 'Mary Kathryn Nagle.' Accessed May 23, 2021. http://www.pipestemlaw.com/attorney/mary-kathryn-nagle.
Robinson, Betsi. 2017. 'Story of the Artist's Journey. *And So We Walked*.' Accessed May 23, 2021. https://www.andsowewalked.com/storyofjourney.
Studi, DeLanna. 2017a. *And So We Walked: An Artist's Journey Along the Trail of Tears*. Typescript.
———. 2017b. 'Author's Note.' In *And So We Walked*, ii. Typescript.
Warrior, Robert Allen. 1995. *Tribal Secrets: Recovering American Indian Intellectual Traditions*. Minneapolis: University of Minnesota Press.
Weaver, Jace, Craig S. Womack, and Robert Warrior. 2006. *American Indian Literary Nationalism*. Albuquerque: University of New Mexico Press.

CHAPTER 37

Diasporic Trauma, Nativized Innovation, and Techno-Intercultural Predicament: The Story of *Jingju* in Taiwan

Daphne P. Lei

The long Chinese civil war that ended in 1949 decided many people's fate: people from the two sides of the Taiwan Strait—under the communist regime in mainland China and the republic government in Taiwan—would not see each other again for about four decades. Estimated over one million mainlanders migrated to Taiwan, following the retreat of the Chiang Kai-shek's Nationalist Party (KMT) government. Soldiers fatigued by the long wars against Japanese and communists, evacuated civilians from all over China, and crestfallen government officials all suddenly found themselves negotiating a space of survival on a small (semi)tropical island laden with complicated colonial and migration history. Along with tears and broken hearts of the refugees were also a living national treasure—*jingju* (Beijing opera, Peking opera), which would take roots and thrive in this new home.

This chapter addresses the evolution of *jingju* in Taiwan from 1940s to early 2020s. As the development of *jingju* is always closely related to national politics, the artistic history of *jingju* in Taiwan *is* a history of the nation; the survival story of *jingju* reflects the difficult negotiations among cultures, ethnicities, politics, and identities of Taiwan. The identity of the large post-1949 migration is ambiguous: are they diaspora, refugees, immigrants, foreign invaders, or new settlers? James Clifford discusses 'roots and routes' related to diaspora and

D. P. Lei (✉)
University of California, Irvine, Irvine, CA, USA
e-mail: dlei@uci.edu

asks, 'how long does it take to become "indigenous"?' (Clifford 2005, 530–31). *Jingju* was an uprooted plant with broken branches trying to survive in the new distressed environment, and the gradual acclimation, hybridization with local cultures, and new stimuli helped grow it into a new 'native' plant—Taiwan *jingju*. National politics and diplomacy, however, are the winds that largely control the direction of the growth of the arts and sometimes present a threat to their new roots. I will first discuss the pre-1949 sociopolitical condition of both *jingju* and Taiwan, and then the development of Taiwan *jingju* in three stages.

JINGJU AND NATIONAL POLITICS

What is *jingju*? *Jing* means capital and *ju* means drama or theatre, and *jingju* literally means capital drama or capital theatre. *Jingju* is known as Beijing opera or Peking opera in the West; however, it is not a native art of Beijing, the national capital of China for most of the time since the thirteenth century. The origin of *jingju* is often linked to a troupe from Anhui province that performed in Beijing on Emperor Qianlong's eightieth birthday in 1790. This 'migrant' art matured and thrived in Beijing and established close relationships with the power centres in the next two centuries. It was first banned but later favoured by many royalties and aristocrats in the Qing dynasty (1644–1911), and in the early Republic, by many government officials, warlords, the rich and the elites, along with the masses. In the early twentieth century, through the effort of some elites and artists, *jingju* was deliberately rid of its vulgar elements and elevated to the status of 'national opera' (*guoju*). Mei Lanfang's 1930 visit to the United States promoted the image of *jingju* as the national symbol of China, *the* Chinese opera (Goldstein 2007, 134–71). His brief encounter with Brecht and Stanislavski in 1935 further secured *jingju* as the *de facto* Chineseness in the international and intercultural context, and this has remained a favourite topic for theatre scholarship till today. The *national* opera continued to be a popular pastime, and the arias were treated like pop songs and famous artists as celebrities.

Aesthetically, all forms of traditional music-based Chinese theatre (*xiqu*) share similar visual elements—elaborate makeup and costume, minimalist props and set, and acting style. 'Acting' in *xiqu* includes stylized singing and recitation, as well as formalized gestures, mime, dance, fighting, acrobatics by well-defined role types—*sheng* (male), *dan* (female), *jing* (painted face), and *chou* (clown), along with numerous sub-types. What distinguishes one genre from another is usually its musical and linguistic element. *Jingju* uses both string and percussion instruments and its singing and music often appear more boisterous and vigorous compared to 'quieter' genres such as *kunqu*, whose music is more melodious and elegant. The traditional repertoire contains stories from histories, legends, and folklores, which are often shared in many genres.

When Chiang Kai-shek decided to make Taiwan the home for the Republic of China (ROC) to counter the new China, the People's Republic of China (PRC), established by Mao Zedong with the Chinese Communist Party (CCP),

Taiwan was already a place layered with ethnic conflicts and traumas resulted from the waves of immigration and colonialization. The indigenous population of Taiwan, which is related to Austronesian peoples and has suffered every type of colonial subjection throughout history, only represents 2% of the entire population today. For centuries, Han Chinese—the largest ethnic group in China—settled in Taiwan and its surrounding small islands from the mainland. Most of the early immigrants were from the southern coastal provinces such as Fujian and Guangdong. In the international context, Taiwan, named 'Formosa' (beautiful island) by Portuguese sailors in the sixteenth century, was partially occupied and colonized by the Dutch and Spanish in the seventeenth century. The Qing regained control of Taiwan in the late seventeenth century but lost the Sino-Japanese War of 1895 and Taiwan was subject to a comprehensive and systematic Japanese colonization for half a century (1895–1945). Despite the anti-Japanese resentment, people in the postcolonial Taiwan did not wholeheartedly welcome the takeover by the ROC government in 1945, and the '228 Incident,' named after the date of its occurrence—February 28, 1947—broke their trust for the new government. 228 originated as a minor conflict between the new KMT police and earlier settlers but quickly evolved into a large protest and subsequent suppression and arrests of political dissent and a long period of martial law. 228 became a symbol of the historical trauma of the earlier Han settlers, who considered themselves the rightful Taiwanese 'natives'; 228 is also a powerful political tool as it can conjure up historical animosity against mainlanders.

Although Chineseness and Taiwaneseness are often pitted against each other in today's political rhetoric, we should understand that both concepts are temporal constructions. There was never a pure 'Taiwanese' identity before the 'Chinese' arrival. Leo Cabranes-Grant's writing on Mexico explains Taiwan's situation well: based on Latour's Actor-network theory, he explains that 'distinctions between pure and impure practices are not produced by intercultural relations—they are already there as part of a complex chain of networking operations that flow through, against, and because of them' (Cabranes-Grant 2016, 5). As both immigration and colonization of different sorts continued for centuries in Taiwan, the various historical and cultural beliefs in Taiwan exist in constantly shifting networks of relationships. Taiwanese identity at any given historical moment could be anti-Dutch, anti-Japanese, anti-communist, anti-Chiang Kai-shek, anti-mainlander, or today's anti-Chinese. There was no pre-intercultural, pre-hybridized Taiwaneseness; the purity of Taiwaneseness needs to be imagined because it has never existed.

'Chinese' Nostalgia and Nationalism

Similarly, a unique 'Chineseness' had to be imagined in the post-war Taiwan as the new mainland migrants came with distinctive linguistic and cultural backgrounds; therefore, *jingju*, a genre that was widely popular on the mainland and not unfamiliar in Taiwan, became a ready-made tool for constructing the new national narrative. Numerous *jingju* troupes from the mainland visited Taiwan in the early twentieth century, and the founding of Yongle Theatre in 1924 to host local and visiting artists indicated a certain popularity of *jingju* before 1949. The most significant migration, however, took place in 1949, when the military-based *jingju* troupes migrated with troops. New military-sponsored troupes—Air Force's Dapeng Troupe (1950–1995), the Navy's Haiguang Troupe (1954–1995), and the Army's Luguang Troupe (1954–1995)—were formally established during the 1950s. Opera schools— Little Dapeng (1954), Little Luguang (1963), and Little Haiguang (1969)— were also formed to train youngsters to carry on the tradition (Wang 2002, 1:55–72).

Most of the soldiers who retreated with the troops—many of whom were very young—lost contact with their family members. Despite the patriotic fervour generated by such inspirational messages as 'defeating communists' and 'recovering homeland,' there was insurmountable sadness, anxiety, and nostalgia in the military. As a familiar pastime from home, *jingju* comforted the tormented souls and broken hearts; traditional repertoire was also a psychological stabilizer and healer, as well as morale booster, as many stories focused on traditional values such as loyalty, filial piety, integrity, and righteousness. The *jingju* troupes both served the soldiers and performed commercially. Despite the harsh economic condition and poor performance venues in the early Cold War era, *jingju* established a solid footing in Taiwan in the 1950s.

The Cultural Revolution (1966–1976) in mainland China provided *jingju* another opportunity to thrive in Taiwan. As early as in 1942, Mao Zedong had indicated that art and literature should serve the 'revolution machine' for the communist struggle (Mao 1971, 250–86). To counter the Cultural Revolution, which sought to discard traditional cultures, the ROC government launched the *Wenhua fuxing* ('Cultural Restoration') movement, putting *jingju* on the political frontline to defend traditional cultures. Beyond the internationally recognized 'Red China vs. Free China' Cold War tension, Taiwan claimed to be the legitimate China forced into temporary exile. Svetlana Boym points out that nostalgia is 'a longing for a home that no longer exists or has never existed'; nostalgia is a 'sentiment of loss and displacement' but also 'a romance with one's own fantasy.' The concerns about restoring lost homes or memories are what she calls 'restorative nostalgia,' which has two narrative plots—the restoration of origins and conspiracy theory (Boym 2001, xiii–xiv). Conspiracy theory presents stark contrast between good and evil, us and them, and in this case, the temporarily displaced real Chinese vs. communist bandits who stole our homes. What could be a better symbol of national nostalgia and orthodox Chineseness but *jingju*, the Chinese opera? Through *jingju*, the national nostalgia and personal nostalgia work together to construct a new national narrative. Although the transplant was rushed and incomplete, *jingju* as an art form nevertheless survived and thrived under the harshest circumstances, largely because of its ability to help narrate the nation.

GANGA AND INNOVATIVE TRANSITION

The façade of the 'real' China in Taiwan faced tremendous challenge in the 1970s. Internationally, while Taiwan was moving up the economic ladder to becoming one of the 'Four Little Dragons of Asia,' diplomatic support was fading. The Dragon Gate in San Francisco Chinatown, a gift from the Chiang Kai-shek government in 1969, was Taiwan's desperate last try to claim a legitimate space internationally (Lei 2006, 179–80). In 1971, the ROC was forced out of the United Nations and replaced by the PRC as the *Chinese* UN member. Richard Nixon visited China in 1972, and in 1979, the United States officially recognized the PRC and terminated its official relations with Taiwan. Domestically, Chiang Kai-shek died in 1975 and the constructed national nostalgia was waning after nearly three decades of separation; meanwhile, the oppositional voice—largely identified with the political positions of the early Han settlers, the so-called 'native' Taiwanese—against the KMT government was growing stronger, which culminated in the 'Formosa Incident' (1979), a large political protest leading to arrests of dissidents. The apparition of the 228 spectre and the new Formosa force helped the oppositional movement gain momentum, which led to the establishment of the Democratic Progressive Party (DPP) in 1986. The DPP is the majority party today.

If the constructed orthodox Chineseness could not be defended both internationally and on the island, how could *jingju*, the ultimate symbol of Chineseness, survive? With the declining of nationalist political power and the older *jingju* aficionados, as well as the increasing force of westernization and globalization, some second-generation mainlander artists sensed an ontological crisis: they needed to sustain the life of the old *jingju* with the new blood from their generation. Although traditional *jingju* continued to be performed until today, in the convention of *zhexixi*, which generally indicates that a program comprises various famous scenes from different plays instead of a full play, younger artists began to experiment with traditional forms and eventually created a unique new genre—innovative Taiwan *jingju*. In the 1980s, traditional plays were reimagined through a lens that was more modern and western, with new dramaturgy and staging, modified scripts and even new music. Guo Xiaozhuang (1951–), a second-generation mainlander trained in traditional *jingju*, was an important pioneer. Her Yaying Ensemble (founded in 1979) began a new phase of *jingju* in Taiwan. Wu Hsing-kuo (1953–) went a step further: his Contemporary Legend Theater (*Dangdai chuanqi*, founded in 1986) staged Shakespeare plays with modified *jingju* style in the 1980s and has continued with his *jingju*-based intercultural experimentation till today.

As the 'native' voice gained more political control and the first native president was elected in 1988, national support of *jingju* declined rapidly in the 1990s. Military-based troupes were disbanded and consolidated into one company, the National Guoguang Opera Company in 1995. To successfully survive the political transition, Guoguang created new plays to comply with the ideology of nativization, such as *Taiwan Trilogy* (1998–1999), telling stories of

Mazu (the goddess widely worshiped in Taiwan) and Taiwanese folk heroes such as Zheng Chenggong (Koxinga 1624–1662) and Liao Tianding (1883–1909) (Lei 2011b, 23–40). Although the performance style (such as singing and acting) largely followed the tradition, there were surprising visual elements such as aboriginal and Dutch characters.

The need for innovation did not only come from political pressure; it was also decided by the market. If *jingju* didn't want to die, it had to change! In the new millennium, it is clear that Taiwan is not China and Taiwanese not Chinese; and yet, Taiwanese are not 'not Chinese,' nor not 'not "not Chinese."' And yet, if Taiwan/ROC is not the orthodox China (claimed by Chiang Kai-shek), a renegade province of China to be reunited (claimed by the PRC), or an independent country (recognized by only twelve UN members and the Holy See), what is it? Is Taiwan's sovereignty always nested in an either/or or neither/nor liminality?

There is a term in Chinese *ganga* that perfectly describes this dilemma of Taiwan. *Ganga* generally describes the sentiment of awkwardness and embarrassment, which is specifically caused by feeling stuck in an uncomfortable neither/nor state. An ancient Chinese dictionary *Shuowen jiezi*, which was compiled around 100 AD, defines *ganga* as 'not straight,' with the extended meaning as not walking straight, crippled, or illegitimate by later commentaries (Xu 2006, 11: 6598–99). Nowadays *ganga* is usually used to describe a type of unnatural and thorny dilemma. *Ganga* is a mental state that one would want to escape from as soon as possible because prolonged liminality posed an existential threat. Taiwan *jingju* was stuck in a situation between tradition and modernization, Chinese and non-Chinese, diaspora and nativization. The *ganga* condition of *jingju* was the product of the *ganga* ontology of Taiwan.

I argue that *ganga* was the major catalyst that initiated the radical revolution of Taiwan *jingju* in the new millennium. *Jingju* scholar and playwright Wang An-Ch'i writes about the famous *ganga* moment in her college class on the subject of the classic *Yubei Ting*: Meng Yuehua, the young wife of Wang Youdao, is caught in a rainstorm on her way home and has to take refuge in a pavilion overnight; a young man is trapped there for the same reason. They—a young man and a young woman—spend a night together alone, although they do not have any personal interaction. However, Wang Youdao divorces his wife because he suspects her 'immoral' conduct. He later learns about her innocence and takes her back. A traditional happy ending!

While Wang An-Ch'i explained how the classical poetry and music beautifully expressed the female pathos, her students burst into loud laughter: the traditional Chinese female virtues such as obedience and chastity all seemed so ridiculously backward in the eyes of the youngsters, and a classical masterpiece became a farce. The shocking reaction of students immediately triggered a *ganga* situation in the classroom, which ruthlessly revealed the misfit of *jingju* classics in the contemporary value system (Wang 2008, 23–5). I imagine the shock, embarrassment, and humiliation she experienced in the classroom as a significant phenomenological moment, not so different from what Frantz

Fanon experienced when a girl uttered, 'Mama, see the Negro! I'm frightened!' (Maman, regarde le nègre, j'ai peur!). Fanon described feeling nauseous: 'I was responsible at the same time for my body, for my race, for my ancestors ... I discovered my blackness' (1967, 109–40). Such physical response to and cognitive reflection of a complicated emotion like embarrassment and humiliation are a cross-cultural phenomenon. Virginia E. Sturm's study on the neurodegenerative disease FTLD (frontotemporal lobar degeneration) perfectly describes such 'universal' human response to a high-intensity moment like Fanon's and Wang's. The complicated self-conscious emotion (such as embarrassment or guilt), automatic physiological response (such as blushing or sweating), and motivation of behavioural change (such as correcting the cause of the embarrassment and repairing social relations) are closely connected, because pgACC (pregenual anterior cingulate cortex) controls both emotional and behavioural regulations. Patients with neurodegenerative illness have a reduction of self-awareness of complicated emotions, motivation to change behaviour, and social dexterity (Sturm et al. 2008, 2013).

Having felt intensely *ganga* in front of her students, Wang realized that getting *jingju* out of the *ganga* dilemma was the only way to save the art. She rewrote the play with a new title *Wang Youdao xiuqi* (Wang Youdao Divorces His Wife). The story itself describes a *ganga* situation with the single man and married woman trapped in a small space. Wang intensified the liminal situation by having two actresses in different role types play the character of Meng Yuehua: as a schizophrenic double of Meng, the *huadan* (the vivacious female role type) expressed her fantasy of sexual adventure, whereas the *qingyi* (the virtuous female role type) defended the female chastity of a wife. Defying the strict rules of role types both pointed out the lack of psychological complexity of traditional *jingju* characters and enhanced theatricality. She also personified the pavilion with a *chou* (clown role type), who offered social commentaries and historical observation (Lei 2011b, 41–46).

Wang Youdao Divorces His Wife (2004) was the trail blazer of innovative *jingju* in Taiwan: generally respecting traditional *jingju* aesthetics (music, singing, acting), the play experimented with non-conventional staging and characters with psychological complexity. In the next decade, besides deconstructed classics like *Wang Youdao*, there were also adaptations from modern literature and popular legends, and completely newly created stories. Although Wang An-Ch'i is still the most important playwright in this movement today, many young playwrights—including her students—also join in the mission of sustaining and reinvigorating *jingju* in Taiwan. These innovative *jingju* productions followed a similar rule: new or deconstructed old stories, largely conventional singing and acting style, traditional music with some new composition and arrangement, new staging, which in general follows the minimalist style of original *jingju*. The decade-long interruption of the Cultural Revolution had caused irreversible harm to the tradition; *jingju* in Taiwan, despite its fragmented origin, was fortunate to continue its practice without any interruption and preserved certain traditional techniques which might have been otherwise lost. It is clear to *jingju* lovers that political ideologies might mean dwindling funding, but the real irreparable damage is the loss of the 'oral and intangible' traditional art due to the lack of proper training and audience support. Cultivating young talent both in writing and in performing and growing young audiences, therefore, are the top priorities of the Guoguang Opera Company. *Sange ren'er liangzhan deng* (*Three Persons, Two Lamps*, 2005), *Jinsuoji* (*The Golden Cangue*, 2006), *Kuaixue shiqing* (Sunlight after Snow, 2007), *Meng Xiaodong* (Meng Xiaodong, 2010), *Shiba luohan tu* (The Painting of Eighteen Lohans, 2015), *Kangxi yu Aobai* (Kangxi and Aobai, 2016), and *Xiaozhuang yu Duo'ergun* (Xiaozhuang and Dorgon, 2018) are just a few examples of the innovative *jingju* productions in Taiwan in the first two decades of the millennium.

The Predicament of Interculturalism and Techno-Globalization

Jingju, under the name of 'Peking opera (China)', was added to UNESCO's 'Representative List of the Intangible Cultural Heritage of Humanity' in 2010, following *yueju* (Yueju opera, Cantonese opera, China, 2009), and *kunqu* (Kun Qu Opera, China, 2001). The international proclamation emphasized tradition and heritage, distinctive from the focus of the blossoming innovative *jingju* in Taiwan. I have used 'the lotus in the mud' as a metaphor to describe the imagined purity of Chinese opera (lotus) despite its hybridized origin (putrid mud); the invented image of Chinese opera is always connected with the performative Chinese identity in different space and time (Lei 2006). While the transplanted art form has inherited a great deal of traditional assets, innovative *jingju* in Taiwan is anything but pure.

Interculturalism has been a way to energize the old *jingju* with new blood in Taiwan since the 1980s. An important milestone was Wu Hsing-kuo's *Yuwang chengguo* (The Kingdom of Desire, 1986), an intercultural performance of *Macbeth*, *jingju*, and modern dance. Wu also played Agamemnon in *jingju* stylization in Richard Schechner's *Oresteia*, an intercultural and environmental performance in a large park in Taipei (1995). In Wu's performances, despite a reimagined Western story with Western-styled staging and a great deal of intercultural experimentation, the *jingju* elements—singing, speaking, movements, all the essential elements embodied by actors—remained largely intact. These early *jingju*-based intercultural performances are varieties of what I call 'hegemonic intercultural theatre' (HIT), which is 'a specific artistic genre and state of mind that combines First World capital and brainpower with Third World raw material and labour, and Western classical texts with Eastern performance traditions.' The power imbalance between East and West creates inequity among the collaborators during the process as well as in the final product. One good example is Robert Wilson's *Oulanduo* (Orlando, 2009), a solo performance adapted from Virginia Woolf's novel of the same name. *Orlando* was commissioned by the Taiwan government with the hope that Taiwan could ascend the world stage by engaging an internationally renowned director and a familiar HIT formula, along with the most celebrated *jingju* diva in Taiwan, Wei Hai-Ming (Wei Haimin). To the Taiwan artists and audience's dismay, the first non-Western version of *Orlando* largely followed the format of the German (1989), the French (1995), and the English (1996) versions in the past, instead of a new work with *jingju* as an equal intercultural partner. *Jingju* was fragmented, displaced, and distorted in the performance; the art was stripped so bare that it was hardly recognizable. This type of deconstructed *jingju*, unlike experimental works such as *Wang Youdao*, was not for the sake of reinvigorating *jingju* with critical self-reflection; it was a decorative element contributing to the grandiose Wilsonesque light show. *Jingju*, a rather boisterous and dynamic art form, looked dispirited, lonely, and sad. The production was coldly received by audience and critics, who generally identified with Wei's discomfort and awkwardness on stage and commented on the wasted money and opportunity. However, since this expensive flagship production was funded by the government, it was best to minimize self-criticism in order to maintain the national *face* and hope for the collective amnesia of a truly *ganga* episode (Lei 2011a, 571–86).

In recent years, Taiwan's *ganga* diplomatic situation has worsened, due to the heightened cross-Strait tension and the oscillation of world superpowers in their pro- or anti-Chinese positions. While innovative Taiwan *jingju* in the 2020s is significantly different from the pre-1949 traditional *jingju* and from the contemporary *jingju* in mainland China today, it is still often regarded as *too Chinese* in the current political rhetoric in Taiwan because 'anti-Chinese' is a national narrative for the current political regime. The effort of innovation also does not translate well in intercultural and transnational settings as Taiwan *jingju* is still regarded as *Chinese* opera in the Western imagination. Taiwanese opera (*gezaixi*) and glove puppetry (*budaixi*), both earlier transplanted folk arts from the mainland, are well established and usually branded as Taiwanese *native* arts today; however, their international exposure and impact are limited. What else can Taiwan do to tell a story that is not based on anti-mainlander trauma (the 228 Incident), anti-communist (Cold War tension), anti-Chinese human right violation (Tian'anmen and Hong Kong) but something less ideology-based and yet distinctively Taiwanese in the eyes of international allies?

Taiwan is well known for its electronics and telecommunication industry. As a matter of fact, Taiwan dominates the semiconductor manufacturing in the world, as TSMC (Taiwan Semiconductor Manufacturing Company) alone controls more than half of the global chip market. Video gaming and esports, a big rising industry, present another opportunity to create a new national image of Taiwan. In 2012, the team 'Taipei Assassins' won the world championship of League of Legends (LoL), one of the most popular esports whose global tournament viewership often surpasses traditional sports like the Super Bowl. In the political realm, Taiwan's government appointed the first digital minister in 2016 to manage big data and digital communication nationally and internationally. It is clear that in the last decade that technology—digital, electronic, telecommunication—is considered the best tool for a small country to connect with the world. The political climate affects the already precarious 'natural' environment for traditional arts like *jingju*.

For instance, the production *Huxian* (Fox Tales, 2021) was a technological upgrade of the 2009 production. Based on traditional ghost stories, *Fox Tales* theatricalizes different realms of existence—human and ghost, reality and fantasy. The 2009 version used traditional techniques to express fantastical theatricality, such as walking with lanterns or swinging a very large flag. In 2021, floating hologram lanterns and haunting motion-captured ghosts intensified the visual effects (Su 2021; Guoguang 2021). While the wowing sensation was undeniable, one cannot help but worry that technology would ultimately steal the show. The essence of *jingju* is to tell all kinds of stories with only the actor's body—singing, speaking, acting, and fighting, all with live music. Actors' symbolic gestures and minimal props and set (a table and two chairs) are more than enough for them to travel from heaven to earth, summon ghosts, or perform miracles. *Jingju* is a fantastical 'poor theatre'! However, do we still have the patience to appreciate the void and to imagine the unsaid? Or are we simply waiting to be fed with computer-generated spectacle? Would the faster, louder, and brighter stimuli in the digital generation eventually kill the slow and analogue art?

Feite'er (Phaedra, 2019) was an ambitious *jingju*-based intercultural performance and example of intra-Asian minor transnational collaboration. As HIT performances often involve at least one major player in the intercultural setting, 'minor transnationalism,' on the other hand, involves minor players that are often neglected in the dominant discourse (Lionnet and Shih 2005). Based on Racine's original, the *jingju* version was a collaboration of Taiwan *jingju*, Singapore *nanyin*, and Taiwan modern dance. Visually, while the Queen and the Lady-in-waiting are traditionally dressed and move according to the stage decorum of *jingju*, the Prince 'shamelessly' exposes his youthful half-naked body through wild modern dance movements. Musically, the bright, sonorous, and powerful sound from the north (*jingju*) is a direct contrast to the restrained, sinuous, and melancholic melodies from the south (*nanyin*). The *nanyin* singing has a hushed, restrained quality, which is used to demonstrate the psychological state of the character. The 'acoustic interculturalism' is more subtle than visual interculturalism and possibly only appreciated by connoisseurs (Tan 2012). The modern dance's energetic and unconstrained movement, along with the hybridized music (traditional music and jazz), truly challenges the conventional concept of *jingju* performance. The female lead, Chu An Li, received the Best Actor award of Traditional Art in 2020.

The rise of Asia in the twenty-first century made transpacific partnership ever more necessary, and the formation of TPP (Trans-Pacific Partnership, signed in 2016) was an attempt to solidify such trade relationship; however,

Taiwan, an important player in the Pacific region, was excluded.[1] To elevate Taiwan's status from a minor intra-Asian transnational partner to a transpacific player, there was an attempt to have *Phaedra* join in the Festival International Cervantino (Guanajuato, Mexico) in 2021. Collaborating with Mexico in the form of 'minor transpacificism' was perhaps an easier first step before engaging a major player like the United States. Unfortunately, COVID-19 crushed the ambitious transpacific dream.

Instead, in 2021, *Phaedra* was remounted as a transpacific intercultural performance in Taiwan by involving the Mexican playwright Ximena Escalante as artistic consultant. The subtle musical intra(Asian)culturalism between *jingju* and *nanyin* was dropped and replaced with a combination of *jingju* and electronic music. Working remotely, Escalante considered the boisterous and thundering *jingju* sound too loud and asked to reduce the 'noise' by 70% and to use sound barriers around the percussion players during the performance. To fully express Phaedra's sexual desire, she repeatedly asked the actress to show more passion, even with some nudity (Wang 2022; Lei 2022). The apparent lack of deep understanding of *jingju* resulted in such unreasonable requests, and the intercultural negotiation ended with the *jingju* Phaedra's removal of her shoes to symbolize the nakedness. The performance received polarized criticism and retraumatized the *jingju* circle with an *Orlando*-like nightmare; it also provoked debates about *jingju*'s future in preferring the HIT-style interculturalism and techno-globalism as a way to raise Taiwan's international status. If embracing techno-globalism is presented as a national policy, *jingju* artists need to sacrifice the essence of *jingju* with their limited resources. Wang An-Ch'i, the innovative *jingju* pioneer and artistic director of Guoguang, witnessed the focus shifted from training the actors' *real* body to coordinating between live and virtual beings; she also criticized the chasm created by technology as actors without motion-capture suits felt like second-class citizens (Wang 2022; Lei 2022). Wang decided to quit her position as protest to such national policy and her action was enthusiastically supported by the artistic circle. Even though a compromise was reached temporarily, the pressure of complying to the image of techno Taiwan by abandoning the 'Chinese' essence of *jingju* is the looming storm that is going to strike anytime in the future. Can the Chineseness and Taiwaneseness coexist within the hybridized new *jingju*?

The aesthetics of Taiwan *jingju* have been mediated by war, market, politics, interculturalism, and technology in the past decades; *jingju* navigated numerous *ganga* situations by being nimble and resilient. I see the politically

[1] The twelve countries are the United States, Canada, Australia, New Zealand, Chile, Peru, Mexico, Singapore, Vietnam, Japan, Malaysia, and Brunei. The United States withdrew its participation in TPP and the remaining eleven countries changed the name to CPTPP (Comprehensive and Progressive Agreement for Trans-Pacific Partnership) in 2018.

motivated techno-globalism a true threat to the arduous training process, which is the soul of traditional performing arts. As an actor's body can never be as spectacular as a virtual being, a minor player on the global stage today needs to choose wisely between a wonderful poor theatre and an impoverished techno wonder.

References

Boym, Svetlana. 2001. *The Future of Nostalgia*. New York: Basic Books.
Cabranes-Grant, Leo. 2016. *From Scenarios to Networks: Performing the Intercultural in Colonial Mexico*. Evanston: Northwestern University Press.
Clifford, James. 2005. 'Diasporas.' In *Internationalizing Cultural Studies*, edited by Ackbar Abbas and John Nguyet Erni, 524–58. Malden: Blackwell Publishing.
Fanon, Frantz. 1967. 'The Fact of Blackness.' In *Black Skin White Masks*, 109–40. New York: Grove Press.
Goldstein, Joshua. 2007. *Drama Kings: Players and Publics in the Re-Creation of Peking Opera, 1870–1937*. Berkeley: University of California.
Guoguang Opera Company. 2021. 'Three-minute Video Abstract of *Fox Tale*.' YouTube Video, 3:05. May 30, 2021. https://www.youtube.com/watch?v=Je5KW-XO_-Q
Lei, Daphne P. 2006. *Operatic China: Staging Chinese Identity across the Pacific*. New York: Palgrave Macmillan.
———. 2011a. 'Interruption, Intervention, Interculturalism: Robert Wilson's HIT Productions in Taiwan.' *Theatre Journal*, 63 (4), 571–86.
———. 2011b. *Alternative Chinese Opera in the Age of Globalization: Performing Zero*. New York: Palgrave Macmillan.
———. 2022. Online conversation with Wang An-Ch'i. January 27, 2022.
Lionnet, Francoise, and Shu-mei Shih, eds. 2005. *Minor Transnationalism*. Durham: Duke University Press.
Mao, Zedong. 1971. 'Talks at the Yenan Forum on Literature and Art.' In *Selected Readings from the Works of Mao Tsetung*, 250–86. Peking: Foreign Language Press.
Sturm, Virginia E. et al. 2008. 'Diminished Self-Conscious Emotional Responding in Frontotemporal Lobar Degeneration Patients.' *Emotion*, 8 (6), 861–69.
———. 2013. 'Role of Right Pregenual Anterior Cingulate Cortex in Self-Conscious Emotional Reactivity.' *Soc Cogn Affect Neurosci*, 8 (4), 468–74.
Su, Hengyi. 2021. 'Retelling the Story of *Fox Tales* with Technology [*Yong keji chongshuo yiduan Huxian gushi*].' *Performing Arts Redefined (PAR)*, May 10, 2021. https://pareviews.ncafroc.org.tw/?p=66887
Tan, Marcus Cheng Chye. 2012. *Acoustic Interculturalism: Listening to Performance*. London: Palgrave Macmillan.
Wang, An-Ch'i. 2008. *Rouge Lips and Pearl-Sewn Sleeves, Both Lonely* [*Jiangchun zhuxiu liangjimo*]. Taipei: INK Publishing.
———. 2002. *Fifty Years of Taiwan Jingju* [*Taiwan jingju wushinian*]. 2 vols. Taipei: Guoli chuantong yishu zhongxin.
———. 2022. Postings from Facebook. https://www.facebook.com/profile.php?id=100002269788158
Xu, Shen. Launched 2006. *Shuowen jiezi. Chinese Text Project* [*Zhongguo zhexueshu dianzihua jihua*] https://ctext.org/shuo-wen-jie-zi/wang-bu2/zh

CHAPTER 38

Our Life Together: War, Migration, and Family Drama in Korean American Theatre

Ju Yon Kim

Recent Korean Americanist scholarship and American theatrical productions about Korean migration converge in their interest in the impact of war and imperialism on the Korean diaspora. Collectively, these works trouble conceptions of Korean American migration as primarily a post-1965 phenomenon involving immigrants seeking opportunities in the United States. War and colonization are relegated in this narrative to a discrete past, one overcome with the aid of Americans. By contrast, scholars and theatre artists have explored how Korean diasporic articulations grapple with the continuing reverberations of multiple global conflicts and occupations on the peninsula, from their effects on migration patterns to their cultural, political, and everyday manifestations. In particular, two contemporary plays—*The Architecture of Loss* by Julia Cho and *Among the Dead* by Hansol Jung—present the American family drama as a global drama where the promise of a multiracial family extends, rather than absolves, the violence of war and occupation.

HISTORICAL OVERVIEW

The first sizeable migration from the Korean Peninsula to the United States took place in the early twentieth century when thousands arrived in Hawai'i, then a US territory, as labourers on sugarcane plantations and as 'picture brides' of those labourers who sought wives from Korea (Min 2011, 2–3). Japan forced Korea into protectorate status in 1905 before making it a colony

J. Y. Kim (✉)
Harvard University, Cambridge, MA, USA
e-mail: juyonkim@fas.harvard.edu

in 1910. While Japanese colonial rule made moving to and settling in Hawai'i more attractive to Koreans, it also curtailed migration from the Korean peninsula because of restrictions put into place both by Japan and by the 1907-1908 'Gentlemen's Agreement', which limited the entry of Japanese subjects, including Korean colonial subjects, to the United States (Hong 2018, 5–6). The US Immigration Act of 1924 subsequently closed most immigration from Asia. During this early period of limited migration, which coincided with Japanese colonial rule, Korean students and exiled political dissidents in the United States constituted an important part of the diasporic network that emerged to advocate for Korean independence.

Japan's defeat in World War II and the subsequent division of the Korean peninsula transformed migration from Korea to the United States, as well as the relationship between these countries. As postwar tensions increased between the United States and the USSR, the division of Korea at the 38th parallel, originally seen as a temporary situation, was formalized in 1948 with the founding of the Democratic People's Republic of Korea (North Korea) and the Republic of Korea (South Korea). For the United States, keeping the communist DPRK from overthrowing the US-backed regime in the south was a vital part of its strategy to contain Soviet influence during the Cold War. When North Korean troops invaded the South in 1950, the Korean War became the first brutal 'proxy war' between the two superpowers. After three years of fighting, a truce was signed in 1953. By that time, millions had been killed, including approximately two million civilians—a significant portion of Korea's population.

The devastation of two wars, US military occupation and political influence, and the ideological struggles of the Cold War all shaped Korean migration to the United States in the second half of the twentieth century. Between the end of World War II and 1965, when the United States enacted major changes to its immigration policy, Korean immigration largely consisted of US military wives and adoptees, particularly those orphaned by the Korean War and fathered by American soldiers. After World War II, the War Brides Act of 1946 made an exception to immigration restrictions for the wives and children of US soldiers. Continued American military presence in South Korea gave rise to increased interactions between American soldiers and Korean women, and beginning in the 1950s, tens of thousands of Korean women immigrated to the United States as 'war brides'.

The establishment of 'camp towns' around US military bases facilitated contact between soldiers and women who, facing severely limited economic opportunity after the Korean War, found much-needed work in the various businesses there that catered to Americans, including clubs and brothels. The South Korean and American governments sanctioned and enabled these brothels, yet sex workers as well as, more broadly, women who developed relationships with American soldiers and their mixed-race children, had to grapple with the stigma associated with prostitution and miscegenation. The children of American soldiers suffered not just marginalization but also abandonment. The latter phenomenon led American evangelicals Bertha and Henry Holt to set up an agency to find homes for these children with American families (after adopting eight into their own family). The Holts' adoption agency played an integral role in popularizing transnational adoption. Even before their efforts, however, the South Korean government had been encouraging the international adoption of orphaned and abandoned children (Yuh 2005, 279). Korean adoptees continued to arrive in the United States, their most common destination, in the decades after the initial wave of 'war orphans', with approximately 100,000 eventually settling in the country.

Examining American state and public reception of Korean 'war brides' and adoptees during the Cold War, Susie Woo observes, 'Stories of model Korean children and rapidly adjusted Korean brides, and the white American families that loved them, relayed ideal visions of racial democracy and internationalism, making these families another useful node in America's cultural Cold War efforts' (2019, 19). According to Woo, such stories extended representations of US military involvement during the Korean War as a kind of 'rescue mission' such that familial metaphors of a benevolent United States saving its Korean brethren were succeeded by the celebration of actual multiracial families as models of American promise during the Cold War. Thus, these stories exemplified what Christina Klein has described as 'Cold War Orientalism', where 'a sentimental discourse of integration … imagined the forging of bonds between Asians and Americans both at home and abroad' (2003, 16).

Immigration from South Korea to the United States became easier with the Hart-Celler Act of 1965, which removed racial quotas on immigration and privileged family reunifications and professionals. Meanwhile, in South Korea, a military dictatorship, rapid industrialization, and urban overpopulation made immigration to the United States appealing. In the half century following the act's passage, about a million South Koreans migrated to the United States, with middle-class couples and families constituting a greater portion of the pool. The preference given to families also meant that military wives, who served as early sponsors for family members who were then able to sponsor others, contributed substantially to Korean American immigration (Yuh 2005, 278). In the late twentieth century, Korean immigrants became associated with the Asian American model minority myth, with the first generation cast as entrepreneurial small-business owners and the second generation cast as diligent students and professionals. At the same time, undocumented migration has been a significant, if often obscured, phenomenon among Korean Americans. Among recipients of the Deferred Action for Childhood Arrivals, a policy enabling those who arrived undocumented as children to avoid deportation and receive employment authorization, South Korea recently ranked sixth among all the countries of birth, and first among countries in Asia (USCIS 2017, 1).

Immigration from South Korea slowed in the 1990s with the success of pro-democracy movements in South Korea and improved economic conditions. Images of burning Korean American businesses during the Los Angeles uprising of 1992 also brought into relief American interracial tensions and the limits of 'model minority' success. Since the 2000s, however, a growing number of South Koreans have arrived in the United States as part of so-called 'wild geese' families. One parent, usually the father, continues to live in Korea while the other parent and children relocate to countries such as the United States, Canada, and Australia so that the children can be educated abroad, rather than go through South Korea's competitive school system. Finally, although most migration from the Korean peninsula to the United States involves immigration from South Korea, a small number of North Korean defectors and refugees have also been settled in the United States.

Over the course of the twentieth century, a complex and changing set of factors have forced or encouraged people of Korean descent to move, temporarily or permanently, to the United States. Recent scholarship on Korean migration to the United States has sought to highlight its deep connections to US imperialism and military involvement in the Pacific. Observing that '[p]ost-1945 Korean migration has been shaped by the division and militarization of the Korean peninsula', Ji-Yeon Yuh proposes that we think of it in terms of 'refuge migrants', those who might be situated between immigrants, typically associated with voluntary migration following economic and social opportunity, and refugees, defined as those urgently escaping persecution and violence (Yuh 2005, 278). Refuge migrants seek relief from the abiding effects of war and colonization, the instability and fear that persist even beyond the immediate postwar period. Building on Yuh's work, Crystal Baik proposes 'militarized migrations' as a framework that highlights 'how subjects seemingly removed from war are always already touched by militarized movements' and points to 'the racialized, gendered, and sexualized conditions underlying Korean diaspora trajectories' (2020, 39). By reframing Korean migration in this way, Yuh and Baik illuminate how a focus on American opportunity has obscured the impact of American imperialism on the movement of people between Korea and the United States.

Overview of Theatrical Practices

Theatrical performances by and about Korean Americans and the Korean diaspora have multiplied and found a range of platforms in the last few decades with the rising number of people of Korean descent living, working, and studying in the United States, as well as the founding of various Asian American theatre companies and the growing interest of regional and experimental theatres in featuring works by people of colour. Yet theatrical activity by Korean migrants extends into the early twentieth century, and shows the impact of both Japanese and American occupations.

The life of Peter Hyun, one of the few Korean Americans who rose to some prominence in American theatre in the early twentieth century, reflects the diverse forces that shaped migration from Korea to the United States in that period, as well as the limited opportunities available to Korean theatre artists.

Born in 1906, as Japan was moving more aggressively to colonize Korea, Hyun spent his early life in Hawaiʻi, Korea, and Shanghai. His father, a minister who had immigrated to Hawaiʻi, returned to Korea with his family to engage in protests for Korean independence. Japanese efforts to crack down on resistance movements forced Hyun and other family members to escape to Shanghai before returning to Hawaiʻi. After moving to Indiana to attend college, Hyun decided to pursue a career in theatre. He began a theatre company in Cambridge, Massachusetts, and directed *The Revolt of the Beavers* for the Children's Theatre as part of the New York Federal Theatre Project in 1935. Yet when the show had the opportunity to move to Broadway, the cast's reluctance to have him continue as director manifested for Hyun the racism that shadowed his career, and ultimately compelled him to leave the theatre (Hyun 1995, 155–158).

Performers of Korean descent also appeared in acts for Asian-themed nightclubs that were popular through the mid-century. Among the early successes was the Forbidden City nightclub in San Francisco, which opened in 1938. Donning 'exotic' costumes as well as flashy burlesque attire, Asian Americans of various ethnicities, including Korean Americans, sang, danced, and performed comedy sketches at these venues (Lee 2011, 19). The largely white clientele of these clubs included US servicemen in transit to posts in the Pacific (Lee 2017, 411). Once abroad, American soldiers could find comparable entertainment in military clubs where they were introduced to local performers like the popular Kim Sisters. The Kim Sisters, who sang and played musical instruments, consisted of sisters Sue and Aecha and their cousin Mia. After the Korean War, the trio began performing as a band for American soldiers stationed in Korea. Their popularity attracted the notice of Tom Ball, a white stage producer who, after seeing the success of nightclubs like Forbidden City, opened a similar venue in New York City called the China Doll and began an associated travelling show, the *China Doll Revue*. The Kim Sisters made their American debut in 1959 as part of Ball's *China Doll Revue* in Las Vegas. Their performances incorporated Korean instruments and *hanboks* (traditional dresses), American popular music, and acts that evoked the Asian-themed nightclubs developed for American audiences on both sides of the Pacific. They later made numerous appearances on the popular television variety show *The Ed Sullivan Show*, which introduced them to a larger American audience. Yu Jung Lee's study of the Kim sisters observes that their depiction by the American media echoed stories of Korean 'war orphans' and adoptees, 'embracing them as their friendly "daughters" even as they were also presented as "dubious, mysterious, and inscrutable" Asians' (Lee 2017, 408). The Kim Sisters were thus made familiar to American audiences through two ostensibly opposing frames, that of exotic Asian otherness and of imagined Cold War kinship, which characterized them as vulnerable Korean brethren saved from communism and brought into Western modernity and liberalism.

The 1965 immigration reforms radically changed the landscape of Korean American theatre and performance. Whereas Peter Hyun, the Kim Sisters, and performers in Asian-themed nightclubs participated in shows primarily meant for white audiences, the arrival of substantial numbers of Korean immigrants after 1965 meant Korean Americans could constitute their own communities of artists and audiences. Korean cultural centres sponsored by the South Korean government opened in 1979 in New York and in 1980 in Los Angeles, and hosted a range of events, including traditional folk performances, concerts, and contemporary plays, thus introducing aspects of Korean culture abroad while also serving the Korean diaspora.

Korean American and Korean diasporic theatre artists have also been vital members of the major Asian American theatre companies that have formed since the 1970s, including the East West Players, Ma-Yi Theater Company, Lodestone Theatre Ensemble, and Mu Performing Arts. Lodestone, a Los Angeles–based Asian American theatre group that focused on new writing, emerged from the Korean American Theatre Ensemble, which sought to stage performances geared towards second-generation Korean American audiences. Located in the Twin Cities, Mu Performing Arts has developed shows featuring the experiences of Korean adoptees, many of whom reside in Minnesota. In *Mask Dance*, one of their most successful productions, Mu took inspiration from Korean shamanistic dance to create a performance about Korean adoptees. In each of these companies, Korean American artists have developed their work in collaboration with other Asian American theatre makers. Korean American theatrical production has thus been deeply, and productively, intertwined with Asian American theatre more broadly.

Korean American playwrights, including Julia Cho (*Aubergine, Office Hour*), Diana Oh (*Clairvoyance*), Diana Son (*Stop Kiss, Satellites*), Celine Song (*Endlings*), and Lloyd Suh (*Charles Francis Chan Jr.'s Oriental Murder Mystery*), have had their works staged by Asian American theatre companies, regional theatres, and off-Broadway theatres. In 2018, Young Jean Lee became the first Asian American woman playwright to be produced on Broadway. Many theatrical works by Korean American artists have delved into stories centring Korean migration to tackle issues such as war and displacement, transnational adoption, and generational struggles within immigrant families. Yet they also defy neat characterization, often exploring issues of race, gender, and representation as they unfold in a range of sites, and evincing formal diversity and inventiveness.

Case Studies: *Architecture of Loss* and *Among the Dead*

Both *Architecture of Loss* and *Among the Dead* explore the intimate and abiding implications of gendered and racialized violence endemic to war and occupation. The plays take advantage of the inherent hauntedness of theatrical simulation and surrogation to stage the Korean woman as a figure whose absence is variously willed and resisted by her American husband and her mixed-race daughter. For the husband, the Korean woman simultaneously troubles and promises to restore faith in American deliverance. For the daughter, the lost

Korean mother brings into relief the particular affective and material burdens born by women not only during times of explicit conflict and subjection, but also in the many displacements and losses that follow.

Staged in regional and off-Broadway theatres, Julia Cho's dramas often feature Korean American families (*99 Histories, Aubergine*) or centre issues of racism and violence (*BFE, Office Hour*). *Architecture of Loss* opens with a wayward husband who returns to the family he abandoned fourteen years ago, only to learn from his wife, Catherine, that his young son went missing several years after his own abrupt departure. First produced in New York City in 2004, the play is set in a suburban home in Arizona and moves among three moments of loss that constitute its 'architecture': the departure of the husband, Greg; the subsequent disappearance of his son, David; and the death of Nora, Catherine's Korean mother. Greg's unexpected return prompts Catherine and their daughter, Carmie, to recall the time leading up to David's disappearance. Catherine and Carmie's stories offer few insights into David, who remains a mysterious, angel-like figure, or what happened to him, and instead trace the shape of Catherine and Carmie's lives in a period of compounding family losses.

Through the characters of Greg and Richard, Catherine's father, the play dwells in the space where the line between saving someone and inflicting harm upon them becomes muddled. Greg's abandonment of his family when he realizes that his alcoholism is leading to destructive behaviour, his impulsive decision to visit years later 'To make amends' and 'To heal this family' (Cho 2005, 13), and his effort to help a hitchhiker who later dies when they get into a car accident all raise questions, some explicitly articulated by other characters, of whether the succour he seeks to provide might in fact be responsible for greater suffering. This dynamic is magnified—globally and historically—through Richard's relationship with Nora.

Nora's death precipitates a material as well as an emotional crisis for Richard, whom Catherine is forced to take in after he loses his home. Explaining his predicament to Catherine, Richard describes how loneliness and boredom after Nora's death led him to a casino on an Indian reservation where he gambled away his home. He insists to Catherine, 'I did not *lose* the house. It was *stolen* from me' (19). Richard's characterization of his house as *stolen* rather than *lost* reflects not just an inability to accept personal responsibility, but also a settler colonial logic. It recalls, if only to erase, the history of stolen indigenous lands upon which the story of his stolen house stands. Richard can only conceive of himself as someone who is stolen from, not as someone who steals from others. Catherine, however, explicitly challenges Richard's understanding of himself and the past. When Richard describes himself as a 'good husband', Catherine interjects:

> No. You can't do this, you can't revise your whole marriage as if I weren't there. I SAW IT. I saw all of it. What you did to her. Hitting her. For nothing. For leaving the light on in the garage. For not rinsing a dish well enough. For laughing, for talking, for *not* talking. All those years of treating her like she was nothing. (23)

Yet if Catherine unsettles Richard's sense that he was a good husband, he also calls into question her relationship with Nora, accusing her of being embarrassed by her mother during her youth and of evading questions about her ambiguous racial appearance. If Richard, according to Catherine, treated her mother like 'nothing', Catherine, according to Richard, wished in her youth to make her mother, or her mother's racial difference, disappear. Richard and Catherine's argument thus lends Nora's absence in the play a significance beyond marking her death: Richard's violent disregard and Catherine's racialized loathing had worked to diminish her presence in their family long before she passed away.

Yet in a play that centres loss, the negative spaces of the home most vitally constitute its form, and Nora's centrality to this architecture is vividly enacted in the play's penultimate scene. One of the key revelations that the drama finally presents to Catherine concerns not her missing son, but her parents' relationship, which was forged in the crucible of the Korean War. In a moment of incoherence caused by dementia, Richard mistakes Catherine for his deceased wife and divulges that he participated in the massacre of Korean refugees at No Gun Ri, an actual incident that took place during the Korean War. Although the details of what occurred remain fuzzy because of the long reluctance of the US and South Korean governments to acknowledge the event, anywhere from a hundred to several hundred Korean civilians (mostly women, children, and the elderly) were killed, ostensibly because of rumours that North Korean soldiers were disguising themselves as peasants.

Recalling to Catherine, whom he believes is Nora, how the two of them met, Richard reminisces:

> That bar at the base, and how there was that song on the jukebox. And you saw me drinking myself into the ground and came to save me. You were trying to save souls…You asked me why I drank and I told you, because I am a soldier. I've seen terrible things. And you said you'd lost your parents and sister in the war, that you'd seen terrible things too, but you didn't need a drink. So I put down my glass and I asked you to dance and you let me hold you. (45)

Holding Catherine's hands, Richard then confesses to 'Nora' that he withheld from her his participation in the massacre: 'I never told you that. What I did. Because then you would've hated me and then how could you have ever let me save you? …I understand now. I shoot you, I save you, I shoot you, I save you. This is what our life together was' (46).

Richard acknowledges that he was drawn to his future spouse because he believed that he might save her, and thus atone for his part in the massacre. Their relationship, in other words, seemed to offer a medium through which the perpetrator of violence might also be the one who offers deliverance to those harmed. Although Nora first expressed a desire to save his soul, Richard instead sees her as offering him absolution by letting him save *her*, that is, through the opportunity she provides to rewrite history by embodying the massacred Koreans. She is thus, in some sense, a ghost to Richard long before her actual death. Richard's confession, however, recognizes the truth of their relationship, and the larger history that brought them together: shooting and saving are not contrary forces that might be set against each other, but form the perpetual cycles of their life together, with each driving the other. If 'shooting' constitutes the Korean woman as a subject in need of 'saving', the act of 'saving' itself constitutes her as a subject that *can be* shot, or, more precisely, as a subject lacking the ability to defend and deliver herself. Richard's acknowledgement that he both saved and shot recognizes that rather than absolve him, his relationship with Nora merely echoed and sustained the logic that enabled the massacre of Korean civilians in the name of saving them. Nora's Korean ethnicity, formerly just a marker of difference, thus becomes imbued in this moment with the larger history of violence that propelled migration. For this family, the repercussions of destructive Cold War struggles in Asia continue to be felt in the present in a suburb of Arizona, in a home where love and care have become inseparable from violence and desertion.

Among the Dead, which Ma-Yi Theater Company produced at HERE in New York City in 2016, similarly centres a Korean woman, a white American soldier, and their mixed-race daughter. Playwright Jung, who lived in South Korea and South Africa before moving to the United States in her twenties, has penned several other dramas that deal with Korean migration, including *Wild Goose Dreams* (2017), about a North Korean defector and a South Korean 'goose father', and *Wolf Play* (2019), about a Korean adoptee. Whereas *Architecture* only lightly touches on the conditions that wrought Catherine's family until the penultimate scene, much of *Among the Dead* delves into the violence that brings together a Korean woman, known as 'Number Four', and an American soldier, Luke, stationed in Myanmar during World War II.

Jung develops a complex structure to tell the story of Number Four, Luke, and their daughter, Ana. Much of the present of the play is set in 1975, when Ana visits South Korea to pick up her father's ashes. Confined to her hotel room because of ongoing student protests against South Korea's military dictatorship, Ana mysteriously receives her father's journal from the bellboy. As she begins to read Luke's account of his time in Myanmar, he appears in her room, reenacting the scenes described. With the help of Jesus, a chimerical figure who advises the three characters at various moments, Ana realizes that Luke can only hear her when she reads Number Four's 'lines' as written in the journal. She thus not only learns about her parents' relationship by reading the journal, but also recreates it by reading the journal as a dramatic script. The play then moves between these hallucinatory scenes in the hotel room and equally dreamlike ones that take place in 1950, at the outbreak of the Korean War, when Number Four talks to Jesus while waiting for Luke on a bridge in Seoul.

Ana, and the audience, learn that Number Four was tricked into sexual slavery by the Japanese military during World War II. When Number Four then saw her younger sister among a new group of 'comfort women' brought to the camp, she devised an escape for them but lost her sister as they were fleeing. While looking for her sister, she instead encountered Luke, lost in the jungle after being separated from his unit. The two formed a precarious alliance, each hoping the other might help them survive. Luke eventually made contact with his battalion using a radio that Number Four found. Number Four, however, left him to continue searching for her sister, and by the time they reunited months later, she was visibly pregnant. Although Luke acknowledged the baby as his after her birth, when his captain gave him the opportunity to marry Number Four and take her and the baby back to the United States with him, Luke balked, lying to Number Four and attempting to convince her to go to a refugee camp instead. Number Four nonetheless forced Luke to take Ana and promise to meet her in a year's time at a bridge in Seoul. At the end of the play, after learning, and inhabiting, this history through her father's journal, Ana calls her mother, Jin-ah, and arranges to meet her, thus finally fulfilling the promise that Luke never kept. Although Ana is neither precisely a war orphan nor an adoptee, her mother's absence and her father's neglect suggest parallels with the experiences of other mixed-race children from Korea who were brought to the United States in the decades after World War II.

Much like *Architecture*, *Among the Dead* troubles characterizations, encouraged during and in the wake of the Cold War, of US-Korea relations in terms of benevolent American saviours and hapless Korean victims. Just as Cho's play undoes the opposition between saving and shooting, *Among the Dead* refuses to treat Luke heroically. When Number Four learns that Luke witnessed her sister's torturous rape and murder by Japanese soldiers but did not intervene, she explicitly compares him to the soldiers, claiming, 'You are the same as them. You are a monster' (52). Although Luke demurs, he later recalls stories where the pilgrim setting out to fight the devil realizes they have the same face, and the hunters who destroy a forest to defend against tigers realize that they themselves are the tigers (54). Much like Richard, Luke emerges from war in the Pacific unsure of which face he wears, that of the one who saves or the one who destroys, and wondering if they might be aligned rather than at odds.

Although Number Four sees Luke's unwillingness to help her sister as a sign of his monstrousness, his relationship with Number Four also blurs the line between partnership and exploitation. When Luke and Number Four first encounter each other, Luke ties her up, afraid she might be an enemy spy. When Jesus seems to question his decision to keep her around, Luke responds defensively:

Luke. I'm not going to be seduced.
Ana. What?
Luke. I'm just not that kind of person.
Jesus. What kind of person?
Luke. I don't need that kind of thing. From you. It's indecent.
Jesus. Who's giving you any kind of 'that kind of thing'? (Jung 2017, 27)

Luke rejects the notion that he might see Number Four as a sexual object, and casts his rebuttal in moralistic terms. Just as Richard describes himself as a 'good husband', Luke insists he is 'just not that kind of person', and even characterizes himself as the possible victim, the one who might 'be seduced'—but for his sense of propriety. Yet after a particularly stressful moment when someone shoots at them, Luke turns to Number Four for solace and begins kissing her:

> Luke. Soft, warm, and tangible.
> Jesus. This is not what she needs. You know this is not what she—
> (Luke *quietly wills Jesus to disappear. He does.*)
> Luke. And now it's all I can think about. (*Sex.*) (31)

Number Four's reaction is noticeably absent in Jung's script, presumably reflecting its absence in Luke's journal. Does she resist? Does she freeze? Only Luke's desire seems to matter in terms of the dialogue. Yet the horror of the scene is powerfully conveyed by the doubling of roles employed throughout the play: because Ana is playing her mother in this scene (and, as performed in the Ma-Yi production, visibly shocked and unwilling), a deep sense of violation saturates their interaction. Luke's account in the dialogue is intensely overshadowed by Ana's silent dread. Forced to be a surrogate for her absent mother, whose reaction she can only imagine, Ana must embody her own conception as a dubious pursuit of 'comfort' that draws Luke closer to the 'kind of people' who might seek sex from a captive woman in a time of war. Although subsequent scenes suggest a warmness between Luke and Number Four (they even briefly imagine sharing a married life in the United States), the visceral effect of the moment infuses the relationship that unfolds, ensuring that the promise of becoming a happy American family remains indelibly linked to a repudiation, however ambiguously presented, of Number Four's self-determination.

In both of these dramas, Catherine and Ana are forced to enact memories in which their fathers attempt to recuperate the wartime violence inflicted on women through a romance of mutual deliverance. Richard and Luke ostensibly offer Nora and Jin-ah, respectively, the promise of a life away from war, or the possibility of becoming 'refuge migrants'. While Catherine's embodiment of her mother in Richard's confused retrospection highlights Nora's persistent absence, her loss in death as well as her gradual erasure by her family, facilitated by racism and misogyny once in the United States, Ana's unsettling surrogation of her mother is laden with the weight of multiple betrayals: Luke's pursuit of sexual relations despite the vulnerability of Jin-ah's situation and the brutal 'comfort' that she had been forced to provide through the war, and his failure to reunite mother and daughter. Ana and Jin-ah together carry the unfulfilled promise of migration and heteronormative union as a vehicle for absolving, and forgetting, the fraught presence of Americans among Koreans that preceded the rise in Korean migration to the United States. Through their deferred and undramatized reunion, however, the play asks what kind of life together might be imagined beyond the cycles of saving and shooting that have forged their precarious family.

References

Baik, Crystal M. 2020. *Reencounters: On the Korean War and Diasporic Memory Critique*. Philadelphia: Temple University Press.

Cho, Julia. 2005. *The Architecture of Loss*. New York: Dramatists Play Service.

Hong, Jane. 2018. 'The Origins and Construction of Korean America: Immigration before 1965.' In *A Companion to Korean American Studies*. Edited by Rachael Miyung Joo and Shelley Sang-Hee Lee. 3–20. Boston: Brill.

Hyun, Peter. 1995. *In the New World: The Making of a Korean American*. Honolulu: University of Hawaii Press.

Jung, Hansol. 2017. *Among the Dead*. New York: Samuel French.

Kim, Eleana. 2010. *Adopted Territory: Transnational Korean Adoptees and the Politics of Belonging*. Durham, NC: Duke University Press.

Klein, Christina. 2003. *Cold War Orientalism: Asia in the Middlebrow Imagination, 1945–1961*. Berkeley: University of California Press.

Min, Pyong Gap. 2011. *Koreans' Immigration to the U.S.: History and Contemporary Trends*. Research Report No. 3. Research Center for Korean Community, Queens College of CUNY. http://www.qc.cuny.edu/Academics/Centers/RCKC/Documents/Koreans%20Immigration%20to%20the%20US.pdf. Accessed June 15, 2021.

Lee, Esther K. 2011. *A History of Asian American Theatre*. New York: Cambridge University Press.

Lee, Yu Jung. 2017. 'From GI Sweethearts to Lock and Lollers: The Kim Sisters' Performances in the Early Cold War United States, 1959–67.' *Journal of Asian American Studies* 20(3): 405–439.

Oh, Arissa. 2015. *To Save the Children of Korea: The Cold War Origins of International Adoption*. Stanford, CA: Stanford University Press.

United States Citizenship and Immigration Services. 2017. 'Approximate Active DACA Recipients: Country of Birth.' https://www.uscis.gov/sites/default/files/document/data/daca_population_data.pdf. Accessed June 15 2021.

Woo, Susie. 2019. *Framed by War: Korean Women and Children at the Crossroads of US Empire*. New York: New York University Press. Kindle edition.

Yuh, Ji-Yeon. 2004. *Beyond the Shadow of Camptown: Korean Military Brides in America*. New York: NYU Press.

———. 2005. 'Moved by War: Migration, Diaspora, and the Korean War.' *Journal of Asian American Studies* 8(3): 277–291.

CHAPTER 39

Chronicles of Refugees Foretold

Hala Khamis Nassar

HISTORICAL OVERVIEW

As a result of the war in 1948 between the Arabs and the Zionists, 750,000 Palestinians were forcefully displaced from their lands and homes only to relocate as refugees inside Palestine, to the neighbouring Arab countries, and beyond. The internally displaced Palestinians whose villages and livelihood were destroyed, are referred to as Arab Citizens in Israel. The dispossession, the destruction, and the rupture in Palestinian cities, towns, villages, and communities are still an ongoing *nakba* (catastrophe).

Narrating the events of the *nakba* of historic Palestine in different locales—within the homeland or in the diaspora—and through various media tells one story of continuous dispersion and loss. The latest onslaught was on 10th May of 2021 when Israeli Defense Forces (IDF) launched air strikes on the Gaza Strip lasting eleven days. While Hamas called the ensuing conflict the Sword of Jerusalem Battle, the IDF officially dubbed the military campaign in the Gaza Strip Operation Guardian of the Walls. The aggression on Gaza comes after Hamas's ultimatum to Israel to remove its security forces from the Temple Mount complex and from Sheikh Jarrah neighbourhood.

The situation quickly deteriorated and 'has been far more devastating, far-reaching and fast-paced than anyone imagined. It has led to the worst violence between Israelis and Palestinians in years—not only in the conflict with Hamas, which has killed at least 145 people in Gaza and 12 in Israel, but in a wave of mob attacks in mixed Arab-Jewish cities in Israel' (Kingsley 2021).

H. K. Nassar (✉)
Bethlehem University, Bethlehem, Palestine

© The Author(s), under exclusive license to Springer Nature Switzerland AG 2023
Y. Meerzon, S. E. Wilmer (eds.), *The Palgrave Handbook of Theatre and Migration*, https://doi.org/10.1007/978-3-031-20196-7_39

Explaining the past and the present of Sheikh Jarrah neighbourhood in occupied Jerusalem, Abu Sneineh writes that 38 Jerusalemite families are living under the threat of Israeli imminent eviction (2021). Less than a kilometre to the north from the walls of the Old City, the once-green plot is named after the Muslim general Saladin's physician who is believed to have settled there after the conquest of Jerusalem in 1187. Sheikh Jarrah residents are either affluent Palestinian families who moved from the narrow lanes of the Old City and built modern villas there, or are refugees as a result of the 1948 war. Hence, they are facing another *nakba* (catastrophe) if Israeli eviction orders are carried out.

The monthly magazine *This Week in Palestine* dedicated its August 2021 issue to West Jerusalem, recalling its past lives, homes, culture, architecture, business, and so on. The western part of Jerusalem is already Judaized; now the eastern part is under the same threat by Israeli settler organizations. While the western part of Jerusalem was seized in 1948, the eastern part fell as a result of the 1967 war. Since then, two settler organizations claimed proprietorship and have filed successful lawsuits to expel Sheikh Jarrah residents, claiming that Sephardic Jews owned the land in 1885, during Ottoman rule, which ended in 1917.

Another Israeli settler group, Ateret Cohanim, is also claiming ownership in Silwan's areas of Batan al-Hawa and Wadi Hilweh in Jerusalem. These neighbourhoods are 'a hotspot for Israeli settler activities, which include archaeological digging underneath Palestinian homes to search for the lost biblical "City of David"' (MEE 2020). Seizing these neighbourhoods is not merely exercising control and power over already marginalized occupied Palestinians, it is part of a larger scheme of not only Judaizing Jerusalem, but, most importantly, erasing any signs of Palestinian claims to the land and their mere existence. Through winning lawsuits and court eviction orders, 'Israel has a grand settlement strategy called the "Holy Basin," which is a set of settler units and a string of parks themed after biblical places and figures around the Old City of Jerusalem. The plan requires the removal of Palestinian houses in the area' (Abu Sneineh 2021).

Therefore, the volatile atmosphere in Jerusalem ignited the already fragile peace of the last seven years since the last aggression on Gaza. The Sword for Jerusalem Battle, the potential displacements of Sheikh Jarrah residents, and the clashes in Damascus Gate and in the Temple Mount paved the way to grassroots activists all over historic Palestine to dominate the political scene in the face of the silent Palestinian National Authority. The Israeli police violence in Jerusalem spilled over into Israel's mixed cities where Arabs and Jews live together. The confrontations quickly spread to cities such as Lod, Acre, and Haifa, and to the Arab towns of the Galilee. Palestinian youths dominated social media by posting live videos of airstrikes on Gaza and the confrontations in Jerusalem and in Israel under the hashtags #WeAreAllGaza and #WeAreAllSheikhJarrah.

The current clashes have driven the generation of the Oslo Peace Accords of the 1990s to reclaim their Palestinian identity and demand an end to occupation and marginalization, and for equal rights in a discriminatory state. The events have also forced the 1948 generation—like my mother—to relive yet again the traumatic events. The late Edward Said writes in 1984 about the siege of Beirut that he was 'obsessively telling friends and family there over the phone, that they ought to record, write down their experiences; it seemed crucial as a starting point to furnish the world some narrative evidence, over and above the atomized and reified TV clips, of what it was like to be at the receiving end of Israeli "antiterrorism"' (Said 1995, 258).

Commemorating the *Nakba*

The ongoing traumatic events in Palestine, unavoidably or not (whether avoidable or not), have always found a stage of their own on the cultural scene in Palestine and its theatre. While the past events of the 1948 *nakba* and the dispersal of Palestinians from their lands remain unresolved and overshadow a gloomier present, enacting the Palestine story on stage might seem monochromatic at first glance. However, it is an act of resilience, steadfastness, and resistance against Israeli annihilation of what is Palestine and Palestinians. As Massad aptly said, the *nakba* is not simply a cataclysm of the past, but 'pulsating with life and coursing through history by piling up more calamities upon the Palestinian people [...] The History of the Nakba has never been a history of the past but decidedly a history of the present' (Massad 2008). Therefore, commemorating the *nakba* on the cultural scene is a political act as well as necessitating documentation. Having dedicated years to surveying and documenting the historical development of Palestinian theatre since the 1850s, I can safely claim that the cultural scene in Palestine was in tune with that of Cairo, Beirut, and Damascus. Theatres in Palestine were concentrated in the Mediterranean coastal cities, in populated areas, and in Jerusalem, where—for instance—al-Guzi professional theatre troupe established itself. At the turn of the twentieth century, besides local newspapers and poetry, plays were written and staged, in spite of the British Mandate's strict censorship rules, warning about the Zionist influx into the land. With the war of 1948, most theatre makers, like al-Guzi, were driven out, as many people were at that time (Nassar 2018b, 100).

What followed is a period of stagnation only to be revived again after the 1967 war and particularly in the 1970s. Many amateur theatres spread among Palestinians in Israel, in the West Bank, and in Gaza. Although the lifespan of these theatres was short, some of their former members paved the way to more professional theatres to claim the artistic scene mainly in Ramallah in the north and in Jerusalem. Throughout the 1970s Palestinian theatre artists, like their predecessors, employed all means to resist Israeli occupation by contributing significantly to an active cultural resistance in Jerusalem, and in the Palestinian Occupied Territories. East Jerusalem theatres were the centre of such remonstrance by creating a broad range of plays accentuating the Palestinian identity and critiquing social taboos. Some of the notable theatres of that era were al-Hakawati Theatre Troupe founded in 1984 in An-Nuzha-Cinema building, under the late artistic director François Abu Salem, and in 1989, George

Ibrahim founded Al-Kasaba Theatre, which moved to Ramallah in the year 2000. Both al-Hakawati and al-Kasaba successfully managed to put the Palestinian theatre and its people's plight on the international cultural scene by touring from Jerusalem to major European cities, all the way to Los Angeles and to Japan. Other theatres were Firqat Al-Amal Al-Sha'bi (People's Hope Troupe), Al-Jawwal Troupe (The Touring Theatre), Al-Kashkul Troupe (The Notebook), and Sanduq al Agab, among many others (Nassar 2006, 18).

With the first *intifada* (uprising) in 1987, theatre makers, such as al-Hakawati, found themselves unable to reach their audience in the West Bank in the face of political upheavals, thus leading to another period of stagnation, only to pick up the pace again after the Oslo Agreement of 1996. In the midst of the peace agreement euphoria between the Israeli government and the PLO, many theatres mushroomed in the West Bank. Since then and under the current Palestinian Authority, significant theatrical spaces and some of the most active theatres dominating the cultural scene today include Ashtar Theatre's two locations: in Jerusalem (1991) and then in Ramallah (1996); Al-Midan Theatre in Haifa (1995); Sanabel People's Theatre in Jerusalem (1998); Al-Rowwad Theatre (1998) in Aida refugee camp near Bethlehem; Masrah Al-Harah (2005) and Inad Theatre in Beit Jala; Freedom Theatre near Jenin camp (2006); Yes Theatre in Hebron (2007), and Khashabi Theater in Haifa (2011). These cultural centres produce and tour their plays locally and internationally, organize festivals, conferences, workshops, and some even include theatre schools. Their presence strengthens the diverse Palestinian cultural productions and their focus and steadfastness are imperatively political.

The Palestinian National Authority rarely supports or builds the necessary cultural infrastructure. Therefore, theatres in Jerusalem and the West Bank constantly face dire financial difficulties and are forced to turn to foreign donors, NGOs, and international collaboration to survive and to forge lasting partnerships. International funders most of the time stipulate the agenda, the direction, the theme of the production, and the imposition of their own practitioners. Despite these challenges, Palestinian theatre practitioners continue to navigate and benefit from cooperating with international theatres (Nassar 2018, 109). The above-mentioned theatres have addressed urgent and relevant issues in Palestinian society such as the Israeli occupation, continuous harassment and dehumanization, gender issues, women's status, sexual harassment and rape, among other taboos.

Presently, on the Palestinian stage the enactment of the *nakba* and its ongoing repercussions is being revisited and is dominating the cultural scene. A very recent example is the Site-Specific Theatre Festival organised by al-Harah theatre in July 2021. Collaborating with the Grid Iron Theatre in the UK and supported by leading countries from the EU, the plays in the festival portrayed life before and after 1948, the brutality of Israeli occupation, and the threats to Sheikh Jarrah residents. Storytellers, independent artists, directors from the West Bank and Israel, and the Freedom Theatre were the main participants in the festival. Yet, one cannot overlook the fact that the most outstanding plays are monodramas documenting Palestinian life pre- and post-1948. The first discerning illustration of such enactments is Amer Hlehel's biographical *Taha*; a play that never ceases to be relevant, nowadays more than ever. For *Taha* documents the Zionist aggression on the northern regions of historic Palestine resulting in the erasure of entire villages, depopulating them, and displacing their inhabitants only to make them become refugees internally or forced to migrate outside the geographical borders of Palestine. The second case study is Samia Qazmouz Bakri's *The Alley*, which also documents Palestinian life before 1948, the ramifications of displacements of refugees, and of the Judaization of the Palestinian landscape, villages, towns, and cities. Both plays delve into the collective memory of Palestinians and use it as a political weapon in the process of a national struggle when wars and peace agreements have proved to be ineffective. They also aim to remind, educate, politicize, and inform the public that the Zionist project is ongoing.

Amer Hlehel's *Taha*—a one-person drama—is a biography about the life of the Palestinian poet Taha Mohammad Ali (1931–2011). Hlehel told me over the phone during the aggression on Gaza that reading Adina Hoffman's book *My Happiness Bears No Relation to Happiness* (2010), a biography about Taha, and interviewing Taha's family, informed him about how to recount the story of a major Galilean resistance poet. Both Hoffman's book and Hlehel's play chronicle the life of the poet and his poetry as a boy from a village in the Galilee, called Saffuriyya. Both narratives end up informing, if not mirroring, one another in an attempt to portray the idle life in the village of Saffuriyya, where breezy groves of fruits, vegetables, and farmers dwelled. It is about Mohammad Ali Taha's village, poetry, and narrative from the ensuing *nakba* to his recent passing.

Taha's first performance in Arabic, directed by Yusef Abu Wardeh, opened at Al-Midan Theatre in Haifa on the 7th of May 2014. The play, which was directed and translated into English by Amir Nizar Zuabi, had successfully toured to the Young Vic Theatre in London, Edinburgh Fringe Festival, The Kennedy Center in Washington DC, and Toronto, Singapore, Belgium, Sydney, Stockholm, and many capitals of the Arab World. In the English version, most of the lines are delivered in English and only Taha's poems are spoken in Arabic, translated on the screen behind the actor. *Taha* opens with Hlehel circling a dimly lit stage, pausing every now and then as if is trying to recollect his thoughts. The prologue to the play reads:

All my life, nothing came easy.
Not even becoming a poet… (al-Saber and English 2020, 219)

These lines, written by Hlehel, depict the harshness of Taha's life. According to a reviewer, 'It's a tumbling of words, engaging and warm, as the audience listens rapt to a master storyteller recounting his life from his near miraculous birth to his experience of the *nakba* (Catastrophe) of 1948 and his later emergence as a renowned poet' (Gill 2018). The avid storyteller describes Taha's idyllic childhood and early schooling. In spite of experiencing poverty at an early age, and with his father being unemployed, Taha excels at school. He gets to know poetry, borrows books from the library school and from Haj Taher's personal library, and later on he learns English by listening to the BBC radio.

Although Haj Taher wanted to educate the people of Saffuriyya, so they are informed in the ways of the world, and kept saying that 'they wanted to steal our land', the villagers were preoccupied with their daily lives toiling in their fields. These lines foreshadow the rest of the scenes in the play (al-Saber and English 2020, 223).

Taha has to grow up fast and become the breadwinner of the family for what remains of his father's land is only three plots, 'one for olives one for wheat, and one for seasonal planting' (224). Taha's father keeps his Diwan (parlour) open where 'all the men in the village would meet, and would gather every night, to tell stories, share the village gossip and the latest news' (224). The Diwan is Taha's father's life and it has to be kept open, even if the remaining plots of land have to be sold. Such a situation drives Taha to become a young entrepreneur. His successful egg-selling takes him all the way to Haifa. Taha is mesmerized by Haifa: the different scents in the air, the shiny new cars and buses, the lit streets at night, the cafes where people are reading newspapers, the cinemas, the theatres, and the mixture of spoken languages and of people walking the streets such as Greeks, Syrians, Germans, and Jews.

The scene describes the hustle and bustle of Palestinian Mediterranean coastal cities, and what made the fabric of Palestinian society and culture rich and diverse before the 1948 war, thus negating Golda Meir's declaration: 'The Palestinian people do not exist' (Giles 1969). In Haifa, Taha sees Jews and Arabs 'speak to one another', although he only has seen them before 'outside of our village […] dressed in uniforms, they were surveying the area with binoculars. They wrote on maps and carried guns', reminding of Haj Taher's warnings that the land will be lost which falls on deaf ears (al-Saber and English 2020, 225).

Hlehel captures the roughness of Taha's early life in a moving and engaging manner. We get to see the young boy's business flourishing, successful at school, a reciter of poetry, and how the men in his father's Diwan appoint him as the BBC radio listener. Taha would listen to the news at his uncle's house and report back to the men in the Diwan. Taha 'hated the Brits', because of the Mandate. When WWII broke out the village of Saffuriyya was divided between the supporters of the British Empire and the Germans, 'and no one thought World War II would change Saffuryeh beyond recognition' (226).

In the aftermath of WWII, people become apprehensive as the Partition Plan of Palestine is being negotiated, and according to Taha's father 'the world is changing. Things are changing. People are fleeing their homes. God knows if we are not next' (229). Like many Palestinians at that time, the 17-year-old Taha has faith that the UN and the British will make sure they are not attacked, as Saffureyh is 'outside of the Separation Lines' (229). But they were attacked and had to flee. Hlehel's voice remembering what happened next becomes sombre and reflective. Taha defies his father and ignores the fact that by May 1948, Zionist forces were on the offensive and had captured several major towns such as Jaffa, Haifa, Acre, and Tiberias, as well as large areas of the proposed Arab state, according to the UN's Partition Plan, particularly in Galilee. He goes to Nazareth to buy lambs to expand his business.

The breaking point in Taha's life happens on 15 July 1948 while herding the lambs under the full moon in the valleys of Saffuriyya:

> I hear a quiet but constant hum of a fly. It begins to envelope the dark skies.
> But this hum is coming from far away. How can I hear a fly from so far a distance?
> The hum comes closer.
> Then there's another. This one. Distant
> Two flies now. Not one.
> (…)
> An Airplane.
> And another airplane. […] My God- BOOM! BOOM! (231)

Taha has seen airplanes before in Saffuriyya's skies.

Terrified, young Taha starts running from the fields towards the village. In 'the alleyways, people are fleeing, desperately trying to leave the village' (231). But Taha runs towards home and finds no one. Taha runs north and tracks his family near the old cemetery. Saffuriyya has been attacked and fallen.

Saffuriyyans flee, leaving their homes, their fields, their livelihood, as Taha leaves his frightened goats behind because Israeli Air Force Auster planes 'pummeled them with bombs from on high, sending up flames and sending down mayhem' (Hoffman 2010, 133).

According to Hoffman's findings in the Tel Hasshomer army archives, Saffuriyya was not the only village that was bombed. Israeli Air Force operations during the summer of 1948 reveal that 'in early July [the Galilee Squadron] had registered 91 bombing sorties and dropped a total in excess of one ton of bombs. All of this had been achieved with four Austers' (Hoffman 2010, 133). The unarmed villagers had to flee for their lives, thus leaving the villages empty, marking the 1948 *nakba* for the Palestinians and the War of Independence for the Israelis.

Walking towards the north with other displaced Galilean villagers for two days Taha and his family leave Palestine and enter Lebanon. In Beint Jbail, Taha's family with tens of thousands of Palestinians 'were living in a refugee camp in Lebanon. Our homes were blue tents issued by the UN'. As the UN inspectors come and go filling reports, Taha declares: 'Some of us were in denial. Others understood something big is happening' (al-Saber and English 2020, 234).

Amer Hlehel continues his story and describes for us the inhabitable conditions in Palestinian refugee camps. While some families venture to Beirut, further north, or to other Arab countries, Taha and his family stay put in the camp and are hit with another loss as his only sister dies of meningitis. Taha's mother, Imm Taha, snaps. She had 'already buried six children [...]. She had no idea if her own mother and sister were alive. She had just lost her house, her belongings, her neighbors, her fruit trees, her village, her country, the only life she had ever known, and she was now exiled' (Hoffman 2010, 168). Sensing the gravity of the situation, Taha's father wants to right the wrong. They should return home.

For Taha's family, like many Palestinians, infiltrating the already well-guarded borders where soldiers are ordered to shoot anything that moves is dangerous and life threatening. Palestinian refugees have been trying for months to cross over to Palestine—now Israel—and on the night the Taha family are waiting anxiously for the smuggler, the number of returnees is almost a hundred. Upon crossing the borders Taha says: 'Our land feels changed. Even the air smells different' (al-Saber and English 2020, 241).

Risking their lives to return to the village of Saffuriyya which they were expelled from, Taha's family finds out that it is now a closed military zone. No Palestinian is allowed to enter the village: 'the church is still there though. The school is gone. The houses gone. And the bakery is gone. [...] the smell of fresh olive oil, thyme and bread that filled the air is gone' (al-Saber and English 2020, 241).

Saffuriyya is gone. 'There is no returning home. The land is no longer called Palestine. Now, it's called Israel' (244). Even though Taha's family manages to return to Palestine, ironically, they end up as refugees in their own land. Once they reach Palestine, the family moves to Reina (a town in the upper Galilee) and eventually settles in Nazareth.

Hlehel told me that his own family shared the same experience as Taha's in 1948 and its aftermath. His grandfather's village was also attacked and destroyed, and he fled to Lebanon and ended up in the Ayn al-Hilweh refugee camp. After a year he sneaked back to Palestine only to find that he was not allowed to live in his village for the rest of his life. Palestinian forced displacement had not been restricted to the northern part of the country as it also reached Jerusalem.

At the time of writing this chapter in 2021, I was sitting at my desk in the town of Beit Jala. All of a sudden, my apprehensive mother rushes in and tells me that the war on Gaza has started. Like her I become paralyzed with fear. The Israeli aggression on the Jerusalemites and on Gaza drove my mother to relive the traumas of 1948. Like Taha, Hlehel's grandfather, and thousands of Palestinians who were driven by force out of their homes, my mother was expelled as a child from her house in Saint Julian's Street, West Jerusalem, with only the clothes on her back. No trace of her parents' house can be found today. As Edward Said eloquently describes, the Palestinian story is 'not a narrative … but rather broken narratives, fragmentary compositions, and self-consciously staged testimonials, in which the narrative voice keeps stumbling over itself, its obligations and its limitations' (Said 1986, 38). Taha, the young boy from Saffuriyya, in spite of a harsh life, trauma, loss, and pain, is the renowned Palestinian poet Mohammed Ali Taha. His own personal saga is the epitome of the Palestinian saga.

While Hlehel's *Taha* chronicles pre-1948 life and the severity of displacement, Samia Qazmouz Bakri's monodrama charts what happened to Palestinians and their homeland post-1948. Bakri wrote and performed the monodrama *az-Zarub* (The Alley), directed by Fuad Awwad, at the Second Jerusalem Theatre Festival Theatre Week, in December 1992, and in Berlin in June 2001, directed by the late Iraqi Awni Karumi. Like Hlehel, Bakri is an avid storyteller. Her stories are not about a prominent Palestinian figure but rather the tragic accounts of five different Palestinian women after the 1948 war. The stories are from the Mediterranean coastal city of Acre, where one can visit the Pasha Palace and its baths, the Jacob's Wednesday Celebrations, the Ramadan feast, and the Palestinian fishermen on the sea front. Similar to Hlehel, Bakri tells stories about the Acre citizens who became Palestinian refugees in Burj al-Barajneh in Lebanon, but she deviates to present-time Acre. Listening to her stories, the audience become aware and reminded of the Israeli attempts to obliterate the remnants of Palestinian heritage, culture, and history by demolishing historical places and renaming the sites of Arab homesteads.

Whilst Taha returns and finds most of his village demolished, in *The Alley* we walk the lanes of the old city of Acre and witness massive Judaization of the landscape. In *Taha* we see young Taha intrigued by the coastal city of Haifa and in *The Alley* we see Bakri immersed in pre-1948 Acre and informed of its present plight. We visit the Inn of the Columns where merchants from Egypt used to rest before continuing their journey to Lebanon and Syria. The inn—which now exists only in old pictures—was full of merchants and surrounded by shops selling silk, carpets, flower, meat, cotton, herbs, and spices (Jayyusi 2003, 83). Suddenly, Bakri abruptly returns to present-day Acre to report that the Inn Column 'is silent now', and the keys are with an Israeli company for urban development (84).

Bakri walks us down memory lane and describes the Casino—The Glass Coffee House where famous Egyptian and Lebanese singers would sing (85). She also reminisces about al-Ahli Cinema—as Masrah as Sayhk al-Lababidi. The cinema-theatre hall hosted in the past many respected Egyptian artists on its stage, like Yusuf Wahbi, Amina Rizq, Ali al-Kassar, and theatre troupes as well as the Lebanese singer Sabah. The beautiful building—with its wooden Arabesque balconies, marble corridors, and coloured glass windows—was torn down, to be replaced with a branch of the Israeli National Bank (Nassar 2006, 26). Bakri also tells us about Acre's well-known Pasha Baths, which in 1954 were turned into an Israeli museum (known in Hebrew as Hanozion Ha-Airani Museum), and how even parts of the seashore, *Satt al Arab*, are suddenly encircled with a fence and turned into a private shore. Acre inhabitants cannot bathe there anymore because this public space is now Israeli private property (27).

Bakri's narrative on Acre reminds the public of important events, places, and people who left an impact on its residents. But all have suffered change, alienation, and displacement from their past. Invoking the collective memory of Acre residents, Bakri recounts the plight of the family who owned a mansion overlooking the Mediterranean. In 1948, the Shuqayris' were forced to flee. Shifting into the present, Bakri reports that there is no trace of the mansion as it was demolished and replaced with a residential compound. Incidentally, Bakri describes how she found among the ruins an engraved stone: 'Dr. Anwar al-Shuqayri: surgeon and obstetrician. Office hours: mornings 8–1, evenings 4–7' (Jayyusi 2003, 100).

Bakri deviates from her chronicles of Acre and either updates or changes her story depending on her audience's Palestinian experience. During the performance in Berlin on the 29th of September 2000, in the audience were Palestinian refugees who fled Palestine to Lebanon, and due to the civil war settled in Germany—they agreed with Bakri's stories. Some spectators corrected Bakri if she mispronounced a name and even gave precise direction to places in Acre. In other words, Bakri not only collects 'memory which consists of past reminiscences that link given groups of people for whom remembered events are important'; she also arouses her audience to relive those tragic events, because their memory did not yet become a 'memory of memory' but still resides in their own unresolved present and living past (Osiel 1997, 18). During the Berlin performance, a niece of the late Dr Anwar al-Shuqayri corrected Bakri on how to get to the clinic and where he is currently buried.

In both plays, Hlehel and Bakri re-enact painful memories and both serve to educate the public on the ongoing Zionist project, this time the Judaization of Jerusalem. I have seen, again, Amer Hlehel performing on 11 July 2021 in Jerusalem at the Palestinian National Theater also known as al-Hakawati. The monumental theatre is just a few blocks away from the Sheikh Jarrah neighbourhood where Palestinians are fighting Israeli court eviction orders. The timely performance of *Taha* informs the audience inside the theatre of what could happen if the Sheikh Jarrah residents comply with Israeli court eviction orders. Their story would be no different than Hlehel's or Bakri's. They will be displaced, again, in their own land.

Similarly, as the resistance of the Sheikh Jarrah residents made it to the international news, their outside presence also informs us through the emblematic figure of Taha on the stage. At this moment the outside/inside, the past/present collide, and merge on stage/the political scene where Hoffman's/Hlehel's/Bakri's texts not only inform one another but complement each other. The rest of the story is about the resilience of the refugees/residents to stay put and resist what might come in the face of continuous annihilation and erasure of not only the landscape, but of memory as well.

References

Abu Sneineh, Mustapha. 2021. 'Sheikh Jarrah Explained: The Past and Present of East Jerusalem Neighbourhood.' *Middle East Eye*, May 6, 2021; https://www.middleeasteye.net/news/israel-palestine-sheikh-jarrah-jerusalem-neighbourhood-eviction-explained. Accessed 5 April 2022.

al-Saber, Samer and English, Gary M. 2020. *Stories Under Occupation and Other Plays From Palestine*. London and Calcutta: Seagull Books.

Giles, Frank. 1969. 'Golda Meir: Who Can Blame Israel.' *Sunday Times*, June 15, p. 12.

Gill, Joe. 2018. 'Playing Palestinian Poet Taha: "I Carry That Nakba on Me 24 Hours a Day."' *Middle East Eye*, July 3, 2018; https://www.middleeasteye.net/features/playing-palestinian-poet-taha-i-carry-nakba-me-24-hours-day. Accessed 5 April 2022.

Hoffman, Adina. 2010. *My Happiness Bears No Relation to Happiness: A Poet's Life in the Palestinian Century*. Yale University Press.

Jayyusi, Khadra Salama. 2003. *Short Arabic Plays: An Anthology*. Northampton: Interlink Books.

Kingsley, Patrick. 2021. 'After Years of Quiet, Israeli-Palestinian Conflict Exploded. Why Now?' *The New York Times*, May 15. https://www.nytimes.com/2021/05/15/world/middleeast/israel-palestinian-gaza-war.html. Accessed 5 April 2022.

Massad, Joseph. 2008. 'Resisting the Nakba.' *Al-Ahram Weekly* 897 (15–21 May). http://weekly.ahram.org.eg/2008/897/op8.htm.

MEE Staff. 2020. 'Israeli Court Orders Eviction of 87 Palestinians from East Jerusalem Neighbourhood.' *Middle East Eye*, November 26. https://www.middleeasteye.net/news/israel-palestine-east-jerusalem-court-eviction-order. Accessed 5 April 2022.

Nassar, Khamis Hala. 2006. 'Stories from Under Occupation: Performing the Palestinian Experience.' *Theatre Journal*, 58 (1), 15–37.

———. 2018a. 'Conflicting Agenda: Post Oslo Theater caught between National Visions and Western Donors.' In *The Freedom Theatre. Performing Cultural Resistance in Palestine*, edited by Ola Johansson et Johanna Wallin, 123–131. New Delhi: LeftWood Books.

———. 2018b. 'Palestinian Theater: Trials and Tribulations.' In *the Freedom Theatre. Performing Cultural Resistance in Palestine*, edited by Ola Johansson and Johanna Wallin, 199–212. New Delhi: LeftWood Books.

Osiel, Mark J. 1997. *Mass Atrocity, Collective Memory and the Law*. New Brunswick: Transaction Publication.

Said, W. Edward. 1995. *Politics of Dispossession*. New York: Vintage.

———. 1986. *After the Last Sky: Palestinian Lives*. New York: Pantheon.

CHAPTER 40

Ukrainian Theatre in Migration: Military Anthropology Perspective

Robert Boroch and Anna Korzeniowska-Bihun

Recent events in Ukraine have shown that modern wars are waged not only on the battlefield but also on a massive scale through cultural means (see Korzeniowska-Bihun 2014; Boroch 2016, 81–94). Since the beginning of the Russian-Ukrainian war in 2014, the Ukrainian theatre has been combatting not only the increasing migration of its internally displaced audiences, but also the ongoing cultural propaganda from Russia that denies the independent status of Ukraine. This chapter develops the theory of anthropological defence whereby a nation wages a cultural war at the same time as a military war. It focuses on two Ukrainian theatre companies: the Theatre of Displaced People (TDP) and the Luhansk Regional Theatre. The TDP was founded in 2014 to provide psychological and organisational aid for people forced to flee their homes in eastern Ukraine. The Luhansk Regional Theatre has shared the fate of the migrants themselves, having to change their place of operation because of the Russian invasion.

In this chapter, we study how theatre—both as an artistic practice and as a cultural institution—can play a unique role in the practices of the anthropological defence.

Theatre's primary functions—we argue—are inextricably linked to culture. As a weapon of the anthropological defence, theatre can enable resistance against negative information from the enemy; and it can provide artistic support and information through its creative work. Moreover, during the time of

---

R. Boroch (✉)
University of Warsaw, Warsaw, Poland

A. Korzeniowska-Bihun
Academy of the East. Independent Research Center, Warsaw, Poland

© The Author(s), under exclusive license to Springer Nature Switzerland AG 2023
Y. Meerzon, S. E. Wilmer (eds.), *The Palgrave Handbook of Theatre and Migration*, https://doi.org/10.1007/978-3-031-20196-7_40

war, theatre can serve as a supporting agency to the residents in their daily lives. It can give them physical and emotional shelter, but also it can create a special place of engagement for leading voices in society, to reinforce the cohesion of local social groups, and to shape a sense of community (see Boroch and Korzeniowska-Bihun 2017; Boroch and Korzeniowska-Bihun 2021; Boroch 2018, Boroch 2020, Boroch 2021).

Historical Background: Ukrainian Theatres in the Face of War

Ukraine did not secure statehood for centuries. Apart from the short period of independence in 1918–1919, it achieved independence only in 1991, after the collapse of the USSR. Historically, the eastern regions of Ukraine had been under the influence of the Russian administration for much longer than the western ones. They were also subjected to intense Russification processes, including the physical destruction of Ukrainian culture and its signifiers. Due to the weakness of the young Ukrainian state from 1991, the eastern territories were heavily influenced by Russian propaganda. The Russian Federation carried out unrestrained anthropological aggression there. The primary objective of the Kremlin was not only to prevent building Ukrainian national identity, but also to promote the regional breakup of Ukraine.

In 2014, the Russian Federation attacked and annexed the territory of Crimea and promoted the formation of two quasi-states: the Donetsk People's Republic and the Luhansk People's Republic. These actions initiated the eight-year war between Russia and Ukraine from 2014 to 2022. The annexation of Crimea by the Russian Federation in 2014 and the first stage of the Russian-Ukrainian war triggered a massive wave of migration. As a result, complete cultural institutions as well as people were forced to relocate to other cities, predominantly in central and western Ukraine. The Ukrainian Ministry of Social Policy registered 1,590,056 internally displaced persons (IDPs) from 2014 to 2017 (Nalyvayko and Furina 2017, 45), while unofficial data recorded about two million IDPs from Crimea and the Donbas area alone.

From the start of the full-scale Russian invasion on 24 February 2022 until July 2022, one-third of the Ukrainian people have been forced to leave their home (UNHCR 2022), and eight million people have been internally displaced within Ukraine (IOM 2022, 1) out of a total of almost fifteen million displaced persons (i.e., IDPs and refugees fleeing across national borders).

The reaction of the Ukrainian theatre to these hostilities should be divided into two stages. The first period (from 2014 to the beginning of 2022), characterised by kinetic military actions in eastern Ukraine and intense hybrid cultural attacks by Russia, was when Ukrainian cultural workers began to intensively develop tools of anthropological defence.

In this phase of the war, the main objective of the Ukrainian theatres—and one of the tactics of their anthropological defence—was the psychological protection of the IDPs and the integration of Ukrainian society, which faced mass migration for the first time in its history as an independent state.

Until 24 February 2022, Ukrainian cultural institutions, among them theatres, took actions aimed at helping IDPs to integrate into a new environment. The theatres created a dialogue and welcoming space where city dwellers could meet newcomers. It was an essential opportunity under Ukrainian conditions that not only helped IDPs feel better in a strange region but also worked to combat mutual stereotypes. For decades, Russian propaganda persuaded eastern and western Ukrainians that their language differences and historical experiences were irreconcilable. Thanks to working with migrants and locals, the Ukrainian theatre put the alleged problems in perspective. It showed that the differences were not as huge and that Ukrainians could overcome them by putting in an appropriately directed effort. This purpose was achieved through various projects involving IDPs. Some companies created joint performances; others invited migrants to existing projects.

A second tactic in anthropological defence was to use theatre as a place for discussion. After the performance, the creators encouraged the audience to exchange opinions. It was important that when the theatre discussed political issues, the audience included representatives from the eastern and western regions of the country. The discussion did not have to lead to consensus, but a moderated debate made it possible to listen to both sides of the argument. Given that a difference of views is a common element of the political landscape in a democracy, disagreement did not imply that the country was torn apart.

In the second phase of the warfare—that is, after the launch of the full-scale Russian invasion on 24 February 2022—workers of Ukrainian mainstream stages concentrated on the physical protection of IDPs and the survival of theatres as state institutions. At the same time, representatives of independent theatres dealt with documenting the war and its victims.

According to the Ukrainian intellectual Maiia Harbuziuk, Ukrainian state theatres began to serve a few functions: (1) *theatre as a volunteer*—for example, collection of humanitarian aid, fundraising, and assistance to IDPs; (2) *theatre as IDPs shelters*; (3) *theatre as a bomb shelter*. Furthermore, Harbuziuk points out that 'the actors became service personnel who enabled the functioning of the shelter.' In the most general terms, 'the theatre as a building' and 'the theatre as an institution,' together with its personnel, performed essential administrative functions, sometimes replacing state institutions (Harbuziuk 2022). In addition, theatre makers also documented current events, focusing on social emotions or the sociocultural context that showed war trauma as it is. There is no doubt that, as a feature of anthropological defence, members of the theatre company acted as high-impact leaders—both by their personal involvement, leading by example, and by taking responsibility for IDPs to build a feeling of security among IDPs and residents. It is therefore not surprising that the enemy would attack theatres. The enemy regarded theatres as crisis management centres and places of asylum for civilians run by social leaders who are the first line of civil defence. Russian actions were aimed at intimidating leaders and civilian residents, leading to unprecedented acts of violence and brutality.

Case Studies: The Theatre of Displaced People and the Luhansk Regional Theatre

Since the beginning of the Russian-Ukrainian war in 2014, the Ukrainian theatre has responded to Russian anthropological aggression, creating a network of grassroots initiatives, many of which were directed at IDPs. In January 2015, the Theatre of Displaced People (TDP) was established. It was an independent initiative founded by two Ukrainian playwrights—Nataliya Vorozhbyt and Maksym Kurochkin—the German theatre director Georg Genoux, and the military psychologist Oleksii Karachynskii.

Vorozhbyt and Kurochkin are representatives of the artistic movement known as the New Ukrainian Drama, a recent initiative that gathers playwrights of various creative temperaments. They began to act not so much in opposition to the official conservative Ukrainian theatres as creating an alternative voice. Both Vorozhbyt and Kurochkin were first associated with the Russian independent theatre community. Vorozhbyt returned to Ukraine before the Revolution of Dignity (2013–2014). Kurochkin did the same a little bit later. Their return became an essential stimulus for the consolidation of contemporary Ukrainian playwrights. Following the outbreak of war, Vorozhbyt and Kurochkin felt that they were morally obliged to assist victims of the Russian invasion. Thus, the Theatre of the Displaced People was born. The word 'displaced' in the name of the theatre, according to Genoux, means more than a fugitive or IDP because it contains an element of alienation (Sopova 2018).

The TDP set itself the goal of helping the IDPs and integrating the inhabitants of the eastern and western regions of Ukraine. During the five years of its operation, it launched eighteen projects, most of which took into account the needs of the IDPs and involved migrants in theatrical productions. Over time, volunteers and soldiers of the Ukrainian Armed Forces (both active and demobilised) also became participants in the actions of the TDP.

The theatre used mainly 'verbatim' techniques. Their documentary performances usually took place in ordinary rooms, on makeshift stages, without set or unnecessary props. Nothing distracted the actors and the audience. The auditorium was often randomly placed, and the viewers' seats were organised in a hurry. Minimal lighting was used, playing with light and darkness, and the TDP experimented with music and video footage.

The first stage of the theatre's work was collecting interviews with IDPs with the help of the psychologist Karachynskii. Then Vorozhbyt and Kurochkin transformed the interviews into dramatic material, and Genoux, the director, adapted them for the stage. As Vorozhbyt claimed, her role as a playwright boiled down to listening to people's stories and picking out those threads which could form a short story. These short stories became parts of the performance. Genoux believed that telling your own stories had a therapeutic effect: 'So from a victim of your story, you eventually become a hero of your story' (Grytsenko 2016).

On 27 October 2015, in Kyiv, the TDP presented the premiere of a verbatim performance, *Gdie Vostok?* (Where Is the West?)—a series of stories about the problems of people who were forced to abandon their homes and everyday lives. The performance took on a therapeutic character. IDPs from eastern Ukraine were invited to participate in it. On stage, they talked about their own experiences. Fifteen actor-migrants came out in front of the audience without rehearsals to avoid losing the spontaneity of the event. After the premiere performance, the line-up of actors changed so that the presented stories changed as well.

The theatre makers paid great attention to child and youth victims of the war. Working with them took many formats. On the one hand, various activities were organised at the places of their resettlement. On the other hand, the TDP travelled to cities on the front line to work with local teenagers and Ukrainian soldiers stationed there.

Many of the TDP's projects took place in Kyiv because many migrants from Donbas and Crimea gathered there. In December 2015, the TDP launched a *Displaced Kids* project dedicated to children who had difficulty adapting to a new place. The theatre company began to organise free activities for them. For example, in September 2017, within the framework of the GOGOLfest theatrical festival, the TDP set up a week of exercises with theatre specialists, including playwrights, actors, and other artists. During the *Displaced Kids* project, the curators and their pupils prepared a cartoon, *I Believe I Can Fly*, using stop-motion technique. The children wrote a screenplay, and the movie's main heroes were their favourite toys which young migrants carried with them while escaping from the war zone.

The migrant issue was treated by the theatre much more broadly than the standard definition of the term 'IDP.' Genoux said: 'It also concerns the general situation in eastern Ukraine, the situation of losing your place in the world. We think people near the front line are displaced because they no longer realise where they live. The war also displaces the soldiers: they are not at home' (Sopova 2018).

Accordingly, the TDP came to towns near the front line where the curators conducted activities to integrate Ukrainian military men and women with inhabitants, mainly young people.

Although Ukrainian troops were stationed on Ukrainian-controlled terrain, they faced the consequences of decades-long Russian propaganda. The propaganda had a powerful impact on Russian-speaking inhabitants in the eastern regions of Ukraine. Above all, it exacerbated stereotypes, making relations between soldiers and locals much more difficult. The soldiers blamed the Russified inhabitants for the war. The inhabitants believed that the war was caused by the soldiers stationed there. However, the curators understood that the youth were looking for dialogue with the soldiers because they were interested in the situation in Ukraine and the front. The TDP wanted to help both sides to overcome fear and stereotypes.

In addition, military personnel also wanted to establish contact with the residents. Many soldiers were conscripts, and in civilian life, they were specialists in various fields (e.g. teachers, athletes). If they were not on duty, they often were willing to use their free time to work with the local youth. However, they were afraid of the reaction.

In 2016 and 2017, the TDP launched the *Dity ta viyskovi* (Children and Soldiers) project, organising verbatim performances in three eastern cities: Popasna, Sloviansk, and Shchastia. The performances were prepared for a week by teenagers and soldiers and then presented to a local audience, mainly the teenagers' families. Due to such actions, both groups—locals and military personnel—ceased to be anonymous to each other. Additionally, they began to understand that despite their differences, they had more in common. The TDP stopped operating in 2019, partly due to its founders' occupational burnout.

The TDP was a theatre that dealt with migration issues. In contrast, there are also theatres in Ukraine that have become migrants themselves because of the war. One such company is the Luhansk Regional Theatre (LRT). This Ukrainian institution experienced migration in both stages of the Russian-Ukrainian war.

The LRT had operated in the eastern Ukrainian city of Luhansk since 1970. For more than forty years, it was part of the cultural map of the region. Although it was the only Ukrainian-language theatre in the area, the LRT was very popular among the Russian-speaking audience. They performed contemporary, modern, and often experimental pieces in their repertoire. Unfortunately, Russian aggression in 2014 forced the company to move to Severodonetsk. Some of the theatre's employees moved to other cultural institutions in Ukraine. Others went to Russia or stayed in occupied Luhansk.

A symbolic delegation consisting of the director, an accountant, and an actor came to Severodonetsk. From this seed a new company was born bearing the name LRT. This was also understood by members of the audience who had fled to Severodonetsk from Luhansk, continuing to treat the LRT as their theatre, although they no longer recognised any of the actors. This symbolic recognition of the continuity of a state institution has become one of the manifestations of statehood during war time.

The Luhansk Regional Theatre took over the building of the local Severodonetsk Drama Theatre, after almost the entire company left for Russia as the result of the Russian invasion in 2014. However, the premises of the Severodonetsk Drama Theatre were in terrible technical condition. Until mid-2015, the LRT in Severodonetsk existed only on paper. In 2015, Serhii Dorofieiev was appointed director of the theatre, and there were less than ten actors in the company: the mentioned actor from Luhansk, art school graduates who had worked there for a few weeks, a married couple of actors from Luhansk who had been students of the former director of the LRT Volodymyr Moskovchenko, and three actresses who had worked for the Severodonetsk Drama Theatre and refused to go to Russia with other members of its company. Several Luhansk actors who had already worked in other Ukrainian cities returned to the company in time. The theatre also began attracting art school graduates, for example, from Dnipro, Kyiv, and Kharkiv. The acting team was very young. Three-quarters of the company were people in their twenties.

During the 2015–2016 theatrical season, the LRT held rehearsals in the wrecked building of the former Severodonetsk Drama Theatre and performed on the stage of the city's Palace of Culture. Each time the company had to transport all its costumes and set. In addition, the Palace of Culture stage did not meet all the requirements of a professional theatre. There were also situations where the LRT could not have a dress rehearsal before the premiere because the stage was occupied for other purposes. In the 2015–2016 season, the LRT created twelve performances but could not present them to the public because the Palace of Culture stage was only available to the LRT for four or five times a month.

In August 2016, a significant renovation of the theatre building began. The team was unable to conduct rehearsals and was forced to leave. It continued its work in a former kindergarten. One of the plays being worked on at the time had two-level sets. Due to the small room size, the actors had to rehearse on all fours. They were only able to practice playing on that set in an upright position on stage in the Palace of Culture. In 2017 the LRT finally moved into its premises in Severodonetsk. As the LRT left its entire technical and material base in Luhansk, it willingly accepted support from other institutions. This was provided, among others, by the Theatre in Kherson, which presented to the Luhansk colleagues costumes and set for a performance that the Kherson company was not staging anymore. Thanks to the Theatre in Kherson, the LRT was able to premiere in 2018 the play *Idzanami* by Tetiana Iwashshenko, directed by Serhiy Pavluk, an artist also associated with the theatre in Kherson. *Idzanami* was advertised as an 'erotic melodrama.' It was pure entertainment and did not touch on the subject of war in any way. However, the donation of this performance by one theatre to another is an excellent example of artistic solidarity in wartime conditions. As the only theatre in the Luhansk region that used the official state language (i.e., Ukrainian), the LRT had to respond to all artistic needs. Therefore, it worked in all genres and addressed various categories of viewers.

When the LRT moved to the renovated building, in addition to the repertoire work, it also started organising a Ukrainian theatre festival called SvitOhlad. As Dorofieiev says: 'One of its purposes was to show Ukraine to the Severodonetsk [people]' (Korzeniowska-Bihun 2022a). Local theatregoers left the region very rarely and hardly knew the theatre arts of other Ukrainian cities. However, due to the festival, they had the opportunity to meet them, while other theatrical companies had the chance to get to know the Luhansk region. Consequently, the Ukrainian-speaking theatre performed the function of integrating the Russian-speaking community with the rest of the state organism. Like all eastern regions of Ukraine, the Luhansk region has long been the target of intensified Russian anthropological aggression. Therefore, the presence of Ukrainian culture in the area, especially high culture, has become truly significant. The repertoire of the festival was vast and included Ukrainian classics and contemporary drama, as well as world classics translated into Ukrainian. This helped to increase the value of Ukrainian culture. Earlier, people in these areas discovered classics of world literature, for example, through Russian interpretations. But unfortunately, this gave the mistaken impression that everything valuable in the civilisation was in the Russian language. For festival participants, all-Ukrainian art events (including theatre festivals) also helped to create a network of personal contacts that work as reliable information sources in wartime.

The migratory fate of the LRT found its stage reflection in a verbatim performance, *Bayky Severa* (Legends from Severo, 2022), with a meaningful subheading, *Pro shcho movchat pereselentsi?* (What the IDPs Are Silent About?) Andriy May directed the play in 2016. It was a story based on the real-life experiences of four actors. Being IDPs, they raised questions such as: 'Run to a bomb shelter, which is unlikely to protect you or not?' 'Will you participate in the illegal and falsified referendum or not?' 'How to maintain relations with parents who categorically support the other side of the conflict?'

It would seem that the similarity of experiences and choices should have created a specific thread of understanding between the actors and the Luhansk audiences. However, that did not happen. On the contrary, the performance was very well received in various cities of Ukraine, whereas the Severodonetsk public rejected it. In the opinion of Dorofieiev (Korzeniowska-Bihun 2022b), this was because people in Severodonetsk were not ready for such open discussions about their own experiences. Therefore, they were not able to rework traumatic emotions themselves. As a result, the project lacked the element of art therapy that, for example, the TDP offered to its viewers.

After the full-scale Russian invasion in February 2022, the LRT was forced to relocate for a second time. As a result, the company has been divided into two groups, operating in two cities: central Ukrainian Dnipro and western Ukrainian Drohobych. In both cases, the LRT actors were received by local theatres that housed them on theatrical premises.

Once again, the LRT left all its technical and artistic facilities behind. On 30 May 2022, the newly renovated theatre building in Severodonetsk was destroyed by Russian occupation troops. The soldier who targeted the theatre knew that civilians were hiding in the theatre's basement (Sluzhba bezpeky Ukrayiny 2022). Their fate is unknown.

Since moving to new locations, the LRT has been engaged in voluntary work. For example, in Dnipro, the company presents concerts for the Ukrainian army. In Drohobych, they also give charity concerts to raise money for products and prepare dinners for Ukrainian military men and women (Ostrohliad 2022).

After the second forced move, the theatre has only one play in its repertoire: *Khto ya?* (Who Am I?) directed by Stanislav Sadakliyev. There are only two actors in the show. Besides, it is undemanding in terms of scenography. It was easy to recreate the performance under new conditions, especially since the version had to be adapted from a large stage to a small one. In Dnipro, the LRT has presented *Who Am I?* a few times, hosting a lot of migrant-viewers from the Luhansk region.

In 2022 a performance took place at the Ukrainian theatrical festival Melpomena Tavriyi, which can also be treated as a kind of migrant. The event is considered to be one of the most famous Ukrainian theatrical events that has been held in Kherson for a very long time. As Russia currently occupies the city, a new festival formula was created. Each participant presented a performance on their stage, and the video recording was made available on the Internet.

The LRT's general director Dorofieiev plans to gather the entire company in one place to resume the work of the theatre. However, his hopes are much more far-reaching. This is how he describes the future of his theatre team:

> I will go to my home city of Luhansk. I haven't been there for eight years, since the war started. We [the theatre team] have decided that we will surely return to our home city. Firstly, we will clean up the debris on the theatre grounds. Then, we will sign up for a volunteer squad to clean up and reconstruct the ruined buildings and infrastructure of the city. Like it was after WWII when culture workers and other state employees performed the reconstruction works. Anyway, we will handle it all after. Now, we have to defeat the enemy. (Ostrohliad 2022)

Summary

Theatre performances, or more generally the activities of theatres and theatre company members, are one of the most effective forms of social activism—entirely positive.

There can be no doubt that armed conflict is any nation's most traumatic social experience. Therefore, it is also no surprise that the art of theatre, theatre as an institution or a building, has significant social and symbolic functions. In this sense, the work of the theatre transforms the trauma of war into collective art therapy. But on the other hand, the institution of theatre plays a leadership and organisational part in the social life of the habitants.

All this results in the theatre becoming a means of spontaneously arranged social defence, an anthropological defence in the paradigm of military anthropology. Finally, and most importantly, and worth noting, theatre art documents, reconstructs, and re-frames social emotions concerning specific events, eternalising them in the collective memory, influencing the strategic culture of a nation, ethnic group, or society. This function cannot be underestimated.

References

Bajki Severa. 'The Luhansk Regional Theatre.' Accessed July 30, 2022. https://ukrlugteatr.com.

Boroch, Robert. 2016. 'Agresja–wojna antropologiczna a nauki o kulturze — wielkie tematy kulturoznawstwa na marginesie krytycznej analizy dyskursu' [Aggression-anthropological warfare and the cultural sciences—the great themes of cultural studies on the margins of critical discourse analysis], *Kultura Bezpieczeństwa. Nauka–Praktyka–Refleksje*, 22: 81–94.

———. 2018. 'Granice agresji i obrony antropologicznej w przestrzeni kultury materialnej Warmii' [The limits of anthropological aggression and defence in the material culture space of Warmia]. In *Wyzwania bezpieczeństwa międzynarodowego w XXI wieku. Bezpieczeństwo społeczno-kulturowe*, edited Marta Gębska and Paweł Majdan, 2: 171–182. Warszawa: Akademia Sztuki Wojennej.

———. 2020. 'Sprzeczności agresji antropologicznej na przykładzie konfliktów kulturowych' [Contradictions of anthropological aggression on the example of cultural conflicts]. In *Wyzwania I zmiany społeczne w XXI wieku*, edited by Aleksandra Surma, Ewelina Chodźko, 40. Lublin: Tygiel.

———. 2021. 'Military Anthropology — Specialisation Frame.' *Wiedza Obronna*, 274(1): 63–73.

Boroch, Robert, and Anna Korzeniowska-Bihun. 2017. 'Ukrainian Theatrical Projects as an Example of Anthropological Defence in Terms of Anthropology as Contemporary Social Warefare.' *Security Dimensions. International & National Studies*, 24: 122–36.

———. 2021. 'Conflict and Performing Arts—Class Act Project—Ukrainian Theatre as an Anthropological Defence.' *Wiedza Obronna*, 274(1): 119–36.

Grytsenko, Oksana. 2016. 'Theatre of reconciliation.' *Kyiv Post*, December 10, 2016. Accessed July 9, 2022. https://www.kyivpost.com/ukraine-politics/theater-of-reconciliation.html.

Harbuziuk, Maiia, 2022. 'Theatre as a Humanitarian Mission: Ukraine's Experience 2022. *Critical Stages/Scènes critiques*, 25. Accessed July 13, 2022. https://www.critical-stages.org/25/theatre-as-a-%ce%b7umanitarian-mission-ukraines-experience-2022/.

IOM UN Migration. 2022. *Ukraine Internal Displacement Report. General Population Survey. Round 4.*

Korzeniowska-Bihun, Anna. 2014. 'Sztuka w czasach zarazy' [Art in the Time of Cholera]. *Teatr*, 10: 12–15.

———. 2021. 'Cultural Projects as a Tool of Anthropological Defence. Ukrainian Example.' *Wiedza obronna*, 274(1): 35–47.

———. 2022a. Unpublished interview with Serhii Dorofieiev. June 30, 2022.

———. 2022b. Unpublished interview with Serhii Dorofieiev. July 26, 2022.

Nalyvayko, L., and A. Furina. 2017. "Pravove zakripleniya statusu vnytrishno peremeshchennykh osib". *Porivnyano-analitychne pravo*, 5: 44–47.

Ostrohliad, Yulia. 2022. 'Serhii Dorofieiev.' *The Théâtre National.* Accessed July 9, 2022. https://www.theatrenational.be/en/articles/2755-serhii-dorofieiev.

Sluzhba bezpeky Ukrayiny. 2022. 'Narodnyj milicioner DNR vojuvav proty vlasnoho syna i rozstriluvav z tankiv budynky v Severodonec'ku'. Accessed July 30, 2022. https://www.youtube.com/watch?v=C5GCg5QOvtw.

Sopova, Alisa. 2018. 'Teatr vijny: psykhodramatychnyy proiekt, yakyy dopomahaye ukrayinciam podolaty travmu.' *Krytyka*, 2. Accessed July 9, 2022. https://krytyka.com/ua/articles/teatr-viyny-psykhodramatychnyy-proiekt.

UNHCR. 2022. 'Internally Displaced Persons (IDP).' *The UN Refugee Agency*. Accessed July 2, 2022. https://www.unhcr.org/ua/en/internally-displaced-persons.

PART V

Refugees

CHAPTER 41

Spaces and Memories of Migration in Twenty-First-Century Greek Theatre: Station Athens's *I_Left (E_Φυγα)*

Marilena Zaroulia

In the autumn of 2015, as thousands of women, children, and men continued crossing from Turkey to the Greek islands, a photograph went viral: in the East Aegean island of Lesvos, three elderly women—Maritsa Mavrapidi, Aimilia Kamvysi, and Eftratia Mavrapidi—were captured bottle-feeding an one-month-old Syrian baby. The three women were hailed as a symbol of solidarity with refugees and were nominated for the 2016 Nobel Peace Prize. Reporters noted that the family of two of the 'Lesvos grannies' had fled Turkey in the 1920s, drawing parallels between two moments of displacement: the 1920s and the current 'European refugee crisis' context. This chapter focuses on a theatre project that aimed to engage with these two moments: *E_Φυγα (I_Left)* featured two promenade performances (*I_Left Elefsina* and *I_Left Mikrasia*) devised by Station Athens Group, conceived for and performed in the city of Elefsina.

The performances engaged with two waves of migration to Greece: the first wave was precipitated by conflicts in the Middle East and Sub-Saharan Africa and gathered momentum in the summer of 2015. The second one, what Greek history books record as the 'Asia Minor Disaster,' refers to the culmination of the 1919–1922 war between Greece and the then newly established Turkish nation-state with the burning of the port of Smyrna (today, the Turkish city of Izmir), a multicultural hub that hosted Greek, Armenian, and Jewish

M. Zaroulia (✉)
The Royal Central School of Speech and Drama, University of London, London, UK
e-mail: Marilena.Zaroulia@cssd.ac.uk

© The Author(s), under exclusive license to Springer Nature Switzerland AG 2023
Y. Meerzon, S. E. Wilmer (eds.), *The Palgrave Handbook of Theatre and Migration*, https://doi.org/10.1007/978-3-031-20196-7_41

communities for centuries. That war forced thousands of Asia Minor Greeks to flee and ended in 1923 with the compulsory exchange and relocation of Greek-Orthodox populations from Asia Minor to Greece and of Muslim populations from northern Greece to Turkey.

I_Left centres the stories of migrants and 'second- and third-generation migrants' locating them in sites of everyday life, challenging perceptions of the migrant as Other. Space and location are crucial for understanding this project. Writing about the figure of the migrant as 'stranger,' Emma Cox draws on Michel de Certeau's definition of space 'as human practices, relations and perceptions within it' (quoted in Cox 2014, 3–4); space is the place that we inhabit and build relations, the place that is '*practiced*' (de Certeau 1984, 117; emphasis original). I follow Cox's conceptualization of migration as a spatialized practice, not only because 'migrant' is someone who moves (by choice or by force) from one country to another. Migration is a spatialized practice because it is intertwined with storytelling, another kind of 'spatial practice.' Stories 'traverse and organize places; they select and link them together; they make sentences and itineraries out of them. They are spatial trajectories' (1984, 115). This chapter reads *I_Left* as performing spatial trajectories in the context of twenty-first-century Greece. It is concerned with how site-specific theatre, a genre that is ostensibly the opposite of mobility and yet 'has the tools to enable a re-imagining of what it means to live in a mobile world' (Wilkie 2012, 204), engenders migrant identities in a specific space and time, negotiating politics and histories of migration.

I begin with a brief overview of the Greek socio-political landscape in the 2010s before I turn my attention to dramaturgies of migration and particularly testimony and documentary theatre. I situate the work of Station Athens Group within this genre, a theatre made *by* and *for* migrants-experts, and I explore how *I_Left* invites audiences to consider migration as a lived experience. I argue that the two productions (as well as an earlier version of *I_Left* that I briefly touch on) mobilize memories as stories, highlighting migrancy as a practice of everyday life, beyond discourses of crisis, and 'state of exception' policies.

Greece as Borderland

According to modern Greek studies scholar Dimitris Tziovas, 'diaspora, exile, immigration represent three successive phases in modern Greek history' and as such they can 'serve as useful vantage points from which to analyse changes in Greek society, politics and culture' (2009, 1). Greek theatre in the second half of the twentieth century mediated these experiences of displacement, including the arrival, slow integration, and intergenerational trauma among Greeks of Asia Minor; playwrights of the 1960s and 1970s represented experiences of political refugees who emigrated to Eastern Europe after the Civil War (1944–1949) or Greek 'guest workers' in Germany, Australia, and the US in the 1950s and 1960s. Since the end of the Cold War, Tziovas observes, Greece transformed from 'a country of emigrants' to a 'host to migrants' (8), largely due to the growing arrivals of people from the Balkans and the former Eastern Bloc, some of whom were Christian Orthodox of Greek ethnic origin, descendants of the Civil War refugees. Plays engaging with the figure of the migrant in the second half of the twentieth and early twenty-first centuries, include Iakovos Kampanellis's *Η αυλή των θαυμάτων* (The Backyard of Miracles), Loula Anagnostakis's *Νίκη* (Victory), *Ο Ουρανός Κατακόκκινος* (Deep Red Sky), and *Σε εσάς που με ακούτε* (To You Who are Listening to Me), Vasilis Katsikonouris's *Το Γάλα* (Milk), and Lena Kitsopoulou's *Άουστρας, ή Η αγριάδα* (Austras or the Couch Grass).

Since the early 2000s, the country saw an acceleration of migrants' arrivals. According to the United Nations Refugee Agency's estimates, 119,700 refugees and asylum seekers have settled in Greece since 2015 (UNHCR 2021) and migrants' main countries of origin were Syria, Afghanistan, Iraq, Eritrea, and Somalia. Most migrants, who undertook perilous sea crossings to arrive in Greece, saw the country as a stepping stone to 'Europe.' However, the European Union's (EU) border policies—and particularly the Dublin Regulation, which determined under what terms any EU member-state should assume responsibility for an asylum application made by a third-country national—meant that asylum seekers often remained in Greece indefinitely, held in unsuitable and overcrowded refugee camps while waiting for their asylum claim to be processed.

The 2015 'refugee crisis' coincided with the so-called 'Greek Eurozone crisis' that had started in 2010 when the Greek government sought the intervention of the International Monetary Fund and the European Central Bank to tackle the country's public debt. The year 2010 marked the beginning of a decade of harsh austerity and unemployment that precipitated other phenomena, including the rise of the far-right, xenophobia, and racist attacks against migrants, as well as a significant increase in grassroots, activist, pro-migrant movements. Writing about this complex decade, political theorist Stathis Kouvelakis approaches the 'refugee' and 'Eurozone crises' as interconnected. He recognizes that, historically, Greece has occupied a borderland position:

> European, but not quite Western; Christian, but neither Catholic nor Protestant; the alleged original site of European culture, but also, for many centuries, part of an Islamic multi-ethnic empire; peripheral and 'backward', but economically inextricable from the Western core of the continent; dependent and dominated, but never part of the modern colonized world—Greece appears as a true embodiment of those tensions. (2018, 5)

That borderland position of the country took on different socio-political significance during the 2010s, not only because Greece was perceived as the 'bridge' to Europe but also because of a new function that was attributed to the Greek state. Kouvelakis argues that debt and dispossession were mobilized in ways that shaped Greece into a 'neo-colonial state,' placing the country in the vanguard of EU border (necro)politics and simultaneously rendering it a testing ground for austerity policies, not too dissimilar to the interventions on Global South economies. The country's geographical location and its history in the Mediterranean Sea, 'an intricate site of encounters and currents' (Chambers 2008, 32), were crucial in this development. Greece's crossroads position became a 'predicament'; as discussed later on, Elefsina, where *I_Left* was staged, exemplifies this predicament. Hence, by writing about the state of play in Greece in the mid-2010s, I am also alluding to broader EU border politics. To borrow Etienne Balibar's words, I approach Europe as 'the name of a problem' and Greece as one of 'Europe's centres,' because of 'the current problems concentrated there' (quoted in Calotychos 2013, 5); Station Athens's work offers insight into these interconnected problems.

DRAMATURGIES OF MIGRATION: THE MIGRANT-EXPERT

Against this background, Greek theatre of the 2010s saw a proliferation of performances that tackled migrant experiences, shifting the narrative from works of fiction, like the plays I mentioned in the previous section, to documentary theatre which often presents the 'migration crisis' beyond the oversaturated narrative of 'humanitarian crisis,' highlighting instead the biopolitical and structural mechanisms that perpetuate the problem. A new generation of theatremakers, including Anestis Azas, Martha Bouziouri, Yolanda Markopoulou, Georgia Mavragani, and Prodromos Tsinikoris, turned their attention to testimonies of displaced Others, attempting to offer some agency to migrant performers to 'express a profound anxiety about belonging as well as a desire for integration into Greek society' (Fragkou 2018, 319). In fact, some of these theatremakers have migrant backgrounds themselves: Tsinikoris was born to a family of *Gastarbeiters* in Germany and returned to Greece in his teenage years; Markopoulou's family is from Asia Minor and the director has recognized that autobiographical element is significant for the development of *I_Left* (Markopoulou 2019). Moreover, in the past, Markopoulou, Tsinikoris, and Azas had all worked with Rimini Protokoll; the German theatre collective's approach to a 'theatre of experts' and the politics of making theatre drawing on everyday life clearly had an impact on the Greek makers' approach to the representation of the migrant as an expert.

Another element that is important to note about this wave of documentary work is that the migrant who appeared on Greek theatre stages after 2010 was often racially marked as Other. In doing so, theatremakers responded to nationalist and fascist propaganda that framed that migrant body as a threat triggering (and, in some cases, legitimizing) racist, anti-migrant attacks. Documentary theatre sets out to challenge the ostensible threat that a dark-skinned migrant body carries by centring them and their stories onstage; in doing so, such works can expose how migrants have always been framed as 'strangers,' 'not as that which we fail to recognize, but as that which we have already recognised as "a stranger" ' (Ahmed 2000, 3).

Station Athens Group is exemplary of this new wave in Greek migrant dramaturgies. The group emerged out of the non-governmental organization AMAKA, which in 2010 set up Synergy-o, a workshop space for applied arts, open to asylum seekers, migrants, and refugees. Drawing on art therapy and led by director Markopoulou, the workshop space offered migrants (particularly, younger generations) an opportunity to develop skills in artistic practice (such as photography, film, and visual arts) as well as to learn the Greek language and build a social network. Participants 'explor[ed] found material, creat[ed] scenes based on source work, [...] and analys[ed] texts' (Fedda et al. 2016). Synergy-o, located in Metaxourgeio, one of the most racially and ethnically diverse neighbourhoods in Athens, offered an experimental space not only for the exploration of migrants' narratives but crucially of what an arts-led intervention for the integration of migrant communities might look like and the impact such an intervention could make. A core of performers emerged and the company explored experiences, themes, and spaces of migrancy, by means of dramaturgies interweaving autobiographical testimonies and dramatic texts—for example, Aeschylus's *The Persians* in *We Are the Persians!* (2015)—or specific locations, like Elefsina in *I_Left*.

Notwithstanding the ethical pitfalls and challenges that documentary theatre posits, theatremaker and anthropologist Bouziouri has argued that this genre can challenge the dominant framing of the refugee as victim, a narrative that is designed to elicit sympathy but ultimately perpetuates problematic conceptions of the refugee as Other. Indeed, in works such as *I_Left*,

> [r]efugees are no longer a distant, abstract or stereotyped amalgam of what we hear, read or watch; they are lovers, relatives, friends, people we admire, like or dislike. In this way, the stage challenges the 'victimhood label' as the only possible identity and can, hopefully, become a space for restored normalcy. (2019, 98)

What distinguishes the work of Station Athens is a desire to offer glimpses into a more hopeful, yet not romanticized, experience of life after the migrants' arrival. Writing about *We Are the Persians!*, Marios Chatziprokopiou proposes that the performers' references to positive experiences since their arrival should not be understood as a simplistic happy end. Drawing on Walter Benjamin's conceptualization of the 'angel of history,' Chatziprokopiou argues that the traumas and mourning of the past transcend the present and become a memory to be carried and reckoned with (2018, 132). For example, in *We Are the Persians!*, one actor sang a lullaby that his grandmother used to sing, transposing that memory of the past on the present, engaging with loss in a new way. I understand this moment in performance, where the song—like a story—works as a 'spatial trajectory' connecting here and elsewhere, as significant because it bears the potential of highlighting a common experience between a (Greek) spectator and performer (migrant 'Other').

That search for a common ground or what Marissia Fragkou calls a 'space for [...] surprising reconfigurations of exile, identity, and belonging that may challenge assumptions about the "stranger" ' (2018, 319) is key in *I_Left*, particularly for examining the work's engagement with the complex entanglement of site, memory, and migration. Both performances highlight the potential of documentary theatre or, more loosely speaking, the theatre that draws on real events and everyday life to stage 'a process of remembrance,' 'to ask how we remember' (Azas and Tsinikoris 2017, 264), and to negotiate the politics of remembering—as individuals and as a nation.

LOCATING MIGRANCY: *I_LEFT*

I_Left Elefsina (June 2018) and *I_Left Mikrasia* (June 2019) were staged as a part of *Synoikismos Festival*, which was established in 2018 as part of the programme of Elefsina 2021 European Capital of Culture. The festival took place in the northern part of Elefsina, in the refugee settlement set up in 1922 to host (initially) 2500 forcefully displaced Greeks of Asia Minor, a term that refers to the Western coast of Turkey and in Greek is called *Mikrasia* or *Anatolia*. This is the geographical space of ancient Ionia, homeland of writers including Homer, Sappho, Thales, and Herodotus; to this day, the refugee settlement remains in the area where their descendants live. The festival aimed to use that space as a trigger for the convergence of past and present histories, considering twenty-first-century issues as well as celebrating the histories of migrant communities. *I_Left* was programmed alongside visual arts and live art projects, performance installations, and workshops, all of which negotiated the relation between memory and history, belonging and displacement. In 2018, performances included *Routes on Roots* by Osmosis theatre group, a work that offered residents the opportunity to tell their stories, considering what has changed in the area in the past century; the site-specific installation *Beforelight* that examined the ruins of the urban environment, particularly deserted buildings; Tania El Khoury and Bazel Zaara's one-to-one performance *As Far as My Fingertips Take Me* and Dictaphone Group's *Bunker*—both these projects stemmed from work alongside refugees from the Middle East, specifically Syria. A similar thematic underpinned the programme in 2019, with more projects examining the impact of the Syrian War (such as El Khoury's *Gardens Speak*). Performances took place either in public space or in people's homes—they were all designed to happen beyond the traditional theatrical frame, making that neighbourhood, the site, the festival's protagonist.

Space is a crucial element for Station Athens, shaping dramaturgy, offering opportunities to complement testimonies and documentary material. Speaking about *I_Left Mikrasia*, Markopoulou recognizes that when attempting to compose a narrative from such rich yet disconnected stories of real people, it is vital to 'reimagine the space, the site, in a dynamic way' and to frame it as 'situation' that triggers people to share their stories (Harami 2020). The site emerged as a dramatic character—because of its history and related memories—or it was framed in a fictional way that served the narrative; in either case, the site became a connecting element in the piece's dramaturgies which relied on the interweaving of the past (in Asia Minor or the Middle East) and the present (in the Elefsina refugee settlement).

I_Left Elefsina (2018) stemmed from an earlier version of the work, created and presented in Synergy-o in 2014. That was the group's first fully formed piece, employing 'dramatization and theatricality—with the assistance of set design—to create a performance that overcame the limitations of documentary theatre'; for the 2018 version, 'the story was re-adapted and reshaped for the historic neighbourhood' inviting people to walk around (Mitropoulos 2018) and encounter the migrants mostly in public, outdoors spaces. Experiences from faraway lands—a home in Kabul, a classroom in Bangladesh, an underground room in Tehran—were transposed in this neighbourhood of migrants, pointing at similarities and differences between then and now, tracing spatial trajectories between here and there. The core cast of the group—Chaljl AliZada, Hossain Amiri, Aidim Joyimal, Reza Mohammadi, and Ramzan Mohammad—all of them refugees from Afghanistan, Bangladesh, Iraq, and Pakistan, invited audience to listen to their stories of persecution, arrival, and new beginnings.

Writing about the 2014 version, Natasha Remoundou draws attention to the performance's title. *Efyga* in Greek means 'I left,' but

> the incongruous hyphenation resulting in 'e' and 'fyga' [...] could be read as 'Hey, (Re)fugee' establishing a vocative hail as well as the hint of a dialogue with someone either mocked or unfamiliar for he/she is defined by his/her status as someone who escaped from a place or a situation. (2019, 300)

This semantic ambiguity that Remoundou identifies is crucial for understanding the politics of this project. The work's title shifts the emphasis from the 'vocative hail' addressed to the migrant-fugitive (*fyga*), an aggressive hail that frames the migrant in passive terms, conjuring their identity as a stranger and potential threat, to the active verb *efyga* (*I left*) that centres the migrant's voice and experience.

The 2014 version of *I_Left* involved the audiences in a journey through the company's five-storey building; audiences met the performers in different rooms and had the opportunity to listen to their stories. The same principle applied to the 2018 Elefsina version; however, the indoors, domestic spaces that featured in the 2014 production were replaced by outdoors spaces. For example, one of the performers spoke to the audiences about his father's illness while standing in the middle of a deserted basketball pitch; Reza narrated his fleeing from Afghanistan while sitting outside a house, playing backgammon (a game that was introduced to Greece by Asia Minor migrants); a family shared food around a table at the terrace outside one of the houses. Meanwhile, veiled women walked around the streets, singing and guiding the audiences through the site and the stories. The memory of the past was transposed to a space that was not behind closed doors, as the performance celebrated a culture where the coming together of the community happens in outdoors spaces. In highlighting open, public, or at least accessible spaces as the setting for encounters, *I_Left* advocated for the migrant's visibility in the community, beyond the moment when a migrant has to share their testimony—a testimony that, outside the theatrical frame, can determine the legal framework of their residence.

I_Left staged the performers' past spatialized in sites and doings of everyday life, in the host country; by narrating their stories, they located them in a lived, 'practiced' space. The stories became 'spatial trajectories' that connected Elefsina with locations in the Middle East, complicating perceptions of the migrant as being 'out of place.' Meanwhile, the performance recognized the weight of memories that migrants often carry, as they continue with their lives elsewhere. By situating these stories in specific spaces, *I_Left* interrupted conceptions of migracy as a constant state of crisis and suffering, framing it as a practice of everyday life.

A similar approach emerged in *I_Left Mikrasia*, which opened a year later, celebrating the legacy of Asia Minor Greeks refugees who settled in that neighbourhood in the 1920s. Audiences started their promenade at the local Asia Minor Greeks Museum, which was established by refugees' descendants in 2013 in one of the settlement's oldest houses. The museum hosts a range of artefacts, documents, and materials telling the story of the century-old displacement. During the performance, audiences heard testimonies of fleeing, arrival, and life in the settlement, by eavesdropping conversations happening around the settlement; they encountered a woman opening a suitcase and finding a poem about the lost 'homeland'; they sat at the churchyard and listened to songs; or they came across Thanos Tsakalidis, a young actor-guide to the piece (who, like the director, was also of Asia Minor heritage), having a haircut and listening to the barber's story. Video recordings of interviews conducted during the lengthy research process were projected on the buildings' walls, hinting at how the settlement is continuously marked by narratives of departure and arrival, past and present.

This exploration-juxtaposition of present and past is directly connected to the choice of situating these performances in Elefsina, a 'borderland' site that distils Greece's current, 'borderland' situation. According to the Elefsina European Capital of Culture website, the ancient Greek etymological root of the city's name *Elevsis* signifies 'the arrival of someone notable' as well as terms including 'appearance, emergence, coming, birth, dawn.' Elefsina was 'one of the five most important sacred cities of antiquity, the city of the Elefsinian Mysteries' that celebrated the reunion of goddess Demetra with her daughter Persephone. After the Greek nation-state was established in 1830, Elefsina became a large industrial centre, and—later—home of the biggest oil refineries. However, the 2008 financial crisis led to factories closing and unemployment rising, while the city's industrial harbour remains disused.

Elefsina is a city in transit, a borderland between the ancient and the modern, nature and industry, life and death. Thus, Elefsina presented an apt location for site-specific work that engages with migracy, an ideal space for situating lives in transit but also bearing the potential of 'transcending the traumatic past and offering some comfort' that, according to theatre director and artistic director of the European Capital of Culture Michail Marmarinos, remains the 'task of artistic practice' (Marmarinos 2021). Indeed, *I_Left Mikrasia* offered that sense of comfort by interweaving memories of loss and suffering with a celebration of the distinct refugee identity that Asia Minor Greeks have built since their arrival a century ago. Women sang, danced, cooked; audiences sat on traditional carpets; artefacts from the museum were shared. Like in the 2018 iteration of *I_Left*, migrancy emerged as an everyday practice, spatialized in this neighbourhood, embedded in the history of the Greek nation.

The history of Elefsina, a key element for the performance's dramaturgy, was highlighted by including footage of Filippos Koutsaftis's documentary film *Αγέλαστος Πέτρα* (Mourning Rock) (2000). The film follows everyday people's lives in Elefsina in a meditative way, juxtaposing them with the archaeological sites. Described as an 'elegy' (Plantzos 2019), it traces the transformation of Elefsina from a natural site for the goddess of fertility to a dystopian site of modernization and urbanization and their failures. Elefsina emerges 'as a land abandoned to soulless Westernization and the cruelties of capitalism, [and] strikes a chord in his viewers' hearts by alluding to the latent humanity of a homeland almost forgotten' (Plantzos 2019, 352). Two decades after the premiere of Koutsaftis's film, *I_Left* attempted to reclaim that humanity by staging hospitable gestures to those who arrived in Elefsina.

Significantly, *I_Left* moved beyond entrusting audiences with migrants' stories, inviting a more proximate encounter with them. Audiences of *I_Left* embarked on a journey of sorts, walking through the streets of the refugee settlement, encountering migrants and their descendants. Although not conceived as 'processional aesthetics,' 'an embodied practice responsive to refugees' that gathered pace in the wake of the 'refugee crisis' (Cox 2017, 479), often enacted through community solidarity marches, *I_Left* had a similar quality: walking through the old refugee settlement, with others, in silence or while listening to music, bear a symbolic significance. This act of walking could both reanimate the location's history, drawing connections with contemporary movements of migrants across borders; when invited to walk along, audiences were invited to take part in the 'spatial syntaxes' (de Certeau, 115) of the migrants' stories, momentarily transcending the imagery of migrants' crossings that had dominated international media. Thus, the promenade, site-specific dramaturgy of *I_Left* questioned the established dynamic, whereby the migrant is the one who moves and seen moving and proposed a different way of encountering and apprehending recent newcomers by remembering past arrivals and the lives they built.

I_Left is an important example of recent Greek 'migration theatre' because it demonstrates the potential that emerge when documentary theatre, a 'public forum for discussion of the recent past as well as a place to expose current issues' (Wilmer 2018, 84), is situated in spaces—like Elefsina—that point at connections across migrant histories. I began this chapter with an instance where the parallel between the 'Asia Minor disaster' and the 2015 'European refugee crisis' was brought up to highlight the across-time continuity between 'human tragedies' and to make sense of people's attitudes towards the migrant. *I_Left* returned to this continuity and the narrative-parallel between the two historical moments not to essentialize or depoliticize the twenty-first-century situation and its specificity. Instead, the project raised the question 'how do we remember?'—a question that, as noted earlier, is key for theatre practitioners who draw on everyday life. *I_Left* spatializes a 'process of remembrance' to suggest a way of moving forward, inviting audiences to commit not only to listening but also to co-habitation. By framing migrancy as a practice that has shaped everyday life, Station Athens's work highlights how new migrants continue to shape the spaces that we—migrants and hosts—(can) all inhabit together.

References

Ahmed, Sara. 2000. *Strange Encounters: Embodied Others in Post-Coloniality*. London: Routledge.

Azas, Azas and Prodromos Tsinikoris. 2017. '"Shifting the gaze": Azas and Tsinikoris in conversation with Philip Hager.' Translated by Philip Hager and Marissia Fragkou. *Journal of Greek Media and Culture*, 3(2): 259–72.

Bouziouri, Martha. 2019. 'Dramaturgies of the "Other": Self-Making and Sense-Making in Contemporary Documentary Theatre.' *FKW*, 66: 87–100.

Calotychos, Vangelis. 2013. *The Balkan Prospect: Identity, Culture and Politics in Greece After 1989*. London: Palgrave.

Chambers, Iain. 2008. *Mediterranean Crossings: The Politics of an Interrupted Modernity*. Durham: Duke University Press.

Cox, Emma. 2014. *Theatre & Migration*. London: Palgrave.

———. 2017. 'Processional Aesthetics and Irregular Transit: Envisioning Refugees in Europe,' *Theatre Journal*, 69(4): 477-96.

Chatziprokopiou, Marios. 2018. 'Είμαστε οι Πέρσες! Επινοώντας εκ νέου τη θρηνητική φωνή του αρχαίου δράματος,' *σκηνή*, 10: 116–38.

De Certeau, Michel. 1984. *The Practice of Everyday Life*. Translated by Steven F. Randall. Los Angeles: University of California Press.

Fedda, Yasmin, Daniel Gorman, and Tory Davidson. 2016. 'Creation and Displacement: Developing New Narratives Around Migration,' *IETM Mapping*. https://www.ietm.org/system/files/publications/ietm_creation-and-displacement.pdf. Accessed 26 July 2023.

Fragkou, Marissia. 2018. 'Strange Homelands: Encountering the Migrant on the Contemporary Greek stage.' *Modern Drama*, 61(3): 301–27.

Harami, Stella. 2020. 'Το θέατρο της ελληνικής πραγματικότητας τώρα δικτυώνεται.' *monopoli*, September 11, 2020. Accessed June 25, 2021. https://www.monopoli.gr/2020/09/11/istories/epikaira/413647/to-theatro-tis-ellinikis-pragmatikotitas-tora-diktyonetai/.

Kouvelakis, Stathis. 2018. 'BORDERLAND: Greece and the EU's Southern Question,' *New Left Review*, 110(2): 5-33.

Markopoulou, Yolanda. 2019. 'Interview with K. Parri.' *elculture.gr*, June 20, 2019. Accessed June 25, 2021. https://www.elculture.gr/blog/article/giolanta-markopoulou-mikrasia/.

Marmarinos, Michael. 2021. 'Η Ελευσίνα είναι ένα παγόβουνο. Βλέπουμε μόνο την επιφάνεια.' *euronews*, February 2, 2021, Accessed June 25, 2021. https://gr.euronews.com/2021/02/02/michael-marmarinos-i-elefsina-einai-ena-pagovouno-vlepoume-mono-tin-epifaneia.

Mitropoulos, George. 2018. 'Ελευσίνα 2021: Πρώτη της δράση το φεστιβάλ «Συνοικισμός».' *euronews*, June 14, 2018. Accessed June 25, 2021. https://gr.euronews.com/2018/06/14/sinikismos-elefsina-festival-politistiki-protevousa.

Plantzos, Dimitris. 2019. 'The Past as Present in the Films of Filippos Koutsaftis.' *Journal of Modern Greek Studies*, 37(2): 327–59.

Remoundou, Natasha. 2019. 'Intercultural Performance Ecologies in the Making: Minor(ity) Theatre and the Greek Crisis.' In *Interculturalism and Performance Now: New Directions?*, edited by Charlotte McIvor and Jason King, 283–309. London: Palgrave.

Tziovas, Dimitris. 2009. *Greek Diaspora and Migration since 1700: Society, Politics, Culture*. London: Ashgate.

Wilkie, Fiona. 2012. 'Site Specific Performance and the Mobility Turn' *Contemporary Theatre Review*, 22(2): 203–12.

Wilmer, S.E. 2018. *Performing Statelessness in Europe*. Cham: Palgrave Macmillan.

UNHCR. 2021. 'Greece.' *Global Focus: UNHCR Operations Worldwide*. Accessed June 25, 2021. https://reporting.unhcr.org/greece.

CHAPTER 42

Troubled Waters: The Representation of Refugees in Maltese Theatre

Marco Galea

INTRODUCTION

Malta is at the centre of one of the most important migration routes through the Mediterranean, and the presence of migrants and asylum seekers in the country is a hotly contested political issue in Malta. As will be explained, there has been very limited integration of migrants into Maltese society, and migrants' participation in cultural life is almost non-existent. One would expect the Maltese artistic community to at least take up the migrants' cause and try to give them a voice. This has happened only to a limited extent through painting, photography, poetry, and fiction. However, and of course this is my main concern, migration is hardly ever taken up as subject matter in theatre, whether in the mainstream or in fringe and experimental theatre. While trying to understand the reasons for this near invisibility, this chapter will discuss a small number of performances which took place in Malta during the last decade that speak directly about the issue of migration in the Maltese islands in the context of political and theatrical realities in the country.

CONTEXT

The small size of the three inhabited Maltese Islands has always been linked with a fragility of the eco-system and vulnerability to any outside intervention, usually in the form of colonization. The population of the islands has lived with

M. Galea (✉)
University of Malta, Msida, Malta
e-mail: marco.galea@um.edu.mt

© The Author(s), under exclusive license to Springer Nature Switzerland AG 2023
Y. Meerzon, S. E. Wilmer (eds.), *The Palgrave Handbook of Theatre and Migration*, https://doi.org/10.1007/978-3-031-20196-7_42

migration for much of their history, whether that be through Malta's population being sold off in other lands as slaves or as economic migrants to North Africa or Australia when the islands could not support all the inhabitants.

During the twenty-first century, however, it has been inbound migration which has often made the news in Malta. Since its accession to the European Union in 2004, the country (a British colony until 1964) has had a remarkably successful economy and has attracted migrant workers, mainly from the EU, to fill vacancies in many economic activities, from construction to gaming, from hospitality to transportation. Besides, like many Western countries, it regularly needs to recruit hundreds of medical professionals and carers from outside the EU, without whose contribution the public health system and old-age care sector would probably collapse. During the same period, Malta has seen a relatively steady flow of migrants reaching the shores on board small boats, or more commonly brought on land after being rescued in Maltese territorial waters by the national armed forces or by vessels belonging to humanitarian organizations working in the Mediterranean. Between 2002 and 2012, 16,617 people arrived in this way, but UNHCR estimated that only around 30% were still in Malta as of 2012 (UNHCR 2015). Numbers of migrant arrivals remained relatively stable during the last decade.

Within the country, citizens consider migration to be one of the major challenges that the country faces, regularly eclipsing corruption or environmental issues in surveys (see European Commission 2016, 6). Mainstream politicians compete to be seen as defenders of the country against migrants, and very little is done to integrate refugees already in the country. They are often underemployed, exploited, and given little protection by the state (Farrugia 2019, 24; *Times of Malta* 2021).

Malta has the habit of turning up at every controversy and tragedy involving migration in the Mediterranean, whether it is for sending back migrants to Eritrea when it was not safe to do so, to end up being tortured (Amnesty International 2004, 30–31) or for its repressive detention policy, for its threat to start a 'pushback' policy, or for its decision to accept the corpses retrieved after tragic crossings, but not any of the survivors. The COVID-19 pandemic made matters worse for asylum seekers as—even when saved in Maltese territorial waters and, therefore, becoming the direct responsibility of the Maltese state—several groups were refused entry into Maltese harbours (Scicluna 2020; Daily Sabah 2020).

Needless to say, migrants are practically invisible in the cultural sphere. Their marginality in Maltese society guarantees that they play no active role in cultural life and are only ever brought in to represent their origins in feel-good multicultural festivities which usually focus on food. The migrant and post-migrant theatre that has become an important voice in the theatrical scene of countries like Germany or Sweden is inconceivable in Malta. It is not an exaggeration to say that the public performances involving migrants that the general Maltese public enjoys most watching are the deportations of failed asylum seekers and the departures of flights resettling migrants and refugees in other countries, spectacles which feature regularly on national television news and in newspaper reports.

HALF-SISTER ISLANDS: MALTA AND LAMPEDUSA

There have been only a handful of Maltese theatrical events dealing with the issue of migration in the last ten years. Most were small-scale productions based on migrant narratives, some using a verbatim theatre method. The notable exception was the Maltese production of Anders Lustgarten's *Lampedusa*, staged in 2016 at the St. James Cavalier Theatre in Valletta, directed by Herman Grech and performed by Mikhail Basmadjan and Pia Zammit. In this full-length play written for British theatre, one of the two speaking characters is a fisherman-turned-lifeguard on the island of Lampedusa, an island very close to Malta but forming part of the Italian Republic. As Lampedusa and Malta both have regular and direct encounters with migration, the play struck a chord with Maltese audiences. It was performed both in the original English and in a Maltese translation, as well as in a version where the Italian coastguard spoke Maltese and the Syrian second-generation migrant in the UK (changed from the original Chinese) spoke English. It is interesting that what was probably the hardest-hitting play about migration to be performed in Malta to date was written by someone who does not live in Malta or in the Mediterranean. When the play was performed in the UK, it was criticized as not considering the economic cost of migration on southern European countries (Billington 2015) and for misrepresenting the agency that the inhabitants of Lampedusa have in their encounter with migration (Zagaria 2015). However, when it was performed in Malta, it was seen as a brave and honest discussion of the issue, especially in the light of the hostility regularly shown publicly towards migrants (Wilmer 2018, 64–65).

The significance of the production of *Lampedusa* in Malta has, therefore, to be understood in the context of the dearth of other performances which discuss the issue. During the past decade, very few other theatrical productions have tackled migration as their main topic. The annual satirical performance *Bla Kondixin* (No Conditions), one of the best-followed theatrical events in Malta, often has skits light-heartedly critiquing the treatment of migrants and refugees in Malta. Other productions have always been small scale and generally involved up-and-coming artists or were led by people who are not directly involved in the arts. One example of this trend is *Limbo*, a verbatim piece about migration and integration created by young artists and performed for free during 2016. Another small-scale production was a performance of Heather Raffo's partly verbatim play *9 Parts of Desire*, as part of a project led by human rights organization Aditus in 2012 (Delicata 2012). This play, about nine women from Iraq or of Iraqi descent, many of whom are displaced, focused on the plight women find themselves in because of war. The larger project also included a photography exhibition of portraits of women, one of whom was an Eritrean migrant who told her story of suffering and migration (Tabone and

Falzon 2012). The performers in the play, however, were all ethnic Maltese, implicitly highlighting the invisibility of migrants from the Maltese stage. In recent years, no other performances of note have taken place in Malta that tackled migration. Indeed, in 2019, the London-based refugee Phosphoros Theatre Company had to cancel its shows in Malta, despite having an official invitation, because the travel documents of one of the performers were not recognized, and the troupe was deemed 'suspicious' (Mallia 2019).

I will, therefore, try to explain, first, why theatremakers are not very interested in discussing issues of migration in Malta, and, second, how this void is filled by a specific type of performance and one particular performer who would not consider himself part of the theatre community. As already hinted, migration is a political hot potato in Malta, with the two major political parties, who together represent around 95% of the electorate, competing over who appears more muscular when faced with the phenomenon of migrants reaching, trying to reach, or ending up in Malta. This included detention in buildings with 'inadequate sanitation and hygiene facilities, and allow[ing] no privacy for the detainees' (Aditus 2021). No efforts for integration were made even after refugees and other persons granted lesser forms of protection were released from detention, as authorities have always assumed that migrants would want to leave Malta and made sure they continued to feel that way. Given very limited access to the labour market, and often reduced to live in very poor conditions, many refugees continued to dream of continuing their journey towards northern Europe, a dream often fuelled by the Maltese government's policies of trying to resettle as many of these refugees as possible (Nimführ et al. 2020, 161). These measures have proved quite popular in Malta among all sectors of the population.

In this context, taking a pro-migrant stand is associated with radicalism, anti-nationalism, and even irresponsibility. Besides human rights NGOs and a few public figures, a few artists have made their voice heard over this matter. There are also a good number of poets who have taken stands, but in fiction the issue is rarely debated. My reasoning is that many artists as individuals do have a strong opinion about migration, but it is very difficult to develop artistic products on migration that require the work of multiple artists or the mobilization of substantial resources. Unlike poetry, the publication of fiction is a commercial risk for publishers who would not want to antagonize a large proportion of their readers; likewise, theatre productions require investment that in Malta is often partly covered by corporate sponsorship and depends on spectators turning up for shows to recover costs. It appears that highlighting the issue of migration is an unpopular choice and one that most cultural producers are not keen on making.

Considering the small population of the country, one would assume that alienating that sector of the captive audience that is not comfortable with accepting asylum seekers in the country results in great financial losses. *Lampedusa* was backed by a production company called Unifaun, which had a faithful spectatorship, one that had been trained to expect being made to feel uncomfortable in the theatre, having watched a series of plays in the 'In-Yer-Face' style and other provocative works (Cremona 2016, 247–248). In its original run, it was considered successful, having had a run of ten performances in a theatre that seats a little over a hundred spectators. It would be difficult to imagine plays with more disturbing content, or which breached subjects that would be more directly related to uncomfortable local experiences, going into production.

The Spectacle of Suffering

In his book *Distant Suffering*, originally published in 1993, Luc Boltanski discusses how difficult it has become in contemporary society to bring about compassion through representation. Our obsession with scientific objectivity has created obstacles to manifesting what he calls 'a politics of pity.' He uses the theatre as a metaphor of how the suffering is given a voice and transmitted from actor to spectator (2004, 26). Reading this idea literally, this transfer requires both the detached and impartial a priori position on the part of the spectator as well as his or her investment of emotional, affective, and sentimental energy to become politically committed. We all know the difficulties this process implies. What Boltanski is suggesting is not a catharsis that can be attained through the representation of tragedy in theatre, but the discomfort that would force the spectator to react. In Malta's case, this is not even the 'distant suffering' that Boltanski has in mind, but an immediate, although not personal, suffering. Taking a stand on this suffering means taking the discomfort that the spectator would have felt in the theatre into their own life. Doing something about it implies doing away with some of the privileges that the spectator enjoys as a Western, probably middle-class human being that allow them to be a theatre-goer in the first place. Seen from this angle it is no wonder that theatremakers and spectators have reached a silent consensus not to approach this subject. When the fisherman-turned-coastguard in the Maltese production of *Lampedusa* shines his torch on individual spectators' faces while searching for migrants, living or dead (Wilmer 2018, 65), the spectator is thrown out of their comfort zone bought through the price of a ticket. Following Boltanski's analysis of the reaction required or expected from the spectator when faced with the representation of suffering, they would need to feel pity, to then become indignant as they are unable to take any course of action that would be meaningful for the sufferer whose plight they are watching. This would then lead to anger as the only possible course of action, but as representation (as in theatre) creates a distance between the spectator and the object in the real world that is being represented, anger can only be expressed verbally, therefore demanding an effort from the spectator to shift from being passive to being not only active but also eloquent—that is, performing action that is meaningful (Boltanski 2004, 57). This is a process that the typical theatre-goer will not willingly undertake.

Taking It to the Street

There is, therefore, a gap in the theatrical scene that cannot be filled in by conventional theatre, and this is where the Passaport project comes in. Poet, translator, and human rights activist Antoine Cassar published the long poem *Passaport* as a booklet in the form and size of a typical passport (Cassar 2016). The poem is a declaration of the author's belief that all humans should be treated equally and allowed to move freely around the world without any discrimination arising from their national or economic background (see Cassar 2017). In very vivid language, it denounces the concept of borders as the root of human trafficking and all the abuse that asylum seekers and migrants go through in search of a better life, or simply of a life. The poem was translated into nine other languages and has been performed at many literary festivals, by the author and by other performers. It has also been used as material for several theatre productions, primarily in French-speaking parts of Europe.

However, I would like to focus on a specific event that can best be described as street theatre that took place in 2015 to coincide with the Valletta Summit on Migration in November 2015. This conference saw European leaders meeting African counterparts in an attempt to solve what they saw as the migration crisis in Europe and billions of euros were pledged to convince African governments to make sure their citizens stayed at home, whatever their reasons for wanting to leave.

Ironically, at the same time it was hosting this summit, the Maltese government was being heavily criticized for a scheme it was publicizing as 'Citizenship by Investment' but which critics consistently referred to as 'the selling of Maltese passports' (Rettman 2020). The Maltese government, especially through regular personal appearances by the prime minister of the time at international 'citizenship' fairs and conferences made a case that acquiring Maltese citizenship was a sensible option for anyone who considered themselves as 'ultra-high net worth' and could afford upward of half a million euro upfront. Beyond the benefits of belonging in a successful pro-business country, the advantages were portrayed as including access to unhindered travel and business opportunities in all EU countries.

Thus, at the same moment that Malta was claiming (like the rest of Europe, but a little more vociferously) that migrants were a burden and had to be repelled, it was offering much more than it was denying to asylum seekers to millionaires who did not appear to be in any immediate danger. This irony prompted Antoine Cassar to stage a short performance, at exactly the same time and very close to where the conference was taking place.

Unlike other performances based on the *Passaport* publication, this performance did not involve the author or any other performer using text from the book. Instead, what spectators encountered was a man standing behind a portable table set up as one would set up a stall in a car-boot sale or a flea market. The items on sale were the *Passaport* publications in several languages, with a hand-written sign hanging from the table: 'MALTA GLOBAL

PASSPORT. ONLY €5 (€649,995 discount). All proceeds go to Integra Foundation.' The discount referred to was the difference between the price of the book and the cost of a Citizenship by Investment passport as advertised by the government. During the performance, Cassar could be seen promoting his passports, in a way that was not dissimilar to how any Maltese hawker would try to attract customers, by shouting a description of the items he had for sale. He could be heard repeating, 'You can go wherever you want. No questions asked. No visa. No deportation. No interrogation. No humiliation. Five euros only.' As a backdrop, Cassar had created the slogan 'No Border,' using revolving tiles which are a permanent fixture of Pjazza Teatru Rjal (Borg 2017, 84). This site used to be Malta's largest theatre until it was bombed during World War II. It was recently transformed into an open-air performance space which has limited possibilities for live theatre. It is the theatre which does not speak, and therefore allows for the theatricality to happen outside its doors, literally on its doorstep.

Conventional theatre has to engage with spectators who form part of society as it is now. Theatre itself is a part of that society and depends on the survival of society as it is for its own existence, or at least it is very difficult to think of an alternative reality. What Cassar's poetry and his street performances do is bypass all these relationships and engage directly with his readers and (few) spectators, as well as the thousands of people who must have watched the performance online as it was picked up by *The Times of Malta* website. Cassar does not need to apply for funding or in any way converse with the agencies that form part of the same state apparatus that he sees as the source of the problem he wants to challenge. In doing so, he is able to move towards what Giorgio Agamben sees as the unavoidable future of the world, one where states no longer exist, where categories of people dissolve and where the only 'thinkable figure' will be that of the refugee (2008, 90).

THE REFUGEE WRIT LARGE

The refugee is also the unlikely protagonist of a theatre production that could not be more different from Cassar's street theatre. As one of the main events of the Valletta European Capital of Culture in 2018, the foundation in charge of the programme commissioned an opera by its own artistic director, Mario Philip Azzopardi. Azzopardi is a successful stage and television director who has been a prominent figure in the Maltese cultural scene during the last decade (Galea 2019, 105–108). However, he has often courted controversy by making public statements that were considered to be Islamophobic or misogynist. One of these statements was a Facebook comment referring to a young woman as 'a sorry bitch' for organizing a protest in central London against the Maltese government's 'Citizenship by Investment' scheme while the Maltese prime minister was attending a gala dinner in the area to advertise the scheme (*The Malta Independent* 2018). A number of comments targeted Islam, equating it with Sharia law and calling Muslims 'idiots' who were 'tied to a set of rules written 1500 years ago' (Martin 2014). His choice as artistic director of the Valletta European of Culture organization was, therefore, criticized from several quarters. His role as librettist and director of the opera *Aħna Refuġjati* (We Are Refugees) was all the more problematic, also as being one of the few offerings in the Valletta 18 programme to seem to be offering clear political content, besides being, by Maltese standards, a very expensive production, costing the Valletta 2018 foundation almost €400,000 and only recouping €16,000 in ticket sales (Parliament of Malta 2018).

The opera is set between an unnamed war-torn country, populated by Muslims, and another unnamed European country, and its plot revolves around a family who witness atrocities within their community and decides to seek refuge in Europe. The general theme is mercy: the mercy that is missing in the refugees' motherland and which they seek in Europe, only to be met with exploitation, walls of indifference, and hostility. The libretto is clearly sympathetic with the plight of refugees and shows them as victims of situations they have no control over. However, the way the refugee problem is framed as an issue that arises simply because of Islamic fundamentalism is problematic. People flee because they see their peaceful neighbours executed in the name of Allah (Azzopardi 2018, 1–2), and this in turn is seen as the absence of mercy in that society. No other explanations are given for the exodus of migrants towards the European coasts of the Mediterranean. The perilous journey of the migrants is condensed into a representation of their crossing the Mediterranean in a crowded boat, where the mother and one of the daughters lose their lives, to be rescued and taken to a facility that seems to be modelled on Malta's infamous detention centres (Global Detention Project 2021), where the little dignity they had left is taken away from them. Further violence and death leads the refugees to make a collective decision to return to their homeland. In the last scene we see the refugees—who after many of the named characters die are seen simply as a crowd and speak as a chorus—perform a very decisive and simple action: 'Refugees enter with their luggage, ready to start their journey back home' (Azzopardi 2018, 18).

Perhaps it is the decision to treat this sensitive material through opera that leads to actions and motivations to be seen as oversimplified and unproblematized. Just like the journey to Europe was represented as a simple, if perilous, trip, the return journey is dramatized just as simply. In terms of text, there are only a few lines between the decision to leave Europe and the final scene with the refugees carrying their luggage. This finale to the opera makes two strong statements, one which is overt and the other which is more covert. The first one is that refugees will never be integrated in European society, as the society they came from and the one they found themselves in are too different. Despite the text repeating utopic slogans about a world where colour and race do not have any significance, the clash between a theocratic non-European society and a secular Europe was highlighted in the first production of this opera, especially through a scene where the refugees were exposed to a series of tableaux depicting clubbing. This difference between cultures is cynically exploited in the opera by a xenophobic character to foment trouble, but it is also reflected fatalistically as a truism. The second claim that the finale of the opera is making is that for refugees it is easy to return home. The war they had escaped from and that would have destroyed whatever was left of their community is no longer considered an impediment. On the contrary, the last surviving member of the family we saw making the journey at the beginning of the opera speaks for the whole refugee community when she states that their place is in the homeland.

These sentiments are admirable coming from a young refugee, but they are also very comforting for those Europeans who believe that each country should solve its own problems. As recently as May 2021, the Office of the United Nations High Commissioner for Human Rights, in a damning report, documented cases where the armed forces of Malta, rather than rescuing migrants in the Maltese Search and Rescue Zone, tried to guide them towards Lampedusa or deterred them from approaching Malta through other ways (UNHRC 2021, 15–16, 23). The army is also entrusted with running detention centres in which migrants are kept, often for many months after their arrival. Claims of inhumane conditions, as well as of physical and mental violence, are made on a regular basis. The report quoted above even records a migrant interviewee declaring 'that some detention centre guards have taunted migrant detainees saying "go ahead, kill yourselves" ' (33). The opera, therefore, while substantially reaffirming the difficulties refugees face in Malta, offers no solution except their return to the homeland, which is exactly the position of anti-migrant activists.

Another issue that one needs to consider when discussing this opera is representation. Edward Said defines 'orientalism' as the body of works created by the West to represent, and ultimately to control, the East. The justification for the creation of this body of works is that the East cannot represent itself, and therefore needs to be represented by the West (Said 1995, ix, 6). This opera seems to be a continuation of the reasoning that created orientalism, even if unconsciously. As we have said, Azzopardi was both librettist and director, while the music was composed by a tandem of a Maltese and a British musician. All the cast is made up of European artists, and there is no reference in the programme to any non-European person (or indeed any person at all) who was consulted with regards to the way refugees are represented. With all its good intentions, the opera becomes another example of the West's perceived superiority over the East, as well as its inability to engage with their problems. The opera's finale, with the refugees deciding to go back home, could even be seen as a triumph for prevalent policies within the EU of trying to displace the refugee problem out of European territory, rather than making a meaningful contribution to address the causes that force people to attempt the perilous crossing across the Mediterranean. That it happens to be the largest-scale (and in many senses the most official) offering about the subject coming from a country that has been at the centre of the discourse on migration in the European continent for decades is even more problematic.

Conclusion

Malta's encounter with refugees in recent decades has been a troubled one. In many ways, refugees and asylum seekers have become society's others, taking the blame for much that is wrong in the country. As I have tried to demonstrate, Maltese theatre has been generally reluctant to address this issue. Thankfully, unlike mainstream media like television and some newspapers, theatre has not been a part of this othering. However, with only a handful of performances which speak about migration over a ten-year period, the difficulty that Maltese theatre has in engaging with migration is evident. This difficulty perhaps reflects Malta's unwillingness to transform itself into a society that is more open to diversity. It is also a reflection of theatre's interrelatedness with society, on which it depends for its existence, whether it comes from funding that is taxpayers' money or from money spent directly and voluntarily by theatre-goers.

References

Aditus. 2021. 'Conditions in Detention Facilities: Malta.' *Asylum Information Database*. Accessed June 6, 2021. https://asylumineurope.org/reports/country/malta/detention-asylum-seekers/detention-conditions/conditions-detention-facilities/.

Agamben, Giorgio. 2008. 'Beyond Human Rights.' *Social Engineering*, 15: 90–95.

Amnesty International. 2004. 'Eritrea: "You Have No Right to Ask"—Government Resists Scrutiny on Human Rights.' Accessed June 6, 2021. https://www.amnesty.org/download/Documents/92000/afr640032004en.pdf.

Azzopardi, Mario Philip. 2018. *Aħna Refuġjati*. Malta: Valletta 2018.

Billington, Michael. 2015. 'Lampedusa Review— A Brave Excursion Into the Dark Waters of Mass Migration.' *The Guardian*, April 12. Accessed June 6, 2015. https://www.theguardian.com/stage/2015/apr/12/lampedusa-soho-theatre-london-review.

Boltanski, Luc. 2004. *Distant Suffering: Morality, Media and Politics*. Translated by Graham Burchell. Cambridge: Cambridge University Press.

Borg, Ruben Paul. 2017. 'A Methodology for the Quality Assessment of the Theatre.' In *Capitalizing on Culture? Malta and the European Capital of Culture*, edited by Vicki Ann Cremona, 77–96. Malta: Mediterranean Institute, University of Malta.

Cassar, Antoine. 2016. *Passport*. Fifth edition. Translated by Albert Gatt. S.L.: S.N.

———. 2017. 'Deportation as marketing.' *Malta Today*, February 2, 2017. Accessed June 6, 2021. https://www.maltatoday.com.mt/news/national/73920/antoine_cassar__deportation_as_marketing#.YL1iHfkzaUk.

Cremona, Vicki Ann. 2016. 'Anthony Neilson's *Stitching* and the High Moral Ground.' In *Global Insights on Theatre Censorship*, edited by Catherine O'Leary, Diego Santos Sanchez and Michael Thomson, 245–58. London: Routledge.

Daily Sabah. 2020. '180 Migrants in Limbo at Sea After Italy, Malta Refuses Entry to Ports.' *Daily Sabah*, July 2, 2020. Accessed 6 June 2020. https://www.dailysabah.com/world/europe/180-migrants-in-limbo-at-sea-after-italy-malta-refuse-entry-to-ports.

Delicata, André. 2012. 'A Senseless Conflict'. *Times of Malta*, March 21, 2012. Accessed June 19, 2021. https://timesofmalta.com/articles/view/A-senseless-conflict.412033.

European Commission. 2016. *Standard Eurobarometer 86: National Report—Public Opinion in the European Union (Malta)*. Accessed May 25, 2021. https://europa.eu/eurobarometer/surveys/detail/2137.

Farrugia, Sarah. 2019. *Working Together: A UNHCR Report On The Employment Of Refugees And Asylum Seekers In Malta*. Acessed May 25, 2021. https://www.unhcr.org/mt/wp-content/uploads/sites/54/2019/12/UNHCR-Employment-report_WORKING-TOGETHER_web.pdf.

The Malta Independent. 2018. 'V18 Artistic Director Mario Philip Azzopardi Describes London Protester "A Sorry Bitch."' *The Malta Independent*, April 23. Accessed May 26, 2021. https://www.independent.com.mt/articles/2018-04-23/local-news/V18-artistic-director-Mario-Philip-Azzopardi-describes-London-protester-a-sorry-bitch-6736188663.

Galea, Marco. 2019. 'Bodies without Organs and Organs without Bodies: The Maltese Experience of Creating National Theatres.' In *Redefining Theatre Communities: International Perspectives on Community-Conscious Theatre-making*, edited by Marco Galea and Szabolcs Musca, 101–13. Bristol: Intellect.

Global Detention Project. 2021. Accessed May 31, 2021. https://www.globaldetentionproject.org/countries/europe/malta.

Mallia, Mathias. 2019. 'London Theatre Cancels Shows in Malta After Visa Issue—PFWS.' *Newsbook*, Februrary 21, 2019. Accessed June 19, 2021. https://newsbook.com.mt/en/london-theatre-cancels-shows-in-malta-after-visa-issue/ Accessed 19 June 2021.

Martin, Ivan. 2014. 'Minister Denounces Rant on Islam by V18 Director'. *Times of Malta*, November 28. Accessed April 1, 2023. https://timesofmalta.com/articles/view/Minister-denounces-rant-on-Islam-by-V18-director.545916

Nimführ, Sarah, Laura Otto, and Gabriel Samateh. 2020. 'Denying, While Demanding Integration: An Analysis of the Integration Paradox in Malta and Refugees' Coping Strategies.' In *Politics of (Dis)Integration*, edited by Sophie Hinger and Reinhard Schweitzer, 161–81. Cham: Springer.

Parliament of Malta. 2018. *Parliamentary Question 7129*. 5 October 2018. Accessed May 31, 2021. https://apq.gov.mt/PQWeb.nsf/7561f7daddf0609ac1257d1800311f18/c1257d2e0046dfa1c125833700402f47!OpenDocument

Rettman, Andrew. 2020. 'EU Declares War on Malta and Cyprus Passport Sales.' *euobserver*, October 21. Accessed June 19, 2021. https://euobserver.com/justice/149810.

Said, Edward W. 1995. *Orientalism*. London: Penguin.

Scicluna, Christopher. 2020. 'Malta Refuses to Let Migrant Ship Dock, Awaits EU Deal.' *Reuters*, May 1. Accessed June 6, 2021. https://www.reuters.com/article/us-europe-migrants-malta-idUSKBN22D5ES.

Tabone, Jo and Neil Falzon. 2012. *9 Parts of Desire*. Accessed June 19, 2021. https://www.um.edu.mt/library/oar/handle/123456789/13115.

Times of Malta. 2021. 'Refugee Council Warns New Policy Driving People Into Poverty and Marginalization.' *Times of Malta*, June 4. Accessed June 6, 2021. https://timesofmalta.com/articles/view/refugee-council-warns-new-policy-driving-people-into-poverty-and.876920.

UNHCR. 2015. *Malta Asylum Trends, 2005–2015.* Accessed June 6, 2021. https://www.unhcr.org/mt/wp-content/uploads/sites/54/2018/05/8_2005-2015_fs.pdf.pdf.
———. 2021. '*Lethal Disregard' Search and rescue and the protection of migrants in the central Mediterranean Sea.* Accessed June 6, 2021. https://reliefweb.int/sites/reliefweb.int/files/resources/OHCHR-thematic-report-SAR-protection-at-sea.pdf.
Wilmer, S.E. 2018. *Performing Statelessness in Europe.* Cham: Palgrave Macmillan.
Zagaria, Valentina. 2015. 'Why the Differences between Lampedusa (the place) and Lampedusa (the play) Matter.' *Allegralab*, May 15, 2015. Accessed June 6, 2021. https://allegralaboratory.net/why-the-differences-between-lampedusa-the-place-and-lampedusa-the-play-matter-2/.

CHAPTER 43

Staging Borders: Immigration Drama in Spain, from the 1990s to the Present

Andrés Pérez-Simón

In the last thirty years, playwrights and directors in Spain have been reacting to the contemporary migratory flows into the country. These flows of foreign-born populations resulted in a changing demographic landscape. A significant number of theatrical productions have portrayed the death of African migrants in their voyage across the Mediterranean Sea. Meanwhile, other productions have focused on the different types of discrimination that migrants suffer once they are on Spanish soil. In order to achieve the artists' goals of conveying a political message and producing an immediate effect on the spectators, both of the above trends are characterized by a predominantly realistic tone.

The first section of this chapter contains a historical review of migratory flows originating in Spain in the late nineteenth century and throughout most of the twentieth century. Additionally, this segment offers a brief analysis of Spain's transformation into a country that received immigrants in the closing years of the past century. The second section is concerned with the figure of the French playwright Bernard-Marie Koltès. Placing special emphasis on how Spanish authors and directors interpreted Koltès' work, this section discusses the development of a type of migration drama that responded to the arrival of African migrants to the Spanish coast in the 1990s and early 2000s. The third section provides synopses of the most characteristic titles of this period, starting with Ignacio del Moral's *La mirada del hombre oscuro* (The Dark Man's Gaze, 1992) and Encarna de las Heras' *La orilla rica* (The Rich Shore, 1993). The fourth section focuses on recent plays written by female playwrights who

A. Pérez-Simón (✉)
Universidad Autónoma of Madrid, Madrid, Spain
e-mail: andres.perezs@uam.es

© The Author(s), under exclusive license to Springer Nature Switzerland AG 2023
Y. Meerzon, S. E. Wilmer (eds.), *The Palgrave Handbook of Theatre and Migration*, https://doi.org/10.1007/978-3-031-20196-7_43

discuss intercultural issues while departing from the tradition of depicting the primal encounter with the African 'Other', typically on Spanish shores. Finally, as a case study, a brief performative analysis discussing Angélica Liddell's *Y los peces salieron a combatir contra los hombres* (And the Fish Rose Up to Make War Against Mankind 2004) will close this chapter.

A Brief History of Emigration in Spain

Spain underwent a rapid transformation, from sending to receiving immigrants, in the last decade of the past century and the early 2000s. Before this period, Spain was a country of emigrants in the nineteenth and the twentieth centuries. The first wave of mass emigration took place in the last third of the nineteenth century, and was directed to the Americas, mainly to Argentina, Brazil, and Cuba. This migratory pattern continued in the first third of the twentieth century. Overall, it is estimated that around three and a half million Spaniards crossed the Atlantic Ocean between 1880 and 1930, to occupy permanent and temporary positions in the industrial and service sectors. The period of highest activity was 1900–1913, with over 180,000 departures a year, mostly to booming Argentina (Sallé Alonso 2009, 16). After the financial crisis of 1929, the pace of this economic migration decreased significantly as job opportunities became scarce. In addition, the 1930s were the most tumultuous decade in the history of modern Spain. This time period witnessed the rise and fall of the progressive Second Republic (1931–1936) and the ensuing Civil War (1936–1939) that caused one million deaths. Economic emigration came to a halt during these years. The only massive exodus was the departure of tens of thousands of political refugees that left Spain during the Civil War, mostly to settle in Mexico.

General Francisco Franco seized power in 1939. Spain suffered from the effects of political isolationism due to the fascist tenets of his regime, and the country remained closed to the outside world until the late 1950s. In 1959, the visit of President Eisenhower to Spain signaled the beginning of a new era in Franco's regime. Thanks to this new strategic alliance with the USA, Spain received economic and logistical support to undertake a series of structural reforms under the umbrella concept of 'developmentalism' (*desarrollismo*). Developmentalism produced a high growth in domestic demand, salary wages and productivity. This rapid development, however, affected regions unequally, as the flow of human and economic capitals tended to concentrate in industrialized Madrid, Catalonia and Basque Country. Industrialized nations in Western Europe, in need of a young male workforce, were now the main destination for Spanish workers. France, West Germany and Switzerland received an estimated total flux of two million people from Spain in the 1960s and early 1970s. This population arrived through 'guest workers' programmes and with the opportunity to later obtain permanent resident status. The international economic crisis of 1973, however, caused a drastic reduction of job opportunities outside Spain. Almost concurrently, the political reforms implemented after the death of Franco in 1975 accelerated Spain's convergence with Western Europe. In this new context, migration ceased to be a mass phenomenon.

Spain's integration into the European Economic Community (EEC) in 1986 formed the last step in Spain's rapid economic and social modernization. African immigrants, mostly from the Maghreb region, constituted the first group that massively immigrated to Spain in the early 1990s. At the end of the 1990s, the number of foreign residents in Spain was approximately 750,000, less than 2% of the total population. Ten years later, the foreign-born population amounted to five and a half million people, or 12% of the total population. With a net flow of 4.1 million, Spain became the second-largest recipient of migrants among OECD countries in the first decade of this century. This very quick reversal of demographic patterns transformed the social and economic fabric of Spain. Meanwhile, the government could hardly improvise one regularization procedure law after another—regularizations of undocumented immigrants were conducted in 1996, 2000, 2001 and 2005. During these years, workers originated mostly from Eastern Europe (Romania, Bulgaria), Latin America (Ecuador, Colombia, Bolivia), Morocco and China.

With enhanced border vigilance over the autonomous Spanish cities of Ceuta and Melilla, in Northern Africa, and the Strait of Gibraltar, migrants searched for the Canary Islands route to enter Europe in the 2000s. Smugglers exploited this West African route in reaction to the increased surveillance along the Mediterranean. Between 2006 and 2009, there were approximately 55,000 irregular entries to the Canary Islands. This occurrence was known as the *cayuco* crisis, a crisis which transformed the migration policy of the European Union as Spain was able to involve the EU member states via Frontex, a joint programme designed to protect the European border. The implementation of the advanced operation Hera, facilitated by Frontex and supported by the European Union, halted the migratory pattern through the West African route. The programme emphasized the detection and containment of the migration flows at their points of origin. After a decade of low arrival numbers, the year 2020 registered 23,000 migrants to the Canary Islands. The rate of arrivals increased in 2021, to make for a total of 55,000 entries in these two years combined. Due to the COVID-19 pandemic, European authorities paid little attention to this humanitarian crisis. The Spanish government interned migrants in camps while proceeding to deport those migrants whose countries of origin were identified. However, the refusal of African countries to receive deportees, out of fear of the coronavirus, resulted in migrants being confined in overcrowded detention centres.

The Influence of Koltès on Spanish Immigration Theatre

The works of Bernard-Marie Koltès (1948–1989) provided Spanish playwrights with a dramatic language to respond to the swift demographic and social changes taking place in their country in the closing years of the past century. Koltès' plays exhibited a repertoire of characters and situations that could be used as a blueprint for a new dramatic subgenre, one that portrayed the arrival of African immigrants on Spanish soil (Pérez-Rasilla 2010, 102–103). In the 1990s, theatrical venues in Madrid and Barcelona predominantly featured the works of Koltès. In 1990, in Madrid, Miguel Narros directed *Black Battles with Dogs* at the National Drama Centre (NDC), and Guillermo Heras directed *In the Solitude of Cotton Fields* at the National Centre of New Stage Trends (NCNST). These productions received generous public funding as the two centres depended on the National Institute for Performing Arts and Music, created by the Spanish Ministry of Culture five years before. A third Koltèsian play, *Night Just Before the Forests*, was staged at the prestigious Teatro María Guerrero in 1992.

The reception of Koltès in Catalonia can be traced back to 1988. This year marked the publication of the Catalan translation of *Black Battles with Dogs*—a text prepared by playwright and theatre director Sergi Belbel. Additionally, in 1988, the play premiered in a small theatrical space in Barcelona under the direction of Carme Portaceli. In 1993, Lluís Pasqual directed Koltès' *Roberto Zucco* at the Teatre Lliure, the leading venue for contemporary theatre in Catalan language. Furthermore, Belbel authored four Catalan translations of Koltèsian texts (*Night Just Before the Forests*, *In the Solitude of Cotton Fields*, the anthology of short pieces *Periphery Koltès*, and *Quay West*) which were staged in Barcelona from 1993 to 2002.

The foundational role of the Koltèsian drama in the creation and development of an immigration theatre in Spain can be better understood by looking at the importance of fictional spaces in his plays. In Koltès' works, dramatic spaces appear tightly connected to the frail identity of the main characters. These characters frequently perceive the arrival of foreigners as a threat against the stability of their (psychological, social) world. Due to this tension, Rodrigo Palacios describes Koltèsian topoi in terms of 'territory, rather than space [...] [one] that is characterized by the existence of material and immaterial frontiers' (2017, 23). A good example of this spatial pattern operates in *Black Battles with Dogs*. In this play, a fence separates Horn and Cal—two Frenchmen in charge of a soon-to-be abandoned construction site in Africa—and the native workers exploited by their multinational company. The spectacle of verbal and physical violence in *Black Battles with Dogs* influenced Ignacio del Moral's *La Mirada del hombre oscuro* (The Dark Man's Gaze). Ignacio del Moral's drama was the first to thematize the opposition between 'civilized' white people and African population in the 1990s in Spain.

The Other Takes the Stage: The Creation of the African Immigration Drama

Del Moral's *The Dark Man's Gaze* (1992) is regarded as the first play to depict the perils endured by African immigrants who risked their lives to get to Spain. The play premiered at the National Centre of New Stage Trends in 1993. Del

Moral's play inaugurated the subgenre of African immigration drama. In addition to gravitating towards the migratory struggles of African males on their journey to Spain, this subgenre tends to highlight the discriminatory treatment the migrants suffered upon their arrival in the promised land. Del Moral wrote *The Dark Man's Gaze* in response to press stories featuring drowned migrants in the Mediterranean. Thus, Del Moral established a precedent for the numerous realistic immigration dramas to come in the 1990s and early 2000s (see Kunz 2002, 214–218 on this issue).

The Dark Man's Gaze features a working-class family from Madrid who has come to spend the weekend on a beach in the southern part of the country. This stereotypical family of four (Father, Mother, Boy and Girl) does not sympathize with Ombasi or, as they refer to him, the *negro* [black]. Ombasi barely reaches the coast, having been forced to jump off the boat by a human trafficker whose aim was to escape the sea patrol's watch. His friend and travel companion dies attempting to reach the Spanish shore. The companion's dead body remains on stage for the entire play.

The basic characteristics of the subgenre of the African immigration drama are present in *The Dark Man's Gaze*. The presence of African male figures is predominant (typically, from the Maghreb or Sub-Saharan Africa) to the detriment of female characters or other ethnicities and nationalities. Inspired by real events as they appeared in the press, the play also emphasizes a sense of the 'reality' of the stories. Moreover, the sea travel constitutes a personal and spiritual journey, and the seashore operates as a locus of tension and negotiation of values between the newly arrived and the native population. In terms of characterization, del Moral's *The Dark Man's Gaze* depicts very shallow Spaniards, inherently ignorant and racist, in stark contrast to a migrant figure who can hardly communicate. Yet, this migrant character's kindness and good intentions are never doubted. Some scholars have criticized this portrayal of immigrants as flawless characters (Kunz 2002, 233).

Del Moral's *The Dark Man's Gaze* found a second life through its very popular film adaptation, *Bwana* (1996, dir. Imanol Uribe). The film won the Golden Shell award at the San Sebastián International Film Festival and was nominated for three categories (Best Film, Best Director, Best New Actor) of the Goya awards. *Bwana* features debuting actor Emilio Buale, born in the former colony of Equatorial Guinea, in the role of Ombasi. After the sensational success of *Bwana*, Buale worked in the television and film industries. Meanwhile, he performed roles in plays that touched on the issue of immigration. Buale was cast in two productions of Koltès' plays, *Black Battles with Dogs* (2000) and *Return to the Desert* (2003). In 2004, Buale played the role of the *morisco* leader Cadí in Pedro Calderón de la Barca's *Amar después de la muerte* (Love After Death, 1634). This play was a production by the National Classical Theatre Company (NCTC) that critics interpreted through the prism of ongoing debates on immigration (Soria Tomás 2010, 191–192). Calderón's play recreates the crushing of the second *morisco* rebellion (1568–1570) in a mountainous region of Granada. This intervention resulted in the prohibition of the *moriscos*' distinct cultural, religious and linguistic status.

In 1993, the year of Del Moral's *The Dark Man's Gaze*, Encarna de las Heras' *La Orilla Rica* (The Rich Shore) premiered in the alternative space of La Cuarta Pared in Madrid. De las Heras' text is an African immigration drama which was the first of these plays to thematize the situation of female migrants. *The Rich Shore* is a dramatic monologue featuring Kawtar, a Moroccan woman who takes the decision to leave her family and country after the death of her mother. Her discourse echoes the voices of absent family members, a lyrical dialogue with the living and the dead. To free herself from her father's authoritarian rule, Kawtar makes the dangerous journey across the Mediterranean. In a quite implausible twist, her father is the one who gives her the money to buy a spot on the raft. Kawtar is eventually detained by Spanish immigration authorities and deported to Morocco. The 1993 production of *The Rich Shore* in La Cuarta Pared received a positive review in the Madrid press. The play's success led to a tour around Spain in 1994. Additionally, this drama was one of the eleven plays produced by the National Women's Institute to celebrate International Women's Day in Madrid that year.

Besides del Moral's *The Dark Man's Gaze* and de las Heras' *The Rich Shore*, a third foundational work of the genre of African immigration drama is Jerónimo López Mozo's *Ahlán* (1996). This drama features the journey of a Moroccan immigrant. The voyage begins with the departure from his own country, includes his journey across the Mediterranean, and concludes with a succession of encounters with racism once the character arrives in Spain. These negative experiences occur in drastically different geographical contexts. Ahlán, the Moroccan immigrant, wanders through towns and urban centres spread across four regions, following an episodic structure that resembles the typically Spanish tradition of the picaresque novel. *Ahlán* merges tragicomic elements to expose the narrowmindedness of Spaniards who see immigration as a new Arabic invasion. López Mozo's work received two highly prestigious prizes awarded by the Spanish Government—the Tirso de Molina Prize and the National Dramatic Literature Prize. However, this drama was never produced on the stage. This lack of production was in large part due to the difficulty of staging a text which was divided into 23 sequences and extended over more than 200 pages. Despite not being performed, the support from government agencies indicated institutional recognition of the role of contemporary playwrights in shaping perceptions on immigration.

In 1992, the killing of Lucrecia Pérez, a Dominican housemaid, presented the first xenophobic hate crime in democratic Spain. This crime received extensive media coverage that sparked a national discussion on the benefits and downsides of immigration. If the images of dead migrants in the Mediterranean Sea inspired numerous playwrights, a similar phenomenon can be observed in the emergence of the subgenre of racist aggressions against immigrants. Episodes of diverse types of violence against vulnerable migrants can be traced back to Del Moral's *The Dark Man's Gaze* and López Mozo's *Ahlán*. However, the presence of neo-Nazi characters is now explicitly present in Yolanda Pallín's *Lista negra* (Black List, 1997), a play described by Luisa García-Manso as 'the first dramatic text with skin heads as main characters' (2016, 138). The production of Pallín's play, under the direction of Eduardo Vasco, took place in the Sala Cuarta Pared of Madrid. The small theatrical venue was the same space where Encarna de las Heras saw *The Rich Shore* staged four years earlier. The presence of skin heads in Pallín's *Black List* was later echoed in José Luis Alonso de Santos' *Salvajes* (*Savages*, 1998), Paloma Pedrero's *Cachorros de negro mirar* (*Puppies with a Dark Gaze*, 1999), Alberto Miralles' *Mongo, Boso, Rosco, N'Goe … Oniyá* (1999) and Fernando Martín Iniesta's *La falsa muerte de Jaro el negro* (The False Death of Black Jaro, 2004).

In the late 1990s and early 2000s, Spanish playwrights tended to focus more of their attention on the challenges of cultural assimilation (García-Manso 2016, 139). David Planell's *Bazar* (Bazaar, 1997) was one of the first plays to move away from the dramatic conflict between two sharply defined types of characters (Spaniards versus immigrants). Instead, this work presents two Moroccan immigrants as the main characters. The plot is set in Lavapiés, famously recognized as the most multicultural neighbourhood of Madrid and, arguably, of Spain. Yet, Planell has no intention of indulging himself in a celebratory story of assimilation. His focus is on the differing ways in which the two Moroccan men negotiate their cultural assimilation to Spanish culture. Hassan, the older of the two, owns a thrift store and represents the immigrant who basically gives up his culture of origin. Unlike other dramatic works from his period, *Bazaar* has had a long stage history. The text obtained the Sanlúcar de Barrameda Comedy Award, and the play premiered in Madrid in 1997. In that same year, *Bazaar* premiered at the Royal Court Theatre of London, in an English translation of the original version. New productions of the play ran in Madrid in 2003 and 2014.

Other plays that explicitly portray the theme of migration are Juan Mayorga's *Animales nocturnos* (*Night Animals*, 2004), Ignacio Amestoy's *De Jerusalén a Jericó* (*From Jerusalem to Jericho*, 2006) and Fermín Cabal's *Maldita cocina* (*Damn Kitchen*, 2007). Also worth mentioning are the two plays premiered in Catalan language in the same year of 2004, Carles Batlle's *Temptació* (*Temptation*) and Sergi Belbel's *Forasters* (*Strangers*). These two dramas merge memories from present and past by connecting the recent arrival of Arab immigrants in Catalonia with past memories of arrivals of migrants from the poorest provinces of Spain in the 1960s and 1970s.

Female Perspectives on Migration, from the 2000s to the Present

Laila Ripoll and Angélica Liddell are two leading females figures of Spain's contemporary theatre scenes. They form part of the same generation, as they were born only two years apart (in 1964 and 1966, respectively). Moreover, they adopt a comprehensive approach towards theatrical performance that is the result of their extensive training and experience in playwriting, acting, directing and scenic design. These actresses are two artists with their own theatre companies. Thus, they maintain a position of relative independence with respect to market forces (García-Manso 2011, 116). Ripoll is the author of *Victor Bevch (blanco, europeo, varón, católico y heterosexual)* (Victor Bevch (White, European, Male, Catholic and Heterosexual)), which premiered in the Basque city of San Sebastián in 2003. In this play, the clownish figure of Spectre appears as a stand-up comedy actor in the prologue and epilogue that frame the play's main plot. The latter consists of fifteen scenes portraying a love story between a Spanish woman and a recently arrived immigrant from Bangladesh. Liddell, who has collaborated with Ripoll on several occasions, was the author, director and single actress in *And the Fish Rose Up to Make War Against Mankind*. (This play, premiered in 2004, will be studied as a separate case later.)

In recent years, female dramatists have published numerous plays on immigration, among them Carmen Resino, author of *Allegro (ma non troppo)* (2004). Resino's drama offers a new perspective on immigration by focusing on the life of migrant female domestic workers from Latin America. Resino is also the author of *Pájaros verdes* (Green Birds), a text published in Concha Fernández Soto and Fernando Checa's anthology of short plays on immigration *Los mares de Caronte* (The Seas of Charon, 2016). This volume includes a total of seventeen plays and features works by renowned female playwrights Antonia Bueno, Juana Escabias, Diana de Paco, Paloma Pedrero, Laila Ripoll and Vanesa Sotelo. This collective volume is an example of the recent use of public funding to support theatrical explorations of the phenomenon of migration through an intercultural and feminist lens. The interdisciplinary research group Centro de Estudios de las Migraciones y las Relaciones Interculturales (CEMyRI), based at the University of Almería, has led numerous initiatives with direct applications to teaching, research and service, with notable contributions in the field of contemporary Spanish theatre. Fernández Soto and Checa, editors of the anthology *The Seas of Charon*, are two members of this group. More recently, Fernández Soto published *Sillas en la frontera* (Chairs on the Border, 2018), an anthology of twenty migration plays written exclusively by women. With contributions by authors from ten different countries, there is a clear emphasis on the commonalities of particular experiences of war and displacement suffered by women in the twentieth and the twenty-first centuries. This volume gives voice to the underrepresented group of emigrée playwrights, as is the case of Bahira Abdulatif, an Iraqi exile who authors a bilingual text in Arabic and Spanish.

Case Study: Angélica Liddell's *And the Fish Rose Up to Make War against Mankind* (2004)

Liddell's *And the Fish Rose Up to Make War Against Mankind* (2004) is the first title of her trilogy *Actos de resistencia contra la muerte* (Acts of Resistance against Death). The trilogy also comprises *Y como no se pudrió... Blancanieves* (And It Did Not Rot: Snow White, 2005), on child soldiers, and *El año de Ricardo* (Richard's Year, 2007), a denunciation of autocratic leaders. These three works constitute Liddell's most explicit take on political theatre to date. The play's title revolves around the image of fish attacking Spaniards while they bask in the sun on the beaches of the Southern coast. The fish mutate into humans after devouring so many bodies of African migrants who die attempting to cross the Mediterranean. Liddell's *And the Fish* … can be defined as 'autobiographical performance,' a term commonly applied to her works. However, this concept should be accepted with theoretical reservations, for the dramatic work does not render full justice to the way Liddell structures her performance.

In this play, Liddell creates a fictional mask, the Whore, that has a counterpart in the imaginary character of Mr. Whore, to whom she addresses her speech. One can identify this imaginary addressee with the actual audience, as the Whore uses diegesis to direct their attention to a reality outside the theatre walls. While Liddell's mask is porous and unstable, these attributes do not eliminate the idea of the dramatic persona in its entirety. Liddle plays with the distance between performing subject and dramatic character by piling up different layers of meaning. The playwright presents this layering as a gesture that she initiates by splitting herself into a recorded voice that is heard offstage and through the portrayal of the character of Whore who remains on stage throughout the whole production. The Whore is a violent and loquacious character who misses the time when there were no immigrants in Spain ('all the construction workers were white') and who openly expresses her disgust at the presence of African migrants on the beach ('this is not what it used to be, Mr. Whore'). She wears a pompous court dress in the colours of the Spanish flag, compulsively drinks from plastic bottles of water, and has a giant Christian cross, made of washing machines, in the background. Her acting partner, Gumersindo Puche, stays mostly in the wings. With his body fully naked and his face painted in black in the style of a minstrel, Puche represents the anonymous men who died in the sea. At times, Liddell exerts physical violence against him, while he remains passive and silent, in accordance with the Whore's view of African migrants as subjects without rights ('the black man, Mr. Whore, cannot protest; the blacks are outside of language').

Approximately halfway through the production, Liddell steps out of the character of the Whore and makes a 15-minute photographic presentation of art interventions carried out by Puche and herself while working on this project. She comments on a series of slides showing photographs documenting their interventions in the cities of Madrid and Cádiz. They also embarked near Cádiz on a ferry trip to Morocco, thus experiencing a pleasurable trip on the same waters where migrants regularly die in their attempts to reach the Spanish shore. When the presentation is over, Liddell announces that it is time 'for the show to go on' and then returns to the character of the Whore. As the play approaches its end, Liddell's language becomes more lyrical, announcing the final transformation of the fish into vengeful creatures who will now devour all of those who felt no great pain when watching reports of dead migrants in the daily news.

Liddell's *And the Fish* … evokes the same sense of urgency that characterized the first migration plays that were composed and staged to denounce the deaths of migrants crossing the sea to arrive at the Spanish Peninsula. Her play also incorporates images and situations taken from news stories published in the media, a common practice in early migration drama (as in Del Moral, for example). What distinguishes Liddell *And the Fish* …, however, is a constructional pattern which is different from the norm. By minimizing the emphasis on the creation of a fictional world, and putting more stress on the ideological tenets behind the performer's discourse, Liddell breaks the previously established standard. She first creates a thin fictional layer and then proceeds to reproduce negative stereotypes about African migrants in order to make the audience aware of their complicit role in the perpetuation of these racist views. Unlike her contemporaries, Liddell only partially relies on a dramatic text.

In Spain, the theatrical responses to mass immigration were largely determined by the impactful images of African migrants. The dramatic subgenre 'immigration drama' first provided playwrights with a common repertoire of situations and tragic characters. This model, however, progressively dried up. A look at recent publications and theatre productions shows the emerging importance of gender and intercultural issues that remained underdeveloped in the 1990s and 2000s. Even in this second iteration, the negotiation between cultures is still presented through a predominantly realistic language that relies on the existence of a dramatic text.

References

Fernández Soto, Concha, ed. 2019. *Sillas en la frontera: Mujer, teatro y migraciones.* Almería: EDUAL.

Fernández Soto, Concha, and Francisco Chjeca, eds. 2018. *Los mares de Caronte.* Madrid: Fundamentos.

García-Manso, Luisa. 2011. 'Teatro, inmigración y género: La identidad del otro en *Victor Bevch*, de Laila Ripoll, y *Los peces salieron a combatir contra los hombres*, de Angélica Liddell.' *ALEC* 36(2): 113–149.

———. 2016. 'El teatro español sobre la inmigración de los años 90: Influencia mediática y procesos creativos.' *Hispania* 99(1): 137–147.

Kunz, Marco. 2002. 'El drama de la inmigración: *La mirada del hombre oscuro* de Ignacio del Moral y *Ahlán* de Jerónimo López Mozo.' In *La inmigración en la literatura española contemporánea*, edited by Irene Andrés-Suárez, Marco Kunz and Inés D'Ors, 215–256. Madrid: Verbum.

Liddell, Angélica. 2004. *Y los peces salieron a combatir contra los hombres.* INAEM. Online. http://teatroteca.teatro.es/opac?id=00006806. Accessed 11 February 2022.

Palacios Ferro, Rodrigo. 2017. *Interculturalidad y conflicto en la obra de Bernard-Marie Koltès.* Doctoral dissertation. Madrid: Autonomous University of Madrid.

Pérez-Rasilla, Eduardo. 2010. 'Representaciones de la inmigración en el teatro español contemporáneo.' In *Imágenes del otro: identidad e inmigración en la literatura y el cine*, edited by Montserrat Iglesias Santos, 87–116. Madrid: Biblioteca nueva.

Sallé Alonso, María Ángeles, ed. 2009. *La emigración española en América: Historias y lecciones para el futuro*. Madrid: Fundación Directa.
Soria Tomás, Guadalupe. 2010. 'Inmigración y novísima dramaturgia española.' In *Imágenes del otro: identidad e inmigración en la literatura y el cine*, edited by Montserrat Iglesias Santos, 117–138. Madrid: Biblioteca nueva.

CHAPTER 44

Performance and Asylum Seekers in Australia (2000–2020)

Caroline Wake

Over the past four decades, five so-called 'waves' of 'boat people' (asylum seekers) have arrived on Australian shores. In the first of these (1976–1981), approximately 2000 arrived from Vietnam. During the second wave (1989–1994), 700 asylum seekers arrived from Cambodia, Vietnam and China. The third wave (1994–1998) comprised 2400 arrivals from China and Vietnam. Then, from 1999 to 2001, more than 9500 arrived from Iraq, Iran and Afghanistan. Most recently, from 2009 to 2013, more than 50,000 asylum seekers arrived by boat; further, at least 1200 people drowned at sea. Relative to the contemporaneous experiences of other countries, these numbers are infinitesimal. However, relative to Australia's historical experience, the numbers have seemed—or have been framed as—exponential. Indeed, the fourth wave was more than the previous three combined, and the fifth more than the previous four combined. Consequently, Australian governments have implemented a raft of ever more punitive policies designed to discourage boats carrying asylum seekers.

In response to the second wave, the government introduced a policy of mandatory detention, which places people who arrive by boat without a valid visa into involuntary—and potentially indefinite—detention. Similarly, in response to the third wave, it introduced a repatriation policy, which forcibly returns all failed asylum seekers to their country of origin. These policies persisted during the fourth wave, along with four new ones collectively referred to as the Pacific Solution: temporary protection, interdiction, excision and

C. Wake (✉)
UNSW Sydney, Sydney, NSW, Australia
e-mail: c.wake@unsw.edu.au

© The Author(s), under exclusive license to Springer Nature Switzerland AG 2023
Y. Meerzon, S. E. Wilmer (eds.), *The Palgrave Handbook of Theatre and Migration*, https://doi.org/10.1007/978-3-031-20196-7_44

offshore processing. These brutal and illegal policies have been criticized by the Australian parliament (via various Senate committees), independent bodies (e.g., the Australian Human Rights Commission), non-government organizations (e.g., Amnesty International) and even the United Nations via its Working Group on Arbitrary Detention and Special Rapporteur on Torture. They have also been contested by asylum seekers themselves, their advocates and artists working both within and beyond detention.

This chapter compares the theatrical responses that emerged during the fourth and fifth waves of asylum seekers. I argue that, while the response to the fourth wave was dominated by documentary theatre, the response to the fifth has been characterized by the rise of more hybrid aesthetics. Further, whereas the former was relatively uniform in terms of participant age, gender and nationality, the latter is far more diverse. Most strikingly, recent responses have embodied and enacted a more ambivalent politics—as if no longer convinced of theatre's power.

THEATRE OF THE FOURTH WAVE (2001–2008)

From 2001 to 2008, more than 40 performances were made by, with and about asylum seekers. These ranged across genres such as circus, comedy, drama and performance art. However, the dominant genre was documentary; within this, subgenres included autobiographical, testimonial, epistolary and tribunal. First came three solo shows loosely based on the author's autobiographical experiences. Some signalled this relationship explicitly; for example, Towfiq Al-Qady's *Nothing But Nothing* (2005) described 'voices, memories, events, thoughts. I lived this; I heard it from friends when we escaped together from one land to another land, and from one airport to another, and from port to port, and in the detention centres' (Al-Qady 2013, 190). Second, testimonial works were based on the ensemble's lived experience. For example, the Fitzroy Learning Network ran a series of workshops with professional writers and directors to devise *Kan Yama Kan* (2002), in which asylum seekers told their stories directly to the audience. Third, plays such as Nigel Jamieson's *In Our Name* and Ros Horin's *Through the Wire* (2004) were based on interviews with refugees and asylum seekers. Some plays were also based on correspondence with detainees, such as Actors for Refugees' *Club Refuge* (2002). Finally, *CMI (A Certain Maritime Incident)* (2004) was a tribunal play based on the transcripts of a 2002 parliamentary inquiry into the rescue of the Suspected Illegal Entry Vessel (SIEV) 4, the sinking of the SIEV X, and the impact of these events on the 2001 federal election.

Regardless of subgenre, these documentary plays typically employed an aesthetics of authenticity. When performed or published, they often opened with a statement such as 'the words which follow are those of asylum seekers and refugees taken from interviews and letters' (Actors for Refugees 2004; see also Goodall 2003, 26). In addition to interviews or letters, these works drew on government documents. *Subclass 26A* (2005) borrowed from 'Form 866C,

Application for a Protection Visa; a [Department of Immigration] letter to Iranian detainees; lists of boat arrivals [and their] nationalities' (Rothfield 2005, 16). These productions also often cast current or former refugees and asylum seekers, who comprised anywhere from the entirety of the cast to the solo cast member—in such cases, they carried a heavier burden of representation. These textual and casting strategies were further buttressed by visual techniques that utilized official images. For example, *CMI* included Royal Australian Navy footage of an asylum seeker boat sinking. Together, such strategies continually reinforced the performances' truth claims.

If the most common genre was documentary, the most common trope was domestic. In both comedy and drama, writers often downsized the national drama to a domestic one and staged asylum seekers arriving at someone's home. For example, in Ben Eltham's satire *The Pacific Solution* (2006), the prime minister and two successive ministers for immigration are recast as housemates watching the cricket when an asylum seeker staggers in. In such plays, the nation is recast as a family; however, the metaphor only extends so far, and Australia is never imagined as part of the 'family of nations'. Further, these plots always cast refugees as invaders rather than visitors or long-lost family members.

The final trend that emerged during fourth-wave theatre was a focus on men in their twenties and thirties, typically from Iraq, Iran, and Afghanistan. This focus reflects both migration trends of the time and refugee studies' habitual framing of the Middle East as a region that produces rather than receives refugees as well as the field's neglect of women and children. *In Our Name* (2004) exemplifies these four core trends: documentary, authenticity, family, and men.

IN OUR NAME (2004)

Premiering in April 2004, *In Our Name* was 'the first mainstream subscription season play to deal with the refugee issue' (Morgan 2004, 21). The play was catalysed when director Nigel Jamieson visited Villawood detention centre and met the Al Abaddi family: father Jasim, mother Nahtha, 15-year-old son Humam and 6-year-old daughter Afnan. When he visited them several months later, he was struck by Humam's deterioration and decided to give him a chance to tell his story (Rose 2004a, 27).

In Our Name focuses almost exclusively on the Iraqi family's experience of detention. Like a 'narrative of terror', the play does not abide by the 'if … then' principle, but rather what Freddie Rokem has called the 'then … then' principle, 'presenting a series of meaningless and even unconnected catastrophes' (2002, 569). The Al Abaddis narrate a series of such catastrophes, from arriving on Christmas Island in December 1999 to being deported in February 2003. Within this family story is the individual story of Humam, who protested, *then* endured 15 days in solitary detention, *then* dug his own grave, *then* stitched his lips, *then* attempted suicide, and *then* attempted suicide again. Each event is traumatic in isolation, but in combination they become too much to bear. On opening night, this 'terrible litany was received by the audience in almost complete silence, except for stifled crying and appalled gasps' (Rose 2004b, 27).

The performance is documentary in the sense that it is a performed oral history. The programme notes describe the play as 'written by Nigel Jamieson in association with the Al Abaddi family' (Belvoir 2004, 3–4), and various reviews describe it as 'taken from transcripts of' (Jaivin 2004), 'scripted [...] from' (Rose 2004a, 27), 'constructed out of' and 'evolved out of' (Hazou 2008, 198, 82) interviews. As indicated by these different verbs, it is unclear how exacting Jamieson was. Nevertheless, he acknowledged that these interviews bestowed upon him a unique set of responsibilities—akin to those Amanda Stuart Fisher called an 'ethical contract' (2011, 197). This contract entailed a duty to maintain the Al Abaddis' voices and their vision, even at the expense of his own. For example, he wanted to include material about the effects of mandatory detention on guards but decided to focus only on the family's tale. He told Linda Jaivin that 'it's the story that these people wanted to tell', from which she surmised that, for Jamieson, 'the urgency of the issue outweighs more literary concerns' (Jaivin 2004). In this way, Jamieson prioritized ethics over aesthetics.

The play's aesthetics emphasized its authenticity in several different ways, but predominantly via casting. In interviews, Jamieson stated that he was anxious to avoid 'a virtuoso performance from an Australian actor trying to put on an Iraqi accent' (Rose 2004a, 27). Instead, he sought what he repeatedly—and perhaps problematically—called a 'sense of authenticity' (Belvoir 2004, 6; Rose 2004a, 27). To this end, he conducted 'an exhaustive search amongst [Sydney's] Iraqi community' and elsewhere to find 'a cast who had shared common experiences with the family' (Belvoir 2004, 6). If we define authenticity as Jamieson did, in terms of the proximity between an actor and their character, the three actors who played the older Al Abaddis each embodied a different degree of authenticity. Haydar Haydari, who played Humam, was very close to his character: both were Iraqi asylum seekers who arrived in Australia by boat and spent significant time in detention. Further, both staged hunger strikes and other protests while detained and were aspiring actors. Majid Shokor, who played Jasim, shared some similarities with his character. Like Jasim, Shokor is from Iraq; however, he arrived in Australia as a refugee rather than an asylum seeker, meaning that he did not spend any time in detention (Zable 2007). He had also worked as a professional actor for the past 25 years. There was an even greater gap between Silvia Entcheva, who plays Nahthta, and her character: Nahthta is Iraqi, and Entcheva is Bulgarian; Nahthta is an asylum seeker, and Entcheva is a migrant who arrived in Australia in 1994; Nahthta is not a performer, whereas Entcheva is a singer. In this way, each actor brought a different combination of national, experiential, and occupational authenticity to his or her role.

Finally, at its core, the play emphasizes family. However, it effectively inverts the most common trope of the era: the single male asylum seeker encroaching on an Australian family. Here, an Iraqi family is centred to the extent that the guards and activists disappear from view. Nonetheless, within the family, it is men whose stories dominate.

Interregnum (2008–2012)

In 2007, the centre-left Labor Party won government after 11 years of conservative rule. The following year, it announced that it would be winding back the Pacific Solution. Both artists and activists felt vindicated—the moment had become a movement, and the movement had effected real change. However, in 2009, boats started arriving again, and by 2012 Labor had lost its nerve. In 2012, the government reintroduced offshore processing and in 2013, it went even further, announcing that refugees would not only be processed but also resettled in Papua New Guinea rather than Australia. When the conservative Liberal-National coalition won government again in late 2013, they named this new suite of policies 'Operation Sovereign Borders'.

Whereas the response to the Pacific Solution was instantaneous, the response to Operation Sovereign Borders was slower. There are several possible explanations for this. First, survivors of the fourth wave were still rebuilding their own lives and did not have the time to make art in response to newer arrivals. Further, many advocates were burned out by their previous efforts and did not have the energy for another campaign. Another explanation is that the government started making its own startling forays into the artistic sphere. For example, the Department of Immigration and Border Protection's *No to People Smuggling* channel on YouTube features several videos, one of which resembles the final scene of *CMI* and another that looks like verbatim theatre. Elsewhere, the government has funded street theatre, a telemovie, and a comic book. Finally, another potential explanation concerns a vastly different media ecology characterized by the rise of smartphones and social media.

To illustrate the differences between these two periods, consider the responses to the SIEV X and the SIEV 221. When the SIEV X sank and 353 people drowned, numerous performances were made in response. The boat is referred to, and several survivors are quoted in the final scene of Version 1.0's *CMI* and their one-off performance *X Marks the Spot*. Survivor Amal Hassan Basry's testimony features in Actors for Refugees' play *Something to Declare* (2003), she collaborated with Steve Thomas on the documentary film *Hope* (2008), and Arnold Zable honoured her in his book *Violin Lessons* (2011). Victims have also been commemorated via the SIEV X Memorial Project, Kate Durham's series of 353 paintings, and sculptures by Bradley Burke, Richard Goodwin, Glenn Morgan, Alex Seton, and Arthur Wicks. By contrast, there was a striking lack of artistic responses to the SIEV 221 or 'Christmas Island tragedy', which occurred on 15 December 2010. Fifty asylum seekers died when their boat smashed onto the reef, out of reach but within view of people standing on the shore. Unlike the SIEV X, which disappeared without a trace, smartphones captured this disaster. The footage entered Australia's visual culture immediately, starting on social media and rapidly moving to broadcast media; the event is now known by several iconic images. Ultimately, the SIEV X produced no images but at least a dozen artistic responses, whereas the SIEV 221 produced a plethora of images and (to my knowledge) only one artistic response—Hilary Bell's short play *Flying Fish Cove*, shown only once in 2015.

If the artist's task during the Pacific Solution was to render visible previously invisible victims and to amplify the inaudible voices of survivors, it has become something altogether more complicated during Operation Sovereign Borders. Rather than seeking to humanize the dehumanized, the task becomes how to intervene in a culture where art has been weaponized. One option is to withdraw, as when artists boycotted the 2014 Biennale of Sydney because one of its key sponsors profits from offshore detention. However, this is not the only way forward.

Theatre of the Fifth Wave (2013–2020)

When it eventually got underway, the response to the fifth wave was far more diverse in three significant ways: the genres it mobilized; the gender, age, and nationality of its participants; and the politics it modelled. The documentary genre has not disappeared completely. Notable recent examples include Katie Green's verbatim play *If You Come to Australia* (2015), Ross Mueller's *Darker Angels* (2015) and Ros Horin's *Baulkham Hills African Ladies Troupe* (2013). However, overall, the genre has waned in favour of others.

Comedy has become much more popular. Several short comic works debuted at the *Asylum* festival (2015), including Tania Cañas's *Three Angry Australians* (2015) and Noëlle Janaczewska's *Going for Gold* (2015). The former is set in the office of a non-government organization, depicting an increasingly frustrated staff replying to an endless stream of emails from artists asking if they and their clientele would be interested in participating in an art project 'about' refugees. The latter commentates Australia's efforts in an 'Olympics of Cruelty'—the US is the obvious favourite for waterboarding, but Australia is way out in front when it comes to mistreating asylum seekers. There has also been a rise in stand-up, including Anh Do's *Happiest Refugee Live* (2012) and Tom Ballard's *Boundless Plains to Share* (2016).

In addition to comedy, there has been an increase in participatory genres. Take, for example, Damara Gieysztor's *Bureau of Worldly Advice* (2014), presented in the Melbourne Town Hall. The piece began in the street, where signage and a spruiker (the Australian term for a tout) invited passers-by in to ask for 'worldly advice' from a panel of eight experts. The panel included an engineer, a chef, a social worker and a visual artist, all of whom had arrived in Australia as refugees. When participants entered, they were handed a menu detailing the advice on offer for the day, with topics ranging from industrial design to cooking, history, volunteering, daydreaming, and stigma. The performance was intriguing due to its recruitment of the general public (as opposed to 'preaching to the converted'), its emphasis on the performers' professional identities and expertise (as opposed to their stories of migrant status), and its reversal of power (placing refugees in the position of authority and citizens in the position of apprenticeship).

The third notable trend has been the rise of meta-theatricality, particularly the play-within-the-play. Dhananjaya Karunarathne's *A Sri Lankan Tamil Asylum Seeker's Story as Performed by Australian Actors Under the Guidance of a Sinhalese Director* (2016) weaves between two realities: a Tamil asylum seeker fleeing Sri Lanka and two white Australian actors rehearsing a theatrical version of this story. Recently, the multi-authored play *The Audition* (2019) advanced the premise that 'a stage is a country in itself, [w]ith its own rules and regulations' and, further, that there are parallels in the processes experienced by actors seeking work and refugees seeking asylum (La Mama 2019). Both find themselves waiting while someone more powerful determines their future, often based on a single encounter. Moreover, those who are both actors and asylum seekers are doubly displaced in Australia, where stages are overwhelmingly white and migrant artists often face discrimination.

Fifth-wave theatre has also exhibited a broader range of gender, age, geography and language. In particular, female-focused projects have been far more visible. For example, Ros Horin's *Baulkham Hills African Ladies Troupe* (2013) featured a cast of seven women. This same play also raised the profile of refugees from Africa, who have never attained the visibility of those from the Middle East. Other performances focusing on African Australian experiences include *Four Deaths in the Life of Ronaldo Abok* (2011), about a South Sudanese refugee resettling in the suburbs of Sydney, and *Prize Fighter* (2015), about a Congolese refugee and former child soldier building a new life in Brisbane.

In addition, a broader range of ages has been seen both onstage and in the auditorium. Since 2010, Sydney's Treehouse Theatre has 'provide[d] a platform for young refugees to share their life stories' via public performances (Treehouse Theatre 2021). In Melbourne, *We All Know What's Happening* (2017) combined particular interests in both children and regionalism. Directors Samara Hersch and Lara Thoms collaborated with seven Australian children, aged between 11 and 17, to tell the history of Nauru, including Australia's own exploitation of the country. Staged in the naïve style of a school play, the performance attracted both junior and adult audiences and effectively highlighted a new generation of citizens who do not remember political life without these policies.

The mention of Nauru brings me to the final and most significant trend of the fifth wave: a much greater awareness of how the detention of asylum seekers relates to the settler-colonial state. There are various exemplary performances from the era; however, several of these trends—the diversity of participants and genres—are exhibited in Powerhouse Youth Theatre's play *Tribunal* (2016).

TRIBUNAL (2016)

Premiering in August 2016, *Tribunal* has been described variously as 'a participatory performance piece [...] fusing of contemporary theatre with legal procedure and intimate conversations' (Powerhouse Youth Theatre [PYT] 2018, 9); 'part verbatim theatre, part curated conversation' (Pham 2016); and 'a makeshift truth and reconciliation commission' (Dow 2017). When the theatre doors open, Aunty Rhonda Dixon Grovenor—a Gadigal/Bidgigal/Darug/Yuin Elder—is already onstage and watches the audience enter. Once we are seated, the other performers enter and take their places behind or beside her. Then Katie Green stomps her heel twice, issuing the order: 'all rise!' (PYT 2017, 1). Dutifully, the audience does so, remaining standing as Dixon Grovenor introduces herself as the convenor of this tribunal and explains that the government's treatment of refugees and asylum seekers causes her great grief: 'this is not our culture, to treat people this way' (2). At this point, Mahdi Mohammadi—a Hazara man in his twenties—steps forward to testify about his experiences of growing up in Iran and Afghanistan before fleeing and travelling via Indonesia to seek asylum in Australia. Notwithstanding their differences in age, gender, nationality, and cultural background, Dixon Grovenor and Mohammadi find themselves united by the experience of forced displacement and discrimination at the hands of the state. In addition, they are bound by a love of the performing arts—during the show, he dances, she sings, and their obvious love for performing shines through. These two main characters are supported by Jawad Yaqoubi, Mahdi's friend and a fellow Hazara refugee who plays himself as well as an interpreter; Katie Green, who testifies to her experience as a Red Cross case worker; Kaz Therese, who voices the regrets of a human rights lawyer; and Paul Dwyer, who plays an immigration official.

Tribunal is a documentary in several familiar ways. Dixon Grovenor provides an opening statement of factuality: 'all people speaking here tonight are speaking their truth from their own personal experiences' (PYT 2017, 1). When not speaking their own stories, the actors often cite official documents; for example, Dwyer reads from the script employed by immigration officers when interviewing asylum seekers (2–4, 11). The presence of Mohammadi and Yaqoubi also serves to authenticate the production. They, in turn, authenticate themselves by sharing their testimonies, speaking to each other in Dari, displaying photographs of life in Afghanistan and Indonesia and demonstrating Hazara dances. Where there is no visual, verbal or corporeal evidence, its absence is highlighted and furnished as further evidence of the story's veracity. For example, Therese states that sharing the lawyer's story is 'tricky [...] for all sorts of reasons,' including the provision of a confidentiality agreement (8). In these ways, *Tribunal*—like *In Our Name* and other fourth-wave productions—continually reiterates that it is telling the truth.

Yet, *Tribunal* is far more participatory than most works from the fourth wave. Rather than simply casting from refugee communities, Therese co-devised the performance, Therese co-devised the performance with them via a process that took 15 hours a week over eight months, as well as six weeks of intensive rehearsals (Artshouse 2017). Further, the final act is designed to facilitate conversation between the cast, experts, other migrant artists and the audience. In the penultimate scene, titled 'Tea Break', the performers sit on stage and drink tea while a guest speaker addresses the audience. On some occasions, the guest was an asylum seeker, on others, it was a psychologist or lawyer who works with refugees. On still other occasions, the tea break would segue into slam poetry delivered by artists who had been seated in the audience. When performed in Fairfield, the Western Sydney suburb where Powerhouse Youth Theatre is located, *Tribunal* also involved the local community via Parents Café—a social enterprise that supports the parents of students at Fairfield High School's Intensive English Centre—with the group serving Iraqi sweets in the tea break scene, and in the theatre foyer. Overall, *Tribunal* involves far more participation for refugees and non-refugees, whether artists, activists or audience members.

Finally, *Tribunal* also exhibited the meta-theatricality that has characterized the work of the fifth wave. In the opening scene, as Dwyer is interviewing Mohammadi, the latter interrupts to exclaim: 'come on, please! These interviews go on for hours and hours. [...] They never let you tell your story in your own words ... (*He turns to Rhonda*) Can I just say it in my own words?' (4). Dixon Grovenor replies, 'Mahdi, this is a theatre—you can do what you like' (4). At different points in the play, he also speaks about Papyrus Theatre, a feminist theatre company he co-founded with two women, and demonstrates a Hazara dance (11). Crucially, it was Papyrus's dancing at a theatre festival in Sweden that caused Mohammadi to become a refugee. When the BBC produced a story about the group and a religious figure in Afghanistan saw it, Mohammadi was called an infidel and threatened with arrest before being ambushed and losing one of his relatives (12).

Performance also appears in *Tribunal* via songs and stories. Dixon Grovenor sings the lullaby 'Mumma Warruno' in response to Green's testimony about a refugee who self-immolated (7) and 'Miss Celie's Blues' in response to Mohammadi's story about life in detention (21). Green tells a story about taking a group of 50 newly arrived refugees to the public art installation 'Sculptures By the Sea'. On seeing the sculptures, they are variously bewildered (Mohammadi says, 'there were [...] piles of wood, old things, mattresses [...] I was wondering "Where is this art they are talking about?" I didn't know that everything around me was actually the art. I thought it was just where people were throwing their junk!'), embarrassed (by a man miming oral sex next to a sculpture of a woman), and retraumatized (by a sculpture of a broken boat) (15–16). While that scene is played for laughs, the final scene is sombre as Yaqoubi and Mohammadi discuss their friend Nabi who is still in a detention centre on Nauru. The show concludes with '*Mahdi lead[ing] Jawad in the singing of a Dari song about friends who have travelled over the seas in search of a better life*' (26).

In each of these meta-theatrical moments—the slideshows, dances, songs, and stories—performance emerges as an ambivalent force. While theatre serves as a progressive feminist influence in Afghanistan, it is also responsible for Mohammadi's status as an asylum seeker. Similarly, while Dixon Grovenor's songs are framed as a source of sustenance in the face of state violence, it is notable that they are predominantly in English rather than Darug. Likewise, Green's anecdote is decidedly mixed—public art is at once trivial and traumatizing. These moments within the production gesture towards an ambivalence regarding the role of theatre that is typical of the fifth wave. Compared to fourth-wave productions, *Tribunal*'s politics are more sophisticated in terms of how it models intersectionality and solidarity between First Nations and migrant communities. Indeed, the performance was one of the first to examine the parallels between these communities. It is also—unusually for the Australian stage—multilingual, featuring both Darug and Dari, often without translations. However, *Tribunal* also seems more modest in its aims and more muted in its assessment of theatre's potential to influence policy. In the final scene, when an audience member would inevitably ask 'what can we do?', the answers would default to 'get to know an asylum seeker, convince three friends to change their minds, demand more from your local and federal government' (Thatcher 2016); 'become aware of cultural diversity [...] talk to people' (Wadewell 2017); or 'listen to the stories' (Dow 2017). Several reviewers noted this lack of ambition, but none more incisively than Lisa Thatcher, who wrote that 'this won't change the situation, but you should do it anyway was the message we walked away with' (2016). For a show that garnered critical acclaim and enjoyed five seasons, including one at the Sydney Opera House, this seems oddly deflating. It is, however, typical of the fifth wave.

Theatre of the fourth wave often demonstrated anti-theatrical aesthetics—productions sought to suppress overt theatricality and instead pursue an austere aesthetic of authenticity—and pro-theatrical politics—artists had faith that theatre could effect change. Conversely, theatre of the fifth wave has often embraced pro-theatrical aesthetics—meta-theatricality demonstrates a profound pleasure in theatre and its mechanisms—and anti-theatrical politics—exhibiting little faith that art will affect change. Perhaps this is only logical, given that theatre of the fourth wave did not change anything, despite what we may have thought in 2008. Or perhaps the difference is temporal—whereas artists of the fourth wave looked to the immediate past to affect the immediate present and near future, artists of the fifth wave have their eyes set on a more distant horizon. Rather than referencing a recent inquiry, as *CMI* did, it stages a tribunal that is currently inconceivable but may yet come into being.

Conclusion

There is now a large body of theatrical work that responds to and represents the experience of seeking asylum in Australia in the twenty-first century. During the Pacific Solution, these responses were dominated by the documentary genre and its associated aesthetics of authenticity and politics of speaking truth to power. Common tropes included foci on the family and men. More recently, however, theatrical responses have become far more diverse in terms of genre and participant gender, age, and nationality. This reflects shifts in media ecologies, government propaganda and artists' own priorities. If the first era was exemplified by *In Our Name* (2004), the second is best illustrated by *Tribunal* (2016). When the two productions are placed side by side, we can see how theatre has moved from re-enactment to rehearsal and from a politics that emphasizes the power of theatre to one that reckons with its inherent impotence.

References

Actors for Refugees. 2004. 'Something to declare.' https://web.archive.org/web/20160227001513/http://actorsforrefugees.org.au/whyframe.html. Accessed 15 February 2022.

Al-Qady, Towfiq. 2013. 'Nothing but Nothing.' In *Staging Asylum: Contemporary Australian Plays About Refugees*, edited by Emma Cox, 185–202. Strawberry Hills: Currency Press.

Artshouse. 2017. *Tribunal*. Programme. http://www.artshouse.com.au/wp-content/uploads/2017/07/Tribunal-by-PYT-l-Fairfield-Show-Program.pdf. Accessed 15 February 2022.

Belvoir. 2004. *In Our Name*. Programme.

Dow, Steve. 2017. 'Tribunal: The Participatory Performance Making Australians Face Up to Forgotten People.' *The Guardian*, June 5. https://www.theguardian.com/culture/2017/jun/05/tribunal-the-performance-piece-linking-the-indigenous-and-asylum-seeking-experiences. Accessed 15 February 2022.

Fisher, Amanda Stuart. 2011. '"That's Who I'd Be, if I Could Sing": Reflections on a Verbatim Project with Mothers of Sexually Abused Children.' *Studies in Theatre & Performance*, 31 (2), 193–208.

Goodall, Jane. 2003. 'Introduction to *Citizen X*.' *Australasian Drama Studies*, 42: 26–30.

Hazou, Rand. 2008. 'Acting for Asylum: Asylum Seeker and Refugee Theatre in Australia, 2000–2005.' PhD thesis, La Trobe University, Victoria.

Jaivin, Linda. 2004. 'Theatre of the displaced.' *The Bulletin* 122 (16). April 20.

La Mama. 2019. 'The Audition.' *La Mama*. https://lamama.com.au/whats-on/winter-spring-2019/the-audition/. Accessed 15 February 2022.

Morgan, Joyce. 2004. 'Behind the Wiring of an Easy Lifestyle.' *Sydney Morning Herald*, April 21. https://www.smh.com.au/entertainment/art-and-design/behind-the-wiring-of-an-easy-lifestyle-20040421-gdirwn.html. Accessed 15 February 2022.

Pham, Stephen. 2016. 'Handle With Care: On White Australian Invisibility in Non-White Dialogues.' *The Lifted Brow*, August 15. https://www.theliftedbrow.com/liftedbrow/handle-with-care-on-white-australian. Accessed 15 February 2022.

Powerhouse Youth Theatre. 2017. *Tribunal*. Unpublished script.

Powerhouse Youth Theatre. 2018. Annual Report 2017. http://pyt.com.au/wp-content/uploads/2018/12/Annual-Report-2017-FINAL.pdf. Accessed 15 February 2022.

Rokem, Freddie. 2002. 'Narratives of Armed Conflict and Terrorism in the Theatre: Tragedy and History in Hanoch Levin's *Murder*.' *Theatre Journal* 54 (4), 555–573.

Rose, Colin. 2004a. 'Locked up, Kicked Out But How Does It End?' *Sun Herald*, 18 April, 27.

———. 2004b. 'Weep On a Journey to Hell and Back.' *Sun Herald*, 25 September, 13.

Rothfield, Philipa. 2005. 'Selves Imprisoned and Released.' *RealTime* 66 (April–May): 16. https://www.realtime.org.au/selves-imprisoned-and-released/. Accessed 15 February 2022.

Thatcher, Lisa. 2016. '*Tribunal*—Face to Face with the Deepest Problem of the Political Left.' *Lisa Thatcher*, August 15. https://web.archive.org/web/20210122151105/https://lisathatcher.com/2016/08/15/tribunal-face-to-face-with-the-deepest-problem-of-the-political-left-theatre-review/. Accessed 15 February 2022.

Treehouse Theatre. 2021. 'Welcome to Treehouse Theatre.' http://treehousetheatre.org.au/. Accessed 15 February 2022.

Wadewell, Natalie. 2017. '*Tribunal*: Realities of The Refugee Crisis.' *State of the Arts*, May 5. https://web.archive.org/web/20180312114031/https://stateofthearts.com.au/tribunal-realities-of-the-refugee-crisis/. Accessed 15 February 2022.

Zable, Arnold. 2007. 'Harmonies in old Iraq.' *The Age*, 22 September. https://www.theage.com.au/entertainment/music/harmonies-in-old-iraq-20070922-ge5vil.html. Accessed 15 February 2022.

CHAPTER 45

Ramadram: Refugee Struggles, Empowerment, and Institutional Openings in German Theatre

Anika Marschall

Migration movements, refugee struggles and racial discrimination in German society and theatre have a long and interwoven history (Sharifi 2011; El-Tayeb 2011; Liepsch, Warner and Pees 2018; Stewart 2021). As Amelie Deuflhard, the artistic director of the Hamburg-based Kampnagel theatre, says, to engage with refugees as a German theatre works only as part of a longer practice and a commitment to deal with issues of coloniality and migration, and new forms of participation (2016, 307). This chapter sheds light on the issue of institutional openings in German theatre in response to the so-called refugee crisis in 2015. I refer to the so-called refugee crisis to underline that the linguistic marker of crises is an inherent part of racial and colonial politics (El-Tayeb 2011, 166). This crisis is as much about forced migration, as it is one of national identity and self-understanding, both in Germany and in Europe at large.

The number of people filing applications for asylum in Germany in 2014 was about 173,000, most having arrived from countries such as Syria, Serbia, Iraq and Eritrea (UNHCR 2014, 3). This was the highest number since 1993 in the German Federal Republic and it increased two-fold one year later, in 2015, in parallel with the increase in deportations. Between 2014 and 2017, more than 1.5 million people filed asylum applications in Germany (Bundesamt für Migration und Flüchtlinge 2017). To name but a few important, self-organized refugee struggles, which came before 2015 and have contributed to today's societal configuration: in 1994, the Voice Refugee Forum was founded in a refugee camp in Thuringia and is still active today. In 1998, the network

A. Marschall (✉)
Utrecht University, Utrecht, Netherlands
e-mail: a.marschall@uu.nl

© The Author(s), under exclusive license to Springer Nature Switzerland AG 2023
Y. Meerzon, S. E. Wilmer (eds.), *The Palgrave Handbook of Theatre and Migration*, https://doi.org/10.1007/978-3-031-20196-7_45

the Caravan for the Rights of Refugees and Migrants coined the slogan 'We are here because you destroy our countries'. The group Kanak Attak has used theatre and political art as specific forms of protest since the turn of the century and from distinct German citizen and postmigrant perspectives (Gürsel 2013). In 2012, the Berlin Refugee Movement formed and gained international media attention, after an asylum seeker from Iran committed suicide and his friends and other asylum seekers protested in solidarity and went on hunger strike. To demand their right to work, to attend school and the right to choose their own place of living, a group of about fifty asylum seekers from across Germany marched more than 500 km from Würzburg to Berlin (Ulu 2013).

In the following, the chapter focuses on the case of Migrantpolitan, which opened in 2015 as an autonomous refugee community centre and creative laboratory on the premises of Kampnagel. Since 2015, a dynamic community of migrants, refugees and asylum seekers have structurally contributed to the theatre programme and produced their own artistic works. In doing so, Migrantpolitan reconfigures the narrative of a German society with its emphasis on migration and cosmopolitanism. The Migrantpolitan community offers an embodied twenty-first century, first-generation refugee perspective on the struggle for the right to stay and make a meaningful life, on questions of representation and decolonial practices. The self-administered Migrantpolitan community works in alliance with the cultural capital of Kampnagel; they have been answering to pressing socio-political and cultural demands for refugee empowerment and institutional openings in German theatre since 2015. In the following, Migrantpolitan's multilingual, diasporic performance series *Ramadram* (2020) takes centre stage and opens the discussion.

'Unter Verdacht'

In the style of a 1990s German TV soap opera aesthetic, *Ramadram*'s intro-theme shows one protagonist after another in close-up on screen. Each of them introduces their character through a poignant gesture and playing with a prop, before turning around and gazing into the camera with a welcoming or witty mimic. At the end of the intro-theme, the episode title appears in a golden frame, the first one reading: 'Unter Verdacht' (New Media Socialism 2020). Translated into 'Under Suspicion', it references a wider culture of disbelief, in which forced migrants seeking asylum are often characterized as bogus, while, paradoxically rendered speechless and being silenced in the public sphere.

The very first scene opens to a green-screened, wide-angled photograph of a German ministry building in Hamburg. The European, the German and the municipal flag are hoisted up on the right hand-side. In the next image, two white middle-aged police officers, who wear white-collar shirts and black sweaters, sit in front of massive beige computers dating back to the early 2000s. In the background, a wallpaper image shows endless rows of ring binders. One of the police officers hangs up the phone and mumbles to his partner the first few lines in the series: 'That was yet another complaint about this *Migrant*...

politan...somehow this woman on the phone says, there are Blacks everywhere... and Nafris... and Arabs... and all' (translated from German and emphasis by the author. Note that 'Nafris' is a racializing, degrading and hateful term used by the police for young men of North African descent). These first lines already make viewers get a sense of the racialized discrimination at the heart of the series' dramaturgical conflict, as well as pointing to the painful and problematic understanding of the refugee as a bogus figure. It is Migrantpolitan, which is under suspicion by the racist police officers. They google its name and read aloud the following description, as it says on the real website of Kampnagel too:

> The Migrantpolitan is a place, a laboratory and a meeting point where new formats of collaboration, co-living and co-celebrating are tested and developed. A place in which the social classification of 'refugee' and 'local' are abandoned and its actors develop shared cosmopolitan visions. (Migrantpolitan n.d.)

The second scene opens up to the main setting of the soap opera: Migrantpolitan, a 100 sqm building in the garden of the Kampnagel grounds, surrounded by lush green trees in spring and summer. Its title 'Migrantpolitan' claims and combines the terms 'migration' and 'cosmopolitanism', because, as it says in its mission statement, Migrantpolitan seeks to move beyond the classification refugee.

> forced migrants find themselves caught in cross-cultural encounters. Migrants are heavily involved in it themselves—both in defining their future roles in our society as well as in intervening in their current presentation on theatre stages. These presentations depict them at times as instrumentalised victims, as narrators of their own biographies, as self-determined agents in future commons. (Migrantpolitan n.d., translated from German by the author)

Further, the German translation of the term 'refugee', *Flüchtling*, often has pejorative connotations due to its particular suffix '-ling', which commonly turns a positive adjective into a belittling noun. In writing this chapter, I am navigating the difficult tension between on the one hand being asked to and interested in critically writing *about* refugees (Sen 2018) and theatre in Germany. On the other, I recognize, listen to and take seriously voices from the Migrantpolitans themselves, who are often cast as refugees but reject this label and seek to emancipate themselves from the structural violence imposed on them, when being described, narrated, and reflected upon by others, by non-refugees such as myself. As a white, German citizen and an academic, my responsibilities and goals lie in constantly making use of my privileges to redistribute spaces in research, writing, teaching, cultural participation and beyond.

For Anas Aboura, the curator of Migrantpolitan, 'refugee' can be a helpful term to describe the first period of arrival in a new host country, as he himself has experienced in Germany. As he has shared in conversation with me (2021), the label refugee to him describes the literal period of seeking refuge, making a home and starting a new life in a different country. Maren Ziese and Caroline Gritschke describe from the perspective of German citizens, respectively, '[w]hen we speak about newcomers, we often do so without thinking critically about collectivizing concepts which facilitate processes of exclusion' (2016, 63). They quote Hannah Arendt's infamous essay 'We Refugees', whose words mirror Aboura's view: 'In the first place, we don't like to be called "refugees" [...] very few individuals have the strength to conserve their own integrity if their social, political and legal status is completely confused' (Arendt 1999, 116). The act of naming people who seek refuge in Germany has implications for the legal process, as well as someone's identity and their own conceptions of self. The act of naming someone as a refugee does not only have perilous consequences in asylum processes, but is rooted in social power dynamics and shapes public perception and the potential to imagine how to be together otherwise. Aboura explains that the category becomes useless and more violent as time passes in a country of arrival, and while people are busy surviving, finding dignity and creating meaning in their new lives. This process to him goes far beyond any cultural representation of refugees he has seen in mainstream German media, which often reinforce common stereotypes of Othering, racialization or victimhood. Throughout my conversation with Aboura and the Kampnagel dramaturge Nadine Jessen (2021), the notion of being fixed in place by others is a strong common theme—be that other voices, images, structures, myths, powers, bureaucratic authorities or policies. For Jessen, what captures the ethos of collaboration and the drive that compels Migrantpolitan to tackle the binary of refugee/non-refugee is the experience that 'being refugee means wanting to not be a refugee anymore' (Larry Macaulay quoted by Jessen, 2021).

In Germany, a refugee or someone eligible for asylum is legally recognized as such, if they are being persecuted based on their race, nationality, politics, or belonging to a particular social group in their homeland. The law grants asylum to people who face the risk of serious harm, if forced to go back to their home country (i.e. capital punishment or inhuman treatment), and respects the European Convention for the Protection of Human Rights and Fundamental Freedoms. Importantly, while finding oneself in the asylum process, people are legally prohibited from earning a living wage, making them dependent on food packages. Only legally recognized refugees are granted access to the labour market, social security, to language classes and cultural introduction courses. What emerges in the political context of asylum and migration in Germany are also housing and residency policies to manage the refugees' rights and movements within national borders, and the transnational EU Dublin regulation, to manage the refugees' rights and movements across borders.

Because of such violent policies and regulations, self-determination is an important means for creating a dignified life and navigating one's presence in a host country in meaningful ways. Self-determination lies at the heart of Migrantpolitan—both in terms of artistic programming and productions, as well as in political responses to specific power dynamics and structures of oppression and discrimination. Abimbola Odugbesan and Helge Schwiertz pinpoint that 'self-organization includes directly affected people becoming active in groups that build collective structures of support, empowerment, and, visible politics' (2018, 186). It is the Migrantpolitans, rather than the Kampnagel director, who identify the issues that they themselves consider a priority, communicate them on their own terms and embody them through a decolonial practice.

Institutional Openings in German Theatre

I put emphasis on self-determination in light of the plethora of German theatre projects emerging since 2015, which have responded to the political situation of refugees (Marschall 2016, 2018). We need to keep asking which roles refugees perform in art projects led by German theatre makers, how their stories are being told and what their agency is behind the scenes. Despite many publications, public discussions and self-determined migrant struggles, there remains a great risk of retraumatization, tokenism and commodification of refugees and their *aestheticized* stories. As Sandrine Micossé-Aikins and Bahareh Sharifi criticize, despite the increase of cultural projects with refugees initiated by white German theatre makers, the structures of cultural institutions and cultural policy at large have not changed much (2016, 79). Despite good intentions from theatres, dramaturges and directors, aesthetic representations of refugees on German stages have reproduced Othering, where a white, non-migrant, German audience is imagined to sympathize or be affected. Stereotypical narratives and images have often placed the responsibility to arrive, integrate and assimilate on the refugees. However, it is of the utmost importance to shift the weight of the responsibility onto the cultural institutions, a change which I and others have called upon them to make along with committing to the work of anti-racism, anti-ableism, anti-classism on all levels (Sharifi 2015; Liepsch, Warner and Pees 2018).

With their dramaturgical choice to start *Ramadram* with a case of racial profiling, the Migrantpolitans position their work politically. They make transparent the flipside of German welcome culture: the increase of hate crimes against refugees, people of colour and at times supporters, as well as racial profiling by the police. *Ramadram* shows what it means to find yourself as racially marked Migrantpolitan within a society, where structural and institutional racism has long been marked and exposed by those directly affected, but which has been belittled and negated by a white-dominant social majority (Micossé-Aikins and Sharifi 2016, 76). Further, racism is being understood by this social majority as an issue located on the political right only, rather than as an all-encompassing historically grown structure, which comprises the art world and theatres too. The Migrantpolitans' art practices are rooted in the practitioners' visible and tangible political positioning and solidarity. Because these artistic narratives and formats speak for themselves, their politics of solidarity is strategically not presented in additional discursive dramaturgical formats as in panel discussions, writings and papers.

Migrantpolitan is funded by the Federal Government Commissioner for Culture and the Media, the Robert Bosch Stiftung and EU's Creative Europe. The Migrantpolitan programme includes concerts, jam sessions, language classes, Golden morning sessions to start the day with Syrian hot beverages, screenings of Arabic series and films, cooking clubs and more. Entry is usually free. One of the capitalist funders of *Ramadram*, the Philip Morris GmbH, has been a point of internal critique at Kampnagel. The company explains their decision to support the production of the soap opera as follows: 'The self-administered Migrantpolitan means for many refugee artists first access to the creative industry and creates realistic long-term career perspectives' (Philip Morris GmbH 2018). With the emphasis on access, long-term practices and professionalization, the description of Migrantpolitan speaks to what I have identified as the importance to practice holistically and enact sustainable structural change within and across cultural institutions, rather than to create temporary *aesthetic* projects only (Marschall 2018).

> It is especially difficult for people, who do not share a similar socio-educational background to access cultural institutions in Germany. To enter and move freely within established cultural institutions, the so-called E-Kultur or higher culture, means to know and perform its specific behavioural and dress codes, the 'right' way of speaking, and to learn and master the 'right' knowledge or canon. [...] Discrimination against migrants and racialised people are still prevalent in these institutions. (Zosik 2020, 22, translated from German by the author)

In the case of Migrantpolitan, we see an actual opening of the much-discussed enclosure and elitist access to German theatre in particular, its hierarchical production system and connected abuses of power, including racist, sexist and ableist discrimination (Diesselhorst et al. 2021; Iyamu 2020). Crucially, Kampnagel's institutional opening is neither part of any neoliberal logic of audience development (Saha 2017), nor about exposing refugees on stage to merely diversify the theatre's artistic programme and elicit sympathy and hope in audiences on the basis of their presumed victimhood (Cox 2012) or deservingness (Holmes and Castañeda 2016).

Refugee Struggles and Empowerment

In light of the asylum policies in the contemporary European-German context and the complex issues surrounding rights, empowerment and self-determination of refugees, it is important to make explicit the connection between Kampnagel and the Lampedusa in Hamburg group, which initiated Migrantpolitan. Lampedusa in Hamburg is a group of 300 refugees mainly from Sub-Saharan Africa who fled the civil war in Libya. The group gained nationwide media attention for their fight for the right to remain in Germany, despite having been given legal status in Italy first. The participants have been actively protesting the Dublin regulation and national German policies since 2013 (Borgstede 2016).

Odugbesan and Schwiertz explain in reference to their own experience fighting from within and alongside Lampedusa in Hamburg, that

> [t]hese movements publicly fight against the exclusion of migrants and the denial of rights in the German-European border and migration regime. Besides relatively invisible everyday acts of claiming the right to mobility and access to resources, different forms of refugee protests have emerged that directly challenge migration policies through public action and campaigns. (2018, 185)

The struggles to move on—literally and metaphorically—to find a place to stay, and everyday survival often remain imperceptible and invisible but are utterly political in that they shift regimes 'without ever intending it' (Papadopoulos et al. 2008, 75).

The refugee struggle of Lampedusa in Hamburg is crucial for mapping the work of Migrantpolitan and identifying the role of Kampnagel therein, as a powerful state-funded German cultural institution. Importantly, when such refugee struggles and grassroots solidarity networks are the main drivers, they make theatres' engagement with refugees and migration meaningful *before and beyond* any temporary event aesthetic (Marschall 2018). Second, I highlight here again the agency, self-determination and long-time migrant and refugee struggles, which date back long before the so-called crisis in 2015 (Jakob 2016). Migrantpolitan, rather than emerging out of a genius idea by an institutional artistic director and his gesture of goodwill, has its (grass)roots in Lampedusa in Hamburg and in refugees' self-determined fight against border mechanisms, and for the right to have rights (Arendt 1968, 296–297). Their powerful slogan 'We are here to stay!' puts emphasis on presence and longevity, and it challenges any assumptions about refugees staying only temporarily and being essentially in transit and mobile subjects.

Over six months during the winter 2014–2015, six members of the Lampedusa in Hamburg group moved into an artistic, temporary, wooden structure on the Kampnagel grounds called *ecoFavela Lampedusa Nord*. *ecoFavela Lampedusa Nord* was an artistic intervention into the legal and political case of Lampedusa in Hamburg and functioned as a temporary space for gathering, discourse and action led by the refugees themselves. Deuflhard describes how Kampnagel framed *ecoFavela Lampedusa Nord* as a durational theatre space to be performed 24/7. Because German theatres are prohibited from officially housing refugees and asylum seekers, Kampnagel made sure to enact their rights to artistic freedom by presenting durational performances instead. Yet, the far-right fascist German party AfD took legal steps against Deuflhard because of Kampnagel's solidarity with and housing of asylum seekers. Only in July 2016 was the criminal investigation closed. Through the cloak of artistic practice, they actually could offer six-month-long living and sleeping arrangements for a refugee community in need. In a newspaper article by Deuflhard, with the telling title 'Time Is of the Essence' (2015), she describes how the building has worked relatively independent from the Kampnagel theatre. To her, it could be seen as a prototype for an alternative housing for refugees, one that is 'compartmentalised, peaceful, connected, active, integrating, open and thus, fundamentally different from regular housing for refugees, which are based on the all-round management by authorities, while at the same time on seclusion and disintegration' (Deuflhard 2015, 11).

Migrantpolitan transformed out of this temporary art project *ecoFavela Lampedusa Nord*, after Hamburg-based refugees communicated their need for a continuous space like this. At the end of the six-month project, Kampnagel was host to the self-organized International Conference of Refugees and Migrants with more than 1000 participants by a European-wide network of refugees (Benbenek and Schäfer 2018, 368). At the conference, the Kampnagel dramaturge Jessen met the later Migrantpolitan curator Aboura; both being in their own words 'creatures of the night and passionate smokers, as well as sharing a love for karaoke singing'. Jessen had long been in touch with different refugee communities in Hamburg, taking seriously responses from the communities themselves to the question of what was missing for them in the city, what they were longing for, what infrastructural shortcomings they identified in the local culture. Aboura confirmed that there was a lack of spaces for more radically diverse nightlife—including karaoke bars with Arabic song titles. Together, Jessen and Aboura have since been driven to address this shortcoming (among others) and initiated Migrantpolitan. Having curated the space since 2015, Aboura reflects that Migrantpolitan to him means a platform to participate in, no matter your background, language and legal status (2021). Migrantpolitan is about bringing together critical, cultural and infrastructural tools to address local and global issues.

RAMADRAM: *MIGRANTPOLITAN'S DECOLONIAL DRAMATURGY*

In the final part of this chapter, I return to *Ramadram* and exemplary artistic practices by the Migrantpolitans. Importantly, they tackle the racialization and marginalization of refugees in Germany through what I identify as a decolonial dramaturgy, which confounds the universalist, modernist and colonialist myths imbued in the concepts of aesthetics and art (Mignolo and Vázquez 2013). Their practices subversively ask who uses these concepts to represent and judge the everyday skills, doing and poetics of racialized and marginalized people, without positioning themselves too. Migrantpolitans' decolonial dramaturgy works both institutionally as detailed earlier, and artistically as a type of empowerment and a form of community-building, as I will now demonstrate in the following.

Ramadram is a soap opera produced by Migrantpolitans, whose first episode 'Unter Verdacht' opened this chapter's discussion and analyses of theatre about, with and by refugees in Germany. At first sight, and in particular from my white, colonial/modernist, German citizen view, *Ramadram*'s aesthetic feels crude, DIY, unfinished and irritating. The genre soap opera, which is a pillar of the so-called U-Kultur (mere popular entertainment industry), seems to be in a cultural chasm in opposition to the theatre as part of the so-called E-Kultur (serious, high culture). It is exactly this colonial/modernist binary of judging popular versus serious culture, good versus bad aesthetics, which *Ramadram* inverts. In doing so, they push the boundaries of the theatre and broach questions about audiences and identity. *Ramadram* allows *us* to explore moments of un-ease, irritation and disconnect with the regime of representation, and thus mark *our* limits of empathy and identification. *Ramadram* demands an unlearning of habitual readings of aesthetic representation, which have been shaped by colonial and heteropatriarchal structures.

Migrantpolitan aims to combine entertainment and empowerment both in front and behind the cameras through storytelling and modes of co-production. The Kampnagel dramaturge Jessen highlights the amount of creative and bureaucratic labour she puts into making sure all participants of productions like *Ramadram* are fairly paid—no matter their legal status, working permit or other political and legal obstacles. Migrantpolitans produce alternative stories which are otherwise not broadcasted on mainstream German TV, in particular those *by* first-generation refugees. Therefore, it is important for the series producers' and this chapter's emphasis on self-determination and empowerment that all of the performers are credited and given space here in this chapter's final lines: Aya Alsamra, Anas Aboura, Moaeed Shekhane, Lenja Busch, Michael Spormann, Bernd Kroschewski, Boye Diallo, Henry Peter, Eric Parfait Francis Tarengue, Daniel Chelminiak, Noor Nael, Wasiu Oyegoke, Larry Macaulay, Linda Marie Moeller, Majd Henna, Nidal Sultan, Abou Jabbie, Nadine Jessen, Gadoukou La Star, Annick Choco, Ordinateur, DJ Meko and Carlos Martinez.

To conclude: the stories the Migrantpolitans tell in *Ramadram* deal with cross-cultural differences, exoticization, racism, stereotypes and prejudices, and, of course, careers, friendships and love. They perform multilingually, including equally Arabic, English, German, Yoruba, Mandinka and different accents, which are heard and represented in their everyday reality. The Migrantpolitans challenge a monolingual and mono-heritage narrative of *Germanness* and present multiple perspectives, cultural references, music, spirituality and narratives. At times, they remind us in *Ramadram* of the stereotypical images they are faced with about themselves, but more often than not, they refuse to represent these and instead invert the white, colonial, German citizen gaze. This refusal is exactly where they counter the heteropatriarchal colonial fantasies of nation, migration and race; that is, presumed hierarchies about what is important to tell in a story from, about and for a *German* public, and how impossible it might be to self-represent as a racialized subject therein.

The dramaturge Jessen explained to me that for the artistic process, there was no written script for the actors, as not all are able to read and speak in the same languages (2021). In preparation, director and actors developed and decided together on a dramaturgical arc and a basic plot, while adding other elements during the filming, including choreographies, dances, songs and jokes. For Jessen, the dramaturgy of *Ramadram* does not revolve merely around one art project only, but sits within a larger, communally embodied, continued process that is Migrantpolitan. In her own words, any 'personal development' throughout the production of *Ramadram* is created through 'time and trust', including self-confidence, new social relations and friendships, skills such as storytelling, directing, filming, acting, singing, dancing, choreographing and organizing.

At the end, each episode of *Ramadram* includes a few blooper scenes. They are vital to the Migrantpolitans' decolonial dramaturgy, because they offer glimpses into the life-enhancing communal spirit and celebration of *making together* behind the scenes. While pointing to the immense real-life labour of the series production, the funny take-outs of someone bursting into laughter, messing up the dialogue or even tumbling over a barrier show moments of levity and humanity. I too giggle in front of the screen, enjoy the bloopers' silliness and relate to the performers in ways where race and the category of refugee or migrant crucially do not factor and become delinked. At the same time, these blooper scenes make me as a white German citizen viewer explore the limits of identification. They encourage the audience to reconfigure the social through a plurality of ways to relate to the world, including these joyful celebrations and dorky moments of simply being human. The affective intensity of *Ramadram* thus lies precisely in these fleeting moments of transmitting intimate encounters from screen to an affirming and deeply felt being-with, which goes beyond any idea of representing authentic plights and experiences of refugees or telling stories of cultural integration.

As it is painted on the walls of Migrantpolitan: 'Refugees Humans welcome.' Crucially, through both its infrastructure and its decolonial dramaturgy, Migrantpolitan reconfigures the struggle for the right to stay in Germany and is exemplary for how institutional theatres can work in solidarity with refugee and racialized communities.

References

Aboura, Anas and Jessen, Nadine. 2021. Interview with Anika Marschall, 22 May.
Arendt, Hannah. 1968. *The Origins of Totalitarianism*. San Diego: Harcourt.
———. 1999. 'We Refugees.' In *Writers on Exile*, edited by Marc Robinson, 110–119. London: Faber and Faber.
Benbenek, Ewelina, and Schäfer, Martin Jörg. 2018. 'Das Spiel mit den Grenzen. Flucht und die Hamburger Theaterszene zwischen 2013 und 2016.' In *Flucht und Szene. Perspektiven und Formen eines Theaters der Fliehenden*, edited by Bettine Menke and Juliane Vogel, 348–373. Berlin: Theater der Zeit.
Borgstede, Simone Beate. 2016. '"We are Here to Stay": Reflections on the Struggle of the Refugee Group Lampedusa in Hamburg and the Solidarity Campaign, 2013–2015.' In *Migration, Squatting and Radical Autonomy*, edited by Pierpaolo Mudu and Sutapa Chattopadhyay, 162–179. London: Routledge.

Bundesamt fur Migration und Flüchtlinge. 2017. 'Jahresbilanz 2016.' https://www.bamf.de/SharedDocs/Anlagen/DE/Downloads/Infothek/Presse/20170111-pressemappe-pk-jahresbilanz.pdf?_blob=publicationFile. Accessed 21 May 2021.

Cox, Emma. 2012. 'Victimhood, Hope and the Refugee Narrative: Affective Dialectics in Magnet Theatre's Every Year, Every Day, I am Walking.' *Theatre Research International*, 37 (2), 118–133.

Deuflhard, Amelie. 2015. 'Die Zeit drängt.' *Stadtlichh* No.18. https://epub.sub.uni-hamburg.de/epub/volltexte/2015/45325/pdf/150306_stadtlichh_nr18_screen.pdf. Accessed 24 May 2021.

Deuflhard, Amelie. 2016. 'Acting in Art and Society. Der Kunstraum als Raum für Geflüchtete.' In *Geflüchtete und Kulturelle Bildung: Formate und Konzepte für ein neues Praxisfeld*, edited by Maren Ziese and Caroline Gritschke, 305–3011. Bielefeld: Transcript.

Diesselhorst, Sophie, Hütter, Christiane, Philipp, Elena, and Römer, Christian, eds. 2021. *Theater und Macht. Beobachtungen und Übergang*. Berlin: Heinrich-Böll-Stiftung.

El-Tayeb, Fatima. 2011. *European Others: Queering Ethnicity in Postnational Europe*. Minneapolis: University of Minnesota Press.

Gürsel, Duygu. 2013. 'Discursive Acts of Citizenship: Kanak Attak in Germany.' In *Wer MACHT Demo_kratie? Kritische Beiträge zu Migration und Machtverhältnissen*, edited by Duygu Gürsel, Zülfukar Çetin, and Allmende e.V., 214–223. Münster: Edition Assemblage.

Holmes, Seth M., and Castañeda, Heide. 2016. 'Representing the "European Refugee Crisis" in Germany and Beyond: Deservingness and Difference, Life and Death.' *American Ethnologist*, 43: 12–24.

Iyamu, Ron. 2020. *Yes, he is black. It's better! Ein Erfahrungsbericht über Rassismus in der deutschen Schauspielszene*. Dissertation University Mozarteum, Salzburg.

Jakob, Christian. 2016. *Die Bleibenden: Wie Flüchtlinge Deutschland seit 20 Jahren verändern*. Berlin: Ch. Links Verlag.

Liepsch, Elisa, Warner, Julian, and Pees, Mathias, eds. 2018. *Allianzen: Kritische Praxis an weißen Institutionen*, Bielefeld: Transcript.

Marschall, Anika. 2016. 'The State at Play? Notions of State(less)ness in Contemporary Interventionist Performances.' *Critical Stages* 14. http://www.critical-stages.org/14/the-state-at-play-notions-of-statelessness-in-contemporary-interventionist-performances/. Accessed 6 March 2022.

———. 2018. 'What Can Theatre Do about the Refugee Crisis? Enacting Commitment and Navigating Complicity in Performative Interventions.' *Research in Drama Education: The Journal of Applied Theatre and Performance*, 23 (2), 148–116.

Mignolo, Walter, and Vázquez, Rolando. 2013. 'Decolonial AestheSis: Colonial Wounds/Decolonial Healings.' *Social Text*. https://socialtextjournal.org/periscope_article/decolonial-aesthesis-colonial-woundsdecolonial-healings/. Accessed 22 April 2021.

Micossé-Aikins, Sandrine, and Sharifi, Bahareh. 2016. 'The Colonial Nature of the Willkommenskultur. Flight, Migration and the White Stains of Cultural Education.' In *Geflüchtete und Kulturelle Bildung: Formate und Konzepte für ein neues Praxisfeld*, edited by Maren Ziese and Caroline Gritschke, 75–86. Bielefeld: Transcript.

Migrantpolitan, n.d. https://www.kampnagel.de/de/programmreihe/migrantpolitan/?programmreihe=47. Accessed 23 May 2021.

New Media Socialism. 2020. *Ramadram.* https://youtu.be/ROQaSEsUDFk. Accessed 20 May 2021.

Odugbesan, Abimbola, and Schwiertz, Helge. 2018. '"We Are Here to Stay"–Refugee Struggles in Germany Between Unity and Division.' In *Protest Movements in Asylum and Deportation*, edited by Sieglinde Rosenberger, Verena Stern, and Nina Merhaut, 185–203. Cham: Springer Nature.

Saha, Anamik. 2017. 'The Politics of Race in Cultural Distribution: Addressing Inequalities in British Asian Theatre.' *Cultural Sociology*, 11 (3), 302–317.

Sen, Somdeep. 2018. 'Writing the "Refugee Crisis": Proposals for Activist Research.' In *Syrian Refugee Children in the Middle East and Europe. Integrating the Young and Exiled*, edited by Somdeep Sen, and Michelle Pace, 101–112. London: Routledge.

Papadopoulous, Dimitris, Stephenson, Niamh, and Tsianos, Vassilis. 2008. *Escape Routes. Control and Subversion in the Twenty-First Century.* London: Pluto Press.

Philip Morris GmbH. 2018. 'Migrantpolitan von Kampnagel Internationale Kulturfabrik GmbH.' https://www.thepowerofthearts.de/migrantpolitan/. Accessed 22 April 2021.

Sharifi, Azadeh. 2011. *Theater für alle? Partizipation von Postmigranten am Beispiel der Bühnen der Stadt Köln.* Frankfurt a. M.: Peter Lang.

Sharifi, Azadeh. 2015. 'Berlin Mondiale—Flüchtlinge und Kulturinstitutionen: Zusammenarbeit in den Künsten.' https://www.kubinaut.de/media/downloads/berlin_mondiale_evaluation_public.pdf. Accessed 21 May 2021.

Stewart, Lizzie. 2021. *Performing New German Realities: Turkish-German Scripts of Postmigration.* London: Palgrave Macmillan.

Ulu, Turgay. 2013. 'Eine Widerstandserfahrung der Flüchtlinge in Deutschland.' In *Wer MACHT Demo_kratie? Kritische Beiträge zu Migration und Machtverhältnissen*, edited by Duygu Gürsel, Zülfukar Çetin, and Allmende e.V., 117–136. Münster: Edition Assemblage.

UNHCR. 2014. 'Asylum Trends 2014', https://www.unhcr.org/551128679.pdf. Accessed 8 April 2023.

Ziese, Maren, and Gritschke, Caroline, eds. 2016. *Geflüchtete und Kulturelle Bildung: Formate und Konzepte für ein neues Praxisfeld.* Bielefeld: Transcript.

Zosik, Anna. 2020. '"Die" kommen doch (nicht) von alleine.' In *Diversitätsorientierte Nachwuchsförderung und Personalgewinnung im Kunst- und Kulturbereich*, edited by Yasemin Akkoyun, 20–25. Genshagen: Stiftung Genshagen.

CHAPTER 46

To Come Between: Refugees at Sea, from Representation to Direct Action

Emma Cox

This chapter concerns itself with a category of migrant that is defined by United Nations covenant and integrated into the laws of 149 nation-states: the refugee. But refugeehood enjoys little categorical neatness in practice. Easily instrumentalised in the service of anti-immigrant sentiment and hard-line policy, many would-be refugees are pejoratively generalised as illegal migrants as they engage the nation-state that, paradoxically, acts as both guarantor and prohibitor of their protection. The following discussion considers how understandings of performance as *intervention* are shaped in relation to refugees. In theatre and performance studies, the concept of intervention describes the instrumentality or efficacy of practices, their disruptive capacity, or their cumulative potential to foment social change. Intervention is often understood to have an ideological dimension, to trouble consciousness, though its formations are also sited spatio-temporally and its general aim is to make some sort of material impact.

Artists concerned with the perilous maritime movements of refugees are perhaps uniquely impelled to stage interventions that come between human life and necropolitical or death-permitting sovereign power (Mbembe 2003), but few interventions in this sphere consist of direct action (activism whose purpose is to directly achieve an objective). And so performative engagements with maritime refugees are shadowed by an overwhelming awareness—for their creators and their audiences—of a geopolitical status quo that is both

E. Cox (✉)
Department of Drama, Theatre and Dance, Royal Holloway, University of London, Egham, UK
e-mail: emma.cox@rhul.ac.uk

© The Author(s), under exclusive license to Springer Nature Switzerland AG 2023
Y. Meerzon, S. E. Wilmer (eds.), *The Palgrave Handbook of Theatre and Migration*, https://doi.org/10.1007/978-3-031-20196-7_46

intolerable and monolithic. It is one of the deep structural violences of our era: that migrant and refugee deaths at sea are extremities nations prepare for but do not prevent (Van Reekum 2016, 338; Pugliese 2014, 579). Practices of non-assistance, interdiction and quasi-legalised boat turn-backs shapes relations between maritime migrants and border forces in the Mediterranean, the Caribbean and the waters between Australia and Southeast Asia (Zoppi 2020; Schloenhardt and Craig 2015). State border surveillance in these regions regularly serves the purpose of non-intervention. Here, on water, lies the vanguard of extra-territorialised state power that Giorgio Agamben describes in terms of external capture, *ex-capere* (Agamben 2000, 40), or what Joseph Pugliese identifies as the neoimperial 'pre-frontier spaces' of powerful states (Pugliese 2014, 579).

Of the wide variety of refugee-responsive performance practices, 'intervention' is a term most readily applied to socially engaged theatre making with refugees that has as its core aim the enrichment and empowerment of participants in contexts of resettlement or shelter (see, e.g., Balfour 2013; Jeffers 2012; Thompson 2009), as well as to performative activism, such as vigils, *die-ins*, street protests, or hunger strikes. For obvious reasons, such projects do not take place during moments of immediate threat to life; indeed, participatory performance interventions often concern what Michael Balfour calls 'little changes' (Balfour 2009) rather than grand gestures. But what might we make of performative interventions whose mode is direct action in extremis? In other words, work that manifests intervention's Latin root of *inter* and *venire*: to come between. This chapter considers one case in order to look more closely at the relationship between symbolic or representational work and direct action: the maritime performance of the M.V. Louise Michel, a 31-metre vessel purchased by the pseudonymous British graffiti artist Banksy. The Louise Michel, named after the French anarcho-feminist, undertook its first, widely publicised migrant rescue operation in the Mediterranean during the summer of 2020.[1] This performative humanitarian gesture, an act of coming between, stands in continuity with non-artistic activism, specifically NGO-led sea rescue operations in the Mediterranean, but Banksy's Louise Michel represents an explicit aestheticisation of rescue in a region that has already rendered migrant transit and death a mediatised spectacle (De Genova 2013). Aestheticisation in this discussion describes both the design elements of the operation and also the political framework it constructs for itself. In this discussion, I consider what the aestheticisation of direct-action activism (in this case, rescue) means for our understanding of refugee-responsive performance intervention.

---

[1] Since this chapter was written, the Louise Michel recommenced maritime missions in the central Mediterranean (2022 onwards).

The Work of Representation and Intervention

Fundamentally, of course, performance offers a representation of the world (at the same time as being of the world). The field of refugee theatre and performance studies is concerned with how representation takes place: who portrays refugees' narratives, how such narratives are constructed, and what the ethical implications are of acts of portrayal and participation. Alongside and sometimes subordinating its elucidation of aesthetics, refugee performance scholarship tends to coalesce around the problem of how the symbolic or imaginative domain intersects with, reflects, or even reshapes the day-to-day conditions and constraints (legal, political, social, territorial) that determine refugees' lives. In turn, theatrical and performative engagements with refugees seek to represent the vast complexities of lives impacted by forced migration. In a conceptual sense, such engagements undertake representational *work*, with work carrying a political connotation insofar as refugee arts are always already bound up with the deep contentions over rights and belonging that shape refugeeness itself. The representational forms considered in refugee theatre and performance studies include theatrical productions, participatory workshops, film and photographic work, live art installations and exhibitions, as well as curated walks or pilgrimages. Scholarly analyses of such work consider, for example, the techniques and ethics of verbatim performance (Wake 2013); the politicisation of crisis and the aesthetics of excess (Zaroulia 2018); the narrative structure of asylum stories (Woolley 2014); normative performances of refugeeness and the ethics of social participation (Jeffers 2012); the work of adaptation and the institutional approach to postmigrancy in arts and cultural organisations (Wilmer 2018; Schramm et al. 2019); artistic subjectivity and cosmopolitanism (Meerzon 2020); ethical philosophy (Farrier 2011); and procession, visibility, and en masse transit (Cox 2017). This scholarship has an interest in the *work* of representation, that is, with how artistic practices connect to the wider, non-representational aspects of the marginalised lives and identities that they seek to portray. As well as shaping perceptions of refugees by framing what may be deemed *representative*, representation is inseparable from the ways contemporary refugees themselves are required to move, as Sophie Nield has shown in her tracing of the disaggregation of bodies and their legal documentation at the political border (2008).

The fact that refugee theatre and performance studies is so preoccupied with the work of representation speaks to the readiness with which refugee responsive performing arts practices are evaluated in terms of their efficacy as *interventions*. As Baz Kershaw demonstrated in his seminal book *The Politics of Performance: Radical Theatre as Cultural Intervention* (1992), a conception of performance as intervention situates performance as a socio-political practice, first and foremost, with concerns of efficacy at its centre. Balfour points out that the notion of efficacious intervention is resisted by many applied or socially engaged theatre practitioners due to its potential rigidity; as he notes, 'The rationale of the useful artist, making creative interventions into a fixed social reality with predictable impacts is problematic' (Balfour 2009, 353). Nevertheless, the pervasiveness of terminology on intervention in theatre and performance studies since Kershaw can bely the complexity involved in grasping what an intervention in the lives of refugees may consist of, what it comes between, what its material impact might be.

This chapter identifies the 2020 maiden voyage of Banksy's Louise Michel as a *humanitarian performance* that stands in continuity with, but is distinct from in crucial ways, NGO-led direct-action rescue activism in the Mediterranean Sea. It also regards Banksy's project as linked with, but divergent from, contemporary artistic work about maritime refugees (much of which has at its core an awareness of its limits in terms of efficacy, when efficacy is most urgently needed). Across Europe in recent years, there has been no shortage of theatre, film, digital media, installation, and ceremony foregrounding the Mediterranean maritime zone as locus for resistance to oppressive migration policies as well as for grief and the commemoration of lives lost. In theatre, Anders Lustgarten's *Lampedusa* (UK) used a storytelling form to narrativize the experiences of a fisherman-turned-migrant rescuer; in film, Gianfranco Rossi's *Fire at Sea* (Italy) offered a perspective on the ways Lampedusan lives have become entangled with the tragedies of desperate strangers attempting to reach its shores; Max Hirzel's *Migrant Bodies* (Italy) was a powerful photo essay on the tragedies suffered across the region, while heat-sensitive images in Richard Mosse's video installation *Incoming* (Ireland) starkly visualised hyperthermic, just-rescued bodies, as well as those of the deceased. Displays of wrecked migrant boats, such as was featured at the 2019 Venice Biennale, have had small- and large-scale iterations across Europe. Meanwhile, activists have worked with religious leaders across the Mediterranean to establish migrant cemeteries, to hold vigils and commemorations and even funerals for some of those lost (see Cox 2017).

Either intentionally or inadvertently, the work of some artist-performers communicates profound anxiety concerning the limits of representational work, and in turn of intervention, concerning forced migration. In both his notorious photographic recreation of the image of 3-year-old Syrian boy Alan Kurdi's drowned body and his various installations in Europe of life-jackets and abandoned personal items (see Zaroulia 2018), as well as his film *Human Flow* (2017), Chinese dissident artist Ai Weiwei probes the function of visual representation in the aftermath of loss. His establishment of a studio at Lesvos in 2015–2016 came out of a concern to document and to be present in the midst of unfolding humanitarian disaster but not to engage in direct action. As far as intervention is concerned, Ai's work evidences a personal commitment to come *closer*, but not to come *between*, by pushing at the limits of his own embodied, empathetic engagement with refugees. Taking a caustic and ironic approach to the question of art's role amid the European refugee *crisis*, two fake direct-action interventions by German art activist collective Center for Political Beauty, both virtual art pieces, pointed to an ambivalent awareness of their own impotence beyond the realm of image making. *The Jean Monnet Bridge* (2015), an enormous virtual sea bridge that would link Tunisia and Sicily, exists as a fevered vision on CPB's website in a series of glamourised images, their mode of presentation drawing on the idealised aesthetics of tourist imagery. The ambitious imagined project is presented in the futuristic language of an infrastructure initiative: 'It will be nothing less than a landmark achievement of humanity: a bridge from North Africa to Europe, a lifeline between two continents and the largest economic stimulus package in the history of the European Union' (CPB). A video accompanies utopian images of a four-lane highway at sunset, its design ultra-modern at road level, its base structure of stone-built arches reminiscent of a classical aqueduct. The second of CPB's fake direct-action interventions at sea consists of rescue platforms 'placed' in the Mediterranean Sea to assist migrants in distress (2015). The CPB's website mocks the faux-visionary tone of state infrastructure project announcements: 'In order to fight this silent dying efficiently, we will install 1000 rescue platforms: 1000 navigation lights as an international commitment to humanity and a monumental symbol of the 21st century' (2015). These strange imaginings of thoroughfares of hospitality between North Africa and Europe are designed to underscore, of course, their absence in reality. Yet, even this conceptual project of non-existence couldn't resist gesturing towards the real when in 2015 CPB had a single rescue platform constructed and placed in the sea. In a section of their website, 'Utopia meets reality', CPB explain: 'In order to bring humanity to the sea, the first rescue platform "Aylan 1" (6 × 6 m) was loaded onto a ship in the harbour of Licata / Sicily and installed in international waters on 4 October 2015. On board: satellite emergency call devices, direction-finding radio transmitters, radar reflectors, a flag pole, navigation lights, life buoys, a box with a steel insert and solar modules for power generation' (2015). There is no suggestion that this realisation of a non-existent intervention has been involved in any form of assistance or rescue at sea.

Humanitarian Performance: The M.V. Louise Michel

On 29 August 2020, Banksy posted a video clip in his Instagram page (which has 10.9 million followers) that satirically drew attention to overlaps as well as contradictions that emerge at the interface of art as a symbolic domain, an inefficacious European rescue system, and Banksy's own hubristic gesture of funding of a maritime rescue project. The video contained subtitles that read: 'Like most people / who make it in the art world / I bought a yacht / to cruise the Med / It's a French navy vessel / we converted into a lifeboat / because E.U. authorities / deliberately ignore distress calls / from "non-Europeans" ' (Banksy 2020). The clip presented a pastiche of grotesque juxtapositions, including bidding at an art auction house, a luxury yacht, refugees scrambling for their lives in the sea, and a member of the coast guard asleep at his desk. The clip ended with the words 'all black lives matter', thereby explicitly racialising the treatment of migrants in the region and connecting this treatment to the Black Lives Matter anti-racist movement, which was dramatically resurgent in the summer of 2020. As of July 2021, Banksy's clip has had 4,724,271 views. The wry representational techniques employed in this clip are also evident on the Louise Michel's website, which announces of the vessel, 'She is as agile as she is pink [...] She runs on a flat hierarchy and a vegan diet' (Louise Michel 2020). The reference to non-hierarchical organisation underscores an ideological affiliation with anarchism, a politics that has traditionally had direct action at its heart, while the whimsical image of pink agility situates aesthetics within an activist domain. A space emerges here for refugee-responsive action that is more-than-art and more-than-activism.

While artists like Ai Weiwei and collectives like CPB have sought to elucidate what the assisting of migrants in the Mediterranean might look and feel like, NGOs have responded to inadequate state and EU search and rescue (SAR) activity. Unlike artistic practice, NGO activity is not first and foremost concerned with narrative or the visual, but as I shall outline, the M.V. Louise Michel prioritises the symbolic along with the actual. The cessation of Italy's military rescue operation, Mare Nostrum, at the end of 2014 and its replacement with the smaller EU-funded operation Triton, overseen by Frontex (the European Border and Coast Guard Agency) (Davies and Nelson 2014) precipitated the need for rescue by other means. Commercial ships undertook a third of these during the first half of 2015 (Mainwaring and DeBono 2021, 8), and for a longer period during the European migrant crisis between 2015 and 2017, NGO operations were responsible for the rescue of more than 110,000 people (Mainwaring and DeBono 2021, 2). The first NGO search and rescue operation in the region was undertaken in 2014 by *M/Y Phoenix*, a vessel funded by American-Italian millionaire philanthropists (Mainwaring and DeBono 2021, 8), which has since undertaken observation and supply missions in the Bay of Bengal and the Andaman Sea. Other operations have been carried out by a number of vessels, including, indicatively, the cargo ship *Ocean Viking* (which undertakes large capacity missions) and the *Aquarius Dignitus*, both chartered by SOS Méditerranée and Médecins Sans Frontières; the Italian vessels *Mare Jonio* and *Alex*, backed by NGO Mediterranea Saving Humans; the Spanish former fishing vessel *Aita Mari*, run by Salvamento Marítimo Humanitario; the Dutch former fishing vessel *Iuventa*, operated until its prosecution by German organisation Jugend Rettet; *Open Arms*, run by the Spanish NGO Proactiva Open Arms; the former trawler *Sea-Eye* and former oceanographic vessel *Alan Kurdi*, both operated by German NGO Sea-Eye; several German Sea-Watch vessels, which have been blocked and detained several times by European authorities; and the surveillance yacht *Josefa* and newer ketch *Nadir*, run by German NGO Resqship. Mainwaring and DeBono trace the emergence from 2017 of an EU-led narrative of NGO collusion with people smugglers, with the maritime activities of NGOs described by Frontex as generating migrant pull factors and several NGO vessels being seized and impounded by state authorities (2021, 2, 9).

In the context of what has become a highly mediatised domain of migrant distress and rescue, the criminalisation of NGO search and rescue operations has shown up some of the contradictions of European humanitarianism.

Mainwaring and DeBono note that the activities of NGOs interrupt 'The social construction of the Mediterranean as an empty space' as well as the 'framing [of] migration flows as an ahistorical "crisis" ' by 'expos[ing] the limits of Europe's humanitarianism and illustrat[ing] the persistence of neo-colonial imaginations of the Mediterranean as *mare nostrum*' (2021, 3, italics in original). Recent proposals for the EU to fund border controls in eastern Turkey (Rankin 2021) represent just the latest example of the *us* that is implied in these neo-colonial imaginings. And at the same time as NGO criminalisation has increased, large numbers of migrants have been intercepted at sea in state-run and UNHCR-supported operations, whereupon they are returned to Libya rather than taken to Europe ('Record Number' 2021). As such, the criminalisation of NGO rescue in the Mediterranean highlights starkly divergent notions regarding safe places and refoulement, which in turn produce what might be termed *maritime dramaturgies of migration*. Such dramaturgies highlight continuities between NGO vessels and Banksy's Louise Michel because of the way SAR *per se* has become politically performative: in her discussion of representations of refugees at sea, Parvati Nair observes that when the NGO boat *Aquarius* languished for several days in 2018 after rescuing 629 migrants, whereupon Italy and France closed their borders to the vessel, 'a new socialist government in Spain offered "sanctuary" by way of a political statement' (Nair 2020, 411). As the political stand-off played out, close-up images circulated in the media of stranded migrants, many in poor condition. This confirmed the degree to which the region's national and supranational debates over unauthorised migration have produced the conditions for the escalation of distress and for spectacularised rescue. A performative circularity binds the capitalist agency of the millionaire owners of *M/Y Phoenix* and the agency of the millionaire visual artist who, as I will discuss below, has frankly rendered his own economic privilege part of his art-activist intervention.

Out of a framework of criminalised NGO rescue emerges the aestheticisation of the M.V. Louise Michel and its associated promotional discourse. More than a week after its departure from Burriana, Spain, on 18 August 2020 (Tondo and Stierl 2020), the Louise Michel received calculated media attention, with reports accompanied by images of the brightly coloured vessel with its recognisable Banksy iconography. The story was broken on 27 August in the *Guardian* (Tondo and Stierl 2020), and numerous global media reports picked it up, repeating details concerning Banksy's initiation of the project. He had reportedly emailed Pia Klemp, the former captain of several NGO rescue missions, writing 'I am an artist from the UK and I've made some work about the migrant crisis, obviously I can't keep the money. Could you use it to buy a new boat or something? Please let me know. Well done. Banksy' (qtd in Tondo and Stierl 2020). While Klemp insists upon a distinction between the work of the boat and that of its artist financier, stating, 'Banksy won't pretend that he knows better than us how to run a ship, and we won't pretend to be artists' (qtd in Tondo and Stierl 2020), the use to which the 31-metre former French navy vessel has been put cannot be disentangled from art practice. Its differentiation from other NGO rescue operations—contextually, visually and in terms of reception—is precisely what clarifies the artistic character of its intervention.

The Louise Michel's iconography stands in conversation with Banksy's body of work, which in recent years has responded to forced migration and other forms of oppression. Typically, he situates his concern with oppression in relation to wealth inequality, sometimes in very obvious ways, with images of obscene luxury placed side-by-side with the abject conditions of the most impoverished. Aside from its more famous characteristics of pseudonymity and clandestine working methods, Banksy's is a practice concerned with citation and ironic repurposing. His rescue vessel project bears this out. Painted white with a lurid pink spray-paint motif running along its sides and the word RESCUE in large letters, the Louise Michel features a repurposed take on Banksy's iconic 'Girl with Balloon' stencils of a young girl holding aloft a heart-shaped balloon (a version of which self-shredded at auction at Sotheby's London in 2018 in an action known as 'Love Is in the Bin'). The Louise Michel riffs on this image, only here the girl holds aloft a life buoy. In the years preceding the Louise Michel project, politicised maritime motifs had become an increasingly central dimension of Banksy's oeuvre. In 2015, he created several murals at Calais, the site of the former 'Jungle' refugee encampment, one of which referenced Theodore Gericault's *Raft of the Medusa* with a depiction of distressed and drowning migrants attempting in vain to draw the attention of a luxury yacht in the far distance (Carrigan 2020). At the 2019 Venice Biennale, Banksy set up an illegal 'street stall' of gilt-framed paintings depicting across several canvasses an enormous luxury yacht, dwarfing its surroundings in Venice and spilling over the frames of each individual painting. The works were displayed in a tight grid formation (referencing old European academy hanging traditions) and accompanied a small hand-painted sign that elliptically referenced the harmful excesses of luxury, 'Venice in Oil'. In the same year, a mural appeared in Venice, presumed to be by Banksy, of a child holding a bright pink rescue flare. This, of course, is an image whose child subject matter and vivid palette would be revisited in the decoration of the Louise Michel.

The project by Banksy that had come closest to the direct-action work of the Louise Michel is his subversive 'theme park' Dismaland, constructed on the site of a former public pool in Somerset, UK, in 2015. One of Dismaland's several 'attractions' were motorised refugee boat sculptures depicting near-identical busts of migrants sitting listlessly aboard a tiny vessel (one of these sculptures was sold in a raffle in 2018 to raise funds for refugees [Thomson 2018]). Upon the dismantling of Dismaland, Banksy transported some of its items to Calais to facilitate the construction of accommodation units and play areas at the Jungle (Kordic 2015). Much like the repurposing of a French navy vessel for Mediterranean SAR, the repurposing of infrastructure from Dismaland to the Calais Jungle, reinforcing a brutally ironic conceptual mirroring of the two sites, operates *both* as direct-action *and* as representational work: in each instance, a politicised identification of a desperate need for items that have elsewhere been classified as no longer of use, detritus—or in Banksy's words, 'crap' (qtd. in 'Dismaland' 2015).

During its first rescue operation in the summer of 2020, the Louise Michel rescued 219 migrants off the coast of Libya. When it became stranded due to overcrowding and the release of a life-raft, authorities of Italy, Malta and Germany were unresponsive. Ultimately, the Italian Coastguard transferred 49 of the most vulnerable on board and transported the body of a deceased man. The NGO vessel *Sea-Watch 4* transferred the remaining people (Sibthorpe and Mercer, 2020). As far as its mission was concerned, the voyage of the Louise Michel was beset by the prohibitions that have faced similar NGO operations that have sent out calls for and belatedly received assistance. As an operation that brought wider public attention to the fraught processes of sea rescue in the region, to the loss of life that occurs regularly as a result of dangerous maritime transit, the operation made its action politically instrumental. The operation was publicised via social media, and in the wake of their assistance, a tweet was sent reporting: 'Just transferred all remaining guests onto #SeaWatch4, who now have about 350 people on board. It's not over: We demand a Place of Safety for all survivors, now' (@MVLouiseMichel, August 29, 2020). In this statement, migrants or refugees are reclaimed as *guests* and as *people* and as *survivors*. The combinatory quality of this rescue—its mode of direct action being inseparable from its visibility and political notoriety—demonstrate the inescapability of representation in such contexts. To put it differently, as much as it was a rescue, the Louise Michel's operation was also an event: framed in time and place, reported on in the media with accompanying images, narrativised with a particular ideological slant by stakeholders. Banksy's project inserted an intervention at sea into the domain of cultural-artistic practice.

The move by some NGO rescue operations into branding and merchandising underscores their continuity with the aesthetic techniques of visibility employed by Banksy and his team of commissioned activists. Open Arms, for example, sell a range of branded 'life saving gifts', including clothing, tote bags, badges, posters, a mug and drink bottle, stationary, and in the Covid-19 era a 'stay safe' face covering. The organisation also markets a book of photographs by Ricardo Garcia Vilanova *The Libyan Crossroads* (2021). But representation is not the key purpose of or point of departure for NGOs and I have sought to distinguish Banksy's intervention as artistic and performative in a way that makes it distinct from NGO operations, even those that pursue practices of visibility that include branding. The distinction does not compromise the political efficacy of the Louise Michel. In his discussion of artistic and non-artistic political activism, Philipp Kleinmichel is clear that 'there is no authentic political activism on the one hand and an inauthentic, failed aestheticized or simulated political activism on the other'. The difference between artistic and non-artistic political activism inheres, Kleinmichel argues, in the way the symbolic operates in artistic political activism:

> There is [...] a minimal yet irreducible difference between nonartistic and artistic political activism that comprises the production of an excessive symbolic surplus that exceeds the symbolic dimension of political activism. While nonartistic political activism may employ aesthetic strategies with disinterest in the fact, whether or not they are recognized as art, artistic political activism is driven by the conscious or unconscious intention to signify and code the specific aesthetic and symbolic forms of nonartistic political activism as art. (2019, 234)

The fact that the Louise Michel's mission was beset by obstruction may situate the intervention as generating what Kleinmichel calls 'symbolic surplus', its publicity attaching to it a spurious aesthetic of gesture (though state interference at sea means that excess here should not imply ineptitude). Kleinmichel argues that the identification of artistic political activism as art is a recognition of its symbolic, aesthetic value, through which it moves 'into the context of the museum' (2019, 235). This 'musealized context', he argues, 'not only allows for, but also forces the viewer into a distance from the immediate effects of direct political action', a framework of 'time and space' (2019, 235) from which to perceive and appraise the intervention's meaning, now and in the future.

#Solidarityandresistance v Benefactors and Beneficiaries

The activists operating the Louise Michel as well as those on various other NGO humanitarian missions in the Mediterranean use social media to articulate a shared ideological project via the hashtag #SolidarityAndResistance, a reclamation of the SAR (Search and Rescue) acronym. This discursive repurposing of SAR aligns the NGOs' actions at sea in terms of the anarchist ideals of horizontal (shared) power. The social media feeds of NGO vessels express broad condemnation of EU border policies, including the prosecution of crew members and blocking or impounding of vessels. On 22 October 2020, the Louise Michel's Twitter account reported that it was being prevented from leaving port. Further tweets noted that several NGO vessels were in a similar position. As widely accessible forms of public communication, social media is deployed here to situate the saving of lives in the Mediterranean in two important and related ways: first, as part of a framework of global anti-racism action, and second, as contingent upon state power. The dual implications of race and state sovereignty underscore the neo-colonial condition of European powers that extend beyond state borders into what Pugliese calls the 'pre-frontier'. Sovereign power exerted beyond its own borders generates, as Pugliese argues, sites of 'externalised externality' in such a way as to 'signif[y] an imperially extended and amplified understanding of geopolitical space' (2014, 578). As noted above, Mainwaring and DeBono identify similar neoimperial underpinnings in the operations of state and EU powers, but they also observe that these operations are strategically ambivalent: in the Mediterranean, they contend, 'criminalization of NGO activity at sea is made possible through an oscillating neo-colonial imagination of the sea as *mare nostrum* and *mare nullius*, *our sea* and *nobody's sea*, respectively' (2021, 3). While a notion of *mare nullius* abdicates responsibility (and erases the sea's historical, political and legal dimensions), assertions of *mare nostrum* are, Mainwaring and DeBono argue, a means by which 'states and the EU [have] reasserted their control over the Mediterranean' (2021, 11).

How far can SAR initiatives by NGOs that are ideologically aligned with ideals of race equality and horizontal power circumvent the neo-colonial state power that determines their very capacity to operate, not to mention their *need* to do so? An obvious feature of the direct-action intervention of the Louise Michel is that the subjects of its intervention cannot legitimately be framed as participants. Certainly, operational attention to terminology, with references (as noted above) to guests rather than migrants, signals a politicised construction of rescue in terms of hospitality rather than citizenship. But hospitality is not the same as equality. Mainwaring and DeBono's observation that NGO vessels are 'an important new form of monitoring on the high seas, where oversight of government activity had previously been limited to migrant accounts, readily dismissed by policymakers' (2021, 8) underscores the differential authority afforded to the accounts of rescuers over those of migrants in the discursive construction of the Mediterranean. With his profile eclipsing that of any NGO activist, Banksy's art-activist intervention both contributes and draws public attention to this monitoring on the high seas, but inevitably it does so by reinforcing the benefactor / beneficiary relation that is built into refugee status.

The persistence of uneven agency in performative refugee representations is not easily rectified. Even artistic projects that are refugee-led can, via an audiencing that is preoccupied with helping refugees, reproduce insidious inequalities. According to the celebrated Iranian writer, activist and former detained refugee Behrouz Boochani, audiences' implicit positive biases are a form of colonial thinking. Following a screening of his feature-length documentary film *Chauka, Please Tell Us the Time* (2017), made clandestinely during his detention by the Australian government on Manus Island in Papua New Guinea, Boochani expressed disappointment that the kinds of questions he would routinely be asked at Q&As were overwhelmingly those oriented towards a kind of interventionist thinking (with questions such as *what can we do to help detainees* and *what can this film do*), as well as generalised expressions of apology by emotionally impacted audience members. What Boochani desired was to be asked about his film as an aesthetic product: for a critical engagement with complex questions of representation, authorship, form and influence. Boochani's film was widely received as a potential springboard to political change, its achievement indexed to its revelation of the conditions of detainees' lives more than to its considerable formal innovation. While Boochani has recently received major plaudits for his art, particularly his writing (for more detail, see Cox 2021), his experience—which he interprets with lucidity—reminds us that refugees struggle to be perceived as producers of aesthetic artefacts, foremost, in the complex, unevenly privileged ecologies of artistic and political intervention through which Bansky moves with comparative ease.

Presented to the public via an ironic Instagram clip imbued with its artist-funder's self-conscious awareness of the extreme contrast between mobilities of wealth and privilege and mobilities that are forced, Banksy's direct-action intervention lends greater clarity to the non-artistic interventions with which it is bound. Banksy brought aesthetics into the domain of SAR, inserting a 'musealized context' (Kleinmichel 235) from which the power relations that govern the neo-colonial zone of the Mediterranean could be framed. As a direct-action work, Banksy's intervention is a spatial and ideological palimpsest, tracing non-artistic SAR missions by NGOs and thus *coming between* migrants and necropolitical power, even as it does so for representational purposes additional to those of coming between. Banksy's humanitarian performative arguably elucidates non-artistic action in the world. And even so, in terms of its capacity as art, the same problems that can limit interventionist ambitions in applied and participatory theatre (Balfour 2009, 355–357), those concerning sustainability, unpredictability, incompletion, and the instrumentalisation of human relationships, pertain to the M.V. Louise Michel, operating as it must within an ecology of state-led maritime surveillance, whereby expulsion is preferable to the facilitation of migration across the sea.

References

Agamben, Giorgio. 2000 [1996]. *Means Without End: Notes on Politics*. Translated by Vincenzo Binetti and Cesare Casarino. Minneapolis and London: University of Minnesota Press.

Balfour, Michael, ed. 2013. *Refugee Performance: Practical Encounters*. Bristol and Chicago: Intellect.

Balfour, Michael. 2009. 'The Politics of Intention: Looking for a Theatre of Little Changes', *RiDE: Research in Drama Education*, 14 (3), 347–359.

Banksy. 2020. Instagram video, August 29. 2020. https://www.instagram.com/p/CEeHxqgF7gU/.

Carrigan, Margaret. 2020. 'Banksy Funds Refugee Rescue Ship in the Mediterranean', *The Art Newspaper*, August 27. https://www.theartnewspaper.com/news/banksy-refugee-ship

Center for Political Beauty. n.d. 'The Jean Monnet Bridge.' Accessed 10 July 2021. https://politicalbeauty.com/rescue.html.

Cox, Emma. 2021. 'Island Impasse: Refugee Detention and the Thickening Border.' In *The Oxford Handbook of Politics and Performance*, edited by Shirin M. Rai, Milija Gluhovic, Silvija Jestrović and Michael Saward, 217–233. Oxford: Oxford University Press.

———. 2017. 'Processional Aesthetics and Irregular Transit: Envisioning Refugees in Europe', *Theatre Journal*, 69 (4), 477–496.

Davies, Lizzy and Arthur Nelson. 2014. 'Italy: End of Ongoing Sea Rescue Mission "Puts Thousands at Risk"', *The Guardian*, October 31, 2014. Accessed 10 July 2021. https://www.theguardian.com/world/2014/oct/31/italy-sea-mission-thousands-risk

De Genova, Nicholas. 2013. 'Spectacles of Migrant "Illegality": The Scene of Exclusion, The Obscene of Inclusion.' *Ethnic and Racial Studies*, 36 (7), 1180–1198.

'Dismaland to be Taken Down and Sent to Calais to Build Shelters'. 2015. *Guardian*, 28 September: https://www.theguardian.com/artanddesign/2015/sep/28/banksy-dismaland-taken-down-sent-calais-build-shelters-jungle-migrants. Accessed 10 July 2021.

Farrier, David. 2011. *Postcolonial Asylum: Seeking Sanctuary Before the Law*. Liverpool: Liverpool University Press.

Jeffers, Alison. 2012. *Refugees, Theatre and Crisis: Performing Global Identities*. Houndmills, Basingstoke: Palgrave Macmillan.

Kershaw, Baz. 1992. *The Politics of Performance: Radical Theatre as Cultural Intervention*. London and New York: Routledge.

Kordic, Angie. 2015. 'What is The Meaning Behind the New Banksy Piece in Calais?', *Widewalls*, December 12, 2015. Accessed 10 July 2021. widewalls.ch/magazine/banksy-steve-jobs-calais

Kleinmichel, Philipp. 2019. 'The Symbolic Excess of Art Activism.' In *The Art of Direct Action: Social Sculpture and Beyond*, edited by Karen Van Den Berg, Cara Jordan, Philipp Kleinmichel, 211–238. Berlin: Sternberg Press.

Louise Michel. 2020. Accessed 10 July 2021. https://mvlouisemichel.org/.

Mainwaring, Ċetta and Daniela DeBono. 2021. 'Criminalizing Solidarity: Search and Rescue In a Neo-Colonial Sea.' *Environment and Planning C: Politics and Space*, 39 (5), 1030–1048.

Mbembe, Achille. 2003. 'Necropolitics', *Public Culture*, 15 (1), 11–40.

Meerzon, Yana. 2020. *Performance, Subjectivity, Cosmopolitanism*. Basingstoke: Palgrave Macmillan.

Nair, Parvati. 2020. 'At Sea: Hope as Survival and Sustenance for Refugees.' In *Refugee Imaginaries: Research Across the Humanities*, edited by Emma Cox, Sam Durrant, David Farrier, Lyndsey Stonebridge and Agnes Woolley, 410–422. Edinburgh: Edinburgh University Press.

Nield, Sophie. 2008. 'The Proteus Cabinet, or "We are Here but not Here."' *RiDE: Research in Drama Education*, 13 (2), 137–45.

Pugliese, Joseph. 2014. 'Technologies of Extraterritorialisation, Statist Visuality and Irregular Migrants and Refugees.' *Griffith Law Review*, 22 (3), 571–597.

Rankin, Jennifer. 2021. 'EU plan to fund Turkey border control "risks refugees' forced return"', *Guardian*, June 23, 2021. https://www.theguardian.com/world/2021/jun/23/eu-proposal-to-fund-turkey-border-control-could-lead-to-syrian-refugees-forced-return

'Record Number of Migrants Returned to Libya, UN Says'. 2021. *Deutsche Welle*, June 13, 2021. https://www.dw.com/en/record-number-of-migrants-returned-to-libya-un-says/a-57870566

Schloenhardt, Andreas and Colin Craig. 2015. '"Turning Back the Boats": Australia's Interdiction of Irregular Migrants at Sea.' *International Journal of Refugee Law*, 27 (4), 536–572.

Schramm, Moritz, Sten Pultz Moslund, Anne Ring Petersen, Mirjam Gebauer, Hans Christian Post, Sabrina Vitting-Seerup, Frauke Wiegand. 2019. *Reframing Migration, Diversity and the Arts: The Postmigrant Condition*. New York: Routledge.

Sibthorpe, Clare, and David Mercer. 2020. 'Hundreds Stranded on Banksy-Funded Migrant Rescue Boat Transferred to Safety', *Sky News*, August 30. Accessed 11 July 2021. https://news.sky.com/story/banksy-funded-migrant-rescue-boat-helped-by-italian-coastguard-after-it-became-stranded-in-mediterranean-sea-12059020

Thompson, James. 2009. *Performance Affects: Applied Theatre and the End of Effect*. Houndmills, Basingstoke, Palgrave Macmillan.

Thomson, Lizzie. 2018. 'Banksy "Dream Boat" Refugee Sculpture is Up for Grabs in This £2 Ticket Raffle', *Evening Standard*, December 12. Accessed 10 July 2021. https://www.standard.co.uk/culture/banksy-sculpture-charity-raffle-refugee-ps2-a4015301.html

Tondo, Lorenzo, and Maurice Stierl. 2020. 'Banksy Funds Refugee Rescue Boat Operating in Mediterranean', *Guardian*, August 27. Accessed 10 July 2021. https://www.theguardian.com/world/2020/aug/27/banksy-funds-refugee-rescue-boat-operating-in-mediterranean.

Van Reekum, Rogier. 2016. 'The Mediterranean: Migration Corridor, Border Spectacle, Ethical Landscape.' *Mediterranean Politics*, 21 (1), 336–41.

Vilanova, Ricardo Garcia. 2021. *The Libyan Crossroads*. Barcelona: Blume.

Wake, Caroline. 2013. 'To Witness Mimesis: The Politics, Ethics and Aesthetics of Testimonial Theatre in *Through the Wire*', *Modern Drama*, 56 (1), 102–25.

Wilmer, S. E. 2018. *Performing Statelessness in Europe*. Cham: Palgrave Macmillan.

Woolley, Agnes. 2014. *Contemporary Asylum Narratives: Representing Refugees in the Twenty-First Century*. Houndmills, Basingstoke: Palgrave Macmillan.

Zaroulia, Marilena. 2018. 'Performing That Which Exceeds Us: Aesthetics of Sincerity and Obscenity During "The Refugee Crisis."' *RiDE: Research in Drama Education*, 23 (2), 179–92.

Zoppi, Marco. 2020. 'The "Three Absences" of Black Africans in European Migration Debates.' *Mediterranean Politics*, 25 (5), 627–649.

CHAPTER 47

Theatre, Migration and Activism: The Work of Good Chance Theatre

Alison Jeffers and Ambrose Musiyiwa

In our case study investigation into theatre and arts practices with refugees and migrants in refugee camps and other locations in Europe, we focus on Good Chance Theatre's work in the Jungle, an informal migrant and refugee camp in the city of Calais in France, and on the company's subsequent work in Britain and France. Primarily, we are interested in questions of activism which we investigate through the prism of structures. This begins with thinking about structures of feeling before moving on to consider the physical structure of the theatre space in the Jungle and beyond. We write against a background of growing xenophobia and extreme distrust of migrants coupled with deliberate policies by many governments in Europe to create a hostile environment for refugees and migrants.

Refugee camps are sites of theatre and performance (Thompson 2004; Thompson and Schechner 2004) but rarely receive detailed scholarly attention as such. Possibly the earliest reflections on these sites come from performance theorist and practitioner Dwight Conquergood in Ban Vinai refugee camp in Thailand in the 1980s (Conquergood 1988). Recent examples of reports on arts activities in refugee camps include Fadi Fayad Skeiker's study on theatre workshops with young Palestinians in the Baqaa refugee camp in Aman, Jordan

---

A. Jeffers (✉)
University of Manchester, Manchester, UK
e-mail: Alison.Jeffers@manchester.ac.uk

A. Musiyiwa
University of Manchester and Community Arts Northwest (CAN), Manchester, UK
e-mail: ambrose.musiyiwa@postgrad.manchester.ac.uk

© The Author(s), under exclusive license to Springer Nature Switzerland AG 2023
Y. Meerzon, S. E. Wilmer (eds.), *The Palgrave Handbook of Theatre and Migration*, https://doi.org/10.1007/978-3-031-20196-7_47

(Skeiker 2011), and Kimberley Clair's accounts of work in Za'atari camp, also in Jordan, where painting and drawing workshops led to the creation of large murals (Clair 2017). Anita Hallewas' accounts of applied theatre practices in Greek refugee camps can be added to this small but growing list (Hallewas 2022).

In her 2011 UNHCR report, Awet Andemicael identifies arts activities in around 21 camps and draws attention to a growing trend in which 'refugees themselves have been actively engaged as initiators, participants and/or participatory audience members' (Andemicael 2011, 1). Andemicael suggests that such activities may provide an effective medium for behaviour change communication and are useful educational tools through which to address psychosocial issues and improve the quality of life for camp residents (Andemicael 2011, 1). To this, we add that, as the Good Chance Theatre (GCT) case study shows, participating in the arts can also be a way for camp residents themselves to reactivate, develop or maintain interest or careers in the arts.

We consider the decision by GCT volunteers to tap into artistic practices that were present in the Jungle and make a direct offer of further creative opportunities to people living there. We also look at the effect of doing this work in a temporary settlement with no fixed infrastructure, and the use and impact of the geodesic dome in which the work took place, first in the Jungle and then in Britain and France. We argue that the dome provided a pole whose magnetic force made the previously unimaginable happen—that there can be a theatre in a refugee camp. And we investigate what happens when this theatre moves out of the camp into communities where large numbers of refugees have settled. We are also interested in the wider implications of this work on a political level and will investigate questions of activism, which we define broadly as encompassing all activities that work towards effecting change.

Ideas about structures, both physical and political, form the common thread through this case study. For the former, we focus on the dome structure that GCT first set up in the Jungle and later used in other locations. We pay attention to the dome's functions and the effect of its actual shape and structure on the activities carried out within. In thinking about the wider social and political structures within which the dome operates, we are guided by Raymond Williams' 'structures of feeling' (1977). We are interested in the ways in which structures of feeling can help articulate processual or 'forming and formative processes' (Williams 1977, 128). Structures of feeling allow us to tie together the thinking that created the dome in the Jungle with the processes of thinking that have seen its reuse in other locations. They provide us with a way of thinking about the unfinished creative work that occurs in and around the structure of the dome. Structure of feeling also allows us to embrace an open sense of everyday activism that is reflected by Williams' concern with 'meanings and values as they are actively lived or felt' before they ossify into 'more formal concepts of "world-view" or "ideology" ' (Williams 1977, 132). This we are calling structures of activism.

STRUCTURES OF ACTIVISM

Reflecting on GCT's work in the Jungle and beyond, we argue that the physical and material potential created by the dome's structure enabled and influenced both the work in the Jungle and GCT's continuing participatory work. We further suggest that the company's work is activist in nature while reclaiming activism from possible negative connotations.

We see clear connections between GCT's work and Cathy Sloan's concept of spaces of potentiality. Sloan, whose work focuses on participants who are addicted to drugs and alcohol, discusses the way in which the people she works with exist within a 'hostile environment' (Sloan 2020, 390), a phrase more commonly associated with Britain's harsh immigration policies put into place in the early 2000s under Theresa May's Conservative government. Sloan is interested in how 'theatrical performance might serve as a mechanism for exploring the ways in which bodies, identities and social relations evolve' (Sloan 2020, 392). Her interest in participatory and collaborative approaches to performance is similar to methods adopted by artists working with GCT in the dome who operate within a 'liminal milieu' in which 'creative practice as a space of potentiality […] also attends to the material conditions or societal systems that impact on practice' (Sloan 2020, 396). The 'space of potentiality' indicates how encounters in a novel temporary environment might enable people with similar experiences to make discoveries about themselves and others in that space.

For theatre maker and cultural theorist Ngugi wa Thiong'o 'the struggle between the arts and the state can best be seen in performance in general and in the battle over performance space in particular' (Ngugi 1997, 11). Writing about the post-independence Kenyan state in the 1970s and 1980s, Ngugi observed that 'the open space among the people is perceived by the state to be the most dangerous area because it is the most vital' (Ngugi 1997, 28). We find it an easy leap of the imagination to move from the open-air performance spaces Ngugi describes to the geodesic dome GCT built in the Jungle and subsequently used in towns and cities in Britain and France. The dome has as much, if not more, value as a symbolic space—a kind of impossible space of performance in a place where the struggle to meet the most basic needs was paramount. It speaks to audiences far beyond the camp, the 'interested watchers outside the gates' (Ngugi 1997, 23), of human suffering and struggle, of the huge injustices that brought people to that site and which kept them there as virtual prisoners.

We suggest that the liminality of GCT's activities in the Jungle makes a spatial analysis compelling because it brings together the material and the symbolic. A liminal space of potentiality was created by building the dome in the Jungle, providing a convivial focal point in an extremely hostile environment. The space created by GCT also occupies a symbolic liminal space, unsanctioned and unsupported by the state, an 'open space among the people' (Ngugi 1997, 28) that at the same time continues to provide a memory or an image that outlasts the structure itself. The memory of the Jungle is evoked every time GCT constructs the theatre dome elsewhere, recalling an important initiative that brought the needs of refugees and migrants sharply into focus. The dome generates an image that reminds us of so many on-going injustices around migration across the globe.

This leads us to consider the work of GCT as a set of activist practices. We wish to make an argument here for reducing the popular stigma often attached to activism. For Williams, 'art and literature are often among the very first indications that such a new structure is forming' seen particularly in 'emergent formations' rather than in more dominant modes of creative expression (Williams 1977, 133). The emergent participatory forms seen in the work of GCT have their roots in older forms, in community arts, theatre in education and processual drama, to name but a few. Placing these forms into the contemporary context of work with forced migrants in places where they settle reflects an 'inclusive, reflexive view of activism' (Maxey 1999, 199) whereby activism can be broadened out and reclaimed as a 'continual process of reflection, challenge and empowerment' (Maxey 1999, 201). Taking this back to GCT's community and participatory work allows us to see the people involved as activists who are contributing and consciously placing themselves in relation to their world with an aim to challenge rather than impose power dynamics (Polonyi 2021, 27). The unique space offered by the dome, its location in 'impossible' spaces of art and within a structure of feeling that is largely anti-immigrant, demonstrates the need for the work of companies like Good Chance Theatre.

GOOD CHANCE THEATRE CASE STUDY

The Jungle, where GCT set up its first geodesic dome, was largely populated by refugees and migrants from different conflict zones in the Middle East and northern Africa who were either travelling with an aim to settle in Britain or were waiting for their asylum applications to be processed in France, which does not provide accommodation for most people during this process (Ansaloni 2020; Stuber 2021). The French state initially tolerated the makeshift camp, which had a fluctuating population of between 4000 and 10,000 people, and had grown on a former landfill site near chemical factories in the eastern part of Calais between January 2015 and October 2016. However, the state soon adopted a hostile approach towards the settlement and its inhabitants and routinely bulldozed structures that overspilled before finally demolishing the camp in October 2016. In the process, the French state destroyed belongings and any identification papers and passports left in the structures (Charlton 2015). Conditions in the Jungle were appalling. According to *Médecins du Monde*, one of very few organizations providing psychosocial support in the camp, the situation constituted 'a humanitarian emergency' with approximately 90 per cent of the people living there experiencing mental health conditions (Clair 2017). Volunteers, non-governmental organizations and an investigation by the French state itself reveal that many of the people living in the camp experienced disproportionately high levels of police violence, including physical and verbal abuse and excessive use of tear gas and force (Boittiaux et al. 2021). Before and after the demolition, the residents of the camp relied almost completely on their own resourcefulness and on volunteer support to improve conditions.

Good Chance Theatre, a geodesic dome that operated in the Jungle between October 2015 and March 2016 was one of the spaces erected by volunteers and residents. The dome housed many kinds of participatory arts, sports, martial arts, meetings, film nights and drama and theatre activities. There was a strong will among the organizers to be responsive to the wishes and needs of the refugees and migrants who came into the space, working with their impulses more than expecting the people, many of whom were in very fragile states of health, to participate in any kind of ready-made or fixed programme (Bailey 2020). The dome provided a space in which activist and community-building arts activities were provided and coordinated by professional artists who worked in a voluntary capacity.

In the Jungle, which was an hour away from both Paris and London, Joe Murphy and Joe Robertson, founders of GCT, found a refugee camp where 'the living standards and the sanitary standards were below a lot of other refugee camps in the world, in some of the poorest, most conflicted areas of the world' (Good Chance 2015). They found a constantly shifting community of people from many different conflict zones living in very basic tents, many of which leaked when it rained. The camp did not have any electricity or adequate drainage, sewage or sanitation facilities (Good Chance 2015). The people in the camp also did not have enough food (Dawnay 2017) or anywhere to dry clothes if they got wet which contributed to the ill-health many of them experienced (Index on Censorship 2016). At the same time, Murphy and Robertson found that the people there had built 'a sort of city, a city full of shops, a bustling market, barbershops, amazing restaurants and cafes like the Kabul Cafe which, for a while, was 5 stars on TripAdviser' (AtlanticLive 2016). There was also a church and mosques and even a sauna, all of which had been built by the people who lived in the Jungle.

Murphy and Robertson envisaged a big physical space that they called a theatre which would be a place where people could tell stories and more in an environment that was safe, relaxed, warm and open to all (Good Chance 2015). The space would be 'sort of a town hall' (Good Chance 2015); 'a cultural space for people who live there [in the Jungle]' (Ministry of Counterculture 2016); 'a space that didn't divide people based on nationality or by faith or by gender'; a space that would have '[n]o categories' (AtlanticLIVE 2016) and 'no judgement' (Good Chance 2015) and which would offer 'something to do in the boredom and the difficulty of life [in a place like the Jungle]' (Index on Censorship 2016). It would be 'somewhere to go to get out of the Jungle' (Index on Censorship 2016) where people could sit, write, talk, share, sing and dance (Good Chance 2015). It would also be 'a place for listening' (Ministry of Counterculture 2016) and connection 'where people on the move can come together with local people and create artistic events, relationships and performances' (Geneva Peace Week 2020) and would reaffirm the humanity of refugees and migrants (Index on Censorship 2016) while the walls of the dome itself would become a space where people could display their artworks (Good Chance 2015).

GCT ran crowdfunding campaigns to fund both the purchase of a second-hand 11 metre geodesic dome and the day-to-day running of the theatre. The Young Vic Theatre, the National Theatre and the Royal Court Theatre offered material support (Good Chance 2015). When asked why they chose a dome, Murphy and Robertson responded, 'It was cheap. It was practical to build. But most importantly, it felt democratic. We needed others to help us build it, and those people then felt invested in it as a space. We wanted people not to feel daunted by whatever it was, but for it to stick out in a compelling way that made you wonder, Why is that here? Then people would have to enter to find an answer to that question' (Personal communication, 3 September 2021).

The shape of the dome was important to the aspirations of GCT, amplifying its functions through its architecture. One member of the company comments on the way in which the shape of the theatre space had a democratizing effect: 'the domes are an incredibly special space because … there is something, physically, about the fact that they are spherical. There are no corners. There is no sense of some people being in a corner and some people being separated out on a stage. It's very equalising' (Interview 16 April 2021). This seems to have been aided specifically also by the acoustics created within the structure: 'The quality of the cover of the dome creates an acoustic effect inside where voices bounce off the walls, so that wherever you are you can hear somebody all the way across the dome as if they are right next to you' (Interview 16 April 2021). The intimacy created by the sonic qualities of the dome had the effect of breaking down barriers: 'There's something almost philosophical about these acoustics that help to create a space where everyone is equal. You can leave labels at the door in the dome. You don't have to be considered through the prism of being "a refugee", or an asylum seeker or a volunteer or an audience member even. All of those things are fluid and, in a way, irrelevant. You are just a human being in that space, making art and participating in art together' (Interview 16 April 2021). This is confirmed by Mazin Saad, an artist with GCT who says the dome gave those working alongside refugees 'the foundation to become close to the refugee, have better understanding and better idea about the refugees, who they are and where they come from' (Geneva Peace Week 2020).

In interviews and public talks they have given on the work, Murphy and Robertson say they called the space a theatre as a provocation because, while they could see no reason why a theatre could not exist in a place like the Jungle (Good Chance 2015), others thought such an offer to be frivolous as it did not attend to the need for food, shelter and other basic necessities which were perceived to be what the people in the camp needed most (Thompson 2016). This is clearly expressed by a volunteer who worked with the company: 'I didn't expect to end up in a theatre. I didn't come here to do artsy fartsy bollocks. I came here to fix stuff and I've built a house. I helped build a school' (Good

Chance 2015). This incredulity was also shared by some camp inhabitants with one of the company members telling the story of Majid Adin, an Iranian artist and animator who 'came into the dome in Calais and kind of looked around and was like, "What is this place? What are you doing? Why are you doing art? People need food. People need shelter here. What… like… this is such a waste of time. I need shoes. I'm going to find shoes"' (Interview 16 April 2021). They report that Adin, who had trained as a visual artist in Iran but had not painted since leaving Tehran, later came back to the dome, started painting again and, on arriving in Britain, went on to sit on the Board of Trustees of Good Chance (Interview 16 April 2021; Good Chance 2022a).

In the day-to-day running of the theatre space, most of the challenges the company faced revolved around navigating linguistic, cultural and related differences. The company worked with these challenges to provide a programme of activities that suited the environment and the people living there. For example, to facilitate arts practices with people who spoke many different languages, GCT often handed out translation sheets during the rare occasions when performances were held in English (Dawnay 2017). They also designed workshops that were physical and which, as Fenella Dawnay, an international theatre producer who volunteered with GCT in Calais and Britain, puts it, could 'connect with people on a much more physical basis and get people to do more abstract work together' (Dawnay 2017). The temporary nature of the refugee and migrant population also meant that 'long-term projects, of even a week long, were almost impossible and very difficult to achieve. Projects had to be short, engaging and beneficial in practical terms. So, it meant that things like games, that might not be given such importance in the UK, were really, really great at bringing people together' (Dawnay 2017). While there was a lot of violence in and around the Jungle, we have found no evidence to suggest that this violence spilled into the dome at any time. The majority of people who lived in the Jungle were young men who were largely the ones who had more access to activities in the dome (Dawnay 2017). There were also 'tens of children in the dome all the time and very often women too' (Personal communication, 14 December 2021).

After the October 2016 demolition of the camp, many of the evicted refugees and migrants were taken to Paris. GCT focused their efforts there and, between 2017 and 2019, built the dome at six locations (Personal communication, 5 January 2022). At each of these sites, GCT offered a multi-genre programme of performances, workshops and discussions that included carpentry, building, puppetry, circus, theatre, poetry and music. They also offered a weekly or fortnightly 'Hope Show', as they had done every week in Calais, which brought together work that had been made throughout the week and which was presented or performed by the people who had taken part in the workshops. In Britain, GCT first set up the dome for a nine-day festival held at Southbank Centre in London in the summer of 2016. This was followed by 'Dome in a Day', which was offered as part of Refugee Week celebrations in Coventry in June 2019. The following year, GCT built the dome for their

FreeDome Festival in Sheffield. On each of these occasions, the company offered a programme of activities that included poetry, puppetry, theatre, music and dance, and more (Good Chance 2022b).

Like the work in the Jungle which took place over an extended period, GCT's community and participatory arts activity in towns and cities in Britain and France is informed by an understanding of the need to work slowly and incrementally in order to effect change. As one company member puts it, 'It takes a huge amount of resource and effort and individual contact and really democratic networking, I think, to understand who the community leaders are in a particular community and reaching out to them and making a strong enough relationship with them that they then want to reach out to their community and say, "Come along to this thing" ' (Interview 16 April 2021). They describe how 'for Change the Word [the company's poetry collective], for example, we spend at least six months in a place before we start the project, trying to get to know everyone, to share a cup of tea with them, to meet partners and to meet individuals—and slowly, slowly, those relationships hopefully mean that people come who wouldn't necessarily know about it or feel comfortable to otherwise' (Interview 16 April 2021). In this way, GCT demonstrates the importance of listening carefully to communities and how this helps build relationships and establish connections between the company and existing networks.

Alongside this participatory work, GCT has developed a public-facing strand of theatrical activity which sits more comfortably within traditional structures. *The Jungle*, a multi-award-winning play by Murphy and Robertson, drew on their experiences and work in the camp. The play was commissioned by the National Theatre and first presented at the Young Vic Theatre in December 2017 as a co-production by the National Theatre, the Young Vic and GCT. It moved to the Playhouse Theatre in London's West End before touring to the US in 2018. In relation to the production, Yana Meerzon and Kimberley Clair have written about the potential, inherent in the play, of 'humanising' refugees through theatrical representation (Clair 2017; Meerzon 2021) while other voices have looked at its transfer to large commercial venues and questioned the political efficacy of the production in this context (Lamont-Bishop 2019; Tyrell 2020; Welton 2020).

For *The Walk*, GCT's second large-scale production (in conjunction with Handspring Puppet Company), GCT turned Little Amal, a child refugee character from *The Jungle*, into a 3.5 m puppet and set her on a journey from Gaziantep near the Turkish-Syrian border, across Europe to Britain, ending in Manchester in November 2021. Described as 'a theatrical show on an 8000 km stage' (Sherwood 2021), *The Walk* was accompanied by 120 events in 65 cities, towns and villages along the way. To make the events happen, the production team worked with 250 partners and thousands of participants along the route. These groups and partners included humanitarian organizations, civic society, the mayors of the cities *The Walk* passed through, faith leaders, grassroots refugee organizations, and refugee artists. According to Amir Nizar Zuabi, Artistic

Director of *The Walk* (and of Good Chance since summer 2021), the events ranged from 'big city-scale installations, participatory performances in the cities, [and] precise meetings with communities or with an artistic work across the journey' (Zuabi 2021).

In most places Little Amal passed through, she was received with enthusiasm, support and goodwill. Examples of this include how, in Gaziantep, refugee children made lanterns as a sign of welcome. In Rome, at the Vatican, Little Amal shook hands with the Pope and in Brussels, among the people who welcomed her were refugees who were on hunger strike demanding a regularization of their immigration status (Gentleman 2021). In Greece, however, she had a mixed reception in that, while most places she passed through welcomed her, others did not. For example, in the municipality of Meteora, councillors voted against allowing her to visit the monasteries of Meteora on the grounds that 'a puppet depicting a Muslim refugee should not be permitted to perform in a space of such importance to Greek Orthodox believers […] while a local heritage group complained that the initiative could bring more refugees to a country that has already hosted tens of thousands' (Kitsantonis and Marshall 2021). In Larissa (also in Greece), Little Amal and about 300 children who had gathered to meet her were pelted with stones by a group of right-wing protesters (Gentleman 2021).

In conclusion, the 'space of potentiality' (Sloan 2020, 396) represented by the dome in the Jungle and, subsequently, in towns and cities with large migrant and refugee communities, can be seen as an impossible space of performance that allows those directly affected by forced migration to share experiences both within their immediate communities and with the 'watchers outside the gates' (Ngugi 1997, 23), those without that direct experience. The diverse theatrical registers GCT utilizes oscillate productively between large public-facing works like *The Walk* and *The Jungle* and the slower, smaller-scale participatory arts work with communities. By utilizing the full fluidity of arts structures at its disposal, GCT's work sets itself against the negative structure of feeling that persists around refugees in Europe and beyond. We suggest that it is only by understanding the full repertoire of the company that we can fully appreciate the activist nature of the work Good Chance Theatre is doing.

References

Andemicael, Awet. 2011. 'Positive Energy. The Role of Artistic Activity in Refugee Camps.' UNHCR, June. https://www.unhcr.org/us/media/positive-energy-review-role-artistic-activities-refugee-camps-awet-andemicael-june-2011. Accessed 16 July 2023.

Ansaloni, Francesca. 2020. 'Deterritorialising the Jungle: Understanding the Calais camp through its orderings.' *Environment and Planning C: Politics and Space*, 38(5): 885–901. https://doi.org/10.1177/2399654420908597.

AtlanticLIVE 2016. 'Under the Klieg Lights of Calais: What Happens When You Start a Theater in a Refugee Camp / CityLab'. *AtlanticLIVE*, 25 October. https://youtu.be/qhpR-EC4ODs. Accessed 14 August 2021.

Bailey, Tom. 2020. 'The Empty Space. Performing Migration at the Good Chance Theatre in Calais.' In *Refuge in a Moving World: Tracing Refugee and Migrant Journeys across Disciplines*, edited by Elena Fiddian-Qasmiyeh, 210–227. London: UCL Press.

Boittiaux, Camille; Gerlach, Fae Mira and Welander, Marta. 2021. *Refugees and Displaced People: A Brief Timeline of the Human Rights Situation in Northern France*. Refugee Rights Europe, Choose Love / Help Refugees and Human Rights Observers (HRO). https://resourcecentre.savethechildren.net/node/19093/pdf/rre_northern-france-timeline-2020.pdf. Accessed 6 August 2021.

Charlton, Joseph. 2015. 'What Life is Really Like Inside the 'Jungle' in Calais.' *The Independent*, September 30. https://www.independent.co.uk/news/world/europe/refugee-crisis-what-life-really-inside-jungle-calais-a6674256.html. Accessed 10 August 2021

Clair, Kimberly. 2017. 'Art-making as Social Justice in Za'atari and Calais.' *Peace Review. A Journal of Social Justice*, 29(1): 40–47.

Conquergood, Dwight. 1988. 'Health Theatre in a Hmong Refugee Camp. Performance, Communication and Culture.' *TDR*, 32 (3), 174–208.

Dawnay, Fenella. 2017. 'A Space for Theatre in the Calais "Jungle" Refugee Camp.' *In Place of War*, February, 17, 2017; https://www.youtu.be/kMY3W-ENS2g. Accessed 13 September 2021.

Geneva Peace Week. 2020. 'The Power of Collaborating Across Borders: Along the Migration Route'. *Geneva Peace Week*, November 2. https://youtu.be/-AWxicY-2S4. Accessed 11 August 2021.

Good Chance. 2015. 'The Good Chance Theatre—Calais.' *Good Chance*, 5 November. https://www.youtu.be/zD-RyGco3kQ. Accessed 8 August 2021.

Good Chance. 2022a. 'Ensemble: Majid Adin.' *Good Chance*. https://www.goodchance.org.uk/ensemble-majid-adin. Accessed 30 March 2022.

Good Chance. 2022b. 'What We Do: Theatres.' *Good Chance*. https://www.goodchance.org.uk/theatres-what-we-do. Accessed 30 March 2022.

Gentleman, Amelia. 2021. '"People Felt Threatened Even by a Puppet Refugee": Little Amal's Epic Walk Through Love and Fear.' *The Guardian*, October 18. https://www.theguardian.com/stage/2021/oct/18/threatened-puppet-refugee-little-amals-epic-walk. Accessed 18 December 2021.

Hallewas, Anita. 2022. 'Responsibility for the Other: An Ethic of Care in Applied Theatre Practice in Greek Refugee Camps'. In *Applied Theatre: Ethics*, edited by Kirsten Sadeghi-Yekta and Monica Prendergast, 171–186. London: Bloomsbury Publishing.

Index on Censorship. 2016. 'The Good Chance Theatre, Calais—Index on Censorship Awards 2016 Arts nominee.' *Index on Censorship*, 16 March. https://youtu.be/loOWcI73XHg. Accessed 9 August 2021.

Kitsantonis, Niki and Alex Marshall. 2021. 'Giant Puppet Ruffles Some Feathers on a Long Walk Through Greece.' *The New York Times*, 27 August. https://www.nytimes.com/2021/08/27/world/europe/greece-syria-refugees-puppet.html. Accessed 18 December 2021.

Lamont-Bishop, Olivia. 2019. 'Four Thoughts on Place and *The Jungle*.' *Performing Ethos: An International Journal of Ethics in Theatre and Performance*, 9(1): 105–110.

Maxey, Ian. 1999. 'Beyond Boundaries? Activism, Academia, Reflexivity and Research.' *Area* 31(3): 199–208. https://doi.org/10.1111/j.1475-4762.1999.tb00084.x.

Meerzon, Yana. 2021. 'From Exile to Migration: Staging (The) Face of The Human Waste.' In *The Oxford Handbook of Politics and Performance*, edited by Shirin Rai, Milija Gluhovic, Silvija Jestrović and Michael Saward, 199–216. Oxford: Oxford University Press.

Ministry of Counterculture. 2016. 'Монолог для двоих: Good Chance Theatre, Кале'. *The Ministry of Counterculture*, 4 March. https://youtu.be/E9ieH1wRRes. Accessed 12 August 2021.

Murphy, Joe and Joe Robertson. 2017. *The Jungle*. London: Faber and Faber

Ngugi wa Thiong'o. 1997. 'Enactments of Power: The Politics of Performance Space.' *TDR. The Drama Review*, 41 (3), 11–30.

Polonyi, Réka. 2021. 'Disrupting the Hierarchy of Knowledge Production: The Case of Documenting Social Theatre in Palestine.' *Studies in Theatre and Performance*, 41 (1), 21–39

Sherwood, Harriet. 2021. 'Little Amal in Britain: Giant Puppet of Syrian Girl Reaches Her Journey's End.' *The Guardian*, October 18. https://www.theguardian.com/world/2021/oct/17/little-amal-in-britain-giant-puppet-of-syrian-girl-reaches-her-journeys-end. Accessed 30 March 2022.

Skeiker, Fadi Fayad. 2011. 'Performing Orphanage Experience: Applied Theatre Practice In a Refugee Camp in Jordan.' *Applied Theatre Researcher/IDEA Journal*, 1, 1–8.

Sloan, Cathy. 2020. '*The Antidote*: Theorising Recovery Engaged Theatre-Making as a Process of Affective Attunement and Agonistic Activism.' *Research in Drama Education: The Journal of Applied Theatre and Performance*, 25 (3), 390–404.

Stuber, Sophie. 2021. 'What's Behind The Housing Crisis for Asylum Seekers in France?' *The New Humanitarian*, April 27. https://www.thenewhumanitarian.org/news-feature/behind-the-housing-crisis-for-asylum-seekers-in-france. Accessed 5 September 2021.

Thompson, Isobel. 2016. 'Art + Aid: The Good Chance Theatre, Calais.' *Suitcase*, 1 November. https://suitcasemag.com/articles/good-chance-theatre-calais. Accessed 10 August 2021.

Thompson, James. 2004. *Digging Up Stories. Applied Theatre, Performance and War*. Manchester and New York: Manchester University Press.

Thompson, James, and Richard Schechner. 2004. 'Why "Social Theatre"?', *TDR—The Drama Review—A Journal of Performance Studies*, 48 (3), 11–16.

Tyrell, Áine Josephine. 2020. 'Representing Calais' Camp: In the heart of *The Jungle* with the Good Chance Theatre.' *TDR—The Drama Review—A Journal of Performance Studies*, 64 (2), 155–162.

Welton, Emma. 2020. 'Welcome to the Jungle: Performing Borders and Belonging in Contemporary British Migration Theatre.' *Theatre Research International*, 45 (3), 230–244.

Williams, Raymond. 1977. *Marxism and Literature*. London: OUP.

Zuabi, Amir Nizar. 2021. 'A Theatrical Journey Celebrating the Refugee Experience.' *TED*, September 22. https://youtu.be/0He5yz8CwuU. Accessed 18 December 2021.

CHAPTER 48

Theatre and Migration in the Balkans: The Death of Asylum in Žiga Divjak's *The Game*

Milija Gluhovic

Filmed over three years along the borders of Syria, Iraq, Kurdistan, and Lebanon, Gianfranco Rosi's latest nonfiction film *Notturno* (2020) explores the aftermath of war in the Middle East, focusing on those who have stayed and directly suffered its effects. Employing a dark palette and an austere soundtrack, scant dialogues, and no commentary, Rosi renders a potent series of sketches of lives and places torn asunder by war: Peshmerga soldiers going about their daily business; a group of grieving mothers and widows wander through an abandoned fort, the prison from which loved ones failed to emerge; a hunter paddles through twilight marshes captivatingly illuminated by the distant fires of the oil wells; a collection of survivors in a Baghdad asylum rehearse a polemical state-of-the-nation play under the direction of their doctor. In another powerful extended sequence, traumatised children from a destroyed Yazidi village share drawings and memories of their life when they were captured by the Islamic State. Among these war children is Ali, who hunts to support his family. In the film's final sequence, we see him shelter from a tempest under a bending tree, his eyes searching the dark horizon for a glimmer of light. While movingly observing the everyday life of people and places across Syria, Iraq, Lebanon, and Kurdistan, Rosi's film also 'moves beyond a sense of perpetual aftermath by picking up threads of continuity in people's resilience' (Rapold 2021, n.p.).

In this chapter, I will explore the plight of asylum seekers, refugees, and migrants, largely from Syria, Iraq, and Afghanistan (but also from African and

M. Gluhovic (✉)
University of Warwick, Coventry, UK
e-mail: M.Gluhovic@warwick.ac.uk

© The Author(s), under exclusive license to Springer Nature Switzerland AG 2023
Y. Meerzon, S. E. Wilmer (eds.), *The Palgrave Handbook of Theatre and Migration*, https://doi.org/10.1007/978-3-031-20196-7_48

Central Asian countries), who have been following the so-called Western Balkan routes from early spring 2015 onward. This is the territory that also saw the dissolution of Yugoslavia in the 1990s and the displacement of thousands of people from its former republics. I begin this chapter with Rosi's lyrical evocation of the maelstrom of the Middle East because it captures so well the despair, insecurities, and lack of basic means of subsistence and survival, which has propelled many migrants to flee to Europe. Furthermore, all too often, we forget how people in flight—seeking refuge, demanding protection, and claiming asylum—are haunted by horrors that remain inaccessible to those who are witnessing their exodus from the position of the onlooker (see Jestrović in this *Handbook*). The trauma that haunts these people on the move—and which is rarely mentioned in any accounts of their perilous journey toward fortress Europe—is perhaps the thread that connects Rosi's stunningly composed mosaic of darkness and displacement to not only Mediterranean crossings from the Middle East and Africa to Europe but also to crossings along the Balkan routes with its prison-like camps. It is these Balkan crossings and migrant encampment sites that I will explore in this chapter. Rosi's film also reminds us that we cannot critically engage with the migration crisis today without engaging thoroughly with the legacies of the colonial past and the enduring inequalities of the postcolonial present.

This chapter will begin by outlining the historical and socioeconomic factors that have contributed to the rise and fall of the West Balkan corridor that made it possible for a large influx of migrants—men, women, and children—from Africa and the Middle East (Syria in particular) to enter Western Europe in 2015 and 2016. This chapter will then briefly survey the ways in which theatre and performance artists have responded to a recent mass migration occurrence in the region before focussing on the performance *Gejm* (The Game), a devised theatre project by the Mladinsko Theatre in Ljubljana, Slovenia, that premiered on 10 June 2020 and which received the grand prix for best performance of the fifty-sixth annual Maribor Theatre Festival in 2021. This testimonial piece of theatre, this chapter argues, builds an archive of the heterogenous biopolitical and spatial tactics deployed by states for pushing back, diverting, and disrupting migrations, as well as denying migrants access to asylum procedures; at the same time, *The Game* also helps in tracing the political legacies of migrant struggles, thus countering the violent erasures of racialised border practices.

The Balkan Corridor

While in the last decade, irregular migration to Europe has primarily been associated with the transit migration via Libya and the central Mediterranean region, this changed with the rise of the Balkan corridor in the summer of 2015. This exceptional situation was related to the humanitarian emergency caused by the war escalation in the Middle East and the millions of refugees fleeing their homes to find protection elsewhere. While most of these refugees found shelter in the neighbouring countries, hundreds of thousands of migrants who arrived from Turkey to the Greek Islands that summer continued their journey further onward towards Western Europe via Macedonia, Serbia, Hungary, Croatia, and Slovenia. During this period, the media was populated with images of this humanitarian disaster: the critical human mass of people passing through the wide fields of the Western Balkans with little more than a bag, or refugees trying to board a train in Belgrade or Budapest. The Balkan corridor lasted from summer 2015 to spring 2016. It is now maintained that a large influx of migrants was not only due to a combination of different push-forces—including political instability and war especially in Syria but also in Iraq, Afghanistan, and Eritrea—but also due to an array of various idiosyncratic responses from both transit and receiving countries in Europe. Prior to the mass arrivals of migrants in 2015, several states in the southern and southeastern regions of Europe served as 'buffer zones' for the core European Union (EU) countries. However, once Germany and Sweden declared that they would grant protection to Syrian asylum-seekers reaching their borders, the Balkan territories defined themselves as transit countries enabling more than one million people to traverse these states.

Several other historical and socioeconomic factors have framed local authorities' response in the region. Most countries in the region were also destinations for hundreds of thousands of migrants from the Yugoslavian republic following the dissolution of Yugoslavia in the 1990s, so 'throughout the whole region, the responses of the local populations and NGOs were often related to their own experiences of conflict and displacement' (Župarić-Iljić and Valenta 2018, 3). West-Balkan countries' policy positions in the EU, and their relations with the EU need to be taken into account too. While Greece, Hungary, Slovenia, Croatia, and Bulgaria are in the EU, Macedonia, Serbia, and Bosnia and Herzegovina are not. All these countries also suffer from high levels of unemployment, which has generated substantial movements to the EU as well. Given this context, it is not surprising that the West Balkan countries—and people on the move—'were in tacit agreement that such countries could not be regarded as destination countries' (Župarić-Iljić and Valenta 2018, 4). While different countries reacted in different ways to the growing arrival of migrants, some opening their borders with a focus on short-term humanitarian aid (Serbia, Croatia), other countries tried to protect their borders with walls and razor fences (e.g., Bulgaria, Macedonia, Slovenia, and Hungary).

This does not come as a surprise. The range of measures that were put in place more than a decade ago by European Union (EU) member states, with deterrence being their key priority, have effectively undermined the right to seek asylum by blocking access to Europe. Their arsenal includes the imposition of visas for all refugee-producing countries, readmission agreements with neighbouring countries that form a 'buffer zone,' immigration intelligence sharing and police co-operation, reinforced border controls, systematic detentions, and sanctions on carriers transporting migrants without the required travel documents and visas.

Practices of internment and detention in dealing with irregular migrants have grown more abundant in recent years. For instance, from 2000 to 2012, the number of detention camps in Europe has increased from 324 to 473, while increasing security concerns have at times compromised even the principle of non-refoulement, as Seyla Benhabib notes in a recent and scathing critique of the EU's failure to live up to its own human rights commitments (2018, 122). This failure was manifest during the so-called European migration crisis: in the removal of refugees from trains headed to Germany and writing numbers on their arms in ink by both the Czech and the Hungarian police; in the use of police dogs, tear gas, and water guns on protesting refugees by the Macedonians, the Slovenians, and the Hungarians; and in the inhumane living conditions and administrative procedures of harassment, incarceration, and deportation that irregular migrants were subjected to in open-air prisons, such as the Moria camp in Lesbos, until it was burned down in September 2020, and the informal, now dismantled, camps of Calais referred to as 'the jungle' (2018, 101–2).

In mid-February 2016, the heads of police forces in Macedonia, Serbia, Croatia, Slovenia, and Austria agreed on the joint adoption of a standardised migrant registration system, supporting FRONTEX activities, and selecting and profiling migrants based on their nationality. These measures, followed by the signing of the EU-Turkey agreement on 7 March 2016, largely contributed to the ending of the Western Balkan corridor as a safe passageway for refugees. The closure of the route caught thousands of refugees stranded in Serbia—the only country along the route that decided not to close its borders and to continue providing humanitarian support. While the number of arrivals in Serbia has decreased significantly after the closure, a flow of people continues to enter the country who are accommodated in hospitality camps.

During the period of mass migrant transit through the Balkan route, the main migration route circumvented the territory of Bosnia and Herzegovina (BiH) and the number of migrants and refugees entering BiH remained low (Kogovšek Šalamon 2020). However, since late 2017, the 'zero tolerance' policies towards migrants practiced by Višegrad countries meant that the route shifted southwest, via Albania, Montenegro, BiH, and Croatia. Consequently, since 2018, the migration route through BiH strengthened considerably. However, many migrants and refugees enroute to the EU are stranded in the city of Velika Kladuša in western BiH without access to asylum procedure and basic care. As Neža Kogovšek Šalamon writes, migrants 'experience difficulties in moving onwards as first the Slovenian, and then also Croatian authorities are continually pushing them back to Bosnian territory, the latter also with violence' (2020, 136–7). During the wintertime of 2021, European media broadcast reports about thousands of irregular migrants freezing in Bosnia's wide fields and ancient forests while in the 'game' of crossing the frontier to Croatia, calling once more upon the European Union to provide an emergency response. In the meantime, the predominantly ethnicised political leadership of BiH failed to create an appropriate legal framework and structures to offer a minimum of living conditions for receiving migrants on the move.

Theatre and Migrations in the (Western) Balkans: The Game

The field of theatre and performance studies in the Western Balkan countries has seen an uptick in research and creative responses because of the migrant crisis (e.g., Barnett 2016; Orel 2017; Dragićević Šešić and Korać-Sanderson 2019). In 2017, the Belgrade International Theatre Festival (BITEF) marked its fiftieth anniversary featuring many performances that addressed the European migration crisis, while also hosting the congress of the International Association of Theatre Critics. The following year, the International Federation for Theatre Research (IFTR) held its annual conference in Belgrade also on the theme of migrations. Some of the projects that were developed by local theatre artists in relation the recent migration crisis included participatory theatre projects implemented in Belgrade by the Group 484 in collaboration with the DAH Theatre (2018–2019) and by the Centre for Cultural Decontamination (CZKD) and Theatre Zoukak from Beirut. Tanja Ostojić's *Mis(s)placed Women?* (2009–2022) is an ongoing collaborative art project—which features performances and workshops by international artists and people from diverse backgrounds—that embodies and enacts some of the everyday activities that thematise displacement experienced by migrants, refugees, homeless people, and victims of family violence, among others. In May 2021, the Living Atelier DK hosted Selma Banich's exhibition *The Passage*, a collection of memorial portraits commemorating the lives of the people who have died on the migrant trail in the Balkans in recent years. The international group Shadow Casters, composed of professionals of various generations and fields of activity—from art through architecture to science—have realised projects addressing this theme in Ljubljana, Zagreb, Belgrade, and other European cities. Finally, in 2017, the Mikser Festival—an annual cultural event promoting innovative, sustainable, and socially engaged ideas in design, architecture, urban planning, arts, and culture—focused on the theme of migrations and created programmes that directly aided and supported incoming migrants and refugees.

Among these artistic responses, Slovenia's Mladinsko Theatre's documentary theatre piece *The Game*[1] most tellingly epitomises the complexities of the Balkan Corridor. The performance is based on migrants' testimonies from the Border Violence Monitoring Network (BVMN) database, an organisation which documents violence at the borders of the European Union.[2] As a Mladinsko Theatre programme note explains, people on the move 'call the last

---

[1] Many thanks to my colleague and friend Barbara Orel from the Academy of Theatre, Radio, Film and Television of the University of Ljubljana and the staff from the Mladinsko theatre for sharing with me the video and other documentation relating to performance of *The Game*.

[2] In 2020, BVMN published two volumes of *The Black Book of Pushbacks*, a collection of hundreds of testimonies of migrants and asylum seekers who have experienced human rights violations at external borders. See *The Black Book* 2000.

stretch of their route, the stretch that takes them from Bosnia and Herzegovina to a safe destination in the European Union, the game' (Mladinsko Theatre 2020). The long journey that would bring them from one country to another 'has no rules, laws don't apply, the powers of the police is limitless, the violence increasingly brutal, the dangers increasingly more dangerous, the possibilities smaller and smaller, and the destination further and further … Many try several times, even twenty or thirty times; it's a numbers game' (Mladinsko Theatre). After many days and nights of walking and sleeping in the woods, most of the people on the move get caught by the Croatian police and are pushed back into Bosnia. Some of those who make it to Slovenia will be captured there, while those who make it to Italy can hope to move forward. Just as in Mladinsko's performance, 'the game has roles, characters, strategies, enemies, and obstacles (Zocchi 2020, 3). This is how one of the asylum seekers describes it: 'Game … It's really a game. If you're there, that's your reality. You have to be smart in what you're doing. Some people go to game to fight, some just to crosswalk. But in the game … once you lose, you're lost' (Divjak 2020, 40). As we shall see later, the game is fatal for many such people on the move.

At the beginning of the performance, the actors remind the audience that '[a]s a party to the Geneva Convention and a member of the European Union, the Republic of Slovenia is required to provide international protection (asylum) to those persons who are not guaranteed such protection in the country of their nationality or permanent residence' (Divjak 2020, 1). We are then told that the first reports about breaches of the human rights of the asylum seekers who tried to apply for the asylum in Slovenia surfaced in June 2018. These migrants made their way from makeshift shelters in Velika Kladuša and Bihać in Bosnia and Herzegovina and transited through Croatia to Slovenia. Their claims for asylum were ignored by the Slovene officials; instead of being taken to the asylum centre, they were returned to Croatia, and from there to Bosnia and Herzegovina. Many of these migrants claimed that they did not even have the possibility to state their intent to apply for international protection during the police procedure in Slovenia, which was corroborated by the NGO reports and official statistical data. The actors also relate to the audience data from both the Slovenian Ministry of the Interior that documents various asylum procedural irregularities, as well as from the Human Rights Ombudsman's report that confirms 'the seriousness of accusations that there may have been irregularities in some police procedures, including the incidents of push-backs' (Divjak 2020, 3). We also learn that their returns are based on the agreement between Slovenia and Croatia on asylum-seeker readmission (a point I will return to later in this chapter), and that readmission procedures are often accompanied by police violence against migrants in Croatia. In these respects, *The Game* speaks directly to how 'the two basic pillars enshrined in the international refugee protection standards, access to territory and access to procedures for applying for international protection, are obstructed and restricted' (Župarić-Iljić and Valenta 2018, 14).

The years following the Second World War saw the emergence of human right treaties, including the two most important international legal documents governing cross-border movement, namely the Universal Declaration of Human Rights (United Nations 1948) and the Geneva Convention of 1951 Relating to the Status of Refugees along with its 1967 Protocol. These and other human rights treaties have arguably allowed human rights to come of age by recognising the rights of a 'person' independent of any legal state's regime; however, state consent remains the basis for protecting said rights. The Convention and its Protocol, for instance, are binding only for signatory states 'and can be brazenly disregarded by non-signatories and, at times, even by signatory states themselves' (Benhabib 2004, 11). The international human rights norms that emerged in the mid-twentieth century did not solve the principal problem of the refugee as identified by Hannah Arendt—the problem of legal protections independent of citizenship or state consent.

The adoption of the European Agenda of Migration (EAM) by the EU and its members in May 2015, which emerged in response to a dramatic increase in arrival figures, defined European policy towards the 'migrant crisis' in terms of security management of people on the move, by means of Frontex and Europol, and their effective criminalization. While the Agenda maps a range of key actions designed not only to 'manage migration better' (European Commission 2015, 6) but also to 'save lives' (European Commission 2015, 3), Divjak's *The Game* highlights its limitations, documenting the violence of contemporary policies in failing to respect the rights of people on the move.

There are several short scenes in *The Game* in which actors provide information on numerous incidents involving migrants over the course of 2018–2019; these scenes are emblematic of many breaches to their human rights and irregularities in handling migrants on the part of the Slovenian police, such as long hours and multiple days of detention in the police stations with no access to interpreters. Additionally, refugees routinely described their complete denial of access to the asylum process, recounting how their asylum claims would not get heard, translated, or otherwise adequately recorded, and how asylum seekers were forcibly compelled to sign documents in a language they did not understand. Once they were handed over to the Croatian police forces, they would often be subjected to various forms of threats, mockery, and humiliation before getting expelled across the Croatian border with Bosnia and Herzegovina.

Spectators of *The Game* follow close to twenty individual, first-person stories of migrants, which are laid out in chronological order. These stories are terribly similar in their depictions of utterly desperate situations, in which the protagonists are trapped, recalling memories of police brutality and overlooked asylum applications. The actors first offer the objective account of an event in a matter-of-fact manner, which is then followed by a personal story. One after another the stories accumulate just like the various objects that are piled on a map on the floor—wet clothes, phones, a shoe.

For instance, the character of Sara tells the story of four migrants from Afghanistan, aged sixteen to thirty-nine, who entered Slovenia near Žeželj nad Vinico on 13 June 2018:

> My friends and I left Velika Kladuša, crossed Croatia and got to Slovenia where Slovenian border police got us. An officer saw that one of us used GPS and accused him of being a smuggler. Then they started yelling at him, hitting him on the head and slapping him repeatedly. They didn't beat others, just him. Then they took us to the police station in a van. We waited there for about seven hours. We had to write down our names, age, names of parents and other info. I told them I wanted to stay in Slovenia, that I didn't want to run anymore, that I'd work here ... The officer said: 'No, no working, no immigration, you go back.' I couldn't even apply for the asylum. (Divjak 2020, 5–6)

Numerous testimonies conveyed by the Mladinsko's actors recount the acts of physical violence performed by the Croatian police against migrants before they would deport them across the Croatia-BiH border. One of the testimonies spoken by the actors tell of the following incident:

> The door of the van opened, and six cops were standing there, all in the blue Croatian uniforms, and they had masks, so that we could only see their eyes. They created a tunnel, and you had to (go) out, one by one, between them, and they beat us. Then we all had to lie down, and all six cops circulated around us, and they beat us with batons. (Divjak 2020, 14–15)

While these stories are terribly similar in their tragic, in their unrelenting exposition of 'the same,' they still display a personal quality that brings these fates closer to the audience. In the non-identity of mirrored events, every pushback from authorities, theft of property, threats, and violence differently affects the lives of people on the move, impinging on their already-precarious sense of safety and limited options for mobility. In between each account of abuse, the actors perform symbolic gestures that evoke the brutality and inhumanity with which the migrants are treated.

These and other testimonies recounted here suggest that there was a clear pattern of denied access to international protection coupled with various forms of violence performed by the Croatian border police. It is evident that given the frequency and patterns of police behaviour, these pushbacks cannot be characterised as isolated and sporadic cases of illegal expulsion but as forms of systemic violence against refugees and the criminalisation of migration. As numerous human rights organisations report, the Croatian police 'behaviour reveals consistent, planned and systematic measures of deprivation of freedom of movement without a legal basis, the denial of access to international protection and violation of the non-refoulement principles' (quoted in Bužinkić and Avon 2020, 162). The technology of pushbacks is not an isolated act of the Slovenian and Croatian police; these expulsions remain an ongoing practice within the border control regimes deployed by all the EU member states and the Balkan countries. However, the border between Croatia and Bosnia and Herzegovina remains one of the most acutely policed spots along the borders of the European Union deploying border violence that needs further critique, and alteration of political action. This current situation represents yet another manifestation of a profoundly broken refugee system whereby pushback get justified through the securitisation paradigm and protected by the law.

On Solidarity

While the scholarship on refugees and many theatrical representations of the migrant crisis abounds with the acts performed by the local populations in solidarity with migrants in need (Marschall 2018; Taylor 2020), Divjak's performance features many migrant accounts where actual solidarity was in short supply. As one of the migrants whose testimony was relayed in the performance stated:

> We walked for nine days (music from the phone) through Croatian forests and mountains. We avoided major roads, settlements, all people, in short. All the time through forests and wilderness, because if anyone sees you, people always call the police, and the police always find you, if not immediately, then the next day. So, we were hiding as much as possible all the time. (Divjak 2020, 31)

Another migrant from Algeria, apprehended by the Slovenian police just twenty kilometres from the Italian border testifies:

> We only had twenty kilometres left before Italy. Only twenty kilometres. We walked along the rails when a local guy in a white car noticed us. We saw how he looked at us, and we knew what would happen. We started walking really quickly. We heard a strange sound, we looked up and above us, there was a small drone with a camera. Soon we saw policemen and soldiers and dogs walk towards us, we wanted to flee, but it was already too late. (Divjak 2020, 30)

There is a sense here of being forced into 'ethical loneliness,' as Jill Stauffer describes, 'the isolation one feels when one, as a violated person or as one member of a persecuted group, has been abandoned by humanity' (2015, 1). The surrounding world exacerbates the individual's feeling of having been forsaken by turning a blind eye to the atrocity by failing to stop it or to acknowledge it. Ethical loneliness is the result of being forsaken not once but twice: 'the experience of having been abandoned by humanity compounded by the experience of not being heard' (Stauffer 2015, 1). While Stauffer's book is primarily about the double abandonment and existential isolation experienced by Holocaust survivors and black South Africans under Apartheid, her argument for the fundamental importance of solidarity is equally relevant in the context of the Balkans and stories of people on the move.

While some people on the move attempted the game many times, their experience of repeated criminalisation and dehumanisation through physical violence and denied access to international protection mechanisms often leads to depression, anger, and even suicide attempts. For some migrants, the game is fatal. At the end of the performance, one of the actors recounts statistical data—gender, the date of their disappearance or death, or when their bodies were found—of the twenty-four persons who died in the game from January 2018 to June 2020 in Slovenia. The actor's repeated, impersonal narration of these migrants' 'ends of life,' which holds the accumulation of human intimate suffering and alienation in nonidentical repetition, becomes the matter of history endlessly gone awry. With this finale, *The Game* also captures the insidious workings of 'necropolitics,' the state's arrogation of the right to determine under what practical conditions some people may live and how some must die at the behest of sovereign power (Mbembe 2003, 11).

In viewing the spectacle of unjust and failed responses to the migrant crisis, 'we' are inevitably implicated in the conditions of its making. As Ariella Azoulay has argued in *Civil Imagination*, 'the central right pertaining to the privileged segment of the population consists in the right to view disaster—to be its spectator' (2012, 1). We live in a radically unequal world. But what can be done with that knowledge? We could argue that performances such as *The Game*, which seeks to 'move' us aesthetically and emotionally, contribute to a process of reframing precarious migrations in terms that promote collective responsibility for violent policing associated with a chain reaction of pushbacks within the border control regime deployed in the Balkan countries and the rest of Europe. The performance also enables the opportunity to reach further and deeper in affecting positive change through promoting a broader shift of consciousness that invokes appreciation of the importance of taking collective action in response to the claims and demands raised by people on the move in precarious conditions. Furthermore, the performance contributes to the creation of conditions for positive change also by provoking discomfort that can prompt action on the part of 'receiving communities.' As Helen Gilbert and Jacqueline Lo argue about the growing corpus of theatre about asylum in Australia, the significance of these performances resides 'in their potential to elicit shame and outrage as a prelude to ethical community,' claiming that their 'efficacy is possible when the immediate and local effects of a particular performance change, however minutely, not just the future action of its audience members but also the structure of their community' (2007, 204). As some of the reviews by Slovenian theatre critics seem to suggest, they have been highly effective in this activist project: '*Gejm* is a performance that outlines facts. By avoiding unbridled sentimentality and moralising, it stirs up emotions in the viewer and provokes a desire for action, a desire for change' (Jenček 2020, n.p.); 'While politics demand tighter border controls, [this] important performance highlights the current state of events that lead to a total collapse of the fundamental principles of legal and ethical acts' (Radaljac 2020, n.p.).

Mladinsko's actors' invitation to their fellow Slovenians to bear witness to the violence of contemporary policy has been critical to the project's overall aim of affecting positive transformation in the field of migration politics. However, this is not to suggest that performances such as *The Game* can provide a quick and easy fix to such violence, nor can they in any straightforward way provide an alternative policy frame to that of the European Agenda and the CEAS. The refugee and migrant 'question' in the European Union, including the wider European space involved in the accession process, cannot be resolved by only documenting the shrinking of the asylum system and appealing to emotions and moral sentiments. The absence of political and structural solutions for the refugee crisis proposed by supra- or transnational European institutions and actors is currently one of the most visible symptom of the deep and multifold dimensions of the EU crisis.

References

Azoulay, Ariella. 2012. *Civil Imagination: A Political Ontology of Photography*. Translated by L. Bethlehem. London: Verso.

Barnett, Dennis, ed. 2016. *Dah Theatre: A Sourcebook*. Lanham: Lexington Books.

Benhabib, Seyla. 2004. *The Rights of Others: Aliens, Residents, and Citizens*. Cambridge: Cambridge University Press.

———. 2018. *Exile, Statelessness, and Migration: Playing Chess with History from Hannah Arendt to Isaiah Berlin*. Princeton: Princeton University Press.

Bužinkić, Emina, and Maddalena Avon. 2020. 'Pushback as a Technology of Crimmigration.' In *Causes and Consequences of Migrant Criminalization*, edited by Neža Kogovšek Šalamon, 157–70. Cham: Springer.

Divjak, Žiga, director. 2020. *The Game*. Co-production: The Mladinsko Theatre and Maska Ljubljana. The text of the performance is based on testimonies from the Border Violence Monitoring Network database. Premiere June 10, 2020.

Dragićević Šešić, Milena, and Korać-Sanderson, Maja, eds. 2019. 'A European Agenda on Migration: Communication from the Commission to the European Parliament, the Council, the European Economic and Social Committee and the Committee of the Regions.' *European Commission*, May 13, 2015. https://ec.europa.eu/homeaffairs/sites/homeaffairs/files/what-we-do/policies/european-agenda-migration/background-information/docs/communication_on_the_european_agenda_on_migration_en.pdf.

European Commission. 2015. A European agenda on migration: Communication from the commission to the European Parliament, the Council, the European Economic and Social Committee and the Committee of the Regions. COM(2015) 240 final, 13 May. https://ec.europa.eu/home-affairs/sites/homeaffairs/files/what-wedo/policies/european-agenda-migration/backgroundinformation/docs/communication_on_the_european_agenda_on_migration_en.pdf.

Gilbert, Helen, and Jacqueline Lo. 2007. *Performance and Cosmopolitics: Cross-Cultural Transactions in Australasia*. Basingstoke: Palgrave Macmillan.

Jenček, Brina. 2020. 'Gejm Over,' *Radio Študent*, June 22, 2020. https://radiostudent.si/kultura/teater-v-eter/gejm-over

Kogovšek Šalamon, Neža. 2020. 'EU Conditionality in the Western Balkans: Does It Lead to Criminalisation.' In *Causes and Consequences of Migrant*, edited by Neža Kogovšek Šalamon, 131–55. Cham: Springer.

Marschall, Anika. 2018. 'What Can Theatre Do about the Refugee Crisis? Enacting Commitment and Navigating Complicity in Performative Interventions.' *Research in Drama Education: The Journal of Applied Theatre and Performance*, 23 (2), 148–166.

Mbembe, Achille. 2003. 'Necropolitics.' Translated by Libby Meintjes. *Public Culture*, (15)1: 11–40.

Mladinsko Theatre. 2020. 'The Game.' 2020. https://mladinsko.com/en/program/98/the-game/.

Orel, Barbara, ed. 2017. *Uprizoritvene umetnosti, migracije, politika: slovensko gledališče kot sooblikovalec medkulturnih izmenjav*. Ljubljana: Znanstvena založba Filozofske fakultete.

Radaljac, Anja. 2020. 'Ocenjujemo: Gejm,' *Delo*, June 11, 2020. https://www.delo.si/kultura/ocene/ocenjujemo-gejm/.

Rapold, Nicolas. 2021. '"Notturno" Review: The Heart of the Middle East,' *The New York Times*, January 21, 2021. https://www.nytimes.com/2021/01/21/movies/notturno-review.html.

Stauffer, Jill. 2015. *Ethical Loneliness: The Injustice of Not Being Heard*. New York: Columbia University Press.

Taylor, Diana. 2020. *¡Presente!: The Politics of Presence*. Durham: Duke University Press.

The Black Book of Pushbacks - Volumes I & II. 2020. Border Violence Monitoring Network.

Zocchi, Benedetta. 2020. 'On the Margins of EU-rope: Colonial Violence at the Bosnian-Croatian Frontier.' *E-International Relations*, June 30, 2020. https://www.e-ir.info/2021/06/30/on-the-margins-of-eu-rope-colonial-violence-at-the-bosnian-croatian-frontier/.

Župarić-Iljić, Drago, and Marko Valenta. 2018. '"Refugee Crisis" in the Southeastern European Countries: The Rise and Fall of the Balkan Corridor.' In *The Oxford Handbook of Migration Crises*, edited by Cecilia Menjívar, Marie Ruiz, and Immanuel Ness, 1-24. New York: Oxford University Press.

CHAPTER 49

Theatre of the Syrian Diaspora

Edward Ziter

In discussing the theatre of the recent Syrian diaspora, two broad categories emerge: work by exiled established theatre makers and projects with formerly untrained actors often with therapeutic goals. These categories often overlap, with established artists working both in professional venues and devising projects with fellow refugees who have no previous theatre experience. Whether or not this varied work specifically addresses the violence of Syria's ongoing civil war, the experience of forced migration is invariably part of the power of this theatre. Even when a production is not explicitly about the experience of fleeing from a war zone, the biography of the theatre makers is present in the room. This chapter provides a selective overview of theatre makers working in both categories and the organizations that support such work. I conclude with a single case study, Omar Abu Saada's trilogy of ancient Greek plays performed with female Syrian refugees without previous theatre training. This body of work addresses or makes manifest shared traumas, territorial belonging, collective memory, and linguistic idiosyncrasies—all of which mark national identity. In this sense, Syrian diasporic theatre is rethinking the Syrian nation in defiance of the Syrian regime, a nation that encompasses a people dispersed across multiple states and a territory held in memory.

E. Ziter (✉)
New York University, New York, NY, USA
e-mail: ebz1@nyu.edu

© The Author(s), under exclusive license to Springer Nature Switzerland AG 2023
Y. Meerzon, S. E. Wilmer (eds.), *The Palgrave Handbook of Theatre and Migration*, https://doi.org/10.1007/978-3-031-20196-7_49

Context

My presentation of diasporic theatre as a national reimagining follows a body of work that has expanded on Benedict Anderson's famous definition of the nation as 'an imagined political community—and imagined as both inherently limited and sovereign' (2006, 6). Whereas Anderson identified 'print capitalism' as the principal engine of nationalistic imagining, theatre historians have identified theatre as a corollary engine (Kruger 1992; Roach 1996). As theatre scholars have demonstrated, occupying the shared space of the playhouse has fostered the 'deep, horizontal, comradeship' that Anderson ascribes to the national community (7). Examining national imaginings in the twentieth-first century requires that we consider theatre alongside deterritorialized mediascapes (Appadurai 1996, 35). My assertion that diasporic theatre can contribute to national imaginings relies on Appadurai's observation that 'the nationalistic genie, never perfectly contained in the bottle of the territorial state, is now, itself diasporic' (1996, 160–161). Anderson defined the nation as 'limited' in membership not geography, allowing for the possibility that members of the nation might carry it with them as they travelled beyond national boundaries. In the case of Syrian diasporic theatre, this decoupling of nation and territory is an originating trauma repeatedly processed through performance. Finally, and most problematically in the case of the Syrian diaspora, Anderson defined the nation as 'sovereign', arising as it did with the waning legitimacy of divinely ordered dynasties. Syria's diasporic theatre circles around the dilemma of sovereignty when a regime holds power through the violent defiance of a large part of national sentiment.

Over 6.6 million Syrians have fled Syria since 2011 according to the UNHCR. In March of that year, the regime of Bashar Al-Assad cracked down on peaceful protests in the southern city of Daraa. Protests spread throughout the country, government violence increased, and by 2012 Syria was embroiled in a civil war with a growing number of militant groups. The majority of Syria's refugees, roughly 5.6 million, have found refuge in neighbouring countries. In addition, another 6.7 million people are displaced within Syria (UNHCR 2021). Among those who fled are many in Syria's artistic communities. Exiled theatre makers have found opportunities and resources to create work that greatly expand on Syrian theatre traditions.

Makers and Funders

A range of NGOs and public theatres in the Middle East and Europe have funded Syrian diasporic theatre, creating opportunities for exiled younger theatre makers and non-professional actors, as well as established artists. Some famous performers have created work drawing attention to the atrocities of the Syrian regime or used their platform to create work with exiled amateurs. Much of this work is attentive to the psychosocial well-being of displaced Syrians, either through their participation in the work or as audience members. In the process, Syrian theatre makers have navigated a variety of funding mechanisms, each with their own social or political objectives. The funding mechanisms, no less than the subject matter of the works, depicts a Syrian identity that includes territorial displacement.

The director Omar Abusaada and the playwright and dramaturge Mohamad Al-Attar are among the most prominent young diasporic theatre makers. In addition to their collaborations on Ancient Greek plays (discussed below), they have worked extensively in a form of theatre that blurs the boundaries of documentary theatre. The combination of verbatim materials in imagined contexts gives the weight of the real to their depictions of Syrian life while at the same time they use fiction to find artfulness in the moral complexities of resistance. Such work, composed in the Syrian dialect and often documenting collective action for political rights, depicts new structures of national belonging beyond allegiance to a state.

In April 2012, Abusaada directed Al-Attar's *Could You Please Look into the Camera* at the Doosan Art Center in Seoul, South Korea, for a two-week run followed by a one-night performance at the Sunflower Theatre in Beirut. The play began as a verbatim theatre piece composed from the testimonies of thirteen individuals who had been held by the security forces during the first year of the Uprising before evolving into a fictional story about a film-maker compiling interviews for a documentary. Abusaada also directed Al-Attar's *While I Was Waiting*, which premiered at the Kunsten Festival, Brussels, in 2016 and was selected for the official program at the 2016 Avignon Theatre Festival, the 2017 Lincoln Center Festival, a 2017 run at Beirut's Sunflower Theatre, and the 2018 OzAsia Festival in Adelaide Australia. This production further complicated the relation between documentary and fiction. At the heart of the play is footage taken by a young man beaten into a coma at a checkpoint for unknown reasons. The man was attempting to create a film about his growing ambivalence towards a resistance movement that had embraced violence and religiosity. That footage, which appears on screens throughout the production, is actually footage taken surreptitiously in Damascus by the show's video designer.

The duo's next collaboration, *The Factory*, which premiered at the Volksbühne in September 2018, examined the French cement company Lafarge which paid more than $5 million to armed groups in Syria and violated international embargoes in order to continue operating a plant in northern Syria. In order to create his script, Al-Attar spoke to workers from the plant who had fled to France and Germany, and spoke via Skype and WhatsApp with others in Syria, Turkey, and Greece. In addition, he spoke with lawyers involved in the case and journalists who investigated. Al-Attar describes the resulting script as 'a combination of documentary and fiction' (Attar 2018). Their next collaboration, *Damascus 2045*, premiered at the Theater Freiburg in January 2022.

Several German theatres, in addition to the Volksbühne, have addressed the refugee crisis by giving platforms to exiled theatre artists. Such projects complicate ideas of national belonging. The work is often in Arabic or English (as a mediating language between Germans and migrants), and the performers are marked as non-Germans even as they reside in Germany. The subject matter varies, but the complexities of one's attachment to a country-of-origin figure prominently. In 2018, the Open Border Ensemble of the Münchner Kammerspiele (an ensemble of five Syrian actors) mounted *Miunikh-Damaskus: Stories of One City* and *What They Want to Hear*. The Gorki Theatre created the Exile Ensemble in 2016. At its core are three Syrian-born actors and two Palestinian-born actors. As of 2021, the ensemble has mounted five productions.

Perhaps the German theatre that has most supported Syrian representations of Syrian life after the Uprising is the Theater an der Ruhr in Mülheim. As early as 2013, Theater an der Ruhr had approached exiled Syrian actress and director Amal Omran with the idea of creating an international theatre lab in residence at the theatre. In 2017, she became the Artistic Director of Ma'louba (Levantine for 'upside down' and the name of a rice dish). The collective is largely composed of Syrians. Now, in its fourth year, the collective recently staged their sixth production, *'auda dāntōn* (The Return of Danton, June 2021), authored by the company member Mudar Alhaggi. (Alhaggi authored four of their six productions.) Outreach to the Arab-German communities has been important for Ma'louba. Omran explains that the theatre has sent representatives to local refugee populations, that teachers of German as a second language routinely bring groups of students, and that the audiences for their productions (which are in Arabic with German supertitles) contain a large number of Arabs and refugees (Omran). Tickets are free for people who claim financial difficulties.

The production of *The Return of Danton* speaks to the range of funding mechanisms supporting Syrian diasporic theatre. The play was staged as part of London's 2021 Shubbak Festival (held virtually that year), the UK's biennial multi-artform festival celebrating Arab voices. A coproduction of the festival and Theater an der Ruhr, the piece was co-presented by several UK-based arts organizations, the Maxim Gorki Theatre, and the Beirut-based NGO Ettijahat, devoted to funding art and culture producers and researchers in the Syrian diaspora. The play's storyline implicitly addresses such complicated funding arrangements; it depicts a troupe of displaced Syrian actors rehearsing scenes from Buchner's *Danton's Death* for a showcase intended to attract German funding for a full production. While the actors struggle to articulate how the play speaks to their own experience of war, the need to please potential sponsors ultimately takes precedence over exploring such questions. The specificities of Syrian identity are put in tension with the need to make that identity legible to European art funders.

Ma'louba associate, Wael Kadour, is one of the most talented playwrights of the Syrian diaspora, and the presentation of his work similarly reveals how European and Middle Eastern organizations collaborate in providing exiled artists platforms for dramatizing the nation. His two major plays since fleeing Syria in 2011 are *al-'aitirāf* (The Confession) and *waqā'ie madīnat lā t'aerifuha* (Chronicles of a City We Never Knew). *The Confession* is set in the early days of the Uprising and depicts a theatre troupe that (improbably) has been given permission to stage *Death and the Maiden* in Syria—Ariel Dorfman's play about political torture and revenge. As in the source text, the storyline turns on the difficulty of identifying war criminals and obtaining justice. *The Confession* was staged as part of the 2018 Redzone festival, a festival funded by the Norwegian record label KKV in collaboration with two Lebanese theatres: The Shams Association (the parent organization of the aforementioned Sunflower Theatre) and Zoukak Studio. *The Confession* was directed by the Syrian exile Abdullah Al Kafri, executive director of Ettijahat with a cast of Syrian and Lebanese actors. *Chronicles of a City We Never Knew* depicts an obscure love story between two women set against increasing state violence as the regime rounds up, interrogates, and tortures demonstrators in the early days of the Uprising. The play's mounting was similarly an international effort; it was developed within the Sundance Theatre Lab in Berlin in May 2017, where it received a reading at the Gorki Theatre. It was produced by the National Theatre of France in January 2019 at La Filature in the city of Mulhouse and the Tandem in the city of Arras. Wael Kadour and Mohamed Alrashi co-directed.

Several famous Syrian performers were forced into exile during the Uprising, and the television stars Mai Skaf and Nawar Bulbul have used their notoriety to draw attention to the violence of the Syrian regime and failure of the world to address the ensuing refugee crisis. On August 20, 2017, Mai marked the four-year anniversary of the Ghoutta chemical attack with a 'chemical dance' experiment, with a theatre troupe in Paris. As both performer and exile, Skaf's performance served as a powerful metonym for the Syrians killed in the chemical attack. Skaf went even further to foreground her precarity as a refugee at the same time that she insisted on her rights as an artist and world citizen in *Eating Refugees*, a performance action staged by the Center for Political Beauty. The group chartered a plane to bring 100 Syrian refugees to Berlin and threatened that if they were refused entry, the group would feed a Syrian refugee, played by Skaf, to the four tigers housed in cages outside the Maxim Gorki Theatre in downtown Berlin. In her press conference during the action, Skaf identified herself as 'maybe' an actress and 'maybe' known to an Arab television audience in the millions, but then noted that she no longer plays the 'role' of actress: 'The only role that I play now is the one assigned to me by the authorities in France: I am a refugee' (Skaf 2016).

Nawar Bulbul's fame contributed to the success of his theatre projects with displaced Syrian children. Twice he staged Shakespeare productions with Syrian children: *Shakespeare in Zaatari* performed in March 2015 at the Zaatari refugee camp in Jordan followed by a performance at the Roman theatre in Amman, and *Romeo and Juliet* performed simultaneously at a makeshift health center for Syrian refugees in Amman and in a private residence in Homs Syria in April 2015. With over one hundred children involved and a four-month rehearsal period, *Shakespeare in Zaatari* was a huge project. The Zaatari camp, created in 2012 in response to the forced migration of tens of thousands of Syrians, housed some 83,000 refugees by March 2015 (Wikipedia). Bulbul, a famous television actor in Syria before the revolution, fled Syria in 2011. Because of his prominent support for the Syrian Uprising, he was unofficially told to choose between arrest and publicly disavowing his anti-regime stance (Hubbard 2014). *Shakespeare in Zaatari* is an adaptation of *Lear* with interpolated text from *Hamlet*, performed by fifteen principal actors with a chorus of several dozen providing commentary and sound effects. When Bulbul's plan for additional theatre productions encountered resistance from camp administrators and the UNHCR, he conceived of a production of *Romeo and Juliet* in which Syrian children in Amman would perform opposite children in besieged and bombed-out Homs via a Skype connection. For three months, Bulbul worked with children at a health center in Amman run by Souriyat Across Borders and, via Skype, with a group in Homs. The script included a number of interpolations referencing the Syrian conflict. The most significant change came at the close when Romeo and Juliet dash their poison to the ground and Juliet's companion declared 'Enough killing! Enough blood! Why are you killing us? We want to live like the rest of the world!' (Taneja 2015).

Bulbul next performed *safīnat al-ḥub* (Love Boat) with six adult refugees with no previous theatre experience at the French Institute of Amman in April 2016. *Love Boat* tells the story of a Syrian acting troupe, disbanded during the revolution and reunited in an unnamed country, that boards a small boat in the hopes of reaching Europe. In the course of their travels, the troupe performs scenes from Aristophanes' *The Knights*, Goldoni's *The Servant of Two Masters*, Molière's *Tartuffe*, Goethe's *Faust*, and a dramatized scene from Cervantes' *Don Quixote*. As in Skaf's work, the performers play refugees as they enact their own status as refugees. In one scene, a character with a prosthetic leg describes staring down the pilot who, high above, dropped a barrel bomb on her. She removes her prosthetic, raises it over her head and triumphantly describes hurling her severed leg at the pilot to bring down his plane. Even the boundaries between classic works and present-day tragedies grow porous. While the troupe is performing the scene in which Tartuffe attempts to seduce Elmire, the character playing Elmire experiences a sudden flashback to being repeatedly beaten and raped in a Syrian prison (Mousilli 2016).

Bulbul then went on to perform two solo pieces: he adapted *Mawlana* (Master) by Alfares Alzahabi so as to examine how the Assad regime used religion to crush civil and humanistic values, and he authored *Egalité*, a piece that incorporates texts by the sociologist Michel Seurat critiquing the barbarity of the Assad regime as a voice-over, into the story of Seurat's fictional neighbour, Omar Abu Michel, a man who survived Assad's prisons only to see his home bombed by Russians supporting the Assad regime. Omar's prized possession is a bicycle, bequeathed to him by Seurat, which he has named Egalité. By incorporating details of Seurat's life and writings into the text, Bulbul blurs the boundaries of the real and fictional.

Bulbul does not use the term 'drama therapy' (which refers to the intentional use of theatre techniques for therapeutic goals) when describing his theatre work with Syrian refugees. However, other practitioners working with Syrian refugees present the work in the context of psychosocial goals. The frequency is remarked on in *The Return of Danton*. At one point one of the characters triumphantly resigns from the production asserting that she has been offered full-time theatre work. In fact, because of her poor German, she does not realize that she was invited to participate in a drama therapy workshop for refugees.

For several years, the Zoukak Studio of Beirut has offered drama therapy workshops to Palestinian refugees and now includes the Syrian refugee population. In 2014, it mounted *ikhtarli bir* (Pick a Land for Me) and *sitti el ʿarja* (My Limping Granny), devised pieces created by Palestinians who fled Syria and Palestinians already in Lebanon (Beirut). In addition, Zoukak has offered multiple trainings for activity leaders in schools and other locations on the Lebanese-Syrian borders and conducted a ten-day workshop and performance with the refugees of the Calais Camp in France. The Campfire Project also provides drama therapy for Syrian refugees. It was conceived by Jessica Hecht and transpired during the summer of 2018 and 2019 at the Ritsona refugee camp in Greece. Hecht assembled an impressive roster of theatre and music professionals who offered workshops to children and young adults at the camp, with the guidance of a psychiatric advisor, culminating in the 2018 performance of an adaptation of *The Tempest*.

Case Study: Omar Abusaada's Greek Trilogy

Between 2013 and 2017, Omar Abusaada mounted three productions that combined text from an ancient Greek drama in classical Arabic with the personal experiences of a cast of female refugees in the Syrian dialect: *The Trojan Women* (Amman Jordan 2013), *Antigone of Shatila* (Beirut 2014), and *Iphigenia* (Berlin 2017). Abusaada incorporated exercises into the rehearsal process to prompt reflections on personal history and then used the material generated in the final production. For example, Abusaada asked the women to create a map of the most important events of their life and to share their map with the rest of the cast. He asked the women to discuss which characters most resembled them, to draw pictures of the characters, and to write letters to these characters (Abusaada 2021). A documentary on the mounting of *The Trojan Women*, titled *The Queens of Syria*, includes footage of the mapping exercise (Fedda 2015).

The performers' movement between classical Arabic and a national dialect marks them as Syrians, as does the act of sharing individual traumas that all figure as part of a larger national trauma. The interpolated text emphasizes the Syrian identity of the performers, even as these stories draw attention to territorial displacement. Abusaada is Syrian, but as the only son of older parents, he is exempt from military conscription. Nor has his work branded him as a conspicuous regime critic. As a result, unlike many Syrians he has achieved relative security, residing part time in Damascus and travelling widely to direct. In this respect he differs from his dramaturge, Mohammad Al-Attar, a Syrian exile and vocal regime critic, and his actors who have all fled regions that have undergone sieges and bombings.

The self-generated material functioned differently in the three productions, reflecting the increasing contributions of dramaturge Mohammad Al-Attar. All three productions mixed live performance and video projections. Abusaada did not work with a dramaturge when mounting *Trojan Women* and this production exclusively featured text generated by the actors and selections from Euripides' play—the former taking precedence. Abusaada limited his use of Euripides' text—sticking mostly to the choral odes which were performed live by the entire cast of twenty-four women. Some of the most gripping passages came when the women recounted their experiences of the conflict. One woman recounted her flight from al-Bayda (site of one of the worst massacres in the war) and her brother-in-law's return to the city to identify the bodies of her male relatives who stayed behind. Another woman, who returned to Syria for her mother's funeral, described the abduction of her brother days later.

The few character speeches were presented as video projections, but even these were framed by women describing their own lives. For example, one sequence focusing on Hecuba featured a projection of an actor facing the camera and another in profile. The actor facing the camera identified herself, gave her age, and then reflected that Hecuba resembles her in that she also once 'desired death and felt that a taste of bitterness would linger in my mouth to the end of my days no matter how long I lived.' She went on to explain that this all changed when a 'great joy' entered her life—her children and husband. Only then did the actor in profile deliver several of Hecuba's lines, in which the character describes seeing her husband cut down before her. Rather than directly confronting loss, this sequence allowed participants to confront trauma through metaphor. Hecuba resembles me in her loss, she announces, but then goes on to emphasize her own resilience by explaining that she overcame depression and embraced joy. Even the staging choices elevated personal experience over Euripides' text; the actor recounted her life facing the camera whereas Hecuba's lines were delivered in profile—first my life and only then Hecuba's lines (Ziter 2017, 183). Here Abusaada used Euripides' play as a projective device, a technique he employed in the other productions in the trilogy. When actors confronted their loss directly, as in the two live monologues described above, choral odes framed the passages. After grappling with trauma, the speaker reintegrated into a community of actors, her own trauma contained by the trauma described in classic literature. *The Trojan Women* ran for two nights in December 2013 at the King Hussein Foundation National Center for Culture and Arts in Amman.

Abusaada used a similar development process with his next two pieces, *Antigone of Shatila* (Beirut 2014) and *Iphigenia* (Berlin 2017), but the final scripts incorporate storylines developed by his dramaturge and long-time collaborator, Mohammad Al-Attar. *Antigone* presents as the rehearsal diary of one of the performers, who introduces us to the other women as part of recalling her experiences on the days leading up to the opening. *Iphigenia* goes even further to create a dramatic context to account for the personal reminiscences interpolated into the source text; the audience witnesses auditions for the role of Iphigenia for a future production of that play and when the performers speak as themselves it is because they are responding to questions posed by an audition judge. (The judge was played by a professional actress, Reham Alkassar, who also served as the cast's acting coach—the only instance in the trilogy when a professional actor took a role.) (Fig. 49.1)

In all three productions, the women speak about their experiences in their host countries, but that was especially the case in *Antigone of Shatila*. Shatila is of course the Palestinian refugee camp, infamous as the location of a civilian massacre in 1982. Since Lebanon chose not to create new refugee camps, the million and a half Syrian refugees in that country have spread over more than 1750 sites (UNHCR 2014). There are an estimated 18,000 Syrian refugees in Shatila, a sizable percentage of that camp's unofficial population of 40,000 (Syam et al. 2019). Squalor and a sense of imprisonment feature in several of the actor's speeches, and there are resonances between Antigone's 'rocky vault' and Beirut's camps as 'enclosures of poverty and misery'; while it's true the camps don't have high walls, one actor remarks, 'once you're inside you feel you'll never get out' (Al-Attar [n.d.-a], 3). Just as Antigone's cave is conflated with Shatila, the women's recent flight out of Syria is conflated with the Palestinian exodus in 1948. In one scene, a woman describes fleeing Yarmouk (a Palestinian camp in Syria) and arriving at Shatila, but before she speaks a

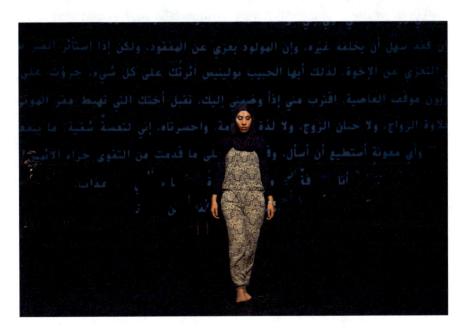

Fig. 49.1 *Antigone of Shatila* (Beirut 2014). Director Omar Abusaada. (Photo: Dalia Khamisy)

video plays in which another woman recounts her husband's flight as a small child from Palestine in 1948. Multiple Arab migrations are layered into Euripides' text. *Antigone of Shatila* was performed at Beirut's Al-Madina theatre from December 10 through 12, 2014.

The conceit that informs *Iphigenia*, that we are watching auditions for the title role in that play, stemmed from a peculiarity in the rehearsal project; when the performers were asked to write about the character that most resembled them, they all focused on Iphigenia. In constructing the script, Dramaturge Mohammad Al-Attar then fashioned these self-reflections into discussions as part of an audition process (Abusaada 2021). The women describe very different relations to their host nation. Some are recent arrivals, one emigrated in 2009; one is more comfortable auditioning in German, another recounts that though aged 17 she is in 9th grade because of her poor language skills. None of the performers recount harrowing migration stories. One complains that she 'can't keep hearing the same story over and over' and describes being interviewed by a journalist who disregarded most of what she said in order to tell a story of a terrifying journey by rubber boat (Al-Attar [n.d.-b], n.p.). *Iphigenia* opened on September 9, 2017, in Hanger 5 of the former Tempelhof airport before transferring to the Main Stage of the Volksbühne.

Abusaada does not describe his work as drama therapy but acknowledges its capacity for healing for both performers and audience. That element no doubt changes when the work is remounted, as when cast members from *The Trojan Women* were invited to perform at the 2014 Tälberg Workshop at CERN, the European Organization for Nuclear Research, or when it was again remounted for a 2016 United Kingdom tour co-produced by the Young Vic. Similarly, *Antigone of Shatila* meant something different in its runs at Beirut's Al-Madina theatre and its mounting in Marseille in 2016 and Hamburg in 2016.

The existence of multiple audiences comprising migrants, citizens of adjacent nations, and Europeans reflects the way that theatre, the most local of art forms, circulates in an age of globalization. While the content of the work discussed has largely focused on the transformations of Syria and the Syrian people both in and out of Syria, the audience for this work is invariably a mix of displaced Syrians and members of host countries. This process is further complicated as news of these productions circulate in the mediascape—in news reports, online extracts, and documentaries. The artist depicts the nation from exile. The depiction takes on new meanings when members of the diaspora are in the audience and still different meanings are generated when news of a production circulates online. This circulation is further complicated by the number of productions described in this chapter featuring Syrians grappling with Western texts. Both fictional and autobiographical work foregrounds the performers' experience of migration, an experience further underscored by the act of adapting Western texts. Today, the nation like the self is an idea that is arrived at in international arenas.

References

Abusaada, Omar. 2021. In discussion with the author, 20 May 2021.
Al-Attar, Mohammad. [n.d.-a] 'Antigone of Shatila.' Translated by Katherine Halls. Unpublished manuscript.
———. [n.d.-b] 'Iphigenie' [sic]. Translated by Anna Galt. Unpublished manuscript.
———. 2018. 'Mohammad Al Attar: "Why did we allow this to happen?" The Syrian author on justice, the relationship between documentation and fiction and his new play "The Factory".' Volksbühne digital. https://www.volksbuehne.berlin/en/news/6416/interview-mohammad-al-attar-why-did-we-allow-this-to-happen-the-syrian-author-on-justice-the-relationship-between-documentation-and-fiction-and-his-new-play-the-factory.
Anderson, Benedict. 2006 [1983]. *Imagined Communities*. London: Verso.
Appadurai, Arjun. 1996 *Modernity at Large : Cultural Dimensions of Globalization*. Minneapolis: University of Minneapolis Press.
Fedda, Yasmin, director. 2015. *The Queens of Syria*. Refugee Productions Limited. 2015.
Hubbard, Ben. 2014. 'Behind Barbed Wire, Shakespeare Inspires a Cast of Young Syrians.' *New York Times*. March 31. https://www.nytimes.com/2014/04/01/world/middleeast/behind-barbed-wire-shakespeare-inspires-a-cast-of-young-syrians.html. Accessed 20 May 2021.
Kruger, Loren. 1992. *The National Stage: Theatre and Cultural Legitimization in England, France and America*. Chicago: University of Chicago Press.
Mousilli, Maan, director. 2016. *Love Boat*. Documentary film. MA3MAL612 Productions.
Roach, Joseph. 1996. *Cities of the Dead: Circum-Atlantic Performance*. New York: Columbia University Press.
Skaf, Mai. (2016) 'Die erste kandidatin stelt sich vor.' https://www.youtube.com/watch?v=JfLLnirY5ak&t=7s. Accessed 28 July 2021.
Syam, H., Venables, E., Sousse, B. et al. 2019. '"With Every Passing Day I Feel Like a Candle, Melting Little by Little." Experiences of Long-Term Displacement Amongst Syrian Refugees in Shatila, Lebanon.' *Conflict and Health* 13 (45). https://doi.org/10.1186/s13031-019-0228-7.
Taneja, Reti. 2015. 'Sweet Sorrow as Star-Crossed Lovers in Syria and Jordan Connect via Skype.' *The Guardian*. April 12. https://www.theguardian.com/stage/theatre-blog/2015/apr/14/romeo-and-juliet-staged-in-amman-and-homs. Accessed 20 May 2021.
UNHCR. 2014. 'Shelter Update Lebanon August 2014.' https://data2.unhcr.org/en/documents/details/42209. Accessed 26 May 2021.
———. 2021. 'Syria Emergency.' https://www.unhcr.org/en-us/syria-emergency.html. Accessed 26 May 2021.
Wikipedia. n.d. 'Zaatari refugee camp.' https://en.wikipedia.org/wiki/Zaatari_refugee_camp. Accessed 25 May 2021.
Ziter, Edward. 2017. 'The Syria Trojan Women: Rethinking the public with therapeutic theater.' *Communication and the Public*, 2 (2), 177–190.

CHAPTER 50

The Finnish National Theatre, Refugees, and Equality

Pirkko Koski

Introduction

Since the turn of the millennium, the Finnish National Theatre has increasingly shifted its artistic focus to social groups that had previously been alienated from the theatre, notably Finland's refugees and asylum seekers. In the beginning of the 2010s, the National Theatre founded a fourth stage, Kiertuenäyttämö ('The Touring Stage'), the mission statement of which was to use art as a way to reach people who had been traditionally excluded from theatres and foster a deeper and broader connection between communities and the artistic establishment.

My study focuses on three Finnish National Theatre Touring Stage productions spanning from 2011 to 2020. Co-created in collaboration with refugees, these productions were heavily influenced by the societal tensions of the time, notably the challenges arising from the 2015 refugee crisis. During this period, the position of refugees underwent significant changes in Finnish society, and the National Theatre not only reflected these changes but also helped shape the social debate on asylum seekers and migrants in Finland.

One of the three refugee Touring Stage productions, *Paperiankkuri* (Paper Anchor) (2011), was performed on the National Theatre's Small Stage. It was

---

This article was translated from Finnish by Kayleigh Töyrä.

P. Koski (✉)
Helsinki University, Helsinki, Finland
e-mail: pirkko.koski@helsinki.fi

part of the Theatre's *Vastaanotto* (Reception) project, which also included workshops and performances at asylum centres. *Toinen koti* (The Other Home) (2017), performed in the Theatre's Omapohja studio space, took on an even stronger and more direct stance on the refugee experience in Finland. It was part of the national arts research initiative *ArtsEqual* (ArtsEqual 2017). *Undocumented Love* (2020) was an intimate Omapohja production co-created with refugee artists (though the COVID-19 pandemic cut the production run short not long after its opening night, preventing the fruition of the project).

The Touring Stage was formed at the instigation of its founder, a National Theatre actor Jussi Lehtonen, who collaborated with disenfranchised communities throughout his theatrical career. By working with refugees, Lehtonen manifested a central tenet of his artistic career: achieving equality and fostering respectful encounters of otherness. Alison Jeffers comes to an important conclusion in *Refugees, Theatre and Crisis* (2012) when she argues that 'the act of creating theatre itself can be seen as a manifestation of the possibilities of generous action, of acting ethically with refugees and people seeking asylum' (Jeffers 2012, 15). I will examine these acts of creating theatre at the National Theatre in the light of the ethical challenges posed by Jeffers: as opportunities to draw attention to refugees and make them centre-stage, free refugees from the invisibility and silence to which they are so often condemned, and welcome strangers with an open mind without asking for reciprocity (Cf. Jeffers 2012, 10–11). The Finnish National Theatre refugee productions were proof that the coming together of different cultures posed both internal and external threats to the accomplishment of mutual artistic aims: societal tensions impacted both performances and their critical reception, and careful negotiations were required in order for working groups to reach mutual goals. As I examine the three National Theatre productions co-created with refugees and gauge their societal impact, I aim to trace how the shifting ideological debates in society, theatre, and academia impacted and shaped the performances, and simultaneously assess whether the National Theatre achieved its goals.

The Cultural and Theatrical Frames Behind the National Theatre's Productions

Immigration is not a new phenomenon in Finnish society, although migration in Finland has been moderate compared to many other European countries. Only a small proportion of people settling in Finland applied for political asylum. Some exceptions included the large groups of refugees arriving from beyond the Eastern border in the years after the Russian Revolution, small groups of Vietnamese boat refugees, as well as Chilean refugees in the 1970s. In the early 1990s, refugees came to Finland from the disintegrating states of Yugoslavia and Somalia, but Finland still had proportionally the lowest immigrant population in Europe, at less than 1 per cent (Korkiasaari and Söderling 1994, 255–256, 261–262).

After the turn of the millennium, the number of refugees in Finland increased, though the figures were still proportionally low in comparison with many other European countries: annually, only 4000 asylum seekers arrived in a country of 5.5 million inhabitants. Finland has committed to welcoming a certain number of quota refugees through the UN Refugee Scheme, whereas other migrants seek asylum when they first enter the country. The number of quota migrants in 2014–2015 was just over a thousand, whereas the annual number was between 620 and 750 during the preceding and following years (Migri 2021).

Up until 2015, the public debate on refugees was divided yet restrained, largely based on pre-existing prejudices as well as information circulated in national and international media. The 2015 refugee crisis radically changed refugee reality in Finland as the number of people seeking asylum in Finland rose to over 32,000. From 2015 onwards, refugees became more visible in Finnish society and their presence became more tangible, although the number of asylum applications to Finland soon fell to one-fifth of 32,000, finally settling at about 2000 to 5000 per annum, fluctuating as a function of the number of renewal applications and including a quota of resettlement refugees (Migri 2021).

As the 2015 refugee crisis unfolded and a populist political party that was openly refugee-critical gained seats in the Finnish parliament, legal considerations on who constituted an asylum seeker were tightened, and it became apparent that Finnish authorities were not adequately equipped to control the potentially volatile migrant situation. Simultaneously, sympathetic stories about refugees and their plight were circulated in the media and, as a counterbalance to anti-immigration discourse, many Finnish citizens (especially artists and researchers) took a firm stance against harsh asylum policies and were inspired to volunteer for refugee causes. Public opinion became increasingly entrenched and polarised, and political divides over the refugee issue deepened. By January 2020, the debate around refugees and asylum seekers had become relatively stabilised. Due to the number of people annually seeking asylum significantly dropping, the conversation had become divorced from many people's everyday realities; the extreme anti-migrant stance upheld by the political far-right was mainly aimed at existing party supporters.

Theatres and the Nordic art scene in general positioned themselves as supporters of the refugees' plight and defenders of their humanitarian rights by criticising public policy. Plays often toured neighbouring Nordic countries, all the while crossing political and metaphorical borders. The report *Actualise Utopia: From Dreams to Reality* (2019) by the Norwegian Arts Council took a closer look at refugees by problematising the questions of inclusion and racial structures in the arts in the Nordic countries.

In Finland, the National Theatre was not the only theatre to touch on the topic of refugees, but the Finnish National Theatre productions stood out from other theatre works due to their versatile background research, the focused way they approached collaboration, and the productions' community ties, as well as the cultural capital inherent to the theatre's central position.

From Invisibility to Centre-Stage

In 2011, the National Theatre's *Vastaanotto* (Reception) project shifted the refugee question from a discursive axis to one of more personal encounters. The *Paperiankkuri* (Paper Anchor) production, staged at the National Theatre, was preceded by the projects created in refugee reception centres. The performers familiarised themselves with the reception centre and its people; they put on small performances, and ran workshops with refugee women, men, and children. They created *Paperisilta* (Paper Bridge)—a one-and-a-half hour touring show with dance and music—and *Paperihiiri* (Paper Mouse)—a workshop-style performance for children under ten years-old. These productions visited more than thirty reception centres and group homes for juvenile asylum seekers in 2011–2012, focusing their messages at asylum seekers rather than traditional theatre audiences, with the aim of building a bridge between the newcomers and native Finns (Finnish National Theatre and Finnish Immigration Service 2011). The project was implemented in cooperation with the Finnish Red Cross and the Central Union for Child Welfare, while the Finnish Immigration Service provided financial support for activities undertaken at reception centres (Fig. 50.1).

Paper Anchor, performed on the Small Stage, was devised by Lehtonen in collaboration with dramaturg Taija Helminen and stage director Hanna Brotherus, with Lehtonen also performing. Mikko Perkola and Sanna Salmenkallio were responsible for the music and sound design. On stage, Lehtonen was joined by several dancers and three performers with personal experiences of the asylum process: Edina Bilajac (Bosnian), Naimo Mahamud (Somali), and Matthew Rahmani (Iranian), two women and one man, all young adults. Lehtonen has used the terms 'documentary theatre' and 'socially minded theatre research' to describe his creative process: the production was pieced together from in-depth interviews with asylum seekers, workshops, newspaper articles, as well as material gathered from migrant-critical online discussion boards and blogs, and even included a video of the men's workshop's (known as Men's group) dance performance. Refugees *themselves* influenced the narrative progress by taking on the roles of subject matter experts and performers. The refugee performers who auditioned and were chosen to participate in the project had already received asylum in Finland. This was done in order to ensure that performers could participate in this work and remain in Finland for the entirety of the five-month performance run, but also to ensure that participation would not jeopardise their application process that was still in process. Out of the seven male performers in the dancing video that had been completed in March 2011, three had already had their asylum applications rejected in the autumn (Helminen and Lehtonen 2012, 54–55, 149–150).

Fig. 50.1 *Paper Anchor* (2011), Finnish National Theatre, directed and choreographed by Hanna Brotherus. In the first row, Alexandros Kotsopoulos. (Photo: Nico Backström)

The production's central theme was crystallised in the prologue and opening scene: the performance began with asylum seekers reading official instructions for entry into asylum centres in front of an iron fire curtain opposite the 311-seat auditorium. As the curtain rose, the light focused on a small boy who was carrying a cardboard box, sitting in a small sled that was hard to move. At the end of the performance, the scene was repeated as the whole cast approached the audience rhythmically and very slowly, each in their own sled propelling themselves forwards with their hands. The asylum issue was made corporeal and visible, and the reviews attest to the significance of the affective experience; the thorough style of theatrical storytelling was deeply affective. For example, the Finnish audience knew from experience how challenging it is to shift a downhill sled on a surface with no snow (Koski 2015, 43–45, 50–52).

The traditional layout of the Small Stage placed *Paper Anchor* performers directly in the audience's line of sight, and, in group scenes, refugees and native Finns performed side by side on-stage. In certain scenes, refugee performers spoke directly to the audience as subjects and witnesses of their stories, unlike in the anxiety-inducing process of applying for asylum where their stories were under scrutiny and potentially being doubted. Narrated stories and direct monologues confronted audiences and reinforced the authenticity of the stories told. Being performed on a stage that was part of the National Theatre supported both the visibility and dissemination of the production's message, and the production's reach went national when the premiere was recorded and shown on national television.

The production took a strong stance in the prevailing political atmosphere of Finland. The critical press reception was positive, and the entire *Reception* project received widespread publicity in different media, though the audience success of *Paper Anchor* dwindled as the number of performances marched on. The initiative left its most indelible mark when dramaturg Helminen and Lehtonen published a book, *Vastaanotto* (Reception) (2012), describing and analysing the project's different phases, including detailed interviews with the project's participants. According to the book, refugee performers found the project empowering and it enabled them to open up to a new culture, but the book also shows how the initiative opened up Finnish artists' eyes to the extent and depth of the refugee problem (Helminen and Lehtonen 2012, 65–77).

WELCOMING A STRANGER: *THE OTHER HOME*

The impact of the influx of refugees to Finland in 2015 was very evident in the next production, *Toinen koti* (The Other Home), staged in 2017 in the adaptable Omapohja studio. The space held only about a quarter of the seats of the Small Stage auditorium, but the National Theatre as an institution still lent the event gravitas. The title of the production, *The Other Home*, can be seen as an ethical statement on theatre as a 'a space of permanence,' acceptance, and somewhere where people can be amongst peers.

The increasingly polarised social debate around refugees had now also taken on increasingly religious undertones, focusing on Muslim provenance and culture. During the 2015 refugee crisis, refugee-critical groups tapped into preconceived notions of an unfamiliar religion and purported extreme fundamentalist groups connected with it. The Finnish Christian Church had national church status and in Finland religion had traditionally been associated with Finnish nationalist movements; this tradition still held sway, despite the church in many ways being alienated from people's everyday realities.

The Other Home was written by Kati Kaartinen and directed by Lehtonen, with the music provided by Salmenkallio. For this production, fifteen refugee artists (found through a variety of intermediary organisations) from Iraq, Syria, and Iran were interviewed, and four of them (Bakr Hasan, Ali Saad, Harith Raad Salih, and Soroush Seyedi) were selected to play the starring roles. The cast also included a group of performers of refugee background who had engaged with the project through an open workshop. The group included ten men and two women ranging from sixteen to over sixty years old. The cast's cultural diversity was vast: amongst the Syrians were people from both government *and* opposition camps of their home country. It included both Sunni and Shia Muslims, and Kurds, Druzes, Iraqis, and Iranians. Out of the sixteen refugee performers in the production, seven were still waiting to hear back on their asylum application, and by the time the play opened, three performers were still awaiting a decision. The production's Finnish performers included Terhi

Panula and Salmenkallio (Lehtonen and Pöyhönen 2018, 39; Lehtonen 2021a, 114).

As the performance began to take shape, the original production theme of settling in and integration was joined by the actual process of seeking asylum and its inherent problems, such as the inability of the Finnish system to acknowledge asylum-seeking artists. The rejection of lead actor Hasan's asylum application is illustrative of the issues the performance sought to bring to light. Hasan's case might be understood as a systemic failure of bureaucrats in the Finish Immigration Service (Migri), including interpreters and other key stakeholders and decision-makers, to understand the language and content of art and its potential political reflection. This kind of failure led to the rejection of Hasan's asylum application. For him, being an artist was seen as a minor matter, secondary to him seeking asylum, as opposed to something that was central to his refugee identity. His story and character became the central nucleus to which all the other refugee stories in the production were compared (Lehtonen and Pöyhönen 2018, 38). Migri, founded in 1995, processes and makes decisions on residency and asylum. The asylum process includes two in-person interviews to support a refugee application. The applicant then has the right to appeal Migri's decision with the administrative court. This final decision can no longer be appealed, and if a negative decision is reached, the applicant must immediately leave the country (Migri 2020).

Hasan was by his own definition an atheist with a Sunni-Muslim background, raised in Iraq in a religious family who rejected the boy who chose a theatre career. Hasan named Antonin Artaud as one of his influences, and his production of Samuel Beckett's *Waiting for Godot* with its questioning of God's existence had become a turning point in his activist work. Before he acted in *The Other Home*, Hasan had already performed in Finland and even visited the National Theatre with his one-man play *Made in Bagdad* in 2016 (Lehtonen and Pöyhönen 2018, 37).

In *The Other Home*, different cultures were signalled by certain visual cues such as the carpets covering the floors, and artistic identities were made evident through the alternation between Finnish music, Iraqi music, and music from the rest of the Arab diaspora. The refugee artists also parodied Finnish politicians and Finnish decision-makers for their lack of cultural knowledge. For example, they parodied the prime minister by rapping out his documented statements in a new multicultural context and performance mode, which revealed the patronising tone of his statements, exposing them to ridicule.

The aim of achieving a sense of equality extended to the relation with the audience. The eighty auditorium seats were arranged over a stepped podium that rose on three sides around the performance space, with no clear demarcation between performers and audience members. The performance ran in Finnish and Arabic, with subtitles in both languages projected on the wall facing the audience. It was consistently sold out.

The publicity surrounding the production was particularly abundant and reactions tended to be very personal. The main national newspaper, *Helsingin*

Sanomat, gave the performance a full five stars on its rating scale. British academic James Simpson provided his opinion in an online blog: 'It's a profound play, intensely moving, and all the more poignant because the stories performed on stage have their origins in the migration narratives that the actors themselves recounted at the beginning of the process eighteen months ago' (Simpson 2018). The extensive archival material of positive feedback praising the experience tells the story of an audience who, to a large extent, already felt themselves allied to the production. Even when criticising Finnish politics, the audience were 'in' on the subject matter, recognising the target of attack and its justifiable critique.

The refugee policy of Finland and the public refugee debate provided reference to a kind of 'other' for all three productions, and they were most evident in the context of *The Other Home* production. The project 'made Migri an agent or "actor" in the artistic process' and resulted in the working group becoming active outside the theatre by contacting the Finnish national newspaper *Helsingin Sanomat*, the national radio station, Yleisradio, and various arts organisations. The production group was also active in preparing a policy brief for officials and other bodies interested in processing artist asylum applications (ArtsEqual). The efforts led to tangible results: Hasan's rejected asylum decision was reversed, as his new asylum application more convincingly argued for the connection between art and political oppression and the importance of artists (Lehtonen and Pöyhönen 2018, 41). The production group joined into political interventions that took a stand against the deficiencies and mistakes inherent to the asylum-seeking process. Making an international comparison, Simpson observed, 'Finland has a well-established bureaucracy of immigration, asylum and deportation. The Finnish Immigration Service […] is fast gaining a reputation to challenge the UK's Home Office, in terms of obstacles, barriers and arbitrary decisions that new arrivals seeking asylum face when attempting to claim sanctuary, to find a foothold in a place they feel safe' (Simpson 2018).

Several members of the artistic group took part in a several months long demonstration named 'The Right to Life' in front of the National Theatre on the Central Railway Station Square and came to rehearsals directly from the protest (Lehtonen 2021a, 114). The protest took shape in February 2017 and was quickly met by a 'Finland First' counterprotest. The Right to Life group tried to affect change in the Finnish asylum-seeking process by engaging Finnish officials in dialogue, whereas the counterprotest's aims centred around ideologically, and even physically, disrupting and harassing refugees. The Right to Life campaign received widespread support from individuals across the religious spectrum, and twenty-four theatres around the country organised events where rejected asylum applications were read out. People in the Finnish cultural and artistic circles handed over a collective petition to Finnish authorities. The theatre director of the Finnish National Theatre, Mika Myllyaho, visited the Right to Life protestors' tent and ended up as one of the day's news items. On opposite sides of the square, the Finnish National Gallery, Ateneum, and the Finnish National Theatre hung their buildings with banners stating

'Refugees Welcome'. The counterprotest camp was dismantled due to antisocial and violent behaviour at the end of April, and the Right to Life protest ended at the end of June.

The Other Home performance also made important interventions into the sphere of academic research, as it was linked with research projects within the Academy of Finland, such as *Crossing Borders—Artistic Practices in Performing and Narrating Belonging* and the *ArtsEqual* project that examined how art as a public service can increase social equality and well-being in Finland. Alongside another Touring Stage production produced with prisoners, the research context of this specific production was the programme named *Socially Responsible Arts Institutions and Artists*, one of six *ArtsEqual* research groups led by specialist researcher Sari Karttunen, with other group members including Lehtonen, and professor of applied language studies, Sari Pöyhönen (Arts Equal). The project's documented objective of making 'strategic steps towards equality' displayed a confidence in the fact that art in and of itself, without any specific application, is a vehicle for equitable encounters between people from different backgrounds.

IDENTITY, REPRESENTATION, AND THE *UNDOCUMENTED LOVE*

Kaartinen and Lehtonen continued their collaboration in the production *Undocumented Love* in the Omapohja studio in 2020, and Salmenkallio and Saad were in charge of the production's soundscape and music. The three performers with refugee backgrounds (Angela al Debs, Mohammad Mandla, and Bakr Hasan) and the two Finnish performers (Kalle Lehto and Marja Salo) were all professional artists. Their professions as dancer, clown, circus artist, and actor were an essential starting point for the production's artistic vision and shaped its performance, which was mainly in English.

In this production the audience were placed on chairs in the middle of an empty space, with actors performing on a raised platform and occasionally moving freely amongst the audience with only scant auditory effects and music bringing in any extra meaning. The political focus was on the refugees' country of origin, on the reasons artists leave their homelands. The project's concern with undocumented identity and the need to understand a refugee's feelings of *belonging* (and *non-belonging*) to the old home country had led to project interviews in different countries, including a fieldwork phase in circus and theatre workshops for refugee children in Istanbul (*Undocumented Love* Programme).

The performance was made up of three scenes. 'Story of the Other' was a story of an African man who was subjected to violent persecution in his native Cameroon because of his homosexuality. The man behind the story wanted to remain anonymous, so two of the cast's women, al Debs and Salo (a Syrian and a Finn; a dancer and an actress; both non-black) were chosen as the story's narrators. 'Death of the Father' told Iraqi Hasan's own account of how he had to witness his father's death over the phone. 'Case Syria' told the stories of Syrian

Mandla and al Debs. The artists joined to (re)present each other's stories, regardless of their origins. The performers all shared the same ideological message and artist identity, but they performed, depicted, and represented the story from different angles: as asylum seekers and refugees, or native Finnish nationals, as storytellers of their own stories, or as a vehicle for someone else's story. The show's planned international tour and the accompanying seminars titled 'Forced Migration and Ethnic Plurality on Nordic Stages' envisioned for the Nordic leg of the tour were cancelled due to the COVID-19 pandemic (Lehtonen 2021b).

Despite the cancellation of the tour, the *Undocumented Love* production was judged to be significant, and reviews were generally very positive. However, the question of refugee representation—who can represent whom, and to what extent native Finnish actors have the right to represent a refugee—remained a hotly debated issue. Critic Maria Säkö wrote about how the stories of the persecuted migrants overawed the viewer, and how the production built an effective bridge with oil and superpower politics, but she felt that the Finnish performers were given too much space at the expense of the migrant performers. The project's creators countered this criticism with the argument that it was important to also depict the 'identity shifts' experienced by members of the welfare state when confronted by these stories (Säkö 2020, 14–15). This topic was also the subject of lively internet debates (Lehtonen 2021b). In the late 2010s, the debate on identity and representation, such as the #MeToo movement, Black Lives Matter, and the discussion on intersectionality gained more momentum, highlighting comments made in relation to this production. From this viewpoint, criticism was especially leveraged at the representation of a black homosexual man by two non-black women who were tasked with telling his story. Theatrical critic Suna Vuori waded in on the representation discussion, arguing that debates centring on who has a right to represent whom had become banal, and in this context the demands placed on art alienated the basic tenets of theatre (Vuori 2020). The COVID-19 pandemic was also an effective silencer of the representation conversation.

Conclusions

According to Lehtonen, a major goal of the Touring Stage productions was to raise awareness about the multifaceted nature of migrant issues without compromising the dignity of individuals (Lehtonen 2021a, 113). His concept of a 'hybrid community of artistic expression' that came out of *The Other Home* production describes 'an imagined community that perpetuates a vision of its inner sameness while also being aware of the phenomenon that causes its members to be different.' The people invited to participate in each project were chosen from vulnerable members of society, and 'the phenomena of communitas, liminality, anti-stigma […] tell something about the quality of the community that it was,' writes Lehtonen (Lehtonen 2019, 31–32). An open invitation for refugees to participate led to tensions between refugees traumatised by political conflict. Some of them had been on opposite sides in their home countries, and observed different cultural practices, such as gender norms and possessed uneven professional skills, which added their own tensions. However, the joint desire to tell stories was able to override the potential for conflict (Lehtonen and Pöyhönen 2018, 34, 39).

Lehtonen's term 'hybrid community of artistic expression' is comparable to A. Barh's concept of 'diasporic space' that Alison Jeffers examines in the context of theatre: ethnicity underpins all groups, and native and diasporic individuals create their own identities as equals. In a diasporic space, 'multiple subject positions are juxtaposed, contested; proclaimed or disavowed.' Jeffers emphasises the importance of theatre in raising the profile of refugees, as the theatre 'allows us to address specifics where diaspora space is small enough to examine moments of encounter; the space between two individuals on a stage, for example, or the space in which an audience and performers meet' (Jeffers 2012, 11).

In the National Theatre, in its diasporic space, the on-stage relationships between performers shifted from production to production in response to the identities of the participants, the physical space, and the meanings created by the surrounding society. In *Paper Anchor*, only three of the performers came from refugee backgrounds, and they had all come to Finland from different continents. In *The Other Home*, the ensemble of refugees could understand each other's national language, but in contrast the political tension between individual characters was more significant. The power of theatre was made manifest: belonging to a theatrical community and a joint purpose served to build bridges across political faultlines and tensions inherent in differing ethnic groups. In the third production, all of the performers were professional artists, creating a greater sense of equality amongst them.

All productions shared a desire to give voice to refugees, placing an emphasis on the authenticity of the messaging conveyed. S.E. Wilmer has observed that '[w]hile the presence of a refugee on stage telling his or her own story adds an additional aspect of authenticity to verbatim theatre, this authenticity is simultaneously undermined by the refugee performing as an actor. The better the craft of the refugee actor, the more effective the delivery might be, but ironically the less authentic the story might seem' (Wilmer 2018, 92). This held especially true in the first production where refugees communicated the stories rather than interpreting them as actors. When later productions looked at artistic identity as a function of, and as a reason for, seeking asylum, the burden of proof doubled and became more complicated: a refugee had to testify of his/her talent as a performing artist and to convince the profession of the political risk that threatened him and he had to deliver his/her story authentically. This was especially complicated in *Undocumented Love* with its coherent but, for the spectators, distant stories, while in *The Other Home* the spectators did not need to be convinced; they already shared the concerns which focused on local Finnish politics.

The growing emphasis on refugees as artists signalled equality, but in the end it also led to new and challenging problematics such as questions of representation at the end of the 2010s that impacted the *Undocumented Love* production. Representation is inherent to all theatre, but the critical discussion around the *Undocumented Love* production (with non-black women representing a black man) led to new questions. If the stronger of the two in a specific power dynamic is the one doing the representation, are we talking about equality or cultural appropriation? There were no final conclusions, but the conversation as such testified to the heightened tensions in the Finnish art world—and of refugee performers being included in that space.

The increased political activism of the National Theatre productions did not incite anti-refugee discourse; it was the visit by the theatre director to the refugee demonstration that created a public stir. The right-wing populist movements did not have a prominent newspaper and their online publishing was mainly focused on existing party supporters, and was not concerned with art. The Touring Stage projects culminated in theatrical performances, but an equally important aim was the building of a new artistic community during their lengthy rehearsals over several years.

References

ArtsEqual. 2017. *ArtsEqual Policy Brief.* https://www.artsequal.fi/documents/14230/0/PB_vainotut_taiteilijat/fbe10926-9fc1-4cbe-beae-daa10ec977d1.

Finnish National Theatre and Finish Immigration Service. 2011. *Bulletin.* Press release, November 29, 2011. NT Archive.

Helminen, Taija, and Jussi Lehtonen. 2012. *Vastaanotto.* Helsinki: Kirja Kerrallaan & Suomen Kansallisteatteri.

Jeffers, Alison. 2012. *Refugees, Theatre and Crisis. Performing Global Identities.* Basingstoke: Palgrave Macmillan.

Korkiasaari, Jouni, and Ismo Söderling. 1994. 'Muuttoliike.' In *Suomen väestö*, edited by Seppo Koskinen et al. Helsinki: Gaudeamus.

Koski, Pirkko. 2015. 'Challenging the Centre. Asylum Seekers Encounter Native Citizens.' *Nordic Theatre Studies*, 27 (1), 43–54.

Lehtonen, Jussi. 2019. 'Imagining What It Is Like To Be You: Challenges of a Hybrid Community.' *Drama—Nordisk dramapedagogisk tidsskrift*, 2, 30–35.

———. 2021a. 'Ilmaisuyhteisö Kansallisteatterissa: eettisiä haasteita yhteisöllisesti suuntautuneessa dokumenttiteatterissa.' In *Yhteisötaiteen etiikka*, edited by Lea Kantonen and Sari Karttunen, 97–127. Helsinki: Taideyliopisto.

———. 2021b. Jussi Lehtonen's email to Pirkko Koski, April 15, 2021.

Lehtonen, Jussi, and Sari Pöyhönen. 2018. 'Documentary Theatre as a Platform for Hope and Social Justice.' In *Critical Articulations of Hope from the Margins of Arts Education*, edited by Eeva Anttila and Anniina Suominen, 31–44. London: Routledge.

Migri. 2020. Accessed October 24, 2021. https://migri.fi/en/home.

———. 2021. Accessed April 3, 2022. https://migri.fi/en/about-the-finnish-immigration-service.

Simpson, James. 2018. 'Toinen koti—Other Home.' *Tlangblog*, February 4, 2018. Accessed April 10, 2021. https://tlangblog.wordpress.com/2018/02/04/toinen-koti-other-home/.
Säkö, Maria. 2020. 'Näin syntyy teatterikritiikki.' *Journalisti*, 3/2020. 14–15.
Undocumented Love. Programme. 2020. Helsinki: Kansallisteatteri.
Wilmer, S. E. 2018. *Performing Statelessness in Europe*. Cham, Palgrave Macmillan.
Vuori, Suna. 2020. 'Teatteri ei ole peili.' *Image*, October 18, 2020.

PART VI

Itinerancy, Traveling, and Transnationalism

CHAPTER 51

Transnationality: Intercultural Dialogues, Encounters, and the Theatres of Curiosity

Pavel Drábek

At the heart of theatre lies encounter—a confrontation with difference, with a new experience, a world unknown or little understood. This, I would argue, is the *dialogue* that occurs in performances—an interaction between different (*dia-*) views or kinds of knowledge (*-logos*). The spoken dialogue on stage is, in a sense, merely the most visible manifestation of this encounter between worlds apart. Dialogue is more than just mere *conflict* or a clash of wills and it comprises 'not only the words and speaking but also the acting of actors' (Zich 1931, 49, 174; all translations from Zich by Pavel Drábek and Tomáš Kačer). What comes to grapple with one another on stage are different values, meanings, and worlds. We could take this idea even further: the quintessential theatrical dialogue takes place both on stage between the performing personas, and—perhaps even more crucially—in the interaction between the stage and the audience, who are confronted with the *logos* of the onstage performance and its world. That world is put on view for the audience to behold (θεᾶσθαι, *theasthai*) and in doing so, it becomes part of their lived experience and cultural life.

However, this analytical dialogic core of the theatre far too often disagrees with Western theatre historiography. Since ancient Greece, theatre has been promoted and celebrated as a civic institution, a nation-, identity- and community-building cultural apparatus, and much of modern theatre history follows suit. Theatre is seen as the manifestation of a civilisation, of a locale, or a community. This theatre is *about* something; it conveys an *idea* or a *political*

P. Drábek (✉)
University of Hull, Hull, UK
e-mail: P.Drabek@hull.ac.uk

message; it plays a role in a *national* context. The tendency towards a singular *aboutness* stems from our cognitive biases: when confronted with a *dia-logos*—clashing worldviews, ideological disagreements, epistemological discrepancies—we tend to come to terms with them, reconcile them or ignore them as outliers, achieve a balance, and by the same token also arrive at epistemic entropy. That, however, doesn't reflect the variety, let alone the cognitive experience that theatre confronts its audiences with. This chapter reflects on the long history of cultural dialogues in theatre, summed up in the concept of *transnationality*. Drawing on a range of dramaturgies, I argue for a historiographic approach that foregrounds the transnational and intercultural encounter, or *metaphysical dialogue*, that takes place in the theatres of curiosity.

In what follows I pursue an alternative version of transnationality: the transnational mindset that places the intercultural dialogue at the forefront of the meaning making. This is not necessarily material, literal transnationality but metaphysical transnationality—sometimes disparagingly referred to as armchair travelling—but when practised fully, metaphysical transnationality is a genuine mode of curiosity in the dialogue—with other nations, cultures, people, identities, customs, behaviours, and viewpoints—without the narcissistic mindset of the colonialist or religious zealot who aspires to convert everyone to *his* ways. The metaphysical transnational theatre maker—or cosmopolitan, to borrow Kwame Anthony Appiah's word—pursues a philosophical agenda: to encounter the unknown and even the unsettling, get to know it and try to understand it—and eventually make it enrich our worldview.

Migration: Itinerancy, Travelling, and the Foreign

'Today, we may associate drama with paid productions mounted on an indoor stage,' writes Claire Sponsler about medieval theatre, 'but during the medieval period it was a medium in motion' (Sponsler 2017, 106). The same can be said about any period in theatre history, from classical antiquity throughout early modernity to the present. Itinerancy has always been an inherent part of performance. Even in ancient Greece, the classical model that has come to define the Western notion of theatre, performance always migrated. As Patrick Hadley observes:

> Though Athens always retained a certain pre-eminence as a centre of dramatic production, all the literary sources attest to a 'circulation' in the truest sense of the word by the fourth century [BCE], at the very latest, with playwrights, actors and playscripts moving readily back and forth between Athens and the cities that had initially emulated her in the production of drama. (Hadley 2017, 87)

It perhaps comes down to 'the spell of Plato' (as Karl Popper has called it) that itinerant theatre and performance outside the metropolis have carried pejorative associations. Plato appeals in his antitheatrical complaint that 'he who thinks he makes tragedy well, doesn't run around showing it in other cities outside Attica, but brings himself straight here and, as is only fitting, shows it to these people' (*Laches* 183a–b, quoted in Hadley 2017, 86). Indirectly, this passage proves not only the transnationality of Greek tragedy from the earliest times but also the early cultural awareness of it. Theatre was transnational, itinerant, and decentralised—which is what provokes Plato's diatribe, I would argue, as it contravened his centralist epistemology. (See also Hadley 2017, 86, for an overview of critical interpretations of this passage.) A rich theatrical culture existed outside Athens and 'less formalized troupes of travelling players […] must have been already active well back in the fourth century' (Taplin 1999, 35). Furthermore, a significant proportion of the known ancient tragedians (authors as well as actors) came from other parts of the empire, not to mention the recorded performances of Athenian plays abroad—such as Aeschylus' *Persians* performed in Syracuse in 470 BCE, two years after its opening in Athens (Hadley 2017, 84). What could have been the appeal of that transnational play with an intercultural conflict at its heart to audiences outside Attica?

Perhaps even more significantly, Greek tragedy was a major cultural export that 'not only "showed the city to herself", but to others as well' (Taplin 1999: 51). It is this inherent, metaphysical transnationality that plays a significant part in theatre history, although it hasn't been given a sufficiently prominent place.

> Homer is, in some sense, the archetypal precedent for this cultural supra-nationalism. The epics were performed everywhere, whether or not the locality in question figured in the poems—indeed, many major centres, including Athens and Chios, had to swallow their pride in this matter. (Taplin 1999: 47)

Arguably, the historiographic model that prioritises Plato's centralism and disparages other venues in the circuit around Attica (ἔξωθεν κύκλῳ περὶ τὴν Ἀττικὴν) as periphery or provincial still survives, nourished by the modernist emancipation of theatre into an artform that looks down upon its itinerant variants.

The centralist pattern replicates colonial ideologies of knowledge and yokes the history of theatre with that of wealth, capital, as well as empire. In that vein, theatre history has prioritised metropolitan achievements manifested by established wealth and architecture, to the detriment of the diversity of theatre cultures. Histories of Early Modern theatre write predominantly of the leading playhouses and court venues in the metropoles like London, Madrid, or Paris, but less so about the less wealthy sites of performance in those cities, and even less about other cities, towns, and itinerant forms of performance. Histories of modern-day theatre fare no better despite the fact that the stationary model of theatre is a rare exception, not the standard—not to mention the migratory working patterns of theatre makers.

Nation and Transnationality

One of the most popular, if not *the* most-performed Early Modern play was *Doctor Faustus*—one of whose versions was written by Christopher Marlowe for the London stage. It was a repertory evergreen and was also popular in print: Marlowe's version first appearing posthumously in 1604, reprinted numerous times, and then again in 1616 in a version revised by Samuel Rowley and William Bird, and reprinted repeatedly again. This impressive record, however, skews the reality. This play about a doctor of philosophy who sells his soul to the devil in exchange for superhuman powers is only one of many variants of a perennial story of insatiable human desire for knowledge and fulfilment here on earth. Moralistic Jesuit plays from all around Europe about a man selling his soul to the devil predate the English play, but Marlowe's inspiration clearly came from Johann Spies' German chapbook *Historia von D. Johann Fausten* (1587), which in turn reworked folk tales about trickster figures from around Central Europe. The Faustian map complicates further since the Marlowe play was also very popular on tour with the English players throughout the British Isles and abroad—unsurprisingly in Germanic Europe, where it survived in countless versions in German, Polish, or Czech on the repertoire of travelling puppeteers well into the twentieth century (Drábek 2014, 185–188).

Why *Faustus*? I would argue that the appeal came not only of its universal theme of the humanistic overreacher but also because the play's episodic qualities—a feature of oral storytelling not unlike Homer's *Iliad* and *Odyssey* and other folk narratives (Ong 1982, 138–144). Narratives structured episodically are malleable enough and lend themselves to retellings that easily adopt homeostatic qualities: the exigencies and opportunities of performing here and now. Besides, one of Faustus' desires is to know the world—to travel to Rome, to meet the great and the good, before coming back home with a vengeance. That wanderlust spikes the audience's curiosity, while firmly embedding it in a readily relatable moral: too much knowledge and boundless straying is potentially forbidden fruit. Yet, the vicarious experience is worthwhile. Archival records of itinerant puppeteers (who mostly used Neapolitan marionettes) show how adaptable and welcoming to novelties *Faustus* was. As such it not only remained the staple of the touring repertoire but also set the pattern for the genre of the transnational puppet play as such (Dubská 2012). It is worth observing that a similar structural, episodic quality in firmly morally anchored narrative can be found in the nineteenth and early twentieth centuries in 'America's most mutable book,' *Uncle Tom's Cabin* (Davis and Mihaylova 2018).

Numerous other plays known from the Early Modern London theatres enjoyed rich stage lives abroad. Throughout England, the anonymous *Mucedorus* (c. 1590) was an all-time favourite performed at least until the 1830s. Thomas Kyd's *The Spanish Tragedy* (c. 1587) found keen audiences in the Netherlands and in Germany (Bosman 2013, 504–515; Cinpoeş 2016), as have many versions and variants of William Shakespeare's (and George Peele's?) *Titus Andronicus* (c. 1591) and *Romeo and Juliet* (c. 1594), probably also nourished by the popularity of Bandello's novellas and its several Spanish dramatisations. *King Lear* (c. 1606) is an interesting case in point due to its affinities with Central European folk tales (Procházka 1988) that could have played a significant role in the play's popular reception. Among the other hits of Early Modern English drama abroad are Thomas Dekker's *Old Fortunatus* (1599), which is based on a German folk tale; William Rowley's *A Shoemaker a Gentleman* (1637) with its hagiographic subplot reworking *The Golden Legend*; and Thomas Dekker and Philip Massinger's *The Virgin Martyr* (1620) about the martyrdom of Saint Dorothea, which survived in numerous versions as a folk play collected in the nineteenth century (Neuhuber 2014, 139–140). None of these plays have anything specifically English about them: while they originated as play scripts for the London stages, they stem from a transnational body of stories and legends. At least some of their authors were very conscious of the theatrical life elsewhere—and not only outside of London but also across the channel: Shakespeare worked from the Italianate culture of the novella (Walter 2019); John Fletcher based most of his plays on Spanish sources; Dekker and Massinger arguably wrote with a pan-European purview, given their dramaturgies inspired by works from Spain, Italy, France, Holland, and Germany. The plays' inherent transnationality made them appealing to a truly transnational audience.

'Theatre often appears to be a fantastical form of tourism,' Susanne L. Wofford argues, 'in which audiences are presented with the awesome and bizarre nature of foreign places and characters' (Wofford 2013, 478). She makes a convincing case for Shakespeare's plays as mediators of transnational conventions, genres as well as emotions, with their Italianate sources, plots, and theatergrams (see also Walter 2019). In turn, Wofford argues, the plays articulate

> a complex English identity, one that was never simply nationalist or native, but hybrid and 'foreign'. […] English national identity in this [Early Modern] period can best be understood through its deep immersion in and growth from foreign performances, foreign plots, and foreign politics. (Wofford 2013, 491)

In a similar way, other national theatres created complex national identities, reflecting specific political and cultural predicaments—as for instance in the imperial imagination of Golden Age Spain which spanned several continents and comprised several religions and races (see Fuchs 2001). Negotiating a *transnational national* identity became a complex dialogical process in which theatre played a crucial role, with its inherent foreignness, diversity, and racialisation at heart (see Ndiaye 2022).

Dialogic Theatre and Monologic Bias

Theatre history offers countless examples of plays that are transnational at their heart. Inevitably, many of them streamline the cultural, religious, or epistemic diversity towards a singular overriding interpretation that monologises the views, eliminates the dissenting voices, and reasserts the status quo. Nonetheless, to settle for the ideological resolution without acknowledging the validity of the alternatives would be to abnegate the entire purpose of theatre. The propositional *what if* that launches the experience of every single play invites its audience into a possible world that confronts its inhabitants as well as the spectators. What would it mean if this happened to us? That curiosity is the heart of the play and without contemplating this *what if*, the theatrical experience fails.

In early 1517, in the chamber of the Portuguese Queen Maria of Aragon, where she was 'ill with the sickness from which she died,' Gil Vicente's morality play *Auto da Barca do Inferno* was performed—as the frontispiece of the first print states (Vicente 1997, 29). In front of the dying queen was presented a rowdy *danse macabre* as the Devil and his ship's crew welcome sinners on board their boat of hell, ready to depart. While the ideological anchoring is self-evident (sinners go to Hell, the virtuous to Heaven), the carnivalesque comedy questions its characters and vicariously its spectators too. What makes the play particularly unsettling is its naval setting: Portugal with King Manuel and Queen Maria at its helm was a leading colonial power with a large navy of ships navigating around the globe. The play's confrontation with the daily reality of seafaring to the end of the world, superimposed over the moralistic script of the journey to Hell for the sinners, is a powerful metaphor that, for the duration of the comedy, turns the status quo upside down. The morality play is used here as an old script to make sense of what Anthony Grafton has called 'the shock of discovery' (Grafton 1992). Throughout the late Middle Ages and early modernity, this was a common strategy of coming to terms with the new world and new realities that were yet to find a place in the Western imagination. In a characteristically logocentric fashion, European discoveries were interpreted and *epistemically colonised* with reference to the foundational scriptures, be it the Bible or the ancient classics, no matter how unsuitable these may have been. This had painfully often tragic consequences for the discovered cultures—not only in the genocides in the New World and in Asia but also in the cruelties in Africa (see, for instance, Olusoga 2016, 34–37) as the European explorers were forcibly trying to make other cultures comply with their vision of the world and *God's creation*. Vicente's *Auto da Barca do Inferno* propositionally confronts its imperial audience and invites the ethical question about Portugal's naval exploits—of course, without daring to infer an interpretation. Overall, the play is firmly rooted within a monologic discourse of Christian morality: the sinners are ordered by the Devil to 'Come on board: | here's the plank, step up on it' (41), whereas the 'four noble knights of the Order of Christ who died in Africa [...] in the power of the Moors' are invited by the

Angel to board the 'boat of glory' (91, 93). And yet, the question about the sea journey awaiting travellers and its morality is constantly there.

Writing for the Madrid stage a century later, Lope de Vega, the most prolific of Early Modern playwrights, created a dramatic version of the antisemitic folk legend of the alleged ritual murder of a ten-year-old boy in 1491. *El niño inocente de La Guardia* (The Innocent Child of La Guardia, c. 1605–1608) features Queen Isabel and King Ferdinand, towns- and village people, a prominent member of the Holy Inquisition (who interestingly fails in his judgement of his neighbour's character), a French rabbi and half a dozen Jews, many of them *conversos*, as well as two Angels and the allegorical personas of Reason and Intellect. While it is beyond question what the overall propagandistic interpretation is, and the status quo of the royally authorised Holy Inquisition remains intact, there are numerous situations in the play that confront us with unsettling voices and viewpoints. It would be specious to argue that Lope de Vega's play subverts the dominant ideology. Nonetheless, the play presents an intercultural dialogue that sits apart from the overriding reading:

> I have lost all will to live, and gladly await my death.
> What sort of monarchs are these who dream up
> all these charges against poor, harmless people
> who keep to themselves, and to their own private beliefs?
> [...]
> What miserable beings are we Spanish Jews,
> stranded at sea without a single port in sight!
> Already a new Inquisition is baying for our blood,
> anxious to expose our every so-called secret.
> (*The Innocent Child*, Act I, trans. Michael Jacobs; Lope de Vega 2001, 113–114)

The Jews' suffering is genuine and their desperate emotions retain their humanity. The dramatic situations of the ritual murder, enacting a dark version of the Easter Passion on a little boy, are harrowing enough, but to write this play off as simply antisemitic would ignore the nuance and the dialogic confrontations that take place within it. The official line—warranted by the ever-present Holy Inquisition that nourished popular antisemitism and cruelties against other religions and races—was too transparent a narrative to accept at face value. When a similar scenario—the reenactment of the Easter Passion—was adopted in the mid-twentieth century by Nikos Kazantzakis in his novel *Christ Recrucified* (adapted for opera as *The Greek Passion* by Bohuslav Martinů), it was prosecuted for heresy. Clearly, the intercultural dialogue, although merely propositional, was a dangerous enough matter. The transnationality of Lope de Vega's play is an indelible part of the audience's experience, irrespective of the monologic interpretation that frames it.

Theatres of Curiosity

The final section of this chapter considers three transnational case studies. These negotiate ancient storylines and motifs, repositioning them in new genres and circumstances and offering their audiences multiple scenarios of engaging with them—as ways of engaging with one's curiosity in the cultural other.

Armida

The cultural memory of the Crusades (1091–1291), the attempts at capturing Jerusalem for the Christian world, was long-lasting and could be seen as a trauma of sorts—a series of failed confrontations with the Middle East and its oriental otherness. The centrepiece that commemorated the campaigns in the cultural imagination was Torquato Tasso's *Gerusalemme liberata* (The Liberation of Jerusalem) (1581), published after what may seem like an immense hiatus of three centuries after the last Crusade. While Tasso's epic poem was immensely influential, one episode in particular inspired tens of dramatic versions, particularly in the opera: that of Rinaldo and Armida. Rinaldo, one of the crusaders, is captured and is enchanted by the Damascan princess and magician Armida, who casts a spell on him. Rinaldo is overwhelmed by the blissful magic of Armida's oriental charms, before he sobers up and resumes his Christian duties. Tasso's story is, in many ways, a Renaissance adaptation of the Medea legend—the story of a foreign *femme fatale* with supernatural abilities; that myth in turn endows the Armida legend with cultural depth. Following from Claudio Monteverdi's (lost) dramatic cantata of 1626, the Armida-Rinaldo story became a staple of the operatic genre in numerous variations of the same pattern: framed by the holy design of the crusaders' Christian mission, Rinaldo and Armida enjoy seemingly boundless moments of bliss in an earthly paradise. It was this allowed enchanted world of enjoying forbidden fruit that created a supreme opportunity for composers, librettists, and scenographers to present theatrical spectacle to their audiences. Numerous versions played out on opera stages from Italy (Marco Scacchi, 1638; Benedetto Ferrari, 1639; Marco Marazzoli, 1641) through France (Jean-Baptiste Lully, 1686), England (George Frideric Handel, 1711), to Austria (Antonio Salieri, 1777) (for a detailed list, see Carter 1992). Sung in Italian, French, German, and even Czech (Antonín Dvořák 1904), the subject matter encapsulated the transnational and intercultural encounter that uproots the foundations of the Western world.

Boccaccio's Punished Adulterers

The generic Early Modern visual portrayal of travelling comedians performing on their trestle stages in a marketplace or at a crossroads shows almost invariably one situation: a man and a woman in lascivious embrace are secretly observed by another man, while yet another person is peeping from a hiding place in a basket or a chest (see Katritzky 2006, for Early Modern visual documentation of the commedia dell'arte). That setup is naturally emblematic and vague enough, encapsulating the scurrility and voyeurism of travelling performance, but there is one family of comedies that fit the bill perfectly. The first known published version of this group is in Czech and forms an interlude attached to *Historia duchovní o Samsonovi* (The Sacred History of Samson, Prague, 1608). Its plot derives from a novella in Boccaccio's *The Decameron*: a husband returns home unexpectedly just as his wife is entertaining two lovers, one of them already hidden in a chest, while the other is sent out with a drawn sword to meet the returning husband under a fabricated excuse of a violent attack. This bawdy comedy enjoyed a popular tradition in Czech folk theatre, performed solely by women under the title *Salička*, and its variants are extant throughout Germanic Europe (see also Drábek 2020, 222–223). Under the title of *Kemp's Jig* it was registered for print in London in 1595, and it was probably thanks to the clown Will Kemp, who was also a well-known comedian in Germany at the time, that a musical version of his jig spread on the European mainland. It was published in German in 1620, in Dutch in 1648, and in Swedish around 1700 (Clegg and Skeaping 2014, 101–103). Arguably the second of Falstaff's escapades in Shakespeare's *The Merry Wives of Windsor* (c. 1597) follow the same plot—and of course, Kemp was likely to have played Falstaff. Whether Kemp was or wasn't responsible for the diaspora of this comedy on the European mainland is moot. Boccaccio's novella was well known, circulating in manuscript copies since its publication in fourteenth-century Italy and reworked countless times by others (by the popular Matteo Bandello for instance). In its emblematic simplicity, it would be recognisable and relatable across linguistic and cultural boundaries. Besides, marketing it as an Italian comedy from Boccaccio would have sparked audience curiosity and given it a veneer of fashion and style.

Aphra Behn's Neglected Play

Aphra Behn (1640–1689) was the first professional female author in the English language. As a prolific playwright, outmatched in her time only by John Dryden, she was an important presence on the London stage, although theatre history hasn't yet given her sufficient attention. Among her least known and least studied plays is *The Young King; or, The Mistake* (1679). Its convoluted, baroque plot defies simple summary; the play features an Amazon warrior princess Cleomena; her brother, an heir to the throne who is hidden away to protect the kingdom from an ominous prophecy; and a semi-mythological military conflict between two warring kingdoms. The fictional dedication from Astrea to Philaster, that Behn attached to the published edition of 1683, alludes to the play as 'this youthful sally of my Pen, this first Essay of my Infant-Poetry' (Behn 1996, 83), and it is often referred to as a juvenilia or imperfect work. However, this tragicomedy is a remarkable play—not only for its accomplished stagecraft but also for its transnational dramaturgy. Having explored and performed the play with students at the University of Hull in October–November 2019, in what was its first revival since the 1670s, I would argue that *The Young King* skilfully combines dramaturgical inspirations of a rich provenance: English tragicomedy, namely John Fletcher and Francis Beaumont's *Philaster, or Love Lies a-Bleeding* (c. 1609) and Shakespeare's *Twelfth Night, or What You Will* (c. 1601); Spanish comedia, with the subplot borrowing from Pedro Calderón de la Barca's *La vida es sueño* (Life is a Dream, c. 1635); Tasso's *The Liberation of Jerusalem*; and, La Calprenède's French novels *Cléopâtre* (1646–1663) (Todd in Behn 1996, 80–81). Theatrically, the Amazon Cleomena is a supreme *diva*, bearing apparent inspirations from the Italian commedia dell'arte and its operatic qualities (for the diva in the commedia and in opera, see Wilbourne 2016), and the framing genre of the play is the most transnational dramatic vessel of all—the Italianate tragicomedy, with its pastoral subject matter and a riches of intercultural explorations of violence, sex and gender, and poetic idealism. Quasi-operatic and truly baroque in its structure and content, Behn's neglected play—allegedly written during her stay in Surinam before returning to England—is a fine specimen of transnationality concentrated in a piece written in a seemingly home-grown fashion (Fletcherian tragicomedy) and for a London theatre (Duke's Company, led by William Davenant, playing at Dorset Garden). As a theatrical experience, though, it offered its audiences a spectrum of cultures, from the literary and dramatic cultures from all over Europe to the imaginary worlds of the late European Renaissance—with its conflict of Dacians and Scythians in a mythical version of the East (in this case the Balkans and the regions of the Black Sea).

Historiography often presents theatre as a shop window of the nation and of the establishment, or its subversive refraction. The ideological framing of historic examples may suggest a more streamlined engagement than would have been the case. I have argued in this chapter that the transnationality inherent in the theatrical experience is not rooted in a singular discourse but rather in a deep cultural dialogue that is often unsettling, confrontational, and uprooting. Predicated on a curiosity of otherness, the cognitive experience of the theatrical performance is in its essence itinerant, confronting the audience with the possible and playful worlds of *what if*, which often offer alternative views, possibilities, and systems of knowledge. In this sense, theatre history needs to acknowledge not only the undoubted, solid facts about performance practice but also its inherent, essential itinerancy: at the heart of the theatre is a journey to that which is not—the speculative, the possible, and the curious Other.

References

Appiah, Kwame Anthony. 2007. *Cosmopolitanism: Ethics in a World of Strangers*. London: Penguin.

Behn, Aphra. 1996. *The Young King; or, The Mistake*. In *Works*, vol. 7, edited by Janet Todd, 79–151. London: Pickering & Chatto.

Bosman, Anston. 2013. 'Mobility.' In *Early Modern Theatricality*, edited by Henry S. Turner, 493–515. Oxford: Oxford University Press.
Carter, Tim. 1992. 'Armida.' *Grove Music Online*. https://doi.org/10.1093/gmo/9781561592630.article.O900189.
Cinpoeș, Nicoleta. 2016. *Doing Kyd: Essays on The Spanish Tragedy*. Manchester: Manchester University Press.
Clegg, Roger, and Lucie Skeaping. 2014. *Singing Simpkin and Other Bawdy Jigs: Musical Comedy on the Shakespearean Stage. Scripts, Music & Context*. Exeter: University of Exeter Press.
Davis, Tracy C., and Stefka Mihaylova, eds. 2018. *Uncle Tom's Cabins: The Transnational History of America's Most Mutable Book*. Ann Arbor: University of Michigan Press.
Drábek, Pavel. 2014. 'English Comedy and Central European Marinette Drama: A Study in Theater Etymology.' In *Transnational Mobilities in Early Modern Theater*, edited by Robert Henke and Eric Nicholson, 177–196. Farnham: Ashgate.
———. 2020. '"Samson Figuru nese": Biblical Plays Between Czech Drama and English Comedy in Early Modern Central Europe.' In *Enacting the Bible in Medieval and Early Modern Drama*, edited by Eva con Contzen and Chanita Goodblatt, 211–231. Manchester: Manchester University Press.
Dubská, Alice. 2012. *The Travels of the Puppeteers Brat and Pratte Through Europe in the Eighteenth and Nineteenth Centuries*. Praha: NAMU.
Fuchs, Barbara. 2001. *Mimesis and Empire: The New World, Islam, and European Identities*. Cambridge: Cambridge University Press.
Grafton, Anthony. 1992. *New Worlds, Ancient Texts: The Power of Tradition and the Shock of Discovery*. Cambridge, MA: Harvard University Press.
Hadley, Patrick. 2017. 'Circulation: Theatre as Mobile Political, Economic and Cultural Capital.' In *A Cultural History of Theatre in the Antiquity*, ed. Martin Revermann, 83–101. Volume 1 of *A Cultural History of Theatre*, edited by Christopher B. Balme and Tracy C. Davis. London: Bloomsbury.
Katritzky, M.A. 2006. *The Art of Commedia: The Study in the Commedia dell'Arte 1560–1620, With Special Reference to the Visual Records*. Amsterdam: Rodopi.
Lope de Vega, F.C. 2001. *The Innocent Child*. Translated by Michael Jacobs. London: Absolute Classics.
Ndiaye, Noémie. 2022. *Scripts of Blackness: Early Modern Performance Culture and the Making of Race*. Philadelphia: University of Pennsylvania Press.
Neuhuber, Christian. 2014. 'Ein Gottesgeschenk für die Bühne Dramatisierungen der Dorothea-Legende im deutschen Sprachraum.' In *Johann Georg Gettner und das barocke Theater zwischen Nikolsburg und Krumau*, edited by Margita Havlíčková and Christian Neuhuber, 131–181. Brno: Masaryk University Press.
Olusoga, David. 2016. *Black and British: A Forgotten History*. London: Macmillan.
Ong, Walter J. 1982. *Orality and Literacy: The Technologizing of the Word*. With additional chapters by John Hartley. London: Routledge, 2012.
Procházka, Martin. 1988. 'Images of *King Lear* in Czechoslovak Folklore.' In *Images of Shakespeare: Proceedings of the Third World Shakespeare Congress*, edited by Werner Habicht et al., 258–268. Newark: University of Delaware Press.
Sponsler, Claire. 2017. 'Circulation.' In *A Cultural History of Theatre in the Middle Ages*, ed. Jody Enders, 105–121. Volume 2 of *A Cultural History of Theatre*, edited by Christopher B. Balme and Tracy C. Davis. London: Bloomsbury.

Taplin, Oliver. 1999. 'Spreading the Word Through Performance.' In *Performance Culture and Athenian Democracy*, ed. Simon Goldhill and Robin Osborne, 33–57. Cambridge: Cambridge University Press.

Vicente, Gil. 1997. *Gil Vicente: Three Discovery Plays. Auto da Barca do Inferno, Exortação da Guerra, Auto da Índia*. Edited and translated by Anthony Lappin. Warminster: Aris & Phillips.

Walter, Melissa Emerson. 2019. *The Italian Novella and Shakespeare's Comic Heroines*. Toronto: University of Toronto Press.

Wilbourne, Emily. 2016. *Seventeenth-Century Opera and the Sound of the Commedia dell'Arte*. Chicago: University of Chicago Press.

Wofford, Susanne. 2013. 'Foreign.' In *Early Modern Theatricality*, edited by Henry S. Turner, 478–492. Oxford: Oxford University Press.

Zich, Otakar. 1931. *Estetika dramatického umění: teoretická dramaturgie*. Praha: Melantrich. Forthcoming as *Aesthetics of the Dramatic Art: Theoretical Dramaturgy*. Translated by Pavel Drábek and Tomáš Kačer. Edited by David Drozd. Praha: Karolinum, forthcoming.

CHAPTER 52

German Theatre and August von Kotzebue's Theatrical Success and Pitfalls in Russia

Maria Berlova

As a cosmopolitan city where various European cultures co-existed in the nineteenth century, St. Petersburg had its own German Theatre, as well as French, Italian, and Russian stages. German Theatre had already taken root in Russia in the seventeenth century, with Russia's first dramatic theatre in German opening during Alexei Mikhailovich's reign in 1672. St. Petersburg's German Theatre lasted nearly a hundred years, having been founded in 1799 and closed in 1890. This unique theatre existed in a cordoned-off world. Its performances were mainly aimed at an audience comprised of German immigrants, with the exception of some Russian spectators interested in German culture and fluent in the language. August von Kotzebue worked as an assistant director of an existing German Theatre in St. Petersburg in 1781–1783, and in 1800–1801 as a director of the German Theatre, which had been founded the previous year. This article explores the special niche that the German Theatre occupied in early nineteenth-century St. Petersburg's cultural sphere, as well as Kotzebue's two periods of work in German theatres in Russia. It focuses on the issues of theatre and migration in the context of the culturally diverse and multinational St. Petersburg of two centuries ago.

It can be argued that the entrenched system of serfdom resulted in limiting the Russian state's territorial expansion. This led to it being necessary to attract foreign entrepreneurs to Russia from the second half of the eighteenth through to the beginning of the nineteenth centuries and to enlist their help in developing the south-eastern and southern territories of the European part of Russia.

M. Berlova (✉)
Washington, DC, USA

Owing to the fact that Catherine the Great hoped to open new lands and enlarge her country's population, she issued decrees and manifestoes in 1762 to entice foreigners to settle in Russia, granting benefits and privileges to immigrant entrepreneurs. These enticements succeeded most in attracting Germans. What persuaded them to undertake the journey was that at the time their country was splintered into multiple states, which—in comparison to other European countries—faced a gruelling socio-economic predicament. Added to this was the fact that their country lacked any legal restraint to keep them from settling elsewhere (German et al. 2005, 31).

By the beginning of Catherine the Great's rule in 1762, Tsar Peter the Great had already 'opened a window to Europe' not only by building St. Petersburg in 1703 and elevating it to be the Russian capital in 1712, but also by inviting battalions of foreign artisans and specialists to fashion it into a cornerstone of urban beauty. Germans, Dutchmen, Frenchmen, Englishmen, Italians, Poles, and other nationalities flocked to the city. From its foundation onward, St. Petersburg always harboured a large German population. Throughout the nineteenth century, an extensive number of immigrant German residents dwelt in special districts of St. Petersburg and Moscow. In 1818, they totalled 6% of St. Petersburg's inhabitants and continued to stand out as the city's major group of foreigners until 1914, all the while ardently preserving their language and customs (Melnikova 2012a, 12).

A Germanic influence could be seen in the ruling House of Romanov's direct genealogical links to the German House of Holstein-Gottorp. Germans also held prominent positions in Russian government and administerial institutions, and they prospered in military service and other nationally significant fields, such as engineering, architecture, medicine, education, and the arts. When Catherine II, who was notably of German origin, ascended to the throne in 1762, she promoted the rise of private companies in St. Petersburg, including German ones, causing many German artisans to become manufacturers (Keller 2001, 11).

German Theatre in St. Petersburg

In the early nineteenth century, migration was also a common attribute amongst Germans in creative professions, including actors. During the first half of the eighteenth century, German Theatre troupes arrived in St. Petersburg and Moscow to perform for different lengths of time. In 1777, Karl Knipper, a German entrepreneur and merchant in St. Petersburg, opened *Volny Rosiysky Teatr* (The Free Russian Theatre). Knipper ran this private theatre as a venue for a German theatrical troupe until 1781. Johann Karl Sauerweid and his wife featured as the German troupe's leading actors. Catherine the Great, who had a keen interest in theatre and was a playwright herself, incorporated Knipper's theatre into the Imperial Theatres, a theatrical organization financed by the Imperial exchequer, which lasted from 1781 until 1791. Following this period, the German Theatre was restructured a couple of times up until Joseph Miré arrived in St. Petersburg in 1799. Being an adventurous entrepreneur and son-in-law of Karl Knipper's leading actor Sauerweid, Miré bought the existing German Theatre along with its costumes and properties and launched a whole new German Theatre enterprise. For this St. Petersburg-based theatrical enterprise, Miré set up a collection of funds from local German merchants, even including some from Emperor Paul I's second son, Grand Duke Konstantin Pavlovitch.

Unfortunately, Miré's funds for the German Theatre only lasted a year. They ran out in 1800, leaving him and the theatre near bankruptcy. This led to the Directorate of Imperial Theatres taking it over. On 1 September, August von Kotzebue was appointed the German Theatre's new director for a year. After that, it again returned to being Miré's private enterprise (1801–1805) and then became Georg Arresto's enterprise that was supported by imperial subsidies (1805–1806). When a fire broke out in the theatre, this caused Alexander I to proclaim on 31 October 1806 that the German Theatre be put under jurisdiction of the Directorate of Imperial Theatres with a government subsidy. This status continued until the theatre's final closure in 1890.

A wide variety of genres comprised the German Theatre's repertoire. According to Austro-German tradition, dramatic and musical performances overlapped in the repertoire, because at the time theatrical genres had not yet been clearly differentiated (Gubkina 2003, 15–16). The German Theatre further distinguished itself as the first to introduce a Russian audience to the masterpieces of Lessing, Schiller, and Goethe, as well as operas by Mozart and Rossini. However, in the early nineteenth century, the plays by August von Kotzebue and August Wilhelm Iffland formed the core of its dramatic repertoire.

The activity of German actors followed a nomadic pattern; they regularly moved to St. Petersburg from Germany, Prussia, and Baltic cities, such as Riga, Reval (now Tallinn), Mitawa, Köningsberg (now Kaliningrad), and elsewhere. Baltic countries played a decisive role of being a connecting bridge between Germany and St. Petersburg (Keller 2001, 5). What proved most attractive in drawing German actors to Russia were the imperial subsidies that supported the German Theatre. This guaranteed stable work for the actors in the form of a contract and a regular salary, while also offering a splendid opportunity to earn a pension (Gubkina 2003, 70).

German actors in St. Petersburg tended to be isolated within an extremely limited social world. This was largely due to the language barrier. It resulted in nearly all German actors marrying within their professional community, and almost every day having to publicly declare their love to their better half in a theatrical context (Karatygin 1970, 53).

In the early nineteenth century, Russian memoirists were the ones mostly writing about the German Theatre. They represented St. Petersburg's artistic elite and gave various opposing perceptions of the theatre. These eyewitness perspectives range from Stepan Zhikharev's enthusiastic admiration to Filipp Vigel's irritable scepticism. Some emphasized the German Theatre's exceptionality, whereas others were comparatively hostile and stressed its total insignificance. From such eyewitness accounts of this theatre's audience, it is apparent that St. Petersburg's German Theatre appealed mostly to Germans. The spectators came not from high society, but rather were regular German folk with modest funds.

Rafail Zotov was a Russian playwright, translator, and theatre critic. He worked for the Imperial Theatres and directed the German Theatre from 1815 until 1818. Regarding the German Theatre's spectators, he wrote in his memoirs:

> And what an archaic audience it was! Ladies came to the boxes in the simplest, most homely attires, and calmly knitted stockings, occasionally wiping their tears with them in pathetic places, or putting off their work for a minute to heartily laugh at Lindenstein's comic antics. There were almost no calls, and applause was rare. But by the audience blowing their noses from tears and laughing in the right places, the actors knew that their acting gave pleasure. (Zotov 1859, 20)

Kotzebue's Life and Work

Among the many Germans working in St. Petersburg for their national theatre, Kotzebue stood out because of his international fame. Born 3 May 1761 in Weimar, Kotzebue didn't come from a noble family, but strove insatiably for recognition in multiple fields, including law, politics, journalism, creative writing, drama, and theatre administration.

In Weimar, when Kotzebue was a boy, Johann Wolfgang von Goethe allowed him to catch birds in a snare in his garden. Goethe also had friendly conversations with the youth and strongly encouraged diligence in him. In Goethe's short play *Brüder und Schwestern* (Brothers and Sisters), which was performed at a private theatre in Weimar, Kotzebue performed on stage for the first time in his life, playing a tiny role of a postman (Kotzebue 1804, 57). Kotzebue was also at this time acquainted with Friedrich Maximilian von Klinger, the German dramatist and novelist whose play, *Strum und Drang* (Storm and Stress), gave its name to the whole artistic epoch. Goethe and Klinger clearly influenced Kotzebue's future decision of becoming a playwright.

From 1777 until 1779, Kotzebue studied law in the German university city of Jena and also in Duisburg. In Jena, he started writing plays for an amateur theatre. In 1780, at the age of 19, Kotzebue became a lawyer in Weimar. The next year, by means of personal connections, he was appointed secretary of the Governor General in St. Petersburg. Four years later, Kotzebue was ennobled, and in 1785 became a president of the Magistrate of the Governorate of Estonia, a province of the Russian Empire. In 1790, he left his government service and travelled around Germany and France. Then he lived on an estate outside of Reval. By the end of the 1780s, he achieved astonishing success with his early dramatic works, such as *Menschenhass and Reue* (Misanthropy and Repentance) and *Die Indianer in England* (The Indians in England).

As mentioned above, in 1800, Kotzebue became a director of the German Theatre in St. Petersburg. That same year he received the title of Court Counsellor. A short while later he was elected to be a member of the Royal Prussian Academy of Sciences in 1806 while also acting as a political writer. An ardent opponent of Napoleon, he wrote pamphlets against the French usurper, doing so from St. Petersburg—a place to which he had relocated again. Then, positioning himself as a German patriot, he returned to Berlin and began publishing a Russian-German newspaper. Travelling between Berlin and St. Petersburg, Kotzebue decided to join the main headquarters of Mikhail Kutuzov's Russian army and reported military news to Berlin. In 1816, he was promoted to State Secretary of the Ministry of Foreign Affairs in St. Petersburg and gained the trust of the Russian Emperor Alexander I. In 1817, he returned to Germany, but worked there for Russia's benefit. It was believed that Kotzebue was a secret agent of the Holy Alliance, a coalition linking the great monarchist powers of Austria, Prussia, and Russia, as well as Alexander I's intelligencer (Ratgauz 2001, 305). In Kotzebue's journal *Literarisches Wochenblatt* that he published in Weimar at the time, he harshly condemned liberals. These activities of his lasted until Karl Ludwig Sand, a fanatical German student, who valued freedom highly, killed Kotzebue in 1819.

By the time of his death, Kotzebue had become a world-renowned figure for his dramatic works. One-eighth of the Weimar Court Theatre's repertoire consisted of his plays. This theatre was influential because Goethe led it for more than 25 years. Along with August Wilhelm Iffland, Kotzebue was thought of as the most successful playwright of his period both in Germany and throughout Europe, including Russia.

Kotzebue's First Stay in Russia

From 1781–1783, Kotzebue worked as a secretary for St. Petersburg's Governor General Friedrich Wilhelm von Bauer and became Bauer's assistant director of the existing German Theatre. Bauer entrusted Kotzebue to take care of the German Theatre's repertoire. Kotzebue not only had an administrative role, but also wrote plays. He composed his dramatic works in German, which were later translated into Russian and Russified—the names of the characters, locations, and realities of life often became Russian.

Kotzebue found St. Petersburg German Theatre's artistic standard as 'very moderate'. Prior to this time, the theatre was on the edge of closure, but Bauer agreed to patronize his German art. Using his influence, Bauer convinced the Empress Catherine the Great to grant the German Theatre an imperial status and get himself appointed as its director.

It is noteworthy that Kotzebue became a Russian citizen in 1781. Throughout the rest of his life, he cultivated his political and cultural links and sense of belonging both to the country and particularly to St. Petersburg. Despite being of origin a German author, he nevertheless called Russia his home country (Dmitrieva 2003, 330; 347). Kotzebue's cosmopolitan nature meshed well with the internationally diverse life of St. Petersburg.

For the German Theatre, Kotzebue decided to write a play that had an opportunistic Russian theme, yet problematic storyline. *Demetrius Ivanowitsch, Zar von Moskau* (Demetrius Ivanovich, Tsar of Moscow) (1782), a tragedy in five acts, was based on the history of Prince Demetrius, the son of Ivan the Terrible, who was alleged to have been killed in the city of Uglich, but later reappeared with Poland's support. Then he dethroned the Russian Tsar, Boris Godunov, and became a Russian ruler himself in 1604. The main question in Kotzebue's dramatic work was whether or not Demetrius was an impostor. Kotzebue's argument against this common accusation was supported by the happy tears of Demetrius's mother, that she shed when she met him during a public meeting and accepted Demetrius as her true son. For Kotzebue, who was an avid schemer and opportunist himself, Demetrius was not an impostor but the victim of unfavourable fate.

Kotzebue first read his new play in public for a small circle of noblemen at the Russian court, including the Prussian envoy who was also the president of the St. Petersburg Academy of Art. Kotzebue's play was approved, and Bauer ordered it to be staged at the German Theatre with lavish scenery and costumes in the ancient Russian style.

As a theatre director appointed by the Empress, Bauer didn't feel the need to go to the trouble of showing Kotzebue's play to the censor. On the morning of the scheduled opening night, the Chief of Police came to the theatre and ordered that the performance be cancelled. Bauer reassured the Chief of Police that the play's content was innocuous.

This incident happened due to a decree of Peter the Great, which was unknown to Kotzebue, that clearly declared Demetrius an impostor. Because of this, it was against the law to present Demetrius as a Moscow tsar and especially to flaunt this status in the play's title. Out of respect for Bauer, the Chief of Police allowed the performance, but required the author to change the tragedy so that Demetrius would be unveiled before all the people and acknowledged as a sneaky cheat. The story ended with Kotzebue admitting that the liberty he took in his tragedy was simply *licentia poetice* (poetic license) (Kotzebue 1804, 94–99).

The only performance of *Demetrius* happened on 23 June 1782, and it was a success. In the spirit of bourgeois drama, Kotzebue's play emphasized the sensibility of its main character and his life story, aiming to provoke spectators' compassion and tears as a main emotional response. Being a German outsider in St. Petersburg, yet sensitive to foreign cultures and traditions and able to assimilate them, Kotzebue succeeded through his play in forming a stereotype of a Russian 'character's' perception among Germans (Dmitrieva 2003, 333).

By writing and staging *Demetrius* in St. Petersburg, Kotzebue sought to position himself not only as a government official but also as a playwright. Situating himself as a German author in the Russian capital, which had become his new hometown, he decided to provoke a scandal. By doing so, he hoped to win the attention of St. Petersburg's literary and theatrical audience, as well as that of high society (Melnikova 2012b, 18). Kotzebue was not only a master of exciting dramatic intrigue in his plays, but also a gambler in life.

Kotzebue's successful stay in St. Petersburg ended with the death of his protector Bauer, who, in his will, asked the Empress to be merciful to his protégée. However, Catherine didn't favour Kotzebue; she promoted him to Titular Councillor but sent him out of St. Petersburg. Kotzebue left for Reval on 18 November 1783. Having been part of the Governorate of Estonia since 1721, the city of Reval belonged to the Russian Empire, and Kotzebue continued his Russian service as Appellate Assessor there. Along with his service, he wrote plays for Reval's amateur theatre with significant success. His play *Menschenhass und Reue* (Misanthropy and Repentance), which premiered in Reval on 23 November 1788, brought Kotzebue international fame. It was staged in Moscow in 1791 and then again in St. Petersburg (Melnikova 2012b, 25). By the early 1790s, Kotzebue lit up the sky as a fashionable celebrity throughout Germany and across Europe, as well as in Russia. Kotzebue's winning bourgeois dramas and comedies appealed to the general public of any nationality. His ingenious and skilfully crafted plots, as well as the rich emotionality of his plays, could easily be perceived by any national audience, and evoke a strong emotional response in most spectators.

While in Reval, Kotzebue made many strides through his connections to acquire a position and return to St. Petersburg, but Catherine the Great blocked his appointment from happening. Instead, Kotzebue moved from Reval to Vienna where he was appointed as dramatist for the Burgtheater in 1798. For two years he wrote plays for this theatre, but then resigned due to the difficulties of working with troublesome actors. In 1800, Kotzebue decided to travel to Russia to visit his sons from his first marriage who studied in the Naval Cadet Corps of St. Petersburg.

Kotzebue's Second Stay in Russia

Kotzebue described his second visit to Russia in his memoir, *Das merkwürdgste Yahr meines Lebens* (The Strangest Year of My Life), which was first published in Germany in 1801. In the memoir, Kotzebue reveals how, without explanation, he was arrested and searched on the Russian border in Polangen, and was then exiled in Siberia. This unexpected turn in Kotzbue's life seems worthy of one of his spectacular dramas. Many reasons could account for why the incident transpired, but none seems to offer enough conclusive evidence.

One cause for Kotzebue's arrest could have been that the Russian government found his play, *Graf Benjowsky oder die Verschwörung auf Kamtschatka* (Count Benyowsky; or, The Conspiracy of Kamtschatka) (1790), inappropriate. In it, Count Benjowsky was exiled by the Russian government and deported to Kamchatka to work as a serf peasant for the rest of his life. Benjowsky became a leader of a prisoners' revolt. The uprising succeeded, and the hero was able to escape with his fellow prisoners. Despite the fact that there is no apparent proof that this play caused Kotzebue's arrest, it is remarkable how this piece foretold the course of future events, such as Kotzebue's exile to Siberia and his attempt to flee. However, unlike Benjowsky's escape in the play, Kotzebue did not succeed.

Another possibility was by arresting Kotzebue and exiling him to the Siberian city of Kurgan, the Russian Emperor Paul I, who promoted terror during his reign, wanted it to be a lesson to all European writers (Melnikova 2012b, 28). As a highly contradictory, hot-tempered, and tyrannical ruler, Paul I could be harsh to those out of his favour, and Kotzebue was among these. During his four-month exile, Kotzebue observed Russian life from its darker, less attractive side. He viewed it as potential material for future plays. At that time, his plays found great favour with Russian audiences. To his immense surprise, he discovered them even being performed in Tobolsk, the capital of Siberia.

Four months into Kotzebue's exile, Paul I signed a decree that set the author free. Just as Kotzebue's arrest and exile doesn't make much sense, neither does his release have much explanation—except one. This would be Kotzebue's play in one act, *Der alte Leibkutscher Peters des Dritten. Eine wahre Anekdote* (The Old Personal Coachman of Peter the Third. A True Anecdote) (1799). The play was inspired by Kotzebue's enthusiasm for a generous act of Emperor Peter III (Paul I's father), supposedly assassinated and succeeded by his wife, Catherine the Great. The latter took the throne instead of her son, Paul, by means of a *coup* and did everything possible to erase Peter III's half-year reign from Russian history.

The play's plot, which touches upon the issue of migration, unfolds in St. Petersburg. Almost all of the characters are German and dwell in the Russian capital. Leberecht, the German carpenter, has a sick wife and a daughter, Anna, whom he can't allow to marry his poor apprentice, Peter, because of his poverty. Leberecht himself doesn't have much money, but provides for his poor and elderly friend, Dietrich, and has been doing so for 34 years. Dietrich worked as a *Leibkutscher* (court coachman) for Peter III's father and used to perform coachman duties for Peter III when he was a child. Now, Dietrich is upset because he realizes he is a burden on his friend. A Russian peasant, Ivan, advises him to visit the Emperor to ask for help, because, according to Ivan, the Emperor's greatest pleasure is 'to be a father of all the poor and oppressed' (Kotzebue 1824, 13). Ivan is surprised that Dietrich hadn't approached the monarch earlier and says that 'living in St. Petersburg, you do not know that it is as easy to reach the Emperor, as it is for a son to reach his father' (Kotzebue 1824, 13–14). What additionally proves the Emperor's merit is that he buried his father in a highly dignified and honourable way, which shows the great love of a son for his parent.

Dietrich follows Ivan's advice and meets the Emperor. He returns from the meeting rejuvenated. What impressed Dietrich was how the Emperor took his headgear off when he saw him: 'Yes, he bows to all honest people. The Emperor bowed to me!' (Kotzebue 1824, 31). With tears of joy, Dietrich describes how the Emperor spoke with him kindly and mercifully and ended up giving him 20 thousand roubles. Leberecht's exclamation follows: 'God Himself sent Him to make all our days feasts' (Kotzebue 1824, 35–36).

Dietrich wants to share the money that he received from the Emperor with Leberecht, but the latter refuses to take his money. The rebuffed Dietrich then gives it to Peter, so that he can marry Anna. Peter is happy that he can now help the poor orphans, who are his nephews in Germany. Regarding the Germans, he says: 'Let them be surprised and envious of the happy lot of such a great Emperor's subjects and let them glorify him' (Kotzebue 1824, 43).

Using his twin skills as a playwright and politician, Kotzebue exemplifies through the adulation of his main character's words how humble he feels in front of the Russian government. Dietrich proclaims: 'Blessed are those subjects who lack the words to glorify and bless their good sovereign!' and, at the play's end, everybody exclaims, 'Long live the Monarch!' (Kotzebue 1824, 44).

Kotzebue not only shows in the play how lucky German immigrants are to live in St. Petersburg under the protection of the Russian ruler, but also makes obvious references to Peter III and his son, the current monarch at the time, Paul I, who dignified his father's relics with royal honour (Shilder 1901, 305–6). In his play, Kotzebue succeeded in conceptualizing an idealized situation of German immigrants in St. Petersburg and an ideal image of a Russian ruler within an emotionally engaging dramatic framework, which linked the Russian past to modern time and appealed to both German and Russian spectators.

According to Kotzebue, who regularly seized every chance to flatter the Russian government, he didn't imagine that this play, which served as royalist propaganda, would so strongly influence his future. The young writer Krasnopol'skij translated it from German into Russian. Aiming to dedicate his translation to the Emperor Paul I, he was advised not to mention Kotzebue's name in his work because the playwright was in disfavour. While performing Kotzebue's plays, Russian and German actors did not dare to include his name on its playbills. Krasnopol'skij couldn't deliver his translation to the Emperor in person but instead sent it by mail. Paul I read the play and liked it very much. He ordered that the translator be rewarded with a precious ring, but at the same time forbade him to publish the manuscript. A few hours later, he asked to see the manuscript again, read it over, and then changed his mind—allowing it to be published with the omissions of a few expressions, such as '[t]he Emperor bowed to me!' As the day proceeded, the Emperor requested the manuscript a third time, read it again, and this time asked for it to be published without any omissions. He also announced that he'd done wrong by Kotzebue and needed to correct his mistake, considering it his duty to give him a gift equal to the one received by the coachman from his father, Peter III (20 thousand roubles). At the same moment a courier was sent to Tobolsk to free Kotzebue (Kotzebue 2001, 228–29). This curious anecdote illustrates that it was a unique tradition of Russian monarchs, especially exemplified by Catherine the Great and passed along to her son Paul, to take an active part in theatre business, lives of actors, and playwrights. In doing so, Russian rulers enacted the role of demiurge and used theatre to reinforce their political power.

On Kotzebue's return to St. Petersburg from Siberia, Paul I granted him the title of Court Counsellor and an estate with 400 serfs, as well as appointing him as director of the German Theatre, starting 1 September 1800.

During his second stay in the Russian capital, Kotzebue found St. Petersburg's German actors 'decent, but still very far from perfect' (Kotzebue 2001, 224) During his leadership, Kotzebue made a number of improvements in the theatre. However, the task was tough because of the competition from the French theatre. As a matter of principle, both St. Petersburg's general audience and the government tended to regard the French theatre with more respect and esteem than the German Theatre. According to Kotzebue, the German theatrical development was also held back in St. Petersburg due to the personal envy and intrigues of Madame Chevalier, the French troupe's leading star. According to Kotzebue, four times the Emperor expressed a desire to see a German performance in his palace, and four times Kotzebue received an order from the Knight Marshal to prepare for the event, and four times Madame Chevalier managed to prevent it from happening (Kotzebue 2001, 232–33). Such brazen competition between foreign national theatres defined a part of the immigrant artists' lives in early nineteenth-century multicultural St. Petersburg.

As the theatre's director, Kotzebue had to stage 11 of his own plays at this time. No other option was available to him due to the fact that foreign books were banned during Paul I's reign (Kotzebue 2001, 247).

The Emperor ordered Kotzebue to have the strictest supervision over the selection of plays and to exclude all suspicious passages. Kotzebue persuaded the Emperor to appoint a censor to oversee him in order to avoid being put into such a precarious situation. However, Kotzebue's position as a playwright in St. Petersburg was very peculiar. In his memoirs, he gives some examples of the severe censorship at that time. According to him, the word *republic* was not supposed to appear in his drama *Octavia*. In another play, it was necessary to exclude the treacherous ideas that caviar came from Russia, and that Russia was a distant country. Kotzebue once had to turn a Russian prince, who in one of his plays was mentioned in passing, into a foreign nobleman, and another character had to wear a Hungarian hat instead of a Polish one. A character known to come from Paris couldn't come from there, nor could the play mention either this city or France. Comte de Buffon's knowledge of the natural sciences, d'Alembert's theory, Rousseau's sensibility, Voltaire's spirit—all of these were excluded with the quick stroke of a pen (Kotzebue 2001, 230–31). Such censorship restrictions in Russia highly limited Kotzebue's freedom as a German playwright acclaimed across Europe. As an artist, he didn't feel at home in his second homeland during Paul I's repressive regime.

After the long and crushing blow to Kotzebue's hopes while he was in Siberia, to his genuine amazement he suddenly found himself set apart as Paul I's confidant in St. Petersburg. The Emperor entrusted Kotzebue to write to all the sovereigns of Europe, inviting them to a knightly tournament that he decided to organize. Kotzebue was also commissioned to create a detailed description of his favourite, newly built Mikhailovsky Castle. However, despite this good fortune, Kotzebue's emotional state was fragile. Fearful of being sent back to Siberia, Kotzebue did not dare to go to Gatchina, the country residence of Paul I, without taking with him a fair amount of money. It might be guessed that he hoped to use these funds to bribe officials. Every evening, Kotzebue went to bed with dark foreboding thoughts in his mind; during the night, he would suddenly wake and leap up in mortal terror at the slightest noise or carriage passing by on the street. During every performance of his plays, he expected the police to come for him (Kotzebue 2001, 230; 235).

Paul I's reign was abruptly cut short on the night of 12 March 1801 when his own officers assassinated him in his bedchamber in Mikhailovsky Castle. Thereafter, his son Alexander I became the Russian emperor.

Kotzebue submitted a petition to the new ruler asking for the financial support without which, in his view, the German Theatre couldn't properly function. At a time when the French theatre received goodly sums from the government, Kotzebue's request was denied. In response, he formally resigned his position, was granted the title of Collegiate Counsellor and a pension. With these in hand, he departed Russia on 29 April 1801.

If St. Petersburg is to be described as an elegant and cosmopolitan European city in the eighteenth and nineteenth centuries, August von Kotzebue would definitely be among its brightest luminaries in regard to the world of theatre. While his plays migrated across the continental realm earning acclaim and applause, he pursued both German and Russian interests. His nomadic embrace of the erasure of geographical borders and acceptance of different cultures thriving together seems an attribute he clearly shared with the mysterious northern city that always attracted him. For an important time in its history, St. Petersburg was not only his home, but also home to the city's unique German Theatre.

References

Dmitrieva, Ekaterina. 2003. 'Peterburg, prigrezivshijsya gradom na Neve, ili Peterburg v sud'be Avgusta Kozebue.' In *Obraz Peterburga v mirovoj kul'ture: materialy mezh. konferentsii*, Edited by V. E. Bango, 324–356. St. Petersburg.: Nauka Fil.
German, A. A., T.S. Ilarionova, and I.R. Pleve. 2005. *Istoriya nemtsev Rossii*. Moskva: MSNK-Press.
Gubkina, Natalya. 2003. *Nemetskiy muzyikalnyiy teatr v Peterburge v pervoy treti XIX veka*. St. Petersburg: Dmitriy Bulanin.
Karatygin, Petr. 1970. *Zapiski*. Leningrad: Iskusstvo.
Keller, Andreas. 1995 [2001]. '*Das Deutsche Theater und die Entwicklung der deutschen Gesellschaft in St. Petersburg im 18. und 19. Jahrhundert.*' Master's thesis, University of Freiburg.
Kotzebue, August. 1804. *Moya uchyonaya zhizn'*. Smolensk: Gubernskaya tipografiya.
———. 1824. *Leib-kucher*. Third Edition. Oryol: v tipografii Cytina.

———. 2001. *Dostopamyatnyiy god moey zhizni*. Moskva: Agraf.
Melnikova, Svetlana. 2012a. *Nemetskiy teatr v Sankt-Peterburge: istoriya, idei, geroi*. Saarbrücken: Lap Lambert.
———. 2012b. 'August Kozebue v Sankt-Peterburge. Linii sud'by nemeckogo dramaturga.' In *Nemcy v Sankt-Peterburge. Biograficheskij aspekt. XVIII–XX vv.*, Edited by T. A. Shrader, 17–36. St. Petersburg: MAE RAN.
Ratgauz, Grejnem. 2001. 'August Kotzebue. Eskiz k portretu chestolyubca.' In *Kotzebue, August. Moya uchyonaya zhizn'*. Smolensk: Gubernskaya tipografiya.
Shilder, Nikolaj. 1901. *Imperator Pavel Pervyj*. St. Petersburg: Izdanie A. S. Suvorina.
Zotov, Rafail. 1859. *Teatralnyie vospominaniya*. St. Petersburg: Tipografiya Yakov Ionsona.

CHAPTER 53

The Itinerant Puppet

John McCormick

In much of the world, puppetry is one of the oldest migrant professions, and European puppetry itself was probably a result of earlier migrations. Such entertainment can be extremely portable and is also a way in which the very poor may scrape a living. Paramount is the need to go where audiences are to be found.

Travelling Circuits

Up to the eighteenth century, groups of entertainers, *skomorokh*, ranged over vast areas of Russia, and puppetry was one of their skills. In Europe there were similar groups of entertainers living in groups on the margins of society, performing on the streets and perceived by sedentary populations as gypsies and semi-criminals. Tomaso Garzoni's wonderful survey of all the different professions, *La piazza universale di tutte le professioni del mondo* (Venice, 1585), includes a chapter in which he describes performers on the piazza and the charlatans. Charlatans, predecessors of the American medicine men of the nineteenth century, often attracted custom with *bagatellieri*, a term in general use for glove-puppet performers, who also did card tricks and other pieces of magic. In 1788, Father Incisa, a priest in Asti (Piedmont), recorded in his diary the visit of a group consisting of 17 or 18 entertainers. Three women sang and danced on the piazza; others, including a glove-puppet performer and a girl who performed conjuring tricks and a balancing act, went through the town and its inns.

J. McCormick (✉)
Trinity College Dublin, Dublin, Ireland

© The Author(s), under exclusive license to Springer Nature Switzerland AG 2023
Y. Meerzon, S. E. Wilmer (eds.), *The Palgrave Handbook of Theatre and Migration*, https://doi.org/10.1007/978-3-031-20196-7_53

Right up to the early twentieth century the edges of larger cities were places where entertainers might congregate with their caravans. In northern Italy in the early 1900s the Niemen family, probably from Lithuania, had a small outdoor circus for acrobatics, sometimes combined with a shooting range. Gualberto Niemen travelled with his solo puppet show and today Bruno Niemen, sometimes referred to as Italy's last itinerant puppeteer, does the same and still lives in a caravan, now on a fixed site in Vercelli.

Not all puppeteers emerged from the travelling community. In Lyon at the end of the eighteenth century the unemployed silk weaver Etienne Mourguet took up street dentistry which he accompanied with glove puppets to draw a crowd. Out of this developed Guignol, first as a street show and later in cafes where, with his regular comments on topical events, he became a sort of living newspaper. Mourguet himself did not travel much outside the city and surrounding countryside, but Guignol, the puppet, became popular in Paris and was soon to replace the Italianate Polichinelle throughout France.

Marionette shows have always been easier to trace than the highly portable street glove-puppet ones, which were not always perceived as theatre and attracted less attention from the authorities. In Reggio-Emilia in Italy, itinerant glove-puppet companies were very common up to the mid-twentieth century. Most had a regular circuit, rather like travelling theatre companies, but seldom moved far beyond the Po valley. Their shows enjoyed a status comparable to marionette ones, and these puppeteers were quite distinct from other groups of itinerant entertainers.

The movements of puppeteers can sometimes be established by trawling through archives. Such work was done for the German-speaking lands by Hans Purschke. Lars Rebehn's valuable research on lodgings used by entertainers staying in Hamburg has revealed the presence of many foreign puppet companies in the city. In the Czech lands and in Russia Jaroslave Bartoš and Anatoly Kulish, respectively, recorded many foreign puppeteers in the eighteenth and nineteenth centuries. In the United States, Paul McPharlin's work is of immense value for the coverage of visiting and immigrant European puppet companies. Newspaper archives are a major resource for researchers, but until more recent years consulting these has been extremely time-consuming. Where these have been digitised, as in the case of the British Library, it is now possible to see the files of local papers where small advertisements may indicate the passing of a puppet company, and provide extra details about the time and place of performance, and, occasionally, the repertoire performed.

Many puppeteers started as emigrants, usually driven by economic necessity, and then settled in a host country. The celebrated Brioché of seventeenth-century France was of Italian origin, In 1825 Enrico Lano, a marionette performer from Milan, came to America and the following three generations of Lanos travelled there with puppets, circuses and medicine shows. Agrippino Manteo emigrated to Argentina in the early twentieth century and then moved to New York where he set up a Sicilian-style Pupi theatre.

The puppet Punch was himself a migrant and is thought to have arrived in England with Pietro Agiomonti of Bologna, whose show was seen in London by Samuel Pepys in 1662. Agiomonti is first heard of in Reggio Emilia in 1655, but a year later was in Munich, visited Vienna and Innsbruck in 1658 and Cologne in 1659, by which time he had become known as Signor Bologna. By the time he reached London he had quite a substantial show with an orchestra and a full dramatic repertoire, but always with Punchinello (Pulcinella) as the central character. In October 1662 he performed for the king at Whitehall and the last mention of him is in 1678 when a Sieur de Bologne appeared at Paris's Foire St Laurent. Bologna's Punchinello was a marionette, but a little over 100 years later Pulcinella returned to Britain on the hand of an Italian immigrant, Piccini, from Piacenza, and became the familiar glove puppet, Punch. Piccini died in the workhouse some 40 years later, poverty and obscurity being part of the condition of the solo puppeteer.

Before 1800 marionette showmen enjoyed similar status to travelling actors, but, once notions of high culture as opposed to popular culture developed, actors dissociated themselves from them. Marionette showmen were not so different from other strolling players, and with their stage, puppets, costumes and scenery together with a vehicle for transport they saw themselves as superior to any street performer.

By the mid-nineteenth century waggons adapted for habitation avoided the need to find accommodation. As late as the 1990s, Dombrowskis in Saxony had a living-waggon and another which took all the equipment. A caravan might be a permanent or seasonal home but it also meant that marionette showmen were easily perceived as vagrants. One German company kept a set of immaculate linen which, on arrival in a village, would be hung up on a washing line to show the resident population that they were not gypsies.

Publicity often reflected a desperate attempt to sound as good as actors' theatre, and sometimes tried to obscure the difference between the wooden actor and the live one. The National Library of Ireland has a bill from the Irish town of Youghal in the 1780s advertising a performance with 'Mr Punch's company of artificial comedians'.[1] Some nineteenth-century showmen called their marionettes living waxworks, and terminology was often used to give added value. The term automata had up-market social implications, and some showmen liked to suggest that they were really men of science, describing themselves as *Mechanikus*. In Germany mechanical shows, or *teatrum mundi*, were added to marionette performances, whilst demonstrations of optical and physical science were another way in which the educational value of the show might be implied.

---

[1] Catalogue of the National Library of Ireland, classified as 'ephemera' without a specific numerical reference, it reads: 'The British Company of Performers From Sadlers [sic, Sadler's] Wells By Permission of the Worshipful David Freeman, Esq; Mayor: means to exhibit their different Pieces of Agility: First the Little Poland...Mr. William Punch...is just arrived from Dublin, with a Large Compnay [sic, Company] of Artificial Comedians...'

In the eighteenth and nineteenth centuries European puppet companies often had a circuit which they followed each year. This might be relatively close to their home base (as in Reggio Emilia), or from one end of a country to another. In Britain the vade mecum of many companies was Owens' *Book of Fairs*, and the circuit was built around the dates of fairs throughout the country. In continental Europe there were companies who travelled readily throughout an area where a common language was spoken, such as the German states and the Austro-Hungarian Empire. What was particularly significant was that puppet companies often brought their shows to audiences who for geographical reasons or because of poverty normally had no access to theatre.

Some companies travelled well-beyond their own linguistic area. Piccini probably had virtually no English when he arrived, but the simple glove-puppet show depends heavily on sound and rhythm for communication, especially when the performer uses a voice modifier or swazzle. There are many references to Italians visiting Russia from the mid-eighteenth century onwards. Companies presenting an extensive theatrical repertoire of plays, such as the Pitous in France, generally remained within their linguistic area. Travelling abroad, larger marionette companies emphasised the visual nature of the show rather than the dramatic, but sometimes managed to insert at least a few words of the language of the host country. When Holdens travelled, they employed a manager with at least one extra language who went ahead, sorted out local requirements and arranged bookings or hire of venues. After 1850 Europe's rail network revolutionised transport and once sailing ships had been replaced by steamers, sea travel became easier, with some companies moving from continent to continent.

Puppets and the Authorities

Suspicion of the travelling community and a general intolerance of theatre often led to negative attitudes, and this was further compounded by an idea that an element of magic might be involved. A Dutch puppeteer and his wife were imprisoned in 1602 and their puppets were burned because of the popular association of puppetry with sorcery, and even in twentieth-century Italy the church was sometimes suspicious.

Part of the nature of puppet theatre, and especially the street show, is the comments on and mockery of those in power, and sometimes showmen such as Gaetanaccio in Rome in the 1820s ended up in prison. However, the idea of the subversive puppeteer is a twentieth-century construct which we may associate with Josef Skupa in Nazi-occupied Czechoslovakia and more recent politically engaged puppeteers from Peter Schumann to Gary Friedman and Ariel Doron.

In nineteenth-century Britain, obtaining a place for performance usually involved negotiation with local authorities, finding a space on a fairground, making arrangements directly with the owner of a site or else renting an available hall or assembly room. In the early 1870s Charles Middleton kept his large portable theatre in Portsmouth for 15 months, changing the programme nearly every day to encourage audiences to pay more than one visit. On the fairground, shows were shorter and could be repeated a number of times during the day. The programme was generally a series of trick or variety acts, but might also include a highly curtailed version of a drama. In Britain no official permit was required, but such was not the case everywhere. In France puppeteers were classed as *forains*, or outsiders. The *statut des saltimbanques* was designed to control travelling entertainers or mountebanks, and involved a little notebook which the showman, before moving on, had to get signed by the prefecture with a statement that he/she had been of good moral behaviour. In Italy available halls were often church property, but a sympathetic priest might be prepared to announce the show from the pulpit. It was quite common for a showman to attend church at the first available opportunity, with children well cleaned-up and respectably dressed.

A dislike of anyone who does not fit into the generally accepted pattern re-asserted itself in a different way in the German Democratic Republic and Czechoslovakia in the 1950s where older travelling companies, usually consisting of very small family groups, were viewed as private enterprise and therefore capitalist and ran into many problems, including a dislike of repertoires that did not promote socialist values. Dombrowskis in Saxony survived, often by performing in a village where official disapproval might be less. The Anderle brothers in Slovakia were less fortunate, being forced to cease operations in 1955 and take up work as dustmen.

Migrancy and Practice

Migrancy did not so much modify the profession of puppetry as shape it. Given the right environment, migrant puppeteers became fixed in their host country and travelling ones might become sedentary. Theatres specifically for puppet (marionette) performance started to appear in the eighteenth century, ranging from a small back room or cellar to a theatre space where puppets rather than live performers appeared. Randal Stretch's theatre in Dublin, recorded by Jonathan Swift, lasted some 40 years. The Lupi family in Turin, having begun as travellers, had the 300-seat San Martiniano theatre, from about 1830, and in 1884 bought the 1200-seat Teatro d'Angennes, where they continued until the late 1930s. None the less, travelling in one form or another has always remained the modus vivendi for most puppet showmen. In the seventeenth and eighteenth centuries, travelling actors sometimes used puppets for economic reasons or when they met hostility to the idea of live actors on a stage. In the German states, the show might also be tailored to the religious denomination of the audience, with plays about the lives of Saints in a Catholic area and stories from the Old Testament in a Protestant one.

The marionette repertoire, related closely to that of the actors' theatre, but was adapted in a way that suited the individual showman, especially with the use made of the comic figure. This character, like its glove-puppet counterpart, regularly broke frame with direct address to the audience, slipping in local references to known people or events. A usual programme was a full drama and some variety numbers, but there might also be a farce or even some form of optical show. A noted feature of the British marionette show was the pantomime which in the nineteenth century concluded with a harlequinade.

Many puppet companies crossed national frontiers. English performers brought their shows to Bohemia in the early seventeenth century. Italians visited Britain in the later eighteenth century and the term *fantoccini* became a common word for marionettes. Imitation of what has brought success or profits to others has always been an incentive to performers, and any new trick, technique or act might be copied directly, or absorbed into the way of working. Migrants might modify their own practice after arriving in a host country, but at the same time any novelty in their work would be rapidly taken up. Today, in more developed countries, touring has ceased and companies travel to take up engagements, whether locally or at international festivals. One result of this is that techniques migrate as much as the puppets or performers and one can, for example, see European puppeteers who have adopted oriental techniques.

Case Studies

The Pitou company in France performed mostly in the department of the Loire, and are an example of a company travelling within a relatively limited geographical range. In contrast, the English Holdens were ready to follow an ongoing pattern of moving from country to country.

Around 1830 a puppeteer from Lorraine named Chok had a small travelling company. In the 1840s he took on an assistant, Emile August Pitou, who had become proprietor of the show by 1864 and this was continued and developed by Pitou's son, also Emile. The surviving Pitou material includes registers covering the years 1874–1896, and these are now in MUCEM (Marseille). They are of immense value for the establishment of the repertoire, but more importantly for the picture they give of the movements and the fragile economy of what was one of France's major travelling companies.

The commonest performance days were Sunday, Monday, Thursday and Saturday, and the registers list the pieces played and the takings for each. Saturday and Sunday had the larger audiences, and productions with more elaborate scenic effects, requiring more setting up, were usually given on both days. The furthest the Pitou company went was to Belgium, but sometimes a move meant no more than shifting their portable theatre from one part of a town to another. In 1874 the theatre was set up in St Etienne from March 5 to May 17, at which point there is a note to the effect that on May 19 it cost 40 francs to transport the show to another pitch in the same town. During this time 26 different plays were presented, starting with *Le Festin* (*Don Juan*, the great classic of the European puppet theatre).

On 18 August 1881 Emile Auguste Pitou collapsed at the end of a performance of the popular melodrama *Victor; ou l'Enfant de la Forêt*, and died the next day. That night the canvas roof of the booth was blown off, but the following day the young Emile with his brother Paul managed to put on the announced performance of *Le Juif errant*. A note on expenditure includes mourning clothes for Emile and his brother Paul, a fee of 6 francs for the grave, rent of 45 francs for the pitch and a baker's bill of 20 francs. The highest takings that month had been 102 francs for a Sunday performance of *Les deux Orphelines* but for weekday shows 20 francs was closer to the norm. Without a booth, Emile and Paul struggled on until November in whatever small venues they could find, but then gave up, having lost their home, sold their carts and abandoned their equipment.

Emile found work as a painter until a small inheritance put him on his feet again in 1884, and the register for April 8 records a list of new clothing and a payment of 20 francs to redeem something from a pawnshop. Takings amounted to 388 francs and expenses 185 francs 10. The latter were the rent of a school hall at Firminy near St Etienne (15 francs), a payment of 5 francs for authors' rights, a daily police payment of 1 franc 50, printing of programmes 10 francs, hire of lamps for two days 8 francs, hire of planks (possibly for seating) 8 francs, ropes 3 francs, town crier (for publicity) 10 francs, music for 2 days 14 francs, food 50 francs, a journey for Paul 11 francs 55, a payment of 8 francs possibly, the repayment of a loan, to a certain Goyet, 5 francs 50 to a day labourer, who may have helped with the moving or erection of the booth, 7 francs (1 franc daily) plus a tip of 5 francs to Louis (probably a boy assistant), official stamps for posters, cards, 1 franc 20, oil (for lamps) 5 francs 75, glasses (for lamps) wicks, paint brushes, resins (for paint), dry-point and paper 6 francs 10, Bengal fire (for red and green firework effects) 1 franc 75 and candles 2 francs 45. A cost that does not appear on this list is the regular poor tax that theatrical entertainments had to pay, but it is referred to elsewhere.

By July 1885 Pitou had an elegant little portable theatre, and as he avoided the fairground, this did not have the typical grand painted facade. The walls consisted of wooden panels and the size could be modified according to the site. He usually remained in one place for about a month, but in 1895–1896 he spent six months on the Place Denis Papin, Montluçon. Playing four or five days a week, with a break in Holy Week and a few days when bad weather meant cancelling the show, Pitou presented some seventy different plays, most receiving one, or sometimes two, performances. There were well-known titles from the repertoire of the popular Parisian theatres such as the Ambigu and the Gaîte or the Châtelet, but also melodramas no longer performed in the theatres of the capital and classic *féeries* (extravaganzas) such as *Le pied de mouton* and *Les pilules du diable*. Opera libretti were staged as spoken operas (*La Juive. Mignon*). The older popular puppet repertoire was retained with the *Passion* and the *Nativity*, together with *Faust*, *Geneviève de Brabant* and *Le Festin*. The signature piece of the company was *l'Enfant prodigue* or *Crasmagne à l'académie*, deriving from a German puppet play, probably in the original Chok repertoire and loosely inspired by the biblical story of the prodigal son.

The Pitous are typical of many nineteenth-century European puppet companies. A small family unit, they were never unduly prosperous and even buying a new hat might be a serious item of expenditure. They ceased to perform with puppets when work of this sort was no longer economically viable and in 1913 settled down in their home town of Rive-de-Gier, opening a cinema as a more reliable way of earning a living.

The Holden family, originally glass-blowers on the fairground, had a travelling marionette show by the mid-1850s and this became one of the largest in Britain. By 1869 they had a portable theatre, the temple of fantoccini, seating about 1000, with a magnificent carved and painted façade, designed to attract and draw in spectators. With its frontage of thirty metres and depth of ten, this theatre was made up of carefully numbered parts and could be dismantled and re-assembled in a very short space of time. The full outfit sometimes required a whole train for transport and can be compared with that of the Schichtl family in Magdeburg who went so far as to have a special railway siding leading to their home.

The eldest son, John Holden, took over the family show around 1872 and after 1876 toured widely in Belgium, France and Spain, where he reaped the substantial rewards which foreign travel could offer. In 1874 his brother Thomas went to the United States with William Bullock's Royal Marionettes and received a baptism of American showbiz and publicity methods which he would later use. In 1876, back in Britain, he set up his own show with his brother James. By the late 1870s he was appearing at the top London music halls and also visiting Belgium and Holland.

Between the later 1870s and 1890 Thomas Holden was rarely in his native Britain. Outside Britain his marionettes were a novelty. Operated entirely by strings they no longer had the older rigid control rod to the head. The figures were also lighter and more flexible than the rather solid wooden ones more common in the rest of Europe, and their movements were closer to human ones. Performance against a background of black corded fabric rendered the strings virtually invisible, and the expressive quality of the manipulation convinced audiences that the figures had a life of their own. Many believed that Holden had some special secret (a notion which he carefully cultivated), and as a result of his performances, the all-string marionette as used in Britain now began to be widely imitated by many European companies. Emile Pitou continued with rod marionettes until the end, but acquired some Holden-style trick figures around 1890.

In early 1879, Thomas rented a disused Paris cafe concert, the little Bolero Star. Performances opened in March once the building had been re-classified as a marionette theatre, and the company took up residence in the two dressing rooms behind the stage. A horrified inspector's report described them as ten or twelve people and their children encamped like strolling players or mountebanks. They were instructed to move out, but no action appears to have been taken.

The success of the Paris season was enormous, and did a great deal for the perception of puppet theatre, drawing audiences from a social level that normally would have looked down on entertainments of this sort. During the summer Holden booked theatres in Bordeaux and Marseille, returning to the Bolero Star for the winter. He had two pantomimes that he could alternate and the rest of the show included a harlequinade with sketches, trick numbers, a black-faced minstrel act and a grand transformation scene.

Publicity on a new scale for a puppet show included coloured lithograph posters, some carrying portraits of Holden, and 3000 copies of a brochure *Thomas Holden et ses fantoches*.

After playing in major towns and cities in France, Holden embarked on a more extensive international tour than had been undertaken by any previous British troupe. He crossed Germany and Austria, regularly using popular theatres with a large seating capacity, such as the ill-fated 1700-seat Ringtheater in Vienna (destroyed with huge loss of life by a tragic fire the following year), and this also raised the profile of marionettes in terms of the theatre industry of the time. In Budapest a temporary theatre was erected close to the opera house and used for a profitable six-month season. Performances in Poland were followed by three months of excellent business in Bucharest. In December 1881 Holden crossed the Black Sea to Istanbul and took a recently erected theatre in the fashionable Levantine suburb of Pera. At first there was resistance to allowing such a low form of entertainment, but opinions changed rapidly once the season opened.

After three months in Istanbul, the company crossed the Black Sea to Odessa and worked their way via Kiev and Kharkov to Nizny Novgorod, where they performed in a *balagan*. Then it was on to Moscow and St Petersburg's Renaissance Theatre where one special performance was given for children at the request of the Tsar and Tsarina, who now joined the extensive list of crowned heads whose names adorned the publicity.

In February 1883 the company paid further visits to Germany, Romania and Turkey, with an autumn season in Greece. By late December 1884 they were in Venice for the start of a period of over a year's touring in Italy. They visited the principal cities, generally stopping for at least a month and using the larger popular theatres. In Livorno nothing suitable was available, so a huge open-air theatre was constructed on the Piazza Mazzini where they remained from July to September 1885. In Naples at the enormous circus-type Politeama the show attracted a far more fashionable public than would normally attend that theatre. In targeting a more middle-class audience, Holden distanced himself from any notion that puppet theatre was entertainment for the popular classes and its practitioners' mountebanks. An astute businessman, he also encouraged the idea that his marionette show was morally appropriate for a more juvenile audience.

On 5 March 1887, Holden set off for South America which offered a new and lucrative market. He performed at major theatres in Argentina, Uruguay and Brazil. His intention had been to go on to North America, but the tour was exhausting and the company returned to Europe in early December. Before resuming touring in Europe, Thomas took a break of about three months in London where he had a house. Then, in 1889, he unexpectedly announced his retirement, possibly because the show had lost its novelty appeal and had many imitators. Continuous touring is demanding, and he now felt the need to settle down. He always said that Turkey was where he made the small fortune which allowed him to live for the next 40 years in middle-class ease in a smart house in Wimbledon.

James continued the company, and when his brother John retired in 1890, he acquired the celebrated portable theatre, using it in France and Belgium. He returned to Italy and South America and was in New York and Boston in 1903, by which time the show was merely an item on a vaudeville programme. In 1911 he settled in Harrogate and converted a former chapel into a little variety theatre. This rapidly became a cinema with marionettes sometimes as part of the cine-variety programme. Up until the late 1920s James continued to give sporadic performances, and he had a small fit-up which could be erected on the stage of a cinema.

In the past, puppetry was first and foremost a means of earning, or scraping, a living and not perceived as an art as it is today. Piccini was an example of the immigrant puppeteer, travelling only with what he could carry. Others had a small cart which later developed into a large fit-up. Mobility remained a key factor. The great travelling booths were cumbersome to transport, and few lasted much beyond 1900. With the twentieth century, better opportunities of regular paid employment led to younger people abandoning the family show, and this decline was further accelerated by the advent of cinema as a cheap and easily accessible form of entertainment. The travelling puppeteer may be an immigrant, an economic migrant or merely a person involved in an itinerant profession, and has frequently brought skills and practices which are unfamiliar to the host country or region and may be absorbed into the work of indigenous performers. In this way the art of puppetry is constantly being renewed and enriched. Today much of the association with poverty has disappeared and it has become a profession embraced out of choice rather than necessity.

Further Reading

Barnard, Richard. 1981. *The Life and Travels of Richard Barnard Marionette Proprietor.* Edited by George Speaight. London: Society for Theatre Research.

Jurkowski, Henryk. 1996. *A History of European Puppetry from its Origins to the End of the Nineteenth Century.* Lampeter: Edwin Mellen Press.

McCormick, John. 1998. *Popular Puppet Theatre in Europe, 1800–1914.* Cambridge: Cambridge University Press.

———. 2010. *The Italian Puppet Theater – a History.* Jefferson: McFarland.

———. 2018. *The Holdens: Monarchs of the Marionette Theatre.* London: Society for Theatre Research.

McPharlin, Paul. 1969. *The Puppet Theatre in America, a History 1524–1948*, with a supplement on *Puppets in America since 1948* by Marjorie Batchelder McPharlin. Boston: Plays Inc.

Pitou, Emile. 2020. 'Émile Pitou's Memorandum The Life of a French Travelling Puppeteer at the Turn of the 19th Century.' *European Journal of Theatre and Performance* 2 (May) 594–605.

Purschke, Hans. 1986. *Die Puppenspieltraditionen Europas Deutschsprachige Gebiete*. Bochum: Deutsches Institut für Puppenspiel.

Purvis, Billy. 1854. *The Life and Adventure of Billy Purvis. Continued to the time of his death*. Edited by J.P. Robson. Newcastle upon Tyne: John Christie.

Rebehn, Lars. 2003. *Rüstige Bursche und martialische Dienstmädchen … Karussellbuden, Karussellwirte und ihr Publikum; Hamburg 1807–1863*. Gerolzhofen: S. Oettermann.

CHAPTER 54

Fin-de-siècle Black Minstrelsy, Itinerancy, and the Anglophone Imperial Circuit

Kellen Hoxworth

Following the end of the US American Civil War, African American performers established themselves on transnational stages by fashioning an alternative to white blackface minstrel performance: Black minstrelsy. In the United States, Black minstrel troupes developed extensive touring circuits throughout the country that catered primarily to Black audiences while simultaneously attaining popularity among Northern white audiences. From 1865 through the early twentieth century, Black minstrelsy was the predominant form of Black performance culture in the United States, constituting 'one of the most popular and generative theatrical forms in the history of US performance culture' (Jones 2021, 130). For several decades, leading African American performers in theatre, music, comedy, and dance made their careers—or, at the very least, their beginnings—in Black minstrelsy, including Bert Williams, George Walker, Aida Overton Walker, W.C. Handy, Bessie Smith, Ma Rainey, and Jackie 'Moms' Mabley, as well as less commonly remembered figures such as James A. Bland, Billy Kersands, Ernest Hogan, Orpheus McAdoo, and the Hyers Sisters, among many others. Yet, since its inception, Black minstrelsy has long been viewed ambivalently by Black cultural critics—particularly those adhering to politics of Black nationalism, racial uplift, and class respectability—who, in the words of Paul Gilroy, have 'little to say about the profane, contaminated world of black popular culture' (1993, 32; cf. Jones 2021). Such critics framed Black minstrelsy as a low, popular form that was merely imitative of white blackface minstrelsy and which therefore confirmed the racist figurations of blackness

K. Hoxworth (✉)
University at Buffalo – State University of New York, Buffalo, NY, USA
e-mail: hoxworth@buffalo.edu

© The Author(s), under exclusive license to Springer Nature Switzerland AG 2023
Y. Meerzon, S. E. Wilmer (eds.), *The Palgrave Handbook of Theatre and Migration*, https://doi.org/10.1007/978-3-031-20196-7_54

common to the white blackface repertoire. By contrast, scholars of Black performance have done much to recuperate Black minstrelsy as a charged site for performing vernacular Black humour, Black music, and the complex racial politics of blackness, freedom, and modernity (Watkins 1994; Southern 1997; Krasner 1997; Sotiropoulos 2006; Brooks 2006; Brown 2008; Jones 2021).

Notably, in his landmark study of blackface and Black minstrelsy, Robert C. Toll observes, 'Minstrelsy was one of the few opportunities for mobility—geographic, social, and economic' available to African American performers in the postbellum era (1974, 223). Toll's emphasis on *mobility* as central to Black minstrelsy underscores the importance of itinerancy to the formation of early Black performance cultures comprised of audiences across disparate regions of the United States. Indeed, Jayna Brown asserts that '[t]he lives of African Americans, and especially African American performers, were inherently itinerant' (2008, 10). Though some scholars have attended to the transatlantic itineraries of African American performers, the vast majority have considered Black minstrelsy within the default frame of postbellum and/or post-Reconstruction US American racial politics and performance histories. Yet, the circuits of Black minstrelsy were not limited to the United States nor to occasional tours to the stages of metropolitan Britain. In the late nineteenth century, leading Black minstrel troupes toured through British colonies in southern Africa, Australia, and New Zealand. As Lynn Abbott and Doug Seroff observe, 'there were nearly as many first-rate black acts in Australia [at the turn of the century] as there were back in the States' (2002, 137). Why did so many prominent Black minstrels engage in colonial tours? How does the prolific transoceanic, imperial travel of Black minstrels affect prevailing theorizations of Black minstrelsy as a mode of performing Black freedom and/or Black vernacular culture?

Itinerancy functioned as a core practice and mode of nineteenth-century minstrel performance economies. As such, transoceanic tours through what I term the *Anglophone imperial circuit* were integral to the success of Black minstrel performers. Exemplifying the colonies' central location in a global performance economy, in 1899, two Black minstrel troupes competed for audiences in Sydney, Australia: The American Negro Minstrels and Orpheus McAdoo's Georgia Minstrels and Alabama Cakewalkers. The former was an all-star ensemble featuring leading Black minstrels, specially formed for a tour of Australia and New Zealand; the latter was a popular troupe founded by McAdoo, a Black impresario who spent a decade touring the Anglophone imperial circuit. Their overlapping itineraries trace the forgotten global routes of Black minstrelsy, the racial politics of late nineteenth-century transnational Black performance, and the integral role played by African American performers in the earliest waves of theatrical globalization. In this expanded political frame, Black minstrels not only resisted and subverted the transnational racial discourses of white supremacy but also staged enactments entangled with colonial discourses and structures. Therefore, in this chapter, I posit that the Black minstrel tours of the Anglophone imperial circuit staged the contradictory imbrications of Black minstrelsy both as what Gilroy terms a 'counterculture of modernity' and as a repertoire of colonial modernity (1993, 1–40).

Minstrelsy and the Anglophone Imperial Circuit

Prior to the advent of Black minstrelsy, blackface minstrelsy as staged by white performers was an inherently transnational phenomenon. In the 1830s, early blackface minstrelsy developed as a solo performance genre that was staged by white actors in the United States, Britain, and throughout British colonies in Australia, India, Jamaica, and southern Africa (Hoxworth 2020). By 1843, the Virginia Minstrels developed a new mode of blackface minstrelsy as an ensemble performance; notably, this troupe followed their New York City debut almost immediately with an extended tour of the British Isles. Contemporaneously, theatremakers in British colonies staged their own local ensemble minstrel shows featuring white colonists. In the 1850s, amidst the Australian gold rush, professional blackface minstrel troupes comprising white performers based in the United States and Britain began touring extensively to the antipodes via what Matthew Wittmann terms the 'Pacific circuit' (Wittmann 2010). In 1862, a troupe of Christy's Minstrels led by Anthony Nish embarked upon a three-year tour of the British colonies in southern Africa, India, and Australia, expanding the 'Pacific circuit' into an Anglophone imperial circuit that encircled the globe. During the remainder of the nineteenth century, white performers of blackface minstrelsy travelled this transoceanic performance itinerary. For such white troupes, the cultural terrain of the British colonial world was not significantly dissimilar from the national theatre circuits of the United States and the British Isles. Blackface minstrel troupes popular in London, New York, and San Francisco performed substantively similar material as they toured the globe, thereby forging a global performance network around a shared repertoire.

Individual African American performers occasionally shared the minstrel stage with white blackface troupes throughout the Anglophone imperial circuit. William Henry Lane ('Juba') was the earliest known African American performer to tour Britain with white blackface minstrel troupes wherein he performed as a speciality dancing act. Another key actor on this transimperial circuit was the famous Black dwarf performer Thomas Dilward ('Japanese Tommy') who attained fame on the antebellum minstrel stage in the United States before touring Britain from 1866 through 1873 with the various white and Black minstrel troupes; he later toured to Australia with white blackface troupes such as Billy Emerson's California Minstrels in 1874 and the Kelly and Leon Minstrels in 1878 (Advertisement 1866, 8; 'Public Amusements' 1866, 1; 'Provincial Theatricals' 1873, 6; 'Amusements,' *Sydney Morning Herald*, 1874, 4; Waterhouse 1990, 62).

Whereas both Lane and Dilward began their minstrel careers prior to the US American Civil War, postbellum African American performers joined together to form Black minstrel troupes that competed with white blackface minstrel companies. In 1865, the Georgia Minstrels established themselves as a leading Black minstrel troupe by touring widely throughout the United States, thereby inaugurating Black minstrelsy as an intrinsically itinerant performance form (Waterhouse 1990, 49–50; Southern 1997, 232). As early as 1866, an offshoot of the Georgia Minstrels performing under the title of Sam Hague's Slave Troupe toured to England, quickly establishing the Anglophone imperial circuit as an extension of Black minstrelsy's emerging touring itineraries ('Public Amusements' 1866, 1; Toll 1974, 199; Waterhouse 1990, 51–52; Southern 1997, 232).

One performer and impresario linked these two companies: Charles B. Hicks. Originally the manager of the Georgia Minstrels, Hicks broke with the company when the white British impresario Sam Hague took over management and led the troupe on its transatlantic tour. Nevertheless, in 1870, Hicks briefly reunited with his former company, performing as a comedian in a racially integrated troupe featuring white singers well-versed in popular British styles and the troupe's Black comic performers. In 1871, Hicks returned to the United States, where he toured with various incarnations of his Georgia Minstrels until he brought the company to Australia in 1877. Hicks's Georgia Minstrels toured Australia and New Zealand for three years (1877–1880); nearly a decade later, Hicks returned for another three-year tour (1888–1891) with the Hicks-Sawyer Minstrels, in which he shared management duties with a Black manager, A.D. Sawyer (Toll 1974, 213; Waterhouse 1990, 57). Hicks's two extended tours demonstrated that the British colonies were profitable venues for Black minstrel performers who could compete with touring troupes of white blackface minstrels. Indeed, the transoceanic itinerancy of Hicks's tours led directly to permanent migrations as several members of his troupes—including star performers such as Hosea Easton and Billy Wilson—elected to remain in Australia and New Zealand where they continued to work in local theatres and with other minstrel troupes that toured the region (Egan 2020, 25–26).

Travel on the Anglophone imperial circuit offered African American performers the opportunity of mobility—even fugitivity—as a mode of provisional freedom and individual agency in the long aftermath of slavery. Following the end of Reconstruction in the United States in 1877, Black minstrels faced reinvigorated antiblack racism in the United States that culminated in what is commonly known as the 'nadir' of US racial politics (Logan 1954, 52). Though Black minstrelsy continued to flourish amidst these disadvantageous conditions, the majority of Black minstrel companies were owned and managed by white impresarios (Toll 1974, 211). Black impresarios faced cut-throat competition with white minstrel company managers in the United States and Britain. Indeed, Hicks's several transoceanic tours were in part attempts to maintain his Black minstrel troupes without interference from white competitors (Toll 1974, 213; Waterhouse 1990, 57). For African American performers and managers seeking to escape such limited prospects for self-direction in their performance ventures, British colonial theatres promised to be comparatively less racially oppressive. As exemplified by Ernest Hogan's Australian tour with the American Negro Minstrels in 1899, Black minstrels often navigated the post-Reconstruction 'nadir' of US American racial politics and the 'Jim Crow' system of segregation through transoceanic travel.

The American Negro Minstrels and the Australian Loophole of Retreat

On 1 July 1899, the Afro-American Minstrel Company organized by M.B. Curtis made its Australian debut in Sydney. Curtis was a white impresario who recruited a star-studded ensemble of Black American performers for a bespoke Australasian tour. The African American performers in the company were well-practiced in the techniques of Black minstrelsy, through which they refashioned blackface minstrelsy into a 'counterculture of modernity' by staging songs, skits, and other material that emphasized Black experiences of plantation life, political perspectives, and the racial paradoxes of Blackness and modernity. The star of the Curtis company was Ernest Hogan, author and performer of the immensely popular song 'All Coons Look Alike to Me' (1895). This comic song epitomized the Black minstrel humour of the era by ironically voicing the song's racist title as its chorus—an 'awfully funny' statement which Hogan first heard when a Chicago policeman uttered it as justification for wrongfully arresting him ('Talks With Theatrical Favorites' 1899, 2; cf. Fletcher 1984, 138). Transposing the policeman's racist phrase into the voice of the singer's erstwhile girlfriend, Hogan smuggled a critique of antiblack racism's absurdities into a song that appeared to be merely about romantic troubles. With 'All Coons Look Alike to Me,' Hogan inaugurated both the vogue in 'coon songs' and popular interest in ragtime music and dancing (Southern 1997, 317–19). Joined by other leading African American performers well-versed in Black minstrelsy's subtle and spectacular reworkings of minstrel material such as comedian Billy McClain and singer Madah Hyer ('The Bronze Patti'), Hogan headlined a spectacular bill that featured 'the largest and best aggregation of Coloured talent ever engaged under one management' ('Amusements,' *Australian Star*, 1899a, 2).

Despite the company's assembled star power, the troupe struggled financially for several months as it toured Australia and New Zealand. On 5 October, in Christchurch, New Zealand, the company abruptly changed its advertised name to Ernest Hogan's American Negro Minstrels and announced that the company's members were seeking legal intervention against Curtis for nonpayment of their salaries ('Amusements &c.' 1899; 'Amusements,' *Press*, 1899b; cf. Egan 2020, 81–83). For the remainder of the company's tour that concluded in February 1900, Hogan managed the troupe along with fellow company member Carl Dante. On one hand, the intracompany conflict between Curtis, a white manager, and the troupe's African American performers typified the racialized power dynamics of most Black minstrel troupes of the era. On the other hand, the company member's turn to self-management and their successful legal actions against Curtis signalled a stark difference governing racial politics in colonial New Zealand and the 'Jim Crow' United States. Whereas Hogan was able to pursue legal modes of redress against Curtis in New Zealand, litigation was often foreclosed to African American performers in the United States, especially in the South. Thus, within months of arriving in the British colonies, the members of Ernest Hogan's American Negro Minstrels seized upon their legal rights to self-representation in court in order to halt Curtis's financial exploitation of the troupe.

Though Hogan and the troupe only remained in Australia and New Zealand for slightly over six months, their tour made a profound impact. Early during their tour, Hogan wrote a letter thanking the Sydney public for their hospitality, specifically noting that 'the citizens of [Sydney] admire ability and do not recognize caste' ('Thanks (To the Editor of the *Evening News*)' 1899, 3). Though this sort of audience flattery was common in the era, it seems likely that Hogan was sincere in his appreciation of Australia's legal protections of racial equality and that he experienced the tour as a respite from 'Jim Crow' racism. Indeed, Hogan was no stranger to the intense, immediate threats posed by 'Jim Crow.' He later recounted a traumatic incident that occurred when he was performing with the Black Patti Troubadours in New Orleans (c. 1897–1899), wherein he accidentally went to the box office reserved for white performers to request money and received instead verbal and physical threats. Hogan responded by punching his assailant before being smuggled out of town to avoid any reprisals. Though Hogan escaped the situation physically unharmed, the encounter was so significant that he stated, 'I didn't get myself together again until I was in Australia with my own company' (quoted in Fletcher 1984, 141). For Hogan, then, Australia represented the epitome of geographic mobility as a means of securing a sense of freedom and psychic repair. Liberated from Curtis's exploitative management and leading '[his] own company,' Hogan seized the opportunities for self-determination furnished by his itinerant tours through the British colonies.

Though Hogan's narrative of his experience of Australia modelled an individual encounter with the colonies as a space unmarked by US American forms of antiblack racism, audience responses to the troupe's performances suggest that the citizens of Sydney were not altogether free of antiblackness. A review of their 8 July performance in Sydney in *The Daily Telegraph* evinced a clear investment in minstrel stereotypes of blackness:

> Almost all the items on the programme are of the pure nigger kind, and their resemblance to the old character of minstrel business is made the more striking by the intensity of gesture and general action which the members of the company employ in their various 'turns.' ('The "Afro-American" Minstrels at the Criterion' 1899, 3)

Asserting a striking 'resemblance' between Black minstrelsy and 'the old character of minstrel business,' the reviewer indicates his nostalgia for white blackface minstrelsy and his enjoyment of its apparent return through Black minstrelsy. Though Hogan and the other members of the American Negro Minstrels fashioned what Daphne Brooks terms 'Afro-alienation acts' in which they 'seized on and re-ordered' minstrel tropes, it is evident that many colonial audiences did not perceive these political acts of self-making as anything other than typical 'minstrel business' (2006, 4). Indeed, Australian racialisations of the Black minstrels even conflated them with Aborigines, as when the troupes were cast as Australian Aboriginal trackers in a 'spectacular drama' about rural outlaws entitled *The Kelly Gang* ('The Criterion Theatre' 1899, 10). This casting indicates that Australians did indeed 'recognize caste,' albeit not in precisely the same ways common in the post-Reconstruction United States. Instead, colonial audiences engaged with Black minstrelsy through local articulations of Anglophone imperial racial orders.

These Australian responses to Black minstrelsy demonstrate the complex entanglements of multiple racial discourses that were animated by African American performers in the colonies. Rather than posit them as counterweights to adjudicate or dismiss Hogan's experience of his Australasian tour, it is more generative to consider how he and other Black minstrels may have reconciled such encounters with colonial racism and their feelings of greater freedom in the colonies. Black minstrels from the United States toured the British colonies amidst a period in which the rights and freedoms of Black American citizens were violently denied. Australia offered touring African American performers with the sort of 'vastly improved yet far from ideal condition[s]' that characterize what Saidiya Hartman terms (after Harriet Jacobs) a 'loophole of retreat—a space of freedom that is at the same time a space of captivity' (1997, 9). As Katherine McKittrick elaborates, Jacobs's retreat into a cramped garret as a space of provisional freedom demonstrates how Black people—and Black women, in particular—make use of the 'possibilities in the existing landscape' to navigate their routes to emancipation (2006, 40). Might Hogan's journey of 'get[ting] himself together again' have required his embarkation on a 'loophole of retreat' to Australia wherein he encountered new possibilities in the existing landscape of the colonial world? And, if so, how does his retreat to Australia's public, colonial theatres complicate the concept of 'retreat?' To answer these questions, let us turn to the primary rivals, and sometime collaborators, of Hogan's American Negro Minstrels in Australia: Orpheus McAdoo's Jubilee and Minstrel Companies.

The Colonial Modernity of Orpheus McAdoo's Jubilee and Minstrel Companies

Though Black minstrelsy was the primary theatrical mode available to African American performers, many Black vocal artists instead joined companies of 'Jubilee Singers' who modelled their choral performances of Black spirituals on the Fisk Jubilee Singers (Graham 2018). The original troupe was founded in 1871 as a fundraising endeavour for the Black educational institution Fisk University, but the most famous troupe of Fisk Jubilee Singers were officially unaffiliated with the university. Rather, the troupe led by Frederick J. Loudin was reconstituted in 1879 as a commercial endeavour that engaged in the modes of Black itinerant performance dominant throughout the period. In 1884, amidst the intensification of post-Reconstruction reactionary racial politics, Loudin took his troupe abroad and Loudin's Fisk Jubilee Singers embarked on a world tour that began with a two-year engagement in Britain (Erlmann 1991, 26). In 1886, they departed for a three-year tour of Australia and New Zealand, which ended with a brief engagement in South Asia (Abbott and Seroff 2002, 4–27; 'The Jubilee Singers' 1889, 3). By contrast to the Black minstrels with whom they shared audiences, the Fisk Jubilee Singers abjured the comic material and blackface make-up endemic to minstrelsy; instead, they centred their performances on their unique arrangements and earnest singing of Black folk spirituals and on their commitment to politics of racial uplift. During their six years touring Britain and the British colonies of Australasia, the Fisk Jubilee Singers expanded the transnational repertoire of Black performance material to include vernacular Christian Black spirituals that gave voice to the tribulations and freedom dreams of Black Americans such as 'Didn't My Lord Deliver Daniel?,' 'Nobody Knows the Trouble I've Seen,' 'Steal Away to Jesus,' 'Turn Back Pharoah's Army,' and 'Swing Low, Sweet Chariot.' Moreover, this extended tour also provided their members with familiarity with the Anglophone imperial circuit as an alternative to transatlantic routes.

One member of Loudin's Fisk Jubilee Singers, Orpheus McAdoo, recognized the opportunity presented by the global touring network and formed his own transoceanic touring troupe. Born under slavery in Greensboro, North Carolina, Orpheus McAdoo attended university at the Hampton Institute, where he joined the Hampton Male Quartet (Erlmann 1991, 21–53). In 1885, McAdoo joined Loudin's Fisk Jubilee Singers during their London tour. He remained a member of the company throughout the ensuing four years of their tour through Australia and New Zealand, though he left the company just prior to their final stop in South Asia. After his departure from the Fisk Jubilee Singers, McAdoo returned to England where he formed his own company named alternately the Virginia Jubilee Singers or the Virginia Concert Company. Despite a lacklustre beginning to his English tour, McAdoo decided to tour his new company to the British colonies in southern Africa. McAdoo's choice to embark on an extended colonial tour may be explained in part from his direct experience of the Anglophone imperial circuit attained during his time with the Fisk troupe. Yet, more to the point, McAdoo also drew directly upon interpersonal connections made during this tour. In Australia, McAdoo befriended the colonial governor of Victoria, Lord Loch; by 1889, Lord Loch had been reappointed as High Commissioner for Southern Africa, a position from which he encouraged McAdoo to visit the Cape Colony (Egan 2020, 58). McAdoo accepted this invitation and, from 1890 to 1891, McAdoo's Virginia Jubilee Singers toured southern Africa. Though the Cape and Natal colonies had been regular stops on the Anglophone imperial circuit for decades, McAdoo's company was the first Black troupe to perform for southern Africa's predominantly white colonial audiences (Thelwell 2020, 96–130). Following a remarkably successful tour of the Cape and Natal colonies, McAdoo and his troupe travelled to Australia and New Zealand for three years (1892–1895) before returning to southern Africa for a two-year engagement (1895–1897). In 1897, he left Cape Town to recruit new members for his company, which toured throughout southern Africa through 1898. After losing several company members to a rival engagement, McAdoo returned to the United States once again to enlist new members for his reconstituted troupe: Orpheus McAdoo's Georgia Minstrels and Alabama Cake Walkers. This new company toured Australia and New Zealand beginning in 1899 and continued in the wake of McAdoo's death (by illness) in Sydney, Australia, in July 1900.

Throughout his experience in the colonies, and especially in his development of relationships with colonial politicians, McAdoo negotiated with the shifting terrain of colonial modernity and its racial politics. During the course of his decade of touring of the British colonies, McAdoo regularly adapted his performance repertoire and the racial politics of his performance to the local particularities of his various audiences. Most notably, despite beginning his tours with a troupe of 'Virginia Jubilee Singers' modelled on his experiences with Loudin's Fisk company and its repertoire of Christian Black spirituals or 'jubilee songs,' by 1899, McAdoo's troupes performed Black minstrelsy and popular items such as the cakewalk and ragtime music. What spurred the transformation of McAdoo's repertoire? Following the initial two-year tour of southern Africa, McAdoo toured his troupe to Australia and New Zealand for three years amidst the transnational popularity of 'coon songs' inaugurated by Hogan. Upon his return to the Cape Colony, he advertised his shows as 'the only true exponent of American Coon Songs in South Africa' (Erlmann 1991, 35; cf. *Grahamstown Journal* 1897). McAdoo was likely motivated in large part by financial considerations—his troupe had performed Black spirituals and other elements of their 'refined' repertoire of jubilee songs for southern African colonial audiences for two years, and Black minstrel material offered novel attractions. Notably, it was McAdoo's time in Australia and New Zealand—where he followed closely after Charles B. Hicks's Black minstrel troupe—that instigated his company's transformation from a troupe of 'Jubilee Singers' into a variation on the Black minstrel show replete with the popular novelty of comic plantation sketches, minstrel burlesques, cakewalks, and 'Coon songs' that were circulating widely throughout the United States and the British

Empire (Erlmann 1991, 37; Thelwell 2020, 97). Moving among sites within the Anglophone imperial circuit, McAdoo modelled how touring Black minstrels updated their repertoires and adapted to the shifting tastes, desires, and racialized expectations of colonial audiences.

McAdoo's adaptability was evident especially in his navigation of colonial racial politics. In 1897, McAdoo returned to the Cape Colony with a new troupe, now called Orpheus McAdoo's High Class Coloured American Minstrel Vaudeville Company. As Chinua Thelwell has outlined, this renamed company emphasized McAdoo's claim to the 'refined' ('High Class') quality of their performance material and, implicitly, the troupe's performers; moreover, McAdoo's choice of the ambiguous term 'Coloured' played upon the ambivalences of Cape colonial racial schemas (96, 104–46). Cape racial discourses imagined a tripartite racial classification system comprising white settlers, Black Africans, and 'Coloured' (i.e., 'mixed-race') colonial subjects. Within this schema, 'Coloured' subjects were understood to have white ancestry and to therefore be more amenable to white imperial civilizational projects than the colony's 'native' Black peoples. Thus, McAdoo's usage of the term 'Coloured' invited white colonial audiences in southern Africa to view his troupe not only as 'refined' but also as essentially different from the colony's majority Black subject population. Positioning the troupe as 'Coloured' performers specializing in 'Negro' material, McAdoo strategically advertised the company as authentic delineators of Black American cultural material and as high-class, refined, 'mixed-race' entertainers. McAdoo also maintained the typical three-part division of the minstrel programme which allowed him to segregate the 'Coloured' jubilee songs and their embodiments of racial uplift and Christian salvation from the low comedy of 'Negro' minstrelsy (Thelwell 2020, 115). Thus, McAdoo's strategic deployment of the ambiguities of 'Coloured' identity facilitated his fusion of two formerly oppositional strands of late nineteenth-century Black performance culture—jubilee singing and Black minstrelsy—thereby playing on while also reinscribing colonial racial orders.

McAdoo's savvy negotiation of colonial racial politics—including his strategic embrace of discourses of racial uplift and imperial racial hierarchies—left a complex and contradictory legacy redolent with the paradoxes of colonial modernity and its racial structures. The adherence of minstrelsy and low comedy to 'Negro' identity animated colonial racial discourses that figured Black ('Native') Africans as uncivilized. Nevertheless, though McAdoo could not tailor his performances to the desires and expectations of Black audiences—as was common in Black minstrelsy's circuits in the United States—his performances nevertheless inspired Black anticolonial figures such as Sol Plaatje and John Dube, and his southern African tour of Jubilee songs played an integral role in the globalization of Black music by prompting the formation of the earliest Black South African choirs in local missions (Erlmann 1991, 46–50; Thelwell 2020, 110). McAdoo's savvy navigation of colonial racial discourses fostered recognition and inspiration for southern Africa's 'Christian Africans,' whose Christianity was associated colonial discourses of European-ness and 'civilization' as well as with the McAdoo troupe's 'High Class' embodiments of respectability and uplift. Here, McAdoo's transoceanic tours functioned as a relay connecting postbellum Black American projects of racial uplift to both colonial evangelism and emergent anticolonial performance cultures.

Thus, whereas Hogan's experiences of the Anglophone imperial circuit figured the colonies as a brief 'retreat' from the racial politics of the United States, McAdoo's sustained tours trace the entanglements of Black countermodernity and colonial modernity. Attesting to these tight entanglements, Hogan's antipodal tour overlapped with McAdoo's final tour of Australia, as both companies performed on Sydney's stages in July 1899. This convergence of itinerant performers in the British colonies invites a reconsideration of the politics of Black minstrelsy that moves beyond analyses of Black minstrelsy as bound to the binary racial politics of the 'Jim Crow' United States and instead considers Black performance within the capacious, shifting, and ambivalent racial discourses of colonial modernity. In this vexed and difficult transnational space, Black artists fashioned complex performances that navigated intersecting structures of race, class, and colonialism to pursue—and, thereby, to complicate—the incomplete global project of emancipation.

References

Abbott, Lynn, and Doug Seroff. 2002. *Out of Sight: The Rise of African American Popular Music, 1889–1895*. Jackson: University of Mississippi Press.
Advertisement. *The Era*. 1866. March 11, 8. Gale British Library Newspapers.
'The "Afro-American" Minstrels at the Criterion.' *Daily Telegraph* (Sydney). 1899. July 10, 3. National Library of Australia Trove.
'Amusements.' *Australian Star*. 1899a. June 30, 2. National Library of Australia Trove.
'Amusements.' *Press* (Canterbury). 1899b. October 5, 5. New Zealand National Library Papers Past.
'Amusements.' *Sydney Morning Herald*. 1874. January 10, 4. National Library of Australia Trove.
'Amusements &c.' *Lyttelton Times*. 1899. October 6, 1. New Zealand National Library Papers Past.
Brooks, Daphne A. 2006. *Bodies in Dissent: Spectacular Performances of Race and Freedom, 1850–1910*. Durham: Duke University Press.
Brown, Jayna. 2008. *Babylon Girls: Black Women Performers and the Shaping of the Modern*. Durham: Duke University Press.
'The Criterion Theatre.' *Daily Telegraph* (Sydney). 1899. July 29, 10. National Library of Australia Trove.
Egan, Bill. 2020. *African American Entertainers in Australia and New Zealand: A History, 1788–1914*. Jefferson: McFarland & Co.
Erlmann, Veit. 1991. *African Stars: Studies in Black South African Performance*. Chicago: University of Chicago Press.
Fletcher, Tom. 1984. *100 Years of the Negro in Show Business*. New York: Da Capo Press.
Gilroy, Paul. 1993. *The Black Atlantic: Modernity and Double Consciousness*. Cambridge: Harvard University Press.

Graham, Sandra Jean. 2018. *Spirituals and the Birth of a Black Entertainment Industry.* Urbana: University of Illinois Press.

Grahamstown Journal. 1897. April 10.

Hartman, Saidiya V. 1997. *Scenes of Subjection: Terror, Slavery, and Self-Making in Nineteenth-Century America.* Oxford: Oxford University Press.

Hoxworth, Kellen. 2020. 'The Jim Crow Global South.' *Theatre Journal,* 72 (4), 443–67.

Jones, Douglas. 2021. '"The Black Below": Minstrelsy, Satire, and the Threat of Vernacularity.' *Theatre Journal,* 73 (2), 129–146.

'The Jubilee Singers.' *Indian Daily News.* 1889. November 26, 3.

Krasner, David. 1997. *Resistance, Parody, and Double Consciousness in African American Theatre, 1895–1910.* New York: St. Martin's Press.

McKittrick, Katherine. 2006. *Demonic Grounds: Black Women and the Cartographies of Struggle.* Minneapolis: University of Minnesota Press.

Logan, Rayford W. 1954. *The Negro in American Life and Thought: The Nadir, 1877–1901.* New York: Dial Press.

'Provincial Theatricals.' *The Era.* 1873. November 2, 6. Gale British Library Newspapers.

'Public Amusements.' *Liverpool Mercury.* 1866. June 25, 1. Gale British Library Newspapers.

Sotiropoulos, Karen. 2006. *Staging Race: Black Performers in Turn of the Century America.* Cambridge: Harvard University Press.

Southern, Eileen. 1997. *The Music of Black Americans: A History.* Third Edition. New York: W.W. Norton & Co.

'Talks With Theatrical Favorites.' *Sunday Times* (Sydney). 1899. July 9, 2. National Library of Australia Trove.

'Thanks. (To the Editor of the "Evening News".' *Evening News* (Sydney). 1899. August 12, 3. National Library of Australia Trove.

Thelwell, Chinua. 2020. *Exporting Jim Crow: Blackface Minstrelsy in South Africa and Beyond.* Boston: University of Massachusetts Press.

Toll, Robert C. 1974. *Blacking Up: The Minstrel Show in Nineteenth-Century America.* Oxford: Oxford University Press.

Waterhouse, Richard. 1990. *From Minstrel Show to Vaudeville: The Australian Popular Stage, 1788–1914.* Kensington: New South Wales University Press.

Watkins, Mel. 1994. *On the Real Side: Laughing, Lying, and Signifying—The Underground Tradition of African-American Humor That Transformed American Culture, from Slavery to Richard Pryor.* New York: Simon & Schuster.

Wittmann, Matthew W. 2010. 'Empire of Culture: U.S. Entertainers and the Making of the Pacific Circuit, 1850–1890.' Ph.D. diss., University of Michigan.

CHAPTER 55

Actor Migration to and from Britain in the Nineteenth Century

Jim Davis

In *Theatre and Migration* Emma Cox states that 'it is important to locate the emergence of conditions of [theatre and migration's] possibility in the popular itinerant and immigrant theatres of the nineteenth century, which didn't necessarily foreground stories of migration' (Cox 2014, 7). Cox goes on to argue:

> If itinerant and immigrant practitioners didn't tend to make migration their topical focus, the cultural and economic transactions initiated by their work represents the beginnings of theatre's globalisation as we recognise it today. These artists' careers also show how theatre and migration can be mutually propelling activities. (8–9)

These are indisputable points, but some of the performers Cox references in support of these statements, such as Dion Boucicault, Charles Kean and J. C. Williamson, are successful touring actor-managers, following or creating transnational networks and circuits, of the sort that Christopher B. Balme, for example, has brought to our attention through his work on Maurice Bandmann. A broader historical sweep might also recognise the arrival of some actors in a new country as a form of economic migration—not always successful financially—and that there is also a line to be drawn, however haphazardly, between touring and migration. Race can also be a factor in determining actor migration. My intention in this chapter, using the career of Ira Aldridge in Britain and the presence of British actors in Australia as case studies, is to consider

J. Davis (✉)
University of Warwick, Coventry, UK
e-mail: Jim.Davis@warwick.ac.uk

some of the reasons for actor migration in the nineteenth century, the points at which touring and migration intersect, and the extent to which we can differentiate between the two processes.

Migration in the nineteenth century does not always fit easily within transnational or intercultural narratives: in fact, colonial narratives are more appropriate to the case studies discussed here. The countries under scrutiny in this chapter—Britain, America and Australia—were linked by complex colonial histories. The American War of Independence (1775–1783) had led to the severance of colonial ties between Britain and America well before the black actor, Ira Aldridge, sailed from New York to Britain. Australia's colonisation by the British commenced in 1788, its penal origins gradually displaced by the arrival of a settler community. In America, a black actor such as Aldridge was not permitted to perform in the legitimate theatre. Migration was the only way in which he could follow his chosen profession, although throughout his career in Britain, Europe and Russia, he still had to cope with racial prejudice. In Australia, Western forms of theatre were enacted first by the convict population and later by settlers and touring actors. Theatre as practiced in Europe and America was still in its infancy in Australia in the early years of the nineteenth century.

As transport both by sea and by land developed during the century, so travel conditions improved, and it was because of this that actors were able to tour and emigrate more easily. British actors visited Australia as part of global or regional tours, sometimes stopping off for long periods or even settling permanently. Touring was economically driven, often because of lack of employment or opportunity in the home country, but most nineteenth-century actors were itinerant a lot of the time, even when performing only in their native countries. Although Aldridge became a British citizen, he toured extensively in Europe and Russia, even stating that he would eventually like to settle in Germany. Sometimes it is difficult to tell where touring ends and migration begins (and vice-versa) when reviewing the lives and intentions of nineteenth-century actors. This issue may be clearer-cut in relationship to those established *stars* for whom touring was simply a circular profit-making trip, but for many actors this was not the case.

On a national basis, travelling companies might be nothing more than barnstorming troupes with portable theatres, moving from location to location in search of new audiences. By the mid-nineteenth century, travelling companies in Britain toured major provincial theatres in new productions of plays originally staged in London's West End. Internationally, travelling theatre companies also endorsed imperial and colonial agendas, imposing a common culture on a range of different countries, as was the case with companies touring the British Empire and with the travelling German companies of the Habsburg Empire. When major actors toured internationally, they often recruited their own travelling company (sometimes supplemented by local talent). Individual actors occasionally left these companies mid-tour to try their luck in one of the venues visited, even remaining there permanently if successful. Other actors might undertake a solo engagement in another country, once again remaining or not according to how successful they were. Mobility was generally more important than migration: even those actors who eventually settled beyond their native country often made temporary return visits or even returned home permanently later in life. However, it would be wrong to focus just on those actors for whom migration was an outcome of economic contingency. For an actor such as Aldridge it was a political necessity.

IRA ALDRIDGE

During the nineteenth century, 'African American travelers, for whom Britain was an imagined space of liberation, crossed the Atlantic as sailors, fugitives from slavery, activists nourishing the anti-slavery movement, preachers and pleasure seekers' (Tuffnell 2020, 20). Many African American migrants settled in areas such as the East End of London or in Liverpool; the majority were engaged in lowly paid occupations, although there were exceptions. One of these was Ira Aldridge. His is not a typical story of black migration to Britain in the early nineteenth century; rather, his experiences are exceptional and unique. Born in New York in 1807, he was the son of a preacher and had been educated at one of the two African Free Schools in New York until 1822. He allegedly acted at the 'African Theatre' which had opened in 1821 with a black theatre group in New York, renamed the American Theatre in 1822. Late that year the company moved to Albany to avoid opposition, eventually returning to New York shortly before its closure in 1824. Although some theatres allowed black spectators seats in the gallery, black actors were segregated from white actors and it was impossible for a black actor to pursue a professional career in America.

Aldridge departed at around the age of 16 for England, where he sought theatrical engagements (possibly helped by letters of introduction from the English actors, William and Henry Wallack). Described on the bills as a 'Gentleman of Colour', he first appeared in London in May 1825 at the Royalty Theatre, located in the East End, and then at the Coburg Theatre located south of the Thames. Subsequently, he secured engagements at several provincial theatres, making a strong impression as Othello and as other black characters, such as the title role in *Oroonoko* and Zanga in *The Stranger*. Initially, he had to overcome the inbuilt racism of his audiences, accentuated at the time by the popularity of the comedian Charles Mathews's travesty of a black Shakespearean actor mangling Shakespeare's verse and breaking off mid-performance to sing 'Opossum up a Gum Tree' at his audience's request in his one-man show *A Trip to America*. Primed by Mathews's depiction, audiences went to the theatre to laugh at Aldridge, unprepared for his professionalism and competency as an actor. In his early years in England, Aldridge was known as F. W. Keene, possibly attempting to draw comparison with the actor Edmund Kean. Sarcastically described as the 'African Roscius' by *The Times* (11 October 1825, 2), which referred to him as a 'blackamoor' and claimed the shape of his lips prevented him from speaking English properly, he turned the newspaper's racism to his advantage by adopting the title, although later in his career he was known as the African Tragedian. Initially, he was advertised as coming from New York, but later emphasised his African lineage, claiming descent from Senegalese royalty. His racial origins became a defining characteristic of Aldridge's public and professional personae, countering prejudice through the quality of his acting, his clearly enunciated articulation of the English language and his intelligence, dignity and gentlemanly demeanour in private. In farewell addresses delivered at provincial theatres from the 1830s onwards he also capitalised on the notion of his status as a 'black man born and bred in Africa' (Lindfors 2011a, I: 189).

Aldridge became a popular provincial actor and subsequently also enjoyed a popular following in Ireland, remaining there for almost six years consecutively in the mid to late 1830s. Nevertheless, a major key to success in this period was an engagement at one of London's two patent theatres—Covent Garden and Drury Lane—and in 1833 Aldridge appeared at Covent Garden Theatre. A year earlier *Figaro in London* (22 September 1832, 168) had described him as 'a stupid-looking, thick-lipped, ill-formed African' (Lindfors 2011a, I: 230), a harbinger of further attacks by the press in advance of his Covent Garden debut. The same journal (6 April 1833, 56) indignantly called his engagement an 'act of insolence', suggesting that the fact that Nature had supplied him with a skin which 'renders soot and butter superfluous' (Lindfors 2011a, I: 257) was no indication that he was competent to play Othello. It felt he should be driven from the stage and find more appropriate employment as a street sweeper or a footman. Many more xenophobic comments were made about Aldridge's physical appearance, while the *Athenaeum* (13 April 1833, 236) complained at the impropriety of 'an interesting actress and lady-like girl, like Miss Ellen Tree [the white actress playing Desdemona], being subjected…to the indignity of being pawed about by Mr Henry Wallack's black servant' (Lindfors 2011a, I: 267). There is no evidence that Aldridge was ever employed as a servant by either of the Wallack brothers and he himself denied it. In direct contrast to the generally laudatory criticisms heaped upon Aldridge by the provincial press, many London critics from newspapers of all political persuasions reacted with hostility and Aldridge's engagement lasted only two nights, although this may have been compounded by the outbreak of a major flu epidemic. Perhaps the most shocking aspect of Aldridge's rejection by the London critics was the overt racism embedded in their commentaries. While such comments were not absent from some provincial accounts, Aldridge's performances, particularly of Othello (but also of other major roles), were often praised in the provinces for their judgement, vocal qualities and intellectual acumen. In London in 1833, however, the year that Parliament passed a bill for the abolition of slavery throughout the British Empire, there were still many anti-abolitionists who believed servitude was the natural condition of native Africans, an attitude belied and even threatened by Aldridge's example (Fig. 55.1).

Fig. 55.1 Ira Aldridge as Othello in *Othello* by William Shakespeare, Oil on canvas. Unknown artist c. 1848. Museum Number S.1129–1986. URL https://protect-eu.mimecast.com/s/Vj2fCL8N8UNMvnliB4TtD/

Although (unlike other black migrants from America) Aldridge was not directly involved in anti-slavery activities, his qualities as an actor and as a gentleman made a compelling case for abolition and gave the lie to notions of racial inferiority perpetuated by the pro-slavery movement. '[H]e has disarmed the lovers of colonial slavery of a favourable argument, "that the poor African possesses not a mind capable of cultivation"', claimed the *Leeds Times*, 28 September 1833 (Lindfors 2011b, II: 21). This viewpoint recurred continually in provincial reviews of Aldridge's performances. He was also adept at re-appropriating and subverting racially stereotyped roles. From an early stage he would follow performances as Othello with the farcical role of the black servant Mungo in Bickerstaff's *The Padlock*, demonstrating not only his versatility as an actor but also the gap between representation and actuality. He often included 'Opossum up a Gum Tree' in his performance of Mungo, while later he impersonated the Jim Crow character first devised by T. D Rice and sang blackface minstrel songs as part of the evening's programme, effectively taking control of and owning such material. In *Stage Mad*, derived from *Stage Struck*, a farce deliberately parodying Aldridge's aspirations to play Othello, he played the stage-struck black footman in intentional self-parody. One role in which he declined to appear, however, was that of Uncle Tom in a Drury Lane adaptation of *Uncle Tom's Cabin*. Over time he added whiteface roles to his repertoire, including Macbeth, Shylock, Richard III and King Lear. He also developed a popular one-man show which commenced with a lecture in defence of the drama, particularly targeting religious bigotry. His arrival in provincial cities, conveyed by his costly carriage and horses, was often commented upon and provided additional advance publicity prior to his performances. Sometimes he travelled with a small company, who assisted with his one-man shows or performed in the plays he chose to present. From the late 1840s he once again began to perform solo engagements in the provinces; he also appeared in London at the Surrey Theatre in 1848 and in 1852 at the Britannia Saloon, where his roles included Aaron (elevated now to a more noble and heroic character) in *Titus Andronicus*, substantially rewritten by C. A. Somerset in collaboration with Aldridge.

Aldridge's career in Britain and Ireland depended heavily on touring, which provided him with a substantial income over time. Major London engagements, however, remained closed to him. It was only from 1852 when he started to tour in Europe that his abilities were fully appreciated. In 1852 he visited Brussels with a small company, subsequently appearing in Germany with great success. By the end of 1853 Aldridge had dispensed with most of his company and subsequently resolved to perform only in Europe, stating that nothing would tempt him to act in England again, given the respect he was achieving and honours he was accumulating abroad, and the prejudice and insurmountable barriers placed in his way in Britain. From 1852–1867 Berlin, Vienna, Prague, Zurich, Krakow, Zagreb, Belgrade, Tallin, Riga, Odessa, St Petersburg, Moscow, Constantinople, Paris and Stockholm were among the cities in which he appeared and over time he was awarded many honours and medals by the European countries he visited. In fact, he alternated between performances in Britain (including a West End engagement at the Lyceum Theatre in 1858) and Europe up until 1860. In Europe, he often acted in English, while other actors performed in their native language. Beyond Europe, he also achieved great acclaim in Russia. In some instances, his presence as a black actor, with a carefully mediatised identity as an African outsider, may also have turned him into a surrogate for the victims of more localised oppression, as in Pest-Buda in thraldom to the Habsburg Monarchy at the time of his 1853 visit. This was probably the reason he was subsequently asked to leave the city (Imre 2020, 75–101). In 1862 and from 1864–1867, he was banned from St Petersburg for similar reasons at a time when many there opposed the emancipation of the serfs in Russia.

In 1825 Aldridge married Margaret Gill, the daughter of a Northallerton stocking-weaver; on her death in 1864 he married his Swedish mistress, Amanda Brandt. Throughout his career he had many affairs. At a period when miscegenation was still frowned upon, the fact that white women were attracted to him caused negative reactions. J. B. Howe, who performed with him at Croydon and admired him as an actor, recalled the feelings of repugnance he experienced 'at the adulatory congratulations bestowed upon him by the fair members of the company' and that it shocked him 'to see a pure blonde with almost angelic features and form, putting on a most bewitching smile, and using every art of feminine blandishment' (Howe 1888, 58) to win Aldridge's notice. Aldridge applied for and was granted British citizenship in 1863, a move that allowed him to own property in Britain which he could eventually leave to his family. On tour in Poland in 1867, he was taken ill and died in Lodz, where he was given an elaborate burial. At the time of his death Aldridge had been planning a return from self-imposed exile to America to perform in New York and Chicago.

Ironically, despite Aldridge's talent and his role in perpetuating the cultural iconicity of Shakespeare both within and beyond his adopted country, racism was a significant factor in preventing his full acceptance as a major actor in Britain. So long as notions of the inferiority of black races, fears around miscegenation and the political expediency of promoting racial stereotypes prevailed, a migrant such as Aldridge was not able to realise his full potential. Thus, his professional career in Britain took on a form of internal migration: he was 'the perennial outsider from English society...always on the move' (Waters 2007, 86). Even his success and popularity in Europe and Russia did not free him from occasional racial slurs in the press: despite his antipathy to Britain, he never settled permanently in any of the other countries he visited.

BRITISH ACTORS IN AUSTRALIA

In 1788 the British invaded what was to become Australia and, using the concept of *terra nullius*, eventually deprived the indigenous population of property and land rights. New South Wales became a convict settlement and in

1789 some of the convicts performed George Farquhar's *The Recruiting Officer*, allegedly the first European play to be performed on the continent. The convicts may have been unwilling migrants, but the cultural consequences of this performance are chillingly implied in Thomas Keneally's novel *The Playmaker*:

> Seen from the immensity of time, Ralph's play might appear a mere sputter of the European humour on the edge of a continent which, then, still did not have a name. This flicker of a theatrical intent would consume in the end the different and serious theatre of the tribes of the hinterland. In the applause at the end of the evening...Arabanoo [the novel's major aboriginal character]—had he still lived—would have heard the threat. (Keneally 1987, 305)

Keneally's novel is very much about dispossession and the mistaken notion that cultural imposition and civilising values are the same thing. Both the aboriginal population impelled into internal migration and the convicts as victims of forced migration suffer different forms of dispossession and loss of identity, a parallel that *The Playmaker* deliberately emphasises. Convict theatres, however, were more widespread and nuanced than Keneally's fiction recognises, according to Robert Jordan in his pioneering study of early Australian convict theatre: 'none of them quite fits Thomas Keneally's picture of an uncouth troupe dependent on an officer and gentleman for polish and understanding' (Jordan 2002, 201). Jordan reveals that convict theatre was far more socially diverse than previously acknowledged and that some of the transported convicts brought theatrical skills first honed in Britain to the colony.

In time, farming opportunities and subsequent labour shortages attracted free settlers to Australia. By the 1850s and 1860s Australia had very much become a settler colony rather than a repository for transported convicts. As the population grew, so did the demand for entertainment and theatres were constructed in many towns and cities. Australia also emerged as a potentially lucrative market for touring actors and as a promising site for relocation for performers who enjoyed only sporadic success in their home country.

One of the first actors to visit Australia for an extended period was the Irish actor Gustavus V. Brooke, who fulfilled a successful series of engagements from 1855–1861. Brooke provides a good example of the touring actor whose sojourn in countries such as Australia hovers on the verge of migration and settlement. He exemplifies the pioneering actors who became identified as part of the Australian theatre—George Coppin, Clarance Holt, Barry Sullivan, the Brough-Boucicault Company, William Hoskins, George Rignold, Roy Redgrave—as opposed to the visiting stars such as Charles and Ellen Kean who identified with Britain far more than Australia. Before returning to Brooke, however, it is important to reference perhaps the most significant migrant of them all, the English-born George Seth Coppin. From his arrival in Sydney on 10 March 1843, Coppin was to have an especially significant impact on the development of Australian theatre in the nineteenth century. After initial success at Sydney's Royal Victoria Theatre, Coppin, who specialised in low comedy characters, and his wife visited Tasmania and then Melbourne in 1845. After a successful sojourn as theatre manager and actor in Melbourne Coppin moved to Adelaide, where he was to remain, even after the death of his wife, until financial collapse and the lure of the Victorian gold-rushes tempted him away in 1851. He resumed his career as a theatre manager first in Geelong and then in Melbourne. In 1854 he engaged Brooke to tour Australia under his management from 1855 and for a time even entered into management with him. He also managed Charles Kean's tours of Australia and America from 1863–1865 before resuming his career in theatrical management in Melbourne early in 1866. He remained a forceful presence in Australian theatre for many years, particularly through his association with the Theatre Royal, Melbourne. Many of his papers and letters survive, providing an abundant source of information on nineteenth-century Australian theatre. Coppin also ventured into politics as a member of the Victorian Legislative Assembly and later of the Legislative Council. Despite financial ups and downs, he typifies the type of actor-migrant who settles and stays rather than the touring actor who is constantly seeking new venues across the globe to enhance their fortune.

The discovery of gold in Victoria was undoubtedly the largest single factor behind the expansion of the Australian population in the 1850s, increased migration and the subsequent need for an increased supply of entertainment. Between 1851 and 1854 Victoria's population rose from 77,345 to 236,776. This inevitably led to the building of more theatres both on the goldfields, in towns such as Ballarat, Bendigo and Castlemaine, and in Melbourne. The Gold Rush began to abate in 1854 at a time when Melbourne was still developing its full potential as a city. Yet it would be wrong to identify the experience of visiting actors purely with specific cities. Moving between cities and touring to more remote communities were experiences common to most actors. Moreover, touring was tough, a fact attested to in many memoirs. Rats, cockroaches, snakes, unbearable temperatures, flea-ridden hotel rooms and uncomfortable modes of transportation were just some of the hazards faced by actors. Clarance Holt and his troupe were held up by six mounted bushrangers, forced to dismount from their carriage and hand over all valuables, while the actress Avonia Jones recalls a madcap drive across the outback with a group of drunken actors. In the smaller towns and communities, accommodation could be primitive with performances taking place in tents and saloons on makeshift stages such as trestles or billiard tables, while barns were used as changing rooms. In many ways the accounts of actor's experiences such as these in 1850s Australia tally with the pioneering spirit and battler myths of early settler narratives. Traversing the outback is an adventure that identifies the actors' own complicity in the formation of a certain facet of Australian national identity, a legitimation of their relationship with the Australian landscape and its inhospitable terrain.

Conversely, while actors such as Brooke might achieve a temporary and partial Australian identity through their pioneering work, they also reasserted British and Irish identity. In securing Brooke to appear in Australia Coppin launched one of the first starring engagements in the colony and one based, moreover, on Brooke's reputation in Shakespearian tragedy. In April 1855 Brooke laid the foundation stone for Melbourne's Olympic 'Iron Pot' Theatre, stating:

> Every Briton must experience a motion of pride as he beholds the city which has arisen as it were by magic, at the command of his countrymen and look forward with hope into the future of these colonies, already rich in the inheritance of British laws, customs and literature. (*Age*, 19 April 1855, 5)

Brooke was much admired by his Australian audiences despite his addiction to the bottle. It is quite possible that he might not only have resurrected his career in Australia but also have remained there permanently if the wreck of the *London*, the boat on which he was returning to a new engagement in 1866, had not forestalled this.

Subsequently, the lure of Australia proved too strong to withstand for many other actors. Robert Brough, an English actor who founded the Brough-Boucicault Comedy Company in Australia in 1886, clearly numbered among those actors who had a primary commitment to Australian theatre in the period during which they performed there. Brough had found, claimed the pro-Republican *Bulletin* (9 March 1905), that 'a long residence in Australia takes the Englishness out of your blood and puts in something different, which leaves you at cross purposes with life when away from Australia'. Many actors chose to settle and retire in Australia, including George S. Titheradge, a member of Brough's company, who according to the *Lone Hand* (X.57, 1 January 1912, 193), 'has identified himself with Australian civic and social life. He is also a learned amateur botanist, well known to the curators of Australian Botanic Gardens'. But perhaps the most representative of English actors to settle in Australia was William Hoskins, who, after a thorough grounding in the English provinces, acted with Samuel Phelps at Sadler's Wells Theatre before leaving for Australia. An 'educated, scholarly man', he arrived in Australia in 1856, remaining there until his death 30 years later. Hoskins, who had instructed the young Henry Irving in acting while still in England, mounted a production of *The Tempest* at Ballarat in the early 1860s and made a speech after the first performance extolling Shakespeare as a civilising force around the globe, 'making his way through distant climes and foreign regions, vanquishing race after race, as our conquerors did of old'. He exhorted his audience to guard Shakespeare's 'throne' in Australia ('Mummer Memoirs', *Sydney Sportsman*, 20 February 1907, 3). Hoskins is a typical instance of the English actor who brought with him to Australia and maintained the cultural capital of English theatrical values.

Having arrived with his production of *Henry V* in 1876, another British actor George Rignold also remained in Australia, apart from brief starring engagements in Britain and the United States. He insisted on the highest possible standards of production and was prepared to take risks. Moreover, his management did not rely on importations from London. According to the

Lone Hand (VII:42, 1 October 1910, 458–460) 'he trained his own actors and actresses—Australians'. His scenery was painted, dresses made and music composed locally, and he genuinely attempted to produce local plays. 'If ever we have a national theatre...then we may salute George Rignold as its pioneer'. The *Bulletin* (17 September 1887), however, sneered at Rignold's encouragement of 'the Anglophilic tendencies of white Australian colonists' through his production of *Henry V*. After Rignold's retirement the standard of Henry V was to be seen on bright days floating on a flagpole amid the eucalyptus trees in his garden, which overlooked Sydney's Middle Harbour. When he died, the standard was draped over his coffin for the funeral procession.

By the 1880s Australia had enjoyed significant economic, social and cultural progress; Melbourne was considered one of the great cities of the southern hemisphere. Australian journalist James Smith celebrated this advance in 1888, demonstrating what migrants and visitors might now experience:

> Thirty years ago men and women migrated to Australia in search of health or fortune with something of the feeling that they were going into exile, and that they must relinquish many of the comforts, most of the social enjoyments, and nearly all the luxuries that had been accessible "at home". That sentiment has pretty well died out. There is nothing in any of the principal cities of Australasia to remind the new-comer that he is in a new country, except the absence of the antiquities, the brightness of the atmosphere, the general air of vivacity and alertness which characterizes the people he meets with in the streets, and the non-appearance of the squalor and mendicancy which obtrude themselves upon your notice in the centres of population in Europe, and even in many of the large cities in the United States. (Stuart 1989, 160)

Smith suggests a more urbane society and culture had replaced that which had been defined by the outback and by the pioneering spirit of earlier settlers or by the madcap adventures of earlier generations of performers such as Holt and Brooke. Yet from Brooke onwards the iconicity of British cultural values, especially those exemplified through Shakespeare, predominated. Whether touring or migrating, British and Irish performers tended to re-affirm the colonial status quo.

Not all actors succeeded in Australia. In 1895 the English actor Arthur Dacre shot his wife, Amy Roselle, and then cut his own throat in Sydney after failing to achieve professional and financial success on the Australian stage. This is a far cry from the experience of a George Coppin or Harry Rickards, the English music hall performer who established the Tivoli chain of vaudeville theatres throughout Australia from the late nineteenth century. Nevertheless, in exploring the mobility of performers throughout the nineteenth century, it is crucial that we recognise not only the global circuits facilitated by actors, managers and agents, but also the implications of extended residency and even total migration for the changing patterns of theatrical exchange in the period and what it meant in human terms.

* * *

Whereas, for many British and Irish actors, migration was economically driven, for Ira Aldridge migration was a consequence of the fact that his race precluded him from following his chosen profession in America. This was also the reason why another African American, Samuel Morgan Smith, set out for London in 1866, following in the footsteps of Aldridge and performing professionally in Britain for the next 16 years. In Aldridge's case, his performances and critical reactions to them, 'were directly entangled with the coterminous history of racialized debates about slavery and abolition in the Caribbean and the United States of America' (Saxon 2020, 275–277). Yet, as with the actors performing in Australia, Aldridge endorsed traditional British theatrical and cultural values. Whether touring or emigrating, these actors also functioned as cultural emissaries, both in the colonies and in Europe and Russia. Exceptionally, perhaps through the sheer physical and emotional force of his stage presence, Aldridge was able to perform effectively in English alongside European and Russian actors using their native languages. Within contexts that encompassed the slave trade and its abolition, racism, transportation and economic uncertainties, the reasons for actor migration in the nineteenth century were multifaceted and inexorably intertwined with both national and international touring. For Aldridge, an African American actor journeying to Britain from America, migration was intentional, but touring became essential; for British and Irish actors visiting Australia, what may have started as touring sometimes metamorphosed into an intentional act of emigration.

References

Cox, Emma. 2014. *Theatre & Migration*. Basingstoke: Palgrave Macmillan
Howe, J. B. 1888. *A Cosmopolitan Actor His Adventures All Over the World*. London: Bedford Publishing.
Imre, Zoltán. 2020. 'Surrogation, Mediatization, and Black Representation On- and Off-stage: When Ira Aldridge, the African Roscius, visited Pest-Buda in 1831.' *Theatre Survey*, 6 (1), 75–101.
Jordan, Robert. 2002. *The Convict Theatres of Early Australia 1788–1840*. Sydney: Currency House Inc.
Keneally, Thomas. 1987. *The Playmaker*. London and Australia: Hodder and Stoughton.
Lindfors, Bernth. 2011a. *Ira Aldridge The Early Years 1807–33*. Vol. I. Rochester, NY: University of Rochester Press.
Lindfors, Bernth. 2011b. *Ira Aldridge The Vagabond Years, 1833–52*. Vol. II. Rochester, NY: University of Rochester Press.
Saxon, Theresa. 2020. 'Ira Aldridge in the North of England: Provincial Theatre and the Politics of Abolition.' In *Britain's Black Past*, edited by Gretchin H. Gerzina, 275–293. Liverpool: Liverpool University Press.

Stuart, Lurline. 1989. *James Smith The Making of a Colonial Culture*. Sydney: Allen & Unwin.
Tuffnell, Stephen. 2020. *Made in Britain Nation and Emigration in Nineteenth-Century America*. Oakland, California: University of California Press.
Waters, Hazel. 2007. *Racism on the Victorian Stage Representation of Slavery and the Black Character*. Cambridge: Cambridge University Press.

CHAPTER 56

Migration and Marathi Theatre in Colonial India, 1850–1900

Kedar A. Kulkarni

During the mid-nineteenth century, western India saw the rise of a vibrant theatrical culture. Within what was then the Bombay Presidency, a colonial administrative unit, this emergent theatre reflected the geographic and linguistic diversity of the region itself, and performances in English, Gujarati, Marathi, Kannada, and Urdu were a common feature of the theatrical climate. Given the close proximity of these various languages and their theatre traditions, they naturally influenced each other. Marathi theatre, the subject of this essay, was no exception; it borrowed freely from and also influenced other traditions in its proximity, especially the Parsi theatre. But, owing to colonial networks of exchange, the theatrical personalities of the time were also well aware of styles and performances from overseas—the colonial metropolis was more connected to the colonizer's metropole than even the hinterlands of the colonizing country. Bombay, for example, emerged as the second largest city in the British Empire, after London, during the 1850s, and it had a theatrical culture fitting its prominence in the economic sphere.

Most importantly, for purposes of this chapter and handbook, the Marathi theatre—much like the Parsi theatre—that developed during this time was primarily itinerant in nature. While individual practitioners of a troupe certainly had hometowns and familial relations, their theatrical practice almost always took them on the road. Dozens of troupes circulated around the Bombay Presidency performing in venues small and large, and sometimes also in

K. A. Kulkarni (✉)
FLAME University, Pune, India
e-mail: kedar.kulkarni@flame.edu.in

© The Author(s), under exclusive license to Springer Nature Switzerland AG 2023
Y. Meerzon, S. E. Wilmer (eds.), *The Palgrave Handbook of Theatre and Migration*, https://doi.org/10.1007/978-3-031-20196-7_56

makeshift tents. Until the early twentieth century, no Marathi-language troupe owned its own performance space, and even after troupes began to build their own playhouses, travel remained a major part of their theatrical practice. This chapter speaks to migration and travel in three separate dimensions: firstly, the migration of theatre artists from smaller cities and principalities (independent kingdoms whose foreign policy was controlled by the East India Company and then the British Crown) in colonial India towards larger urban settlements, thereby ensuring a more democratic form of patronage, relying on individual ticket sales, rather than a feudal kind of patronage; secondly, the transformation of performance genres as these theatre artists travelled from smaller towns to larger ones, in accordance with their patron's desires; and finally, professionalization of the theatre troupe itself during this era.

Vishnu Amrut Bhave, regarded as the father of modern Marathi drama and the progenitor of the *Marāṭhi saṅgīt nāṭak*, or Marathi music drama, died in 1901. By the time of his death, an active critical discourse about Marathi theatre had emerged, and the theatre scene was well into the golden era of the Marathi Music Drama (approximately defined from 1880–1920). But what remained constant was the facticity of travel, and of course, Bhave's own travels. Bhave, like many theatre personalities of subsequent generations, started his career within a system of patronage and performance that can hardly be considered professional. He was, early in his career, pandit at a small aristocratic court in Sangli, Maharashtra, India. His patron, Chintamanrao Patwardhan (d. 1851), was a wealthy landlord who was known for supporting the arts, from painters to artisans of various stripes, and of course, owing to Bhave, performers as well. Bhave had served as a minor court pandit to the Patwardhan, but also had creative inclinations. In 1842, the Patwardhan had the opportunity to see a Kannada-language *yakṣagāna* performance—a kind of folk theatre whose plots included selections from the Indian epics, the *Rāmāyaṇa* and *Mahābhārata*, as well as the *Bhāgvata Purāṇa*. Knowing of Bhave's creative endeavours, the Patwardhan asked him to compose something similar to what he had seen with the *yakṣagāna* performance. The play Bhave staged, *Saṅgīt Svayaṃvar* (*Sita's Choice, the Musical*; *Sita's Choice* hereafter), based upon the marriage of Sītā to Rāma in the *Rāmāyaṇa*, was presented at the court to a very limited audience of other courtly officials, in 1843. Nissar Allana's *Painted Sceneries* contains a photograph of the venue (Allana 2008, 15). And so, Bhave's theatre practice began in a settled way, within a structure of patronage and performance that recalls feudal ties rather than commercial ones. With sufficient financial assistance and without much hardship for recruiting talent and procuring spaces to perform, he only needed to please one patron.

An intimate courtly setting was a comfortable place to inaugurate a career in theatre. Living quarters in which to stay, dressing rooms, ample money for costume and set design, and most importantly, an audience that maintained composure during the performance—all these were the luxuries of having a prince as one's patron. To the best of my knowledge, from the time Bhave staged *Sita's Choice* in 1843, until Chintamanrao Patwardhan's death in 1851,

Bhave did not travel outside the court to perform: he was at the Patwardhan's behest. After *Sita's Choice*, Bhave also composed ten more plays based on the *Rāmāyaṇa*, according to one critic (A. Kulkarni 1903, 12), which one finds in Bhave's 1885 *Nātya Kavitā Saṃgraha* (1885). As I explain below, many of Bhave's actors were illiterate, in terms of being able to read and write, but highly literate from another point of view, and in a society that valued the knowing-by-heart more than book knowledge. For the most part, Bhave was successful, until his patron died. After the Patwardhan died in 1851, Bhave's practice took off in a different direction, marking an important transitional moment from a courtly to commercial performance culture. This point is crucial to keep in mind when considering patronage and audience later, when performing for a commercial stage demanded broad popular appeal rather than the idiosyncrasies of an Indian prince or aristocrat.

From the time Bhave left the court of Chintamanrao Patwardhan in 1851, we can say that his activities were forced to become commercial ventures, relying on a more democratic kind of patronage. Migration—prompted by losing his patronage at court—occasioned a monumental shift in the theatrical experience, both for performers and audiences alike. Unlike the controlled environment of a court, or even the potentially raucous performance venue of a village square—for many performers, the village square was the predominant site of performance—something new happened when the Patwardhan's heir refused to patronize Bhave. Indeed, when the patron was not a single wealthy potentate, Bhave's productions became beholden to multiple contingencies. Upon departing the court, Bhave had to negotiate for all the things that were provided while he was in Sangli. He had to find appropriate venues and procure materials and sponsorship for set and costume design. He not only had to recruit talent to perform, but moreover, had to retain that talent that may have sought employment elsewhere for better compensation, or simply refused to travel.

Travelling Theatre

Where, and how, did the troupes travel though, and how did travel affect their makeup and the professionalization of theatre? With Bhave's troupe, few archives remain to indicate a complete history of their travels. S.N. Banhatti (writing in 1952) provides us a brief itinerary in his work on Marathi theatre (107–115). From Banhatti's work, it's evident that Bhave travelled predominantly in Mumbai and Pune. But perhaps the most complete record of travel of a major troupe in the latter nineteenth century concerns *Kirloskar Nāṭak Maṇḍalī* (the Kirloskar Drama Troupe), established first in 1880. It's founder, B.P. Kirloskar, was, initially, a *kīrtankār*, a kind of performer who would deliver sermons based upon stories from India's epics, accompanied by music. Often performed in village squares and adjacent temple sites, his beginnings were akin to Bhave's: functioning within different systems of patronage than a commercial one. Even though the Kirloskar Drama Troupe's repertoire and performance style were quite different from Bhave's Sangli Drama Troupe—Kirloskar scripted his plays, unlike Bhave's, which contained only a dramatic poem for the narrator to recite while actors improvised—its travel schedule is quite instructive, and speaks to the continuing relevance of travel for theatre practice, even decades after Bhave had inaugurated his professional career.

Some scholarship has provided us a record of the Kirloskar Drama Troupe's travels from 1884–1890—an itinerary much more complete than we see with Bhave's theatre troupe. The itinerary gives us just a sense of how much and how widely the troupe travelled in western and central India, in Marathi-speaking regions (roughly the size of contemporary Italy today), and beyond. The troupe quickly established itself amongst the middle-class intelligentsia owing to its reliance on carefully scripted drama and a dramaturgical structure imported and observed in a number of travelling theatre companies that frequented the colonial circuits through Bombay. Unlike in Bhave's illiterate actors who improvised their roles, here actors all memorized lines and were given active roles within the structure of a five (or more) act drama. From the troupe's incipience, it relied heavily on taking its productions to audiences scattered between the expected locations—Bombay (and its nearby cities such as Thane, Kalyan, and Vashi) and Pune, but also to cities in (contemporary) southern Maharashtra such as Satara, Kolhapur, Pandharpur, Miraj, Solapur; to border towns in Karnataka such as Belgaum, Dharwad, Hubli; to towns in north and central Maharashtra such as Nashik, Akola, Nagar, Amravati, Jalgaon; as well as towns that were historically associated with Marathi-language courtly culture such as Indore, Gwalior, and Jhansi (in Madhya Pradesh); as well as one visit to Kashi (Benares). Looking over their itinerary, it seems as though the troupe was nearly always on the move for a period of those six years. While these travels persisted, the troupe supported itself solely on its fare of three music dramas—something between an opera and a Broadway musical, in which there was abundant dialogue, but the many verse numbers were composed in accordance with Hindustani classical music.

Why only three? Perhaps because travel ensured that audiences would not tire of the same productions, as they might were they a troupe situated within a theatre of their own, with their own urban audience. Perhaps also Kirloskar's verse numbers, sung with accompanying music, provided differing levels of entertainment than a drama simply based on a plot, and audiences back then, as listeners today, also wanted to listen to songs more often than simply once. One of their productions, a translation of the Sanskrit play *Abhijñānaśākuntalam* (Kalidasa, fourth century CE), as *Saṅgīt Śākuntal* (1880) is the only time in modern history that a Sanskrit play has been revived with widespread popular appeal: while many of India's myriad theatre and performance forms adapt materials from the Indian epics, these forms rarely restage Sanskrit drama in the way performance cultures elsewhere often adapt and restage Greek drama. Nor is Sanskrit drama usually restaged outside of academic confines. The company's second major success, *Saṅgīt Saubhadra* (1882), about the central epic hero of the *Mahābhārata*, Arjun, and his marriage to Subhadra, has remained a popular fixture to this day for the way it treats romance and love.

Travel also affected the professionalization of Indian theatre, marking a point of transition from performers who performed within a caste group, as a hereditary profession, to performance of a more volitional and professional nature, irrespective of traditional occupation. Once Bhave began to take his troupe on tour, theatre became quite popular and commercially viable. Various people founded dozens of other troupes—up to thirty-six according to Sudhanva Deshpande (2009, 181). Facing what proved to be a competitive environment, Bhave found it necessary to enter into contracts with his actors to prevent them from leaving to join other troupes, among other things (Deshpande 2009, 177; Mehta 1960, 130; Desai 1975, 9–10). The contract contained in Desai's collection is for a period of ten years, and is signed by the actors in exchange for singing tuitions. Bhave taught them songs that they would perform in various plays. The contract is written on stamp paper, making it official and legally binding. The contract contains some noteworthy terms: the first item, for example, demands that actors take parts they are assigned, go where Bhave takes them, without complaint. Item four states explicitly, 'We will not deceive you as we did when we previously went to Mumbai and we shall not teach others as you have taught us without your permission'. Meanwhile, the last paragraph mentions that the penalty for breaking the terms of the contract will be one hundred rupees, in addition to an eighth part of the monies earned from teaching the materials elsewhere (Desai 1975, 9–10). Without a doubt, this contract indicates that there must have been a fierce competition amongst troupes seeking an audience, and also that managers had to negotiate quite a bit with unruly actors who may not have been too pleased with the roles they were given. Furthermore, since the plays themselves were not original productions, and plots were well known to their audiences, anything beyond the ordinary, anything innovative that would give one troupe the upper hand, or anything that would make the troupe known within the performing circuit must have been a valuable commodity. In another way, this contract, and Bhave's attempts to rein in actors, suggests an emergent culture of stardom in which troupes with known actors with specific talents would also become more popular in the public eye. Most of all, the transition from traditional and hereditary performers whose caste determined their occupation as performers into a more professional one required a new structure of affiliation. The contract, a legal technology, seems to have filled that void. None of these changes were immediate, but they certainly gradually became part of a culture of traveling theatre during this time, structuring the performance in various ways.

Dramaturgy

Wallposters—advertisements glued to walls—contained in a volume entitled *Marāṭhi Raṅgabhūmicā Itihās* (History of Marathi Theatre) by S.N. Banhatti (1957), and republished elsewhere (K. A. Kulkarni 2015; K. A. Kulkarni 2022), give us a glimpse of what performing for a popular stage meant during this time, rather than the courtly setting in which Bhave's career began. Once again, the archival remains of Bhave's troupe are quite sparse, but those of one other troupe, the Altekar Troupe, provide some interesting parallels and complementary materials. These wallposters, presumably, would have been affixed to the walls of buildings throughout cities and towns, and read aloud as they were distributed. The wallposters provide us with information about the program, audiences, the imagery associated with performances, as well as a tangible way to approach discourses about the theatre, such as notions of respectability, sexuality, class, and aesthetics. While none of these posters advertise Bhave's troupe, the toponymical *Saṅglikar Nāṭak Maṇḍaḷī* (Sangli Theatre Troupe hereafter), they do give a glimpse of how the experience of theatre began to gradually change in the mid-nineteenth century.

The evening's performance would not have begun right away with the show's contents. As indicated by the imagery of Saraswati, Goddess of Knowledge, and Ganapati (Ganesha), remover of obstacles and patron of the arts, the performance would begin with a prayer to each. Appaji Kulkarni, an early enthusiast, details this opening process in his 1903 work. He writes of Bhave's plays:

> First and foremost, the *sūtradhār* [troupe leader], coming out of the curtains and standing to the side will offer an invocation. He will offer some verses in song praising God. Then, in the guise of a forest-dweller, the *vidūṣak* [comic] will come out [of the curtains]. After he dances in a foolish manner, the *sūtradhār* and *vidūṣak* will have a humorous discussion. After a common introduction, the *sūtradhār* will tell which play will be performed…Then, after a praise/*pujā* of Ganapati, the curtain will open. (A. Kulkarni 1903, 13; my translation)

The initial dialogue between the *sūtradhār* and the *vidūṣak* is often very important even in contemporary folk traditions—and folk traditions comprise the bulk of non-urban performance genres in India; the *vidūṣak* played the joker, while the *sūtradhār* tried to convey the plot and moral of the story to the audience. The procedural dimension of these plays, in addition to their obvious marketing on the wallposters, does consciously draw on folk traditions, but it employs a visual and ritual idiom to initiate a performance—that of worship—recreated on the wallposter at the top of the page. While these plays were not performed specifically during religious occasions like forms of folk theatre such as *daśāvatāra* (literally, 'ten avatars' [of Vishnu]) or *yakshagāṇa* (folk theatre of Karnataka), invoking Ganapati to ensure a smooth and problem free performance would have made these plays legible as more than entertainment, at least partially framed by religious and ritual practice.

Reading the wallposter further, we gain a sense of how the performance contained an episodic structure, without an integrated narrative—or perhaps integrated by the ritual presence of Ganapati and Saraswati. It lists several episodes from various epics including a battle, defeat, a biography, and a historical drama, of Narayan Rao Peshwa; it advertises a decapitation, a sword fight, and a disembowelling, replete with rice and beans—a real gut buster! And, it tells us how we ought to feel. While we do not have written scripts of the episodes themselves, S. N. Banhatti provides us with reviews from the *Bombay Times*, just prior to and following a performance at the Grant Road Theatre. Both reviews concern a performance staged by none other than Vishnu Amrut Bhave on Wednesday 9 March 1853, his troupe's performances would have resembled those of the Altekar Troupe:

> The play commences with the appearance of a reciter and a clown (an imitation of the old Greek chorus), and the recitor, having described to the clown all the particulars regarding the play, Gunputtee [Ganesha] and Sarasvatee [Saraswati]; 'the God and Goddess of Wisdom' appear. They are soon followed by two angels, who by their performances [sic] endeavor to please the deities. The play commences with a battle between Luxuman [Laksman], 'the Brother of Rama' and Indrajit the 'son of Ravan, the giant King of Ceylon' in which the latter being killed, his head is carried off to Rama by his monkey followers, while the arm of Indrajit, cut off by an arrow from Luxuman, flies through the air to the apartment of 'Sulochana,' the wife of Indrajit. The dead limb writes for the information of the lady of the sad fate of her husband, Sulochana resolves to burn herself on the funeral pile of her husband and goes, with her father-in-law Ravan's permission, to Ramchandra [Rama] for the recovery of her husband's head. The monkeys around, to put her virtue to the test, request Sulochana to make the dead head smile. The head smiles and it is restored to her. A great many events that followed are omitted, and the next part of the play commences with the accession of Rama to the throne of Ayodhya after exile of Sita, his wife, to a forest on account of certain imputations cast upon her conduct.... (Banhatti 1957, 394–395)

Two days later, this review appeared:

> The performance seemed to us very creditable, as far as we could judge—utterly ignorant as we were of the language used, which was Mahratta [Marathi]. The actors were all Hindoos—those of them who performed the chorus being Brahmins in their ordinary dress, and the others—the real actors—the representatives of Gods, Goddesses, demi-Gods and Monkey Soldiers being Khutrees [*kṣatriya*, 'warrior'] The clown was a leading character throughout the play, and thought nothing of standing on his head, or making a summersett [sic] while Rama or Ramchundra [Rāma] or Indrajit were delivering heroic orations. The God and Goddess of wisdom seemed quite at home, too, while sitting on chairs and couches, and the combat between Luxuman [Laksman] and Indrajit was

carried on (the weapons being bows and combatants dancing fiercely round and round each other) in an English looking parlour. These things we mention, however, with no wish to detract from the merit of the performance, which was such, upon the whole, as agreeably to disappoint us [sic]. The grotesque feats of the clown amused even those who did not know even a word of what he was saying, and his jests and repartees were received with hearty laughter and loudly applauded by the native portion of the audience, [sic] The actor who represented Ramchundra bore himself with part and dignity becoming such a hero, and the two boys who performed the female characters, moved, spoke and lamented after the most approved fashion of eastern women. The various costumes were doubtless quite as appropriate.... (Banhatti 1957, 396–97)

Neither Banhatti nor Appaji Kulkarni cites descriptions from the Marathi language press, and I too was unable to find much of anything from my own searches, excepting some limited plot summary in Kulkarni's work. While the descriptions above provide richer details than the Altekar Troupe's wallposter, they also reaffirm several tropes I would like to discuss—emotion, music, the caste of actors, the terminological approximations of the reviewer to make this performance comprehensible to the Anglophone readers of the *Bombay Times*, and the episodic nature and mode of narrative. Value judgments about 'eastern women' aside, these reviews, combined with the Altekar wallposters, enable us to visualize the spectacle, which included heroic orations, comical interruptions, and bizarre and 'grotesque feats'. Something for everyone—ensuring that the performance would attract the widest possible variety of clientele.

It is apparent that the comic, heroic, grotesque, and erotic are all bound up in the language of *rasa* on the Altekar wallposter. The wallposter explicitly says, 'There being four *rasa*s herein, the mourning *rasa* will be complete'. The advertisement, perhaps, includes these terms as an appeal to the emotional understanding of the audiences, informing them what they will feel during the performance. In the nineteenth century, commentators, critics, members of the elite, and the laity all were aware of *rasa* (emotional modality) theory, presumably from various scattered sources containing parts of the *Nāṭyaśāstra* ('Treatise on Drama' 200BC–200CE) and its interpretations over time, such as the *Kāvyaprakāśa* of Mammaṭa (eleventh century CE). Sometimes, these texts were taught in colleges (Kulkarni 2022, 64–66). While the laity and elite educated Indians may not have understood *rasa* in the same way, at the very least, everyone seems to have had an understanding of the eight *rasa*s: *sṛṅgāra* (erotic), *vīra* (heroic), *hāsya* (comic), *karuṇa* (pathetic), *raudra* (furious), *bhayānaka* (terrible/horrible), *adbhūta* (marvellous), and *bībhatsa* (grotesque/disgusting). If a play had any element that made us feel horror, for example, it was said to have the *bhayānaka rasa*. A Sanskrit play could have all or just a few of these *rasa*s, but generally would privilege one or two over all others—but the performance above is not of a Sanskrit play, but rather contingent upon various performance traditions in which it was common to navigate many *rasa*s; above one finds heroism, comedy, pathos, marvel, and grotesquery.

Visual Literacy

What interests me further is how a night's performance was assembled, through the internal logic of a troupe—such as the desires of star actors—to produce such an interrupted, piecemeal, and multifarious emotional journey, presumably so that many different actors could be featured in roles that suited them. Just as Bhave's play, *Sita's Choice* was based upon the marriage of Sītā, from an episode in the *Rāmāyaṇa*, most plays staged by traveling theatre troupes were plays that were adapted from popular religious traditions as well as from the *Rāmāyaṇa* and the *Mahābhārata*. All the stories that would have been performed were known from numerous religious festivals and practices, from a particular region—western India broadly—in this case. Glancing at the plays Kulkarni (A. Kulkarni 1903, 27) lists as being performed, we need only to read their titles to glean their content. All the plays in the list derive from sources that were part of a living performance or religious tradition during the time, and were performed in the vernacular. Those partaking in the performance would not have to memorize lines since the stories themselves were not the original works of a playwright, but rather part of a cultural repertoire, being recited or performed in a variety of ways during various festivals—especially with troupes such as Bhave's and the Altekar Troupe that were, significantly, different from the Kirloskarite scripted drama.

Owing to these historical conditions, I suggest that the traditional boundary between literate and illiterate, playwright and actor was particularly porous. Sudhanva Deshpande's comment on this point is particularly enlightening: 'Modern theatre in Maharashtra radically altered the relationship between the actor and the audience; it now entailed new ways of representing, new ways of looking [as]...the audience, from being participants, became spectators or onlookers' (2009, 181). It becomes clearer that the performer-audience divide too was somewhat blurry, with a knowing audience that attended the theatre not for an unknown plot, but rather for how the known plot unfolds through the quality of song and representation—gestures, costume, movement, recognizable actions. While actors and the audience may not have been literate, they certainly were aware of religious narratives, and of the iconography associated with various gods, goddesses, and heroic figures. In short, these were non-literate forms of knowing and contain the imagination of 'expressive movements as mnemonic reserves, including patterned movements made and remembered by bodies' (Roach 1996, 26–27).

We have to think of this kind of performance as a negotiation between the manager, actor, and the audience, as a precursor to early Indian (and Hindi) cinema's 'heterogeneous form of manufacture' (Prasad 1998, 42–45). The actor's ability to realize his roles based upon practice and experience was very valuable to the troupe, and also expected by the audience. If the actor portrayed his character well, it would be consistent with the broad cultural repertoire of known representations and meet audience expectations, while also offering some individual flair. Thus, the audience played a vital role in mediating the qualities of the performance, not simply by their patronage, but also by virtue of their cultural repertoire, rather than literate knowledge. While the stage itself was not literate owing to the unschooled actors as well as the audience, it was visually sophisticated, legible to audiences, but subject to their legislation as well. Brahmans did not need to bring any specifically literate knowledge to this kind of production. Instead, thinking about the stage this way is something akin to Sandria Freitag's analysis of the inter-relatedness of reading, print, and oral culture, in which visual and aural/oral literacy remains important to the acceptance of theatre, the enjoyment of it, and its spread (Freitag 2001, 38–39).

Actors and the managers knew how to insert themselves into this domain of visual literacy and the cultural repertoire. They must have actively tried to do so in order to appeal to their audiences, who came from all castes, creeds, and classes of society. This is precisely Kulkarni's point when he speaks of conventional ways to depict certain gods and goddesses, and the illiteracy of the vast majority of actors (A. Kulkarni 1903, 27–33). From the perspective of iconography, gesture, procedure—such as the Ganapati *pujā* prior to performance—however, I would insist that most theatre troupes were not in a situation to dictate their content to their audiences, even if their managers and actors were Brahmin elites or from other upper-castes, such as the Khutrees or noble caste that the reviewer for the *Bombay Times* mentions. In fact, the audience's cultural literacy combined with their expectations and purchasing power at the ticket booth prevented Brahmins from usurping the conventions of itinerant musical theatre and refining its content to suit their more respectable, upper-caste idiom.

The shows that attempted to cater to an upper-caste aesthetic were not profitable. An interesting anecdote from Mehta's work adds valence to this notion. She evaluates student amateur theatre from the same time thus: 'Considering that these plays were produced barely once or at the most twice a year by the students, the newspapers gave them far more attention than was perhaps warranted. There were full-length reviews with names of the cast and usually the talents of actors were highly commended' (Mehta 1960, 189). As with the student amateur theatre, upper-caste domination of literary, documentary, and official governmental channels cannot be taken as evidence of actual conditions of the theatre scene, which was far more expansive and heterogeneous than newspaper accounts imply. Leaving aside the student amateur theatre, even the major troupes such as the Ichalkaranjikar Troupe, Naregal concedes (2010, 90), though reputed for performing prose plays that were staged from written scripts that actors had to memorize, had to rely on their repertoire of pauranic khels or plays inspired by the *Purāṇa*-s (religious texts containing cosmologies, genealogies, hagiographies, and other religious lore), in non-urban areas. Most importantly, however, I want to emphasize the ambiguous relationship between staging and writing a play. Writing a play was not the sole domain of the playwright, but rather a cooperative exercise in composition based upon the interaction between one such as Vishnu Amrut Bhave and the actors in his troupe.

This interaction sought to create a play that capitalized on the visual as a medium, in which the audience would see their own cultural repertoires interpolated and elaborated, and the unique abilities of the actors. Taking into account all these practices, a more complex period of Marathi theatre history emerges than one of ideological and caste struggle. Even if we only account for the major theatre troupes, it is clear that the commercial success of the play and upper caste ideals were not necessarily synonymous, certainly not outside urban areas, nor were the two synonymous during the period of this study, from the 1850–1880s. These issues too speak to questions of patronage and the desires of a wider spectatorship than within an aristocratic court, or in middle-class drama.

One of the biggest questions raised by these theatre troupes, and one relevant across time and into our present day, concerns the practice of travel and itinerancy: wasn't travel the norm during the time period covered in this chapter, very roughly 1850–1900? These travels enabled performing artists to reach wider audiences, and thereby generate more income. While such travel was common then, and even earlier in the form of travelling performer-poets in India, as elsewhere, importantly, travel is also a common condition for performers today. Performing artists generate more income while on tour than in any one location, and for musicians especially, whether popular or operatic singers, travel and contractual agreements are the norm rather than exception.

As I've indicated throughout this brief chapter, theatre in colonial India entailed a new orientation towards performance itself. Migration was central to this new orientation in a number of ways. In the simplest instance of migration, artists departed from smaller cities and rural locations to establish themselves in urban areas—and travelled incessantly to many urban centres. In doing so, they sought patronage differently, requiring some kinds of theatre to transition into a commercial venture. In the process, its aesthetics, too, became something else, departing from the folk traditions which had inspired them. But in moving to urban locations, outside the fold of folk traditions, this theatre also took on a new social function, no longer part of and beholden to the ritual calendar, nor reliant upon performers from performing castes. Company theatre, with actors bound by legal contracts, became a new normal. Eventually, as troupes such as Bhave's gave way to scripted drama akin to what the Kirloskar troupe performed, Marathi theatre became a medium, in one scholar's opinion, for the newly forming middle-class to imagine itself as torchbearers for a growing national sentiment (Kosambi 2015).

Acknowledgments I would like to thank the University of Hawai'i Press for granting me permission to reprint large parts of an article of mine, first published in *Asian Theatre Journal* 32.2, 2015.

References

Allana, Nissar. 2008. *Painted Sceneries: Backdrops of the 19th Century Marathi Sangeet Natak*. New Delhi: Theatre and Television Associates.

Banhatti, Shrinivas. 1957. *Marāṭhi Raṅgabhūmīcā Itihāsa*. Pune: Vhīnasa Prakāśana.

Desai, Vasant Shantaram, ed. 1975. *Vishrabdha Sharada*. Mumbai: H.V. Bhate Prakashan.

Deshpande, Sudhanva. 2009. 'Excluding the Petty and the Grotesque: Depicting Women in the Early Twentieth Century Marathi Theatre.' *Theatre in Colonial India: Play-House of Power*, edited by Lata Singh, 173–193. Oxford: Oxford University Press.

Freitag, Sandria. 2001. 'Visions of the Nation: Theorizing the Nexus between Creation, Consumption, and Participation in the Public Sphere.' *Pleasure and the Nation: The History, Politics and Consumption of Public Culture in India*, edited by Rachel Dwyer and Christopher Pinney, 35–75. Oxford: Oxford University Press.

Kosambi, Meera. 2015. *Gender, Culture and Performance: Marathi Theatre and Cinema before Independence*. London: Routledge.

Kulkarni, Appaji. 1903. *Marāṭhī Raṅgabhūmi*. 'Āryabhūṣaṇa' Chāpākhānyānta.

Kulkarni, Kedar A. 2015. 'The Popular Itinerant Theatre of Maharashtra, 1843–1880.' *Asian Theatre Journal*, 32 (1), 190–227.

———. 2022. *World Literature and the Question of Genre in Colonial India, 1790–1890*. Bloomsbury.

Mehta, Kumud. 1960. *English Drama on the Bombay Stage in the Late Eighteenth Century and in the Nineteenth Century*. A Thesis Submitted to the University of Bombay for the Degree of Doctor of Philosophy in the Faculty of Doctor of Philosophy in the Faculty of Arts.

Naregal, Veena. 2010. 'Performance, Caste, Aesthetics.' *Contributions to Indian Sociology*, 44 (1–2), 79–101.

Prasad, M. Madhava. 1998. *Ideology of the Hindi Film: A Historical Construction*. Oxford: Oxford University Press.

Roach, Joseph R. 1996. *Cities of the Dead: Circum-Atlantic Performance*. New York: Columbia University Press.

CHAPTER 57

The Dybbuk: Wandering Souls of The Vilna Troupe and Habimah Theatre

Ina Pukelytė

This chapter will consider three perspectives on migration in relation to Jewish theatre from the first half of the twentieth century. The first perspective is concerned with the concept of transmigration—the Hassidic belief that a person's soul can migrate from a dead body to a living one. The second perspective addresses the question of migrating identities. Indeed, there were probably very few groups of people in Europe at the beginning of the twentieth century who were as concerned about their identity, and the use of language to express it, as the Jews. Russian, Yiddish, and Hebrew writers and theatre artists migrated from one language to another in an effort to legitimize their belonging to these respective cultures. If we categorize these first two perspectives on migration as symbolic, we might view the third perspective as material. This third perspective concerns the travel that Jewish artists undertook from one country, or continent, to another. The way these artists moved or migrated can be considered nomadic in part because Jewish artists travelled only to the places where audiences and possibilities to survive were assured. These three perspectives on migration and Jewish theatre are exemplified by the activities of The Vilna Troupe and the theatre of Habimah, two of the most exciting case studies in Jewish theatre history. Both troupes gained their popularity and importance due to their staging of *The Dybbuk (Between two Worlds)*. This play, written by S. An-sky (Shloyme Zanvl Rappoport), brought fame and recognition to these two troupes. Using An-sky's work, we shall trace through the

I. Pukelytė (✉)
Vytautas Magnus University, Kaunas, Lithuania
e-mail: ina.pukelyte@vdu.lt

© The Author(s), under exclusive license to Springer Nature Switzerland AG 2023
Y. Meerzon, S. E. Wilmer (eds.), *The Palgrave Handbook of Theatre and Migration*, https://doi.org/10.1007/978-3-031-20196-7_57

three identified notions of migration, and their relation to these influential theatre companies.

Transmigration: *The Dybbuk*

The term *transmigration* is used in this chapter in a phytagorical sense. It relates to discussions about the immortality of the soul, and about the pathways of the 'return to the divine' (Luchte 2012, 14). These discussions presume that 'transmigration is a potent medicine for the disease and division of the soul' (28). This concept of transmigration identifies the imaginative forms tied to the phenomenon, forms that can be found throughout various cultures. In Jewish culture explicitly, the act of transmigration is represented by a *dybbuk*. The term *dybbuk* comes from the Hebrew root *Dabak*, which means to attach, to cling (Atlas-Koch and Cohen 2011, 242). Traditionally, stories of *dybbuks* were designed to reestablish normative power relationships in society. An-sky's *dybbuk*, according to Rachel Elior, on the contrary, tears these relations apart and 'reveals the complexity of the encounter between worlds by describing it from the unexpected perspective of soulmates whose loving desire for each other undermines a coerced match' (Elior 2008, 123).

The stories about *dybbuks* drew An-sky's attention when he was on his ethnographic journeys in Galicia between 1912–1913, the former part of the Pale of Jewish settlement (the area of the Russian empire where Jews were allowed to live), and divided between, what is now, Ukraine and Poland. Even in his fifties, the established writer was still concerned with his identity and was eager to find roots of Eastern European Jewishness in the folklore and relatively simple lives people lived. An-sky chose to study Galician Jews, inhabitants of Volynia, Podolia, and Kyiv provinces, which he found more exotic than Litvaks, who lived in the territories of modern-day Lithuania, Belarus, and northeastern Poland. Together with his companions, he travelled from one village to another, collecting tales, songs, customs, and making audio recordings. This material helped him and the modern Jewish intelligentsia produce a new contemporary art that would find inspiration in the rich and unique Jewish past. Although the first version of the play appeared in 1914, An-sky continued to develop the text for the next six years. The development of the work was halted by his death in 1920.

The title of the play *The Dybbuk (Between two Worlds)* suggests multiple meanings An-sky likely wanted to reveal. A *dybbuk* is not only a tormented soul which seeks to attach itself to a living person, demanding to be freed and buried properly. To An-sky a *dybbuk* was also a living being, such as himself, constantly on the move, tormented between multiple identities, never settled in his perception of self. An-sky's intention to create a love story that would last eternally was, in all likelihood, due to his failed relationships with women. As history shows, he started to work on the play when he was still married to his second wife, Edia Glezerman, who wanted to become an actress. It is thought that she insisted that An-sky create a love story and thus a role for her. However, the couple split up before it was finished.

The plot of the play is organized around two characters, Leah and Khanan, who were promised to each other by their fathers in early childhood. As the story reveals, Leah's father forgets this marriage promise after his friend (Khanan's father) dies. Instead he negotiates his daughter's marriage into a rich family. Having returned to his native village after years of wandering and learning, Khanan receives the news of the marriage of his beloved one to another man, and dies. Just as Leah is about to say 'yes' to her groom during the wedding, Khanan's *dybbuk* enters her body and, possessing her, opposes the marriage. Although the *tsadik* (the sage) of the village succeeds in chasing the *dybbuk* out of Leah's body, she nevertheless dies and reunites with Khanan, her promised one.

What distinguished this story about *dybbuks* from more traditional renditions is An-sky's choice to forgo traditional narratives, which would have society return to an orderly state after the *dybbuk* leaves, and instead looks towards eternal consequences. This approach resonated with the intellectual society An-sky frequented at that time, and the play was read in many places. An-sky's first intention was to offer the play to a Russian theatre, so despite the Hassidic content it was written in Russian. Indeed, it was read by the leaders of the Moscow Art Theatre—Leopold Sulerzhitsky and Konstantin Stanislavsky. After several workshops, the play was approved by the Moscow Art Theatre board with the role of the *tsaddik*, the sage, intended for Mikhail Tchekhov. However, times were difficult and the theatre refused it under the pretence that audiences needed plays that would be 'joyful, light fare, so as not to see or hear what is happening' (An-sky 2016, 139). Following this refusal, An-sky wrote a Yiddish version of the play. He also began to search for the possibilities of translating the play into Hebrew and approached the most talented promoter of the Hebrew language—the poet Chaim Nahman Bialik.

One can presume that the subject of *The Dybbuk* and its artistic representation onstage are directly related to *l'air de temps* or the general expectations of the postwar and postrevolutionary audiences. The play itself was not considered a well-written play, and An-sky was prompted by the heads of the Moscow Art Theatre to ameliorate this issue many times. Bialik, who finally agreed to translate the play, considered it not worthy of being performed in a sacred language and Mukdoni, one of the most influential Jewish theatre critics, treated An-sky as a 'fifth-rate writer' who became popular among Jews only because he had made a career in Russian (Safran 2010, 166). However, both linguistic versions of the play attracted spectators and generated intrigue.

The Dybbuk was, first and foremost, a love story dear to all kinds of audiences and nationalities. But it was also imbued with different elements belonging to the world of transmigration: mysticism, rituals of exorcism, and the belief in external forces that are stronger than rational human will. These transmigratory beliefs were still present in Jewish folkloric heritage and could still be detected in the remote corners of the Pale, even though they were not common anymore among those living in the cities. The play allowed non-Jewish audiences to witness the exotic environment depicted by the interpretations of the actors and shown in the scenographies, whereas the assimilated Jews in different countries were provided with a deeper knowledge of their roots and could thus construct a more solid identity.

Migrating Identities: An-Sky

The Dybbuk, as noted, revealed not only the transmigratory issues that interested the Jewish society of the time, but also addressed the inner conflicts and contradictions of human life. It can be suggested that the character of Khanan reveals the torments that An-sky himself was going through while searching for his own identity and peace.

An-sky's life and the evolution of his professional name are a perfect illustration of the inner identity conflict that Russian Jews were experiencing. In a speech delivered on the 25th anniversary of his first publication he declared: 'A writer has a difficult fate, but a Jewish writer has an especially difficult fate. His soul is torn; he lives on two streets, with three languages. It is a misfortune to live on this sort of "border," and that is what I have experienced' (Safran 2010, 171). Born Shloyme Zanvl Rappoport into a Yiddish-speaking family in the province of Vitebsk in 1863, he learned Hebrew and Russian in his early childhood. His father left the family when he was a small boy, and the historical record indicates that Shloyme searched for comfort and education in the rich merchant family of his friend Chaim Zhitlovsky. As teenagers, both Rappoport and Zhitlovsky were inspired by reactionary Russian writers. While Shloyme's first literary texts appeared in Yiddish, in 1884 he switched to the Russian language. The subsequent years, which he spent with peasants and miners of the Donets Basin, led him to the decision of changing his Jewish name into a Russian one, and he began to sign his texts not as Shloyme (Solomon in Russian) but as Semyon Akimovich. It was in St. Petersburg, at the beginning of 1892, that he began his literary career and decided on the pseudonym of S. A. An-sky, arguably aligning him further with the Russian radical writers. An-sky moved to Paris at the end of the same year and remained for eight years in total. Among the many reasons for relocating to France, one of the most influential was his unhappy relationship with Zhitlovsky's cousin Masha Reinus. While abroad An-sky continued to self-educate and write for different publishers in Russia. Soon he realized that Yiddish was gaining popularity and began to use it for writing his novels. At the same time, he became part of a newly created Agrarian Socialist League that published pamphlets defending the rights of the international peasantry.

Rising anti-Semitism, exemplified by the Dreyfus Affair, which was widely covered by the Parisian and European press, caused An-sky to think anew of his Jewish identity. If before An-sky identified himself as a suffering Russian peasant or a member of the working class, he now found it necessary to fight against anti-Jewish sentiment. In 1901 An-sky moved to Switzerland, where he rejoined his childhood friend Zhitlovsky, who was by then a pro-Yiddishist and leader of the Union of Russian Socialist Revolutionaries. In a turbulent and productive period An-sky published poems, novels, plays, and articles in Russian and Yiddish, became an associate of the Bund and other parties fighting for Jewish rights in Russia, and continued to fight for the rights of Russian peasants and workers. By the end of 1905, he was finally able to return to Russia, though his political engagement resulted in a short arrest in 1907 in his native Vitebsk. Constant quarrels between political parties resulted in An-sky embracing activities that would be less short-lived, and his interests pivoted to the study of Jewish folklore. However, his ethnographic work was interrupted by the German-Russian war and An-sky became actively engaged in helping Galician Jews survive its atrocities. The war and the October revolution threw him into such a political maelstrom that at the end of summer in 1918 he was forced to run from Bolsheviks to Vilnius, at that time controlled by the Germans. The Red Army entered Vilnius in January 1919, and three months later Vilnius was occupied by the Poles. Being in poor health An-sky moved to the Otwock resort, then to Warsaw where he died in November 1920.

'He lived as if he were camping', concludes Gabriella Safran in her book dedicated to An-sky's works and life (Safran 2010, 248). Indeed, An-sky's turbulent life is an example of the nomadic condition into which Eastern European Jews were often thrown by the political circumstances at the turn of the century. This condition allowed not only a more profound understanding of the international political environment but also of the inner life common to the peasant and working-class people. This life was based on folklore, stories, songs, and beliefs, and An-sky strove to capture them for the generations to come. These stories influenced the writer profoundly and inspired him to create a play, which revealed not only the complex transmigratory environment influenced by external forces, but also the complexity of an individual's inner life.

THE VILNA TROUPE AND HABIMAH THEATRE: *BETWEEN THE WORLDS*

Despite the many writings that An-sky left in Russian, Yiddish, and Hebrew, he is primarily remembered for *The Dybbuk*, the play that not only encompassed Jewish folklore but also spoke to the personal conflicts that An-sky faced and those issues that his generation encountered in established society. The play became the cornerstone of, what are often considered, the two most important Jewish theatres of the time, the Yiddish language theatre The Vilna Troupe and the Hebrew theatre Habimah. The realities of touring and living for these two troupes and their members can be compared to the lifestyle of nomads described by Deleuze and Guatarri in their chapter '1227: Treatise on Nomadology—The War Machine':

The nomad has a territory; he follows customary paths; he goes from one point to another; he is not ignorant of points (water points, dwelling points, assembly points, etc.). But the question is what in nomad life is a principle and what is only a consequence. To begin with, although the points determine paths, they are strictly subordinated to the paths they determine, the reverse of what happens with the sedentary. The water point is reached only in order to be left behind; every point is a relay and exists only as a relay. (Deleuze and Guatarri 2005, 402)

By conducting an analysis of The Vilna Troupe and Habimah Theatre, we can better understand how these two troupes chose their 'points' and used them in their survival.

Though the name The Vilna Troupe suggests a strong relationship to Vilna (now known as Vilnius, the capital of Lithuania) this city was only the point of departure for a substantial and long-lasting undertaking by this company. It started when the Kadison family (real name Shusters) were forced to leave their native city Kovno (now known as Kaunas, the second-largest city of Lithuania) at the outbreak of the First World War. In May 1915, the Russian government ordered Jews who lived in the border zones with the German Empire to abandon their homes within twenty-four hours. Leyb Kadison, who was already an established arts practitioner in Kaunas, fled to Vilnius with his wife and three children. It was there, according to Leyb's daughter Luba Kadison, that he was approached by local Jewish actors Alexander Azro and Jacob Sherman (Kadison and Buloff 1992, 6). The latter knew that Kadison was an experienced theatre maker (indeed, he had worked as a decorator at the Kaunas City Theatre and as an active member of Kaunas Jewish Theatre Society) and asked him to help create a Jewish theatre in Vilnius. The adventure only intensified at the end of 1915, and the premiere of the newly created Federation of Yiddish Dramatic Actors (FADO) took place in February 1916 in an abandoned and poorly heated circus. The play, *Der Landsmann* (The Compatriot) by Sholom Asch, was a success and the company of fifteen actors continued with *Farvorfen Vinkel* (A Remote Corner) by Peretz Hirschbein. The reception of both plays was so favourable that the German authorities ruling the city at that time allowed the troupe to play in the Vilnius City Theatre starting in November 1916.

From the very beginning, the troupe agreed that they would base their acting on the notion of an ensemble: there would be no stars, and the language used on stage would be unified and in that of the literary Litvak style, with the particular pronunciation of vowels common to the Jews living in Lithuanian territory. Kadison was backed by Mordechai Mazo—a reputable manager—and the duo succeeded in creating performances of high artistic quality. The troupe performed in Vilnius until May 1917, and followed this with a tour to Kaunas, Bialystok, Grodno, Łódź, and finally to Warsaw where conditions for Yiddish theatre were more favourable than in the provinces. It was in Warsaw that the FADO group received the name of The Vilna Troupe. The troupe rose in fame, with the actors gaining celebrity status. As Debra Caplan notes, during the second tour in 1918 'they were courted by admirers in cities and towns across

Eastern Europe, where they were treated to lavish banquets in their honour and provided with luxurious accommodations' (Caplan 2018, 78). It was at this time that the troupe split into two. This was due to internal conflicts and because actors Azro and his wife Alomis decided to work on their own. However, even after their separation, the two groups managed to share the same label—The Vilna Troupe.

While the Kadison-Mazo branch of The Vilna Troupe was continuing to work in Warsaw, An-sky was at the nearby Otwock resort. As Luba Kadison recalled, she went with her father to see the famous writer and her father obtained permission to stage *The Dybbuk* (Kadison and Buloff 1992, 28–29). However, when the troupe started the stage readings of the play, An-sky suddenly died. The play was staged thirty days later, for a one month commemoration of An-sky's death. By many accounts the performance was a revelation. If earlier performances by the company were appreciated for their naturalistic approach to characters and the ensemble work, *The Dybbuk* now revealed the troupe's capacity to integrate multiple artistic styles. As Caplan sums up, the performance fused Moscow Art Theatre's ensemble style, German expressionism, and the modernist neo-romanticism of the Young Poland movement: 'all blended together within a decidedly Jewish framework' (Caplan 2018, 88). This was due to David Hermann, a stage director who not only had the Hassidic background needed for the mystical play but who was also influenced by the modernist Polish, German, and Austrian theatres. The poetic and sombre sets of the performance were created by Leyb Kadison himself.

The performance became a hit and the earlier splintered members of The Vilna Troupe, who had not found as much success, invited Herman in 1921 to recreate the same performance. The result was an omnipresent Vilna Troupe. *The Dybbuk*, played by the two groups, was shown in Poland, Lithuania, Germany, Austria, England, France, Belgium, the Netherlands, and Romania. Although the performances were praised by the critics for their artistic quality, which had originally been tied to their cohesive performance, the actors were no longer an ensemble. Urged by everyday needs, actors moved from Mazo's to Azro's group and vice versa; many of them also tried their luck in North and South America. Most of them profited from The Vilna Troupe label and even when they performed solo they identified themselves as Vilners. As Caplan's research shows, there were at times upwards of ten official Vilner troupe branches in Europe and the United States, with several hundreds of actors engaged (Caplan 2018, 224). The Vilna Troupe phenomenon existed until 1936, the date when Mazo officially disbanded the troupe with the last performance of *The Dybbuk* in New York.

Constant migration from one country to another was at the core of existence for the Vilners. And there were many successful moments when actors could benefit from their popularity and live at ease. Yet even so, most of the time the members of the ensemble struggled for their daily existence. One can observe similar signs of activities in the development of another Jewish theatre—Habimah. Contrary to The Vilna Troupe, this theatre did not disband and fade into history but eventually found its home in Tel Aviv.

The founder of Habimah, Nahum Zemach, was a young Hebrew language teacher. Around 1911 he organized an amateur Hebrew theatre in Bialystok, modern-day Poland, and in 1912 the first performance of the group was shown in Vilnius. Following this first performance, the theatre then moved to Warsaw, performed at the Zionist congress in Vienna, and then returned to Vilnius in 1914 (Agranovsky 2014, 220). By this time, the troupe had come to possess the name Habimah. Although the work of the company was gaining momentum, their activities came to a halt due to Zemach's illness and the outbreak of the First World War. Following this disruption, Zemach undertook the same theatre initiatives in Moscow. Yet, this time he was supported by Stanislavsky and the Moscow Art Theatre, and opened Habimah Theatre Studio in October 1918. As Habimah's historian Mendel Kohansky noted years later, '[i]t still remains a mystery how he succeeded in not only obtaining permission for the studio to exist in Moscow, where Hebrew was otherwise banned but in gaining official recognition for it' (Kohansky 1969, 25). After presenting its first performances to the Moscow-elite audiences in 1918 and 1919, the studio started working on An-sky's play *The Dybbuk*. The script was already well known to the regulars of the Moscow Art Theatre and Stanislavsky encouraged its realization in the Hebrew language. He proposed that the play be directed by his pupil Evgenii Vakhtangov, who later became the head of the studio. Unlike The Vilna Troupe, the rehearsals of the performance lasted not thirty days, but more than three years. It took Vakhtangov an extended period of time to unlock the secrets of staging the Hassidic play. In fact, most fortuitous was that Vakhtangov had an opportunity to meet a Jewish rabbi while staying in hospital and used their interactions to learn Hassidic customs and life. It was during these conversations, and after having observed the rabbi, that Vakhtangov found the key gesture for the performance. This gesture was then integrated into the dances and movements of the actors. Help also came from the composer of the performance, Yoel Engel, who had accompanied An-sky in his folkloric trip to Galicia and was well acquainted with Hassidic music. Rounding out the presentation of the show, the sets of the performance were created by a Soviet Avant-garde painter Nathan Altman.

As in the case of *The Dybbuk* performed by the Vilners, Habimah's performance also became a sensation. The troupe was first invited to Leningrad to perform *The Dybbuk*, and then returned to Moscow and continued to stage other plays in Hebrew. However, audiences were limited, and the troupe decided to go on a world tour in 1926. As in the case of The Vilna Troupe, the actors of Habimah were received as stars of the modern Jewish theatre in Riga, Kaunas, Warsaw, and Łódź. The group continued to Austria, Germany, France, and finally moved to the United States at the end of 1927. The tour in America began with success but, as with The Vilna Troupe, ended in considerable losses. This led to internal conflicts and, like with The Vilna Troupe, a split. Zemach and a small group of his followers stayed in the United States, while the majority of the troupe returned to Europe, though not to the Slavic nations, but to Berlin. With the help of the German Jewish community, Habimah succeeded in collecting the necessary amount of money for the journey to Palestine where it sought to find its home. This dream was, however, challenging to fulfil; the Jewish community in Palestine was small and struggled with the difficulties of everyday life. In 1929, after a year and a half, the troupe returned to Berlin, where tours to other European cities were organized. New performances of the group did not stimulate the expected interest, and the penniless troupe returned to Palestine in 1932 (Lewy 2016, 62). Although the situation in Europe started to deteriorate, Habimah continued to organize tours. The troupe performed in Kaunas in 1938, where it was positively received by the press and the Jewish community. Finally, in 1945, after years of wandering and struggle, Habimah had the opportunity to build its theatre in Tel Aviv, and in 1954 it was given the status of National Theatre of Israel.

As the travel itineraries of both theatre companies show, Jewish troupes moved to places where the largest Jewish communities could be expected. And the parallels do not end there. The most important stops for both troupes were Kaunas in Lithuania, Warsaw and Łódź in Poland, Berlin in Germany, Vienna in Austria, London in Great Britain, and New York in the United States. Numerous other less significant stops helped spread the word about these extraordinary troupes. These two theatre companies, one producing in Yiddish and the other in the Hebrew language, reflected two conflicting ideologies that nurtured the Jewish nation at the beginning of the twentieth century. The Yiddishists sought to maintain the Jewish diaspora across the world, whereas the Hebrewists strove to establish their homeland in Palestine and help with the creation of a state. The activities of these two theatres illustrate the tensions of this turbulent period and allow for an understanding of Jewish theatre activities *between the worlds*.

As the descriptions of both performances show, Herman, of The Vilna Troupe, and Vakhtangov, of Habimah, were primarily concerned with revealing the symbolic, transmigratory elements of the play, and did so in their own, yet quite similar, ways. Herman, for instance, added a prologue and an epilogue to the play, whereas Vakhtangov added a long Beggar's Dance to the second act and thus changed the overall structure of the piece (Fishman 1980, 43–58). Both directors merged the third and the fourth act and thus shortened An-sky's version. Both were also interested in the form of the performance, so the roles of the set designer and the composer were given higher status than was typical of the time. As descriptions of the sets indicate, an important role was attributed to the opening scene of the performance, especially regarding the choice of the curtains. The Vilna Troupe used two curtains to open the performance, the second one being a replica of the Jewish prayer shawl, which served as a frame for the interiors of a synagogue. Alternatively, Habimah's performance started with the opening of a heavy grey/off-white curtain which also revealed a small traditional synagogue. Both stage designers, Kadison and Altman, used a palette of sombre colours, thus adding to the mystical atmosphere of the action. As the images of the performances reveal, both artists avoided any realism on stage and used distorted, expressionistic forms in the set design.

The interpretation of the costumes was also of significance. Kadison integrated references to Jewish religious rituals in the costumes and thus achieved a poetic visual effect. Altman, on the other hand, concentrated on creating a distorted, grotesque image. His characters were distinctly expressionistic, with exaggerated makeup. This visual interpretation of Altman demanded from the actors a certain stylization of their movements. Not only did the movements have a particular rhythm and expressiveness, but they also amplified the way that the actors were speaking. It resembled singing, more than anything else, and thus a stronger emotion could be extracted from the text. The biblical *Song of Songs* also played an important role in both performances. In Herman's performance this song was used for the final scene, where actors sang together, hand in hand, and addressed the audiences as if affirming the possibility of a reconciliation between the past and the modern world, as well as between the nations. Such a scene had all the necessary elements to create a strong emotional relationship with the audiences and to leave them transfixed and transported into the performance. Habimah's performance was not only about reconciliation, but also transmitted a political message. The Beggar's Dance served to juxtapose two ideologies, the proletarian and the bourgeois one. This message was also identifiable in the decoration. As Pearl Fishman noted, a translucent wedding canopy hanging above stage left represented 'both the joyousness of the occasion and the revolution' (Fishman 1980, 51).

The creative impact of the stage directors Vakhtangov and Herman refined the play in significant ways. They both achieved success in broadening its appeal for the various audiences they encountered. The two directors also succeeded in creating a story where theatricality played the most important role and led audiences to experience the *between two worlds* that was encoded in An-sky's text.

The Transmigratory and Transcendent

The success of *The Dybbuk*, as well as its recognition in Yiddish and Hebrew languages, confirms that despite the choice of the language the play was first and foremost recognized as a love story gesturing to the complexities of transmigratory backgrounds. Full of mysticism, rituals, and exorcism, it intrigued European and American audiences because of its transcendent aspects, which were revealed through An-sky's interpretation of Jewish folklore. The play was also a story about a search for personal identity. The events of An-sky's life show that this search was complicated and led the writer into dangerous environments and situations numerous times. His personal identity can be seen as possessing a liquid quality and tended to transform itself according to the material conditions that life presented. In An-sky's case his identity was torn between his Jewish origins and the Russian environment, and between the choice of three languages, Russian, Yiddish, and Hebrew. The character of

Khanan revealed these inner torments that An-sky and the Jews of his generation were confronted with.

The Vilna Troupe and Habimah, as with many other Jewish artists, were forced to live as nomads, migrating from place to place to survive. Although the troupes performed *The Dybbuk* successfully in all places where the Jewish community had significant presence (Kaunas, Warsaw, Łódź, Berlin, Vienna, London, New York) their success was temporary and did not lead to more secure lives. One can conclude that migration was, for the Jewish troupes in the first half of the twentieth century, a natural and necessary condition of existence.

References

Agranovsky, Genrikh. 2014. *Oni zdes zhili*. Vilnius: Versus Aureus.

An-sky, S. A. 2016. *1915 Diary of S. An-sky: A Russian Jewish Writer at the Eastern Front*. Translated by Polly Zavadivker. Bloomington: Indiana University Press.

Atlas-Koch, Galit and Leonard Cohen. 2011. 'The Bad Father, the Sinful Son, and the Wild Ghost: A Psychoanalytic Exploration of the Dybbuk.' *Psychoanalytic Perspectives*, 8 (2), 238–251.

Caplan, Debra. 2018. *Yiddish Empire. The Vilna Troupe, Jewish Theater, and the Art of Itinerancy*. Ann Abor: The University of Michigan.

Deleuze, Gilles and Félix Guattari. 2005. *A Thousand Plateaus*. Translated by Brian Massumi. Minneapolis: University of Minnesota Press.

Elior, Rachel. 2008. *Dybbuks and Jewish Women in Social History, Mysticism and Folklore*. Jerusalem: Urim Publications.

Fishman, Pearl. 1980. 'Vakhtangov's "The Dybbuk".' *TDR: The Drama Review*, 24 (3), 43–58.

Kadison, Luba and Joseph Buloff. 1992. *On Stage, Off Stage. Memories of a Lifetime in the Yiddish Theatre*. Cambridge: Harvard University Press.

Kohansky, Mendel. 1969. *The Hebrew Theatre: Its First Fifty Years*. Jerusalem: Israel Universities Press.

Lewy, Tom. 2016. *Zwischen Allen Bühnen: Die Jeckes Und Das Hebräische Theater 1933–1948*. Translated by Sebastian Schirrmeister. Berlin: Neofelis Verlag.

Luchte, James. 2012. *Pythagoras and the Doctrine of Transmigration: Wandering Souls*. London: Bloomsbury Academic.

Safran, Gabriella. 2010. *Wandering Soul: The Dybbuk's Creator, S. An-Sky*. Cambridge: Harvard University Press.

CHAPTER 58

Indian Circus: A Melting Pot of Migrant Artists, Performativity, and Race

Aastha Gandhi

In this chapter, I delve into understanding the unique cosmopolitan identity of Indian circus artists, which necessarily developed through living and performing in the circus community, and that existed beyond the binaries of colonizer/colonized and local/global. Of particular relevance to this discussion are the different positions and socio-economic status occupied by individuated groups within Indian circus's changing cultural milieu. I examine this cosmopolitan identity through Indian circus's changing performance idioms, which have been shaped by interactions between different racial groups. Acts and group repertoires evolved through travel, exchanges of artists and trainers between circuses, and artist co-habitation. For instance, individual artists working in Indian circuses, who carried with them a certain skillset learnt from their traditional communities, were part of local networks, which in turn connected them to the larger global network of circuses through international artists. Here, I evoke 'network' in a Latourian sense of the term in his Actor-Network Theory (Latour 1996). With more mobility and exposure, artists gained greater access and exposure to a diverse range of skills. The circus renewed its identity, even if in minutiae, with each encounter of a different skill and a diverse art form.

The circus, since its inception in the colonial period, has always been a space for migrant and travelling performers. From Europeans in 1880s and Russians in 1990s to Africans, Mongolians, East Europeans, and other Asians in 2000s, the presence of different ethnicities in Indian circuses has been a major factor in its rise and acceptance as a popular form. However, each successive ethnic group to join the Indian circus has found itself peripheral to other ethnic

A. Gandhi (✉)
Ambedkar University, Delhi, India

© The Author(s), under exclusive license to Springer Nature Switzerland AG 2023
Y. Meerzon, S. E. Wilmer (eds.), *The Palgrave Handbook of Theatre and Migration*, https://doi.org/10.1007/978-3-031-20196-7_58

groups that occupied already established presence within the community throughout the last century. This dynamic has defined racial interactions within Indian circuses, including in the earliest established circuses of the 1880s in which performers belonged to different ethnic groups from the subcontinent.

The cosmopolitan identity of the Indian circus artist has been especially shaped by racial interactions throughout the last century: firstly, local Malayalee artists with European artists in both Indian and colonial circuses; secondly, Indian artists with Nepalese artists; and thirdly, Indian artists with African, European, and Mongolian artists. Focusing my analysis through the differing migration trajectories of the groups identified above, I will examine how the presence of dominant racial groups in Indian circuses continues to define the cosmopolitan identity of the circus artist.

A Cosmopolitan Performing Identity: Beyond the Colonizer-Colonized Binary

Circus artists who travelled extensively worked within diverse groups. Performances evolved when itinerant artists encountered a different community of artists. These artists then embodied a hybrid identity, rather than a singular one. The embodied experiences of hybridity are defined by what Royona Mitra terms as *new interculturalism* (2015, 15). Yana Meerzon further developed this concept and suggests that cosmopolitan theatre 'represents a conceptual, processual, embodied lived condition driven by one's own multiple affiliation to cultures, nations and faiths' (2020, 19). Can circus then be seen as what Meerzon terms as a 'cosmopolitan performance' with the performer as the 'cosmopolitan subject' (2020, 4)? What is the subjectivity of this cosmopolitan identity which is 'neither local/national nor international/global, but both at once' (2020, 13)? What are the transcultural modes of experience that these contact zones create?

Even when there was a majority of Indian artists performing in Indian circuses, there was also the presence of Europeans in both local and colonial circuses. For example, Chiarini's Circus, Harmston's Grand Circus, Wilson's Circus, Cooke's Circus, and others were some of the colonial circuses regularly touring India from late nineteenth century. Most circuses travelled on the same circuits and had exchanges of artists and trainers, and it was not uncommon for international artists to perform with local circuses and local artists (and vice versa). Amongst the international artists who were running colonial circuses in India, S.O. Abel, a gymnast and animal trainer, was also performing with a local circus, the Great Bengal Circus (Ghosh 2014). Similarly, Kannan Bombayo, an Indian tight-rope walker, travelled with the Canestrallis, an Italian circus family, through India in 1920s.

What was the identity performed by the local artists? How was their cosmopolitanism reflected in their performative presence inside the ring and received by a cosmopolitan audience outside of it? The local Indian artist was trained in multiple indigenous physical cultures. By indigenous, I refer to the traditional performance practices which were imbibed from one's community. These practices and knowledge systems were passed on only to the members of that particular community. The blending of skills made the local artist uniquely hybrid (in comparison to their international artist colleagues) and also cosmopolitan—essentially local, but also made global through their exchanges with international artists and performances in international circuses. This cosmopolitan identity created a unique experience inside the ring. Bombayo, for instance, kept redefining his rope act with newer elements, tricks, equipment, and costumes picked up during his travels. Octavio Canestralli, a friend and co-artist of Bombayo, replaced the coir rope in Bombayo's performance with Manila rope, which was more flexible and more popular in Europe. He also replaced the bamboo frames with A-shaped metallic frames, which were sturdier, and (unlike the bamboo frames) the metallic frames were rigged with bungees at each end (Jando 2007).

Seeing the circus artist through Meerzon's concept of the cosmopolitan subject of the hypermodern world, I find that such artist is also 'always in the process of being re-fractured and redefined,' undergoing a transformation where the sense of self is always being redefined through the act of encounter (2020, 5). This process, in which self-identity undergoes re-fracturing and redefining, is relevant to study the relationship between the colonizer and the colonized. But can the cosmopolitan identity of the circus artist be confined to these binaries? The circus artists travelling and performing with diverse circus communities refuse to be perceived through a singular lens. As the example of Bombayo suggests, performers added to their repertoire of skills through their performing, living, and working within the diverse communities of travelling circuses. With more mobility, artists gained greater access and exposure to a diverse range of skills, enhancing the cosmopolitan character of the performance. They challenged binary notions of the colonizer/colonized and pushed beyond the confines of racial and nationalistic perception. The artist, who is a colonial subject, when performing a cosmopolitan identity, is neither limited to that self nor bound by the collective memory of a colonized nation. The artist's subjectivity, emerging through experiences of diverse circus communities, lies in the hybrid and outside the binary of colonizer-colonized. It forms a parallel colonial history of a nation that is absent from recorded and documented histories.

Kerala: The Breeding Ground for Trainers, Artists, and Owners (1880s to 1980s)

In this section, I will lay out the historical trajectory of circus identity through macro shifts in migration patterns. I examine three different periods of migration and use case studies of performance to illustrate the cosmopolitan identity of the Malayalee circus artist.

Indigenous circus practice in India, from the establishment of the earliest local circuses in 1880s, evolved to create a unique identity that was distinct from colonial practices. Local circus practice did not wholly negate colonial methods but rather encompassed their techniques. The form grew as an amalgamation of Western gymnastics, circus acrobatics, and hybrid indigenous forms. The formative years of Indian circus practice emerged in the circus *kalari* (traditional gymnasium) of Kerala, which disseminated knowledge of physical, dietary, medicinal, and martial training regimes. The circus *kalari* grew into a space where a multitude of physical forms were taught to artistes from different backgrounds, irrespective of their caste and community. This is an example of the diverse milieu from which a new, hybrid circus language grew.

In 1888, Keeleri Kunhikannan established the first circus training institute, the All India Circus Training Hall, located in Thalassery on the coast of Malabar region of northern Kerala. The training method devised by Kunhikannan for circus acts combined *kalaripayattu* (a traditional martial arts form from Kerala) and his knowledge of indigenous systems together with Western gymnastics (Nisha 2020, 46). He was trained in indigenous physical sports and in Punjabi wrestling forms and practices (Nisha 2017, 19). Gradually, Kunhikannan added single and double trapeze, weightlifting, forehead pole, shell on parallel bar, cycle feats, slanting wire, and various somersaults to his repertoire (Champad 2013, 14). He increased the number of horizontal bars to three instead of one. The young circus enthusiasts, though trained in Indian forms, primarily followed the methods of colonial circuses by watching and learning Western drills. I speculate that the training process must have involved reworking what they witnessed in European circuses, using their own technique in Indian martial arts along with other forms of specialization and improvisation. This created a unique experience inside the ring with the presence of indigenous bodies trained in foreign performance practices. The artists' performative presence inside the ring was confined neither to the local nor to the global but became 'cosmopolitan.'

Kunhikannan's circus *kalari* shaped the circus as a commune. Living in an artistic commune is another example of a cosmopolitan lifestyle. In India, circuses were unique among other performance practices by being the only space where people from different caste backgrounds lived and worked together. The foundation of circus is that it thrives on communal and inclusive living, giving equal status to all: performers, technicians, and assistants, most of whom were from lower castes (Skidmore 2014, 224). Kunhikannan transformed the caste-based space of traditional *kalari* into a secular space by training and recruiting students from underprivileged castes (Nisha 2017, 19).

The circus was soon adopted as a sub-culture in the Indian subcontinent and the city of Thalassery particularly boasted of providing the highest number of circus artists from 1880s to 1980s. By 1920s, the artists trained under Kunhikannan had accumulated the infrastructure and capital to either buy or establish their own circuses. Many of these Malayalee artists went on to create some of the biggest circus companies in India, thus establishing their monopoly in this art form. Prof C. Ambu and K. M. Kunjikannan Nair (Great Bombay Circus), Gemini Sankaran (Gemini Circus), Bal Gopalan and K. K. Achuthan (Great Oriental Circus), and Prof. K. Damodaran (Kamala Circus) were the first of many stalwarts (Gopalan 1966, 8; Champad 2013, 22–25). Almost '20,000 out of an estimated 35,000 circus artists nation-wide and 90 per cent of the major circus companies originated from Tellicherry [now Thalassery] and neighbouring areas' (Pillai 1987).

Migration to the Gulf and Deterioration of Circus: 1970s Onwards

Gradually, the presence of Malayalee artists in circuses witnessed a decline. By the 1970s, even highly skilled Malayalee artists were leaving circuses, opting to work in local *beedi* (handmade cigarettes) factories for half the pay to lead a more settled life closer to family. The situation worsened through the 1980s, as working in a circus became a stigma for Malayalees in Thalassery (Pillai 1987). The scenario had acutely changed from 1940s and 1950s when many parents used to send their children to circus camps to make an earning (Radhakrishnan 1996). In the 1980s, the children who lived and trained in circuses in their formative years refused to pursue it as a career, often opting for a job in the Middle East or to pursue a university degree. Kunhikannan's centre continued to exist in name but for all purposes was non-functional. There were limited measures taken by the state government to improve the condition of the circus (Vaidyanathan 1981). Kandi Kumaran, a circus agent in Thalassery of the time, states in a news article that 'up to the late '70s, hundreds of people used to swamp my house with requests to join some circus or the other. Today, even after a house-to-house search, we can attract barely 100 people in a year. The circus companies today are getting their people from Nepal' (Pillai 1987). In the late 1970s, there were twenty-six Thalassery-based circus companies, but only fourteen survived into the following decade. Well-known names like Kamala Three Ring Circus and Bharat Circus had to pull down their tops permanently by the 1980s (Pillai 1987). With the Left Democratic Front forming a coalition government led by the Communist Party of India (Marxist), its welfare-driven, pro-people policies placed greater emphasis on the education of the youth and children in Kerala, and generally created more employment opportunities in the area. These factors are understood to have impacted the numbers of those opting for circus careers within Thalassery district.

Migration to the Arabian Gulf had become a significant feature in Kerala as a whole, a common response to an economic slump and chronic unemployment. The economic boom within the Gulf countries gave international migration a considerable boost and acted as a big economic liberating force, and Thalassery, like other small towns, had become just another 'Gulf town' (Pillai 1987). The educated artists opted for more lucrative jobs in the Middle East, or for government jobs within India, both of which were considered to be more reputable than the circus, even if it did not pay as well in comparison. Beginning in 1960s, migration reached its peak in terms of both numbers and remittances between 1979 and 1984. Filippo Osella and Caroline Osella note that these migrants were exclusively young males, the majority of whom were in unskilled or semi-skilled jobs and with an education level at or below SSLC (Secondary School Leaving certificate); this was similar to the class earlier opting for circus employment, but now opting for contractual jobs in the Gulf given the chance of 'rapid and vast accumulation of wealth by village standards' (2000, 119). Simultaneously, the number of Malayalees joining circus as performers or other casual labour drastically reduced, opting instead for professions which involved more skilled work. Even if there is no direct data to mark this shift, a larger connection between migration of labour towards the Gulf and the loss of creative labour in circuses is suggested by interviews and reports of the period.

In parallel to these changes to employment circumstances in circuses, the post-1970s generation of artists from Thalassery were unwilling to perform risky tricks (Pillai 1987). This can be read as one of the causes for deterioration in the skills and techniques of the performers. Even though newer and more innovative acts had replaced earlier ones, I conjecture that one of the primary causes for a change in circus acts and repertoire could be because of the changing demography of circus artists. By the 1980s, some of the most scintillating and daring acts had ceased to be performed in the ring. Daring acts put the body at a higher risk, had visible danger to the performer, or challenged the body to its utmost limit. For instance, jumping, leaping, and somersaulting on a single horizontal bar is routine, but doing these gymnastics across seven horizontal bars would be a daring act. Clutching the trapeze bar by the feet would put the performer's body in a more precarious position than the one where it was held by the knees, thus creating a heightened visceral experience for the audience. Such skills and techniques were gradually disappearing from the circus ring. Sreedharan Champad and various circus managers whom I met during my field work informed me that this moment marked the entry of the artists from Nepal. Articles appearing in dailies (Vegas 1988; Radhakrishnan 1996) as well as my other interlocutors from Thalassery confirmed the same. Even though it cannot be proven as either a direct effect of growing employment opportunities and economic liberation (whether in the Gulf or at home), the reduction of Malayalee artists in circuses—which is not to say owners, who continued to remain majority Malayalees—can be read as a symptomatic of worsening economic conditions.

Nepalese Migrants and the Changing Demography of Circus: 1980s Onwards

Nepalese artists had started replacing Malayalee artists in Indian circuses since the 1980s (*The Times of India* 1989, 8). Newspaper reports from 1980s reason that this was economically beneficial for the circus, as the former would work for less wages and were reported to be more hardworking than the latter.

A crucial question follows: given the socio-economic status of Nepalese artists, who facilitated their movement across the border? Champad states that some Nepalese artists and other workers who had already established ties within Indian circus became agents for circus companies and established headquarters in Kolkata for the purposes of facilitating new Nepalese migration. These artists-turned-agents 'brought hundreds of children aged between ten and fifteen from Nepal, especially from Hettoda [sic], which became a name like Thalassery in the history of Indian circus' (Champad 2013, 120). Often, these agents are referred to as 'uncle-figures' who arrange movements across the border. Khushi and Sita, originally from Solapur, Nepal, informed me that they joined the circus in India with the help of one middle-man whom they referred to as their *maama* (maternal uncle) (interviewed at Great Apollo Circus on May 18, 2016). So too did Pinky and Shiny, from Hetauda, Nepal, at Global Circus in Kerala (interviewed on May 5, 2018).

India is considered a preferred destination for Nepalese migrants because of its proximity, open border, cultural affinities, easily convertible currency, easy and affordable travelling options, and histories of migration within families and villages (Bhattrai 2007). Nepal and India share an 'open' border as per the agreements of a bilateral treaty signed in 1950. According to the treaty, Nepalese and Indians can travel and work across the border and are to be treated at par with the Indian citizens. The 1991 Census of Nepal recorded that absentee population from Nepal towards India constituted 89.2 per cent of the total migrants, the first choice for a large illiterate or lowly literate, unskilled, and marginal population of rural Nepal (Bhattrai 2007). Most of these migrants constitute 'unskilled,' 'skilled,' and seasonal labour.

The open border between Nepal and India also became a major factor for a continuous flow of Nepalese migrant artists to Indian circuses which began in the latter half of 1980s (Champad 2013, 120). Even though no specific records exist in any state migration records, it is known that circus was a lucrative option. Champad offers that, in Indian circuses, artists from Nepal, in addition to middle-men and agents, found their network through Nepalese cooks and guards already working in the circus in the 1970s (interviewed at Thalassery on May 7, 2016). My findings and interviews with artists revealed that while women migrants from Nepal were trained in acrobatics and other acts, the men continued to serve as assistants, guards, and general labour on the circus grounds. The women performers blended in with the circus commune and were trained in multiple acts such as tight rope, cycling, equestrian act, shooting, and performing with hoola-hoops.

The circus is seen as the one remaining performing arts industry in India that recruits artists from the poorest regions. The present demography of circus artists constitutes some middle-aged Indian artists, but mostly young performers. These are the first-generation artists who have migrated from Bihar, North-East India, and other eastern states, or are from Nepal or Bangladesh, with all of them assimilating into a singular identity—that of a cosmopolitan circus identity. They perform similar acts, live in the same tents, marry artists from different communities, thus living their cosmopolitanism not only through the performance aesthetics within the ring but also outside of it.

The circus performer is placed on the lowest rung of artists of performance forms in India, with their identity often fluctuating between a performer, labourer, and gymnast/acrobat. Most first-generation circus artists that I interviewed belonged to impoverished regions with minimal or no education. Many of them were forced by their financial predicament to migrate to India, where the circus provided them with minimum means of survival. Basanthi Kumari, a successful circus artist from Nepal, had already made her mark in the circus through her exemplary performances in flying trapeze, rocket trapeze, contortion, and cycle feats in the 1980s. She is quoted in a newspaper article as saying, 'I can never dream of making so much money in Nepal. Every time I go back home, my sister, cousins, and others want to come back with me to join the circus' (Pillai 1987).

There is a marked presence of different racial and gendered bodies in these performances. Therefore, reading the bodies, expressions, postures, and gestures becomes relevant. As E. Ravindran (a circus trainer) notes, 'the fact that they [Nepalese artists] are fair also helps' (Pillai 1987). Ravindran's observation hints towards the preference for a certain body type, complexion, and racial features in this commercially driven entertainment form. It is imperative to note that even though the first generation of artists from Kerala rose up in class status and went on to establish their own circuses, or bought circuses of other owners, this has not been the case with artists from Nepal, as most of them were women who have remained socioeconomically marginalized. Moreover, they have no professional status in the Indian context. Most often, the real names of female circus artists are not even revealed to the audiences. This was often reiterated by many performers and circus managers during the field work. They keep pseudo-names which often change as they move from one circus to the other. What is eliminated through this is the association of their skill with their identity, and thus the absence of star status and popularity for the female artists which pushes them into oblivion.

It bears to mention here that since the early 2000s, when NGOs in both India and Nepal were becoming more proactive against trafficking, there was a major shift in the discourse around circus. Having received complaints of child trafficking primarily from the regions of Hetauda and Makwanpur in Nepal, where allegedly over 700 girls from a small region had left to work in Indian circuses, Bachpan Bachao Andolan (an India-based children's rights movement) conducted child rescue raids in a few circuses in 2004. This culminated in filing a petition against child labour in circuses in 2006 and resulted in a total ban on child labour in circuses by the Supreme Court of India in a landmark judgment (Bachpan Bachao Andolan vs. Union of India and Others 2011). The discourse around the ensuing public campaign against trafficking and child labour made the circus appear like an exploitative entity. As a result, the circus has disappeared from the urban public imagination with a diminishing audience, an indifferent state, and declining skills that have further pushed it to the point of extinction. The celebratory narrative of these villages in Nepal producing circus stars in 1980s had changed to that of victimization and exploitation by 2000s (Gandhi and Dutt 2017).

Neoliberal Policies and International Migration: 2000s

In recent times, after the ban on child labour from circuses, an economic and artistic crisis in the Indian circus has led to a desperate effort to survive through showcasing more and more acts by African performers. Different types of migration and assimilation are determined by economic, racial, and ethnic relationship. Globalization and neoliberal policies hastened the flow of migrant artists into India, and international performers from Kenya, Ethiopia, Vietnam, Mongolia, and eastern Europe were hired by Indian circuses. Mongolian and European troupes are mainly hired for the high season, whereas African troupes are present throughout the year. In Indian circuses, Africans are usually the star performers except when eclipsed by Europeans in the high season.

I stipulate that there must be a hierarchy of income amongst the international artists. Within this hierarchy, artists from Nepal (as discussed earlier) appear to be the lowest paid, even below the rate paid to Indian artists. Comparatively, African artists appear to receive higher salaries than those paid to Indian artists. They perform on annual contracts and are seen more frequently in Indian circuses. However, Mongolian, Russian, or European artists are only seen in big circuses and during the high season when there are more audiences and thus higher box office sales, indicating that they must occupy the highest rung in terms of pay scale. With the general decline in Indian circus, and therefore reduced earnings even in the peak season, the presence of European artists in Indian circus is on the decline. This is indicative of the fact that training, skill, and expertise play a significant role while determining the salary of an artist, but race and ethnicity might also serve as important criteria.

It bears mentioning that cultural exchange has been an integral part of China's 'package strategy' in generating and increasing its international relations with developing countries (Shinn and Eisenman 2012, 3). Training in circus arts provided by Chinese masters to artists in developing countries is one such part of its diplomatic agenda. The training programs of African performers in circus skills has its historical origins in Cold War-era performance networks: either the Chinese masters visit African countries to teach them the skills, or selected students from Africa are invited to training schools in China. Jessica Kendall notes that growing political connections between China and various African countries have led directly to cultural exchanges between the two primarily over the past forty years (2018). However, a popular cultural form like circus makes itself available to be adopted by any group or community that takes it up. Even if the practices imbibed and embodied by troupes of African artists are derived from traditional Chinese acrobatics forms, this engagement lends a new identity to the emergent form: the circus act remains neither exclusively Chinese nor becomes absolute African, but rather represents a globalised culture.

In this context, Meerzon's self-as-other formulation for modelling the identity of the cosmopolitan subject (2020, 6) is a particularly potent vehicle for probing how the differential aesthetics of the Indian circus' form are received by an alien group of artists. In my observation, the African body in performance does not exhibit the circus act as something imposed; instead, the self intermingles with the other by allowing it to assimilate. The subjectivity of the artist further determines how this aesthetic encounter in a circus is received by the artist. How does this aesthetic encounter affect the artist's self and his subjectivity? Shifting the discussion from self (us) and other (them) paradigm to the self-as-other formula, I find that the cosmopolitan persona of the circus artist is constructed out of a divided self. It is the subjectivity of this divided self which is staged inside the ring. It is imperative to ask why these figures of a divided self are obscured from circus history. Why do they not find any space in the larger performance archives? Their multiple subjectivities could not be bracketed into a singular subjectivity. The archives, however, follow a linear method of categorization which has no place for complexities. Archives derive from knowledge of a singular subjectivity and not multiple or divided subjectivities. The everchanging complex circus body therefore does not fit into this order.

This raises additional pertinent questions: What are the forces which dominate the cultural spaces? Does the performing body display and perform a certain nation-ness? Does it perform the politics underlying the creation of state-driven and state-monitored intercultural exchange? What are the state-drawn boundaries inscribed on the performing body of the artists? Even if the boundaries were so, they seem to have been erased from their performance. Instead of typical circus costumes, African performers opt for a costume with animal prints or one with a local flavour. Clearly the music, distinctly African with fast beats and rhythm, brings an ethnic character to the act, but does not always remain specific to its source culture, replacing it with other upbeat rhythmic Western music thus pushing beyond the boundaries of nationality. Within Indian circuses, the African troupes may still be identified as a certain racial community which is unfamiliar and international. However, this identity does not remain confined to a racial type, as it is integrated into the cosmopolitan character of circus. In Chinese diplomatic relations with African countries where circus creates the dialogue, it is imperative to ask where the performing body is placed in these politically driven programs. Is the performance only shaped by the nationalist agenda, or does it create a 'performing identity' beyond the hegemonic ideas of the state? In the case of African artists, the norms of possible hegemonizing of one culture by another are overturned and the progressive and disruptive potential is retained.

International artists carry a different cultural capital. It is the same socio-economic conditions which forced them to migrate to India to work as a circus artist that are experienced more or less equally in different places in the world (Nepal, Mongolia, East Europe, and Africa) which now bring them together through professionalism, despite belonging to different ethnicities which usually divide rather than unite other communities. In my reading, these negotiations between communities across networks do not carry a national or racial characteristic anymore. When taken up by performers from different racial, national, and/or ethnic groups, performance vocabularies change in form and identity and become a part of the universal circus identity. The process of cultural exchange is not a mere swapping of certain aesthetics under imposed structures of state diplomacy, as in the case of Chinese diplomatic exchanges with African troupes, but also, at other times, a process willingly taken up by artists.

Conclusion

In this article, I have discussed how circus practice in India has always been constituted by multiple identities, regionalities, and ethnicities, and situated these conversations within larger debates about how a cultural form might be seen as one regional or national entity. Circus artists are compelled to join or leave the circus because of demographic changes, labour, economic migration, and changing laws. Migration of circus artists to India has taken various forms, whether it be the Malayalees who ruled the circus ring from the late nineteenth century onwards, the migration of Nepalese artists throughout the 1980s, or African circus artists who have risen to dominate the ring during the current period of globalization. These artists are driven not by a choice, but by the necessity to migrate and find newer audiences and markets for their skill.

The encounters between circus artists are configured by multiple forces: state, commercial, diplomatic, and others. The performing bodies which travel across these networks stage the underlying socio-political crosscurrents through the many cosmopolitanisms which they perform inside the circus ring and live outside it. Circus takes an alternate position with respect to political and economic network structures that are propagated between nations. Culture is not a fixed practice, but a porous arrangement, which makes these multiple interactions and interjections plausible. Circus displays the openness to other influences, urges to move across cultural boundaries, and challenges 'more traditional perceptions of national cultures as integrated and bounded' (Gilbert and Lo 2009, 8). Circus, thus, in many ways can be said to be one space that has constantly pushed the boundaries of nation, ethnicity, race, and gender, and it continues to do so.

References

Bhattrai, Raju. 2007. 'Open Borders, Closed Citizenship: Nepali Labour Migrants in Delhi.' Paper presented at *International Migration, Multi-Local Livelihoods and Human Security: Perspectives from Europe, Asia and Africa*, August 30–31, 2007, Institute of Social Studies, Netherlands.

Champad, Sreedharan. 2013. *An Album of Indian Big Tops*. Houston: Strategic Book Publishing.

Gandhi, Aastha and Bishnupriya Dutt. 2017. 'Laws and Marginalized Bodies: Sex Trafficking, Child Labour and Circus as a Site for Negotiations.' In *Gendered Citizenship Manifestations and Performance*, edited by Bishnupriya Dutt, Janelle Reinelt, and Shrinkhla Sahai, 291–308. London: Palgrave Macmillan.

Ghosh, Anirban. 2014. 'The Tropic Trapeze: Colonial Circus in India.' Unpublished Ph.D. Dissertation. Maximillians Universität, Munich.

Gilbert, Helen, and Jacqueline Lo. 2009. *Performance and Cosmopolitics: Cross-Cultural Transactions in Australasia*. London: Palgrave Macmillan.

Gopalan, Keezhanthy. 1966. 'The Indian Circus. Decline of a Great Tradition.' *The Times of India*, January 23, 1966.

Supreme Court of India. 2011. 'Bachpan Bachao Andolan v. Union of India and Others Writ Petition (C) 51 of 2006.' *Supreme Court Cases*.

Jando, Dominique. 2007. *Kannan Bombayo*. Accessed November 15, 2020. http://www.circopedia.org/Kannan_Bombayo.

Kendall, Jessica. 2018. 'Training Like a "Native": Alternative Acrobatic Practices of Sudanese Circus Performers on Cultural Exchange in China.' Working Paper presented at *Circus Histories and Theories Conference*. Johannesburg: Centre for Indian Studies in Africa, University of Witwatersrand. June, 2018.

Latour, Bruno. 1996. 'On Actor-Network Theory: A Few Clarifications.' *Soziale Welt* 47 (H.4), 369–381.

Meerzon, Yana. 2020. *Performance, Subjectivity, Cosmopolitanism*. Cham: Palgrave Macmillan.

Mitra, Royona. 2015. *Akram Khan: Dancing New Interculturalism*. London: Palgrave Macmillan.

Osella, Filippo, and Caroline Osella. 2000. *Social Mobility in Kerala: Modernity and Identity in Conflict*. London: Pluto Press.

P.R. Nisha. 2020. *Jumbos and Jumping Devils: A Social History of Indian Circus*. New Delhi: Oxford University Press.

———. 2017. 'The Circus Man Who Knew Too Much.' *Economic and Political Weekly*, LII(34): 18–19.

Pillai, Sreedhar. 1987. 'Tellicherry: Times Change in The Once Booming Circus Town.' *The Times of India*, December 15.

Radhakrishnan, M. G. 1996. 'Hard Life Forces Inhabitants Of a Kerala Circus Town Off the Profession.' *India Today*, October 15. Accessed April 2, 2020. https://www.indiatoday.in/magazine/offtrack/story/19961015-hard-life-forces-inhabitants-of-a-kerala-circus-town-off-the-profession-833305-1996-10-15.

Shinn, David H, and Joshua Eisenman. 2012. *China and Africa: A Century of Engagement*. Philadelphia: University of Pennsylvania Press.

Skidmore, Jamie. 2014. 'Defying Death: Children in the Indian Circus.' In *Entertaining Children: The Participation of Youth in the Entertainment Industry*, edited by Gillian Arrighi and Victor Emeljanow, 219–233. Hampshire: Palgrave Macmillan.

The Times of India. 1989. 'Circus Rings Face Closure.' *The Times of India*, January 31.

Vaidyanathan, P. S. 1981. 'Circus: The Big Top is Dying.' *India Today*. July 31.

Vegas, Savia. 1988. 'Women of Steel.' *The Times of India*, January 2, 1988.

CHAPTER 59

Contemporary (Post-)Migrant Theatre in Belgium and the Migratory Aesthetics of Milo Rau's Theatre of the Real

Janine Hauthal

Introduction: Towards a Migratory Aesthetics

Mobility and migration within and beyond Europe have become central themes of artistic production around the globe. Both features also often directly impact on the aesthetics, production, reception, and institutionalization of contemporary theatre, giving rise to performance practices that reflect the changing realities of our world. To capture these newly emerging forms, researchers have started to explore what they variously call minority, multicultural, intercultural, (post-)migrant, or transcultural theatre, performance, or dramaturgy (see e.g. Gonzalez and Laplace-Claverie 2012; Kovacs and Nonoa 2018; Lei and McIvor 2020; Sharifi 2018). In this chapter, the notion of 'migratory aesthetics' (Durrant and Lord 2007) will be put forward as a way to expand the focus of analysis beyond shifts in the ethnicities of theatre makers or in the themes of (their) theatre productions—a focus which has often led to appreciating such intercultural theatre exclusively for its educational, pedagogical, or sociocultural value rather than (also) as an aesthetic expression in its own right, thus fuelling the reduction of 'social' or 'community' arts to their ethnic content and their separation from allegedly universal professional (state/city/national) theatre. '[D]raw[ing] attention to the ways in which aesthetic practice might be constituted by and through acts of migration' (Durrant and Lord 2007,

J. Hauthal (✉)
Vrije Universiteit Brussel, Brussels, Belgium
e-mail: Janine.Hauthal@vub.be

© The Author(s), under exclusive license to Springer Nature Switzerland AG 2023
Y. Meerzon, S. E. Wilmer (eds.), *The Palgrave Handbook of Theatre and Migration*, https://doi.org/10.1007/978-3-031-20196-7_59

12), the term migratory aesthetics, by contrast, deliberates primarily on the form rather than the content of these works. 'The modifier "migratory,"' as Mieke Bal puts it, neither 'refer[s] to migrants or actual migration of people' (2007, 23), nor does it concern the accuracy of representing a particular history or experience of migration. Rather, it denotes 'a ground for experimentation that opens up possible relations with "the migratory," rather than pinpointing such relations' (Bal 2007, 23).

Multilingualism is an important factor in the realization of a migratory aesthetics. According to Yana Meerzon and Katharina Pewny (2020), it is one of the most prominent cultural transformations brought forth by the mobility of people and lends itself to be used on stage as a tool to represent and make the experience of migration tangible for spectators. Centring text and national language, dramatic theatre traditionally conceives of the stage and auditorium as one homogenous national space, united by a shared mother tongue. It is precisely this received idea of a national or city theatre that polyglottal plays and performances displace or question by decentring the national language of spectators who are expecting to be addressed in their mother tongue and by potentially impeding their understanding. Bal, moreover, conceptualizes one's mother tongue as an important 'tool of self-realization' (2007, 32) as well as 'a key component of what it is to be human' (32) which is why having actors speak in their (different) mother tongues plays a crucial role in realizing a migratory aesthetics. This requires, however, that multilingualism is not used to showcase difference, as this would reduce actors to their ethnicity, but rather to offer both actors and audiences an experience of displacement and allow for a friendly encounter with the migratory. At the basis of such a use of multilingualism lays the 'ethical imperative [...] to provide a congenial, friendly soundscape in which mobility—the migratory—is not the despised exception but the valued norm' (Bal 2007, 33).

This chapter studies theatre and migration in a Belgian context. Section "Multicultural Performance and the 'Flemish Wave': 1990s Theatre in Belgium" briefly focuses on multicultural and multilingual performance in Belgium and the internationalization of the Belgian theatre and dance scene during the 1990s 'Flemish wave.' Section "Belgian Post-Millennial 'Theatre of the Real': Thomas Bellinck and Action Zoo Humain" turns to two Belgium-based post-millennial exponents of the 'theatre of the real,' before section "Provincializing Europe? The Migratory Aesthetics of Milo Rau's *Empire* (2016) and *Orestes in Mosul* (2019)" zooms in on the work of Milo Rau, a Swiss-born writer, theatre, and film maker who became artistic director of the Nederlands Toneel Gent (NTGent) in 2018. The overall aim is to investigate the complex relations between theatre, migration, and the ethics of form by exploring the migratory aesthetics of Rau's theatre as a case in point.

Multicultural Performance and the 'Flemish Wave': 1990s Theatre in Belgium

Studies of European (post-)migrant theatre that specifically focus on Belgium are scarce. Manfred Brauneck's seven-volume history of European theatre (2007), for instance, includes a chapter on Belgium theatre in the second half of the twentieth century but does not specifically account for (post-)migrant forms, and neither do the field analyses commissioned by the Flemish Theater Institute VTi (Janssens and Moreels 2007; Janssens 2011; Performing Arts in Flanders 2013). Azadeh Sharifi (2017), in turn, adopts a specific focus on post-migrant theatre, but Belgium is not among the seven Western European countries she analyses. In 2003, the Informal European Theatre Meeting, an international network for contemporary performing arts, published a report, authored by Jude Bloomfield, in which Belgium features as one out of ten Western European 'country snapshots of multicultural theatre and dance scene' (23). The report acknowledges the emergence of new kinds of multicultural theatre in the Flanders in the 1990s and mentions independent theatre and dance groups such as Dito'Dito and Les Ballets du Grand Maghreb in Brussels, Victoria in Ghent, and Hush Hush Hush in Antwerp (Bloomfield 2003, 73–74). In addition, the Kunstenfestivaldesarts (KFDA), set up in Brussels in 1994, is said to have served as a 'spearhead for the development of intercultural arts' (Bloomfield 2003, 74) by creating international collaborations and providing a showcase for international theatre from Europe and overseas as well as the local arts scene. According to Bloomfield, it was the KFDA that first addressed a bilingual audience (2003, 74). A few years later, the close connection with, and fascination for, the multilingual and multicultural city of Brussels prompted the Dutch-speaking theatre company Dito'Dito (1984–2005) to start collaborating with their French-speaking counterpart Transquinquennal, and, together, they started to perform bilingually in Dutch and French. Over the years, Dito'Dito developed into a more and more inclusive company, extending membership and collaboration to (migrant) artists belonging to different non-Flemish ethnicities and cultures. Yet, while, as Bloomfield cautions, companies collaborating with (post-)migrant artists or communities have experienced pressures and misrecognition, and although independent (post-)migrant artists and companies remain few and often only thrive with the support of their established Flemish counterparts, their breakthrough nevertheless enhances 'the prospects for the second generation' (2003, 83).

Bloomfield's analysis is certainly correct; however, parallel developments in the Belgian theatre and dance scene, especially in the Flanders, may have—albeit indirectly—also contributed to cultural diversification and thereby may have prepared audiences for the widespread acceptance of recent attempts to create, and experiment with, a migratory aesthetics. One of these noteworthy developments concerns the relatively early and wide-reaching internationalization of the Flemish theatre and dance scene. In the 1990s, the so-called Flemish wave, referring to a group of Belgian choreographers and postdramatic theatre makers including, for example, Jan Fabre, Jan Lauwers and Needcompany, Anne Teresa de Keersmaeker, Alain Platel, and Wim Vandekeybus, gained international recognition. Significantly, bi- and multilingual expression abounds in their works. Partly resulting from the international make-up of their casts and deployed to facilitate international touring, multilingualism often serves to foster their productions' international appeal. Moreover, as I have shown elsewhere for the work of Jan Lauwers and Needcompany (Hauthal 2018), the performers' accent-laden expression lends their artistic creations a multicultural quality.

However, while the use of different languages in performance, to which companies such as Dito'Dito and Needcompany testify, can be ascribed to the historical, geographical, and cultural context of the Belgian trilingual state, the aesthetics of their productions do not yet qualify as 'migratory.' Nevertheless, they may have paved the way for post-millennial theatre productions whose migratory aesthetics allow spectators to relate to entangled migratory histories, and the linguistic and cultural complexities resulting from them, not just in Belgium but in contemporary Europe and our globalized world at large. Departing from documentary material but placing it in a fictional frame in ways that blur the boundaries between fact and fiction, these works belong to the newly emerging strand of documentary theatre called 'theatre of the real' (Martin 2013).

Belgian Post-Millennial 'Theatre of the Real': Thomas Bellinck and Action Zoo Humain

Since the 1990s, the performing arts have witnessed a '"new" documentary revival' (Forsyth and Megson 2011, 1). Various contemporary theatre makers working in the Flanders (e.g. Thomas Bellinck, Chokri and Zouzou Ben Chikha/Action Zoo Humain, Elly Van Eeghem, Milo Rau) or Wallonia (e.g. Nimis Groupe) participate in this movement. Their often complex and hybrid works cover an array of theatre practices and styles that variously connect theatre to personal, social, political, or historical realities but commonly depart from documentary sources, which they place in a fictional context and investigate in a way that deliberately and self-reflexively blurs the boundaries between fact and fiction. In so doing, this new generation of documentary theatre makers—in contrast to predecessors such as Erwin Piscator and Bertolt Brecht—'both acknowledges a positivist faith in empirical reality and underscores an epistemological crisis in knowing truth' (Martin 2013, 14). In other words, the theatre of the real is (self-)critical about striving to reveal 'the objective truth' behind a perceived reality; rather, it 'proceeds from acts of the imagination in the forms of reiteration, representation and narration' (Martin 2013, 74). Notably, its latest exponents have expanded the re-evaluation of Europe's cultural memory and amnesia to include migrant and decolonial testimonies as two (post-)migrant theatre productions by Belgian-based artist Thomas

Bellinck and the performance group Action Zoo Humain demonstrate in an exemplary way.

Addressing mobility and migration on a European scale, Bellinck's series of performances and installations entitled *Simple as ABC* (2015–) scrutinizes the apparatus of the European Union's (EU) border control and 'mobility management.' The series' third and fourth episodes, *The Wild Hunt* and *The Museum of Human Hunting*, are particularly relevant in the context of this chapter as they confront spectators with the surtitled snippets of recordings in Arabic, English, Farsi, French, and Greek that Bellinck collected from around the Mediterranean in interviews with refugees trying to enter the EU as well as with journalists, border control guards, and people traffickers. *The Wild Hunt* is set in a museum-like stage space, in which several objects—including a European passport—are displayed that symbolize the EU's violence against migrants. The performance begins with an introduction by Bellinck himself, in which he traces the discursive origins of today's fortress Europe, with its digitized border technologies and outsourced border controls, back to Aristotle. Reflecting on his own privilege as a white European man, he then leaves the stage to allow the 'disembodied voices from the borders of Europe to paint another picture of reality with their own words' (Rees 2019). In confronting audiences with a theatre without bodies, Bellinck's staging of stories from the borders of Europe makes both audible and visible the impact of migration and of the exclusionary practices of EU border policing on the lives of those speaking. In 'mimic[king]—at the level of form rather than content—that which it sets out to represent' (Durrant and Lord 2007, 13), *The Wild Hunt* conforms to a migratory aesthetics.

De Waarheidscommissie (The Truth Commission; 2013–2018) by Action Zoo Humain, in turn, highlights stereotypical images of the black 'other' and the humiliating discourses and cultural traumas pertaining to the (neo-)colonial practice of the human zoo. The company was founded in 2009 by Chokri Ben Chikha who—together with his brothers, actor Zouzou and musician Walid, actresses Marijke Pinoy and Dahli Pessemiers-Benamar as well as actor Maxime Waladi—form the core artistic team. *De Waarheidscommissie* is a series of site-specific performances of which five editions exist to date. Starting out in a former Court House in Ghent in 2013, one hundred years after 128 Senegalese and 60 Filipinos were exhibited under harrowing circumstances at Ghent's 1913 World's Fair, the production travelled to Cape Town (2014) and, after that, to Antwerp (2016) and Mechelen (2017), before the fifth and final edition to date was performed in the Belgian Senate in Brussels (2018) on the occasion of the sixtieth birthday of Expo '58, the World's Fair in Brussels, which showcased Congolese people enacting supposedly 'authentic' rituals in mock huts.

De Waarheidscommissie draws attention to the human toll of exhibiting exotic others as attractions. Throughout the performance, historians, scientists, artists, and witnesses 'play themselves' and engage the audience in a debate about the ethics and aesthetics of the human zoo. According to Karel Arnaut, this early form of 'intercultural performance' (2011, 344) articulates diversity and alterity through subjugation and, thus, perpetuates racist-colonial discourses. Moreover, as Arnaut rightly claims, by 'widening the gap and reinforcing the inequality between actors and spectators' (2011, 357), human zoos truncate the inter-subjectivity of performance: they lack 'performative reflexivity' (359) and can therefore 'also be repudiated on aesthetic grounds' (359). Action Zoo Humain's negotiation of the human zoo in *De Waarheidscommissie*, by contrast, is highly self-reflexive. On the one hand, the performance repeatedly highlights that it takes place in 'real' spaces, displays 'real' evidence, and features 'real' people, while, at the same time, it also alludes to its own theatricality when thematizing the company's implication (and that of their collaborators) in replicating stereotypes (Kuyl 2013, 56). Ben Chikha, for instance, is blamed for exploiting the descendants of the Senegalese that he cast in the role of witness, and the choreographer of the Saartje Bartman re-enactment by dancer Chantal Loïal is accused of voyeurism. Through such self-reflexive acts, *De Waarheidscommissie* subverts the clear-cut binarism of 'victim vs. perpetrator' and points to the irreducible complexities of debating the postcolonial condition.

These complexities also find expression in how the performance shifts the debate from moralizing discourses about guilt to questions of ethic accountability concerning the ongoing legacy of (Belgian) colonialism. Towards the end of the performance, the audience is asked to take an ethically charged decision (in the case of the Ghent edition, about whether (or not) Ben Chikha should return the passports to the Senegalese performers)—a decision that potentially confronts spectators with their own racial prejudices. By involving audiences in this way, *De Waarheidscommissie* could be said to offer 'a ground for experimentation [...] with "the migratory"' in the sense of Bal (2007, 23), relating in this case to the after-effects of colonization. Hence, while both Bellinck's multi-voiced but actorless engagement with the so-called European refugee crisis and Action Zoo Humain's decolonial interventions can be classified as documentary theatre, they simultaneously renew this tradition by confronting the aesthetic limits of theatrical realism through a migratory aesthetics. In their works, presenting (responses to, or effects of) migration on stage is therefore intricately linked with confronting the ethics of theatrical representation. This is a characteristic they share with Milo Rau, whose aesthetic approach to the global 'real' has been internationally hailed for 'problematiz[ing] the continual negotiation between reality and its inevitable representations (by the media, technology, historiography or politics)' (Le Roy 2017).

Provincializing Europe? The Migratory Aesthetics of Milo Rau's *Empire* (2016) and *Orestes in Mosul* (2019)

The remainder of this chapter studies two exemplary cases from the work of Milo Rau, *Empire* (2016) and *Orestes in Mosul* (2019). Both works critically scrutinize Europe's relations to its 'Others' and 'provincialize Europe' in the sense of Dipesh Chakrabarty (2000). Crossing Europe's border in southerly direction (to Syria in *Empire* and to Iraq in *Orestes in Mosul*), they demonstrate how Europe's imperial history continues to create caesuras that deeply affect those countries as well as the wider region. The exploration of the two works is guided by the manifesto that Rau wrote upon his appointment as NTGent's artistic director. This so-called Ghent manifesto delineates his artistic mission in ten rules, relating to, for instance, the casting of actors and non-actors (rule seven), collaborative modes of production, and the democratization of authorship (rules three and four; Rau 2018, 281). Together, they indicate how Rau steps away from the Western European tradition of working with a fixed local ensemble to realize what he calls 'global realism' and a 'global ensemble.'

Empire and *Orestes in Mosul* substantiate Rau's tendency to employ intertextuality and metatheatre as a political strategy. Both productions are metatheatrical in that they exclusively feature actors playing themselves. Rau's actors are already on stage when the audience enters the auditorium and remain there for the entirety of the performance, thus inhabiting the stage in a typically postdramatic fashion (Lehmann 2006, 110). Transitions between scenes are marked by actors switching places (rather than a black-out), having a friendly (inaudible) chat and drinking some water, tea, or coffee, while they are waiting for the next scene to start. Seeing actors rest on stage in this way is implicitly metatheatrical as it blurs the distinction between actor and role and foregrounds theatre as a process.

Moreover, all three parts of *The Europe Trilogy* (2014–2016) are intertextual as they refer to well-known classics from the canon of western drama. *Empire* specifically draws on the 'giant tableaux of exile' (Rau 2016, 235) of Euripides' *Medea* (431 BC) and even features two actors performing a dialogue from the original on stage (322–25). The intertext of *Medea* mirrors *Empire*'s thematic thrust in demonstrating how imperial quests cause migration and how tragedy emanates from excluding a migrant (Medea) as 'foreigner.' At the same time, it also reveals that actors and audiences share a transnational (European) frame of reference and, by testifying to the cross-cultural travelling of cultural forms, this shared cultural space oddly contrasts with the experience of imprisonment, exclusion, and discrimination that the four actors—two from Greece, one from Syria, and one Romanian actress—relate.

Orestes in Mosul similarly attests to Rau's employment of intertextuality as a political strategy. Adapting Aeschylus's trilogy *Oresteia* (458 BC), Rau superimposes Mosul and Troy, the city destroyed by the Greek army in the *Oresteia*, and uses the latter to reflect on whether (or not) to pardon or kill the captured fighters of IS, the Jihadi terrorist organization that seized control of Mosul in

2014 and brought heavy damage on the city, when the Iraqi government recaptured the city three years later. By relocating the *Oresteia* to Mosul and by introducing Mosul as a place with a history older than that of ancient Troy, Rau's production participates in the project of 'provincializing Europe' in the sense of Chakrabarty: presenting Mosul in this way undermines the Eurocentric ideology of 'first in Europe, then elsewhere' (2000, 7).

Rau 'provincializes Europe' also through his use of multilingualism. In *Empire*, each actor speaks in her/his mother tongue (Arabic, Greek, Kurdish, and Romanian), and in their acts of self-expression they authenticate the autobiographical nature of their storytelling. Validating the actors' agency as creators of their own text, *Empire*'s multilingualism additionally attests to Rau's collaborative mode of production and democratization of authorship. Hence, Rau's multilingual theatre clearly accords with Marvin Carlson's idea of the 'macaronic stage,' that is, a heteroglossic theatre characterized by 'voices that speak a language not that of the author or the presumed audience' (2006, 20).

With its international cast of European and Iraqi performers, *Orestes in Mosul* integrates not just three different languages (Arabic, Dutch, and English) but also various acting styles. Rau thus stimulates intercultural understanding in (and demands it from) those involved in the production as well as from its audience. As the presence of translators in the pre-recorded videos filmed in Iraq and the live projection of surtitles reveal, translation forms an integral part of both artistic process and onstage performance. The surtitles prompt audiences to choose (or oscillate) between either focusing on understanding the actors' verbal utterances (by reading the surtitles) or on what Meerzon calls 'paralinguistic cues vital to speech-making: changes in rhythm and intonation, speed of delivery, pauses, gestures, postures, facial expressions, movements, and so on' (2018, 260). By separating the visibility and audibility of language from its meaning, Rau's multilingual mise-en-scène extends the experience of cultural complexity to his collaborators and audiences alike. His insistence on foreignness and impenetrability in cross-cultural encounters results in an aesthetic that continues the play's critique of Eurocentrism in the act of performance. Pointing to the transformations brought forth by migration in our globalized world, *Empire* and *Orestes in Mosul* can be seen to subscribe to Bal's following claim: 'an aesthetic that is migratory [...] endorses and explores the mobility of the current social world' (2007, 31).

Rau's departure from the monolingual tradition of the city theatre has resulted in a highly sophisticated performance style. The integration of pre-recorded audio(visual) material, live recordings as well as cinematic front, inter-, and end titles contribute to the distinctly intermedial aesthetic which has become a trademark of his theatre. The huge projection screen hanging above the stage (which also displays the surtitles) 'create[s] real-time repetitions of what happens on stage,' thus turning 'a personal story into an allegory of a historical problem field that both surpasses and influences the personal' (Le Roy 2017). Even though the use of hand-held cameras and different angles in *Orestes in Mosul* is clearly different from *Empire*'s static camera position and fixed visual framing of the actors in close-up, both productions evoke documentary frames (i.e. embedded journalism in *Orestes in Mosul* and an interview situation in *Empire*). The filmic doubling of the actors prompts spectators even more forcefully to look at the screen rather than the stage—not just for the purpose of reading the surtitles but also because of the emotional appeal of the filmic images. In both cases, the camera brings the actors visually closer: they often look straight at the camera and seem to directly speak to the audience. The camera thus turns the actors' speeches into an address to, or an encounter with, the audience and enhances the illusion of immediacy and intimacy in performance.

Having said that, critics of *Orestes in Mosul* found that the intimate quality of the video and live recordings made the onstage action unappealing or simply redundant. Indeed, when scenes are partly repeated or enacted parallel on stage and screen, the resultant doubling has potentially distancing functions (in a Brechtian sense). Accordingly, the filmic frame potentially yields both reflexive and emotional effects. Most importantly, however, the doubling of verbal utterances on stage and visual text in the surtitles as well as of moving images and life action serves a crucial function in Rau's 'theatre of the real' as it is precisely the remediation of theatre through film that enhances the experience of the 'real.' Notably, as Jay David Bolter and Richard Grusin have argued, remediation enables the experience of the real by way of replacing reproduction with acts of production (2000, 53). Rau's theatre, rather than reproducing the actors' stories through a mimesis of action (representation), uses live recording to continuously produce reality in performance (presentation). The filmic medium transforms the actors' performances into an encounter with the (linguistic) other by transferring the ethic accountability of empathetic listening from the (fellow) actors to the audience. In so doing, Rau's theatre reshapes the ethics of spectating.

Indeed, both *Empire* and *Orestes in Mosul* were internationally praised for their 'multicultural democratic quality' (Carlson 2006, 143). Critics, nevertheless, complained that the latter production had failed to meet its own ethical standards because the intertext of the *Oresteia* evokes a Eurocentric frame. Many also found fault with the fact that the production relegated the Iraqi actors to the collective role of the chorus, while western actors exclusively performed individualized characters, that is, Agamemnon, Orestes, Clytemnestra, and her lover Aegisthus. This imbalance increased when authorities prevented the Iraqi actors from travelling to Europe which is why they solely feature in the videos filmed on location while western actors are present on both stage and screen. This unequal distribution of stage and screen presence among Iraqi and western actors renders visible the politically forced immobility of the former and juxtaposes it with the unrestricted movement of the latter. Hence, in the complex and potentially lopsided intercultural context in which Rau's production was created, 'intermediality is charged with political meaning' (Neumann 2015, 512). Seen from this angle, Rau's intermedial theatre is steeped in questions of ethics and exposes the power relations and inequalities in processes of creation in particularly striking ways. In other words, Rau's theatre is not just *about* migration but itself *migratory* as it is 'anchored in movement, not just of people, but also of media, of images, and of voices' (Bal 2007, 24). It is in this sense that Rau's multicultural and multilingual 'theatre of the real' forms a major tendency of contemporary dramaturgies of migration.

Conclusion

With the appointment of Milo Rau as artistic director, NTGent became one of the most influential contemporary theatres, not just in Flanders and Belgium but also in the world. Yet, while Rau's European and wider international recognition is clearly remarkable, the local and national success of his multilingual, intermedial, and postdramatic theatre may not be altogether unexpected in the Belgian context. Rather, as section "Multicultural Performance and the 'Flemish Wave': 1990s Theatre in Belgium" of this chapter has argued, the use of different languages in performance, which has become a trademark of Rau's theatre, has a relatively long history in Belgium and resonates with the historical, geographical, and cultural context of the Belgian trilingual state. The fact that multilingualism forms an integral part of everyday life and of cultural production and reception in Belgium (see also the standard practice of subtitling—rather than dubbing—cinema and television) potentially prepared audiences for the first collaborative bilingual productions by Dito'Dito and Transquinquennal as well as for the internationalization of the postdramatic theatre and dance scene in Flanders during the 1990s Flemish wave. These early multicultural and multilingual productions, in turn, may have paved the way for post-millennial theatre productions, in which multilingualism plays a crucial role in realizing a migratory aesthetics, and could possibly explain what attracted Rau to the relatively small city of Ghent.

However, broadly speaking, it is not until the post-millennial 'theatre of the real' by Rau and other Belgian-based theatre makers that the use of bi- or multilingualism which already characterized multicultural performances in Belgium during the 1990s is no longer primarily connected to Belgium as a trilingual state, or serves to facilitate international touring, but points to Belgium's and Europe's colonial history as well as to the global present of (forced) mobility and (post-)migration. Indeed, the similarly 'migratory' works by Thomas Bellinck and Action Zoo Humain discussed in section "Belgian Post-Millennial 'Theatre of the Real': Thomas Bellinck and Action Zoo Humain" demonstrate that the intricate interlacement of ethics and aesthetics in the engagement with the migratory in Rau's work is no exception among Belgium-based theatre makers. Rau's success therefore rather indicates that (post-)migrant theatre in Belgium may have finally overcome the earlier separation of social and community theatre from the mainstream of professional theatre.

All the works discussed in this chapter, but especially those by Milo Rau, testify to entangled histories and an aesthetics in which the migratory is the 'valued norm' (Bal 2007, 33). Together, they reshape the ethics of acting and spectating, thus preventing that their works are reduced to the ethnicities of those involved in their production or to their ethnic content. Yet, while, with Rau, migratory aesthetics may have arrived in the middle of Belgian theatre and society, in that middle, more so than in the aesthetic and social fringes, power relations and inequalities in processes of production and reception show very clearly that aesthetic practices that are constituted by and through acts of migration do not happen in a political vacuum. Ultimately, they testify to the need to further decentre Eurocentric attitudes and traditions in ways that stimulate intercultural understanding and offer experiences of displacement and complexity to all those involved, allowing for friendly encounters with, and emphatic listening to, (linguistic) others.

References

Arnaut, Karel. 2011. 'The Human Zoo as (Bad) Intercultural Performance.' In *Human Zoos: The Invention of the Savage*, edited by Pascal Blanchard, Gilles Boëtsch, and Nanette Jacomijn Snoep, 344–65. Arles: Actes Sud.

Bal, Mieke. 2007. 'Lost in Space, Lost in the Library.' In *Essays in Migratory Aesthetics: Cultural Practices Between Migration and Art-making*, edited by Sam Durrant and Catherine M. Lord, 23–35. Amsterdam: Brill.

Bloomfield, Jude. 2003. *Crossing the Rainbow – National Differences and International Convergences in Multicultural Performing Arts in Europe*. Brussels: Informal European Theatre Meeting.

Bolter, Jay David, and Richard Grusin. 2000. *Remediation: Understanding New Media*. Cambridge: MIT.

Brauneck, Manfred. 2007. 'Belgien.' In *Die Welt als Bühne: Geschichte des europäischen Theaters. Fünfter Band: Die Geschichte des Europäischen Theaters in der zweiten Hälfte des 20. Jahrhunderts*, 861–72. Stuttgart: Metzler.

Carlson, Marvin. 2006. *Speaking in Tongues: Languages at Play in the Theatre*. Ann Arbor: University of Michigan Press.

Chakrabarty, Dipesh. 2000. *Provincializing Europe: Postcolonial Thought and Historical Difference*. Princeton: Princeton University Press.

Durrant, Sam, and Catherine M. Lord. 2007. 'Introduction.' In *Essays in Migratory Aesthetics: Cultural Practices Between Migration and Art-making*, edited by Sam Durrant and Catherine M. Lord, 11–20. Amsterdam: Brill.

Forsyth, Alison, and Chris Megson, eds. 2011. *Get Real: Documentary Theatre Past and Present*. 2009. Houndmills: Palgrave Macmillan.

Gonzalez, Madelena, and Hélène Laplace-Claverie, eds. 2012. *Minority Theatre on the Global Stage: Challenging Paradigms from the Margins*. Newcastle: Cambridge Scholar.

Hauthal, Janine. 2018. 'Multilingual Expression and Postnational Frames in *100% Brussels* and *Isabella's Room*.' *Modern Drama*, 61(3): 271–300.

Janssens, Joris, and Dries Moreels. 2007. *Metamorphoses: Performing Arts in Flanders since 1993*. Brussels: VTi.

Janssens, Joris, ed. 2011. *Ins & Outs: A Field Analysis of the Performing Arts in Flanders*. Brussels: VTi.

Kovacs, Teresa, and Koku G. Nonoa, eds. 2018. *Postdramatisches Theater als transkulturelles Theater: Eine transdisziplinäre Annäherung*. Tübingen: Narr.

Kuyl, Ivo. 2013. 'De Waarheidscommissie: Expo Zoo Humain van Chokri & Zouzou Ben Chikha.' Etcetera, 133, 55–57.
Lehmann, Hans-Thies. 2006. Postdramatic Theatre. London: Routledge.
Lei, Daphne, and Charlotte McIvor, eds. 2020. The Methuen Drama Handbook of Interculturalism and Performance. London: Methuen.
Le Roy, Frederik. 2017. 'The Documentary Doubles of Milo Rau & the International Institute of Political Murder.' Etcetera, 148. https://e-tcetera.be/the-documentary-doubles-of-milo-rau-the-international-institute-of-political-murder/.
Martin, Carol. 2013. Theatre of the Real. Houndmills: Palgrave Macmillan.
Meerzon, Yana. 2018. 'The Theatres of Migration and Cosmopolitanism.' Modern Drama, 61 (3), 257–62.
Meerzon, Yana, and Katharina Pewny, eds. 2020. Dramaturgy of Migration: Staging Multilingual Encounters in Contemporary Theatre. London: Palgrave.
Neumann, Birgit. 2015. 'Intermedial Negotiations: Postcolonial Literatures.' In Handbook of Intermediality, edited by Gabriele Rippl, 512–29. Berlin: de Gruyter.
Performing Arts in Flanders. 2013. Perspective Dance. Brussels: VTi.
Rau, Milo. 2016. Die Europa Trilogie/The Europe Trilogy: The Civil Wars, The Dark Ages, Empire. Berlin: Verbrecher Verlag.
———. 2018. Globaler Realismus/Global Realism. Berlin: Verbrecher Verlag.
Rees, Liam. 2019. 'Simple as ABC #3: The Wild Hunt – Thomas Bellinck/ROBIN.' Etcetera, 157. https://e-tcetera.be/simple-as-abc-3-the-wild-hunt-thomas-bellinck-robin/.
Sharifi, Azadeh. 2017. 'Theatre and Migration: Documentation, Influences and Perspectives in European Theatre.' In Independent Theatre in Contemporary Europe. Structures – Aesthetics – Cultural Policy, edited by Manfred Brauneck and ITI Germany, 321–415. Bielefeld: Transcript Verlag.
———. 2018. 'Multilingualism and Postmigrant Theatre in Germany'. Modern Drama, 61 (3), 328–51.

CHAPTER 60

Belarus Free Theatre: Political Theatre in Exile

Margarita Kompelmakher

The Belarus Free Theatre (BFT) was founded in 2005 in Minsk, Belarus, by a husband-and-wife team, Nikolai Khalezin and Natalia Koliada. Their early work was instrumental in the formation of the Belarusian wave of 'New Drama,' which largely eschewed scripts in favour of devised texts from sources such as interviews, photographs, blog posts, and documents. These found texts were intended to offer access to everyday reality that was silenced, or glossed over, under the state-sponsored system of theatre production. In Belarus, the political content of the Belarus Free Theatre's work was rooted in the concept of 'alternative-ness,' which refers to a form of representation that surfaces the voices of marginalised identities as well as a mode of production that works outside of the official system.

Following the post-election crackdown in 2010, the artistic leaders of the company went into exile in the United Kingdom and the company began a period of binational production, with a season produced in Minsk, Belarus, and in London, England. They continued to work binationally for almost ten years. Their mode of production during this time was multi-pronged: there were productions created in underground spaces in Minsk that were never shown abroad; there were productions developed in Minsk that toured to Western Europe; and there were also productions that originated in London, featuring an international and multilingual cast, that were never shown in Belarus.

In the late 2000s, the company was catapulted to international fame as a human rights theatre company and it garnered a variety of human rights awards such as the French Republic's Human Rights Prize (2007) and the Atlantic Council Freedom Award (2011). These awards were as much for their theatre

M. Kompelmakher (✉)
Alliance Theatre in Atlanta, Atlanta, GA, USA

© The Author(s), under exclusive license to Springer Nature Switzerland AG 2023
Y. Meerzon, S. E. Wilmer (eds.), *The Palgrave Handbook of Theatre and Migration*, https://doi.org/10.1007/978-3-031-20196-7_60

work as they were for their work as activists in the Belarusian political opposition. However, when addressing Western audiences, the company's repertoire and their notion of political theatre did not travel smoothly across national borders.

This chapter focuses on the political and aesthetic strategies of the Belarus Free Theatre as a company in exile in London, England. I examine how their approach to political theatre changed as they encountered international audiences in the West, first in the immediate moment of exile and then in its later stages. To understand this change, I look at the production of the geopolitical notion of 'Belarus' in their work and the ways that the concept of 'Belarus' was understood, or mis-understood, by Western critics. While described chronologically, the strategies the company employed were not developmental or teleological in nature. On the contrary, the opposite is true: each strategy emerged from a unique historical relationship of pressures, struggles, and opportunities faced by the Belarus Free Theatre at different moments in time.

The first part of this chapter establishes a political meaning of the Belarus Free Theatre's work *in* Belarus for local audiences. In the second part, I illuminate three artistic strategies that position BFT as a theatre company in exile. The first strategy, '(en)gendered politics,' looks at the gendered body politics that the Belarus Free Theatre deployed to gain international attention for their work. This strategy is exemplified in their 2012 production *Minsk 2011: A Reply to Kathy Acker*. The second strategy, the 'politics of sensation,' emerges in reaction to the Western gaze that fuelled a sensational narrative about the company and limited their ability to speak beyond a concept of 'Belarus' that I describe as 'illiberal Belarus.' 'Illiberal Belarus' is a production of a specific knowledge of Belarus premised on the country's lack of civil liberties and human rights under the current authoritarian regime of President Aleksandr Lukashenko. To dislodge themselves from this overdetermined narrative, the Belarus Free Theatre utilised sensation as a strategy in their 2013 production of *Trash Cuisine*. Lastly, I demonstrate how the company expanded on the earlier strategy of (en)gendered politics, but with a regional twist. From 2015 to 2020, the company formed regional alliances with other expats and exiled artists from Eastern Europe to address not just the political situation in Belarus, but the increasingly intertwined political landscape between Belarus, Ukraine, and Russia.

As exilic figures with resources and support from British and American allies, the Belarus Free Theatre has benefited from an appeal to human rights that other collectives have not. Elsewhere, I discuss their privilege as a White refugee company in the United Kingdom that benefits from the status of the 'perfect Other.'[1] However, the company has also been criticised for reproducing familiar tropes of Cold War era human rights discourse between a repressed

---

[1] For my discussion of the racial imaginary at play in human rights theatre, see Margarita Kompelmakher (2019), 'The Perfect Other,' in *Staging Postcommunism: Alternative Theatre in Eastern and Central Europe After 1989*, edited by Vessela S. Warner and Diana Manole, 195–207, Iowa City: Iowa University Press.

Eastern Europe and a freer, albeit money-hungry, West. When, in response, they have ventured beyond this trope, they have been criticised for not speaking about what they know best—illiberal Belarus. Their story reveals many paradoxes of political theatre that contemporary theatre companies negotiate in exile.

Belarus: Historical and Political Context

Belarus is a country of around ten million people, geographically situated between Russia to the east, Poland and Lithuania to the west, Latvia to the north, and Ukraine to the south. Between the fourteenth and eighteenth centuries, the current territory of Belarus was part of the Grand Duchy of Lithuania, a political entity that included modern day Poland, Lithuania, and Belarus. In the nineteenth century, it was part of the Russian Empire. Belarus first became a political entity in the twentieth century after the Treaty of Riga in 1921, however, independence lasted for only a short while and Belarus soon became a Soviet Republic. Until 1991, Belarus was one of the sixteen Soviet Republics and gained independence after the dissolution of the Soviet Union.

Whereas Belarus's neighbouring countries have actively sought to rewrite their national histories in the post-Soviet moment, Belarus's path to self-determination has followed a different trajectory. This different trajectory is attributed to the regime of current President Aleksandr Lukashenko (in power since 1994). Economically, Lukashenko has propped up the economy through oil subsidies from Russia. Politically, Lukashenko has consolidated power by dissolving parliament and other forms of opposition. Socially, Belarussian identity under Lukashenko has reconciled its Soviet past rather than broken away from it.

All of these factors contributed to a discourse on national identity in the 1990s and 2000s that talked about a 'weak' Belarusian national identity and a stronger civic notion of identity. Later, this discourse was re-framed as a situation of two spheres of social and political life: the official and the alternative. The alternative sphere applies to life that happens outside of the state-owned institutions in underground cultural spaces and in pockets of privatization such as the country's emerging IT sector and pursuit of multinational business.

When I first came to Belarus in 2011 for research, Lukashenko had won the presidential election, but few of my acquaintances in Minsk said they voted for him. The possibility of a rigged election was raised in local circles and in the Western media, which often referred to Lukashenko as the 'last dictator in Europe.' Lukashenko's popularity waned heading into the election of 2020, and his re-election that year sparked the largest pro-democratic demonstration in Belarusian history, with protests erupting in major cities across Belarus.

The protests were overwhelmingly peaceful. The response by the government was not. Just like in the aftermath of the 2011 election, the government cracked down on protestors. Lukashenko managed to retain power in the midst of mass demonstrations and international sanctions with the help of Vladimir

Putin, the president of Russia. Putin brought in Russian military and cultural workers as proxies and kept the country running amidst strikes, walk-outs, and protests. Lukashenko's debt to Putin placed Belarus in the position of collaborator with Russia and paved the way for their alliance in the War in Ukraine (2022) that Putin would launch less than one year later.

The Meaning of Political Theatre in Belarus

The Belarus Free Theatre emerged from within the crucible of debates about Belarus's national identity in the early 2000s. The company was founded by journalist and playwright Nikolai Khalezin and his wife Natalia Koliada, a member of a prominent theatre family and a communications strategist. Soon after its founding, the duo partnered with Vladimir Scherban, a director at the Yanka Kupala National Theatre in Minsk.

The company adopted documentary theatre practices in their work whose primary political function was to represent marginalised positions within Belarus. Their first devised piece in 2005, *My. Samoidentifikaciya* (We. Self-Identification), was made through verbatim-style dialogues recorded 'from below' at the construction site of the National Library of Belarus. The piece gave voice to subjectivities within the nation that were erased from sight in the homogenous, unified, and purified vision of the country embodied in the grand project of the National Library. Their 2007 production, *Zona molchaniya* (Zone of Silence)—which artistic director Scherban considers to be the piece that 'solidified' their approach to theatre—expanded their devising methodology to include oral histories, newspaper articles, autobiographical stories from the actors, and statistical research.

The Belarus Free Theatre's early work was described by Belarusian political scientist Nelly Bekus as an 'alternative theatre' because it represents an alternative Belarusian national identity in juxtaposition to the official images distributed through the state apparatus (Bekus 2010, 235–41). Most of the company's work was in Russian, the dominant language in Belarus. The Belarusian language would appear in references to Belarusian cultural traditions and, in some later work, deployed as a strategy of resistance to the colonial language of Russian.

Additionally, the Belarus Free Theatre's alternative theatre has to do with what Belarusian theatre scholar Taciana Arcimovič identifies as their 'free' mode of production, referring to the independent creation of theatre in relation to state models (Arcimovič 2013). While most alternative companies in Belarus must negotiate with the state apparatus to secure legal status, funding, and rehearsal space, the Belarus Free Theatre was an independent player within the system and drew on private forms of support, including award winnings at international festivals.

The company and its audience were periodically pressured by the state and the police. The original group of actors and the artistic director Scherban, all of whom simultaneously held stable jobs at state theatres, were squeezed out of their government jobs and became unemployable for other projects. Their underground, or vagabond, existence led scholars such as Kathleen Elphick to point out that the political nature of the company lies in their attempt to reconfigure the spaces that delimit who can speak within the public sphere and who is relegated to silence (Elphick 2014, 124). In this way, their alternative-ness has less to do with whether or not the content of their work represented a political position (i.e. anti-Lukashenko), but the way that it functioned to produce an alternative public sphere.

(EN)GENDERED BODIES: GAINING INTERNATIONAL ATTENTION

While most of their theatre projects can be described as 'alternative,' the work that the Belarus Free Theatre toured abroad in the late 2000s had more direct political content, including stories of political violence and testimonials from disappeared persons and political prisoners in their 2008 production *Postigaya lubov'* (Discover Love) and their 2006 production *Byt' Garol'dom Pinterom* (Being Harold Pinter). *Being Harold Pinter*, in particular, drew a lot of attention from international audiences when it toured to the United States in the immediate aftermath of the 2010 election crackdown.

Following the tour to the United States, the Belarus Free Theatre's co-directors (and the actor Aleh Sidorchyk) defected to the United Kingdom and gained residency at the Young Vic Theatre in London. This moment marked the end of exclusively Belarus-made theatre. From 2011 onwards, the Belarus Free Theatre held performance seasons in both London and Minsk every year with actors traveling between the two cities to perform.

In the UK, the Belarus Free Theatre was mostly welcomed by elite artistic institutions and crowned darlings of the human rights theatre scene. The artistic directors focused on capitalising on their status as a world-renowned human rights theatre to further raise awareness about the political situation in Belarus. A new strategy emerged at the critical moment of their migration. The company adopted a strategy that foregrounded the female body as the site for state-enforced violence. The figure of the woman became emblematic of the disregard of the Belarusian state for its people. The Belarus Free Theatre worked with, and against, feminist and queer theories of the body to demonstrate the patriarchal and misogynistic forms of violence undertaken by the Belarusian state, with the hope that their theatre would push European publics and policy stakeholders to intervene in the situation.

This strategy is evident in the final moments of *Minsk 2011: A Reply to Kathy Acker*, the first production from the company post-exile. *Minsk 2011* was produced during a three-week residence in the UK with a good deal of travelling of actors back and forth between Belarus and the United Kingdom. The play, performed mostly in Russian, tells the story of the Belarusian capital in 2011 and produces a narrative of the city through two intertwined prisms: political repression and sexuality. Referencing the deceased feminist punk icon Kathy Acker, the production uses the lens of gender and sexuality to mark violent interactions in Belarus on multiple levels—between people in Minsk, between the Belarusian state and the people, and finally between the country of Belarus and other countries.

The monologue towards the end of the play establishes a powerful metaphor between a young woman (played by Yana Rusakevich) and Belarus, which lacks 'sexy' qualities because it is a land-locked and resource-poor country. Faced with limited economic and political power, the young woman, like Belarus, is forced to appeal to the international public by using her naked body. The message underscores the violence of international relations between Belarus and other countries that led to an inevitable act of prostitution to gain attention on the world stage.

Minsk 2011 drew a mix of support and criticism from audiences and theatre critics in the United Kingdom. Michael Billington of *The Guardian* praised the production's evocative aesthetics that he felt circumvented a 'polemic' retort against the political climate in Belarus (Billington 2012). Other reviewers were less impressed with the production and described the work as aesthetically backward. An unidentified reviewer wrote:

> If it weren't for the title one might easily mistake 'Minsk, 2011' for a show *from 1979*: this is an exercise in old school agit-prop, and there are moments when, regardless of the message, the media of nudity, screaming and bodypaint feel like unhelpful clichés from a bygone age of radical theatre. But context is everything: Belarus is Europe's last dictatorship and this banned theatre company does come from an extreme time and place. (*Time Out London* 2012)

The sentiment in this review is striking. The reviewer depicted the company's aesthetics as backward but justified this backwardness by pointing to the Belarusian context, presumably a place where a by-product of political repressions is out-of-date aesthetics.

Neither Billington's review nor the far more problematic review from *Time Out London* registers the (en)gendered strategy in *Minsk 2011*. They focused on the representation of Belarus and its 'extreme' conditions of repression. In doing so, they helped re-enforce the problem that the Belarus Free Theatre critiqued in the play. These reviewers latched onto the narrative of 'illiberal Belarus' and the meaning that they extracted from the production—that is its 'sexy-ness'—was ultimately rooted in the Belarus Free Theatre's banned status. What caught the attention of the reviewers, and became the evaluative criteria, was not the company's aesthetic choices but their bravery for existing in a country that seemed years removed from theirs. This framework for reception is referred to by Belarusian art historian Svetlana Poleschuk as a persistent interest in the 'Belarusian trouble'—a tendency that Poleschuk first identified in her assessment of the reception of Belarusian artists abroad (Poleschuk 2011). 'Belarusian trouble' as a receptive framework creates a distinction between 'liberal' and 'illiberal' places and it provides for a reading of Belarusian cultural productions as 'exotic' by dint of existing.

The lack of artistic appreciation concerned the Belarus Free Theatre's co-artistic directors, who worried that the failure of critics to recognise them as artists would lead to a reductive interpretation of their form of political theatre. Paradoxically, the company was turning into victims of their own (en)gendered politics: international audiences saw them through the prism of a banned theatre company from Belarus whose artistic and political purpose was only to speak about oppression at home.

Sensation: Going Global

The problem of aesthetic appreciation grew in the years following the company's exile. A sensational narrative amassed around the company that positioned them as victims of state-enforced violence in Belarus and called on them to perform this role for a Western public that saw their role as the company's rescuers. The company's mission to call out injustices in Belarus was falling squarely into a familiar Cold War trope premised on the lack of artistic freedom, and other freedoms, in the East. In some artist circles in Belarus, and in left-leaning circles abroad, the company was criticised for 'selling' an overly troubled picture of Belarus to Western media for their own benefit.

To counteract this development, the company found it necessary to find a new theatrical language that could dislodge them in the minds of their new Western audiences from the marker of 'illiberal Belarus.' They pursued a global human rights project that would work not just with Belarusian topics of human rights, but other human rights topics across the globe. The production of *Trash Cuisine* (2013) was a critical juncture in this phase.

Trash Cuisine was directed by co-artistic director Nikolai Khalezin and choreographed by Australian-British choreographer Bridget Fiske. It featured an international cast of Belarusian, UK, US, and Australian actors from different racial and ethnic backgrounds. Unlike *Minsk 2011*, it was performed mostly in English with the inclusion of other languages. The play is structured through a series of vignettes, or 'dishes,' that relate stories of capital punishment and state-enforced violence from places around the world and across historical periods. These scenes are about the genocide in Rwanda, a case of capital punishment in the United Kingdom in the 1970s in relation to the IRA resistance, the 'Dirty War' in Argentina in the 1970s and 1980s, and others.

Trash Cuisine presents a unique culinary tour across national borders. Most of the scenes place a recipe for a national dish alongside a story of state-enforced violence in that country. This thematic juxtaposition produces a provocative message about the production of global knowledge: beyond the seductive national narrative on the 'table' are 'trash' bins, bags, and vessels full of discarded human carcasses kept hidden from sight by the ruling regimes of nation-states.

Taken together, these scenes in *Trash Cuisine* connect different places and people through the extra-national narrative of human rights abuses. This connectivity is produced through an aesthetic and political strategy I call the 'politics of sensation,' which uses sensation to rupture sedimented representations of nation-states that divide people and places from one another. In *Trash Cuisine*, the politics of sensation are produced through the relationship between food and the human body, and they are staged through strong choreographic choices, food-centric object art, and 'extreme' forms of body art that rely on virtuosic performances from the actors. The strategy is powerfully evoked in the final sequence of the production where actors chop bags of onions in front of the audience to the music of a fast-paced mazurka. The audience is moved to tears, but not from an empathetic response to the story of political violence in Belarus, that concludes the production. It is the sweat of the onion that stings the eyes.

In this way, the politics of sensation situates the audience into a different affective mode than what is conventionally expected in theatricalised depictions of human rights violations. The onion chopping is deployed by Khalezin and the ensemble as an affective trigger to emphasise the automatic, involuntary, and ultimately vacant emotional responses that are part and parcel to sensationalised narratives of 'illiberal Belarus'—a type of emotional alienation that is premised on real and imagined separations between people and places. In using sensation as a strategy to relate different people and places to one another in the metatheatrical manner described, the Belarus Free Theatre was also engaging in an act of criticism that posed a 'vote of no confidence' to frameworks of reception that circumscribed the scope and meaning of their political theatre to just 'one place.'

In general, the UK reviews applauded the production's theatrical imagination (Coveney 2013) and sense of urgency in dealing with capital punishment. Many of the reviews picked up on the way that the production was an 'assault on every one of our senses' (Brantley 2015) and that the 'sensuous theatricality' of the production was able to 'stir our consciousness' about the state of world affairs, in particular the murder, decapitation, and general violence inflicted by state institutions on civilians (Billington 2013). A common line of critique also emerged: the production's watered-down effect. This critique referred to the Belarus Free Theatre's expanded view of violence outside of Belarus and the inclusion of 'arbitrary' stories of atrocities from the last forty years enacted in places like Argentina, Thailand, and the UK (Lukowski 2013). Similarly, Ben Brantley of the *New York Times*—who generally admired the production—noted that the show 'overloads its plate and dilutes its potential strength' (Brantley 2015).

The critique of the production's dramaturgy also carried a sentiment that prior productions that dealt with the specifics of Belarus avoided, because they stayed within the borders of the Belarusian context: '[t]he grisly, fascinating specifics of their little-known homeland have always been one of the BFT's strongest suits but here they wander aimlessly from Northern Ireland to Rwanda before only belatedly going home' (*The Evening Standard* 2013). The review exemplifies how the sensational narrative presented itself again in the reception of the Belarus Free Theatre's work, calling on them to deliver 'fascinating' specifics about Belarus and challenging their ability to speak beyond the Belarusian particular.

Paradoxically, the perceived failure of the show—a watered-down message and too little focus on Belarus—was precisely what the Belarus Free Theatre hoped to achieve. *Trash Cuisine* was an experiment, however fragile, that sought a strategy of sensation to create a more inclusive picture of human rights violations around the world and to challenge the sensational narrative of 'illiberal Belarus' that the company encountered. It responded directly to the conditions of cultural production in the West that trapped the Belarus Free Theatre in the Belarusian context and continued to cast them as Cold War caricatures.[2]

STAGING A REVOLUTION: A MULTI-STRATEGY FESTIVAL

In 2015, the Belarus Free Theatre produced a two-week retrospective of their work in London as part of commemorations for the company's ten-year anniversary. The event, *Staging a Revolution*, featured ten productions, including a world premiere of a *Time of Women* (2014), which was created and directed by Nikolai Khalezin with actors in Belarus. *Staging a Revolution* registered the Belarus Free Theatre's multiplicity of strategies of political theatre. In addition to the presentation of productions at the Young Vic Theatre, the festival gestured to the company's alternative mode of production in Belarus by staging 'secret' shows in clandestine venues across London. Each production also included a 'Let's Act' post-show conversation that departed from the themes in each production to examine a global human rights topic. Similar to *Trash Cuisine*, these conversations located the Belarus Free Theatre's politics within a broader discussion and asserted that the company could speak to, and about, global human rights issues rather than just the Belarusian particular.

Time of Women is a quintessential Nicolai Khalezin and Natalia Koliada production in that it featured their network of influential Belarussian activists and showcased the pair's commitment to telling stories that could hold the Belarusian state accountable. The Russian-language play features the story of Irina Khalip, a Belarusian journalist and wife of a 2010 oppositional candidate for president in Belarus, who was also in exile in the UK. The production was created through digital technologies with actors in Minsk. It first premiered in an apartment in Minsk and later travelled to London for the *Staging a Revolution Festival*.

Time of Women is based on the real stories of three Belarusian women journalists and their experience living in one cell together in a Belarusian prison following the 2010 protests. The play critiques a political system that naturalises the biological differences between men's and women's bodies—a gendered assertion that the ruling party uses in order to issue a threat against the

---

[2] Following *Trash Cuisine*, the Belarus Free Theatre created a similar production, *Red Forest* that suffered from critique similar to *Trash Cuisine* and was less favourably received.

opposition by depicting women as physically unsuitable for political struggle. This tactic is powerfully depicted in a scene where the prison warden pressures one of the women to sign a document, saying that she will spend her childbearing years in prison if she refuses to comply. By putting the story of women in the Belarusian opposition at the centre of the conversation, *Time of Women* accomplishes an important intervention in the Belarusian political discourse that heavily privileges the contributions of men. It presents a parallel story—a 'time of women'—that disrupts the totality of political time constructed in a patriarchal manner.

Time of Women had a positive, if lukewarm, reception as part of the *Staging a Revolution Festival*. The inclusion of the female body and female perspective in *Time of Woman* drew on the gendered politics that the company had successfully employed in *Minsk 2011*. However, the production itself—though consumed by an international public—did not address international relations between Belarus and other countries and was instead reminiscent of the documentary style theatre of the company's earliest works in Belarus. What made it an exilic production was its inclusion within the festival: the 'Let's Act' conversation that followed the production featured female journalists that discussed comparative notions of freedom in the media in the UK, Belarus, and Saudi Arabia. This conversation included Irina Khalip, the exiled journalist, whose story was featured in the play.

Conclusion

From 2015 to 2020, the Belarus Free Theatre's work was marked by a few key developments. First, the co-artistic directors drifted in different directions as they continued to build a life for themselves in the United Kingdom. The husband-and-wife team and Vladimir Scherban parted ways. Scherban continued to live in London and pursued his own projects, eventually forming his own company with a British collaborator. Khalezin and Koliada continued to oversee the company. In Minsk, they supported the work of the company, now led by a group of original Belarus Free Theatre artists such as Maryna Yurevich, Pavel Haradnitski, Sveta Sugako, and a new generation of student performers trained at Fortinbras, the Belarus Free Theatre's acting programme.

Second, the political life of Khalezin and Koliada in the United Kingdom became increasingly regional and coalitional over time. They formed an alliance with other artists and activists from Ukraine and Russia. The regional solidarity that emerged had to do with the reality of their exile as they found support from a group that shared their native language and understood their historical and political context. It also had to do with the increasingly connected political situation in Ukraine, Russia, and Belarus. For Khalezin and Koliada, the political focus of the company in the United Kingdom shifted to being advocates for the region as a whole. Their production *Burning Doors* (2016) is an example of a regional form of gendered politics that featured the story of Russian artist and activist Maria Alyokhina, a member of the persecuted performance group in Russia called Pussy Riot.

On 24 February 2022, with Russia's invasion of Ukraine, the Belarus Free Theatre's work gained a new significance. When their production *Dogs of Europe* (2020) was presented at Barbican Centre in London in March 2022, it was a shocking reprimand to UK and European policy makers that had failed to take the company's earlier warnings seriously. Based on the 2017 novel by Belarusian author Alhierd Baharevich, *Dogs of Europe* is a dystopian play that imagines a grim future for Europe. According to Alex Marshall of the *New York Times*, the production depicts a continent cut in half by (another) wall: on one side sits a Russian superstate, where a dictator has eliminated almost all opposition and absorbed Belarus, Ukraine, and other states; and on the other side sits a Europe that failed to realise the Russian threat (Marshall 2022).

Dogs of Europe was originally created in Minsk in 2020, in Russian and Belarusian, under a slightly different, albeit related, context. It was an opportunity for the Belarus Free Theatre to get in front of the upcoming election in Belarus. After living through two 'failed' Belarusian elections, in 2011 and 2015, the company intended to use the production to raise awareness about the unchecked power of Russia in the region. *Dogs of Europe* was presented in Minsk and foretold a story that would unfold months later in Belarus after the August 2020 election. The failure of Europe to intervene beyond limited sanctions in Belarus took the continent one step closer to the reality depicted in *Dogs of Europe* as Putin and Lukashenko further locked arms.

When *Dogs of Europe* was presented in the UK in 2022, after a two-year delay because of the COVID-19 pandemic, it was less of a premonition of a future than an urgent (maybe too late) call for international intervention to support Belarusian and Ukrainian democratic movements. By this time, most of the company that had been living in Minsk, Belarus had left the country and gone into exile in Warsaw, Poland.

Once again, amidst a great uncertainty about the future of the company and its members, the Belarus Free Theatre was called on to speak to the human rights situation in Eastern Europe—this time about the consequences of a war unfolding in the neighbouring country of Ukraine.

References

Arcimovič, Taciana. 2013. 'Alternative Theater in Belarus in the Period of Transition (from 1980s Through 2000s).' Unpublished.

Bekus, Nelly. 2010. *The Struggle Over Identity: The Official and Alternative 'Belarusianness.'* Budapest: Central European University.

Billington, Michael. 2013. 'Trash Cuisine—review.' *The Guardian*, June 6, 2013. https://www.theguardian.com/stage/2013/jun/06/trash-cuisine-review.

———. 2012. 'Minsk 2011: A Reply To Kathy Acker review.' *The Guardian*, June 17, 2012. https://www.theguardian.com/stage/2012/jun/17/minsk-2011-belarus-free-review.

Brantley, Ben. 2015. 'Belarus Free Theater's Trash Cuisine Serves Politics with Teeth.' *New York Times*, April 29, 2015. https://www.nytimes.com/2015/04/30/theater/review-belarus-free-theaters-trash-cuisine-serves-politics-with-teeth.html.

Coveney, Michael. 2013. 'Theater Review–Trash Cuisine, Young Vic, London.' *The Independent*, June 6, 2013. https://www.whatsonstage.com/london-theatre/reviews/trash-cuisine_30903.html.

Elphick, Kathleen. 2014. 'The Belarus Free Theatre: Performing Resistance and Democracy.' *45°F: Electronic Journal of Theory of Literature and Comparative Literature*, 10, 111–27.

Kompelmakher, Margarita. 2019. 'The Perfect Other: Performing Artistic Freedom in Solidarity with the Belarus Free Theatre.' In *Staging Postcommunism: Alternative Theatre is Eastern and Central Europe After 1989*, edited by Vessela S. Warner and Diane Manole, 195–208. Iowa City: University of Iowa Press.

Lukowski, Andrzej. 2013. "Trash Cuisine." *Time Out London*, June 6, 2013. https://www.timeout.com/london/theatre/trash-cuisine.

Marshall, Alex. 2022. "An Exiled Theatre With a Warning for Europe." *New York Times*, March 10, 2022. https://www.nytimes.com/2022/03/10/theater/belarus-free-theatre-exile.html.

Poleschuk, Svetlana. 2011. 'Being Political: The Heavy Duty of Belarusian Art.' In *Opening the Door? Belarusian Art Today*. Warsaw: Zachęta National Gallery of Art Catalog.

'Trash Cuisine, Young Vic—theater review.' *The Evening Standard*, July 6, 2013.

'Review of Minsk 2011: A Reply to Kathy Acker'. *Time Out*. London, June 18, 2012. https://www.timeout.com/london/theatre/minsk-2011-a-reply-to-kathy-acker.

Index[1]

A

Abolitionists, 690
Abramović, Marina, 105, 108–113
Abusaada, Omar, 21, 613, 617–620
Accent, 15, 95, 99, 100, 138, 139, 315–320, 322, 323, 330, 333, 431, 433, 552, 569
  accented actors, 319
Acharnians, 13, 209
Acrobatics, 220, 255, 260, 262, 264, 464, 664, 728, 731, 734
Act of walking, 521
Action Zoo Humain, 742–744, 748
Activism, performative, 574
Adigun, Olabisi, 98, 99
Aeschylus, 13, 40, 73, 196, 198, 200–204, 201n2, 202n3, 203n4, 517, 641, 745
Aesthetics, intermedial, 746
Afiba and Her Daughters, 429
African diaspora, 18, 132, 428, 429, 436
African indigenes, 17
Afropeanism, 18, 444–446, 448
  Afropean identity, 18, 444, 448
Afrophobia, 17, 404
Agamemnon, 13, 196, 198, 201, 470, 747

Ahlán, 542
Ahna Refuġjati (We are Refugees), 532
Ai Weiwei, 576, 578
Aidoo, Ama Ata, 429
Aitmatov, Chingiz, 339, 345, 346
Ajax, 196, 202
Alabama Cake Walkers/Alabama Cakewalkers, 676, 683
  See also Minstrelsy
Al-Attar, Mohammad, 613, 617–620
Alcestis, 197
Aldridge, Ira, 23, 687–693, 698
Aliens, 116, 200, 244, 245, 270, 734
  Alien Act, 245
All Coons Look Alike to Me, 679
Alley, The, 491, 495
Almafuerte, 283
Alon, Chen, 310, 312
Al-Qady, Towfiq, 550
American dream, 682
American Negro Minstrels, 676, 679–681
American Sunrise, 453, 454
American War of Independence (1775–1783), 688
Amnesty International, 73, 382, 526, 550

---

[1] Note: Page numbers followed by 'n' refer to notes.

Among the Dead, 475, 480–485
Anarchism, 578
Ancient Mesopotamia, 173–175
And the Fish Rose Up to Make War against Mankind, 20, 544–546
Andromache, 201
Anglophone imperial circuit, 22, 675–685
Angura (underground) theatre, 237
An-sky, S., 23, 713–717, 719–723
Antigone in New York, 298
Antigone of Shatila, 617–620
ANU Productions, 99, 100
Aoi no Ue (*aka The Lady Aoi*), 232–236, 238
Aqyn-opera, 339, 341–343, 349
Arambe Productions, 379
Architecture of Loss, The, 475, 480–485
Aristophanes, 13, 207–210, 212, 616
Arthaśāstra, 190
Asia Minor Disaster, 513, 521
Aspis, 215
Asylum, 1, 3, 4, 10, 17, 21, 24, 35, 40, 68–70, 72, 75, 85, 98, 100, 103, 106, 144, 197–199, 202, 204, 305, 312, 313, 370, 377–381, 386, 501, 515, 555, 556, 558, 561, 562, 564, 566, 575, 590, 599–609, 624–630, 633
  asylum-seekers, 3, 5, 6, 8, 14, 16, 20, 21, 40, 70–73, 75, 76, 84, 106, 108, 195, 196, 202, 205, 210, 303, 304, 307, 309–312, 377, 378, 380, 381, 385, 515, 517, 525, 526, 528, 530, 534, 549–559, 562, 567, 592, 599, 603n2, 604, 605, 623, 625–627, 632
Asylum Monologues and *Asylum Duologues*, 74
Ausnahme und die Regel, Die (*The Exception and the Rule*), 49
Ausnahmezustand
  a state of emergency, 49
  a state of exception, 46
Australian Human Rights Commission, 550
Authenticity, 99, 111, 282, 445, 550–552, 558, 559, 627, 633
  aesthetics of, 550, 558, 559

Auto da Barca do Inferno, 644
Autothanatography, 105, 111
Ayan theatre, 344–345, 349
Ayivi, Simone Dede, 80, 85–87
Azas, Anestis, 74, 516

B

Babilonia, 285
Babylonians, 207, 210
Bacchae, 196, 201, 445
Bahok, 395–397
Bakri, Samia Qazmouz, 491, 495, 496
Balkan Baroque, 105, 109, 110, 113
Balkan Corridor, 600–603
Ballhaus Naunynstrasse, 82–85
Banishment, 9, 107, 198, 243–250, 256, 299, 443, 449
Banksy, 21, 574, 576, 577, 579–581, 583, 584
Banlieue, *see* French banlieue
Bare life, *see* Biopolitics
Basilea, Samuel "Shlumiel," 274
Baudhāyana Dharmasūtra, 190
Bazaar, 543
Behn, Aphra, 647–648
Beier, Ulli, 417, 418, 420, 421
Belarus Free Theatre (BFT), 23, 751–761
Bellinck, Thomas, 742–744, 748
Belonging, 2, 4, 12, 37, 87, 89, 105, 108, 115, 116, 118, 120, 122, 131, 145, 149, 190, 292, 320, 347, 390, 391, 398, 432, 435, 436, 458–460, 494, 516–518, 526, 530, 564, 575, 590, 611, 613, 631, 633, 655, 713, 715, 735, 741
  beyond belonging, 80–85 (*see also* Migration)
Ben Chikha, Chokri, 742–744
Benjamin, Walter, 10, 43–53, 107, 517
Berliner Theatertreffen, 84
Bharata, 184–186, 189, 193
Bhave, Vishnu Amrut, 702–707, 709–711
Biopolitics, 3, 38, 67, 76, 119, 160
  See also Bare life
Birds, 13, 210–212

Black Battle with Dogs, 441–443
Black diasporic, 132
Black Lives Matter (BLM), 327, 577, 632
Black migration, 689
  migratory blackness, 12, 131–141
Blackface minstrelsy, 22, 675, 677, 679, 681
Black minstrelsy, 22, 675–685
Boal, Augusto, 310
Boat people, 549
Border identity, 440
Border Violence Monitoring Network database, 603
Bourekas cinema, 319
Brahma, 185, 186
Brecht, Bertolt, 34, 48–51, 355, 442, 464, 742
British Mandate, 305, 317, 489
Brokentalkers, 16, 377, 381, 383, 385, 386
Brook, Peter, 94–97, 322
Brooke, Gustavus V., 23, 694–697
Brough, Robert, 696
Buddhist priests, 219, 221
Buenos, Maya, 304, 311, 312
Buffoni, 268, 274
Bulbul, Nawar, 615, 616
Bwana, 541

C
Calderón de la Barca, Cadí in Pedro, 541, 648
Campfire Project, The, 617
Camps
  concentration camps, 38, 57, 70, 307
  death camps, 56
  labour camps, 56
  refugee camps, 6, 70, 76, 209, 484, 490, 493, 494, 515, 561, 587, 588, 591, 615, 617, 619
  transit camps, 56
"Camp town," 476
Caravan for the Rights of Refugees and Migrants, The, 562
Cärer, Maria Ursula, 263
Caribbean migration, 429
Carvalho, Wagner, 85

Case Farmakonisi or the Justice of the Water, 74
Cassar, Antoine, 530, 531
Catherine the Great, 652, 655, 657–659
Celtic Tiger, 378, 379, 381
Censorship, 291, 294, 489, 660
Center for Political Beauty (CPB), 576–578, 615
Charlatans, 211, 663
Cherkaoui, Sidi Larbi, 16, 17, 389–398
Cherokee, 451, 453, 455–461
Childhood Arrivals, Deferred Action, 477
Child labour, 733
Children and Soldiers, 504
Child's Dream, The, 307, 312
Chilton, Noah, 324
Chin, Staceyann, 430–433, 436
Cho, Julia, 475, 480, 481, 484
Circus, 2, 7, 23, 172, 237, 238, 282, 308, 550, 593, 631, 664, 718, 725–735
Citizen of the world, 103, 109
Climate Change, 1, 2, 5, 8, 12, 24, 120, 143, 144, 146, 148, 150–153, 158
Cocoliche, 282, 283, 288
  See also Gringo
Cold War, 367, 466, 471, 476, 477, 479, 483, 484, 514, 733, 752, 757, 759
Come Good Rain, 74, 75, 330
Comici, 267–271, 274, 275
Commedia dell'arte, 2, 14, 258, 267–275, 647, 648
Compassion, 3, 9, 34, 37, 38, 41, 272, 286, 304, 529, 656
Con-fusion, 243–245, 250, 391–394, 413
Contemporary Legend Theater, 467
Coppin, George Seth, 23, 694, 695, 697
Cosmopolitanism, 11, 23, 93, 103–113, 122, 305, 398, 562, 563, 575, 726, 732, 735
Could You Please Look into the Camera, 613
Covid-19 pandemic, 3, 13, 157, 158, 161, 179, 526, 539, 624, 632, 761
Creolization, 447
Crimea, 500, 503
Criollos, 281–284, 288
Criollos (native-born Argentines), 281

D

Danaids, 203, 210
Dance of the Forests, A, 421, 423
Danse macabre, 644
Dark Man's Gaze, The, 537, 540–542
Darwish, Mahmoud, 308, 309
Dead Centre Theatre Company, 159, 162, 163
Death and the King's Horseman, 418, 422
Declaration of the Rights of Man and of the Citizen, 68
Decolonization, 11, 121, 124, 126, 439, 443, 445
Defilippis Novoa, Francisco, 281, 284, 286–288
De las Heras, Encarna, 537, 542, 543
Del Moral, Ignacio, 537, 540–542, 546
Dembélé, Bintou, 440, 446–449
Demes, 209
Demetrius Ivanowitsch, Zar von Moskau, 656
Demokratia, 196
Dengaku (rice field dancing), 221
Deportation, 1, 21, 55, 57, 60, 67, 69, 71, 175, 283, 359–362, 369, 370, 435, 439, 447, 477, 526, 531, 561, 602, 630
Dernier Caravansérail, Le, 74, 97
Detention, indefinite, 549
Deterritorialization/ deterritorializing, 309
Dialogue, metaphysical, 22, 640
Diaspora
  diasporic space, 633
  digital diaspora, 157
  Syrian diaspora, 611–620
Dilemma of a Ghost, 429
Direct Provision system, 379, 381
Discépolo, Armando, 281, 284–286
Dislocation, 12, 115, 123, 126, 132, 157, 177, 396
Displaced Kids project, 503
Displacement, 3, 9, 10, 17–20, 34, 36, 42, 52, 83, 105, 108, 120, 143, 144, 176–177, 201, 208, 217, 243, 271–274, 297, 300, 303–313, 354, 403–413, 428, 433, 436, 466, 480, 481, 488, 491, 494–496, 513, 514, 518, 520, 544, 556, 600, 601, 603, 613, 617, 740, 749
Dispossession, 5, 19, 115, 116, 118–120, 124, 405, 487, 515, 694
Dissensus, 40, 76
Divjak, Žiga, 599–609
Doctor Faustus, 642
Documentary theatre, 35, 36, 341, 350, 383, 514, 516–519, 521, 550, 603, 613, 626, 742, 744, 754
Domba, 193
Dorofieiev, Serhii, 504–507
Draft-Dodgers, 210
Drama therapy, 616, 617, 620
Dramaturgy
  decolonial dramaturgy, 568–570
  dramaturgy of migration, 12, 226, 514, 516–518, 748
  land-based dramaturgy, 116, 123
Dream, 159, 162–163, 165
Dreams of Babel, 394
Drury, Jackie Sibblies, 429
Dybbuk, The (Between two Worlds), 23, 713–723

E

EcoFavela Lampedusa Nord, 567, 568
Electra, 196, 198, 201
Elefsina, 513, 516–521
Elias, Aryeh, 15, 315–324
Eliáš, Zdeněk, 61, 62, 64
Elizabethan drama, 245
Elmina's Kitchen, 131–141
El organito, 285, 287, 288
Eltham, Ben, 551
Emigrant, 16, 18, 377–386, 427, 515, 538, 664
Empire, 23, 745–748
Empire Windrush, HMT, 12, 131, 132, 134–137, 139, 433, 435
  empire crossings, after, 131
  See also Windrush
Engelische Comedien und Tragedien Sampt dem Pickelhering, 261, 262
English Comedy, 255–265
Enslavement, *see* Slavery
Erasure, 120, 236, 317, 334, 385, 485, 491, 496, 600, 661

Erpulat, Nurkan, 84
Ethics, 36, 38, 73, 94, 105–108, 126, 158, 552, 575, 743, 744, 747, 748
  See also Spectating, ethics of
Eupolis, 209, 210
Euripides, 13, 196–202, 204, 445, 618, 620, 745
European Convention for the Protection of Human Rights and Fundamental Freedoms, 564
Europe Trilogy, The, 745
Exile
  eternal exile, 12
  exiled established theatre makers, 611
  external exile, 10
  intellectual in exile, 107
  internal exile, 10
  self-imposed exile, 103, 422–424, 693
Expatriates, 18, 106, 208, 427
Expulsion, 122, 451, 606
External capture, ex-capere, 574

F
Factory, The, 613
Farmers, 209
Farquhar, George, 694
Fasshauer, Catharina ("Catrin"), 263
Festin, Le, 668, 669
Fisk Jubilee Singers, 682
Flaneur, 43, 107
Flight of the Turk, The (*il volo del Turco*), 274
Forbidden City nightclub, 479
Foreigner, 8, 16, 34, 73, 80, 86, 106, 193, 195, 196, 199–204, 207, 208, 211, 245, 271, 282–284, 320, 342, 353, 394, 442, 443, 448, 540, 652, 745
Forum theatre, 36
French banlieue, 439
  See also Banlieue
Fronteras Americanas, 37, 327, 331

G
Game, The, 21, 599–609, 603n1
Ganga, 468, 469, 471, 473
Gaucho hero, 282

Gauchos y gringos, 283
Gently, 303, 311
Georgia Minstrels, 676, 678, 683
  See also Minstrelsy
Gerusalemme liberata, 646
Ghetto, 10, 55–64, 331, 332, 448
Gilgamesh, 12–14, 171–180
Globalization, 2, 7, 8, 10, 97, 99, 100, 103, 104, 467, 620, 676, 684, 687, 733, 735
Globe theatre, 246
Głowacki, Janusz, 15, 297–299
Gomara, Justo López de, 281, 283
Good Chance Theatre (GCT), 21, 74, 587–595
Graf Benjowsky oder die Verschwörung auf Kamtschatka, 657
"Grande Nation," 18, 440
Greek tragedy, 13, 97, 195–205, 416, 641
Gringa, La, 283
Gringo, 15, 281, 283, 284, 288
Gringo-criollo drama, 281
Grinshtein, Nana, 340, 342, 346, 347
Guatemalan Mayans, 368, 369
Guatemala's Civil War (1960–1996), 365, 369, 372
Guest
  guesting, 115, 124, 126
  guest worker, 79, 368, 390, 514, 538
Guignol, 664
  See also Puppets/puppetry
Guzmán, Jacobo Árbenz, 366

H
Habima theatre, 312
Hamlet, 45, 51, 52, 324, 616
Harjo, Joy, 18, 453, 454, 460, 462
Hasan, Bakr, 628–631
Helen, 196, 201
Helots, 209
Heracles, 199
Hesiod, 195
Heteroglossia, 17, 37, 397, 398
  heteroglossic theatre, 397, 746
Heterotopia, 10, 33–35, 42, 448
Hicks, Charles B., 678, 683
Hlehel, Amer, 491–496

Hofmann, Maria Ursula, 263
Hogan, Ernest, 675, 679–681, 683, 685
Holden family, 670
　See also Puppets/puppetry
Holocaust, 10, 15, 55, 57, 81, 230, 298, 303, 304, 306–307, 312, 317, 607
Holocaust journeys, 55
Holot theatre, 310
　Holot Legislative Theatre (HLT), 310–312
Home
　homecoming, 16, 115, 120, 309, 393, 394
　homeland, 9, 12, 18, 61, 107, 109, 122, 124, 126, 132, 135, 139, 147–149, 166, 202, 215, 230, 292, 295, 308, 331, 340, 343, 360, 361, 368, 432, 444, 451–461, 466, 487, 495, 518, 520, 521, 532, 533, 564, 631, 660, 721, 758
　homelessness, 121, 166, 291, 292, 309, 445
Homer, 195, 196, 518, 641, 642
Hoskins, William, 694, 696
Hospitality, see Philoxenia
Host, 24, 34, 69, 72, 73, 125, 145, 149, 196, 198, 243, 245, 251, 258, 309, 320, 329, 340, 344, 349, 390, 392, 466, 515, 518, 520, 522, 563, 564, 568, 619, 620, 664, 666–668, 672
Hsing-kuo, Wu, 467, 470
Human rights, 1, 2, 10, 67–73, 103, 105, 113, 160, 161, 366, 372, 405, 471, 527, 528, 530, 556, 602, 603n2, 604–606, 751, 752, 752n1, 755, 757–759, 761
　universal human rights, 67, 68, 76
Humanitarian crisis, 4, 158, 381, 516, 539
Humanitarian performance, 576–582
Human zoo, 743, 744
Hybridity
　hybrid community of artistic expression, 632, 633
　hybrid identity, 18, 333, 336, 449, 726
Hyun, Peter, 478, 479

I
I-Kiribati, 146, 148–150
I_Left (Ε_Φυγα), 513–522
Illegale Helfer (Illegal Helpers), 67, 74
Immigrantes, Los, 286, 287
Immigrants
　first generation immigrants, 334–336
　gringos (European immigrants), 281, 283, 284, 288
　1.5 generation immigrants, 332, 336, 337
　second generation immigrants, 332, 333, 335, 336, 389, 390
　working-class immigrants, 284
Immigrant theatre, 17, 327–337, 687
In-between cultures, 17, 389, 391
Indigeneity, 11, 115–120, 123, 126
Innocent Child of La Guardia, The, 645
In Our Name, 550–553, 556, 559
Interculturalism
　acoustemological interculturalism, 99
　Hegemonic Intercultural Theatre (HIT), 96, 98, 101, 470
　interculturalism from below, 96
Intercultural theatre, 2, 11, 91, 95–97, 337, 739
Interrelatedness, 453–456, 458–460, 462, 534
Intertextuality, 23, 37, 40, 83, 231, 413, 745
Intervention, 21, 37, 39, 40, 50, 80, 83, 88, 96, 158, 311, 366–368, 370, 371, 515–517, 525, 542, 545, 567, 573–577, 579–584, 630, 631, 679, 744, 760, 761
Interweaving, 80, 96, 455, 457, 517, 519, 521
Iphigenia, 617–620
Iphigenia in Aulis, 196
Itinerancy, 22, 640–641, 648, 675–685, 711
Itinerant performers, 217, 274, 685
　itinerant puppeteers, 22, 642, 664 (see also Puppets/puppetry)
Izutsu (play), 220, 226–227

J
Jamieson, Nigel, 550–552
"Japanese Tommy" (Thomas Dilward), 677

Jelinek, Elfriede, 40, 67, 73
Jetñil-Kijiner, Kathy, 150–152
Jewish performers, 14, 267, 268, 275
Jewish theatre, 23, 713, 715, 717–721
Jim Crow character, 692
Jingju (Beijing opera, Peking opera), 18, 19, 463–474
Jiutai (the chorus), 224, 227
Jolly, George, 262–264
    Jolly's Migrant English Troupes, 262
Juan Moreira, 282, 288
Juba, 677
    See also Lane, William Henry
Jung, Hansol, 475, 483–485
The Jungle, 21, 37, 74, 594, 595, 602
Jūrō, Kara, 236–238

K

Kabuki, 231, 235, 237
Kafka, Georg, 62–64
Kampnagel, 21, 561–569
Kanak Attak, 562
Kanata, 98
    Kanata–Episode 1–the Controversy, 98
Kan Yama Kan, 550
Kanze troupe, 221, 222
Kathak, 392
Kayoi Komachi, 221
Kean, Edmund, 689
Kemp's Jig, 647
Kemp, Will, 259, 647
Keneally, Thomas, 694
Khalezin, Nikolai, 751, 754, 757–760
Khan, Akram, 12, 17, 145, 389–398
Kiertuenäyttämö ("The Touring Stage"), 623
Kim Sisters, 479
The Kingdom of Desire, 470
King Lear, 14, 643
Koliada, Natalia, 751, 754, 759, 760
Koltès, Bernard-Marie, 20, 440–445, 448, 537, 539–541
Korean War, 19, 361, 476, 477, 479, 482, 483
Kotzebue, August von, 22, 651–661
Krieg der Hörnchen (War of the Squirrels), 80, 85
Kurochkin, Maksym, 502

Kuśīlava, 189
Kwahulé, Koffi, 440, 444–447, 449
Kwei-Armah, Kwame, 131, 139

L

Ladipo, Duro, 416–418, 420–422
Lampedusa, 21, 33, 37, 73, 527–529, 533, 566, 567, 576
Lane, William Henry, *see* Juba
Langhoff, Shermin, 82–85
Laugh with Us [*Smějte se s námi*], 59, 60
Leave Taking, 131–141
Legends from Severo, 506
Legislative Theatre, 311
Lehtonen, Jussi, 21, 624, 626, 628–633
Leibkutscher Peters des Dritten. Eine wahre Anekdote, Der alte, 658
Lepage, Robert, 98, 104
Letters Home, 67, 75, 76
    See also Refugee Club Impulse
Leukadia, 213
Levin, Hanoch, 306
Levy, Andrea, 429–431, 434–436
Liddell, Angélica, 20, 538, 543–546
Life and Death of Marina Abramović, The, 105, 110, 113
Lilienthal, Matthias, 81
Liquid Africa, 446
Lisovsky, Vsevolod, 342–344
London Calling, 430
Longing, 308
López Mozo, Jerónimo, 542
Love Boat, 616
Luhansk Regional Theatre (LRT), 19, 499, 502–507
Lukashenko, Alexander, 23, 752–754, 761
Lustgarten, Anders, 527, 576
Lustig, Josef, 60, 64

M

Mad about Layla, 322
Madmen and Specialists, 423
Mahabharata, The, 94, 97, 184, 188, 702, 705, 709
Majok, Martyna, 15, 299

Marāṭhi saṅgīt nāṭak, 702
Marathi theatre, 23, 701–711
Mare Nostrum, 70, 578, 579, 583
Maribor Theatre Festival, 600
Markopoulou, Yolanda, 516–518
Marlowe, Christopher, 642
Marronage culture, 18, 448
Marson, Una, 430
Marys Seacole, 429
Massacre, 366, 482, 483, 618, 619
MASS MOVEMENT FOLAU: The Arrival, 152, 153
Matka Ojczyzna, 292
Maxim Gorki Theater, 74–76, 85, 614, 615
Mayan migrants, 372
Ma-Yi Theater Company, 480, 483
McAdoo, Orpheus, 675, 676, 681–685
Medina Onrubia, Salvadora, 283
Melancholy, 60, 62, 63
Memory, 309
Menaechmi, 13, 214, 215
Menander, 208, 212, 213, 215
Menschenhass und Reue, 654, 657
Mensch mit Migrationshintergrund (person with a migration background), 79
Merchant of Venice, The, 16, 243, 315, 318, 324
Merry Wives of Windsor, The, 647
Metatheatre, 745
Metics, 200, 201, 201n2, 204, 208, 211
Metoikountas xenous, 201
Midsummer Night's Dream, 159, 162
Migrancy, 11, 22, 117, 255, 257, 260, 262, 394, 514, 517–522, 667–668
  transnational migrancy, 260
Migrant
  melancholic migrant, 281
  migrant day labour, 370
  migrant-expert, 516–518
  migrant performers, 255, 261, 516, 632
  migrantpolitan, 21, 562–570
  second generation migrant, 17, 390–394, 398, 527
Migrating identities, 23, 713, 716–717

Migration
  African migration, 429
  climate migration, 10, 12, 143–154
  conflict migration, 23, 91, 97
  cultural migration, 268–269, 274, 275
  digital migration, 12, 157–166
  economic migration, 8, 91, 103, 538, 687, 735
  elite migration, 212
  forced internal migration, 57
  forced migration, 18, 24, 55, 56, 119, 201, 205, 208, 209, 212, 383, 561, 575, 576, 580, 595, 611, 615, 632, 694
  happy migrants, 281, 283
  horizontal migration, 230, 231, 237
  illegal migration, 8, 573
  Indigenous migrations, 11, 115–126
  intercultural migration, 101
  intercultural migration 'from below,' 98, 101
  intracultural migration, 424
  inward-migration, 98, 99, 377, 379, 380, 384
  labour migration, 8, 339, 341, 342, 349, 350
  Migration mainstreaming, 138
  rural migration, 123, 404
  social migration, 88, 211
  transmigration, 23, 257, 713–716
  transnational migration, 91, 368
  undocumented migration, 365, 369, 374, 477
  urban migration, 23, 119–123, 126, 404
  vertical migration, 14, 229–240
Migratory aesthetics, 23, 739–749
Migratory subjectivities, 17, 18, 427–437
Military anthropology, 19, 499–508
Minority
  audible minority, 333
  minority-becomings, 7
  model minority, 477, 478
  visible minority, 81, 333, 339
Minsk 2011: A Reply to Kathy Acker, 752, 755–757, 760
Minstrelsy, 676–679, 682, 684
Mishima, Yukio, 235–238, 240
Misterioso 119, 445

Mitterrand, François, 18, 440, 441, 446
Mizrahim, 316n1, 318, 321
    Mizrahi character, 318
Mladinsko Theatre, 600, 603, 603n1, 604
Mnouchkine, Ariane, 94–98
Modernity, liquid, 107
Moriscos, 542
Motherlessness, 292, 295, 297–300
Mothers, hopeful, 281, 283, 288
Motherstruck!, 430–433, 436
Mother tongue, 328, 396, 397, 740, 746
Mothertongue Project, The, 429
Mouawad, Wajdi, 327, 328, 330
Mouth of a Shark, 16, 377, 378, 380–386
Mugen (dream vision), 220, 224–228
Multiculturalism, 319, 321, 329, 331, 335, 337, 424, 440, 441
Multilingualism, 16, 23, 108, 270, 319, 332, 342, 740, 742, 746, 748
Murasaki Shikibu, 14, 231–238, 240
Murphy, Joe, 37, 74, 591, 592, 594
Murphy, Oonagh, 16, 377, 381–383
M.V. Louise Michel, the, 574, 577–582
My Right is Your Right, 67, 75, 76

N
Nāgarika, 187, 190
Nagle, Mary Kathryn, 455–461
Nakba (catastrophe), 305, 487–496
Nārāyana, Bhatta, 188
Narihira, Aniwara no, 225
Narrative of terror, 551
Narrow lane, the, 488
National Guoguang Opera Company, 467
Nationalism, 3, 15, 23, 97, 105, 106, 132, 139, 317, 349, 397, 405, 413, 416, 435, 436, 675
    liberatory nationalism (Europhobia), 17, 404
Natour, Salman, 309
Nātya, 184–188, 191
Nātyaśāstra (NŚ), 14, 184–187, 189–193, 708
Naufragés du Fol Espoir, Les, 97
Neformat, 340
Neuber, Caroline Friederike, 264

Nihon rōmanha, 236
Nomad, 6, 7, 104, 113, 208, 718
    nomadism, 10, 108
Non-citizens, 1, 20, 67, 196, 200, 208, 216, 217, 311
Nostalgia, 9, 133, 236, 282, 295, 331, 345, 406, 466, 467, 681
Nō theatre, 14, 219–228, 232
Nothing But Nothing, 550

O
Obexer, Maxi, 67, 74
Oceanic Africas, 446
Octopus, 365–374
Odyssey, 174, 195, 444, 642
Oedipus at Colonus, 73, 197, 198
Oedipus Tyrannus, 45, 51, 52, 196
Ogunde, Hubert, 416, 417, 419–421
Ogunmola, Kola, 416, 419–421
Okina, 220
Okón, Yoshua, 365–374
1948 War, 15, 308, 323, 488, 495
Oral history, 552, 754
Orestes, 13, 196, 198, 201, 747
Orestes in Mosul, 745–748
Orientalism, 92, 93, 95, 533
Orisun Theatre, 421, 423
Orpheus, 61–64
Othello, 243, 691
Other/otherness, 34, 37, 39, 41, 73, 81, 82, 91–101, 110, 111, 178, 244, 335, 397, 442, 443, 445, 448, 514, 516, 517, 538, 630
Ottoman Empire, 68, 305

P
Pacific Solution, The, 551
Paperiankkuri (Paper Anchor), 623, 626
Passport, 31, 99, 119, 341, 394, 530, 531, 590, 743, 744
Passaport project, 530
Patlay, Anastasiya, 340, 342, 346, 347, 349
Pericles, 14, 244, 250–253
Persecution, 5, 44, 52, 55, 68, 75, 120, 144, 203n4, 245, 267, 342, 381, 383, 416, 478, 519, 631

Phaedra (Fete'er), 472, 473
Philoctetes, 198
Philoxenia, 3, 4, 13, 15, 24, 37, 41, 67, 73, 74, 158, 195–198, 244, 251, 398, 526, 577, 583, 602, 680
Phoenician Women, 201, 210
Pickelhering, 14, 257, 260, 262
Pillai, Abhilash, 729, 730, 732
Pinnock, Winsome, 12, 131, 137, 138, 141
Pitou company, The, 668
Plakha, 339
Planell, David, 543
Plato, 198, 442, 640, 641
Plautus, 13, 208, 213–217
Playmaker, The, 694
Podestá, José, 281–283
Poenulus, 214, 215, 217
Postdigital
　postdigital condition, 157, 158, 165, 166
　postdigital theatre, 157, 159, 161
Postdramatic theatre, 741, 748
Postmigrant theatre, 11, 79–89, 741
Post-pandemic culture, 161
Precarious labour, 339–350
Prince, Mary, 428, 429
Processional aesthetics, 35, 521
Puppets/puppetry
　glove puppets, 471, 663–667
　marionettes, 642, 664, 667
Pūrvāraṅga, 185, 192

Q
Queens of Syria, The, 617

R
Race/racism, 12, 17–19, 23, 69, 74, 76, 80–82, 84–86, 88, 89, 92, 121, 131, 132, 136–140, 144, 148, 202, 229, 268, 269, 283, 311, 317, 322, 333, 384, 392, 404, 409, 413, 423, 427–437, 439, 441–443, 461, 469, 476, 479–481, 483–485, 532, 542, 564, 565, 569, 570, 582, 583, 643, 645, 678–681, 684, 685, 687, 689, 690, 693, 696, 698, 725–735

Ramadram, 561–570
Rau, Milo, 23, 739–749
Recruiting Officer, The, 694
Re-enactment, 108, 110, 112, 165, 365–367, 369–374, 405, 645, 744
　war reenactments, 366, 373, 374
Refrain, 55–64, 133
Refugee Club Impulse, *see Letters Home*
Refugees, 1, 33, 43, 55, 67–76, 80, 106, 143, 144, 175, 195, 196, 207, 251, 303, 329, 378, 390, 403, 463, 478, 487–496, 500, 513, 525–534, 538, 550, 561–570, 573–584, 587, 599, 611, 623–634, 743, 752
　maritime refugees, 573, 576
Regimes, 23, 42, 81, 109, 134, 159, 211, 221, 299, 367, 463, 471, 476, 538, 567, 569, 605, 606, 608, 611, 612, 615–618, 660, 728, 752, 753, 757
　of mobility, 103
Remediation, 747
Repatriation, 70
Resident-aliens, 200
Resurrection plays, 261
Reterritorialization (reterritorialising), 6
Return to the Desert, 441, 443, 541
Rice, Thomas "Daddy," 692
Rich Shore, The, 537, 542, 543
Rignold, George, 694, 696, 697
Rise: From One Island to Another, 151
Robinson, Joe, 37
Romeo and Juliet, 14, 244, 247–250, 615, 616, 642
Ronen, Yael, 306
Rosi, Gianfranco, 599, 600
Royal Court Theatre, 145, 341, 421, 543, 592
Royal Shakespeare Company, 159, 162, 251
Rudens, 13, 215, 217

S
Sackville, Thomas, 256, 257
Safe Shore, Concerto for Refugee and Orchestra, 311–312
Sainetes (short farces), 283–285, 288
　sainete grotesco, 284

Salička, 647
Sánchez, Florencio, 281, 283, 368
Sanctuary City, 299
Saṅgīt Svayaṃvar, 702
Sanskrit theatre, 183, 184, 186
Sarugaku (miscellaneous entertainments), 219–224, 226
Schechner, Richard, 93, 133, 470, 587
Schuster, Yaffa, 310
Schutzbefohlenen (The Charges), Die, 73, 74
Sears, Djanet, 330
Seremba, George, 74, 75, 330, 377
Settlers, 22, 115–120, 122, 123, 330, 393, 404–406, 409, 451, 452, 460, 461, 463, 465, 467, 481, 488, 684, 688, 694, 695, 697
  settler colonialism, 11, 18, 19, 116, 118, 119, 124
7 Deaths of Maria Callas, 105, 111–113
ŚhakāŚhailūṣ, 189
Shakespeare in Zaatari, 615, 616
Shakespeare, William, 14, 45, 51, 95, 97, 134, 162, 231, 243–253, 259, 315, 320, 337, 467, 615, 642, 643, 647, 648, 689, 691, 693, 696, 697
Shawqi, Ahmed, 323
Shikibu, Murasaki, 14, 231–232, 240
Shilappadikaram, 189
Shingeki, 235, 237
Shinto rituals, 234
Sikyonioi, 212, 213
Simple as ABC, 743
Simultaneity, 11, 104, 108
Site-specific theatre, 490, 514
Slavery
  non-citizen slaves, 196
  slave narratives, 428, 429
  slave tourism, 133
  slave trade, 85, 135, 417, 428, 698
  slave trade in Britain, 417
Small Island, 430, 431, 433–436
Smith, Samuel Morgan, 698
Smoke of Home (Dým domova), The, 61–64
Sons of Heracles, 13
Sophocles, 48, 51, 196–199, 201, 202, 443

Sovereignty, 18, 19, 106, 115, 118, 119, 147, 149, 251, 409, 441, 448, 452–461, 468, 582, 612
Soyinka, Wole, 17, 310, 415, 416, 418, 419, 421–425
Spectating, ethics of, 747, 749
Spencer, John, 256
Stage clowns, 14, 257, 261, 262
State of exception, 10, 43–53, 160, 514
  state of emergency, 49, 71
  See also Ausnahmezustand
Station Athens Group, 513, 514, 517
Stein, Jiří, 61, 62, 64
Stereotypes, 15, 19, 37, 98, 101, 123, 124, 207, 230, 319, 320, 322, 347, 348, 409, 430, 460, 501, 503, 546, 564, 569, 656, 680, 693, 744
Stone, Maeve, 16, 377, 381–383
Stranger, 13, 34, 51, 106, 107, 148, 175, 177, 195, 196, 199, 224, 243–253, 303, 308, 354, 384, 395, 396, 444, 514, 516, 518, 519, 576, 624, 628–631, 680
Street show/street performance, 20, 531, 664, 666
Structures of feeling, 118, 587, 588
Studi, DeLanna, 455, 457, 459–461
Suffering, distant, 529
Suppliants, The, 73
Suppliant Women, 13, 15, 195, 199–202, 204
Supplication (*hiketeia*), 73, 258, 259, 263
  suppliants, 195, 196, 199, 200, 202–204, 203n4, 443

T
Taha, 19, 491, 495, 496
Taha, Mohammed Ali, 491–496
Takeshi, Kawamura, 238–240
Tale of Genji, The, 14, 15, 231–232, 235
Tasso, Torquato, 646, 648
Taumoepeau, Latai, 152, 153
Teatr.doc, 16, 339, 341–344, 347, 349
Tempest, The, 14, 617, 696
Terence, 14, 208, 213, 216, 217
Terezín/Theresienstadt Ghetto, 10, 55–64

INDEX

Testimonial theater, 600
Thalia Theatre, 73
Théâtre du Soleil, 74, 94, 95, 97, 98
Theatre of Displaced People (TDP), 19, 499, 502–507
Theatre of the Oppressed, 310
Theatre of the Real, 739–749
This Beach, 377, 378, 380–386
Time of Women, 759, 760
To Be A Machine, 159, 163–166
Toinen koti (*The Other Home*), 624, 628
Touring
  touring abroad, 261
  touring companies, 247
Tourism, 2, 103, 133, 382, 643
Trafficking, 13, 17, 36, 72, 99, 100, 208, 212, 213, 310, 345, 428, 445, 530, 732, 733
  human trafficking, 17, 36, 212, 213, 428, 530
Trail of Tears, 18, 451–462
Transhumance, 196
Transnationalism, 14, 22, 416, 472
  transnationality, 22, 639–648
Transnational Travel
  traveling actors, 755
  traveling theatre companies, 688, 704
Trash Cuisine, 752, 757–759, 759n2
Tribunal, 555–559
Trip to America, A, 689
Trojan Women, The, 201, 617, 618, 620
Tsaddik, The, the sage, 715
Tsuina, a ceremony for driving out demons who carried plague, 220
Turkish, 14, 20, 70, 82, 84, 267, 273–275, 513
  Türkisches Ensemble (Turkish ensemble), 82
Two Women, 236–238

U

Uhambo: Pieces of a Dream, 429
Uncle Tom's Cabin, 642, 692
Undocumented Love, 624, 631–634
U.N. Refugee Convention, The 1951, 143, 203n4, 311
Uprooting/uprootedness, 35, 56, 120, 134, 396, 648

U.S. Immigration Act of 1924, The, 476
Utvandrarna (*The Emigrants*), 436

V

Vagrancy laws in England, 260
Vakhtangov, Eugeniy, 720–722
Vardo, 99, 100
Vega, López de, 645
Veṇīsamhāra, 188
Verbatim theatre, 341, 408, 527, 553, 556, 613, 633
  testimony theatre, 613
Verdecchia, Guillermo, 327, 328, 331
Verrücktes Blut (*Mad Blood*), 84
Vicente, Gil, 644
Victim, 3, 14, 24, 42, 46, 50, 81, 97, 98, 150, 212, 285, 286, 306, 343, 359, 385, 484, 485, 501–503, 517, 532, 553, 554, 563, 603, 656, 693, 694, 744, 757
  victimization, 98, 733
Vigil for Roxie, A, 429
Vilna Troupe, 713–723
Visitor(s), 57, 173, 209, 211, 246, 251, 551, 697
Voice Refugee Forum, The, 561
Vorozhbyt, Natalka, 502

W

Waarheidscommissie, De (The Truth Commission; 2013–2018), 743, 744
Waiting for Godot, 321, 629
Waki character, 224, 225, 228
Walker, George, 675
Wang Youdao Divorces His Wife, 468, 469
War Brides Act of 1946, 476
War reenactment, 366, 369, 373, 374
  See also Re-enactment
Wasted lives, 104
We. Self-Identification, 754
While I was Waiting, 613
Who am I?, 507
Wilkins, George, 244, 251
Williams, Bert, 675

Windrush, 131, 132, 134–137
  Empire Windrush, 131, 132, 433
  Windrush generation, 12, 131, 136, 137, 139, 433, 435
Winterreise (Winter Journey), 74
Wolf, Alfred, 49
Works and Days, 195

X

Xenia (guest-friendship), 13, 197, 198, 204
Xenophobia, 76, 81, 105, 195, 348, 349, 404, 429, 436, 515, 587
Xiaozhuang, Guo, 467

Y

Yaying Ensemble, 467
Years of Exile, 310
Yoruba travelling theatre, 17, 415–425
Young King; or, The Mistake, The, 647, 648
Young Vic Theatre, 491, 592, 755, 759

Z

Zeami
  Zeami Motokiyo, 220, 232–234
Zero Degrees, 394
Zionism, 315, 317–319
Zone of Silence, 754
Zon-Mai, 395

Printed in the United States
by Baker & Taylor Publisher Services